BIOLOGY
Principles, Patterns, and Processes

890021

Co-ordinating Author:

DON GALBRAITH
Faculty of Education
University of Toronto

Author Team:

TOM DICKINSON
University of Toronto

NANCY FLOOD
University of Toronto

WILLIAM G. FRIEND
University of Toronto

JANET GARDEN
Thornlea Secondary School

WILLIAM HOPKINS
University of Western Ontario

NORMAN HUNER
University of Western Ontario

NILS PETERSEN
University of Western Ontario

JAMES RISING
University of Toronto

IRV TALLAN
University of Toronto

RON WEEKS
Banting Secondary School

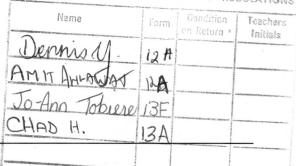

VAUGHAN ROAD COLLEGIATE INSTITUTE
TEXTBOOK AGREEMENT

THIS TEXTBOOK IS THE PROPERTY OF
THE BOROUGH OF YORK BOARD OF EDUCATION

1. Students must not mark or deface the text in any way.
2. Books are to be returned to the school office if the student leaves this school during the year.
3. Books are to be returned on request in good condition or the student will be charged the value of the book.
4. Credit for this course will not be given until this book is returned and/or settlement made.

I WILL COMPLY WITH THE ABOVE REGULATIONS.

Name	Form	Condition on Return *	Teachers Initials
Dennis Y.	12A		
Amit Ahlawat	12A		
Jo-Ann Tobiere	13F		
Chad H.	13A		

*Good. Fair. Poor

WILEY

John Wiley & Sons
Toronto · New York · Chichester · Brisbane · Singapore

Canadian Cataloguing in Publication Data

Main entry under title:

Biology : principles, patterns, and processes

Includes index.
ISBN 0-471-79629-8

1. Biology. I. Galbraith, Donald I., 1936– .

QH308.2.B56 1989   574   C88-095071-4

Design: Michael van Elsen Design Inc.
Illustration: Acorn Illustration & Art Studio
Typesetter: Compeer Typographic Services Limited
Printer: John Deyell Company

Cover:
*The cover photograph is a close-up of the eyespot found
near the underside tip of the front wing of a Cecropia or
robin moth (Hyalophora cecropia). These moths, of the
family Saturniidae, are found throughout Canada, the
United States, and Mexico. They are the largest and most
common of all silk moths. In fact, they are so large,
having a wingspan of 13–16 cm, that they are often
mistaken for bats!*

*The caterpillars (larval moths) are usually about 10 cm in
length. They feed on a variety of common plants,
including willow and maple trees. They are green in
colour and spin brown silk cocoons.*

*The abundance of Cecropia moths and the ease with which
they are kept and bred make them a popular choice among
collectors and breeders.*

Printed and bound in Canada

10 9 8 7 6 5 4 3 2 1

TABLE OF CONTENTS

Breakdown of glucose in the presence of O_2 (fermentation.)

ACKNOWLEDGEMENTS

No book can be written without the hard work and expertise of many dedicated individuals. First, we would like to extend our sincere thanks to all of the staff of John Wiley & Sons Canada Limited for their support throughout this project. We thank Trudy Rising, who initiated the project, and Ann Adair, who directed development of the project. Lee Makos, the associate editor for the project, ensured that we developed the material as it should be developed. We sincerely thank her for her patience and skill. Thanks also to Cynthia Young, editorial assistant.

We would like to extend a word of appreciation to Joan Kerr and Zane Kaneps and their able production staff, especially Lisa Stacey and Jeff Aberle. Thank you also to Michael van Elsen for his innovative design, Vernon Freer for his photo research, and Donna Coburn for writing the glossary.

Our thanks go as well to Bruce Bartlett and Cecilia Chan, Wiley's copy editors for the project, and to Gillian Bartlett and Mary Kay Winter for their critical reviews of specific units of the book.

The following classroom teachers served as consultants for various portions of the manuscript during its development. We thank them for their valuable recommendations.

Donna Coburn, Sutton District High School, York Region Board of Education

William MacPherson, Glendale Secondary School, Hamilton Board of Education

Henry Pasma, Cawthra Park Secondary School, Peel Board of Education

Jacinta Sheppard, Holy Heart of Mary High School, St. John's, Newfoundland

Silvio Tallevi, Earl Haig Secondary School, North York Board of Education

Robert Whitney, Jarvis Collegiate Institute, Toronto Board of Education

Maxine Widmeyer, Milliken Mills Secondary School, York Region Board of Education

The Authors

TO THE INSTRUCTOR

Biology: Principles, Patterns, and Processes is a text designed to provide a solid foundation of knowledge and insight into the study of biology at the senior level. At the foundation of biology are basic concepts that tie facts and terms into a meaningful and integrated whole. You will see that we have used many examples to support each concept as it is developed. By balancing concepts and facts, we have strived to provide students with a better understanding of the integrated processes of life.

The material is presented in a manner that allows you to introduce concepts from a number of viewpoints, placing a variety of curriculum emphases on the material. Some of these emphases may include a solid foundation, the nature of science, practical applications, communications, and science, technology, and society.

A solid foundation of factual knowledge is critical. It is important, however, that the solid foundation not be the only emphasis placed upon the material.

Throughout the text, students are exposed to the processes of science, including model building, hypothesizing, inferring, communicating findings, etc. All of these processes relate to the *nature of science* —the ways in which scientists approach and carry out their craft. Students are made aware that scientific models are subject to change as new evidence and observations come to light. We have tried to show that biology is not a rhetoric of conclusions but rather an ongoing, dynamic search for solutions to many of humankind's problems.

Many aspects of biology have obvious *practical applications*. At appropriate points, these are addressed throughout the text. For example, transmission and scanning electron microscopes enable scientists to pinpoint sites of cellular chemical activities and to identify structures not normally present in an organism. Knowledge of the endocrine and nervous systems assists physicians in recommending treatments for hormonal and nervous disorders.

Today, it is impossible to imagine a study of biology without a consideration of how the discoveries in our laboratories and field studies impact on society as a whole. Throughout the text, within the textual material itself and in the accompanying special features, we remind students constantly of the interaction between *science*, *technology*, and *society*.

By emphasizing knowledge, science skills, and the interactions of science, technology, and society, we hope that we have provided both student and teacher alike with a text that is a valuable resource and one which is seen to promote scientific literacy.

TO THE STUDENT

For most students, this will not be your first course in biology. For many, it will be a stepping stone into the dynamic realm of advanced biology. Regardless of your future goals, this course will provide you with the solid foundation necessary for examining biological issues in the world around us. These issues could include such things as genetic engineering, the use and abuse of drugs in our society, solid waste disposal, and pollution of our environment. Regardless of the issue, we require a solid information base on which to make ''real-life'' judgements as modern biology takes on greater significance in everyday life.

Biology: Principles, Patterns, and Processes is organized to increase your appreciation of the interactions which occur within an organism, between organisms, and between an organism and its surroundings.

Firstly, an understanding of biology includes the study of the organisms themselves, such as their anatomies—the parts of the organisms, and their physiologies — the chemical and physical interactions that take place within the organisms.

A second important aspect of biology is the study of the change of organisms over time—the evolutionary history of organisms. Studies of the remains of organisms which inhabited the earth many centuries ago have revealed much about the development of life on earth.

Biology also includes the study of how organisms interact with one another and their environment. This interaction becomes increasingly important as organisms, including humans, compete for diminishing space and natural resources, both renewable and nonrenewable. Behaviour—the study of how organisms react and respond to their surroundings — is another field of current biological research.

As you can see, the scope is enormous. However, the organization of this book is designed to make your task an enjoyable one. In the final analysis, you will have succeeded if, as a result of using this book, you gain an understanding of the nature of life itself and can better deal with issues involving living things and their environment.

As you work your way through your course in biology with the aid of this text, you may ask yourself the following questions:

- What are the main concepts or objectives which I should learn in this chapter?
- What other concepts must I first understand in order to be able to benefit most from this new material?
- Where does the material in this chapter fit into my overall understanding of biology?
- How is the content of this chapter related to the world around me?
- How is the content related to other subjects which I am studying?
- What new skills have I learned from this chapter?
- What issues have been raised in this chapter which merit further study?
- How can I best summarize the material in this chapter?
- How shall I prepare myself to be evaluated on the content of this chapter?

Good luck in your study of biology. We hope you enjoy it as much as we do.

The Authors

FEATURES OF THE TEXT

The following are some of the features of the text designed to make your study of biology both a stimulating and a rewarding experience.

- Each chapter begins with a stimulating photo and/ or quotation relating the content of the chapter to the world around us. These serve as a constant reminder of the importance of science in society.

- As new terms are introduced, they are printed in **boldface** type. These words also appear in a list at the end of the chapter under the heading **Vocabulary**. A review of these terms will ensure a solid understanding of the concepts of the chapter. These terms are also defined in the **Glossary** which appears at the end of the text.

- Throughout the text, there over 40 special interest features. These are designed to extend your level of understanding and to tie the topic to a current issue outside the classroom. A list of these features can be found following the Table of Contents.

- Each chapter concludes with a **Chapter Summary**, a concise synopsis of the content and concepts of the chapter.

- A basic list of major **Objectives** appears at the end of each chapter. This is not intended as a complete list but rather a statement of the ''key ideas'' covered in the chapter.

- A set of questions, entitled **Review Questions**, also appears at the end of each chapter. Much of the material required to answer these questions will be found in the chapter.

- **Advanced Questions** is a section of questions at the very end of the chapter, designed to encourage you to apply your new-found knowledge to solving biology problems. Many of these problems relate to societal issues.

INTRODUCTION

The content of this text covers a wide range of topics which fall within the subject Biology. Not only is the content far-reaching, but the extent to which we use this knowledge is substantial. A set of case studies follows which will illustrate the extensive impact the study of biology has on our day-to-day decisions. The answers to the questions posed within each situation are not always completely known. Researchers are working toward the *correct* answer to these questions. In some cases, however, answers are known and you will be exploring aspects of these cases at different points throughout the academic year

Situation 1   New Corn Variety

Mexican researchers have developed a new maize (corn) variety with double the protein of conventional varieties. Over 200 million people worldwide rely on maize as their primary or sole source of protein. The new variety is referred to as QPM, which stands for quality-protein maize (*BioScience*, November 1988).

Why is this discovery so important? What type of research would scientists pursue to develop a new crop variety? Traditional maize varieties lack two essential amino acids — lysine and tryptophan. What is so important about these amino acids in terms of human nutrition? Both chemistry and biology are involved in answering the above questions. More important, though, is the fact that this knowledge is being applied to addressing the worldwide issue of malnutrition.

Situation 2   World Food Issue

In the past four years, India, China, Indonesia, and Mexico have failed to increase their food production. Since these nations represent a large part of the total world population, the global per capita food production has decreased. This has occurred in spite of a ninefold increase in the use of chemical fertilizers since 1950.

How can this situation be altered? What part, if any, could genetic engineering play in alleviating this situation? When land is cleared for agricultural use, single kinds of crops tend to be grown. Because of this, there has been a worldwide reduction in the variety of plants produced. This, in turn, has resulted in a reduction in the gene pool from which new varieties of useful plants can be developed. The above issue requires much further study to secure the food reserves necessary to maintain an ever increasing world population.

Situation 3   The Use and Abuse of Drugs

A person entered a bar and consumed four alcoholic beverages within the space of one hour. This individual had not eaten for three hours prior to the first drink. Although it is against the law, the person left the premises, attempted to drive home, and had a serious accident.

What effect, if any, does eating have on the absorption of alcohol? How is it that alcohol works so quickly once it is swallowed? How does the alcohol enter the bloodstream? What parts of the nervous system are affected by the presence of alcohol? How can one convince another person to avoid drinking and driving? All of the above questions relate, in some measure, to an understanding of the digestive, circulatory, endocrine, and nervous systems. Some of these systems, in turn, trigger the movement and co-ordination of muscles. Thus, this situation requires a knowledge of a number of biological and chemical concepts.

Situation 4   Amazon Rain Forests

The Amazon River Basin in the northern part of South America represents approximately 30 percent of the rain forest remaining on earth. Largely for economic reasons, the forest is being cut and burned to make way for new crops and industrial developments. Biologists have suggested that the rain forest be maintained for a number of reasons.

Why is the maintenance of rain forests so important to the biosphere? Why is the forest ecology described as being ''fragile''? How are the rain forests related to the ''green house'' effect? What right, if any, do citizens of other nations have to expect or demand that the government of a country with rain forests maintain the rain forets? (Rain forests, including those in the Amazon, cover just seven percent of the earth's land surface but contain an immense variety of organisms.) These are but a few of the many questions which might be asked about the destruction of global rain forests — the answers to which will have a definite bearing on our own well-being.

Situation 5   Toxic Waste Disposal

Newspapers are filled with debates over what to do with toxic wastes. Government agencies select waste disposal sites and local municipal groups fight to prevent the agencies from locating such a site in their region. No one wants toxic wastes in their own backyard.

What exactly are toxic wastes? Where do they come from? Why are they considered toxic? Are they toxic to all organisms? What is meant by tolerance levels? What effects do specific toxins have on organisms? Why are lead and mercury wastes considered toxic? This issue points out the need to understand both chemistry and biology to even begin to address the problem.

As you work your way through this text, constantly try to see ways in which the material might be applied to a general understanding of the world around you. By doing so, you will become a better informed, more scientifically literate citizen.

THE
CHEMICAL BASIS
OF LIFE

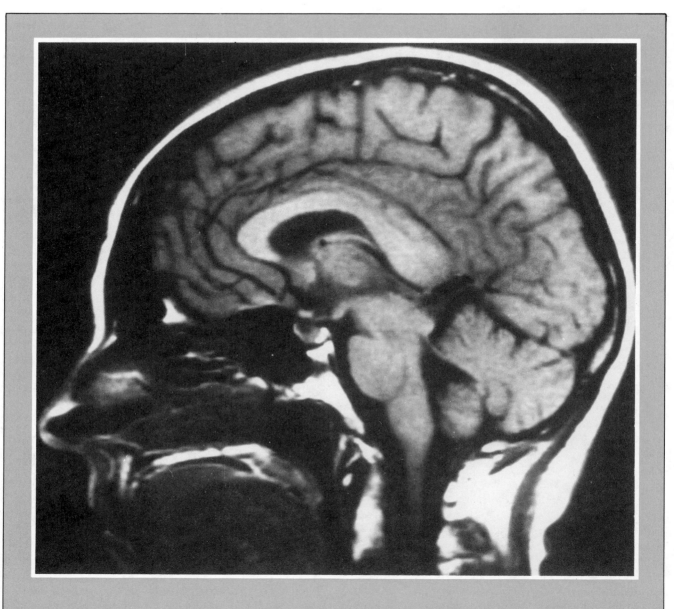

CHAPTER 1

A CHEMICAL BASIS OF LIFE

These are the days of miracle and wonder . . .

from 'The Boy in the Bubble'
by Paul Simon, 1986

Catch that thought! Is it in the picture? No, we cannot photograph the thinking process—not yet. Not too many years ago, it was impossible to photograph the interior of a living organism without cutting it up. Now modern techniques such as computerized tomography and magnetic resonance imaging do just that. These tools can capture, in seconds, a picture of the brain or other internal organs of living beings. In this particular picture, the various regions of the brain are seen by magnetic resonance imaging of water and fats. As these techniques develop, they will become rapid enough to get sub-second snapshots of the brain in action. Imagine a movie of your brain as you are thinking. Perhaps we will capture that fleeting thought.

One of the important developments in modern science has been, and continues to be, the gradual unveiling of the molecular basis on which life works. Continued success in this venture depends on a thorough understanding of biology at the level of interactions among molecules within organisms. It is, therefore, necessary to provide a rudimentary introduction to the chemical basis of life.

This chapter presents only those concepts in chemistry that are essential to the study of biology. At first you may feel the topics discussed are as far removed from biology as the moon is from the earth. Without an understanding of them, however, we cannot make sense of the structures and interactions of the simplest molecules found in living organisms, which are the topics of Chapter 2.

It is the intent throughout this book to introduce the relevant background when and where it is needed.

You will, therefore, see new applications of chemical principles in many of the subsequent chapters. The introductory chapters form the basis for these more detailed developments. In many ways, you should view Chapters 1 and 2 as resource material to be referred to as you find the need, rather like you would use a dictionary.

1.1 CONSTITUENTS OF MATTER: MOLECULES

Molecules are the smallest units of a substance that still possess the fundamental chemical and physical properties of the substance. We may, for example, take a tablespoon of water (approximately 18 mL or 18 g) and repeatedly divide it in half. At each division we would still have a substance with the properties of water. However, after about 79 such halvings, we would end up with *one* molecule of water, which can no longer be subdivided, and which still retains those properties.

If you apply a large amount of energy, it is possible to break down molecules into their constituent **atoms**. These are generally highly reactive and therefore short-lived. Atoms, as individual entities, play virtually no role in biological systems. For example, the hydrogen atom (H) is never encountered except for extremely short times in a chemical laboratory, or as an isolated species in outer space.

Somewhat confusingly at times, we also use the word atom to describe a constituent of a molecule when the molecule is intact. For example, we say that the water molecule is a triatomic molecule consisting of two atoms of hydrogen bonded to one atom of oxygen (H—O—H). It must be made very clear that the atom as a component of a molecule is chemically very different from that of the isolated atom. Some examples of molecules are listed in Table 1.1.

Table 1.1   Examples of Small Molecules

SUBSTANCE	SYMBOL	TYPE
helium	He	monatomic molecule
oxygen	O_2	diatomic molecule
carbon dioxide	CO_2	triatomic molecule
ammonia	NH_3	tetratomic molecule
methane	CH_4	pentatomic molecule

An **element** is a substance which consists of atoms of only one kind. The most important elements associated with living systems are listed in Table 1.2. These are but a small fraction of the more than one hundred elements which have been discovered to date.

Table 1.2   Most Abundant Elements in Living Matter

ELEMENT	SYMBOL	MASS (see the text)	ABUNDANCE (by mass)
oxygen	O	16.0	62.0
carbon	C	12.0	20.0
hydrogen	H	1.0	10.0
nitrogen	N	14.0	3.3
calcium	Ca	40.0	2.5
phosphorus	P	31.0	1.0
sulfur	S	32.0	0.25
potassium	K	39.0	0.25
chlorine	Cl	35.5	0.2
sodium	Na	23.0	0.1
magnesium	Mg	24.5	0.07
iron	Fe	56.0	0.01

Although the Greek word *atomos* means indivisible, modern day nuclear physicists are able to break down the atoms of elements into a large array of *subatomic particles*. The most important of these, for our understanding of chemical processes, are the **electrons**, **protons**, and **neutrons**. Electrons and protons have equal but opposite charges, with the proton being positive and the electron therefore negative, while neutrons have no charge. Protons and neutrons have approximately equal mass, while the electron mass is negligible by comparison. The protons and neutrons combine to form the *nucleus* which constitutes more

than 99.99 percent of the mass of the atom, but occupies less than one percent of its volume. The electrons occupy regions of space around the nucleus called *orbitals*. The electron orbitals are responsible for the interaction of atoms to form molecules.

All the atoms of an element have the same number of protons in the nucleus. This number is different for different elements. It is called the element's **atomic number**. Thus, each element has a unique atomic number. The number of neutrons in the nucleus of the atoms of an element can vary, but it is generally close to the number of protons. The **atomic mass**, which is the sum of the number of neutrons and protons, is therefore close to twice the atomic number. An element can consist of a mixture of atoms each having the same number of protons but a different number of neutrons. These atoms have the same atomic number but have different atomic mass. They are called **isotopes**. All isotopes of an element have similar *chemical* properties, but vary in their *physical* properties, most obviously in mass. Some isotopes are unstable and disintegrate spontaneously in nuclear fission reactions which emit high energy radiation. Scientists have found invaluable use of such isotopes in studying chemical reactions in biological systems. Other isotopes have special properties in magnetic fields. This has permitted the development of modern magnetic resonance imaging techniques for diagnosis and treatment of many diseases.

The number of electrons in a neutral atom is always equal to the number of protons. If electrons are added to or removed from an atom, it becomes an **ion**. The difference in the number of electrons and protons determines the net charge of the ion. A sodium atom (Na) can, for example, give up one electron to become a sodium ion which is positively charged (Na^+). Correspondingly, a chlorine atom (Cl) can take up an electron and become the negatively charged chloride ion (Cl^-). Molecular ions are formed when one of the atoms in the molecule takes up or gives up electrons. Table 1.3 lists a number of the most important ions in living systems.

1.2 FROM MICROSCOPIC TO MACROSCOPIC

Although molecules represent the fundamental units of matter, they are virtually impossible to observe individually because they are extremely small. As indicated above, if we divide a tablespoon of water in half for about 79 times, we end up with a single water

Table 1.3 Some Common Ions in Living Systems and Their Functions

SYMBOL	NAME	FUNCTIONS
Cations:		
H^+	proton	maintains acid-base equilibria
Na^+	sodium ion	provides membrane potentials
K^+	potassium ion	provides membrane potentials
Ca^{2+}	calcium ion	regulates enzyme activity
Mg^{2+}	magnesium ion	regulates enzyme activity
Fe^{3+}	ferric ion	takes part in oxidation-reduction reactions
Anions:		
HO^-	hydroxide ion	maintains acid-base equilibria
Cl^-	chloride ion	provides membrane potentials
HPO_4^{2-}	phosphate ion	maintains acid-base equilibria
Ionic groups:		
$-NH_3^+$	ammonium group	provides protein charge
$-COO^-$	carboxylate group	provides protein charge
$-OPO_3^{2-}$	phosphate group	provides nucleic acid charge

molecule. This may not appear to be a large number of subdivisions, but beware the power of two! The halving process results in an object which is of a size equal to ½ multiplied by itself 79 times — more precisely, to $(½)^{79}$ its original size. This number equals 1.66×10^{-24}, which is almost too small to imagine. As a comparison, if one were to try to divide the earth in half 79 times, in the end each piece would have a mass of only about 10 kg (or about ten times the mass of this book). Correspondingly, we may say that the original spoonful of water contained about 2^{79} or 6×10^{23} molecules of water. This is a very large number. If one considers the width of a match (about 2 mm) as a unit of measure, then 6×10^{23} matches laid side by side would cover the distance from the earth to the Andromeda Galaxy (one of the closest galaxies to the Milky Way).

Because we most often work with objects the size of the tablespoon of water, or perhaps a few factors of two smaller or larger, it is more convenient to have a unit of matter on the macroscopic scale instead of the microscopic scale of atoms and molecules. Accordingly, we define a **mole** as the number of carbon atoms in *exactly* 12 g of carbon-12, the isotope of carbon that has 6 protons, 6 neutrons, and 6 electrons. This leads to the number of atoms per mole, also called *Avogadro's Constant*, of $6.022\,05 \times 10^{23}$.

The mass (recall that mass is a measure of the amount of matter in an object and differs from the weight which is a measure of the attractive force between the earth and the object: weight = mass × acceleration due to gravity) of a single atom of carbon-12 is taken as exactly 12 *atomic mass units* which means that one atomic mass unit is equal to 1.6606×10^{-24} kg. The mass given in Table 1.2 can then be interpreted either as the mass in atomic mass units per molecule, or as the mass in grams of a mole of the elements. Thus the mass of an atom of potassium is 39 atomic mass units (about 64.8×10^{-24} g) while the mass of a mole of potassium ions is 39.0 g. Since the atomic mass unit is defined relative to carbon-12 having a mass of 12 units, it is frequently called the relative molecular mass or the relative molar mass. To calculate the molar mass of any molecule is simply a matter of adding the molar masses of each of the constituent atoms in the molecule.

1.3 BONDING: FORCES HOLDING MOLECULES TOGETHER

In general, we distinguish the forces which hold the atoms together in a molecule from those holding different molecules together. The former are called **intramolecular forces** and they determine the strength of bonds within the molecule. This is what is generally understood as **chemical bonding**. In contrast, **intermolecular forces** determine how molecules interact to form liquids or solids through **physical bonding**. In some cases, the distinction becomes difficult, but in general terms, we can say that more than 100 kJ of energy is needed to break the chemical bonds in a mole of substance whereas less than 10 kJ of energy is needed to break the physical bonds in the same quantity of substance (1 kJ of energy is the amount of energy needed to heat up a cup of water by one degree, or the amount of energy required to climb a 15 step flight of stairs).

Chemical Bonding

Chemical bonds are formed when the electron orbitals on different atoms interact. The details of how bonds are formed are complex, and are only understood in full detail for the simplest bonds. In fact, as recently as 1986, Dr. John C. Polanyi at the University of Toronto shared the Nobel Prize in Chemistry with two chemists from the United States for his contributions to our understanding of how small molecules react.

The interaction of two hydrogen atoms, each with only one proton and one electron, to form a molecule of hydrogen (H—H) is the simplest example of the formation of a chemical bond. In this case, the bond is formed by the two electrons interacting in the region of space between the two nuclei. When the electrons interact to form an electron pair, it turns out that the energy of the molecule is less than the energy of the two isolated atoms. The molecule is therefore more stable than the individual atoms. This type of bond, where each atom provides one electron to form the bond, is called a **single bond**.

Elements with larger atomic number contain more electrons and are therefore, in principle, able to form more than one bond. In general, it is only the electrons that occupy the region of space furthest away from the nucleus that are able to interact to form chemical bonds. These electrons in the outermost orbitals are the **valence electrons**. Table 1.4 lists the number of valence electrons in the biologically most important elements along with the typical number of bonds each element can form. For example, oxygen has six valence electrons, two of which readily form bonds. Hence when two oxygen atoms interact to form the oxygen molecule, they each provide two electrons and form a **double bond**, denoted by a pair of lines in O=O. In nitrogen, three of the five valence electrons readily form bonds. Hence, molecular nitrogen is formed when two nitrogen atoms form a **triple bond** by sharing three pairs of electrons. These single, double, and triple bonds are all examples of **covalent bonds**.

Atoms with more than four valence electrons can in some cases use all those electrons in covalent bonds. Examples include phosphorus (in H_3PO_4) and sulfur (in H_2SO_4) as shown in Table 1.4. More often than not, however, the number of bonds is fewer. As a rule, these atoms form the more stable molecules when the numbers of valence electrons add up to eight. Hence oxygen and sulfur most frequently form two bonds while chlorine forms one.

Table 1.4   Valence Electrons and Bonding in Biologically Most Important Elements

ELEMENTS	NUMBER OF VALENCE ELECTRONS	NUMBER OF CHEMICAL BONDS	EXAMPLES
H, Na, K	1	1	H—H; H—O—H
Mg, Ca	2	2	Cl—Ca—Cl
C	4	4	(see structure)
N	5	3	N≡N; (see structure)
P	5	3 or 5	(see structure)
O	6	2	O=O; H—O—H
S	6	2 or 6	(see structure)
Cl	7	1	H—Cl

Atoms with a small number of electrons in their valence shell have a tendency to give up those electrons to form positively charged ions, **cations**. Thus H^+, Na^+, Mg^{2+}, and Ca^{2+} are commonly encountered cations. In contrast, atoms that have a large number of electrons in their valence shell are more likely to take up additional electrons to form negatively charged ions, **anions**. The tendency to attract electrons is referred to as the **electronegativity** of the atom. Usually, the maximum number of electrons that can be accepted by an element is that number which brings the total number of valence electrons to eight. Thus the Cl⁻ ion is formed by addition of one electron to the seven already present. The doubly charged anions, O^{2-} or S^{2-}, are much less stable and are never observed in biological systems. However, singly charged anions such as HO^- are very common. These arise from a combination of bonding and addition of electrons to the oxygen atom.

When a chemical bond is formed between two identical atoms, the electrons in the bond are shared equally by the two component atoms. However, when atoms that have a tendency to give up electrons form bonds with atoms that have a tendency to take up electrons, then the electrons in that bond spend more time closer to the latter. The bond is said to be **polarized**. For example, in the molecule H—Cl, the pair of electrons in the bond spend more time close to the chlorine atom than at the hydrogen atom. The chlorine is said to be more **electronegative** than the hydrogen. Similarly, in the molecule H—O—H, the bonds are polarized such that there is more negative charge close to the oxygen atom than at the two hydrogen atoms. As the electronegativity of the two atoms gets closer, the bond polarization decreases. The C—N bond in molecules, for example, is only slightly polarized.

When atoms of sodium and chlorine form bonds, the tendency for the sodium atom to give up its electron and the tendency for the chlorine atom to take up an electron are so great that the electrons stay almost exclusively on the chlorine atom. In this case, the chemical bonding is, in effect, between the two ions, Na^+ and Cl^-. Accordingly, this bond and others similar to it are called **ionic bonds**. Molecules made up by ionic bonds are generally called salts, because they easily dissociate in solution into the constituent ions.

Physical Bonding

Intermolecular forces are usually attractive, so molecules will tend to associate. These attractive forces are, however, weak enough that collisions among molecules frequently can supply sufficient energy to overcome the intermolecular interactions and separate the molecules. As an analogy, you can think of molecules behaving in much the same way as a set of snooker or billiard balls with sticky surfaces. When the balls are first spread on the table, some of them would stick together in pairs. If such a pair of balls is hit by the cue ball, they might well separate. The chance that the cue ball will separate a pair of other balls depends on the speed it has when it hits. Similarly, the chance that

a pair of molecules attracted to each other will be separated by a collision with a third molecule depends on the speed of the latter. While the speed of the cue ball depends on how hard you hit it, the speed of molecules depends on the temperature. Molecules have much higher speeds at high temperatures than at low temperatures. This is basically the reason that many substances at high temperatures become gases, in which the molecules move about independently of one another. At low temperatures, substances are either liquids or solids in which the molecules are in much closer contact.

The temperature at which intermolecular interactions are broken depends on the magnitude of the intermolecular forces. These in turn depend on the mass of the molecules, on the polarization of the bonds in the molecules, and on whether the molecules are charged ions or neutral. Consequently, small neutral molecules with non-polar bonds, such as hydrogen, oxygen, and nitrogen are gases at room temperature. Larger molecules or molecules with polar bonds, such as water, tend to be liquids, and salts are solids at room temperature.

In living systems, there are two particularly important intermolecular interactions which largely determine the shape and assembly of large molecules. These are *hydrogen bonding* and *hydrophobic interactions*.

Hydrogen Bonding

Bonds between hydrogen and oxygen, between hydrogen and nitrogen, and to some extent between hydrogen and sulfur are highly polarized. As illustrated in Figure 1.1, there is a net positive charge on the hydrogen atom and a net negative charge on the other atom. Because of the strong polarization in these bonds, there is a particularly strong interaction between the positive atoms and negative atoms on neighbouring molecules. This is depicted in the case of water in Figure 1.2.

Figure 1.1
The partial charges on the atoms in water, ammonia, and hydrogen sulfide due to bond polarization

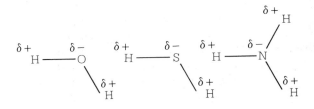

Figure 1.2

The dashed lines indicate hydrogen bonding between water molecules. The wedge-shaped bonds in the lower structure indicate that these hydrogen atoms are above the page.

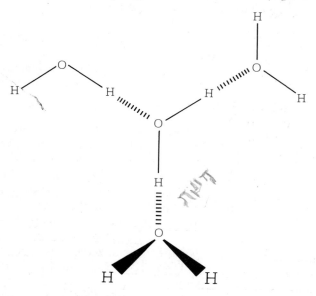

Figure 1.3

Hydrogen bonding between water and methanol, water and ammonia, water and acetic acid. Note that acetic acid can form hydrogen bonds in more than one way.

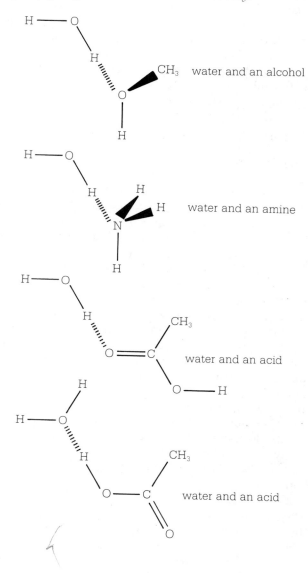

water and an alcohol

water and an amine

water and an acid

water and an acid

The bond formed between the hydrogen of one molecule and the oxygen (or nitrogen or sulfur) of another molecule is called a **hydrogen bond**. While it is not nearly as strong as the chemical bond between the corresponding atoms in the same molecule, the hydrogen bond is a significant factor which gives water some of its special properties. The hydrogen bond in water is much stronger than that in hydrogen sulfide (H_2S). This accounts for the fact that at room temperature water is a liquid, while hydrogen sulfide is a gas even though the molar mass of water is much less. As you will see in Chapter 2, hydrogen bonding is critical in forming the particular shapes of complex macromolecules. Hydrogen bonds can form between many types of chemical groups. Figure 1.3 shows some important examples.

Hydrophobic Interactions

Oil and water do not mix. This is because oil molecules have non-polar bonds (C—H bonds) which do not interact well with the highly polar bonds in the water molecules. In fact, the presence of an oil molecule forces the water in the immediate vicinity of the surface to become more structured, more like a solid. This is not favourable, and can only be minimized if the surface area of contact between the oil and water mol-

ecules is decreased. One way this may happen is for the oil molecules to interact specifically with one another, forming small droplets of oil (Figure 1.4). The surface area of these droplets is smaller than that which would be exposed to the water if the molecules were dispersed. The larger the droplets, the smaller the contact area per molecule, and ultimately, the best situation is attained when all the oil molecules float on top of the water.

Figure 1.4
The hydrophobic effect—an attempt to minimize the surface contact between non-polar molecules (here propane) and water.

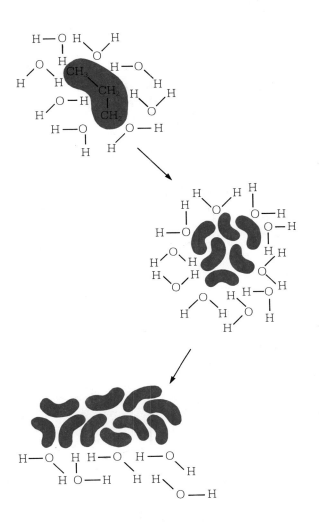

The composition of molecules is represented by their **molecular formula**. The molecular formula of water is H_2O, and it indicates that there are two atoms of hydrogen for every atom of oxygen. Similarly, the molecular formula of ethanol, C_2H_6O, tells us that there are two carbon atoms and six hydrogen atoms for every oxygen atom. Unfortunately, these molecular formulae do not tell us which atoms are bonded to which.

The **structural formula** describes explicitly how the various atoms are bonded. In the case of water, the structural formula is $H-O-H$. This shows that the hydrogen atoms are each bonded to the oxygen atom by a single bond. The structural formula of ethanol is shown in Figure 1.5. It shows that the two carbon atoms are linked by a single bond, that one of these carbon atoms has three hydrogen atoms attached, while the other carbon has two hydrogen atoms and an oxygen atom attached, and that the last hydrogen atom is attached to the oxygen by a single bond. Note that for each carbon atom, there are four bonds. Clearly, the structural formula provides much more information. It is also unambiguous. The molecular formula for dimethyl ether is the same as that for ethanol, namely, C_2H_6O. The structural formula as shown in Figure 1.6, however, clearly shows that in dimethyl ether, the carbon atoms are each bonded to the oxygen and to three hydrogen atoms. Dimethyl ether and ethanol are two very different chemicals with very different properties. Figure 1.6 also shows the molecular and structural formulae of several other chemicals.

Figure 1.5
The molecular formula for C_2H_6O can correspond to the structural formula for ethanol.

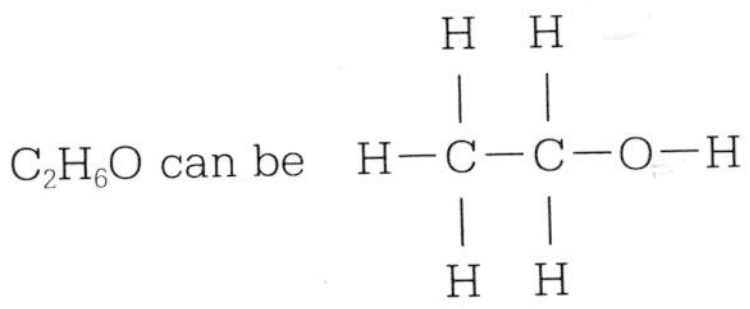

$$C_2H_6O \text{ can be } \quad H-\overset{\displaystyle H}{\underset{\displaystyle H}{C}}-\overset{\displaystyle H}{\underset{\displaystyle H}{C}}-O-H$$

This effect, whereby oil molecules are prevented from mixing with water molecules because they would tend to cause too much ordering of the water molecules, is termed the **hydrophobic** effect. The word hydrophobic means "water fearing" (from the Greek words *hydros* meaning water, and *phobos* meaning fear). It describes the phenomenon that non-polar molecules, or non-polar regions of molecules, prefer to segregate so as to avoid contact with water. As you will see in Chapter 4, this is an important factor in determining the structure of cell membranes.

A useful way to express the composition and structure of a molecule is to write in sequence the units or groups of atoms that are attached. For example, the formula for ethanol can be written as CH_3CH_2OH to indicate how the atoms are grouped. This is less ambiguous than writing simply the molecular formula, C_2H_6O, but is simpler than drawing the detailed

Figure 1.6
Examples of molecular and structural formulae for some common chemicals

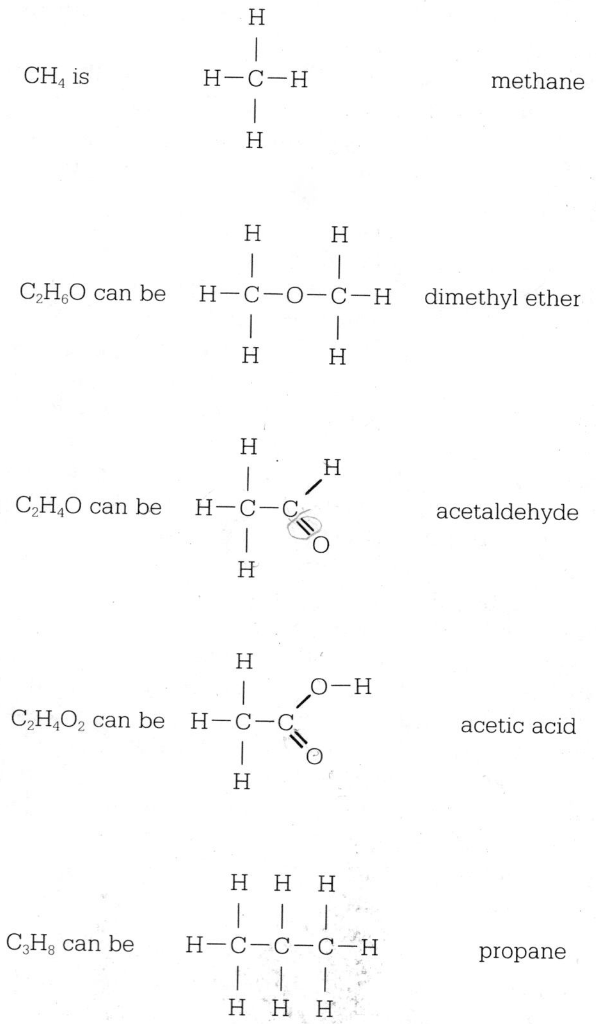

CH₄ is

H—C—H   methane

C₂H₆O can be   H—C—O—C—H   dimethyl ether

C₂H₄O can be   H—C—C   acetaldehyde

C₂H₄O₂ can be   H—C—C   acetic acid

C₃H₈ can be   H—C—C—C—H   propane

Figure 1.7
Simplified diagrams of structures omit the symbols for carbon and hydrogen and assume bonds that are not drawn are to hydrogen atoms. Recall that each carbon must have four bonds.

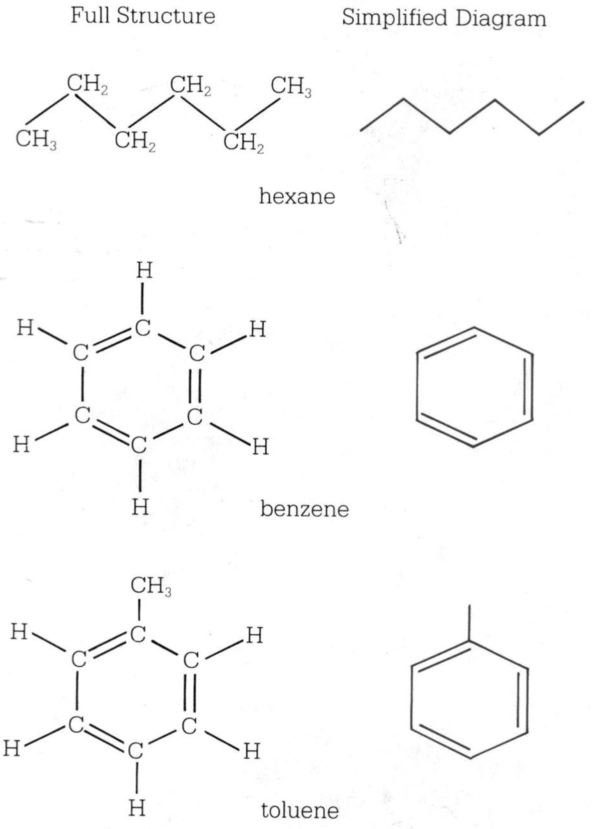

Full Structure   Simplified Diagram

hexane

benzene

toluene

1.5 SHAPES OF MOLECULES

Even though the structural formula adequately represents the bonding between the various atoms in a molecule, it does not show the shape of the molecule. It must be recognized that in most cases molecules are not flat, but fill up space in three dimensions. The four bonds in methane (CH₄) are not all in the same plane, as implied by the structural formula in Figure 1.6. Rather, the four hydrogen atoms bonded to the carbon atom are positioned in space so as to be as far apart as possible. This is achieved if they each occupy an apex of a tetrahedron. The shape of the methane molecule is shown in Figure 1.8.

structural formula. Other simplified diagrammatic representations are also frequently used. You will encounter some of them in later sections or chapters. In most of these, the symbols for carbon and hydrogen atoms and the bonds to the hydrogen atoms are omitted for clarity. Figure 1.7 shows some examples.

Figure 1.8
The tetrahedral shape of methane

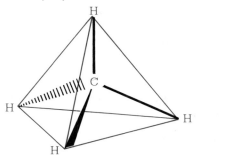

In general, oxygen and sulfur atoms with two single bonds, nitrogen atoms with three single bonds and carbon atoms with four single bonds all have the bonds arranged in tetrahedral shapes (Figure 1.9).

Figure 1.9
Shapes of three simple molecules in three dimensions

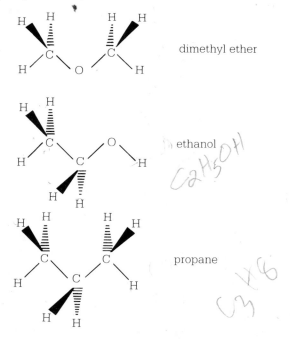

dimethyl ether

ethanol

propane

Molecules that have atoms bonded by double bonds become planar in the vicinity of the double bond. For example, formaldehyde, CH_2O, has the structure shown in Figure 1.10, in which the carbon is approximately at the centre of an equilateral triangle, and the hydrogen and oxygen atoms are at the apexes. Similar flat structures are observed whenever there are C=O, C=N, or C=C bonds in a molecule, as shown in the other examples in Figure 1.10.

Figure 1.10
Examples of molecules that are flat because of a double bond

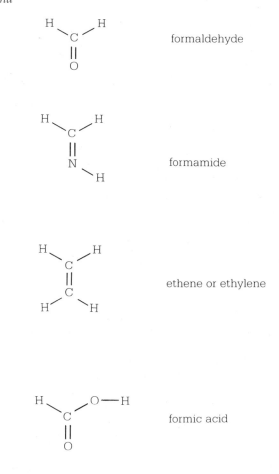

formaldehyde

formamide

ethene or ethylene

formic acid

Triple bonds are rare in biologically important molecules, but when they occur, the molecules are linear in the region of the bond. Hydrogen cyanide (HCN) is a simple example of a linear molecule with a triple bond between the carbon atom and the nitrogen atom.

The geometry of molecules plays an important role in most chemical reactions, and particularly so in biological systems. As you will see in later chapters, the shape of molecules can make all the difference in the world. For example, pheromones are molecules emitted by certain insects to attract mates. If the shape is right, the molecule can bind to receptors in the insect's antennae and be recognized. If the shape is wrong, the receptor will not notice its presence. Thus the shape of the pheromone ensures that mates of the correct species of insects are attracted.

1.6 PHYSICAL TRANSFORMATIONS OF SUBSTANCES

Substances can exist either as solids, liquids, or gases. Solids are characterized by the property that they resist deformation when pressure is applied. This implies that the intermolecular interactions in solids are sufficiently strong that the applied forces cannot pull the molecules apart. This is typical of substances that consist of large molecules, of salts where intermolecular forces are dominated by strong attraction among the charged ions, and of molecules that can pack into crystal structures very easily. Liquids are different from solids in that the molecules can easily slide by each other when pressure is applied, and the entire structure deforms. The intermolecular forces are still strong enough to keep the molecules in close contact—their separation is smaller than their molecular radius. Gases are different from liquids in that they are much less dense. In the gas state, molecules move freely in space over long distances without encountering other gas molecules. Their separation is much greater than their size.

If enough heat is supplied to a solid, it will *melt* to form a liquid. This is an example of a phase transition. If heat is removed, the liquid will re-form the solid. Liquids can *vaporize* to form the gas. The reverse process is called *condensation*. The process whereby a solid transforms directly into the gas without melting is called *sublimation*. Examples of this are easily observed in cold, dry climates (for example, in the Rocky Mountains) where the snow frequently sublimes rather than melts.

Intermolecular interactions can also be broken if in the process other more favourable physical bonds can be formed. For example, when ethanol is added to water, the two liquids mix completely. This indicates a disruption of the physical bonds among ethyl alcohol molecules and among water molecules. These disruptions require energy, which is provided by the favourable cross-interactions of ethanol molecules with water molecules. *Miscibility* of liquids therefore is determined by the balance of the intermolecular interactions among like and unlike molecules. Two liquids are immiscible if the attractions of like molecules are greater than those of unlike molecules. These concepts of miscibility are important for understanding the formation of membranes and will be encountered again in Chapter 4.

Miscibility can be viewed as solubility of one liquid in another. Solubility of solids in liquids is determined

by exactly the same principles. If the attractive interactions between the solvent molecules and the solute molecules are large enough, they can overcome the attractive interactions between the solute molecules in the solid, allowing the solid to dissolve.

1.7 CHEMICAL TRANSFORMATIONS OF MOLECULES: REACTIONS

Chemical reactions are processes in which the structure or bonding of molecules changes. This may occur in three ways:

1. by transfer of electrons between molecules in reduction and oxidation reactions;

2. by transfer of protons between molecules in acid–base reactions; or

3. by transfer of atoms between molecules in breaking and making chemical bonds.

It has been estimated that 40 percent of all chemical reactions occur by transfer of electrons, another 40 percent by transfer of protons, and only about 20 percent by transfer of atoms or groups of atoms exclusively. Nevertheless, most reactions are in fact combinations of these three types of processes, and the classification is merely for convenience in the discussion of them.

Reductions and Oxidations

The removal of an electron from an atom or a molecule is called an **oxidation**. This term arises from the observation that adding oxygen to a molecule has the same effect as removing electrons from the affected bonds. For example, adding oxygen to the hydrogen molecule to form water has the effect of drawing the electrons further away from the hydrogen atoms to make the polarized bonds in the water molecule. The reverse process of adding an electron to an atom or a molecule is a **reduction**.

Electrons are highly reactive and do not exist for long periods of time as isolated entities. When an electron is removed from one molecule, it is immediately transferred to another. Consequently, oxidations and reductions always occur simultaneously. You cannot have one without the other. Reactions involving transfer of electrons are frequently called **redox reactions**. The equations in Figure 1.11 show some examples of separate oxidation and reduction processes and of a few redox reactions.

Figure 1.11
Electrons are used *in reductions and released in oxidations, but are transferred in redox reactions.*

Reductions
$$Cl_2 + 2e^- \longrightarrow 2Cl^-$$
$$O_2 + 4H^+ + 4e^- \longrightarrow 2H_2O$$

Oxidations
$$H_2 \longrightarrow 2H^+ + 2e^-$$
$$Na \longrightarrow Na^+ + e^-$$

Redox Reactions
$$Na + H_2O \longrightarrow Na^+ + HO^- + \tfrac{1}{2}H_2$$
$$2H_2 + O_2 \longrightarrow 2H_2O$$
$$CH_4 + O_2 \longrightarrow CH_2O + H_2O$$

Some of the best known redox reactions are those involved in combustion reactions in which molecular oxygen reacts with a molecule to form the fully oxygenated compounds such as carbon dioxide, nitrogen dioxide, sulfur dioxide, and water (Figure 1.12). In these types of reactions, oxygen is being reduced while the carbon, nitrogen, sulfur, and hydrogen atoms are being oxidized.

A specific example is the combustion of propane in a gas-operated barbecue. Here, propane reacts with oxygen to form carbon dioxide and water:

$$CH_3CH_2CH_3 + 5O_2 \longrightarrow 3CO_2 + 4H_2O$$

This balanced chemical equation tells us that in the reactants, for every mole of propane oxidized, five moles of oxygen are reduced, giving a product mixture of three moles of carbon dioxide and four moles of

water. Most importantly, the reaction releases a lot of energy, 2050 kJ to be exact. An average propane container for a barbecue contains 10 kg or just over 200 mol of propane. In theory, this quantity of propane, when burnt, can release more than 400 000 kJ of energy, which is sufficient to heat 40 000 steaks to an average temperature of 125°C. Of course, much of the heat is wasted in the barbecue — it literally disappears into the surrounding air.

As you can see, burning propane in a flame produces *heat* and the rather harmless carbon dioxide gas and water vapour. Propane is therefore useful for cooking and heating purposes. In recent years, it has become more and more popular to use propane in the combustion engine of cars. In this case, a large fraction of the energy is used to do *work*, namely, to move the car. If all the 400 000 kJ of energy from burning 10 kg of propane could be used to produce work, it could move a 2 t car a distance of 2000 km. However, since the engine is not perfectly efficient, and since we have to overcome friction with the air and the road, the actual travel distance would be much less.

All living matter can be viewed as combustion engines. In cells, nutrients such as sugars are oxidized in a series of controlled redox reactions in which the energy is harnessed and stored in the chemical bonds of special molecules. In a series of similarly controlled chemical redox reactions, the energy from the sun is captured in photosynthetic plants and stored in the form of reduced carbon compounds such as the sugars. The combustion of the sugar glucose is capable of producing about 2800 kJ of energy for every mole that is reacted:

$$C_6H_{12}O_6 + 6O_2 \longrightarrow 6CO_2 + 6H_2O$$

Figure 1.12
Combustion reactions correspond to burning the chemical in pure oxygen, thereby producing carbon dioxide, water, nitrogen dioxide, and sulfur dioxide.

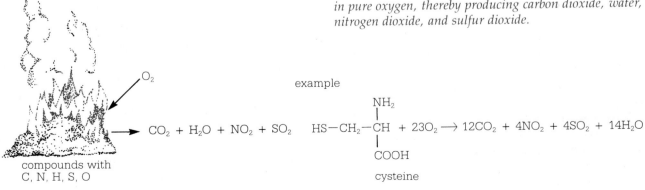

$$O_2$$
$$CO_2 + H_2O + NO_2 + SO_2$$
compounds with
C, N, H, S, O

example

$$\underset{\text{cysteine}}{\overset{\displaystyle NH_2}{HS-CH_2-\underset{\displaystyle COOH}{CH}}} + 23O_2 \longrightarrow 12CO_2 + 4NO_2 + 4SO_2 + 14H_2O$$

The reverse process corresponds to photosynthesis in which carbon dioxide is utilized to produce glucose in plants. The details of these essential biological processes will be considered in Chapters 5 to 9.

Acid–Base Reactions

A molecule from which a proton is easily removed is called an **acid**. A molecule which readily binds a proton is a **base**. Water is unique in that it can react both as an acid and as a base. Hydrochloric acid is a *strong acid* relative to water so that when the two are mixed the following reaction occurs:

$$H-Cl + H_2O \longrightarrow Cl^- + H_3O^+$$

A proton has been transferred from the hydrochloric acid to the oxygen atom in water. The resulting cation, H_3O^+, is called the *hydronium ion*. There is no molecule of hydrochloric acid left. In contrast, acetic acid is a *weak acid*, which can donate a proton to water, but the reaction progresses only slightly:

$$CH_3COO-H + H_2O \longrightarrow CH_3COO^- + H_3O^+$$

Even though the equation of the reaction is written in the same way as in the case of hydrochloric acid, only a small fraction of the acetic acid molecules in the solution actually lose their proton. In both these reactions, the water is the proton acceptor, in other words, it reacts as the base.

Molecules containing nitrogen atoms with three single bonds are the most common proton acceptors in biological systems. For example, methyl amine reacts with water as follows:

$$CH_3NH_2 + HO-H \longrightarrow CH_3NH_3^+ + HO^-$$

Here water has acted as a proton donor (an acid) in the transfer of a proton to the nitrogen atom. Amines are *weak bases* in the same sense that acetic acid is a weak acid—the reaction does not go to completion.

Mixtures of weak acids and weak bases are common in biological systems. For example, carboxylic acids, of which acetic acid is an example, will react completely with amines, such as methyl amine, to form the corresponding ions:

$$CH_3COO-H + CH_3NH_2 \longrightarrow CH_3COO^- + CH_3NH_3^+$$

Since water can act both as an acid and a base, water molecules can react with one another to form a mixture of hydronium ions and hydroxide ions:

$$HO-H + H_2O \longrightarrow HO^- + H_3O^+$$

This reaction between water molecules is extremely important because it controls the final concentration of hydronium ions in an *aqueous solution* (solution in water). Water is both a weak base and a weak acid, so the reaction does not proceed to completion. In fact, only one in ten million molecules of pure water will react in this way.

The concentration of hydronium ions in aqueous solutions $\left(\dfrac{c}{H_3O^+}\right)$ can vary over at least 14 orders of magnitude. Strong acids produce very high hydronium ion concentrations, easily one or more moles per litre of solution. Strong bases reduce the concentration of hydronium ions by forming hydroxide ions which react with hydronium ions to yield water (the reverse of the reaction shown above). The hydronium ion concentration can be reduced to below 10^{-14} mol/L. Because of the very small numbers involved, it is convenient to introduce a scale for describing the hydronium ion concentration with numbers ranging between 0 and 14. This scale, called the **pH scale** (from *power* of *Hydronium* ion concentration), is defined as the negative of the logarithm to the base ten of the numerical value of the hydronium ion concentration, provided that this is expressed in units of mol/L.

$$pH = -\log_{10}\left(\frac{cH_3O^+}{mol/L}\right)$$

At first sight this may seem an awkward definition, but it serves two purposes. First it expresses the hydronium ion concentrations as small positive numbers which are easier to communicate and remember. Second, it makes all concentration measurements relative to a standard concentration of mol/L. For example, a 10^{-8} mol/L solution has a $pH = -\log\left(\dfrac{10^{-8}\ mol/L}{mol/L}\right) = 8$ (note that there are no units within the logarithm). It should be clear that solutions with high hydronium ion concentrations have low pH values. We usually classify solutions as acidic if the pH is less than about 6, as neutral if the pH is between 6 and 8, and as basic if the pH is greater than about 8. The pH of the solutions inside cells and in tissues is close to 7, so these solutions are neutral. Low pH values (as low as 2) are found in the stomach where acids are present for digestion.

Breaking and Making Bonds

The redox reaction discussed earlier, in which propane is oxidized by oxygen to produce carbon dioxide and water, clearly involves breaking all the bonds in the propane molecule and making new bonds with oxygen atoms. This is an extreme example of rearrangements of bonds during a reaction. Most chemical reactions proceed with the breaking and making of only one or two bonds. A simple example is the oxidation of ethanol to ethanal and then to acetic acid:

$$2CH_3CH_2OH + O_2 \longrightarrow 2CH_3CHO + H_2O + \tfrac{1}{2}O_2$$
$$\longrightarrow 2CH_2COOH + H_2O$$

There are two important classes of reactions which do not involve reductions or oxidations. These are as follows:—

1. **condensation reactions** in which a molecule of water is removed

$$CH_3O-H + HO-CH_3 \longrightarrow CH_3-O-CH_3 + H_2O$$

2. **hydrolysis reactions** in which a molecule of water is added

$$CH_3-O-CH_3 + H_2O \longrightarrow CH_3O-H + HO-CH_3$$

It will become evident in later chapters that these reactions are extremely important for the functioning of living organisms. The condensation reactions permit assembly of small molecules into larger units. This type of reaction is the basis of the biosynthesis of macromolecules such as proteins and nucleic acids (Chapter 2). Hydrolysis reactions are important in breaking apart the macromolecules into smaller molecules during metabolism.

Condensation reactions require energy from some source to proceed to any appreciable extent. It is therefore costly to organisms to produce macromolecules. On the other hand, hydrolysis reactions always produce energy. Living organisms take advantage of this as a means of *storing* energy as chemical energy. Central to this process is the use of the complex molecules **adenosine diphosphate (ADP)** and **adenosine triphosphate (ATP)** as sinks and sources of chemical energy. The condensation of a free phosphate group (often called (P) for inorganic phosphate) to the phosphate group in ADP produces ATP (Figure 1.13). This requires about 30 kJ per mol of ATP formed. The

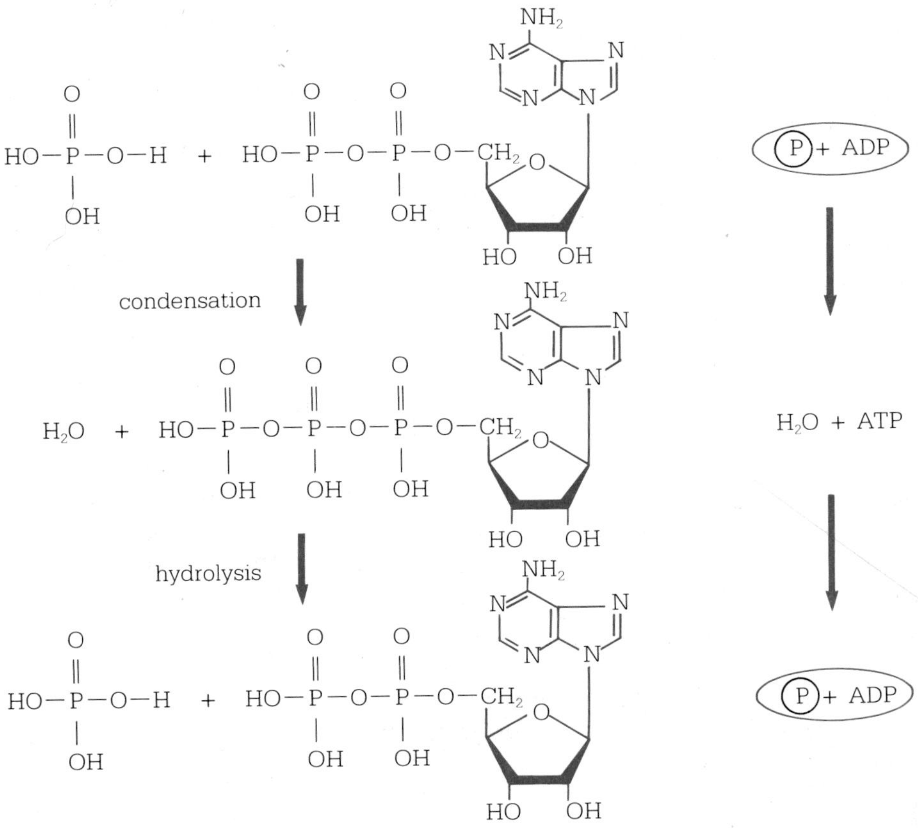

Figure 1.13
Condensation of phosphate (P) and ADP gives ATP. Hydrolysis of ATP yields phosphate and ADP. In this figure, the phosphates are shown as the corresponding acids for simplicity.

hydrolysis of ATP produces ADP and free phosphate molecules, which releases about 30 kJ of energy per mole of ATP hydrolyzed. Living organisms use ATP as a molecule in which to store energy for use in other reactions or at other times. The production and utilization of ATP is discussed in detail in Chapters 5 to 9.

1.8   INTERCONVERSION OF ENERGY: THERMODYNAMICS

Energy is a measure of the potential to do work. If a rock is sitting at the top of a hill, it has the potential to do work when it falls down the hill. If a string is attached between the rock and a small wagon that has a smaller mass, the wagon will be pulled to the top of the hill when the rock rolls down the other side (Figure 1.14). The rock has **potential energy** because it is in a gravitational potential, being attracted to the earth.

Figure 1.14
A rock on a hill has the potential to do work as it falls. Here the work involves pulling the wagon up the hill.

Chemical energy is similarly a measure of the potential of molecules to do work when they undergo chemical reactions. We have already mentioned that redox reactions such as combustions can release a lot of energy. In fact, you saw that the energy could be used to provide heat, as in the barbecue, or to do work, as in a car.

Although we place different labels on energy — mechanical energy, electrical energy, chemical energy, nuclear energy and so on—depending on the source, they are in fact different forms of the same thing. Energy is a quantity which has no absolute value, and we only know it exists because we can see the effects of *changes in energy* in the form of heat or work, or a combination of both. It makes no sense to say that the rock on top of the hill contains a specific amount of energy. If it rolls down the hill to the right, it can roll further than if it rolls to the left. It can therefore do more work if it rolls one way than another. *Relative* to the bottom of the hill on the right side, the rock has more energy—more potential to do work—than relative to the bottom of the hill on the left side. It is in fact only relative energies that are important.

This is true for chemical reaction as well. We cannot state a specific amount of energy that one mole of ATP has. We can only say that *relative* to one mole of ADP and one mole of phosphate ions, one mole of ATP and one mole of water have 30 kJ more energy. Therefore, if one mole of ATP is hydrolyzed, 30 kJ must be released to the surroundings.

From many years of experience, scientists have observed that any process that releases or absorbs energy does so as either heat or work. If the process is isolated so that it can neither transmit heat nor do work, then there cannot be a change in energy. This principle of conservation of energy is also called the *first law of thermodynamics* (Figure 1.15).

When a rock is pushed from the bottom of a hill to the top of the hill, a certain amount of work must be performed. If the rock is then allowed to fall freely, no work is done, and the energy is released as heat when the rock hits the bottom. In the process, all the work performed to push up the rock has been converted into heat. Now imagine that you were clever enough to capture all the heat produced during the fall of the rock. You could use this heat to produce steam and use the steam to do work, raising the rock again. However, it is impossible to convert all the heat into work, so that the rock can only be lifted part of the way up again (Figure 1.16). Some of the heat available must be used to raise the temperature of the hill and the rock while it is being lifted. Even though the total energy of the rock and the hill is the same as it was before the rock fell down the hill, the *quality* of the energy in terms of doing work is less. The principle that the quality of the energy degrades is called the *second law of thermodynamics*.

Figure 1.15
The change in energy is equal to the work done (pushing the rock up the hill) plus the heat released (when the rock hits the bottom). If the two sides of the hill are at the same elevation, the change in potential energy of the rock is zero.

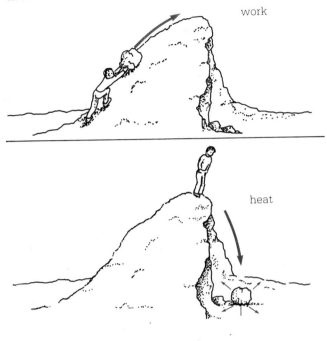

Figure 1.16
Even if all the heat released when the rock falls can be captured and used to do work, it cannot raise the rock to its original elevation. The quality of the energy to do work has decreased.

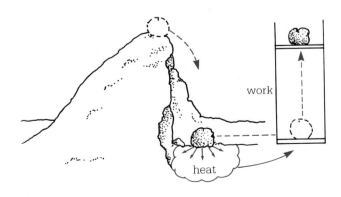

1.9 RATES OF REACTIONS

Although it may be energetically favourable for a chemical reaction to occur, it may proceed very slowly. The rate of a chemical reaction is measured as the increase in the number of moles of products per litre per second, or as the negative of the decrease in the number of moles of reactants per litre per second. The rate of reaction is always a positive number.

When a chemical reaction takes place, it always requires a certain amount of energy to start it. This is the **activation energy**. It corresponds to the energy needed to get a rock to start rolling down a hill, which is the energy needed to overcome the initial friction between the rock and the earth it sits on.

If the activation energy for a chemical reaction is large, then it is hard for the reaction to proceed. Again, you can use the analogy of snooker balls with sticky surfaces. In this case, the chemical reaction corresponds to the cue ball hitting a pair of attached snooker balls and separating them. Suppose that you can shoot the cue ball once every second, so that there is a collision between the cue ball and a pair of snooker balls once every second. The rate of the chemical reaction corresponds to the number of pairs of snooker balls separated per second (which is a number necessarily less than or equal to one). If the glue holding the snooker balls together is weak, almost every collision would successfully separate the pair, and the chemical reaction is fast. If the glue is strong, then only one of many collisions would have enough energy to separate the pair, and the reaction is slow. The strength of the glue represents the activation energy of the chemical reaction — the greater it is the slower the reaction.

It is possible to speed up chemical reactions by increasing the temperature — hitting the cue ball harder on average—but that is not possible in biological systems, where the temperature is strictly controlled in most cases (for example, the temperature of the human body is 37°C). To enhance the rates of chemical reactions, living organisms use **catalysts**, which decrease the activation energy (Figure 1.17). In the snooker balls analogy above, the catalyst will be something that can make the surface less sticky.

Biological catalysts are in almost all cases proteins. By interacting with the small molecules of the reactant, these proteins make the reaction happen with a higher frequency. They are called **enzymes**. Examples of enzymes will be discussed in Chapter 2.

Figure 1.17
The energy barrier to a reaction—the activation energy—
is reduced in the presence of a catalyst.

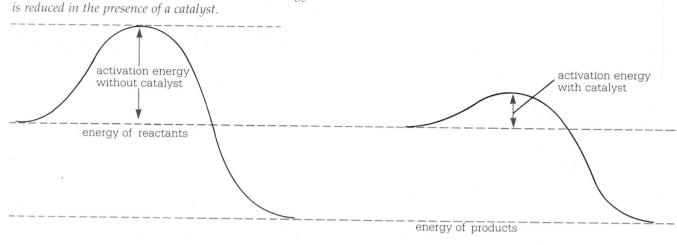

1.10 WATER: THE CHEMICAL BASIS OF LIFE

Water is a unique chemical. Its special properties have shaped the way life has evolved to the point that it is hard to picture living organisms in an environment without water. Living matter consists of mostly water, and many of the physical properties of organisms are in fact those of water.

Properties of Water

Solvent Properties of Water
Ions and polar molecules readily dissolve in water. Since many of the most important biological molecules are either charged or highly polar (Chapter 2), they are soluble in water. The exceptions are the lipids, which form special structures as membranes without which life could not have evolved as self-contained replicating units (Chapter 4).

Thermal Properties of Water
It takes a great deal of energy—almost 75 J—to heat one mole of water up by one degree Celsius. The large amount of water in an organism absorbs or releases heat without drastically changing the temperature of the organism. The organism is therefore able to maintain a steady temperature.

Water also readily transmits heat from one region to another. Large variations in temperature within an organism are therefore unlikely.

The intermolecular interactions of water molecules are dominated by strong hydrogen bonding. These interactions are so strong that in spite of its very small molar mass, water has relatively high melting and boiling points. Most importantly, there is a large difference (100°C) between the melting and boiling temperatures. Living organisms are found in the wide range of temperatures from freezing, such as in the arctic climates, to boiling, such as in hot springs in Banff, Alberta.

The strong intermolecular attractions also mean that it requires a lot of energy, in the form of heat, to evaporate water. This is vital for temperature regulation in an organism. For many organisms, evaporation of water from the surface is an important mechanism for keeping cool on hot days. Examples include perspiration in humans and panting in dogs.

Cohesive Properties of Water
Again because of the remarkably strong intermolecular attractions between water molecules, they are **cohesive**. Since water forms strong hydrogen bonds with other polar or charged substances, it can also be very **adhesive**. The net result is that water can move through fine pores and crevices even against gravitational forces. The movement of water by the process of capillary action is essential to the movement of water up the stems of plants and trees.

Density of water
Water has a density of 1 kg/L at 4°C. At the freezing point, the density of water is slightly less than 1 kg/L. Water is one of the few substances for which the

density of the solid is less than that of the liquid. While most liquids when compressed become solid, water does not. In fact, if you put pressure on ice, it melts. This is probably important for the existence of the oceans. As you may realize, the pressure increases at increasing depths in the oceans at the rate of about 100 kPa for every 10 m. If water were like most other substances, it would not require very deep oceans for solidification to occur. There probably would not be a body of water deeper than a few hundred metres! Furthermore, the fact that ice melts as pressure is applied, makes it possible for water to remain liquid at the depth of several thousand metres even though the temperature could be less than 0°C. Considering that life probably originated in the oceans, and that by far the largest amount of living matter is present in the oceans today, this peculiar property of water is quite significant.

CHAPTER SUMMARY

One quest in modern biology is to understand the processes of life at the molecular level. We must, therefore, begin by appreciating that molecules consist of one or more atoms bonded through interactions of their valence electrons. The number of chemical bonds that a given atom can form depends on the number of valence electrons: hydrogen forms one bond, oxygen two, and carbon four. The molecular formula shows the composition of a molecule and the structural formula shows both its composition and chemical bonding.

Molecules interact with one another through physical bonding such as hydrogen bonds and hydrophobic effects. These interactions play a role in determining the shapes of molecules as well as their physical state. Strong intermolecular attractions are present in liquids and solids, whereas weak interactions permit molecules to escape into the gas phase.

The foundation for life processes is the transformation of molecules through chemical reactions. These may, in simple terms, be considered as redox reactions in which electrons are transferred, as acid–base reactions in which protons are transferred, or bond breaking and making in which groups of atoms are transferred. In actual fact, most reactions are combinations of these. Two extremely important reactions in biological systems are the condensation and hydrolysis reactions, one being the reverse of the other.

All chemical processes are accompanied by transfer of energy between the reacting molecules or between the reacting molecules and the surroundings. For example, a hydrolysis reaction results in products with overall less energy content, and heat is transferred to the surroundings. The rate at which a chemical reaction occurs depends on its activation energy. The lower the activation energy, the faster the reaction. In biological systems, the activation energy of many chemical reactions is lowered significantly by enzymes. These are special proteins which act as catalysts for the reactions.

The unique features of water for life include its properties as a solvent, its ability to act as both an acid and a base, its thermal properties, its cohesive properties, and its physical properties.

Objectives

Having completed this chapter, you should be able to do the following:

1. Explain the difference between molecules, atoms, elements, and isotopes.
2. Describe the differences between chemical and physical bonding, give examples of each type, and explain the physical basis on which the bonds of various types depend.
3. Classify chemical reactions according to whether there is a transfer of electrons, protons, or other atoms.
4. Describe the difference between oxidation and reduction.
5. Define an acid and a base and give examples of each.
6. Explain the concept of pH and use it in calculations.

7. Give examples of hydrolysis and condensation reactions.
8. Describe the concepts of heat and work, and explain why it is the relative energy of reactants and products which are important.
9. Explain what is meant by the rate of a reaction and how it depends on the activation energy.
10. Describe some of the unique features of water as a biological fluid.

Vocabulary

molecule
atom
element
electron
proton
neutron
atomic number
atomic mass
isotope
ion
mole
intramolecular force
chemical bonding
intermolecular force
physical bonding
single bond

valence electron
double bond
triple bond
covalent bond
cation
anion
electronegativity
polarized
electronegative
ionic bond
hydrogen bond
hydrophobic
molecular formula
structural formula
oxidation
reduction

redox reaction
acid
base
pH scale
condensation reaction
hydrolysis reaction
adenosine diphosphate (ADP)
adenosine triphosphate (ATP)
potential energy
activation energy
catalyst
enzyme
cohesive
adhesive

Review Questions

1. How is an atom different from an element ?
2. Carbon consists of the three isotopes carbon-12, carbon-13 and carbon-14. State the number of electrons, neutrons, and protons in each.
3. How does the atomic mass relate to the atomic number?
4. Explain the relation between a molecule and a mole of molecules.
5. Calculate the molar mass of each of the following compounds:
   (a) acetic acid
   (b) ethanol
   (c) water
   (d) propane
6. How does physical bonding differ from chemical bonding?
7. How do single, double, and triple bonds arise?
8. What is the distinction between a covalent and an ionic bond?

9. (a) Calculate the molar masses of water and hydrogen sulfide.
   (b) Explain why water is a liquid while hydrogen sulfide is a gas at room temperature.
10. Draw all the possible structural formulae corresponding to each molecular formula, keeping in mind that each carbon atom forms four bonds, each oxygen atom two bonds, and each hydrogen atom one bond.
    (a) C_3H_6O
    (b) C_4H_{10}
11. Define oxidation and reduction.
12. Define an acid and a base.
13. Write equations for two examples of each type of reaction:
    (a) condensation reaction
    (b) hydrolysis reaction
14. Describe how a catalyst enhances the rate of a chemical reaction.

Advanced Questions

1. Trichloroacetic acid is a stronger acid than acetic acid. Account for this observation in terms of polarization of bonds in the two molecules.

2. For each of the following, make a molecular model. Then draw, as carefully as possible, the three-dimensional structure of each molecule in the shape you think is most likely. Keep in mind that the largest groups try to be as far apart as possible.
   (a) propane
   (b) ethanol
   (c) acetic acid
   (d) formaldehyde

3. Find, in appropriate resource materials, the boiling points of methanol, propanol, propane, and hexane. Calculate the molar mass of each compound. For each of the following pairs, compare the boiling points and the molar masses, and explain why one boils at a lower temperature than the other.
   (a) methanol and propanol
   (b) propanol and propane
   (c) propane and hexane

4. Classify each of the following reactions as redox, acid–base, condensation, or hydrolysis reaction.
   (a) $NaOH \longrightarrow Na^+ + HO^-$
   (b) $Mg + 2H_2O \longrightarrow Mg^{2+} + 2HO^- + H_2$
   (c) $CH_3COOCH_3 + H_2O \longrightarrow CH_3COOH + CH_3OH$
   (d) $CH_3NH_2 + HCOOH \longrightarrow CH_3NHOCH + H_2O$
   (e) $H_2NCH_2COOH \longrightarrow H_3N^+CH_2COO^-$

5. (a) Methane, propane, and hexane are all hydrocarbons which can react with oxygen in combustion reactions. These reactions can be represented by the general equation:

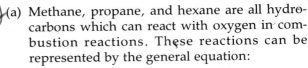

$$CnH_{2n+2} + \left(\frac{3n+1}{2}\right)O_2 \longrightarrow n\, Co_2 + (n+1)\, H_2O$$

where n represents the number of carbon atoms in each molecule of the hydrocarbon. Write the equation of the combustion reaction for each compound.

   (b) The energy released in the combustion is 804 kJ per mole of methane, 2050 kJ per mole of propane, and 3867 kJ per mole of hexane. Which fuel, methane, propane, or hexane, is more efficient for use in an automobile, where only the fuel needs to be carried? Which is more efficient in a rocket where both fuel and oxygen need to be carried? (Hint: Calculate the energy released in each reaction per kilogram of hydrocarbon and per kilogram of reactants including oxygen.)

6. Write a brief essay describing the special properties of water that are relevant to life as we know it.

— dilutes blood stream
— coolant for the body
— can serve a source of oxygen for the body.
— anomalie behavior
— hydrogen bonds (polarized molecules)

CHAPTER 2

BIOLOGICALLY IMPORTANT MOLECULES

Life is a great bundle of little things.

from 'The Professor at the Breakfast Table'
Oliver Wendell Holmes sen., 1859

You seldom see this relative of the poison ivy in North America, yet the juicy, yellow cashew apple is a delicacy in its native Brazil. The more familiar product, the cashew nut, is inside the dark brown shell at the tip of the fruit. You cannot buy cashew nuts in the shell since it contains an oil which is highly irritating and slightly poisonous. The oil is driven off through heating before the nut is extracted, and is recovered for use in paints or varnish. This is but one example of the complexity and ingenuity of nature. It offers an attractive fruit to ensure that animals collect and eat it, thereby carrying the fruit and seed away from the parent plant. Yet, the seed is protected in its unattractive shell from being eaten. Only through the inventiveness of humans, is it possible for us to enjoy the nut. It is interesting to wonder what prompted the first person to think that inside the repulsive shell there would be a delicious nut.

In this chapter, you will explore the molecules of life. They contain mostly carbon, hydrogen, and oxygen, together with small amounts of nitrogen, phosphorus, and sulfur. The ingenuity of nature reveals itself over and over in the ways these few elements have been utilized to make literally millions of structurally and functionally different molecules. You will see that by using relatively few simple and small molecules in long chains, living organisms are able to make large molecules as varied as silk, hair, rubber, or wood. In fact, the most spectacular large molecule of all, deoxyribonucleic acid, or DNA, is a long chain made up of only four different types of small molecules, yet within the sequence in the chain rests all the genetic information needed for life. The chapter starts with an overview of the characteristic chemical groups and the reactions they undergo in living systems, and continues with a detailed description of the most important large molecules, namely, the carbohydrates, the proteins, and the nucleic acids. The chapter concludes with a discussion of the characteristics of fatty acids and several other interesting vital molecules.

2.1 FUNCTIONAL GROUPS AND THEIR REACTIONS

In all molecules, some bonds are more reactive than others, and are therefore more likely to be involved in chemical transformations. A group of atoms which tend to react in a particular way is collectively called the **functional group** of the molecule (Figure 2.1). It usually also contributes to the chemical or physical properties of the molecule.

Figure 2.1
The alcohol group in ethanol and the carboxylic acid group in acetic acid are examples of functional groups.

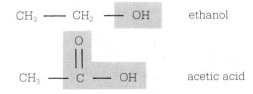

Some of the most important functional groups are listed in Table 2.1 along with selected examples.

Table 2.1   Examples of the Most Important Functional Groups in Biological Systems

NAME	STRUCTURE	EXAMPLE
alcohol	$-\overset{\textstyle\mid}{\underset{\textstyle\mid}{C}}-OH$	CH_3OH methanol
aldehyde	$-\overset{\textstyle O}{\underset{\textstyle H}{\overset{\textstyle \|\|}{C}}}$	CH_3CHO acetaldehyde
ketone	$C-\overset{\textstyle O}{\underset{\textstyle C}{\overset{\textstyle \|\|}{C}}}$	CH_3COCH_3 acetone
carboxylic acid	$-\overset{\textstyle O}{\underset{\textstyle OH}{\overset{\textstyle \|\|}{C}}}$	CH_3CH_2COOH propanoic acid
amine	$-\overset{\textstyle\mid}{\underset{\textstyle\mid}{C}}-NH_2$	CH_3NH_2 methyl amine
thiol (sulfide)	$-\overset{\textstyle\mid}{\underset{\textstyle\mid}{C}}-SH$	$CH_3CH_2CH_2CH_2SH$ butathiol
phosphate	$HO-\overset{\textstyle O}{\underset{\textstyle OH}{\overset{\textstyle \|\|}{P}}}-O-$	$HO-\overset{\textstyle O}{\underset{\textstyle OH}{\overset{\textstyle \|\|}{P}}}-OH$ phosphoric acid

Many molecular properties are frequently dominated by a single functional group which, through reactions such as redox reactions, acid-base reactions, or condensation reactions, can generate new functional groups or linkages between molecules. You have already seen examples of these reactions in Chapter 1. **Alcohols** and **aldehydes** are easily oxidized to the corresponding **carboxylic acid**. For example, ethanol is oxidized to ethanal, which is further oxidized to acetic acid:

$$CH_3CH_2OH + O_2 \longrightarrow$$

$$CH_3CHO + \tfrac{1}{2}O_2 + H_2O \longrightarrow CH_3COOH + 2H_2O$$

The reverse reductions are also possible, and these redox reactions are of basic importance to cellular respiration and photosynthesis, as you will see later in Chapters 5 to 9.

Thiols form **disulfide** linkages upon oxidation.

$$CH_3SH + HSCH_3 \longrightarrow CH_3S-SCH_3 + H_2$$

This, and the reduction in reverse, are very important in cross–linking the individual chains of proteins, thereby generating stable three-dimensional structures.

Double bonds in hydrocarbons are susceptible to both reduction and oxidation. Hydrogenation, the reduction of these hydrocarbons, is important in commercial applications involving fats and oils, which will be described later.

$$CH_3CH{=}CHCH_3 + H_2 \longrightarrow CH_3CH_2CH_2CH_3$$

In biological systems, however, the oxidation is far more important since it acts to break down lipids (Chapter 4) in membranes.

$$CH_3CH{=}CHCH_3 + O_2 \longrightarrow CH_3CHOHCHOHCH_3$$

Carboxylic acid groups are weak acids, relinquishing protons to water to a limited extent only. Correspondingly, amines are weak bases which only accept protons from water to a limited extent (Chapter 1). When these functional groups are found in the same molecule the weak acid and the weak base interact such that there is a proton transfer from the carboxylic acid group to the amine group. This transfer is virtually complete, so that in solutions in water, the predominant species is the doubly charged species.

$$H_2NCH_2COOH \longrightarrow H_3N^+CH_2COO^-$$

This type of ion, containing both a positively charged and a negatively charged ion, is called a *zwitter ion*. Zwitter ions are very common in biologically important molecules.

Condensation reactions can occur whenever a molecule of water can be eliminated. Table 2.2 shows some examples, along with the names of the linkages that are formed. In addition, there are two examples of straight addition reactions, in which a carbon–oxygen bond is formed without the elimination of water or without oxidation. All of these are essential in a variety of biological molecules.

Table 2.2 Selected Examples of Condensation and Addition Reactions

REACTION	LINKAGE FORMED
Condensations	
$CH_3-O-H + H-O-CH_3$	ether $CH_3-O-CH_3 + H_2O$
$CH_3-O-H + H-O-CO-CH_3$	ester $CH_3-O-CO-CH_3 + H_2O$
$CH_3-NH_2 + H-O-CO-CH_3$	amide $CH_3-NH-CO-CH_3 + H_2O$
$CH_3-CO-O-H + H-O-CO-CH_3$	acid anhydride $CH_3-CO-O-CO-CH_3 + H_2O$

Phosphoric condensation:

$$HO-\overset{\overset{O}{\|}}{\underset{\underset{OH}{\|}}{P}}-O-H + H-O-\overset{\overset{O}{\|}}{\underset{\underset{OH}{\|}}{P}}-OH$$

phosphoric anhydride

$$HO-\overset{\overset{O}{\|}}{\underset{\underset{OH}{\|}}{P}}-O-\overset{\overset{O}{\|}}{\underset{\underset{OH}{\|}}{P}}-OH + H_2O$$

Additions

$CH_3-O-H +$ $\overset{O}{\underset{H}{\diagdown}}C-CH_3$ acetal $CH_3-O-\overset{\overset{OH}{|}}{\underset{\underset{H}{|}}{C}}-CH_3$

$CH_3-O-H +$ $\overset{O}{\underset{H_3C}{\diagdown}}C-CH_3$ ketal $CH_3-O-\overset{\overset{OH}{|}}{\underset{\underset{CH_3}{|}}{C}}-CH_3$

2.2 FORMATION OF POLYMERS

A **polymer** is a molecule formed by linking a large number of small molecules of the same type together in long chains or networks. The small molecule units which make up the polymer are called **monomers**.

Molecules with a single functional group are able to link to form a **dimer**. Once the reaction has taken place, the linkage formed will generally not be reactive. Thus one of the prime requirements for the formation of polymers is that each of the monomers must have at least two functional groups. Rubber is one of the simplest polymers found in nature. It consists of repetitive units of five-carbon segments derived from the polymerization of isoprene as shown in Figure 2.2.

Gutta-percha has the identical chemical composition and is also made from isoprenes, but the groups are arranged differently around the double bond as shown in Figure 2.2. Gutta-percha is much harder than rubber and less elastic. It is the material used in making the covering of golf balls.

Figure 2.2
Natural polymers, rubber and gutta-percha are derived from linking of many monomers of isoprene.

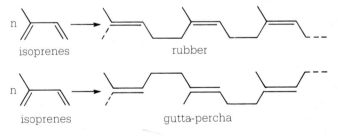

2.3 CARBOHYDRATES

Carbohydrates are molecules whose composition is principally carbon, hydrogen, and oxygen in the proportion 1:2:1. The general molecular formula is $(CH_2O)_n$, where n is some integer. They are more commonly known as *sugars*. All carbohydrates contain a number of alcohol groups and one aldehyde or ketone group. The names of sugars share the ending -ose, as in aldose and ketose which are sugars containing aldehydes and ketones respectively.

Monosaccharides

Monomer units of carbohydrates, called **monosaccharides**, have either five or six carbons and are consequently called either **pentoses** or **hexoses**. The pentoses have five functional groups, namely, four alcohols and one aldehyde or ketone; the hexoses have five alcohols and one aldehyde or ketone. As indicated in Figure 2.3, the terminal carbon at the end containing the aldehyde or the ketone is labelled by the number 1, the next by 2 and so on. This way it is easy to keep track of which of the many functional groups are involved in chemical reactions.

Because rings of five or six carbon atoms are very stable, hexoses easily react *intramolecularly* such that the alcohol on carbon number 5 adds to the aldehyde or ketone. The aldehydes then form six-member rings whereas the ketones form five-member rings (Figure 2.4). The pentoses only form five-member rings.

Figure 2.4 also includes the schematic representation of the cyclic structure in which the symbols for the carbon atoms in the ring, and many of the hydrogen atoms attached to them, are omitted for simplicity. Note also that the numbering of the carbons in the ring is consistent with those in the linear form of the molecule.

Individual monosaccharides, such as glucose, galactose, and mannose, differ only by the relative orientation of some of the alcohol groups. As Figure 2.5

Figure 2.3
General structure of a hexose. This is also an aldose.

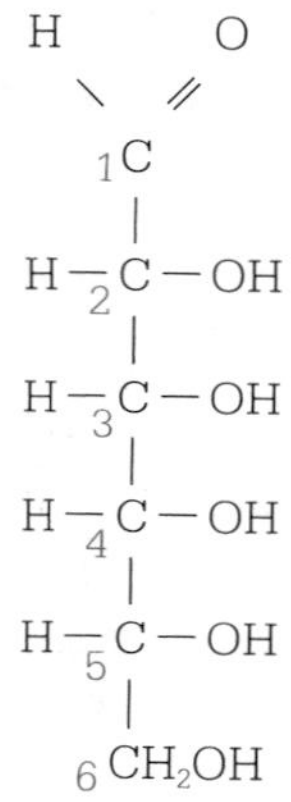

Figure 2.4
Rings with either six or five atoms can be formed from aldoses (a) and ketoses (b) respectively. The schematic drawings at the right show the relative orientations of the −OH groups.

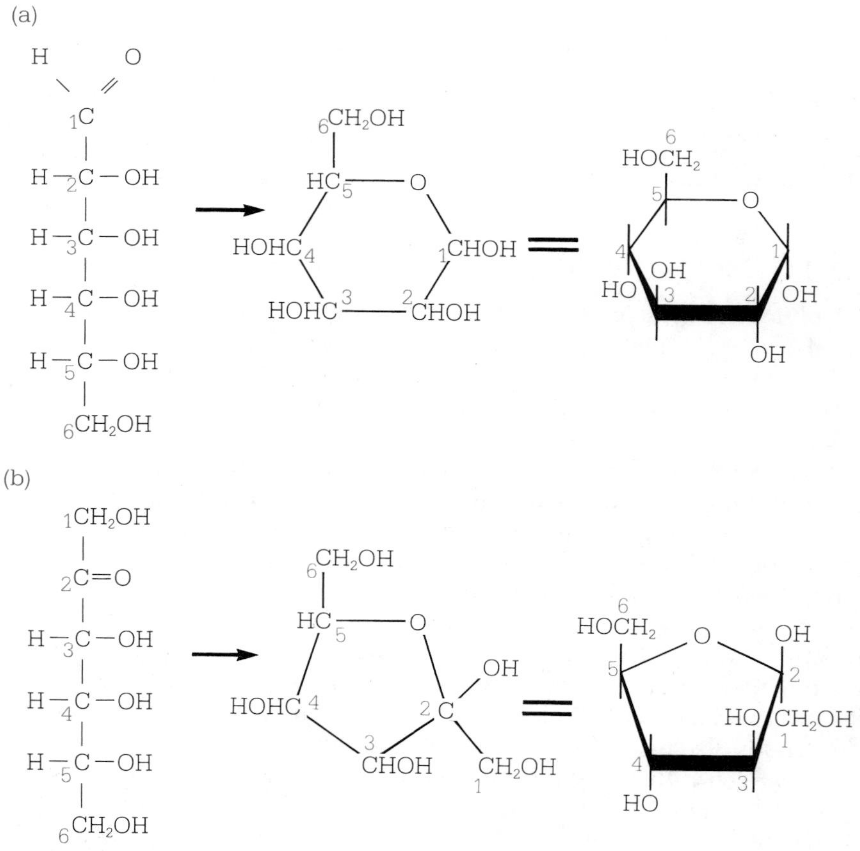

(a)

(b)

Figure 2.5
Structures of glucose (a), mannose (b), and galactose (c).
Notice the relative positions of the alcohol groups in both
sets of structures.

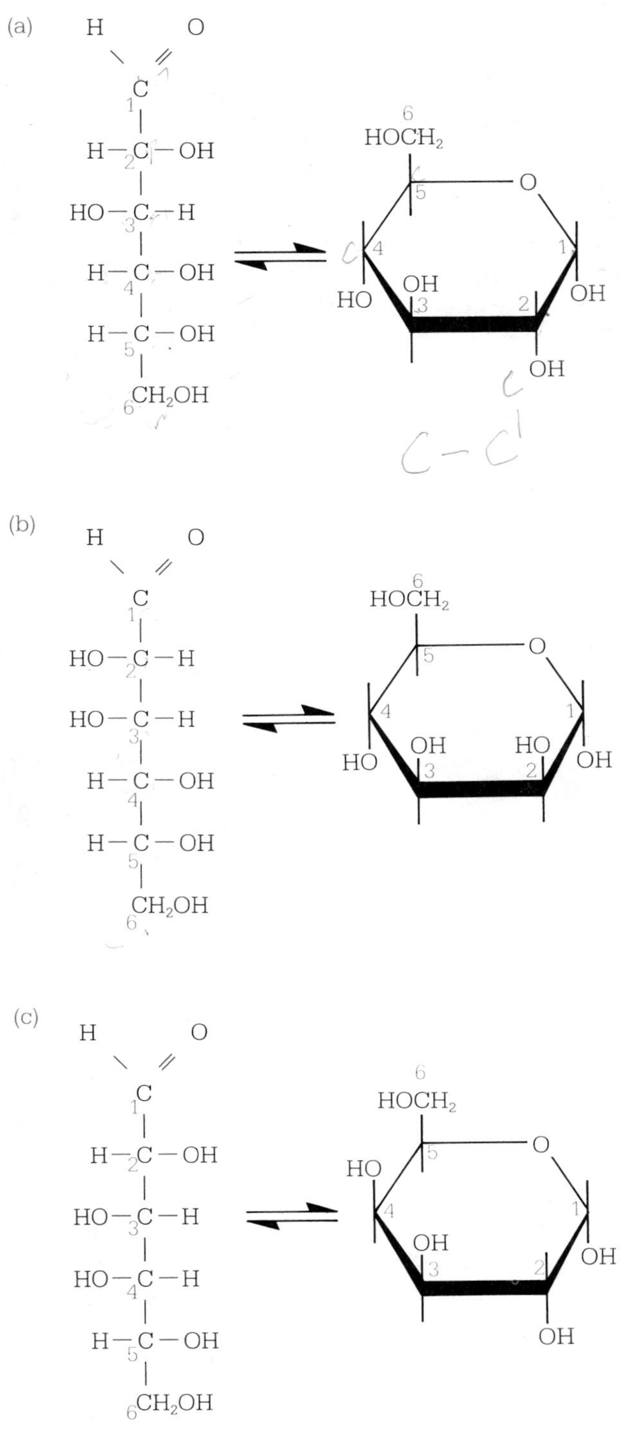

Figure 2.6
Structures of disaccharides sucrose (a) and lactose (b).

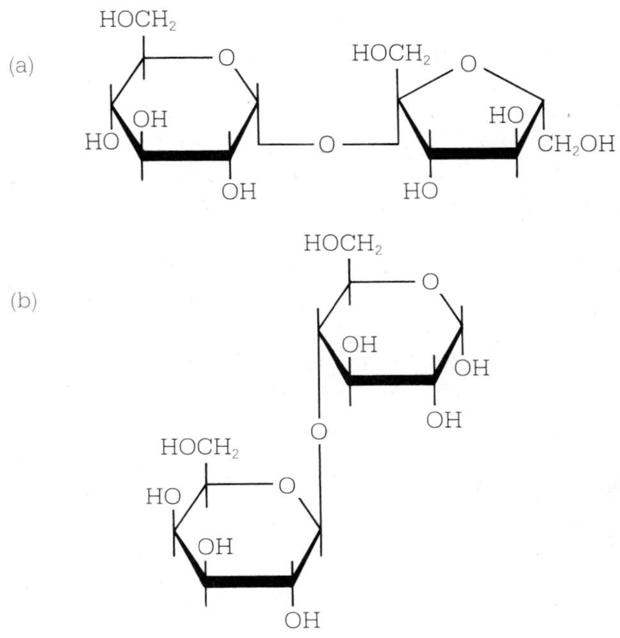

shows, in glucose, only the alcohol on carbon number 3 is on the same side of the ring as the $-CH_2OH$ group. In mannose, the alcohols on carbon numbers 2 and 3 are on the same side of the ring as the $-CH_2OH$ group, while galactose has the alcohols on carbons 3 and 4 on the same side of the ring as the $-CH_2OH$ group.

Disaccharides

Even though monosaccharides tend to form ring structures, or cyclic structures, there are still four or five functional groups available for further reactions. The monosaccharides are therefore able to react further to form **disaccharides** containing two linked sugars, or **polysaccharides** containing a large number of monosaccharides linked together. The most common linkages occur by a condensation reaction between carbon number 1 on one monomer and either carbon 4 or carbon 6 on another. These are referred to as 1–4 linkages or 1–6 linkages respectively.

Disaccharides are very common. The sugar in your kitchen is sucrose, which is formed by linking carbon 1 in a glucose molecule to carbon 2 in a fructose molecule. The dimer formed from the 1–4 linking of galactose to glucose is lactose, the most abundant sugar in milk (Figure 2.6).

Milk and dairy products are valuable components of the human diet because of the high levels of calcium and other minerals. Lactose accounts for almost half the energy potentially available in mammalian milk, but through a quirk of nature it cannot always be utilized. Hydrolysis of the 1–4 linkage between the galactose and the glucose requires an enzyme called lactase—found in the digestive tract. The maximum concentration of this enzyme is found in infants immediately after they are born, and the level tends to decrease to a low level within the first few years of life. This happens because mammals normally do not encounter lactose in the diet after they have been weaned from mother's milk. Mammalian milk is the only known source of lactose except for the flower of the forsythia and a few tropical shrubs.

Most human adults have extremely low levels of lactase in their digestive systems. The undigested lactose reaches the colon where bacterial cultures rapidly utilize this energy source, producing large amounts of carbon dioxide gas (Chapters 5 to 8) which can cause severe intestinal discomfort. Interestingly, a similar problem exists with the sugar raffinose, which is a trisaccharide consisting of galactose, glucose, and fructose. This is a major component of peas and beans, which if consumed in excess can also cause stomach pains.

Throughout the world, the majority of people have low levels of lactase. It was not until fairly recently that milk became part of the diet of anyone but the youngest children.

There are relatively few populations which consume fresh milk regularly, and therefore only few have developed lactose tolerance. Among them are peoples of northern European descent.

In many cultures, people eat a large number of dairy products in which the lactose is already hydrolyzed. These include cheeses, yogurt, and specially treated milk products such as Lacteeze, which have been exposed to bacterial culture of various types. Heated milk, and therefore milk used in cooking and baking, also contains less lactose and presents fewer problems. Still, even people with low lactase levels can frequently drink one or two glasses of milk daily without difficulty.

It is important to recognize that lactose intolerance is not an allergy. A small number of people are allergic to milk, but in these cases, it is the protein constituents of milk which are to blame.

Milk products

Figure 2.7
*Structures of amylose (a) and cellulose (b) differ only by
the orientation of the alcohol group on carbon 1 in each of
the glucose rings.*

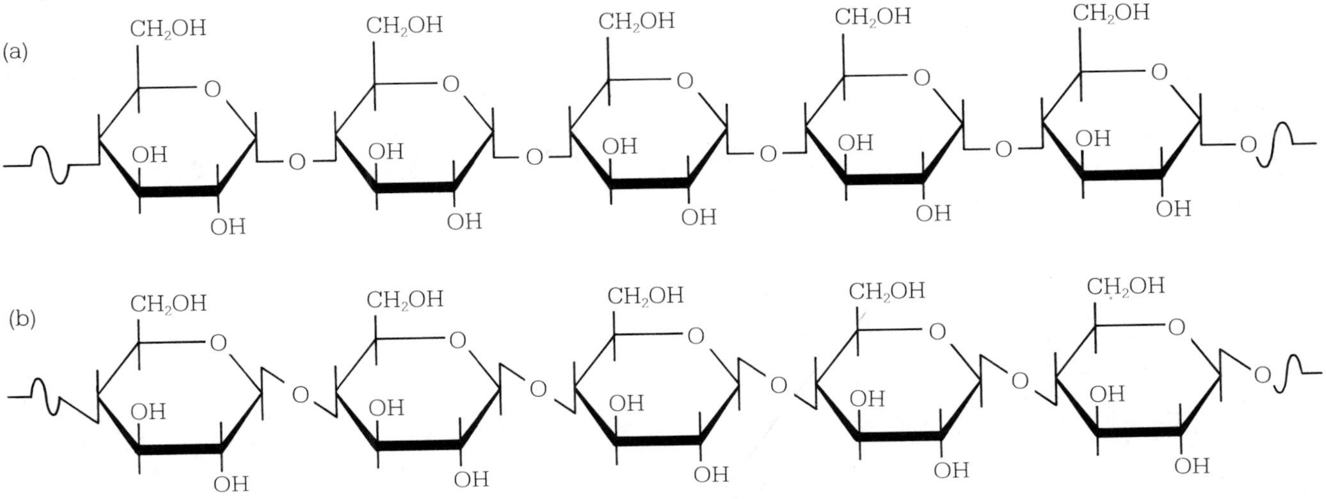

Polysaccharides

Polymers of monosaccharides, called polysaccharides, are formed from the condensation between the alcohols on carbon 1 in one molecule and carbon 4 or 6 in another. They are therefore long chains of 1–4 or 1–6 linked sugars. In some polysaccharides, it is also possible to generate a 1–6 condensation on a monosaccharide unit which already has a 1–4 link to a third sugar. This way branching can occur. The polysaccharides are the only natural polymers that exhibit branching.

Simple polysaccharides serve principally to store energy. Amylose is a long chain of 1–4 linked glucose molecules, while amylopectin is a highly branched polymer of glucose. Starch, as produced from corn or potatoes, is a mixture of amylose and amylopectin. The use of starches in the kitchen to thicken sauces depends on the ability of the amylopectin to form large networks of polysaccharides through hydrogen bonding between the alcohol groups. If the starch contains too much amylose, the sauce will set as a gel rather than remain as a viscous fluid. Bread goes stale when water is lost as the amylose forms stronger and stronger networks through hydrogen bonding.

Cellulose is also a polymer of glucose produced in plant tissue and is of prime importance in generating the plant cell walls. The principal component of wood is cellulose. Curiously, the 1–4 condensation of the glucose in cellulose occurs with the alcohol on carbon 1 on the same side as the —CH$_2$OH group, while that in amylose occurs with the alcohol group on the opposite side (Figure 2.7). This appears to be a trivial difference, but it is the only reason why most mammals cannot digest cellulose and use it directly as a food source. For humans, the cellulose in fruits and vegetables is for the most part wasted as an energy source, but it serves an important function as roughage (fibre) in the diet. Herbivores, which rely entirely on plant material for their energy, frequently contain bacterial cultures in their digestive systems (for example, in the appendix of the rabbit). These bacteria break down the cellulose to the monomeric glucose in a hydrolysis reaction. The glucose can then be absorbed and used by the host animal (see Chapters 5 to 8).

Glycogen is the most common carbohydrate found in animals. It consists of a branched polymer of glucose, similar to amylopectin, but with more highly branched structures.

In addition to these simple polysaccharides, there are a large number of more complex polymers which are usually attached to lipids or proteins. The sugar units in these glycolipids and glycoproteins are typically much more complicated and serve very different functions. In some cases, the polysaccharides serve as stabilizing structures on the surface of cells. The major blood groups (A, B, AB, and O) arise because of different types of polysaccharides on the glycolipids in the membrane of red blood cells.

2.4 AMINO ACIDS AND PROTEINS

Amino Acids

Amino acids contain two reactive functional groups attached to the same carbon atom, namely, an **amine** and a carboxylic acid. In addition, there is a third group, generally referred to simply as the **side chain**, attached to the same carbon. The fourth bond is always formed with a hydrogen atom. The structure of the side chain is different for each amino acid. There are 20 different major amino acids, the structures of which are shown in Figure 2.8. The side chain can be neutral and non-polar, neutral but polar, positively charged, or, negatively charged. Ultimately, the properties of the side chains collectively determine the properties of the protein polymers they form.

The bonds to the carbon in the amino acid bearing the amine, the carboxylic acid, and the side chain are tetrahedral, which means that those groups are pointing in different directions in space as indicated for the methane molecule (see Figure 1.8). The relative orientation of the group is, however, always the same in naturally occurring amino acids.

OPTICAL ACTIVITY

Optical activity arises when a molecule can exist as two structures which are mirror images of each other. Your hands are mirror images of each other, but are in all other respects the same. A tetrahedral molecule with a carbon atom attached to four different groups can exist as two mirror-image structures.

Many of the chemical and physical properties of these mirror-image structures are identical, except for the way they interact with polarized light. They are therefore also called *optical isomers*. When chemists make the compounds in the laboratory, both isomers are formed with equal ease, and the compound exists as a fifty-fifty mixture of the mirror-image compounds. When nature produces those compounds, only a single isomer is formed. For example, in amino acids, only one optical isomer is ever found in nature.

The biological effects of two mirror-image compounds can be quite different. In the mid 1950s, a popular sedative, called thalidomide, was produced chemically as a mixture of the two possible mirror-image compounds, and was sold widely in Europe. A decade later, it was found that the drug was directly responsible for a large number of babies born with congenital defects to mothers who had taken the drug during the early parts of pregnancy. We now know that only one of the two mirror-image forms of thalidomide causes the congenital defects.

The two possible structures of alanine are mirror images of each other—they are optical isomers.

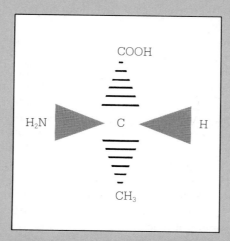

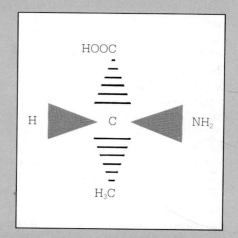

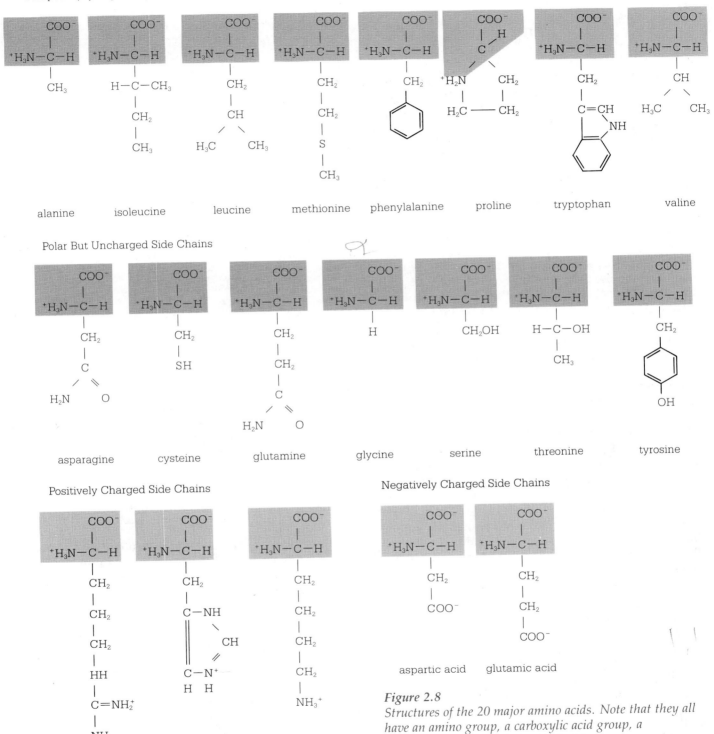

Nonpolar (Hydrophobic) Side Chains

alanine   isoleucine   leucine   methionine   phenylalanine   proline   tryptophan   valine

Polar But Uncharged Side Chains

asparagine   cysteine   glutamine   glycine   serine   threonine   tyrosine

Positively Charged Side Chains

Negatively Charged Side Chains

aspartic acid   glutamic acid

arginine   histidine   lysine

Figure 2.8
Structures of the 20 major amino acids. Note that they all have an amino group, a carboxylic acid group, a hydrogen, and a side chain attached to the same carbon atom.

Figure 2.9
The amide linkage is formed by condensation of a carboxylic acid and an amine. Note that the resulting molecule still has a free carboxylic acid and a free amine.

Figure 2.10
Protein shape is determined by the sequence of amino acids, the formation of a chain, the folding of the chain, and the interaction of different chains.

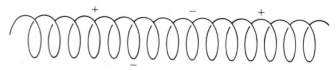

(a) primary structure = sequence of amino acids ($R_1 \longrightarrow R_5$)

(b)   secondary structure = formation of a chain

(c)   tertiary structure = folding of the chain

(d)   quaternary structure = association of two
or more protein chains

Condensation of amino acids can occur by the reaction of the amine from one amino acid molecule with the carboxylic acid group of another, forming an *amide linkage* (Figure 2.9). Note that the resulting product still has one amine and one carboxylic acid group. It is still a bifunctional molecule which can react further, in either end, with a third amino acid. The two ends are, however, different and are often referred to as the amino and carboxy terminals of the chain.

Proteins

Proteins are polymers of amino acids. Some typical proteins contain as many as a few hundred amino acids. While polysaccharides very often are polymers made up of a single type of monosaccharide, polymers of a single type of amino acid are rare outside of the research laboratory. It is, in fact, the sequence of the different types of amino acids which is of prime importance in determining the function and properties of the polymer. Because of the large number of monomers in a typical protein, and because there are 20 types of monomers to choose from, a very large number of different proteins can be formed. For example, it is possible to make 20^{18}, which is about 3×10^{23}, different protein molecules with only 18 amino acids in each. Since one mole consists of 6×10^{23} molecules, this would correspond to half a mole of mixture in which every molecule would be different!

As you will see later, the sequence in which the amino acids are added to the polymer chain is controlled very strictly during its synthesis. The sequence of amino acids in a protein is also referred to as the *primary structure* of the protein. See Figure 2.10(a).

The primary structure of a protein determines whether there are regions of the protein which are either highly charged, because of a large number of charged amino acids, or very poorly soluble in water, because of a large number of non-polar amino acids. The effect of the asymmetric structure, and of hydrogen bonds being formed between various parts of the same chain, is to produce particular three-dimensional arrangements of the amide bonds in the proteins. These are referred to as the *secondary structures* of the protein. See Figure 2.10(b).

Amino acid chains can also fold in various ways into large globular arrangements which represent the *tertiary structure*. See Figure 2.10(c). These are particularly sensitive to the groups present in the side chains. They can interact through hydrogen bonding, ionic attractions, or hydrophobic effects to form particularly

Figure 2.11
Structure of an antibody molecule. Each small circle represents an amino acid unit. Each large circle represents a monosaccharide unit. The antibody can recognize the shape of specific molecules, antigens, at each of two sites.

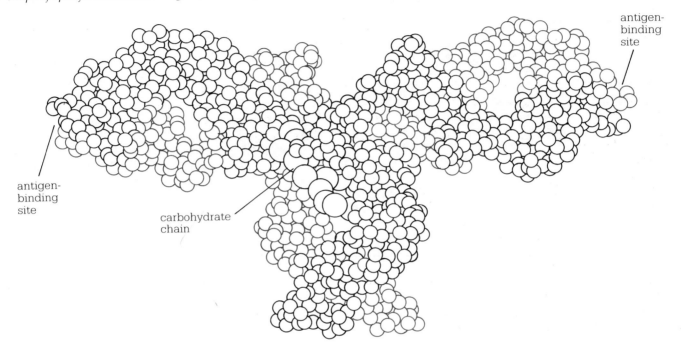

antigen-
binding
site

antigen-
binding
site

carbohydrate
chain

stable arrangements of the chains. An additional important factor is the ability of the —SH groups on the cysteine side chain to oxidize to the —S—S— group (section 2.1). Proteins which are soluble in water typically have a three-dimensional structure which exposes the charged amino acids on the surface and buries the other amino acids inside. Proteins which need to be imbedded in a membrane must have regions of non-polar amino acids. These can then interact favourably with the long chains of the fatty acids as you will see later in Chapter 4.

Many large proteins exist as complexes of two or more polymer chains, which are held together by the same types of forces that cause a chain to fold in unique ways. The complexes form the *quaternary structure* of the proteins. See Figure 2.10(d).

Proteins are perhaps the most versatile constituents of the cell. They have a wide range of functions. Some serve as messengers (hormones), some as sites of recognition (surface receptors on cells), some as structural building blocks (muscle proteins), and some serve as catalysts (enzymes). If there is a common theme in these functions, it is probably shape. The

protein structures result in surfaces that have specific shapes and which therefore can recognize special shapes. The best example of this is the structure of the antibodies. These proteins contain a region that can recognize small structural differences, for example, the difference between glucose and galactose. The diversity in amino acid sequence makes possible a very large number of different types of shapes. These proteins, therefore, allow for specificity, selectivity, and diversity in recognizing different shapes associated with different foreign materials.

Hair is made of a protein called α-keratin, which consists mostly of glycine and leucine amino acids. The secondary structure is that of a long helix. Three helices wrap around each other in a coil; 11 coils bundle together in a microfibril. Hundreds of microfibrils align to form macrofibrils which make up the hair cells. A hair fibre is made up of many hair cells. The shape of hair depends on the cross-linking among the protein chains by disulfide linkages. In doing a permanent, the disulfides are reduced while the hair is shaped, and then reoxidized to maintain the new shape.

33

ENZYME KINETICS

Enzymes act as catalysts, which means that they enhance the rate of chemical reactions. Because of their ability to recognize only specially shaped molecules, enzymes are highly selective in the kinds of chemical reactions that they catalyze. Recall from earlier discussion that the hydrolysis of lactose required a particular enzyme, lactase. The specificity is so great that lactase is the one and only enzyme for the hydrolysis of lactose, which in turn is the one and only reaction catalyzed by lactase.

The reagents in an enzyme-catalyzed reaction are called the substrates of the enzyme. The rate of the reaction depends on a number of factors such as the pH and the temperature, but more importantly, it depends on both the substrate and the enzyme concentrations. If a large amount of substrate is present, the rate of reaction is increased.

The efficiency of the enzyme can frequently be controlled or regulated by the presence of other substances, particularly the products of the reaction. For example, large amounts of products may indicate that sufficient amounts have been produced, and the substrate can then inhibit the catalysis and slow down the reaction. The inhibition may be *competitive*, which means that the inhibitor acts by binding to the same part of the enzyme where the substrate binds, or it may be *non-competitive*, which means that the inhibitor acts at a different site. It is thought that non-competitive inhibition works because the binding causes a change in the shape of the enzyme, so it less readily binds and reacts with the substrate. This is called *allosteric regulation* of enzyme function. It is also possible for other substances to enhance or activate the enzymatic function through allosteric regulation.

Silk is made of a protein called β-keratin, consisting mostly of glycine and alanine. In contrast to α-keratin, β-keratin forms three-dimensional structures that are like flat sheets stacked on top of one another. Because of the protein structure, silk will not stretch as easily as wool (which is hair). However, it feels very soft, because the flat sheets can glide past one another and give a high degree of flexibility.

Enzymes form one of the most important groups of proteins. These are proteins that accelerate specific biochemical reactions. They function by allowing reagents to be in close proximity and appropriate orientation for a sufficiently long time during which a reaction takes place. An important point to note is that the enzyme is not altered or consumed in the process, so a small amount of enzymes can accelerate the reaction for a large amount of reactant.

Proteins are an essential component of our diet because some of the amino acids we need cannot be produced by our cells. The only source of these essential amino acids is the hydrolysis of proteins in our digestive tract. This hydrolysis is catalyzed by peptidases, examples of which include trypsin and chymotrypsin.

2.5 NUCLEOTIDES, NUCLEOSIDES, AND NUCLEIC ACIDS

Nucleotides and Nucleosides

The **nucleotides** consist of three chemical entities, namely, a **purine** or **pyrimidine** base, a pentose, and a phosphate group. The purine bases are **adenine** (A) and **guanine** (G), and the pyrimidine bases are **cytosine** (C), **thymine** (T), and **uracil** (U). Figure 2.12 shows their structures.

These bases react, via a N–H group, with the alcohol on carbon 1 of the pentose in its ring form to form a N–C bond. The resulting compound is a **nucleoside**. The pentose may be either ribose or deoxyribose (the latter differs by lacking an alcohol group at carbon 2), giving either ribonucleosides or deoxyribonucleosides (Figure 2.13).

Nucleotides are generated from nucleosides by reacting phosphoric acid with the alcohol on carbon 5 (the $-CH_2OH$ group), thereby creating a phosphate ester. These compounds are also referred to as nucleoside 5'-monophosphates. Note that in the nucleoside and the nucleotide shown in Figure 2.14, the numbers on the carbons in the pentose ring are indicated with a prime. Ribonucleotides and deoxyribonucleotides differ only in the structure of the pentose ring.

Figure 2.12
Structures of purine (a) and pyrimidine (b) bases

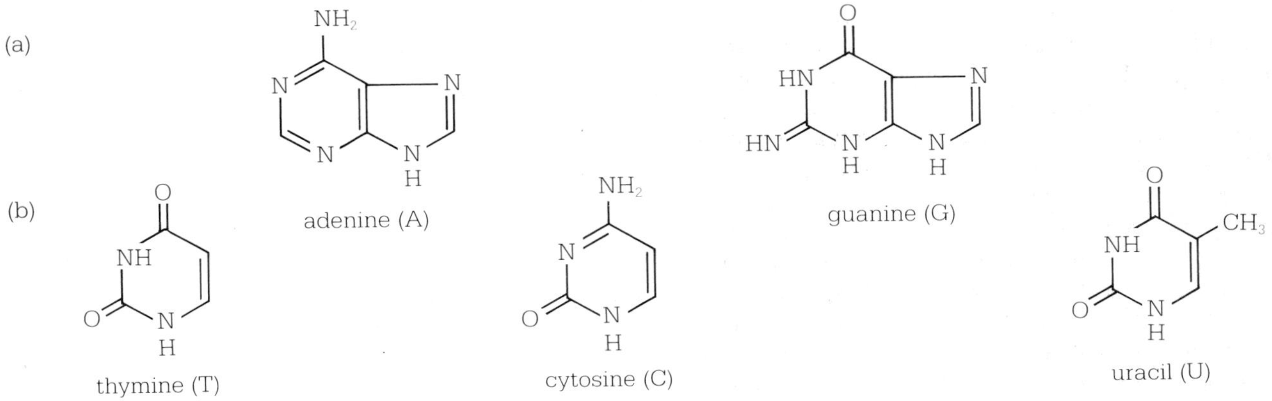

(a)

adenine (A)

guanine (G)

(b)

thymine (T)

cytosine (C)

uracil (U)

Figure 2.13
The condensation of a base and a ribose yields a ribonucleoside. Deoxyribonucleosides lack an −OH group at the 2′ position in the pentose ring.

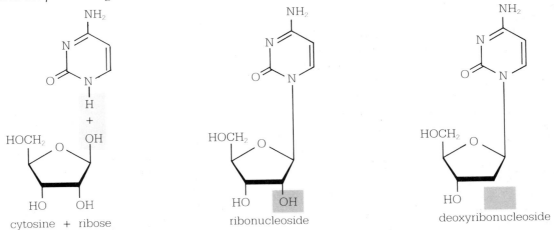

cytosine + ribose

ribonucleoside

deoxyribonucleoside

Figure 2.14
Nucleotides are formed by condensation of phosphoric acid at the 5′ alcohol group in the pentose ring.

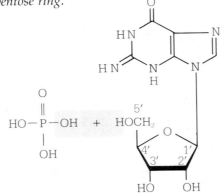

Nucleic Acids

Nucleotides are the monomeric building blocks of dinucleotides, which are made by formation of a second ester bond between the phosphate on one nucleotide and the alcohol on carbon 3′ of the pentose of another nucleotide. The single phosphate then acts as a bridge between the two pentoses attaching to the 5′ and 3′ positions (Figure 2.15).

The dinucleotide maintains two functional groups, so it is capable of reacting further to give a chain of alternating pentoses and phosphate groups with either purine or pyrimidine bases as side chains. This polymer of nucleotides is called a **nucleic acid**. The sequences of purine or pyrimidine bases are the distinguishing factors among the nucleic acids. As in the case of proteins, the side chain sequence determines the properties of the polymer chain. Unlike proteins, however, the side chains are sufficiently similar that the overall structure of the nucleic acids are fairly independent of that sequence.

Ribonucleotides and deoxyribonucleotides never co-exist in the same polymer. The ribonucleotides condense to form **ribonucleic acid**, or **RNA**, while the deoxyribonucleotides condense to give *deoxyribonucleic acid*, or **DNA**.

Base Pairing

The purine and pyrimidine bases have special hydrogen bonding properties which play important roles in determining the structure and function of nucleic acids. The guanine and cytosine entities can form three parallel hydrogen bonds, while the adenine and thymine or adenine and uracil groups can form one pair of hydrogen bonds (Figure 2.16). It is, however, not possible for stable hydrogen bonds to form between any other pairs, and no entities form more than one hydrogen bond to themselves. These paired entities are, therefore, special pairs that fit particularly well across from each other. This is the secret to the genetic code which will be discussed in much more detail in Chapters 14 to 18.

The hydrogen bonds can form between different parts of the same chain, which therefore folds. They can also form between different chains, which thereby form a double stranded helical molecule. The requirement for stable interactions to occur is that there are several complementary base pairs which can interact along the chains. Thus if one DNA chain consists of the sequence 3′—ACCGATC—5′, it turns out that the

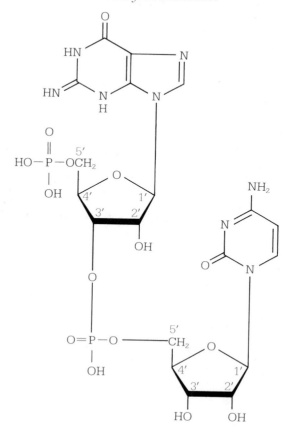

Figure 2.15
An example of a 3′–5′ linked dinucleotide. Is this a diribonucleotide or a dideoxyribonucleotide?

other chain segment must be 3′—GATCGGT—5′ in order for the chains to interact in opposite directions:

$$5'-TGGCTAG-3'$$
$$3'-ACCGATC-5'$$

This is the basis for the double helix structure of DNA (Figure 2.17). The details will be discussed in later chapters.

Nucleoside Triphosphates

In addition to their tremendously important role in forming nucleic acids, the nucleoside monophosphates (nucleotides) are extremely important biological molecules. The most thoroughly studied is adenosine monophosphate (AMP). By further reaction with phosphoric acid, it is possible to make the phosphoric anhydrides (refer to Table 2.2) corresponding to ADP and ATP as discussed in Chapter 1.

Figure 2.16
Base pairing occurs by multiple hydrogen bonds between cytosine and guanine bases (a) or thymine and adenine bases (b).

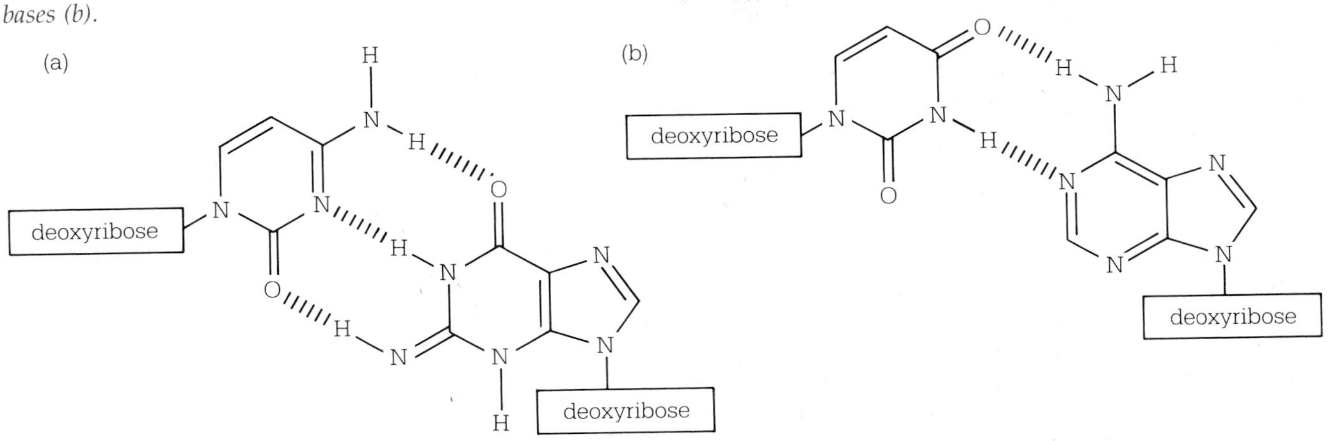

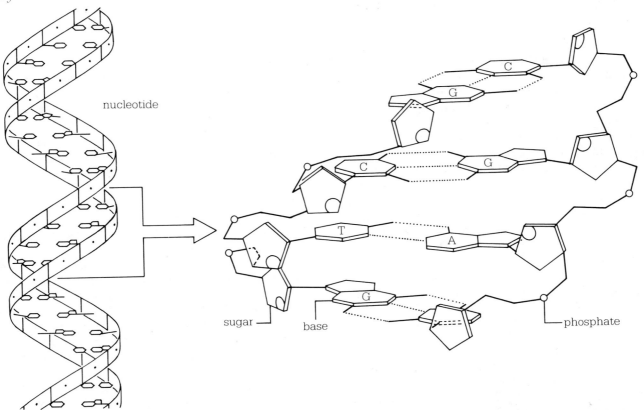

Figure 2.17
The double helix. This shows the base pairing in DNA which leads to formation of a pair of intertwined chains of polynucleotides.

Figure 2.18
Structure of cyclic AMP

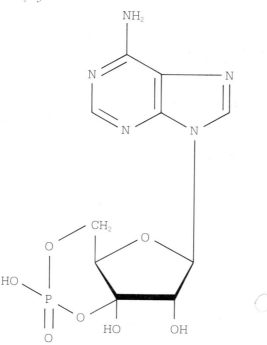

Figure 2.19
Structure of myristic acid—a simple fatty acid. Note the long hydrophobic chain of CH_2 units and the polar end with the carboxylic acid group.

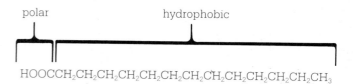

These are most important intermediates in the flow of energy throughout the cell. The corresponding guanosine derivatives (GMP, GDP, and GTP) are important regulators of the functions of a large number of proteins. Cyclic AMP (Figure 2.18) is thought to act as a chemical signal which is generated inside cells in response to a large number of external stimuli, such as hormones binding to the surface.

The concentration of ATP is very high in muscles, where it is used as the energy source for driving muscle contraction. When an animal is slaughtered, the ATP is quickly hydrolyzed to AMP, which in turn is easily oxidized to inosine monophosphate, IMP, which differs only by having a $C=O$ group instead of the $C-NH_2$ group on the purine base. IMP is responsible for the flavour we typically associate with meat, and is in many cases used as an artificial flavour ingredient.

2.6 FATTY ACIDS

Fatty acids are long chains of carbon atoms with hydrogen atoms attached and contain a carboxylic acid group at one end (Figure 2.19). They have only one functional group and are therefore incapable of form-ing polymers. They do, however, react with **glycerol** (Figure 2.20) to form either the **triglycerides**, which serve mainly as storage of energy in the form of fat, or **diglycerides**, which form the building blocks for **phospholipid** molecules.

Fatty acids are not soluble in water even though they have a very polar group at one end, because the molecules also have a large hydrophobic region. As a consequence, they tend to associate into large aggregates held together mostly by hydrophobic interactions. The organization of these assemblies depends on the structure of the molecules. Fatty acids are almost cylindrical in shape and contain a polar and a non-polar end. They assemble to form *micelles* of molecules, which are like small drops of oil with polar groups at the surface.

Fats and oils are very efficient molecules for storing energy. The oxygen content is low, so that there is a large amount of energy released when the molecules are oxidized. Glucose ($C_6H_{12}O_6$) and decanoic acid ($C_{10}H_{20}O_2$) have approximately the same molar mass, but the amount of energy released when the fatty acid is oxidized is about twice the amount released when glucose is oxidized. For this reason, nature uses fats for storage of energy when space or weight is important as in the case of seed pods or mobile animals, but can make use of carbohydrates for energy storage in large plants.

Some fatty acids are unsaturated, that is, they contain carbon–carbon double bonds in the chain. These are readily oxidized and can also form cross-links among themselves in the process. We make use of this in preparation of paints, which contain large amounts of triglycerides with unsaturated fatty acids. Upon drying, oxidation causes extensive cross-linking which results in the hard film of paint.

The structures and functions of fatty acids and lipids, which are relevant to biological membranes, will be discussed in much greater detail in Chapter 4.

Figure 2.20
The structures of tri- and diglycerides also reveal the long hydrophobic chains of CH_2 units and the polar region of the glycerol.

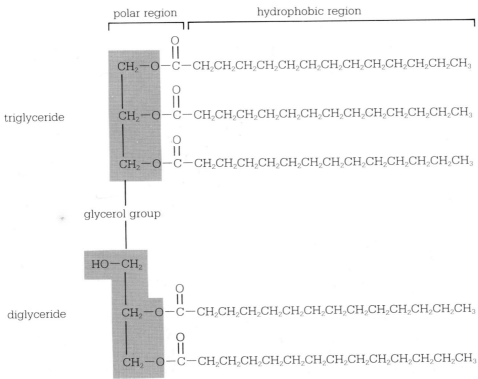

2.7 EXAMPLES OF OTHER BIOLOGICALLY IMPORTANT MOLECULES

Carotene and Its Relatives

You are what you eat. This statement is clearly exemplified with the carotenoids. These are a class of closely related molecules containing a large number of double bonds in a chain (Figure 2.21). These double bonds are capable of absorbing light of a certain colour, depending on the number of double bonds and on the functional groups attached to them. For example, carotene absorbs blue-indigo light and, therefore, looks orange, but the more oxygenated form, astaxanthin, appears pink. Carotene is responsible for the orange colour of carrots and persimmon fruits, whereas astaxanthin absorbs light in the yellow to green region and is responsible for the pink colour of cooked salmon and shrimp. The yellow-orange colour in butter arises from carotenes eaten by the cow, and the slightly yellow tone in the fat of a steak is also due to carotenes. Flamingos have a beautifully pink plumage when their diet is rich in shrimp which supplies astaxanthins.

In humans, carotenes are oxidized to produce retinol (vitamin A) and retinal. The retinal combines with a protein in the membranes of the cells in the retina of the eye. When light strikes the retinal in the protein, it is absorbed and causes the membrane to momentarily become leaky to ions. The first step in vision has occurred. Next, a nerve signal arises from the retina and is transmitted to the optic centre at the back of the brain where it is interpreted as a burst of light. Carotenes are therefore essential components of our diet. Indeed, if you eat too many carrots, your skin will turn orange, but if you don't eat enough, your vision will be affected.

Figure 2.21
The carotenoids are chemically similar to vitamin A and retinal.

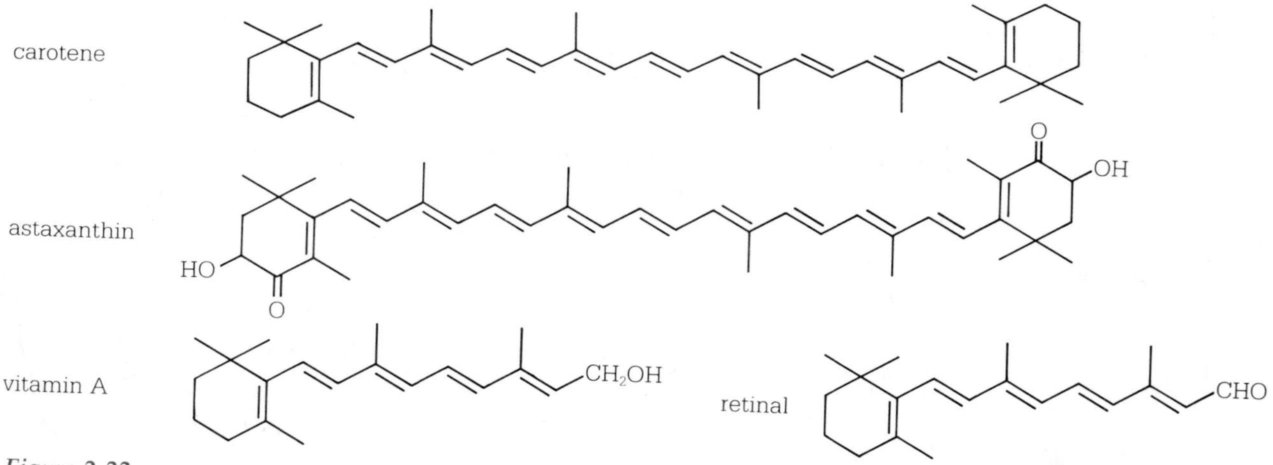
carotene
astaxanthin
HO
O
O
OH
vitamin A
CH2OH
retinal
CHO

Figure 2.22
The red colour of hemoglobin arises from the iron-containing porphyrin (a), while the green colour of leaves comes from the magnesium-containing porphyrin (b).

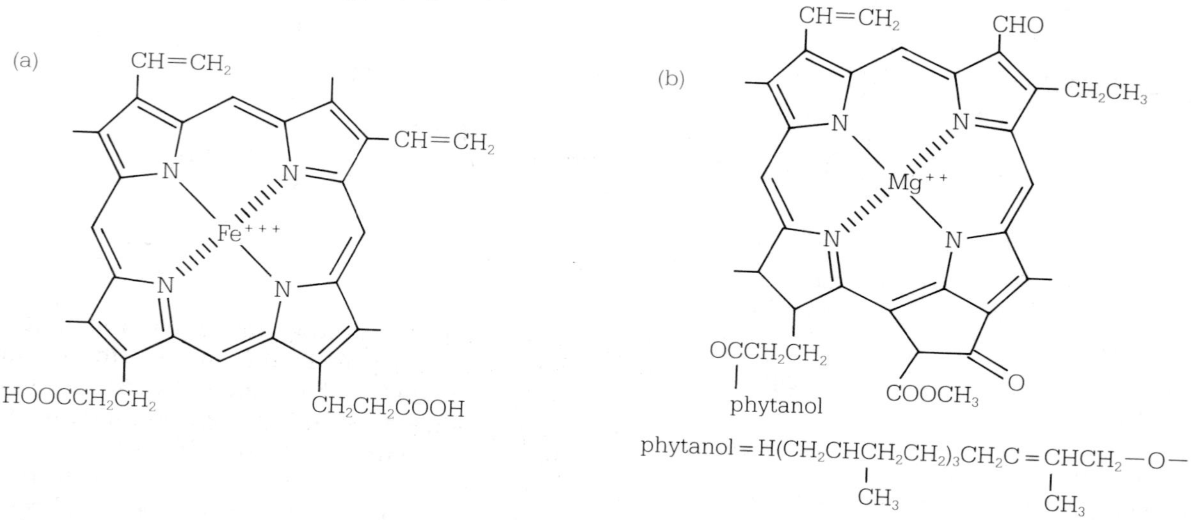
(a)
CH=CH2
CH=CH2
N
N
Fe+++
N
N
HOOCCH2CH2
CH2CH2COOH
(b)
CH=CH2
CHO
CH2CH3
N
N
Mg++
N
N
OCCH2CH2
phytanol
COOCH3
O
phytanol = H(CH2CHCH2CH2)3CH2C = CHCH2—O—
CH3
CH3

Porphyrins

What do red blood and green leaves have in common? Their typical colours arise from the absorption of light by molecules belonging to the class called **porphyrins**. These consist of a large ring system at the centre of which N—H groups can bind with a metal ion. The protein in red blood cells, hemoglobin, contains a porphyrin group which binds with iron. It is designed to bind oxygen and transport it through the blood stream from the lungs to the body tissues. The chlorophyll in green leaves is a large porphyrin group which binds with magnesium, and it has a long fatty acid side chain which anchors it firmly in the membrane. It is designed to absorb light and convert it into chemical energy during photosynthesis.

The proteins in the mitochondria of all cells, called cytochromes, are responsible for the orderly oxidation of chemicals and the production of ATP. The redox reactions are controlled by oxidation–reduction cycles of iron centred in a porphyrin ring within the proteins. These processes will be explained in more detail in Chapters 5 to 9.

Steroid Hormones

Estradiol, a major female sex hormone, and testosterone, a major male sex hormone, differ only in chemical structure by an extra methyl group in the latter, and in the state of oxidation of one of the ring structures (Figure 2.23). It is remarkable that such a small chemical difference can result in such a large physiological difference between females and males. Perhaps this is testimony to the fact that females and males are, in almost all other respects, equal.

The sex hormones belong to a class of compounds called steroids, which serve a multitude of functions in the body. One of the precursors, cholesterol, is extremely important in the structure and function of biological membranes (Chapter 4). A related compound, vitamin D, is a precursor to a steroid that is important in the transport of calcium ions. Deficiency in vitamin D can lead to the disease rickets, and may be related to osteoporosis, a condition in which the bone structure becomes very brittle because of poor utilization of calcium and phosphate in the bone.

Figure 2.23
The steroid hormones differ only by small changes in the groups attached to the same four-ring structure.

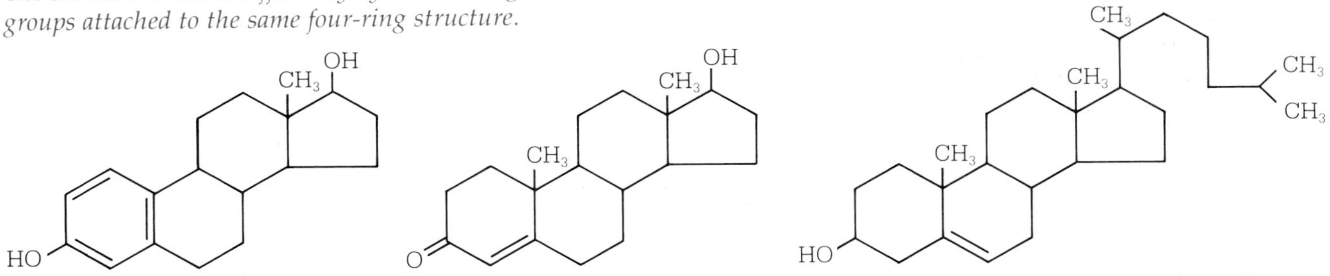

estradiol   testosterone   cholesterol

CHAPTER SUMMARY

Functional groups are the most reactive parts of molecules. The most important functional groups in biologically relevant molecules are the alcohol, the aldehyde and ketone, the carboxylic acid, the amino group, and the phosphate group. These react to form characteristic linkages, which allow many small molecules, monomers, to join into long chains, forming polymers.

Monosaccharides, which are either pentoses or hexoses, join to form polysaccharides such as amylose, cellulose and glycogen. These are used essentially for storage of energy and as structural components.

Amino acids, of which there are about 20 major ones, link by amide bonds to form proteins. Proteins constitute the most diverse group of polymers. They serve as messengers, antibodies, structural components, and catalytic agents. The last, the enzymes, are critical in providing both specificity of reaction and control of the rate at which critical compounds are made.

Nucleotides, which are a complex assembly of a base, a sugar, and a phosphate group, link by phosphate esters to form the nucleic acids. These are the basic components in the genetic material passed on from generation to generation.

Fatty acids, linked with glycerol as triglycerides, are the most efficient means of storing energy, since there are relatively few oxidized groups. The energy content of fats is comparable to that of gasoline. Fatty acids play an important role in the formation of membranes. This will be discussed in Chapter 4.

The diversity of molecules in nature appears to be endless. From a few simple elements — carbon, oxygen, hydrogen, nitrogen, phosphorus, and sulfur — life has generated an arsenal of chemicals with very specific functions and unique characteristics. By small modification of chemical structures, colours may change from yellow to pink, and males develop differently from females. The subtlety with which nature works is perhaps best appreciated when you realize that the bright red colour of blood and the green colour of leaves arise from similar molecules called porphyrins.

Objectives

Having completed this chapter, you should be able to do the following:

1. Name and draw the structures of some of the most important functional groups, and write equations for the most important reactions they can undergo.
2. Compare condensation and hydrolysis reactions and describe their roles in the synthesis and degradation of polymers.
3. Describe the characteristics of carbohydrates and the properties and functions of some of the polysaccharides.
4. Describe the general features of amino acids, and draw at least four different amino acid structures.

5. Describe in general terms the structure of proteins and explain its significance.
6. Draw and describe the structure of at least one nucleotide and indicate how several can be linked to form a nucleic acid.
7. Outline the differences between DNA and RNA, and indicate the major function of nucleic acids.
8. Describe in general terms the structure of fatty acids and outline its importance in relation to storage of energy.

Vocabulary

functional group
alcohol
aldehyde
carboxylic acid
thiol
disulfide
polymer
monomer
dimer
carbohydrate
monosaccharide
pentose
hexose

disaccharide
polysaccharide
amino acid
amine
side chain
protein
nucleotide
purine
pyrimidine
adenine
guanine
cytosine

thymine
uracil
nucleoside
nucleic acid
ribonucleic acid (RNA)
deoxyribonucleic acid (DNA)
fatty acid
glycerol
triglyceride
diglyceride
phospholipid
porphyrin

Review Questions

1. Draw the structure of each molecule. Circle and name all the functional groups on each.
   (a) ethanol
   (b) glycerol
   (c) glucose
2. Write equations for all the chemical reactions you have encountered that involve an alcohol functional group.
3. Give one example of biological significance of each of the following. In each case, indicate why the reaction is important.

   (a) oxidation–reduction reaction
   (b) acid–base reaction
   (c) addition reaction
   (d) condensation reaction.
4. State the minimum requirement that allows molecules to form polymers.
5. State the differences between each pair and give an example of each.
   (a) aldoses and ketoses
   (b) pentoses and hexoses

6. (a) Draw the structures of glucose in both linear and cyclic forms.
   (b) What type of reaction is responsible for the formation of the ring, and which functional groups are involved?
7. Describe the structural differences between the major polysaccharides found in plants.
8. Draw the characteristic structure of an amino acid.
9. Draw the structure of each molecule and indicate on each the number and type of functional groups.
   (a) alanine
   (b) lysine
   (c) glutamic acid
   (d) tyrosine
   (e) cysteine
10. Draw in three-dimensional perspective the structure of the amide bond.
11. Describe how the shape of a protein arises.
12. Define an enzyme. Give an example.
13. Show by examples the difference between a purine and a pyrimidine base.
14. Describe the differences among a nucleoside, a nucleotide, and a nucleoside triphosphate.
15. What are the key differences between the chemical make-up of DNA and RNA?
16. Show in a diagram the pairs of bases which form the best hydrogen bonding, and indicate why adenine and cytosine do not form stable hydrogen bonding.
17. Draw the structure of palmitic acid ($C_{16}H_{32}O_2$) and explain why this molecule is incapable of forming polymers.
18. Why are fats better for storing energy than carbohydrates?

Advanced Questions

1. Draw a segment of the polysaccharide, amylopectin, showing at least five monosaccharide units and one branch point.
2. The enkephalins are polymers of five amino acids. Met-enkephalin has tyrosine, glycine, glycine, phenylalanine, and methionine in that order. The enkephalins are released in the brain in response to pain, and act as pain killers by binding to nerve cells. They are believed to bind to the same receptors as do morphine, the principal component of opium.
   (a) Draw a structure of met-enkephalin.
   (b) Do you have to make any assumptions in order to make this drawing?
3. Optical activity arises whenever there are *four different* chemical groups attached to the same carbon atom.
   (a) Draw an example of a monosaccharide, an amino acid, a pyrimidine base, a nucleoside, and a fatty acid, and indicate which of these are optically active.
   (b) Circle the carbon or carbons that are responsible for the optical activity.
   (c) Is it true that *all* amino acids are optically active? Give reasons.
4. In an experiment, the rate of hydrolysis of lactose to galactose and glucose using lactase was measured as a function of the concentrations of both lactose and lactase. The results are summarized in the table below.

LACTOSE CONCENTRATION mol/L	LACTASE CONCENTRATION mol/L	HYDROLYSIS RATE (mol/L)/s -
10^{-4}	10^{-6}	10^{-6}
5×10^{-4}	10^{-6}	5×10^{-6}
10^{-3}	10^{-6}	8×10^{-6}
2×10^{-3}	10^{-6}	10^{-5}
10^{-4}	10^{-7}	10^{-7}

(a) Draw a graph of the rate of hydrolysis as a function of lactose concentration.
(b) Note that at low concentrations, the rate increases proportionally with the lactose concentration, but at higher concentrations, the rate reaches a maximum level. Explain why there is a maximum rate.
(c) The rate is also proportional to the concentration of the enzyme. How is this supported by the data?
(d) What would you expect to happen if the enzyme concentration were raised to 10^{-4} mol/L in the last experiment? Would it be easy to do that experiment?

UNIT TWO

ENERGY
AND THE
LIVING CELL

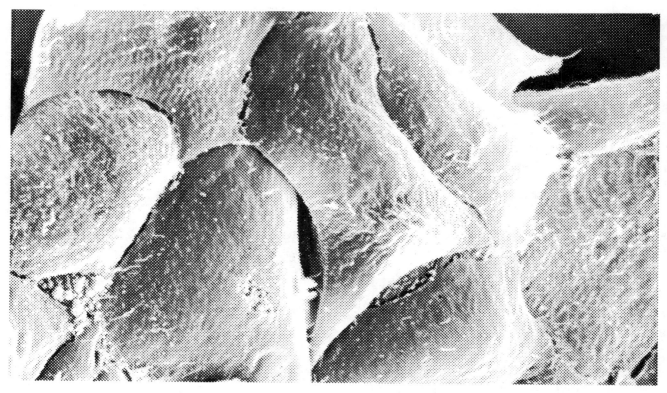

CHAPTER 3

THE FUNCTIONAL CELL

*. . . all organized bodies are composed of essentially
similar parts, namely, of cells; these cells are formed
and grow in accordance with essentially similar laws . . .*

Theodor Schwann

The picture on the top shows the normal connective tissue cells from a rat. The one on the bottom shows cancerous ones. The normal cells are irregular in shape and flat. They are also quite sticky and adhere to the surface on which they are growing. The cancerous cells have become round and are relatively nonadhesive. They easily break away from the growing surface and surrounding cells. In general, the growth, differentiation, and replication of the normal cells in plants and animals are strictly controlled. They become cancerous when they lose this control and they begin to grow and divide in an uncontrolled fashion. It is as if the body simply becomes a growth chamber for the cancerous cells. Eventually, a large mass of cancer cells results and this is called a tumour. Cancer cells also lose their ability to differentiate, that is, to become specialized in structure and function. Cancerous liver cells, for example, no longer generate blood proteins or bile, or dismantle red blood cells. When a normal cell becomes cancerous, it is said to be *transformed*.

During this decade, cancer has claimed the lives of approximately 50 000 Canadians each year. In addition, cancer will strike one in every three Canadians sometime during their lives. Because it is such a serious disease, millions of dollars and countless hours have been spent on research into the causes, prevention, and cure for cancer. A lot is known but there are still many unanswered questions. It is known, for example, that cancer is a disease of the genetic material in the cell. It is, therefore, a heritable defect in cellular control mechanisms. Although scientists agree that there are several steps involved in cell transformation,

the mechanics of how cancer actually begins in the cell are still not fully understood. It is generally believed that tumours are monoclonal, that is, they evolve from a single cell. Cancers spread throughout the body by cancerous cells breaking away from the tumour and moving to another part of the body. This process is called *metastasis*.

A variety of cancer-causing or *carcinogenic* agents have been identified. Several forms of radiation such as X rays and ultraviolet rays have been shown to promote cancers. Various chemicals such as hydrazine and vinyl chloride, both of which are present in cigarette smoke, and organic solvents such as carbon tetrachloride and benzene have been shown to be carcinogenic agents. Viruses have also been implicated in some plant and animal cancers. Although viruses are highly suspect in causing some human cancers, there is as yet no conclusive proof that they are directly involved.

As you follow this chapter, you will become aware of the marvellous control mechanisms and the relationship between structure and function in cells. These factors are all the more fascinating when you realize how completely they can be disrupted by cancer.

3.1 WHAT IS A CELL?

''We have seen that all organisms are composed of essentially like parts, namely, of cells.'' This profound statement is part of the cell theory and was first articulated by Theodor Schwann and Matthias Schleiden in 1839. Twenty years later, Rudolph Virchow pointed out that all cells come from pre-existing cells. They do not arise spontaneously as some people at the time, including Schwann, believed. The cell theory indirectly defines what a cell is. It also points out that in addition to being the basis of life, the cell is also the functional unit of life.

In its complete form, the <u>cell theory</u> can be stated as follows:

1. All living things are made up of one or more cells and the products of those cells.
2. Cells are the functional units of life.
3. All cells come from pre-existing cells.

The actual study of the cell and the attempts to uncover its mysteries began almost two hundred years before the formulation of the cell theory. Robert Hooke was the first to use the term cell. He described a variety of cells and other microscopic objects in his book entitled *Micrographia* published in 1665.

Quite understandably, the beginnings of cell research coincided with the invention of the microscope. The lenses of the first microscopes were not very good, however, and only provided fuzzy images. Hooke, for example, used a simple two-lens microscope and was only able to discern the walls of plant cells and not much more. As the capabilities of microscopes improved, more and more of the structure of cells could be seen. Figure 3.1 shows the improvement of microscope images over the years.

As the structure of the cell was revealed, questions concerning the function of cell organelles became important. Now with sophisticated electron microscopes, elaborate tissue preparation techniques, and effective chemical analysis procedures, scientists are able to investigate the structure and function of cells at the molecular level. The <u>study of the cell is called</u> <u>cytology</u>. The <u>questions</u> that are now being asked in this important area of science are: <u>How are the activities of the cell controlled?</u> How are proteins synthesized, modified, and moved around the cell? How do cells differentiate, grow, and age?

With the extensive knowledge that is now available, the definition of the cell has become considerably more complex. At present, a generally accepted definition for the cell might be stated as follows:

A cell is a confined system of potentially self perpetuating linked organic reactions that are catalyzed stepwise by enzymes that are themselves produced by the system.

It is the purpose of this chapter to unravel the meaning and significance of this elaborate definition.

Figure 3.1

Progress in seeing the structure of the cell. A first representation of cells was drawn by Hooke in 1662 (a). Schwann's diagram in 1839 showed more details of the cell (b). A micrograph of part of a cell taken with an electron microscope contains a lot of details (c).

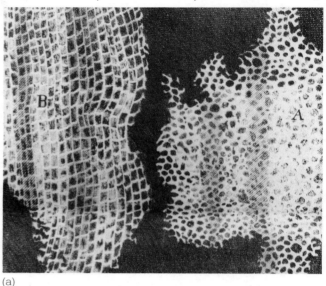

(a)

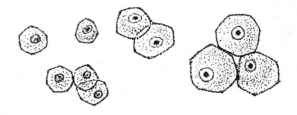

(b)

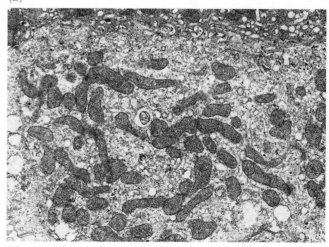

(c)

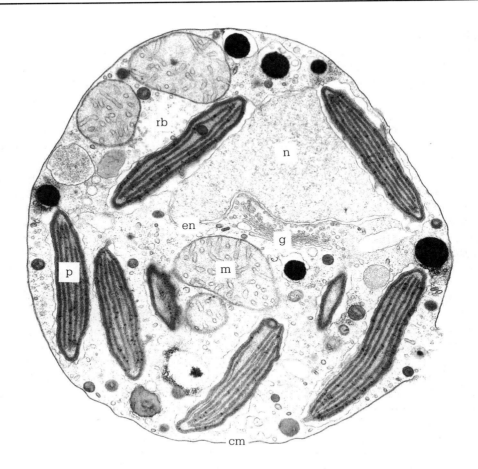

Important Characteristics of Living Cells

Figure 3.2
A plant cell in an embryo. The following can be identified: nucleus (n), ribosomes (rb), mitochondria (m), early Golgi apparatus (g), nuclear envelope (en), cytoplasmic membrane (cm), and plastids (p).

Cells Are Complex

Since cells are living things, they are complex. You can realize the complexity from the fact that plant and animal cells are made up of more than fifteen different **organelles**. Cells also contain a great variety of complex molecules and other particles. These, and the organelles, constitute the structural complexity of the cell. There are, in addition, the highly sophisticated interactions between organelles and between molecules and organelles that constitute the functional complexity of the cell. This aspect of the cell is the focus of this chapter and will be described in some detail.

An electron micrograph of a cell such as that shown in Figure 3.2 will reveal some of this complexity. You must keep in mind, however, that many cellular components and all of the chemical reactions are hidden even from the most powerful electron microscope.

Cells Are Extremely Small

Most cells are so small that they cannot be seen with the naked eye. The average diameter of cells is approximately 20 μm (micrometres). Human red blood cells are smaller and are typically 7.5 μm in diameter. As a comparison, take the average width of a thumbnail, which is approximately 15 mm. It would take a chain of about 20 000 red blood cells to stretch across the nail!

The micrometre is the unit of measure used to describe the larger parts of the cell, that is, the cell organelles. The other unit of measure commonly used in cytology is the nanometre (nm). The nanometre is 1000 times smaller than a micrometre. The size of protein molecules and the thickness of the cell membrane are measured in nanometres. For example, the thickness of the cell membrane is 7 nm to 10 nm.

Cells Are Self-replicating

This is an extremely important characteristic that was noted in the cell theory. Somehow cells are able to grow and, when new cells are required, divide. The control mechanisms for this process are not fully understood. Certain cell organelles such as the chloroplast and mitochondria are also able to reproduce themselves through division. As you will see later in this chapter, a particularly important part of this process is the ability of the DNA molecules in the nucleus to self-replicate.

Cells Can Live as Autonomous or Semiautonomous Entities

A number of organisms such as bacteria and protozoa live their lives as separate cells. As single-celled organisms, each cell must be able to perform all the functions required for life. In multicellular organisms, cells co-exist and depend on other cells. Cells become specialized in their function. For example, some cells in plants conduct water and minerals up the stem while others are designed for photosynthesis in the leaf. In animals, heart cells play a different role from skin cells and so on. You should note, however, that a number of cells that normally live in multicellular organisms retain the ability to live as separate organisms.

Cells Can Regulate Their Internal Environments

Through complex processes of chemical recognition and feedback, cells can control what happens inside them. They are also able to control what enters and leaves. Since many of a cell's activities require relatively constant conditions in order to proceed effectively, this ability to regulate its internal environment is extremely important.

Types of Cells

It is important in the search for an accurate description of cells to realize that all cells have the characteristics described above. At the same time, you must realize that there is a great variety of cells all with different shapes, sizes, and organelles. Two categories of cells have been recognized. The cells of all organisms can be categorized as either **eukaryotic** or **prokaryotic cells**. The eukaryotic group is by far the largest and it includes all of the fungi, protozoa, plant and animal cells. A typical eukaryotic cell is the plant cell shown in Figure 3.2. Prokaryotic cells are thought to be more primitive than eukaryotic cells because the fossils of these cells are older and because they are considerably simpler in structure. This category includes all of the bacteria and blue-green algae cells.

Prokaryotic cells are different from eukaryotic cells in that they do not have organelles that are separated from the rest of the **cytoplasm** (contents inside the cell other than the nucleus) by membrane(s). This was first noticed in terms of the nucleus and gave rise to the distinguishing names prokaryotic, meaning "before nucleus," and eukaryotic, meaning "true nucleus." There is, however, usually a recognizable area in prokaryotic cells that contains the nuclear or genetic material. This area in prokaryotes is called the **nucleoid**. No nucleoli are apparent in the nucleoid. Also, the ribosomes are smaller in prokaryotic cells. The photomicrograph of *Escherichia coli* shown in Figure 3.3 demonstrates many of the typical traits of prokaryotic cells—the presence of a cell wall and a nucleoid and the absence of membrane-bound organelles.

Another categorization of cell types that is often used is plant versus animal cells. Many cytologists, however, will argue that the separation of plant and animal cells into different groups is an artificial one. On the one hand, you probably already know that only plant cells possess a cell wall and chloroplasts; animal cells do not. Plant cells also have fewer but larger vacuoles than animal cells, and there appear to be differences in cell division. These differences are small, however, when you consider that in both plant and animal cells, the basic cell structure, 90 percent of the organelles, and most of the chemical processes are the same.

3.2 CELL FUNCTIONS AND STRUCTURES

The life processes in all living things are dynamic and interdependent. Each of your organ systems is continuously working to perform its own vital role while interacting in a complementary way with other organ systems. For example, you need oxygen to live. Your respiratory system delivers oxygen to your lungs. The needed oxygen then diffuses across the thin walls of the lungs to enter the blood stream. At this point, the circulatory system takes over. The molecules of oxygen attach to the hemoglobin molecules in the red blood cells and are transported throughout the body.

Figure 3.3
A prokaryotic cell, the bacterium Escherichia coli

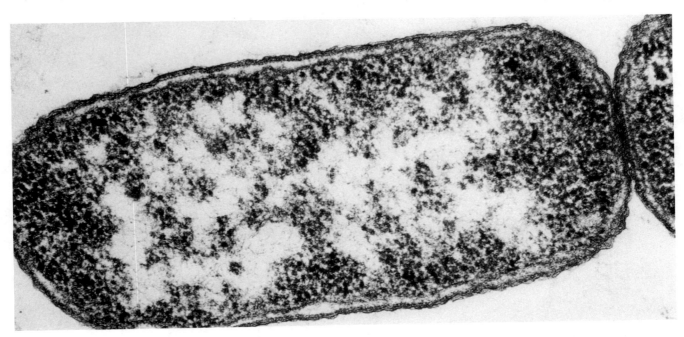

Similarly, the activities of the cell are integrated. Each part of the cell has a variety of functions and works in concert with other cell parts.

In previous studies you have probably considered the structure and function of each cell organelle as a separate entity. In this section, organelles are considered in isolation but are described in terms of their role in various cell activities. You will learn about organelles in groups according to their functional similarities.

Barriers and Defence
To exist as a living thing the cell must be able to maintain itself as a discrete object that is separate from its environment. It must also be able to detect and accumulate the material that it needs for its life processes. To accomplish all of this, it is necessary for the cell to have a barrier that separates it from, but still allows it to be sensitive to, its surrounding environment. The **cell membrane** serves this role. Membranes also separate cell organelles from the rest of the cell's contents.

Although the cell membrane is an effective barrier, it is not thick and rigid enough to provide the cell with much protection against mechanical injury. A form of protection is provided, however, by the chemical nature of the membrane. In this regard, the cell membrane is able to detect and restrict the entry of chemicals that might harm the cell.

Cell membranes in larger organisms also play a key role in providing internal protection for the organisms. The internal cells of multicellular organisms, particularly of animals, possess a chemical label in their membranes which identifies the cell as part of a specific organism. This makes it possible for agents whose job it is to defend the organism, such as the white blood cells and antibodies, to do their job. White blood cells, for example, can use the chemical identity tags on cell membranes to identify and destroy foreign cells and chemicals that have gained entry into the multicellular organism. Other cells of the same organism are left unharmed.

The existence of a cell membrane is the one structural characteristic that is common to all living cells. Although membranes of different cells vary somewhat in their chemical constituents, a major component of all membranes is a fat molecule called phospholipid. Various proteins and carbohydrates are also present. Figure 3.4 shows the structure of the cell membrane. The details of the structure of the cell membrane and how it performs all of its vital functions is one of the most important areas in cytology and will be discussed in detail in Chapter 4.

Figure 3.4
Structure of the cell membrane

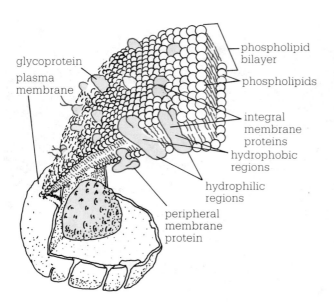

glycoprotein

plasma
membrane

phospholipid
bilayer

phospholipids

integral
membrane
proteins

hydrophobic
regions

hydrophilic
regions

peripheral
membrane
protein

Figure 3.5
Cellulose microfibrils in the cell wall of a green alga

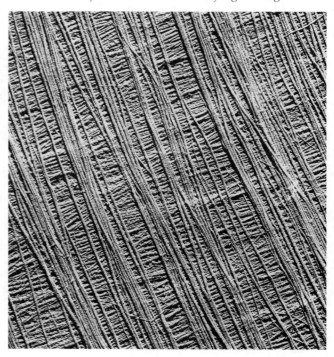

In addition to the cell membrane, plant cells and almost all prokaryotic cells have an additional surrounding barrier just outside of the cell membrane. This additional shell is called the **cell wall**. Among other things, cell walls function to link cells into colonies, prevent cells from bursting due to osmotic pressure, and protect cells from infection by viruses. In plants, the cell wall is composed largely of microscopic fibres, or **microfibrils**, of a chemical called cellulose (Figure 3.5). Although it is an effective barrier, the cell wall contains a number of pores which allow the plant cell to exchange material with its environment and to communicate with other cells.

Structure and Support
The cell membrane also functions to give the cell its shape. This is accomplished not so much by its rigidity but by its adhesive properties. Many cell membranes are sticky and form loose attachments to surrounding cells and structures.

Similarly, in addition to their protective role, plant cell walls function to give the cell its shape, and provide support for the whole plant. Plant cells typically have a large fluid-filled central vacuole. As water moves into the vacuole the vacuole expands. This expansion creates a pressure, called **turgor pressure**,

against the plant cell wall. The plant cell becomes rigid. The rigidity of thousands of cells in the body of the plant helps provide the support required to hold up the plant against gravity.

Until recently it was thought that only the cell membrane and, in the case of plant cells, the cell wall, gave the cell its shape and provided support. It is now known that cell components called **microtubules** and **microfilaments** play an important role in this regard. A number of observations have suggested that the interior of the nucleus is also quite structured. It would appear that there is a proteinaceous skeleton or a nuclear matrix present.

Microtubules appear to be tubular in construction and have a thickness of about 20 nm to 25 nm. Microfilaments are solid and much thinner, averaging about 6 nm in diameter. Both are made up of protein molecules but these are of different types. These structures radiate throughout the cell to form a *microtrabecular network*, or **cytoskeleton**. A matrix of microtubules has been shown to lie just below the cell membrane with attachments formed between the tubules and the protein complexes of the membrane (Figure 3.6). Both microtubules and microfilaments probably form loose attachments with various organelles as well.

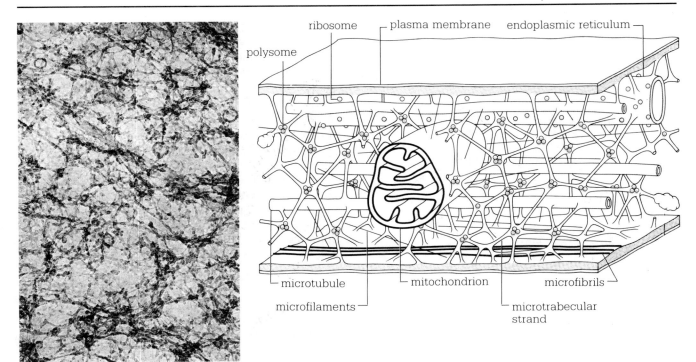

ribosome — *plasma membrane* — *endoplasmic reticulum* —
polysome —

— *microtubule* — *mitochondrion* — *microfibrils* —
microfilaments — — *microtrabecular strand*

Figure 3.6
A micrograph and a model of microtrabecular network found at the periphery of a kidney cell. The darker areas and circular objects in the micrograph are organelles. Points of attachment between the organelles and the microtubules are evident.

Movement

The mechanisms for the movement of the entire cell and the materials within the cell, and for changes in cell shape, were until recent times a mystery. Improved cell study techniques have revealed that the microfilaments and microtubules are responsible for most of these activities.

The movement of organelles within the cells probably results from filaments and tubules sliding against one another and against organelles.

Microtubules are a main structural component of **cilia** (sing. *cilium*) and **flagella** (sing. *flagellum*). Cilia and flagella are external extensions of a variety of cells. Both are hairlike, but flagella are longer than cilia. When present, flagella are usually few in number. Cilia, on the other hand, occur in greater numbers and cover all or large sections of the cell surface (Figure 3.7). Both cilia and flagella are cylindrical with a membrane wall. Both have the same basic internal structure —a central pair of microtubules surrounded by a ring of nine microtubule doublets.

Figure 3.7
Flagella on a bacterial cell (a) and cilia near the opening of the oviduct of a mouse cell (b)

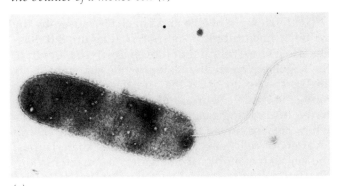

(a)

(b)

Figure 3.8
Various stages in the wave action of a cilium (a) and a flagellum (b)

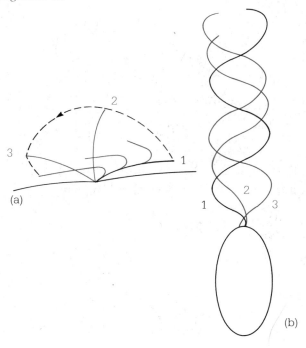

The movement of cilia and flagella is caused by the action of microtubules. As shown in Figure 3.8, flagella use a wave action that moves down the length of the flagella to create movement while cilia move back and forth like an oar. Cilia and flagella are used to move the entire cell or to move material past the cell. In the case of single celled organisms, cilia or flagella when present can be used to move the whole cell. In a variety of cells, cilia are used to move material past the cell. An example of this latter use occurs in our own breathing system. The cells that line our wind pipe or trachea have cilia that beat in such a way as to move foreign debris and mucous up the wind pipe so that it can be expelled from the body.

Control of Cell Activities and Manufacture of Molecules

Control Mechanism

The ability of the cell to control its activities is essential. Imagine what would happen, for example, if there was no mechanism to control cell growth and the cell just kept growing! Your activities are controlled by your brain, the rest of your nervous system, and your hormonal system. But the cell does not have these systems—how does it control its activities?

All cell activities such as growth, repair, movement, and cell division depend on the production of certain necessary chemicals. For example, the growth and repair of the cell membrane depend on the availability of phospholipids, and the production of ATP (adenosine triphosphate) can occur only when ADP (adenosine diphosphate) and an inorganic phosphate group are present. It follows from this that cell activities can be controlled through the manufacture or "nonmanufacture" of chemicals. Normally, living cells can manufacture chemicals only when three factors are present—the reacting chemicals, a source of energy, and enzymes. Control of chemical activities usually results from the control of the availability of the necessary enzymes—this is the basis for the control of cell activities.

Production of Enzymes

If cell activities are controlled by the production of enzymes, what controls enzyme production? How are enzymes manufactured? The topic of enzyme production will be discussed in some detail in Chapter 17 and will be described only briefly at this point.

The control mechanism for the manufacture of enzymes resides in the **nucleus** of the cell. The nucleus is a prominent cell organelle that is found, with few exceptions, in all eukaryotic cells. The equivalent structure in prokaryotes is the nucleoid. The key to the control of enzyme production is the genetic information which is encoded on the molecules of DNA (deoxyribonucleic acid). The code on the DNA consists of a series of molecules with specific patterns. Each pattern contains the blue print for a specific enzyme. Normally, during the growth phase of the cell, the chromosomes are extended in long fibres called **chromatin** (Figure 3.9). In this form the molecular code on the DNA is available to begin the production of enzymes as they are needed.

The mechanisms for the control of enzyme production rely on the movement of molecules into and out of the nucleus. As Figure 3.10(a) shows, a double membrane surrounds the nucleus. This double membrane is called the **nuclear envelope** and it is quite complex. Much of the research on the nuclear envelope has focussed on the pores which are shown in Figure 3.10(b). These pores are quite large (40 nm to 100 nm) and although how they operate is not fully understood, they probably account for the movement of large molecules into and out of the nucleus.

Figure 3.9 ▶
Chromatin fibres from the root cell in the onion, Allium
cepa. *The dark beadlike structures are coiled segments of
chromatin and are called nucleosomes.*

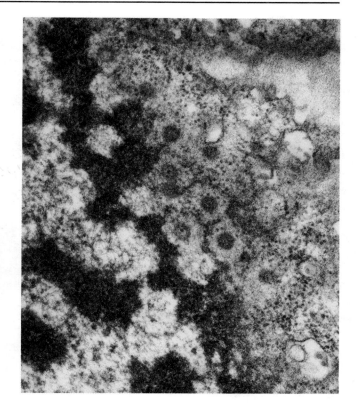

Figure 3.10 ▼
*In the electron micrograph of the nuclear envelope of an
onion root cell (a), the arrow points to a pore in the
nuclear envelope. The nuclear side is denoted by N and the
cytoplasmic side by C. The pores can be seen more clearly
on the electron micrograph of the surface of the nuclear
envelope (b).*

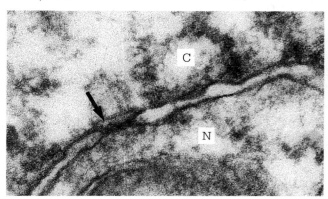

(a)

(b)

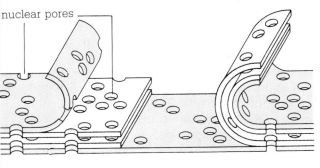

nuclear pores

Figure 3.11

Nucleus in an intestinal cell with a large prominent nucleolus (Nu)

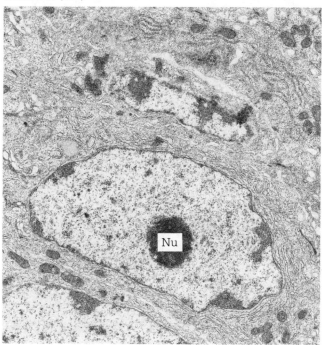

Figure 3.12

A model of a ribosome showing the smaller piece (S) on top of the larger section (L). The two parts of the ribosome fit together so that a tunnel-like space is left between them. It is theorized that the RNA molecule is threaded through this tunnel and is translated as enzymes are assembled.

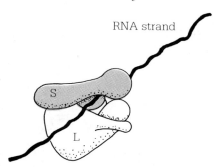

RNA strand

in the cytoplasm. Still others are found within the mitochondria and chloroplasts of cells. Ribosomes are so small (less than 30 nm in diameter) that even the electron microscope cannot show much structural detail. It is evident, however, that ribosomes are made up of two parts, a large and a small section, each having distinct but complementary roles in protein synthesis (Figure 3.12).

Manufacture of Molecules

The site of the initial production of enzymes and other proteins such as hormones is restricted to ribosomes. Lipids and carbohydrates are manufactured elsewhere in the cell, usually in association with membrane surfaces. One system of membranes that is associated with the production of many different chemicals is the **endoplasmic reticulum** (often abbreviated ER). Endoplasmic reticulum is a system of tubules and channels that is formed by membranes and that radiates throughout the cytoplasm. It separates the cytoplasm into two compartments, one which is enclosed within the ER and one which is not. It has been shown in a number of studies to be continuous with the nuclear envelope. In addition to providing a site for chemical reactions, the channels of the ER allow chemicals to move easily from one location in the cell to another.

There are two types of ER. One type is covered with ribosomes and is called **rough endoplasmic reticulum** (RER). As you might guess from the presence of the ribosomes, the RER is involved in the production of proteins. Endoplasmic reticulum without ribosomes is called **smooth endoplasmic reticulum** (SER).

Also suspended within the nucleoplasm of non-dividing cells are one or more dark spherical masses called **nucleoli** (sing. *nucleolus*). A single nucleolus can be seen in the nucleus shown in Figure 3.11. Nucleoli are not surrounded by a membrane. The nucleoli are thought to be the centres where **ribosomes** are assembled.

Scientists have theorized that when a specific enzyme is required, molecular messengers enter the nucleus and switch the control mechanism for that enzyme into the production mode. In the first step of production, the appropriate molecular blueprint on the DNA molecule is used to make a similar molecule of RNA (ribonucleic acid). The required molecular code on the DNA is actually transferred to the RNA molecule. When complete, the RNA molecule carries the molecular code or blueprint for the enzyme out of the nucleus to a ribosome. It is at the ribosome that the information on the RNA, in combination with molecular building blocks that are available in the cytoplasm, is used to assemble the required enzyme.

Ribosomes are small, roughly spherical organelles that are found throughout the cell. Some are attached to membranes of other organelles and others float free

Figure 3.13
An area in a liver cell showing rough endoplasmic reticulum (RER) and smooth endoplasmic reticulum (SER)

Figure 3.14
A Golgi apparatus with its associated vessels

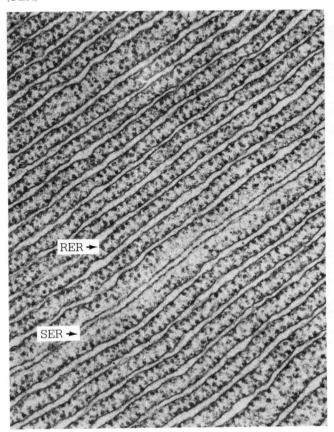

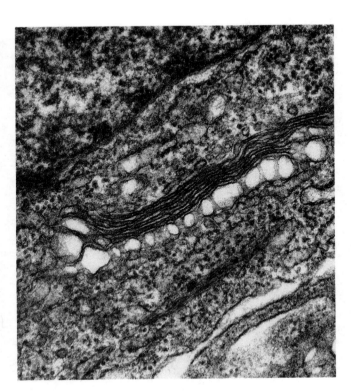

Smooth endoplasmic reticulum is involved in a variety of chemical activities which are described below. Both rough and smooth ER are shown in Figure 3.13.

Depending on their functions, cells vary in the amount of the two ER types. For example, cells that are active in secreting proteinaceous materials, such as the cells of the pancreas that produce insulin and digestive enzymes, have a lot of RER. The relationship between RER and ribosomes seems straightforward. The proteins synthesized by the ribosomes can enter the ER for further modification and for transport throughout the cell. In addition to moving through the ER, sacs containing the proteins can pinch off from the ER and move around the cell. If the role of the cell is to produce secretions, as in the case of salivary gland cells, then the sacs containing the secretory material move to the cell membrane in order to expel their contents out of the cell.

SER is involved in the production of such chemicals as steroids and phospholipids. For this reason, SER is much more prominent than RER in steroid-producing cells such as those of the gonads and the adrenal cortex. In the liver, the SER is specialized for the detoxification of a wide variety of chemicals including several types of drugs. Scientists have observed that when a laboratory animal is injected with a drug such as phenobarbitol, there is a massive increase in the amount of SER in the animal's liver cells.

Closely associated with the ER and the synthesis of molecules is the **Golgi apparatus**. This often takes the form of a complex of closely stacked flattened sacs. As Figure 3.14 shows, there can be more than one Golgi apparatus in a cell. The Golgi apparatus seems to be particularly involved with the modification of protein molecules that occurs through the addition of fat and sugar molecules. The modified protein molecules collect in sacs that pinch off from the Golgi complex. These sacs remain in the cytoplasm or move to the cell membrane for inclusion in the cell membrane or for expulsion out of the cell.

Figure 3.15

This series of micrographs shows the formation of a food vacuole in a human white blood cell. The cell membrane forms a pit around food molecules, the dark dot in (a); the membrane pinches off (b and c) to form the vacuole (d).

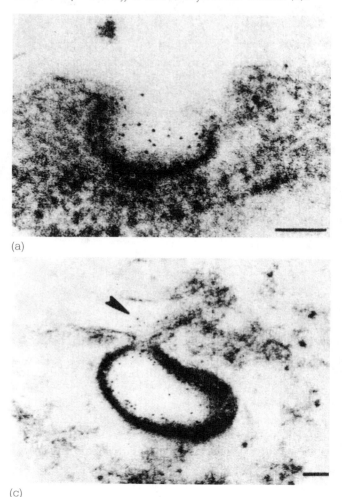

(a)

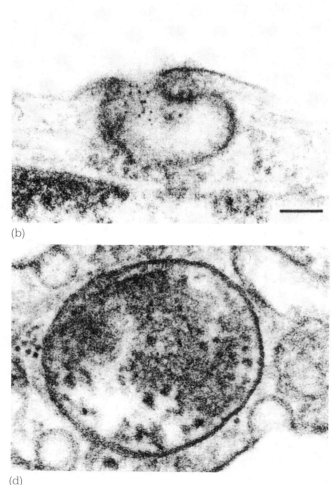

(b)

(c)

(d)

Intake and Use of Nutrients

To perform all of its activities, cells must have a constant supply of nutrients to provide the energy and the raw materials required. Cells extract the necessary nutrients from the liquid environment that surrounds them. Once inside the cell, chemical processes break down the nutrient molecules and extract the energy and chemicals required. A variety of cell organelles are involved in this process.

To begin with, nutrients enter into the cell through the cell membrane. As you will learn in Chapter 4, the cell membrane uses a variety of processes to accomplish this. A number of small molecules enter and leave the cell through simple diffusion. In the case of larger molecules and food particles, the cell membrane actively pursues and surrounds the desired materials or forms channels through which the nutrients pass.

Where the cell membrane is actively involved, the food material is incorporated into a **food vacuole** that pinches off from the cell membrane (Figure 3.15). Once in the cytoplasm, digestive juices enter the vacuole to break down the nutrients enclosed. Useful chemicals leave the food vacuole and move to other organelles for direct use or for further breakdown. The waste material that remains in the vacuole is eventually released from the cell.

Lysosomes can act as "suicide bags" for the cell. When the cell is old and begins to malfunction, many of the lysosomes in the cell break down and release their digestive enzymes into the cytoplasm. When the concentration is sufficiently high, these enzymes break down the entire cell. The products of this process move into the extracellular fluid and are used by other cells that are still viable.

Since lysosomes contain enzymes that are capable of digesting the cell, it is obvious that these enzymes must somehow be confined to protect the cell. The membrane surrounding the lyso-some provides this protection. Normally, all the digestive action of the lysosome is carried on within the confines of its membrane. It is still not known why the membrane of the lysosome is not affected by the enzymes it contains.

For some time it has been proposed that the malfunction of lysosomes might be the major cause of some diseases. Although this proposal has been difficult to verify, some examples are known.

The damage in the joints of those suffering from rheumatoid arthritis is believed to result partly from lysosomal enzymes that have been released from surrounding cells. The symptoms of the miner's disease called silicosis are also attributed to lysosome malfunction. Miners breathe in silica fibres into their lungs, which are then taken in by macrophage cells in the lung tissue and incorporated into lysosomes. But the silica fibres cannot be broken down by the enzymes in the lysosomes and instead, they cause the lysosomes to leak. This causes considerable cell damage in the affected person.

Figure 3.16
A variety of lysosomes (L)

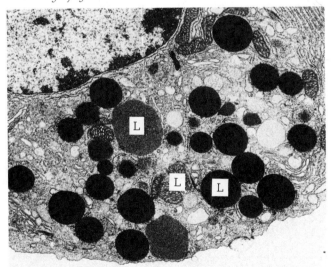

As part of the digestive process, vacuoles that contain food particles often join with **lysosomes**. Lysosomes are approximately spherical organelles which can vary considerably in size (Figure 3.16). Like vacuoles, lysosomes are bounded by a single membrane and lack any visible significant internal structure. They are formed in the region of the Golgi apparatus and contain a variety of enzymes that are derived from the rough endoplasmic reticulum.

Energy Production and Release
In addition to raw materials, the cell must have a continuous supply of energy to drive all its chemical activities. As with raw materials, cells obtain energy by breaking down nutrients. The chemical most frequently involved with the energy supply for the cell is the carbohydrate, glucose. The two cell organelles involved here are **chloroplasts** in the production of glucose and **mitochondria** in its breakdown.

As you are aware, plants have the ability to capture light energy and use it to manufacture glucose. This process, called photosynthesis, occurs in the chloroplasts of plant cells. Chloroplasts are found in plant cells, algal cells and some protozoan cells, but not in animal cells. In higher plants, chloroplasts are generally oval in shape and are 2 μm to 4 μm wide and 5 μm to 10 μm long. They have a double membrane construction (Figure 3.17). The outer membrane surrounds the organelle. The inner membrane forms stacks of flattened membrane sacs called grana. It is in the grana that the chlorophyll molecules are found and it is here that photosynthesis takes place to produce glucose. Chloroplasts are important in cell energetics. The structure and function of the chloroplast will be discussed in greater detail in Chapters 6 to 8.

Chloroplasts are the sites for the manufacture of glucose. The sites for the breaking down of glucose in order to extract the chemical energy from it are the mitochondria. These are large prominent organelles

Figure 3.17
An electron micrograph (a) and a model (b) of a
chloroplast. The double membrane around the outside of
the chloroplast and the internal stacks of membranes
called granum are evident.

stroma

stroma
granum
thylakoids

granum

outer
inner

(a)

(b)

Figure 3.18
An electron micrograph (a) and a model (b) of a
mitochondrion in a pancreas cell of a bat. The inner layer
of the surrounding double membrane can be seen infolded
to form the fingerlike cristae.

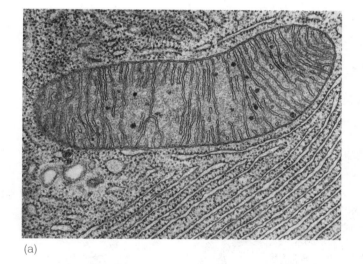

(a)

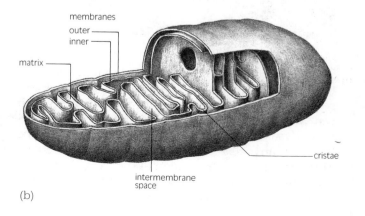

membranes
outer
inner
matrix

cristae

intermembrane
space

(b)

that are found in almost all eukaryotic cells. The number of mitochondria in each cell varies dramatically with the cell type. For example, several species of colourless algae have no mitochondria. Some sperm cells have only a hundred or so wrapped tightly around the sperm cell tail. Liver cells have one to two thousand and some egg cells have as many as 500 000 per cell. The number of mitochondria in a cell is often related to the energy requirements of the cell.

Mitochondria assume a variety of shapes in different cells. Typically they are oval or sausage-shaped with a cross sectional diameter of 0.2 μm to 1.0 μm and a length of 1 μm to 4 μm. They have a double membrane construction with the inner membrane infolded to form **cristae** (Figure 3.18).

Mitochondria are the sites for most of the extremely important chemical processes in which energy is extracted from glucose and made available to the cell. This usable energy is incorporated into ATP. The molecules of ATP move out of the mitochondria and through the cytoplasm to the locations in the cell where energy is required. Like chloroplasts, mitochondria are very important in cell energetics. They will be investigated in greater detail in Chapter 5.

Figure 3.19
Stages of the cell cycle

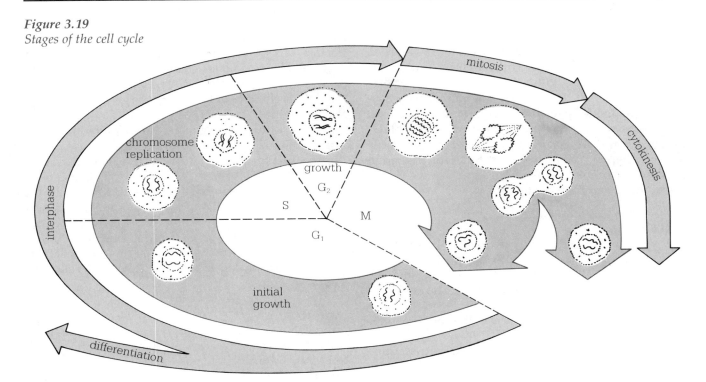

3.3 CELL DIVISION AND GROWTH

You began your existence as a single fertilized egg cell and now your body is made up of approximately 6×10^{13} cells. Within this number, there are approximately 100 different types. Under normal conditions, all of your cells have specialized jobs to do and they work in harmony with one another. Also, in each second, millions of your body cells die. If they were not replaced, you would shrivel up and eventually cease to exist. It is obvious that cells must have an efficient but controlled way to reproduce and grow and indeed they do. Certainly, an overview of cell structure and function would be incomplete without a consideration of cell reproduction.

The Cell Cycle

All living cells can be thought of as going through a cycle of division, chemical and organelle production, growth, and then division again. The knowledge of the phases of this cycle has been valuable to cytologists as they attempt to unravel such mysteries as DNA replication, cell growth and differentiation, and the mechanisms controlling cell division, as well as the reasons for the loss of this control when cells become cancerous.

The stages of the cell cycle, shown in Figure 3.19, are named according to a system first suggested by Alma Howard and Stephen Pelc in 1951. Cell reproduction which includes the division of the nucleus, or **mitosis**, and the division of the cell, or **cytokinesis**, is a key part of the cycle and is often considered in isolation. This phase of the cycle is shown as M in Figure 3.19. Indeed, mitosis is very important. Each new daughter cell that results from a cell division must receive an exact copy of each of the chromosomes that was in the nucleus of the parent cell. Without all of the genetic information contained in the chromosomes, the daughter cells would eventually malfunction and die.

The stage between one cell reproduction and the next is called **interphase** and it has typically been considered as a single event. In the cell cycle, however, interphase is split into three separate phases. The major focus of interphase is the duplication of the chromosomes and the DNA contained in them. If each daughter cell is to receive an exact copy of the chromosomes of the parent cell, there must be two duplicate chromosome sets at the beginning of mitosis. This duplication occurs during the S or synthesis phase of the cell cycle.

After the M phase in the cycle, there is usually a period during which the cell grows but there is no DNA synthesis. This period is labelled G1 where G stands for a gap in DNA synthesis. It is also during G1 that some cells differentiate in order to perform specialized jobs. If they become specialized they usually do not divide again but instead, they age, die and are replaced. After DNA replication is complete, another phase, G2, occurs before mitosis begins. Little seems to happen during G2 except that the triggering mechanism for mitosis occurs. In some cases, cells can arrest in G2 and then fail to divide.

Cell Growth

The mechanisms for growth are essentially the same in all cells. Growth occurs mainly during the G1 phase of the cell cycle. It results from the synthesis and use of all of the major classes of molecules. The energy to promote growth is obtained from glucose in the mitochondria and delivered to the site of the chemical reaction in the form of ATP.

It was noted earlier that the chemical reactions involved with the manufacture of different molecules in cells are initiated and controlled by a variety of enzymes. Cell growth is, therefore, also controlled by the presence or absence of enzymes. Although the mechanics of enzyme production have been described, little is known about what triggers the beginning and end of enzyme synthesis. It is postulated that chemical messengers are somehow involved and indeed several growth regulating agents have been identified. For example, adrenocorticotrophic hormone (ACTH) and interferon are known to restrict growth while insulin and somatomedin are known to stimulate growth.

Variability in the Cell Cycle

The analysis of cell cycles in a large variety of cells has revealed a great deal of variability between different types of cells and also between cells in the same organism. For different cells, the length of time required for the various phases and the presence or absence of phases vary. For example, human cells that are growing in culture, typically complete the entire cycle in approximately 24 hours. Cells in some early non-mammalian embryos can complete a cycle every 20 minutes. Also, in some early embryonic development, G1 may be missing. The cells in these embryos simply divide without growing. The size of the cells diminishes at each division.

The control of the cell cycle is of particular interest to many cytologists. It would appear that a variety of factors can cause mature cells to arrest in G1. For example, in investigating how cell division speeds up to heal wounds in the skin, researchers have discovered that cells in healthy skin tissue give off chemicals which inhibit mitosis. However, damaged cells around a wound stop making these inhibiting chemicals. This enables the cells around the wound to replicate quickly in order to heal the wound. Other chemicals which inhibit cell division have also been discovered and these have proven useful both in the general study of cells and in the treatment of cancer through chemotherapy. Since cancer cells divide continually and rapidly, any chemical which blocks cell division or kills cells when they are dividing will have a much more profound effect on cancerous cells than on normal ones.

Mitosis

Once DNA synthesis is complete and the cell has gone through a relatively brief G2 stage, interphase ends and mitosis begins. Mitosis can be thought of as having four distinct stages: **prophase**, **metaphase**, **anaphase**, and **telophase**.

You will recall that in interphase the chromosomes are in the form of a mass of elongated, loosely associated strands called chromatin. The beginning of prophase occurs when the chromosomes start to condense into distinct recognizable threads. It is the appearance of these chromosomal threads that gives the name mitosis to this process (from the Greek word *mitos* meaning thread). The chromosomes continue to coil and condense until each chromosome appears as two distinct short rods joined at one or more points (Figure 3.20). These rods are called **sister chromatids** and they are the result of DNA replication during interphase.

Several other events occur during prophase. First the nucleolus becomes smaller and by late prophase or early metaphase it disappears. Also during prophase a system of microtubules, called a **spindle**, begins to form outside of the nucleus. Most animal cells and the cells of many of the more primitive plants contain a pair of **centrioles**. As Figure 3.21 shows, centrioles are short rod-like structures and are arranged at right angles to each other. Their internal structure is similar to cilia in that it consists of an array of nine microtubule triads. The centriole pair is called a **centrosome**. Each new cell begins with a single centrosome. It duplicates during interphase.

Figure 3.20
An electron micrograph of a human chromosome showing the two sister chromatids

Figure 3.21
This cross section through a centriole shows that each centriole is made up of nine triplets of microtubules.

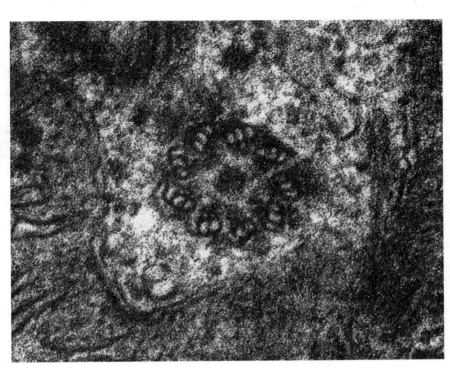

As prophase begins, the centrosomes take up positions close to the nucleus. A number of microtubules have already formed around each centrosome and they are now called **asters**. Early in prophase, the asters move in opposite directions and take up positions on either side of the nucleus. As the asters separate, the microtubules elongate and assemble to form a complete spindle which goes around the outside of the nucleus from pole to pole (Figure 3.22). The term pole is often used for the end of the spindle because the spindle is reminiscent of the globe with lines of longitude running around it.

In cells without centrioles, the spindle appears to be assembled in a clear area that forms around the nucleus. As this clear area forms, it becomes packed with microtubules which lie parallel to one another to converge at either end of the nucleus.

The end of prophase and the beginning of metaphase is marked by the fragmentation and disappearance of the nuclear envelope. Three other events occur during metaphase. As the nuclear envelope disappears, the spindle fibres move in to occupy the space formerly within the nucleus. The chromosomes then

Figure 3.22
A micrograph of a cell at the beginning of metaphase showing the spindle fibres stretching from pole to pole

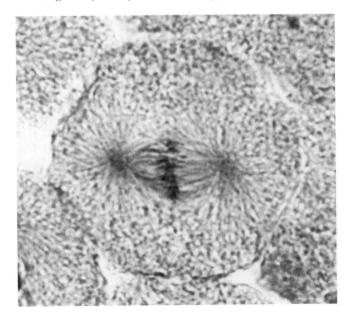

Figure 3.23
In the metaphase of mitosis (a), the centrosomes at both ends of the spindle with the chromosome mass in the middle are evident as dark areas. As depicted in the simple diagram in (b), separate chromosome pairs are often evident during metaphase.

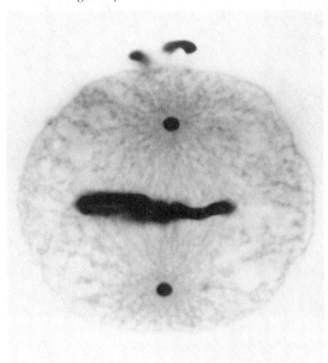

(a)

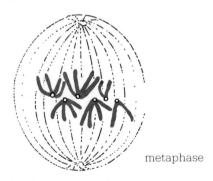

metaphase

(b)

Figure 3.24
Anaphase in mitosis

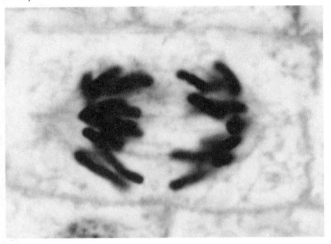

(a)

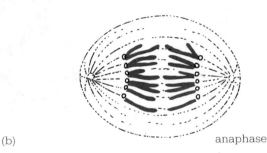

(b)   anaphase

move to the centre of the spindle (Figure 3.23). Finally, each of the chromatids attaches to a spindle fibre in such a way that each sister chromatid is facing the opposite pole. The point of attachment of the spindle fibre to each chromatid is a plate-like structure called a kinetochore. This event is extremely important for it provides the mechanism which ensures that the sister chromatids will separate and travel to the location

in the cell where the new nucleii are being formed. In this way each of the new nucleii will have all the necessary chromosomes and only one of each type.

Anaphase begins the instant that the chromatids begin to separate. The motive force that causes the movement of the chromosomes is still a matter of speculation. It has been suggested that the microtubules either push or pull the chromatids toward the poles. The kinetochores are important; experiments have shown that when the connection between the kinetochores and the spindle fibres is broken, chromatid movement stops. As shown in Figure 3.24, the kinetochore leads the chromatids toward the poles.

Anaphase ends and telophase begins when the chromatids reach the poles of the spindle. At this stage, the condensed chromatids begin to elongate to become chromatin again. The spindle fibres begin to disappear. Also, segments of a new nuclear envelope appear around the chromosome mass and eventually a complete envelope is formed. A new nucleolus forms inside the new nucleus.

(a)

(b)

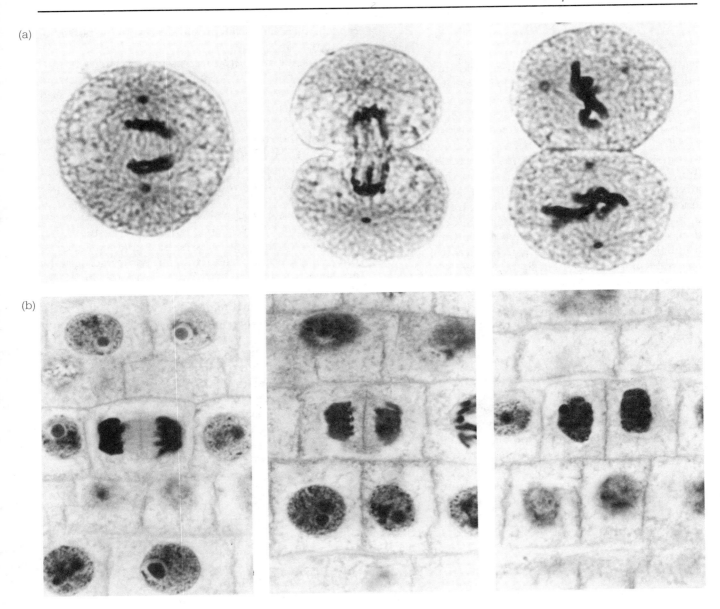

Cytokinesis

In most cells, mitosis and cytokinesis occur simultaneously. Usually division of the cell cytoplasm is initiated during mitotic anaphase. In animal cells, protists, and many fungal and algal cells, cytokinesis is accomplished through the formation of a furrow which deepens to eventually pinch the cell into two pieces. In higher plants, a plate of microtubules, called a phragmoplast forms in the central region of the spindle. The phragmoplast begins to form at the centre of the cell and grows out toward the cell wall. As it forms, the cell membrane and the primary cell wall are laid down in its path. Eventually a new cell wall and membrane split the original cell in two. Figure 3.25 shows cytokinesis in a plant cell and an animal cell.

Figure 3.25
Cytokinesis in a plant cell and an animal cell. In (a) the steps in the splitting of an animal cell are obvious. The three micrographs in (b) show the stepwise accumulation of microtubular material down the centre of the cell and the eventual formation of a new cell wall.

3.4 MODERN TECHNIQUES IN CYTOLOGY

Thousands of scientists around the world are studying the cell and producing thousands of research papers each year. This amount of effort is all the more unusual when you realize that these scientists are working with something that cannot be seen with the naked eye. Cytologists must rely on a variety of techniques that make cell parts and functions detectable and visible. These techniques are so important to the advancement of cell biology that a considerable amount of the research in this area centres on developing improved methods of studying the cell. In addition, cytological techniques have proven useful in a number of other areas, notably in medical testing and research laboratories and in such new fields as genetic engineering. In this section, you will learn about some of the modern techniques that are being used in cytology laboratories around the world.

Microscopy

As it has been for many years, the microscope continues to be a central tool in biology. Many different types of microscopes are in use today ranging from simple monocular light microscopes which are used in elementary schools to sophisticated high voltage electron microscopes which are available only in a limited number of laboratories around the world. You have probably learned from previous science courses about the characteristics of the light microscope and the general operating principles of the electron microscope. This section will deal with a few selected aspects of microscopy.

Light Microscopes

For some time, manufacturers of light microscopes have been able to produce instruments capable of providing the best magnification and resolving power possible. Good light microscopes can provide magnifications in the range of 1500× and can resolve points of an object that are as close as 0.2 μm. This ability to distinguish objects that are close together is called the *resolving power* of the microscope. Resolving power is determined by the wavelengths of the light that are used to illuminate the specimen. The shorter the wavelength, the greater the resolving power. Blue light has the shortest wavelength in the visible spectrum; it is approximately 0.45 μm. Since the best potential resolution is approximately half of the wave-

length, blue light can provide a resolving power of about 0.2 μm.

The use of basic light microscopes is called bright-field light microscopy. Simple light microscopes are used for observing the shapes and size of cells and large organelles such as nuclei, and vacuoles. However, the light microscope is severely limited when it comes to the study of very small organelles that are beyond its resolving power.

Before turning to the electron microscope, it should be mentioned that several other more elaborate types of light microscope have been developed. Two of these microscopes, the phase contrast microscope and the Nomarski microscope, use optical systems that make use of the light interference characteristics of different parts and areas of the cell. Three micrographs are shown in Figure 3.26. The micrograph in 3.26(a) was taken with a bright-field microscope. It shows that thin, unstained living material such as the cell absorbs very little light and is not easy to see. The micrograph in 3.26(b) is of the same cells but was taken with a phase-contrast microscope. In this case, the thicker, denser sections of the cell are made darker and more visible. The Nomarski microscope was used to produce the picture in 3.26(c). Here the image takes on a three-dimensional appearance. Although the image is enhanced using the latter two microscopes, these instruments are more difficult to use and are considerably more expensive.

Electron Microscopes

Just as the invention of the first simple light microscope made microscopic objects visible to early scientists, the development of the electron microscope has made a whole new level of cell structure available to cytologists. The first simple electron microscope was invented in 1932 by Ernst Ruska. Two Canadian scientists, Albert Prebus and James Hillier, made significant improvements on Ruska's original design and developed an instrument that was the forerunner of today's powerful microscopes.

The electron microscope has a resolving power which is about 200 times greater than the light microscope. Magnification can reach levels of 300 000×. With these capabilities, cytologists can see objects as small as protein molecules or strands of DNA.

The electron microscope uses a beam of electrons rather than light to illuminate the specimen. Two types of electron microscopes are available, the *transmission electron microscope* (TEM) and the *scanning electron microscope* (SEM).

Figure 3.26
*Light photomicrographs of cells as taken with bright-field
(a), phase-contrast (b), and Nomarski interference (c)
microscopes.*

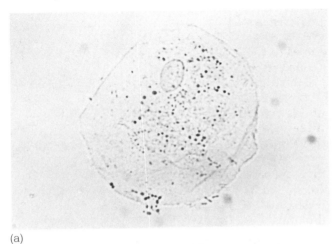

(a)

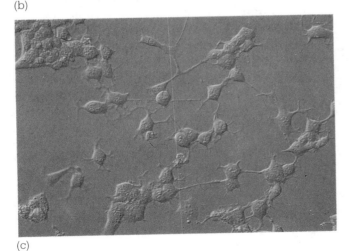

(b)

Figure 3.27(a) shows a transmission electron microscope. A beam of electrons emanates from a tungsten
filament which acts as a cathode. The electrons then
pass down through a tube to an anode. They are accelerated by a high voltage, commonly between 50 000 V
and 100 000 V, which is applied between the anode
and the cathode. The column through which the electrons travel is evacuated to remove the air molecules
which could interfere with the flow of the electrons.
As the electron beam travels down the tube it is
focussed by means of electromagnets placed in the
column.

The specimen to be viewed is placed in the path of
the electrons. The electrons are deflected by the molecules of the specimen and some are deflected more
than others. Immediately below the specimen is an
aperture which allows for the passage of the electrons
that have not been severely deflected. These electrons
continue through the aperture and are further
focussed and allowed to strike a viewing screen. An
image of the specimen is produced because the elimination and emission of electrons create a pattern of
light and dark areas on the screen.

Specimens to be viewed by the TEM must be
extremely thin, less than .1 μm in thickness. This is
necessary because a thicker specimen will absorb all
of the electrons, thus eliminating the image. Since
most cells are 5 μm to 20 μm thick, only an extremely
small portion of the cell can be seen. Recently a new
high voltage TEM which uses 10^6 V to accelerate the
electrons has been developed. This high voltage TEM
makes it possible to view thicker specimens. It gives
cytologists a better view of the depth in the cell.

A scanning electron microscope is used to view the
surface of specimen. Some of the images produced by
the SEM are quite spectacular since it provides a sense
of depth and shows surface features. Figure 3.28
shows the structure of brewers' yeast as seen under
the SEM. As the name suggests, the SEM produces
an image by scanning the surface of the specimen with
a beam of electrons. Some of the electrons may be
reflected or they may cause the emission of electrons
from the material examined. The electrons that are
emitted from the surface of the specimen are called
secondary electrons. Some of the secondary electrons
are captured by a detector and used to create an image
on a video screen.

Specimen Preparation and Staining
You probably already have some knowledge of the
preparation procedures for viewing specimens under

(a)

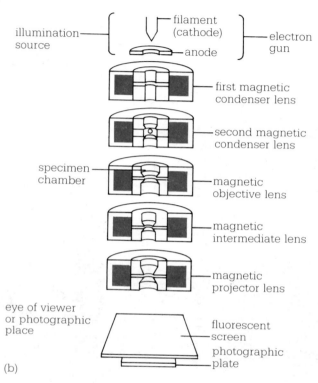

Figure 3.27
A transmission electron microscope (a) and a diagram showing the basic elements of the TEM tube (b)

illumination source

filament (cathode)

anode

electron gun

first magnetic condenser lens

second magnetic condenser lens

specimen chamber

magnetic objective lens

magnetic intermediate lens

magnetic projector lens

eye of viewer or photographic place

fluorescent screen

photographic plate

(b)

the light microscope. Thin sections that are only a few cells thick are cut from the tissue being studied. Normally these are mounted on a glass slide. The specimen is often stained to highlight some of its parts. Sometimes the tissue is macerated to produce a suspension of single cells.

The preparation of materials for examination under the electron microscope is similar but more complex and more exacting. As was pointed out earlier, the specimen for examination under the electron microscope must be very thin — .1 μm or less in thickness. In addition, the material to be viewed must be fixed. This means that the tissue must be immersed in a chemical that kills the cells but also maintains the structure of the cell in its most natural configuration. Gluteraldehyde is the most common chemical fixative and is often used in conjunction with osmium tetroxide which acts both as a fixative and a stain. The material must first be dehydrated. This is done in a variety of ways but often involves immersing the tissue in increasing concentrations of alcohol or acetone. To dry the material even further it can be impregnated with

liquid carbon dioxide. The carbon dioxide drives out any water that might be left.

Once the tissue has been fixed, it must be embedded in a resin that will support the tissue as it is cut. The specimen is then sliced from the resin block and placed on a metallic grid. This grid is much like a small screen; it provides support for the section but has "windows" through which the electrons can pass. The tissue is coated with an ultra-thin layer of heavy metal particles and then the grid with its specimen is placed in a chamber in the column of the electron microscope for viewing.

Separating and Identifying Cell Constituents

Using microscopes, cytologists were able to see the intriguing variety of organelles and other cell constituents. Quite understandably they wanted to learn more about them. For example, they wanted to know what they were made of, how they reacted to different situations, what happened to chemicals that entered them, and so on. But how was this to be accomplished? How could different molecules be separated

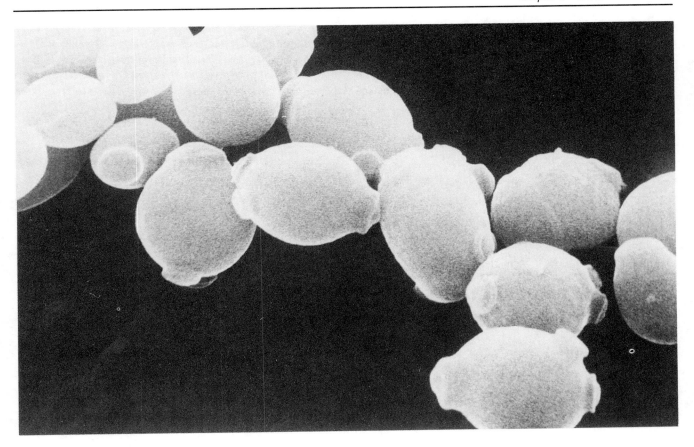

Figure 3.28
A micrograph taken with a scanning electron microscope. This picture shows buds of brewers' yeast.

out for analysis? To test and chemically analyze a specific part of the cell, it would be necessary to separate it from all the other parts. Although they could be surgically removed from a cell, single organelles were much too small to provide enough material for chemical analysis. Somehow, sufficient quantities of specific cell constituents had to be obtained.

A variety of ingenious techniques have been designed for the separation, identification, and analysis of cell components. The first three techniques described below are essentially separation processes. Separation is accomplished by forcing cellular components to move through some material in such a way that the components will separate into groups as they move. In each procedure, a different motive force and a different separating medium is used. The final technique that is described is designed for the identification and mapping of different molecules.

Centrifugation

Differential centrifugation is a powerful technique for the separation of cell parts. First, the tissue containing the cells to be examined is cut into very small pieces. Some of this finely cut tissue is then homogenized in a cold isotonic medium (Figure 3.29). The pestel of the homogenizer fits so tightly to the sides of the glass tube that many of the cells are broken into pieces. This cell homogenate is then placed in the tubes of the **centrifuge** (Figure 3.30) and the tubes are spun to create a centrifugal force on the homogenate. The principle upon which the centrifuge works is simple. In the centrifugal field, cell particles move toward the bottom of the tube at different speeds depending on their density. The denser particles settle more quickly and this makes it possible to separate the homogenate into fractions of different particle densities.

The steps in a simple differential centrifugation are shown in Figure 3.31. At each successive step, the homogenate is spun at an increased speed for a longer time. Each time, particles of a different cell constituent settle out of the homogenate to form a pellet at the bottom of the tube. At the end of each step, the super-

Figure 3.29
A cell homogenizer

pestle of
homogenizer

close-fitting
glass tube

ice

homogenate (suspension
of material from
broken cells)

Figure 3.30
The swinging bucket (a), fixed angle (b) and oil-turbine driven (c) ultra-centrifuge are different types of centrifuge. The different angles of the buckets and tubes in (a) and (b) provide a different effect of the centrifugal force.

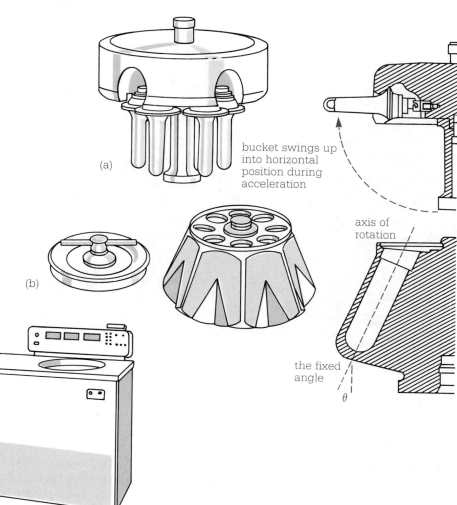

(a)

bucket swings up
into horizontal
position during
acceleration

axis of
rotation

(b)

the fixed
angle

θ

(c)

natant (the homogenate material that is left) is poured into another tube and centrifuged again. As Figure 3.31 shows, in the first step, the homogenate is spun for ten minutes at a rate that creates a centrifugal field that is 700 times the force of gravity. This treatment is sufficient to cause the nucleii and the unbroken cells to settle out of the homogenate. In the next step, the remaining material is centrifuged at 20 000 times the force of gravity for fifteen minutes. This time the larger organelles such as the mitochondria, chloroplasts, and lysosomes settle out.

In another technique, a liquid or a gel which forms a density gradient is placed in the centrifuge tubes first. The cell sample is then placed on top of the density gradient. During the centrifugation, the cell constituents move down through the density gradient and come to rest in the section corresponding to its own density. To extract the sample for analysis, a hole can be made in the bottom of the tube and the material extracted bit by bit.

Normally, the centrifugation process is not able to separate molecular constituents of cells. Some large

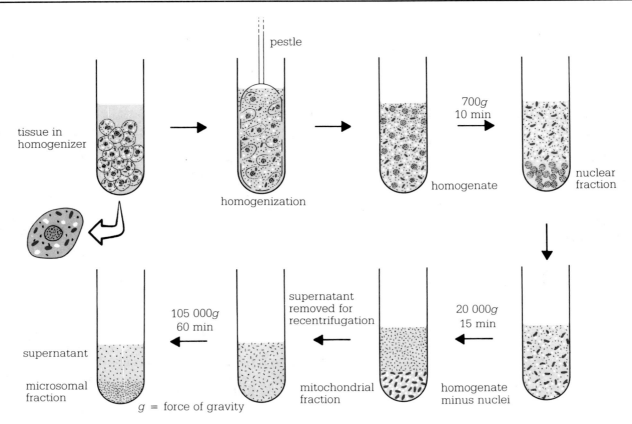

pestle

tissue in homogenizer

homogenization

homogenate

700*g*
10 min

nuclear fraction

105 000*g*
60 min

supernatant removed for recentrifugation

20 000*g*
15 min

supernatant

microsomal fraction

g = force of gravity

mitochondrial fraction

homogenate minus nuclei

homogenate minus nuclei

Figure 3.31
Stages in differential centrifugation: nuclei (pale colour), mitochondria (solid colour), lysosomes (white), microsomes (black) and cytosol (gray)

Figure 3.32
Electrophoresis apparatus. In this type of electrophoresis, the protein molecules to be separated are first embedded in a disc of gel (sample gel). The pore size in the sample gel is large and does not influence the rates of migration of the molecules. The pore size in the separating gel is much smaller and provides the required sieving effect.

molecular species can, however, be extracted using an ultracentrifuge (Figure 3.30). The ultracentrifuge can rotate very quickly, some in the range of 75 000 revolutions per minute. Such speeds create a centrifugal force which is 500 000 times the force of gravity.

Electrophoresis
Another technique capable of separating different types of molecules is **electrophoresis**. In this technique, different types of cellular molecules are separated from one another as they move at different rates through a column or a layer of material. A typical electrophoresis apparatus is shown in Figure 3.32. The material or medium that the molecules move through is often a gel of starch or polyacrylamide. Paper is sometimes used as well. The molecules move in response to an electrical field that is set up across the medium.

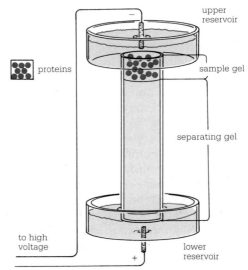

upper reservoir

proteins

sample gel

separating gel

to high voltage

lower reservoir

71

Figure 3.33
An electrophoretic column showing the bands of different molecules that have been separated and then stained

Complex organic molecules, such as those found in a cell homogenate, usually have a net positive or negative charge. Since an electric field is set up in the electrophoresis material, the molecules will move toward the end of the gel column with the opposite charge. The greater the charge on the molecule the more quickly it will move. The gel acts as a complex molecular sieve; the movement of the molecules is affected by their size and shape and their ability to thread through the gel network.

As with centrifuging, the molecules are allowed to migrate for a specific length of time. Since they move at different rates and in different directions, different molecules will take up various positions in the gel and form bands. For further clarification and study, these bands of molecules can be stained (Figure 3.33). This will reveal the number of different types of molecules in the original cellular material. Finally, the gel column can be sliced into sections and the chemicals in each section can be extracted.

Chromatography

Chromatography is another technique for the separation of different types of molecules. In chromatography, the motive force for the migrating molecules is a moving liquid or gas phase. The molecules from the cell extract are dissolved in the liquid or gas solvent. As the solvent moves through the medium the molecules are carried along. The medium or substance through which the solvent and molecules are moving impedes the movement of the cellular molecules. This impedance results from the nature of the medium and its interaction with the size, charge, and attraction of the molecules. The solvent can move through the medium by gravity, capillary action, or by being pumped.

A simple example of chromatography which is often done in high school laboratories is the separation of leaf pigments using paper chromatography. Leaf tissue is first macerated. A drop of leaf pigment is placed at one end of a strip of filter paper. The end of the paper with the pigment spot is placed in an organic solvent such as alcohol. As the solvent moves up through the paper, the various pigments in the spot of the leaf extract dissolve and move up at varying rates. Since the pigments are of different colours, they can be observed as different coloured bands on the paper.

In ion exchange chromatography, molecules are separated by their differences in charge. In this case, the medium through which the molecules move often consists of a resin made up of small charged particles. If the molecules to be separated are positively charged, then a column of negatively charged particles is used. The positively charged molecules will be captured in the column while negatively charged and neutral molecules will pass right through. Chemicals are then added to the column of resin in such a way that the bound molecules are released sequentially according to the strength of their net charge. Figure 3.34 shows an ion exchange apparatus.

Radioactive Labelling

The introduction of radioactive isotopes into biological molecules has proved to be a very useful technique in tracking biochemical reactions and the chemical participants in the cell. Generally, the radioactive isotope is introduced into molecules that will take part in the process to be analyzed. These reagent molecules are then said to be *labelled*. The isotopes most commonly used are ^3H, ^{14}C, ^{32}P, ^{35}S, ^{125}I, and ^{131}I. As these decay, they emit a high energy electron, called a β particle.

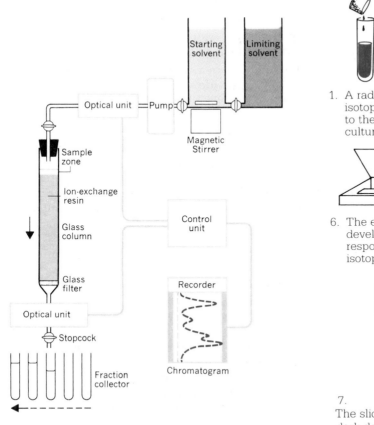

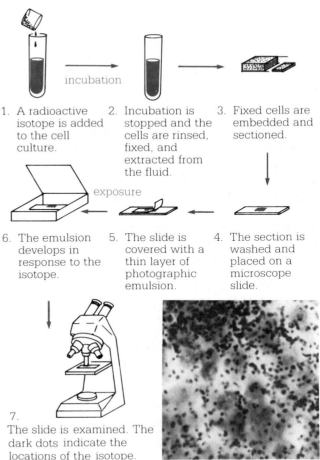

1. A radioactive isotope is added to the cell culture.

2. Incubation is stopped and the cells are rinsed, fixed, and extracted from the fluid.

3. Fixed cells are embedded and sectioned.

6. The emulsion develops in response to the isotope.

5. The slide is covered with a thin layer of photographic emulsion.

4. The section is washed and placed on a microscope slide.

7. The slide is examined. The dark dots indicate the locations of the isotope.

Figure 3.35
Autoradiography

Figure 3.34
Ion exchange apparatus. The sample of protein molecules to be separated is usually dissolved in the starting solvent. As the starting solvent moves through the resin, the protein molecules attach to the charged resin particles. When a solvent is introduced into the column, it causes some of the protein molecules to be released. These molecules are then carried out of the column and are collected for analysis. Different molecules are released when a second solvent is introduced and so on. The optical units detect and record the passage of different solvents and hence, different fractions through the apparatus.

This enables the presence of the molecule containing the isotope to be detected.

The radioactive labelling technique was used to track the path of carbon through the various steps in photosynthesis. In this case, labelled carbon dioxide molecules were produced using ^{14}C. To track the proc-

ess of photosynthesis, plants were exposed to the labelled CO_2. At various times after introduction, leaf tissue was analyzed to identify the chemical constituents that contained the carbon isotope.

In a process called **autoradiography** (Figure 3.35), isotopes are used to determine the sites of chemical processes in the cell. In this technique, living cells are first exposed to the labelled molecules. After an appropriate time to allow the labelled molecules to incorporate, the cells are embedded and then sectioned so that single, intact cells can be plated out on a slide. The cells are then coated with a photographic emulsion and placed in the dark for several days. The β particles that are emitted from the isotopes will develop the photographic film and create an image of the cell showing their locations in the cell.

CHAPTER SUMMARY

The cell has been of major interest to biologists for the last 300 years. Initial attempts at uncovering the mysteries of the cell were hampered by the low quality of the microscopes that were available. By the mid 1800s, improved light microscopes had enabled biologists to observe the basic structure of cells and the cell theory was proposed. This theory, one of the most important in science, states that the cell is the structural and functional unit of all living things and that cells come from pre-existing cells. Within the last 50 years, the development of the electron microscope and sophisticated cytological techniques have allowed biologists to study the detailed structure of cell organelles and their chemical characteristics.

There is a variety of different types of cells. These are mainly divided into two groups — the prokaryotic cells and the eukaryotic cells. However, despite the variety, all cells exhibit a number of similar characteristics. Cells are complex, small, and self-replicating; they can live as autonomous or semiautonomous entities and they can regulate their internal environments.

Cells are made up of 15 or more different parts or organelles. These organelles work together to perform a variety of functions that are essential for life. The cell membrane and, in the case of the plant cell, the cell wall, maintain a system of barriers and defence. They, along with a system of microtubules and microfilaments, provide structure and support for the cell. Cilia and flagella allow the entire cell or materials in the cell to move. The nucleus, DNA, nucleolus, ribosomes, endoplasmic reticulum, and Golgi apparatus play key roles in the control mechanisms of the cell and in the manufacture of molecules. The process of taking in and using nutrients is accomplished by the vacuoles, lysosomes, chloroplasts, and mitochondria. An important feature of the cell is the ability to grow and reproduce. The process of growth, nuclear division or mitosis, and cell division or cytokinesis is described in terms of a cell cycle. The key organelles involved are the nucleus, chromosomes, and the centrosome.

Knowledge of the cell is increasing rapidly. This increase in knowledge depends on the development of sophisticated means of studying the cell. The microscope and, in particular, the electron microscope, contine to be the main tools in cytology. Other techniques centre on the separation and identification of cell parts. These include centrifugation, electrophoresis, chromatography, and radioactive labelling.

Objectives

Having completed this chapter, you should be able to do the following:

1. Provide a modern definition of the term cell.
2. Describe five characteristics common to all cells.
3. Describe the different aspects of all activities, and explain the involvement of the cell organelles in these activities.
4. Explain how the cell grows and reproduces itself.
5. Name and describe four modern cytological techniques.

Vocabulary

cytology	turgor pressure	nucleolus
organelle	microtubule	ribosome
eukaryotic cell	microfilament	endoplasmic reticulum (rough
prokaryotic cell	cytoskeleton	and smooth)
cytoplasm	cilium	Golgi apparatus
nucleoid	flagellum	food vacuole
cell membrane	nucleus	lysosome
cell wall	chromatin	chloroplast
microfibril	nuclear envelope	mitochondrion

crista	anaphase	aster
mitosis	telophase	centrifuge
cytokinesis	sister chromatid	electrophoresis
interphase	spindle	autoradiography
prophase	centriole	
metaphase	centrosome	

Review Questions

1. How does the cell theory describe what a cell is?
2. The definition of the cell has changed over the years. Why has it changed? What is a modern definition of the term cell?
3. List and briefly describe five characteristics of all cells.
4. Compare prokaryotic cells with eukaryotic cells.
5. Why do many cytologists feel that the separation of cells into plant and animal categories is not appropriate?
6. What organelles are involved in providing the cell with a mechanism of barriers and defence?
7. How does the cell membrane provide defence for the cell?
8. Where are microtubules found in the cell and what is their function?
9. In general terms, describe how the activities of the cell are controlled.
10. How do lysosomes function in the intake and use of nutrients by the cell?
11. (a) Why are lysosomes suspect in the cause of some diseases?

(b) Describe how lysosomes are thought to cause one type of disease.
12. Draw and briefly describe the cell cycle.
13. Name and briefly describe the stages of mitosis.
14. Use diagrams to compare cytokinesis in plant and animal cells.
15. Describe the roles of the following in mitosis and cytokinesis:
    (a) centrosome
    (b) phragmoplast
    (c) kinetochore
16. Compare the operation of the transmission electron microscope with that of the scanning electron microscope.
17. Why is it so important for cytologists to be able to separate cell constituents?
18. Describe the process of differential centrifugation.
19. Compare the means of particle separation in electrophoresis with that in chromatography.

Advanced Questions

1. As a cytologist, you suspect that a certain molecule is one of the digestive enzymes that are found in the lysosome of a cell. You wish to verify its location and its activity. Which cytological techniques would you use in your study and why would you use them?
2. Why does cell differentiation have to occur during G1 and not G2 of the cell cycle?
3. It is determined that two objects in a cell are approximately 1 nm apart. Why would it be useless to try to magnify these objects 10 000 times using a light microscope?
4. As a world famous forensic scientist you are given the task of determining whether a deceased person

was a drug addict or not. You are not satisfied that the blood sample you analyzed provided conclusive proof. What other tissue might you examine and what would you look for?
5. Why must there be mechanisms of control over cell activities?
6. A fellow cytologist suggests to you that the nuclear matrix plays a role in the formation of the mitotic spindle. Accept or reject this idea and state your reasons.
7. The main function of an animal cell is the secretion of a proteinaceous chemical. What would be the key structural features of such a cell?

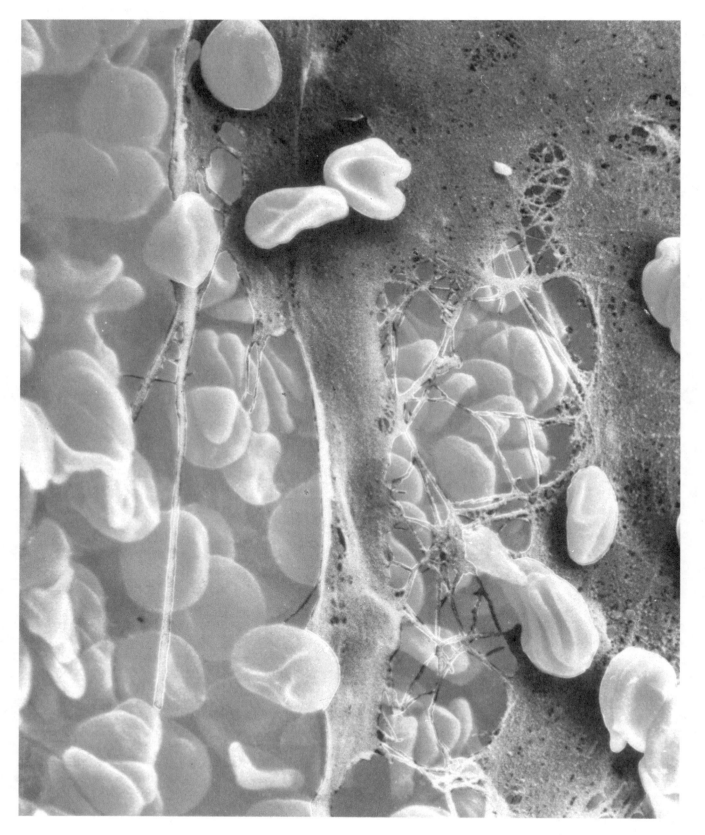

CHAPTER 4

CELL MEMBRANES: A STUDY OF STRUCTURE AND FUNCTION

The road to wisdom? — Well, it's plain and simple to express:
Err and err and err again but less and less and less.

Piet Hein in
Runaway Runes, 1968

You just got a small paper cut on your finger. For a short while you feel a little pain and it bleeds slightly. Soon the bleeding stops and, even though a minor infection might develop, in a day or two the cut will be completely healed. A commonplace occurrence which at first seems simple enough. Still, as a curious person, you may wonder what happens at the level of the individual cells. How is the pain registered? What causes the bleeding to stop? What is an infection and what fights it? The answers to these and related questions are becoming clearer as a result of our increasing understanding of the structure and function of the membrane of individual cells. In fact, the cell membranes serve an important role in most of the complex events that take place after the cut has occurred.

The initial sensation of pain arises from nerve impulses which are caused by rapid movements of certain ions (potassium and sodium) across the plasma membrane of the nerve cell. The clotting process is a result of a sequence of chemical reactions involving proteins circulating in the blood. Some of the first reactions occur in the membranes of blood platelets— small blood cells which have no nuclei. The infection is quickly brought under control by white blood cells. These cells have, in their membranes, proteins which can recognize foreign material such as bacteria. Once alerted to the infectious invasion, the white blood cells communicate signals to one another via their cell membranes. The immune system has begun to function. The ultimate process of healing involves tissue cells migrating into the wound, dividing and forming new tissue. When the dividing cells become too crowded, the cell–cell contact through the membrane, in ways which are not yet understood, inhibits further growth.

The cell membrane is central to a large number of biological processes. The above example illustrates a few of the diverse functions of cell membranes: transport (involved in pain sensation), reaction site (for formation of blood clotting agents), recognition site (to identify invaders), and communication surface (to alert the immune system).

This chapter introduces you to the general structure and functions of membranes. You will study the constituents of the membrane and see how their structure and shape determine the structure of the membrane and the way it is assembled. You will learn about the developments that led to the most modern models of the structure of cell membranes, and about the important features of the models for understanding the functions of the membranes. The chapter will focus on one of the most important functions, namely, control of transport across the membrane. As you come to the end of the chapter, you should have developed an appreciation of the simplicity of the membrane

77

structure and the complexity of the membrane functions. One of the exciting aspects of membrane research is reconciling these two aspects.

Table 4.1 Typical Functions of Membranes

FUNCTION TYPE	FEATURE
permeabilty barrier	occurs in all cells
selective transport	for nutrients and ions
site of reactions	synthesis of protein and ATP, absorption of light
site of recognition	of hormones, other cells
site of communication	by nerve signals, by cell–cell contact

4.1 MEMBRANE CONSTITUENTS

All cell membranes contain a mixture of **lipids** and *proteins*. The proportion and the nature of the mixture depend on the particular membrane and its functions. In plasma membranes, which form the envelope of the entire cell, some of the lipids and proteins have carbohydrate groups attached to them. These are *glycolipids* and *glycoproteins*. Except for the very special case where ribosomes are attached to the endoplasmic reticulum, there are no nucleic acids associated with membranes.

Lipids

The lipids found in membranes are conventionally grouped as *neutral lipids* and *other lipids*. Neutral lipids are soluble in hydrocarbon solvents such as hexane. Of these, **sterols** such as **cholesterol** are the most important. Other lipids are not soluble in hydrocarbon solvents. The predominant classes of other lipids are **phospholipids** and *glycolipids*. Phospholipids are usually the most abundant and important constituents of cell membranes (Table 4.2).

Table 4.2 Composition of the Human Red Blood Cell Membrane

CONSTITUENT	% BY MASS
proteins	50
lipids	50
cholesterol	25
glycolipids	0.5
phospholipids	25
phosphatidylcholine	9
phosphatydylethanolamine	5

Phospholipids

All phospholipids have a common set of building blocks (Figure 4.1). They contain a pair of long *fatty acids* attached to *glycerol* by ester linkages thereby forming a large hydrophobic region in the molecule. The glycerol also contains an ester linkage to a phosphate group, which in turn is connected to the rest of the lipid *head group*. It is this head group which differs among different types of phospholipids.

There are three major classes of phospholipid (Figure 4.2). Phosphatidyl*choline*, which contains the choline unit, is the most abundant phospholipid by mass. It is always both positively and negatively charged (a *zwitter ion* as discussed in Chapter 2). The cross sectional area of the head group is comparable to that of the lipid chains, so the molecule is almost cylindrical in shape. Phosphatidyl*ethanolamine* has a smaller head group because the four methyl groups are replaced by hydrogen. This lipid is generally a zwitter ion also. Phosphatidyl*serine* is normally negatively charged. It is believed that this lipid changes the properties of the membrane in important ways when it is present.

The length and type of fatty acid on the phospholipid can dramatically affect its properties. The fatty acid at the end almost never contains any carbon–carbon double bonds in the chain and is called a **saturated fatty acid** (Figure 4.3). The fatty acid at the middle carbon in the glycerol frequently contains one or two double bonds and is called an **unsaturated fatty acid**. The difference is important, since the more unsaturated fatty acids tend to have lower melting points. You are probably more familiar with this in the context of oils and fats. Corn oil is liquid at room temperature because it contains a large number of unsaturated fatty acids. Certain soft margarines are made from corn oil by hydrogenation, that is, by converting the double bonds to single bonds. The margarines contain more saturated fatty acids and are more solid.

Glycolipids

Glycolipids are similar in structure to phospholipids in the sense that they contain a pair of hydrocarbon chains and a polar head group. The head group, however, consists of one or more carbohydrate groups instead of the phosphate or glycerol group. The neutral glycolipids contain sugar residues such as glucose and galactose and have no charge. They are particularly important components of the membranes of nerve cells and are abundant in the brain.

Figure 4.1
Chemical structure and schematic representation of a phospholipid molecule—phosphatidylcholine

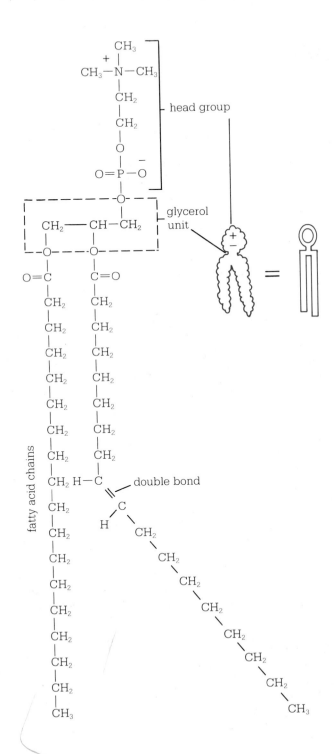

Figure 4.2
The three major classes of phospholipids

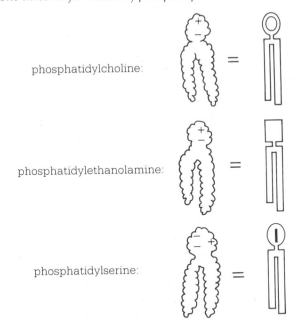

phosphatidylcholine:

phosphatidylethanolamine:

phosphatidylserine:

Figure 4.3
Palmitic acid (a) and stearic acid (b) are saturated fatty acids. Oleic acid (c) and arachidonic acid (d) are unsaturated fatty acids.

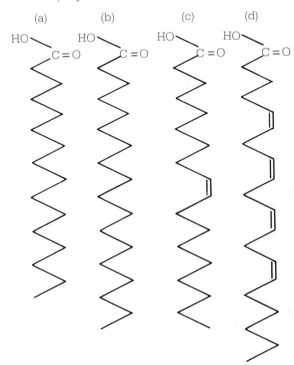

(a)   (b)   (c)   (d)

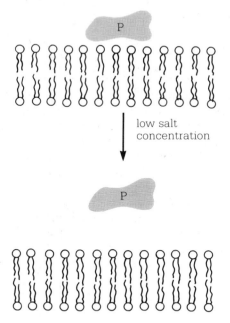

Figure 4.4
Comparison of the ease of dissociation of peripheral and integral proteins from a membrane

low salt
concentration

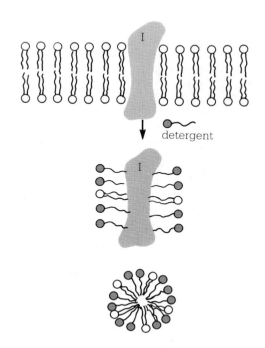

detergent

Neutral Lipids

The most important neutral lipid is cholesterol. It is an important constituent of the membranes of *mammalian* cells. It contains a small polar head group (the —OH group), a rigid and flat system of rings, and a long hydrocarbon chain (see Figure 2.23). The molecule is rigid in the part that contains the ring system but quite flexible in the long tail part. These properties of cholesterol cause a membrane to be more rigid toward the surface and more fluid toward the interior.

Plant cells do not produce cholesterol or similar sterols. Their membranes do, however, contain a greater variety of phospholipids, some of which serve structural functions that are provided by sterols in animal cells. In many fungal cells, the sterol is not cholesterol, but closely related molecules.

Membrane Proteins

Proteins associated with membranes are classified according to how easily they can be removed. *Peripheral proteins* are easily removed and tend to be fairly soluble in water. In some cases, they are bound directly to the membrane lipids (perhaps glycolipids), but in many cases, they are bound to other proteins in the membrane. The *integral proteins* can only be removed when the whole membrane is broken apart by molecules similar to lipids or fatty acids which are called detergents. They are insoluble in water and tend to precipitate when the detergent is removed (Figure 4.4).

4.2 SPONTANEOUS ASSEMBLY OF MEMBRANES

All the natural components of membranes share a common structural feature — the molecules contain regions that are **hydrophilic** (water loving) and other regions that are **hydrophobic** (water fearing). These molecules therefore do not mix with water or oil. They are **amphoteric** (or **amphophilic**) molecules. Moreover, all membrane components tend to be shaped as cylinders, with the polar hydrophilic regions of the molecule at one end. This is particularly evident for the phospholipids and the sterols. As a result of this structure, amphoteric molecules cluster to form a surface containing the polar head groups and an interior consisting of the fatty acid chains. The shape of the cluster depends on the structure of the lipid (Figure 4.5).

Figure 4.5

Amphoteric molecules associate with the polar groups close to each other and with the hydrophobic regions in contact.

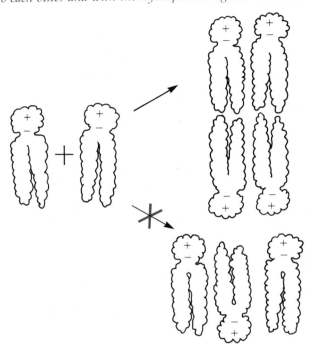

Monolayers and Soap Bubble Bilayers

If amphoteric molecules are added to water, they quickly form a *monolayer* on the surface (Figure 4.6). You can demonstrate this for yourself using soap as the amphoteric molecules. Fill a clean tray with water and clean the water surface by passing a teflon or plas-

tic bar across it a few times. Sprinkle pepper evenly on the surface. Place a bar of soap at one corner of the tray for a few seconds and observe how the pepper gets swept to the side by the spreading monolayer.

It is possible to spread a lipid monolayer on a clean surface of water. The hydrophilic head group is in the water surface, while the hydrophobic tail is extended into the air. If you compress the monolayer by moving a rod across the surface, the long tails are forced to align closely. The area occupied by the lipid monolayer can be measured directly at different pressures. If you know the number of moles of lipids added to the surface, you can calculate the surface area of each lipid molecule. Experiments of this type with lipids from red blood cells provided the first clues about the structure of membranes.

Monolayers are extremely important in lungs. The surface of the lung tissue where it makes contact with the air in the lungs is lined by a phospholipid monolayer. Without the monolayer, the surface tension of water is too high to permit the very small alveolar sacs to exist in the lungs.

If you pull a ring through a surface containing a monolayer of lipids, such as soap molecules, two layers of lipids are drawn out along with some water. The lipid molecules now have the two head groups facing each other with water between them, and the fatty acid chains remain extended into the air (Figure 4.7). These bilayers can form big spherical structures — soap bubbles. The multitude of colours that can be seen in soap bubbles come from refraction of light in the very thin film of lipid molecules. The structure of soap bubbles was first understood in the late 1800s. Their structure turned out later to provide scientists with a clue of how the cell membrane might look.

Figure 4.6

Structure of a monolayer film at the air–water interface

Figure 4.7

Structure of a soap bubble film

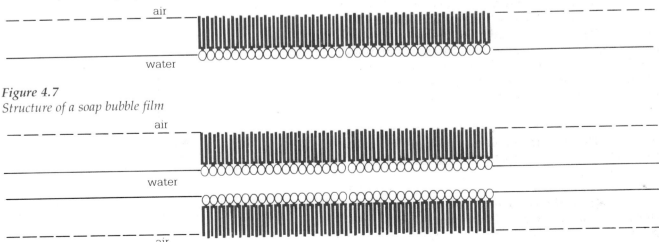

The human lung is designed to exchange gases, notably oxygen and carbon dioxide, between the air and the circulating blood. To accomplish this rapidly and efficiently, the surface area needs to be very large (as large as a basketball court in a typical adult). Yet, the volume of the lungs is only a few litres. This high surface-to-volume ratio is achieved by the existence of millions of small air compartments called alveoli. During inhalation, the volume of each alveolus increases by about a factor of two. If the surface of the alveoli were covered by water only, then due to surface tension, the pressure needed to expand the alveoli thereby increasing the surface area of the lung would have to be many times greater than that available during inhalation. To overcome this problem, the surface of the lung tissue is covered by a lipid mono-layer, which sufficiently reduces the surface tension. Thus the alveoli can expand without difficulty each of the 600 or so times you breathe in an hour.

When a healthy baby is born, the alveoli are collapsed, and must initially be expanded with a great deal of effort. The first cry from the infant is part of the mechanism whereby the lungs are forced to expand. As they do, the lipid monolayer forms, and once it is in place subsequent breathing is much easier.

Babies born prematurely, for whatever reason, frequently have not developed the cells that produce the necessary lipids. As a result, the monolayers do not form and the lungs remain collapsed.

Since the collapsed alveoli are much less efficient at absorbing oxygen from the air, physicians must provide air with a larger proportion of oxygen so that the infant can survive. Over a period of weeks as the newborn develops, the lungs eventually begin to expand and function normally. In severe cases, the exposure to high levels of oxygen for long periods of time may interfere with the proper development of vision. In the worst cases, blindness may result.

The understanding of the formation and the role of the lipid monolayer has raised some hope that it might become possible to treat the premature infant with a spray containing an appropriate lipid that can keep the lungs from collapsing. Several research laboratories around the world are actively studying this prospect.

Micelles and Bilayer Membranes

When amphoteric molecules are forced into contact with water, the hydrophobic portions of the molecules will tend to associate, leaving the surface covered with the polar region. If the cross sectional area of the head group is as large or larger than that of the fatty acid chains, then the surface will tend to curve and form a sphere. The cluster formed this way is a **micelle** (Figure 4.8). Micelles are formed by soaps and detergents as well as by fatty acids. It is not clear how important micelles are in biological systems, if at all. There are some speculations that perhaps micelles form when membranes merge during cell fusion. At this time the evidence is not complete.

Micelles of soaps and detergents are important in washing. The micelle is able to make soluble small particles of dirt or stains which are not normally soluble in water.

Phospholipids have two fatty acid chains for each head group, so the cross sectional area of the head group is smaller than that of the fatty acids. Phospholipids cannot, therefore, form very stable micelles. As

Figure 4.8

Micelles can form spontaneously from single chain amphoteric molecules such as fatty acids, soaps, and detergents.

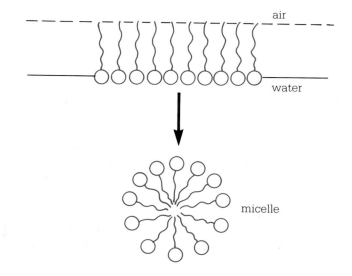

Figure 4.9
Basic structure of a phospholipid bilayer membrane

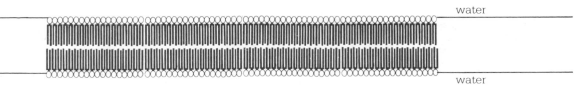

a result of their molecular structure, the phospholipids must assemble with the long hydrocarbon chains parallel to one another. The structure that forms is therefore flat rather than curved or spherical. The only way to avoid exposure to the water is to have the hydrophobic tails together in a *bilayer* (Figure 4.9). This bilayer structure is the reverse of that in the soap films because the water surrounds the bilayer. The bilayer structure is the simplest model of a cell membrane. It achieves one of the most important functions of membranes by virtue of its structure — it separates two regions of water into two compartments, the "outside" and the "inside."

4.3 DEVELOPMENT OF MODELS OF MEMBRANE STRUCTURE

You must realize that the current model of cell membrane structure did not come from a sudden inspiration. Rather, it has developed through many years of experimentation and observation. The present picture is not likely to be the final one as research in this field continues.

The **bilayer hypothesis** for membrane structure arose in 1925. Scientists E. Gorter and F. Grendel extracted lipids from red blood cells (erythrocytes) and spread these as a monolayer on the surface of water. The area covered by the lipids in the monolayer was measured. For comparison, the surface area of the cell was estimated, and found to be about one half of the area occupied by the lipid monolayer. The investigators inferred from this that there were twice as many lipid molecules per unit area in the cell as there were in the monolayer, which led them to propose the bilayer model. As it now turns out, this is an interesting example of "two wrongs being right." We now know that not all the lipid was extracted in those experiments, so the lipid monolayer area was too small. Coincidentally, the surface area of the cell was also underestimated with the net result that the factor of two was maintained.

The bilayer hypothesis immediately raised many questions: Where are the proteins? Do hydrophobic molecules pass more readily through the membrane? What determines permeability? Is the inside of the bilayer like an oil or like margarine? How does the bilayer link to the rest of the cell? Is it simply a bag to contain the cytoplasm or does it serve other functions? Not all the answers to these questions are known yet.

In the period from 1930 to 1940, the membrane proteins were found to be either peripheral (easily extracted) or integral (hard to remove). Nobody knew the three-dimensional structures of proteins, so the models for the membrane were crude. During the same period, it became evident that proteins were necessary for some compounds to pass through the membrane. It was proposed by J.F. Danielli and H. Davson that proteins formed **transmembrane pores** by wrapping around the edges of bilayers (Figure 4.10). Although the detailed structural picture is now thought to be incorrect, the concept of proteins spanning the membrane is still an important feature of cell membrane models.

As the three-dimensional structure of proteins became understood in the early 1950s, the details of the membrane models improved. In particular, it became clear that many proteins in solution were globular (shaped like a sphere) rather than long chains of amino acids. It was therefore proposed that membrane proteins were also more likely to have a structure close to that of a sphere. Still little was known about the properties of the membrane itself.

In 1972, some very important experiments were performed. C.D. Fry and M. Edidin showed that proteins in one cell could mix with those of another cell when their cell membranes were fused to make one large membrane. This apparently simple experiment proved for the first time that the interior of membranes are fluid. In other words, it became clear that the molecules in membranes could move and mix, as in a liquid, rather than being stationary in a solid matrix. The results greatly changed the models of membranes from static structures to dynamic fluids.

Figure 4.10
Development of models of cell membranes

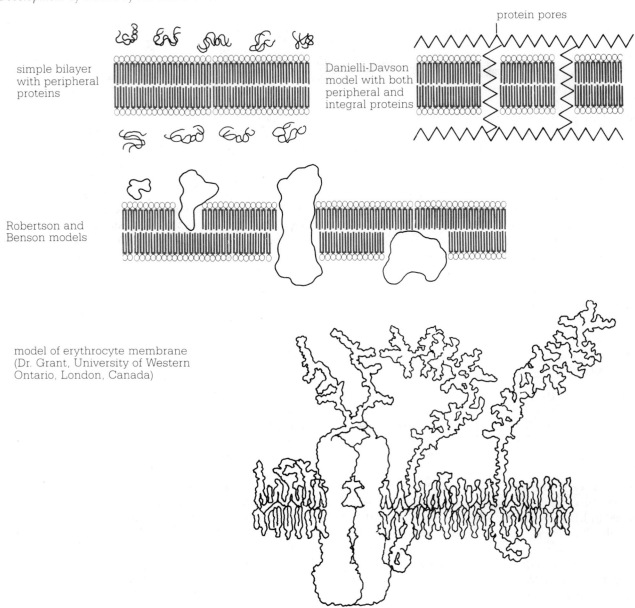

simple bilayer
with peripheral
proteins

protein pores

Danielli-Davson
model with both
peripheral and
integral proteins

Robertson and
Benson models

model of erythrocyte membrane
(Dr. Grant, University of Western
Ontario, London, Canada)

The **fluid mosaic model** of cell membranes incorporates most of what is now known about the cell membrane structure (Figure 4.11). As the name implies, the liquid properties are considered an important feature. Some of the questions that are now slowly being answered are related to how proteins interact with one another both within the membrane and at the surface. In 1980, V. Bennett showed that a large network of proteins inside the membrane of red blood cells is connected to the membrane proteins by a specific protein called *ankyrin*. More recently, evidence is accumulating that proteins often exist as large clusters within the membrane. Future work will undoubtedly require more updates of the model.

Figure 4.11
Fluid mosaic model

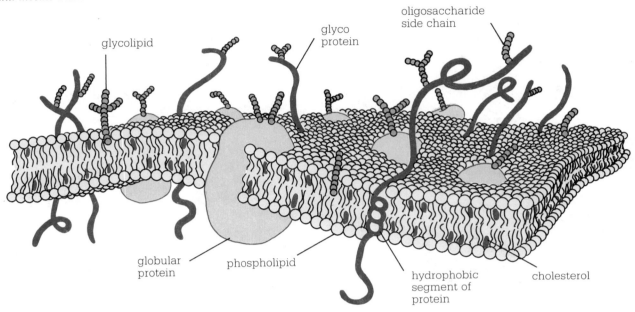

4.4 SPECIAL PROPERTIES OF MEMBRANES

The concepts of a bilayer structure of lipids with integral and peripheral proteins have persisted in the models of membrane structure. The newest pictures of the membrane differ mostly in the added details, many of which are very important for the function of the membrane.

Membrane Asymmetry

A given membrane contains a large variety of lipids. These differ both in the nature of the head group and in the make-up of the fatty acid chains. In most plasma membranes, the lipid bilayer consists of two monolayer halves with different lipids. The extracellular (outer) half of the membrane has a larger proportion of phosphatidylcholine and is the only site of the glycolipids. The cytoplasmic (inner) half contains a larger fraction of phosphatidylserine and phosphatidylethanolamine. As a result of this asymmetric distribution of lipids, there are more negatively charged lipids on the inner half.

Integral proteins are always oriented in one specific direction. Glycoproteins have the carbohydrates attached on the extracellular side (Figure 4.12). Those proteins whose structure in the membrane is known, have so far been found to be transmembrane proteins.

Figure 4.12
Representations of membrane asymmetry

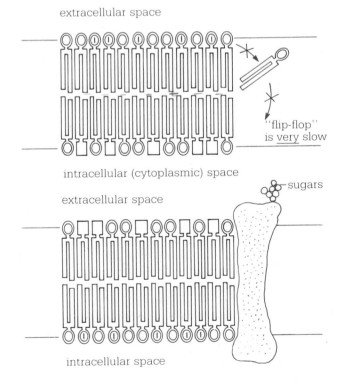

Figure 4.13
Interactions between membrane proteins and the network of proteins inside the cell

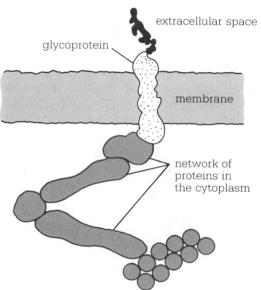

Figure 4.14
Lateral diffusion of both lipids and proteins is rapid.

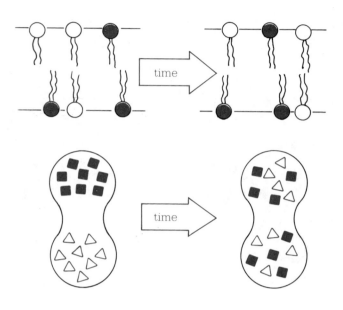

This implies that a portion of the protein chain passes through the entire membrane at least once but in some cases several times. The portion imbedded in the membrane contains a large number of hydrophobic amino acid residues. Frequently, the residues adjacent to the hydrophobic segment of amino acids are charged, possibly so that they interact more strongly with the polar surface of the membrane. Presumably, the transmembrane structure provides the extremely strong binding of the integral proteins to the membrane.

Peripheral proteins are asymmetrically associated with the membrane. There are many extracellular proteins which help the cell anchor to the surface on which it grows. They form an exoskeletal matrix which strengthens the membrane structure. Likewise, there are networks of cytoskeletal proteins associated with the interior of the membrane (Figure 4.13). These also serve structural functions in the cell.

The asymmetric orientation of both lipids and proteins is produced when they are synthesized and placed in the membrane. The asymmetry is maintained because the rate of "flip-flop," that is, the rate at which a phospholipid molecule is transported from one side to the other, is very low (Figure 4.12). It is not known what function the asymmetric distribution serves. It may be that the lipid asymmetry helps to orient the proteins.

Membrane Fluidity

The lipids move rapidly within the plane of the membrane (Figure 4.14). This means that the bilayer is *fluid*. Measurements of the rate of the movement suggest that the interior of the membrane has the consistency of a heavy oil. It would flow about as fast as cold maple syrup.

The membrane fluidity is important since it also permits the movement of proteins in the plane of the membrane. It appears that this mobility is critical in a large number of membrane functions. For example, a number of hormone receptors are present in the surface of cells. When the hormone binds, the receptors appear to diffuse together and stick in larger clusters. It is possible that this clustering is the means whereby the cell recognizes that the hormone is bound.

The lipids in the membrane form a fluid in which the proteins are dissolved. The analogy of icebergs of proteins floating in a sea of lipids is frequently used. The important point is that the lipids serve as a solvent for the proteins in much the same way that water serves as a solvent for salts. The diversity of lipids in the membrane probably helps provide the best type of solvent for the proteins.

The lipid composition of certain cells can be changed by changes in the growth environment. For example, if the growth temperature of the micro-organism *Acholeplasma ladlaawi* is decreased, the cell incorporates a larger number of unsaturated fatty acids into the membrane lipids. This allows the fluid properties of the membrane at the lower temperature to remain very similar to those originally present at the higher temperature. Similar experiments with mammalian cells indicate that if one component is removed, the membrane composition changes so as to provide a nearly constant environment for the membrane proteins at a given temperature. The membrane functions are then not severely affected by gross changes in the environment.

While the lipid forms the fluid and provides the general function of compartmentalization, the proteins are responsible for the special functions of each type of membrane. They serve to selectively transport ions or other small molecules. They act as receptors for hormones or light, and can produce energy in the form of ATP (Chapter 5). While it is very important to understand the role of the lipids in the function of the membrane, the proteins are of more interest for understanding the special biological functions such as transport and receptor.

4.5 TRANSPORT ACROSS MEMBRANES

The formation of membranes was likely one of the crucial steps in the formation of life. Obviously there is a need to keep biological molecules, which must react and interact, together. Without the membrane, the individual molecules in the cytoplasm of the first cells would have quickly dispersed into the vast body of water where they are likely to have been formed. The first essential function of the membrane is therefore containment of the cellular constituents. In effect, the membrane is a bag in which the important molecules for life can be kept at a high concentration.

If the membrane were completely sealed, the cell would be a closed or isolated system. There would be no way for new molecules to enter or excess molecules to exit the cell. The membrane would be too restrictive if it provided a complete seal. In fact, cell membranes are partly leaky and allow **passive transport** of non-polar molecules and small polar molecules, such as water, across it. Large polar molecules and charged molecules cannot penetrate the membrane. Yet, some of these are important to the cell. These can cross the membrane by **facilitated diffusion** through protein pores as long as the concentration differs on the two sides of the membrane. In certain cases, ions need to be transported against the concentration gradient.

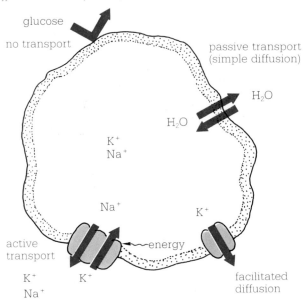

Figure 4.15
Different classes of transport in a cell

This requires energy and is called **active transport** (Figure 4.15).

Transport of molecules across the membrane is an important function of some of the proteins in the membrane. The type of molecule that is transported can, in many cases, be regulated by the cell in response to changes in the environment. In this way a cell may increase the efficiency of the uptake of nutrients when these are sparse. The response to the environment requires that the membrane is also able to transport information. For example, many cells are able to respond to a high concentration of a nutrient by migrating toward the source. This involves a complex processing of signals into action. The way this works is as yet less understood than the transport of molecules.

What Determines the Direction of Transport?

You all know from experience that a rock will roll down a hill if there is nothing to hold it. This is because the rock is in a *gravitational potential* created by the earth. You also may have observed the movement of a magnetic object in a *magnetic potential* (for example, a compass needle responding to a magnet), or the flow of charged particles in an *electric potential* (for example, ions moving through air when large charges build up as in lightning or sparking). In all cases, the objects (the rock, the needle, and the ions) move from a region

Figure 4.16
Movement of objects in various potentials

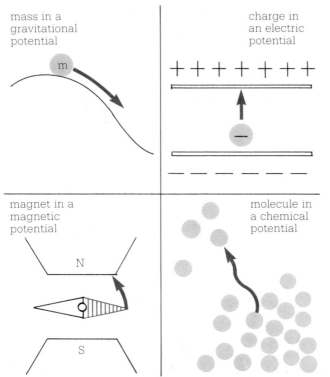

mass in a gravitational potential

m

charge in an electric potential

+ + + + + + +

−

magnet in a magnetic potential

N

S

molecule in a chemical potential

Figure 4.17
The balance between chemical and electric potentials for charged molecules gives a uniform electrochemical potential.

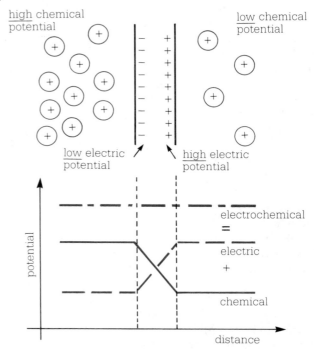

high chemical potential

+

low chemical potential

+

low electric potential

high electric potential

potential

electrochemical

=

electric

+

chemical

distance

of higher potential to a region of lower potential (Figure 4.16).

Molecules that are in a region of high concentration are at a higher *chemical potential* than those in a region of low concentration. In fact, the chemical potential of a molecule is dependent on the ratio of the number of molecules of that type to the total number of molecules of all types present. This ratio, the mole fraction, is often a convenient measure of the concentration of molecules. As with the other potentials described above, molecules will tend to move to regions where their chemical potential is lower—they tend to move toward lower concentrations.

Molecules are not particularly sensitive to gravitational potentials because their masses are very small. Except for a few unusual molecules, they are not sensitive to magnetic potentials either. If they are charged, that is, if they are ions, then they will always move toward the region with the lowest electric potential. In all cases, they will tend to move to a region of lower chemical potential. In the absence of electric potential and chemical potential (no difference in concentration), then there is no net transport of molecules or ions. The system is at equilibrium.

Ions respond to both electric potentials and chemical potentials. These may act in opposite directions. Thus an ion may tend to move in one direction because the electric potential is lower in that direction, but may tend to move in the opposite direction because the chemical potential is lower in the other direction. The net transport is zero when the effect of the difference in chemical potential is equal, but opposite, to the effect of the difference in electric potential. The system is at equilibrium when the two potentials balance. This effect is extremely important for cells, because it is possible to generate an electric potential across a membrane (a membrane potential) by maintaining a concentration difference of ions between the two sides. As you will see later in Chapters 5 and 6, this is essential for generating ATP molecules from other sources of energy.

It is often convenient to consider the combination of the electric potential and the chemical potential. The result, when the two are added together, is the *electrochemical potential* (Figure 4.17). Ions will always move in the direction of decreasing electrochemical potential. When the electrochemical difference between two regions of the solution is zero, there is

Figure 4.18
Illustration of diffusion by random motion

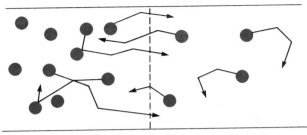

Figure 4.19
Mixing can occur unimpeded in the absence of a membrane, but requires permeability through the membrane when this is present.

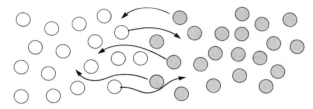

permeable
molecules

non-permeable
molecules

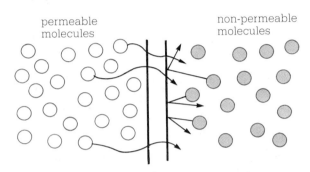

no net movement of ions. Notice that if there is no charge on the molecule, the electric potential difference does not affect the transport. The electrochemical potential is therefore the same as the chemical potential for neutral molecules but not for ions.

Random Motion, Diffusion, and Permeability

Molecules in liquids and gases continuously move. The motion of a particular molecule appears random, because the direction and speed of the molecule changes whenever it collides with other molecules. However, if there is a difference in concentration of a solute between two regions of a solution, there will be a net movement of solute toward the region with lower concentration. Consider the simple case illustrated in Figure 4.18, where the solution to the left of an imaginary line is more concentrated. The probability that solute molecules will cross the line from left to right is greater than the reverse simply because there are more molecules available. There will, therefore, be more molecules moving from left to right in a given period of time. This will continue to be true until the concentration is the same on both sides.

Diffusion is the bulk movement of molecules because of a difference in chemical potential or concentration between two regions in space. The larger the gradient (difference) in chemical potential or concentration, the faster the movement of molecules. In other words, the rate of movement of molecules is higher when the chemical potential changes by a large amount over a short distance. As an analogy, a mass moves faster down a steeper hill.

Diffusion of molecules is unimpeded in solution. If a solution of a dye is added to water from the top, the dye will eventually mix completely in the entire volume of water. The mixing will continue until the concentration of the dye is the same everywhere. At this time, there will be no further net transfer of molecules from one region of the solution to any other. However, any specific dye molecule will continue to move.

Given enough time the molecule will, by random motion, move throughout the entire volume. Even though the system of dye molecules in the water is at equilibrium, individual molecules continue to move. The system is said to be dynamic.

Two solutions separated by a membrane can only reach equilibrium if the molecules can permeate (cross) the membrane. The membrane must be permeable to the molecules of interest (Figure 4.19). If there is a difference in the chemical potential of the molecules in the two solutions and if the membrane is permeable, there will be a net transport from the solution of higher chemical potential to that of lower chemical potential. The rate of transport will depend both on the gradient in chemical potential and on the **permeability** of the molecule through the membrane.

The permeability of a molecule is related to how soluble it is in the interior of the membrane relative to its solubility in water. Hydrophobic molecules are more soluble in the membrane and therefore have higher permeabilities. Ions are less soluble in the membrane and have low permeabilities in pure lipid membranes. Dimethylsulfoxide (DMSO) is a small polar molecule which penetrates membranes with ease. It also has the property that it will carry with it other molecules with low permeability through the membrane. This has its advantage and disadvantage.

Figure 4.20
Comparison of the effects of hypertonic, isotonic, and hypotonic solutions on cells with and without cell walls

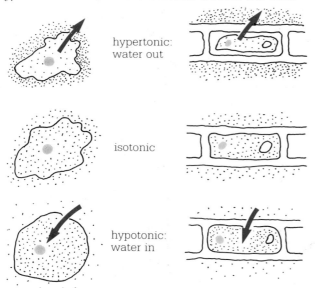

hypertonic:
water out

isotonic

hypotonic:
water in

Figure 4.21
Stages of cell lysis

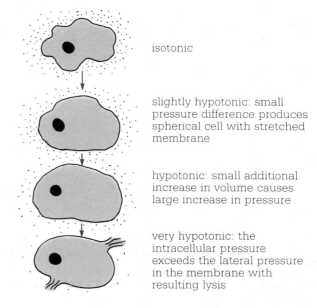

isotonic

slightly hypotonic: small pressure difference produces spherical cell with stretched membrane

hypotonic: small additional increase in volume causes large increase in pressure

very hypotonic: the intracellular pressure exceeds the lateral pressure in the membrane with resulting lysis

For example, DMSO was once used as a solvent for antiarthritic drugs, which were applied directly to the skin and were adsorbed by the action of DMSO. It is no longer used for this purpose, because in addition to carrying the beneficial drug, the molecules can also carry potentially hazardous compounds that may be present on the skin into the underlying cells.

Water Transport and Osmosis

Diffusion of a solvent through a selectively permeable membrane is called **osmosis**. Since the solvent in all biological systems is water, osmosis usually refers to the movement of water across a cell membrane. Although water is not very soluble in hydrocarbons, its permeability through cell membranes is large, partly because water molecules are very small. The chemical potential of water in a solution containing mixtures of many molecules depends only on the total solute concentration. The type and structure of the solute is immaterial. Note that a high concentration of solutes corresponds to less water in a given volume of solution. Thus a high solute concentration means a low chemical potential for the water. As long as the total concentration of all ions and other solutes is the same on both sides of the membrane, there will be no net water transport. There is no osmosis. In this case, the two solutions are said to be *isosmotic* or **isotonic** (Figure 4.20).

If water in the extracellular solution has a lower chemical potential (a higher concentration of solutes) than that in the cytoplasm, then water will leave the cell. The extracellular solution is said to be **hypertonic**. It causes osmosis such that water moves out of the cell, raising the cytoplasmic concentration until it becomes equal to that of the extracellular solution.

Conversely, if water in the extracellular solution has a higher chemical potential (a lower concentration of solutes) than that in the cytoplasm, then water will enter the cell. The extracellular solution is **hypotonic**. In this case, water will enter the cell to lower the cytoplasmic concentration.

In most cases, the volume of the cell can only increase by a small amount to accommodate the additional water. This is because the membrane has a limited surface area. Unlike a balloon, which can stretch, membranes cannot stretch as easily or as much. As more water enters, the pressure inside the cell quickly increases. The increase in the pressure increases the chemical potential of the water in the cytoplasm. If the pressure rises sufficiently to prevent more water from entering, the chemical potentials are equal. This pressure is the **osmotic pressure**. For very dilute extracellular solutions, the osmotic pressure is greater than the maximum pressure the membrane can tolerate. The membrane will burst and all the cytoplasm disperses. The cell is said to have been **lysed** (Figure 4.21).

Figure 4.22
Relative permeability across the bilayer

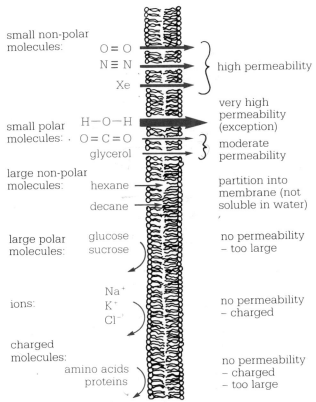

small non-polar
molecules: O = O
              N ≡ N   } high permeability
              Xe

small polar   H—O—H   → very high
molecules: O = C = O   permeability
              glycerol   } (exception)
                           moderate
                           permeability

large non-polar
molecules: hexane —   partition into
              decane —   membrane (not
                          soluble in water)

large polar   glucose   no permeability
molecules: sucrose   – too large

              Na⁺
ions: K⁺   no permeability
              Cl⁻   – charged

charged
molecules: no permeability
    amino acids   – charged
    proteins   – too large

Figure 4.23
Modes of transport across cell membranes

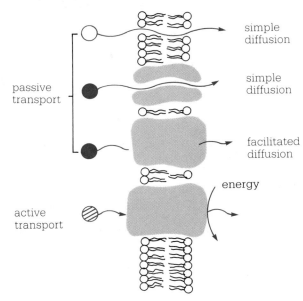

                    → simple diffusion
                    → simple diffusion
passive
transport   → facilitated diffusion
                          energy
active
transport

Plant cells are subjected to much larger osmotic pressures than most animal cells. However, they are protected from lysis since they are often surrounded by a cell wall made of cellulose. This can withstand very large pressures. Osmotic pressures are often used to the advantage of the organism. Some plants must, when they germinate, break through very hard surfaces. Have you ever seen a weed break through the asphalt of a paved driveway? The force needed to crack the asphalt surface is generated by osmotic pressures when water enters the plant cells.

Solute Transport

In order to cross a pure lipid membrane, solute molecules must penetrate both the very polar region produced by the lipid head groups and the non-polar region in the interior. Experiments have shown that small non-polar molecules (such as oxygen, nitrogen, and xenon) and small polar molecules (such as carbon dioxide and ethanol) diffuse rapidly across most artificially prepared lipid membranes, but larger ones move more slowly (Figure 4.22). Large, uncharged

polar molecules such as the sugars (glucose and sucrose) have low permeabilities. Ions, which are of course charged, cross membranes about ten billion times more slowly than water. The charges dramatically decrease the permeability of the molecules. Protein molecules are both large and charged; they, and even their amino acid components, do not cross membranes that are composed of only lipids.

Passive Transport

Spontaneous movement of solute molecules across a membrane in response to a gradient in the electric or chemical potentials is referred to as *passive transport* (Figure 4.23). Passive transport of small uncharged molecules may occur through the lipid bilayer by simple diffusion. Larger polar molecules and ions require special channels or pores in the membrane. Many such channels are created by transmembrane proteins called *transport proteins*. They are believed to contain a narrow channel which is filled with water. The hydrophilic molecules can move through the channel without ever getting exposed to the hydrophobic interior of the membrane. Since the protein channels are really just like holes in the membrane which allow simple diffusion to occur, the transport will only occur in the direction of decreasing electrical and chemical potentials. More precisely, transport will only occur in the direction of decreasing electrochemical potential.

Transport of large molecules would require large channels. This could present problems for the cell. Imagine that the membrane was filled with a number of large channels. All molecules that are smaller than the channel could easily diffuse through the holes. There would be no selectivity. There would be no mechanism whereby the cell could control the type of molecules that would enter or leave the cell. For example, a channel large enough to allow the important nutrient, glucose, to enter the cell would be large enough also to permit amino acids produced inside the cell to escape. The beneficial effect of getting the nutrient would be countered by the negative effect of losing essential molecules from the cytoplasm. For this reason, most channels are small, and can transport only small ions such as sodium ions and potassium ions by simple diffusion.

Larger molecules are transported by *facilitated diffusion*. This does not occur through permanently open channels. Instead, the channels open only when the right type of molecule binds to the surface of the transport protein (Figure 4.24). It is thought that, upon binding of the molecule to be transported, the protein structure changes so that the bound molecule is carried through to the other side of the membrane. Since its concentration on the other side is lower, the molecule is likely to be released — that is, it is effectively transported across the membrane. Once the molecule has been released, the transport protein returns to its original shape and is ready to accept another molecule for transport. This type of transport is selective since the change in protein structure can only occur when the right type of molecule binds.

Passive transport of molecules through permanent channels in the membrane will be faster if the concentration difference between the two sides of the membrane is increased. Facilitated diffusion through transient channels made in transport proteins will also be faster when the concentration difference is increased, but is limited by how rapidly the protein can change between its different structures. There will be an upper limit to how fast facilitated diffusion can occur. This difference between simple and facilitated diffusion is the only way we can experimentally determine by which mechanism the passive diffusion takes place.

Active Transport

Simple and facilitated diffusion of molecules can occur in the direction of decreasing electrochemical potential because it does not require energy. *Active transport* is

Figure 4.24
Facilitated transport is selective. Only molecules with the correct shape or charge are transported.

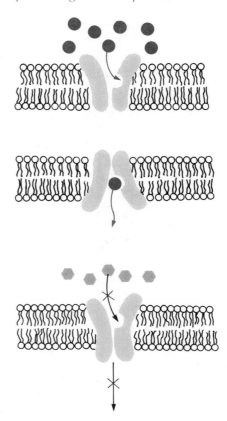

a net transfer of molecules in the direction of increasing electrochemical potential. The molecules are being moved ''uphill.'' Rolling a rock up a hill requires energy in the form of work on your part. Likewise, active transport requires energy from the cell.

The proteins that are able to actively transport molecules against a concentration gradient are called *pumps*. (These are analogous to the pump that transports water from the basement to the upper levels in a building.) Molecular pumps are highly selective for the molecules they transport (Figure 4.25). This way, only the right molecules are transported and there is no or very little waste of energy.

A well studied active transport system is the **sodium–potassium pump** (Na^+–K^+ pump). It is found in plasma membranes as well as in many other types of membranes. Its function is to transport *sodium ions* (Na^+) *out* and *potassium ions* (K^+) *in*. Normally, the sodium concentration is about ten times greater in the extracellular fluid than in the cytoplasm. Conversely,

Figure 4.25
Active transport is selective, but requires
energy since it moves molecules against
a concentration gradient.

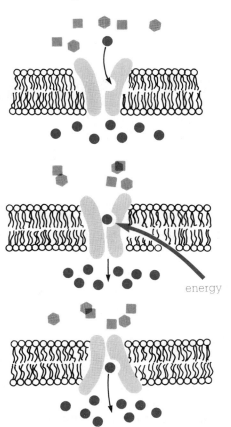

Figure 4.26
Schematic model of how the sodium–potassium pump might work

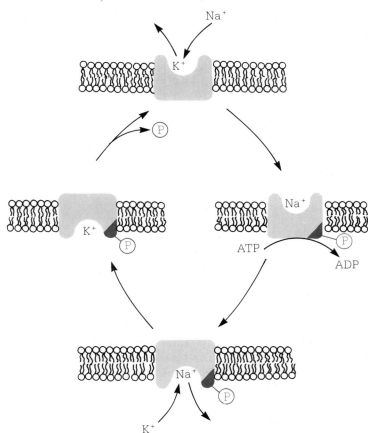

the potassium ion concentration is about ten times higher in the cytoplasm. Both ions are therefore transported against their respective chemical potentials.

Partly because of the differences in the sodium ion and potassium ion concentrations, there is a membrane potential which is positive on the outside (this will be discussed later). The sodium ions are therefore also pumped against the electric potential across the membrane.

The sodium–potassium pump gets its energy from the chemical reaction in which ATP is hydrolyzed to give ADP and phosphate (Chapters 2, 5 and 6). The amount of energy released in the chemical reaction is sufficient to transport three sodium ions out and two potassium ions in. There are many models of how this might occur. One of these is shown in Figure 4.26. It is not important that you understand the details at this point as they are beyond the scope of this text. The

model does, however, show a few interesting points. First, it illustrates one of the important principles of biological energy use—use as little as needed, and in several steps. Here the energy gained from the hydrolysis of the ATP molecule is used in two steps—part of it is used to change the shape of the protein to allow transport of the sodium ion and part of it is saved as a protein–phosphate chemical bond. This latter part is used later to allow the protein to change back to the original shape while it transports potassium ions in.

Another interesting feature of the sodium–potassium pump is that it can run *backward*. This turns out to be important because it allows the cell to use the energy released in the transport of the ions down their chemical potential gradients to *make* ATP. The concentration differences of the ions can, when needed, be used as a source of energy. In a sense, the membrane potential is like a battery in which energy is stored.

Figure 4.27
In addition to simple transport — uniport — there can be co-transport of molecules.

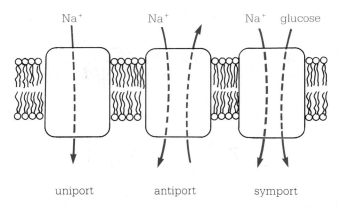

uniport   antiport   symport

Figure 4.28
Glucose–sodium ion symport is coupled to sodium–potassium pump activity. Glucose transport does not directly require ATP hydrolysis, but it is an active transport because it uses the energy stored in the chemical potential derived from the gradient of sodium ions.

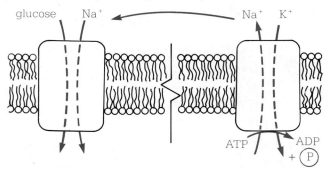

Because the chemical reaction and the transport properties are linked, this system is also called the sodium–potassium ATPase. You will learn more about this system in Chapters 5 and 6.

The sodium–potassium pump system transports two types of ions in opposite directions. This type of transport is called *antiport* (*anti* meaning against). There are also cases in which the transport of one molecule toward lower chemical potential can cause co-transport of another molecule against its chemical potential gradient. This is called *symport* (*sym* meaning with or together). For example, glucose is transported into the cell along with sodium ions (Figure 4.27). The ions are moving to a lower chemical potential inside. This energetically favourable process is coupled to the energetically less favourable uptake of glucose, which is usually at lower concentration outside (Figure 4.28).

Regulated Transport
Many of the transport systems in cell membranes are regulated or controlled. This serves to control when and for how long the transport systems are to function. In nerve cell membranes, there are channels which open or close depending on the electric potential across the membrane. When the potential is high (the membrane is polarized) the channels are closed. When the membrane potential decreases below a certain level (the membrane is depolarized) the channels open. These are called voltage-gated channels (Figure 4.29). In other cell membranes, the channels respond to the binding of molecules. The channels open when the concentration of a desirable molecule is high, and close when this compound is absent. These are ligand-gated channels. In many cases, the regulated channels

are important for facilitated diffusion. Active transport channels are also regulated, but usually by the energy available rather than by the concentration of transported molecules.

Macromolecule Transport
Large molecules, such as proteins, are not typically transported through the membrane. They are either taken up by cells by means of **endocytosis** (also called pinocytosis) or released from cells by **exocytosis**. Both processes involve dramatic reorganization of the membrane into small *membrane vesicles*. These are like small bags of lipids used to transport selected material to various regions of the cell (Figure 4.30).

Endocytosis is important in many cellular responses to hormones. By forming small invaginations (sheaths) of the membrane the cell engulfs the material in the immediate environment of the membrane which ends up in an intracellular vesicle. This in turn fuses with other vesicles (lysosomes) in which the protein material is hydrolyzed to amino acids. These are recycled for use as energy or as building blocks for new proteins.

The receptor mediated endocytosis is an important example of how small peptide hormones such as insulin are taken up by cells. Upon binding to the insulin receptor in the cell membrane, the hormone clusters with its receptor in particular regions on the surface. These invaginate and form an intracellular vesicle. In the liver, the lipoproteins circulating in the blood are taken up by liver cells by a similar mechanism. After endocytosis, the cholesterol contained in the lipoprotein is released and binds to the nuclear membrane, thereby altering the metabolism of the cell.

Figure 4.29
Schematic examples of gated channels

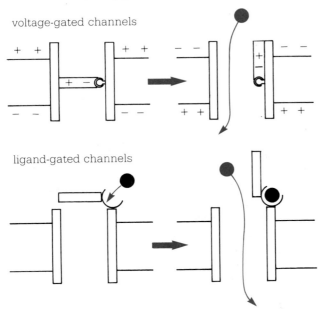

Figure 4.30
Endocytosis (a) and exocytosis (b) are transport mechanisms for macromolecules such as proteins.

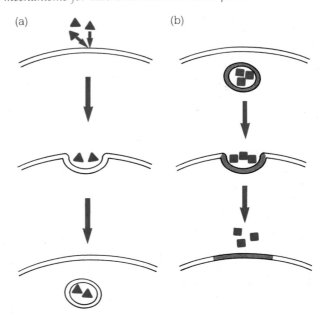

Neurotransmitters, such as acetylcholine, and peptide hormones, such as the encephalins (Chapter 2), are released by exocytosis. These agents are either synthesized or concentrated in small vesicles which accumulate at the inside surface of the membrane. Upon stimulation, by a nerve signal for example, the vesicles all fuse with the membrane and cause a rapid release of all the material within. Similarly, histamine is released by mast cells when they encounter foreign material such as pollen, thereby initiating the allergic response.

Membrane Potentials

A difference in concentration of ions may produce a difference in electric potential across a membrane. In most cells, this **membrane potential** is determined by the relative concentrations of sodium ions and potassium ions in the cytoplasm and the extracellular fluid. In most animal cells, the membrane potential is around −40 mV to −60 mV. The membrane potential is maintained by the sodium–potassium pump at the expense of the hydrolysis of ATP. It has been estimated that as much as one third of all the ATP generated in the cell is used to transport these ions in order to maintain the membrane potential. It is not totally clear why the cell spends this large fraction of

its energy resources on this task. Perhaps the membrane potential is much more important than we recognize at the present.

The role of the membrane potential in nerve cells is well understood. A nerve cell transmits its nerve impulse as a transient change in the membrane potential. The sequence is complex, but very effective. At the cell body, neurotransmitters bind to receptors causing a rapid change in passive permeability of the sodium ion. As a result, the membrane potential increases above the normal value of about −60 mV. If the change is large enough, the voltage sensitive sodium ion channels open fully to produce a rapid change in membrane potential toward +100 mV. At this very large positive potential difference, the potassium ion channels open as the sodium ion channels start to close. The efflux of potassium ions repolarizes the membrane toward the initial −60 mV. Meanwhile the very large positive membrane potential, which occurred for a brief moment, is conducted along the cell membrane. At another site along the nerve, it causes other voltage sensitive sodium ion channels to open and depolarize the membrane at that site. The cycle is repeated as the nerve impulse travels along the membrane. In nerve cells it has been estimated that as much as two-thirds of the total energy is used to pump sodium ions and potassium ions.

4.6 SPECIAL MEMBRANES

Plasma Membranes
Most of the properties of membranes described so far are best understood in the plasma membrane. This is the membrane that separates the cytoplasm of the cell from the extracellular environment. It is the membrane for which it has been possible to measure membrane potentials. Of all membranes, the plasma membrane has the greatest variety of functions. It encloses the cell and keeps the cell content concentrated. It serves as the communication link between the inside of the cell and the outside. For this function, the plasma membrane has a large number of specialized proteins, the receptors, which are capable of recognizing particular messenger molecules such as hormones. This is the most active transport system of all the membranes and is intimately linked with the structural components of the cell. Together with the cytoskeleton and the exoskeleton of the cell, the plasma membrane is responsible for maintaining and changing the shape of cells. Even though it is the membrane about which most is known, it is actually the least abundant membrane in a cell.

Mitochondrial and Chloroplast Membranes
In the cytoplasm there are several organelles which are themselves separated from the cytoplasm by membranes. Mitochondria are found in all eukaryotic cells. They are the sites of release of most of the energy in the cell (Chapter 5). Chloroplasts are found in certain plant cells in addition to mitochondria. They are the sites of photosynthesis (Chapter 7). Mitochondria and chloroplasts are both enveloped by a double membrane. The special significance of the double membrane construction will become clearer as you learn more about the intricate biochemical reactions that occur in these organelles.

The Endoplasmic Reticulum
The endoplasmic reticular membrane system runs throughout the cell and constitutes between one-third and one-half of the membrane mass of a cell. This membrane system is the site of synthesis of many of the proteins. The rough endoplasmic reticulum (ER) appears as it does in electron micrograph pictures because it is pebbled with ribosomes. The smooth ER does not have ribosomes attached; it serves the function of producing small membrane vesicles for transport of glycoproteins during their synthesis. The Golgi apparatus is a large network of membranes which is intimately involved in the control and production of transport vesicles.

Membrane Vesicles
Throughout the cell there are a large number of highly specialized, small spherical membrane vesicles. In recent work it is becoming clear that these vesicles act as small shuttles which transport material from one region of the cell to another. They also serve to keep particularly obnoxious reactions or chemicals from the rest of the cell. Lysosomes, for example, have an interior at a very low pH and seem to function as the site of degradation of proteins ingested from the cell surface. How the intracellular traffic of vesicles is controlled is one of the great mysteries of the cell — how does a vesicle destined to go to the plasma membrane know which way to go?

4.7 THE EFFECT OF DRUGS ON MEMBRANES

Polyene Antibiotics
Polyene antibiotics are drugs which can act at the membrane level. These drugs are used to fight fungal infections (or yeast infections). They are able to kill cells because they bind to sterols in the membrane and form large pores. The pores are large enough to allow ions to permeate freely. The result is a rapid influx of sodium ion and a rapid efflux of potassium ion. The cell soon loses control of the osmotic balance, and water enters the cell. Eventually the cell lyses and dies. The polyene antibiotics kill all types of cells. They are effective as antifungal agents because they appear to bind much more strongly to ergosterol, which is the major sterol in yeast cells, than to cholesterol, the major sterol in human cells. However, if we were to administer too much of the drug, it would quickly kill our own cells as well. It is evident that the drugs have no effect on bacteria, which have no sterols at all.

Anesthetics
If you go to the dentist, you will often be given a local anesthetic to decrease the pain the dentist is about to inflict. This anesthetic, typically lidocaine, is injected directly into the nerve bundle where the effect is needed. If, on the other hand, you go to the hospital to have more extensive surgery, you will be given a general anesthetic. General anesthetics are typically hydrophobic gases. In the older days, physicians used ether or even chloroform. A common gas used in dental surgery was nitrous oxide, also known as laughing gas because it induces uncontrollable fits of laughter

in the patient. Xenon, cyclopropane, and ethanol also work as anesthetics. The detailed mechanism whereby general anesthetics work is still not known, but it is becoming clear that they can act by physically disrupting the membrane structure. Experiments show that all the compounds that work as effective general anesthetics also can disrupt membranes to the point where they become very leaky. Although it is not necessarily because the nerve cells become leaky that the anesthetic works, it is likely that the disordering effect of the anesthetic on the membrane structure affects the normal function of all the proteins in the plasma membrane of the nerve cell. Modern anesthetics are chloro- and fluorocarbons similar to the gases used in the compressors of refrigerators and as aerosol propellants which are a major cause of the depletion of ozone in the atmosphere.

4.8 VARIATIONS ON A BASIC THEME

There is one fundamental lesson in this chapter which is relatively simple — all membranes are structurally very similar, yet each membrane has adapted the basic structural theme to provide for its specialized functions. The membranes resemble each other because they all consist of a bilayer of lipids with a mixture of proteins either integrally or peripherally associated with it. Yet each type of membrane is unique in the composition of both lipids and proteins. Different membranes within any given cell differ in composition so that they can perform different functions. The composition of corresponding membrane types, plasma membranes for example, in different kinds of cells of the same organism varies also because the cells perform different functions. The liver cell, for example, needs to respond to different hormones and perform different functions than the brain cell. Correspondingly, the protein receptors in these cells are different.

Cell membranes are wonderful subjects of study in science. On the one hand, the similarities allow us to formulate general hypotheses about both structure and function. These hypotheses or models apply to all membrane systems. They allow us to simplify and unify our thoughts and allow us to generalize. On the other hand, the dissimilarities remind us that although unifying models are tremendously educational and can be used to make predictions for new experiments, they may also be dangerously misleading. We must always examine the results of our experiments both in the context of the general and unifying scheme and in the context of the particular system being studied.

CHAPTER SUMMARY

Cell membranes are composed of lipids and proteins, which in some cases have sugar residues attached. The principal lipids are the phospholipids which form a bilayer structure in which the polar head groups face the water and the fatty acid chains face one another. The bilayer phospholipid structure also contains sterols such as cholesterol, which tend to make the centre of the bilayer more fluid and the edges more rigid. Proteins are associated with the bilayer either as peripherally attached units or as transmembrane, integral proteins.

The bilayer structure of the membrane is in part determined by the amphoteric structure of the phospholipid molecules. The properties of the membrane depend on the type of the head group and the extent of unsaturation of the fatty acids. The fluid mosaic model of membranes stipulates that the bilayer is dynamic — the lipid and protein molecules can move in the plane of the membrane and the various components intermix freely. In all membrane systems studied, the distribution of lipids and proteins is asymmetric. The exact functional role of the membrane asymmetry is not known.

One of the most important functions of membranes is to control transport of molecules across it. The driving force for passive transport is a difference in electrochemical potential for the molecules on the two sides of the membrane. On the one hand, molecules will tend to move in the direction of lower concentration. On the other, if they are charged, they will also tend to move in the direction of lower electric potential. The balance between the two makes it possible to establish a membrane potential from a concentration difference. Large molecules and ions must be transported by facilitated diffusion in which specific transport proteins selectively permit a particular molecule to permeate the membrane.

Water transport across a membrane is called osmosis. It results from a difference in chemical potential of the water because of differences in the total solute concentration. Hypertonic solutions cause water to leave the cells, while hypotonic solutions cause water to enter the cells. In extreme cases, hypotonic solutions lead to lysis because the pressure inside the cell exceeds the forces which hold the membrane together.

Active transport involves pumping small ions or large molecules across the membrane against the gradient in electrochemical potential. This requires the expenditure of energy. In the case of the sodium– potassium ATPase, the energy needed to move three sodium ions out and two potassium ions in is obtained from the hydrolysis of ATP. This protein transport system can be made to work backward, such that the energy inherent in the electrochemical potential difference is used to make ATP. This is an example of interconversion of the energy in chemical bonds with that in concentration and electric gradients.

Objectives

Having completed this chapter, you should be able to do the following:

1. Describe the major constituents of membranes, and draw the structure of a typical phospholipid.
2. Distinguish between saturated and unsaturated fatty acids.
3. Describe what is meant by an amphoteric molecule and outline how the shape of amphoteric molecules determine whether they form micelles or membranes.
4. Briefly outline how the fluid mosaic model of membranes is different from earlier models such as the Danielli-Davson model.
5. Outline each of the special properties of the most modern model of cell membranes, with emphasis on membrane asymmetry and fluidity.
6. Describe the factors that might cause transport to occur, the concept of diffusion and its relationship to permeability, and the concepts of osmosis, isotonic, hypertonic, and hypotonic.
7. Distinguish among passive transport, facilitated transport, and active transport, and describe the factors that determine which type of transport might take place.
8. Describe endocytosis and exocytosis, and give an example in each case.
9. Describe a few of the different membranes that are found in a typical cell.

Vocabulary

lipid	amphoteric	active transport	lysed
sterol	amphophilic	diffusion	sodium–potassium pump
cholesterol	micelle	permeability	endocytosis
phospholipid	bilayer hypothesis	osmosis	exocytosis
saturated fatty acid	transmembrane pore	isotonic	membrane potential
unsaturated fatty acid	fluid mosaic model	hypertonic	
hydrophilic	passive transport	hypotonic	
hydrophobic	facilitated diffusion	osmotic pressure	

Review Questions

1. List and describe several fundamental functions of a cell membrane.
2. (a) What are the principal constituents of a cell membrane?
   (b) Which common class of biochemicals is not usually found in membranes?
3. (a) What is the general structure of a phospholipid molecule?
   (b) Which parts of the molecule differ among different phospholipids?
4. In what way does the degree of unsaturation of the fatty acid chains affect the properties of membranes?

5. How does the structure of cholesterol influence the membrane structure?
6. Describe the difference between peripheral and integral proteins.
7. Define each term.
   (a) hydrophilic
   (b) lipophilic
   (c) amphoteric
   (d) hydrophobic
8. Draw schematic representations of the following.
   (a) a monolayer
   (b) a micelle
   (c) a bilayer
9. What are the important features of membrane asymmetry?
10. Why is membrane transport necessary?
11. What is the major distinction between passive and active transport?

12. How does the electrochemical potential determine the direction of transport of ions across a membrane? Your answer should include an illustrative example.
13. What factors might affect the permeability of a molecule?
14. (a) Compare and contrast solutions which are hypertonic and isotonic relative to a cell.
    (b) What type of solution is used to lyse cells?
15. How do simple diffusion and facilitated diffusion through a protein pore differ? Use a diagram to help your explanation.
16. Why does the sodium–potassium ATPase require energy to transport sodium ions out of and potassium ions into the cell?
17. What are the distinctions among uniport, symport, and antiport?
18. Describe the two types of regulated transport.

Advanced Questions

1. Fats extracted from plant sources typically produce oils. (Try to list at least four.) Fats from animal sources (butter, lard) tend to be more solid. In fact, you may well have noticed that goose or duck fat melts at temperatures just above room temperature while beef fat remains solid even in hot tap water. Rationalize these observations in terms of your understanding of the structure of fatty acids. Why do you suppose plant fats tend to be more fluid?
2. Outline the key features of the fluid mosaic model of a membrane and its development from the bilayer hypothesis.
3. One of the early models of membranes suggested that the lipids in the membrane were in the shape of micelles and that the proteins were layered on the surface as indicated in the diagram below. Explain why this model is inferior to the currently accepted model.

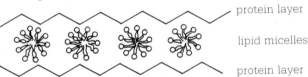

protein layer

lipid micelles

protein layer

4. The table below shows the ratio of calculated permeabilities to experimental values. A small ratio indicates that the true permeability is much greater than expected, as in the case of urea and glucose.

Explain why the calculated and measured values agree reasonably well for glycol and propionamide but disagree severely for urea and glucose.

Propionamide	$(CH_3CH_2CONH_2)$	1.0
Glycol	$(HOCH_2CH_2OH)$	4.0
Urea	(NH_2CONH_2)	0.0025
Glucose	$(C_6H_{12}O_6)$	0.00001

5. In many types of tissues, neighbouring cells are in sufficiently close contact that specialized proteins can span the membrane of both cells. The proteins exist in large clusters called gap junctions and provide a continuous pore from one cell to the other. Experiments show that ions and small molecules can move freely from cell to cell. It has been estimated that the largest molecule that can pass through the gap junctions has a relative molar mass of about 1000. Describe briefly what factor(s) you think will determine the transport between the cells.
6. Many drugs act by interfering with properties of the membrane. This may well be how the general anesthetics work. It is also believed that the insecticide DDT acts by dissolving in the membrane and perturbing the transport functions. Describe as clearly as possible which properties of a molecule you would look for if you were to design a drug molecule that is likely to disrupt the cell membrane.

CHAPTER 5

CELLS AND ENERGY

"Order is Heaven's first law."
Alexander Pope

Whatever the activity in which you participate, you know that it requires *energy*. You may even follow special diets or eat *high energy* foods. But what is energy? Where does energy come from and how is it made available to your body? This chapter will examine the concept of energy and its significance in biology. It will focus on those processes which make the energy stored in the food you eat available to the cell.

5.1 THERMODYNAMICS AND BIOENERGETICS

Gasoline is a familiar example of stored chemical energy. You know that when gasoline reacts with oxygen in air, the result can be a violent explosion. This happens because most of the stored energy in the gasoline is released as heat. The sudden release of heat causes an explosive increase in the volume of the gases. In a gasoline driven automobile, this reaction occurs within the enclosed space of the cylinder in the engine. The increased pressure created by the expanding gases causes the piston to move rapidly downward. The motion of the piston then causes the driveshaft to rotate which, in turn, causes the automobile to move forward. During this process, the stored chemical energy of the gasoline undergoes several transformations. Chemical energy is converted to the mechanical energy of the piston movement and eventually to the movement of the automobile. Actually, only about 25 percent of the energy of the gasoline eventually ends up in the forward motion of the automobile—the balance is dissipated to the environment in the form of heat.

Figure 5.1
The release of stored energy. When the gas–air mixture is ignited by the spark, the sudden release of energy as heat causes expansion of the gases and drives the piston downward.

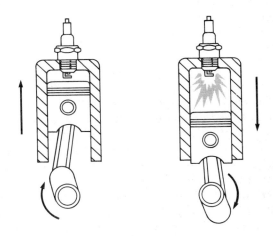

Similar energy transformations occur in biological systems. Plants, for example, use the radiant energy of sunlight to drive the synthesis of sugar molecules. Sugar, like gasoline, is a form of stored chemical energy. Plants use some of this energy to do additional synthetic work (build and maintain structure), electrical work (move ions across membranes), or osmotic work (take up nutrient ions and water from the soil). When an animal eats a plant, it uses the energy previously stored by the plant to perform many of the same kinds of work and for mechanical work such as the contraction of muscle.

101

As you can see, energy continually flows through both the physical and biological worlds. The physical chemists have given the study of energy flow a name —**thermodynamics**. Thermodynamics describes all of the energy transformations which accompany all of the physical processes and chemical reactions in the universe. The science of thermodynamics applies equally well to both physical and biological processes. There are two thermodynamic principles or laws which are of particular importance to the study of biology. The *first* **law of thermodynamics** makes a relatively simple statement about the conservation of energy. The *second* **law of thermodynamics** enables us to predict the direction of various chemical and physical events. These ideas, first articulated by Isaac Newton, have been demonstrated time and again to be useful explanations of how energy is transformed. The study of thermodynamic principles as they apply to energy transformations in biology is given a special name—**bioenergetics**.

Thermodynamics can be a very difficult and even intimidating subject, involving the extensive use of physical chemistry and mathematics. You should not be intimidated, however. In this chapter, the subject will be reduced to a few simple, basic concepts that will help you understand energy transformations in biology.

The First Law: Energy Conservation

The *first law of thermodynamics* states that: Energy can be neither created nor destroyed, but can be converted from one form to another. In the examples cited above, one might easily visualize how the chemical energy of the gasoline is converted to the mechanical energy of the engine, or how the radiant energy of the sun is converted to the chemical energy of sugar by the plant. But the first law also tells us that all of the energy available at the start of the reaction can be accounted for when the reaction has gone to completion. In other words, for the combustion of gasoline, if we were able to add up all of the energy, including the energy in all the product molecules (such as carbon dioxide and water) and the energy lost as heat, in addition to the mechanical energy of the motion of the automobile, we could theoretically account for all of the energy present in the original quantity of gasoline.

Now consider the oxidation of glucose to carbon dioxide and water, which is what happens during respiration in a cell.

$$C_6H_{12}O_6 + 6O_2 + 6H_2O \longrightarrow 6CO_2 + 12H_2O + \text{energy}$$

Virtually all of the energy given off in the right-hand side of this equation is in the form of heat. By reacting glucose with oxygen in a calorimeter (an instrument which measures the heat of a reaction) you can show that 2831 kJ of energy are given off for each mole of glucose oxidized. The first law of thermodynamics tells us that the combined energies of six moles of carbon dioxide and twelve moles of water is less than the combined energies of one mole of glucose, six moles of oxygen, and six moles of water by 2831 kJ. This can be expressed as follows:

$$E_{\text{glucose}+O_2} = E_{CO_2+H_2O} + 2831 \text{ kJ}$$

The change in energy for this reaction is −2831 kJ. The *negative* sign indicates that the energy level of the combined products is *less* than the energy level of the combined reactants.

Now consider the reverse reaction, which is a summary equation for photosynthesis:

$$6CO_2 + 12H_2O + \text{energy} \longrightarrow 6C_6H_{12}O_6 + 6O_2 + 6H_2O$$

By measuring the energetics for this reaction under the same conditions as above, you will find that the energy change for this reaction is +2831 kJ. The *positive* sign indicates that the energy of the products is *greater* than the energy of the reactants. As predicted by the first law, the energy of synthesis of glucose is precisely the same as the energy released when glucose is oxidized.

The Second Law: Biochemical Probability

The first law of thermodynamics tells us only that all of the energy can be accounted for in any reaction. In the study of bioenergetics, it is also important to know how probable it is that a reaction will actually occur. You can predict with some certainty, for example, that the oxidation of glucose *will* occur. All that is required is that the reaction be initiated with a small flame or a strong oxidizing agent such as nitric acid (Figure 5.2). The oxidation of glucose is said to be **spontaneous**. This means that once the reaction is initiated, it will proceed to completion without any further input of energy. But how probable is the reverse reaction? The atmosphere contains ample supplies of carbon dioxide and water. Yet you know intuitively that carbon dioxide and water will not spontaneously combine to form glucose, even on a warm, sunny day!

When attempting to make predictions about complex cellular events, without prior experience, you cannot rely upon intuition. Fortunately, the second law of thermodynamics provides a way to measure

Figure 5.2

The oxidation of glucose. Sugars readily oxidize to produce carbon dioxide and water. But how probable is the reverse reaction?

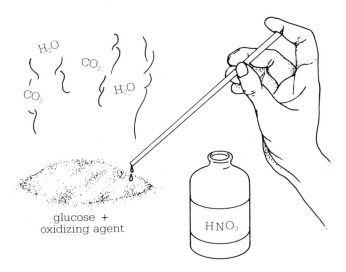

glucose + oxidizing agent

HNO_3

spontaneity. There are two thermodynamic quantities that measure spontaneity: **free energy** and **entropy**. Both free energy and entropy are complex mathematical quantities, the details of which are best left to the physical chemists. However, because of the relative ease with which free energy can be calculated and because of its predictive value, free energy is one of the most important concepts in bioenergetics. Free energy is also important because it is that portion of the total energy which is available to do useful work. The balance of the energy, which is not available to do useful work, is called entropy.

The relationships among free energy, entropy, and total energy may be summarized in this expression:

$$H = G - TS$$

where H is the total energy of the system (also called enthalpy), G is free energy, S is entropy, and T is the temperature of the system in degrees Kelvin. (Free energy is assigned the symbol G in honour of Josiah Gibbs, who is credited with having originated the concept.)

Absolute values of energy, as indicated in this equation are difficult to measure and, for our purposes, not very instructive. In the case of glucose oxidation, for example, we do not know the absolute values for the energies of the reactants or for the products. We can, however, measure the *change* in energy as the reaction

proceeds and that is useful information. We can restate the relationship between total energy, free energy and entropy in the following way:

or, $$\Delta E = \Delta G + T\Delta S$$
$$\Delta G = \Delta E - T\Delta S$$

The delta symbol signifies "change in." The second equation tells us that the change in free energy (ΔG) of a system is equal to the change in total energy (ΔE) minus the change in entropy ($T\Delta S$). The change in free energy can be calculated from easily measured variables, such as the concentrations of reactants and products in a chemical reaction. It is the *change* in free energy that gives us the required measure of spontaneity. A spontaneous reaction, for example, will be accompanied by a *decrease* in free energy, that is, ΔG will be *negative*. We can now state the *second law of thermodynamics* in this way: A reaction will occur spontaneously if it is accompanied by a decrease in the free energy of the system.

The oxidation of glucose is a spontaneous reaction. The 2831 kJ of energy released is, in fact, the *standard free energy change* for that reaction. This is the free energy change determined under certain carefully defined *standard* conditions. It is indicated by the symbol °.) Stated in thermodynamic terms, the standard free energy change for the complete combustion of one mole of glucose is 2831 kJ, or, $\Delta G° = -2831$ kJ. Such a reaction is also said to be **exergonic**, which means that energy is given off. Note that exergonic refers specifically to a negative free energy change, not to total energy. The reverse reaction, the synthesis of glucose, has a positive $\Delta G°$ and is **endergonic**—it will not occur spontaneously. In other words, a *minimum* requirement for the synthesis is the input of at least 2831 kJ of energy from an outside source.

The designation of a reaction as spontaneous means only that the reaction is capable of proceeding in the indicated direction. It does not mean that it will necessarily proceed. As you know, glucose is quite stable, in spite of its negative $\Delta G°$. The breakdown of glucose will normally proceed only if a small amount of energy is provided to initiate the reaction. On the other hand, the synthesis of glucose, as you have seen, is not a spontaneous reaction. It is, indeed, a highly improbable event. Yet the synthesis of glucose can and does proceed in plants at extremely rapid rates. This is because plants are able to use free energy from the sun to drive the reaction. In fact, a singularly unique characteristic of living organisms generally is that they possess the information necessary to *couple* energy-requiring biochemical reactions with energy-yielding reactions. The principle of biochemical coupling will be discussed in a later section.

Order and Disorder

The other side of the thermodynamic coin is entropy. What is entropy? You may think of entropy as a mathematical measure of randomness or disorder. Again, consider the oxidation of glucose. The carbon, hydrogen, and oxygen atoms in a glucose molecule are arranged in a highly ordered, non-random fashion. Furthermore, energy is concentrated in the bonds of the glucose molecule. When glucose is burned (that is, oxidized), the atoms of carbon, hydrogen, and oxygen become more randomly distributed. Some of the bond energy is also dispersed through space. This more random distribution of molecules and energy represents a higher state of entropy. Consequently, the decrease in free energy as glucose oxidizes is offset by an increase in entropy. The second law of thermodynamics can now be expressed in an alternative way: In the course of all reactions, the entropy of the universe tends toward a maximum. Note the key word, universe, in this definition. It is true that some reactions do lead to a decrease in entropy, an apparent contradiction of the second law. This is particularly true of living organisms which, in the course of growth and development, produce striking increases in order. However, it has been shown that a decrease in entropy within the organism is achieved only with an increase in entropy elsewhere in the universe. In our universe, of course, the ultimate source of free energy is the sun.

From the above discussion, you can see why entropy, in contrast to free energy, is that portion of the total energy which is *not* available to do useful work. It is for this reason that the focus of the biologist is, for the most part, on free energy changes which accompany cellular reactions and not entropy changes.

5.2   COUPLED REACTIONS AND THE CENTRAL ROLE OF ATP

In order to build and maintain structure or perform biological work, all cells require a constant input of matter and energy. The primary input of energy into the biosphere is through the process of **photosynthesis**. (This topic will be discussed in detail in later chapters.) Through photosynthesis, plants and some bacteria use the energy of the sun to build complex organic molecules from inorganic precursors. Non-photosynthetic cells and organisms, such as fungi and animals, depend on the products of photosynthesis for their supply of both matter and energy. Complex carbohydrates, fats, and proteins can be broken down by cells to make smaller molecules, or carbon "skeletons," such as sugars, organic acids, and amino acids. This process by which larger molecules are broken down into smaller molecules is known as **catabolism**. These carbon "skeletons" are the building blocks which cells use to synthesize the macromolecules required for their growth and development. This process of synthesis is known as **anabolism**. Together, the two processes of catabolism and anabolism constitute **metabolism.** Metabolism is the sum total of all the degradative and synthetic chemical reactions in the cell. In addition to providing the building blocks for anabolism, a second important function of catabolism is to provide the energy for it and for other forms of cellular work.

Biochemical coupling of reactions is the key to building thermodynamic order in the cell. It is the means by which the free energy released from spontaneous, exergonic reactions can be used to drive energy-requiring, endergonic reactions. In order to illustrate this principle, consider the conversion of 1,3-bisphosphoglycerate (1,3PGA) to 3-phosphoglycerate (3-PGA) and inorganic phosphate ((P)). This is a key reaction in the biochemical pathway known as glycolysis (section 5.5). It is a *spontaneous, exergonic* reaction:

$$1,3\text{-PGA} \longrightarrow 3\text{-PGA} + (P) \qquad \Delta G° = -49 \text{ kJ}$$

A second reaction, the synthesis of ATP from ADP and (P), is an *endergonic, energy-requiring* reaction:

$$ADP + (P) \longrightarrow ATP \qquad \Delta G° = +31 \text{ kJ}$$

In the cell, these two reactions occur simultaneously on the same enzyme. The enzyme catalyzes the direct transfer of the phosphate from 1,3-PGA to ADP. The products of the reaction are 3-PGA and ATP. This coupled reaction may be described as the sum of two partial reactions:

$$
\begin{array}{ll}
1,3\text{-PGA} \longrightarrow 3\text{-PGA} + (P) & \Delta G° = -49 \text{ kJ} \\
ADP + (P) \longrightarrow ATP & \Delta G° = +31 \text{ kJ} \\
\hline
1,3\text{-PGA} + ADP \longrightarrow 3\text{-PGA} + ATP & \Delta G° = -18 \text{ kJ}
\end{array}
$$

Note that the energy change of the coupled reaction is the sum of the energy changes of the two partial reactions. The coupled reaction is spontaneous because the sum of the two free energy changes turns

Figure 5.3
The chemical structure of ATP. ATP is a nucleotide
triphosphate. It is composed of adenine, the five-carbon
sugar ribose and three phosphate groups. The oxygen–
phosphorus bonds which are involved in energy transfer
are shown in colour.

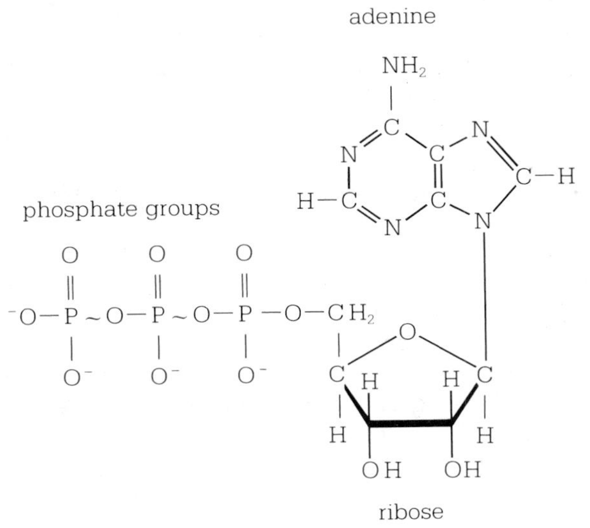

adenine

NH$_2$

phosphate groups

$$^-O-P\sim O-P\sim O-P-O-CH_2$$

ribose

Why does ATP appear to assume such a special role in the energy metabolism of the cell? The answer to this question lies in the amount of free energy that is released when the terminal phosphate is transferred from the ATP molecule:

$$ATP + H_2O \longrightarrow ADP + H_3PO_4 \qquad \Delta G° = -31 \text{ kJ}$$

The free energy released (-31 kJ per mole) is more than enough to drive most of the energy-requiring reactions in cells, from synthesis of nucleic acids and proteins, to the movement of solutes across cell membranes, or the contraction of flagella and muscle myofibrils. On the other hand, there are numerous *phosphorylated compounds* for which the free energy of phosphate transfer is even more negative than that of ATP. One example, 1,3-bisphosphoglycerate, was introduced in the earlier discussion of coupled reactions. The significance of ATP in the cell appears to reside in the fact that its free energy of phosphate transfer is intermediate. ATP thus serves to mediate the transfer of energy between energy-yielding reactions, which normally have high free energies of phosphate transfer, and energy-consuming reactions with normally lower free energies of phosphate transfer (Figure 5.4). These latter reactions may also include activities such as active transport of molecules across cell membranes or muscle contraction.

out to be negative. In the overall reaction, then, the free energy which accompanies the release of the phosphate group from 1,3-PGA is coupled to the energy requirement for the addition of phosphate to ADP.

In the cell, it is frequently necessary for energy to be transported, such as when the energy-consuming reactions (for example, muscle contraction or membrane transport reactions) are spatially removed from the energy-yielding reactions (for example, transfer of phosphate from 1,3-PGA). Some form of mobile carrier is required. The most common mobile energy carrier in the cell is ATP (Figure 5.3). This chemical was first isolated from extracts of muscle in 1929. F. Lipmann was one of the first scientists to recognize the significant role played by ATP in the energy metabolism of the cell. He called it a *high energy molecule* and designated the terminal phosphate bonds by the symbol $\sim$. Actually, the designation of ATP as a high energy molecule is somewhat misleading, because it implies that ATP is somehow a unique molecule. It isn't. The two terminal phosphate bonds of the ATP molecule are normal, covalent bonds.

Figure 5.4
Energy coupled reactions. The terminal phosphate of ATP carries energy between an energy-yielding reaction and an energy-consuming reaction elsewhere in the cell.

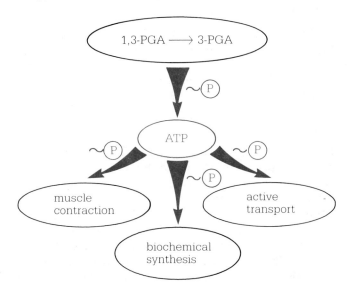

5.3 OXIDATION REDUCTION REACTIONS

As you learned in Chapter 1, oxidation reactions are a very common type of spontaneous reaction in cells. Along with ATP, oxidation reactions are intimately involved in energy metabolism. Recall that oxidation involves the transfer of an electron from a donor molecule to an acceptor molecule. The molecule from which the electron is removed is said to be *oxidized*. The molecule which accepts the electron is said to be *reduced*. Recall too that an oxidation cannot occur without a corresponding reduction. Redox (*reduction–oxidation*) reactions follow this general form:

$$\text{electron donor} \longleftrightarrow e^- + \text{electron acceptor}$$

An electron donor is also known as a **reducing agent** because, by donating electrons, it causes a reduction. Conversely, an electron acceptor is known as an **oxidizing agent**. As a general rule in the bioenergetics of redox reactions, strong reducing agents mean a high potential negative free energy change.

Many of the more important redox reactions in the cell are mediated by **coenzymes**. Coenzymes are non-protein components which are not substrates but which must be present in order for an enzyme to act. **Nicotinamide adenine dinucleotide (NAD)** and **flavin adenine dinucleotide (FAD)** are two common coenzymes involved in redox reactions of cellular respiration (Figure 5.5). The coenzyme nicotinamide adenine dinucleotide phosphate (NADP), closely related to NAD, will be encountered later in the study of photosynthesis (Chapter 6).

The participation of NAD in a redox reaction is illustrated by the following example:

$$\begin{array}{l} \text{malate} \longrightarrow \text{oxaloacetate} + 2e^- + 2H^+ \\ \underline{NAD^+ + 2e^- + 2H^+ \longrightarrow NADH + H^+} \\ \text{malate} + NAD^+ \longrightarrow \text{oxaloacetate} + NADH + H^+ \end{array}$$

Note that as malate is oxidized to oxaloacetate, NAD is also reduced to NADH. NADH is important for two reasons. First, NADH is a strong reducing agent and thus represents the conservation of a large amount of energy. Second, NADH, like ATP, is a mobile energy carrier within the cell. NADH can be used as a reducing agent for synthesis reactions elsewhere in the cell.

The cellular organelle that is responsible for generating the largest amounts of reduced NAD is known

as the mitochondrion. The following section will focus on some of the more significant features of this important organelle.

5.4 THE MITOCHONDRION

Mitochondria were discovered late in the nineteenth century by cytologists studying cells with the light microscope. These early microscopists observed small organelles having similar properties but in a variety of shapes and sizes, from granular to threadlike. One unifying characteristic of these organelles was their ability to stain with oxidation-reduction dyes. They called these organelles mitochondria (from the Greek word *mitos* meaning thread). The small sizes of mitochondria and the limitation of the light microscope hampered early studies of these organelles. However, early in the twentieth century, a subcellular fraction containing mitochondria was isolated by differential centrifugation (Figure 5.6), and work on the biochemistry of these organelles began in earnest. These early biochemical studies clearly indicated that the mitochondria were the principal sites of energy metabolism in the cell. When it was later discovered that the mitochondria were also the sites of ATP production, they were appropriately labelled ''the powerhouse of the cell.'' Still, because of their small size, a study of the structure of mitochondria was not possible until the development of the electron microscope.

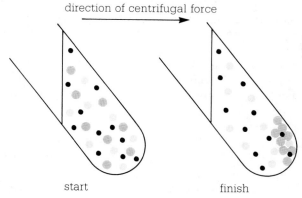

direction of centrifugal force

start   finish

Figure 5.6

Separation of cellular organelles by differential centrifugation. Subjecting a cell homogenate to centrifugation at low speed causes the larger, denser particles to settle on the bottom of the tube. The remaining fluid, or supernatant, can then be poured off and centrifuged at a higher speed to cause smaller particles to settle. By selecting the proper speed settings, different cellular organelles can be separated.

Figure 5.5
The chemical structures of nicotinamide and flavin adenine nucleotides. Nicotinamide adenine dinucleotide (a) may occur in the oxidized form (NAD^+) or the reduced form ($NADH + H^+$). The oxidized and reduced forms of the nicotinamide portion of the molecule are shown. Flavin adenine dinucleotide (b) undergoes oxidation and reduction on the riboflavin portion of the molecule. Both molecules are important energy carriers in the cell.

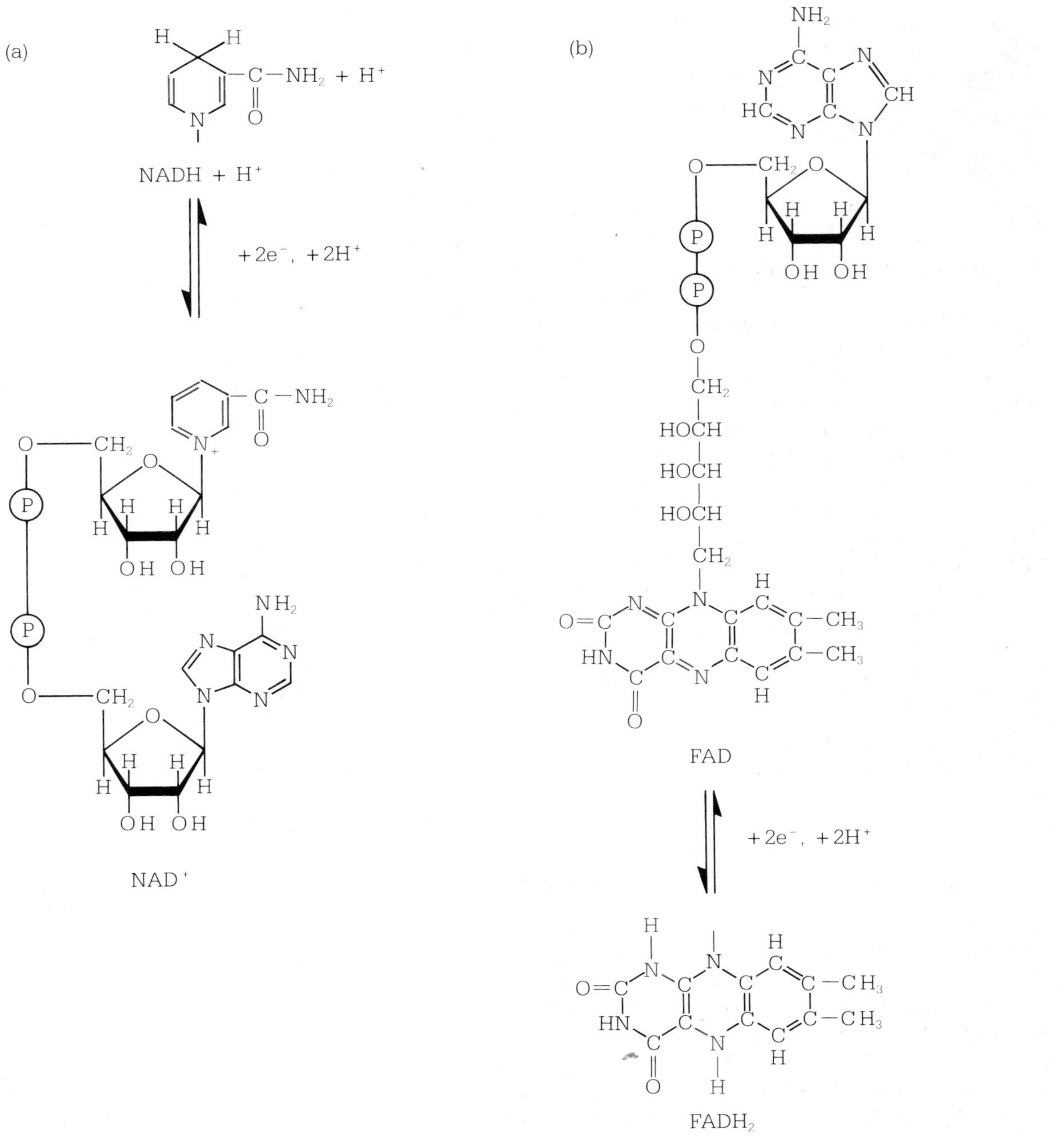

(a)

(b)

$$NADH + H^+$$

$$+2e^-, +2H^+$$

$$NAD^+$$

FAD

$$+2e^-, +2H^+$$

$$FADH_2$$

107

Figure 5.7
An electron microscope image of a mitochondrion

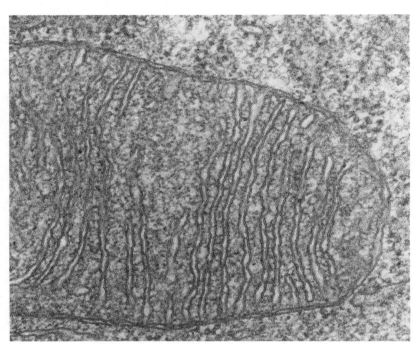

Figure 5.8
The mitochondrion in three dimensions

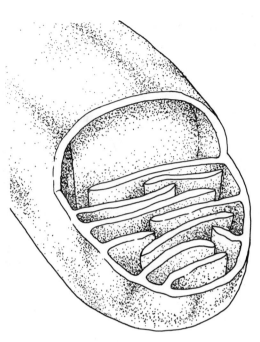

Mitochondria (Figure 5.7) are small, often threadlike organelles found in nearly all eukaryotic cells, both plant and animal. Prokaryotic cells (for example, bacteria) do not have mitochondria. Their respiratory activities occur on the plasma membrane. The mitochondria of plant cells are typically spherical or near-spherical in shape and 1 μm to 2 μm in diameter. Animal cell mitochondria are more varied in size and shape. A liver cell mitochondrion, for example, is typically 0.5 μm to 1.0 μm in diameter and 2 μm in length. But in other cells, mitochondria may reach lengths of 8 μm to 10 μm or more.

The number of mitochondria and their distribution in the cell generally correlates with the metabolic demand of the cell. Normal liver cells contain 1000 to 1600 mitochondria per cell while a single öocyte (egg cell) may contain as many as 300 000. Within some cells the mitochondria move about freely, while the long threadlike mitochondria of kidney cells tend to concentrate in the region where the active movement of solutes and water takes place — where energy is required. In skeletal muscle (especially insect flight muscle) and mammalian heart muscle, the large mitochondria are found in intimate association with the A-bands, the contractile segments of the myofibril.

Sperm typically have a few elongated mitochondria coiled in springlike fashion around the base of the energy-consuming flagellum.

Although there is no uniformity in the size and shape of mitochondria from cell to cell, the structural details, as revealed by the electron microscope, are remarkably similar. Each is composed of four distinct metabolic regions or compartments (Figure 5.8). These are the **outer membrane**, the **inner membrane**, the **intermembrane space**, which lies between the two membranes, and the central **matrix**. Not only can intact mitochondria be isolated from other cytoplasmic constituents of the cell in order to study their chemical and enzymatic composition, but scientists can also separate the four compartments in order to study their individual composition and function. From these studies, scientists are able to learn a great deal about the role each compartment plays in the overall function of the mitochondrion.

The outer membrane is a smooth membrane. It is freely permeable, allowing molecules with a mass of 10 000 daltons or less to pass through without hindrance. It also contains enzymes that convert fatty acids to forms that can be further metabolized inside the mitochondrion.

The inner membrane is characteristically folded into the interior of the organelle. These folds, called cristae, serve to increase the total surface area of the membrane. Compared with most membranes, the inner membrane is exceptionally rich in protein. In fact, as much as 75 percent of the mass of the membrane is protein. Some of these proteins make up the respiratory electron transport chain (Section 5.5), some make up the enzyme that synthesizes ATP and others are specific transport proteins that regulate the passage of metabolites into and out of the mitochondrion. As you will see later, it is important that the inner membrane, in contrast to the outer membrane, is impermeable to most small molecules or ions. The number of cristae and the oxidative capacity of the mitochondrion are very closely correlated. This reflects the significant role assumed by the inner membrane in energy metabolism. It has been estimated, for example, that the inner membrane from a muscle cell or a brown fat cell mitochondrion, both of which are metabolically very active, has a surface area which is nearly ten times that of a liver or epithelial cell mitochondrion.

The intermembrane space is an unstructured region which contains enzymes that use ATP. It also serves as a proton reservoir during the synthesis of ATP.

The matrix is the unstructured central region of the mitochondrion. It is a highly concentrated mixture of proteins including the enzymes for the oxidation of foodstuffs such as proteins, lipids, and carbohydrates.

5.5 AEROBIC CELLULAR RESPIRATION

The molecules synthesized during photosynthesis and subsequently ingested by animals are particularly important because they are chemically reduced. As discussed earlier, the amount of free energy available in a molecule is a direct function of the level of chemical reduction. The free energy is derived from these energy-rich molecules by the process of chemical oxidation. This oxidative breakdown of foodstuffs by the cell is known as **aerobic respiration**. As an example of aerobic respiration, consider the oxidation of glucose. The overall reaction for the complete combustion (that is, oxidation) of glucose in air is:

$$C_6H_{12}O_6 + 6O_2 + 6H_2O \longrightarrow 6CO_2 + 12H_2O + 2831 \text{ kJ/mol}$$

Oxidation in the cell, however, could not occur all at once. A sudden release of all that energy would be far more than the cell can handle at one time (Figure 5.2)! If this were to happen, the cell would literally burn up. In the cell, the complete oxidation of glucose

occurs as a series of smaller steps. Each step is catalyzed by a separate enzyme and serves to release only a portion of the total free energy available from glucose oxidation. In certain specific steps, some of the energy released is conserved in the form of ATP. In this way the foodstuffs are subjected to a *controlled oxidation* which releases energy in amounts and forms that are useful to the cell.

The overall process of respiration can be conveniently divided into three major stages, as shown in Figure 5.9. The initial stage, in which glucose is converted to pyruvic acid, is known as **glycolysis** (from the Greek words *glycos* meaning sugar, and *lysis* meaning loosening or setting free). The reactions of glycolysis occur outside the mitochondrion in the cytoplasm of the cell. For some time, it was thought that the enzymes for glycolysis were simply dissolved in the cytosol (the soluble aqueous portion of the cytoplasm), but recent evidence suggests that the enzymes may be more organized, perhaps in association with the microtubular network of the cell. The process of glycolysis will proceed when no oxygen is available, a condition said to be **anaerobic**. As a means of producing usable energy, glycolysis is not very efficient. Nevertheless, glycolysis alone can support life as it does in many bacteria.

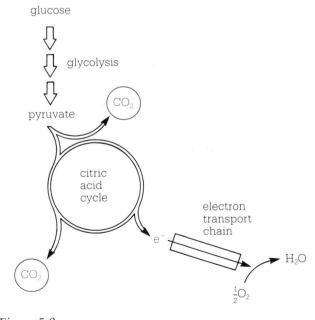

Figure 5.9
Aerobic respiration. When oxygen is available, glucose may be completely broken down into carbon dioxide and water. This process occurs in three major stages.

When oxygen is available, that is, under **aerobic** conditions, the pyruvic acid produced by glycolysis may be metabolized further through the second stage, the **citric acid cycle**. Here the pyruvic acid is completely oxidized to carbon dioxide. The reactions of the citric acid cycle occur *within* the matrix of the mitochondrion. Again, little energy is conserved as ATP. Most of the energy of oxidation is conserved as electron pairs in the form of the reduced electron carriers, NADH and $FADH_2$. NADH and $FADH_2$ in turn donate electrons to the third stage of respiration, the **electron transport chain,** where the largest quantities of ATP are produced. The electron transport chain, which is the principal site of ATP synthesis in the cell, is located within the inner mitochondrial membrane.

Each of the three stages of respiration is a rather complicated series of biochemical reactions. In order to simplify the process and focus on the overall principles, only the more important steps will be considered in the following discussion.

Glycolysis

The principal raw material, or **substrate**, for glycolysis (Figure 5.10) is glucose. Glucose may be derived from several sources, depending on the organism or metabolic state. Plants and animals both store excess carbohydrate as polymers of glucose—as starch in plants and as glycogen in animals. These storage carbohydrates may be enzymatically broken down into glucose-phosphate. Alternatively, glucose may be ingested directly as a component of foodstuffs or as part of a carbohydrate molecule such as table sugar (sucrose) in your soft drink or coffee. (Sucrose is made up of two simple sugars, glucose and fructose.) Proteins and fatty acids may also be metabolized through these same series of reactions in order to provide both carbon skeletons and energy. The metabolism of glucose will be used here to illustrate the respiratory process.

Glucose is a rather stable molecule; it is not easily broken down into simpler molecules. Earlier you examined the analogy of energy conversions in an automobile, in which the potential energy stored in the gasoline is converted into the kinetic energy of forward motion. Energy is also required to start the engine. Automobiles once came equipped with a hand crank for this purpose, although we now depend on electric starters. In a similar way, energy must be supplied in the form of *activation energy* in order to initiate the breakdown of glucose. Not surprisingly, the activation energy for glycolysis is supplied in the form of ATP. In the first reaction of glycolysis, a glucose molecule is **phosphorylated**. This is accomplished by transferring a phosphate from an ATP molecule to a glucose molecule. The product of this reaction is called glucose-6-phosphate (Figure 5.10). The glucose-6-phosphate is then rearranged to form fructose-6-phosphate, a related six-carbon sugar. A second phosphate is transferred from ATP to the fructose-6-phosphate. At this point, the six-carbon fructose-1,6-bisphosphate is split into two three-carbon units called phosphoglyceraldehyde (PGAL). Each PGAL molecule retains one phosphate.

$$\text{Fructose-1,6-bisphosphate (C6)} \longrightarrow$$
$$\text{(2) 3-phosphoglyceraldehyde (C3)}$$

In the complicated reaction which follows, two things are accomplished. First, PGAL is oxidized; the electrons removed from PGAL are transferred to nicotinamide adenine dinucleotide (NAD). Secondly, at the same time, another phosphate group is added. This time the source of phosphate is inorganic phosphate (Ⓟ)

$$\text{PGAL} + Ⓟ + \text{NAD}^+ \longrightarrow \text{1,3-PGA} + \text{NADH} + \text{H}^+$$

drawn from the surrounding medium. Thus, some of the energy released in the oxidation of PGAL to glycerate is conserved as NADH and some is used to add inorganic phosphate to the glycerate.

The net effect of the reactions up to this point has been to *rearrange* the glucose molecule so that subsequent transformations will release sufficient free energy to drive the synthesis of ATP. In other words, the glucose molecule has been modified to an energetically favourable form. In the next step, a phosphate group is removed from 1,3-bisphosphoglycerate to form 3-phosphoglycerate.

$$\text{1,3-PGA} + \text{ADP} \longrightarrow \text{3-PGA} + \text{ATP}$$

The phosphate group is transferred directly to ADP, forming one molecule of ATP. Because this ATP is synthesized through the action of an enzyme directly on a respiratory substrate, this process is known as *substrate level phosphorylation*. The next step is a rearrangement, in which the phosphate is shifted from the terminal carbon to the central carbon. This is followed once again by the transfer of the phosphate group to ADP to make ATP. As before, the rearrangements are necessary in order that the subsequent reaction will release sufficient free energy to drive the synthesis of ATP. Thus for each molecule of glucose which entered glycolysis, four ATP molecules have been generated.

Figure 5.10
The intermediates of glycolysis. Glycolysis may be subdivided into two stages. The first stage is a series of preparatory reactions in which six-carbon sugars are converted to two molecules of the three-carbon glyceraldehyde-3-phosphate (GAP). In the second stage,

the two molecules of GAP are degraded to two molecules of pyruvate, coupled with the formation of ATP. Under aerobic conditions, pyruvate may be further degraded to CO_2 through the citric acid cycle. Under anaerobic conditions, pyruvate may be reduced to ethanol or lactate.

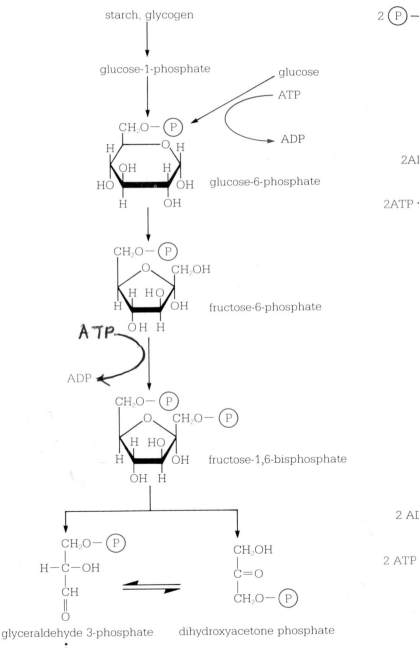

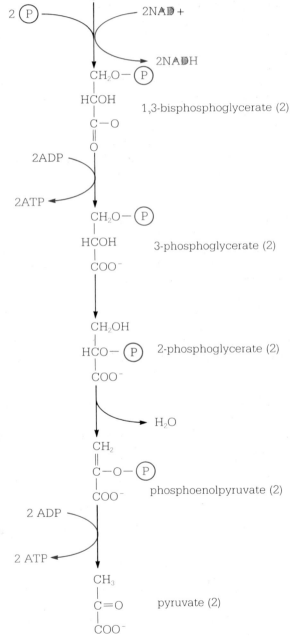

The overall result of glycolysis may be summarized as follows:

1. The six-carbon glucose molecule is broken down into two molecules of the three-carbon pyruvic acid.

2. An initial expenditure of energy in the form of two molecules of ATP results in the conservation of energy as four molecules of ATP. Thus the net gain is two molecules of ATP.

3. An additional quantity of energy is conserved as two molecules of NADH.

The overall energetics of glycolysis are depicted in the scheme shown in Figure 5.11.

The Citric Acid Cycle

The next stage in glucose metabolism is the citric acid cycle (CAC). The CAC is also known as the Krebs cycle, in honour of Hans Krebs whose research in the 1930s was responsible for elucidating this important metabolic process. Krebs was awarded the Nobel Prize in medicine in 1953 for his outstanding contribution.

Entry of pyruvic acid into the citric acid cycle begins with a complicated series of reactions involving a derivative of vitamin B_1 (thiamine) and a coenzyme called **Coenzyme A** (abbreviated CoA). In the process, the three-carbon pyruvic acid molecule is split into a carbon dioxide molecule and a two-carbon acetate unit. These reactions also involve an oxidation. As before, some of the energy released by oxidation is conserved as a molecule of NADH. The acetic acid unit is not free, but is bound to a molecule of CoA. The complete complex is called **acetyl-CoA**. Since there are *two* molecules of pyruvic acid formed for each glucose which enters the system in the first place, two molecules of NADH and two molecules of acetyl-CoA are formed. The overall reaction is shown in the following equation:

2 pyruvic acid + 2NAD$^+$ + 2CoA $\longrightarrow$
$$2CO_2 + 2NADH + H^+ + 2 \text{ acetyl-CoA}$$

Remember that the pyruvic acid is produced in the cytoplasm of the cell, *outside* the mitochondrion, and therefore must be transported *across* the membranes of the mitochondrion before it can be converted into acetyl-CoA. Once in the matrix of the mitochondrion, the acetate group is transferred from the acetyl-CoA to the four-carbon molecule oxaloacetate (OAA). The product of this reaction is a six-carbon molecule, citrate (hence the designation, citric acid cycle). The CoA

Figure 5.11

Free energy changes during glycolysis. Some energy, in the form of ATP, must first be supplied to prime the system. Subsequent release of free energy, as the fructose-1,6-bisphosphate is converted to pyruvate, may be used to phosphorylate ADP and reduce NAD$^+$. The energy level of pyruvate is substantially lower than that of glucose.

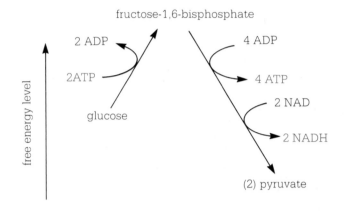

released is free to return to the cytoplasm in order to react with another molecule of pyruvic acid. The citrate then enters into a series of oxidation reactions (Figure 5.12) which release two molecules of carbon dioxide. Most of the energy of the acetyl group is conserved as one ATP (by substrate level phosphorylation) and four reduced electron carriers (one FADH$_2$ and three NADH). Finally, one molecule of oxaloacetate is regenerated. The oxaloacetate is then ready to accept another acetyl group and thus continue the cycle. The overall reaction for *one* turn of the citric acid cycle is shown in the following summary equation:

acetyl-CoA + ADP + (P) + 3NAD + FAD $\longrightarrow$
$$\text{CoA} + \text{ATP} + 3\text{NADH} + \text{FADH}_2 + 2CO_2$$

Since the original glucose molecule is split into *two* three-carbon units, this equation must be multiplied by two in order to express the results of the cycle as equivalent to one glucose molecule.

Notice that, although the citric acid cycle has completely broken down the glucose molecule to carbon dioxide, little ATP has been produced and no molecular oxygen consumed. You will find it useful to review at this point the conservation of energy through the first two stages of respiration. The summary equation above shows that the citric acid cycle generates two ATP by substrate level phosphorylation. To this can be added the four ATP produced in

Figure 5.12
The citric acid cycle. Under aerobic conditions, the pyruvate from glycolysis is oxidized further through the citric acid cycle. Pyruvate is first converted to acetyl-coenzyme A which then reacts with the four-carbon oxaloacetate to form the six-carbon citrate (citric acid). The principal products of the cycle are ATP, reduced electron carriers (NADH, FADH$_2$) and CO$_2$. In the process, the oxaloacetate is regenerated in order to accept another acetate group and continue the cycle.

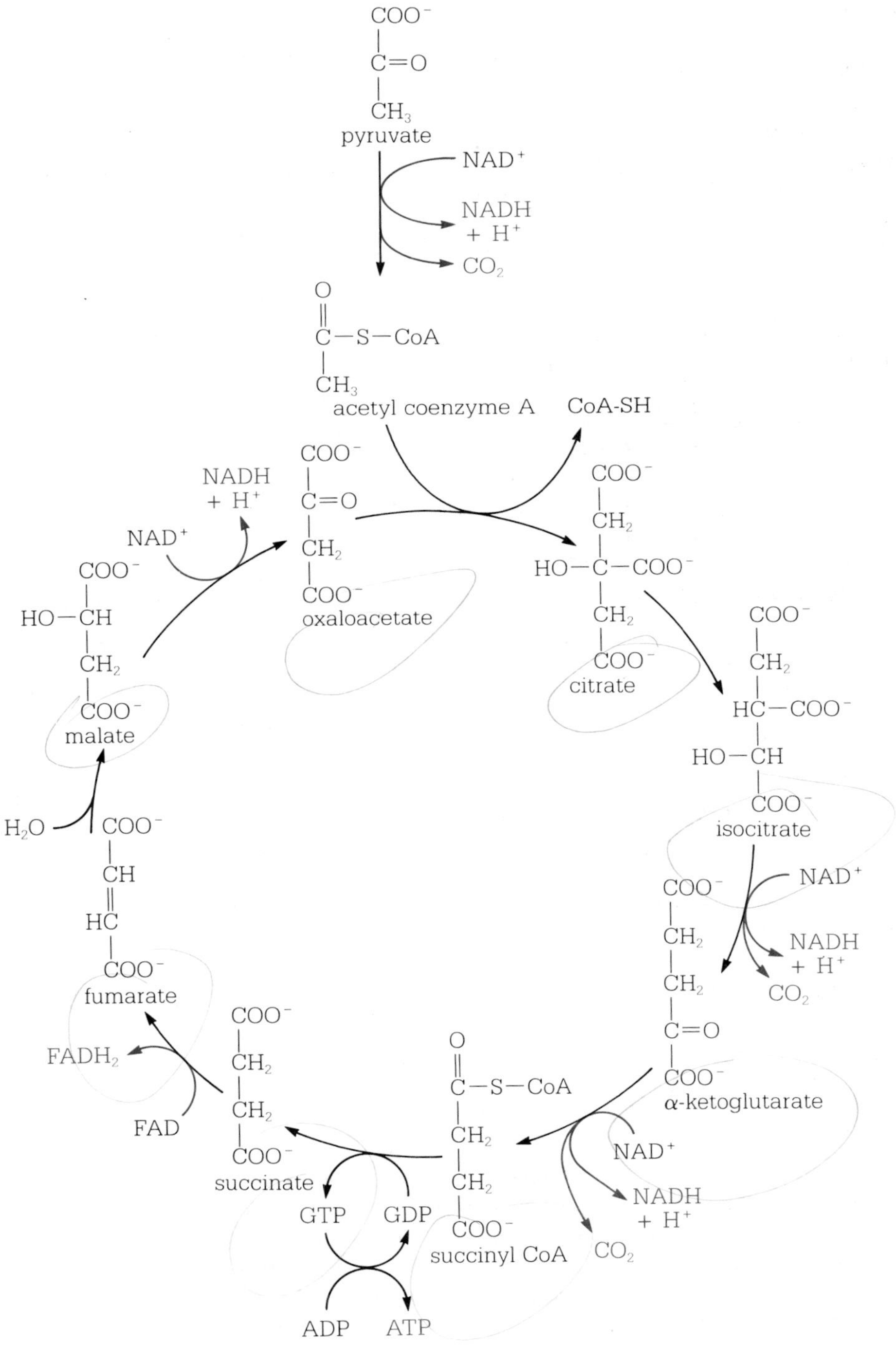

COO$^-$
|
C=O
|
CH$_3$
pyruvate

NAD$^+$
NADH + H$^+$
CO$_2$

O
||
C—S—CoA
|
CH$_3$
acetyl coenzyme A   CoA-SH

NADH + H$^+$
NAD$^+$

COO$^-$
|
C=O
|
CH$_2$
|
COO$^-$
oxaloacetate

COO$^-$
|
CH$_2$
|
HO—C—COO$^-$
|
CH$_2$
|
COO$^-$
citrate

COO$^-$
|
CH$_2$
|
HC—COO$^-$
|
HO—CH
|
COO$^-$
isocitrate

NAD$^+$
NADH + H$^+$
CO$_2$

COO$^-$
|
HO—CH
|
CH$_2$
|
COO$^-$
malate

H$_2$O

COO$^-$
|
CH
||
HC
|
COO$^-$
fumarate

FADH$_2$
FAD

COO$^-$
|
CH$_2$
|
CH$_2$
|
COO$^-$
succinate

GTP   GDP

ADP   ATP

O
||
C—S—CoA
|
CH$_2$
|
CH$_2$
|
COO$^-$
succinyl CoA

COO$^-$
|
CH$_2$
|
CH$_2$
|
C=O
|
COO$^-$
α-ketoglutarate

NAD$^+$
NADH + H$^+$
CO$_2$

glycolysis, but you must subtract the two ATP originally expended to activate the glucose. The net gain is four ATP. You can also see that the citric acid cycle yields six molecules of reduced NAD (three NADH for each turn of the cycle). To this, add two NADH generated in the oxidation of pyruvate to actetate plus the two NADH produced in glycolysis. The total is ten NADH produced. Finally, two molecules of FADH$_2$ are generated in the citric acid cycle. These numbers can now be multiplied by the amount of free energy released when these molecules are either hydrolyzed (as in ATP) or re-oxidized by molecular oxygen (as for the electron carriers). These calculations, which summarize the efficiency of energy conservation through glycolysis and the citric acid cycle, are shown in Table 5.1.

Table 5.1   Free Energy Conserved in the Products of Glycolysis and the Citric Acid Cycle

	NUMBER		ENERGY (kJ/mol)		
ATP	4	×	31	=	124
NADH	10	×	221	=	2210
FADH$_2$	2	×	180	=	360
	total			=	2694

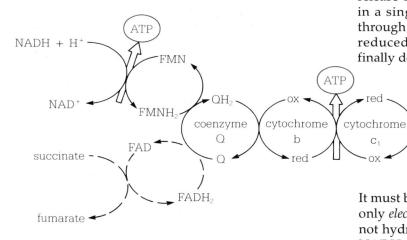

Figure 5.13
The electron transport chain. The chain is composed of a series of electron carriers, arranged in order of decreasing redox potential. The passage of electrons from one carrier to the next is accompanied by a drop in free energy. At three positions in the chain, the energy drop is sufficient to drive the synthesis of ATP.

Since the free energy of oxidation of glucose is 2831 kJ/mol, the efficiency of energy conservation *at this stage* is

$$2694/2831 \times 100 = 95\%$$

Thus, with completion of glycolysis and the citric acid cycle, the glucose molecule is broken down into six molecules of CO$_2$, but approximately 95 percent of the energy of the glucose molecule is conserved as ATP and reduced electron carriers. Most of the energy is in the form of high energy electrons transferred to NAD and FAD during the oxidation steps. This exercise helps to emphasize the significance of reduced electron carriers in the energy exchange reactions of the cell. It also serves to focus our attention on the third stage of respiration, the electron transport chain. It is in this stage that NADH and FADH$_2$ are oxidized at the expense of molecular oxygen, with the simultaneous production of large quantities of ATP.

The Electron Transport System
In the presence of oxygen, NADH may be oxidized to NAD$^+$ and water according to the following equation:

$$2NADH + 2H^+ + O_2 \longrightarrow 2NAD^+ + 2H_2O$$

As indicated in Table 5.1, this reaction releases 221 kJ of free energy for each mole of NADH. As before, the release of this amount of energy is not accomplished in a single step. Instead, the electrons are passed through a series of electron carriers, each alternately reduced, then re-oxidized, until the electrons are finally donated to oxygen to form water (Figure 5.13).

It must be stressed that, through this entire sequence, only *electrons* are passed from one carrier to the next, not hydrogen ions (protons). Protons given up when NADH passes electrons on to the next carrier in the chain are simply released into the pool of protons in the surrounding aqueous medium. When the electrons are finally donated to oxygen at the end of the electron transport chain, the protons required to make water are taken up from this same proton pool. The principal carriers in the middle of the electron transport chain, the **cytochromes**, accept only electrons when they are reduced.

It can be shown by experiment that, for every pair of electrons which moves through the electron transport chain from NADH to oxygen, *three* molecules of ATP are generated from ADP and inorganic phosphate. For electrons donated to the chain from $FADH_2$, only *two* ATP are generated. This process, by which ATP is formed at the expense of molecular oxygen is known as **oxidative phosphorylation**. The mechanism by which this ATP is formed will be better understood if you first consider how the components of the electron transport chain are organized within the membrane.

As pointed out earlier, the electron carriers which make up the electron transport chain are associated with the inner membrane of the mitochondrion. They are, in fact, multiprotein, transmembrane complexes. This means that they extend right across the membrane. Remember that the inner membrane is extensively folded. The folds in the membrane, the cristae, provide a large surface area which, in turn, provides space for a large number of electron transport complexes. This correlation between the amount of folding and the number of electron transport complexes is supported by the observation that mitochondria in insect flight muscle cells and other cells with a high

energy requirement typically have an extensively folded inner membrane. On the other hand, the mitochondria of cells with a relatively low energy requirement have comparatively few folds. The electron transport chains of prokaryote organisms are located in the plasma membrane.

Biologists have used a variety of physical and chemical techniques to carefully disassemble the inner membranes of isolated mitochondria. By doing so they have been able to show that the membrane contains five different multiprotein complexes. Four of these complexes (Figure 5.14) are involved in the transport of electrons while the fifth complex is responsible for the synthesis of ATP.

By comparing Figure 5.14 with Figure 5.13, you will see that each of the four membrane complexes is capable of transferring electrons through a portion of the electron transport chain. It should be pointed out that Figure 5.14 is only a schematic diagram. It does not mean that the four complexes are necessarily rigidly arranged in such an orderly fashion in the membrane. Indeed, each complex is free to diffuse laterally within the plane of the membrane, receiving or passing on electrons only when it encounters an appropriate donor or acceptor complex. Such encounters occur hundreds of times every second for each complex!

Experiments which use inhibitors of electron transport or artificial electron donors have identified three sites in the chain where electron transport is coupled to ATP synthesis. These three sites correspond to protein complexes I, III, and IV identified in Figure 5.14. Coupling in this sense means that the energy released as electrons are transported from NADH (or $FADH_2$) can be used to drive ATP synthesis.

Figure 5.14
The multiprotein complexes of the electron transport chain. The electron transport chain is composed of four multiprotein complexes which extend across the mitochondrial inner membrane. The paths of electrons from NADH or succinate are shown by the solid arrows. Dashed arrows indicate proton pumps which move protons from the matrix into the intermembrane space.

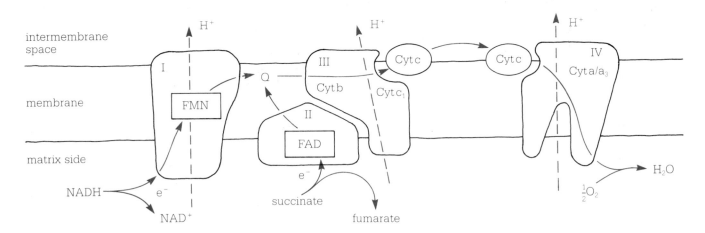

What is the maximum yield of ATP that may be expected from glycolysis and the citric acid cycle? How much ATP is actually produced if a glucose molecule is completely oxidized to carbon dioxide and water? A theoretical maximum yield is summarized in the table below. This yield takes into account all of the ATP that might be produced by substrate level phosphorylations in both glycolysis and the citric acid cycle. To this is added all of the ATP that could be produced by oxidative phosphorylation if all of the electron pairs were passed through the electron transport system.

Note that a yield of *three* ATP molecules is assigned to each electron pair derived from the citric acid cycle that enters the electron transport system as NADH + H$^+$. On the other hand, the table indicates that each NADH derived from glycolysis is able to generate only *two* ATP molecules. This apparent anomaly is based on two observations. First, the citric acid cycle enzymes and the electron transport system are both located inside the mitochondrion while the enzymes of glycolysis are located in the cytosol, outside the mitochondrion. Second, the inner membrane of the mitochondrion is impermeable to NAD$^+$ and NADH + H$^+$. Consequently, any NADH generated in glycolysis does *not* have direct access to the electron transport chain.

Cytosolic NADH + H$^+$ can be oxidized by the electron transport chain, but only indirectly. One way to accomplish this is by the *glycerophosphate shuttle* shown below. NADH + H$^+$ generated during glycolysis may be re-oxidized by a cytosolic enzyme which reduces dihydroxyacetone phosphate to glycerol-3-phosphate. The glycerol-3-phosphate is free to diffuse through the outer mitochondrial membrane to the outer surface of the inner membrane. There, a second enzyme re-oxidizes the glycerol-3-phosphate to dihydroxyacetone phosphate. The electrons are accepted by FAD, rather than by NAD$^+$. Electrons entering the electron transport chain via FAD are donated directly to the coen-

Theoretical Maximum Yield of ATP

SOURCE OF ATP		NO. OF ATP
Glycolysis		
1. ATP consumption in glucose activation		− 2
2. substrate level phosphorylations		+ 4
3. election pairs (2) (as NADH + H$^+$)		+ 4
Citric Acid Cycle		
4. electron pairs (8) (as NADH + H$^+$)		+24
5. electron pairs (2) (as FADH$_2$)		+ 4
6. substrate level phosphorylations		+ 2
	Grand Total	+36

5.6 A MODEL FOR ATP SYNTHESIS

The question of how ATP synthesis is coupled to electron transport has puzzled scientists for many years. Many scientists have researched a variety of possible mechanisms without success. The puzzle appears finally to have been solved by Peter Mitchell when, in 1961, he published the **chemiosmotic hypothesis** for ATP synthesis. Although not readily accepted by many biochemists in the beginning, Mitchell's hypothesis is now firmly supported by experimental results. In honour of his pioneering work, Mitchell was awarded the Nobel prize for chemistry in 1978.

Mitchell's hypothesis is based upon two fundamental requirements. First, the inner membrane is impermeable to protons (hydrogen ions, H$^+$). Second, the electron transport complexes serve a dual purpose. In addition to transporting electrons, each complex also serves as a **proton pump**. A proton pump is a mechanism for using energy to move protons from one side of the membrane to the other. In the case of the mitochondrion, the protons are moved from the matrix side of the inner membrane to the intermembrane space. In bacteria, which do not have mitochondria, the protons are instead moved across the cell membrane. The effect of the proton pump is to establish an unequal distribution of protons across the membrane. The difference in proton concentration across the membrane may be as much as ten-fold. Since the proton carries a positive charge, a proton

zyme Q (Figure 5.13), bypassing the first of the three possible phosphorylation sites. Thus only two ATP molecules are generated.

The glycerophosphate shuttle, commonly found operating in skeletal muscle and brain tissue, is only one of several shuttle mechanisms which have been studied. Other shuttles, such as the *malate-aspartate shuttle* found in heart muscle and liver cells, pass electrons to NAD^+ and so can produce the full complement of three ATP. In those tissues, the maximum yield of ATP would be 38. Since the electron transport chains of aerobic bacteria and other prokaryotes are not localized in mitochondria, these organisms would also be capable of producing 38 ATP.

ATP yields discussed above are *theoretical maximum yields* which are probably never achieved in practice. This is because glycolysis and the citric acid cycle, in addition to being responsible for the *oxidative breakdown* of glucose, are also the starting points for the *reductive synthesis* of other cellular constituents (section 5.7). For this reason, glycolysis and the citric acid cycle together are often called *intermediary metabolism.* Carbon skeletons are drawn from both glycolysis and the citric acid cycle to be used in the synthesis of, for example, lipids, proteins, and nucleic acids. The reduction potential required for the synthesis of these compounds is often supplied in the form of $NADH + H^+$. Consequently, much of the glucose entering glycolysis and the citric acid cycle is not completely oxidized and much of the NADH generated does not donate electrons to the electron transport chain. It is important to remember that glycolysis and the citric acid cycle are not isolated from the rest of metabolism and that ATP production is not the sole function of aerobic respiration.

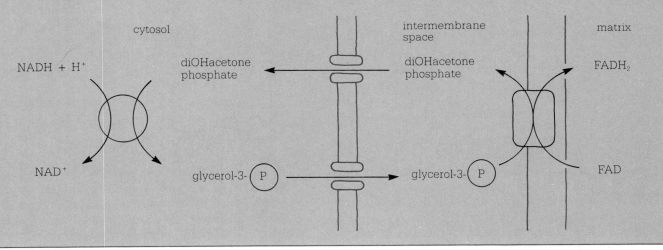

concentration gradient also contributes to the electrical potential gradient across the membrane. The normal potential gradient across the inner membrane is approximately -160 mV (Figure 5.15). A proton gradient of one pH unit contributes another -60 mV.

Figure 5.15
The electrochemical proton gradient across the inner mitochondrial membrane. The proton motive force consists of two components: the large (-160 mV) membrane potential ($\Delta\psi$) and the smaller pH gradient (ΔpH). Because protons are positively charged, the pH gradient also contributes to the charge difference. Both the charge difference and the differential proton concentration tend to force protons back into the matrix space.

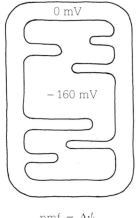

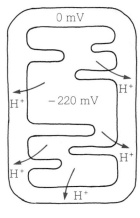

Figure 5.16

The ATP synthetase complex. The ATP synthetase is a transmembrane protein complex which couples ATP synthesis to proton diffusion. The diffusion of protons from the intermembrane space to the matrix is directed through the channel-forming proteins in the membrane. The energy released by proton diffusion is used to drive ATP synthesis from ADP and inorganic phosphate.

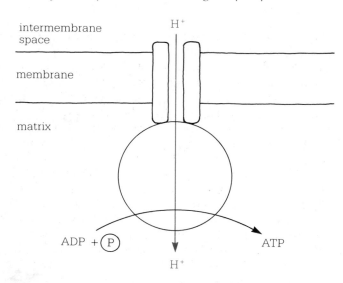

Figure 5.17

The chemiosmotic hypothesis: A model for ATP synthesis. The energy released during electron transport is used to establish an electrochemical proton gradient required. The energy of that gradient is used to drive ATP synthesis as the protons return to the matrix through the ATP synthetase.

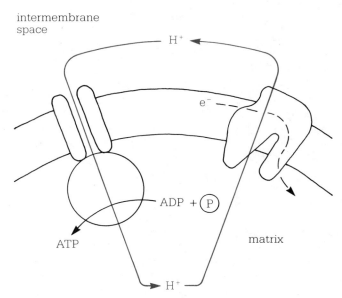

Together the membrane potential and the proton gradient constitute a **proton motive force** of -220 mV. Energy must be supplied in order to pump protons out of the matrix *against* a proton motive force of this magnitude. This energy is provided by electron transport. The direction of the proton motive force also favours the return of protons to the matrix, but the inner membrane will not allow the protons to simply diffuse back. In fact, the return of protons to the matrix is restricted to highly specific, protein-lined channels which extend through the membrane and which are a part of the ATP synthesizing enzyme, **ATP synthetase** (Figure 5.16).

When the electron transport complexes and the ATP synthesizing complex are both operating, a proton circuit is established (Figure 5.17). The electron transport complex pumps the protons from the matrix into the intermembrane space and thus establishes the proton gradient. At the same time, the ATP synthetase allows the protons to return to the matrix. The energy of electron transport is conserved initially in the proton gradient. As this energy-rich electrochemical proton gradient collapses, the conserved energy is available to drive the synthesis of ATP.

5.7 RESPIRATORY CONTROL

Cells regulate the rates of glycolysis, the citric acid cycle, and electron transport along with the production and use of ATP through a mechanism known as **respiratory control**. This regulation ensures that cells oxidize only enough substrate to satisfy their immediate metabolic demands. A high rate of metabolic activity will be accompanied by a rapid use of ATP. The resulting increased availability of the substrates ADP and Ⓟ stimulates ATP synthetase to work faster. As the enzyme works faster, more protons are allowed to flow back into the matrix, thereby dissipating the electrochemical gradient more rapidly. The collapse of the gradient in turn stimulates electron transport and more rapid re-oxidation of NADH (or $FADH_2$). Finally, the activities of certain critical enzymes in glycolysis and the citric acid cycle are sensitive to the relative levels of NAD and NADH. Activities of these enzymes are accelerated as the NADH level falls or the NAD level rises.

Conversely, if metabolic demand *decreases* and ADP is in short supply, the electrochemical proton gradient will not be dissipated by the demand for ATP. Instead,

Figure 5.18

Uncoupling ATP synthesis. Chemicals such as dinitrophenol (DNP) provide an alternative path for protons through the inner membrane, thereby uncoupling ATP synthesis from electron transport.

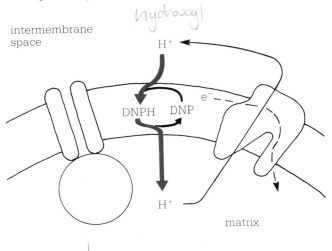

the proton gradient may reach very high levels. NADH oxidation will then cease because too much energy will be required to pump additional protons against the existing gradient. The ultimate result in this event would be to bring the oxidation of glucose to a halt. Respiratory control works because both ATP synthesis and electron transport are *obligatorily coupled* to proton pumping.

Some poisons are known to interfere with respiratory control by *uncoupling* oxidative phosphorylation (Figure 5.18). The compound 2,4-dinitrophenol (DNP), for example, is known to accelerate NADH oxidation and consequently oxygen consumption without synthesis of ATP. DNP acts by transporting protons across the inner membrane, bypassing the ATP synthetase proton channel. By providing an alternative route for dissipation of the proton gradient, DNP has uncoupled ATP synthesis from electron transport.

In some cases, the uncoupling of oxidative phosphorylation can be biologically useful. Brown fat is a form of adipose (fatty) tissue which contains abundant mitochondria, enough in fact to give the tissue a dark brown colour. Brown fat mitochondria have a unique protein in the inner membrane which functions as a natural proton transporter. This protein, like other uncouplers, accelerates electron transport while blocking the synthesis of ATP. In the absence of ATP synthesis, virtually all the energy of respiration is con-

verted to heat. This method of **thermogenesis** can be vital to the survival of some organisms. Newborn infants and hibernating animals have abundant brown fat. Mitochondria of rats which are adapted to cold temperatures have larger quantities of the uncoupling protein; likewise in fur seals and other mammals that are adapted to cold environments.

5.8 ANAEROBIC METABOLISM

The citric acid cycle, electron transport, and ATP synthesis are involved in cellular respiration in the presence of molecular oxygen. What happens, however, when molecular oxygen is in short supply or not available at all? To begin, the citric acid cycle effectively shuts down. Oxygen, or rather the lack of it, has an effect on the citric acid cycle and electron transport similar to the effect of the ADP/ATP supply already described. Under anaerobic conditions, all of the carriers in the electron transport chain become fully reduced. They become saturated with electrons. NADH then accumulates, since there is no oxidized carrier available to accept electrons from the NADH. This reduces the supply of NAD which in turn slows down or brings to a halt the oxidation of citric acid cycle intermediates. Of course, since the electron transport system is no longer operating, no ATP is produced by oxidative phosphorylation.

Under the conditions described above, pyruvate, the product of glycolysis, cannot enter the citric acid cycle. It is instead diverted to the production of a secondary product. The nature of the product will depend on the organism and the presence of the appropriate enzymes. Usually the product is ethyl alcohol or lactic acid. The metabolism of glucose under anaerobic conditions is known as **fermentation** (Figure 5.19). Yeasts of the genus *Saccharomyces* convert glucose to ethanol by a process known as **alcoholic fermentation**. Various bacteria of the genus *Lactobacillus* convert glucose to lactic acid; the process is known as **lactic acid fermentation**. total breakdown in O_2

In alcoholic fermentation, the pyruvate is first decarboxylated to form acetaldehyde and carbon dioxide. The acetaldehyde is then reduced to ethyl alcohol at the expense of NADH. In lactic acid fermentation, the pyruvate is directly reduced to lactic acid. In either case, the source of reducing potential is the NADH which is generated at an earlier step in glycolysis (Figure 5.10). The NAD regenerated in the terminal step is then available again to accept electrons in glycolysis and to keep glycolysis going.

A POSSIBLE LINK BETWEEN MITOCHONDRIA AND OBESITY

Have you ever seen a mouse shiver? Mice, like all mammals, use metabolic heat to regulate their body temperature at a specific level. At times, the heat generated by normal metabolism may not be sufficient to maintain proper body temperature. In such a case, most mammals, including humans, respond by shivering. This is one means of generating heat, a process known as *thermogenesis*. Some animals, such as mice, take advantage of an alternative method for generating heat which is called *non-shivering thermogenesis* (NST). Jean Himms-Hagen of the University of Ottawa, a leading researcher of thermoregulation in animals, believes there may be a link between NST and obesity.

NST is due largely to the distinct metabolic activity of specialized fat storage tissue called brown adipose tissue. In contrast to the cells of normal, white fat storage tissue, the cells of brown adipose tissue have large numbers of mitochondria. When an animal senses a drop in the temperature of the environment (as little as 2° is sufficient), the sympathetic nervous system responds by releasing noradrenalin, a neurotransmitter. This, in turn, stimulates the oxidation of fatty acids by the mitochondria in the brown adipose tissue. These mitochondria, however, contain a unique protein which "short circuits" proton flow across the inner membrane, thus uncoupling ATP synthesis from electron transport. Instead of producing ATP, the energy of fatty acid oxidation is released as heat.

Small mammals, such as mice, do generate heat by shivering when first placed in a cold environment. However, within a few weeks, they will stop this mechanism and maintain body temperature entirely with non-shivering thermogenesis. This ability of mice to acclimate to cold stress is correlated with an increase in the mass of brown adipose tissue and the synthesis of uncoupling protein. While other researchers concentrated on the unique properties of brown adipose tissue mitochondria, Himms-Hagen studied the physiological role of brown adipose tissue itself. Studies involving genetically obese (ob/ob) mice have led Himms-Hagen to hypothesize that NST and obesity share a common root—namely, brown adipose tissue.

Unlike their genetically normal (and lean!) counterparts, genetically obese mice are unable to acclimate to low temperature. They are, in fact, so cold sensitive that they will die within a short time if the temperature drops to about 4°C. Himms-Hagen has shown that the ob/ob mouse is incapable of developing NST and therefore low temperature tolerance because the genetic defect prevents the animal from accumulating sufficient levels of uncoupling protein. Defective regulation of uncoupling protein also contributes to the development of obesity. Animals with the defect are unable to use brown adipose tissue effectively to burn off excess calories (or joules!) in the diet.

It is still not known whether or not defective thermogenesis might contribute to obesity in humans. Brown adipose tissue is highly developed in the newborn of many mammalian species, including human infants, but probably contributes no more than 2 percent of body mass in adults. Yet it has been shown for the adult rat that brown adipose tissue can account for as much as 60 percent of the maximum metabolic response to cold. Unfortunately, present experimental methods for estimating the contributions of brown adipose tissue to thermogenesis are not applicable to human subjects. Further advances in this field may require the development of more indirect methods for assessing the relative contributions of different tissues to the overall energy balance in daily life.

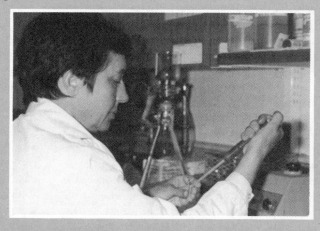

Figure 5.19
Fermentation. Under anaerobic conditions, pyruvate derived from glycolysis may be converted to lactate (e.g., in muscle) or to ethanol (e.g., in yeast). NADH + H⁺ is provided from the oxidation of glyceraldehyde-3-phosphate to 1,3-bisphosphoglycerate earlier in glycolysis. The yield of usable energy from fermentation is very low.

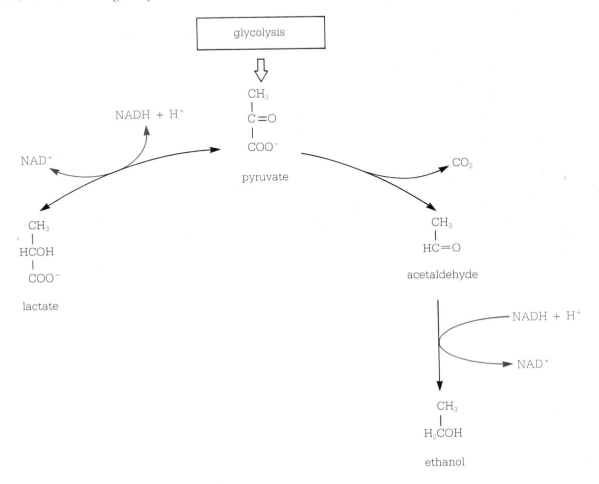

Note that, as a means of producing ATP, both fermentation processes are far less efficient than aerobic respiration. In fact, the only ATP produced is the net gain of two substrate level phosphorylations. Since each mole of ATP is equivalent to 31 kJ of energy and each mole of glucose is equivalent to 2831 kJ, the total yield for fermentation is 62/2831, or 2.2 percent. On the other hand, one cannot help but notice that in spite of the low energy yield of fermentation there are a large number of organisms, especially micro-organisms, that live in anaerobic environments.

Alcoholic fermentation produces alcohol. Reduction of pyruvic acid to alcohol is necessary in order to regenerate NAD so that glycolysis may continue to produce even the small but necessary amounts of ATP.

Yet alcohol is a poison, even to the micro-organisms that produce it. Most yeasts are killed by alcohol concentrations of 12 to 14 percent, although some strains of wine yeasts will survive alcohol concentrations as high as 18 percent. This explains why table wines normally contain 12 to 14 percent alcohol. Natural sparkling wines, such as champagnes, are bottled while the yeasts are still actively fermenting, thus trapping both the alcohol and the carbon dioxide.

Lactic acid fermentation produces lactic acid. Like alcohol, lactic acid is also toxic, as you may be able to attest after a period of physical exertion without proper conditioning! Runners often experience lactic acid toxicity in muscle. At top speed, the lungs and blood cannot deliver sufficient oxygen to the muscle cell mitochondria in order to supply ATP as fast as it is required. Sprinters generally have a large bulk of muscle in order to deliver maximum power over short distances. Over those short distances, glycolysis and lactic acid fermentation can keep the muscles functional. Over longer distances at full speed, however, the runner would soon succumb to fatigue and cramps due to the toxic effects of lactic acid. Long distance runners, on the other hand, are usually small and wiry; it is inefficient to carry excess bulk over long distances. They must also maintain a slower pace in order to keep oxygen delivery balanced against ATP consumption. Training programs for the long distance runner are designed to build up efficient oxygen delivery. With an adequate supply of oxygen, the muscles can continue to operate at peak efficiency without switching to anaerobic which brings about lactic acid fermentation.

Fermentation does have practical uses. It has long been used as a means of preserving foods before the widespread use of refrigeration and other more modern methods. Foods preserved by alcohol include fruits, which are preserved as wine. Milk products (yogurt, sour cream, and cheese), vegetables (pickles and sauerkraut), and silage for animal feed are preserved by lactic acid. Fermentation by the bacterium *Acetobacter aceti* produces another preservative, acetic acid (vinegar). Various cheeses are preserved by bacteria that produce propionic acid. In each case, the accumulation of fermentation products prevents the growth of other decomposing bacteria.

5.9 METABOLISM OF FATS AND PROTEINS

Like carbohydrates, both fats and proteins can be catabolized by aerobic respiration and their energy conserved as ATP. Long chain fatty acids, which are components of lipids (Chapter 2), can be oxidized by removal of two-carbon acetate units from the carboxyl end of the chain, a process known as β-*oxidation*. The cleavage of acetate units is accomplished by enzymes associated with the *outer* membrane of the mitochondrion. Coenzyme A is a necessary cofactor for these enzymes and the resultant acetyl-coenzyme A enters the citric acid cycle in the same way as does the acetyl-coenzyme A derived from the oxidation of glucose. The details of the process do not concern us but, as the name β-oxidation implies, the stepwise degradation of the fatty acid chain by removal of the acetate units is an oxidative process. During the process, two

moles of NAD are reduced for each mole of acetate removed. This additional NADH production may give rise to additional ATP through the electron transport chain. Fatty acids are more highly reduced than carbohydrates and consequently their oxidation can result in larger quantities of ATP. For example, 45 moles of ATP are produced during complete oxidation of the six carbon fatty acid hexanoic acid compared with 36 moles of ATP for the six-carbon carbohydrate, glucose. Since fats appear to be a more concentrated source of energy, it is understandable that so many organisms store food reserves as fat. This is particularly true for animals such as migratory birds and insects which must sustain muscular activity over exceptionally long distances!

Proteins also may be metabolized through the citric acid cycle. They, like other large molecules in the cell, are subject to *turnover*, that is, they are continually degraded into their component amino acids and then resynthesized. Unlike fatty acids and carbohydrates, amino acids in excess of what is required for protein synthesis cannot be stored. Normally, the amino group is removed by an enzymatic process called *deamination* and the resulting carbon skeleton is metabolized through the citric acid cycle. For example, the amino acid glutamate is converted to the organic acid α-ketoglutarate, which is an intermediate in the citric acid cycle.

$$glutamate + NAD^+ + H_2O \longrightarrow$$
$$\alpha\text{-ketoglutarate} + NH_4^+ + NADH + H^+$$

In terrestrial vertebrates, the NH_4^+ is converted into urea and excreted. The α-ketoglutarate is then further metabolized by the citric acid cycle. In a similar fashion, the carbon skeletons derived from other amino acids enter the citric acid cycle as pyruvate, succinate, fumarate, or oxaloacetate.

5.10 THE CENTRAL ROLE OF GLYCOLYSIS AND THE CITRIC ACID CYCLE

The discussion so far has focussed on the catabolic role of the pathway from glucose to carbon dioxide and water. The ATP that is produced is, of course, used in part to provide energy for the synthesis of other molecules that are required by the cell. But what of the carbon skeletons that are used in the assembly of these molecules? Where do they come from? Fatty acids and lipids such as cholesterol and the steroid hormones are derived from acetyl-coenzyme A. Since acetyl-

Figure 5.20
The central role of glycolysis and the citric acid cycle. The intermediates of glycolysis and the citric acid cycle are the principal source of precursors for the biosynthesis of other molecules required by the cell. Only a few of the many possible interactions are shown here.

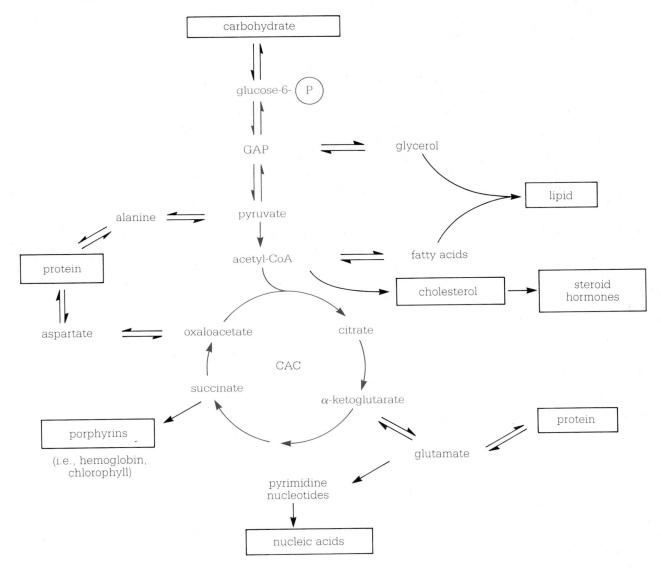

coenzyme A is derived from glucose through pyruvate, this provides a route for the synthesis of fat from sugar. It should not be difficult, then, to understand how carbohydrate consumed in excess can result in increased body fat. The carbon skeletons for amino acids and, subsequently, protein biosynthesis are similarly derived from the several intermediates of glycolysis and the citric acid cycle (Figure 5.20). For example, the amino acid glutamate is synthesized from α-ketoglutaric acid by the reverse of the reaction shown in the last section. Through the catabolic breakdown of various foodstuffs such as carbohydrates, fats, and proteins, these pathways provide the energy to drive a variety of cellular functions. At the same time, these pathways also provide both the energy and the simple carbon skeletons which are used as starting points for the assembly of many of the cell's macromolecules. Thus the glycolytic pathway and the citric acid cycle assume a truly central role in the general metabolism of the cell.

CHAPTER SUMMARY

Energy transformations in cells may be explained in terms of two thermodynamic laws. The first law of thermodynamics tells us that all of the energy available at the start of a reaction may be accounted for when the reaction has gone to completion. The second law enables us to predict the direction of a reaction. The application of thermodynamic rules to the study of energy transformations in cells is known as bioenergetics. Cellular metabolism is the sum of all degradative reactions (catabolism) and synthetic reactions (anabolism). Catabolism provides both carbon skeletons for synthesis and energy to drive cellular activities. ATP plays a significant role in energy metabolism by linking energy-yielding reactions with energy-consuming reactions.

Aerobic respiration is the principal catabolic pathway in the cell and may be subdivided into three stages. The first stage, glycolysis, occurs in the cytoplasm. The products of glycolysis are pyruvate and small quantities of ATP and reduced NAD. Under aerobic conditions, pyruvate is transported into the matrix of the mitochondrion and, through the citric acid cycle, oxidized to carbon dioxide and water. A small amount of ATP is formed while most of the energy of the pyruvate is conserved as reduced NAD or FAD. Large amounts of ATP may be generated by oxidative phosphorylation as the reduced NAD and FAD are re-oxidized through the membrane-based electron transport system. Peter Mitchell's chemiosmotic hypothesis explains the coupling of ATP synthesis to electron transport through a transmembrane electrochemical proton gradient.

Under anaerobic conditions, pyruvate is commonly reduced to ethyl alcohol or lactic acid. Pyruvate does not enter the mitochondrion; the citric acid cycle and electron transport system are not operative and there is no ATP production by oxidative phosphorylation.

Objectives

Having completed this chapter, you should be able to do the following:

1. Describe the relationship between bioenergetics and thermodynamics.

2. State the first and second laws of thermodynamics and discuss the information they can provide about energy transformations.

3. Define free energy and discuss its importance in biochemical reactions.

4. Define catabolism, anabolism, and metabolism.

5. Discuss the central role of ATP in energy metabolism.

6. Describe the structure of the mitochondrion and identify its major metabolic compartments.

7. Distinguish between aerobic and anaerobic respiration.

8. Describe the relationships among glycolysis, the citric acid cycle, and the electron transport system.

9. Describe the breakdown of glucose by glycolysis and summarize the principal products.

10. Describe the overall scheme of the citric acid cycle and show how energy is conserved as ATP and reduced electron carriers.

11. Describe the organization of the electron transport system in the membrane of the mitochondrion.

12. Distinguish between substrate level phosphorylation and oxidative phosphorylation.

13. Describe the chemiosmotic hypothesis and show how it can explain oxidative phosphorylation.

14. Describe how metabolic demand for ATP regulates the rate of respiration.

15. Describe alcoholic and lactic acid fermentation and discuss their relationship to glycolysis.

16. Describe the central role of glycolysis and citric acid cycle in metabolism.

Vocabulary

thermodynamics	coenzyme	phosphorylate
first law of thermodynamics	nicotinamide adenine	Coenzyme A
second law of thermodynamics	dinucleotide (NAD)	acetyl-CoA
bioenergetics	flavin adenine dinucleotide (FAD)	cytochrome
spontaneous	outer membrane	oxidative phosphorylation
free energy	inner membrane	chemiosmotic hypothesis
entropy	intermembrane space	proton pump
exergonic	matrix	proton motive force
endergonic	aerobic respiration	ATP synthetase
photosynthesis	glycolysis	respiratory control
catabolism	anaerobic	thermogenesis
anabolism	aerobic	fermentation
metabolism	citric acid cycle	alcoholic fermentation
reducing agent	electron transport chain	lactic acid fermentation
oxidizing agent	substrate	

Review Questions

1. What is bioenergetics?
2. What is meant by the thermodynamic term spontaneous?
3. Distinguish between free energy and entropy.
4. Distinguish between anabolism and catabolism.
5. Explain how living organisms appear to operate contrary to the laws of thermodynamics by decreasing entropy.
6. (a) What are coupled reactions?
   (b) What role do they serve in the cell?
7. Outline the principal steps in the oxidative breakdown of glucose. Identify the steps in which energy is conserved.
8. Describe the central role of ATP in metabolic reactions.
9. Draw a diagram of a mitochondrion and identify the outer membrane, intermembrane space, inner membrane, and matrix.
10. How many mitochondria may be found in a cell?
11. Name four electron carriers found in the mitochondrion.
12. List three principal results of glycolysis.
13. Describe the flow of energy through the electron transport system.
14. Distinguish between substrate level phosphorylation and oxidative phosphorylation.
15. Why must glucose be phosphorylated at the beginning of glycolysis?
16. Outline the essential features of Mitchell's chemiosmotic model for ATP synthesis.
17. Trace the path of carbon in aerobic respiration.
18. How did Hans Krebs contribute to our understanding of cellular respiration?
19. What are the products of fermentation in
    (a) muscle?
    (b) yeast?
20. What must be done to a fatty acid before it can be metabolized through the citric acid cycle?
21. List two important functions of the citric acid cycle.

Advanced Questions

1. When fermentation is used as a means to preserve food products, preservation is maintained only so long as anaerobic conditions prevail. Why?

2. Barbiturates are one of several classes of drugs which act by preventing the transfer of electrons through the electron transport chain. Why is the uncontrolled use of barbiturates dangerous?

A STUDY OF PHOTOSYNTHESIS

CHAPTER 6

LIGHT-INDEPENDENT REACTIONS OF PHOTOSYNTHESIS

"It's the light reaction about which we are most in the dark."

Melvin Calvin

About three billion years ago a major evolutionary innovation occurred which was to have such an enormous impact that it would alter completely the environment of the earth. This evolutionary advance was to pave the way for the development of totally new forms of life. For the first time, certain unicellular, aquatic organisms living in the primeval oceans developed the capacity to utilize the energy of sunlight to synthesize their own organic food, that is, the first **autotrophic** organisms appeared. The process of synthesizing carbohydrates using the sun's energy is called *photosynthesis*. These primitive organisms represent the evolutionary ancestors of all autotrophic organisms such as higher plants, algae, cyanobacteria, and photosynthetic bacteria. Animals, fungi, and most protists are **heterotrophic**. This means that they obtain their organic food stuffs from the environment by consuming, directly or indirectly, autotrophic organisms or their remains. They are unable to synthesize their food from atmospheric carbon dioxide.

Life requires energy. Directly or indirectly, the process of photosynthesis is the source of energy which sustains all life on this planet. Since photosynthesis derives its energy from sunlight, you may conclude that all life is ultimately dependent on sunlight. It is through the process of photosynthesis that all life on the earth is linked to the sun.

6.1 BRIEF HISTORY OF THE DISCOVERY OF PHOTOSYNTHESIS

The scientific study of photosynthesis was really initiated by Joseph Priestley in 1772. It had been known that a candle burning in a sealed container would extinguish itself after a period of time (Figure 6.1). Priestley was the first to demonstrate that the presence of green plants enabled the candle to continue to burn. Shortly thereafter, a Dutch physician, Jan Ingenhousz showed that light was also a requirement for this effect. Antoine Lavoisier, the famous French chemist, was able to demonstrate that the result of Priestley's experiment was due to the ability of green plants to enrich the surrounding atmosphere with oxygen. In 1782, Jean Senebier, a Swiss clergyman, showed that the ability of green plants to produce oxygen in the light also required the presence of "fixed air" or carbon dioxide. Thus, by the early part of the nineteenth century, the major components of the photosynthetic process were known. The process can be expressed in a word equation as follows:

$$\text{carbon dioxide} + \text{water} + \text{light} \xrightarrow[\text{plant}]{\text{green}}$$
$$\text{oxygen} + \text{organic material}$$

Figure 6.1
Priestley's experiments. A candle burning in an air-tight jar (a) went out after a short time; likewise, a mouse kept in an air-tight jar (b) shortly died. A mouse was able to survive when kept in an air-tight jar with a green plant (c).

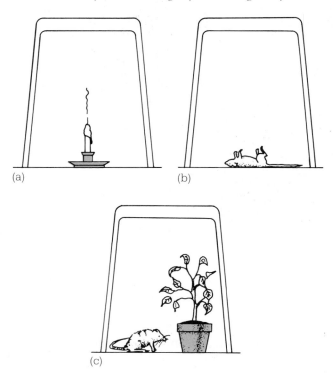

(a)   (b)

(c)

We now know that the chloroplast within the plant cell is the specialized organelle that controls photosynthesis.

6.2 THE CHLOROPLAST

All eukaryotic, autotrophic organisms have highly specialized, intracellular organelles called *chloroplasts* (Chapter 3). The primary function of this organelle is to convert light energy into a useful chemical form, ATP and NADPH (reduced nicotinamide adenine dinucleotide phosphate). This chemical energy is subsequently required for the conversion of carbon dioxide to carbohydrates. These processes take place completely within the plant chloroplast. Palisade and spongy mesophyll cells of higher plant leaves typically contain a large number of chloroplasts (Figure 6.2).

A typical chloroplast from higher plants is ellipsoid in shape (Chapter 3). The average diameter of a chloroplast is about 0.005 mm. This means that a chloroplast is approximately 5 to 10 times larger than a mitochondrion. Like mitochondria, chloroplasts also contain their own DNA and their own protein-synthesizing machinery.

Like nuclei and mitochondria, the chloroplast also has an outer, limiting membrane called the **envelope membrane**. However, unlike the single limiting membrane of other eukaryotic organelles, the envelope membrane in chloroplast is a *double* membrane. The principal role of the envelope membrane is to control and regulate the transport of metabolites from the cytoplasm into the chloroplast as well as the transport of the products of photosynthesis from the chloroplast into the cytoplasm of the cell.

Chloroplasts are filled with an aqueous solution called the **stroma**. Dissolved in the stroma are all the enzymes necessary for the conversion of carbon dioxide to carbohydrate. These biochemical reactions of photosynthesis do not utilize light energy directly. They are, however, dependent upon the products, ATP and NADPH, which are produced by the conversion of light energy into chemical energy in the **thylakoid membrane** (Figure 6.3). Thus, the biochemical reactions involved in the conversion of carbon dioxide to carbohydrate are referred to as **light-independent reactions**. The photochemical reactions of the thylakoid membrane resulting in the biosynthesis of ATP and NADPH are referred to as the **light-dependent reactions** of photosynthesis.

Thylakoid membranes are highly specialized membranes that form an intricate network embedded within the stroma. These chloroplast membranes are unique in that they contain all of the pigments involved in the light absorption processes of photosynthesis, **chlorophyll** and **carotenoids**. These membranes, in fact, appear green in colour due to the predominant presence of chlorophyll pigments. The chloroplast envelope membrane does not contain any chlorophyll. Thus, the green colour of plants is due to the presence of chlorophyll in the thylakoid membranes of the chloroplasts.

The thylakoids of higher plants are usually organized into regular, inter-connected, closely packed stacks called **grana** (sing. *granum*). See Figure 6.4. When viewed from above, these grana are roughly circular and might be likened to a pile of coins. They are joined or interconnected by single, non-appressed or separate membranes called **stromal thylakoids**. The primary function of the specialized, green, thylakoid membranes is the conversion of visible light energy into ATP and NADPH—the *light-dependent reactions* of photosynthesis (Chapter 8).

Figure 6.2
Structure of a leaf (a), mesophyll cell (b), and chloroplast (c)

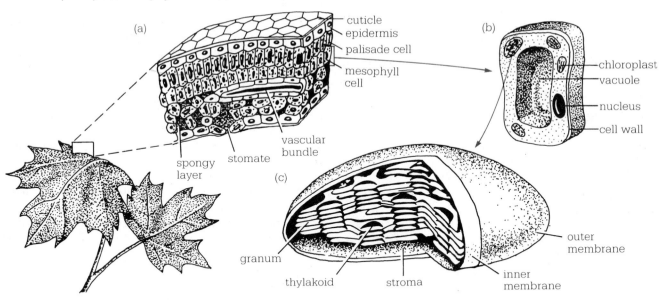

(a)

cuticle
epidermis
palisade cell
mesophyll cell

spongy layer
stomate
vascular bundle

(b)

chloroplast
vacuole
nucleus
cell wall

(c)

granum
thylakoid
stroma
outer membrane
inner membrane

Figure 6.3
Interrelationships between the photochemical stage of photosynthesis and the carbon fixation reactions

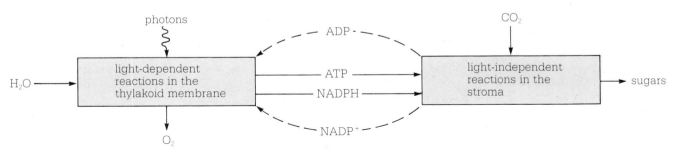

photons

CO_2

ADP
ATP
NADPH
NADP$^+$

H_2O → light-dependent reactions in the thylakoid membrane → light-independent reactions in the stroma → sugars

O_2

Figure 6.4
Diagram (a) and electron micrograph (b) showing chloroplast structure

(a)

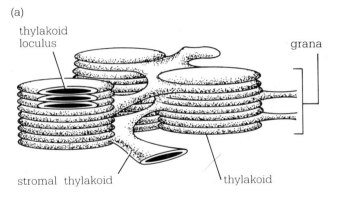

thylakoid loculus
grana
stromal thylakoid
thylakoid

(b)

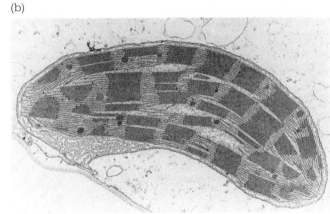

6.3 THE FIXATION OF CARBON DIOXIDE (CALVIN CYCLE)

The following balanced chemical equation summarizes the photosynthetic process in higher plants:

$$6CO_2 + 12H_2O \xrightarrow[\text{light}]{\text{chloroplasts}} \underset{\text{(glucose)}}{C_6H_{12}O_6} + 6O_2 + 6H_2O$$

The minimum free (available) energy (ΔG) required to produce one mole of glucose from six moles of carbon dioxide is approximately 2800 kJ. This energy is provided by sunlight and is stored in the covalent bonds that make up the glucose molecule. This section describes the general mechanism by which chloroplasts are able to utilize the energy derived from sunlight to convert six one-carbon molecules of carbon dioxide into one six-carbon molecule of glucose (Figure 6.5).

The light-independent reactions refer to those biochemical, enzyme-catalyzed reactions involved in the synthesis of carbohydrate from carbon dioxide. These reactions, which occur in the chloroplast stroma, are collectively termed the Calvin cycle in honour of Melvin Calvin who received the Nobel Prize for the elucidation of this series of reactions.

The primary reaction in the Calvin cycle involves the fixation of a single molecule of carbon dioxide and the subsequent formation of two molecules of phosphoglycerate. Thus, for every one-carbon molecule of carbon dioxide that is joined to a five-carbon molecule of ribulose bisphosphate, two three-carbon molecules of phosphoglycerate are produced. This reaction is catalyzed by an enzyme called ribulose bisphosphate carboxylase-oxygenase or "Rubisco." This enzyme can constitute up to 50 percent of the total soluble

Figure 6.5

A summary of carbon flow through the Calvin cycle reactions. For every carbon dioxide molecule that is joined to a five-carbon ribulose bisphosphate, two molecules of phosphoglycerate are produced. These phosphoglycerate

molecules are subsequently phosphorylated using ATP and then reduced to PGAL by NADPH. Some of the three-carbon PGAL combine to form six-carbon sugars and the remainder is used to regenerate the five-carbon carbon dioxide–acceptor molecule, ribulose bisphosphate.

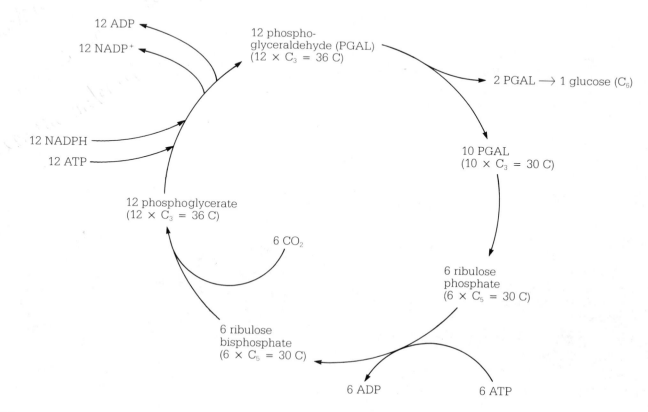

protein in the leaves of higher plants and, as such, is by far the single most abundant protein in all of nature. Next time you eat your green salad, remember that you are basically consuming Rubisco!

$$\text{carbon dioxide} + \text{ribulose bisphosphate} \longrightarrow$$
$$(C_1) \qquad\qquad (C_5)$$
$$2 \text{ phosphoglycerate}$$
$$(C3)$$

The phosphogylcerate molecules formed as a result of this initial reaction are subsequently phosphorylated using ATP and then reduced by NADPH to the three-carbon molecule, phosphoglyceraldehyde (PGAL), which is a type of triose phosphate and is a very important intermediate compound. Some of the PGAL is eventually converted to glucose but a significant portion of this intermediate is used to regenerate the initial carbon dioxide–acceptor molecule, ribulose bisphosphate. As illustrated in Figure 6.5, the series of stromal reactions involved in the regeneration of this important five-carbon intermediate is dependent on the presence of ATP and NADPH. Thus the Calvin cycle reactions provide two important metabolic functions: first, they lead to three-carbon intermediates used to synthesize glucose, a major building block and energy source for all plant cells; second, they lead to three-carbon intermediates used to regenerate the initial carbon dioxide–acceptor molecule. The capacity of chloroplasts to continuously regenerate ribulose bisphosphate ensures that green plants have the capacity to synthesize carbohydrate continuously in the presence of light, water, and carbon dioxide. This is the advantage of the cyclic nature of these reactions.

Where do the ATP and NADPH come from? These molecules are two important products of the light-dependent, photochemical reactions which take place in the chloroplast thylakoid membranes. Their formation will be discussed in detail in Chapter 8. In the absence of the light-dependent formation of ATP and NADPH, the conversion of carbon dioxide to glucose cannot occur effectively. As shown in Figure 6.5, ATP and NADPH are *absolute* requirements for the formation of PGAL and the subsequent regeneration of ribulose bisphosphate. Although the reactions that convert carbon dioxide to glucose are not directly dependent upon light, this series of reactions is intimately linked to the light-dependent reactions of the thylakoid membrane through the absolute requirement for ATP and NADPH. Therefore the overall process for the conversion of carbon dioxide to carbohydrate in higher plants is indeed light-dependent.

6.4   THE UTILIZATION OF GLUCOSE

As discussed in section 6.3, the three-carbon phosphorylated compound, PGAL (a triose phosphate) is a very important intermediate compound since it represents an essential branch point in the photosynthetic carbon metabolism of higher plants. This triose phosphate eventually gives rise to the six-carbon glucose molecule and is involved in the regeneration of the five-carbon carbon dioxide–acceptor molecule, ribulose bisphosphate.

Why does a plant produce glucose? To answer this important question, you must examine the metabolic fates of glucose, that is, you must understand how a plant utilizes glucose.

First, within the chloroplast stroma, glucose can be converted to *starch* through a series of enzyme-catalyzed reactions. Starch is a polysaccharide composed of many hundreds of glucose molecules linked together, usually forming a large branched polymer. The formation of starch provides a temporary storage of carbohydrate for the plant. If there is a metabolic imbalance within the plant such that carbon dioxide is converted to glucose faster than carbohydrate is being consumed by the plant, the surplus glucose can be converted and stored in the chloroplast in the form of starch. The starch will appear as large starch granules within the chloroplast (Figure 6.4). Such a metabolic imbalance typically arises when the plant is actively photosynthesizing at maximum rates, such as in bright daylight. The storage of glucose in the form of a large carbohydrate polymer in plants is analogous to the formation of glycogen, which is another type of glucose polymer, in the liver of higher animals. Glycogen is a storage form of carbohydrate in animals (Figure 6.6).

Conversely, when the metabolic requirements of the plant are such that glucose levels are too low, starch will be converted back to glucose in the chloroplast stroma. Such conditions can prevail when plants are in the dark. Although plants obviously do not photosynthesize in the dark, it is important to appreciate that they actively metabolize glucose and grow in the dark as well as in the light. Thus, starch is an important carbohydrate reserve for plants.

A second metabolic fate of glucose is its conversion to sucrose. Plant cells, like all living cells, require

Figure 6.6
The structure of glycogen, starch, and cellulose. The glucose units of glycogen and starch are joined by $\alpha(1 \rightarrow 4)$ linkages. Branches arise in glycogen and starch by $\alpha(1 \rightarrow 6)$ linkages. In cellulose, the glucose units are joined by $\beta(1 \rightarrow 4)$ linkages. Cellulose forms a straight chain. Hydrogen bonding between cellulose chains produces cellulose fibres.

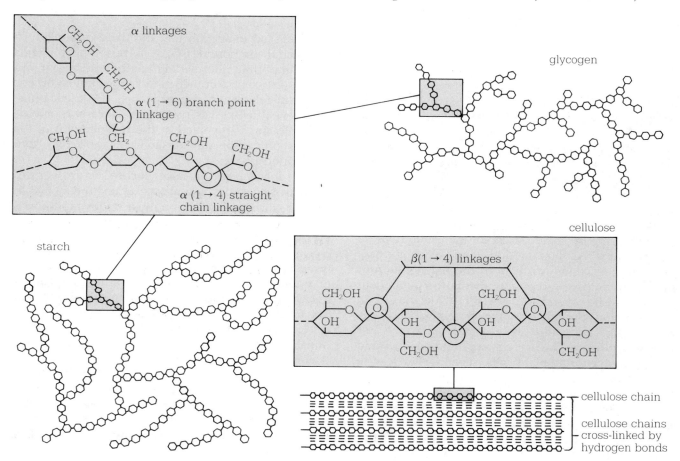

energy to function properly. These include the photosynthetic mesophyll cells of leaves as well as the non-photosynthetic cells of roots and stems. The energy is supplied by glucose metabolism by way of glycolysis in the plant cell cytoplasm and cellular respiration in the mitochondria. The glucose produced by photosynthesis in the leaves must first be transported by way of the phloem cells of the vascular bundle to other plant tissues and cells. It is translocated in the form of sucrose. This is a disaccharide composed of one glucose molecule covalently linked to one fructose molecule. The synthesis of sucrose takes place in the cytoplasm of plant cells, *not* in the chloroplast. Triose phosphates (including PGAL) produced by photosynthesis in the chloroplast stroma are exported from the chloroplast and into the cytoplasm of leaf mesophyll cells. It is in the cytoplasm that the triose phosphates are converted through a series of reactions to sucrose. The sucrose is then actively transported and loaded into the phloem cells of the vascular bundle for translocation to other tissues and cells within the plant that are actively metabolizing glucose.

The third major metabolic fate of glucose is the formation of **cellulose**, the basic building block for the cell walls in higher plants. The synthesis of cellulose from glucose also takes place within the cytoplasm. Cellulose is chemically similar to starch. However, the individual glucose units of cellulose are chemically linked together in a different manner than in starch (Figure 6.6).

Figure 6.7
Possible metabolic fates of photosynthetic triose phosphates (TP)

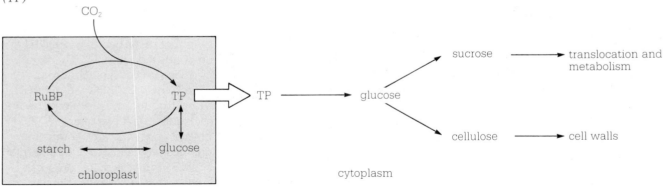

Thus, triose phosphates produced by photosynthesis in the chloroplast stroma are critical biochemical intermediates in overall plant carbohydrate metabolism. They are involved in the regeneration of the primary carbon dioxide–acceptor molecule, ribulose bisphosphate, and in the biosynthesis of starch, sucrose, and cellulose (Figure 6.7). It is also important, at this point, to remember that the glucose which is metabolized by cellular respiration is also ultimately derived from the triose phosphate produced in photosynthesis. Mitochondria metabolize carbohydrate to produce the intermediates of tricarboxylic acid cycle (Chapter 5). Several of these intermediates, in turn, provide the carbohydrate skeletons for amino acids used in protein synthesis as well as the precursors to nucleic acids and lipids.

6.5 LIGHT REGULATION OF THE CALVIN CYCLE

Under normal environmental conditions, plants undergo a daily transition from periods of light to periods of dark. In the dark, all conversion of atmospheric carbon dioxide to carbohydrate in the plant will eventually stop because the chloroplast is unable to synthesize ATP and NADPH which, in turn, prevents the regeneration of ribulose bisphosphate and the synthesis of PGAL. Thus, when the chloroplast has consumed all of the available ribulose bisphosphate and PGAL in the dark, no further fixation of carbon dioxide can take place. When the plant is subsequently exposed to light, maximum rates of carbon dioxide fixation cannot take place until all the intermediates of the Calvin cycle have been replenished to an optimal level. Thus, there is usually an initial lag time prior

to the onset of maximum photosynthesis during a dark to light transition (Figure 6.8). This lag time represents the time taken to replenish the Calvin cycle intermediates to a level which will allow maximum rates of photosynthesis to occur. This phenomenon is called **photosynthetic induction**. Light is obviously an important factor which regulates the concentrations of the various intermediates in the chloroplast stroma which, in turn, influences the rate at which the plant can convert carbon dioxide to glucose.

Figure 6.8
A graph illustrating photosynthetic induction. The maximum rate of photosynthetic carbon dioxide uptake occurs after a short lag time, x, after the plant has been exposed to light.

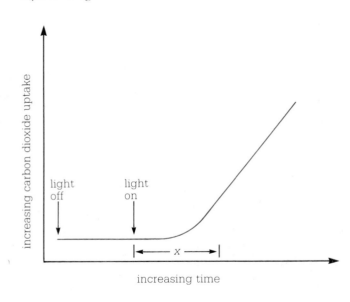

All higher plants which produce the three-carbon phosphoglycerate molecule as the first product of light-dependent carbon dioxide fixation (Figure 6.5) are called C_3 plants. These include such plants as wheat, spinach, and tobacco. These plants are also able to release carbon dioxide under light conditions. This process is called *photorespiration*. While photosynthesis is the light-dependent uptake of carbon dioxide in C_3 plants and its subsequent conversion to carbohydrate, photorespiration is the light-dependent release of carbon dioxide from C_3 plants. Clearly, photosynthesis and photorespiration are antagonistic processes. This perplexing charac-teristic of C_3 plants is due to the fact that Rubisco, the enzyme that converts carbon dioxide plus ribulose bisphosphate to two molecules of phosphoglycerate, is also capable of utilizing oxygen as a substrate. In fact, oxygen and carbon dioxide compete for the same binding sites in this enzyme. When Rubisco fixes oxygen, a two-carbon molecule of phosphoglycolate is produced which is subsequently metabolized by plant cell mitochondria and peroxisomes, resulting in the release of carbon dioxide. However, Rubisco exhibits a greater preference for carbon dioxide than for oxygen. This is extremely important since the normal oxygen concentration in the air (20 percent) is significantly greater than that of carbon dioxide (0.03 percent). Nevertheless, C_3 plants may lose up to 50 percent of the carbon they assimilate in photosynthesis through the process of photorespiration. A positive physiological role for photorespiration has been elusive. Experimental control of photorespiration poses a challenge to plant physiologists, biochemists, and molecular biologists since it might be possible to double the yield of some important C_3 crops such as wheat if this drain on the plants' potential carbon reserves were diminished or eliminated.

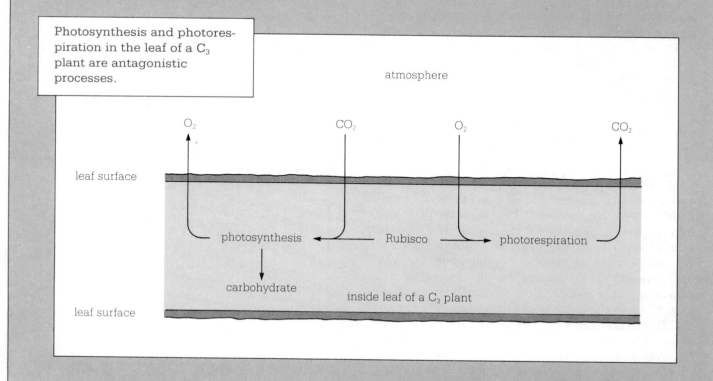

Photosynthesis and photorespiration in the leaf of a C_3 plant are antagonistic processes.

Figure 6.9
Calvin cycle enzymes are regulated by light.

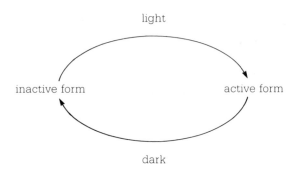

The reactions of the Calvin cycle are all enzyme catalyzed. Certain enzymes of this pathway, such as fructose bisphosphatase, can exist in an active or an inactive form. The inactive form is incapable of catalyzing its particular reaction whereas the active form can. It has recently been shown that products of light-dependent electron transport are also required to convert these light-sensitive enzymes from the inactive to the active form. Thus, light not only regulates the Calvin cycle by its direct involvement in the synthesis of ATP and NADPH, but also in the production of the chemicals needed to convert certain inactive enzymes to their active forms. The conversion of these inactive enzymes to their active forms also ensures that the Calvin cycle will operate at maximum capacity.

When a plant undergoes a dark to light transition, changes in the hydrogen ion (H^+) concentration of the stroma can cause its pH to change from 6 in the dark to 8 in the light. The mechanism for this change will be discussed in detail in Chapter 8. All enzyme-catalyzed reactions are pH sensitive. The enzymes of the Calvin cycle operate at their maximum rate when the pH of the stroma is alkaline (pH > 7.0). For example, Rubisco operates optimally at pH 8 and minimally at pH 6. Thus, light also influences the rate at which the Calvin cycle reactions occur by regulating the pH of the stroma. In addition, light influences the magnesium ion (Mg^{2+}) concentration of the stroma. This ion is an important cofactor in many of the reactions involved in the conversion of carbon dioxide to glucose.

Clearly, light regulates the overall rates of photosynthesis not only by controlling the availability of ATP and NADPH, the primary products of the light-dependent reactions, but also by ensuring that the enzymes of the Calvin cycle are operating under optimal conditions. Taken together, these factors ensure that the net synthesis of carbohydrate, in the form of glucose, from carbon dioxide occurs with maximum efficiency.

CHAPTER SUMMARY

Photosynthetic carbon dioxide fixation occurs by the light-independent reactions which take place within the stroma of the chloroplast. The net result of these reactions is the conversion of six one-carbon molecules of carbon dioxide to one six-carbon molecule of glucose, and the regeneration of one molecule of ribulose bisphosphate (RuBP). The capacity to regenerate RuBP continuously allows the plant to fix carbon dioxide continuously. The synthesis of glucose and the regeneration of RuBP have an absolute requirement for ATP and NADPH which are products of the light-dependent reactions in the chloroplast thylakoid membranes. Glucose can be converted to the disaccharide, sucrose, or the polysaccharide, cellulose, within the cell cytoplasm or to the polysaccharide, starch, within the chloroplast. The overall efficiency of carbon fixation in C_3 plants is generally limited by photorespiration which results in the light-dependent evolution of carbon dioxide.

Objectives

Having completed this chapter, you should be able to do the following:

1. Describe the structure of chloroplast indicating where the light-dependent and light-independent reactions of photosynthesis take place.

2. Explain the roles played by ATP and NADPH in photosynthesis.

3. Describe three metabolic fates of glucose.

4. Define photosynthetic induction.

5. Describe how light regulates the Calvin cycle.

6. Define photorespiration and describe its impact on photosynthesis.

Vocabulary

autotroptic
heterotrophic
envelope membrane
stroma
thylakoid membrane

light-independent reaction
light-dependent reaction
chlorophyll
carotenoid
grana

stromal thylakoid
cellulose
photosynthetic induction

Review Questions

1. (a) What is photosynthesis?
   (b) Where does it take place in a leaf?

2. How are autotrophic organisms different from heterotrophic organisms? Give examples of each.

3. Describe and illustrate with a diagram the structure of a chloroplast.

4. What are the light-dependent and light-independent reactions of photosynthesis?

5. What are the two most important metabolic functions of the Calvin cycle reactions?

6. Why is photosynthetic carbon dioxide uptake by a green leaf light-dependent?

7. Describe the four metabolic fates of glucose in green plants.

8. Describe the roles of PGAL as a critical biochemical intermediate in the photosynthetic process.

9. (a) What conditions are favourable for starch formation in higher green plants? Explain your answer.
   (b) Precisely where in a leaf mesophyll cell would you find this starch?

10. Describe four ways in which light regulates the overall rate of photosynthesis.

11. (a) What is photorespiration?
    (b) How does it affect photosynthesis?

Advanced Questions

1. Imagine that you are a research biochemist studying the properties of the photosynthetic enzyme, Rubisco. You dissolve your enzyme in a solution in a test tube. The solution contains only carbon dioxide, magnesium ions, and a hydrogen ion concentration of 10^{-8} mol/L. What must you add to this reaction mixture in order to be able to convert the substrate carbon dioxide to phosphoglycerate? Does this reaction need light to proceed? Why or why not?

2. The accompanying graph illustrates the net carbon dioxide uptake in a green leaf as a function of time in the dark and the light.

   (a) Why is net carbon dioxide uptake extremely low in the dark?

   (b) Why does carbon dioxide uptake increase significantly in the light?

   (c) Calculate the *maximum rate* of carbon dioxide uptake from the accompanying graph.

   (d) Why is there a lag in the attainment of maximum rate of carbon dioxide uptake during the first minute in the light?

   (e) What physiological phenomenon does this graph illustrate?

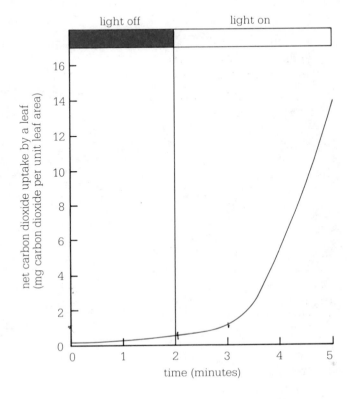

CHAPTER 7

LIGHT-DEPENDENT REACTIONS OF PHOTOSYNTHESIS

. . . Chlorophyll . . . is the real Prometheus,
stealing fire from the heavens.

K. Timiryazev

I n 1952, on the Eniwetok atoll in the South Pacific, a few hundred grams of hydrogen were fused to form helium. In the process, a very small amount of matter was annihilated, a massive amount of energy was released, and a brilliant mushroom cloud rose into the sky. The world had witnessed the detonation of the first hydrogen fusion bomb. While this event represents the release of a massive amount of energy, it pales by comparison to the events which occur on the sun. About 150 million kilometres from the earth, some 596 million tonnes of solar hydrogen is converted to 591 million tonnes of helium *every second*. An immense amount of energy released by hydrogen fusion in the core of that distant star works its way to the surface and radiates out into space. A very small portion of this radiant energy eventually reaches the earth where it is converted by green plants to the chemical energy on which we depend for our very existence. It is paradoxical that a simple nuclear transformation like the conversion of four atoms of hydrogen to one atom of helium can be one of the most destructive forces known to humans and yet, at the same time, is the very source of energy upon which life is so dependent. This chapter will examine the photochemical processes which enable green plants to capture this radiant energy from the sun and convert it to the chemical forms which are so important to life on earth.

7.1 ENERGY CONVERSION BY CHLOROPLASTS

In the previous chapter, it was shown that for carbon to be fixed by the Calvin cycle, energy must be supplied in the form of reduced nicotinamide adenine dinucleotide phosphate (NADPH) and ATP. These important energy carriers are made in the chloroplast by the light-dependent reactions of photosynthesis. A photosynthetic electron transport chain in the chloroplast thylakoid membrane uses light energy to reduce NADP and generate ATP. The purpose of this chapter is to examine the organization of this electron transport chain and, in general terms, the mechanism for the synthesis of NADPH and ATP. First, however, since the principal function of photosynthesis is to convert light energy to chemical energy, it is important to have some understanding of the nature of light.

7.2 THE NATURE OF LIGHT

Waves and Particles
Light is a form of radiant energy which makes up a very small part of the electromagnetic spectrum (Figure 7.1). Like other forms of energy, light is most easily described by the ways in which it interacts with matter. For example, when light is transmitted through space, reflected by an object, or refracted by a lens, it

Figure 7.1

The electromagnetic spectrum. Radiation is propagated as a continuous wave (a). The distance between adjacent wave crests or troughs is known as the wavelength (λ). Visible light, shown on an expanded scale in (b), is a very small portion of the total electromagnetic spectrum.

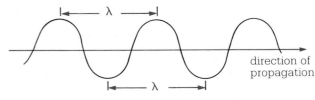

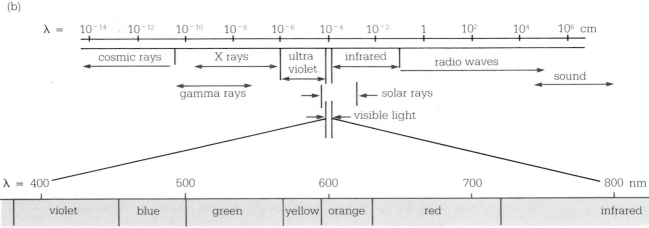

behaves as a wave phenomenon. The distance between wave crests, known as **wavelength**, is the most useful means for identifying the colour of light (Figure 7.1). On the other hand, when light is being emitted or absorbed by a substance, it behaves as though it were a stream of discrete particles. A particle of electromagnetic radiation is called a **quantum** (pl. quanta). A quantum of light may also be called a **photon**. An individual quantum of light carries a precise quantity of energy which is inversely proportional to its wavelength. For example, a quantum of red light, with a wavelength of 660 nm (1nm = 10^{-9}m), carries less energy than a quantum of blue light which has a wavelength of 450 nm.

Excitation of Atoms and Molecules

When light encounters a molecule, any one of three events may occur. It may be *reflected* (bounced off), *transmitted* (passed right through), or it may be *absorbed*. Neither of the first two events causes any change in the molecule and so neither has any lasting or significant biological consequence. However, changes do occur if the photon is absorbed. What happens when a photon is absorbed? The process of absorption is the same for atoms as for more complex molecules. For simplicity, the discussion here will refer to atoms but it equally applies to molecules.

According to a current model, an atom consists of a nucleus surrounded by one or more negatively charged electrons (Figure 7.2). Each electron occupies a discrete region of space called an *orbital*, which is defined by its distance from the nucleus. Normally, an atom exists in a state in which each electron occupies an orbital as close as possible to the nucleus. This is the lowest energy state for that atom and is called its *ground state*. When a photon is absorbed, it effectively disappears but its energy remains associated with the absorbing atom (or molecule). This additional energy causes an electron to move to an orbital position further out from the nucleus. The atom is now in a higher energy state and is said to be *excited*.

Only certain orbitals are allowed and quanta cannot be subdivided. Therefore, the energy of the quantum to be absorbed must exactly match the difference in energy between the ground state of the atom and one of its allowed excited states. If the energy content of the quantum is too large or too small, the transition of the electron cannot occur and the quantum will not be absorbed. In other words only certain wavelengths, which correspond to the correct energy level, can be absorbed by a particular atom or molecule.

An atom may remain in the excited state for only a small fraction of a second before it must give up this additional energy. Some of the energy will always be

Figure 7.2

Absorption of light energy. A photon may be absorbed by an atom in its ground (non-excited) state (a). The absorbed energy causes an electron to move to a higher orbital (b). The electron may return to the ground state (c), re-emitting the excess energy as a photon of light. The emitted photon has a longer wavelength than the absorbed photon. Alternatively, the energized electron may be used to reduce a suitable electron acceptor (d). The symbol hν denotes a quantum or photon.

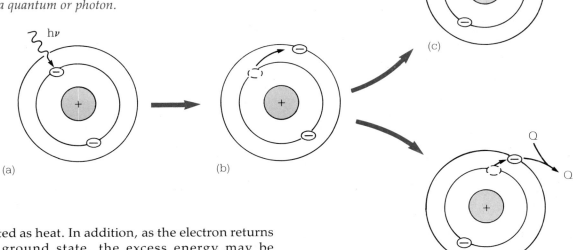

dissipated as heat. In addition, as the electron returns to the ground state, the excess energy may be "repackaged" as a quantum and emitted as light. This phenomenon is known as fluorescence. See Figure 7.2(c). This series of events, like all physical processes, is not 100 percent efficient. Consequently, the emitted photon of fluorescent light contains less energy and has a longer wavelength than the photon originally absorbed by the atom. Alternatively, as indicated in Figure 7.2(d), the energized electron may be passed to another atom or molecule.

7.3 PIGMENTS AND ABSORPTION SPECTRA

Chlorophyll

A molecule that absorbs light is called a **pigment**. A quick survey of your environment will serve to remind you that plants have many different kinds of pigments. Each pigment absorbs light in different regions of the spectrum and so appears a different colour. The dominant colour of most plants, however, is green. This is because they contain large amounts of the pigment, chlorophyll. Chlorophyll is actually a family of pigments with similar chemical structures (Figure 7.3). Each chlorophyll molecule has two parts: a complex porphyrin ring and a long, hydrocarbon tail. The por-

phyrin ring of the chlorophyll molecule is very similar to the heme structure found in the blood pigment, *hemoglobin*, and the respiratory pigments of the mitochondria, the *cytochromes*. However, the porphyrin rings of both hemoglobin and cytochrome contain a central iron atom. In chlorophyll, it is replaced by a magnesium atom.

The porphyrin part of the chlorophyll molecule is responsible for the absorption of light. The long hydrocarbon tail of the chlorophyll molecule is very hydrophobic. This is why chlorophyll is not water soluble and is found only in the lipid membranes of the chloroplast.

Absorption Spectra

Why is chlorophyll green? Like all pigments, chlorophyll selectively absorbs only certain wavelengths of light. It absorbs predominantly in the blue and red regions of the spectrum but is transparent to green light (Figure 7.4). Light that is transmitted or reflected by the chlorophyll will therefore be depleted of both the blue and red wavelengths and will be perceived by the observer as green.

Figure 7.3

Molecular structure of chlorophyll. The cyclic porphyrin group, which contains a magnesium ion, is responsible for the absorption of light. The long hydrocarbon tail is very hydrophobic and renders the molecule soluble in the lipid membrane. The molecule shown is chlorophyll a. A second form of chlorophyll, chlorophyll b, contains a formyl group (—CHO) in place of the encircled methyl group.

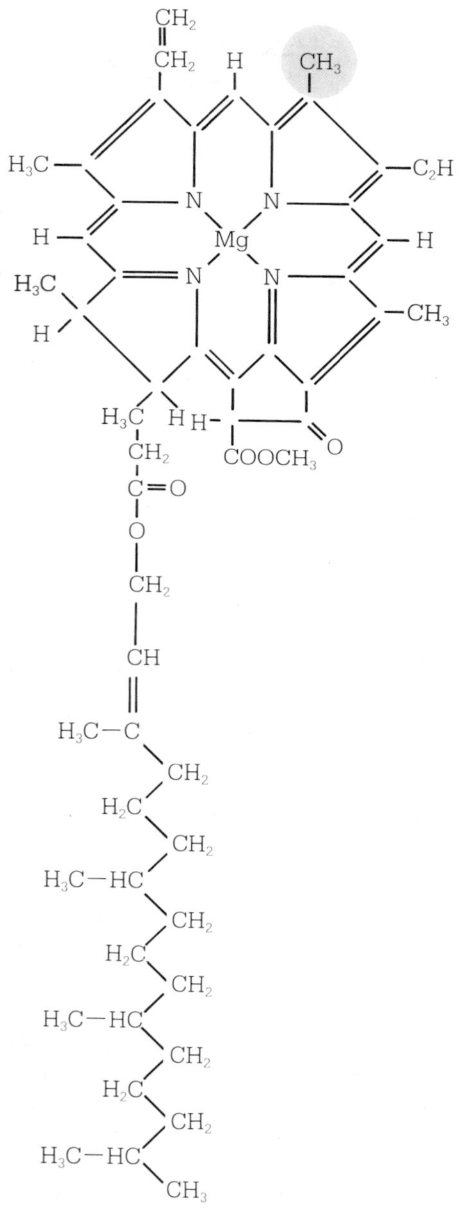

Figure 7.4

Why is chlorophyll green? Chlorophyll appears green because the red and blue portions of the spectrum are absorbed, leaving only light from the green region to be transmitted.

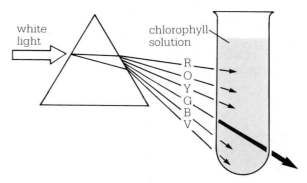

The principle of light absorption by a molecule such as chlorophyll is illustrated in Figure 7.5. Figure 7.5(a) is a simplified *energy level diagram*. It shows the differences in energy levels between the ground state of a chlorophyll molecule and two different excited states. Note that the highest excited state, requiring the most energy, is achieved with quanta from the blue end of the visible spectrum. A lower excited state is achieved with quanta from the red end of the spectrum. These excited states correspond to the relative energy contents of the quanta of blue and red light, respectively.

Figure 7.5(b) is a graph which shows relative light absorption as a function of wavelength. This kind of graph, which plots the efficiency of light absorption as a function of wavelength, is known as an **absorption spectrum**. In the figure, the absorption spectrum has actually been turned 90° from its normal orientation. This has been done in order to emphasize the correspondence between the possible excitation states of the molecule and the principal bands in the absorption spectrum. An absorption spectrum is very much like a "fingerprint" of the absorbing molecule. Each pigment has a unique absorption spectra which is a key to its identification.

Figure 7.5 also shows the spectrum of the fluorescence emission from chlorophyll. Fluorescence will occur when the pigment is unable to use the energy in any other way. Green leaves do not appear to fluoresce because most of the energy absorbed by the chlorophyll is used in the chloroplast. On the other hand, a solution of chlorophyll extracted from leaves is unable to participate in any useful chemical reactions and will fluoresce a deep red colour when illuminated.

Figure 7.5
Relationship between energy of absorbed light and absorption spectra. Only certain quanta of light corresponding to specific energy levels or excited states may be absorbed by a given molecule. Molecules may drop to a lower excited state by giving off heat (a). The symbol hν designates a *quantum. The wavelengths of bands in an absorption spectrum (solid line) correspond to the energy levels of possible excited states (b). The fluorescence emission spectrum is shown by the dashed line. The spectra are turned 90° from their normal orientation in order to illustrate this relationship.*

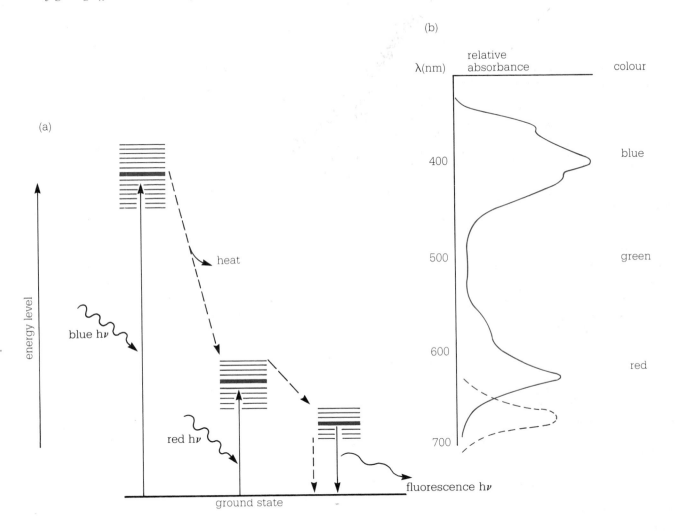

Photo-oxidation

In some circumstances, the absorption of light by a molecule will impart sufficient energy to an electron such that it moves far enough away from the nucleus to be captured by another molecule, as shown in Figure 7.2(d). The absorbing molecule will then have lost an electron and, consequently, is oxidized. The molecule which captures the electron becomes reduced. This process of light-dependent oxidation is called **photo-oxidation**. Later in this chapter, it will be shown that photo-oxidation of chlorophyll is a central feature of photosynthesis.

7.4 IS CHLOROPHYLL THE PHOTOSYNTHETIC PIGMENT?

The discussion up to this point has assumed that chlorophyll is the pigment which absorbs photosynthetically active light. Is this a valid assumption? What evidence is there to support this assumption?

Action Spectra

Circumstantial evidence for the role of chlorophyll in photosynthesis was noted as long ago as the late eighteenth century. In 1779, for example, the Dutch physician J. Ingenhousz observed that photosynthesis did not occur in tissues or plants which have no chlorophyll. Today, a more direct approach to identifying the pigment responsible for any photosensitive process is to obtain an **action spectrum**. An action spectrum is a graph which shows the efficiency of the process as a function of wavelength. For photosynthesis, this is determined by comparing the amount of photosynthesis produced when a plant is subjected to light of different wavelengths. Note the similarity between the definition of an action spectrum and the definition of an absorption spectrum given above. It is a fundamental rule of photobiology that for light to be active in a process, it must first be absorbed. The pigment responsible for a photosensitive process can often be identified, then, by comparing absorption spectra of the putative pigment with the action spectrum for that process.

A typical action spectrum for photosynthesis in a green plant is shown in Figure 7.6. It is compared with the absorption spectrum for chlorophyll extracted from the green leaf. Note that the action spectrum for photosynthesis has pronounced peaks in the red and blue regions of the spectrum and that these action maxima correspond to the absorption maxima for chlorophyll. This result is strong evidence that chlorophyll is the principal photosynthetic pigment.

Accessory Pigments

In addition to the chlorophylls, green plants contain several other kinds of pigment molecules. Of special interest with regard to photosynthesis are the orange and yellow pigments known as *carotenoids*. One common carotenoid, β-carotene, gives the orange colour to carrot roots. This is also found in the chloroplasts of green plants and gives leaves their orange colour in the autumn. The carotenoid pigments absorb light exclusively in the blue region of the spectrum. Experiments have demonstrated that energy trapped by the carotenoids can be passed on to chlorophyll for use in

Figure 7.6

The action spectrum of a green plant (a) shows that photosynthesis occurs most efficiently in red and blue light. Green light is less effective. The peaks in the action spectrum correspond to the principal absorption bands for chlorophyll in the chlorophyll absorption spectrum (b).

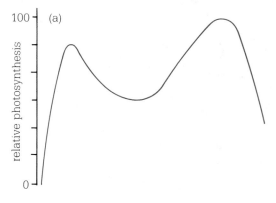

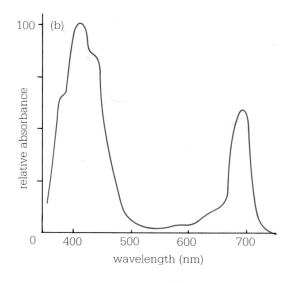

photosynthesis. This allows the plant to absorb light of a wider range of wavelengths and, consequently, more energy, than would be possible with the chlorophylls alone. It is because of this accessory role in gathering light for photosynthesis that the carotenoids are known as *accessory pigments*.

A striking example of the role of accessory pigments is illustrated by a particular group of marine algae known as the red algae. Some representatives of the red algae survive at depths far greater than any other known photosynthetic organism does. An action spectrum for photosynthesis in the red algae is shown in Figure 7.7. Note that, unlike green plants, red algae

Figure 7.7

Red algae contain the light harvesting pigments phycocyanin and phycoerythrin. These pigments absorb green light and pass the energy on to chlorophyll. Consequently, photosynthesis in red algae is efficient in green light. Green plants, on the other hand, cannot use green light.

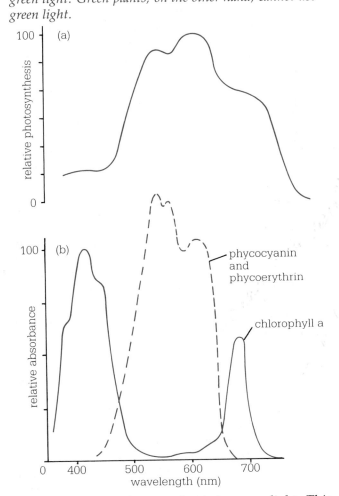

7.5 ELECTRON TRANSPORT IN CHLOROPLASTS

The Photosynthetic Unit

Current understanding of the role played by chlorophyll in energy conversion and the organization of the pigment in the chloroplast began with the work of Robert Emerson in the 1930s. Emerson and his coworkers were studying photosynthesis in green algae. Their results indicated that only a small proportion of the chlorophyll molecules in the chloroplast, perhaps 1 in 2500, appeared to be *directly* involved in the conversion of radiant energy to chemical energy. Emerson's discovery gave rise to the concept of a **photosynthetic unit**.

The current model of a photosynthetic unit is that of an organized collection of several hundred chlorophyll molecules which work together to process the energy of a single photon (Figure 7.8). Within each photosynthetic unit is a single chlorophyll molecule which functions as the catalytic site, called the **reaction centre**. It is the reaction centre chlorophyll where the photochemical transformation of light energy to stable chemical energy actually takes place. The remaining chlorophyll molecules in the photosynthetic unit appear to serve as **antenna chlorophyll**. In the same way that the antenna of a radio picks up a signal and sends it on to the radio receiver, the antenna chlorophyll molecules in the photosynthetic unit absorb photons and pass the energy to the reaction centre.

Figure 7.8

The photosynthetic unit. Energy absorbed by an antenna chlorophyll molecule is passed energetically downhill to the reaction centre where the actual photochemical conversion takes place.

show very active photosynthesis in green light. This action spectrum reflects the large amounts of red and blue accessory pigments, *phycoerythrin* and *phycocyanin*, found in the red algae. Phycoerythrin and phycocyanin absorb predominantly in the green region of the spectrum where there is virtually no absorption by chlorophyll. The presence of these pigments, which gives these algae their characteristic red color, enables the red algae to utilize energy from almost the entire visible spectrum. This factor is also believed to be important in the ability of the red algae to grow at much greater depths in the oceans where light intensity is much lower.

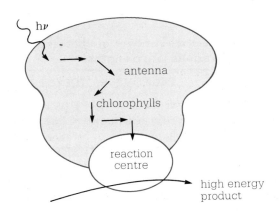

The transfer of energy from antenna chlorophyll to reaction centre chlorophyll is possible because not all chlorophyll molecules have the same absorption characteristics. Chlorophyll molecules do not occur free in the membrane of the chloroplast. Each chlorophyll is instead bound to a protein to form a *chlorophyll-protein complex*. The binding of protein to the chlorophyll introduces small but significant changes in the capacity of the chlorophyll to absorb light. Each chlorophyll-protein complex absorbs slightly different energy levels. Chlorophyll molecules will therefore exhibit slightly different absorption spectra, depending on the nature of the protein to which they are bound or where they are located within the complex. These minor differences allow the absorbed energy to migrate between neighbouring chlorophylls and appear to *direct* energy flow to the reaction centre. The reaction centre chlorophyll is always the longest wavelength, lowest energy absorbing form in the photosynthetic unit.

Two Photosystems in Photosynthesis

In another series of experiments, Emerson investigated the action spectrum of photosynthesis. Surprisingly, Emerson found that the efficiency of photosynthesis decreased rather abruptly with light of wavelengths longer than 680 nm, a region of the spectrum where chlorophyll still absorbs. Emerson was able to explain this unexpected result with a simple but very elegant experiment. He subjected the plant to long wavelength light (>680 nm) simultaneously with short wavelength light (<680 nm). He found that the efficiency of photosynthesis at the long wavelength was markedly increased when supplemented with short wavelength light. In fact, the amount of photosynthesis when long and short wavelength light were combined proved to be greater than the sum of the amounts when either wavelength was presented individually in separate trials (Table 7.1).

Table 7.1   Relative Amount of Photosynthesis at Various Wavelengths

WAVELENGTH (nm)	RELATIVE PHOTOSYNTHESIS	
	Without supplementary light	With supplementary light (650 nm)
660	1.00	1.24
680	0.94	1.25
700	0.06	1.18

These results, called the **Emerson enhancement effect**, can be explained if it is assumed that there are two different **photosystems**. One photosystem is driven by short wavelength light (680 nm or less) and the second photosystem is driven by long wavelength light (longer than 680 nm). In order for photosynthesis to operate most efficiently, both photosystems must be driven simultaneously (Figure 7.9). The validity of this theory has subsequently been confirmed by a variety of experiments, including the physical isolation of the two photosystems from chloroplast membranes.

The two photochemical systems are now known as *photosystem I* (PSI) and *photosystem II* (PSII), respectively. Each photosystem consists of a reaction centre chlorophyll a molecule which is surrounded by approximately 40 to 70 antenna chlorophylls. The antenna chlorophylls are also chlorophyll a. In addition, each photosystem has associated with it numerous protein molecules and electron carriers.

In order to understand how a photosystem operates, examine the diagram of PSI (Figure 7.10). The reaction centre for photosystem I is a species of chlorophyll a–protein that has an absorption maximum near 700 nm. Consequently, the PSI reaction centre is identified as P700. When a photon arrives at P700, one of the molecule's electrons is raised to an excited state (P700*). This electron is sufficiently energetic to be captured by a protein called *ferredoxin*. In the process, P700 is photo-oxidized (it loses an electron) and ferredoxin is reduced (it gains an electron). The energy required for ferredoxin reduction is, of course, supplied by light.

Now turn your attention to the diagram of PSII shown in Figure 7.11. The reaction centre chlorophyll-protein for PSII is identified as P680, since it absorbs maximally at 680 nm. The initial excitation in PSII is similar to that in PSI except that in this case, the high-energy electron (P680*) is captured by a protein-bound quinone, Q. This protein is important not only because it serves as a primary electron acceptor for PSII, but also because it appears to bind an herbicide called *atrazine*. Atrazine is one of several commonly used herbicides which block electron transport through PSII and thus interfere with photosynthesis. Some plants have developed resistance to atrazine, apparently by developing a modified protein which does not bind the herbicide.

Non-cyclic Electron Transport

The photo-oxidation of either P700 or P680 leaves that reaction centre chlorophyll lacking in one electron.

Figure 7.9
In photosynthesis there are two sequential photoacts. Electrons derived from the oxidation of water are excited twice, gaining sufficient energy to reduce CO_2 to sugar.

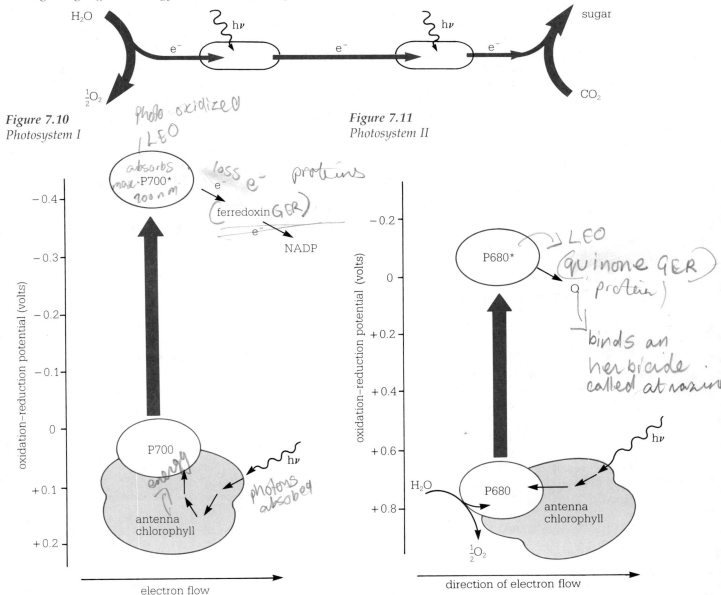

Figure 7.10
Photosystem I

Figure 7.11
Photosystem II

This is an unstable configuration and an electron must be found in order to satisfy this deficiency. In the case of PSII, the electron deficiency in P680 is satisfied by coupling the photo-oxidation of P680 with an enzyme complex which oxidizes water:

$$H_2O \longrightarrow \tfrac{1}{2}O_2 + 2H^+ + 2e^-$$

This reaction will not proceed spontaneously. It needs an input of energy and is tightly coupled to the photo-oxidation of P680. The mechanism is not well understood, but clearly some of the energy absorbed by P680 is used to drive this oxidation of water. It is this reaction which gives rise to the oxygen evolved in photosynthesis (Chapter 6).

PHOTOSYNTHESIS AND CHEMICAL WEED CONTROL

Since the dawn of agriculture, humans have waged war against weeds. Weeds compete with crop species for moisture, nutrients, and light and ultimately reduce crop yields. Traditional methods of weed control, such as manual hoeing or tractor-drawn cultivators, were largely replaced in the 1940s by labour-saving, chemical weed control. The production and distribution of herbicides (chemicals which kill plants) is now a multibillion dollar industry.

Many herbicides work by inhibiting photosynthesis, usually by interfering with electron transport. Two major classes of such herbicides are the urea derivatives, such as monuron and diuron, and the triazine herbicides, atrazine and simazine. Both urea and triazine herbicides are taken up by the roots and transported to the leaves. They appear to bind to a particular protein associated with PSII and block the reduction of plastoquinone.

Atrazine is used extensively to control weeds in cornfields. Corn roots contain an enzyme which breaks down triazine herbicides, so corn is tolerant to atrazine. However, many weed species have also developed a resistance to triazine herbicides. Chloroplast mutations in the resistant strains produce a modified PSII protein which is effective in electron transport but which no longer binds the herbicide.

Since triazines are active in the soil for one to two years, heavy applications on a cornfield may make it difficult to grow an alternate crop on the same soil in the following year. In addition, although atrazine itself has been thoroughly tested and found safe, recent evidence indicates that the products of atrazine breakdown in the plant may cause mutations in microbial and plant test systems.

Another class of herbicides which interfere with photosynthesis are the viologen dyes, diquat and paraquat. These compounds interfere with electron transport through PSI and, in very low concentrations, quickly cause cell death. Because viologen dyes are also very toxic to humans, their use is banned or tightly controlled in many jurisdictions. Chemical herbicides have become an essential component of modern agriculture, but their value simply as a labour-saving device must be carefully weighed against potentially harmful side-effects.

The electron deficiency in PSI caused by the photo-oxidation of P700 may be satisfied by linking PSII and PSI, as shown in Figure 7.12. This is done through an intermediate chain of electron carriers which includes *plastoquinone*, a *cytochrome b_6/f complex*, and *plastocyanin*. The flow of electrons from water to NADP through linked PSI and PSII is known as *non-cyclic electron transport*. When PSI is excited, the electron is passed from P700 through ferredoxin to NADP. The resulting electron deficiency in P700 is then satisfied by re-oxidizing a molecule of plastocyanin. Plastocyanin, in turn, receives an electron from the cytochrome b_6/f complex which receives electrons from plastoquinone. A pool of reduced plastoquinone is maintained through the action of PSII. In this way, a continual flow of electrons is established through both photosystems.

The overall effect of non-cyclic electron transport is to remove a low-energy electron from water and raise its potential (voltage) sufficiently to reduce NADP. A

Figure 7.12
The interaction of photosystem I and photosystem II in non-cyclic electron transport. The two photosystems are linked in sequence by a chain of electron carriers similar to that found in the mitochondrion.

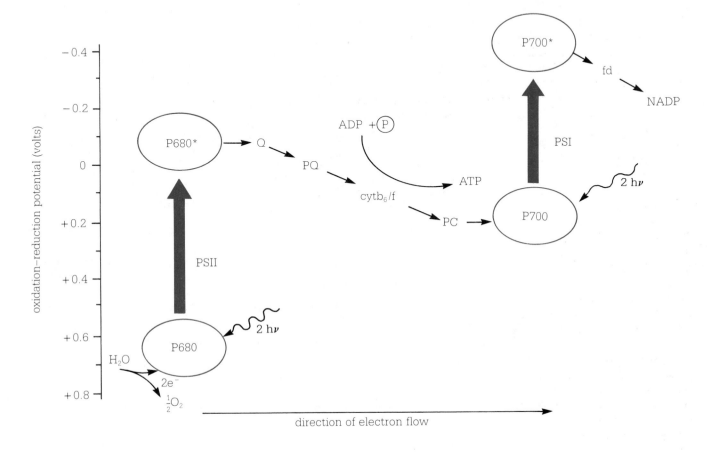

Figure 7.13
The use of two sequential photosystems is like using two batteries in a flashlight.

single excitation would not provide the electron with sufficient energy (that is, impart sufficient voltage) to achieve this reduction. Linking the two photosystems together is very much like using two batteries in series to produce a higher voltage in a flashlight (Figure 7.13). As electrons move between PSII and PSI, the energy of electron transport may be used to generate ATP. ATP generation associated with non-cyclic electron transport is known as **non-cyclic photophosphorylation**.

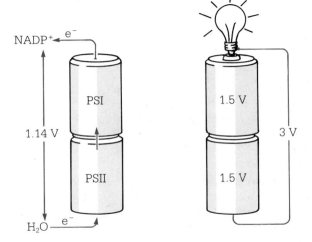

Figure 7.14

Cyclic electron transport. A cyclic flow of electrons from ferredoxin back to the reaction centre of photosystem I occurs when a photosystem I unit does not have access to a photosystem II unit. Cyclic electron transport results in the synthesis of ATP but no $NADP^+$ is reduced.

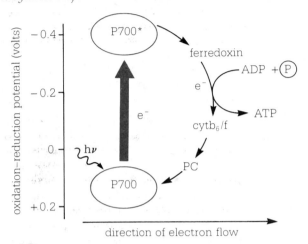

Cyclic Electron Transport

PSI may operate alone, that is, without interacting with PSII. In this situation, PSI has no access to an external source of electrons, such as water. The electron deficiency in P700 must be satisfied by returning the electron to P700 through cytochrome b_6/f and plastocyanin (Figure 7.14). This pathway is known as *cyclic electron transport*. Note that cyclic electron transport may also be accompanied by the production of ATP, *but not NADPH*. ATP formation accompanying cyclic electron transport is called **cyclic photophosphorylation**.

7.6 ATP SYNTHESIS IN CHLOROPLASTS

Electron transport in the chloroplast is very similar to electron transport in the mitochondrion (Chapter 5). Recall that, in the mitochondrion, electron transport begins with *high energy* electrons provided in the form of reduced NAD. These electrons are passed through a series of membrane-bound electron carriers. At three of these steps, some of the energy is used to pump protons across the membrane. The energy in this proton gradient may then be used to drive the synthesis of ATP in accordance with Mitchell's chemiosmotic hypothesis. In the chloroplast, high energy electrons provided by the excitation of PSII are passed down a chain of membrane-bound electron carriers which link PSII with PSI. It should not be too surprising, then, that photosynthetic electron transport can also be used to establish a proton gradient and synthesize ATP according to the same principles.

Figure 7.15 shows the arrangement of the principal components of non-cyclic photosynthetic electron transport within the thylakoid membrane. PSII, the cytochrome f/b_6, and PSI are all transmembrane complexes which extend across the thylakoid membrane between the stroma and the intrathylakoid space. Plastoquinone is a small, mobile carrier which transports electrons between PSII and the cytochrome com-

Figure 7.15

Non-cyclic photosynthetic electron transport and photophosphorylation. The synthesis of ATP is linked to electron transport by a proton motive force across the thylakoid membrane.

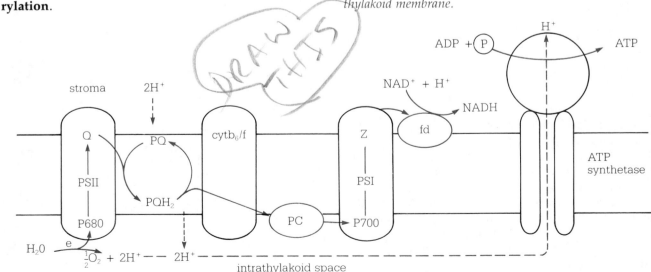

plex. Plastocyanin is a peripheral protein which mediates electron transfer between the cytochrome f/b₆ complex and P700.

As plastoquinone is alternately reduced and re-oxidized during the course of non-cyclic electron transport, protons may be pumped from the stroma into the intrathylakoid space. Plastoquinone thus establishes a proton gradient across the thylakoid membrane. The protons produced by the oxidation of water also contribute to the gradient. Since the water-splitting enzyme is located on the intrathylakoid space side of the membrane, the protons from the splitting of water accumulate in that space. It is not necessary for protons to be physically transported from one side of the membrane to the other in order to establish a gradient provided that a difference in concentration is maintained. By either mechanism, it is possible to establish and maintain a proton gradient because, like the inner mitochondrial membrane, the thylakoid membrane is generally impermeable to protons.

As pointed out in Chapter 5, the proton motive force across the inner mitochondrial membrane is composed of both a membrane potential and a proton gradient of approximately one pH unit. In the chloroplast, virtually all of the proton motive force may be attributed to a proton gradient. An actively photosynthesizing chloroplast in bright sunlight can establish a pH difference of nearly 3.5 across the thylakoid membrane, equivalent to an electrochemical proton gradient of 210 mV. This represents a nearly 5000-fold difference in proton concentration between the stroma and the intrathylakoid space!

The large proton motive force established by the light-driven proton pump favours the return of protons to the stroma. An ATP synthetase in the thylakoid membrane, which is virtually identical to the ATP synthetase of the mitochondrion, provides the necessary proton channel for the flow of protons back into the stroma and accompanying synthesis of ATP.

ATP synthesis is achieved in a similar manner by cyclic electron transport, except that the proton gradient is established by pumping protons through the cytochrome complex as the electron cycles back to P700 (Figure 7.16).

A most convincing demonstration of the application of Mitchell's chemiosmotic hypothesis to ATP synthesis in the chloroplast has been provided by A. Jagendorf. In a very elegant experiment, Jagendorf demonstrated the synthesis of ATP in the dark when a suitable proton gradient was imposed across the membrane (Figure 7.17). He used isolated chloroplasts which were allowed to equilibrate with an acid solution (pH 4) for several hours in the dark. At equilibrium, the concentration of protons in the intrathylakoid space was the same as that surrounding the chloroplasts. By rapidly transferring the chloroplasts to a basic solution (pH 8), a proton gradient from the intrathylakoid space to the stroma side of the membrane was established. Jagendorf demonstrated the synthesis of ATP as the protons were transported across the membrane and the proton gradient disappeared.

Figure 7.16
Cyclic photosynthetic electron transport and photophosphorylation. Cyclic photophosphorylation is not accompanied by reduction of NADP⁺.

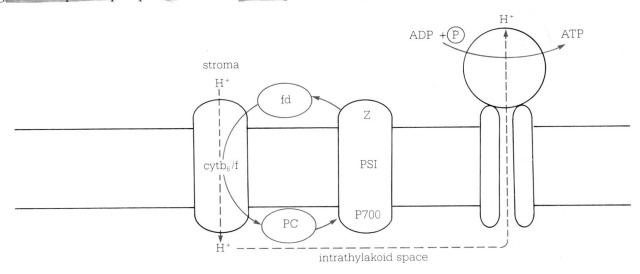

Figure 7.17
Jagendorf's experiment shows that isolated chloroplast thylakoids can use an artificial proton gradient to synthesize ATP in the dark.

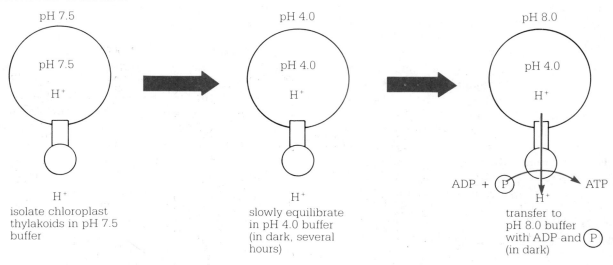

isolate chloroplast thylakoids in pH 7.5 buffer

slowly equilibrate in pH 4.0 buffer (in dark, several hours)

transfer to pH 8.0 buffer with ADP and (P) (in dark)

7.7 LOOKING TOWARD THE FUTURE

Understanding the molecular processes by which radiant energy is converted to chemical energy in the chloroplast has its own intrinsic value. It is, above all, intellectually satisfying to understand how these intricate chemical processes work, especially a process so essential to our existence as photosynthesis. Furthermore, it is possible that, by combining this knowledge with modern techniques in recombinant DNA and biotechnology, scientists and technologists may be able to improve the efficiency of energy conversion in crop plants and thereby improve our capacity to produce food.

It is possible that better understanding of the light-dependent reactions of photosynthesis could lead to a source of energy self-sufficiency. The past decade has witnessed an increasing awareness of limitations imposed by our dependency on fossil fuel or nuclear sources of energy. Some scientists have urged that we should pay more attention to the elegant way in which green plants convert sunlight into chemical energy. Chloroplasts produce storable chemical energy in two forms — the hydrogen (protons) generated when water is oxidized and the electricity of electron flow from water to NADP. Hydrogen is a clean, non-polluting fuel. The product of hydrogen combustion is simply water. True, there are engineering difficulties associated with the utilization of hydrogen as a fuel,

but these could be overcome. The real problem lies in the inefficiency and cost of hydrogen production. Theoretically, however, an almost limitless supply of hydrogen is available by photochemical splitting of water, as in photosynthesis. It would be necessary to modify the system slightly in order to encourage the electrons to recombine with the protons to form hydrogen atoms. It has been estimated that if the photochemical conversion were only 10 percent efficient, 78 000 km^2 of solar collector could supply the energy needs of the world. Others encourage the direct generation of electricity, using organic solar cells. Such cells could be constructed with chorophylls and quinones supported on artificial membranes. The feasibility of both approaches has been established on a small scale in the laboratory. The major challenge appears to lie in the engineering technology needed to develop the full potential of these innovative ideas.

EUKARYOTIC CELLS

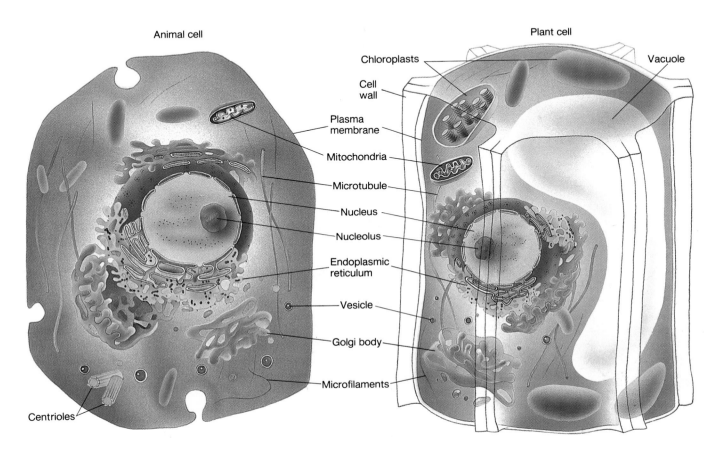

Animal cell

Plant cell

Chloroplasts

Cell wall

Plasma membrane

Mitochondria

Microtubule

Nucleus

Nucleolus

Endoplasmic reticulum

Vesicle

Golgi body

Microfilaments

Centrioles

Vacuole

Generalized structure of eukaryotic cells. Plant and animal cells both have a plasma membrane, nucleus, cytoplasm, and cellular organelles. They differ in the types of organelles they contain and by the presence of cell walls in plant cells. (See Section 3.1.)

PLASMA MEMBRANES

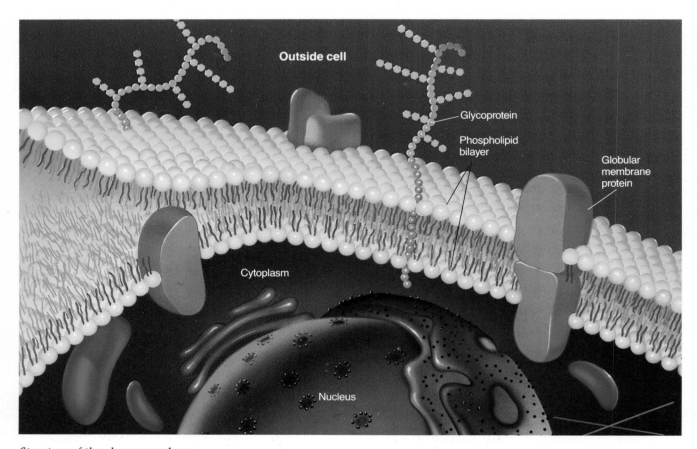

Structure of the plasma membrane
(See Section 4.2.)

The plasma membrane: a fluid
mosaic. The plasma membrane is
composed of two layers of
phospholipids. Globular proteins
float in the phospholipid bilayer, and
carbohydrate groups project out from
the proteins and phospholipids. (See
Section 4.2.)

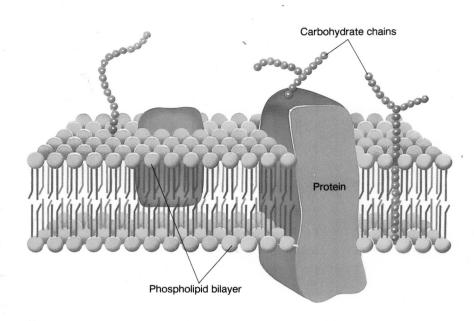

RESPIRATION

The three parts of respiration.

Step 1. Glycolysis converts glucose to pyruvic acid in the cytoplasm, generating NADH and a small amount of ATP.

Step 2. Pyruvic acid is moved into the mitochondrion as it is converted to acetyl CoA, which is then completely oxidized by the Krebs cycle to Co_2, generating several molecules of NADH and one $FADH_2$. The NADH molecules from glycolysis also move into the mitochondrion.

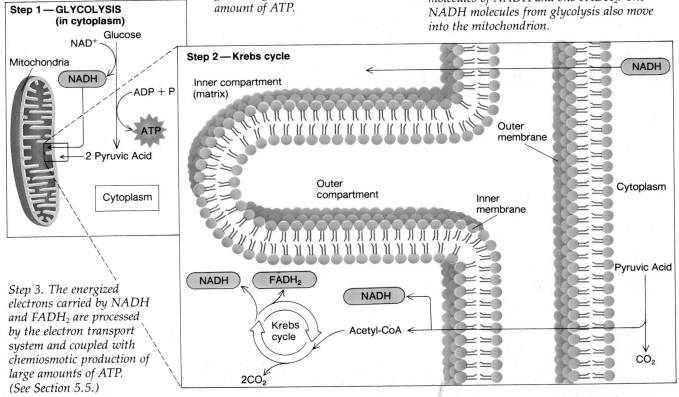

Step 1 — GLYCOLYSIS (in cytoplasm)

Glucose

NAD⁺

Mitochondria

NADH

ADP + P

ATP

2 Pyruvic Acid

Cytoplasm

Step 2 — Krebs cycle

Inner compartment (matrix)

NADH

Outer membrane

Outer compartment

Inner membrane

Cytoplasm

NADH

FADH₂

NADH

Pyruvic Acid

Krebs cycle

Acetyl-CoA

2CO₂

CO₂

Step 3. The energized electrons carried by NADH and $FADH_2$ are processed by the electron transport system and coupled with chemiosmotic production of large amounts of ATP. (See Section 5.5.)

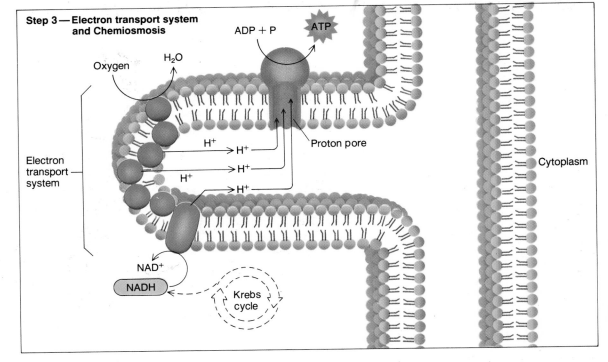

Step 3 — Electron transport system and Chemiosmosis

ADP + P

ATP

Oxygen

H₂O

H⁺ → H⁺

Proton pore

Electron transport system

H⁺ → H⁺

H⁺

H⁺ → H⁺

Cytoplasm

NAD⁺

NADH

Krebs cycle

PHOTOSYNTHESIS

Organization for photosynthesis. Photosynthesis takes place in the chloroplasts of plant cells. A leaf cell may contain as many as 60 chloroplasts. The thylakoid system of the chloroplast is the site of the light reactions, whereas the stroma is the site of the synthesis reactions. Photosynthetic pigments are precisely arranged in the thylakoid membranes to form light-harvesting photosystems. The reaction center of each photosystem receives energy from surrounding antenna pigments. When sufficient energy is absorbed by the reaction center, its electrons are boosted to a higher energy level and are then passed to an electron-acceptor molecule. This starts a chain of chemical reactions that leads to the formation of ATP and NADPH, and ultimately energy-rich carbohydrates. (See Section 6.2.)

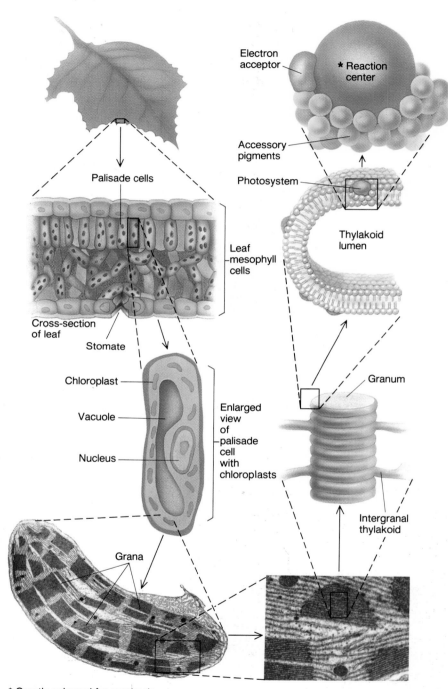

Palisade cells

Electron acceptor

* Reaction center

Accessory pigments

Photosystem

Thylakoid lumen

Leaf mesophyll cells

Cross-section of leaf

Stomate

Chloroplast

Vacuole

Nucleus

Enlarged view of palisade cell with chloroplasts

Granum

Grana

Intergranal thylakoid

* Greatly enlarged for emphasis

NERVOUS SYSTEM

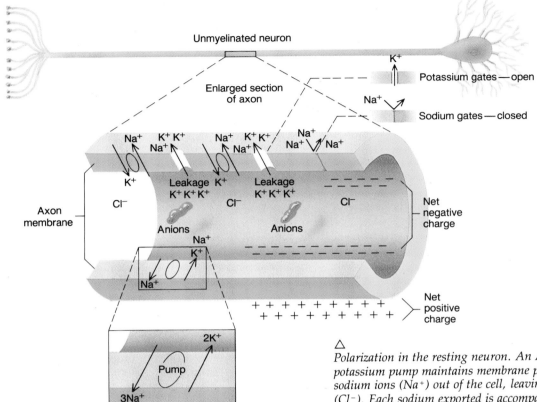

Unmyelinated neuron

K+

Potassium gates — open

Na+

Sodium gates — closed

Enlarged section
of axon

Axon
membrane

Na+   K+ K+   Na+   K+ K+   Na+
Na+   Na+   Na+   Na+

K+   Leakage K+   Leakage
Cl−   K+ K+ K+ Cl−   K+ K+ K+   Cl−

Anions   Anions

Na+
K+

Na+

Net
negative
charge

+ + + + + + + +
+ + + + + + + +

Net
positive
charge

2K+

Pump

3Na+

△
*Polarization in the resting neuron. An ATP-driven sodium-
potassium pump maintains membrane polarity by pumping
sodium ions (Na^+) out of the cell, leaving behind chloride ions
(Cl^-). Each sodium exported is accompanied by the import of a
potassium ion (K^+). Unlike large sodium ions however, the
potassium ions are small enough to leak back through the
membrane, diffusing out of the cell where the K^+ concentration
is lower. The result is an overall positive charge outside the cell
(Na^+ and K^+), and a negative charge inside the cell. Large
organic anions (negatively charged ions) cannot escape the cell,
so they remain in the cytoplasm, intensifying the ionic
gradient. The strength of the electrical potential produced by
this gradient is measured as voltage. (See Section 11.1.)*

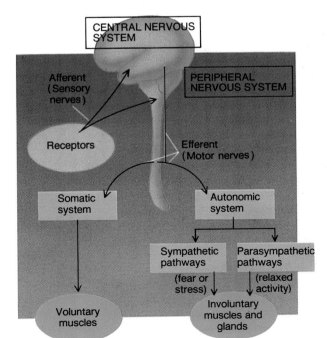

CENTRAL NERVOUS
SYSTEM

Afferent
(Sensory
nerves)

PERIPHERAL
NERVOUS SYSTEM

Receptors

Efferent
(Motor nerves)

Somatic
system

Autonomic
system

Sympathetic
pathways

Parasympathetic
pathways

(fear or
stress)

(relaxed
activity)

Voluntary
muscles

Involuntary
muscles and
glands

◁ *Interplay between central and peripheral nervous systems.
Receptors relay information about the internal and external
environment to the central nervous system by way of afferent
(incoming) nerves. The central nervous system responds to this
input by sending impulses to target cells through efferent
(outgoing) nerves. Efferent nerves are divided into two
systems: (1) the somatic system that acts on voluntary
muscles, and (2) the autonomic system that either excites or
inhibits involuntary muscles and glands. The exact effect of
autonomic activity depends on whether the sympathetic or
parasympathetic pathways are activited. (See Section 11.2.)*

ENDOCRINE SYSTEM

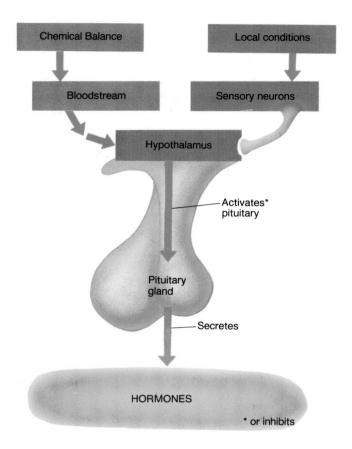

*The major neuroendocrine connection
(See Section 12.1.)*

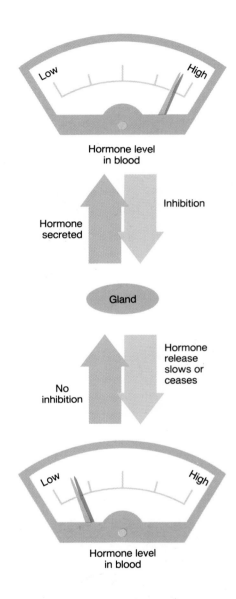

*Negative feedback provides one way
to regulate hormone concentration in
the blood. Higher concentrations of
hormone inhibit the gland that
secretes it, which resumes activity
again as levels decrease. (See Section
12.1.)*

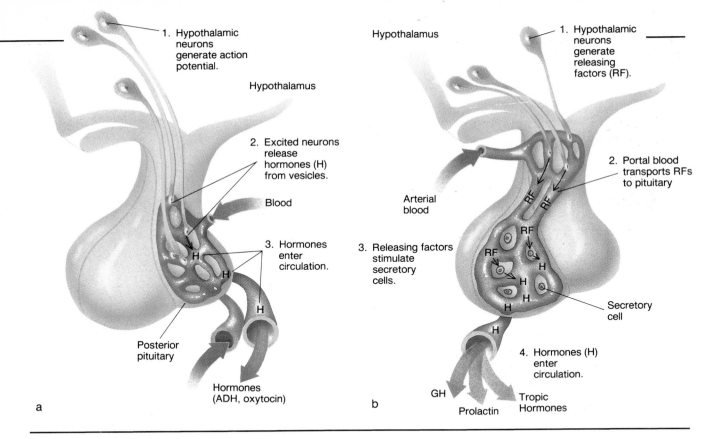

1. Hypothalamic neurons generate action potential.

Hypothalamus

2. Excited neurons release hormones (H) from vesicles.

Blood

3. Hormones enter circulation.

Posterior pituitary

Hormones (ADH, oxytocin)

a

Hypothalamus

1. Hypothalamic neurons generate releasing factors (RF).

2. Portal blood transports RFs to pituitary

Arterial blood

3. Releasing factors stimulate secretory cells.

RF

H

Secretory cell

4. Hormones (H) enter circulation.

GH

Prolactin

Tropic Hormones

b

△ *The pituitary-hypothalamic linkage. The hypothalamus is functionally linked by neurons to the posterior pituitary (a) and by the bloodstream to the anterior pituitary (b). (See Section 12.2.)*

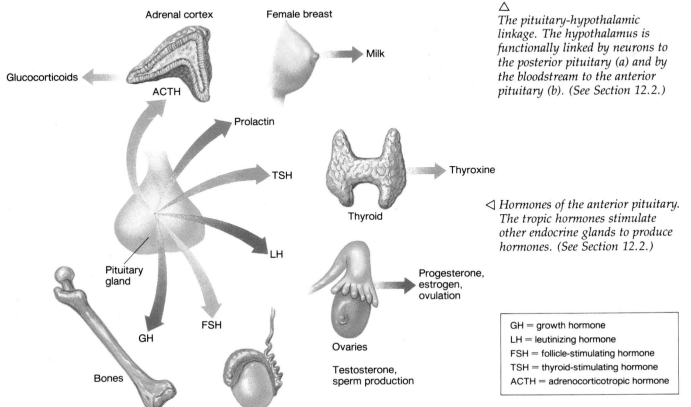

Adrenal cortex

Female breast

Milk

Glucocorticoids

ACTH

Prolactin

TSH

Thyroxine

Thyroid

◁ *Hormones of the anterior pituitary. The tropic hormones stimulate other endocrine glands to produce hormones. (See Section 12.2.)*

LH

Pituitary gland

Progesterone, estrogen, ovulation

FSH

Ovaries

GH

Testosterone, sperm production

Bones

Testes

GH = growth hormone
LH = leutinizing hormone
FSH = follicle-stimulating hormone
TSH = thyroid-stimulating hormone
ACTH = adrenocorticotropic hormone

ENDOCRINE SYSTEM

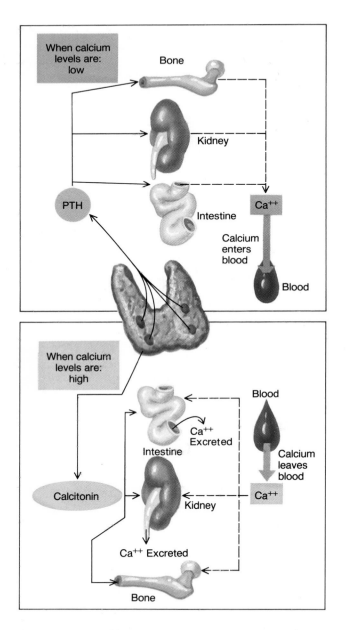

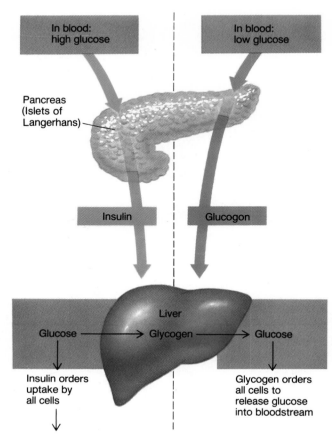

Control of blood sugar concentration by the islets of Langerhans in the pancreas. When blood glucose is high, insulin is secreted, promoting glucose uptake by all cells and storage as glycogen in liver and muscle. Glucagon, produced when blood glucose is low, has the opposite effect. (See Section 12.2.)

Balancing calcium. A low calcium concentration in the blood stimulates PTH secretion by parathyroid glands (shown in green) and inhibits calcitonin secretion by the thyroid gland (in red). A high calcium concentration has the opposite effects. (See Section 12.2.)

CHAPTER SUMMARY

Light behaves as a wave function when it is being transmitted through space, reflected, or refracted. Light being emitted or absorbed behaves as a stream of discrete particles. A particle of light is called a quantum or a photon. The energy content of a photon is inversely proportional to its wavelength.

Pigments are molecules that absorb light. The green pigment, chlorophyll, absorbs light from the sun and produces NADPH and ATP, which in turn supply energy to the Calvin cycle for the synthesis of sugar from CO_2. Chlorophyll is characterized by its absorption spectrum which shows maximum absorption in the blue and red regions of the spectrum. The participation of chlorophyll in photosynthesis may be demonstrated by comparing the action spectrum for photosynthesis with the absorption spectrum for chlorophyll.

The principal function of the light reactions of photosynthesis is to use the energy of sunlight, absorbed by chlorophyll, to reduce NADP and generate ATP.

The NADPH and ATP are in turn used to reduce carbon dioxide to sugar in the Calvin cycle.

The photosynthetic electron transport chain is part of the chloroplast thylakoid membranes and consists of two photosystems, PSI and PSII. PSI and PSII are linked by a chain of electron carriers similar to those found in mitochondria. Each photosystem contains a reaction centre chlorophyll and 40 to 70 antenna chlorophylls. The transport of electrons from water to NADP through linked PSII and PSI is known as non-cyclic electron transport. ATP synthesis that accompanies non-cyclic electron transport is known as non-cyclic photophosphorylation. PSI may also operate independently of PSII, a process known as cyclic electron transport. No NADPH is formed, but ATP is generated by cyclic photophosphorylation. ATP synthesis in the chloroplast is linked to electron transport by an electrochemical proton gradient according to Mitchell's chemiosmotic hypothesis.

Objectives

Having completed this chapter, you should be able to do the following:

1. Discuss the nature of light and explain what happens when a photon is absorbed.
2. Discuss the relationship between an absorption spectrum and an action spectrum.
3. Discuss the concept of a photosynthetic unit.
4. Describe non-cyclic electron transport and explain how its components are organized in the membrane.
5. Describe cyclic electron transport and explain how its components are arranged in the membrane.
6. Show how the chemiosmotic hypothesis explains ATP formation in chloroplasts.

Vocabulary

wavelength
quantum
photon
pigment
absorption spectrum

photo-oxidation
action spectrum
photosynthetic unit
reaction centre
antenna chlorophyll

Emerson enhancement effect
photosystem
non-cyclic photophosphorylation
cyclic photophosphorylation

Review Questions

1. Describe a quantum.
2. Describe the changes a molecule undergoes when it absorbs a quantum of light.
3. Why are chlorophylls green?
4. Distinguish between an action spectrum and an absorption spectrum.
5. How do you determine that chlorophylls are the pigments responsible for absorbing the light which drives photosynthesis?
6. What is the role of accessory pigments in photosynthesis?
7. Describe how a photosynthetic unit functions.
8. What are the principal differences between photosystem I and photosystem II?
9. How does the herbicide, atrazine, kill plants?
10. Distinguish between cyclic and non-cyclic photophosphorylation.
11. What roles does plastoquinone play in photosynthesis?
12. Describe two mechanisms by which a transmembrane proton gradient can be established during photosynthesis.
13. Compare the mechanism for synthesis of ATP in the chloroplast with the mechanism for synthesis of ATP in the mitochondrion (Chapter 5).
14. Identify two practical applications that could arise from the study of photosynthesis.
15. What is the relationship between the light-dependent reactions and the light-independent reactions (Chapter 6) of photosynthesis?

Advanced Questions

1. Why is it possible for P680*, but not P680, to reduce the electron acceptor Q? (Recall the thermodynamic principles introduced in Chapter 5.)
2. Investigators are currently attempting to use techniques of genetic engineering to insert genes for atrazine resistance into certain crop species. Why might this be advantageous?
3. Compare mitochondria and chloroplasts. What are their structural similarities? What are their functional similarities?
4. It is generally known that plants do not, as a rule, grow very vigorously under ordinary fluorescent lighting. Many people who enjoy growing plants indoors will use, instead, fluorescent tubes that are specially formulated for plant growth. The figure shows the spectral output of these two types of lamps. For clarity, the mercury emission lines have been omitted. The solid line represents an ordinary fluorescent lamp, while the dashed line represents the output of a special plant growth light. Use this figure to explain why plants would not be expected to grow well under ordinary fluorescent light, but would grow well when illuminated with the special plant growth lights.

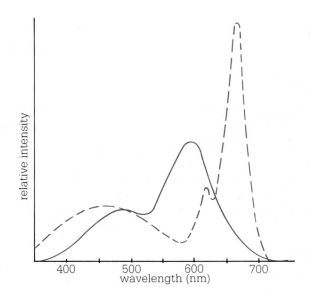

5. Which plant appears to make more effective use of available visible light—a green plant or a red alga? Explain.

CHAPTER 8

PLANTS: THE GREEN MACHINE

*The whole of nature is a trillion,
trillion chemical machines . . .*

H. H. Seliger and W. D. McElroy
Light: Physical and Biological Action

A plant is a sugar factory. The chloroplast is an assembly line. No assembly line operates efficiently unless the entire factory, indeed the entire manufacturing system, is properly organized and functioning in an efficient manner. The supply of raw materials and parts, maintenance of the factory, and delivery of the finished product are all key points to be considered when designing a successful operation. In the previous two chapters, photosynthesis has been considered primarily as a biochemical process. It is an important biochemical process. In fact, despite the great diversity of plant form, the structure and organization of all green plants appear to be designed specifically as photosynthetic machines. Understanding the relationships between structure and function is a major challenge in biology. This chapter will discuss the structure of green plants as it relates to the efficient conduct of photosynthesis.

8.1 DEFINING THE REQUIREMENTS

Photosynthesis requires carbon dioxide, water, light, mineral nutrients, and a transport system. Carbon dioxide and water are, of course, the raw materials of photosynthesis. Water is important also because it forms the milieu in which *all* of the cellular reactions take place. Light is the source of power which drives photosynthesis. A shortage of any one of these three substrates will limit the proceeding of photosynthesis.

All plants require a supply of mineral elements or nutrients. The nutrients are required in order to build and to maintain the chloroplasts and other cellular constituents. Most plants require a minimum of 16 elements for normal growth and development. Three of these elements — carbon, hydrogen, and oxygen — are supplied in the raw materials carbon dioxide and water. Of the remaining 13 elements, seven are required in large quantities and so are called **macronutrients**. They are nitrogen, phosphorus, potassium, sulfur, calcium, iron, and magnesium. The other six nutrients — boron, copper, manganese, cobalt, zinc, and chlorine — are required in very small quantities and are called **micronutrients**. With the exception of carbon, hydrogen, and oxygen, the essential plant nutrients are obtained from the soil or, in aquatic organisms, from the bathing solution.

In a complex, multicellular plant body, there must be a transport system for delivery of the nutrients to the photosynthetic cells and for export of the products of photosynthesis to non-photosynthetic cells. Finally, there must be a means to void the cell of waste products, such as oxygen.

8.2 PHOTOSYNTHESIS IN AQUATIC AND TERRESTRIAL PLANTS

Photosynthesis began in the oceans, early in the history of life on the earth. The first photosynthetic organisms were probably similar to present day photosynthetic bacteria (Chapter 3). These primitive beginnings gave rise to three major groups of photosynthetic plants: unicellular algae, liverworts, and vascular land plants. Each of these three groups represents a different level of structural complexity. Each group must carry out photosynthesis in a unique environment. This section will examine these three groups as photosynthetic machines. You will see how each group satisfies the requirements for photosynthesis within the constraints imposed by the demands of its particular environment.

Algae: Photosynthesis in an Aquatic Environment

Algae make an important contribution to the carbon economy of the earth. It is estimated that algae account for between 50 and 90 percent of the photosynthesis on this planet! Some of this photosynthetic activity is due to beds of kelp and other large seaweeds which grow in the shallow coastal waters and some is due to the microscopic, single-celled algae distributed across the surface of the oceans.

Water is not a limiting factor for photosynthesis in a single-celled alga (Figure 8.1) since the cells are bathed in it. The free exchange of water across the cell boundary is governed only by the principles of osmosis. Moreover, less than one percent of the water taken up by the cell is actually used in all biochemical reactions, including photosynthesis. The rest of the water makes up the bulk of cellular protoplasm.

Carbon dioxide and mineral nutrients are dissolved in the water which bathes the cells and may be taken directly into the cell by active transport across the cell membrane. However, the supply of both carbon dioxide and mineral nutrients frequently limits aquatic photosynthesis. The concentration of carbon dioxide in the earth's atmosphere is relatively low — about 350 parts carbon dioxide per million parts of air (or 0.035 percent by volume). Atmospheric carbon dioxide is made available to the alga by first dissolving in the water and then diffusing through the water to the cell surface. Solubility of carbon dioxide is not a problem

Figure 8.1
Cross section of a single-celled alga (Chlamydomonas). The dominant feature of the cell is a large, cup-shaped chloroplast.

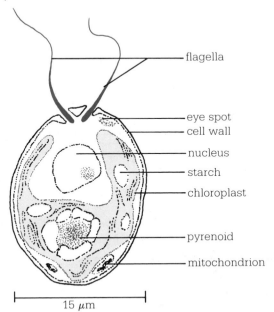

Figure 8.2
Diffusion of carbon dioxide in water is much slower than in air.

since carbon dioxide freely dissolves in water to about 10 ppm. However, diffusion of carbon dioxide through water is very limited (Figure 8.2). In fact, the rate of diffusion of carbon dioxide in water is about one ten-thousandth of its rate of diffusion in air. Because carbon dioxide diffuses so slowly in water, a single-celled alga actively consuming carbon dioxide in photosynthesis might easily use up carbon dioxide more rapidly than it could be replenished from the air. Fortunately for most algae, this potential problem is largely alleviated by wave action and other forms of turbulence. The constant turnover of the water serves to bring fresh supplies of dissolved carbon dioxide and mineral nutrients to the cell. Therefore, the cell is not dependent simply upon diffusion of carbon dioxide from the surface.

Water turbulence also assists in the removal of oxygen, a by-product of photosynthesis. It is necessary to remove oxygen since high concentrations of oxygen can inhibit photosynthesis in many species.

The availability of light frequently limits photosynthesis in aquatic organisms. In the first place, a single-celled alga presents a very small target for light. Second, natural bodies of water contain dissolved and suspended matter which cause light to be absorbed or scattered. Consequently, light cannot penetrate very

deeply into most bodies of water. This is one of the reasons that algae are found almost exclusively in the shallow waters over the continental shelves or in the surface waters of deep lakes and oceans. Few algae are able to grow in deeper water where light is generally inadequate for photosynthesis. Those which do grow at greater depths, such as some red algae, are able to do so only because they have pigments which can utilize blue-green light (Chapter 7). Light from the blue-green portion of the spectrum penetrates more deeply into water than does red light.

Liverworts: The Invasion of Land
At some point in evolution, certain plants made a successful attempt to invade land. Biologists believe that plants called liverworts exhibit many features of those primitive land-dwellers. Liverworts are small, leafless, green plants which measure 2 cm to 3 cm across. They are commonly found growing on moist soils and are early colonizers in regions which have been burned over by fire. The name liverwort arose from the times of the early herbalists who believed that the flattened plant bodies with lobes resembling those of the human liver would be useful in treating ailments of that organ.

Figure 8.3
A liverwort (Marchantia)

Figure 8.4
Cross section of a liverwort thallus (Marchantia)

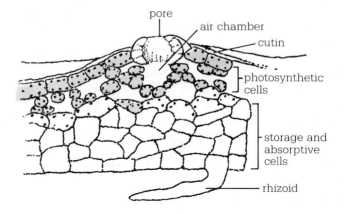

One representative liverwort is the genus *Marchantia* (Figure 8.3). The flattened, lobed, but leafless body (called a thallus) of *Marchantia* lies prostrate on the soil. The upper surface of the thallus appears to be divided into polygonal segments. Each segment reflects the division of the interior of the thallus into a series of air chambers (Figure 8.4). In the centre of each segment is a pore which opens into the air chamber below. The cells which make up the walls and "roof" of the chamber contain chloroplasts and, hence, are photosynthetic. Within each chamber are a number of upright, branching columns of photosynthetic cells. Below the air chambers is a group of cells which make up the bulk of the thallus and contain few, if any, chloroplasts. These cells probably function primarily in the storage of photosynthate (products of photosynthesis) from the photosynthetic cells above. The lowermost layer of cells is an epidermis with projecting **rhizoids**. Rhizoids are lower surface cells with extensions which penetrate and anchor the thallus to the soil.

Liverworts illustrate two major themes which have emerged throughout the evolutionary history of plants — exploitation of light and protection against water loss. The flattened, spreading thallus of the liverwort provides a particularly effective surface for intercepting light and maximizing photosynthesis. It is similar in principle to the large arrays of solar cells which intercept light energy to provide power for satellites orbiting in space (Figure 8.5).

Although the liverwort effectively maximizes interception of light, the broad exposed surface also enhances potential water loss. Water is essential to life. All organisms are dependent on a supply of water

Figure 8.5
A satellite with solar panels. The large area of the solar panels maximizes interception of light.

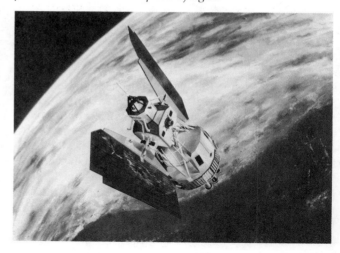

for their very existence. Terrestrial environments are particularly hostile to life because water so readily evaporates into the surrounding air. In *Marchantia*, evaporation of water from the exposed upper surface of the thallus is restricted by a layer of **cutin**. Cutin is a waxy substance which is impermeable to water. It is also impermeable to carbon dioxide, which could have a serious impact on photosynthesis, but this is remedied by the presence of pores in the upper surface of the thallus. Air moves freely through the pores, so that every photosynthetic cell in the thallus, even those inside the chamber, has immediate access to atmospheric carbon dioxide. In this case, the restricted movement of carbon dioxide through water is limited to the relatively short distance between the cell surface and the chloroplast itself. Liverworts exhibit the first signs of compromise in the need to balance access to light and carbon dioxide against the competing tendency toward water loss.

In spite of their multicellular nature, liverworts require no specialized transport system. They obtain nutrients by direct absorption into the epidermal cells or through the rhizoids. Since the thallus is relatively small, no cell is more than about 15 cells distant from the absorptive cells. Similarly, non-photosynthetic cells are only a few cells away from the nearest photosynthetic cells. The cell-to-cell movement of nutrients and photosynthetic product over such short distances imposes no serious limitations.

Vascular Plants: Photosynthesis in a Hostile Environment

The **vascular plants** include the familiar angiosperms (flowering plants) and the gymnosperms (for example, conifers). These plants are characterized by extensive vascular (conducting) tissues known as the **xylem** and **phloem**. The success of vascular plants in colonizing the terrestrial habitat is amply evident from your surroundings. In temperate and tropical regions of the world, vascular plants are a dominant feature in the landscape. Their success is at least in part due to their highly successful exploitation of light. They have also developed some rather interesting and effective ways to protect the photosynthetic cells against desiccation (water loss).

With a spreading, prostrate form, liverworts live in what is essentially a two-dimensional world. Vascular plants, on the other hand, occupy a three-dimensional world. Liverworts are limited in the number of individuals that may inhabit a given area. As more individuals crowd into an area, their thalli will overlap and compete for available light, nutrients, and carbon dioxide. The photosynthetic capacity and growth of the shaded thalli will naturally be reduced as light becomes less available. The successful invasion of terrestrial habitats by vascular plants was accompanied by the development of three major organ systems— stems, roots, and leaves. In an evolutionary sense, the stem functions to separate the photosynthetic organs (leaves) from the absorptive organs (roots). The stem elevates the leaves into an aerial environment, away from the soil surface and away from direct competition with other leaves or organisms for light (Figure 8.6).

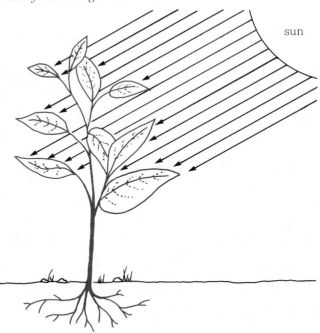

Figure 8.6
The aerial form of vascular plants reduces shading of the photosynthetic organs (leaves).

At the same time, the absorptive tissues, the roots remain anchored in the moist soil and continue to supply the plant with water and nutrients. Conducting tissues in the stem facilitate the long-distance transport of water and nutrients from the roots to the leaves. The leaves, in turn, supply the root system with carbon and energy in the form of carbohydrate produced by photosynthesis.

The vascular tissue is continuous from the tip of the root to the edge of the leaf. In the leaf, the strands of vascular tissue branch out into smaller and smaller veins, much like the capillaries of the mammalian circulatory system. The result is that no photosynthetic cell in the leaf is more than two or three cells distant from the principal transport tissues of the plant (Figure 8.7). Both delivery of nutrients to the photosynthetic cells and removal of the photosynthate is rapid and efficient.

Compared with the moist habitat in which liverworts thrive, the environment surrounding aerial leaves of vascular plants is particularly hostile. Vascular plants have developed some interesting structural features which enable them to balance photosynthetic requirements with protection against water loss. The rest of this chapter will focus on some of those distinctive features.

Figure 8.7
Pattern of vascular tissue in a leaf. The network of small veins brings transport tissues close to the photosynthetic cells.

8.3 GAS EXCHANGE BY LEAVES

There are striking similarities between the anatomical features of a vascular plant leaf (Figure 8.8) and those of a liverwort thallus (Figure 8.4). There are also some very significant differences. Unlike the liverwort, the photosynthetic cells in the interior of the leaf are separated from the carbon dioxide in the surrounding air by a layer of **epidermal cells** on both the upper and lower leaf surfaces. These epidermal cells are not photosynthetic and are coated with an impermeable waxy layer, the **cuticle**. The cuticle (composed of cutin) serves the extremely important function of preventing evaporation of water from the epidermal cells. The epidermal cells in turn protect the underlying photosynthetic **mesophyll cells**. As in liverworts, the cuticle of vascular plant leaves is impermeable to both water vapour and carbon dioxide. If carbon dioxide is prevented from crossing the cuticle, how does the carbon dioxide reach the photosynthetic cells in the interior of the leaf?

Figure 8.8
Three-dimensional section of a vascular plant leaf

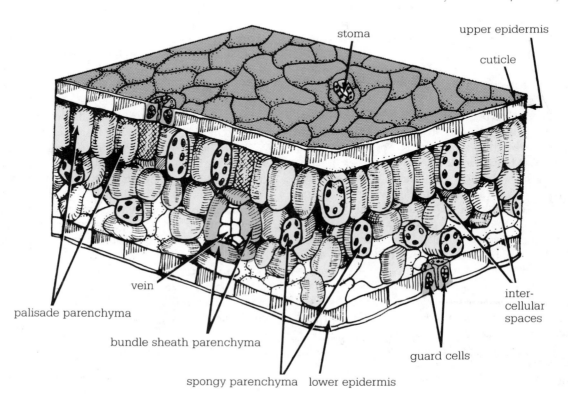

Figure 8.9
Scanning electron micrograph of guard cells on the bottom surface of a maple leaf

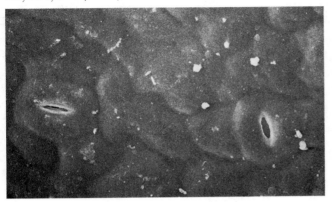

Carbon Dioxide Uptake

Just as in liverworts, all gas exchange between the leaf and its surrounding environment, including exchange of carbon dioxide, is accomplished through pores in the leaf surface. Leaves contain large intercellular air spaces which border the photosynthetic mesophyll cells. These spaces open into external environment through the pores in the leaf surface. In higher plants, these pores are called **stomates**. Each stomate is bordered by a pair of specialized epidermal cells called *guard cells* (Figure 8.9). The guard cells are able to open or close, thus regulating the size of the stomatal opening.

The evolution of stomates is considered one of the most important structural innovations that enable plants to adapt to the aerial habitat. When open, carbon dioxide enters the leaf to satisfy photosynthetic requirements. On the other hand, when water loss threatens the essential water status of the leaf, the guard cells reduce the size of the opening or close down entirely and thus prevent further water loss.

Movement of carbon dioxide into the leaf through the open stomates is remarkably efficient. The aggregate area of the stomates when fully open is generally no more than one to two percent of the total area of the leaf, yet it has been estimated that diffusion of carbon dioxide into the leaf can exceed by some 50 to 70 times the rate expected on the basis of the area of the open stomates alone. In fact, experiments with artificial, perforated septa have confirmed that movement of gases through small pores is indeed far more rapid than can be accounted for on the basis of area alone. Before attempting to discuss this paradox, it would be useful to review the process of diffusion.

Diffusion

Diffusion is the *directed* movement of molecules from a region of high concentration to a region of lower concentration (Figure 8.10). It results from the *random* motion of molecules, which is a manifestation of the average kinetic energy of the molecules. Although the focus of this discussion is the movement of gases, diffusion applies equally well to the movement of molecules in solution.

The rate and direction of movement of individual molecules is not predictable. The direction and rate of movement of a *population of molecules* is, however, predictable so long as certain measurable parameters are known. These parameters are summarized in the general law of diffusion, known as *Fick's Law*. Fick's Law may be stated mathematically as:

$$J = -DA \, (dc/dx)$$

Figure 8.10
Before diffusion, molecules are concentrated in the left chamber (a). There is a high probability that molecules will pass through the opening into the right chamber. Random motion causes a net movement of molecules into the right chamber. Net movement will cease when there are equal numbers of molecules in each chamber and when the probability that molecules will pass through the opening in either direction is the same (b).

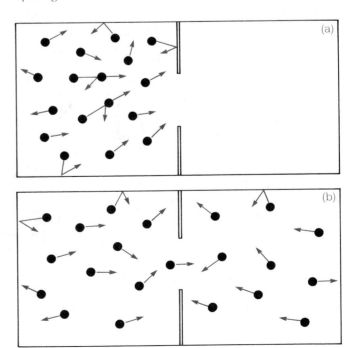

The symbol J stands for the rate of diffusion, or, the quantity of a substance that moves through an area of 1 cm² in one second. The term dc/dx is known as the *concentration gradient*. It expresses the difference in concentration (dc) of the diffusing substance over the length of the diffusion path (dx). A is the cross sectional area of the diffusion path and D is a proportionality constant called the diffusion coefficient. Fick's Law tells us that the rate of diffusion of a substance is directly proportional to the difference in concentration and to the cross sectional area of the diffusion path, but is inversely proportional to the length of the diffusion path. A large concentration difference over a short distance would be considered a steep diffusion gradient. A steep diffusion gradient favours a high rate of diffusion, or a large value of J. A small difference in concentration over a long distance would be considered a shallow diffusion gradient. A shallow diffusion gradient favours a low rate of diffusion, or a small value of J.

Diffusion Through Small Pores

According to Fick's Law, diffusion is directly proportional to the area of the diffusion path. When a gas diffuses through small pores, however, the rate is proportional not to the area but to the diameter. This apparent discrepancy from Fick's Law can be explained by the diagrams in Figure 8.11. When molecules diffuse from a large open surface, mutual interference of adjacent molecules forces them to follow parallel paths. Over small pores, the diffusing molecules fan out to form a *diffusion shell*. The dashed contour lines in Figures 8.11(b) and (c) represent regions of equal concentrations, decreasing outward from the pore. The length of the diffusion path is determined by the distance between contour lines. Note that the length of the diffusion path is directly proportional to the *diameter* of the pore, and molecules diffusing from near the perimeter of the pore experience a shorter diffusion path length than those diffusing from the centre of the pore.

Small pores have a higher perimeter to area ratio than large pores. This is because the area decreases with the *square* of the radius while the perimeter decreases in direct proportion to the radius. As a result of this trend, diffusion from the perimeter becomes more significant with smaller pore diameters. In other words, with smaller pores a larger proportion of the molecules diffusing through the pores do so by the *shorter, more rapid* path. This phenomenon of high dif-

Figure 8.11
Molecules diffusing from an open surface (a) follow parallel paths. Over small pores (b and c) the length of the diffusion path is proportional to the diameter of the pore. Note that the pore diameter in (b) is twice that in (c).

(a)

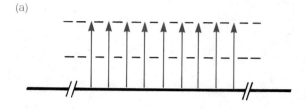

(b)

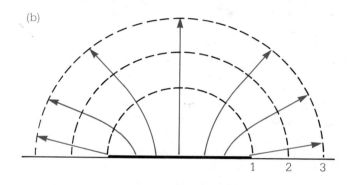

(c)

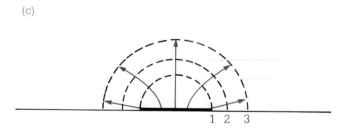

fusive capacity of small pores is commonly known as the *perimeter effect*.

The above model applies best to an ideal septum with a circular pore. Most stomates, however, are elliptical in shape, especially in the partially open condition. This factor probably contributes to an even larger perimeter effect and proportionately larger gas exchange in leaves. Spacing of the pores is also important. If the pores are separated by about twelve diameters or less, adjacent diffusion shells begin to overlap and the advantages of pore size and the perimeter effect are lost. It is interesting to note that stomates are usually separated by an average about 15 to 20 diameters!

Transpiration

As any home gardener or farmer can attest, an efficient architecture for carbon dioxide uptake by the leaf is not without penalty. A design which is efficient for the diffusion of carbon dioxide into the leaf will also allow efficient movement of water vapour out of the leaf (Figure 8.12). Plants can lose extraordinarily large amounts of water. It has been estimated, for example, that a single, mature maple tree can lose as much as 250 kg of water in an hour. A hectare of hardwood forest may lose 75 000 kg in a year. Over a growing season, a stand of corn may lose enough water to cover an area of a hectare to a depth of 52 cm! Most of this water (probably 90 percent) is lost as water vapour through open stomates, a process known as **transpiration**.

Water lost by transpiration actually evaporates at the surface of the mesophyll cells surrounding the air space within the leaf. The water vapour subsequently diffuses through the stomates into the surrounding air. The diffusion gradient for water vapour is normally much steeper than it is for carbon dioxide. At 21°C and 50 percent relative humidity, for example, the diffusion gradient for water out of the leaf is some 40 times greater than the diffusion gradient for carbon dioxide into the leaf!

Water loss by transpiration is enhanced by any condition that influences the steepness of the vapour pressure gradient between the interior of the leaf and the surrounding air. Since the interior air space is always saturated with water vapour, both higher ambient air temperature and lower relative humidity outside the leaf will steepen the diffusion gradient and encourage more rapid transpiration. Air movement also steepens the diffusion gradient by sweeping away the accumulated water vapour on the surface of the leaf. It is not difficult to see that when the stomates are open to admit carbon dioxide and the leaf is actively carrying out photosynthesis, the potential for water loss also becomes very high. The rate of water loss may at times exceed the rate at which it can be replenished from the soil and the plant will tend to wilt. Closure of the stomates will normally prevent further water loss and allow recovery. However, if water loss is extremely severe, recovery may not be possible and the plant will die.

Regulating Water Loss

Water loss from the leaf is regulated by stomatal opening and closure. When carbon dioxide is not required for photosynthesis or under conditions of extreme

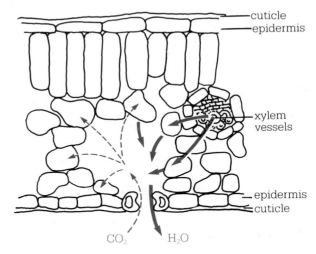

Figure 8.12
When stomates are open to admit carbon dioxide for photosynthesis, water vapour is free to move from the substomatal air space into the atmosphere.

cuticle
epidermis
xylem vessels
epidermis
cuticle
CO_2 H_2O

water stress, the stomates will close. Stomatal opening and closure is known to be under the control of both environmental and internal factors. Stomates are normally open during the daylight hours and closed at night. High concentrations of carbon dioxide inside the leaf also stimulate closure. Light and carbon dioxide appear to interact in the following way. In the light, carbon dioxide is rapidly consumed by photosynthesis in the mesophyll cells adjacent to the air chamber. This lowers the internal carbon dioxide concentration and stimulates stomatal opening. In darkness, however, carbon dioxide is not consumed by photosynthesis and carbon dioxide will accumulate in the substomatal space due to continued respiration of the leaf cells. The resulting high internal carbon dioxide concentration stimulates closure of the stomates.

Closure of the stomates will also occur under conditions of extreme water stress, even in light. Stomatal closure in the light will, of course, cut off the carbon dioxide supply and effectively shut down photosynthesis. This is a compromise which is sometimes necessary for survival.

One of the more perplexing problems in plant biology concerns the mechanism which regulates the movement of the guard cells. Although this problem has been studied for decades, there is still not a completely satisfactory answer. It is known that the driving force for guard cell movement is the osmotic flow of water between the guard cells and the surrounding epidermal cells. There are two special features of the guard cells which account for this behaviour. Each guard cell has a thickened cell wall in the region adjacent to the stomatal pore and special, inelastic fibres which encompass the cell and prevent expansion in the radial dimension (Figure 8.13). When water moves from the surrounding epidermal cells into the guard cells, the guard cell walls expand and the cells become turgid. The heavy wall and accompanying fibres, however, resist expansion, causing the opposing guard cells to ''buckle'' and an opening to appear between them. Conversely, when water is lost by the guard cells, the cells become flaccid, the thickened walls relax and the stomate closes.

Many different theories have been proposed to account for the movement of water between the guard cells and adjacent epidermal cells. More recent evidence favours an ATP-dependent, active transport of potassium ions. It can be shown that, under conditions which favour stomatal opening, potassium moves into the guard cells from the surrounding epidermal cells. The resulting increase in the osmotic potential of the guard cells stimulates the uptake of water and the cells become turgid. Under conditions favouring stomatal closure, the potassium returns to the epidermal cells and the guard cells lose water. Stomatal guard cells, unlike other epidermal cells, contain chloroplasts. It is assumed, although not yet proven, that the energy (in the form of ATP) needed to drive potassium movement is provided by the photosynthesis in the chloroplasts of the guard cells.

Role of Transpiration

Transpiration is a major source of atmospheric water vapour and thus plays a significant role in the earth's water cycle. Interference by humans in the process could result in serious global consequences. Large-scale deforestation, such as that ongoing in tropical regions of South America, may well lead to significant changes in global water economy and climate.

Is there any positive advantage to be gained by the plant itself from the movement of such large amounts of water? This question has generated considerable discussion among plant physiologists. One idea which appears to have some merit is that transpiration helps to dissipate excess energy from the leaf. A leaf fully exposed to the sun absorbs far more energy than can be used in photosynthesis (Figure 8.14). The additional energy may cause the temperature of the leaf to exceed that of the surrounding air by as much as 5°C. If the leaf were not able to dissipate this excess energy, leaf temperatures could reach even higher and poten-

Figure 8.13
A model of a pair of guard cells. The tape represents inelastic cellulose fibres which restrict expansion of the cell in the radial dimension. When the balloons are relaxed (flaccid) as in (a), the stomate is closed. When the balloons are inflated (turgid) as in (b), the stomate is open.

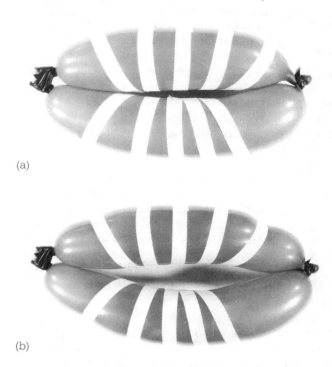

(a)

(b)

Figure 8.14
Only a small proportion of the energy absorbed by a leaf is actually used in photosynthesis.

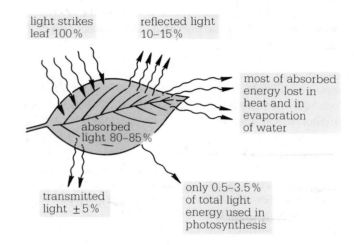

light strikes leaf 100%

reflected light 10–15%

most of absorbed energy lost in heat and in evaporation of water

absorbed light 80–85%

transmitted light ±5%

only 0.5–3.5% of total light energy used in photosynthesis

tially lethal levels. Some excess heat may be dissipated by convection or re-irradiation to the environment. However, a significant amount appears to be consumed by the evaporation of water from the mesophyll cells. A second possibility is that transpiration assists in the distribution of dissolved minerals throughout the plant. Minerals are brought into the xylem through the roots and will be carried in the transpiration stream (section 8.4). It has been observed, however, that minerals will continue to move throughout the plant even when the plant is not transpiring. Both of these apparent advantages may be coincidental. Many scientists are forced to conclude that transpiration is a necessary evil. It is simply an unavoidable consequence of the need to maintain adequate gas exchange for photosynthesis in a terrestrial habitat.

While the opening and closure of stomates is the principal way to regulate water economy, many plants have developed other morphological or biochemical adaptations which further reduce water loss. Some species, especially those that live in exceedingly dry habitats, have developed heavy cuticles and thick, fleshy leaves to store extra water. An extreme example is the cacti, in which the leaves have been reduced to thorns and large quantities of water are stored in the thick, photosynthetic stem. In other plants, the stomates are sunken below the epidermis, thus lengthening the diffusion path, or are surrounded by hairs which trap an insulated area of water-saturated air. A particularly interesting adaptation to dry habitats is seen in those plants which open their stomates at night when the air is cool and the opportunity for water loss is minimal. The carbon dioxide taken in during the night is stored in the form of organic acids. During the daylight hours, the stomates are closed in order to prevent water loss but photosynthesis proceeds as the stored carbon dioxide is released inside the leaf.

8.4 ASCENT OF SAP

A plant undergoing rapid transpiration will require substantial amounts of water to replace that lost by the leaf. The long-distance transport of sap (water and dissolved minerals) between the roots and leaves or other aerial organs is accomplished through that portion of the vascular tissue known as xylem (Figure 8.15). This complex tissue is comprised of two major types of conducting cells, **vessels** and **tracheids**. The precise organization of the xylem will vary from spe-

Figure 8.15
Cross section of a stem showing the relative positions of the vascular tissues, xylem and phloem

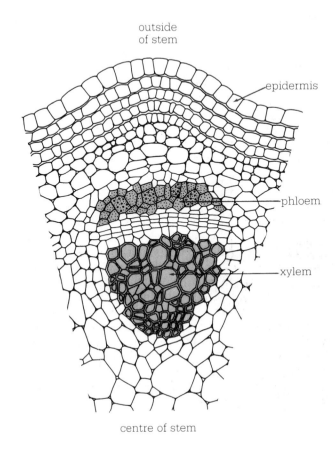

cies to species but the characteristic vessels and tracheids are consistent in all species. Vessels and tracheids are joined both end to end and laterally through open spaces or perforation plates in the cell walls (Figure 8.16). Mature, functional xylem vessels and tracheids are also devoid of protoplasm. These specialized conducting elements thus provide a continuous, interconnected pipeline of non-living cells through which water may be carried from the tips of growing roots through the stem to the lateral margins of leaves and other organs.

It was pointed out earlier that large volumes of water move through the plant, sometimes to great heights. What is the mechanism for water movement in a plant? How are water columns maintained in tall plants? Atmospheric pressure alone will not suffice, since the height of a water column due to atmospheric pressure alone is limited to 10.4 m (Figure 8.17).

Figure 8.16
Vessel members and tracheids. A vessel is composed of many vessel members joined end to end. Vessels may reach lengths of up to 3 m in some species.

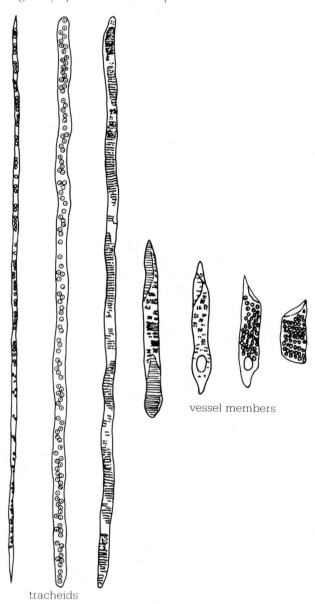

tracheids

vessel members

Figure 8.17
Atmospheric pressure can maintain a column of water to a maximum height of 10.4 m.

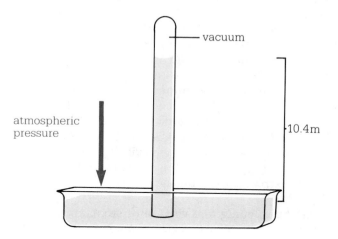

vacuum

atmospheric
pressure

10.4m

According to the *Guinness Book of World Records* (1985 edition), the tallest living tree is the Howard Libby *Sequoia* in northern California. Its height is estimated to be 110.3 m. Woodcutters have reported *Eucalyptus* trees in Australia and Douglas fir trees in British Columbia in excess of 125 m. Any general theory that attempts to explain water movement in plants must therefore account for rapid water movement in trees exceeding 125 m in height. To maintain a water column of 125 m would require a minimum pressure 12 times the atmospheric pressure. Perhaps an additional pressure of equivalent magnitude would also be required to overcome the frictional resistance encountered by the column of water in the narrow xylem vessels. Clearly some other forces must be involved.

In 1894, an Irish botanist, H. H. Dixon, and his colleague J. Joly, a physicist, proposed what has come to be known as the Dixon-Joly **cohesion-tension hypothesis**. This hypothesis suggests that two basic forces account for the ascent of sap—a *driving force* and the *cohesive force of water*. The driving force is evapo-transpiration, or more precisely, the difference in the chemical potential of water which exists between the soil and the atmosphere. Water, like any other chemical system, will tend to flow from a region of high chemical potential to a region of low chemical potential. The chemical potential of water is often identified as *water potential*.

A familiar example of water movement due to differences in water potential is the phenomenon of *osmosis*. A demonstration of osmosis is shown in Figure 8.18. When a solution of sucrose in water is separated from pure water by a selectively permeable membrane, a net movement of water into the sucrose solution will occur. This occurs because the chemical potential of pure water is higher than the chemical potential of water in the sucrose solution. The net

Figure 8.18
A demonstration of osmosis

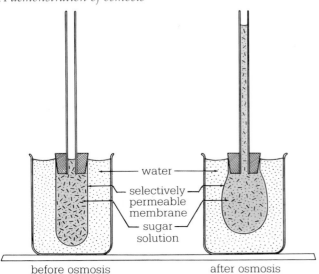

before osmosis   after osmosis

Figure 8.19
The soil–plant–atmosphere water system. There is a continuous gradient in water potential from the soil to the atmosphere. Values for water potential are given in mega pascals (MPa) relative to pure water, which is zero.

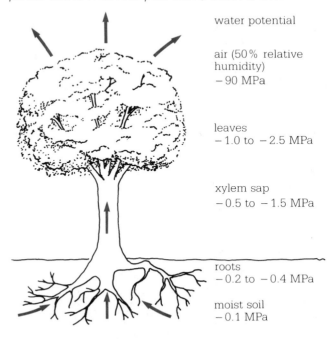

water potential

air (50% relative humidity)
−90 MPa

leaves
−1.0 to −2.5 MPa

xylem sap
−0.5 to −1.5 MPa

roots
−0.2 to −0.4 MPa

moist soil
−0.1 MPa

movement of water in this example will continue until other factors, such as the hydrostatic pressure generated by the weight of the water column, cause the water potential to equalize on both sides of the membrane. In a similar manner, the water potential of air saturated with water vapour is greater than that of air which is less than saturated. An example is the diffusion of water vapour from a substomatal air chamber into the surrounding atmosphere. In fact, the soil, plant, and atmosphere together may be considered a single system with a continuous gradient of decreasing water potential from the soil to the atmosphere (Figure 8.19). Water lost by evaporation from mesophyll cells in the leaf is ultimately replaced by the uptake of water from the soil. This results in a continuous stream of water moving from the soil through the xylem system into the atmosphere. The water column is maintained intact, especially in larger trees, because of the large cohesive force of water. The cohesive force of water is due to hydrogen bonding between adjacent water molecules.

The cohesion-tension theory has not been extensively tested in large trees, principally because plants of that size do not easily lend themselves to experimentation. However, the pull of transpiration can be demonstrated in physical models as illustrated in Figure 8.20. Evaporation of water from a porous clay cup will pull a column of mercury higher than can be expected on the basis of atmospheric pressure alone. The same phenomenon can be demonstrated when the porous clay cup is replaced by a leafy branch.

Figure 8.20
A demonstration of transpiration pull. Evaporation of water from a porous clay cup (a) or a leafy shoot (b) will pull the mercury up the glass capillary tube.

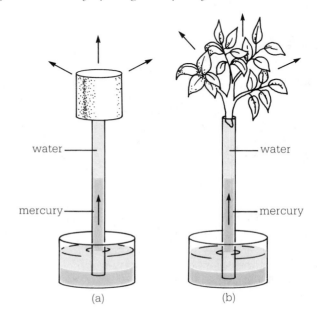

water

mercury

water

mercury

(a)   (b)

Other experiments have demonstrated that the cohesive force of water in capillary columns may exceed 31.4×10^3 kPa, a force more than enough to maintain a column of water in the tallest known trees.

Additional evidence in support of the cohesion-tension theory is obtained by demonstrating that the xylem stream in actively transpiring plants is under tension. By using very sensitive instruments, it can be shown that the diameter of large trees actually decreases during periods of active transpiration (Figure 8.21). It can also be shown by microsurgery that, when a xylem vessel is severed, the cut water column snaps apart. Both of these observations support the theory that the water column being pulled up through the plant by evaporative forces in the leaf is under tension.

Figure 8.21

Daily variations in the diameter of a tree. Small changes in diameter can be measured with a sensitive dendrometer. Minimum diameter is seen in mid-afternoon, when transpiration would be most active. This experiment demonstrates that the water column in the trunk is under tension when transpiration is occurring.

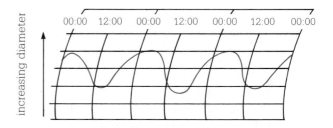

THE SUGAR FACTORY

Every year in late winter, maple trees throughout southern Canada and northeastern United States appear to sprout pails (or plastic tubing)! A pungent odour of wood smoke fills the air as the sugary sap collected from the xylem is boiled down to make maple syrup. The flow of xylem sap occurs in many trees at this time of year, but the sugar maple (*Acer saccharum*) is most popular because of its high sugar content and distinctive flavour.

Sap flows because of a positive pressure which develops in the xylem. The xylem solution does not normally contain large amounts of sugar and, in actively transpiring plants, is usually under tension.

The flow of sap in late winter represents a special case. It occurs before the leaves emerge, usually during periods of alternating cold nights and warm days. Low temperature at night stimulates the enzymatic breakdown of starch, which is stored in xylem parenchyma cells, to glucose. The glucose is actively transported into the adjacent vessels. Warm days then raise the temperature of the xylem solution, causing a release of dissolved carbon dioxide and thereby creating a positive pressure. The sugary solution is forced up the tree, providing energy and nutrients to the growing buds. Or, if the xylem is tapped, the sap is forced instead into the pail to begin its trip to the sugar shack.

8.5 TRANSPORT OF PHOTOSYNTHETIC PRODUCT

The sugars produced by photosynthesis in the leaves must be transported from the photosynthetic mesophyll cells to other tissues and organs in the plant that are not capable of carrying out photosynthesis. Here they are either used directly as a source of energy and carbon for metabolism and growth or stored for future use. The targets for transport of the photosynthate may be regions of active growth and development such as stem tips and developing flowers or fruits, or they may be storage tissues in the stem or roots.

Phloem Sieve Tubes

Transport of sugar and other organic solutes occurs in the **sieve tube** cells of the phloem (Figure 8.22). Individual sieve tubes are connected end to end through structures known as **sieve plates**. Unlike xylem vessels, functional sieve tube elements are living cells filled with cytoplasm. Moreover, the perforations in the sieve plates are much smaller than those in the end walls of the xylem vessels and are filled with strands of cytoplasm. Clearly, transport through the phloem presents some unique problems. Since phloem sieve tubes are living cells, transport in the phloem cannot be explained in purely mechanical terms as in the case of xylem transport.

A great deal of the knowledge of transport in the phloem has originated from insect physiologists who were studying aphid nutrition. Aphids are insects which feed on plants by inserting a long mouthpart (stylet) into individual phloem sieve tubes (Figure 8.23). The insect physiologists were interested in

Figure 8.22
As its longitudinal section (a) shows, the phloem sieve tube is flanked by a companion cell and a phloem parenchyma cell. In the face view of the sieve plate (b), the dark spots shown are actually holes filled with strands of cytoplasm which connect adjacent sieve tubes.

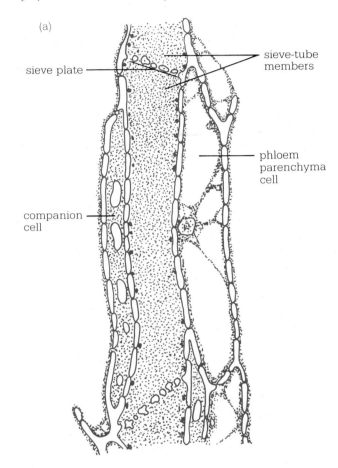

Figure 8.23
Aphids feeding on the stem of a Spirea *plant. The insect inserts its stylet into an individual phloem sieve tube.*

knowing whether the phloem sap was actively sucked up by the aphids or whether it was passively forced into their body by positive pressure within the sieve tubes. They did an experiment in which the feeding aphids were anesthetized with a stream of carbon dioxide and the stylet carefully severed with a razor blade. It was observed that the phloem sap continued to exude from the cut stylet for up to four days. Plant physiologists now make use of this phenomenon to obtain pure phloem sap from individual phloem sieve tubes. This technique has proven very beneficial for studies of phloem transport.

Contents of Phloem Sap

Approximately 90 percent of the dry material of phloem sap (that is, excluding water) is carbohydrate. In most plants, this is sucrose or a closely related sugar. The balance of phloem sap is comprised largely of nitrogen-rich compounds such as amino acids and alkaloids. Alkaloids are a heterogeneous group of compounds containing at least one nitrogen atom. The alkaloids have no known function in the plants which produce them, but many are used as drugs in animals. Nicotine (from cultivated tobacco), caffeine (coffee beans and tea leaves), morphine (a pain killer from opium poppy), and the highly toxic atropine (from deadly nightshade) are some common examples of the several thousand alkaloids known from over 4000 species of plants.

Rate of Phloem Transport

Sieve tubes constitute a very small proportion of the total cross sectional area of a stem, yet remarkably large amounts of organic solute can move through the phloem. One convenient method for estimating the quantity of material that moves through the phloem is to monitor the growth of rapidly growing fruits such as pumpkins. In one such experiment (Figure 8.24), the average gain in mass of pumpkins was 482 g of *dry material* over 33 days. This means that the material (mostly sucrose) moved through the pumpkin stem at an average rate of 0.61 g/h. The average area of cross section of the phloem sieve tubes in the stem was estimated to be 3.72 mm². The material thus had to move through the sieve tubes with a mass transfer rate of 0.164 (g/mm²)/h. In addition, the velocity of movement, that is, the distance traversed by a molecule per unit time, was calculated to be 1.1 m/h. More refined studies using radioactively labelled sugars have confirmed rates of this order of magnitude, although actual mass transfer rate and velocity may vary from species to species or with the substance being transported and the time of day.

Figure 8.24

Volume of transport in the phloem. If the phloem sap is equivalent to a ten percent sucrose solution, the sieve tubes would deliver an average of 6.1 mL/h to the growing pumpkin.

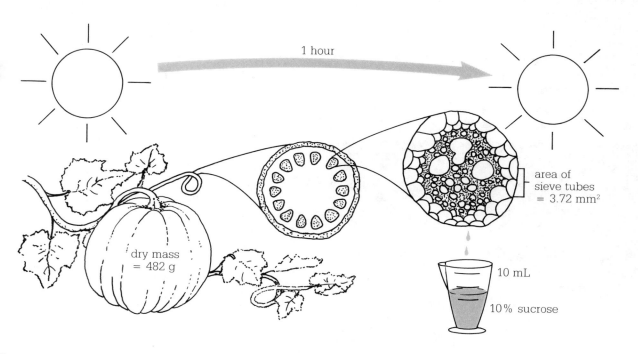

1 hour

area of
sieve tubes
= 3.72 mm²

dry mass
= 482 g

10 mL

10% sucrose

Direction of Phloem Transport

The direction of transport in the phloem has long been an area of some controversy. The traditional view held that transport in the phloem was restricted to the downward direction. However, it is now clear that transport in the phloem occurs both downward and upward (Figure 8.25). It has also been observed that movement in adjacent sieve tubes may be in the opposite direction or that movement in a single sieve tube may periodically reverse.

Mechanism of Phloem Transport

The most widely accepted hypothesis that explains transport in the phloem is known as the **Münch Pressure-Flow hypothesis** (Figure 8.26). This hypothesis suggests a mass flow of water and solute through the sieve tubes along a pressure gradient. In the leaf, which can be considered a *source*, sucrose produced by photosynthesis is loaded into the phloem. Since sucrose is an osmotically active solute, water will also enter the sieve tube by osmosis. Elsewhere in the plant (for example, a rapidly growing fruit), sucrose is actively withdrawn from the phloem, lowering the solute concentration at that end of the sieve tube. The fruit may be considered a *sink*. Here the water will move out of the sieve tube by osmosis. Movement of water *into* the phloem in the leaf establishes a high hydrostatic pressure at the source. At the same time, water movement *out of* the phloem in the developing fruit maintains a low hydrostatic pressure at the sink.

The water movement in and out at opposite ends of the sieve tube, and the consequent hydrostatic pressure gradient, cause a bulk flow of water between the source and the sink. Any dissolved solute would naturally be swept along with the bulk flow of water. So long as the pressure difference is maintained between the source and the sink, the bulk flow of water and solute will continue.

The relationship between source and sink as suggested in the pressure-flow hypothesis explains the bi-directional movement in the phloem. It is only required that different combinations of source and sink be connected by different series of sieve tubes. Moreover, a young rapidly expanding leaf may function as a sink and draw upon photosynthate from other sources. As it matures, this leaf will itself begin to overproduce sugars and thus serve as a source for sinks developing elsewhere in the plant.

Figure 8.25
Direction of sucrose transport in the phloem. The length of the arrows indicates the relative amount of sucrose transported in each direction.

Figure 8.26
Pressure-flow hypothesis for transport in the phloem. Sucrose is loaded into the sieve tube in the leaf (source) and is withdrawn in a root or developing fruit (sink). Transfer of sucrose into the sieve tube is accompanied by the osmotic uptake of water. The resulting hydrostatic pressure gradient establishes a mass flow of sieve tube contents. Water returns through the xylem vessel.

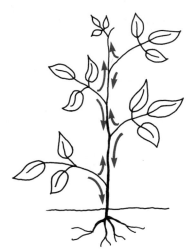

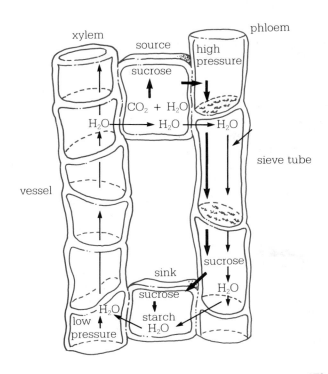

CHAPTER SUMMARY

Photosynthesis requires a supply of carbon dioxide, water, mineral nutrients, adequate light, and a transport system. The structure of the plant may be considered in light of these needs. In the evolutionary history of plants, two major themes have emerged — the exploitation of light and the protection against water loss. The innovation of the stem with its accompanying vascular transport tissue has permitted vascular plants to occupy the aerial habitat, thereby reducing direct competition with other species for light and carbon dioxide while maintaining contact with the water and nutrient supply in the soil. The epidermal cells of leaves are covered with a waxy cutin which prevents water loss from the leaf surfaces, but at the same time also prevents the uptake of carbon dioxide. Carbon dioxide is admitted through pores in the leaf called stomates. Stomates are bordered with specialized epidermal cells called guard cells which can close the pores to prevent escape of water vapour from the surfaces of the mesophyll cells. The driving force for guard cell opening and closure is the osmotic flow of water into and out of the guard cells in response to movement of potassium ions. Diffusion of both carbon dioxide and water vapour through the small stomatal pores is very efficient, one factor which accounts for the very large amounts of water which move through plants. Water lost from the leaf is replaced from the soil through xylem vessels or tracheids. The cohesive force of water is the principal factor responsible for maintaining the continuous column of water in the xylem. Sugars produced by photosynthesis in the leaves are transported to storage tissues or regions of active growth through the phloem sieve tubes. The pressure-flow hypothesis explains the movement in the phloem.

Objectives

Having completed this chapter, you should be able to do the following:

1. List the principal requirements for photosynthesis.
2. Describe unicellular algae, liverworts, and vascular plants as photosynthetic machines.
3. Discuss gas exchange by leaves and explain why diffusion through stomates is so efficient.
4. List the factors which influence transpiration and describe how vascular plant leaves regulate transpirational water loss.
5. Describe the Dixon-Joly cohesion-tension hypothesis and show how it explains water movement through tall trees.
6. Describe the Münch pressure-flow hypothesis and show how it explains sugar transport in the phloem.
7. Define source and sink and describe how the relationship between source and sink determines the direction of sugar transport in the phloem.

Vocabulary

macronutrient	epidermal cell	vessel
micronutrient	cuticle	tracheid
rhizoid	mesophyll cell	cohesion-tension hypothesis
cutin	stomate	sieve tube
xylem	diffusion	sieve plate
phloem	transpiration	Münch Pressure-Flow hypothesis

Review Questions

1. What conditions must be satisfied in order for an a green plant to carry out photosynthesis?
2. What contribution do algae make to the total photosynthesis on the earth?
3. Describe the limitations imposed by the supply of carbon dioxide on photosynthesis.
4. Describe the organization of a liverwort thallus.
5. In what way are liverworts and the leaves of vascular plants similar to a space satellite?
6. What special feature characterizes a vascular plant?
7. Describe one evolutionary significance of a plant stem.
8. How do guard cells regulate gas exchange in a leaf?
9. Describe the role played by potassium ions in regulating stomatal opening and closure.
10. What is Fick's Law?
11. What is the contribution of the "perimeter effect" to the supply of carbon dioxide for photosynthesis in a leaf?
12. Which is a steeper diffusion gradient, the gradient of carbon dioxide into the leaf or the water vapour gradient out of the leaf?
13. What are three possible roles for transpiration?
14. Describe one theory that accounts for the movement of water in tall trees.
15. Describe the mass flow hypothesis for transport of sugars in the phloem.

Advanced Questions

1. Horticulturalists recommend that evergreen trees should be watered thoroughly in the fall before the ground freezes. Why?
2. The leaves of many plants have large numbers of stomates on their lower surfaces but few or none on their upper surfaces. Why?
3. The growth of a fruit is dependent on the amount of photosynthate that can be transported to it. How could you encourage a fruit tree to produce larger fruits?
4. Corn plants have been bred with leaves at an angle to the stem of approximately 45°. This morphology allows the corn plants to be planted very close together and gives the highest possible yields per hectare. How does this morphology encourage maximum yields? Would yields improve if the leaves were more vertical? Explain your answers.

CHAPTER 9

PHOTOSYNTHESIS AND THE ENVIRONMENT

Greater stability of food production can be achieved by manipulating both crops and their environment.

Sylvan H. Wittwer

In Chapter 6 you learned that the following balanced equation summarizes the overall photosynthetic process in higher plants.

$$6CO_2 + 12H_2O \xrightarrow[\text{chloroplasts}]{\text{light}} C_6H_{12}O_6 + 6O_2 + 6H_2O$$

As this equation indicates, photosynthesis is an endergonic process, that is, an energy input is required to convert carbon dioxide to glucose. The ultimate source of this energy, of course, is the sun. This energy is received by the plant in the form of electromagnetic radiation which can be described as packages of light energy, called *photons*. The chloroplast is able to convert this energy into biologically useful forms, ATP and NADPH, by the *light-dependent* electron transport system of the chloroplast thylakoid membrane. Without light, no ATP or NADPH can be generated which, in turn, would eliminate the ability of autotrophic organisms to convert carbon dioxide to glucose. Thus, the conversion of carbon dioxide to glucose in higher plants has an absolute requirement for light. Obviously, carbon dioxide is another important requirement for photosynthesis. For land plants, this comes from the surrounding air. At the present time, the approximate concentration of carbon dioxide in the air is 0.03 percent or 300 ppm. The net conversion of carbon dioxide to glucose depends upon the ability of plants to integrate the light-dependent reactions of ATP and NADPH formation with the energy-consuming reactions involved in the conversion of six one-carbon molecules of carbon dioxide to one six-carbon molecule of glucose.

Environmental factors such as light intensity and the amount of carbon dioxide available in the air may influence the rate at which a plant consumes carbon dioxide and produces oxygen and carbohydrates. Another important environmental factor which influences photosynthesis is temperature. Enzyme-catalyzed reactions are temperature sensitive, that is, their reaction rates are affected by the temperature. Therefore, ambient temperature will influence the rate at which a plant converts carbon dioxide to glucose. In this chapter, you will learn how these environmental factors affect the capacity of a plant to photosynthesize. In addition, you will learn how higher plants modify the mechanism of photosynthetic carbon dioxide assimilation as they adapt to life in different environments, and relate these modifications to their geographic distribution.

9.1 MEASUREMENT OF PHOTOSYNTHESIS

You can see from the balanced chemical equation for the photosynthetic process that six molecules of carbon dioxide are consumed and six molecules of oxygen are evolved for each molecule of glucose produced. Therefore the ratio of the number of moles of carbon dioxide consumed to the number of moles of oxygen evolved during the formation of one mole of glucose theoretically should be one. You can determine the rate of photosynthesis by measuring either the *light-dependent* rate of carbon dioxide uptake from the surrounding air or the *light-dependent* rate of

Figure 9.1

The first reaction of carbon fixation incorporates radioactive-labelled carbon into a molecule of phosphoglycerate (PGA).

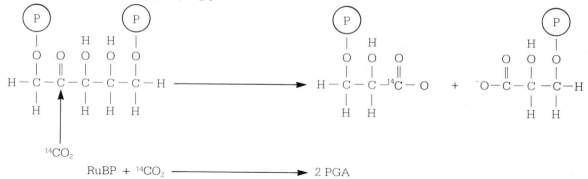

$$RuBP + {}^{14}CO_2 \longrightarrow 2\ PGA$$

oxygen evolution into the surrounding air. In other words, you can measure rates of photosynthesis by measuring the rates of gas exchange between the green plant and its surrounding environment.

If you do an experiment using radioactive-labelled carbon dioxide ($^{14}CO_2$), you can measure the rate of uptake of carbon-14 and at the same time trace the metabolic fate of the carbon dioxide taken up (Figure 9.1). By determining the order of appearance of radioactively labelled compounds during photosynthesis, Melvin Calvin and his associates worked out the sequence of the reactions in carbon fixation. Calvin received the Nobel Prize in 1961 for this work.

All living organisms, including green plants, take up oxygen and evolve carbon dioxide through *mitochondrial respiration* which is independent of light (Chapter 5). In addition, C_3 plants actively take up oxygen and evolve carbon dioxide by the process of *photorespiration* which is light-dependent (Chapter 6). Conversely, photosynthesis results in the light-dependent uptake of carbon dioxide and the light dependent evolution of oxygen. The gas exchanges due to photosynthesis are therefore opposite to the gas exchanges due to mitochondrial respiration and photorespiration (Figure 9.2). Thus, when you measure gas exchange in a plant, you are actually measuring the *net gas exchange* of the plant. This is expressed in the following word equations.

net CO_2 uptake = photosynthetic CO_2 uptake − photorespiratory CO_2 evolution − respiratory CO_2 evolution

net O_2 evolution = photosynthetic O_2 evolution − photorespiratory O_2 uptake − respiratory O_2 uptake

In later sections, you will examine how environmental factors such as light intensity, carbon dioxide concentration, and temperature affect photosynthetic gas exchange.

Figure 9.2

Gas exchanges in the leaf of a C_3 plant

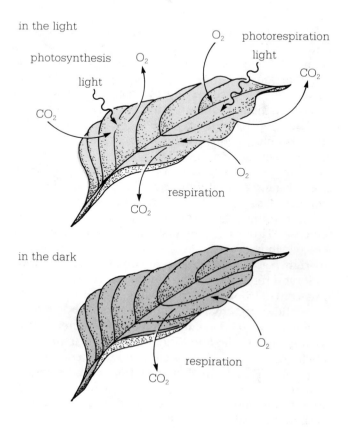

$$6CO_2 + 12H_2O \xrightarrow[chloroplast]{light} C_6H_{12}O_6 + 6O_2 + 6H_2O$$

9.2 INFLUENCE OF LIGHT INTENSITY ON RATE OF PHOTOSYNTHESIS

For any biological process consisting of a series of interdependent reactions, the rate at which the overall process can occur will be limited by the rate of its slowest component reaction. This reaction is the *rate-limiting reaction* (Figure 9.3).

Figure 9.3

Principle of rate-limiting reactions. The conversion of compound A to compound E occurs through a series of four reactions. Reaction 1, 2, and 4 occur very quickly whereas reaction 3 occurs very slowly. The rate at which A can be converted to E cannot occur any faster than the rate at which the slowest reaction proceeds. Thus, reaction 3 is the rate-limiting reaction for the overall conversion of compound A to compound E.

$$A \xrightarrow[(1)]{fast} B \xrightarrow[(2)]{fast} C \xrightarrow[(3)]{slow} D \xrightarrow[(4)]{fast} E$$

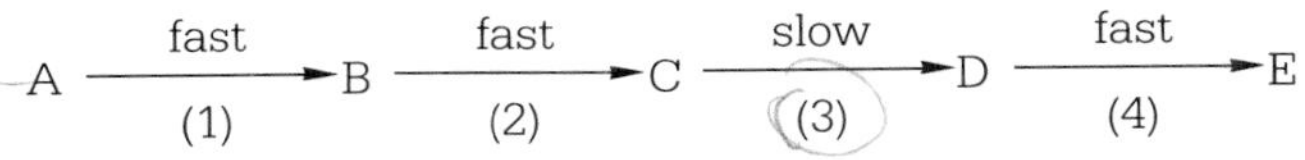

The graph in Figure 9.4 illustrates the effect of light intensity, that is, the amount of light per leaf area, on the rate of photosynthesis which is measured as the rate of *net carbon dioxide uptake*. The data were collected under conditions of constant carbon dioxide concentration (300 ppm) and constant temperature (20°C). At low light intensities, that is, light intensities less than X (Figure 9.4), the rate of net carbon dioxide uptake increases linearly with the increase in light intensity. You can say that the rate of net carbon dioxide uptake is directly proportional to light intensity at all light intensities less than X. Within this range, net carbon dioxide uptake is *light limited*. The reason for this is that at low light intensities, the biochemical reactions in the stroma of the chloroplast are consuming ATP and NADPH, in the conversion of carbon dioxide to carbohydrate, faster than the light-dependent reactions of the thylakoid membrane can produce them. As illustrated in Figure 9.5, this means that the rate of the reactions (b) exceeds the rate of the reactions (a). Thus, at low light intensities, the photochemical reactions (a) limit the overall rate of photosynthesis. The light intensity at which the rate of net carbon dioxide uptake is zero (W in Figure 9.4) is called the **light compensation point**.

As light intensity increases beyond X (Figure 9.4), the rate of net carbon dioxide uptake continues to increase but subsequently levels off at Y. At light intensities greater than Y, the graph shows that

Figure 9.4

Effect of increasing light intensity on net carbon dioxide uptake in C₃ plants

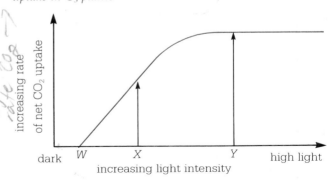

Figure 9.5

Interdependence of the photochemical reactions and the carbon dioxide fixation reactions of photosynthesis

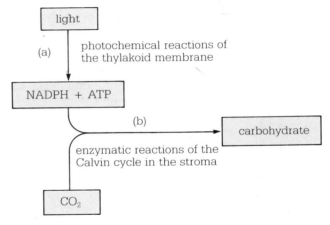

increasing the light intensity no longer affects the rate of net carbon dioxide uptake. Thus, we can say that at light intensities greater than Y, the rate of net carbon dioxide uptake is maximum and is *independent* of light intensity. At the outset, this may seem somewhat perplexing. How can photosynthesis suddenly become independent of light intensity? Now, at high light intensities, ATP and NADPH are produced in abundant amounts by the light-dependent reactions of the thylakoid membrane. The rate at which carbon fixation consumes ATP and NADPH is less than the rate at which they are produced. This means that, in Figure 9.5, the rate of reactions (a) exceeds the rate of reactions (b). Therefore, at high light intensity, it is the rate of carbon dioxide fixation (b) that limits the overall rate of carbon dioxide uptake. At light intensities greater than Y, photosynthesis is said to be *light saturated*.

179

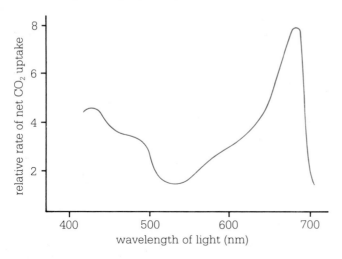

Figure 9.6
An action spectrum for photosynthesis

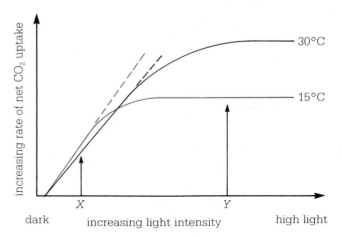

Figure 9.7
Effect of temperature on rate of net carbon dioxide uptake in C_3 plants

9.3 INFLUENCE OF LIGHT QUALITY ON RATE OF PHOTOSYNTHESIS

The graph in Figure 9.4 illustrates the effect of the intensity of *white* light on the rate of photosynthesis. What effect would you observe on the rate of photosynthesis if you used light of different colours instead of white light? The results of such an experiment can be graphed to obtain an *action spectrum* (Chapter 7). As illustrated in Figure 9.6, the light quality or wavelength to which the plant is exposed also has a marked influence on the rate of net carbon dioxide uptake. The highest rates of photosynthesis generally occur in the blue (400 nm to 500 nm) and red (600 nm to 700 nm) regions of the visible spectrum. The shape of the action spectrum is very similar to the absorption spectrum of chlorophyll (Chapter 7). This indicates that it is these pigments found in the chloroplast thylakoid membrane that absorb the light required for the uptake and fixation of carbon dioxide in higher plants.

9.4 INFLUENCE OF TEMPERATURE ON RATE OF PHOTOSYNTHESIS

The rates of thermochemical reactions increase as the temperature increases. This is because molecules have higher kinetic energy, and therefore move faster, at high temperature than at low temperature, which increases the probability that molecules will collide and cause a reaction to occur. However, all biological reactions exhibit limits with respect to the temperature range to which they can be exposed and still proceed normally. For example, at extremely high tempera-

tures (greater than 50°C), many enzymes will denature and become inactive, causing the corresponding biochemical reactions to stop. Thus, you can increase the rate of photosynthesis by increasing the temperature as long as it is within a biologically acceptable temperature range (10°C to 40°C). As shown in Figure 9.7, the maximum or light-saturated rate of net carbon dioxide uptake is increased as the temperature is increased from 15° to 30°C. Remember that under conditions of light-saturation, photosynthesis is limited by the rate at which the carbon dioxide fixation consumes ATP and NADPH. Raising the temperature allows these reactions to proceed faster, thus increasing net carbon dioxide uptake in the plant.

Photosynthetic efficiency can be defined as the amount of net carbon dioxide taken up per unit of light energy absorbed. This can be determined by calculating the *initial slope* of the graph of rate of net carbon dioxide uptake versus light intensity as shown in Figure 9.7 (dotted lines). The initial slope is greater at 15°C than at 30°C, that is, the photosynthetic efficiency for the C_3 plant is greater at 15°C than at 30°C. Why is this so? In C_3 plants such as wheat, spinach, and tobacco, the rate of light-dependent photorespiration (Chapter 6) increases more rapidly than photosynthesis as the temperature increases (Figure 9.8). Thus, at higher temperatures, there is less carbon dioxide taken up by photosynthesis relative to the increased release of carbon dioxide through photorespiration. Therefore, at higher temperatures the net carbon dioxide uptake per unit of light absorbed is less than at lower temperature in most C_3 plants.

Figure 9.8
Temperature dependence of photosynthesis and photorespiration in C₃ plants. The ratio of photosynthesis to photorespiration is higher at lower temperatures.

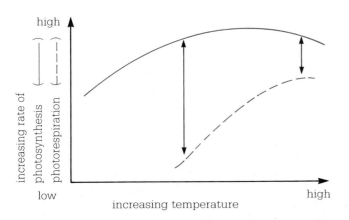

Figure 9.9
Effect of oxygen and carbon dioxide concentrations on rate of net carbon dioxide uptake

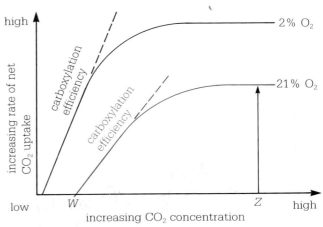

9.5 INFLUENCE OF CARBON DIOXIDE AND OXYGEN CONCENTRATION ON RATE OF PHOTOSYNTHESIS

Carbon dioxide is a primary substrate for photosynthesis. As the carbon dioxide concentration increases under constant temperature and saturating light conditions, the rate of photosynthesis increases steadily up to a certain concentration (Z in Figure 9.9) beyond which the rate of photosynthesis levels off and becomes independent of carbon dioxide concentration. The conversion of carbon dioxide to carbohydrate is enzyme catalyzed. As you learned in Chapter 6, the enzyme Rubisco catalyzes the initial carbon dioxide fixation step of the Calvin cycle. All enzymes exhibit the property of *substrate saturation*. This means that there is a maximum amount of substrate that an enzyme can consume per unit time. Thus, in Figure 9.9, Rubisco has become saturated for its substrate, carbon dioxide, at carbon dioxide concentration greater than Z. Under these conditions, photosynthesis is said to be *carbon dioxide saturated*. The carbon dioxide concentration W at which no net carbon dioxide uptake is observed is called the *carbon dioxide compensation point*. At this concentration of carbon dioxide, the rate of carbon dioxide uptake due to photosynthesis is exactly offset by carbon dioxide evolution due to mitochondrial respiration and photorespiration.

The maximum rate of net carbon dioxide uptake can be increased in a C₃ plant by reducing the amount of oxygen present. As illustrated in Figure 9.9, not only is the maximum rate of net carbon dioxide uptake increased when the amount of oxygen is reduced from 21 percent to 2 percent, but the carbon dioxide compensation point is shifted to a lower carbon dioxide concentration and the initial slope of the curves increases.

What do these changes indicate about photosynthesis under conditions of low oxygen? In Chapter 6, you learned that the initial carboxylation reaction in C₃ plants is catalyzed by Rubisco which can utilize both carbon dioxide and oxygen as substrate. When Rubisco fixes oxygen, phosphoglycolate is produced which is the primary substrate for photorespiration. Thus, if the level of oxygen available is reduced relative to carbon dioxide, less carbon dioxide is evolved by photorespiration while the plant is actively photosynthesizing. This raises the maximum rate of net carbon dioxide uptake in C₃ plants. Because more carbon dioxide will be fixed per unit of carbon dioxide available in the surrounding air under conditions of low oxygen concentration, the initial slope of the graph of net carbon dioxide uptake versus carbon dioxide concentration is greater (Fig. 9.9). Thus, the *carboxylation efficiency*, which is defined as the number of moles of carbon dioxide fixed per mole of carbon dioxide available, increases as the oxygen concentration in the air decreases because photorespiration is preferentially inhibited under these conditions. The next section describes two specific photosynthetic adaptations in certain plant species which, by reducing photorespiration, have resulted in an increased capacity to fix carbon dioxide.

181

ALTERNATIVE PATHWAYS FOR THE FIXATION OF CARBON DIOXIDE

Plant species such as spinach, tobacco, and wheat exhibit C_3 *type metabolism* whereby the enzyme Rubisco catalyzes the formation of the initial product of carbon dioxide fixation—a three-carbon organic acid, phosphoglycerate (Chapter 6). However, not all plant species utilize this reaction exclusively for the fixation of carbon dioxide. Most plants also contain an enzyme, phosphoenolpyruvate carboxylase (PEPCase), which catalyzes the formation of a four-carbon molecule, oxaloacetate, from three-carbon phosphoenol pyruvate (PEP) and carbon dioxide. The capacity to utilize PEPCase as the primary reaction for carbon dioxide fixation is especially prevalent in agriculturally important plants such as corn, sugar cane, and sorghum as well as many weedy species such as crabgrass. These plants exhibit C_4 *metabolism*, and hence, are called C_4 plants.

The different metabolic pathways for carbon dioxide fixation in C_3 and C_4 plants are also reflected in characteristic differences in leaf anatomy. In the leaves of C_4 plants, each vascular bundle is surrounded by a layer of large bundle sheath cells whose chloroplasts contain the enzyme Rubisco. Carbon dioxide fixation reactions take place in these cells. The bundle sheath cells are, in turn, surrounded by a layer of smaller mesophyll cells which can contain large amounts of PEP-Case but no Rubisco. This spatial arrangement of mesophyll and bundle sheath cells is termed *Kranz* (German word meaning halo) *anatomy*. In contrast, the carbon dioxide fixation reactions take place in the chloroplasts of all *spongy mesophyll* and *palisade cells* in C_3 plants.

Comparison of leaf anatomy of C_3 and C_4 plants

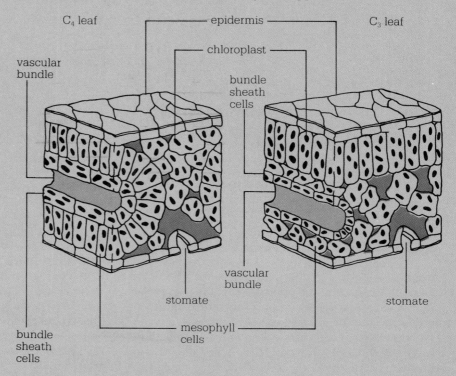

Initial carboxylation reaction in mesophyll cells of C_4 plants

$$\text{phosphoenol pyruvate} + CO_2 \longrightarrow \text{malate}$$
$$(C_3) \qquad\qquad\qquad\qquad (C_4)$$

What advantage does this unique cellular arrangement and mode of carbon dioxide fixation impart to C_4 plants? Bundle sheath cells contain the enzyme Rubisco and therefore have the potential to evolve carbon dioxide through photorespiration. The carbon dioxide released by bundle sheath cells is trapped within the leaf by the enzyme PEPCase in the surrounding mesophyll cells which convert it into malate. The malate is, in turn, transported back to the bundle sheath cells. Thus, in C_4 plants, photorespiratory release of carbon dioxide from leaves is virtually absent or occurs at extremely low rates. As a consequence, C_4 plants exhibit extremely low carbon dioxide compensation points. The diagrams below compare the fates of carbon dioxide in C_3 and C_4 leaves.

Comparison of fates of carbon dioxide in C_3 and C_4 leaves

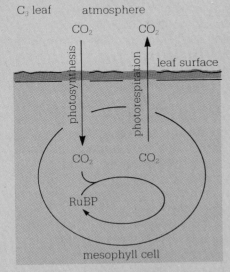

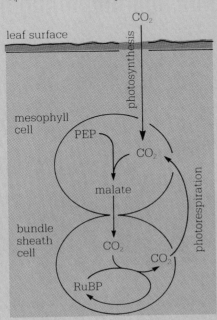

Plants from the family *Crassulaceae* such as cacti also have adapted an alternative mechanism of fixing carbon dioxide, called *Crassulacean acid metabolism* (CAM). The biochemical pathway for the fixation of carbon dioxide that these plants use is virtually identical to that in C_4 plants. Both CAM and C_4 plants store carbon dioxide in the form of malate for later use. However, there is one very important difference. In C_4 plants, the synthesis of malate and its subsequent conversion to pyruvate and carbon dioxide occur in two physically separate compartments, the mesophyll cells and

Temporal separation of metabolic events for carbon dioxide fixation in mesophyll cells of CAM plants

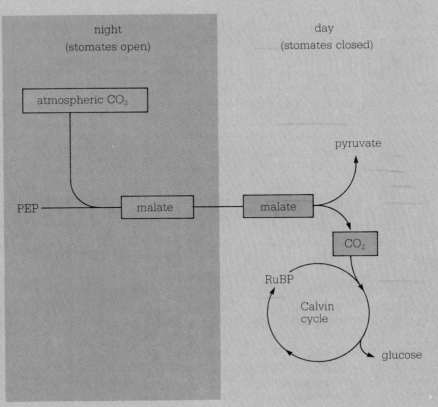

bundle sheath cells. In CAM plants, these two processes are not physically separated but are separated in time. At night, the stomates of CAM plants are open and carbon dioxide is initially fixed by the conversion of PEP to malate by PEPCase. With stomates closed during the day, the carbon dioxide is released from malate and the carbon dioxide is converted to glucose in the chloroplasts by Rubisco and the Calvin cycle reactions. You will learn more about why CAM plants keep their stomates closed during the day in the next section.

9.6 ECOLOGICAL SIGNIFICANCE OF PHOTOSYNTHETIC ADAPTATIONS

The alternative pathways for carbon dioxide fixation have significant consequences with respect to the natural geographic distribution of different types of plants. C_3 plants are found in greater abundance in cooler climates of the temperate regions where the availability of water is not usually a limiting environmental factor. In contrast, C_4 photosynthesis has generally evolved in plant species adapted to areas of high temperature, high light, and limited water supply such as tropical and subtropical grasslands. Plants such as cacti, from the family *Crassulaceae*, have adapted the Crassulacean acid metabolism (CAM) method of carbon dioxide fixation (see box on preceding pages). CAM plants are generally succulent, that is, they have fleshy stems and leaves used for water storage and are found in habitats such as deserts which are too dry for most other higher plants.

What is the relationship between C_4 and CAM photosynthesis and the fact that these plant species are typically associated with hot dry habitats? All forms of life require a source of water to live. In vascular plants, water is taken up by the roots and travels through the vascular system to the leaves. Water is drawn through the vascular system by the process of *transpiration* (see chapter 8). Water is forced or "pulled" through the vascular system by the evaporation of water through the leaf stomates. Stomates therefore regulate gas exchange as well as transpiration. Under conditions where water is limited, such as those found in hot, dry environments, the plant must prevent excess water loss by transpiration in order to survive. The rates of transpiration will be greater at high light intensities and high temperatures. To reduce water loss a plant theoretically could close its stomates. However, the plant must open its stomates to photosynthesize. In attempts to overcome this paradox, C_4 plants have evolved an efficient mechanism for fixing carbon dioxide under conditions of high temperature such that photorespiration is virtually eliminated. This allows C_4 plants to maximize photosynthetic efficiency and at the same time minimize water loss due to transpiration.

CAM plants have adapted to the hot desert environment in quite a different way. They keep their stomates open during the cool desert nights when water loss due to transpiration is minimal. During the night, carbon dioxide is fixed and stored in the form of malate. During the hot day, CAM plants close their stomates to prevent water loss and carbon dioxide is removed from malate in the chloroplasts and refixed by the Calvin cycle to produce carbohydrates. Since the stomates are closed during the day, photorespiratory loss of carbon dioxide is minimal. Again, this allows for maximum photosynthetic efficiency and minimum water loss due to transpiration. Since C_3 plants typically exist in habitats where water is *not* a limiting factor, excess water loss through transpiration will not have a significant impact on photosynthesis.

C_4 plants typically exhibit higher photosynthetic rates (net carbon dioxide uptake) than those observed for C_3 plants at high temperatures. This is primarily due to the fact that photorespiration in C_3 plants results in the release of about 40 percent of the carbon dioxide taken up by photosynthesis. Photorespiratory loss of carbon dioxide is virtually absent in C_4 plants. Thus, it would appear that C_4 plants are more efficient at converting carbon dioxide to carbohydrate than C_3 plants. However, this is true only under conditions that favour C_4 photosynthesis, that is, under conditions of high temperature and high light intensity (Figure 9.10). This is why corn grows best during hot summers but does not grow well under cool conditions. Similarly, crabgrass infestations of lawns are always worst during hot, dry summers. Under these conditions, the crabgrass (C_4) out-competes the C_3 grasses that make up most lawns.

Figure 9.10

Comparison of photosynthetic efficiency in C_3 and C_4 plants as a function of temperature

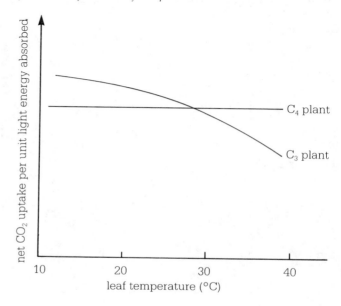

Under environmental conditions that favour C_3 plants, that is, cooler temperatures, C_4 plants are less efficient at converting carbon dioxide to carbohydrate than C_3 plants. Thus, C_4 plants are at a disadvantage in cool habitats whereas C_3 plants are at a disadvantage in hot, dry habitats. However, C_3 and C_4 plants can co-exist in habitats where neither has a noticeable edge in photosynthetic efficiency.

9.7 GLOBAL CARBON BALANCE

The emergence of photosynthetic organisms about 3.4 billion years ago completely changed the face of the earth. By converting carbon dioxide to larger organic molecules, these organisms gradually reduced the high levels of carbon dioxide present in the atmosphere. This reduction helped to cool the earth's surface because atmospheric carbon dioxide can trap heat which causes the so-called **greenhouse effect**. The cooling of the earth's surface led to an increase in the size of the polar ice caps, thus lowering sea levels and exposing new terrestrial habitats.

The simultaneous actions of photosynthesis and respiration constitute the *carbon cycle* (Figure 9.11). The carbon cycle illustrates how all life on the earth is ultimately linked to the energy of the sun. Autotrophic organisms fix carbon dioxide in carbohydrates. All organisms eventually consume these photosyntheti-cally derived carbohydrates and break them down by respiration which leads to the release of carbon dioxide back into the atmosphere. It is estimated that about 136 billion tonnes of carbohydrates are generated each year by the photosynthetic process. Eighty to ninety percent of this is produced by *phytoplankton* (aquatic plant life). The rest is produced by terrestrial plants. It is this continuous recycling of carbon dioxide and oxygen that maintains the very delicate ecological balance on which all organisms, including humans, depend. That is why unrestricted burning of fossil fuels or large-scale deforestation should not be allowed. These processes would significantly affect the global carbon balance, causing more carbon dioxide to be released into the atmosphere than can be consumed by photosynthesis.

Figure 9.11

The carbon cycle. Most photosynthetic organisms fix carbon dioxide into larger organic molecules and release oxygen in the presence of sunlight. The organic molecules represent the ultimate source of metabolic energy of all organisms. In the presence of oxygen, these molecules are broken down by the process of cellular respiration, and carbon dioxide is released back into the atmosphere. Oxygen is also used up in the burning of fossil fuels derived from dead organisms.

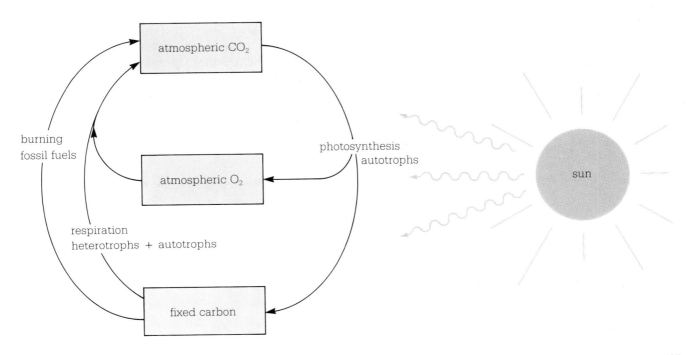

CHAPTER SUMMARY

The rate of photosynthesis in higher plants can be conveniently determined by measuring the rate of carbon dioxide gas exchange in the leaf. Both the quality as well as the quantity of light available to the plant can affect the rate of photosynthesis. At low light intensities, it is the light-dependent production of ATP and NADPH that limits the overall rates of photosynthesis. However, at high saturating light intensities, it is the rate of the light-independent reactions that limits the overall rates of photosynthesis. The light-saturated rate of photosynthesis can be increased by increasing the temperature. This occurs because the rate of the light-independent Calvin cycle reactions is higher at higher temperatures. The carbon dioxide–saturated rate of photosynthesis and the carboxylation efficiency can be increased by decreasing the oxygen concentration. This occurs because the rate of photo-respiration becomes minimal at low oxygen levels.

C_4 and CAM plants exhibit alternative pathways of carbon dioxide fixation which minimize carbon dioxide losses due to photorespiration. This is accomplished by specific biochemical and anatomical adaptations. These photosynthetic adaptations enable C_4 and CAM plants to minimize water loss during photosynthesis. The different photosynthetic pathways largely determine the ecological distribution of C_3, C_4, and CAM plants. The simultaneous activities of photosynthesis and respiration maintain the global carbon cycle. All organisms, including humans, are dependent upon the continuous recycling of carbon dioxide and oxygen to maintain the delicate ecological balance.

Objectives

Having completed this chapter, you should be able to do the following:

1. Describe three ways to measure the rate of photosynthesis.
2. Describe the net gas exchange processes in a C_3 plant in the light and in the dark.
3. Describe the processes that limit net carbon dioxide uptake at low and high light intensities.
4. Describe how temperature can influence the light-saturated rate of net carbon dioxide uptake as well as photosynthetic efficiency.
5. Describe how carbon dioxide and oxygen concentrations can influence the maximum rate of net carbon dioxide uptake as well as the carboxylation efficiency.
6. Explain how C_4 and CAM plants minimize the loss of carbon dioxide due to photorespiration.
7. Discuss the relationships between the mode of carbon dioxide fixation and the ecological distribution of C_3, C_4, and CAM plants.
8. Discuss the ecological importance of the global carbon cycle.

Vocabulary

light compensation point
photosynthetic efficiency
greenhouse effect

Review Questions

1. (a) Describe the net leaf gas exchange in a C_3 plant that is exposed to light.
   (b) Describe the net leaf gas exchange for the same plant kept in the dark.
2. Write a word equation to illustrate the net leaf gas exchange in a C_3 plant in the light.
3. Describe the principle of rate-limiting reactions.
4. In a gas exchange experiment, you determined that the rate of net carbon dioxide uptake by the leaf of a C_3 plant was 20 μmol of carbon dioxide taken up per hour per unit leaf area. In addition, you determined that the rates of carbon dioxide evolution due to photorespiration and cellular respiration were 10 and 5 μmol of carbon dioxide evolved per hour per unit leaf area, respectively. Calculate the *actual rate* of carbon dioxide uptake due to photosynthesis.
5. (a) Why does an increase in temperature cause an increase in the carbon dioxide–saturated rate of net carbon dioxide uptake? (see point X on the graph.)
   (b) Define carboxylation efficiency. Why does this decrease at higher temperatures? (Note that a C_3 plant was used in this experiment.)

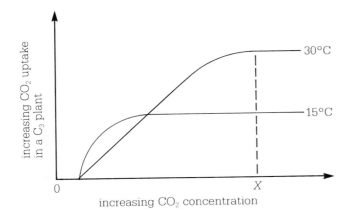

Use the graph below to answer questions 6, 7, and 8.

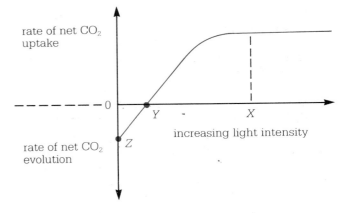

6. Which point on the graph represents the rate of respiration? Explain.
7. (a) Define light compensation point.
   (b) Which point on the graph represents the light compensation point?
8. (a) Define light-saturated rate of photosynthesis.
   (b) Which point on the graph represents light saturation?
9. This graph illustrates an action spectrum for photosynthesis.
   (a) Copy the graph in your notebook and label the axes.
   (b) What does this action spectrum tell you about photosynthesis?

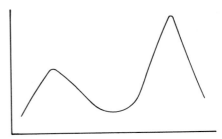

10. Compare and contrast the C_3 and C_4 modes of carbon dioxide fixation.
11. Why did C_4 and CAM plants evolve alternative pathways for the fixation of carbon dioxide?
12. Why is it important for humans to limit excessive use of fossil fuels?

Advanced Questions

1. The summer of 1987 in Ontario was hotter and drier than usual. Although this was ideal for vacationers, many people complained that much of the grass in their lawns turned brown but that the crabgrass thrived. Use the information from this chapter to explain this phenomenon.

2. In the graph below, the rate of net carbon dioxide uptake is plotted as a function of air temperature for two green plants, A and B, under conditions of constant light intensity and constant carbon diox- ide concentration. One was a C_3 plant and the other a C_4. From the data provided, which was the C_3 plant and which was the C_4 plant? Explain your answer.

3. The graph below illustrates the relationship between the occurrence of C_4 grasses and climatic temperature.
   (a) What does this graph tell you about C_4 plants?
   (b) Provide an explanation for the results illus- trated in the graph.

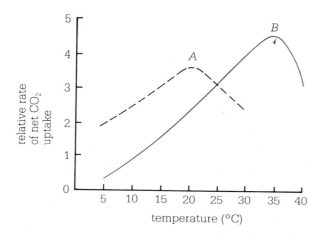

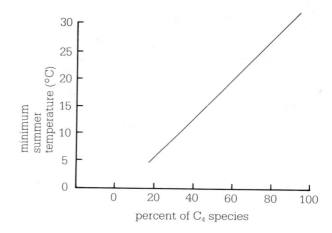

PRINCIPLES OF HOMEOSTASIS

CHAPTER 10

HOMEOSTASIS

La fixité du milieu interieur est la condition de la vie libre.
(The constancy of the internal environment is the necessary condition of the free life.)

Claude Bernard

Control of balance is essential for an athlete. This control is a dynamic process requiring a constant input of information and energy. The athlete continuously makes slight adjustments to counteract the forces acting on him, adjustments which must be well coordinated. If you stand balanced on one foot, you will get some idea of just how much energy and coordination this process involves. Now close your eyes as you balance. Notice how this limitation affects the process.

This chapter deals with the ways that the body maintains its biological balance. Living cells can survive and function only within a very narrow range of conditions; consequently, the internal environment of any organism must be precisely controlled within that range. A special term, **homeostasis**, is used to describe this internal control. The term comes from the Greek *homoios*, meaning same, and *stasis*, meaning standing.

In this chapter some of the homeostatic control mechanisms that operate within the cells, tissues, organs, and organ systems of vertebrate animals are examined. Specific examples are used to illustrate the principles involved. Special attention is given to the role of the kidney in the maintenance of human homeostasis.

10.1 PRINCIPLES OF CONTROL OF COMPLEX SYSTEMS

Both physical and biological systems are governed by principles of control. These principles are sometimes the same for both kinds of systems and sometimes different.

Many complicated physical systems are "rigid," having a high degree of determinism. Such systems are non-correcting. A gasoline engine is an example of a rigid system. When it operates, its parts follow pathways that are determined by the design of the motor. If something goes out of control the motor cannot compensate to correct the flaw.

Although they all have some degree of determinism, most biological systems are much more "flexible" than physical systems. Living organisms are self-corrective and can adjust to certain errors. Wound healing and the recovery from ingestion of toxic materials are two examples of this capacity for self-correction. Cell division (mitosis) and DNA replication by base pairing are examples of biological systems that are relatively rigid in their operation. Yet even here, there are repair mechanisms that can fix some defects. Flaws that do occur during these processes usually give rise to systems which do not operate properly. Cells with serious flaws — for example, faulty DNA replication — usually die and are eliminated from the organism. Only very rarely does a mistake in DNA replication give rise to successful mutant cells.

Living systems must constantly respond to **stress**. The environment provides various forms of external stress such as changing light and temperature conditions, lack of food, and predators and other harmful agents. Internal stresses arise because of metabolic activities: substrate concentrations constantly change as do concentrations of waste materials; parts of tissues wear out as a result of excessive activity; the body ages.

To maintain homeostasis the system must be able to recognize stress and to respond to it in a self-preserving manner. The stress provides the **stimulus**; by applying an appropriate response, the system exercises control.

Most homeostatic systems operate by means of **negative feedback** control loops; that is, the stimulus produces a reaction that ultimately reduces the stimulus or its effects.

The most common example of negative feedback control in a non-living system is the operation of a thermostat attached to a heating device. A *rise* in temperature causes the heater to be turned *off* and a *drop* in temperature causes the heater to be turned *on* (Figure 10.1).

Simple thermostats consist of a **receptor** (usually a strip made of two different metals arranged in a coil). As the temperature changes, the metals in the sensor expand differently, causing it to bend. Electrical contact points are located on the end of the sensor and on the body of the thermostat. When the temperature drops, the sensor bends so that the contact points touch one another. This contact completes an electrical circuit and the heater (the **effector**) is turned on. The heater causes the air around the thermostat to heat up. This rise in temperature loops back and is detected by the sensor, causing it to bend away, open the electrical contacts, and shut off the heater. The entire process then begins again.

The gap between the electrical contacts can be adjusted to set the temperature at which contact is made and broken. This adjustable part of the thermostat is the **regulator**. As the bimetallic strip moves one way and then the other, the temperature cycles around the *set point*.

Figure 10.1
The process by which the feedback causes a reduction in the stimulus is known as negative feedback.

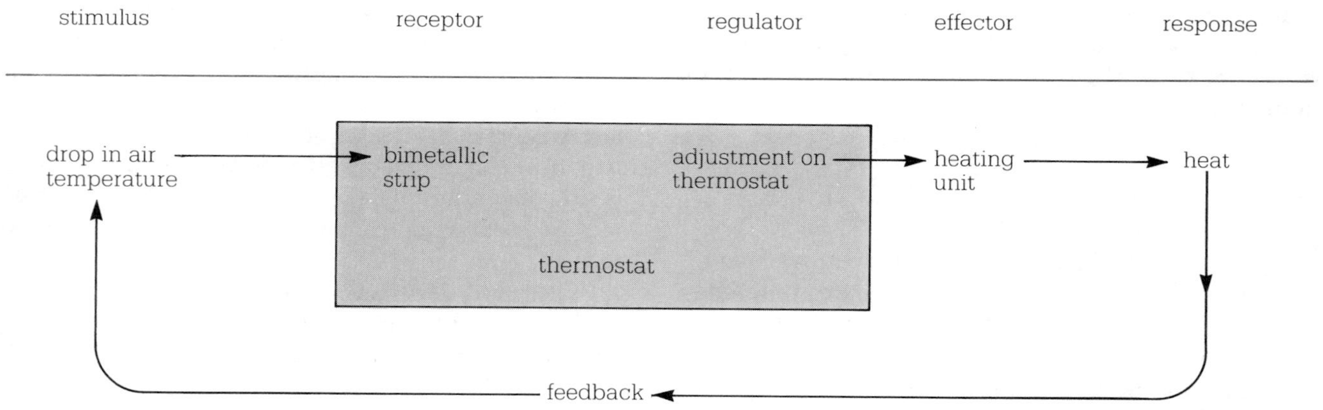

stimulus	receptor	regulator	effector	response
drop in air temperature	bimetallic strip	adjustment on thermostat	heating unit	heat

thermostat

feedback

Figure 10.2

In one of the many complex feedback systems that operate in vertebrate animals, light provides a stimulus to produce responses such as muscle contraction or glandular secretion. These responses then loop back to become new stimuli which inform the regulator (the brain) of the *extent of the response to the original stimulus, the light. The stimuli which are fed back into the system may or may not cause a new response. Because the brain can integrate massive amounts of information, its ability to act as a regulator surpasses that of any mechanical device.*

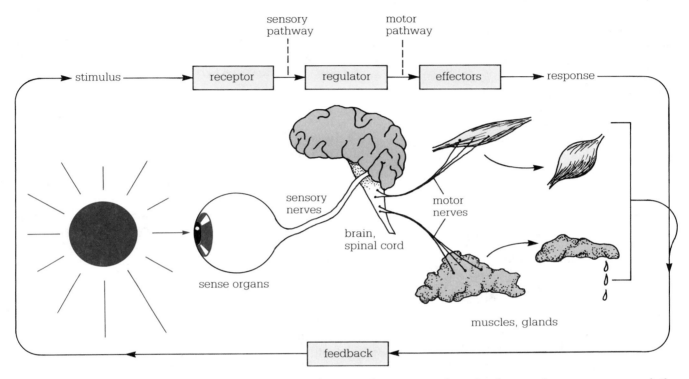

Both physical and biological systems require the same components in order to operate their negative feedback controls successfully. These components are the *stimulus, receptor, regulator,* and *effector.* In biological systems, a *sensory pathway* links the receptor and the regulator and a *motor pathway* links the regulator and the effector (Figure 10.2). The components of biological systems have a far greater capacity for adjustment than do those of physical systems. For example, the eye can respond to light in many more ways than a bimetallic strip can respond to temperature change. Since the brain can integrate massive amounts of information, its ability to act as a regulator far surpasses that of any mechanical device.

The working of the heart is another example of homeostatic control by negative feedback. The rate at which the heart beats is closely coordinated with many homeostatic systems in the body. This coordination is maintained by a double system of feedback loops (Figure 10.3). The walls of the major blood vessels connected to the heart, the vena cava and the aorta, contain special patches of nerve tissue which act as *stretch receptors*. As the heart pumps large quantities of blood into these vessels, their walls bulge, thus activating the stretch receptors. When so activated, the stretch receptors send nerve signals to the heart rate centre in the brain. Impulses from the vena cava cause the heart rate centre to accelerate the beating of the heart. Impulses from the aorta have the opposite effect. This double "check-and-balance system" automatically helps to ensure that the heart delivers the volume of blood required to maintain homeostasis in the body (Figure 10.3).

Two essential points should be noted about biological negative feedback systems. The first is that either the nervous system or the endocrine (glandular) system, or both, can be involved. The second is that the response is fed back into the system and used for further adjustments. The role of both systems in homeostasis will be treated more fully in following chapters.

Figure 10.3

Acceleration and deceleration of heart rate. When muscles are active, many veins are compressed and much blood returns to the heart through the vena cava. Stretch receptors in the vena cava are activated and signal the heart rate centre. In turn, the heart rate centre increases the accelerating signals in the motor nerve and decreases the inhibitory signals in the vagus nerve. The acceleration of heart rate removes more blood from the vena cava, thus decreasing the stretch in this vessel. At the same time, the increased outflow of blood stretches the walls of the aorta, activating stretch receptors in the aorta and signalling the heart rate centre. These signals in turn cause the heart rate centre to decrease the accelerating signals in the motor nerve and increase the inhibitory signals in the vagus nerve. As the heart rate decelerates, the walls of the aorta are not stretched as much.

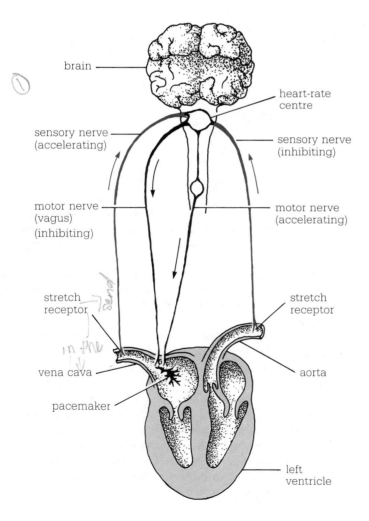

10.2 PROPERTIES OF CONTROL SYSTEMS

The operation of a thermostat and the control of heart rate illustrate four properties common to all control systems, whether physical or biological. First, they must operate within their *limits*. Second, they require *operating energy*. Third, they use *feedback*; that is, part of the output is recycled to modulate the system. Fourth, they can experience *overshoots*. Biological systems (if not physical ones) often have a fifth property: the ability to correct *errors*.

Limits

Homeostatic systems all have limits. There comes a point where the effectors cannot maintain the system in a steady state. During its lifetime, every biological organism has a finite amount of metabolic energy to invest in survival and reproduction. Time and energy invested in one aspect of life are not available for other aspects. The organization of animals and plants consequently must be a compromise.

This restriction leads to the evolution of homeostatic mechanisms that can withstand environmental extremes normally encountered in their natural habitat, but not much more. For example, humans are tropical animals; at 20°C a naked person will start to shiver to produce additional body heat. A species adapted to the cold, such as an arctic fox, has a basal rate of heat production that keeps it comfortable down to −20°C, yet this animal would be unable to function normally in a tropical climate.

Both of these examples show that environmental selection has produced remarkable specialists, organisms able to maintain homeostasis under extreme environmental conditions. However, these organisms consequently have to live with other limitations.

Energy Requirements

Efficient control systems are arranged so that the small amount of energy required to activate the sensor is greatly amplified by the effector. For example, the thermostat in a house requires heat energy to operate the bimetallic strips in its sensor. It requires electrical energy to have the regulator activate the effectors (the furnace and the air conditioner). Some form of energy is needed to run these effectors; in turn, they supply much more energy than does the electrical signal coming to them from the regulator. In other words, the effectors *amplify* the signal energy so that the house can be heated or cooled.

Figure 10.4
A human (a) must shiver to produce extra heat at temperatures as high as 20°C. The use of clothes can extend the temperature range within which a human can survive. An Arctic fox (b), however, is well enough insulated that its normal metabolic heat keeps it comfortable at temperatures as low as −20°C.

(a)

(b)

Biological systems operate on identical principles. Their highly sensitive receptors, regulators, and connecting pathways require only small amounts of energy supplied by ATP to operate. The effectors (muscles and glands) amplify this energy by using much larger amounts of ATP.

Figure 10.5
The regulators supply only a small amount of energy to the effectors when they stimulate them. The effectors can amplify this energy by activation of large amounts of ATP, the cell's energy storage molecule.

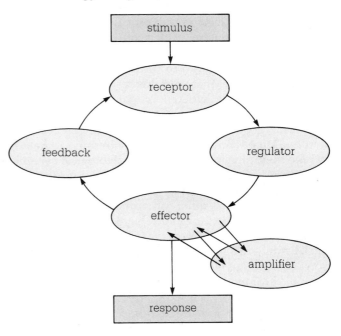

Feedback

Homeostatic systems do not respond to a stimulus with a sudden, single response, but in a series of small, repeated responses. Each response becomes a new stimulus. When "fed back" through the receptor-regulator-effector system, this new stimulus causes the effectors to continue, stop, or reverse their operation. It is both the feedback and the regulator, then, which control the direction, amount, and duration of the effector's output. Effective homeostasis is achieved only when appropriate feedbacks are operative. As an example, consider again the beating of the heart (Figure 10.3). There is a balance between *stimulus* (the stretching of the blood vessels connected to the heart), *reception* (activation of the stretch receptors), *regulation* (the activities of the heart rate centre), and *effector output* (the rate of heart beat). Without feedback, the regulator could not monitor what the effector has been doing and consequently it could not send out appropriate new commands. In other words, the heart rate centre must balance the acceleration of heart rate (caused by the stretching of blood vessels) with the decelerating signal (resulting from increased rate of heart beat).

There are two types of feedback control, negative and positive. All of the controls discussed to this point have been of the *negative feedback* type, where the stimulus produces a reaction that ultimately reduces the stimulus or its effects. In **positive feedback** control loops, the stimulus evokes a response that *increases* the stimulus. A good example of this second type is the sound distortion in an electronic system when the microphone gets too close to its speakers. The microphone picks up a sound from the speaker and sends it to the amplifier; that sound is reamplified and sent back to the speaker, where it is again picked up by the microphone and sent back for even more amplification. This positive feedback loop rapidly escalates to a full-volume whine that is very distressing to hear.

Like their physical counterparts, biological systems operating with positive feedback control are usually associated with something going wrong. Control by positive feedback is inherently unstable.

Addiction to chemicals such as nicotine, alcohol, or other addictive drugs is an example of positive feedback leading to a breakdown in homeostasis. The person takes the chemical to feel better; after a short initial period, during which time the chemical may produce the desired effect, the toxic effects of the chemical cause the user to feel much worse. More chemical is taken to recapture the better feeling and the toxic effects are amplified. Eventually this cycle of positive feedback leads to serious breakdowns in other homeostatic systems in the body.

High blood pressure is another example of a positive feedback loop. Abnormally high pressures cause damage to the walls of arteries and arterioles. The damaged areas can form scar tissue capable of trapping lipid material. Accumulation of lipids reduces the cross sectional area of the blood vessel, causing a further increase in blood pressure.

Overshoots

Continuous feedback gives rise to another property of control systems: they can "overshoot" as they strive for the optimal condition. Control systems functioning with negative feedback loops oscillate to either side of the optimal point. Excessive reduction of a stimulus is termed a negative overshoot, while insufficient reduction of it is termed positive overshoot. For example, rooms remote from a thermostat can often be either too cold or too warm. These large swings in temperature are an example of negative and positive overshoots.

Homeostatic control is best achieved when the amplitude of overshoots is minimized. Some poorly adjusted control devices can have the positive and negative overshoots increase in amplitude until homeostasis is lost. The lurching walk of a person who has consumed too much alcohol is an example. Alcohol causes the nervous system's control over locomotion and balance to become maladjusted, and overshoots occur. For example, swaying too far in one direction would be a negative overshoot, while swaying too far in the opposite direction would be a positive overshoot. When a person is sober, such oscillations are so small that they are not noticed. What sort of oscillations do you experience when you try to balance on one foot?

Errors

Control systems have limits which, if exceeded, result in errors. These can be errors in sensing stimuli, in regulation, or in effector function. In complex biological control systems, functional or structural failures of control systems cause disease. The effects of disease can act as a stimulus which activates other regulating systems. Repair of the disease condition may then occur. This ability to self-repair is one of the special features of living organisms.

10.3 THE ROLE OF THERMOREGULATION IN VERTEBRATE HOMEOSTASIS

Thermoregulation is the ability of an organism to maintain its internal body temperature at a suitable level despite the temperature of the external environment. In short, thermoregulation is the homeostasis of body temperature. This form of homeostasis is the result of internal physiological behaviours that minimize the environmental impact. It is important even in vertebrates that are **poikilotherms** or cold blooded (fish, amphibians, and reptiles), and much more so in **homeotherms** (birds and mammals).

Thermoregulation is a biochemical process; that is, it involves chemical reactions taking place at the cellular level. If an animal gets too cold, the teams of enzymes working together in its cells lose their coordination. Each biochemical reaction that takes place in living cells is affected by the temperature of the cell. A ten degree drop in temperature can slow the rates of reactions two to three times over. Since different reactions have different temperature coefficients, a change in internal temperature can slow one reaction

Figure 10.6
Thermoregulation in humans

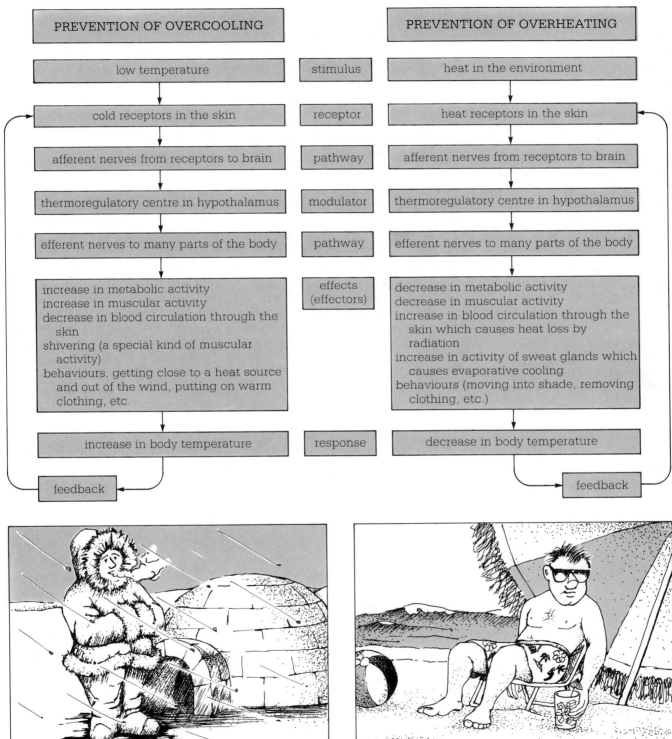

more than another. This uncoupling of reaction rates can seriously affect sequential reactions such as the Krebs cycle. This uncoupling is far more serious for homeotherms than for poikilotherms. Homeotherms cannot tolerate swings in body temperature of more than a degree or so.

A drop in internal temperature slows the biochemical processes down, causing the animal to become sluggish or immobile. Poikilotherms are particularly affected, but a drop in the core temperature of homeotherms has the same effect. Many vertebrate animals have developed measures to conserve metabolic heat and to retain it in the most critical parts of the body. Such conservation mechanisms, which usually involve control of blood circulation, allow the animal to operate under severe weather conditions. If the environment becomes too cold for a given species, a positive feedback loop can become established and lead to the death of the animal. The low temperature causes the animal to lose too much heat from its body. As the animal's core temperature drops, its heat-producing metabolic processes slow down, initiating a further drop in core temperature. Eventually the animal dies from hypothermia. For humans, death occurs when the core temperature of the body drops to about 13°C.

As might be expected, the brain is the human organ that can tolerate the least amount of temperature variation. The temperature of the hands and feet can vary over a much wider range. There are temperature sensors in the skin for both heat and cold. These relay information to a special part of the brain, the **hypothalamus** (chapter 11). It contains the nerve cells that function as the main thermoregulatory centre of the body. Figure 10.6 shows how humans prevent overheating and overcooling.

10.4 THE ROLE OF THE KIDNEYS IN HUMAN HOMEOSTASIS

The functioning of the kidneys provides an excellent example of homeostasis in the form of **osmoregulation**, the control of water and ion balance in the body. With the exception of sharks, all vertebrate animals are **osmoregulators**. Regardless of the animal's environment, the osmoregulator maintains an internal water concentration that varies little. This level must be constantly monitored and adjusted. Terrestrial animals such as humans must conserve water to avoid dehydration.

Humans have two kidneys, each about the size of a fist. They are located just below the ribs on the posterior wall of the abdominal cavity. Their structure is shown in Figure 10.7(a). The functional unit of the kidney, illustrated in Figure 10.7(b), is the **nephron**. Each kidney contains between one and one-and-a-quarter million of these tiny tubular structures, tightly packed together as the **cortex** and **medulla** of the organ.

Research on kidney function and on methods of overcoming the effects of kidney diseases is being carried on very intensively. This research has led to a modification of the hypothesis used to explain how the kidneys work. The *countercurrent multiplier hypothesis* used to be the accepted explanation. Its validity depended on the active pumping of sodium and chloride ions out of the ascending arm of the tubule and the salt permeability of the descending arm. Careful examination of the cells making up the walls of the lower portion of the ascending arm revealed no such active ion transport channels. In addition, the descending arm was shown not to be permeable to salt. The hypothesis, which had appeared in a great many text books, required modification—an example of the type of change that is constantly happening as the scientific method is applied to the study of living things.

In 1972 the *two-solute hypothesis* was proposed to explain how the kidneys work (Figure 10.8). To understand this hypothesis, you must first review the structure of a nephron.

Each nephron consists of a complex tube made up of specialized cells that perform different functions in different parts of the tube. The nephron begins with Bowman's capsule, which wraps around a knot of capillaries called the glomerulus. Coming off Bowman's capsule is the proximal tubule. It leaves the cortex (the outer layer of the kidney) and descends into the deeper layers of the kidney, the outer and inner medulla. As the tube enters the outer medulla it changes into the descending arm. At the bottom it turns up to form the ascending arm. The U-shaped structure formed by the lower parts of the descending and ascending arms is known as the loop of Henle. In the cortex, the ascending arm changes into the distal tubule, which enters a collecting duct. The collecting ducts join together and carry the urine to the bladder.

Figure 10.8 explains the function of the nephron in terms of the two-solute hypothesis. The two solutes involved are urea and sodium chloride. The task that must be performed is the recovery of the proper

Figure 10.7

A longitudinal section through a human kidney is shown in (a), while the relationship between a nephron and the circulatory system is represented in (b).

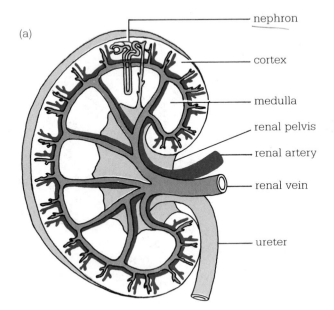

amounts of water and ions from the glomerular filtrate. This controlled recovery is accomplished by two factors. One is the differential permeability of tubule cells to water and ions as the filtrate moves along the kidney tubule. The other is the variations in the concentrations of the two solutes outside the tubules, variations which affect water movement.

The first step of the process is **glomerular filtration**, which occurs between the glomerulus and Bowman's capsule. See Figure 10.8(a). Forced filtration pushes certain constituents of the high pressure blood in the glomerulus out into the space in Bowman's capsule. This filtration is not very selective; the large ''formed bodies'' (blood cells and platelets) and most blood protein molecules are too large to be pushed through the capillary-capsular barrier. But a great deal of water (about 180 L every 24 h!) is forced out of the circulatory system into the excretory system. This water contains many useful molecules such as glucose, amino acids, and some proteins. Waste materials such as urea are also contained in this filtrate. The nephrons recover almost all of the water (about 178–179 L every 24 h) through **tubular reabsorption** and the protein molecules through pinocytosis.

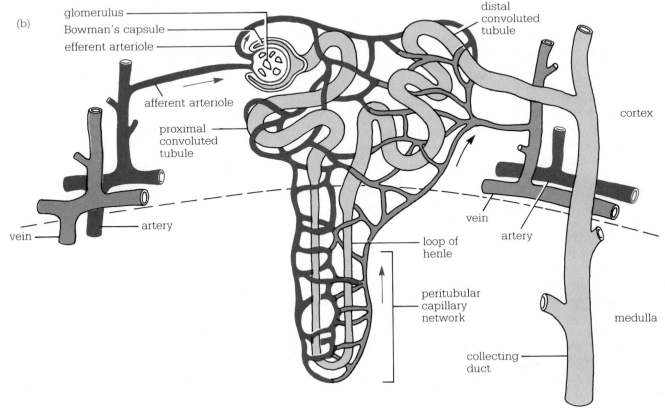

Figure 10.8
*Highly simplified drawing of a nephron, showing how it
functions according to the two-solute hypothesis*

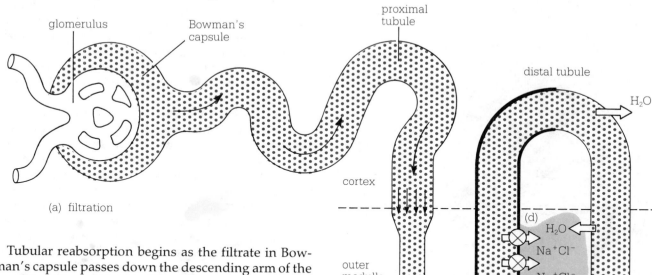

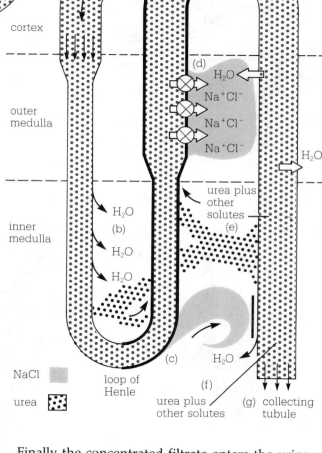

(a) filtration

Tubular reabsorption begins as the filtrate in Bowman's capsule passes down the descending arm of the loop. See Figure 10.8(b). The cells forming the walls of this arm are permeable to water but not to salt or urea. Because they contain high concentrations of urea, the surrounding tissues are hypertonic to the liquid in the tubules. This hypertonicity causes water to diffuse out of the tubule, thus concentrating the remaining filtrate. In the loop of Henle, the tubule cells lose much of their water permeability but become permeable to sodium and chloride ions. See Figure 10.8(c). As the concentrated filtrate moves up the ascending arm, salt diffuses out into the surrounding tissue.

In the outer medulla portion of the kidney, the tubule cells use active transport to pump out even more sodium and chloride ions, thus setting up conditions for water to move out of the tubules by osmosis. As this water leaves, the urea and other waste materials in the tubule become highly concentrated. See Figure 10.8(d). The tubule then empties into a collecting duct which passes back through the outer and inner medulla. See Figure 10.8(e). The lower portions of the collecting duct are permeable to urea. Some of the highly concentrated urea diffuses out into the tissue surrounding the descending arm, increasing the concentration of urea in this tissue and thereby allowing water to move out of the descending arm by osmosis. As the filtrate passes down the collecting duct, which is surrounded by tissue with a high urea and ion content, even more water passes outward by osmosis. See Figure 10.8(f).

Finally the concentrated filtrate enters the urinary bladder and is eventually eliminated from the body. See Figure 10.8(g). The useful substances in the filtrate, such as glucose and amino acids, are completely reabsorbed in the tubule cells through active transport. The water that moved out of the tubules into the surrounding kidney tissue is collected by blood vessels permeable to water but impermeable to urea. This water is returned into general circulation.

Homeostatic Interactions Between the Kidneys and the Nervous and Endocrine Systems

The control of water balance in the kidney is regulated by activities within the hypothalamus that involve a feedback loop (Figure 10.9).

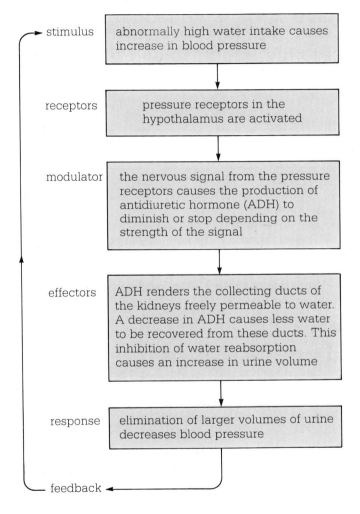

NOTE: When water intake is low the blood pressure is not elevated and so ADH levels are high and consequently much water is reabsorbed.

Figure 10.9
In the control of water balance, the hypothalamus functions as part of both the nervous system and the endocrine system.

Chemicals such as caffeine and alcohol act on the hypothalamus to inhibit the production of **ADH** (the **antidiuretic hormone**). Since ADH causes the nephrons to become *more* permeable to water, a reduction in ADH levels renders the urine *less* concentrated. More water is thus lost from the body. Substances that increase the amount of water excreted are **diuretics**. Caffeine acts as a diuretic in two ways, not only inhibiting the production of ADH but also increasing the filtration rate of the glomeruli by raising the blood pressure. Cold weather can also have this second effect, insofar as the surface capillary beds may constrict when cold, leading to a rise in the blood pressure.

Once ADH is produced by the hypothalamus, it moves down nerve fibre tracts to the posterior pituitary. Damage to either of these structures can cause a loss in ADH secretion. This rare condition is called *diabetes insipidus*. The low water permeability of the collecting ducts resulting from this lack of ADH allows the loss of large volumes of very dilute urine (5 L to 10 L every 24 h instead of the normal 1 L to 2 L). Even under these conditions about 96 percent of the water in the glomerular filtrate is reabsorbed. People with this condition must drink large volumes of fluids to prevent serious dehydration.

The regulation of sodium and potassium ions is extremely important. About 90 percent of these ions in the glomerular filtrate is reabsorbed before the filtrate reaches the distal tubule. This reabsorption occurs at a constant rate and is not regulated by hormones. However, the final concentrations of these ions in the distal tubule are hormonally adjusted by *aldosterone*, a steroid hormone secreted from the adrenal cortex. It in turn stimulates the secretion of potassium from the blood into the distal tubule. This secretion is the only means by which potassium can be eliminated in the urine. An increase in potassium ion levels in the blood directly stimulates the secretion of aldosterone—another example of a negative feedback loop. Aldosterone has the reverse effect on sodium ions; it causes the distal tubule to *reabsorb* them from the filtrate back into the blood. When maximal amounts of aldosterone are released, the urine contains no sodium ions. A decrease in the concentration of sodium ions in the blood promotes aldosterone release, but not directly.

By fine-tuning the concentration of materials returned from the glomerular filtrate into the blood, the kidneys act as one of the most important homeostatic organs of the body.

CHAPTER SUMMARY

Control systems must be established and maintained within the body in order to keep it within the narrow range of conditions within which living cells can survive. The better this homeostasis, the greater the range of life activities available for the animal in question.

Biological homeostatic control systems operate almost exclusively by means of negative feedback loops. A typical feedback system consists of a recep-

tor, a regulator, and an effector. In biological systems, many feedback loops can be interconnected; very precise controls are thus possible. All of the organ systems in the body cooperate to maintain homeostatic balance. The nervous, endocrine, and excretory systems are especially important. Thermoregulation and kidney function are two outstanding examples of mammalian homeostasis.

Objectives

Having completed this chapter, you should be able to do the following:

1. Define homeostasis and explain its importance to biological systems.
2. Describe the principles of control of complex systems and how such systems operate.
3. Differentiate between negative and positive feedback control systems.
4. Outline the feedback control of heart rate and body temperature.
5. Explain how temperature regulation in mammals allows complex enzyme systems to operate as teams.
6. State how the two-solute hypothesis explains the functioning of the kidney nephrons.

Vocabulary

homeostasis
stress
stimulus
negative feedback
receptor
effector
regulator

positive feedback
thermoregulation
poikilotherm
homeotherm
hypothalamus
osmoregulation
nephron

cortex
medulla
glomerular filtration
tubular reabsorption
antidiuretic hormone, ADH
diuretic

Review Questions

1. Define the term homeostasis as it applies to vertebrate animals.
2. (a) Define stress as it applies to biological homeostatic systems.
   (b) Select a system and describe how it responds to stress.
3. Living organisms have control systems that have been described as ''rigid'' and as ''flexible.'' Explain the differences in these two systems, giving examples of how they operate in organisms.

4. Using the control of heart rate as the example, explain how feedback is used to keep the regulator informed of the performance of the effector.
5. (a) Name the parts of a negative feedback loop.
   (b) Outline the function of each part.
6. Using the role of ATP as the example, explain how the small amount of energy produced by biological sensors is amplified by biological effectors.
7. Relating your answer to Figure 10.3, discuss the properties of biological control systems under the following headings:
   (a) limits
   (b) energy requirements
   (c) feedback
   (d) overshoots
   (e) errors.
8. (a) Describe the mechanisms used for temperature control in humans.
   (b) Why is temperature control necessary? Use as your example the control of either overheating or overcooling.
9. Using models of feedback systems, describe the effects on cell survival of changes in

(a) temperature
(b) ion concentrations
(c) toxicity levels.
10. During each 24 h period, how much
    (a) water is filtered from the blood into the kidneys?
    (b) urine is normally eliminated?
11. State the source and the action of
    (a) the antidiuretic hormone (ADH) in osmoregulation;
    (b) the hormone aldosterone in the control of sodium and potassium ion concentration in the body.
12. In the human kidney, water moves out of the tubules in the region of the loop of Henle, where the surrounding tissue has a very high salt content. Most of this water is then picked up by blood capillaries in the tissue and carried back into the general blood circulation.
    (a) What causes the water to move out of the tubules?
    (b) Why doesn't this blood have a very high salt content?

Advanced Questions

1. Why would it not be a good idea to drink alcohol or coffee in the desert?
2. In humans, much of our overall homeostasis depends upon our behaviours. List three behaviours that help keep you in homeostatic balance.
3. (a) Give three examples of biological stresses that effect you.
   (b) Describe how to minimize the effects of one of these stresses.
4. Select an animal that is highly specialized and can maintain homeostasis under an extreme environmental condition.
   (a) What are its specializations?
   (b) In what ways do these specializations limit the animal?

5. (a) Select a disease that causes a breakdown in a homeostatic control system.
   (b) Describe how this disease causes the activation of another system to repair the effects of the disease.
6. If you had to design a machine that would take the place of the kidneys, what homeostatic controls would you have to include for it to operate properly?

CHAPTER 11

THE NERVOUS SYSTEM: ITS ROLE IN HOMEOSTASIS

Cogito, ergo sum.
I think, therefore I exist.

Descartes

Thinking is one of the activities of the nervous system. The human brain constantly creates and manipulates concepts. Its ability to do so has allowed humans to create cultures.

The nervous system does many things. As you read this page, millions of your nerve cells are active, exchanging information in the form of transient electrical and chemical signals known as nerve impulses. The nervous system works closely with the endocrine system. Some nerves actually produce and secrete hormones. Other nerves carry signals that activate endocrine glands, causing them to produce and/or release their hormones.

The nervous system operates rather like a telephone system in a town. It provides a rapid short term system by which information about conditions in and around one part of the body can be sent to other parts of the body. This almost instantaneous flow of information is necessary for the body to maintain its homeostatic balance. Yet the nervous system does more than just pass messages around. It also coordinates and regulates many of the body's functions, particularly those involving active tissues such as muscles.

11.1 THE NEURON: THE FUNCTIONAL UNIT OF THE NERVOUS SYSTEM

The nervous system consists of many millions of specialized cells. Certain ones, the **neurons**, are specialized to carry messages. In vertebrate animals such as

humans, neurons have many shapes and sizes. Neurons have been classified on the basis of this morphology (Figure 11.1).

Figure 11.1
A morphological classification of neurons. The classification is based on the number of nerve processes entering the nerve cell body; bipolar neurons have two, unipolar just one. The multipolar neurons are of two types, with axons and without. The latter carry signals only to cells in their immediate vicinity.

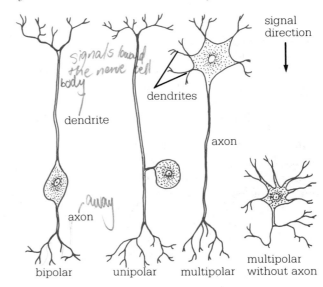

Although neurons differ in many details, they do share certain basic features. All have a *nerve cell body* that contains the nucleus of the nerve cell. Most have long projections, sometimes several metres long, extending out from the nerve cell body. Under normal conditions, the nerve impulse only travels one way in a neuron. The projections that carry signals *toward* the nerve cell body are known as **dendrites**; those carrying signals *away*, as **axons**. If a dendrite or an axon is stimulated under experimental conditions at some point along its length, the signal will travel in both directions.

Another way of classifying neurons is according to the job that they do. On this basis, there are three different types of neurons: sensory, motor, and association or interneurons. Each type has a characteristic structure which allows it to perform its specialized task. **Sensory neurons** are usually associated with receptor cells that are in contact with the environment and can detect changes in it. See Figure 11.2(a). **Motor neurons** activate muscles and glands. See Figure 11.2(b). **Association neurons** connect the sensory neurons to the motor neurons. See Figure 11.2(c).

Neurons work together to form millions of neuron chains in the body. Neurons do not make direct connections with one another; rather, they are separated by a small space known as the **synaptic cleft**.

Despite their different shapes, sizes, and roles, all neurons operate in the same way. They *receive, process,* and *transmit* information. Each of these activities occurs in a specific part of the neurons. Each one relies on the operation of electrical impulses. In turn, these impulses are created by the movement of ions in and out of the neuronal cytoplasm via the nerve cell membrane. This membrane is *excitable*; that is, it can carry an electrical signal.

Reception involves the response of the neuronal membrane to external changes in its immediate environment and its initiation of a nerve impulse. Although all neurons are capable of reception, sensory neurons are specialized to respond to environmental signals such as changes in temperature, light, and sound. *Processing* takes place when neurons interact in ways that either induce or suppress the initiation of nerve impulses. *Transmission* is the movement of nerve impulses down the membrane from the dendritic to the axonal end of the neuron.

Neurons operate on the basis of just two types of electrical signals: weak signals (graded potentials) and strong signals (nerve impulses). The graded potential usually travels in the dendrite to the nerve cell body.

The nerve impulse then travels from the nerve cell body down the axon. When the nervous signal arrives at the end of its neuron, chemicals are released which cross the synaptic cleft in an activity known as *transfer*. These chemicals start the nervous signal in the next neuron in the chain.

Neuron function involves a complex process by which positively charged potassium and sodium ions and other, negatively charged organic molecules interact across the neural membrane. Central to this process is the establishment of the *resting potential* and the *action potential*.

Resting Potential

Neurons that are not transmitting nerve impulses are described as *resting neurons* (even though many metabolic activities are being conducted just to keep the cell alive). The membrane of a resting neuron must continually work at pumping sodium ions out and pulling potassium ions into the neuron (Figure 11.3). The activities of these pumps establish an electrical potential difference across the membrane known as the resting potential.

Numerous factors are involved in the establishment of the resting potential. These factors are all related to a shifting balance of sodium and potassium ions across the neural membrane. Inside each resting neuron, the cytoplasm has a high concentration of potassium ions (K^+) and a low concentration of sodium ions (Na^+). The cytoplasm also contains many negatively charged organic molecules. By contrast, the fluid that surrounds each neuron has a low concentration of potassium ions and a high concentration of sodium ions. The neural membrane is very slightly permeable to potassium ions, about 50 times even less permeable to sodium ions and wholly impermeable to the negatively charged organic molecules.

Because of these concentration differences, some potassium ions diffuse out through the membrane. However, because the membrane is impermeable to them, the negatively charged organic molecules inside the membrane do not diffuse out. The diffusion of potassium ions, which carry a positive charge, causes an excess of positive charges outside the membrane. This difference in charges causes a voltage—the resting potential—to be established across the membrane. In most resting neurons this voltage is about −70 millivolts (mV). The membrane is said to be *polarized* because of this difference in electrical charges.

Figure 11.2
Sensory neurons (a), which conduct nerve impulses from the sense organs to the spinal cord, have dendrites with endings in specific sensory receptor cells. Both their dendrites and their axons are usually wrapped with Schwann cells, as are the axons of most motor neurons

(b). These latter axons conduct nerve impulses from the spinal cord to the muscles and glands. Association neurons (c) are found within the brain and spinal cord. They usually have an elaborate array of extensively branched dendrites.

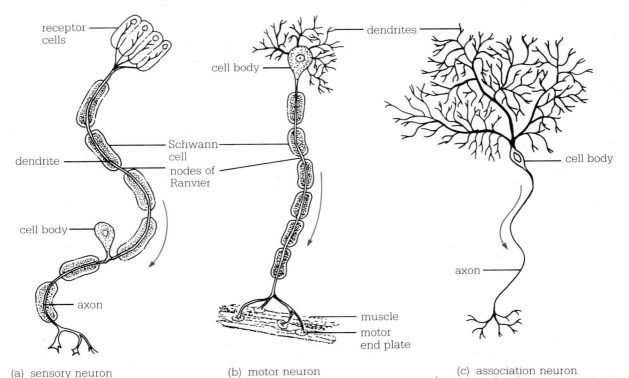

receptor cells

dendrites

cell body

dendrite

Schwann cell

nodes of Ranvier

cell body

cell body

axon

axon

muscle
motor end plate

(a) sensory neuron

(b) motor neuron

(c) association neuron

Figure 11.3
The sodium-potassium pump plays a major role in the establishment of the resting potential. <u>Because three sodium ions are moved out for each two potassium ions that move into the neuron, the pump removes a positive charge from the neuronal interior each time it acts.</u> The high concentration of potassium ions inside the neuron and its membrane's high permeability to potassium ensure that there is a continuous diffusion of potassium ions out of the neurons. It is this outward diffusion which creates the resting potential. The outward diffusion of potassium ions continues until it is balanced by the negative charges left behind in the cell.

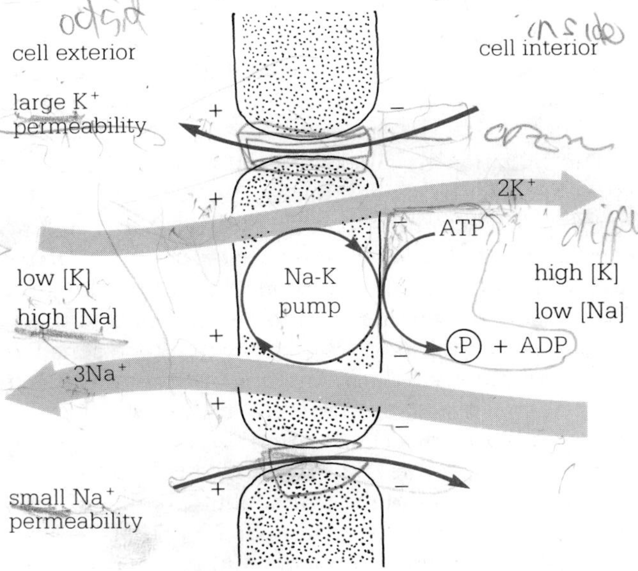

DRAW DIAGRAM

cell exterior

cell interior

large K^+ permeability

$2K^+$

ATP

low [K]
high [Na]

Na-K pump

high [K]
low [Na]

P + ADP

$3Na^+$

small Na^+ permeability

WRITE UP FOR DIAGRAM

diffusion

207

Figure 11.4

The operation of a nerve impulse. In (a), the axon has a resting membrane potential before initiation of the nerve impulse. In response to a stimulus (b), the permeability of the neural membrane changes. Voltage-sensitive channels in protein molecules that form parts of the membrane open and admit sodium ions. This change is confined to a small localized area. Sodium ions suddenly flow in through the membrane and potassium ions flow out. A wave of depolarization then sweeps down the membrane. This action potential (c) moves down the axon in a self-perpetuating manner. It can be measured electrically. Within milliseconds of the depolarization passing, the membrane pumps out sodium ions and the resting membrane potential is reestablished (d).

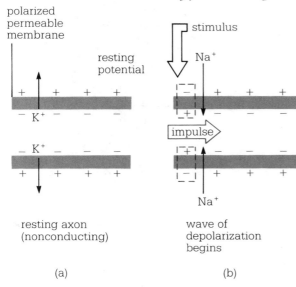

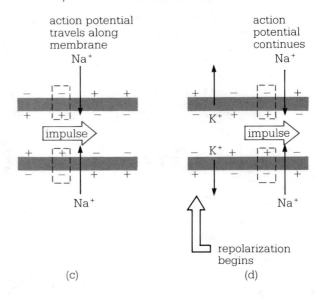

Action Potential

Action potentials, also known as nerve impulses or as "spikes," occur in the axons of neurons and in the dendrites of certain sensory cells. The nerve impulse is a combination of self-propagating chemical and electrical events. Put in its simplest term, a nerve impulse is established once the resting potential voltage is altered or *depolarized*, creating an electrical current that travels across the neural membrane (Figures 11.4 and 11.5).

The initiation of a nerve impulse takes place as a stimulus adds positive charges to the inside of the neuron. This stimulus can be physiological, such as the actions of other neurons, or experimental, such as the application of current by an electrode. The stimulus raises the voltage around the membrane to the *threshold potential*, at which point the voltage-sensitive sodium channels in the membrane open. Sodium then flows into the neuron, creating an inward electrical current. This process, which involves very few sodium ions, produces the depolarizing "spike" (Figure 11.5). The peak of the overshoot is about +120 mV above that of the resting potential. Note that the spike is always of the same strength. Either a full signal is sent, or no signal is sent. This wave of depolarization next travels along the membrane. See Figure 11.4(c).

Once the action potential has peaked, the sodium channels begin to close and potassium channels begin to open. Potassium ions diffuse rapidly outward, removing positive charges from the inside of the neuronal membrane and causing repolarization of the membrane. See Figure 11.4(d). Once the repolarization is completed, the number of potassium ions that have left the axon equals the number of sodium ions that have entered. There is a refractory period of a few milliseconds after the passing of a nerve impulse. During this period, insufficient sodium channels can be activated to produce another nerve impulse. The neuron is then ready to fire again.

In nerves that are wrapped with Schwann cells (Figures 11.6 and 11.9), the nerve impulse jumps from one node of Ranvier to another. The process of ion flow and recovery only has to take place at a limited number of sites on the nerve membrane. This process, known as **saltatorial conduction**, is therefore very rapid and efficient. Most motor axons in vertebrates work in this way.

Figure 11.5
The changes in potential show the difference between the inside and the outside of the nerve membrane during the passage of a nerve impulse.

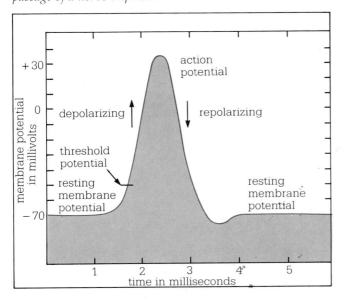

Figure 11.6
The vertebrate spinal motor neuron provides a good example of how various regions of a neuron are involved in the reception, processing, and transmission of information.

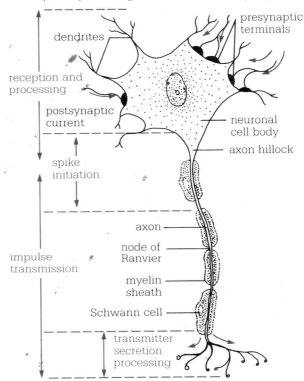

Reception
The dendrites and certain areas on the neuronal cell body are specialized to receive information. Sensory neurons differ from other neurons in the way that they receive information (Figure 11.2). Their dendritic endings are often buried in special receptor cells which can stimulate the dendrites. This stimulation initiates a nerve impulse which sweeps down the dendrite and axon, passing the neuronal cell body. In most other neurons, various branches of the dendrites of a single neuron can receive inputs from many different sources. Some inputs may cause stimulation; some, inhibition. Often branches (presynaptic terminals) from the axons of one neuron will terminate very close to the neuronal cell body of the next neuron in the chain. Under these circumstances, the neuronal cell body itself acts as the receptor. When a dendrite or the nerve cell body is stimulated, information in the form of a very weak electrical current (a graded potential) moves down the membrane of the nerve cell body. It quickly reaches the axon hillock, the area where the nerve cell body gives rise to the axon. Here, much of the information processing takes place (Figure 11.6).

Processing
Information processing is similar in all types of neurons, including sensory ones. The dendrites, or parts of the neuronal cell body near dendrites, act in con-

junction with the presynaptic terminals of other neurons. When synaptic transmission occurs, some of these synapses cause excitation and others cause inhibition of the motor neuron. If the membrane excitation reaches the threshold level at the axon hillock region, a nerve impulse is initiated and then transmitted along the neuronal axon by self-propagation.

The following analogy may help to explain the processing procedure. Think of the dendrites as a series of wires, some connected to sources of heat, others to sources of cold. (The wires that are heated provide stimulatory signals; the ones that are cooled, inhibitory signals). All of these wires lead to a nerve cell body which has an axon connected to it. Think of the axon as the fuse found on a firecracker. If inputs from the heated wires are stronger than inputs from the cooled wires, the heat increases. Likewise, if the heat at the axon hillock region goes over a certain threshold level, the ''fuse'' is lit. The action potential then sweeps down the axon in a self-propagating reaction, similar to the burning of a fuse. Processing also takes place at the neuronal synapse. (Figure 11.7).

Figure 11.7

Neurotransfer at a synapse. In this example, acetylcholine is the neurotransmitter. It is made in the presynaptic knob and stored in small vesicles. When the action potential arrives at this knob (a), the change in membrane potential causes acetylcholine to be released from the vesicles (b). The acetylcholine diffuses across the gap and binds to a receptor molecule (c) which is part of the postsynaptic membrane. The membrane of the receptor dendrite thus depolarizes and initiates a new action potential (d). After the acetylcholine has done its job it is rapidly destroyed by an enzyme, acetylcholineesterase, which is found in the synaptic cleft (e). The cycle recommences once the acetylcholine has been resynthesized (f). The rapid removal of the neurotransmitter allows as many as 1000 impulses per second to cross the synaptic cleft. Only the axonal presynaptic knob releases the acetylcholine and only the dendritic postsynaptic membrane contains the receptor sites. Traffic at the synapse is therefore one-way, from axon to dendrite.

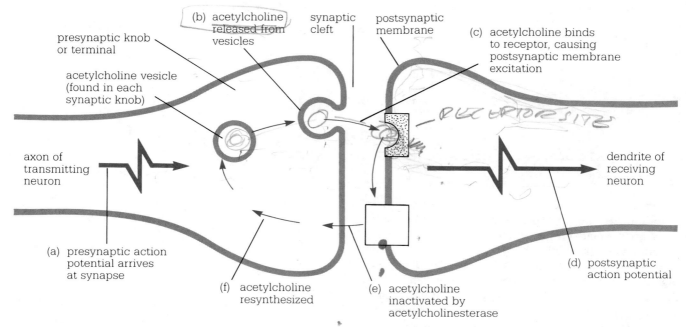

Transmission

Nerve impulses move along the axons of the neurons at great speed over long distances. The information they carry is used to control activities such as muscle contraction and the expulsion of specific material through cell membranes (exocytosis). These activities play major roles in the maintenance of homeostatic balance.

Transfer

As earlier noted, nerve cells do not make direct contact with one another but are separated by the synaptic cleft, a gap between the axon of one neuron and the dendrite or nerve cell body of the next neuron in the neuron chain. The synaptic cleft and the immediate area on either side of it are called the **synapse** (Figure 11.7).

Nerve impulses (action potentials) do not jump the synaptic clefts; rather, they are carried across the cleft by chemicals known as *neurotransmitters*. These chemicals rapidly cross the synaptic cleft and affect the state of membrane potential in the dendrite or nerve cell body of the next neuron in the chain. Figure 11.7 explains the role played by the neurotransmitters. Vertebrate nervous systems use a variety of neurotransmitters. Some cause depolarization of the postsynaptic membrane, while others cause the postsynaptic membrane to become resistant to depolarization. In the first case, an *excitatory synapse* is said to exist; in the second case, an *inhibitory synapse*. The highly complex interplay of excitatory and inhibitory synaptic functions is another mechanism for processing information within the nervous system. In this way, part of the transfer system is part of the processing system (Figure 11.6). In those motor neurons where the axon ends in a muscle, the release of acetylcholine from the motor end plates initiates muscle contraction. See Figure 11.2(b).

Figure 11.8
This representation of a neuron chain is highly simplified.
Thousands of association neurons may be involved in the
linking of sensory and motor neurons.

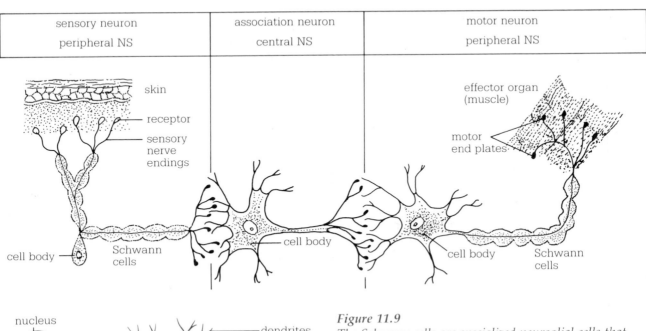

sensory neuron	association neuron	motor neuron
peripheral NS	central NS	peripheral NS

skin
receptor
sensory nerve endings
cell body
Schwann cells
cell body
effector organ (muscle)
motor end plates
cell body
Schwann cells

nucleus

dendrites
cell body
nucleus

Schwann cell
axon

axon
node of Ranvier

development of myelin sheath (Schwann cell) around axon

neurilemma
myelin
direction of impulse

axon
neurilemma
myelin sheath

myelinated nerve fibre

nerve endings

Figure 11.9
The Schwann cells are specialized neuroglial cells that
form the myelin sheath.

A typical neuron chain involves the three types of neurons. In Figure 11.8, the sensory and motor neurons are part of the peripheral nervous system. The association neuron is located in the brain or spinal cord and is part of the central nervous system.

Maintenance of the Neuron
Neurons depend on **neuroglial cells** for much of their nutrition. Taking up about half of the volume of the nervous system in vertebrates, these cells help the neurons maintain their metabolic activities. The **Schwann cells** are specialized neuroglial cells. They wrap around the axon and form a **myelin sheath**. The area where one Schwann cell ends and another begins is a **node of Ranvier**. An axon with its Schwann cells forms a **myelinated fibre**, so named because the neuroglial cells contain much of a white, fatty lipoprotein known as **myelin**. The white matter of the brain and spinal cord is made up of myelinated fibres. The grey matter consists of unmyelinated fibres and nerve cell bodies.

11.2 THE GENERAL PLAN OF THE VERTEBRATE NERVOUS SYSTEM

At each level of its organization, the vertebrate nervous system can be divided into two sections, each of which has contrasting activities. A binary tree can be drawn to describe the general plan of this extremely complex system.

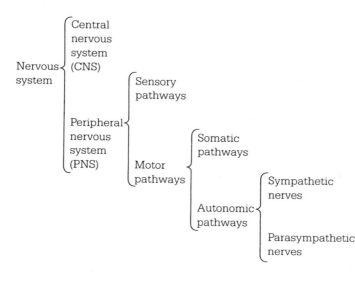

Figure 11.10

The voluntary nervous system contains the somatic pathways. They consist of a network of nerves, many of them myelinated, and carry commands to the striated muscles. The autonomic nervous system contains the autonomic pathways, a network of nerves that carry commands to the smooth muscles such as those encasing the intestines. The neuroendocrine system is a network of endocrine glands controlled by nervous signals from the CNS.

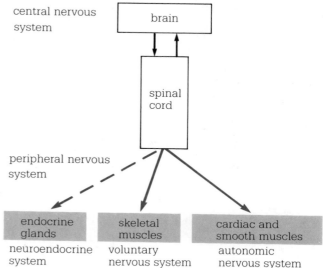

The **central nervous system** (CNS) consists of the brain and spinal cord. Its major function is the processing of information. The **peripheral nervous system** (PNS) consists of all the nerve pathways in the body. Its major function is the communication of information between the body and the CNS. The PNS consists of *sensory* and *motor* pathways. The former carry information *to* the CNS; the latter, *from* the CNS.

In turn, there are two kinds of motor pathways. *Somatic* pathways carry information to the voluntary muscles, that is, to the voluntary nervous system (Figure 11.10). *Autonomic* pathways carry information to the involuntary muscles (that is, to the autonomic nervous system), the glands and the neuroendocrine system (Figure 11.10).

Finally, the autonomic pathways are divided into *sympathetic nerves* which stimulate tissue and *parasympathetic nerves* which inhibit tissue.

Figure 11.10 shows how the central nervous system integrates with the peripheral nervous system. Bear in mind that the central nervous system also integrates with the endocrine system.

11.3 THE CENTRAL NERVOUS SYSTEM: BRAIN AND SPINAL CORD

The central nervous system consists of the brain and the spinal cord. Most of the trillions of neurons in the CNS are association neurons which couple the sensory and the motor pathways and interact with each other (Figure 11.8). This vast neuronal network integrates and controls many of the body's activities. The CNS thus plays a major role in homeostasis. The brain acts as the central command post and the spinal cord as a complex signal relay system.

The CNS is protected by enclosure in bone: the brain by the skull and the spinal cord by the vertebrae. In addition, both the brain and the spinal cord are wrapped in three protective membranes, the **meninges**. Cushioning the CNS is **cerebrospinal fluid**. It fills the spaces between the meninges, the central canal of the spinal cord, and the **ventricles** (spaces) in the brain.

The brains of all vertebrates have the same basic plan. They increase in complexity as one progresses from fish to amphibians through reptiles to birds and mammals. The human brain is the most complex; humans have more brain mass per unit of body weight than any other animal. The special feature of the human brain is the enormous development of the cerebrum. Many biologists maintain that this feature is what makes us so different from other animals. The functioning of the human brain is one of the great mysteries of life. We have learned how parts of this 1.7 kg mass of trillions of cells operates, but there remains much more to learn.

Oxygen and nutrients (particularly glucose) are delivered to the brain cells by a network of blood vessels and capillaries. No nerve cell is more than a few cells away from a capillary. Interruption of the supply of oxygen or glucose to the brain very rapidly leads to a disruption of the brain's activities and a state of unconsciousness. A blockage in the brain's circulatory system causes cerebrovascular accident (CVA), commonly known as a **stroke**. The loss of blood supply causes death of brain cells and a loss of control over the body parts associated with that part of the brain.

Parts of the Brain

The boundary between the brain and the spinal cord is where the first pair of spinal nerves comes off the spinal cord. This area is also very close to where the spinal cord enters the skull. The mature brain has three major divisions: hindbrain, midbrain, and forebrain (Figure 11.11).

Hindbrain

The **hindbrain** is the part of the brain most closely associated with the spinal cord. It is considered the "primitive" brain because its parts are well developed in the brains of fishes and amphibians. In this part of the brain are the control centres for most basic life activities such as breathing, heartbeat, and the control of blood pressure. The hindbrain is made up of a series of interconnected parts: medulla oblongata, cerebellum, and pons.

The **medulla oblongata** is the first extension of the spinal cord. It contains many association neurons and acts like a complex relay centre, sorting incoming and outgoing information. It connects the higher parts of the brain and the sensory pathways to the motor nerves. Nerve impulses that control the diaphragm and the muscles involved in breathing originate here. As well, the medulla controls the heart rate and regulates the diameter of blood vessels.

Figure 11.11
This lateral view, in which the brain has been bisected from front to back, shows the major functional areas.

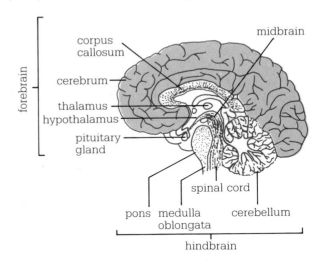

Located just behind the medulla is the **cerebellum**. It contains both white matter (myelinated nerve tissue) and an outer cortex of grey matter (unmyelinated nerve tissue) that has many folds. The cerebellum is connected by nerve tracts to the motor area of the cerebral cortex and receives inputs from almost all of the sensory areas in the body. It coordinates and maintains fine control over all motor actions. Along the motor area of the cerebrum, it controls posture and equilibrium. If you try to balance on one foot, your cerebellum is very actively involved in helping you to maintain your balance. Damage to the cerebellum affects the precision of motor activities. Jerky, abrupt movements, difficulty in keeping balance and slurred speech are typical symptoms of such damage.

The **pons**, named after the Latin word for bridge, is located between the medulla and the midbrain. Its nerve fibres connect the two sides of the cerebellum. The pons also connects the cerebellum to parts of the cerebrum, to the midbrain, and to lower brain centres such as the medulla. In addition, it contains parts of the breathing control system.

Midbrain

The **midbrain**, located above the pons, consists of four small bundles of grey matter which are relay centres for some of the reflexes associated with the eyes and ears. Below this grey matter is some white matter made up of myelinated nerve tracts that form connections between the pons, the cerebellum, the spinal cord, and parts of the cerebrum.

Figure 11.12
This lateral view of the external surface of the human brain shows the four cerebral lobes and the major functional regions of the cerebral cortex.

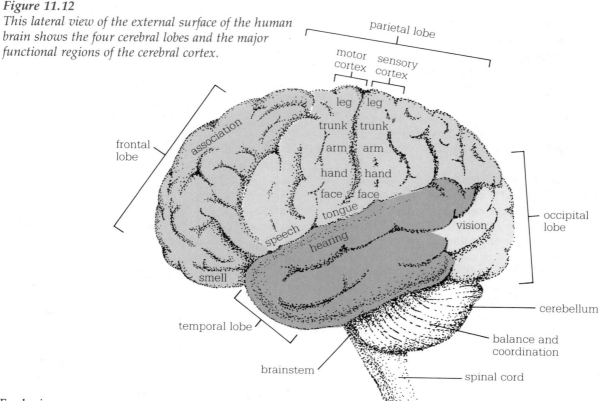

Forebrain

The **forebrain** contains the thalamus, hypothalamus, and the cerebrum (Figures 11.11 and 11.12).

Located above the midbrain, the **thalamus** acts as a relay centre for nerve impulses going to the cerebrum. It affects consciousness and the perception of pain levels.

The **hypothalamus** is the control centre for many vital functions of the autonomic nervous system. Its role in temperature regulation and water balance was described in Chapter 10. The control centres for hunger, thirst, and sexual drive are also located in the hypothalamus. By releasing a series of neurohormones, the hypothalamus also regulates the activity of the anterior part of the pituitary gland. This hormonal action is a good example of close cooperation between the nervous system and the endocrine system. (The importance of the pituitary gland to many of the body's vital functions is discussed in Chapter 12.)

The **cerebrum** is the largest part of the human brain. It seems to envelope all the other parts. In humans and other primates, the cerebrum is split into two hemispheres by a longitudinal fissure. Each one is divided by two deep groves into four lobes: the fron-

tal, parietal, occipital, and temporal (Figure 11.12). The hemispheres are connected only by a nerve tract, the **corpus callosum**.

The cerebrum has an outer layer, the **cerebral cortex**, and a core made up of the inner white matter of the brain. In humans, the cerebral cortex contains over ten billion nerve cells, about ten percent of all the neurons in the brain. The surface of the human cerebral cortex is highly convoluted, thus creating a surface area three times that of a uniformly smooth surface. This increase in surface area is necessary to contain all of the cortical nerve cells. Only a small portion of the cerebral cortex is occupied by the motor and sensory cortexes (Figure 11.12). The remainder is known as the associative cortex.

The associative cortex is the site of mental activities such as conceptualization, planning, and contemplation. Associative memory (the ability to recall information and to fit it in with new ideas) is also an activity of the associative cortex. Humans have the highest proportion of associative cortex in the entire animal kingdom. Intelligence and personality appear to be controlled in an area at the very front of the frontal lobes.

Figure 11.13
Motor signals from the left side of the brain control muscles on the right side of the body.

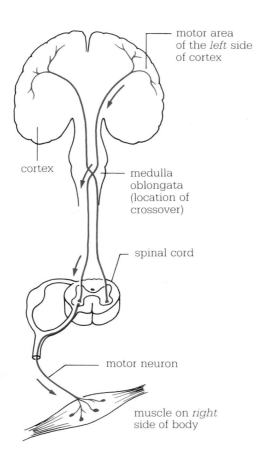

- motor area of the *left* side of cortex
- cortex
- medulla oblongata (location of crossover)
- spinal cord
- motor neuron
- muscle on *right* side of body

The **motor cortex**, consisting of a narrow band of nerve tissue just in front of the central fissure, controls the voluntary movement of the skeletal muscles. A separate patch of nerve tissue controls each group of motor neurons. Body parts involved in many subtle movements, such as the hands and the mouth, are controlled by relatively large areas of the motor cortex. By contrast, body parts involved in a more limited range of movement, such as the ankle or forehead, are controlled by relatively small areas. Impulses from motor nerves affect muscles on the side of the body *opposite* to the side of the brain from which the impulse travels (Figure 11.13). Thus, a stroke occurring on one side of the brain affects the operation of the opposite side of the body.

The **sensory cortex** in the parietal lobes lies in a band behind the motor cortex (Figure 11.12). Different parts of it receive inputs from different areas of the body.

Some of the neurons associated with sense organs are located adjacent to the sensory cortex; for example, neurons for vision on the occipital lobe, those for hearing on the temporal lobe, and those for smell on the frontal lobe (Figure 11.12). Stimulation of parts of the sensory cortex by a blow to the head can sometimes cause sensations such as ''seeing stars'' or a ''ringing in the ears.'' Coordination of the input from several senses takes place in the association areas located on the associative cortex.

Lying just under the cerebral cortex is the inner white matter of the brain. Because its nerve fibres are myelinated, this part of the brain is white. There are three kinds of fibres each doing a different task. Commissural fibres carry impulses from one hemisphere to the other. Association fibres connect other fibres in the same hemisphere. Projection fibres connect to areas in the spinal cord that are relatively remote from the brain.

The Spinal Cord
The spinal cord extends from the brainstem down to the end of the backbone. See Figure 11.14(a). It is divided into 31 segments, each of which gives rise to a pair of *spinal nerves*. Part of the peripheral nervous system, these nerves pass through small openings in the lateral arms of each segment. Originating where the dorsal and ventral roots join, the spinal nerves carry nerve impulses to and from the spinal cord. Sensory nerve fibres enter by way of the dorsal root, which is located in the dorsal surface of the cord (the afferent path). The nerve cell bodies of these sensory neurons are located in the dorsal root ganglia, a bulge in the dorsal root. See Figure 11.14(c). Motor impulses are carried from the cord in the ventral root (the efferent path).

The white matter in the spinal cord consists of bundles of myelinated axons of sensory and motor neurons. The grey matter, by contrast, is made up of the unmyelinated association neurons and the unmyelinated dendrites and nerve cell bodies of motor neurons. Connecting the sensory and motor neurons, the association neurons carry messages up and down the spinal cord.

There are two major functions of the spinal cord and associated parts of the peripheral nervous system. One is to carry sensory signals from the periphery of the body to the brain and to carry motor signals in the opposite direction. The other is to provide the neural pathways for reflex action that does not need to involve the brain directly.

Figure 11.14
The connection of the brain and spinal cord (a), a cross section of the spinal column (b), and a cross section of the spinal cord (c). The spinal cord contains association neurons that link the sensory pathways with the motor pathways. In addition, neurons in the spinal cord carry information to and from the brain.

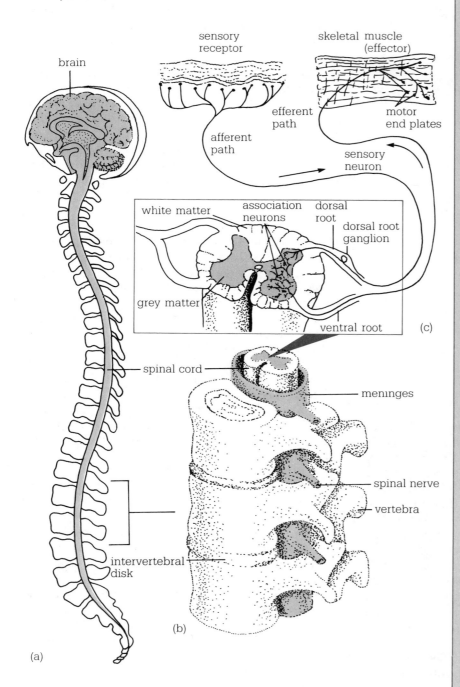

Survival demands that an organism be constantly aware of its external environment. Animals have evolved specialized sensory structures that both respond to environmental stimuli and detect the movement and balance of the body.

Depending on the particular stimulus–receptor interaction, the stimulus is received in a variety of ways. Except where reflex arcs are involved, the stimulus causes the receptor or receptors to initiate a series of nerve impulses that are fed in through the sensory pathways of the PNS into specialized parts of the brain. This information allows the animal to act in ways that maintain homeostasis.

Sensory perception involves responses to a number of things. Among them are *light, sound, chemicals, temperature, and touch,* plus *gravity, balance,* and *motion. Proprioception* is a special form of sensory perception that enables an organism to detect the location and rate of movement of one part of the body relative to other parts.

Light. Specialized epithelial cells in the eye (rods and cones) contain a photosensitive pigment (rhodopsin). When light strikes rhodopsin, it changes its chemical configuration in a way that triggers a nerve impulse. This impulse is transmitted by way of the visual neural pathway (optic nerve) to the visual area of the cerebrum. The eye can do much more than just perceive the difference between light and dark. Its light-sensitive cells work in conjunction with the lens and other parts of the eye to feed complex visual information into the brain. In turn, the brain interprets this information as sight.

SENSORY PERCEPTION

Sound. Vibration in the air causes a vibration in the membrane of the eardrum. When transmitted to the fluid in the inner ear, this membranal vibration causes specialized receptor hair cells to move into contact with a membrane, initiating nerve impulses in them. These impulses are conducted to the auditory area of the brain, where they are interpreted as specific sounds.

Chemicals. Both taste and smell depend upon the arrival of chemicals at the surface of cells that have parts of their membranes specialized for reception. These receptor cells are located on the tongue and in the roof of the nasal cavity. The stimulating molecule dissolves in the liquid coating of the receptor cell membrane. In doing so, it attaches to a receptor protein molecule within the membrane. Usually this attachment is very precise, involving specific parts of the stimulating molecule. The receptor cell then initiates nerve impulses which are interpreted by the brain as a specific taste or smell.

Temperature and Touch. The receptors for these stimuli are part of the cutaneous sensory system. The human skin acts as a sense organ capable of responses to a great many stimuli. The intensity of the stimuli can change the interpretation of the message. For example, if a gentle handshake turns into a squeeze, the sensation goes from one of mere touch to one of pain. The receptors are naked nerve endings on the skin surface or nerve endings within specialized cellular structures. They are scattered over the entire body surface.

The receptors in the human skin have different structures. Pain receptors are the free nerve endings. Pacinian corpuscles are pressure receptors. Merkel's disks, Meissner's corpuscles, and the nerve endings surrounding the hair follicle are all touch receptors.

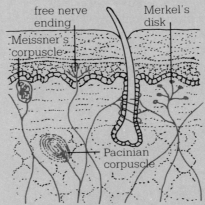

free nerve ending Merkel's disk Meissner's corpuscle Pacinian corpuscle

The various stimuli cause physical changes in the receptors in the skin and initiate nerve impulses. Nerve processes from these receptors are not collected into specialized bundles, instead, the afferent fibres form part of many nerves entering the CNS.

Balance, Gravity, and Motion. Our sense of balance or dynamic equilibrium depends on nerve impulses from hair cells in the semicircular canals in the inner ear. These canals are oriented in different planes: vertical, horizontal, and oblique. When the head rotates, liquid in one or more of the semicircular canals moves, activating the hair cells, which then send messages to the brain. In turn, the brain sends out messages to the skeletal muscles required to maintain balance. Rotational acceleration also affects the semicircular canals.

Two parts of the inner ear, known as the saccule and the utricle, are involved in sensing the pull of gravity and the movement of the body when it is travelling in a straight line. These organs contain small lumps of calcium carbonate (otoliths) which rest on hair cells and are pulled down on these cells by gravity. When you move your head, the otoliths shift their position, thus stimulating the hair cells. When your head is accelerated, the otoliths shift and allow you to detect straight line motion. The hair cells send their signals into the brain, where they are interpreted as sensations of head position and motion. Mechanical stimuli, such as that provided by otoliths, initiate nerve impulses by twisting the membrane of the sensory neuron. This twisting causes ion channels in the membrane to open and thus initiates membrane depolarization.

Proprioception. Without proprioception, you could not remain standing or move your body with precision. Proprioception allows you to estimate weight and to control the movements of your limbs. It works cooperatively with the balance and motion organs of the inner ear. The actual sensing is done by receptors in the muscles, tendons, and joints. Muscle spindles are buried in skeletal muscles and are activated when the muscle changes its length. Golgi tendon organs are located in the tendons that attach skeletal muscles to bones. These organs are activated when the tendon is stretched and they measure the tension in the tendons. Similar sensors detect the movement in the joints. Most proprioceptive action operates by means of reflex arcs without the involvement of brain.

Reflex Action and the Reflex Arc

A **reflex action** is an involuntary response to a stimulus. You usually have little or no control over such actions because the neurons involved in the reflex start the action before the conscious part of your brain can be activated. Common examples are snatching the hand away from a hot object before the pain is felt, blinking when anything touches the surface of the eyeball, or jerking the lower leg when the tendon below the kneecap is tapped.

Actual reflex action involves the simultaneous action of many **reflex arcs**. However, the principles of reflex action can be understood by looking at the action of single arcs. At least five components are usually involved in a simple reflex pathway or reflex arc. They are a sensory receptor, a sensory neuron, an association or interneuron, a motor neuron, and an effector. Figure 11.15 shows the reflex arc involved when one touches a hot object and then snatches the hand away.

Figure 11.15

This reflex arc involves five components. Sensory heat receptors in the skin (a) initiate a nerve impulse in the sensory neuron (b) which synapses with an association neuron (c) in the nerve cord. The association neuron stimulates a motor neuron (d) which stimulates the muscle acting as the effector (e). All of the synapses involved are stimulatory. Another neuron, which synapses at the junction between the sensory neuron and the association neuron, carries the heat signal to the sensory cortex of the brain. This particular neuron is not part of the reflex arc.

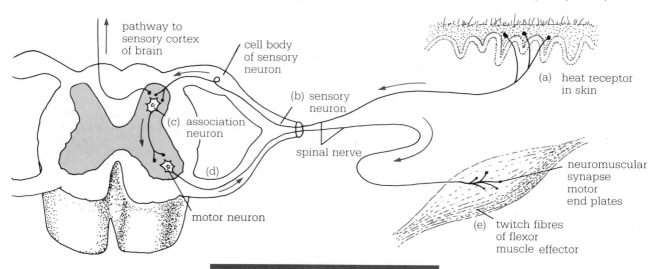

DAMAGE TO THE SPINAL CORD

The vertebral column and the membranes and fluid that surround the spinal cord provide protection. A severe blow can damage these protective devices. The spinal cord may thus become partially or completely severed. The disruption of the nerve paths causes a loss of both sensation and voluntary control of those motor muscles served by neurons located below the point of injury. The farther up the spinal cord the injury occurs, the more extensive the injury is. Damage in the cervical region, near the head, can cause paralysis of almost the entire body. A person who has all four limbs so affected is said to be quadriplegic. If the injury occurs in the middle of the spinal cord, only the legs will be affected. People with this condition are said to be paraplegic.

Caution. If you ever are asked to help at an accident and you suspect that the accident victim may have injury to the spinal cord *do not move them.* Get help from people with training in such matters. Certain types of movement can increase the injury significantly. If you are the victim of an accident, you may rightly suspect spinal cord injury if a part of your body has lost sensation. If so, tell anyone who is trying to help you of your suspicion. Do not let them move you unless they know the proper procedures.

Figure 11.16

A complex reflex arc is involved when one steps on a sharp object and jerks the foot away. Pain receptors in the skin, activated by the sharp object, initiate a nerve impulse in a sensory neuron. Axonal branches from the sensory neuron synapse with three association neurons within the nerve cord and stimulate (+) each of them. Association neuron 1 stimulates a flexor motor neuron (F) on the right hand side. This motor neuron causes the flexor muscle to contract. Association neuron 2 inhibits (−) the right extensor motor neuron (E) and so this motor pathway is not activated. There are no inhibitory nerves to mammalian striated muscle; consequently, if such a muscle is not stimulated, it relaxes. The contraction of the
right flexor muscle and the relaxation of the right extensor muscle causes the right leg to flex, removing it from the sharp object. Association neuron 3 has its axonal processes cross over to the other side of the spinal cord, where one branch stimulates the left extensor motor neuron (E), leading to contraction in the left extensor muscle. Association neuron 3 also has an axonal process which stimulates (+) association neuron 4 in the spinal cord. In turn, association neuron 4 inhibits (−) the action of left flexor motor neuron (F) and so this muscle stays in a relaxed state. The contraction of the left extensor muscle and the relaxation of the left flexor muscle cause the left leg to straighten out. The flexed right leg is thus lifted away from the sharp object.

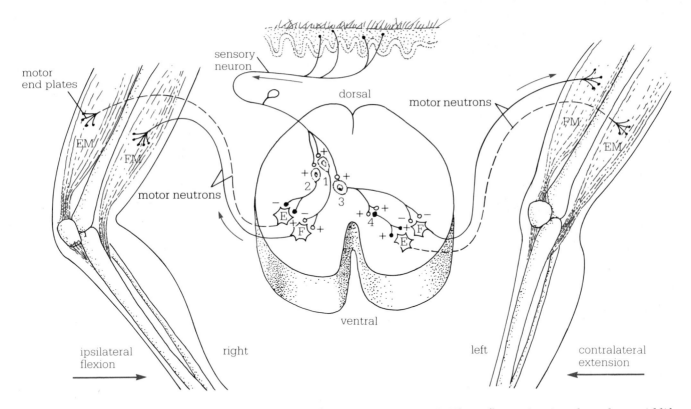

In this and other similar reactions, a pain signal is transmitted to the sensory cortex of the brain by way of another set of neurons. The sensation of pain is not experienced, however, until *after* the reflex action has caused the hand to move. The reflex action provides homeostatic protection at a very basic level, one without the direct involvement of the brain.

A more complicated reflex arc would be involved if you stepped on a sharp object with your right foot

(Figure 11.16). The reflex action involves the rapid lifting of the foot, requiring the right leg to bend and the left leg to straighten out. Both stimulation and inhibition are thus involved. Complex reflex arcs such as these are used to maintain our upright posture. The constant adjustments required depend on the action of many proprioceptors. These adjustments are managed without consciousness of the activities.

11.4 THE PERIPHERAL NERVOUS SYSTEM

The peripheral nervous system (PNS) has many sub-divisions and consists of neurons with long dendrites and/or long axons. The nerve cell bodies are found in the brain, in the spinal cord, and in **ganglia** (sing. *ganglion*), collections of nerve cell bodies. The neurons of the PNS are bundled up into nerves which can be classified on the basis of their activity, as sensory, motor, or mixed nerves. *Sensory nerves* consist of long dendrites of sensory neurons. They carry messages from the peripheral receptors (sensory structures) to the CNS. *Motor nerves* are made up of long axons of motor neurons. They carry signals from the CNS to the effectors (muscles and glands). *Mixed nerves* contain both sensory and motor neurons and carry messages to and from the CNS. Figure 11.17 shows a cross section of a typical mixed nerve.

The nerves of the PNS can also be classified in terms of their anatomical location as either cranial or spinal.

Figure 11.17
Cross section of a mixed nerve. One axon is shown extended to illustrate that each neuronal process is enclosed in its own myelin sheath, thus insulating each process from the others. In a sensory nerve, the axons would be absent; in a motor nerve, the dendrites would be absent.

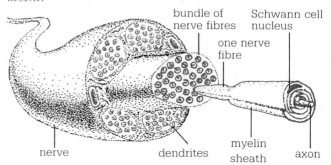

Figure 11.18
The cranial nerves are identified by number and by the name of the organ they innervate.

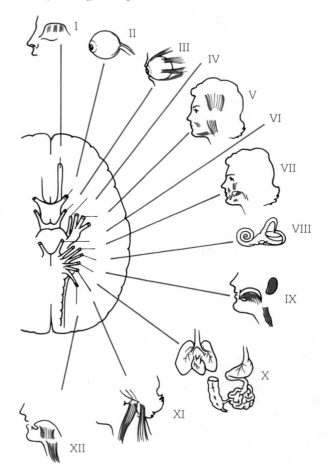

I	OLFACTORY the sense of smell
II	OPTIC the sense of vision
III	OCULOMOTOR most eye muscles, iris, and ciliary muscle
IV	TROCHLEAR superior oblique muscle
V	TRIGEMINAL mastication muscles and sensations from eye, face, teeth, sinuses
VI	ABDUCENS external rectus muscle
VII	FACIAL facial muscles, salivary glands, taste, and tongue
VIII	ACOUSTIC cochlear, sense of hearing vestibular, sense of balance
IX	GLOSSOPHARYNGEAL Parotid gland, sense of taste, tonsils, pharynx
X	VAGUS motor nerves to heart, lungs, digestive tract; sensory from most of the intestinal organs
XI	ACCESSORY mastoid, rear neck muscles, larynx, and pharynx
XII	HYPOGLOSSAL muscles in front of neck and to tongue

The Cranial Nerves

Although the brain is part of the CNS, the **cranial nerves** are classified as part of the PNS. Leaving the underside of the brain, they pass out through small holes in the skull. There are 12 of them, each one named according to the organ or the function of the organ to which it connects (Figure 11.18). For example the optic nerve connects to the eye. Some of these nerves are sensory, some motor, and some are mixed. One of them, the vagus nerve, innervates many of the body's internal organs. Most of the others innervate structures in the head region.

Spinal Nerves

As noted earlier, the spinal cord gives off 31 pairs of **spinal nerves** (Figure 11.14) which are distributed throughout the body (Figure 11.19).

All spinal nerves are mixed nerves; the motor information is carried by both somatic pathways and autonomic pathways (section 11.2).

Somatic Pathways and Neuromuscular Control

Coordination of striated muscles is essential for homeostasis. Somatic pathways carry the information that is used for this control. The network of motor nerves connects to individual striated muscles; as impulses are delivered down these nerves, the release of acetylcholine at the motor end plates of the motor axons causes the muscles to contract.

Neuromuscular control is established by means of feedback loops, the sensors for which are **stretch receptors** located within the muscles. When a muscle extends or contracts, the stretch receptors are depolarized, causing a nerve impulse to go through nerve paths similar to those shown in Figure 11.16. The signal can cause complex feedback signals to be transmitted back to the muscle. The association neurons may interact to produce either stimulation or inhibition. In the former case, the outgoing signal will cause the muscle to remain contracted; in the latter case, to stay relaxed. In this way, the CNS modifies feedback information and controls the activity of voluntary muscles.

Voluntary muscles occur in opposing sets. One set is the *flexors*; the other, the *extensors*. Muscles can only pull; they cannot push. Limb movement is accomplished by contraction of one set of muscles while there is relaxation and stretching of the opposing set. Feedback information, initiated by stretch receptors in the muscles, keeps the CNS informed. In this way, the flexor–extensor muscle pairs are coordinated and neuromuscular control is achieved.

Figure 11.19
Only the major peripheral nerves are shown.

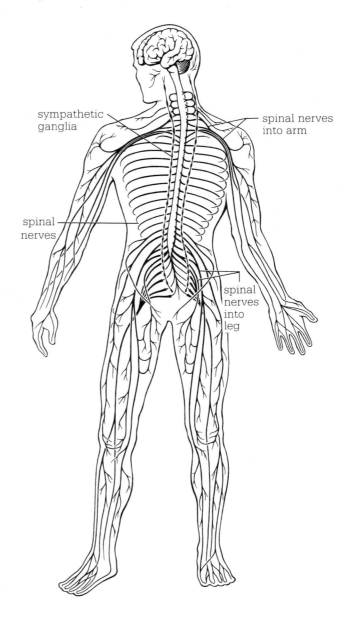

Autonomic Pathways and Neurovisceral Control

The autonomic nervous system works automatically, without conscious control. Its major controlling centre is the hypothalamus but the medulla and the spinal cord are also involved.

The autonomic system has two parts, the sympathetic and the parasympathetic (Figure 11.20). Both of these systems have nerve cell bodies that are located outside the CNS and are usually clumped together as ganglia. In the sympathetic system, the ganglia lie close to the spinal cord, and are accordingly known as the *sympathetic chain ganglia*. In the parasympathetic system, each ganglion lies close to the organ that is being innervated.

The autonomic system controls the body's internal environment by regulation of the glands, smooth muscles, and cardiac muscles. This neurovisceral control is achieved by a combination of feedback loops and antagonistic controls.

The nature of the feedback varies with the type of target tissue. The feedback loop for smooth muscle depends on stretch receptors. It operates in a manner

similar to the neuromuscular control of striated muscle. Many of the feedback loops involving the glands and the heart involve chemical feedback (Chapter 12).

Antagonistic control is achieved in the autonomic system by the opposing action of the sympathetic and the parasympathetic systems (Figure 11.20). The sympathetic system is usually stimulatory, its actions prepare the body for stress (fight or flight responses). The chemical released at the terminal end of the last axon in a sympathetic nerve path is epinephrine (commonly known as adrenalin) or norepinephrine (also called

Figure 11.20
The two parts of the autonomic nervous system balance one another to achieve homeostatic control.

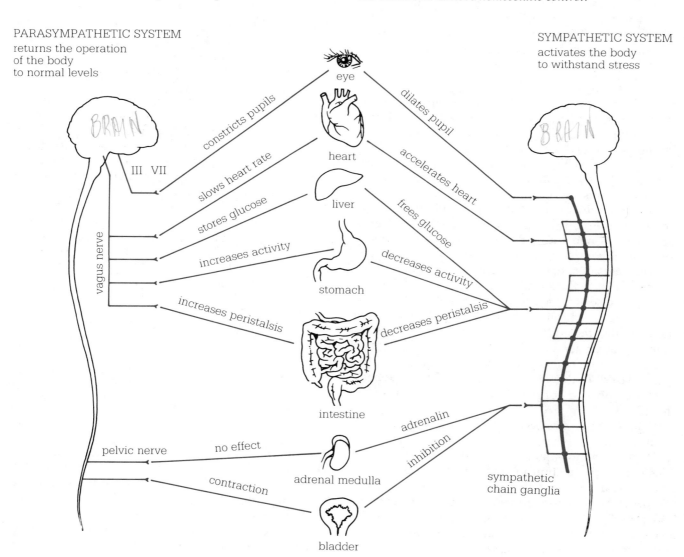

PARASYMPATHETIC SYSTEM
returns the operation
of the body
to normal levels

SYMPATHETIC SYSTEM
activates the body
to withstand stress

noradrenalin). The parasympathetic system is usually inhibitory; it reverses the effects of the sympathetic system. The interaction of the two systems maintains homeostatic balance in the organism.

Some of the nerves of the parasympathetic system arise in the midbrain, the pons, and the medulla.

Important connections between these brain regions and the viscera are made via some of the cranial nerves. Particularly important is the vagus nerve. It has connections to the heart, the bronchi in the lungs, the esophagus, the pancreas, the stomach, the intestines, and the liver.

CHAPTER SUMMARY

The nervous system plays a major role in integrating the functions of multicellular animals. Its basic unit is the neuron. There are three types of neurons: sensory, motor, and association. Neurons are specialized to receive, process, and transmit information. The diffusion of ions across the excitable membrane of the neuron allows electrical signals to be sent. There are just two types of signals, weak (graded potentials) and strong (nerve impulses). Since neurons are separated from one another by synaptic clefts, the signal is transferred from one neuron to another by neurotransmitters.

The vertebrate nervous system consists of a central nervous system, consisting of the brain and spinal cord, and a peripheral nervous system, consisting of all the other nerves in the body. The CNS is the central information-processing system, while the PNS innervates all parts of the body and transmits information to and from the CNS.

The brain has three major parts: hindbrain, midbrain, and forebrain. The various parts of the hindbrain control basic life activities such as breathing and heartbeat. The midbrain contains relay centres for reflexes associated with the eyes and ears. The forebrain, particularly the cerebral cortex, is very highly developed in humans.

The spinal cord and associated parts of the PNS carry sensory signals from the periphery of the body to the brain and carry motor signals in the opposite direction. They also provide neural pathways for reflex action which does not directly involve the brain.

The PNS has both sensory pathways which carry information to the CNS and motor pathways which carry information from it. The motor pathways are in turn divided into somatic pathways that innervate striated muscles and autonomic pathways that innervate smooth muscles and glands. In their turn, the autonomic pathways consist of sympathetic nerves, which activate the body to withstand stress, and parasympathetic nerves, which return the body to normal levels.

Objectives

Having completed this chapter, you should be able to do the following:

1. Describe the structure and function of sensory, motor, and association neurons.
2. Explain how information is received, processed, transmitted, and transferred by neurons.
3. Describe the organization of the vertebrate central nervous system and the functioning of its various parts.
4. Outline the structure and function of a complex reflex arc.
5. State how the various parts of the peripheral nervous system help maintain the homeostatic balance of the body.
6. Describe the mechanisms of neuromuscular and neurovisceral control.

Vocabulary

neuron
dendrite
axon
sensory neuron
motor neuron
association neuron
synaptic cleft
saltatorial conduction
synapse
neuroglial cell
Schwann cell
myelin sheath
node of Ranvier
myelinated fibre

myelin
central nervous system (CNS)
peripheral nervous system (PNS)
meninges
cerebrospinal fluid
ventricle
stroke
hindbrain
medulla oblongata
cerebellum
pons
midbrain
forebrain
thalamus

hypothalamus
cerebrum
corpus callosum
cerebral cortex
motor cortex
sensory cortex
reflex action
reflex arc
ganglion
cranial nerve
spinal nerve
stretch receptor

Review Questions

1. (a) Describe the structural and functional characteristics of a neuron.
   (b) Explain how a sensory neuron differs from a motor neuron.
2. (a) What is a nerve impulse?
   (b) How is it initiated and sent?
   (c) Why does it normally travel only in one direction?
3. Describe the following aspects of neuron operation:
   (a) reception
   (b) processing
   (c) transmission
   (d) transfer
   (e) maintenance
4. Using binary classification, diagram the general plan of the vertebrate nervous system.
5. Draw a diagram of a lateral view of the human brain. Show the location and describe the function of the following parts:
   (a) medulla oblongata
   (b) cerebellum
   (c) pons
   (d) midbrain

   (e) thalamus
   (f) hypothalamus
   (g) cerebrum
6. Why is the hindbrain considered the "primitive" part of the brain?
7. What role is played by
   (a) the associative cortex?
   (b) the motor cortex?
   (c) the sensory cortex?
8. How does the motor area on the left side of the cortex control muscles on the right side of the body?
9. Describe the functioning of a reflex arc.
10. (a) How are the nerves of the PNS classified according to function?
    (b) What is the function of each type?
11. Compare the structure and function of
    (a) cranial nerves and spinal nerves
    (b) somatic pathways and autonomic pathways
    (c) the sympathetic system and the parasympathetic system.
12. Describe a feedback system that operates in neuromuscular control systems.

Advanced Questions

1. Nerve poisons can block the enzyme that removes the neurotransmitter substance at the synaptic cleft. What would happen to the operation of the nervous system if this enzyme were immobilized?
2. (a) What happens to incoming sensory information in the central nervous system?
   (b) How can the way you feel affect this process?
3. (a) Why is it that many of the body's functions operate without your being conscious of them?
   (b) What are some of the advantages of this automatic functioning?
4. (a) How do some of the activities of the left cerebral hemisphere differ from those of the right?
   (b) Is there any good evidence that the two sides of the brain are really different?
5. Why does the human ability to conceptualize allow us to live lives very different from those of other animals?
6. Research the effects on the nervous system of one of these disorders:
   (a) multiple sclerosis
   (b) Parkinson's disease
   (c) Alzheimer's disease
   (d) meningitis

CHAPTER 12

THE ENDOCRINE SYSTEM: ITS ROLE IN HOMEOSTASIS

*Without molecular regulatory agents,
the functions of living tissue
would be chaotic.*

Roger Eckert

The endocrine system consists of organs, tissues, and cells that secrete hormones to regulate the activities of target cells. In doing so, it helps coordinate the homeostatic balance of the organism. Improper functioning of the endocrine system can have profound effects. For example, when the pituitary gland produces irregularly high levels of human growth hormone, an individual can reach an extremely abnormal size.

While the nervous system is somewhat like the telephone system, the endocrine system resembles the mail system. The "letters" are specific hormones produced in endocrine glands. The blood stream is the delivery service. Just as the mail system works more slowly than the telephone system, the endocrine system works more slowly than the nervous system. Hormones provide long term, persistent regulation and homeostatic controls.

12.1 THE ENDOCRINE SYSTEM AND ITS HORMONES

The endocrine system works in close cooperation with the nervous system. For the most part, the nervous system adjusts for short term change while the endocrine system controls long term processes such as growth and sexual maturation. Nevertheless, certain parts of the endocrine system such as the adrenal glands can cause relatively rapid changes.

The functional units of the endocrine system are the **endocrine glands**. These glands secrete their products, known as **hormones**, directly into the blood stream. They do not have ducts or tubes which are characteristic of exocrine glands such as the sweat glands or the salivary glands. Specific endocrine glands release their specific hormone or hormones in response to a stimulus from another part of the body. This stimulus can come from the nervous system or it can be caused by chemicals circulated in the blood to the endocrine gland. These signal chemicals can be other hormones or can be chemicals resulting from metabolism. Only minute amounts of hormones are released; nevertheless, they can produce very large effects.

Substances secreted by cells, carried in the bloodstream, and used by another cell are classified as *humoral agents*. Carbon dioxide is an example of a humoral agent that has many effects. Hormones constitute a special set of humoral agents. They have certain characteristics that distinguish them from other chemicals in the body.

To be considered a hormone, a molecule must meet four conditions. First, it has to be produced by a specialized gland or by an organized group of cells and

In 1971 the American scientist Earl W. Sutherland won the Nobel Prize for his discovery that certain hormones act by means of a "second messenger." Certain hormones such as epinephrine stimulate their target cells without crossing their plasma membrane. Instead, they induce the formation of another molecule (the second messenger) within the cell.

The hormone is circulated in the blood. As shown in (a), it binds to a receptor molecule which is part of the plasma membrane of the target cell. This binding causes the receptor molecule to change its shape, and thus to bind with inactive G-protein which is located on the inside of the plasma membrane. See (b)(i). This binding activates the G-protein. A receptor site for the nucleotide *guanosine triphosphate* (GTP) is consequently formed. See (b)(ii). The GTP, which is present in the cytoplasm, then binds with the newly formed receptor site. See (b)(iii).

Next the GTP-G-protein complex activates an enzyme (*adenyl cyclase*) on the inner side of the plasma membrane. See (c)(i). This activation causes ATP in the cytoplasm to change into *cyclic adenosine monophosphate* (cAMP) and

two inorganic phosphate groups ($\textcircled{P}$). See (c)(ii). This adenyl cyclase activity greatly increases the concentration of cAMP in the cytoplasm.

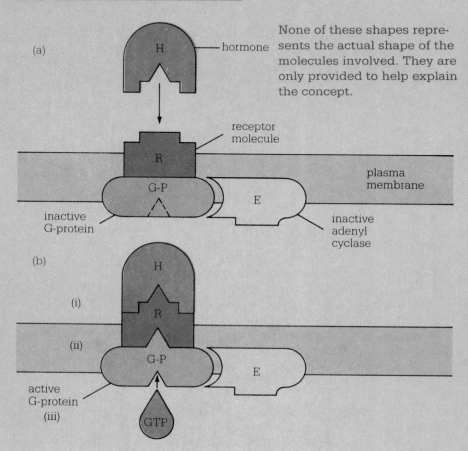

(a) hormone — receptor molecule — plasma membrane — inactive G-protein — inactive adenyl cyclase

(b) (i) (ii) (iii) — active G-protein — GTP

None of these shapes represents the actual shape of the molecules involved. They are only provided to help explain the concept.

secreted directly into the bloodstream. As well, it must exert its effect on a part of the body elsewhere than the place where it was produced. Third, because it is a "trigger" molecule that just supplies information to the target cells, it has to be required in very small amounts. Last, it must act upon specific target cells by regulating the rate of metabolism of a metabolic pathway. Such regulation usually involves modulation of the activities of a specific enzyme. Depending on the concentration of the hormone and the physiological state of the target tissue, the effect may be to speed up or slow down the enzyme.

The link between the hormone and its specific target tissue involves the fit of the hormone molecule into a specific receptor which is usually part of the membrane of the target cells. When the hormone-receptor connection has been made, enzyme systems in the cell are affected. Because of the specificity of the hormone-receptor fit, hormones can only affect tissue cells that have the appropriate receptors.

On the basis of their chemical composition, hormones can be divided into three categories: catecholamines, peptide hormones, and steroid hormones.

The cAMP is the second messenger. It can activate certain enzymes within the cytoplasm of the target cell and deactivate others. Only a few hormone molecules need to bind to receptor molecules to cause large amounts of cAMP to be formed. In this way the effect of the hormone is greatly amplified.

The following figure shows how the cAMP second messenger is involved in the liberation of glucose in response to epinephrine.

When epinephrine binds with receptor protein on the target cell, a chain of events is initiated that leads to an increased concentration of cAMP in the target cell and, in turn, to activation of the enzyme protein kinase A. This protein in its turn activates phosphorylase and inactivates glycogen synthetase. The final result of all of these reactions is the conversion of glycogen to glucose which is then released into the blood and provides energy for the "fight or flight" response.

More recent research has revealed other molecules that act as second messengers. *Cyclic guanosine monophosphate* (cGMP) is found in heart and liver cells. *Inositol tryphosphate* (IP_3) has been shown to act in the release of calcium ions from storage sites within cells.

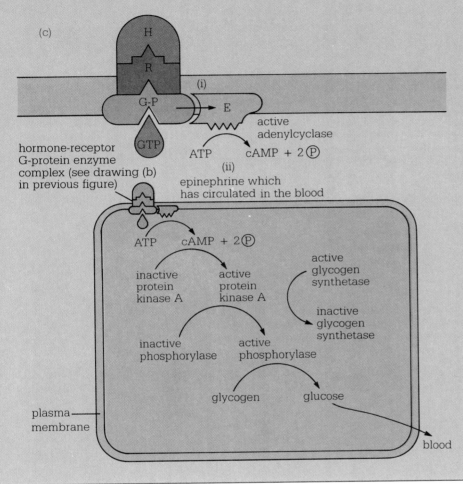

(c)

hormone-receptor G-protein enzyme complex (see drawing (b) in previous figure)

active adenylcyclase

epinephrine which has circulated in the blood

plasma membrane

blood

Epinephrine is a hormone that works by inducing the formation of a second-messenger molecule.

Catecholamines consist of relatively simple molecules which are modifications of the amino acid tyrosine. Epinephrine and norepinephrine are examples of this type.

Peptide hormones are divided into three different groups according to the number of amino acids in the chain. One important group consists of short chains of five or more amino acids linked together in very specific sequences. These "short chain" hormones have many different functions. Oxytocin is a good example of a short-chain hormone. A second group of peptide hormones, known as *endorphins* and *encephalins*, consists of chains of 32 amino acids. These hormones regulate emotional responses in the brain. The release of certain endorphins causes the "runner's high," the feeling of exuberance that sometimes results from intense exercise. Still other peptide hormones are proteins, consisting of even longer amino acid chains; insulin is such a protein.

Steroid hormones are all derived from cholesterol, a complex molecule with four carbon rings. The sex hormones belong in this category. As these hormones enter the target cell and penetrate its nucleus, they turn certain genes on and turn others off.

12.2 THE ENDOCRINE GLANDS

A great many organs in the body can release hormones and could therefore be classified as endocrine glands. The pituitary, thyroid, parathyroid, and adrenal glands, as well as the pancreas, occur in both sexes. Ovaries are specific to females and testes to males (Figure 12.1).

It is commonly believed that certain hormones are specific either to males or to females. For example, testosterone is usually regarded as an exclusively male hormone and estrogen as a strictly female hormone. In fact, *both* of these hormones are produced in *both* sexes. However, the estrogen present in males is produced in very low quantities. The same condition holds true for the testosterone in females. In practical terms, it is therefore still reasonable to talk of "male" hormones such as testosterone and "female" hormones such as estrogen.

The Pituitary Gland and Neuroendocrine Control

About the size of a pea, the **pituitary gland** is located in the brain and is attached to the hypothalamus by a thin stalk. It is actually two glands, an anterior lobe and a posterior lobe, each very different in its structure, function, and embryological origin. The former consists primarily of glandular cells; the latter, of few glandular cells but many nerve cells connected to the hypothalamus in the brain (Figures 12.2 and 12.3).

Neuroendocrine Control

The cooperative actions of the hypothalamus and the pituitary gland illustrate how nerve signals and hormones are mutually involved in a neuroendocrine control system. Home of the major coordination centre of the body, the hypothalamus receives and processes information about various vital activities such as the regulation of body temperature, the intake of food and water, the response to pain and emotional

✳ *Figure 12.1*

The human endocrine glands and their functions. Note that the brain, the heart, and the intestinal organs can also be considered as part of the endocrine system.

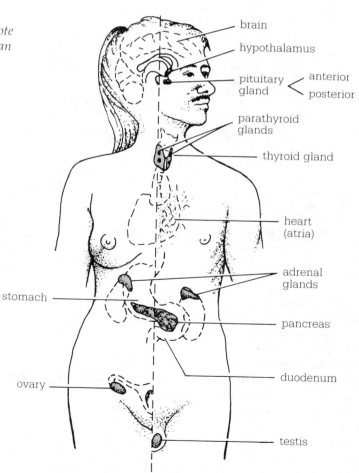

PITUITARY: the master gland; controls or influences all the other endocrine glands

THYROID GLAND: influences the metabolic rate, decreases blood calcium

PARATHYROID GLANDS: increase blood calcium

ADRENAL GLANDS: help to prepare the body for stress

PANCREAS: endocrine function is to control the blood sugar

OVARIES: produce the female sex hormones; influence the secondary sex characteristics

TESTES: produce the male sex hormones; influence the secondary sex characteristics of the male

Figure 12.2

The structure and function of the pituitary gland is highly complicated. The hormones released by the posterior pituitary are actually produced in the hypothalamus. They travel down nerve axons to nerve endings associated with blood capillaries in the posterior lobe, then from these nerve endings into the blood within the capillaries for distribution to target tissues. The hypothalamus also produces tropic hormones which in turn activate the anterior lobe to produce and release its specific stimulating hormones to other endocrine glands and tissues.

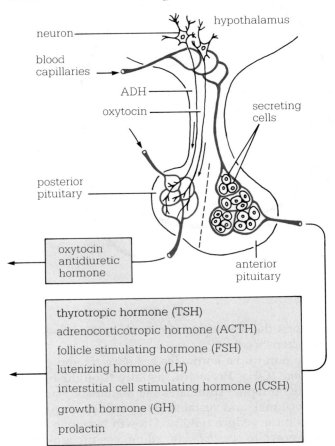

Figure 12.3

The hormones released by the anterior lobe of the pituitary affect many different target organs.

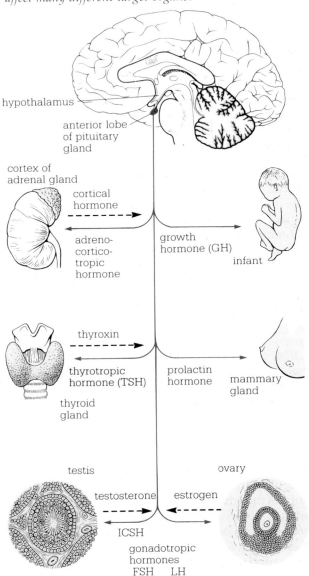

stress, and reproductive behaviour. Specialized *neurosecretory cells* in the hypothalamus then manufacture and release specific chemical messenger molecules to the pituitary gland. Acting both as neurons and as secretory devices, these cells provide the basis for neuroendocrine control.

The Hormones of the Anterior Pituitary

The anterior lobe of the pituitary secretes seven specific hormones. Five of them are *tropic hormones*, which specifically activate other endocrine glands. The other two are *non-tropic hormones*, which stimulate tissues other than endocrine glands. The release of tropic hormones is affected by feedback systems (Figure 12.4).

The tropic hormones are the *thyrotropic hormone* (TSH), the *adrenocorticotropic hormone* (ACTH), the *follicle stimulating hormone* (FSH), the *lutenizing hormone* (LH), and the *interstitial cell stimulating hormone* (ICSH). The last of these is usually regarded as a male hormone. TSH stimulates the thyroid gland to pro-

THE MODE-OF-ACTION OF STEROID HORMONES

The steroid hormone has circulated in the blood. In (a), it enters the target cell and goes to the nucleus where it associates with and activates a specific receptor molecule. As represented in (b), the active hormone-receptor unit binds to a specific part of the DNA in a chromosome. This binding activates a gene or set of genes in the chromosome, thus causing the cell to synthesize a specific protein or proteins. See (c).

The protein or proteins that are made can have many different effects. One is to change the patterns of growth and differentiation. Another is to change the activities of the target cell. The newly synthesized protein can be secreted into the bloodstream and affect other cells or it can form more receptor protein.

After a short period of time the hormone-receptor unit comes off the DNA, as indicated in (d), thus inactivating the gene. The hormone-receptor unit is then broken down into its component parts.

Steroid hormones cause the activation of genes.

duce triiodothyronine (T_3) and thyroxin (T_4). These chemicals in turn both stimulate oxidative respiration and regulate the level of calcium in the blood. ACTH stimulates the adrenal cortex to produce corticosteroid hormones, some of which regulate the production of glucose from fat and others of which regulate the balance of sodium and potassium ions in the blood. The two **gonadotropins**, FSH and LH, act on the ovaries and testes. In females, FSH stimulates the development of a follicle and the production of estrogen in the ovary. In males, it stimulates the development of the seminiferous tubules and the maturation of sperm. In females, LH continues the process initiated by FSH in the ovary and causes release of the ovum. As well, it supports the development of the corpus luteum from cells left in the ovary after ovulation. The corpus luteum in turn stimulates the production of progesterone. In males, both LH and ICSH stimulate the gonads to produce testosterone, which initiates and

supports the development of male secondary sexual characteristics.

The non-tropic hormones are *prolactin* and *growth hormone* (GH). Prolactin, usually thought of as a female hormone, stimulates the mammary glands to produce milk and sustains milk production. At high levels it can reduce fertility. Growth hormone (GH), also known as *somatotropin*, stimulates the growth of cells in juveniles. Excessive amounts in adults produce characteristic overgrowths, particularly in parts of the skeleton.

The Hormones of the Posterior Pituitary

Two hormones, *antidiuretic hormone* (ADH) and *oxytocin*, are released by the posterior pituitary; the latter is regarded as a female hormone. These hormones are actually produced by neurosecretory cells in the hypothalamus and are transported to the posterior pituitary lobe in nerve axons (Figure 12.2.)

Figure 12.4
Hormonal activity here functions as a simple negative feedback system. The stimulus, TSH, ultimately causes a reduction in its own level in the blood. Thus the anterior pituitary and thyroid glands, with their hormones, form an automatic control system with negative feedback. Sex hormones and adrenocortical hormones are controlled by similar feedback systems.

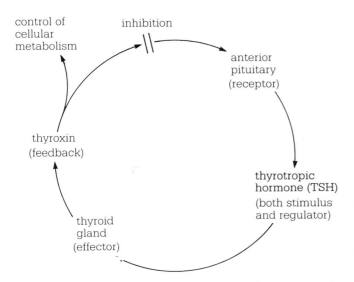

Figure 12.5
A person with goiter

ADH causes the collecting ducts of kidney nephrons to become more permeable to water. As it moves out of the nephrons, this water concentrates the urine and thus reduces water loss from the body. As well, ADH induces contraction of smooth muscles in the wall of blood vessels, thus increasing blood pressure. This latter effect explains the alternative name, *vasopressin*, that is given to ADH.

Oxytocin stimulates contraction of the uterine muscles during labour. The dilation of the cervix causes nerve signals to go to the hypothalamus, which initiates the release of the hormone. Oxytocin also stimulates contraction of smooth muscles in mammary glands, allowing milk to be expressed through the nipple when a baby sucks.

The Thyroid Gland

The shape of the thyroid gland resembles the letter H, with the uprights consisting of two masses of glandular tissue lying on each side of the trachea, just below the larynx. The thyroid gland is 3 cm to 4 cm high and about 2.5 cm wide. When stimulated by TSH, it produces and releases several hormones, the most important of which are *triiodothyronine* (T_3, which

has three iodine atoms) and *thyroxin* (T_4, which has four iodine atoms). Both are derivatives of the amino acid tyrosine and they produce similar effects on target cells. When either is circulated to the rest of the body by the blood, the resulting increase in oxidative respiration, in turn, leads to an increase in energy for cellular metabolism.

As shown in Figure 12.4, thyroxin feeds back to regulate the release of TSH. If iodine supplies are too low, normal amounts of thyroxin cannot be produced. The consequent lack of thyroxin causes the negative feedback system to falter. The uninhibited anterior pituitary then greatly increases the supply of TSH. These high TSH levels stimulate an enlargement of the thyroid and a bulge in the neck, a condition known as iodine-deficiency **goiter** (Figure 12.5).

Abnormally low levels of thyroxin in young children can retard growth and cause the underproduction of other hormones. Serious hormonal imbalance can cause **cretinism**, a condition in which the child has abnormal mental and physical development (Figure 12.6). Iodized salt or marine fish contain ample supplies of iodine; their presence in the diet helps reduce the risk of iodine-deficiency goiter or cretinism.

Figure 12.6
A child showing cretinism

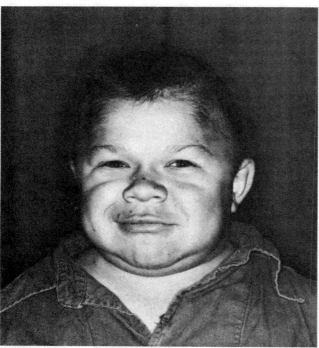

Figure 12.7
Before and after treatment for myxedema. Note the puffy facial features and the general appearance of exhaustion prior to treatment with thyroid extract.

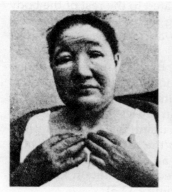

Insufficient thyroxin in adults causes **myxedema**, a condition characterized by thickening and puffiness of the skin and by a slowing of mental and physical responses such as heart and breathing rates (Figure 12.7). Both myxedema and cretinism respond positively to treatment with thyroid extracts.

Too much thyroxin production causes an increase in oxidative respiration. Individuals with this condition (*hyperthyroidism*) are nervous and irritable. Their body temperature is abnormally high and they metabolize abnormally high amounts of nutrients. This condition has been adjusted surgically by removal of part of the thyroid gland or by the use of radioactive iodine to inactivate part of the gland. After either of these treatments, hormone balance is maintained by taking thyroid extract.

The thyroid gland also produces calcitonin, a peptide hormone that helps control the ion content of the blood. Again, a negative feedback loop is at work. The release of calcitonin is stimulated by high levels of calcium ion in the blood. The calcitonin then causes excess amounts of calcium from the blood to be deposited in the bones.

The Parathyroid Glands

The **parathyroid glands**, very small and usually four in number, are located immediately behind the thyroid gland and produce *parathormone* (PTH). PTH works in a way opposite to calcitonin. Low levels of calcium ions in the blood stimulate the parathyroid glands to release PTH, which in turn stimulates bone cells to release calcium ions. The consequent raise in the level of blood calcium feeds back and shuts off the release of PTH. An excessive release of calcium into the blood then stimulates the thyroid gland to release calcitonin. This interplay of PTH and calcitonin regulates calcium ion levels in the blood within narrow limits (Figure 12.8).

The Pancreas

The **pancreas**, a large gland located just below the stomach, acts both as an exocrine and as an endocrine gland. The exocrine function is the secretion of pancreatic juice containing digestive enzymes which act in the small intestine. The endocrine function involves the regulation of blood glucose levels by hormones produced in small circles of cells known as the **islets of Langerhans**. Interspersed among the cells that produce the pancreatic juice, these cells are of three types: alpha cells that produce glucagon, beta cells that produce insulin, and delta cells that produce somatostatin.

Glucagon acts rapidly to induce the breakdown of glycogen into its component glucose units by activation of an enzyme (phosphorylase). The level of blood glucose is thereby raised. Glucagon also causes the protein and fat stores of the body to modify some of their molecules into glucose which is released into the blood.

Figure 12.8
This double feedback system prevents blood calcium ion *levels from fluctuation beyond very narrow limits. The kidneys are also involved in calcium regulation.*

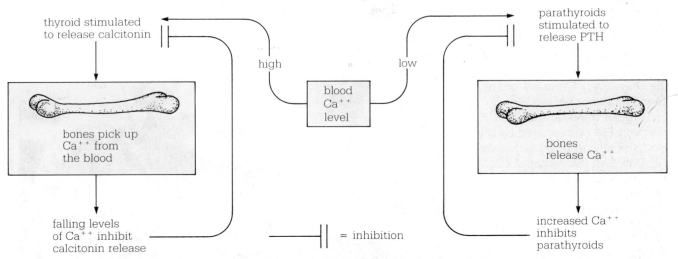

Insulin is slower in its action and has effects that are antagonistic to those of glucagon. It promotes protein storage and inhibits fat metabolism. Insulin causes blood glucose to be changed into glycogen molecules in the liver and muscles. Consequently, glucose is removed from the blood. The mechanism of insulin action is quite complex; it affects glucose metabolism in four ways. First, it makes the cell membrane transport glucose molecules inside the cell more easily. Once inside, a phosphate group is added to the glucose. This phosphorylated glucose can then be metabolized or polymerized into glycogen molecules. In the absence of insulin, very little glucose enters cells. As well, insulin activates glucokinase, the enzyme that does the phosphorylation. Third, it activates the enzymes that make glycogen out of glucose units. Finally, it inhibits phosphorylase.

Somatostatin is released when blood glucose or amino acid levels are high; its effect is to lower these levels. It suppresses both glucagon and insulin secretion. Somatostatin also inhibits growth hormone secretion.

Diabetes Mellitus
Diabetes mellitus results from insufficient insulin secretion by the pancreas or defective reception of insulin by target cells. Its chief symptom is a high concentration of glucose in the blood. Excessive sugar appears in the urine; the afflicted person lacks energy and drinks very large amounts of water. There are two forms of diabetes mellitus, juvenile-onset (type 1 or insulin-dependent) diabetes and maturity-onset (type 2 or non-insulin dependent) diabetes mellitus. Type 1 diabetes results when the beta cells are destroyed by a virus or some other pathological agent. Only about one of every ten diabetics has this type of the disease. People with type 1 diabetes must take insulin on a regular basis.

The symptoms of Type 2 diabetes usually do not manifest themselves until after the age of 40. This form of the disease is usually slow to develop. Its causes are unclear; however, it is hereditary and occurs most commonly in overweight individuals. It is not necessarily associated with low insulin levels in the blood but can result from defective reception of insulin by the target cells. Exercise appears to cause an increase in the sensitivity of the target cells to insulin. Many individuals with type 2 diabetes can thus regulate themselves with a proper diet and exercise programme, avoiding the need to take insulin. The insulin deficiency may be caused by overstimulation, leading to exhaustion of the beta cells. This overstimulation can be induced by factors released by the pituitary or it may be provoked by maintaining high blood sugar levels for long periods of time.

The liver and muscles of diabetics are low in glycogen because glucose cannot enter the cells. The glucose is thus not available for metabolism in the cells. Blood glucose levels can go as high as ten times their normal level. If too much insulin is administered, glucose can drop to one fifth of the normal level and the person will lose consciousness. This condition is known as **diabetic coma**.

THE DISCOVERY OF INSULIN

In October of 1920, Dr. Frederick Banting got the idea that an internal secretion of the pancreas could be isolated and that this extract would benefit people suffering from diabetes mellitus. His research proposal was accepted by the University of Toronto and he began working there in May of 1921 under the direction of Dr. J.J. Macleod. He was assisted by C.H. Best and helped by a biochemist, J.P. Collip. In the winter of 1921–22 this team of researchers discovered insulin.

When pancreatic cells are disrupted, digestive enzymes are released that destroy insulin. The research team therefore had to find a way to render those enzymes inactive. Using dogs as experimental animals, Banting and his team tied off the pancreatic ducts and waited several weeks before attempting to extract this insulin. This time period was sufficient to cause the enzyme-producing cells to atrophy. In the absence of the digestive enzymes, active insulin could then be extracted.

Insulin quickly proved to provide life-saving therapy for sufferers of this disease. Because it was his original idea that had started the research, Banting received most of the credit. In 1923 the Nobel prize for physiology and medicine was awarded to Banting and Macleod. Banting gave half his prize money to Charles Best.

Dr. Frederick Banting (right) and Dr. Charles Best (left), the discoverers of insulin.

Insulin administration must be coordinated with carbohydrate intake and with energy output so that carbohydrate metabolism is kept balanced. Because insulin is a fairly large peptide, it is usually administered by intramuscular injection. Until recently, pork insulin was used; it sometimes triggered allergic reactions. Recent techniques allow the transfer into bacteria of the gene for human insulin. The bacteria make human insulin, which is then extracted and used in diabetes therapy.

Two methods are used to diagnose diabetes mellitus: the oral glucose tolerance test and the insulin sensitivity test.

The first of these methods measures the body's response to the ingestion of glucose. It is given at the dose of one g per kg of body weight. In a normal individual, this intake will cause the blood glucose level to rise from about 5 mmol per L to 7.8 mmol per L and then fall to normal in about 3 h. The drop-off in the level is attributable to the fact that some of the glucose is being used to induce the release of insulin. In a person with diabetes mellitus, the drop-off is much slower and usually does not go below 10 mmol per L (Figure 12.9). Blood glucose levels are reported on the basis of mg per 100 ml in most medical texts. To convert to SI units, divide by 18.01 and the mg/ 100 ml value will be converted to mmol glucose per L.

In contrast, the insulin sensitivity test measures the body's response to the injection of insulin. In normal individuals, injection of small amounts of insulin causes only a slight reduction in blood sugar concentration. People with diabetes, however, are extremely sensitive to insulin. Very small amounts cause a rapid and extreme drop in their blood sugar concentration.

The Adrenal Glands α

There are two adrenal glands, one located on top of each kidney. These glands consist of an outer cortex and an inner medulla.

The **adrenal cortex** produces steroid hormones called *corticoids*, which are released when adrenocorticotropic hormone (ACTH) is circulated by the blood from the anterior lobe of the pituitary to the adrenal cortex. These corticoids are of three major types: mineralcorticoids, glucocorticoids and androgen-like steroids. Each type has its own functions.

Mineralcorticoids such as aldosterone regulate water and ion balance in the body. The secretion of the hormone is regulated by negative feedback of levels of sodium and potassium ions. High hormone levels cause water retention.

Glucocorticoids such as cortisol affect the balance between carbohydrate and protein metabolism by stimulating the formation of glucose from protein. Secretion is regulated by ACTH. Lack of glucocorticoids causes Addison's disease, the characteristics of which are weakness and weight loss. Cortisone, a derivative of cortisol, is used as an anti-inflammatory drug.

Androgen-like steroids cause the development of masculine features. Some androgens are produced by the adrenal cortex in both males and females. A portion of the adrenal cortex normally found only in the fetus and in infants produces these steroids and normally atrophies soon after birth. The growth of a hormone producing tumour in this region can lead to excessive secretion of this hormone, resulting in premature virilism in males or masculinization in females.

Figure 12.9

The blood glucose levels of the diabetic show a different pattern from those of a normal person after ingestion of one g of glucose per kg of body weight.

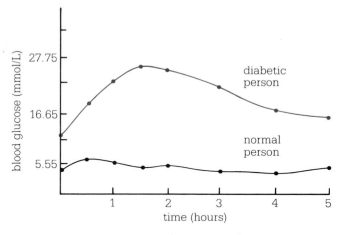

The substances secreted by the adrenal cortex help the body to adjust to pregnancy, illness, and other forms of long term stress.

The secretions of the **adrenal medulla** help the body to adjust very rapidly to short term stress. The adrenal medulla produces two hormones: *epinephrine* (also known as adrenalin) and *norepinephrine* (also known as noradrenalin).

The adrenal medulla is highly innervated. Its activities are controlled by nerves from the hypothalamus and by sympathetic nerves. Epinephrine and some norepinephrine is released into the blood either in response to signals from the sympathetic system or by a drop in blood glucose concentration. Unlike most other hormones, both epinephrine and norepinephrine act very quickly. Emotional stress such as a fright, excitement, pain, or anxiety triggers the secretion of epinephrine. Stress due to cold, on the other hand, increases the liberation of norepinephrine. Both hormones cause the body to adjust for "fight or flight" by inducing the following changes:

1. an increase in heart rate and blood pressure;
2. a contraction of the arteries to organs other than muscle, shifting the blood supply to the muscles, heart, lungs, and brain;
3. a breakdown of glycogen in the liver and a consequent release of glucose into the blood;
4. an inhibition of the release of insulin by the pancreas, thus stimulating a release of glucagon and further increasing the supply of glucose to the blood (muscles that are required to work hard dur-

Figure 12.10
The glucose supply is adjusted to meet the body's ever-changing needs. When blood glucose levels are low (a), glucagon from the pancreas and epinephrine from the adrenal medulla are released into the bloodstream. Once they reach the liver, these hormones increase the rate of conversion of glycogen to glucose. The release of this glucose into the bloodstream increases the level of blood

glucose. One molecule of epinephrine causes the release of millions of molecules of glucose. When blood glucose levels are high (b), as just after a meal, insulin is released from the pancreas and stimulates the liver and the muscles to convert glucose into glycogen. The level of glucose circulating in the blood is thus lowered. The amount of insulin released and the level of blood glucose form a feedback loop.

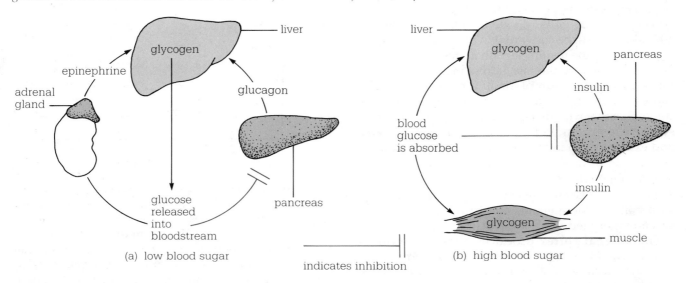

(a) low blood sugar

(b) high blood sugar

indicates inhibition

ing "fight or flight" are supplied with extra sources of energy by the shift in the blood circulation pattern and the elevated amount of glucose in this blood;

5. a decrease in the clotting time of the blood, with consequent reduction of bleeding in case of injury;
6. a relaxation of the smooth muscles in the walls of the bronchioles in the lungs allowing more air to be processed by the lungs (the increased supply of oxygen supports increased energy release through the process of cellular respiration);
7. a dilation of the pupil of the eye, allowing it to admit more light;
8. a contraction of the ureters and sphincter muscles of the bladder and a consequent retention of urine until after the emergency.

Hormonal Control of Blood Glucose Levels
Many hormones interact to control the level of glucose in the blood. Glucagon, epinephrine, and the glucocorticoids all induce increases in blood glucose levels; only insulin induces decreases. Since glucose supplies the energy for cell metabolism, the supply of it must constantly be adjusted to meet the body's ever-chang-

ing needs. This adjustment is an excellent example of homeostasis (Figure 12.10).

The Testes and Ovaries
The testes in the male contain cells which secrete **testosterone** when stimulated by the interstitial cell stimulating hormone (ICSH) from the anterior pituitary. Testosterone induces the development of the male secondary sex characteristics and is necessary for the normal functioning of the male reproductive organs. This hormone causes the deepening of the male voice and the growth of facial and pubic hair; as well, it affects the general shape of the male body. The use by athletes of testosterone-based steroids is discussed in the next chapter.

The ovaries produce **estrogen**. Its release is controlled by the follicle stimulating hormone (FSH) from the anterior lobe of the pituitary. Estrogen controls the growth and development of the female reproductive system. At puberty, it stimulates the growth of mammary tissues and the deposition of fat in the breasts as well as the growth of pubic and underarm hair. Continuous release of estrogen is necessary for the maintenance of these characteristics during adult life.

The nervous system and the endocrine system must maintain internal conditions in the body constant within fairly narrow limits. Complex feedback loops use neurovisceral control to adjust the activities of many organs. One of the many adjustments that must be made during exercise is to the heart rate and blood pressure. Chemical, physical, and neural signals all play a role in this complex feedback loop system.

During exercise, the blood supply to the digestive system is reduced and the blood supply to the skeletal muscles, heart, lungs and brain is increased. This redeployment is accomplished by a balance of the controls exerted by the sympathetic and parasympathetic nervous systems acting in co-operation with the endocrine system, particularly the adrenal glands. The adrenal hormones epinephrine and norepinephrine act as extensions of the sympathetic nervous system.

Exercise uses up glucose in the muscles, causing a drop in the glucose levels in the blood; however blood glucose levels must be maintained within very close tolerances. Glucose is stored in the body as *glycogen*, a complex molecule made up of many glucose units joined together. Excess glucose is stored in the muscles and in the liver as glycogen. Exercise soon depletes the muscles of their glycogen and the glycogen stores of the liver are called on to hold the blood glucose level within its normal limits. The endocrine system acts to control the level of glucose in the blood. A level of 5.5 mmol/L is considered clinically normal; overshoots of about 20 percent above and below this level are common.

HOW THE NERVOUS SYSTEM AND THE ENDOCRINE SYSTEM ADJUST FOR THE EFFECTS OF EXERCISE

Exercise causes increased CO_2 to be released into bloodstream (a). The rising level of carbon dioxide in the blood stimulates receptors in the arteries of the neck to send nerve impulses to the coordination centre in the brain that controls the sympathetic nervous system. (Merely) thinking about exercising can cause the brain to activate this pathway. The sympathetic nervous system sends stimulatory signals down sympathetic nerve fibres to the pacemaker of the heart (b). At the pacemaker the nerves release norepinephrine; it causes the pacemaker to increase heart rate (c) and the force of contraction of the heart's ventricles, thus increasing blood pressure. Note that in this case, the noradrenalin is acting not as a hormone but as a neurotransmitter; it has not circulated in the blood to get to the target cells. Pressure receptors in the aorta respond to increasing blood pressure (d) by sending nervous impulses to a second coordination centre in the brain, one which controls the parasympathetic system. This centre signals the parasympathetic system, causing signals to be sent out via the vagus nerve to the pacemaker (e). There, the release of acetylcholine inhibits the activities of the pacemaker, leading to a reduction in heart rate (f).

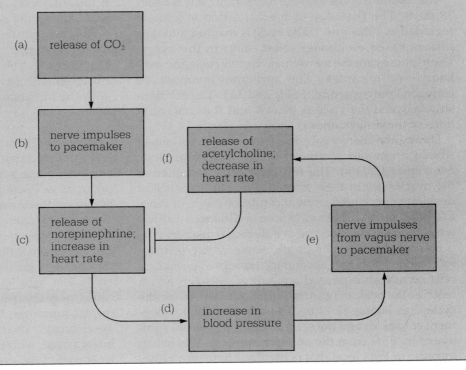

(a) release of CO_2

(b) nerve impulses to pacemaker

(c) release of norepinephrine; increase in heart rate

(f) release of acetylcholine; decrease in heart rate

(e) nerve impulses from vagus nerve to pacemaker

(d) increase in blood pressure

The **corpus luteum** is a specialized group of cells located in the ovary. The luteinizing hormone (LH) from the anterior pituitary causes the corpus luteum to release **progesterone**. This hormone increases the secretory activity of the uterus and stimulates the development of blood capillaries in it. The uterus is thus prepared for the implantation of a fertilized egg and can nourish the egg as it develops into an embryo. Progesterone also works with estrogen to continue the development of the mammary glands during pregnancy.

Hormones and the Menstrual Cycle

Humans and certain other primates have cycles of ovarian activity that occur at intervals of approximately one month. This periodicity has given rise to the name **menstrual cycle** from the Latin term *mensis* for month. The term **menstruation** is used to describe the shedding of the inner epithelial lining of the uterus (the endometrium). In primates, this shedding is accompanied by bleeding. During the normal menstrual cycle, the secretion of ovarian hormones rises and falls in a regular fashion. These changing hormone levels cause cyclic changes in the endometrium and other tissues that are affected by sex steroid hormones.

The duration of the average menstrual cycle is about 28 days. The first day of menstruation is usually regarded as "day one." The cycle is divided into four phases based on changes that occur in the ovary. These phases are the menstrual, the follicular, the ovulatory, and the luteal. The hormones involved are estrogen, progesterone, FSH, and LH. The relationship between the various phases and the concentrations of these hormones is shown in Figure 12.11.

During the menstrual phase, the concentrations of steroid hormones produced by the ovaries are low. See Figure 12.11(a). The **follicular cells** contained in the ovaries are in their *primordial* or *primary* stage of development. Under normal conditions, one of these follicular cells will develop into a **Graafian follicle** which will produce an egg cell during ovulation.

During the follicular phase, some of the primary follicles develop into secondary follicles. Specialized cells secrete an increased amount of estrogen which reaches its peak concentration about day 12 of the cycle. See Figure 12.11(b). The growth and development of follicles and the secretion of estrogen are stimulated by FSH from the anterior pituitary. It is *not* an increase in FSH level that is involved here, but rather an increase in the number of FSH receptors in the estrogen-producing cells.

The rapid rise in the concentration of estrogen in turn causes a jump in LH secretion from the anterior pituitary. See Figure 12.11(c). Taking place on the last day of the follicular phase, this *LH surge* is the result of positive feedback of estrogen on the pituitary and hypothalamus. The LH surge begins about 24 h before ovulation and reaches its peak about 16 h before ovulation. There is a simultaneous though smaller peak in FSH secretion.

The Graafian follicle grows very large under the influence of FSH stimulation. The LH surge causes the wall of the Graafian follicle to rupture, releasing the egg cell. This process is known as ovulation. Normally only one ovary ovulates per cycle. The right and left ovaries alternate during successive cycles.

After ovulation, the empty Graafian follicle is stimulated by LH and changes into the corpus luteum. The corpus luteum secretes estrogen and a new hormone, progesterone. Progesterone concentrations rise rapidly after ovulation and reach a peak about a week after ovulation. See Figure 12.11(d). The combination of high levels of estrogen and progesterone that occur during the luteal phase cause a reduction in FSH and LH secretion — an example of negative feedback. The reduced levels of FSH and LH retard the development of other follicles, so that further ovulation does not occur during the cycle.

The corpus luteum stops functioning and estrogen and progesterone levels begin to drop by about day 22 of the cycle. The levels are very low by day 28. These low levels of the ovarian steroids cause menstruation. With the initiation of menstruation, the cycle begins again.

Oral Steroid Contraceptives

It is estimated that on a world-wide basis, 60 million women are using oral steroid pills to avoid unwanted pregnancy. These pills usually consist of a combination of synthetic estrogen and synthetic progesterone. The pills are taken once each day for three weeks after the end of the menstrual period. The pill causes an elevated level of the two ovarian steroids in the blood that persists for the normal duration of a menstrual cycle. The high levels of estrogen and progesterone cause negative feedback inhibition of the gonadotrophic hormones FSH and LH. As a result, ovulation never occurs. The body is maintained in a sort of false luteal phase, with high levels of estrogen and progesterone and low levels of FSH and LH.

Figure 12.11
The activity of hormones involved in the menstrual cycle

is highly coordinated. The concentration of each shows a rhythmic pattern of changes.

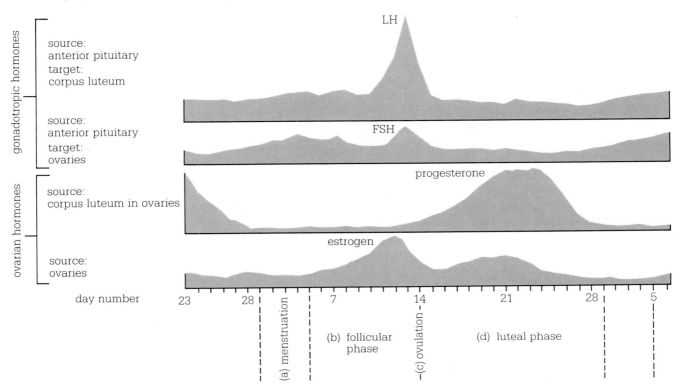

12.3 THE HEART AS AN ENDOCRINE ORGAN

Recent research has revealed that heart muscle cells in the wall of the atria produce short peptide molecules that circulate in the blood and increase urine production. This *atrionatriuretic factor* (ANF) meets all four criteria for a molecule to be considered a hormone. The major signal for ANF release is the extra stretching of the atrial walls caused by elevated blood pressure. ANF acts on the kidneys, inducing them to excrete sodium ions and water. It also causes dilation of blood vessels leading to the glomeruli, which in turn leads to lowering of the blood pressure.

The effects of ANF are directly opposite to the effects of the antidiuretic hormone, ADH. ANF and ADH thus balance one another, raising or lowering the blood pressure and helping to maintain blood pressure homeostasis. ANF plays another role in fluid homeostasis in that it helps govern the volume of fluid that fills the cavity in the central nervous system.

CHAPTER SUMMARY

The endocrine system consists of a number of diverse glands, each of them producing and releasing hormones that act as messengers between various parts of the body. The blood carries these hormones to all of the cells in the body; however, a particular hormone affects only those cells which have the correct receptors for it.

Many parts of the endocrine system interact both with each other and with the nervous system; the pituitary gland exemplifies this close interaction. Its anterior lobe releases seven hormones; five of them are tropic hormones — ones that specifically activate other endocrine glands — while the two remaining ones are non-tropic. The posterior lobe releases two hormones, ADH and oxytocin; the former affects the kidneys; the latter, the muscles.

The thyroid gland produces and releases two hormones containing iodine. This gland also secretes a hormone that regulates calcium levels in the blood, one that acts antagonistically to the calcium control hormone released by the parathyroid glands. The interaction of these two hormones provides an excellent example of homeostatic control.

Present in the pancreas are three types of cells, all of them involved in the production of hormones that help to regulate blood glucose levels. One of these hormones is insulin; insufficient secretion or defective reception of it causes diabetes mellitus.

The adrenal glands have two functional parts, an outer cortex and an inner medulla. The former releases a series of steroid hormones called corticoids. The lat-

ter releases epinephrine and norepinephrine. They trigger the "fight or flight" response.

The testes produce testosterone, necessary for the proper functioning of the male reproductive organs and for the development of the male secondary sexual characteristics. The ovaries produce estrogen, necessary for the growth and development of the female reproductive system. The corpus luteum, a specialized group of cells in the ovary, releases the hormone progesterone. The interplay of estrogen, progesterone, and the gonadotropic hormones FSH and LH is responsible for the menstrual cycle.

A peptide molecule known as ANF is released by the heart. This molecule meets all the criteria essential for a hormone. Therefore, the heart can in this sense be considered an endocrine organ.

Objectives

Having completed this chapter, you should be able to do the following:

1. Explain the role that the endocrine system plays in maintaining homeostasis in vertebrate animals.
2. Describe the activities of the various endocrine glands.
3. Outline some of the interactions between the endocrine system and the nervous system.
4. Describe the endocrine control of blood glucose levels.
5. State the role of hormones in the menstrual cycle.

Vocabulary

endocrine gland
hormone
catecholamine
peptide hormone
steroid hormone
pituitary gland
gonadotropin
goiter
cretinism
myxedema

parathyroid gland
pancreas
islets of Langerhans
glucagon
insulin
somatostatin
diabetes mellitus
diabetic coma
adrenal cortex
adrenal medulla

testosterone
estrogen
corpus luteum
progesterone
menstrual cycle
menstruation
follicular cell
Graafian follicle

Review Questions

1. (a) What is
      (i) an endocrine gland?
      (ii) a hormone?
   (b) What is the relationship between an endocrine gland and its target organ?
   (c) How do hormones differ from other humoral agents?
   (d) What causes the specificity of hormone action?
2. (a) List the three categories of hormones.
   (b) Give one example of each.
   (c) Name the endocrine gland that produces it.
3. Explain how the interaction of the hypothalamus and the pituitary gland exemplifies neuroendocrine control.
4. (a) Using a specific example, outline the action of a tropic hormone.
   (b) Show how this action is controlled by a negative feedback mechanism.
5. What is the source and action of
   (a) the antidiuretic hormone (ADH)?
   (b) thyroxin (T_4)?
   (c) parathormone hormone (PTH)?
6. Describe the normal control of blood glucose levels.
7. (a) What is diabetes mellitus?
   (b) What two tests can be used to diagnose it?
   (c) What does insulin do to relieve its symptoms?
8. (a) Name the two adrenal glands.
   (b) Indicate the hormones produced by each one.
   (c) Outline the action of these hormones.
9. (a) What four hormones are involved in the menstrual cycle?
   (b) How is the interplay of these hormones an example of negative feedback control?

Advanced Questions

1. Compare the nervous and endocrine systems as
   (a) communicating systems
   (b) coordinating systems.
2. How do the nervous and endocrine systems prepare the body for sudden emergencies?
3. Research the role of
   (a) Earl. W. Sutherland in the establishment of the second messenger concept of hormone action
   (b) Dr. Frederic Banting in the discovery of insulin.
4. Many diseases result from abnormal levels of a particular hormone. Select one such disease and research its causes, symptoms, and cure.
5. Research the role of one or more of the following as an endocrine organ:
   (a) brain
   (b) heart
   (c) duodenum
   (d) stomach

CHAPTER 13

YOUR PERSONAL BALANCE: BEHAVIOURAL HOMEOSTASIS

Est modus in rebus . . .
(Things have their due measure)

Horace

The two opposing principles of Chinese philosophy are yin and yang. This opposition represents the balance of feminine with masculine, or of light with dark. The symbol, like the words of the poets of antiquity, is a reminder that there must be balance in all aspects of life. This chapter discusses the use of appropriate conscious behaviours that can help you maintain a healthy homeostatic balance. How you use — or abuse — food and drugs is vital to your personal homeostatis.

13.1 SPECIAL FEATURES OF HUMAN BEHAVIOUR

The natural habitat keeps animals living under wild conditions in a sort of automatic balance. Environmental factors such as available food, seasonal temperature, and humidity conditions are imposed on them. If the balance of these factors is upset by reduction of the food source, early freezing conditions, or drought, many of these animals may die.

The human species has a style of life different from that of all other animals. It lives in an environment that is not only natural but also cultural. Humans use fire, tools, clothing, shelter, and other technological devices which help protect them from the effects of changes in the natural environment. They can use

these devices because, unlike other animals, they can conceptualize and imagine — in short, they can think. Other animals, unable to do so, must therefore respond to real events and must adjust their activities as these events take place. The ability to think allows humans to anticipate future events; in doing so, they can plan their lives in very complex ways.

Cultural change has carried the human species farther and farther away from the natural environment. For most of its existence, *Homo sapiens* led a life of hunting and food gathering. Only about 10 000 years ago, with the first development of agriculture, did hunting and gathering become less important. Less than three centuries ago, the industrial revolution began to bring more and more people from the land into cities where they became even more detached from the natural environment. This trend continues as human societies move further into the information age of the late twentieth century.

Because so many humans live detached from the natural environment, instinctive behaviours appropriate for life in the wild are not very useful to them. Instead, they must use consciously controlled behaviours in order to survive their extremely diverse cultural environments, behaviours that allow them to respond appropriately to new stimuli or new arrangements of old stimuli.

Figure 13.1
We tried hunting and gathering but now we just order in a pizza.

Figure 13.2
Our prehistoric ancestors did not have to balance conflicting nutritional claims.

The system of values in which you were raised does much to determine your behaviours. As you gain knowledge, your behaviour often changes. For example, the more you learn about proper nutrition, the more your decisions about what you should eat are affected. Most Canadians now live in an environment greatly removed from nature. When you get hungry, you do not go out into the natural environment to hunt and gather food. Instead, you go to a supermarket. Many of the foods there are highly processed, containing heavy concentrations of nutrients such as sugar and salt. Eating too many of them can overload your biochemical homeostatic controls. The natural food available to early human ancestors contained almost no simple sugars and had a very low salt content. Yet you must consciously weigh the claims of an advertising industry that may be influencing you to eat nutritionally unsound products.

To achieve healthy homeostatic balance, you must make responsible decisions. What is considered normal by the people you live with on a day-to-day basis greatly affects these decisions. Young people in particular want to be "part of the group"; peer pressure can often lead you to make decisions harmful to yourself. The way you feel about yourself can greatly affect these decisions. A person with a positive self-image usually attempts more and succeeds more than does a person with a negative self-image.

Figure 13.3
As you mature, your self image must change.

"I will *never* get to be like that."

Interactions Between the Brain and the Body
If you imagine a thing to be true, your body generally responds accordingly. For example, you have probably imagined things that frightened you enough to trigger a "fight or flight" response (Chapter 12). When in this condition, your body is adapted for emergency action. "Fight or flight" is an appropriate response if you are facing a genuine physical threat. If the trigger for the response is imaginary, no physical action is required and your body has stimulated you unnecessarily.

Figure 13.4
Our lifestyle has changed but our bodies have not.

the fight-or-flight reaction   the stress reaction

The cultural environment that you live in provides many stressful situations for which the "fight or flight" response is inappropriate. For example, if your car skids on ice, all that is required to correct the skid is some gentle movements of your hands and feet. Yet your body will have adjusted for much more vigorous activity. Research has established that repeated inappropriate stimulation of the stress response can lead to high blood pressure, heart attacks, and strokes. The environment has changed but the human body has not. From a physiological point of view, humans are prehistoric hunters and gatherers who must cope with an environment for which they are not well adjusted.

The control that the mind can exert over the body has recently become a very active area of research; exciting new discoveries have come forth. Dr Herbert Benson and colleagues at the Harvard Medical School have found that a simple meditative technique known as the **relaxation response** can counteract the effects of the "fight or flight" response. Such meditation techniques have been practiced for centuries in eastern civilizations; there is now clinical evidence to support their usefulness to western society. The technique involves sitting comfortably in a quiet place and repeating a simple phrase over and over, a practice that can lower blood pressure significantly.

Some of the best proof that mental attitude affects health is provided by the "placebo effect" (from the Latin verb meaning to please). When medicine is being tested, some of the test subjects are given the medicine while others are secretly given a **placebo**, an inert substance given in place of the drug. Often the test subjects receiving the placebo respond as though they have received the active substance! In recent tests of a drug used to reduce fever, subjects receiving placebos of sugar tablets showed almost the same reduction in fever as those that received the actual drug.

Unfortunately, your beliefs can also work against you. If you believe that your condition is worse than it really is, your condition may deteriorate even further. A positive mental attitude is often the best medicine.

By learning **biofeedback** techniques, you can train your conscious mind to control certain physiological processes. The technique involves the use of an apparatus that continuously monitors one or more physiological processes such as heart rate, blood pressure, muscle tension, or skin temperature. When biofeedback is used to control heart rate, the monitor shows a red light shining when the heart rate is normal and a green light shining when the heart is going too fast. Subjects are trained to think of something that relaxes them when the green light is on. Gradually, they learn how to lower their heart rate and consequently their blood pressure. After the technique is learned, the biofeedback apparatus is no longer necessary.

Biofeedback techniques have also been used to control migraine headaches, an ailment caused by the distension of blood vessels in the head. The subjects are taught to ''think their hands warm.'' By consciously causing the blood vessels in the hands and skin to dilate, they divert blood from the head. The increased circulation of blood in the skin causes the skin temperature to rise. A temperature monitor is attached to the right index finger while the subjects repeat phrases such as ''my whole body is relaxed and my hands feel warm . . . my hands are warm, warm.'' When the temperature monitor shows a rise in temperature there is positive reinforcement of the behaviour. After a period of successful practice, the subject can do without the monitor.

Other research has established that the mind can affect the immune system and vice versa. Dr. Reginald Gorczynski of the University of Toronto and Dr. Alistair Cunningham of the Ontario Cancer Institute are working on how the mind can influence the immune system. Through the use of relaxation and creative imagery techniques, the patients imagine that their immune system is defeating the cancer. The patient's stress level is reduced and there is better appetite, an improvement in sleep patterns, and a reduction of pain.

The current hypothesis used to explain these results is that the brain releases small protein-like molecules called **neuropeptides**. These substances are active in the limbic system, the area of the brain associated with emotion. The neuropeptides attach to *macrophages*, immune cells that gather at sites of infection and destroy invading micro-organisms. The attached neuropeptide affects these cells by increasing or decreasing their activity. The hypothesis goes on to speculate that the brain releases different combinations of neuropeptides as it experiences different moods. If each neuropeptide has a different effect on the macrophages, moods could affect the way the body fights disease.

Can anything be done to control moods? Fortunately, the answer is yes. Dr. Aaron T. Beck and colleagues at the University of Pennsylvania Mood Clinic have pioneered a branch of psychiatry known as **cognitive therapy**. It is based on the hypothesis that your moods are a product of your thought processes; therefore, by learning to control your thoughts, you can consequently control your moods. The original research was done on the control of depression. The approach was to convince patients that they were depressed because they were thinking in an illogical

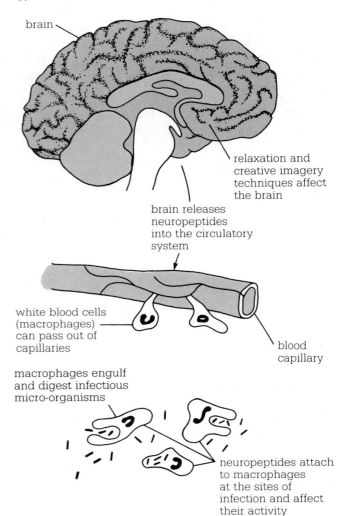

Figure 13.5
How the mind may influence the immune system. Much research is being done at present to test this hypothesis.

brain

relaxation and creative imagery techniques affect the brain

brain releases neuropeptides into the circulatory system

white blood cells (macrophages) can pass out of capillaries

blood capillary

macrophages engulf and digest infectious micro-organisms

neuropeptides attach to macrophages at the sites of infection and affect their activity

and negative manner—in effect, they were depressing themselves. The patients learned how to recognize their negative cognitive behaviours and how to substitute positive ones. For example, a successful novelist became upset whenever his writing was praised. His cognitive error was to have convinced himself that his writing was mediocre; he thus interpreted positive statements about his work as insincerity. This conviction that people who complimented him were lying made him depressed. When his cognitive error and its effects were made clear to him, he recovered from his depression.

Maintaining Chemical Balance

The following sections are about chemicals available in our society. Some of these chemicals are nutrients that you ingest every day. Others alter the way that you think. Knowledge of proper nutritional balance and of psychoactive substances can help you maintain your unique homeostatic balance.

13.2 NUTRITIONAL BALANCE

It has been said "you are what you eat." Nutritionists have shown that your culture greatly affects the way you think about food and, consequently, your eating habits. It might, then, also be said "you eat what you are." From a biochemical point of view, you eat to obtain the chemicals that provide energy and materials necessary to support life activities (Figure 13.6).

Nature has adapted the human body for heavy physical activity but the cultural environment has tended to make such activity less and less necessary. Most jobs in our society do not involve hard physical labour. People don't even play as long and as hard as they used to; instead, they spend much of their time watching television. Changes in diet and a more sedentary life style are thought to be responsible for the increased size of modern people and for the prevalence of obesity, early maturity, cardiovascular disorders, and certain types of cancer.

Figure 13.6
Nutrients and the life processes

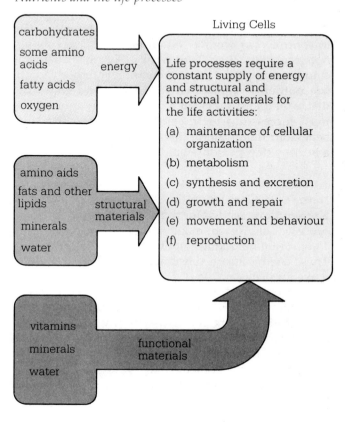

249

Energy Requirements

Your eating habits should reflect your lifestyle. If you ingest nutrients that contain more energy than your body requires, you will gain weight. **Obesity** is North America's major malnutrition problem.

Tables listing your ideal weight according to your height, body type, and age are readily available. Being overweight is a sign that you probably have exceeded the homeostatic control systems associated with your particular energy metabolism. Eating less while eating well and exercising properly is the recommended way to control your weight. When reducing, you should not lose more than 1 kg/week. ''Crash'' dieting is counterproductive; you merely train your body to utilize nutrients more efficiently; when you go off the diet, you gain weight on a lower energy intake. The most successful weight control programmes include behaviour modification that trains patients to eat like a healthy thin person would.

Nutrient Requirements

Nutrients are needed for the body to carry out the life processes of growth, maintenance, and repair (Figure 13.6). Humans require about 40 essential nutrients. These chemicals are substances that the body cannot make for itself.

Obesity is just one aspect of a larger nutritional problem, **malnutrition**, or an imbalance in the diet. Malnutrition can be brought about by a failure to eat a proper variety of foods or by an overuse of diet supplements such as vitamin pills. Dietary balance is not hard to achieve. Canadians have access to a very wide variety of high-quality foods; Canada's Food Guide, a readily available, free document, provides all of the information needed for diet balance. The guide specifies four categories of food:

- Milk and milk products
- Meat, fish, poultry, and alternates
- Breads and cereals
- Fruits and vegetables

As a general rule, you should have something from each category at each meal. The guide specifies the size of a serving and the number of such servings required each day according to the age and sex of the individual. Recommendations concerning energy balance are also given. Although proper nutrition is important all through life, it is particularly critical when the body is maturing and during pregnancy and lactation.

Recent studies of still-existing hunting and gathering societies, such as the Bushmen of the Kalahari Desert in southern Africa, suggest that their diet is healthier than ours. Compared to the average modern diet, the Bushman diet contains about half of the fat, three times the fibre, and four times the vitamin C. Their diet is also very high in calcium and almost all of the sugar is in the form of complex carbohydrates such as starch. A staple of their diet is fibre-rich tubers such as yams and sweet potatoes.

Dietary fibre is indigestible plant material that provides bulk to the food and helps it move through the digestive system. The human metabolic and digestive system demands high levels of fibre. North American diets tend to be high in fat and refined sugar but low in dietary fibre. The connection in our society between dietary imbalance and rates of cancer is presently an active area of research, even if definitive links have yet to be made.

PSYCHOLOGICAL EATING DISORDERS

In the past quarter century or so, two psychological eating disorders have emerged. Both occur only in the wealthy, developed nations and both are primarily associated with young women. These disorders are bulimia (binge-eating followed by purging) and anorexia nervosa (self-starvation).

Bulimia is difficult to detect. People with this disorder tend to be secretive and so it is hard to determine its incidence. In some college settings, up to one in every five women students are believed to be affected. Binge-purge eaters isolate themselves and then eat enormous quantities of food. The foods chosen can vary, but they are usually sweets or starches. Since sweet taste acts as an immediate positive reinforcer it is especially easy to binge on sweet foods. Purging is accomplished by vomiting, laxatives, or enemas. The vomiting may be induced physically or by the use of various non-prescription drugs. In addition, diuretics are sometimes used to increase water loss by excessive urination.

People with this disorder usually have high ambitions and self-expectations that are blocked by low self-esteem, depression, displaced anger, or feelings of self-hate. Most bulimia victims realize that their behaviour is abnormal.

Teenage girls can be very poor judges of obesity.

"I've *got* to lose weight"

Because they do not wish to make their condition known, they are reluctant to seek help. Yet they may be unable to stop their self-destructive behaviour on their own.

Bulimia is difficult to treat. Psychotherapy, group and family therapy, and behaviour modification techniques are the most usual treatments. Nutritional education is of great importance, as is the patients' realization that their *behaviour*, not their weight, is the problem.

The characteristics of anorexia nervosa are severe, prolonged weight loss and an intense fear of becoming overweight. Complicating the problem is the cultural value placed on being thin. The most easily detectable physical symptoms are a wasting away of the entire body, including muscle tissue, and a drying and yellowing of the skin. Even when well below the optimum body weight for their age, sex, and height, people with this disorder continue to diet. Victims of anorexia literally starve themselves to death. The condition is found primarily among females in their mid-teens from success-oriented, weight-conscious families. The victim is usually a perfectionist who becomes more and more obsessed with weight loss. When someone with anorexia drops below a certain weight, starvation affects the brain and it is impossible to reason with the person.

There is controversy over the proper treatment. If the condition seems to be life-threatening, hospitalization and, if necessary, force-feeding are usual first steps. After the patient has gained back enough weight and can again think clearly, family counselling and psychotherapy are often made available. Later, nutritional education and behaviour modification techniques may play a role in recovery.

Figure 13.7 Bushman diet compared to modern diet

Bushman Diet ——— PROGRESS ??? ——→ Modern Western Diet

high	CALCIUM	low
low	FAT	high
high	FIBRE	low
low	SALT	high
high	VITAMIN C	low
low	SIMPLE SUGAR	high
high	COMPLEX SUGAR	low

Another form of malnutrition affects great numbers of people in many parts of the world. **Undernutrition** is caused by insufficient energy in the diet to satisfy the body's metabolic demands. This lack is often complicated by insufficient supplies of one or more essential nutrients. When severe undernutrition is widespread in a society, leading to high death rates, famine is often involved. Famine is usually associated with overpopulation, drought, or crop destruction by insects. Attempts to provide famine relief are often hampered by the difficulties of shipment, storage, and distribution of the food required. As famine illustrates, humans really are not wholly independent of the natural environment.

13.3 PSYCHOACTIVE CHEMICALS AND ADDICTION

Because they can *think* about how they feel, humans are very interested in anything that can alter the way that they feel. Certain chemicals can change the way your brain functions and consequently can affect the way you feel. These chemicals range all the way from seemingly innocuous substances like sugar and caffeine to "hard drugs" like heroin and cocaine. Substances that act on the brain and affect our thought processes are classified as **psychoactive chemicals**.

Psychoactive drugs *can* help relieve many problems, such as the control of pain. To a considerable extent, modern medicine depends on their use. But improper use of drugs may create more problems than it solves. While some degree of stress is part of normal life, it is not an ill to be treated by chemically altering your state of awareness. Any drug should be used only when both the risks and the benefits are clearly understood.

People who regularly use psychoactive substances often develop a dependency on these chemicals ranging from habitual use, which the individual can control, to **addiction**, which the individual cannot control. The Addiction Research Foundation of Ontario (ARF) has described some of the conditions associated with drug dependence. The following definitions are based on those descriptions. (The various tables in this chapter are also adapted from material supplied by the ARF.)

- **Psychological dependence** is a condition whereby a person has a compelling emotional need for periodic or continuous use of a drug, and feels lost or desperate without it.

- **Tolerance** is a condition whereby continuous use of a drug causes the body to need more and more of it to produce the desired effect.

- **Physical Dependence** is a condition whereby a person comes to need a drug for normal functioning after adapting to its presence in the body and develops physical disturbances or illnesses if the drug is stopped.

- **Withdrawal Reaction** is the physical disturbance or illness that ensues when the use of a drug on which a person is physically dependent is stopped. The range of severity of the disturbance and its characteristics vary with the drug used.

Recent studies suggest that people only become addicted to sugar, caffeine, nicotine, alcohol, narcotics, or prescription drugs when certain of their biochemical pathways do not function in a normal manner. The precise nature of this biochemical defect is not known at the present time; it is a subject that is being investigated very intensively. Studies of family histories and of twins have revealed links between the genotype of an individual and susceptibility to addiction. The dangerous genotype is the opposite of what you might expect. Individuals who can "handle" their drinks or drugs are the most likely potential addicts. Initially, such people are much less affected by their chemical of choice than an average person. They often take this high initial tolerance as a good sign, whereas it is actually very bad news. Because it takes much larger doses to achieve the effect, the system of a pre-addict is challenged much more drastically than that of a normal person. Tolerance, which started off at a high level, increases rapidly. The realization that one has become addicted comes as a surprise. Many addicts deny that they have a problem, even though there is clear evidence that they have lost control over the use of their chemical of choice. If you have a high tolerance for any mood-altering chemical, you should consider it an early warning signal, particularly if there is a history of addiction in your family background. If you are in this situation, you should use none of these chemicals because you are probably predisposed to use too much.

Addiction is always associated with a compulsive and uncontrolled use of a chemical substance; characteristic withdrawal symptoms show when use of the chemical is stopped. Addiction is a psychological "drive" and it is often linked with depression. Current medical thinking holds that, for an addiction to

Figure 13.8

The addiction spiral: positive feedback control in action. The number of cycles in an individual's addiction spiral will depend on the chemical used (and whether or not it was used in combination with other chemicals), the amount and frequency of use, the genotype of the individual, and the environment in which the individual lives.

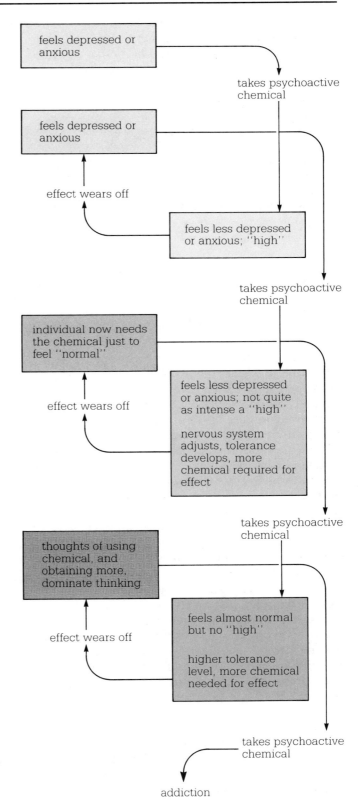

become established, two factors are needed: a genetic defect (nature) and exposure to an addictive substance (nurture). You can do nothing about the first factor but you *can* control the second.

The specifics of addiction vary with the particular chemical or combination of chemicals involved. However, the basic pattern is always the same. Addiction is a classic case of *positive feedback* (Chapter 10); the stimulus resulting from the use of the chemical causes an increased requirement for the chemical. This positive feedback occurs both with drugs that act as stimulants and with those that act as depressants. Initially, use of the addictive substance causes the individual to feel better, more relaxed, less inhibited, less anxious. Addictive people can go for long periods using a more or less fixed amount of their chemical of choice. During this time, the symptoms of their addiction build up; addiction is a progressive disease. Eventually, the person gets less and less effect from their chemical and starts to use more and more of it. This increase in intake is a clear warning sign of addiction. Higher levels of use eventually lead to compulsive, uncontrolled intake levels which seriously damage the homeostasis of the body. Not only the body's biochemical systems but also the brain's thought processes become disrupted.

Alcoholism provides a classic example of the addiction process (Figure 13.8). Typically, a potential alcoholic has a high initial tolerance and uses alcohol to relax and to lose inhibitions. For a time the alcohol works well, giving relief from stress. The user comes to depend more and more on alcohol and always makes sure that there is a supply available. Meanwhile, tolerance is building up and larger and larger amounts are required to achieve the desired effects. Eventually the person cannot operate without alcohol. The toxic side effects are now destroying liver and brain function. The addicted person continues to deny that there is a problem. Very few people recover from alcoholism or other addictions without outside help. (The effects of alcohol are further outlined in Table 13.2.)

A few decades ago, people with an addiction to a drug such as alcohol were considered to be beyond help. There were no successful medical or psychological treatments; indeed, addiction was thought to be the result of immorality, not a disease. This attitude has changed greatly; addiction is nowadays recognized as a disease and is successfully treated as such.

A Canadian, Dr R. Gordon Bell, has had much to do with this change in attitude. He has pioneered the development of treatment for alcoholism. His methods have been adopted all over the world and have been applied to the treatment of addiction to many other chemicals. Dr. Bell's treatment is holistic; it combines intensive counselling, group therapy, behaviour modification techniques, and a three year follow-up programme. The treatment teaches the addict how to enjoy a drug-free lifestyle.

Among the many awards and honours Dr. Bell has received for his contribution are the Canadian Centennial Medal (1967), the Queen's Silver Jubilee Medal (1977), Officer of the Order of Canada (1979), Senior Member of the Canadian Medical Association (1980), Royal Bank Award (1985), and Honorary Doctor of Laws Degree from York University (1986).

Addiction to Sugar

Many people are unknowing victims of sugar addiction, a condition which involves the compulsive use of refined sugar. In this form, sugar is rapidly absorbed into the bloodstream. The victims eat sugar in some form or other all day long or are binge eaters who gorge on sweet food. Often these disruptive eating patterns are associated with ingestion of large amounts of caffeine.

These addicted people do not metabolize sugar in the normal way. When they are given the glucose tolerance test (see Chapter 12), their blood glucose levels fall well below the normal fasting level after 3 h. There are also behavioural changes. The glucose taken at the start of the test produces a feeling of mild euphoria. Three or more h into the 6 h test, this feeling usually changes to unfocused anxiety and irritability.

Not everyone who enjoys sweet food is addicted to sugar. However, people who consume large quantities of sugar as part of their daily diet should try to go sugar-free for a week and see how it affects how they feel and act. Such people are frequently malnourished, their diets being low in iron and the B vitamin thiamine. Lack of these nutrients can cause emotional disorders. The constant challenge to the homeostatic systems that control the level of glucose in the blood can cause exhaustion of the beta cells in the pancreas. Diabetes may result.

Figure 13.9
Some teenagers in Canada eat almost half a kilogram of sugar every day.

Addiction to Stimulants

Stimulants are chemicals that speed up the activity of the muscular and nervous systems to abnormal levels. They cause constriction of the blood vessels and force the heart to beat more rapidly. These changes cause the blood pressure to increase dangerously. Stimulants induce a sense of euphoria, increased physical capacity, and reduced need for sleep. This acceleration of mental and physical activity has led to the street name ''speed'' for such compounds, particularly the amphetamines. Stimulants such as amphetamines, methylphenidate, and cocaine are highly addictive substances. During the 1960s and 70s amphetamines were often prescribed as antidepressants and as drugs that reduced the appetite and thus were helpful to dieters. As their addictive properties became better known, their legal use was sharply curtailed and placed under much stricter controls. Nicotine and caffeine are also potentially harmful stimulants.

Table 13.1 Stimulants

AMPHETAMINES	COCAINE	TOBACCO	CAFFEINE
(Benzedrine*, Dexadrine*, Neodrine*, Preludin*) **Methods of Use** • taken by mouth • sniffing • injection into veins	(Chemically, it is not related to amphetamine and is legally classified as a narcotic; however, it has reactions so closely similar that it is considered a stimulant.) **Methods of Use** • inhalation (sniffing or snorting) • injection into veins • combination with methamphetamine, heroin, morphine, barbiturates • free-basing	**Active Ingredients** • some 500 compounds in smoke, including nicotine, tars, and carbon monoxide	**Extent of Use** In Canada about 5 percent of adults use the caffeine equivalent of more than 7 cups of coffee each 24 h. **Average Contents** • instant coffee, per cup 30-120 mg • brewed coffee, per cup 40–180 mg • decaffeinated coffee, per cup under 5 mg • tea, per cup 10–80 mg • cocoa, per cup under 50 mg • cola drinks, per can 20–45 mg • compound headache-cold preparation, per pill 15–65 mg • ''stay awake'' pills, per pill 100–200 mg
Short Term Effects • reduced appetite • increased energy and postponement of fatigue • increased alertness • faster breathing • increased heart rate and blood pressure (risk of heart failure) • dilation of pupils • risk of infection if taken by injection	**Short Term Effects** • see *amphetamines* • acts as powerful local anesthetic	**Short Term Effects** • increased pulse rate • rise in blood pressure • drop in skin temperature • relaxed feeling in regular smokers • increased acid in stomach • reduced urine formation • stimulation then reduction of brain and nervous system activity • loss of appetite, physical endurance	**Short Term Effects** • increased alertness and sleeplessness • spontaneous tremor of hands • increased pulse rate and blood pressure • irregular heart beat in some individuals continued

Table 13.1   Stimulants *continued*

AMPHETAMINES	COCAINE	TOBACCO	CAFFEINE
With Larger Doses • talkativeness, restlessness, excitation • sense of power and superiority • frequent illusions and hallucinations • irritability, aggressiveness, paranoia, panic, or violence with frequent use • high blood pressure, dry mouth, fever, sweating, and sleeplessness	**With Larger Doses** • stronger, more frequent "highs" • bizarre, erratic, sometimes violent behaviour • paranoid psychosis (disappears if discontinued) • occasional sensation of something crawling under the skin • risk of convulsions • see *amphetamines*		
Long Term Effects • malnutrition • increased susceptibility to infections • development of tolerance with high doses • psychological dependence • long sleep, depression, and ravenous appetite after effects wear off	**Long Term Effects** • strong psychological dependence • destroyed nose tissues with frequent sniffing • see *amphetamines*	**Long Term Effects** • narrowing or hardening of blood vessels in heart, brain, etc. • shortness of breath, cough • more respiratory infections (e.g. colds, pneumonia) • chronic bronchitis • emphysema • risk of cancer of lungs, mouth, larynx, esophagus, bladder, kidney, pancreas • stomach ulcers • risk of thrombosis in users of birth control pills	**Long Term Effects** (More than 8 cups/24 h) • caffeine dependence (withdrawal symptoms include irritability, restlessness, and headache) • insomnia, anxiety, stomach and duodenal ulceration • possibly heart disease, bladder cancer, or damage to fetus in pregnant women

*Registered Trademarks (these trademarks do not necessarily represent all the trademarks under which these generic drugs are sold).

Addiction to stimulants leads to positive feedback reinforcement. The increased and persistent stimulation of the nervous system has been shown to have profound effects on the chronic user's thought processes and personality, eventually leading to psychotic and paranoid behaviour. The symptoms of withdrawal are opposite to the effects. Instead of euphoria, there is depression; instead of rapid mental activity, sluggishness and sleepiness.

Cocaine is an alkaloid, derived from the leaves of the coca plant. It is an extremely powerful, highly addictive stimulant of the central nervous system. Because it is so expensive, cocaine addicts frequently have to resort to crime to support their habit. Street supplies of cocaine are usually heavily diluted with such substances as sugar, starch, strychnine, aspirin, or other chemicals. Cocaine is sniffed up the nose through a straw, mixed with a solvent and injected, or extracted with a solvent, dried, and then smoked (free-basing). Chronic use leads to the same effects and withdrawal symptoms as encountered with amphetamines. The belief that cocaine can be used for recreation without danger of addiction is totally unfounded.

Recently a new cocaine-based street drug known as "crack" has come into use. It is cocaine treated with an alkaline substance such as baking soda and then dried. The resulting powder is smoked. Crack is a very dangerous form of cocaine.

CRACK: THE MOST ADDICTIVE DRUG

Crack is much less expensive than most other drugs. A user can purchase enough to get high for as little as $10.00. Because it is not snorted or injected like other forms of cocaine, but is smoked, it reaches the brain in great concentrations seconds after being absorbed by the lungs, causing an incredibly intense high. Although strong, this high lasts only a few minutes and is followed by feelings ranging from restlessness and irritability to severe depression. These after-effects produce an irresistible craving for another high; after several cycles of highs and crashes, a user can become addicted to crack—within days or weeks. Because the highs and lows are so intense and follow one another so rapidly, there is no such thing as recreational use of crack. Many experts consider it to be the most addictive drug known.

Young people are especially vulnerable to crack because of its availability and because of a misconception that smoking crack is less harmful than snorting or injecting cocaine. Crack may be a cheap drug to try, but in the long run the costs are more than anybody can afford. Since the effects of each "hit" last only a few minutes, addicts may quickly work their way up to an unaffordably expensive habit. They often must resort to stealing or dealing to get the money to support their habit. Crime and crack go hand in hand.

The emotional costs of crack use are harder to measure. A user's health deteriorates, his or her family becomes alienated, and addicted friends die. These experiences are common to all crack victims—regardless of who they are, where they come from, or how much money they have.

Free-base cocaine, crack, and pure nicotine are the most highly addictive substances known. Three or four exposures can induce a full-blown addiction. The street warning that "speed kills" is as true now as it was in the 1960s.

When used normally, nicotine does not have the same drastic effects as cocaine; it is nevertheless a very addictive chemical. Smokers who have also been hard drug addicts say that it is more difficult to get off cigarettes than off hard drugs. Along with the nicotine, cigarette smokers receive tars, phenols, hydrocarbons, arsenic and 15 or more other chemicals that have been shown to cause cancer. Health and Welfare Canada estimates that over 30 000 Canadians die annually from preventable, tobacco-related diseases; about 12 000 from lung cancer, 6000 from emphysema, and 14 000 from coronary heart disease. Smoking has also been related to bronchitis and liver disorders.

Caffeine is thought by many people to be non-addicting; almost all of us drink coffee, tea, and colas. Caffeine does, however, meet the criteria for an addictive substance. When ten or more average-sized cups are drunk each day the use has reached levels that should cause concern. People become addicted to caffeine in the same way as to any other chemical. It temporarily makes a person feel much better because of its stimulatory effect on the central nervous system. These effects include acceleration of mental activity, a mild sense of euphoria and a feeling of vigour. Caffeine's mood-altering effects also enhance other addictive responses—to sugar and to nicotine in particular. One chemical encourages the use of another.

In addition to its effects on the mind, caffeine affects the body. Its physiological effects include an increase in both heart rate and blood pressure. It stimulates the release of insulin into the bloodstream, causing a drop in the blood glucose level. It raises the level of fat in the blood, prolongs the action of epinephrine, and causes an increase in gastric acid in the stomach. It also acts as a diuretic, causing the kidneys to pass large volumes of liquid.

Like other stimulants, withdrawal symptoms include a feeling of depression and general irritability. These symptoms are not nearly as severe as those found in withdrawal from stimulants in the "speed" category. If the effects are so relatively minor, why be concerned about addiction to caffeine at all? At the present time the long term effects of heavy, chronic use of caffeine are not definitively known, but they may be linked to heart damage and high blood pressure.

Addiction to Depressants

Depressants (downers) act in the opposite fashion to stimulants (uppers). The most frequently used depressants are alcohol, barbiturates, and tranquilizers. Opiates such as opium, heroin, codeine, methadone, Percodan and Demerol are more difficult to obtain and, consequently, are used less frequently. All of these chemicals depress the activity of the central nervous system and induce in the user a sleepy, mentally relaxed state. By acting chemically to slow down parts of the brain's activities, these chemicals can effect a change in mood. It is worth noting that both stimulants and depressants produce euphoria.

Depressants are all addictive to susceptible individuals. The easy availability of tranquilizers and alcohol creates a real threat. These depressants can make such individuals feel more relaxed and normal for a brief period, thus inducing a dependency. Many people who have had tranquilizers prescribed for "nerves" have found that continued use has produced addiction. Recovery from such addiction is extremely difficult because these chemicals enter the fatty tissue of the brain and persist for many months after use of the drug has stopped.

Table 13.2   Depressants

ALCOHOL	SEDATIVE HYPNOTICS	OPIATES	TRANQUILIZERS
Alcohol is both a depressant and sedative	(Sleeping Pills) **BARBITURATES** (Amytal*, Seconal*, Nembutal*)	(Opium, Morphine, Codeine, Heroin)	(Equanil*, Vallium*, Vivol*, Librium*)
Extent of Use 80 percent of Canadians over 15 drink.	**NON-BARBITURATES** (Placydil*, Dalmane*, Doriden*)	**Methods of Use** • if opium, eating or smoking • if others, usually injection but also sniffing or oral or rectal intake	
Short Term Effects • initial relaxation • loss of inhibitions • impaired coordination • slowing down of reflexes and mental processes (reactions) • attitude changes, increased risk-taking to point of bad judgement, danger in driving a car or performing other complex tasks • in acute overdose, possible fatality due to respiratory depression • enhancement of above effects if consumed along with sedative hypnotics, minor tranquilizers, opiates, or antihistamines	**Short Term Effects** • in small doses, relief of anxiety and tension, producing calmness and muscular relaxation • in larger doses, behaviour similar to alcohol intoxication • production of sleep in a quiet setting; otherwise sleep may not occur • danger in driving a car or performing other complex tasks • in very large doses, production of unconsciousness • in acute overdose, possible fatality due to respiratory depression • enhancement of above effects if consumed along with alcohol, opiates or minor tranquilizers	**Short Term Effects** • relief from pain • state of detachment from depressing emotions • in large doses, euphoria • occasional nausea and vomiting • in acute overdose, possible fatality due to respiratory depression	**Short Term Effects** • calming of hyperactivity, tension, and agitation • lowering of emotional responses to external stimuli; e.g. pain • muscle relaxation • reduced alertness • short term relief of anxiety • easing of severe withdrawal effects of other depressant drugs • in larger doses, possible impairment of muscle coordination, dizziness, low blood pressure, or fainting • enhancement of effects of alcohol, sedatives, and opiates

continued

Table 13.2 Depressants *(continued)*

ALCOHOL	SEDATIVE HYPNOTICS	OPIATES	TRANQUILIZERS
Long Term Effects • possibility of gastritis, pancreatitis, cirrhosis of the liver, certain cancers of the gastrointestinal tract, heart disease, brain and nerve damage • suppression of sex hormone production, especially in males • convulsions and delirium tremens upon withdrawal	**Long Term Effects** • rapid development of tolerance and dependence if large doses used • possible tiredness and irritability, since drug does not produce completely normal sleep • temporary sleep disturbances upon withdrawal, possibly leading the user to incorrectly decide that more of the drug is required • progressive restlessness and anxiety; possibly delirium, convulsions, and death upon abrupt withdrawal	**Long Term Effects** • rapid development of tolerance dependence • moderate to severe cramps, diarrhea, gooseflesh, running nose etc. upon abrupt withdrawal • in regular high doses, loss of weight, reduction in sex hormone levels, frequent infections	**Long Term Effects** • physical dependence • withdrawal reactions like those of sedative hypnotics

*Registered Trademarks (These trademarks do not necessarily represent all the trademarks under which these generic drugs are sold).

As addiction to any of these drugs progresses, there is the typical loss of control over the amount used. Escalation of use leads to toxic side effects and to psychological disruption.

Abuse of alcohol is one of the most expensive and disruptive problems of our society. Drinking drivers are the cause of the vast majority of fatal automobile accidents. Figure 13.10 shows how even a little alcohol can impair judgement. It has been estimated that, at some time in their life, over one in every ten Canadians will have alcohol-related problems.

Addiction to Hallucinogens

Hallucinogen is the term used to describe drugs that transform the *kinds* of sensations you experience. These drugs are also called psychedelic or "mind altering" drugs. They produce radical distortions of reality. An individual's response is much less predictable to a hallucinogen than to other types of drugs. The effects of using hallucinogens depend on many factors: the type and amount of drug used, the past drug experience of the user, the mood that the person is in prior to use, and the manner in which the drug is taken. Another major complicating factor is the purity of the drug. With street drugs, you never know. It is thus impossible to predict where the mind will wander when under the influence of a hallucinogen.

Figure 13.10

The relationship between the amount of alcohol consumed and its concentration in the blood

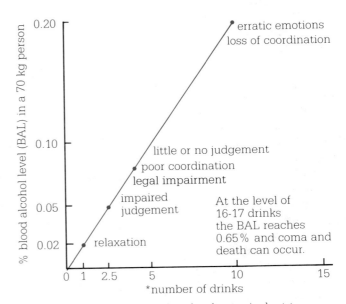

*One drink is considered to be equivalent to:

• 14.2 mL of pure alcohol
• 28.4 mL (1 oz) of 80-proof hard liquor
• 340 mL (12 oz) of 5% beer

Table 13.3 Hallucinogens

CANNABIS	LSD	PCP
(Marijuana, Hashish, Hash Oil)	(Lysergic acid diethylamide)	(Phencyclidine, "angel dust")
All forms derived from the hemp plant *Cannabis sativa*; preparations vary widely in potency; in general, marijuana is the least potent and hash oil the most) **Methods of use** • smoking or swallowing, either alone or mixed with food.	**Methods of Use** • swallowing • sniffing • injection	**Methods of Use** • smoking • injection • intake of tablets or capsules in many sizes, colours and doses
Short Term Effects • euphoria • increased pulse rate • reddening of the eyes • in later stage, quiet, reflectiveness, and sleepiness • in combination with alcohol and certain other drugs, increased impairment of thinking and behaviour • impairment of short term memory, logical thinking, and ability to drive a car or perform other complex tasks	**Short Term Effects** • see *amphetamine* (Table 13.1) • risk of infection if taken by injection • in later stage, distortions of perceptions • exhilaration or "mind expansion," or by contrast anxiety and panic, depending on user • occasional prolonged depression or psychosis • occasional convulsions • rapid development yet disappearance of tolerance	**Short Term Effects** • risk of infection if taken by injection • euphoria • increase in rate of breathing • shallow breathing • increase in blood pressure and heart rate • flushing and profuse sweating • poor muscular control • generalized numbness of hands and feet
With Larger Doses • distorted perceptions of sound, colour, and other sensations; slow and confused thinking • in very large doses, confusion, restlessness, excitement, and hallucinations, leading to anxiety and panic, or even an attack of psychosis		**With Larger Doses** • fall in blood pressure, heart rate, and respiration • nausea, vomiting, blurred vision, rolling movements and watering of eyes, loss of balance, and dizziness • in large amounts, possible convulsions, coma, and sometimes death • symptoms like those of schizophrenia • hallucinations • delusions, mental confusion, and "black-outs" • feeling of detachment

Long Term Effects
• moderate tolerance
• possible psychological dependence
• loss of drive and of interest in sustained activity
• with regular heavy use, increasing risk of
  –chronic bronchitis, lung cancer
  –reduction of sex hormone levels
  –impairment of learning ability and memory
  –lowered immunity against infections
	Long Term Effects
	• possible "flashbacks"— spontaneous recurrences of a prior LSD experience
	• medical repercussions not presently known
		Long Term Effects
		• possible flashbacks, prolonged anxiety or severe depression

Chronic users may become psychologically dependent as the drug becomes central to the user's thoughts, emotions, and activities. Although most drugs affect the brain to some degree, the hallucinogens are particularly disruptive. Some users believe that they can fly and throw themselves off high places, or engage safely in other types of dangerous behaviours.

Inhalants

Inhalants are volatile hydrocarbons produced from petroleum and natural gas. They are used by some people to alter their state of consciousness. Because they evaporate quickly, these chemicals are often incorporated into industrial and household preparations as solvents. The user inhales the fumes, often by holding over the face a bag or cloth containing the solvent. The most widely used chemicals include plastic cement, airplane glue, lacquer thinners, nail polish remover, lighter fluid, cleaning fluid, and gasoline.

Various reasons are given for using solvents and aerosols as inhalants. Curiosity, social pressure, and ready availability are often major factors in the initial use. Use often begins at a very early age but then stops after curiosity has been satisfied. Some of those who continue to use inhalants do so for the "high." Others use these chemicals for a temporary reduction of anxiety or depression, or for relief from boredom, shyness, or insecurity. These positive effects are very temporary and are usually followed by negative after-effects.

The vapours that are inhaled pass through the lungs into the bloodstream, where they are rapidly distributed to organs such as the brain and the liver. Most of these substances are fat-soluble. Consequently, they are easily absorbed through cell membranes into the fatty tissue of the central nervous system. There, they cause an altered state of consciousness and a slowing of the breathing and heart rate. These reactions are unpredictable; if respiration and heart rate are reduced too far, "Sudden Sniffing Death" (SSD) occurs. SSD is a common enough occurrence to constitute a real hazard.

Drugs and Sports

Some athletes take "sports drugs" in the belief that the drugs will improve their performance. Even if not physically addicted to drugs, such athletes can easily become psychologically addicted. Because of the belief that their competitors are using drugs, there is a feeling that they must also take them. Once usage has

Table 13.4   Inhalants

Short Term Effects
• exhilaration and disorientation
• confusion, slurred speech, and dizziness
• distortions of perception
• visual and auditory hallucinations
• poor muscular control

With Larger Doses
• drowsiness and unconsciousness
• increased risk with fume concentration
• possible death by suffocation in unconscious user if solvent has been sniffed from a plastic bag
• in very large doses, possible death from heart failure

Long Term Effects
• dependence, including craving and habituation
• possible restlessness, anxiety, and irritability upon withdrawal
• possible damage to liver and kidneys

begun, it is easy to become convinced that the drugs are essential. There are two groups of sports drug, *restorative* and *additive*.

Restorative drugs are taken to enable the athlete to compete despite injuries or stress. Substances in this class include painkillers (from aspirin to morphine), muscle relaxants, sedatives, anti-inflammatory substances, and anesthetics applied to the skin. Quite apart from the pharmacological damage that can ensue, athletes who are artificially "propped up" by restorative drugs can carry on and injure themselves still further. Pain, stiffness, fatigue, and other such signals should be taken seriously. Playing on when injured may be great for the team but is very bad for the individual.

The additive or **ergogenic drugs** are used to allow the athlete to increase performance beyond his or her normal limits. In this group are the most dangerous drugs — amphetamines and **anabolic steroids**. (*Anabolic* is a term used to describe substances that promote growth or repair.) Much has been written recently about the use of anabolic steroids. Some very prominent athletes have been barred from their sport for life because their urine tested positive for this drug.

The anabolic steroids used by athletes are derivatives of male sex hormones such as testosterone (Chapter 12). Such steroids produce male sex characteristics and are known as **androgens**. As a secondary effect, androgens stimulate the development of muscle mass. There is, however, no such thing as a strictly body-building drug; they all have side effects. A female using anabolic steroids is particularly at risk. She is taking a masculine growth substance that is antagonistic to her own estrogens. The undesired effects include disruption of normal growth patterns and the menstrual cycle, deepening of the voice, development of male hair patterns, and a greatly increased risk of breast cancer. These changes are usually irreversible.

In both men and women, anabolic steroids increase the body's insulin activity, break down DNA in the nuclei of body cells, upset enzyme systems, affect the absorption of calcium in the bones, and lead to liver dysfunction and high blood pressure. In young people who have not reached full height, bone growth can be stopped.

In addition to the physical effects listed above, anabolic steroids also cause behavioural disorders such as increased excitability, irritability, and insomnia. There can be mood changes that range from depression to psychotic behaviour. If calcium metabolism is disrupted, listlessness and fatigue may develop.

Some young people who are not athletes but who wish to build muscle mass to look good turn to anabolic steroids. Because of the effects on bone growth,

particularly bone lengthening, such individuals may end up with bulging muscles but may be very short and subject to other metabolic disruptions.

With all of the known negative effects of this group of drugs, it is amazing that individuals still use them. Not only is winning through the use of drugs unethical, it is very dangerous!

13.4 YOUR PERSONAL BALANCE

Unless you have an identical twin, there has never been a human with an exact duplicate of your genetic information. Although in many ways you may resemble your parents, or your brothers or sisters, you differ from them. As you mature and develop, you form associations with other people that affect you in special ways. This unique combination of "nature" and "nurture" causes every single individual human to be unique. Because no one is exactly like you, you have to take responsibility for your own personal balance.

Achieving a healthy, positive balance in our society is not easy and does not come naturally. Unlike other animals, humans cannot depend on instinctive behaviours. The freedom and choice that you have presents both positive and negative opportunities. You must live by making decisions. The better you understand your own strengths and weaknesses, the better your chances of success.

CHAPTER SUMMARY

Humans differ from all other animals. They exist in a cultural environment. Living in such an environment demands a great deal of decision making. Some of these decisions have profound effects on the quality of your life.

Even if culture surrounds human beings, they are by no means outside of the demands of nature. Good nutritional balance is still essential. Much of the mod-

ern human diet has negative effects on the health.

Another problem in modern culture is how to handle the many mood-altering chemicals that are available. Addiction to these substances presents a real danger. Stimulants, depressants, hallucinogens, and inhalants all carry considerable risks. You are responsible for your own personal homeostasis.

Objectives

Having completed this chapter, you should be able to do the following:

1. Describe how the relationship that humans have with their environment differs from that of other animals.

2. Describe how interactions between the brain and the body affect human physiology.

3. Explain why certain diets are better than others and describe two serious eating disorders.

4. Describe how addiction to mood-altering drugs develops and what dangers are associated with use of these substances.
5. Identify the various types of mood-altering chemicals and describe their effects.
6. Explain why the use of anabolic steroids should be avoided.
7. Explain why each individual must establish a personal balance.

Vocabulary

relaxation response
placebo
biofeedback
neuropeptide
cognitive therapy
obesity
malnutrition

undernutrition
psychoactive chemical
addiction
psychological dependence
tolerance
physical dependence
withdrawal reaction

stimulant
depressant
hallucinogen
inhalant
ergogenic drug
anabolic steroid
androgen

Review Questions

1. Suppose you ate whatever you wanted to. Would your homeostatic systems make all of the necessary adjustments to keep you in balance? Why or why not?
2. Why is a good self-image important?
3. (a) Describe how the biofeedback technique is learned.
   (b) Select a physical condition that can be affected by biofeedback control.
   (c) Describe how the effect is obtained.
4. (a) What is the current hypothesis as to how the mind might influence the immune system?
   (b) How has this hypothesis been applied to the control of cancer?
5. (a) What is cognitive therapy?
   (b) On what hypothesis is it based?
6. (a) Describe how your cultural environment affects your eating habits.
   (b) List five foods that are closely related to your normal cultural pattern.
   (c) List five foods that you consider unacceptable and explain why.
7. (a) Why is "crash" dieting counterproductive?
   (b) What is the best way for a person to lose weight?

8. (a) In what ways does the "Bushman" diet differ from the average modern diet?
   (b) What harmful effects may be induced by the diet eaten by the average North American?
9. Explain the following conditions associated with drug use:
   (a) psychological dependence
   (b) physical dependence
   (c) tolerance
   (d) withdrawal reaction
10. Describe the addictive process in terms of the operation of a positive feedback loop.
11. (a) In what ways is nicotine addictive?
    (b) What effects does smoking have on health?
12. Under the Federal Criminal Code it is an offence to drive with a blood alcohol level (BAL) greater than 0.08 percent. How many drinks would it take for a 70 kg person to reach this level?
13. How do inhalants get to the nervous system?
14. (a) Name two categories of drug used by athletes.
    (b) List two specific drugs in each category.
15. Why is the taking of androgenic drugs particularly dangerous for women?

Advanced Questions

1. The average female (163 cm tall; 64 kg) requires 8800 kJ per day to maintain her body weight. The average male (176 cm tall; 69 kg) requires 11 800 kJ per day. Calculate how many kJ you require for your height and weight and, with the aid of a calorie counter, work out what your energy intake has been over the last week. Are you in energy balance?
2. Research one of the drugs listed in this chapter and describe how it affects the body.
3. Research the law associated with drinking and driving.
   (a) What are the penalties?
   (b) What happens to your car insurance if you are convicted of drunk driving?
4. If your friends use drugs, how will you go about saying no when they put the pressure on? How will you keep saying no? Work out a game plan for this situation and use it as a basis for a discussion group.

5. The following signs might tell you that a friend has started to use drugs: school problems, depression or weird behaviour, rapid weight loss, new drug-oriented friends, stealing or other petty crime, suddenly wanting to be alone a lot. What can be done to help such a person? What would *you* do?
6. Select one of the following topics and prepare a report on it:
   - the law and the use of drugs (prescribed and/or non-prescribed)
   - the connection between genotype and susceptibility to addiction
   - hypertension and the relaxation response
   - cognitive therapy
   - biofeedback technique
   - alcohol problems among teenagers
   - the use and dangers of "crack"
   - stress and the "fight or flight" response
   - the work of a drug or alcohol addiction clinic

GENETICS: THE NATURE AND EXPRESSION OF GENETIC INFORMATION

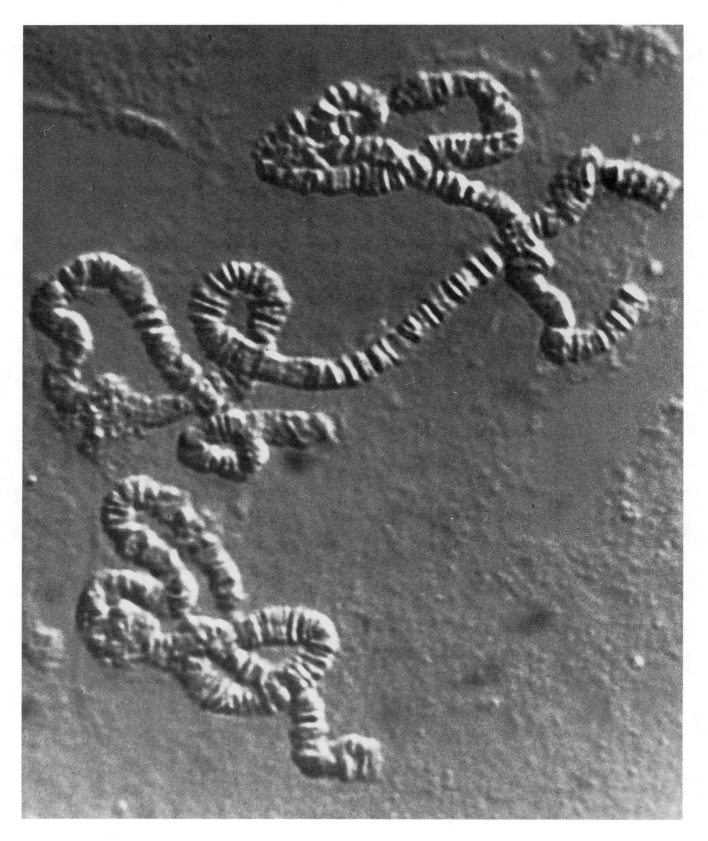

CHAPTER 14

CONCEPT OF THE GENE

*The value and utility of any experiment
are determined by the fitness of the material
to the purpose for which it is used . . .*

Gregor Mendel

Dating back at least to the ancient Greeks and up until the seventeenth and eighteenth centuries, much of the debate about inheritance centered upon the relative contributions of each parent. For example, the famous French naturalist Georges Buffon (1707–1788) believed that the appearance of an offspring's head and limbs was determined by the male parent, whereas the character of the rest of the body, external and internal, was inherited from the female parent. Many of these early views were based upon misconceptions of the fertilization process. With improved microscopes and better staining techniques, the events of cell division and gamete formation were observed in the latter part of the nineteenth century. The chromosomes could be seen to pull apart during the process of cell division, distributing themselves equally in each of the newly formed cells. Consequently, some biologists were quick to suggest that the chromosomes of the nucleus played a roll in inheritance.

This chapter deals with a methodology that revolutionized all prior thoughts about heredity, one that was to result in the concept of the gene. This methodology dominated all genetic studies for the first half of the twentieth century and has continued to be an essential tool in the field. It involves no expensive or elaborate scientific equipment, but is merely a way to analyze and interpret data from breeding experiments.

Although other biologists had carried out breeding experiments, Gregor Johann Mendel, an Austrian monk, (Figure 14.1) was the first to use them successfully to explain the hereditary process. As is the case

with many other scientific advances, few people were aware of the magnitude of Mendel's contribution when he published his analysis in 1866. Indeed, Mendel's findings lay virtually dormant until the beginning of this century. Thereafter, advances would lead over the next half-century to the chromosome theory of heredity. How did Mendel demonstrate the existence of genes? How were genes shown to be located in the chromosomes? The answers to these questions provide a basis for the chapters that follow.

Figure 14.1
Gregor Johann Mendel (1822–1884)

14.1 MENDEL'S DISCOVERY OF THE GENE

Despite the passage of time and the vast number of new insights, many biologists still like to use Mendel's experiments to introduce their students to the field of genetics. They do so because Mendel's work exemplifies how a great many fundamental concepts can be deduced from relatively simple experiments. It also exemplifies the features of a well-designed experiment. Four features in particular stand out.

First of all, Mendel used the experimental approach at a time when most biological studies were descriptive. He restated the general problem into a series of simple, specific questions that could be answered by designed experiments. His appreciation of statistics was reflected in a quantitative approach. Large numbers of offspring were observed and recorded, providing greater validity to his results. The interpretation of these results was framed into hypotheses that were tested in further breeding experiments. To test his predictions, Mendel often extended his studies into the third and fourth generations.

Second, Mendel's choice of the garden pea as an experimental specimen was excellent. Perhaps Mendel was lucky, choosing the garden pea simply because different varieties of pea seeds were readily available. There is an element of luck in most scientific advances; the good scientist can recognize and seize such opportunities. Mendel was aware that although the garden pea is normally self-pollinating, he could cross-pollinate different plants. To do so, he cut off the anthers from one plant (to prevent self-pollination) and transferred pollen to it from another plant (Figure 14.2). Note that the F_1 offspring or progeny (*first filial generation*) are the products of a cross-pollination, whereas his F_2 progeny (*second filial generation*) are the products of a self-pollination (Figure 14.3).

Third, Mendel restricted his studies to specific contrasting characteristics, readily distinguishable from each other; for example, he contrasted round with wrinkled seeds (Figure 14.4). The classification of the progeny was thus easy and unambiguous.

Fourth, Mendel did not start his cross-pollination experiments until he had confirmed that each of the varieties used was *true-breeding*. A plant is true-breeding if all the offspring produced by self-pollination (or by cross-pollination within that variety) are identical to the parent. These results also provided control data which could be contrasted with the experimental findings when different varieties were cross-pollinated.

Figure 14.2

Cross Pollination. In (a), the anatomy of the garden pea plant flower is shown. Note the pollen-bearing anthers and the stigma, which is the receptive surface for the pollen grains. The germinated pollen grains grow down the style to the ovules, where fertilization takes place. The pea plant normally reproduces by self-fertilization because the petals completely enclose the anthers and stigma until after fertilization. Note in (b) how cross-pollination can be done by first removing the anthers of the flower and then dusting the stigma with pollen collected from another plant.

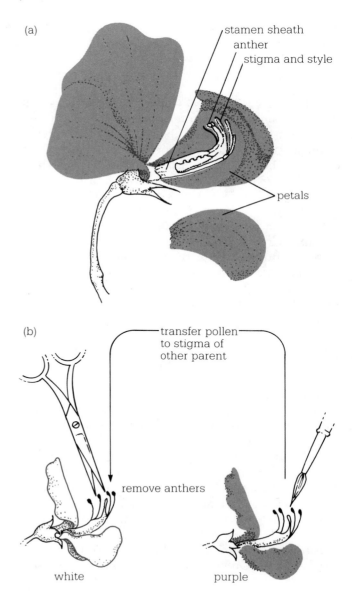

Figure 14.3
A representative cross between tall and dwarf pea plants, with the F₁ and F₂ results obtained by Mendel

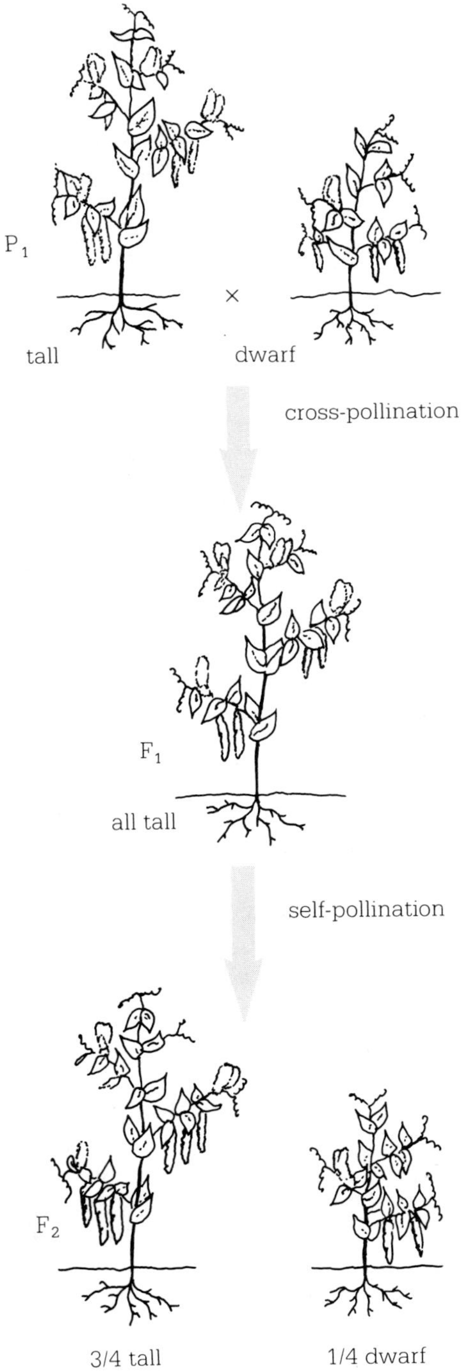

P₁

tall   ×   dwarf

cross-pollination

F₁

all tall

self-pollination

F₂

3/4 tall   1/4 dwarf

Figure 14.4
Mendel studied the inheritance of seven characteristics in the pea plant. Each is represented by two contrasting traits.

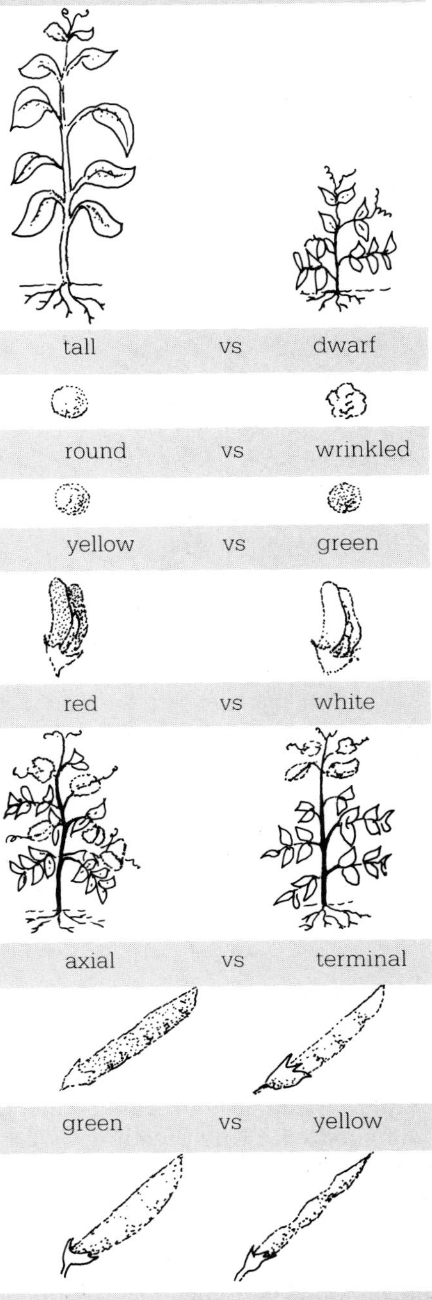

CHARACTERISTICS	TRAITS		
height	tall	vs	dwarf
seed shape	round	vs	wrinkled
seed colour	yellow	vs	green
flower colour	red	vs	white
flower position	axial	vs	terminal
pod colour	green	vs	yellow
pod shape	inflated	vs	constricted

Figure 14.5
A diagram of a typical experiment done by Mendel.
Testing the genetic purity of his source peas required two

years. The F₁ and F₂ analysis took two more years. A fifth
year was needed to test the predictions of his analysis.

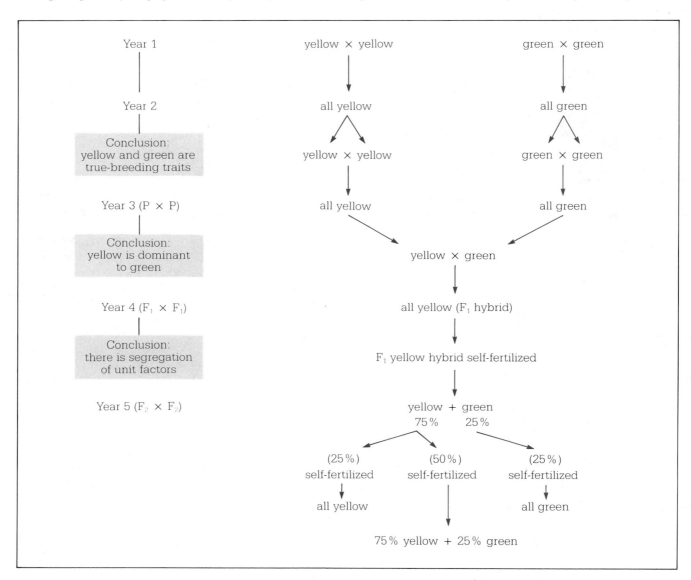

Unit Factors: Toward the Concept of the Gene

Figure 14.5 shows a representative set of Mendel's results. When true-breeding tall plants were cross-pollinated with true-breeding dwarf plants, all of the F₁ hybrid progeny were tall. However, unlike their tall parents, these hybrids did not breed true. Self-pollination of F₁ hybrids yielded F₂ progeny that were mixed: some tall, others dwarf. By far the most significant observation was the reappearance of plants in the F₂ generation similar in appearance to the original dwarf parent. This observation suggested that the character was determined by a **unit factor** which must have been present unaltered in the hybrid F₁ individuals in order to be transmitted intact to the F₂ progeny. Here was a clear statement of what was later to be called the *concept of the gene*. The name **gene** would only later be applied, but the concept of discrete units of heredity had been clearly stated. For simplicity, the term *gene* will be used in these chapters to describe Mendel's work.

Two individuals, both with the same genotype for a given gene, often show some variation in their phenotypes. Mendel used inbred strains and chose traits that showed minimal variation under normal environmental conditions. However, certain other factors can cause inherited traits to be more evident in one individual than another. Part of any difference between individuals lies in their overall genetic makeup. Although two individuals are similar for a given gene, they likely differ in many of their other genes. Some of these other genes may modify the internal environment of the cell and/or individual, thereby affecting the trait. Baldness and gout are two cases in point.

The gene for pattern baldness shows greater expression in males than in females. Indeed, heterozygous males show baldness, whereas heterozygous females do not. The difference is attributed to the much higher levels in males of the sex hormone testosterone.

Gout results from excessive levels of uric acid in the bloodstream. The excess may be deposited as crystals at the joints, causing severe pain. Because it is expressed in some heterozygotes, the allele for gout is considered to be dominant. However, only about 10 percent of all heterozygous individuals develop the condition. Even among those who do, there is considerable variation in the location of uric acid deposition and the intensity of the associated pain. These differences do not only vary from individual to individual; even within the same individual, severity of pain can differ from day to day. External factors such as diet play an important role. Equally important are internal factors such as the individual's rate of metabolic production of uric acid and/or the breakdown of uric acid.

The study of twins is used to show the relative contributions of heredity and environment to human traits. Twins reared together likely share a relatively common environment. *Monozygotic twins* (MZ) arise from a single fertilized egg and should be genetically identical. *Dizygotic* twins (DZ) arise from two different fertilized eggs and are genetically as similar as brothers or sisters. Comparison of monozygotic and dizygotic twins can give some indication of the importance of heredity. Comparison of monozygotic twins reared together with those reared apart can give some insight into the contribution of environment. Such studies often help evaluate whether there is a heritability component in the expression of complex traits such as height, weight, diabetes, schizophrenia, and epilepsy.

With the notion of a unit factor established, Mendel could start to develop a formal hypothesis to account for his results. The hybrid F_1 individuals had to have a gene for tall from one parent and a gene for dwarf from the other parent. Therefore, Mendel assumed each individual carried *paired* genes. The gene for tall (*T*) and the gene for dwarf (*t*) represent alternative forms of the same gene. All such alternative forms of the same gene are known as **alleles**; genes *T* and *t* are thus said to be *allelic*. If the paired factors are identical, as must be the situation for true-breeding individuals, the individual is said to be **homozygous**. They could be homozygous for *T* (*TT*) or homozygous for *t* (*tt*). If the paired factors are not the same, the individual is said to be **heterozygous** (*Tt*).

Dominance and Recessiveness
Despite the presence of the two different alleles (*Tt*), the heterozygous F_1 hybrid was tall. To describe this situation, Mendel said that tall was **dominant** to dwarf and that dwarf was **recessive** to tall. A dominant allele or trait is expressed in both the homozygous and heterozygous state, whereas a recessive allele or trait is expressed only in the homozygous state. These terms describe only what is observed, without offering any explanation or possible mechanism (see Chapter 16). Nevertheless, the concept of dominance and recessiveness was significant because it was contrary to the concept of *blending inheritance*. This concept interpreted the fact that offspring show some features of each of the parents by assuming that there were changes in the inherited information, much like the change in an artist's colours when paints are mixed. Unlike the notion of blending inheritance, the unit factors concept successfully explains how traits retain their integrity in the heterozygote and are transmitted unchanged to the next generation. The interpretation for cases of nondominance based upon unit factors is given in the next chapter (section 15.1).

With the concept of dominance, new terminology was needed to describe the genetic information. The homozygous tall parent and the heterozygous hybrid are similar in appearance, yet different in genetic makeup. The term **phenotype** is used to describe the appearance of the individual. **Genotype** is used to describe the genetic makeup of the individual. Thus plants that are TT or Tt have different genotypes, but the same phenotype (tall).

Individuals with the recessive phenotype must be homozygous. On the other hand, individuals with the dominant phenotype must have at least one dominant allele, but could be homozygous or heterozygous. When you are doing a genetics problem, or when a genetic counsellor is recording a family history, the uncertainty about the genotype can be indicated by use of a dash (e.g., T–), where the dash represents either T or t.

Segregation

The notion of unit factors led Mendel to hypothesize that **segregation** must occur; that is, that the paired genes must separate or segregate during the formation of gametes. If an individual has a pair of genes, then the egg or sperm should receive only one or the other gene of that pair. At fertilization, fusion of male and female gametes into a zygote would then restore the paired condition of genes for the offspring or *progeny*. It is noteworthy that Mendel's interpretation anticipated the later finding of chromosome distribution during meiosis (section 14.2).

As can be seen in Figures 14.3 and 14.5, the concept of the gene explains both the qualitative and the quantitative aspects of Mendel's results. The homozygous tall parent (TT) produces gametes with a single copy of the T gene. The dwarf parent (tt) produces gametes with a single copy of the t gene. Fertilization restores the paired condition, with all of the F_1 offspring being heterozygous. Segregation is more apparent in the formation of gametes by the heterozygotes. Each gamete has one or the other of the alleles (either T or t).

To determine the expected progeny for the F_2 generation, a **Punnett square** can be used (Figure 14.6). This device is a grid or matrix that provides a convenient, systematic way to consider all possible random combinations for the gametes. The vertical columns represent the gametes produced by the male parent; the horizontal rows, those produced by the female parent. A Punnett square allows you to systematically consider all possible random combinations resulting

Figure 14.6

Punnett squares. To determine the expected results of a cross, a Punnett square can be constructed. Each possible type of pollen (male gamete) is assigned to a column along the top and each possible type of ovum (female gamete) is assigned to a row along the side. By filling in all of the squares, all possible combinations of random fertilization are considered.

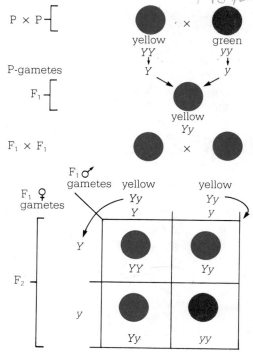

from fertilization. The completed Punnett square here shows that both tall and dwarf progeny should be expected. As well, it predicts at least three other results.

First, if segregation yielded gametes with T or t in equal numbers and if fertilization is random, then 3/4 of the progeny should be tall and 1/4 dwarf. This prediction is consistent with the data collected by Mendel. He obtained 787 tall and 277 dwarf, results approximating the predicted 3:1 ratio.

Second, both homozygotes and heterozygotes should be found among the tall progeny. One-third of the tall progeny should be homozygous and breed true when self-pollinated. The remaining 2/3 of the tall progeny should be heterozygous and not breed true when self-pollinated. This prediction was tested and confirmed.

Third, all of the dwarf progeny should be homozygous and breed true when self-pollinated. This prediction was also tested and confirmed.

Figure 14.7
A dihybrid cross involving seed shape and seed colour in the pea plant. R represents the gene for round seed; r, its allele for wrinkled seed. Y represents the gene for yellow seed; y, its allele for green seed.

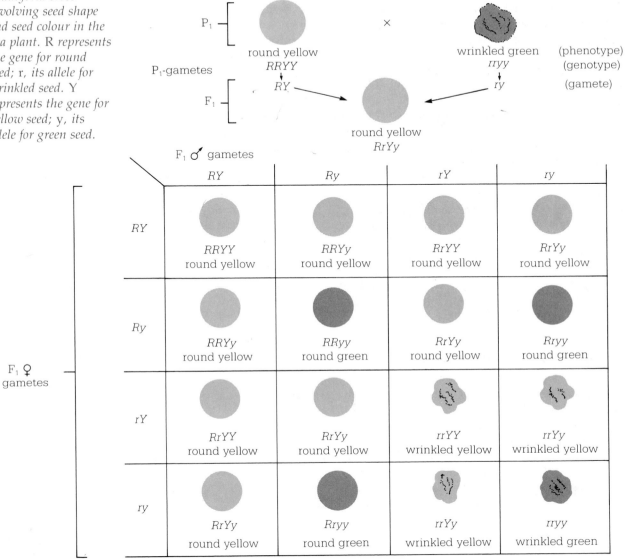

Independent Assortment

Monohybrid crosses involve only one pair of contrasting alleles. In a monohybrid cross, you consider only one of the tens of thousands of different genes present in the individual. Mendel extended his studies to **dihybrid crosses**, experiments where two pairs of genes were considered simultaneously.

Figure 14.7 shows the results of one of the dihybrid crosses done by Mendel. It involved round vs. wrinkled seeds and yellow vs. green seeds. The phenotype of the heterozygous F_1 progeny showed dominance of round to wrinkled and of yellow to green. The

gametes of the heterozygote show segregation for each of the pairs of genes. Each gamete has either R or r. The gamete must have only one member of the pair, never both or neither. Similar conditions hold for the Y and y alleles. Thus each gamete has one member from the R-r pair and one member from the Y-y pair.

Note in Figure 14.7 that there are four possible types of gametes. Random combinations of the different gametes gives 9/16 round yellow, 3/16 round green, 3/16 wrinkled yellow, and 1/16 wrinkled green.

The actual numbers obtained by Mendel in one of his experiments were 315 round yellow, 108 round green, 101 wrinkled yellow and 32 wrinkled green. Mendel noted that each pair of genes behaved as predicted in a monohybrid cross (that is, 3/4 round to 1/4 wrinkled and 3/4 yellow to 1/4 green). Mendel realized that his results could be explained by assuming that the segregation of one pair of genes is independent of the other pair of genes. As a result, all four types of gametes are produced in equal frequencies. This result is referred to as **independent assortment**. Again, it is noteworthy that Mendel anticipated the findings of chromosome distribution during meiosis (Figure 14.16).

The Use of Test Crosses in Genetic Analysis

A key element in Mendel's analysis is the demonstration of how unit factors segregate during gamete formation. Mendel inferred what types of gametes were produced by the F_1 individuals from his F_2 data.

To analyze the genetic makeup of the gametes, Mendel also used another, more direct approach called the **test cross**. F_1 individuals were crossed to individuals known to be homozygous recessive for all of the corresponding genes being studied (Figure 14.8). The homozygous recessive parent can contribute only *recessive* alleles to the test cross progeny. These recessive genes cannot mask the expression of the genes contributed by the F_1 individual. Thus, the relative frequencies for the different phenotypes among the test cross progeny should correspond directly to the kinds and frequencies of gametes produced by the F_1 individual.

In a monohybrid cross, the test cross progeny should provide a 1:1 ratio reflecting the two types of gametes produced by the F_1 individual. See Figure 14.8(a). In a dihybrid cross, the test cross progeny should provide a 1:1:1:1 ratio reflecting the four types of gametes produced by the F_1 individual. See Figure 14.8(b). If you know the kinds of gametes an individual produces, you can determine its genotype (Table 14.1).

Figure 14.8

Test crosses of F_1 heterozygous offspring with the corresponding homozygous recessive parent in a monohybrid cross (a) and a dihybrid cross (b)

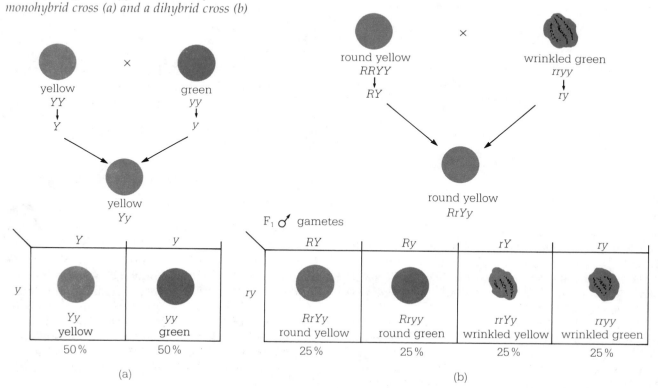

Table 14.1   Some Examples of How a Test Cross is Used to Determine the Genotype of the "Other" Parent

KNOWN TEST CROSS PARENT	OFFSPRING	GAMETES OF TEST PARENT	GAMETES OF OTHER PARENT	CONCLU-SION OTHER PARENT WAS
yy	All yellow	all *y*	all *Y*	*YY*
yy	50% yellow 50% green	all *y*	50% *y* 50% *Y*	*Yy*
rr yy	25% round yellow 25% round green 25% wrinkled yellow 25% wrinkled	all *ry*	25% *RY* 25% *Ry* 25% *rY* 25% *ry*	*Rr Yy*
rr yy	50% round green 50% wrinkled green	all *ry*	50% *Ry* 50% *ry*	Rr yy
rr yy	50% round yellow 50% wrinkled yellow	all *ry*	50% *RY* 50% *rY*	*Rr YY*

14.2 THE CHROMOSOME THEORY OF HEREDITY

There are some strange ironies in the history of science. Darwin derived his concept of natural selection as the primary mechanism of evolution (Chapter 20) without knowledge of genes or the mechanism of heredity. Mendel derived his concept of genes and segregation without knowledge of chromosomes or their pattern of distribution during gamete formation. However, unlike the immediate recognition accorded to Darwin's *On the Origin of Species*, Mendel's publication went largely unnoticed and unappreciated for over three decades. A major factor in this neglect was the fact that Mendel completed his work before there was a corresponding advance in the study of cells.

Without a thorough understanding of cells, Mendel's findings could not really be applied to the study of inheritance.

By the turn of the century, however, the significance of Mendel's work was becoming noticed. New hybridization experiments were showing results strikingly similar to those of Mendel. At the same time, the significance of chromosomes was unfolding. In 1902, Walter Sutton in the United States and Theodor Boveri in Germany independently published papers noting the marked correlation between Mendel's proposed segregation of genes and the segregation of homologous chromosomes during cell meiosis. They also discussed how an independent orientation of the pairs of homologous chromosomes in meiosis could account for Mendel's observation of independent assortment. The postulate that genes are located in chromosomes is called the **chromosome theory of heredity**. In this section you will consider the nature of chromosomes and their behaviour during cell division (mitosis) and gamete formation (meiosis) to better understand the physical basis of Mendel's principles.

The Nature of Chromosomes

The most distinctive structures of the cell during cell division are the chromosomes (Figure 14.9). More significantly, the chromosomes show certain regularities to be expected of material responsible for the transmission of inherited characteristics. Each species has a specific chromosome number. This constancy goes beyond mere number. When the chromosome complement of a *somatic* or body cell is characterized, it can be seen that the chromosomes are present in pairs that are structurally similar. For example, humans have 23 pairs of chromosomes for a total of 46 chromosomes (Figure 14.10).

The fruit fly, *Drosophila melanogaster*, an organism often used in genetic experiments, has four pairs or eight chromosomes in total (Table 14.2). The paired condition is a consequence of its acquisition of one set of chromosomes from the maternal parent and another set from the paternal parent. Thus there are two sets of chromosomes, just as Mendel postulated two sets of genes. A **genome** would be one complete set of genes, that is, one member from each of the paired chromosomes. A genome is often designated by the symbol N. The gamete with only one set of chromosomes is said to be **haploid** (N). The somatic cell, with two sets of chromosomes, is said to be **diploid** (2N).

Figure 14.9

Chromosome structure is clearly seen during cell division. As a result of replication, each chromosome consists of two chromatids held together at the centromere. The replicated chromosome is considered to be two chromosomes only after the two chromatids separate during anaphase.

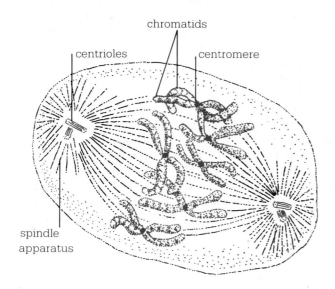

Figure 14.10

Karyotype of human chromosomes (male). A photograph is taken of the chromosomes in a cell. Then each chromosome is cut out of the picture and realigned in the orderly arrangement shown below. The specific banding on each chromosome is the result of special staining techniques.

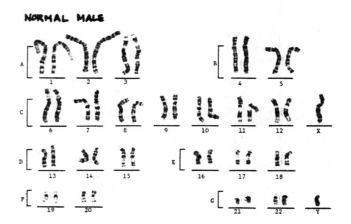

Table 14.2   The Number of Chromosomes Found in Some Representative Organisms

ORGANISM	COMMON NAME	HAPLOID NUMBER (N)	DIPLOID NUMBER (2N)
Drosophila melanogaster	Fruit fly	4	8
Vicia faba	Broad bean	6	12
Neurospora crassa	Bread mold	7	14
Pisum sativum	Garden pea	7	14
Aspergillus nidulans	Mold	8	16
Saccharomyces cerevisiae	Yeast	9	18
Zea mays	Corn	10	20
Lycopersicon esculentum	Tomato	12	24
Rana pipiens	Frog	13	26
Felis domesticus	Cat	19	38
Mus musculus	Mouse	20	40
Homo sapiens	Human	23	46
Gallus domesticus	Chicken	39	78
Canis familiaris	Dog	39	78
Nymphaea alba	Water lily	80	160

Mitosis

Mitosis is a process whereby each daughter cell, following cell division, maintains the proper diploid condition. In other words, not only is the constant number of chromosomes maintained, but the *specific* chromosome composition is maintained. Associated with each cell division is a replication of each chromosome. This replication must be followed by an orderly distribution such that one copy of each chromosome goes to one daughter cell, while the other copy goes to the other daughter cell. In this way, the two daughter cells have identical chromosome complements and are genetically identical (Figure 14.11).

Studies using microscopic observations have provided a well-documented description of how this process happens. When the cell is metabolically active, the chromosomes appear as very fine, barely visible threads. See Figure 14.11(a). They are in an extended state, thereby making the genes more accessible for use. It is during this stage (**interphase**) that

Figure 14.11
A diagram of the major stages of mitosis in an animal cell with diploid number of 4

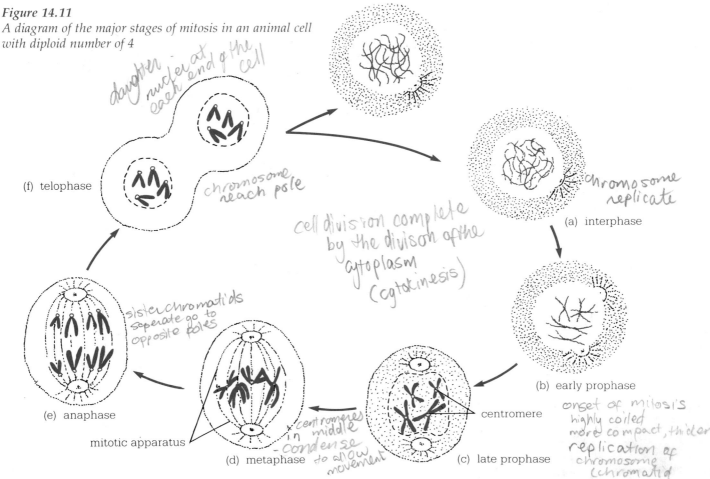

(f) telophase

daughter nuclei at the end of the cell [handwritten]

chromosome reach pole [handwritten]

chromosome replicate [handwritten]

(a) interphase

cell division complete by the division of the cytoplasm (cytokinesis) [handwritten]

(e) anaphase

sister chromatids seperate go to opposite poles [handwritten]

mitotic apparatus

(d) metaphase

centromeres in middle - condense to allow movement [handwritten]

centromere

(b) early prophase

(c) late prophase

centromere

onset of mitosis highly coiled more compact, thicker replication of chromosome (chromatid) [handwritten]

the chromosomes replicate. At **prophase**, the stage which marks the onset of mitosis, the chromosomal threads become highly coiled; as a consequence, the chromosomes become more compact and appear thicker and shorter. Their replication is now apparent. See Figure 14.11(b). Each resulting copy of the chromosome is termed a **chromatid** and retains this designation as long as it remains connected to its partner at the **centromere**. See Figure 14.11(c). Throughout both mitosis and meiosis, the centromere will be essential for chromosome movement.

During prophase, the nuclear membrane disappears and a **mitotic apparatus** is formed that will facilitate the orderly distribution of chromosomes. The apparatus is a series of parallel spindle fibres extending to the two opposite poles of the cell. Each chromosome is attached to one or more of the fibres at the centromere. In a stage referred to as **metaphase**, the chromosomes become oriented within the cell such that their centromeres are in the middle region of the

mitotic apparatus. See Figure 14.11(d). During metaphase, the chromosomes are in their most condensed state to facilitate their movement; it is usually in this stage that the chromosomes are counted and described. In order that the genetic material be distributed in the proper way, the chromosomes must stay aligned and the chromatids must be kept together. The stage in which the sister chromatids separate and begin to go to opposite poles is called **anaphase.** See Figure 14.11(e).

With this separation, the chromatids are recognized as independent chromosomes. As they move apart, the chromosomes appear to be pulled by spindle fibres. The centromere leads the way, with the rest of the chromosome trailing behind. In **telophase**, the chromosomes reach the poles; nuclear membranes reform to create daughter nuclei at each end of the cell. See Figure 14.11(f). Cell division is completed by the division of the cytoplasm (**cytokinesis**) to yield genetically identical cells.

Figure 14.12

*Fertilization without a compensating mechanism (a) would
lead to an increase in chromosome number with every
generation. Fertilization with a compensating mechanism
(b) such as meiosis maintains a constant chromosome
number.*

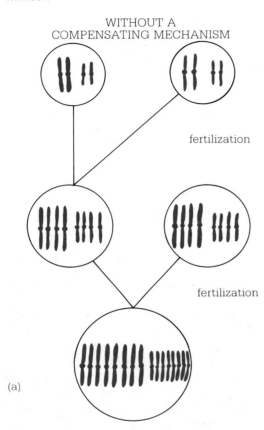

WITHOUT A
COMPENSATING MECHANISM

fertilization

fertilization

(a)

WITH A
COMPENSATING MECHANISM

reduction division

fertilization

reduction division

fertilization

fertilization

(b)

Meiosis

Although meiosis shares a number of features with
mitosis, the outcome is different. The fusion of
gametes creates a problem if the chromosome number
is to be maintained from one generation to the next.
See Figure 14.12(a). There must be a reduction in
chromosome number to compensate for the potential
doubling created by the union of two gametes. Simply
halving the number of chromosomes in the gamete is
not good enough. A haphazard distribution would
likely leave the gamete with both copies of some chromosome pairs and no copies of others. Such upsets in
the genome are highly detrimental and usually result
in the death of the cell (Chapter 18). Therefore, when
the chromosome number is halved, *one member from
each of the paired chromosomes must be retained*! Meiosis
achieves this reduction from the diploid condition

(2N) to the haploid condition (N) by a process involving two successive nuclear divisions, with only *one*
chromosomal replication. It is prior to the first division
(meiosis I) that the chromosomal replication occurs.
There is no chromosomal replication between the first
and second meiotic divisions. See Figure 14.12(b).

Meiosis I and meiosis II can each be described in
four stages comparable to those of mitosis. However,
the details of the stages vary for meiosis I and meiosis
II (Figure 14.13).

Prophase I is quite complex, involving a number of
events. One of the most significant is **synapsis**, the
lengthwise pairing of homologous chromosomes. If
homologous chromosomes are kept together, the
members of an homologous pair will go to opposite
poles during anaphase I.

Figure 14.13
A diagram of the major stages of meiosis in an animal cell

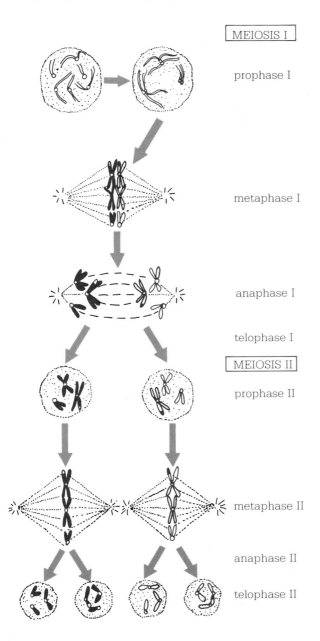

The association of two homologous chromosomes during synapsis is termed a **bivalent**. See Figure 14.14(c). At this stage the synapsed chromosomes actually consist of four homologous chromatids (a **tetrad**), since each chromosome consists of two sister chromatids. The bivalent moves as a unit when the centromeres align at the midline (metaphase I).

Figure 14.14
Shown in (a) are a pair of homologous chromosomes. After DNA replication, each chromosome contains two chromatids (b). After synapsis the paired chromosomes are called a bivalent (c). Since each chromosome consists of two chromatids, the bivalent consists of four chromatids (a tetrad).

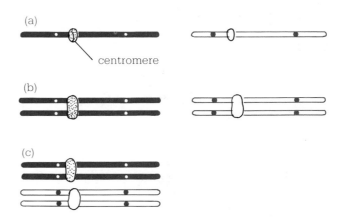

Note how metaphase I of meiosis differs from mitotic metaphase (Figure 14.15). In mitosis, each chromosome is aligned independently of the others. In the fruit fly, with four pairs of chromosomes, there would be eight chromosomes independently aligned. In contrast, there would be four bivalents aligned in meiotic metaphase I. The centromeres of the bivalent remain undivided, so that the two chromatids of each chromosome remain associated and *migrate together* to the same pole during anaphase I.

This process is how Mendel's segregation of alleles is achieved. Simply assume that the pair of genes, for example *R* and *r*, are located in the members of a pair of homologous chromosomes (Figure 14.16). Note that when the homologous chromosomes separate during metaphase I, the two alleles are separated. Sutton and Boveri (page 275) noted that independent assortment of genes could be explained by a random orientation of the bivalents in metaphase I of meiosis. Assume that the two pairs of genes are on different pairs of homologous chromosomes. Let the *R/r* alleles be in the pair of large chromosomes; the *Y/y* alleles, in the pair of short chromosomes. Note that if the orientation of the second pair of chromosomes is independent of the first pair, then two orientations are possible. All daughter cells must receive one chromosome member from each bivalent. However, within this limiting constraint, there should be equal numbers of all four possible combinations.

279

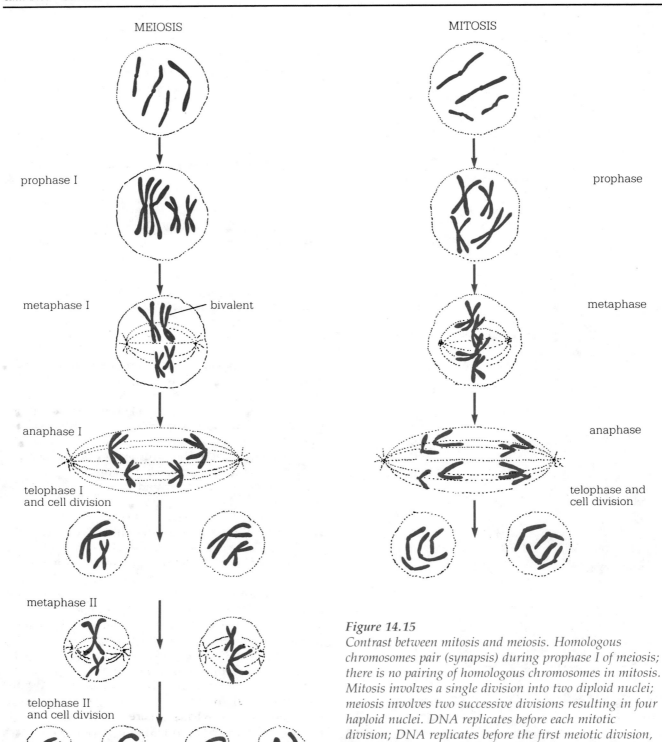

MEIOSIS

MITOSIS

prophase I

prophase

metaphase I

bivalent

metaphase

anaphase I

anaphase

telophase I
and cell division

telophase and
cell division

metaphase II

telophase II
and cell division

Figure 14.15

Contrast between mitosis and meiosis. Homologous chromosomes pair (synapsis) during prophase I of meiosis; there is no pairing of homologous chromosomes in mitosis. Mitosis involves a single division into two diploid nuclei; meiosis involves two successive divisions resulting in four haploid nuclei. DNA replicates before each mitotic division; DNA replicates before the first meiotic division, but not before the second. Mitosis produces two daughter nuclei with genotypes identical to that of the parent; the four haploid nuclei produced by meiosis can have different genotypes.

Figure 14.16
Alternative orientations of two pairs of chromosomes at metaphase I result in independent assortment.

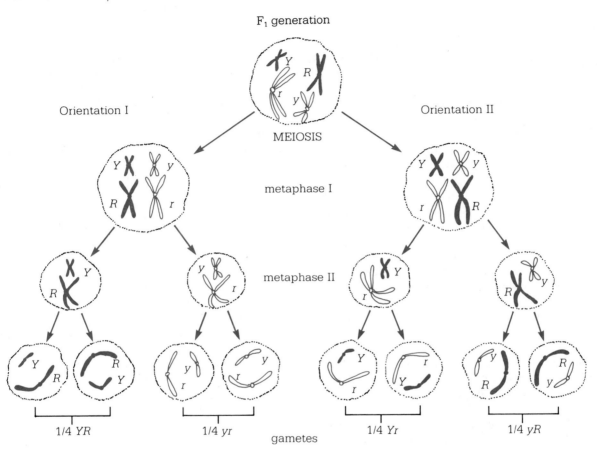

At telophase I, the two nuclei are effectively haploid, having one member of each bivalent. Each chromosome still consists of two chromatids associated by their centromere regions. No chromosome replication occurs in the time interval between meiosis I and meiosis II. Indeed, in many organisms this time interval is so short that no nuclear membrane re-forms during telophase I. Instead, the two daughter cells rapidly go into the second meiotic division, in which the two chromatids will be separated.

The Genetic Consequences of Meiosis

The genetic consequences of meiosis are very profound. The cells are reduced from the diploid (2N) to the haploid (N) condition. As previously stated, organisms which reproduce sexually must undergo this reduction in order to prevent doubling the chromosome number every generation. Meiosis also makes an important contribution to the genetic variation in the population. The meiotic products are all haploid, but need not be genetically identical. The random orientation of the bivalents at metaphase I permits numerous combinations, depending upon the number of chromosome pairs present. The number of possible combinations would be 2^n, where n equals the number of chromosome pairs. Two chromosome pairs would yield four combinations; three pairs, eight combinations; four pairs, 16 combinations; and 23 pairs (as in humans), over 8×10^6 combinations. These figures help explain why there are both similarities and differences between parents and their offspring. If independent assortment alone creates over 8×10^6 combinations for each human gamete, then fertilization would yield $(8 \times 10^6)^2$ or about 6.4×10^{13} combinations!

14.3 EXPERIMENTAL PROOF OF THE CHROMOSOME THEORY OF HEREDITY

By showing a physical basis for the segregation and precise transmission of genes, Sutton and Boveri greatly facilitated the acceptance of Mendelian genetics. Their evidence was impressive, but still only circumstantial.

How could other scientists further validate the findings of Sutton and Boveri? One often hears that "the exception proves the rule." This cliché is often misinterpreted as meaning that every rule must have an exception. In fact, it means that an exception provides an opportunity to prove or test the rule. Showing that the apparent exception is really consistent with the hypothesis would increase confidence in the validity of the hypothesis. If the exception cannot be so explained, then the hypothesis must be changed or discarded.

This section will consider how some early results helped test the chromosome theory of heredity. These studies came from the so-called "fly room" at Columbia University, where T.H. Morgan and his students, Alfred Sturtevant, Calvin Bridges, and Hermann Muller were studying the genetics of the fruit fly *Drosophila melanogaster*. During the decade from 1910 to 1920, this group established an impressive number of additional fundamental genetic principles. This section deals with only one of them, *sex linkage*. As you will see, sex linkage involves some seemingly exceptional results that are explained by the behaviour of a unique pair of sex chromosomes.

Sex Chromosomes

The determination of the sex of an individual is a complex process involving the interaction of many different genes. The most obvious genetic difference between males and females can be seen in their chromosomal make-up. In the decade prior to the work of Morgan's team, it was shown that in several insect species males and females differ in one unique pair of chromosomes. The condition is true for many animals, including humans. The human male has two chromosomes that are morphologically very different, yet segregate like a pair of chromosomes during meiosis and gamete formation. They are referred to as the X and Y chromosomes. Sperm receive only one member of the pair, either the X or the Y chromosome. Females, in contrast, have a pair of X chromosomes, so that the

ovum (egg) has one X chromosome. The other 22 pairs of chromosomes are similar in males and females and are referred to collectively as the **autosomes**. The XY chromosomes in the male and the XX chromosomes in the female are referred to as the **sex chromosomes**. Since the human male produces two types of gametes, he is said to be *heterogametic*. By contrast, the female, who produces only a single type is said to be *homogametic*.

Although this pattern of sex determination is typical of mammals and many other animals, there are some significant variations. In some insects the males have a single, unpaired X, the Y chromosome being absent. This condition is designated as XO. The female is XX. In birds and moths it is the female who is heterogametic, whereas the male is homogametic. Where the female is the heterogametic sex, the sex chromosomes are designated WZ for females and ZZ for males.

Sex-linked Genes

T.H. Morgan began his genetic studies of the fruit fly in 1909. Thirty-five years later, he received the Nobel prize for his contributions to the field. To begin his breeding studies, he needed mutants with easily distinguishable differences from the normal phenotype. Among the mutants that he found was a male fly with white eyes, in contrast to the normally found bright reddish-brown eyes. When normal females were mated with white-eyed males all the F_1 progeny had normal eyes, indicating that the allele for white eyes is recessive. However, reciprocal crosses did not give the same results. When white-eyed females were crossed with normal males, all the female progeny were normal, but all of the male progeny had white eyes (Figures 14.17 and 14.18). Such results implied two possibilities. One was that the two parents did not contribute equally, since the reciprocal crosses differed. The other was that the two sexes did not receive the same genetic information, since the phenotypes of the progeny differ according to their sex.

This correlation between the gene for white eyes and the sex of the F_1 progeny — **sex linkage** — suggested an association with the sex chromosomes. Morgan found he could explain his results with two assumptions. The first was that the gene for white eyes is located in the X chromosome. The second was that the Y chromosome does not carry an allele corresponding to the gene for white eyes. Some consequences of these two assumptions are shown in Figure 14.17. The P_1 females with two X chromosomes have two copies of the gene for white eyes, the P_1 XY males

Figure 14.17
Cross of females with normal eye colour × white-eyed males in Drosophila. Note the differences among male and female F₂ offspring.

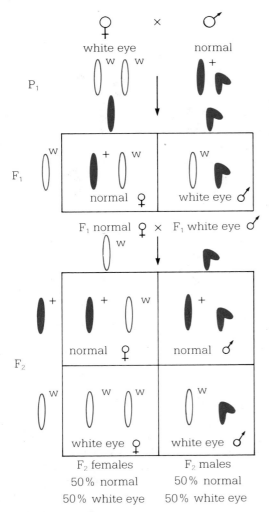

F₂ females
50% normal
50% white eye

F₂ males
50% normal
50% white eye

Figure 14.18
Cross of white-eyed females × males with normal eye colour in Drosophila. Note the differences among male and female F₁ offspring.

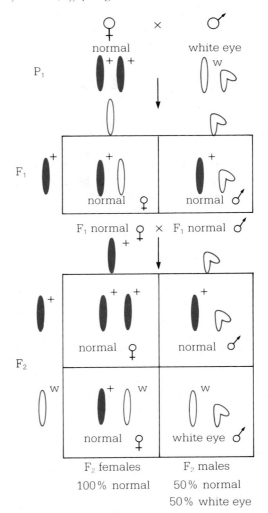

F₂ females
100% normal

F₂ males
50% normal
50% white eye

have only one copy of the normal allele. All the male F₁ progeny must receive a paternal Y and a maternal X chromosome carrying the gene for white eyes. They have white eyes. On the other hand, the female F₁ progeny receive an X chromosome from each parent and are therefore heterozygous with normal eye colour.

Figures 14.17 and 14.18 also show the predictions for the F₂ progeny. Here, too, any atypical predictions corresponded to the results obtained by Morgan. Other genes were found to behave in this sex-linked manner, both in *Drosophila* and in other organisms. Red-green colour blindness was one of the first sex-linked traits to be demonstrated in humans. At present, over 100 human genes have been shown to be sex-linked and located in the X chromosome.

Morgan's interpretation led to another important prediction. To reflect the fact that the female is the heterogametic sex (WZ), birds and moths should have a related yet different pattern of sex-linked inheritance. Such results had been reported earlier by others, but without an adequate explanation. Morgan's predictions fit these cases when the W chromosome was assumed to be genetically inert. There seemed little doubt for many biologists that sex-linked genes were located in the sex chromosomes.

Figure 14.19
Abnormal distribution of sex-linked genes associated with abnormal distribution of sex chromosomes (nondisjunction). In (a), the results are as predicted when normal males are crossed with white-eyed females. Note the expected absence of normal males and white-eyed females among the *offspring. In (b), note the chromosomal basis of the few exceptional normal males and white-eyed females among the offspring. Failure of the pair of X chromosomes to segregate (nondisjunction) in the female parent yields the abnormal genotypes and unexpected phenotypes.*

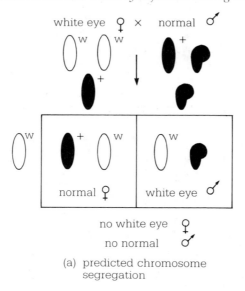

(a) predicted chromosome segregation

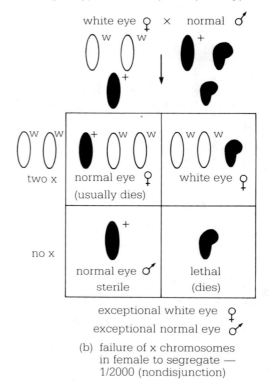

(b) failure of x chromosomes in female to segregate — 1/2000 (nondisjunction)

Definitive Evidence

The parallel patterns of inheritance between sex-linked genes and sex chromosomes were very convincing, but some biologists still considered the evidence only circumstantial. Could the genes be in another unseen structure that also segregated like chromosomes? An exception was needed to further test the proposed rule. When the failure of sex-linked genes to segregate was shown to be paralleled by the failure of sex chromosomes to segregate, there was considered to be definitive evidence that the sex-linked genes were located in the sex chromosomes. It is unlikely that two such rare events would correlate. From this evidence, it was extrapolated that all genes are located in the chromosomes.

The failure of chromosomes to segregate is referred to as **nondisjunction**. Calvin Bridges, one of Morgan's students, detected this situation in crosses between white-eyed female and normal male fruit flies. Among the predicted white-eyed male progeny there were some exceptional normal-eyed males. Similarly, among the predicted normal-eyed female progeny there were some exceptional white-eyed females. The frequency of these exceptions was about 1 in 2000.

Figure 14.19 illustrates how Bridges explained these results on the basis of nondisjunction of the X chromosomes during meiosis in the female. This interpretation was verified by a direct examination of the chromosomes of exceptional flies. The white-eyed females were indeed XXY and the normal-eyed males XO. The XXY white-eyed females developed when a Y-carrying sperm fertilized an ovum with two X chromosomes. The XO male developed when an X-carrying sperm fertilized an ovum without any X chromosome. With these findings, the validity of the chromosome theory of heredity was considered beyond reasonable doubt. The acceptance of the chromosome theory of heredity represented a landmark in biology. It was the beginning of modern genetics.

CHAPTER SUMMARY

Mendel used breeding analysis to demonstrate that inherited traits are determined by unit factors or, as they would come to be called, genes. The analysis was based upon showing the segregation of the alleles during gamete formation. Mendel also found that in dihybrid crosses the two pairs of genes can show independent assortment. The mechanism of genetic transmission was recognized as an orderly process in which the inheritance of both similarities and differences followed predictable patterns. These patterns came to be explained by the finding that the genes are located in the chromosomes. The segregation of alleles is similar to that of the members of a pair of homologous chromosomes. Genes located on different pairs of chromosomes show independent assortment, a result of the independent alignment of the bivalents during meiosis. The acceptance of the chromosome theory of heredity marks the beginning of modern genetics.

Objectives

Having completed this chapter, you should be able to do the following:

1. Outline how breeding analysis established the fundamental concepts of genetics.
2. Discuss the concepts of genes as units of heredity, of the segregation of homologous chromosomes and of alleles, and of the independent assortment of different pairs of genes.
3. Outline the chromosome theory of heredity.
4. Describe how the experiments of Mendel, Sutton and Boveri, Morgan, and Bridges contributed to our understanding of genetics.

Vocabulary

unit factor	dihybrid cross	metaphase
gene	independent assortment	anaphase
allele	test cross	telophase
homozygous	chromosome theory of heredity	cytokinesis
heterozygous	genome	synapsis
dominant	haploid	bivalent
recessive	diploid	tetrad
phenotype	interphase	autosome
genotype	prophase	sex chromosome
segregation	chromatid	sex linkage
Punnett square	centromere	nondisjunction
monohybrid cross	mitotic apparatus	

Review Questions

1. The garden pea was an excellent choice as an organism to study inheritance. Why?
2. Describe Mendel's experimental evidence for his conclusion that inherited characteristics were determined by unit factors or genes. Why did Mendel conclude that the unit factors were paired?
3. Distinguish between the following terms:
   (a) heterozygous and homozygous
   (b) phenotype and genotype
   (c) monohybrid cross and dihybrid cross
   (d) F_2 offspring and test cross offspring
4. List all possible types of gametes that each of the following individuals could produce:
   (a) *A a*
   (b) *A a B b*
   (c) *A a b b*
   (d) *A a B b C c*
5. What is the difference between segregation and independent assortment?
6. How does meiosis ensure that each of the meiotic products will receive a complete set of chromosomes at the same time as the total number of chromosomes is reduced in half?
7. How do the two meiotic divisions differ from two successive mitotic divisions?
8. How did studies of nondisjunction of chromosomes contribute to the acceptance of the chromosome theory of heredity?
9. A summer squash plant homozygous for white fruit is crossed to one that is homozygous for yellow fruit. All of the F_1 offspring have white fruit.
   (a) What predictions would you make for the genotypes and phenotypes of the F_2 offspring? What ratios would you predict?
   (b) What predictions would you make for a cross between a F_1 plant and a plant with yellow fruit?
10. The ability to taste phenylthiocarbamide (PTC) is dependent upon a dominant gene, *T*. The recessive allele, *t*, is associated with the inability to taste the substance.
    (a) What are the possible genotypes for tasters? non-tasters?
    (b) Two parents, both tasters, have a non-taster offspring. What are the genotypes of the two parents? Explain.

(c) Two parents, one a taster and the other a non-taster, have a taster offspring. What is the genotype of the offspring? Explain.

11. Brachydactyly is an autosomal dominant condition in which the affected individual has abnormally short, stubby fingers. A man and woman, both afflicted with brachydactyly, have a child with normal fingers. What are the genotypes of the child and both its parents?

12. Individuals afflicted with hemophilia often suffer from excessive bleeding or hemorrhaging due to the failure of the normal blood clotting mechanism. The disease is associated with a sex-linked recessive gene. Two parents, seemingly normal, have two sons that are hemophiliacs.
    (a) What is the genotype of each hemophiliac son?
    (b) What are the most likely genotypes of the two parents? Explain.
    (c) What are the possible genotypes of any other sons?
    (d) What are the possible genotypes of any daughters?
    (e) A third son is phenotypically normal. Should he be concerned about transmitting the gene for hemophilia to his offspring? Explain.

13. In *Drosophila*, the gene for brown eyes (*b*) is recessive to its normal allele for red eyes (*b⁺*); curled wings (*c*) is recessive to its normal allele for straight wings (*c⁺*).
    (a) Homozygous males with brown eyes and curled wings are mated with females homozygous for the normal red eyes and straight wings.
        (i) Give the genotypes and phenotypes of the F_1 offspring.
        (ii) If F_1 males were mated with F_1 females, what phenotypes would be expected in the F_2 and in what proportions?
    (b) Homozygous males with brown eyes and straight wings are mated to females homozygous for red eyes and curled wings.
        (i) Give the genotypes and phenotypes of the F_1 offspring.
        (ii) If F_1 males were mated with F_1 females, what phenotypes would be expected in the F_2 and in what proportions?

(iii) If test crosses were done with the F_1 females, what phenotypes would be expected in the test cross progeny and in what proportions?

(c) You are given specimens with red eyes and straight wings and told that they all have the same genotype.

(i) List all possible genotypes for these flies.
(ii) A test cross with these flies yields 257 flies with brown eyes and straight wings and 268 flies with red eyes and straight wings. What was the genotype of flies tested?

Advanced Questions

1. Mendel did not encounter any exceptions such as sex-linked traits. Why?
2. Most genes associated with genetic diseases in humans are recessive rather than dominant. Why?
3. If a gene were located in the Y chromosome (and is not present in the X chromosome), what predictions would you make about its patterns of inheritance?
4. There is a popular belief that marriage between first cousins leads to a high risk of having children with genetic defects. What, if any, is the genetic basis of this belief?
5. Why do most organisms have both mitosis and meiosis as mechanisms of cell division? Could an organism have only one of these processes in its life cycle? Explain.
6. Is there a relationship between the physical size or complexity and an organism's diploid chromosome number? Discuss.

CHAPTER 15

MENDELIAN GENETICS IN THE 20TH CENTURY

Beneath the imposing structure called Heredity,
there has been a dingy basement called Mutation.

H.J. Muller 1921

The mark of most great advances in knowledge is that they stimulate a vast array of related studies. Mendelian genetics is certainly a case in point. There were many new findings in which the F_2 ratios differed from the classic 3:1 and 9:3:3:1. For example, consider the different comb shapes found on the heads of chickens. Such genetic diversity cannot be explained by a single gene difference. Is there more than one pair of genes determining this trait? If so, how do different genes interact when affecting the same trait? What can be said about dominance in such cases? Are the different genes located in the same chromosome? Such questions logically follow from Mendelian genetics and the chromosome theory of heredity. This chapter deals with how the extension of Mendelian analysis has refined the concept of the gene.

15.1 DOMINANCE RELATIONSHIPS

Mendel's definition of dominance was based upon the heterozygote's resemblance to one parent and not the other. The terms dominant and recessive were only descriptive terms. It would take further breeding and biochemical studies to determine the mechanism of gene expression that would explain the results. To help you better understand why some genes are dominant and others recessive, a number of points should be considered.

The key point is the kind of information carried by each gene that permits that gene to determine the traits of the individual. Most traits are a consequence of a complex series of developmental steps and interactions. At the molecular level, development is largely dependent upon the presence of certain proteins in the right place, in the right amounts, and at the right time. Many of these proteins function as enzymes to catalyze critical biochemical reactions. Other proteins have other functions. Hormones have a regulatory role; hemoglobin has a role in transport; actin and myosins have a role in contraction; antibodies have a role in protection. Proteins such as collagen act as structural components. As will be discussed in section 15.9, genes carry the information to make these specific proteins and thereby to determine the final outcome.

Albinism, a condition in which the individual cannot make the pigment melanin, will serve as a useful example. Why is albinism a recessive trait? Individuals with normal pigmentation must be able to make all of the enzymes needed to synthesize melanin. The albino individual typically lacks the enzyme tyrosinase and thus cannot carry out one of the essential reactions in the production of melanin. In other words, the normally pigmented individual carries the gene (*A*) for tyrosinase, whereas the albino carries an altered form of that gene (*a*). When the *a* allele is expressed, an altered protein lacking tyrosinase activity will be made. Heterozygous individuals, having one *A* allele and one *a* allele, still possess the needed information to make the enzyme tyrosinase. As long as some tyrosinase is made, melanin can be made and the heterozygote is pigmented. The phenotype of the *homozygous recessive* individual — an albino — results from the total absence of dominant allele, *A*.

Figure 15.1
Monohybrid cross in carnations showing incomplete dominance for flower colour

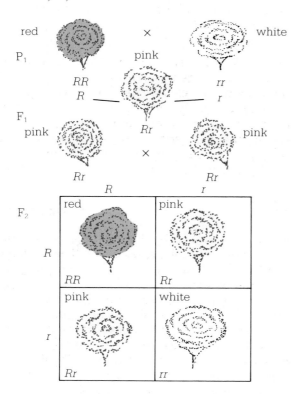

Examples of incomplete dominance are found in the flower colour of many plants. If carnations true-bred for red are crossed with ones true-bred for white, all of the F$_1$ progeny are pink. The colour is intermediate, suggesting that only one copy of the gene for pigment (red) makes less pigment than would two copies. The compliance with Mendelian genetics is reflected in the F$_2$, where the ratio is 1/4 red: 1/2 pink: 1/4 white (Figure 15.1). Clearly there has been a segregation of the alleles. The phenotypic ratio corresponds to the classic genotypic ratio because all three genotypes can be distinguished. Note, however, that when Mendel crossed pea plants having red flowers with plants having white flowers, all the F$_1$ progeny had red flowers —a case of complete dominance. The dominance relationship therefore must be tested and established for each case and cannot be inferred from other species.

Another type of dominance relationship is seen in studies of the human blood group genes, which determine the antigens located on the surface of the red blood cells. Such antigens are detected by their interaction with specific antibodies. For example, two of the blood groups are called M and N. Table 15.1 shows all possible parental combinations and their offspring.

If one copy of the functional allele (*A* −) is as effective as two copies (*AA*), then dominance is said to be complete. *Complete dominance* is the situation described by Mendel. But do heterozygous individuals make as much pigment as homozygous individuals? The difference, if there is any, is not very striking compared to the difference between the heterozygote and an albino. The allele for melanin production, *A*, is therefore expressed as a complete dominant.

For many human conditions, "normal" is simply defined as not requiring medical attention. Yet there are clinical tests that can distinguish between the heterozygote and homozygous normal for many genetic disorders such as sickle-cell anemia and Tay-Sachs disease. For example, there is often a difference in the enzyme levels between the homozygote and heterozygote. This ability to detect the heterozygote can be extremely important in genetic counselling (Chapter 18). Such situations, where the phenotype of the heterozygote is readily seen to be intermediate between the two parent phenotypes, are referred to as partial or **incomplete dominance**.

Table 15.1   All Possible Matings Involving the M and N Blood Group Series and the Resulting Types of Offspring

POSSIBLE MATINGS INVOLVING M AND N BLOOD GROUPS	BLOOD TYPE OF OFFSPRING		
	M	MN	N
M × M	100%	—	—
M × MN	50%	50%	—
M × N	—	100%	—
MN × MN	25%	50%	25%
MN × N	—	50%	25%
N × N	—	—	100%

Note that offspring of type M × type N parents are all type MN. That is, they express both blood groups M and N. Here the heterozygote expresses both alleles, a condition referred to as **codominance**. The column of the table showing offspring blood type demonstrates how Mendelian analysis can establish the genetic basis of certain phenotypes. The demonstration of segregation indicates that the M and N blood groups are determined by a pair of alleles. The observed ratios show that there is a single pair of alleles involved in MN inheritance.

Designating Alternative Forms of the Same Gene

The features necessary when using symbols are simplicity and clarity. That is why upper and lower case letters (e.g., *A* and *a*) are commonly used to designate dominance relationships. However, this convention is inadequate in many situations. What designations should be used in the case of codominance? The problem can be even more complex. Alleles, as alternative forms of the same gene, arise by changes (called *mutations*) in the gene. Such changes are not restricted to only two alternatives! There can be *many* different alternative forms of the same gene.

How can you designate the common relationship of three or more allelic forms of the same gene? The most common approach is to use the same letter designation for all of the alleles, but to distinguish them by superscripts (e.g., c^+, c^h, c^{ch}). The use of "+" as a superscript always denotes the "normal" allele. Some biologists will simply use "+" for the normal allele and the letter for the mutant allele.

15.2 GENETIC ANALYSIS FOR ALLELISM

Genetic analysis often involves the isolation and characterization of numerous mutants. When two mutants with related phenotypes are compared, it is not certain

Figure 15.2
Segregation test with mutations that are alleles. Since neither mutant carries the normal allele, no F_2 offspring with the normal phenotype occur.

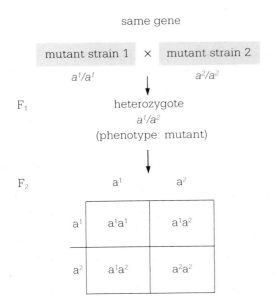

whether or not the mutations are alleles. Did the two mutants arise by mutation of the same gene (alleles) or different genes (nonalleles)? Two genetic methods are used to test for allelism: the **segregation test** and the **complementation test**.

The Segregation Test

Crossing the two mutants to create the heterozygote is the first step in genetic analysis for allelism. If the two mutations are alleles, then the hybrid should be heterozygous for only one gene (Figure 15.2). The one-gene difference between the two mutants will be revealed if the segregation of the alleles gives a version of the 3:1 ratio for F_2 progeny and a 1:1 ratio in a test cross. Note that the absence of the normal allele in

Figure 15.3
Segregation test with mutations that are nonalleles. By the process of segregation and independent assortment, the presence of normal alleles in the mutants permits the occurrence of F_2 offspring with the normal phenotype.

different genes

mutant strain 1	×	mutant strain 2
$a/a \ b^+/b^+$		$a^+/a^+ \ b/b$

F_1 heterozygote
$a^+/a \ b^+/b$
(phenotype: normal)

F_2	a^+b^+	$a^+ b$	$a b^+$	$a b$
$a^+ b^+$	$a^+a^+b^+b^+$ *normal*	$a^+a^+b^+b$ *normal*	$a^+a \ b^+b^+$ *normal*	$a^+a \ b^+b$ *normal*
$a^+ b$	$a^+a^+ \ b^+b$ *normal*	$a^+a^+ \ bb$	$a^+a \ b^+b$ *normal*	$a^+a \ bb$
$a b^+$	$a^+a \ b^+b^+$ *normal*	$a^+a \ b^+b$ *normal*	$aa \ b^+b^+$	$aa \ b^+b$
$a b$	$a^+a \ b^+b$ *normal*	$a^+a \ bb$	$aa \ b^+b$	$aa \ bb$

either parent precludes the occurrence of normal offspring.

On the other hand, if the two mutations are non-alleles, then the hybrid should be heterozygous for two different genes (Figure 15.3). This situation would be reflected in a version of the 9:3:3:1 ratio for the F_2 progeny and a 1:1:1:1 ratio in a test cross. Here, the presence of normal alleles permits the occurrence of normal offspring by segregation and independent assortment. In this way, breeding ratios can be used to decide whether or not the two mutations are alleles.

The Complementation Test

The complementation test involves no segregation ratios; rather, it involves simply looking at the phenotype of the heterozygote. As shown in Figures 15.2 and 15.3, the predicted phenotype of the heterozygote differs according to whether there is a one-gene difference (alleles) or a two-gene difference (non-alleles). The predictions are based upon the assumption that each mutation is recessive to its normal allele.

If the two mutations are alleles, then the hybrid is heterozygous for only one gene, with one copy of each mutation. The hybrid still lacks a normal form of the gene and should have a mutant phenotype. On the other hand, if the two mutations are nonalleles (Figure 15.3), then they are defective for different genes. Each mutant should carry the normal alleles for the defect of the other mutant. The hybrid is heterozygous for two genes. Each mutant has contributed the normal allele that will compensate for the defective gene contributed by the other parent. In other words, the two mutants complement each other. Assuming that the normal alleles are dominant, the resulting phenotype of the heterozygote should be normal.

15.3 MULTIPLE ALLELES

A diploid organism, with paired homologous chromosomes, carries paired (two) alleles for each gene. Any one individual can have only two different forms of a gene. In contrast, there can be many alternative forms of the gene in the general population, a phenomenon known as **multiple alleles**. The list of such alternative forms is called an *allelic series*.

One of the earliest known examples of multiple alleles, which came at the turn of the century from the research of the French scientist Lucien Cuenot, involved coat colour in mice (Figure 15.4). Another early example was eye colour in *Drosophila*. T.H. Morgan found a male mutant with an altered eye colour

Figure 15.4
A multiple allelic series affecting coat colour in mice. The normal coat colour (agouti) is determined by the A gene; A^h for the Himalayan allele; and a for the albino allele.

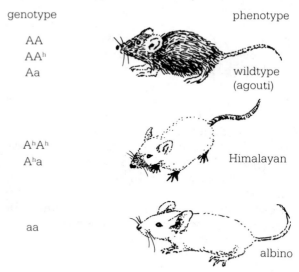

genotype	phenotype
AA AA^h Aa	wildtype (agouti)
A^{h}A^h A^{h}a	Himalayan
aa	albino

in his stock of white-eyed fruit flies. He analyzed the new mutant, which he called eosin, by crossing it with white-eyed females. The F_1 heterozygotes had the eosin mutant phenotype. The absence of the normal phenotype indicated that the genes for eosin and white are alleles (complementation test). The eosin phenotype indicated that eosin is dominant to white. Crosses of the F_1 heterozygous females with white-eyed males in a segregation test yielded a 1:1 ratio of eosin and white, again indicating that they are alleles. Crosses of eosin-eyed flies with normal flies showed that eosin is recessive to normal. Thus Morgan had found an allelic series with three alleles, designated w^+ (normal), w^e (eosin), and w (white). The relationships thus established were the dominance of normal to both eosin and white and the dominance of eosin to white. Since then, many other mutations have been reported that belong to this same allelic series.

ABO Blood Types

Genes usually have multiple alleles. The ABO blood groups in humans are a typical example, worth examining. It is a relatively simple allelic series with three alleles, I^A, I^B and i. (They are not allelic with the blood groups M and N previously discussed.)

Recall that individuals will have only two copies of the *I* gene and that the individual may be either homozygous or heterozygous. The six genotypes listed in Table 15.2 represent all possible combinations.

Table 15.2   All Possible Genotypes for the ABO Blood Group Multiple Allelic Series and Their Corresponding Phenotypes

GENOTYPE	A Antigen	B Antigen	PHENOTYPE (blood group)
$I^A I^A$	+	−	A
$I^A i$	+	−	A
$I^B I^B$	−	+	B
$I^B i$	−	+	B
$I^A I^B$	+	+	AB
ii	−	−	O

Figure 15.5

A,B,O blood typing. Small samples of blood are mixed with anti-A and anti-B sera. The clumping of blood cells reflects a positive reaction, indicating the presence of the antigen.

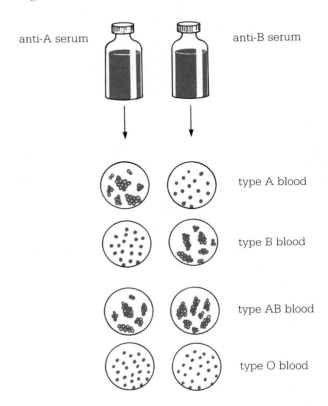

The blood groups can be detected because there are antigens which elicit and react with specific antibodies. When the red blood cells are mixed with the corresponding antibodies, the cells clump together. For example, when anti-A serum is mixed with blood containing A-antigen, clumping results. For the ABO series, the phenotype of the individual is determined by tests with anti-A and anti-B antibodies. This procedure for blood typing restricts the number of phenotypes to only four: A, B, AB and O (Figure 15.5).

With six genotypes and four phenotypes, what are the dominance relationships? A and B show codominance, so the heterozygote $I^A I^B$ is type AB. A and B are both dominant to O, since anti-O antibodies were not used in the tests. Thus type A individuals could be either $I^A I^A$ or $I^A i$. Similarly, type B individuals could be either $I^B I^B$ or $I^B i$.

Predictions for all possible crosses can thus be seen to be simple extensions of Mendelian genetics. The two alleles segregate during gamete formation and, if necessary, a Punnett square can be used to determine the possible types of progeny. Consider a few examples where the genotypes of the parents are given.

1. $I^A I^A \times I^B I^B$

Crosses between these two homozygotes must yield only heterozygous $I^A I^B$ offspring, who are type AB.

2. $I^A i \times I^A i$

Crosses between these similar heterozygotes should yield 1/4 $I^A I^A$, 1/2 $I^A i$, and 1/4 ii, that is, offspring either type A or type O.

3. $I^A i \times I^B i$

Crosses between these different heterozygotes should yield 1/4 $I^A I^B$, 1/4 $I^A i$, 1/4 $I^B i$, and 1/4 ii; that is, all four blood types.

Consider these further examples where you know the phenotype, but not necessarily the genotype. Remember that if the individual is type O or type AB, then the genotype is known. On the other hand, if the individuals are type A or type B, then they could be either homozygous or heterozygous (carrying the recessive i allele). Observe what types of offspring are possible from the following matings:

4. type AB × type O

The parents must be $I^A I^B \times ii$ and the offspring can be either $I^A i$ or $I^B i$; that is, either type A or type B.

5. type A × type O

If the type A parent is homozygous, only type A offspring are possible. However, the type A parent could be heterozygous, so that both type A and type O offspring are possible (see example 2).

6. type AB × type B

The parent AB parent must be I^AI^B, but the type B parent could be heterozygous, in which case the predictions are 1/4 I^AI^B, 1/4 I^Ai, 1/4 I^Bi, and 1/4 I^BI^B. The offspring can be types A, B, or AB, but cannot be type O. If the mother is type A and the baby is type O, what are the possible blood types for the father? Such questions have obvious legal implications in paternity cases.

15.4 LETHAL GENES

Among the alleles for coat colour in mice studied by Cuenot was one for a light coat colour he called yellow. Crosses involving yellow mice yielded seemingly unusual results. When yellow and normal (agouti) mice were crossed, half of the offspring were yellow and half were normal. Moreover, true-breeding yellow mice could not be obtained. Yellow × yellow matings always gave ratios of 1/3 normal:2/3 yellow. The yellow mice behaved as if they were always heterozygous! Cuenot correctly inferred that the yellow allele was a **lethal gene**, one which caused the homozygous mice to die in some embryonic stage of development. This explanation accounted for the 1/3:2/3 ratio. The normal Mendelian ratio would be 1/4 AA, 1/2 AA^Y and 1/4 A^YA^Y (Figure 15.6). Failure of the homozygous yellow mice to survive should leave twice as many yellow heterozygotes and homozygous normals among the *surviving* progeny. Here is another case where the exception proves the genetic rule.

Is the allele for yellow dominant or recessive? In terms of coat colour, it behaves like a dominant. In terms of viability, it behaves like a recessive. Clearly the gene affects more than one feature of the individual. In this case, the mutant gene affects an essential step in the embryonic development of the mouse, as well as the coat colour. This phenomenon is called **pleiotrophy**. A classic example is the mutant gene for sickle cell anemia (section 15.9).

There are numerous examples of lethal mutations in all organisms. Most typically, they reflect a mutation in a gene that is essential to the organism's survival. The age at which the individual dies can show considerable variation. In humans, most lethal alleles influence development and the effect occurs *in utero*. Such cases often are not recognized, being included in misconception or early miscarriage totals. The more obvious cases are those where the child is born but dies in infancy. How much of the life span must be shortened for the mutation to be considered lethal?

Figure 15.6

Inheritance pattern of a lethal gene in mice. Note that the mutant gene for yellow (A^Y) behaves dominantly to the agouti allele (A) in determining coat colour. On the other hand, it behaves as a recessive lethal allele since the heterozygote is viable. Is the A^Y allele a dominant or a recessive gene?

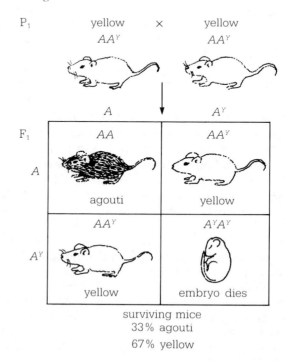

surviving mice
33% agouti
67% yellow

Individuals with Tay-Sachs disease first express the condition at the age of 6 months and die at about age 4 years. Huntington's disease is not expressed until the individual is about 40 or 50 years of age.

15.5 GENIC INTERACTIONS (EPISTASIS)

You have seen that a gene can affect more than one trait of the individual. Equally important is the finding that more than one gene pair can affect the same trait. The interaction between nonallelic genes such that one set of genes interferes with or prevents the expression of another gene is called **epistasis**. This is an important extension to Mendel's conclusions. Despite the difference in ratios obtained, the breeding results remain consistent with the expectations for gene segregation.

Consider an example involving coat colour in mice. There is one recessive mutant associated with black colour (*a*) compared to the normal agouti colour (*A*).

A recessive mutant of another nonallelic gene is associated with the absence of all coat colour (*c*). The homozygous *cc* mouse is white (albino). The mouse must have at least one *C* allele to express any colour, agouti or black.

How do these genic interactions affect the results of the cross *CC aa* × *cc AA*? The *CC aa* parent is homozygous *aa* and would be black. The *cc AA* parent would be albino. The F₁ hybrid *Cc Aa*, having both the dominant *C* and *A* alleles, would be agouti. Crossing two heterozygotes to obtain F₂ progeny (Figure 15.7) yields the following progeny (the dash indicates the presence of either the dominant or the recessive allele):

F₂ ratio	genotype	phenotype
9/16	*C – A –*	agouti
3/16	*C – aa*	black
3/16	*cc A –*	albino
1/16	*cc aa*	albino

The last two groups have the same phenotype, giving a final phenotypic ratio of 9:3:4. This is just a variation of the classic 9:3:3:1 ratio. Note that you still get a 3:1 ratio for coloured:albino. Among the coloured mice, there is a 3:1 ratio for agouti:black. Consider the expected ratio if *Cc Aa* mice were test crossed.

You have seen one example of epistasis, but there are many other examples that yield variations of the 9:3:3:1 ratio. For example, consider the expected F₂ ratio if the two pair of alleles were duplicate genes and performed the same function. Only the double heterozygous recessive (*aa bb*) would be defective and the ratio of normal: mutant would be 15:1. Table 15.3 gives some other examples of epistatic ratios.

Figure 15.7
Epistatic interaction between two pairs of genes affecting coat colour in mice. The gene for agouti (A) is dominant to its allele for black (a). The gene for colour (C) is dominant to its allele for albino (c).

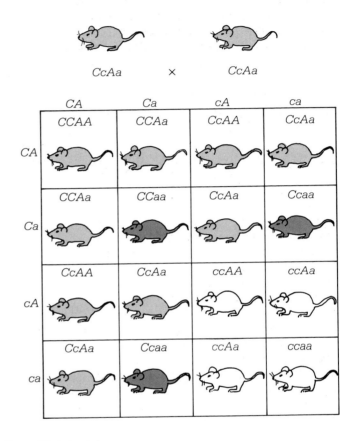

Table 15.3   Some Typical Examples of Gene Interactions (Epistasis)

ORGANISM	CHARACTER	F₂ GENOTYPES AND PHENOTYPES						
		AABB 1/16 *AABb* 2/16 *AaBB* 2/16 *AaBb* 4/16	*AAbb* 1/16 *Aabb* 2/16	*aaBB* 1/16 *aaBb* 2/16	*aabb* 1/16	
chicken	comb	walnut	pea	rose	single	9:3:3:1
pea	flower colour	purple	white			9:7
squash	fruit shape	disc	sphere		long	9:6:1
chicken	colour	white		coloured	white	13:3
squash	colour	white		yellow	green	12:3:1
shepherd's purse	seed capsule	triangular			ovoid	15:1

15.6 GENES IN THE SAME CHROMOSOME

Mendel's conclusions anticipated many of the consequences of the chromosome theory of heredity, but not all of them. One can only speculate on what additional experiments he might have done if he had known about chromosomes. One consideration might have been the consequences of nonallelic genes being located in the same chromosome. Certainly a typical chromosome must carry hundreds, often thousands, of genes. How are they arranged in the chromosome? Do they show independent assortment? What can breeding analysis tell us?

Linkage

In their studies with *Drosophila*, T.H. Morgan and his students went a long way in the discovery of answers to these questions. One such study involved a cross between two autosomal recessive mutants. One of them had shortened wings called vestigial (*vg*), while the other had purple eyes (*pr*). A complementation test showed that the F$_1$ heterozygotes had the normal phenotype, an indication that the mutations were nonallelic. When the heterozygotes were crossed with homozygous recessive vestigial-winged, purple-eyed flies, the test cross progeny should have shown the 1:1:1:1 ratio, *if there was independent assortment*. The results, listed below, were dramatically different from that expectation:

   1067 *vg$^+$ pr* (normal wings, purple eyes)
    965 *vg pr$^+$* (vestigial wings, normal eyes)
    157 *vg$^+$ pr$^+$* (normal wings, normal eyes)
    146 *vg pr* (vestigial wings, purple eyes)

Morgan suggested that the tendency of certain gene combinations to stay together might reflect the fact that the two genes were in the *same* pair of homologous chromosomes. If that is true then the F$_1$ heterozygote should have *vg$^+$ pr* in one chromosome and *vg pr$^+$* in the other. See Figure 15.8(a).

Figure 15.8
Test cross results involving two linked genes in Drosophila. *The test distinguishes between the two arrangements, trans (a) and cis (b).*

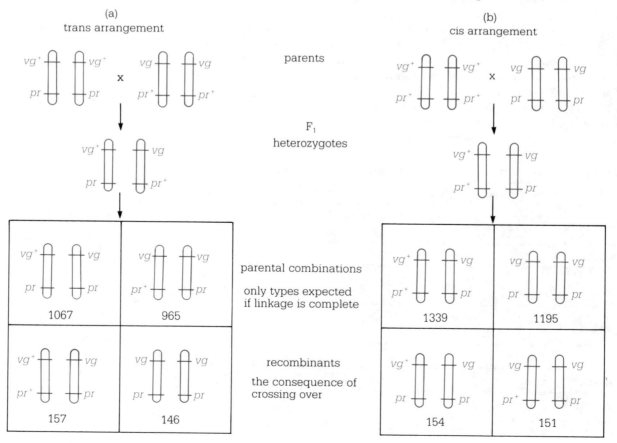

Crosses between vestigial-winged, purple-eyed flies and normal flies gave data consistent with this interpretation. The F₁ heterozygote is again phenotypically normal. However, the combination of genes in the homologous pair of chromosomes should be different. See Figure 15.8(b). One chromosome should have $vg^+ pr^+$, the other $vg\ pr$. These *parental combinations* are now the ones in excess among the test cross progeny.

    1339 $vg^+ pr^+$ (normal wings, normal eyes)
    1195 $vg\ pr$ (vestigial wings, purple eyes)
    154 $vg^+ pr$ (normal wings, purple eyes)
    151 $vg\ pr^+$ (vestigial wings, normal eyes)

These two crosses, each a test cross of the heterozygote, yield different results depending upon the parental combinations. Therefore, it is necessary to indicate the specific genetic constitution of each chromosome when giving the genotype of linked genes in the heterozygote. The conventional notation is to write the genetic constitution of each chromosome on opposite sides of a line. Thus the alternative genotypes are:

$\dfrac{vg^+\ pr^+}{vg\ \ pr}$ referred to as the *coupling* or *cis* configuration, because the two mutants are on the *same* chromosome (*Cis* is Latin meaning on the near side.)

$\dfrac{vg\ \ pr^+}{vg^+\ pr}$ referred to as the *repulsion* or *trans* configuration, because the two mutations are on *different* members of the homologous pair of chromosomes (*Trans* is Latin meaning across.)

Note that linked genes are given in the same order for both chromosomes. For convenience, the genotype can be written in a single line, using a slash (e.g., $vg + pr + /vg\ pr$).

The unexpected aspect of the results was **recombination**; that is, the presence of the non-parental combinations or *recombinants*. The segregation of a pair of homologous chromosomes should yield *only two* types of gametes (Figure 15.8). Morgan suggested the recombinants arise from a physical exchange of corresponding parts of homologous chromosomes. He called this phenomenon **crossing over** (Figure 15.9).

Visible Evidence for Crossing Over
The structures of homologous chromosomes appear identical. Any exchange of corresponding parts would leave them still morphologically identical. The consequences of crossing over can be represented (as in

Figure 15.9

A representation of a crossover event between linked genes during meiosis. The exchange of homologous parts of homologous chromosomes results in recombination.

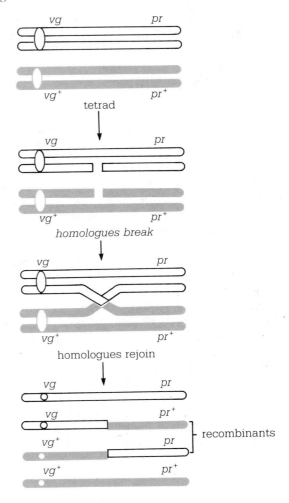

Figure 15.9) by the respective use of black and white coloration to distinguish between the two homologous chromosomes. However, colour obviously cannot be used to mark the chromosomes when actually doing crosses. Morgan could detect crossing over only because the exchanged parts differed *genetically*. He observed a recombination of linked genes, comparable to the recombination of colours seen in Figure 15.9. The only morphological evidence Morgan could cite was the reported observation made by others that synapsed homologous chromosomes were wrapped around each other at some sites. The cross-shaped configuration was called a **chiasma** (Figure 15.10). Could chiasma be the site of crossing over?

Figure 15.10
A tetrad showing two chiasmata during meiosis in a salamander spermatocyte

Definitive physical evidence came 20 years later in 1931 in two independent studies. One, by Curt Stern at the University of Rochester, used *Drosophila*. The other, by Harriet Creighton and Barbara McClintock at Cornell University, used corn. They used heterozygotes in which two members of a chromosome pair were different both genetically and morphologically. In the Creighton and McClintock experiment, one member of the chromosome pair had a dark staining knob at one end and an extra piece of chromosome at the other end (Figure 15.11). Neither of these features was present in the other chromosome. At the same time the two chromosomes could be distinguished by genetic differences at two gene loci (the sites of the genes for colour and starchy or waxy), so that genetic recombinants could be isolated. As Morgan had predicted, individuals showing genetic recombination also carried chromosomes with a physical recombination of the morphological features. These studies were conclusive and the existence of crossing over inescapable.

15.7 MAPPING THE DISTANCE BETWEEN GENES

The incomplete linkage of genes located in the same chromosome results from the phenomenon of crossing over. To put it another way, the observed frequency of recombination reflects the occurrence of crossing over. The frequency of recombination is calculated by the ratio of the two recombinant classes to the *total* number of all offspring. This value is typical of given pairs of linked genes and independent of the parental combinations used in the cross (Figure 15.8). Moreover, each pair of linked genes has its own characteristic frequency of linkage and recombination (Table 15.4).

Figure 15.11
The Creighton and McClintock experiment with corn demonstrating crossovers as a physical exchange of chromosome parts. They used a pair of homologous chromosomes that was heterozygous both genetically and physically; that is, one member of the pair had a knob present at one end and a visible addition on the other end. Note that crossing over creates a physical recombination that can be seen.

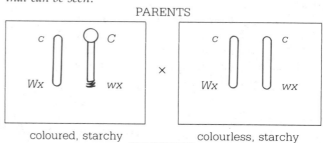

PARENTS

coloured, starchy   colourless, starchy

OFFSPRING

colourless, starchy	colourless, starchy
colourless, starchy	colourless, waxy
coloured, starchy	coloured, starchy
coloured, waxy	coloured, starchy
NONRECOMBINANT (PARENTAL) OFFSPRING	RECOMBINANT (CROSSOVERS) OFFSPRING

* unique recombinant phenotype

Mapping genes, based upon recombination data, requires large numbers of offspring from crosses between parents differing in two or more linked genes. These conditions are not very applicable to studies of human genes. "Arranged marriages" for scientific studies are unacceptable and the human family size is too small. Early attempts at mapping human genes could only designate whether the gene was sex-linked or autosomal.

Special staining procedures that made it possible to identify each specific chromosome (Chapter 18) helped provide an alternative method of mapping. The method, independent of recombination data, is based upon finding a correlation between the presence or absence of a given gene with the presence or absence of a specific chromosome. The work is done with cell samples grown in the laboratory. To increase the likelihood of some chromosome loss in specific cell lines, *somatic cell hybridization* is used; that is, human cells are fused with mouse cells. In such fused cells, most of the human chromosomes tend to

get lost. The question then posed is which human genes are retained in the fused cell when a specific human chromosome is retained.

Accompanying the numerous recent technological advances has been the mapping of a great many human genes. However, the task is difficult and still limited to those genes that can somehow be identified in cell culture. There are two principal methods used to determine whether or not a specific gene is present.

The first method involves *identification of the gene product*, either by the product's enzymatic activity or by its reaction with specific antibodies. For example, there is a gene associated with the nervous disorder Lesch-Nyhan syndrome. This gene is known to determine the enzyme hypoxanthine phosphoribosyl transferase. When the normal allele of this gene is present, the enzyme is produced by the cell culture. On the other hand, the biochemical basis of many disorders, such as muscular dystrophy

or Huntington's disease, is unknown.

The second method involves *identification of the gene itself*. This approach is largely dependent upon the technology associated with recombinant DNA and genetic engineering (Chapter 18). A small fragment of nucleic acid whose sequence will pair with a portion of the gene is needed. This method also is limited to those situations where there is considerable previous knowledge about the gene and/or its product.

There are many applications for knowledge of linkage relationships. For example, the dominant gene for myotonic dystrophy (*MD*) is known to be closely linked to another gene, *Se*. Individuals with the dominant allele, *Se*, secrete the A and B antigens in a water-soluble form. Myotonic dystrophy has a late onset of expression. In some instances, based upon the family history, the likely presence of the *MD* allele can be determined by testing for the more easily detected and linked *Se* allele. Such tests are especially valuable in prenatal diagnosis (Chapter 18).

Table 15.4   Representative Recombination Percentages between Pairs of Linked Genes of the X Chromosome of *Drosophila*

fu-B	2.5%
fu-car	3.0%
B-car	5.5%
B-sd	5.5%
fu-sd	8.0%
car-sd	11.0%

By 1911, Morgan had speculated that closely linked genes are close to each other in the chromosome and that more loosely linked genes are further apart. How-

ever, it was his student, Sturtevant, who realized how these values could be used to determine the sequence of genes in the linear dimension of a chromosome. He used the frequency of recombination as a quantitative estimate of the distance. The values from percent recombination could be converted into distance values by letting each **map unit** (m.u.) be equivalent to a one percent recombination.

Consider the genes for bar-shaped eyes (*B*), carnation-coloured eyes (*car*), fused veins in the wing (*fu*) and scalloped wings (*sd*) in Table 15.4. To put them in a linear sequence, start with the two genes closest together (*B* and *fu*). The map distance would be 2.5 m.u., corresponding to the percent recombination. To add a third gene *car* to the map, we know the distance from *car* to *fu* is 3.0 m.u. With this limited information, two different sequences are possible:

```
            fu    2.5    B
        _____|_____|_____
   car  ◄──────────────► car
            3.0    3.0
```

Using the map distance between *B* and *car*, the correct sequence can be determined. If *car* is to the left of *fu* and *B*, then the map distance between *car* and *B* should be greater than 3.0. If *car* is to the right, then the map distance between *car* and *B* should be less than 3.0. Table 15.4 shows the distance to be 5.5, so the sequence must be *car-fu-B*.   The same type of reasoning can be used to map a fourth gene, *sd*. The map distance between *B* and *sd* is 5.5 m.u., but the sequence could be *sd-fu-B* or *fu-B-sd*.

```
   car   3.0   fu   2.5   B
   _____|_____|_____
   sd  ◄──────────────► sd
          5.5          5.5
```

If *sd* is to the left, then the map distance between *fu* and *sd* should be less than 5.5 m.u. If it is to the right, then that distance should be greater than 5.5 m.u. The map distance between *fu* and *sd* is 8.0 m.u., so the sequence is *fu-B-sd*. Putting all this information into one map, the sequence and the map distances would be:

```
   car   3.0   fu   2.5   B      5.5      sd
   _____|_____|_____|____
   0          3.0   5.5             11
```

The distances between neighbouring genes are indicated above the line. An accumulative map distance value, starting at zero, is given below the line. The map is based upon recombination data, not measurements of physical distance. However, it seems reasonable to assume the greater the physical distance between genes, the greater the probability of a crossover event occurring. Mapping illustrates that each gene occupies a specific site in the chromosome, which is referred to as the **gene locus**.

15.8 MENDELIAN RATIOS AND FREQUENCIES OF GENES IN POPULATIONS

Attempts to extend Mendelian genetics from particular matings to the general population can lead to some erroneous conclusions. Consider the frequency of individuals homozygous for the recessive allele for albinism among residents of Canada. Does Mendelian genetics predict 1/4 of the population will be homozygous recessive? The 3/4:1/4 ratio is a prediction for a specific type of mating, i.e., heterozygote × heterozygote. It is *not* a predictor for the general population.

Consider how many albinos you know. How many people with sickle-cell anemia or hemophilia do you know? These are rare conditions, reflecting the low frequency of these recessive alleles in the general population. Their frequency is low not because they are recessive, but because they are detrimental and natural selection eliminates them from the population. Detrimental dominant alleles are just as rare; for example, the alleles for achondroplasia (dwarfism), Huntington's chorea (a disorder of the nervous system), and Retinoblastoma (cancer of the eye).

15.9 GENES AND THE SPECIFICITY OF PROTEINS

Mendelian analysis demonstrated the existence of genes and the manner of their transmission from one generation to the next. These breeding experiments also provided information about the effect of genic interaction on the phenotype of the individual. However, in order to have a better understanding of how the gene works, more information was needed about the chemistry of cells. This section will deal with studies done prior to the realization that DNA is the genetic material. The methodology was largely dependent upon isolating mutations affecting known metabolic pathways. These mutations were then characterized, combining both biochemical and genetic (breeding) analyses. In this manner, it was established that genes determine the specific amino acid sequence of the proteins. In turn, these proteins, play an important role in determining which metabolic reactions can occur and which structures can be formed.

The field of molecular genetics, which arose from these studies, is chiefly concerned with how genes determine protein specificity and how gene expression is regulated. It is the key to the understanding of normal development, as well as of the many inherited disorders. Such topics will be dealt with in the next three chapters.

Garrod and his Study of Metabolic Disorders
At the turn of the century, Archibald Garrod, an English physician, became the first to suggest a relationship between gene action and the presence of

functional enzymes. He was interested in several disorders that seemed to be inherited, including albinism and alkaptonuria. Individuals afflicted with alkaptonuria accumulate homogentisic acid in their cells and tissues, especially in cartilaginous areas. These areas often darken because the acid's oxidation products are black. The condition is not very serious, but it does have an obvious and disconcerting symptom. Since some of the excess homogentisic acid is excreted, the urine turns very dark after exposure to air.

By studying the family histories of his patients (pedigree analysis), Garrod concluded that alkaptonuria was associated with a recessive gene. The question remained as to why these individuals accumulate homogentisic acid, when normal individuals do not. In Garrod's time the chemical nature of enzymes was unknown. Nevertheless, he appreciated that this genetic condition was caused by some defect in the body chemistry. His suggestion that the affected individual could not break down homogentisic acid was later proven correct. His insight is embodied in the title he chose in 1909 for his classic work, *Inborn Errors of Metabolism*.

The One Gene-One Enzyme Concept

Geneticists sought out many different morphological differences as traits to study. These traits were not very suitable for biochemical studies. The molecular reactions necessary to form a normal wing in *Drosophila* presumably are many and remain obscure. There seemed little hope for clarification. In the 1930s there were some pioneer studies on the metabolic pathway in the synthesis of pigments in plants and the *Drosophila* eye.

Then in the early 1940s George Beadle and Edward Tatum at Stanford University made a major breakthrough with their studies on the bread mold, *Neurospora*. This is a very favourable organism for biochemical studies. It can be grown on a relatively simple, minimal medium. Using simple carbon and nitrogen sources, it can synthesize all the needed amino acids and many of the vitamins, purines, and pyrimidines. Beadle and Tatum selected mutants unable to synthesize one or another of these important compounds. Since *Neurospora* is a haploid organism, mutations are expressed and readily isolated. Mendelian analysis of the mutants showed that each defect was associated with a single gene. The inability to synthesize the needed metabolite was attributed to the mutant's inability to make the required functional enzyme. The concept became known as the *one gene-one enzyme concept*.

As a representative example, consider the mutants unable to synthesize the amino acid arginine. The mutants were identified by two facts. The first was that they could grow on the minimal medium supplemented with arginine. The second was that they could not grow on minimal medium which lacked arginine (Figure 15.12). Each of these arginine-requiring

Figure 15.12
Isolation of arginine-requiring mutants in Neurospora, *following the procedure used by Beadle and Tatum. Following irradiation to increase the general frequency of all mutations, spores are grown on complete medium. Samples are transferred to a minimal medium to identify nutrient-requiring mutant cultures. Arginine-requiring mutants are identified by their growth on a minimal medium supplemented with arginine.*

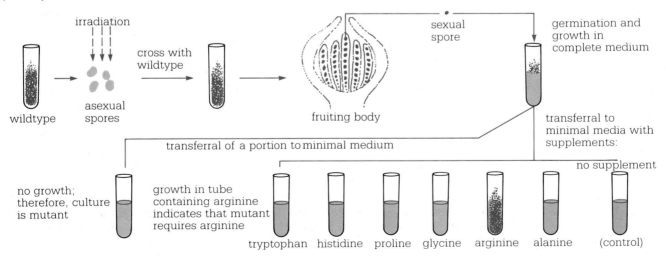

Figure 15.13

The biosynthetic pathway for arginine synthesis in Neurospora *as determined by three classes of arginine-requiring mutants*

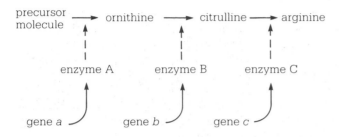

The One Gene-One Polypeptide Concept

How an enzyme is altered in the mutant was determined by work on the hemoglobin produced by victims of sickle-cell anemia. The hemoglobin molecule is a protein lacking enzymatic activity. How then, can information about hemoglobin relate to the one gene-one enzyme concept? By changing the rule to the *one gene-one polypeptide concept*, all proteins can be included; that is, genes determine proteins, many of which (but not all) are enzymes.

In 1949, James Neel at the University of Michigan showed that individuals with sickle-cell anemia differed from the normal by a single gene difference. Moreover, he showed that the heterozygous individuals could be detected by clinical tests. Although they did not have the disease, they are said to have the *sickle-cell trait* as distinct from the anemia. In the same year, Linus Pauling at the California Institute of Technology showed that the hemoglobin from individuals with sickle-cell anemia (Hb^S) differed from normal hemoglobin (Hb^A) in its net electrical charge. The heterozygote makes both types of hemoglobin molecules. The change in net charge suggested a chemical change in the hemoglobin molecule.

The hemoglobin molecule consists of four subunits, two alpha polypeptide chains and two beta polypeptide chains. These two types of chains are determined by two different genes. In the mid 1950s Vernon Ingram at Cambridge University showed that Hb^S differed from Hb^A only in the beta chain, which contains 146 amino acids. Ingram further showed that beta chain of Hb^S differed from the beta chain of Hb^A in only one amino acid (Figure 15.14)! The amino acid normally found in the sixth position of the chain, glutamic acid, is replaced with a valine. This single amino acid change in the beta polypeptide has a profound effect. It happens to distort the shape of the deoxygenated hemoglobin molecules such that they stack into narrow crystals within the red blood cell. This distortion in turn causes the formation of protoplasmic projections from the cell called sickling (Figure 15.15). Sickling cells have an increased fragility, leading to their rapid destruction and a severe anemia. As can be seen in Figure 15.16(a), there are a number of possible symptoms associated with anemia. The possible symptoms shown in Figure 15.16(b) are associated with the tendency of sickling cell to clump and create obstructions in the smaller blood vessels. All of these symptoms illustrate how a single gene can have many potential secondary effects. An individual afflicted with sickle-cell anemia would not express all these

mutants was crossed with the normal strain to demonstrate a one-gene difference from the normal. Complementation tests between the mutants, together with mapping studies, showed that at least three different genes were involved in the biosynthetic pathway for arginine (Figure 15.13). Mutants of gene *a* would grow if the medium were supplemented with ornithine, citrulline, or arginine. Mutants of gene *b* would grow if the medium were supplemented with citrulline or arginine, but not ornithine. Mutants of gene *c* would grow if the medium were supplemented with arginine, but not ornithine or citrulline.

Beadle and Tatum reasoned that if the mutation caused a block in only one step in the biosynthetic pathway, the rest of the pathway should be unaffected and intact. Supplementing the medium with an intermediate substrate *before the block* would not help. Supplementing the medium with an intermediate substrate *after the block* removes the need for the earlier steps. For example, providing mutant *b* with ornithine does not help, since the mutant cannot convert ornithine to citrulline. On the other hand, if citrulline is supplied, then mutant *b* can still convert citrulline to arginine.

In this way, Beadle and Tatum were able to deduce the intermediates and the sequence of the steps in the pathway. The isolation of mutants provided biochemists with specific metabolic blocks for the elucidation of many different biosynthetic pathways. For the geneticist, metabolic pathways provided the explanation for the various types of interactions between genes (epistasis). However, key questions still remained. How does the gene determine the specificity of the different enzymes? When the gene is altered, how is the enzyme altered?

Figure 15.14
Comparison of hemoglobin A and hemoglobin S amino acid sequence. They differ in only one of the 146 amino acids present in the beta chain. In hemoglobin S, the glutamic acid in the sixth position is replaced by valine.

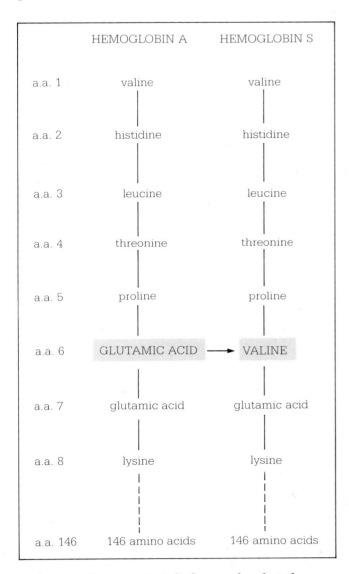

	HEMOGLOBIN A	HEMOGLOBIN S
a.a. 1	valine	valine
a.a. 2	histidine	histidine
a.a. 3	leucine	leucine
a.a. 4	threonine	threonine
a.a. 5	proline	proline
a.a. 6	GLUTAMIC ACID →	VALINE
a.a. 7	glutamic acid	glutamic acid
a.a. 8	lysine	lysine
a.a. 146	146 amino acids	146 amino acids

Figure 15.15
Abnormal red blood cells associated with hemoglobin S. The normal red blood cell (a) has a disk shape. In contrast, the red blood cells of individuals having sickle-cell anemia (b) can show a characteristic elongated 'sickle' shape.

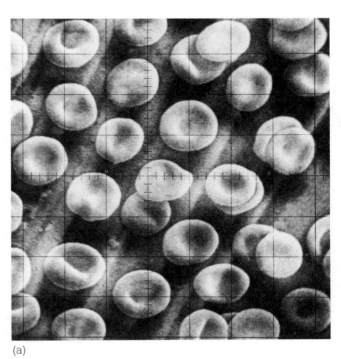

(a)

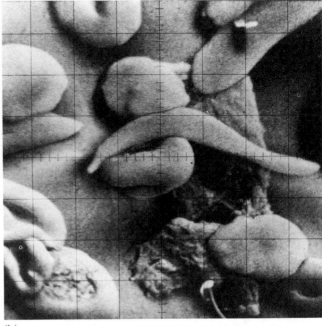

(b)

symptoms. Even so, it is little wonder that the condition is associated with early death.

Not all mutations have such drastic effects. The consequence of the change depends upon the importance of the specific amino acid residue in the functioning of that particular protein. Mutants with drastic effects are the most obvious, but there are many mutants whose effects seem slight and they therefore go undetected.

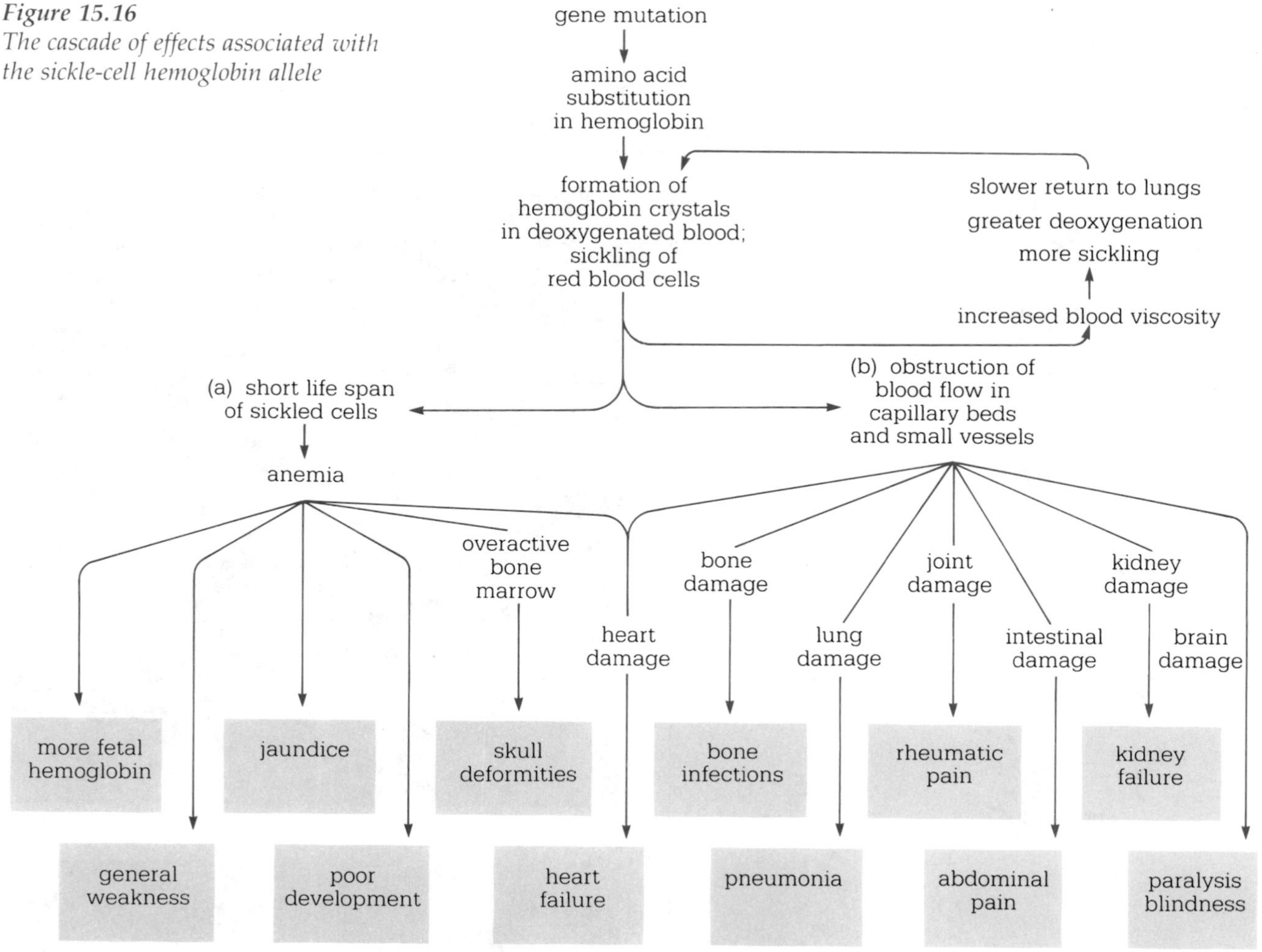

Figure 15.16
The cascade of effects associated with the sickle-cell hemoglobin allele

gene mutation

↓

amino acid
substitution
in hemoglobin

↓

formation of
hemoglobin crystals
in deoxygenated blood;
sickling of
red blood cells

slower return to lungs
greater deoxygenation
more sickling

↑

increased blood viscosity

(a) short life span
of sickled cells

(b) obstruction of
blood flow in
capillary beds
and small vessels

anemia

overactive
bone
marrow

bone
damage

joint
damage

kidney
damage

heart
damage

lung
damage

intestinal
damage

brain
damage

| more fetal hemoglobin | jaundice | skull deformities | bone infections | rheumatic pain | kidney failure |

| general weakness | poor development | heart failure | pneumonia | abdominal pain | paralysis blindness |

CHAPTER SUMMARY

The concepts considered in this chapter all are consistent with the chromosome theory of heredity. They merely extend Mendelian genetics to include a number of other genetic phenomena. Complete dominance, described by Mendel, was extended to include partial and codominance. Consideration of only two alternative alleles was extended to multiple alleles. Breeding experiments also showed that one gene can affect more than one trait (pleiotrophy) and that more than one gene can affect the same trait (epistasis). As expected, it was shown that genes located in the same chromosome tend to segregate together (linkage). The linkage is not complete and the frequency of crossing over can be used to map the genes in a linear sequence.

Despite these findings, the fundamental question of how the gene works still remained. The answer required combining genetic and biochemical studies. An important insight was provided by the one gene-one polypeptide concept. Nevertheless, little further progress in biochemical genetics could be made until the chemistry of the gene itself became known.

Objectives

Having completed this chapter, you should be able to do the following:

1. Outline how breeding analysis contributed to our understanding of the following concepts: incomplete dominance, codominance, multiple alleles, pleiotrophy, epistasis, linkage, and crossing-over.

2. Describe how to construct a gene map of linked genes from test cross information.
3. State the relationship between genes and protein specificity.
4. Describe how the experiments of Morgan, Creighton and McClintock, Garrod, and Beadle and Tatum contributed to our understanding of genetics.

Vocabulary

incomplete dominance
codominance
segregation test
complementation test
multiple alleles

lethal gene
pleiotrophy
epistasis
recombination
crossing over

chiasma
map unit
gene locus

Review Questions

1. Distinguish between
   (a) complete dominance, codominance, and incomplete dominance
   (b) pleiotrophy and epistasis.

2. An example of codominance involves the blood types M and N. The heterozygote is type MN.
   (a) If the mother is type M and the child is type MN, give the possible blood types of the father.
   (b) If the mother is type M and the father is type MN, the offspring cannot be type N. Explain why.

3. An amateur flower fancier is trying to produce a true-breeding variety of *Mirabilis* (the four-o'clock) with pink flowers. However, each time the plants with pink flowers are self-fertilized, only half of the progeny have pink flowers. The rest have either red or white flowers.

(a) What is the most likely explanation for these results?
(b) Do you think he would have better success getting true-breeding varieties with red flowers? Why?
(c) What would be the expected results if plants with red flowers were crossed to plants with pink flowers?
(d) Can you recommend how to get the maximal production of plants with pink flowers?

4. Give all possible genotypes and phenotypes of a parent for each of the following offspring:
   (a) *i i*
   (b) *I^A I^A*
   (c) *I^A i*
   (d) type A
   (e) type B
   (f) type AB

5. In *Drosophila* the gene for pink eyes (p^-) is recessive to its normal allele (p^+) and the gene for absence of large bristles or spines (s^-) is recessive to its normal allele (s^+). The two genes are linked and found in the third chromosome.
   (a) Assume that the genotype of a hybrid was known to be $p^+ s^+ / p^- s^-$.
      (i) What types of gametes would be produced if there was no crossover?
      (ii) What type of gametes would be produced by crossing over?
      (iii) If p and s are 10 m.u. apart, what types of gametes would be produced and in what frequencies?
   (b) Assume that the genotype of the heterozygote was $p^+ s^- / p^- s^+$ and that p and s are 10 map units apart.
      (i) What types of gametes would be produced?
      (ii) In what frequencies would these types appear?

6. In tomatoes the gene for round fruit (R) is dominant to its allele for long fruit (r) and the gene for simple flowering shoot (S) is dominant to its allele for branching flowering shoot (s). When F_1 plants were crossed to plants with round fruit and branching flowering shoots, the following progeny were obtained:

round, simple	112
round, branched	407
long, simple	383
long, branched	98

(a) Determine whether the results indicate independent assortment or linkage.
(b) Construct a genetic map based upon the above data.
(c) Determine the genotype of the F_1 plants.

7. On the basis of test cross data given below, construct a genetic map for the four genes.

genes	% recombination
A—B	7%
A—C	18%
A—D	10%
B—C	25%
B—D	17%
C—D	8%

8. Two arginine-requiring mutants were isolated in *Neurospora*. The first would grow if the growth medium was supplemented with arginine, citrulline, or ornithine. The second mutant would grow if the growth medium was supplemented with arginine or citrulline, but not if ornithine was added. Why? Is this an example of pleiotrophy or epistasis?

Advanced Questions

1. When phenomena such as incomplete dominance and epistasis were first demonstrated, the results were considered to be contrary to Mendelian genetics. Today they are considered to be simply extensions of it. They were exceptions that prove the rule. Which Mendelian rules are supported by incomplete dominance and epistasis?

2. Farmer A and Farmer B each found an albino chicken in their flock. As amateur breeders, they did the appropriate tests to show that the gene determining albino is recessive to the gene for expression of pigment.

(a) What crosses did they most likely make?
(b) As a professional geneticist, you have been consulted to determine whether Farmer A and Farmer B are dealing with mutants of the same gene or different genes. What cross or crosses would you make? Why?

3. Brown eyes and scarlet eyes are two mutant varieties of *Drosophila*. When crosses were made between flies with brown and scarlet eyes, all of the offspring had the normal reddish-brown eye colour. The F_2 offspring obtained when the F_1 were crossed is given below:

normal (reddish-brown eyes)   96
brown eyes   31
red eyes   35
white eyes   11

(a) These results do not fit an explanation involving a single pair of genes showing incomplete dominance. Explain.

(b) Determine how many pairs of genes likely are involved.

(c) Devise a genetic hypothesis for the mode of inheritance of eye colour that is consistent with the above results. You can choose any symbols you wish to designate the genes involved, but be sure to explain them in your system. According to your hypothesis, what were the genotypes of
  (i) the parental mutant varieties?
  (ii) the F_1?
  (iii) the white-eyed flies in the F_2?

(d) Predict the results if the F_1 offspring had been crossed with flies having the same genotype as the F_2 white-eyed flies.

4. A breeder crossed a grey mouse with a black mouse and obtained a litter of five: three grey, one black, and one white. She expected only grey or black offspring and therefore believes the white mouse must be a mutation. Can you give an alternative genetic explanation? How could you test your hypothesis?

5. Do some further investigation of the contributions to genetics made by one of the following:
  (a) McClintock
  (b) Garrod
  (c) Beadle and Tatum

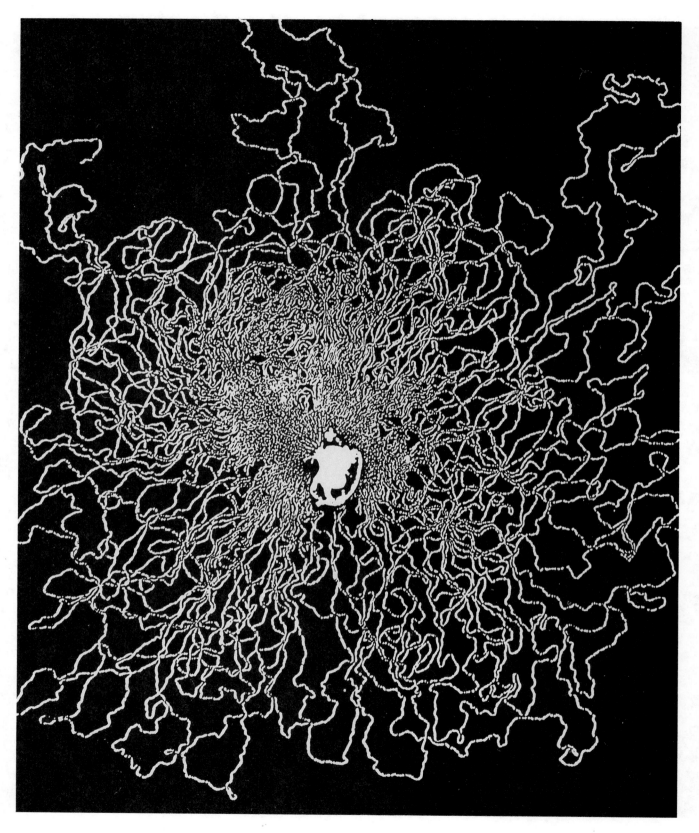

308

CHAPTER 16

MOLECULAR BASIS OF THE GENE

Genetic investigation is by no means confined to breeding experiments . . .

Joshua Lederberg

The electron micrograph shows a disrupted *E. coli* cell, with its single chromosome extruding into the surrounding medium. What you see is a long continuous molecule of deoxyribonucleic acid (DNA). The DNA molecule is about 1.1 mm in length or about 500 times as long as the *E. coli* cell. This molecule contains the genetic information of the cell.

What was the experimental evidence that first suggested that DNA is the genetic material? How was the hypothesis tested? How do the genes replicate prior to cell division? How is the biological information stored within a chemical structure? How may DNA be altered? This chapter deals with such questions.

16.1 BIOLOGICAL PROPERTIES OF GENETIC MATERIAL

By the middle of this century, breeding experiments had well established the concept of the gene. Yet there was little understanding of the gene's chemical nature. Indeed, the biological properties of the genetic material seemed to defy any simple explanation. Three factors were crucial to any such explanation.

First, the genetic material would have to be able to replicate itself with a high degree of accuracy in order to provide continuity between generations. Mitosis yields two genetically identical cells.

Second, the material would have to be able to determine the production of specific proteins and enzymes. (Recall the one gene-one polypeptide concept, section

15.9). This determination would involve not only the storage of the information, but also a mechanism to access it.

Third, the material would have to be able to mutate occasionally. Biological mutation implies more than simply a change. The altered form of the genetic material must still be able to replicate; in other words, to make copies of the mutated form of the gene. If the stored information has been altered, then the mutant will determine an altered form of the protein. Although the rate of mutation must be low in order for biological systems to remain stable, mutation provides the genetic variation needed for survival in changing environments.

What kind of chemical compound could have such biological features? When the chemical nature of genetic material was being investigated in the early years of this century, two major facts were known. The first was that since the genes are in the chromosomes (Chapter 14), one of the chemical components of the chromosome must be the genetic material. The second was that the two main chemical constituents of the chromosome are nucleic acid and protein. These facts suggested that the genetic material was either a nucleic acid or a protein.

Because of their known complexity and diversity, the research initially centered attention on the proteins. However, the more that was learned about proteins, the more difficult it became to explain how any protein could self-replicate. In fact, proteins cannot self-replicate.

In 1953, when the American James Watson and the Englishman Francis Crick, working together at Cambridge University, published a paper on the structure of DNA (a nucleic acid), the chemical basis of the gene's biological properties suddenly became clear. DNA-related studies have dominated most genetic studies since then.

16.2 DNA: THE GENETIC MATERIAL

Why had DNA not been recognized earlier as the genetic material? It had been known since 1868, when it was isolated from cell nuclei by the Swiss chemist Friedrich Miescher. Early thoughts about its biological role were hampered by some erroneous conclusions about its structure. It was falsely assumed that the size of the DNA molecule was only four nucleotides (Figure 16.1). Each tetranucleotide molecule was thought to be the same, with the two purines, adenine (A) and

guanine (G), and the two pyrimidines, cytosine (C) and thymine (T). Even after DNA was shown to be a very long chain, it was assumed to be a repeating series of identical tetranucleotides. This *proposed* structure could hardly account for the complexity of genetic material.

Bacterial Transformation

One of the early lines of evidence for DNA as the genetic material began with the work of the British scientist Fred Griffith in 1928. He was working with a bacterium (*Streptococcus pneumoniae*) that causes pneumonia in mammals. In addition to the *virulent* strain — one causing the disease — he had an altered strain which was *avirulent*, not causing the disease. These two strains were further distinguished by a genetic difference in a surface antigen; this difference served as a "genetic marker." In one type of experiment, he injected mice with both the living avirulent bacteria plus a preparation of heat-killed virulent bacteria. See Figure 16.2(d). Most of the injected mice died within two days; live virulent bacteria was recovered from their blood. Most significantly, these virulent bacteria expressed the genetic marker of the heat-killed bacteria!

Figure 16.1

The tetranucleotide molecule proposed in 1904 to be the structure of DNA. It was ultimately replaced by the Watson-Crick model.

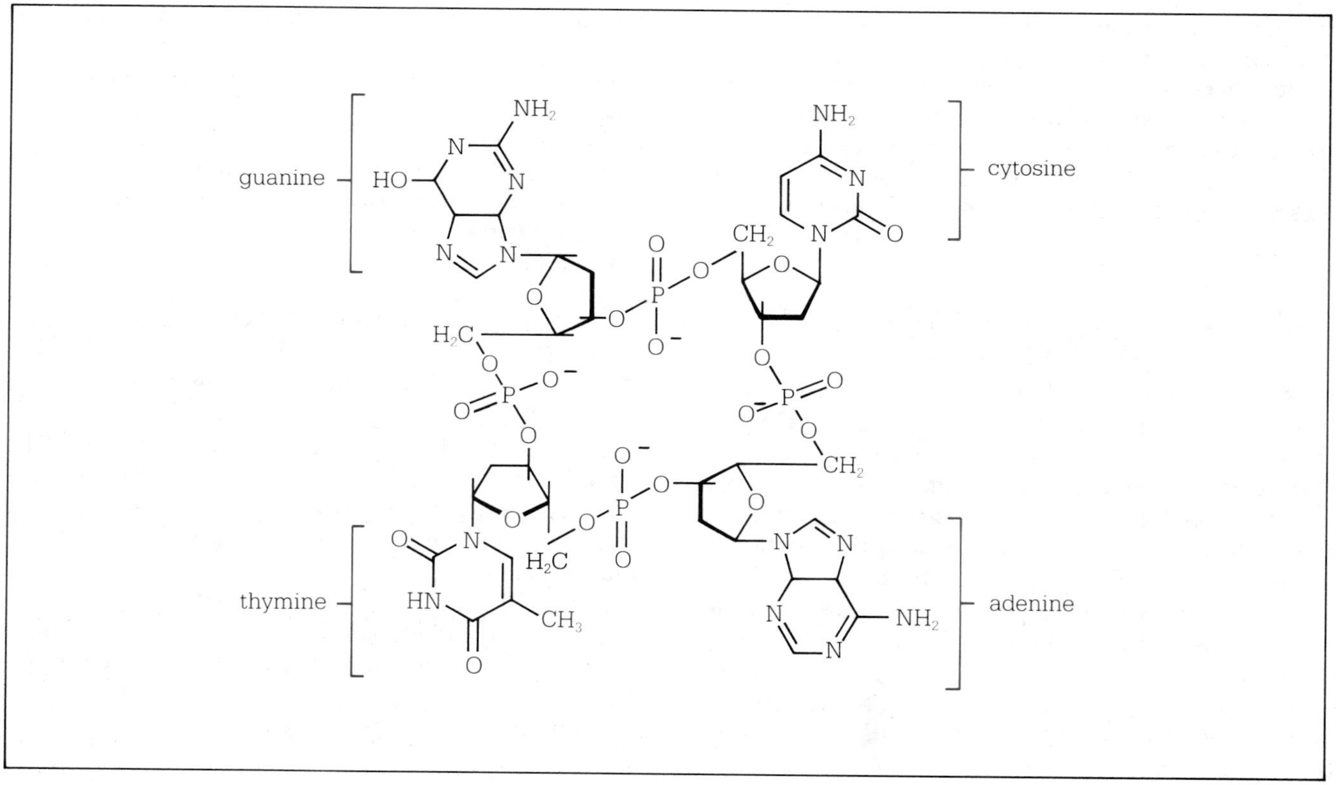

Figure 16.2
Griffith's experiment demonstrating bacterial transformation. In contrast to results of (a) using the avirulent strain alone and the results of (c) using the heat-killed virulent strain, their combination in (d) killed the injected mice.

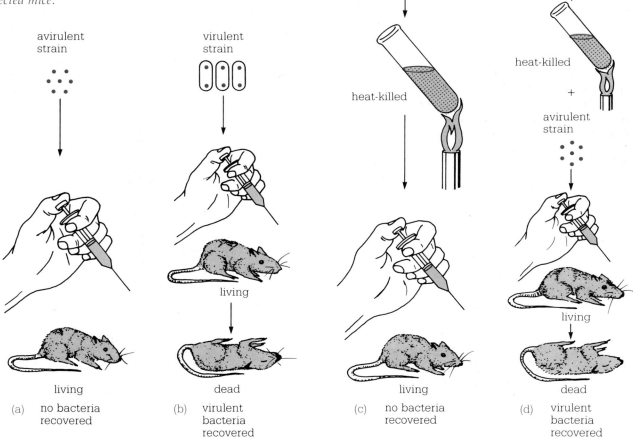

(a)   living
      no bacteria recovered

(b)   dead
      virulent bacteria recovered

(c)   living
      no bacteria recovered

(d)   dead
      virulent bacteria recovered

Griffith interpreted these results to mean that genetic material from the dead bacteria had somehow entered the living bacteria and changed them. What additional work could he have done to test this interpretation? Could some of the virulent bacteria have survived the heat treatment in the experiment above? Controlled experiments showed that mice survived when injected with the heat-killed virulent strain alone. The results ruled out this possibility. Mice also survived when injected with the living avirulent bacteria alone, but did not show the genetic marker of the virulent strain. These results showed that the avirulent bacteria did not change in the absence of the dead virulent cells. Later work showed that extracts from the virulent bacteria were sufficient to cause the change.

This phenomenon was called **transformation**. It involved the uptake of genetic material from the extract of the virulent strain. This genetic material was expressed by the recipient cell and transmitted to the progeny. If the component in the extract responsible for transformation could be chemically identified, then the identity of genetic material would be revealed. In the meantime, this component was referred to as the *transforming principle*.

In 1944, Oswald Avery, Colin MacLeod, and MacLyn McCarty carried out a series of experiments at the Rockefeller Institute in New York City. Their results led them to propose that the transforming principle was DNA. They had obtained and characterized highly purified preparations of the transforming principle. It had all of the physical and chemical properties expected of DNA. Furthermore, the transforming activity was destroyed by enzymes that attack DNA (DNAase), but not by enzymes that attack RNA (RNAase) or protein (protease). Because the structure of DNA was believed to be too simple, this hypothesis was not accepted by many scientists. They still believed that the genetic material must be protein. Nevertheless, Avery had convinced some investigators that DNA had to be studied more intensively.

Virus Infection

Strong supporting evidence for DNA as the genetic material came from studies of virus infection. Bacterial viruses are commonly called bacteriophage, or simply **phage**. The phage consists of DNA contained within a protein coat. See Figure 16.3(a).

Figure 16.3
In (a), the virus contains only DNA and protein. The DNA is packaged within the protein head. The Hershey-Chase experiment is shown in (b). By labelling the protein with ^{35}S they showed that the protein coat remains outside the cell during infection. It can be sheared off and left in the fluid. On the other hand, the DNA labelled with ^{32}P enters the cell.

In 1952, Alfred Hershey and Martha Chase, working at Cold Spring Harbour Biological Lab, published their study of the roles of protein and DNA in phage infection. See Figure 16.3(b). They selectively labelled the phage protein with ^{35}S (a radioactive isotope of sulfur). DNA was not labelled because it contains no sulfur. When these labelled phage were used to infect unlabelled bacterial cells, most of the ^{35}S was found to remain *outside* the cell. This finding was consistent with observed empty phage coats that remain attached to the outside of the bacterial cell wall. By use of a Waring blender, the empty coats were sheared

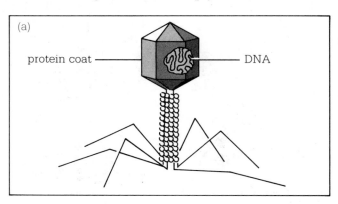

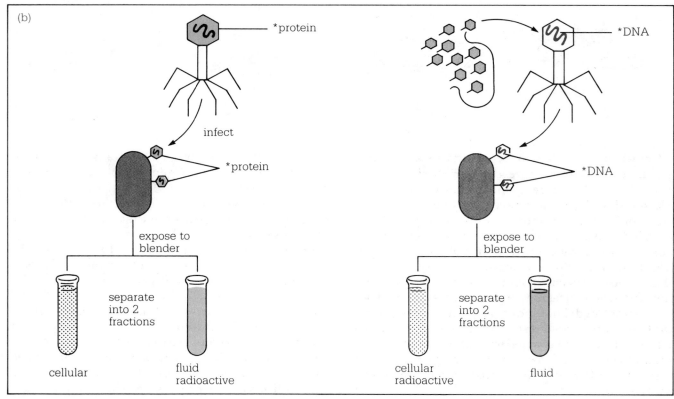

off without interfering with phage multiplication within the infected bacterial cell.

In a similar experiment, the DNA was selectively labelled with ^{32}P (a radioactive isotope of phosphorus). In this case, the labelled DNA was found *within* the infected cell. Indeed, significant amounts of the ^{32}P-labelled DNA were transferred to the progeny phage. This transfer did not take place with ^{35}S-labelled protein.

These results were completely consistent with the hypothesis that DNA is the genetic material. The functions of the protein coat were to protect the DNA and facilitate the injection of the DNA into the bacterial cell. After injection of the DNA, the protein coat has no further role. The injected DNA would be all that is necessary to make phage progeny. If DNA were the genetic material, it could self-replicate to make more phage DNA, as well as determine the specific proteins needed to make more phage coats.

16.3 THE STRUCTURE OF DNA

Following the work on bacterial transformation and phage infection, the foundation for the acceptance of DNA as the genetic material was in place. The remaining doubt was based upon uncertainties of DNA structure. There was considerable knowledge about the individual nucleotides that serve as the building blocks of the DNA chain. What were needed were the details of the structure that could account for the *biological* properties of genetic material.

Nucleotides: the Building Blocks of DNA

DNA is a **polynucleotide**; that is, a long chain of nucleotides. Each nucleotide consists of a *nitrogen base*, a 5-carbon sugar (*deoxyribose*), and a *phosphate*. See Figure 16.4(a). The five carbons of the sugar are numbered 1' to 5'. There are only four kinds of nitrogen bases and therefore only four kinds of nucleotides normally found in DNA. Two of the nitrogen bases are double-ring structures of a class called purines, adenine (A) and guanine (G); whereas the other two nitrogen bases are single-ring structures of a class called pyrimidines, thymine (T) and cytosine (C).

Figure 16.5 shows how the components of a nucleotide are linked together. The nitrogen base is covalently linked to the 1' carbon; the phosphate, to the 5' carbon. Note the availability of the hydroxyl (—OH) group at the 3' carbon. The linkage between two nucleotides involves the 3' hydroxyl group of one

nucleotide and the 5' phosphate of the adjacent nucleotide (a 3',5' phosphodiester linkage). No matter how many nucleotides are linked together, one end of the chain has a 5' phosphate and the other end a 3' hydroxyl group. The DNA chain has a *sugar-phosphate backbone* made of repeating phosphodiester linkages, with a nitrogen base attached to each sugar.

Base Composition of DNA

Chemical differences between DNAs of different species were first reported by Erwin Chargaff of Columbia University in 1949. Note in Table 16.1 that the four types of nucleotides are not present in equal amounts. In some organisms A and T predominate; in others, G and C do. Chargaff derived several important generalizations from his data.

Table 16.1 Base Composition of DNA from Various Organisms

The values represent the molar concentration of each base in the DNA (Chargaff's data).

SOURCE	A	G	C	T	A+G / C+T	A+T / G+C
B. tuberculosis	15.1	34.9	35.4	14.6	1.00	0.42
Rat	28.6	21.4	21.7	28.3	1.00	1.32
Vaccina virus	29.5	20.6	20.3	29.9	1.00	1.45
Human	31.0	19.1	18.4	31.5	1.00	1.67
Yeast	31.7	18.8	17.4	32.6	1.01	1.77
Sea urchin	32.8	17.7	17.7	32.1	1.01	1.83

1. For each species, the molar concentration of purines equals or approximates that of pyrimidines; i.e., A + G = C + T.
2. For each species, the molar concentration of A approximates that of T.
3. For each species the molar concentration of G approximates that of C.
4. The molar concentration of A + T often does not equal that of G + C; i.e., the ratio A + T/G + C varies between species.
5. The A + T/G + C ratio is the same for all tissues of a species, but varies for different species.

These findings replaced the tetranucleotide model with a concept of species-specific DNA that could have a complex and diverse structure. The significance of Chargaff's general rules soon became apparent in the work of Watson and Crick.

Figure 16.4
In (a), a DNA nucleotide is shown as composed of a nitrogen base, a 5-carbon sugar, and a phosphate. Note the numbering system of the sugar and how the three components are linked together. Note in (b) the two kinds of nitrogen bases: pyrimidines and purines. Thymine and cytosine are pyrimidines; adenine and guanine are purines.

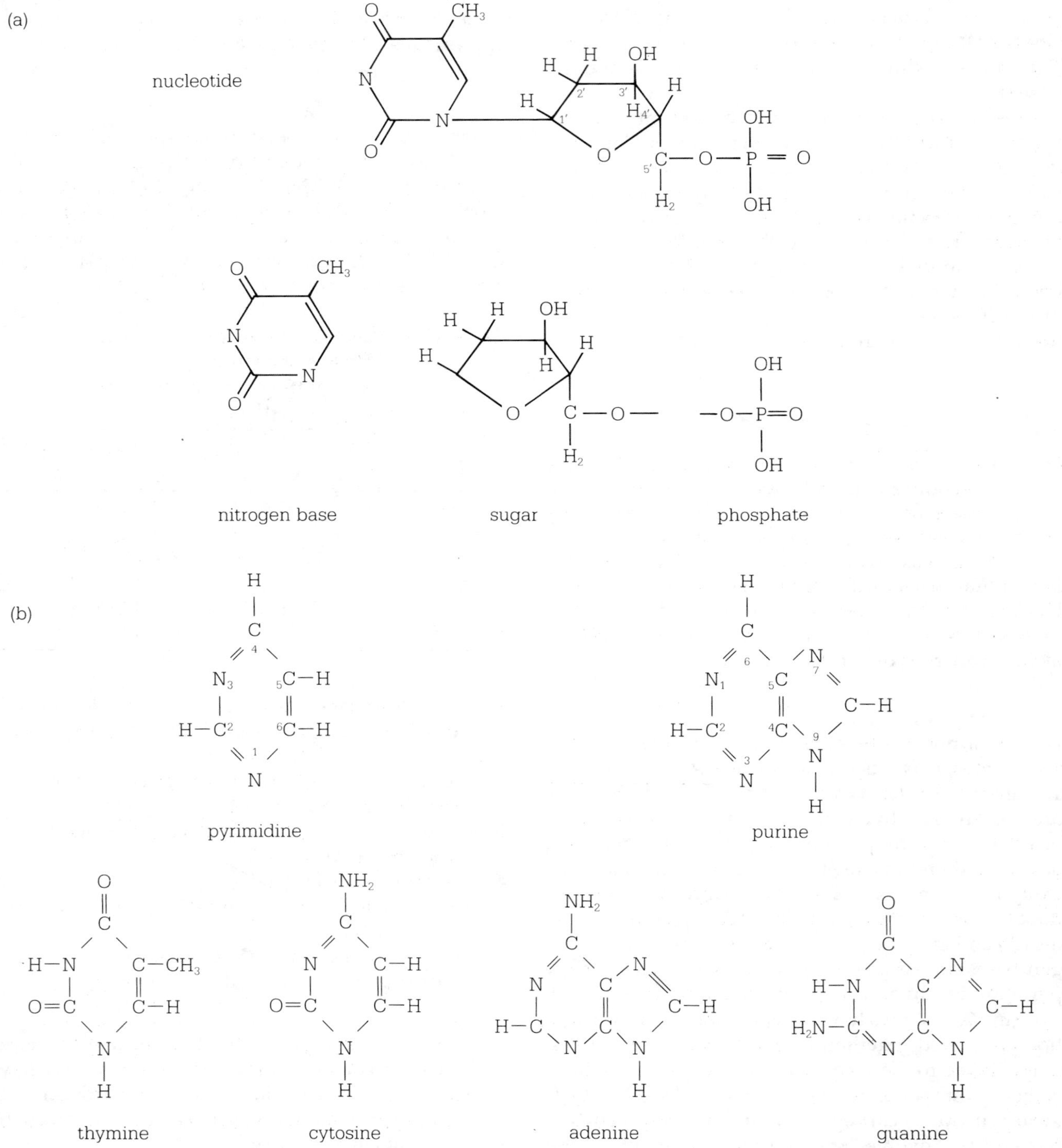

(a)

nucleotide

nitrogen base   sugar   phosphate

(b)

pyrimidine   purine

thymine   cytosine   adenine   guanine

Figure 16.5

A polynucleotide chain with its sugar-phosphate backbone and attached bases. The link between nucleotides is a 5',3' phosphodiester bond. Note the 5'-phosphate at one end and the 3'-hydroxyl (—OH) group at the other end.

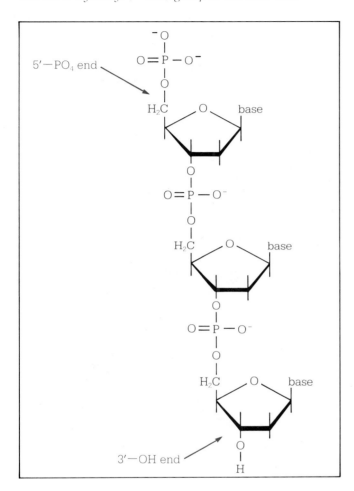

Figure 16.6

The Watson-Crick double helix model of DNA structure. The ribbons represent the sugar-phosphate backbones. The two chains are held together by the pairing of the bases. Each chain has a 3'—OH end and a 5'—P end. Note that the two chains are oriented in opposite directions with reference to the location of their 3'- and 5'-ends.

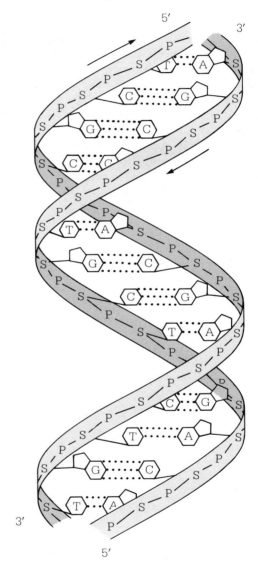

The Double Helical Structure of DNA

The scene was set for Watson and Crick to establish the physical structure of DNA. In addition to Chargaff's chemical findings, they had access to important physical characterizations of DNA. Rosalind Franklin, working in Maurice Wilkins' laboratory at Cambridge, had X ray diffraction data that provided critical information on the spatial arrangement of atoms in the DNA molecule. The X ray data showed DNA contained two (or more) chains wound around each other in a helical manner. While others were working on models with three chains, Watson and Crick in 1953 proposed the **double helix** model. There are several crucial features in their model, shown in Figure 16.6.

1. The DNA molecule consists of two right handed helices (clockwise turns) coiled around a common axis. Because the DNA molecule contains two chains, it often is referred to as a *duplex* or *double helix*.

2. The sugar-phosphate backbone of each chain is the outer portion of the molecule.

3. The nitrogen bases extend inward and are at right angles to the long axis of the chain.

4. The two chains are held together by hydrogen bonds between the bases. A *hydrogen bond* is a weak interaction between two electronegative atoms sharing a common proton.

5. Based upon the physical dimensions of DNA determined by Rosalind Franklin, effective hydrogen bonds would be restricted to A—T, T—A, G—C and C—G pairs (Figure 16.7). Two hydrogen bonds are formed between adenine and thymine; three hydrogen bonds are formed between guanine and cytosine. Note how these **base pairings** are consistent with Chargaff's data.

6. The two chains are oriented in opposite directions; that is to say, they are **antiparallel**. The orientation of each chain is apparent by the presence of a 5'-phosphate at one end and a 3'-hydroxyl at the other end. If one of the chains is oriented in 5'→3' direction, then the other chain must be oriented in the 3'→5' direction (Figures 16.5 and 16.8).

Figure 16.7
Base pairings found in DNA. Such pairings are restricted to hydrogen bonding between adenine and thymine and between guanine and cytosine.

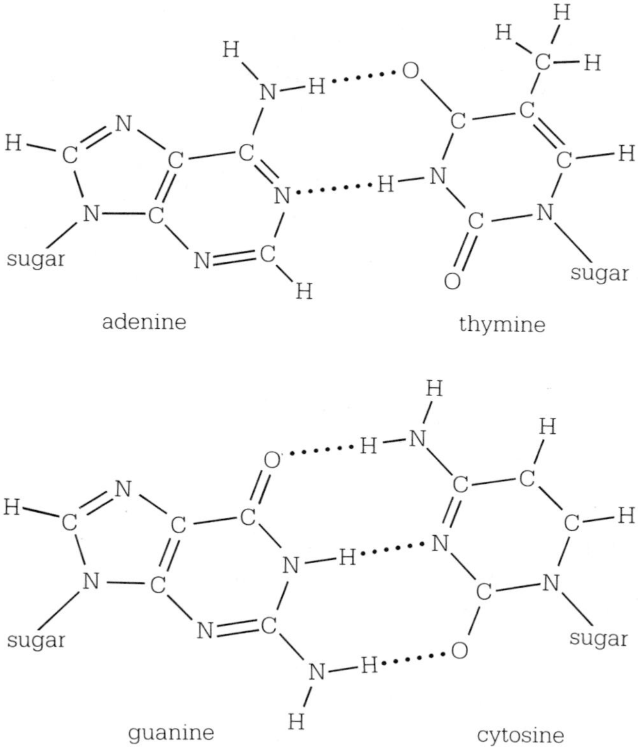

Figure 16.8
DNA replication. After strand separation, each strand can serve as a template for the synthesis of its complementary strand. The mandatory base pairing provides the specificity of this synthesis. The two resulting daughter DNA molecules are identical to the parental DNA.

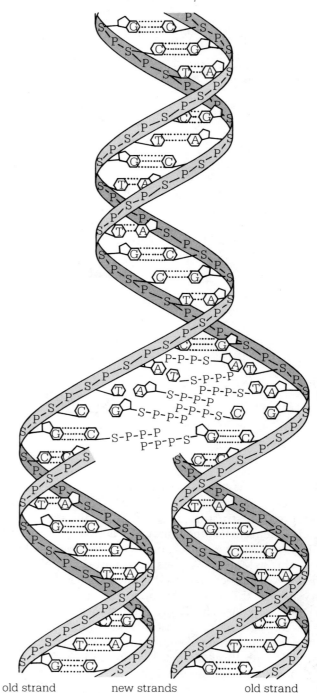

old strand   new strands   old strand

adenine   thymine

guanine   cytosine

The genetic implications of this model were clearly stated by Watson and Crick. The restrictions on base pairing are such that, given the nucleotide sequence of one chain, the sequence of the other chain is fixed. Although not identical, the two chains are strictly complementary. Replication can be achieved by breaking the weak hydrogen bonds to separate the two complementary chains. Then each chain could serve as a template for the synthesis of its complementary partner. The result would be *two* DNA molecules *identical* to the original DNA duplex (Figure 16.8 and section 16.5).

There are no restrictions on the linear sequence of the base pairs in the molecule. The variation in linear sequence is used to store information that will determine the amino acid sequence of proteins (section 16.6). Mutations in the base pair sequence can alter the specific information stored without a loss of the capacity for self-replication (section 16.7).

Using their proposed structure of DNA, Watson and Crick were able to provide a chemical mechanism for each of the biological features of genetic material. Their work removed any lingering doubts that DNA was the genetic material.

Figure 16.9

The association between histones and DNA in eukaryotic chromosomes. The basic unit is called a nucleosome. As shown in (a), the core consists of eight histone molecules (two each of histones 2A, 2B, 3, and 4). The DNA wrapped around this core is stabilized by a fifth kind of histone (histone 1). In (b), a model is shown of the chromatin fibre structure. Note the repeating nucleosomes with the intervening DNA stretches.

16.4 MOLECULAR ORGANIZATION OF EUKARYOTIC CHROMOSOMES

The main component in any chromosome is DNA, which carries the genetic information. The electron micrograph at the beginning of this chapter shows a typical prokaryotic chromosome. The DNA is a circular molecule, folded into a more compact structure by the formation of numerous loops emerging from a central region. There is a small amount of simple, histone-like protein present, likely responsible for the looping structure.

The chromosomes in eukaryotes share many basic features with those found in prokaryotes. However, they show a greater complexity in structure to accommodate their greater size and the changes in organization that the chromosomes undergo during cell division.

Experimental evidence suggests that a single, continuous DNA molecule runs the entire length of each eukaryotic chromosome. The length of the DNA molecule in a typical chromosome is about 50 000 μm, which will contract to about 5 μm in the condensed chromosome. Such packaging suggests a high degree of organization. The histone proteins play an important role in this extensive coiling and folding of the DNA thread.

In the mid-1970s DNA was shown to be wrapped around a core of eight histone proteins. The core consists of four types of histone: H2A, H2B, H3, and H4. See Figure 16.9(a). The **nucleosome**, a bead-like structure, consists of about 145 base pairs of DNA wrapped about one and three quarter times around the histone

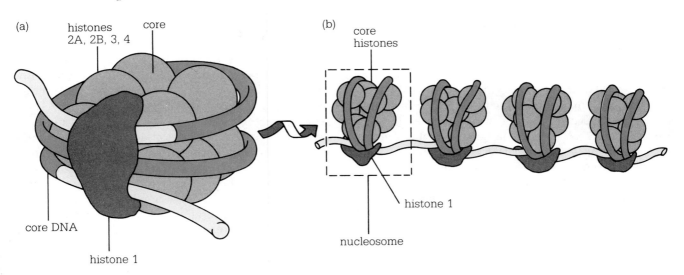

(a) histones 2A, 2B, 3, 4   core
core DNA
histone 1

(b) core histones
histone 1
nucleosome

core. Nucleosomes are repeating units typically separated by about 60 base pairs of DNA. See Figure 16.9(b). A fifth kind of histone, H1, is not part of the nucleosome but binds to the intervening region of DNA; it is also likely involved in the maintenance of chromosome structure.

By coiling DNA around the histone core, nucleosomes condense the DNA thread length to about a tenth of what its uncoiled length would be. During mitosis and meiosis, much greater condensation must be achieved. The detailed nature of such additional coiling and/or folding remains to be determined. Some of the nonhistone proteins may provide a scaffold structure for this condensation.

16.5 DNA REPLICATION

Unwinding of the two DNA chains permits each single chain to determine the sequence of the new chain being synthesized. "A" must pair with "T"; "G" must pair with "C". Several models were suggested for the mechanism of DNA replication. If replication occurs as illustrated in Figure 16.8 and 16.10(a), each daughter duplex will contain one of the parental chains paired with a newly synthesized chain. In this case, the mechanism is described as **semiconservative replication**. It is "semiconservative" in that each of the two original chains conserves its complete integrity, but the original duplex does not. A *completely conservative model* is one in which the daughter duplex retains both parental chains and the other duplex has two newly synthesized chains. See Figure 16.10(b). Watson and Crick proposed that replication was semiconservative, but either mechanism illustrated in Figure 16.10 could be consistent with the DNA structure. Which mechanism is correct? How can the models be tested?

In 1958, five years after the Watson-Crick model was proposed, Matthew Meselson and Franklin Stahl at the California Institute of Technology demonstrated semiconservative replication of DNA. They labelled the DNA of *E. coli* with ^{15}N (a heavy isotope of nitrogen). By using *density gradient centrifugation* at high speeds for a long period of time, they were able to distinguish the ^{15}N-labelled DNA from normal ^{14}N-DNA. See Figure 16.11(a). The centrifugal forces pull down the DNA until it reaches a level in the gradient where the solution density is equal to the buoyant density of the DNA. The DNA will remain at that level in the tube and can be detected as a distinct band.

Figure 16.10

Comparison of (a) semiconservative and (b) conservative models of DNA replication. In each the newly synthesized DNA is indicated by the white ribbon. How do the models differ after the first round of replication? After the second?

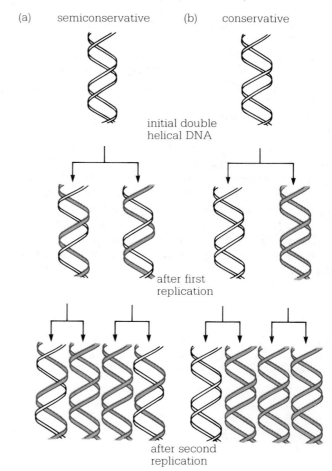

(a) semiconservative   (b) conservative

initial double helical DNA

after first replication

after second replication

When ^{15}N-labelled *E. coli* is grown in a medium containing ^{14}N, the newly synthesized DNA chains should be labelled with ^{14}N. Meselson and Stahl found that all of the DNA had an intermediate buoyant density after one generation of growth in ^{14}N. These results are consistent with the predictions made for semiconservative replication and contrary to those made for a fully conservative mode of replication. DNA fully labelled with ^{15}N is no longer present after replication. Further evidence for the semiconservative mechanism was obtained when the cells were grown for two or more generations in ^{14}N. Two distinct bands of DNA were recovered. One was the same intermediate as seen before and the other was the same as normal ^{14}N DNA.

Figure 16.11

The Meselson-Stahl experiment showing the semi-conservative replication of DNA. In (a), parental DNA was labelled with ^{15}N, which can be distinguished from ^{14}N-labelled DNA by density gradient centrifugation. In (b), bacterial cells with ^{15}N-labelled DNA were transferred to ^{14}N medium for further growth. After one round of replication only a single intermediate band was detected. Why was its position intermediate? Two bands were detected after two rounds of replication. Why?

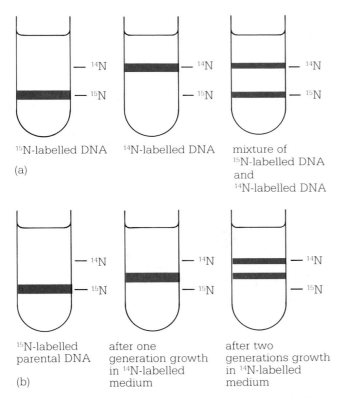

^{15}N-labelled DNA

(a)

^{14}N-labelled DNA

mixture of
^{15}N-labelled DNA
and
^{14}N-labelled DNA

^{15}N-labelled
parental DNA

(b)

after one
generation growth
in ^{14}N-labelled
medium

after two
generations growth
in ^{14}N-labelled
medium

In the same year that Meselson and Stahl made their discovery, another American scientist, Herbert Taylor, confirmed semiconservative replication of DNA in a study of chromosome duplication in bean root-tip cells; he used ^3H-thymidine as the radioactive ''label.''

DNA Polymerase and DNA Synthesis at the Replication Fork

The enzyme responsible for DNA synthesis is called **DNA polymerase**. It catalyses the formation of the sugar-phosphate bond between adjacent nucleotides (Figure 16.12). Such synthesis requires the presence of some pre-existing DNA and all four types of nucleotides. The pre-existing DNA serves as the **template**, each single strand dictating the nucleotide sequence of its complementary newly synthesized chain. If one of the four types of nucleotides is not available, synthesis comes to a halt as soon as the sequence demands its presence. The energy needed to form the chemical bond between adjacent nucleotides is provided by the use of nucleoside triphosphases as the building blocks; that is, the nitrogen base, sugar, and *three* phosphates. Breakage of the phosphate-phosphate bond provides the chemical energy in a manner similar to the use of ATP in metabolism.

However, in the presence of only single-stranded DNA as a template, DNA polymerase cannot start a new chain to form a duplex. In addition to a template, it requires at least a short region of duplex. The short chain serves as the **primer strand**. The enzyme can only add nucleotides onto the free 3'-OH end of one existing chain (while using the other chain as a template). Because it only adds nucleotides to the 3'-OH end, growth of the new chain is only in the 5'→3' direction. Considering the antiparallel nature of the duplex, this fact is highly significant. Figure 16.13 shows the **replication fork**, the region of unwinding of the duplex DNA.

The new chain on the left is called the **leading chain**. Its direction of growth is in the same direction as unwinding so that synthesis can be continuous. In contrast, the other chain, termed the **lagging chain**, must grow in a direction opposite to the direction of unwinding. It can only do this in a *discontinuous* manner, repeatedly synthesizing a new **primer** as more of the DNA unwinds.

These primers are very short segments of RNA (about ten nucleotides) and are synthesized by another enzyme called **primase**. The RNA primer is then used by DNA polymerase to fill in the remaining gaps between primers. When DNA synthesis reaches the preceding RNA primer, the RNA is removed and replaced with DNA nucleotides. In this way, the lagging chain is made up of short segments, each from about 1000 to 2000 nucleotides long in prokaryotes (from about 100 to 200 nucleotides long in eukaryotes). These short segments are covalently linked together by a third enzyme, **DNA ligase**.

Other Components of the Replication Machinery

There are several other kinds of proteins and enzymes that play important roles in the replication process. Some are involved in controlling the *initiation* of DNA replication, while others contribute to the ongoing elongation process. Unwinding the duplex requires breaking hydrogen bonds that are weak yet numerous. This unwinding is achieved by an enzyme called **helicase** which uses ATP as the energy source. The unwound single-stranded DNA chains are protected from degradation by so-called *single-stranded DNA-binding protein* (SSB).

Because one chain is wrapped around the other in the duplex, unwinding can cause twisting and knotting in other regions of the duplex. To avoid such physical problems, there is an enzyme called **gyrase**

(or topoisomerase) that can make transient breaks to relieve the stress and then rejoin the ends.

There is evidence that many of these components are associated together into a larger complex called a **replisome**. The activities of these various proteins and enzymes can be coordinated within the complex so as to function as one machine. Located at the replication fork, the replisome also coordinates the synthesis of the leading and lagging chains of DNA.

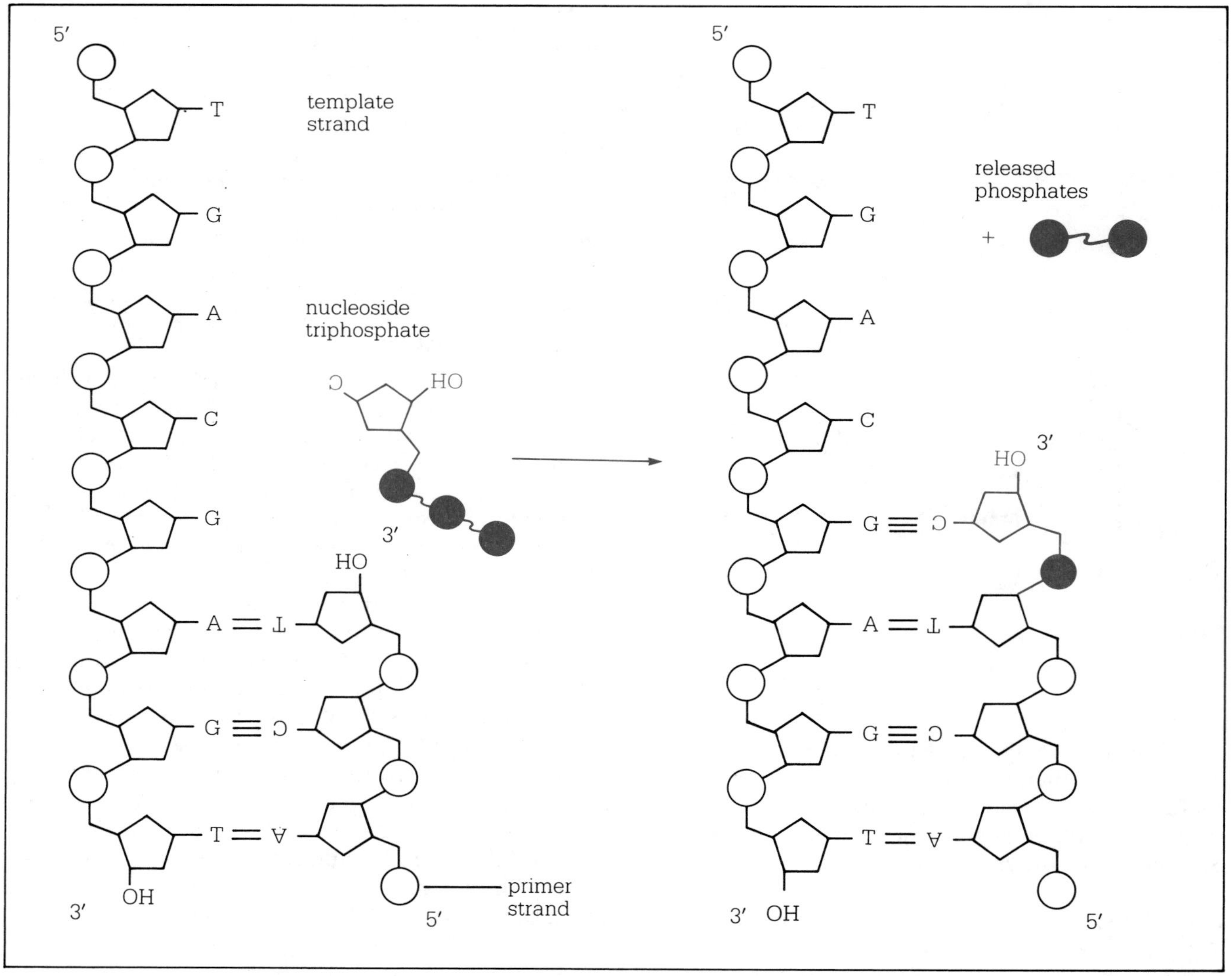

Figure 16.12

DNA replication by DNA polymerase. Nucleotides are added to the 3′—OH end of the primer strand, using the other strand as the template. The building blocks used are nucleoside triphosphases, each consisting of a nitrogen base, 5-carbon sugar, and three phosphates. Breakage of the phosphate-phosphate bond provides the chemical energy for linking the nucleotide to the primer strand. The released phosphates are recycled in the synthesis of additional building blocks. Why are the bases on the primer strand printed upside down?

Figure 16.13

The replication fork. Note in (a) how the opposite polarities of the two DNA chains results in a "leading chain" synthesis for one chain and a "lagging chain" synthesis for the other chain. Note in (b) how the lagging chain synthesis is discontinuous and involves synthesis of RNA primers. The fragments must then be linked together by the enzyme DNA ligase.

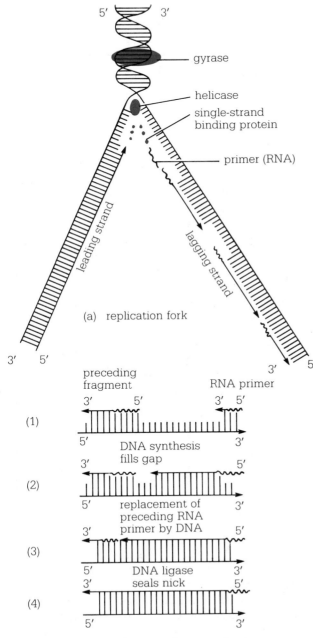

16.6 THE GENETIC CODE

In addition to its ability to replicate, the DNA has the capacity to determine the production of specific proteins. How can this type of information be stored in the nucleotide sequence of DNA? Storage of information for amino acid sequence in a sequence of nucleotides can be viewed as a simple coding problem. The situation is comparable to encoding the letters of the alphabet into dots and dashes (Morse Code) or a series of numbers. DNA contains only four kinds of nucleotides, but must encode the 20 different amino acids used in the formation of proteins. This encoding is accomplished by using a combination of nucleotides to specify each amino acid. Each such sequence of nucleotides is called a **codon**. A gene (which determines a polypeptide) would be a long series of codons, much like this paragraph is a long series of words (Figure 16.14). The number of codons in different genes would vary, depending upon the size of the polypeptide chain being determined.

How many nucleotides are there in each codon? If each codon consisted of only two nucleotides, there would not be a sufficient number of codons ($4 \times 4 = 16$). To encode 20 different amino acids requires codons containing at least three nucleotides ($4 \times 4 \times 4 = 64$).

The Triplet Code

In 1961 Francis Crick and Sidney Brenner at Cambridge University provided experimental evidence that the genetic information is read in frames of three nucleotides. These experiments involved mutations in which varying numbers of base pairs were deleted or added. For example, addition of one or two base pairs upset the reading of frames and disrupted all subsequent codons in that gene. On the other hand, addition of three base pairs resulted in an extra amino acid residue, but left subsequent codons in proper frame and intact (see page 324).

Shortly afterwards, a series of equally ingenious biochemical studies not only confirmed the triplet nature of the code, but also established the specific nucleotide composition of each codon! The biochemical approach involved a variety of *in vitro* protein-synthesizing systems. These systems recombine subcellular components extracted from cells in a test tube. The role of each component can be studied by the effect of its presence or absence on the reaction. The cellular machinery necessary for protein synthesis will be considered in Chapter 17.

Figure 16.14

Storage of information for amino acid sequence of proteins in DNA. A short segment of DNA is shown in (a). Each DNA codon consists of three nucleotide pairs. For gene expression, one strand of the DNA will serve as a template to make a transcription product called messenger RNA (mRNA). Observe in (b) how the segment of mRNA corresponds to the DNA segment above. Note that the mRNA is single-stranded and that thymine (T) is replaced by uracil (U). These differences are discussed in Chapter 17. Observe in (c) a segment of protein corresponding to the codons above. Shown in (d) is a diagram of gene expression in the cell.

(a)   DNA codons   TAG   TCA   CCG   AAG   CGT
                          ATC   AGT   GGC   TTC   GCA

                transcription

(b)   mRNA codons   UAG . UCA . CCG . AAG . CGU

                translation

(c)   protein   MET . SER . PRO . LYS . ARG

(d)

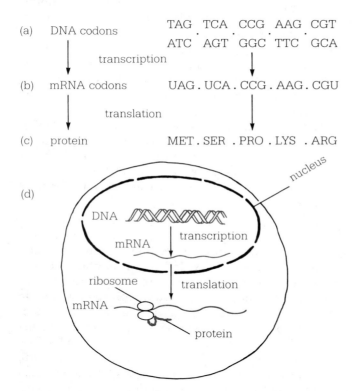

Table 16.2   The Genetic Code: The mRNA Codons for Amino Acids

The genetic code is given in terms of the messenger RNA (mRNA), which is a single-stranded RNA. Amino acids are coded by three nucleotides (a codon). Note the pattern in which several related codons code for the same amino acid. Three codons (UAA, UAG, and UGA) cause termination of or stop translation.

		SECOND BASE				
		U	C	A	G	
FIRST BASE U		UUU UUC } phe UUA UUG } leu	UCU UCC UCA UCG } ser	UAU UAC } tyr UAA –STOP UAG –STOP	UGU UGC } cys UGA –STOP UGG – trp	U C A G **THIRD BASE**
	C	CUU CUC CUA CUG } leu	CCU CCC CCA CCG } pro	CAU CAC } his CAA CAG } gin	CGU CGC CGA CGG } arg	U C A G
	A	AUU AUC AUA } ileu AUG – met	ACU ACC ACA ACG } thr	AAU AAC } asn AAA AAG } lys	AGU AGC } ser AGA AGG } arg	U C A G
	G	GUU GUC GUA GUG } val	GCU GCC GCA GCG } ala	GAU GAC } asp GAA GAG } glu	GGU GGC GGA GGG } gly	U C A G

To consider the characteristics of the code, it is sufficient to note just a few points. Foremost of these is that the DNA is not translated directly (Figure 16.14). An RNA copy of the genetic information is made first. The process is called **transcription** and the RNA is called **messenger RNA (mRNA)**. It is the mRNA that is then translated, using cellular machinery. One method of deciphering the code was to add RNA of known composition to the protein-synthesizing systems. As a consequence, the DNA codons deciphered were listed in terms of their *mRNA counterparts* (Table 16.2).

Characteristics of the Genetic Code

The same genetic code is found in virtually all organisms, including bacteria, yeast, plants, insects, and mammals. Some minor differences have been found in mitochondrial DNA. These exceptions can provide some insight into the evolution of the genetic code and/or the mitochondria. They do not affect the general characteristics of the genetic code outlined in

Table 16.2. Those characteristics could be summarized as follows:

1. All 64 possible codons have a specific meaning. Three specific codons are analagous to the periods that mark the end of a sentence. UAA, UAG, and UGA each cause the translation to stop and the newly formed polypeptide to be released. The remaining 61 codons determine a specific amino acid. This determination results in some redundancy, with several different codons coding for the same amino acids. In contrast, note that there is no ambiguity, as no codon corresponds to more than one amino acid. For example, both UUU and UUC code for phenylalanine (phe); yet UUU corresponds only to phenylalanine, not to any other amino acid.
2. Where several codons correspond to the same amino acid, a pattern can be seen. Table 16.2 is organized to stress that pattern. Redundant codons (for example, UUU and UUC) typically are very similar, sharing the first two nucleotides and differing only in the nucleotide in the third position. Could there be an evolutionary significance to these similarities?
3. The codon AUG has a dual function. It codes for methionine and also helps signal where translation should start.

16.7 MUTATION

In Chapter 14, you saw that Mendelian analysis is based upon the study of mutants. Since every normal cell carries a full complement of genetic material, a mutation can occur in either a *somatic* (body) cell or a *germinal* (reproductive) cell. Of course only the mutations that occur in germinal cells are transmitted to subsequent generations. Mutations which alter a single gene are commonly called **point mutations**. In contrast, **chromosomal mutations** are gross alterations which visibly affect the structure and/or number of chromosomes.

These genetic changes are rare, random events. The high level of accuracy of replication is indicated by the low frequency of point mutations. The likelihood of a specific gene mutation is about 10^{-6}/generation. However, if one considers the total number of individuals in the population and the fact that each individual likely has about 100 000 genes, then many mutations do occur in each generation. The nature of each mutation is independent of the needs of the organism, and most detectable mutations are detrimental. Neverthe-

Figure 16.15
Base substitution mutations. The arrow indicates the site of the mutation. Silent mutations (a) do not change the amino acid sequence. Missense mutations (b) change one of the amino acids in the protein. Chain termination mutations (c) cause translation termination.

normal DNA:	ATG TAC	TGT ACA	CAA GTT	CTG GAC	TCT AGA	GTC CAG
	met	cys	gln	leu	ser	val
			↓			
(a) silent mutation:	ATG TAC	TGT ACA	CAG GTC	CTG GAC	TCT AGA	GTC CAG
	met	cys	gln	leu	ser	val
			↓			
(b) missense mutation:	ATG TAC	TGT ACA	CAT GTA	CTG GAC	TCT AGA	GTC CAG
	met	cys	his	leu	ser	val
			↓			
(c) chain termination mutation:	ATG TAC	TGT ACA	TAA ATT	CTG GAC	TCT AGA	GTC CAG
	met	cys	chain termination			

less, by providing a large source of genetic variation, mutations enable populations to adapt to changes in the environment (Chapter 21).

The Molecular Nature of Point Mutations
Point mutations are of two principal types: base pair substitutions and frameshift mutations.

Base Pair Substitutions
The most common type of mutation involves a change in only a single base pair; for example, a single G—C pair might be replaced by an A—T pair. This change would affect only a single codon of the gene. The general consequences of an altered codon are seen in Figure 16.15. There are, in turn, three types of base pair mutations.

The first type is **silent mutation**. Because of the redundancy in the code, a change of a nucleotide in the third position of the codon could have no apparent effect on the amino acid sequence of the protein. See Figure 16.15(a).

The second type is **missense mutation**. The altered codon could code for a different amino acid from the original codon. See Figure 16.15(b). This alteration

Figure 16.16
The base substitution mutation that causes sickle-cell anemia. The change of the sixth codon from GAG to GUG alters only the sixth amino acid in the globin protein chain.

GAG codon

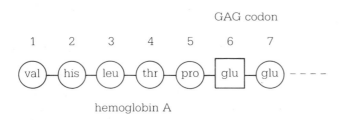

hemoglobin A

GUG mutant codon

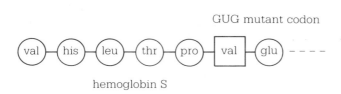

hemoglobin S

Table 16.3   Some Examples of the Consequence of Base Substitution Mutations

The normal hemoglobin (Hb A) is compared to several mutant hemoglobins (Hb S, Hb C and Hb E), altered in their beta-chain. The beta-chain has 146 amino acid residues, but only the two pertinent amino acid residues are shown below. Note that a codon can be changed in several different ways; e.g., in amino acid #6 (Hb S and Hb C). On the other hand, different codons can be altered, affecting different amino acid residues, e.g., in amino acid #26 (Hb S and Hb E).

BETA-CHAIN OF HEMOGLOBIN	AMINO ACID #6	AMINO ACID #26
Hb A (normal)	glu	glu
Hb S	val	glu
Hb C	lys	glu
Hb E	glu	lys

would be reflected in one, and only one, of the amino acid residues in the protein being altered. Sickle-cell anemia is an example of such a mutation. The sixth amino acid residue in beta globin (the beta chain of hemoglobin) is changed from glutamic acid to valine (Figure 16.16). Mutations in other codons cause amino acid substitutions at other positions in the protein (Table 16.3). Most such mutations come to our attention only if they cause disease. However, the consequence of an amino acid substitution often is not so drastic and the mutation goes undetected.

The third type is **chain termination mutation**. Three of the 64 codons code for a stop in the translation process. A chain terminating codon occurs at the normal end of each gene. If the mutation alters an internal codon to one of these three stop codons, then an incomplete protein would result. See Figure 16.15(c). Such incomplete proteins usually lack some or all of their biological activity.

Any of these three types of base pair substitution mutations should be able to revert back to the original form by a second mutation event. If the original G—C pair changed to A—T, the second mutation could return it to G—C. The second mutational event is called a **reversion mutation**.

Frameshift Mutations
The deletion or addition of one or more base pairs (but not three or a multiple of three) causes **frameshift**

mutations. The information stored in the genetic material is translated by starting at a fixed point and "reading" the nucleotide sequence in frames of three. No form of punctuation exists to delineate each separate codon. Accuracy is dependent upon all codons being triplets, so that the translation machinery can move in discrete common steps of three nucleotides.

Addition or deletion of a single base pair disrupts the reading of the nucleotide sequence in proper frames. See Figure 16.17(a). All the codons from the point of the mutation to the end of the gene are also affected. This change is very drastic. How likely is restoration of the normal phenotype by a reverse mutation? A base pair substitution would not be effective, since it could not restore the proper reading of frames. One possibility would be to compensate an addition by a deletion or *vice versa*. See Figure 16.17 (b).

The second mutation need not occur in the original codon. Note that the codons bracketed by the two mutants are still affected, but that the codons beyond to the second mutation are now restored. The consequences of such a double mutant are dependent upon the importance of the affected segment to the functioning of the protein. Crick and Brenner used frameshift mutants in their genetic studies that showed that the code involved triplets. Consider in Figure 16.17(c) what the effect would be of three separate nucleotide deletions on the reading of frames.

Figure 16.17
Frameshift mutations. These mutations result from the addition (+) or deletion (−) of one or more nucleotides. They cause a shift in the reading of all frames beyond the mutation. This shift is most readily seen in (a), where an extra nucleotide was inserted at the third codon position.

In a double mutant (b), + and − , the second mutation compensates for the first to restore the reading frames. However, the codons between the two mutations remain affected. A triple mutation (c) can also restore the reading frames. Why?

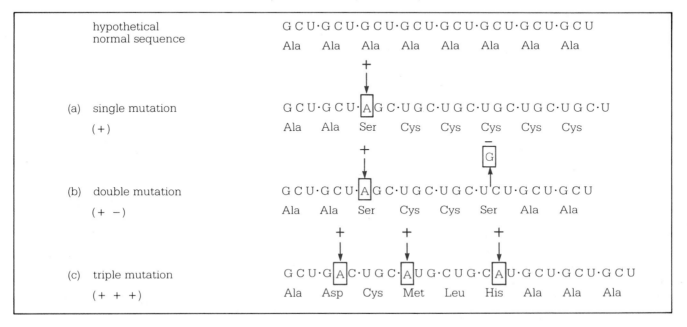

The Induction of Mutations

Mutations that occur under normal conditions are referred to as *spontaneous mutations*. Some of them are caused by mispairing mistakes during replication. For example, Watson and Crick suggested that the reversible change in the location of a hydrogen atom in the nitrogen base could change its pairing specificity (Figure 16.18). A common change causes a shift between an amino group ($-NH_2$) and an imino group ($=NH$). Another typical change causes a shift between a keto group, $=O$ (keto form), and a hydroxyl group, $-OH$ (enol form) (Figure 16.19).

Although the hydrogen atom has alternative locations in the molecule, the hydrogen has a decidedly preferred and stable location. Adenine is usually in the amino form, rather than the imino form (A_I). That is why adenine normally pairs with thymine and not cytosine! A mutation occurs when adenine happens to be in the imino form at the time of replication. The imino form is unstable, and the adenine would return to its stable form. However, the rare mispairing remains. What would happen at the next round of replication?

Other mutations are caused by agents in the environment, both physical and chemical. Agents that increase the frequency of mutations are called **mutagens**. The first mutagen to be demonstrated was ionizing radiation (X ray). In 1927 Hermann J. Muller, then working in Texas, devised an elegant and efficient breeding scheme for measuring the frequency of lethal mutations occurring in the X chromosome of fruit flies. The method permitted him to quantify the number of spontaneous sex-linked recessive lethals and to show significant higher frequencies following X ray irradiation.

Since 1942, when Charlotte Auerbach demonstrated that nitrogen mustard was a mutagen, numerous and varied chemical mutagens have been found. Some mutagens act during replication. For example, *base analogues* are nitrogen bases that resemble the normal bases enough to be *incorporated during replication*. Once incorporated, they differ enough to increase the probability of mistakes being made during later replications. Examples are 5-bromouracil and 2-aminopurine (Figure 16.19).

Figure 16.18

Mutations occurring during DNA replication. A hydrogen atom can undergo reversible changes in its location in the nitrogen base. The arrows in (a) indicate the shift of the hydrogen atom as well as the effect on the neighbouring double bond that can occur in adenine. All four nitrogen bases of DNA can undergo similar shifts. In (b), the shift from the amino form ($-NH_2$) to the imino form ($=NH$) has a significant effect on the potential base pairings. Note that the imino form of adenine pairs with cytosine instead of thymine. Note in (c) how the temporary presence of the imino form of adenine (A_I) causes mutation during DNA replication.

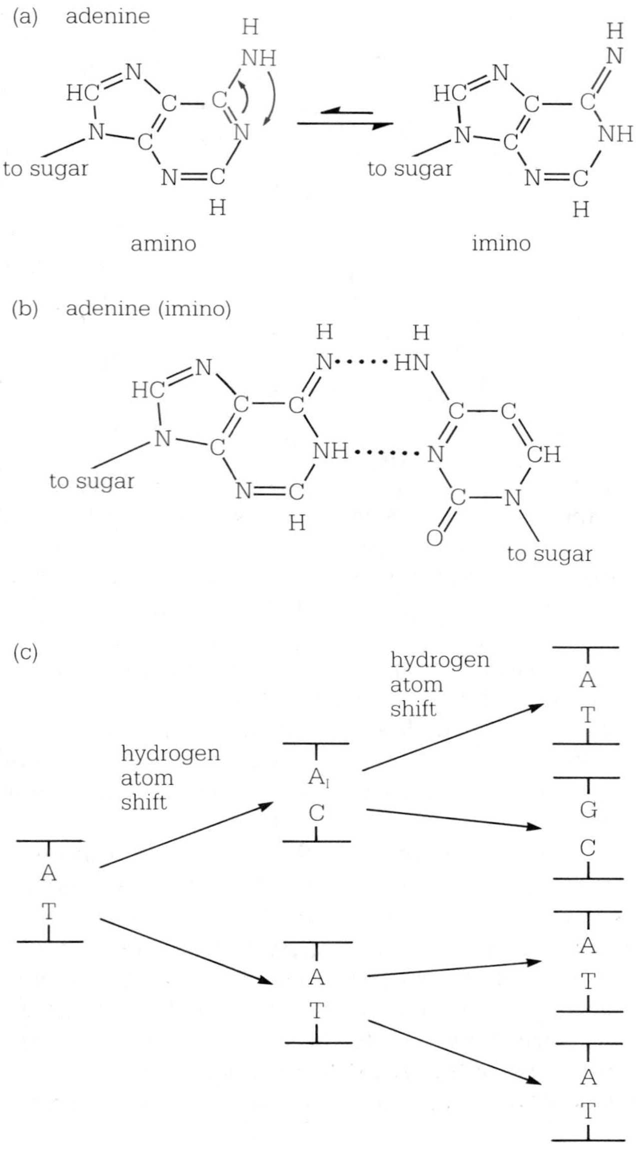

Figure 16.19

Mutagenic action of base analogues. Similar to thymine, the keto form ($=O$) of 5-bromouracil (5-BU_K) pairs with adenine. However, the alternative enol form ($-OH$) of 5-bromouracil (5-BU_E) is more common than for thymine, resulting in more chances of mutation at each DNA replication.

(a)   adenine

amino ⇌ imino

(b)   adenine (imino)

(c)

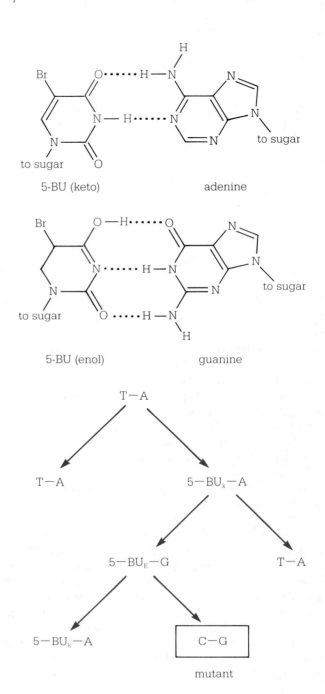

Figure 16.20
Chemicals having a mutagenic effect. In (a), nitrous acid oxidatively deaminates nitrogen bases, replacing an amino group ($-NH_2$) by a keto group ($=O$). Cytosine is converted to uracil, which can then pair with adenine. Mutations occur because the base modified by nitrous acid has a different pairing partner during DNA replication. In (b), ethylmethane sulphonate (EMS) adds an alkyl group (CH_3-CH_2) to the nitrogen base, thereby altering the pairing partner. Proflavin (c) is a flat molecule that can insert between two base pairs, causing frameshift mutations during DNA replication.

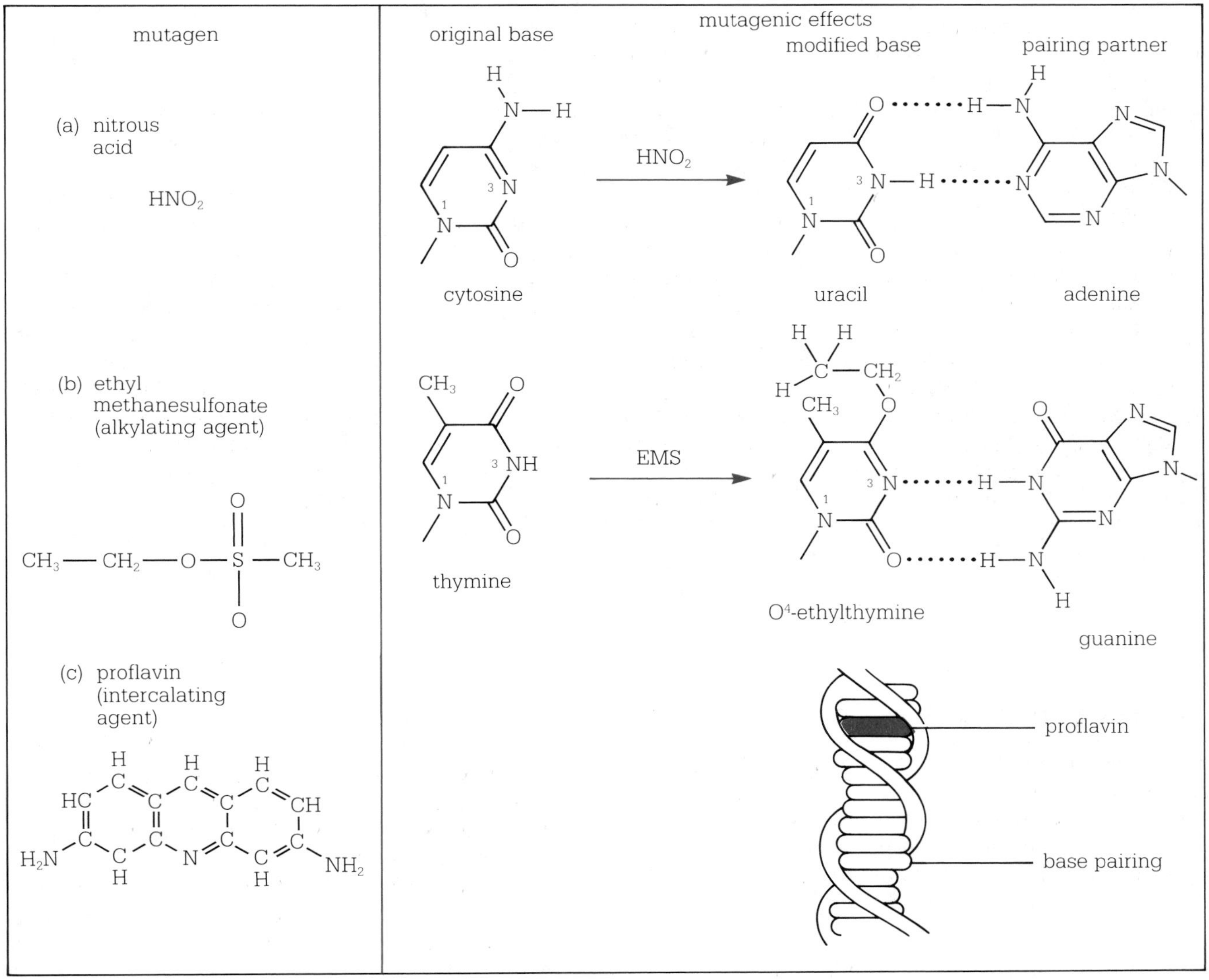

Other chemical mutagens act directly on the DNA. These chemicals cause changes that affect the hydrogen bonding properties of the nitrogen base. For example, *nitrous acid* (HNO_2) oxidatively deaminates nitrogen bases, replacing an amino group ($-NH_2$) by a keto group ($=O$) (Figure 16.20). Hydroxylamine specifically affects cytosine by adding an hydroxyl group ($-OH$) to the amino group of the nitrogen base.

Ethyl methanesulfonate is an *alkylating agent* that can add an ethyl group ($-CH_2CH_3$) to guanine or thymine.

Addition or deletion of base pairs (frameshift mutations) can be induced by *intercalating agents*. For example, *proflavin* is a flat molecule that can insert or intercalate between the stacked bases of the duplex DNA (Figure 16.20).

16.8 DNA REPAIR

The duplex nature of DNA provides a mechanism for repair as well as for replication. If one DNA chain remains intact, there is the potential to use it as a template to repair the altered partner chain. The cell possesses several different repair systems to keep mutation rates at a very low level.

Proofreading Repair During Replication

DNA polymerase has a remarkable accuracy in replication, but it does make mistakes. About one in every 100 000 base pairings is initially a mispairing. Before adding the next nucleotide to the growing chain, DNA polymerase has the capacity to remove the preceding mistake (*proofreading*) and try again. This is an opportunity of the moment. Once replication adds the next nucleotide, it cannot go back. Proofreading increases replication fidelity about a thousand times.

Repair of Mutations

A major mechanism of repair involves the excision of altered nitrogen bases. Many of the more common modifications are recognized by specific repair enzymes and removed. Following *base excision repair* a gap is created, but DNA polymerase can fill in the missing nucleotides. DNA ligase then completes the repair. Another type of repair system recognizes any modification that causes a general distortion in duplex structure. The recognition is less specific, but the net effect is similar. A segment of DNA strand containing the alteration is removed. The resulting gap is repaired through the use of the other DNA strand as the template.

These types of repair must be done before DNA replication. Why? Replication involves separation of the two strands of the duplex. This separation would remove the strand needed as a template. Excision repair enzymes will only act upon duplex DNA.

If replication does occur, still other repair systems exist. One mechanism involves ''borrowing'' from a homologous DNA. The product of such repair is genetic recombination. Indeed, this repair process is related to the mechanism of crossing over.

Xeroderma pigmentosum

Mutant strains of bacteria, defective in one or another of the repair systems, can be isolated and studied in the laboratory. Are there comparable mutants in human populations? Xeroderma pigmentosum is an autosomal recessive disease associated with a defect in the excision repair process. Afflicted individuals are highly sensitive to UV and sunlight. They cannot repair some of the changes in the DNA caused by the UV irradiation. Here, the problem is the accumulation of mutations in the somatic cells. Characteristic symptoms include very heavy freckling with open sores, skin cancer, and often death before adulthood.

CHAPTER SUMMARY

The work of several scientists contributed to the conclusion that DNA was the genetic material. This conclusion profoundly affected genetic studies. The physical structure of DNA could now explain the biological properties of the gene. A scientific revolution was created by asking questions in terms of how DNA functions. Answers were provided at the molecular level for how genes replicate, how genes can determine the specificity of proteins, how mutations arise and are transmitted, and how the mechanisms of DNA repair work.

Objectives

Having completed this chapter, you should be able to do the following:

1. Describe the molecular structure and configuration of DNA.
2. Give two examples of early evidence that DNA is the genetic material.
3. Describe the molecular organization of eukaryotic chromosomes.
4. Outline the process of DNA replication.
5. Describe the genetic code.
6. Explain how mutagens can change the DNA in cells by causing point and frameshift mutations.
7. Give two ways by which the cell could repair mistakes in DNA.
8. Describe how the experiments of Griffith, Hershey and Chase, Chargaff, Watson and Crick, Meselson and Stahl, and Muller have contributed to our understanding of genetics.

Vocabulary

transformation
phage
polynucleotide
double helix
base pairing
antiparallel

nucleosome
semiconservative replication
DNA polymerase
template
primer strand
replication fork

leading chain
lagging chain
primer
primase
DNA ligase
helicase

gyrase
replisome
codon
transcription
messenger RNA (mRNA)

point mutation
chromosomal mutation
silent mutation
missense mutation
chain termination mutation

reversion mutation
frameshift mutation
mutagen

Review Questions

1. Describe
   (a) how the phenomenon of bacterial transformation provided early experimental evidence supporting the hypothesis that DNA is the genetic material;
   (b) how another early experiment also supported this hypothesis.
2. List
   (a) the three components of a nucleotide and describe how they are linked together;
   (b) the two kinds of purines and the two kinds of pyrimidines found in DNA.
3. How are the findings reported by Chargaff consistent with the structure of DNA proposed by Watson and Crick?
4. In comparing the DNA base composition of *E. coli* and human liver cells the A + T/G + C ratios are significantly different, whereas the A + G/C + T ratios are quite similar. Why?
5. Describe the structure of a nucleosome in eukaryotic chromosomes.
6. (a) How did Meselson and Stahl distinguish newly replicated DNA from parental DNA?
   (b) Could Meselson and Stahl distinguish between the conservative and semiconservative modes of replication after

(i) one round of replication?
(ii) two rounds of replication?
   (c) What results would you predict after three rounds of replication and why?
7. (a) List the ingredients needed for a complete DNA replication system.
   (b) Give the function for each.
8. (a) What is a codon?
   (b) What is the size of each codon?
9. (a) What is the maximum number of codons possible if each codon contained
     (i) two base pairs?
     (ii) three base pairs?
     (iii) four base pairs?
   (b) How many codons are there in the genetic code?
10. Distinguish among the three types of point mutations.
11. (a) What is the difference between a base pair substitution mutation and a frameshift mutation?
    (b) Which is likely to be the more potentially harmful and why?
12. Give two ways by which the cell could repair mistakes in DNA created during replication.

Advanced Questions

1. Do you consider the concept that DNA is the genetic material still only an hypothesis? Why?
2. How could bacterial experiments be used to map the bacterial genes? Consider these hints.
   (a) The DNA molecules are broken into fragments during extraction for bacterial transformation.

(b) Uptake of a specific DNA fragment by a recipient bacterial cell occurs at a low frequency.
3. Describe the nature of the 5′ → 3′ polarity found in a polynucleotide chain.
4. DNA was extracted, the two DNA strands separated, and the base composition of each strand determined. The molar concentrations for the

bases of one strand were found to be A (22), G (22), T (28), and C (28).

  (a) Would you expect the same values for the other DNA strand and why?

  (b) If not, what values would you expect and why?

5. Robert Sinsheimer isolated the DNA from the virus φX174 and found the A/T ratio is 0.75, the G/T ratio is 1.31, and the A + T/G + C ratio is 1.35. He later showed that the DNA of virus φX174 is single-stranded!

  (a) Consider whether these exceptional findings disprove the Watson-Crick model for DNA structure.

  (b) Speculate on how virus φX174 could replicate itself.

6. Compare "leading" chain synthesis with "lagging" chain synthesis. Why are there different modes of replication for the two strands of DNA?

7. Why is the genetic code usually given in terms of mRNA codons?

8. Explain how shifts in the location of a hydrogen atom in adinine can cause mutations.

9. Compare how a base analogue such as 5-bromouracil causes mutation with how nitrous acid does so.

10. (a) Speculate on why most point mutations that can be detected phenotypically are

    (i) deleterious.

    (ii) recessive.

  (b) Consider why mutations are essential to the process of evolution.

11. Describe the nature of the human disorder *xeroderma pigmentosum*.

CHAPTER 17

GENE EXPRESSION

Within the past few years researchers have finally begun to be able to peer inside a hitherto impenetrable black box, namely, the development of complex organisms.

Jean L. Marx, 1984

This fruit fly has leg-like structures instead of antennae, making it look like a mutant out of a science fiction movie. Such things normally do not happen during development. The normal fertilized egg grows and differentiates with amazing regularity. In the second half of this century biologists have made significant progress in their knowledge and understanding of how genetic information is expressed in the proper way at the proper time. They now know how the cell can translate the nucleotide sequence of DNA into specific proteins and how it can turn off the activity of some genes while turning on the activity of others. This chapter considers such aspects of gene expression.

17.1 GENE EXPRESSION

The essential points developed so far in this unit might be summarized as three. First, Mendelian analysis shows how genetic information is transmitted from one generation to the next. Second, the DNA molecule serves as a storehouse of the genetic information. Third, DNA replication provides the means of creating additional copies of this information.

However, key questions remain. How is the genetic information *used* in the individual? As discussed in section 15.9 (the one gene-one polypeptide concept), genes determine specific proteins. In some way, the nucleotide sequence of DNA must be translated into the amino acid sequence of the protein. How is this translation achieved? Where in the cell does it happen?

The most direct way of using the information in the DNA would be to synthesize the proteins in the nucleus of the cell. However, studies of eukaryotic cells have shown that the proteins are synthesized *outside* the nucleus (in the cytoplasm). On the other hand, the DNA remains *inside* the nucleus. Clearly then, copies of the genetic information must be made in the nucleus and transported out into the cytoplasm for later use.

As an analogy, consider a reference library where books can be used but not borrowed. These books could represent DNA. When specific information is needed, photocopies can be made and circulated. In the cell, the equivalent of the photocopying process makes a type of RNA called *messenger RNA (mRNA)* as the copy of DNA. The synthesis of RNA, *using the DNA as a template* is called transcription (Figure 17.1). Just as one normally photocopies only a few pages of a book, the mRNA copy represents only a small discrete portion of the genetic information. Note that these events occur within the nucleus.

The process of deriving the amino acid sequence of a protein from the nucleotide sequence of the mRNA is called **translation**. The cellular machinery for translation is found in the cytoplasm.

As discussed later in this chapter, that machinery includes a variety of enzymes, transfer RNAs (tRNAs), and cellular organelles called ribosomes.

Figure 17.1
DNA in the nucleus determines proteins that are synthesized in the cytoplasm. Through the process of transcription, the DNA serves as a template for the synthesis of messenger RNA (mRNA). The mRNA, functioning like a photocopy of the DNA, exits from the nucleus and goes into the cytoplasm. There, it serves as a template for the synthesis of proteins.

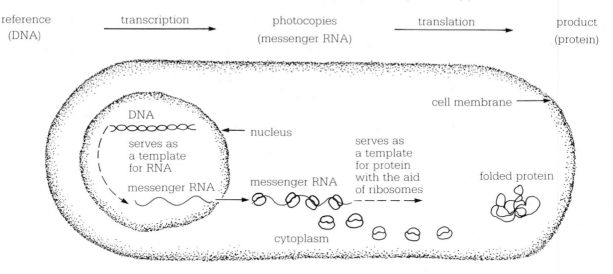

17.2 TRANSCRIPTION

Transcription can be understood by a consideration of four points: how the structures of DNA and RNA compare, how RNA is synthesized, how the transcription process is initiated, and how this same process is then elongated and terminated.

Comparison of DNA and RNA Structure

As a transcript copy of DNA, RNA must be structurally similar to DNA so that it too can carry the genetic information. Like DNA, RNA is a polynucleotide chain containing only four different types of nucleotides. There are three major differences between DNA and RNA. First, RNA is a single-chained molecule, whereas DNA is a double-chained molecule. See Figure 17.2(a). Second, in RNA the five-carbon sugar in each nucleotide is *ribose*, whereas in DNA it is *deoxyribose*. See Figure 17.2(b). Third, in RNA the pyrimidine uracil (U) replaces the pyrimidine thymine (T) found in DNA. Note in Figure 17.2(c) that the absence of the methyl group ($-CH_3$) in uracil does not alter its capacity to form hydrogen bonding to adenine (similar to thymine).

Such differences are considered minor in contrast to the striking similarities. Most significantly, the genetic information stored in the sequence of A, G, C, and T in DNA can be stored in the sequence of A, G, C, and U in RNA.

Synthesis of RNA

The information for all RNAs is stored in the DNA. This includes all of the messenger RNA (mRNA), as well as other specific RNAs to be discussed later: transfer RNA (tRNA), ribosomal RNA (rRNA), and small nuclear RNA (snRNA). The enzyme that catalyzes the synthesis of RNA (transcription) is called **RNA polymerase**.

Transcription bears many similarities to DNA replication. There must be some local unwinding of the double helix of DNA to make it available as a template (Figure 17.3). Similar to DNA replication, RNA synthesis involves adding one nucleotide at a time to the 3′ end of the growing chain. Thus the process begins at the 5′ end of the new RNA chain and proceeds in the 5′→3′ direction. Again the sequence is determined by the complementary pairing with the DNA template. The building blocks for RNA are the four ribonucleoside triphosphates (A, G, C, and U), with uracil (U) replacing the thymine (T) found in DNA.

In transcription, unlike in DNA replication, only one of the DNA chains is used in the unwound region (Figure 17.3). The two DNA chains are not identical, only complementary. If both chains were transcribed, the two DNA chains would determine different mRNAs coding for different amino acid sequences. Although mRNA is transcribed off only *one* DNA chain for a given gene (asymmetric transcription), dif-

Figure 17.2
The structural differences between DNA and RNA. The arrows indicate the sites at which they differ in the sugar and in one of the pyrimidines.

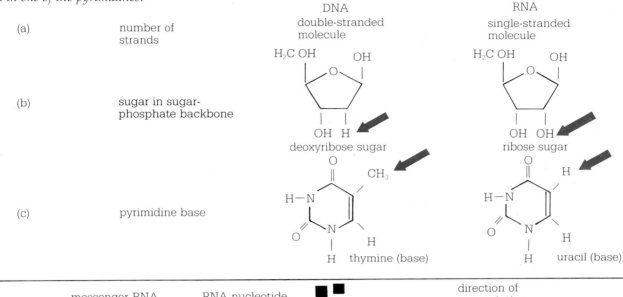

(a)   number of strands

(b)   sugar in sugar-phosphate backbone

(c)   pyrimidine base

DNA
double-stranded molecule

RNA
single-stranded molecule

deoxyribose sugar

ribose sugar

thymine (base)

uracil (base)

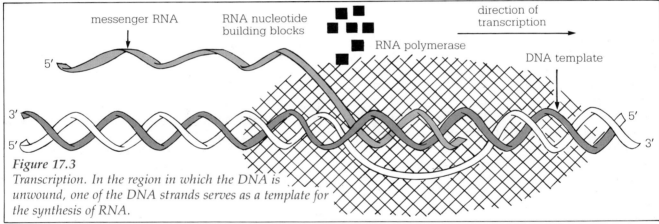

messenger RNA

RNA nucleotide building blocks

RNA polymerase

direction of transcription

DNA template

Figure 17.3
Transcription. In the region in which the DNA is unwound, one of the DNA strands serves as a template for the synthesis of RNA.

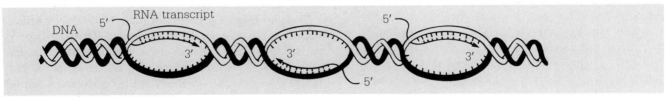

RNA transcript

DNA

Figure 17.4
In any given region only one of the two DNA strands is transcribed (asymmetric transcription). However, for genes in different regions, the strand that is transcribed can vary according to the orientation of the binding site for the RNA polymerase.

ferent DNA chains can be used as the template for different genes (Figure 17.4).

Even if one DNA chain were sufficient to carry the genetic information, there are still advantages to the presence of a double helical structure in DNA. The paired structure likely provides increased stability for DNA. Moreover, as discussed in Chapter 16, the second chain functions in DNA replication and repair.

Initiation of Transcription

How does the RNA polymerase know where to start RNA synthesis? The answer is coded into the DNA. Located in front of each starting site for transcription, there is a binding region for RNA polymerase called the **promoter**. The nucleotide sequence of over 150 different promoter regions in the bacterial cell *E. coli* have been compared and a number of common features found.

All *E. coli* promoters contain two short sequences that are very similar, although not completely identical (Figure 17.5). One sequence, TATAAT, is centered about 10 base pairs in front of the transcription start (the − 10 box). The other sequence, TTGACA, is centered about 35 base pairs in front of the transcription start (the − 35 box). Both the − 10 sequence and the − 35 sequence must be present and spaced the proper distance apart for the region to serve as a promoter.

Shortly after the RNA polymerase binds to the promoter, the two DNA chains in the vicinity of the starting site unwind. Usually, only from 12 to 18 base pairs unwind. The polymerization of the RNA molecule can then begin with the binding of the first nucleotide triphosphate.

How does the RNA polymerase know which DNA chain to transcribe? This answer too is coded into the nucleotide sequence of the promoter. Remember that the two DNA chains are not identical. Transcription always proceeds in the 5′→3′ direction, using as the template the chain with the TATAAT sequence in the − 10 region. The other complementary chain would have an ATATTA sequence in this region.

In eukaryotic cells, there are three different kinds of RNA polymerases, each one responsible for synthesis of different kinds of RNA. RNA polymerase I makes ribosomal RNA; RNA polymerase II makes mRNA;

RNA polymerase III makes tRNA. Each of these RNA polymerases has its own type of promoter region. The promoter region for eukaryotic RNA polymerase II is much larger than its prokaryotic counterpart. There is evidence that an important part of the binding site for eukaryotic RNA polymerase II (the TATA box) is centered about 25 base pairs in front of the transcription start.

Transcription Elongation and Termination

As the *E. coli* RNA polymerase moves along, transcribing the DNA template, the unwound region remains about only 17 nucleotides. Thus, as fast as the DNA chains are unwinding in front, they are rewinding behind. Associated with this rewinding is the continuous release of the RNA chain from the DNA template (Figure 17.3).

The size of typical *E. coli* mRNA ranges from 500 to 5000 nucleotides. Just as there is a specific signal to initiate transcription, there must be specific termination signals called *terminators*. Part of the termination process involves causing the enzyme to stop moving, or at least to pause, at the terminator region. At some terminators, additional protein factors such as rho factor are required.

17.3 TRANSLATION

Transcription copies the genetic information from DNA to RNA. The information for the amino acid sequence of a specific protein is still stored in a sequence of nucleotides. Recall the analogy of the reference library. If you photocopy a book written in German, the photocopy is still in German. Translation into English requires another step. How is the nucleotide sequence of mRNA translated into the amino acid sequence of the protein?

To synthesize a protein, amino acids must be linked together in a specific sequence. The linkage is achieved by the creation of a **peptide bond** as the amino group of one amino acid reacts with the carboxyl group of the adjacent amino acid (see Chapter

Figure 17.5

Typical E. coli *promoter region. When RNA polymerase binds to the promoter region, it covers about 60 base pairs. The two sequences, TTGACA and TATAAT, play critical roles in the specific binding of the enzyme.*

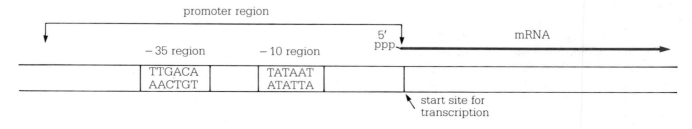

2). The specific sequencing of amino acids is achieved by the use of the mRNA as a template. (The triplet genetic code was described in section 16.6.) A specific sequence of three nucleotides (codon) in the mRNA determines an amino acid. The overall sequence of codons in the mRNA determines the overall sequence of amino acids. However, amino acids show no recognition or affinity with their RNA codons. How, then, are the pieces held together to facilitate the needed reactions? When and where is energy required?

Transfer RNA (tRNA)

A match between the mRNA codon and its corresponding amino acid is achieved through an intermediate, the **transfer RNA (tRNA)**. Each tRNA has both a triplet sequence of nucleotides (the **anticodon**) complementary to a mRNA codon and a binding site for an amino acid. When the tRNA anticodon pairs with the mRNA codon, the tRNA brings in a *specific* amino acid. Each of the 20 different amino acids is associated with specific tRNAs. Thus the sequence of mRNA codons, by determining the sequence of tRNAs, indirectly sequences the attached amino acids (Figure 17.6). Before considering this process, some discussion of tRNA structure is necessary.

Transfer RNAs are polynucleotide chains ranging in length from 73 to 93 nucleotides; the usual one is about 75. Although single-stranded, the tRNA chain can fold back to form intrastrand base-pairings. See Figure 17.7(a). This cloverleaf configuration is typical of all tRNAs. The anticodon is located in one of the unpaired regions; the binding site for the amino acid is found at the 3' end of the tRNA chain.

Xray crystallographic studies have revealed an L-shaped tertiary structure for the tRNA. (See Figure 17.7(b). Again, note the location of the anticodon and acceptor site for the amino acid at *opposite* ends of the L-shaped tRNA. There is nothing specific about the attachment site that would permit recognition of a specific amino acid. A CCA-OH sequence is present at the 3' end of all tRNAs. How, then, does a tRNA become associated with a specific amino acid?

Figure 17.6
The function of tRNAs. Each tRNA is associated with a specific amino acid. The tRNA recognizes a specific mRNA codon by having a complementary triplet of nucleotides, the anticodon. As the tRNAs are sequentially brought in according to the mRNA codons, the amino acids are linked together to form the specific protein.

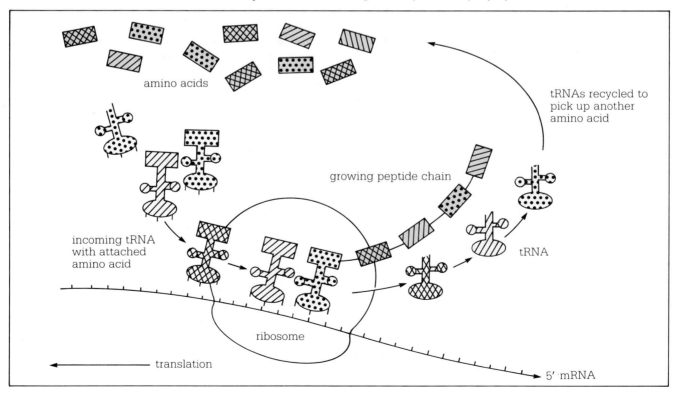

337

Figure 17.7

The structure of tRNA. In (a), base pairings between different regions of the single stranded tRNA result in a cloverleaf secondary structure. The 3' end serves as the binding site for the amino acid. Note the location of the anticodon as part of an unpaired loop of nucleotides. These are features shared by all tRNAs. Observe in (b) the tertiary structure of tRNA, showing the amino acid acceptor arm and the anticodon loop at opposite ends of an ''L''-like structure.

(a)

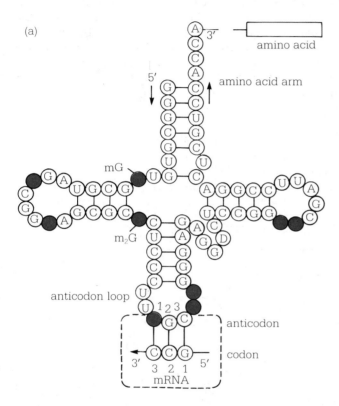

(b)

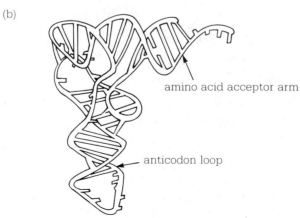

Aminoacyl-tRNA Synthetase

The specificity needed to covalently link specific amino acids to specific tRNAs is provided by a set of 20 enzymes. Each enzyme, called an **aminoacyl-tRNA synthetase**, can recognize and bind only one of the 20 amino acids. Similarly, each tRNA is recognized and bound by only one of the enzymes. By selectively binding only certain tRNAs, this enzyme becomes decisive in the formation of specific aminoacyl-tRNA complexes. That is, each specific enzyme serves to link together a specific amino acid to specific tRNAs.

These enzymes play a second important role. The ultimate formation of peptide bonds between the amino acids requires energy. At the time of formation of the aminoacyl-tRNA complex, this energy is supplied by ATP. The bonding energy released by the hydrolysis of ATP activates the amino acid and is retained in the chemical bond between the amino acid and the tRNA (Figure 17.8). Later, when this bond is broken, the energy is used to form the peptide bond between amino acids.

Ribosomes

The assembly of the amino acids into the peptide chain occurs on the surface of organelles called ribosomes. The ribosome is a complex piece of cellular machinery with several tasks. It must hold the mRNA and tRNAs in a proper position so that the codons are read accurately. As well, it has to catalyze the formation of the peptide bonds between adjacent amino acids (bound to adjacent tRNAs). Furthermore, it must facilitate ribosome movement along the mRNA so that all the codons can be translated.

Ribosome Structure

All ribosomes are composed of two subunits of unequal size. Each of the subunits contains both **ribosomal RNA (rRNA)** and a number of *ribosomal proteins* (Figure 17.9). In bacteria, the smaller ribosomal subunit contains a rRNA molecule about 1500 nucleotides in length plus 21 proteins. The larger subunit has two different rRNA molecules, one about 3000 nucleotides in length and the other only about 120. In addition, the larger subunit has 34 proteins. Eukaryotic ribosomes are very similar but larger.

Recent electron micrographs have provided more detailed information on the shape of the subunits and how they interact. Each subunit has its own characteristic protuberances, clefts, and/or flat surfaces. The smaller subunit is flatter and sits like a cap on the flat surface of the larger hemispheric subunit. Current

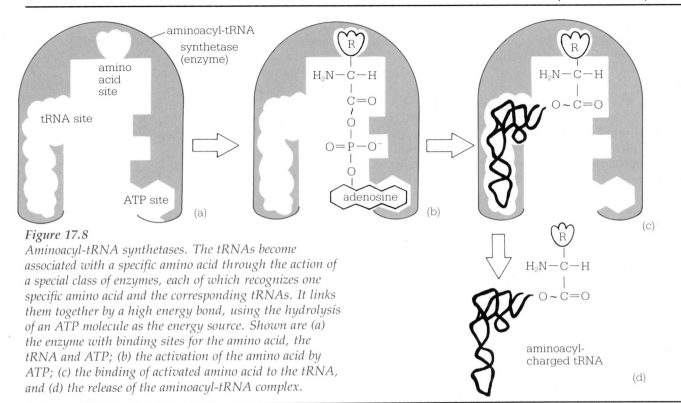

Figure 17.8
Aminoacyl-tRNA synthetases. The tRNAs become associated with a specific amino acid through the action of a special class of enzymes, each of which recognizes one specific amino acid and the corresponding tRNAs. It links them together by a high energy bond, using the hydrolysis of an ATP molecule as the energy source. Shown are (a) the enzyme with binding sites for the amino acid, the tRNA and ATP; (b) the activation of the amino acid by ATP; (c) the binding of activated amino acid to the tRNA, and (d) the release of the aminoacyl-tRNA complex.

Figure 17.9
Ribosome structure. The functional ribosome consists of two subunits of unequal size. Each subunit contains both ribosomal RNA (rRNA) and many different proteins. The shape of the ribosomal subunits was determined by electron microscopy.

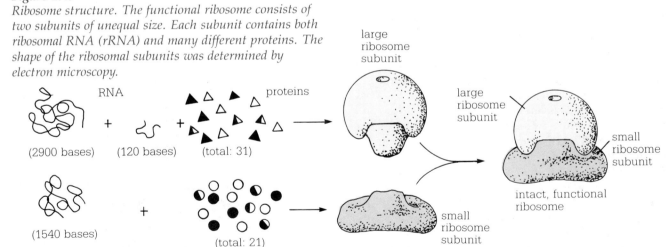

studies have successfully identified the sites for some of the ribosomal functions on the surface of these shapes.

Function of the rRNAs
The rRNAs serve as structural scaffolds upon which the ribosomal proteins are assembled and held in proper position. In addition, the rRNAs, together with the ribosomal proteins, play an important role in binding the mRNA and tRNAs and determining where translation starts and ends.

Perhaps equally important is what rRNAs do *not* do. They do not carry genetic information, as was once believed; rather, it is the mRNA that does so. The ribosome is a non-specific machine that can bind and translate any mRNA made by the cell.

Protein Synthesis

Protein synthesis can be examined in three phases: initiation, elongation, and termination.

Initiation

The specificity of proteins requires that the translation process both start and end at specific sites. In bacteria, translation always begins at an AUG codon (Section 16.6), which codes for methionine. A special *initiator tRNA* that carries a modified methionine (*N-formyl-methionine* or *fMet*) also is required. Protein synthesis begins with the formation of a complex, including the smaller ribosomal subunit, the initiator fMet-tRNA, and the mRNA. The key is to find the proper starting site in the mRNA. To prevent false starts, the signal must involve more than the simple AUG sequence; otherwise, there could be initiation in the middle of genes having an internal methionine codon. The greater specificity required is achieved by an interaction between the 3'-end of the rRNA of the smaller subunit and a purine-rich sequence in the mRNA situated about 10 nucleotides in front of the initiator codon. This interaction helps align the initiator codon of the mRNA with the anticodon of the initiator tRNA (already bound to the smaller ribosomal subunit). Only after this complex is formed does the larger ribosomal subunit bind to form the functional ribosome (Figure 17.10).

Several additional proteins, called *initiation factors*, are also required. GTP must be present as well; it is necessary as an energy source for conformational changes in the ribosome related to tRNA binding.

Formation of Peptide Bonds (Elongation)

Each ribosome has two separate binding sites for tRNA (Figure 17.11). They are the aminoacyl site (**A site**) and the peptidyl site (**P site**). Only the initator tRNA can enter the P site as an aminoacyl-tRNA. The second aminoacyl-tRNA must enter the A site, as specified by the second codon. By means of the enzyme *peptidyl transferase* (located in the larger subunit), the two amino acids can now be linked together.

Note in Figure 17.11 that the formation of the dipeptide involves the release of f-Met from its tRNA. The dipeptide is now bound to the second tRNA, which becomes a *peptidyl-tRNA complex*. To continue synthesis, the initiator tRNA must be released from the P site. Then the ribosome can move one codon down the mRNA. This movement places the peptidyl-tRNA in the P site, leaving the A site empty and positioned for the third codon. Thus, the next aminoacyl-tRNA

Figure 17.10

Translation initiation. In (a), the initiation complex includes a special initiator tRNA, the mRNA, and the smaller ribosomal subunit. Only when the three are complexed at a proper initiating sequence of the mRNA (which includes an initiating codon, AUG, and a binding site for the ribosomal subunit) does the larger ribosomal subunit join in the assembly (b), completing the functional ribosome.

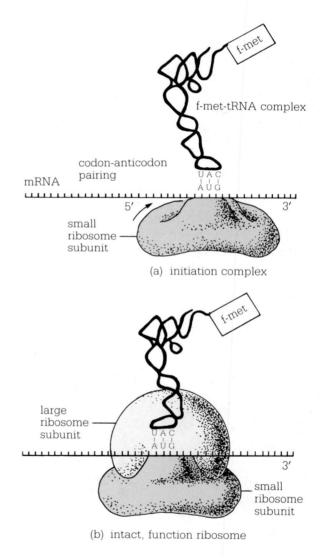

(a) initiation complex

(b) intact, function ribosome

can be bound in accord with the codon sequence of the mRNA. This process is repeated as the ribosome moves along the mRNA in a 5'→3' direction. In this way, the polypeptide is synthesized by the addition of amino acids onto the carboxyl end of the growing protein.

Figure 17.11

Ribosomes and protein synthesis. In (a), the incoming aminoacyl-tRNA complex is bound at the A site of the ribosome. When the peptide bond is formed (b), the growing peptide chain becomes bound to the tRNA in the A site and the tRNA in the P site is uncharged (without

an attached amino acid). In (c), release of the uncharged tRNA from the P site allows for ribosomal movement in relation to the mRNA codons. In (d), the peptidyl-tRNA complex is now positioned in the P site and the A site is empty and free to bind the next incoming aminoacyl-tRNA.

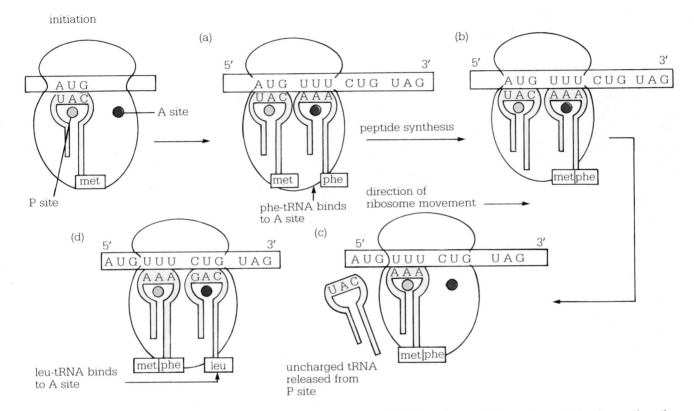

The energy needed to form the peptide bonds was supplied earlier by ATP during the formation of the aminoacyl-tRNAs. The additional energy required for both binding each tRNA to the ribosome and for ribosomal movement is supplied by GTP hydrolysis.

Termination

As described in the previous chapter, there are three mRNA codons (UAG, UAA, and UGA) that cause translation termination. There are no tRNAs corresponding to these codons. Instead, they are recognized by proteins called *release factors*. They cause the release of the polypeptide chain from its tRNA and from the ribosome. The mRNA has determined the primary structure of the protein; that is, the amino acid sequence. The polypeptide chain folds up spontaneously (even while it is being synthesized) into its tertiary structure (Chapter 2).

With the release of the polypeptide chain, the ribosome dissociates from the mRNA. These ribosomal subunits are then available to recommence the translation process for another mRNA.

17.4 COUPLING OF TRANSCRIPTION AND TRANSLATION

There is no nuclear membrane in prokaryotes to separate transcription from translation. In prokaryotes, ribosomes attach to the still-growing mRNA as soon as the ribosome-binding site in the mRNA becomes available. Thus, translation of the mRNA begins while the mRNA is still being synthesized. The ribosome, translating the mRNA, moves along just behind the transcribing RNA polymerase. Electron micrographs provide visual evidence of these events (Figure 17.12).

Figure 17.12
Coupling of transcription and translation in prokaryotes. Electron micrograph (a) of E. coli *DNA being transcribed by several RNA polymerases acting in tandem (arrows). As the mRNA is released from the DNA, ribosomes immediately start the translation process. A labelled drawing (b) interprets the electron micrograph. The direction of transcription is inferred from the increasing length of the mRNAs. A string of several ribosomes associated with the same mRNA is called a polysome. Note that translation begins before the synthesis of the mRNA is completed.*

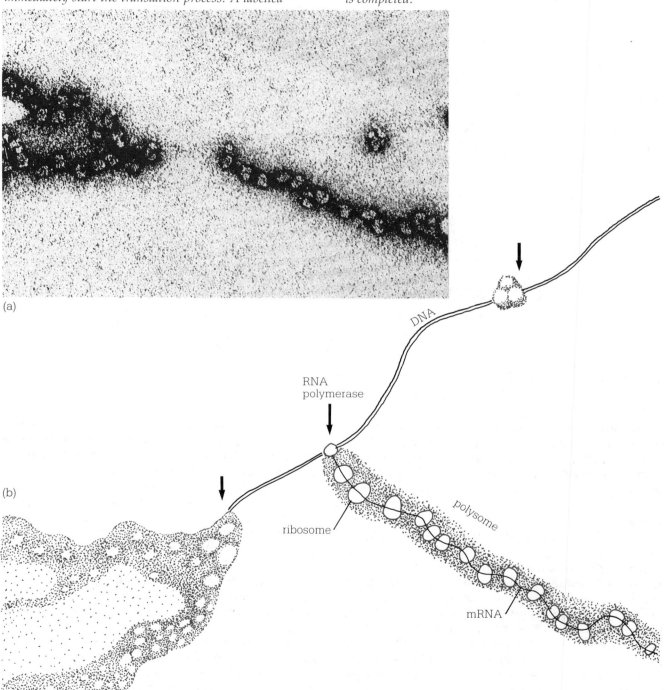

(a)

(b)

DNA

RNA polymerase

ribosome

polysome

mRNA

Figure 17.13

The presence of intervening sequences (introns) in eukaryotic genes. In (a), the DNA encoding the chicken ovalbumin gene contains seven introns (A-G) that are not found in the mature mRNA and therefore are not part of the coding sequences (exons) for the ovalbumin protein.

The exons are represented as boxes and the intervening introns as lines. In (b), all of the exons and introns are transcribed. In (c), the introns are removed from the primary transcription product by a process called RNA splicing. The introns are precisely removed, leaving the exons linked together as a continuous message.

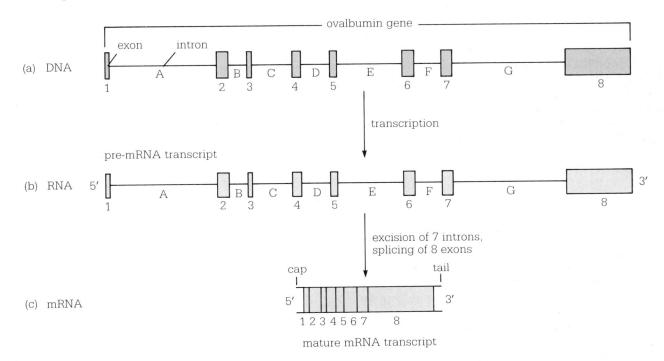

mature mRNA transcript

Note that there is more than one ribosome attached to the mRNA. After the first ribosome vacates the translation start site, a second ribosome can bind. Two or more ribosomes attached to a common mRNA are called **polysome**.

This coupling of transcription with translation is well suited to the short life cycle of prokaryotes. Typically, there is little storage of mRNA for later use. Control of gene expression is primarily done by regulating transcription (Section 17.6). However, when a protein is needed, it must be produced with minimal delay.

In contrast, the mRNA in eukaryotes must move *out* of the nucleus to be translated. Eukaryotic mRNA is much more stable and is often stored. A striking example is the mammalian erythrocyte (the red blood cell). The differentiated cell has lost its nucleus (and DNA), but continues to use its stored mRNA molecules to synthesize hemoglobin. Stored mRNA also allows gene expression to be controlled in eukaryotes at the level of translation.

17.5 MODIFICATION AND PROCESSING mRNA IN EUKARYOTES

The previous section noted some differences between prokaryotes and eukaryotes. However, the genetic machinery of the two share many fundamental features. In each, the DNA is transcribed by an RNA polymerase to make mRNA, which is translated using tRNAs and ribosomes. All the codon assignments are the same in both. Thus, biologists did not at all expect to discover that eukaryotic genes are interrupted by nucleotide segments that are *not translated*. See Figure 17.13(a). Instead, they found that there are intervening sequences *within a gene* present in the DNA that are not within the gene present in the mRNA! The noncoding segments within the eukaryotic gene are called **introns**. Their functions, if any exist, are uncertain (see page 344). Those segments that are retained in the mRNA are called **exons**.

The number, size and locations of the introns are very specific for a given gene but vary greatly for different genes. The size of an intron often is hundreds, even thousands, of nucleotides. Indeed, the introns may represent up to 90 percent of the total nucleotide sequence of the gene.

The presence in the DNA of introns within genes did not fit easily into what was then known about transcription and translation. In transcription, the RNA polymerase proceeds from its start to finish points, adding one nucleotide at a time to the growing RNA chain. It cannot know the possible effect of any nucleotide on the ultimate protein product. Similarly, the mechanism of translation provides no way of dealing with such introns. The ribosome proceeds from the starting AUG codon to the terminal codon, reading the triplets without any discrimination. Transfer RNAs (tRNAs) are brought into place in accord with the next triplet, and without regard for their affect upon the protein product.

Removal of Introns (RNA Splicing)

As shown in Figure 17.13(b), the entire DNA sequence is transcribed, including the introns. The introns are then removed from this large transcription product to yield the smaller mRNA. This step was confirmed by isolation and comparison of the initial transcription product with the mRNA for the same gene.

Removal of introns from the "precursor" RNA is called **splicing**. RNA splicing occurs within the nucleus, shortly after transcription. Only mature mRNAs that have been processed to remove the introns are transported out of the nucleus into the cytoplasm, where they can be translated.

Spliceosomes

The splicing mechanism involves another piece of cellular machinery called the **spliceosome**. Although smaller than the ribosome, the spliceosome resembles it in that both contain both RNAs and proteins. The unique RNAs in the spliceosome are called **small nuclear RNA (snRNA)**. As is true of all specific RNAs, they are encoded in the DNA and synthesized by a transcription process. The complex of snRNA with its specific proteins is called *small nuclear ribonucleoprotein* or *snRNP*. There are different snRNP particles responsible for recognizing and binding to different parts of the intron. One type of snRNP particle binds to the 5′ end of the intron and another type to the 3′ end, whereas other snRNP particles bind to an internal site. The assembly of these snRNP particles into one struc-

Figure 17.14

The spliceosome. The precise removal of introns involves several different snRNP particles. They recognize and bind to the 5′ and 3′ splice sites, as well as to a site within the intron, to form the complex called a spliceosome. Splicing leaves the two exons joined and the excised intron in the form of a lariat.

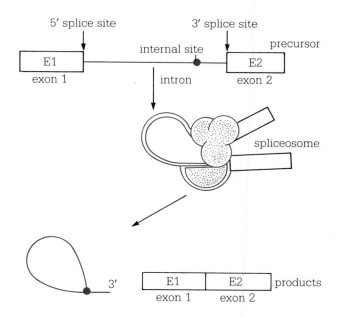

ture, the spliceosome, then brings the splice sites of the intron together (Figure 17.14). The spliceosome may contain the enzymes necessary for the splicing process. On the other hand, there is some evidence suggesting that spliceosome folds the intron RNA into a configuration that makes the RNA self-splicing.

Modification of the 5′ and 3′ Ends of mRNA

In addition to the removal of the introns, the eukaryotic transcription product is modified at both its 5′ and 3′ ends (Figure 17.15). These modifications are characteristic for eukaryotic mRNA and not found in prokaryotes. At the 5′ end, a methylated guanosine derivative is added by a very uncommon 5′-5′ linkage. This structure, called a **5′ cap**, plays an important role in binding the ribosome and in initiation of translation in eukaryotes.

Processing also involves the removal of a terminal segment from the 3′ end. As many as 200 adenines are then added to the newly created end. The function of this **poly(A) tail** is uncertain; however, it likely contributes to the stability of the mRNA.

Introns are noncoding sequences of nucleotides found *within* the eukaryotic gene. Why are they there? They are removed from the transcription product *prior to translation*. What possible function(s) could they serve? Speculation on these questions focussed on the absence of introns in prokaryotes, in contrast to the situation in eukaryotes. Two explanations were proposed. The first was based on the assumption that prokaryotes never possessed introns, and that introns originated only in the eukaryotes. This scheme holds that introns were somehow inserted into pre-existing genes at a later stage of evolution. The alternative explanation suggested that the introns might have been present in the primordial forms of life and then discarded by prokaryotes, yet retained by eukaryotes.

Supporters of the first explanation hypothesize sophisticated roles for the intron, consistent with an "advanced" status for eukaryotes. Regulation of splicing and the processing of the transcription product could serve as a means of regulating gene expression. Alternative patterns of splicing (joining together different combinations of exons of the same gene) can provide several related but different genetic messages from a common genetic locus.

Supporters of the second explanation stress the advantages of a splicing mechanism in the early evolution of living systems. At such a primordial stage, the genes likely were very short (comparable to the exon). Splicing that joined together different coding regions would permit the testing of larger proteins and would thus greatly hasten the evolution of larger and more complex proteins. Presumably, the prokaryotes discarded the advantages of a splicing mechanism in adapting to a very short life span. Elimination of the need to process and modify transcription products permitted more rapid translation of the mRNAs. Indeed, prokaryotes start translation while the mRNA is still in the midst of being synthesized.

Although many molecular biologists support the view that introns are very ancient, it is not possible to conclusively choose between the two models. Even if introns are ancient, they could have evolved additional new functions in eukaryotic organisms over the long course of time. Such changes would further obscure the origin of introns.

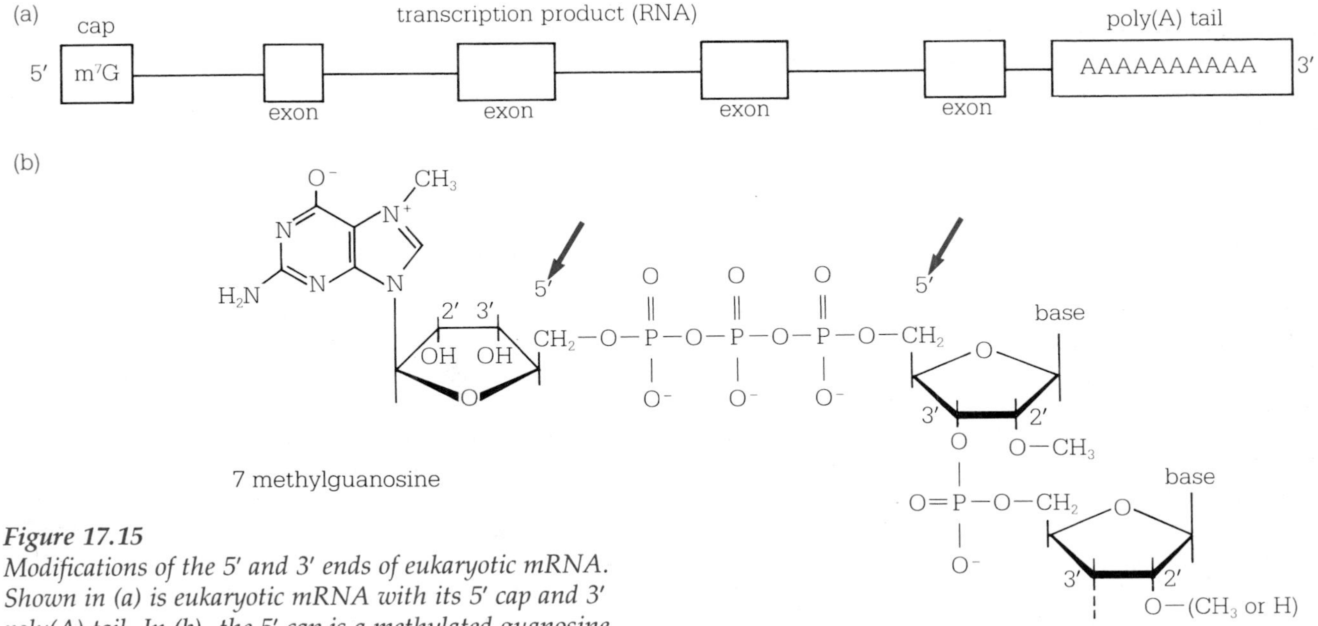

Figure 17.15
Modifications of the 5' and 3' ends of eukaryotic mRNA. Shown in (a) is eukaryotic mRNA with its 5' cap and 3' poly(A) tail. In (b), the 5' cap is a methylated guanosine added to the 5' end of the transcription product by an uncommon 5'–5' linkage.

17.6 REGULATION OF TRANS-SCRIPTION IN PROKARYOTES

Controls are a normal part of most machines or processes. The genetic machinery is no exception. It would be extremely wasteful of the cell's energy supply to continue to transcribe and translate genes when they are not needed. The ability to turn on or turn off specific genes as needed also provides the potential for cellular differentiation. Such control mechanisms can occur at either the transcription or the translation levels.

Prokaryotic cells, having a very short life cycle, are characterized by a regulation at the transcription level. Messenger RNAs are made only as needed and then rapidly degraded. If they are still needed, transcription continues. In contrast, eukaryotic cells have a much longer life cycle. After processing, their mRNAs are stable and often stored for later use. In this situation, post-transcriptional regulation is more likely at the level of processing (for example, splicing) or translation.

A major contribution to the understanding of transcription regulation in *E. coli* was made by François Jacob and Jacques Monod at the Pasteur Institute in Paris in 1961. They integrated the results of their genetic studies of lactose metabolism into a comprehensive model, which they called the **operon** model. The operon is a unit of transcription; it includes the genes that are transcribed together, along with their control elements. This model became the focal point for many studies by other scientists; the description below incorporates these later studies.

The Operon
Jacob and Monod studied three genes that were neighbours in the genetic map of *E. coli* and were regulated as a unit. These genes and the enzymes they determine are *lac z* (determining *beta-galactosidase*, the enzyme which converts lactose to glucose and galactose); *lac y* (determining a *permease*, an enzyme used in the transport of lactose into the cell); and *lac a* (determining a *transacetylase*, whose biological role in lactose metabolism is uncertain). The model proposed, as was later confirmed, that these three genes were transcribed as a unit so that the resulting single mRNA contains all three genes.

The Repressor
Based upon the nature of mutants affecting regulation of transcription, Jacob and Monod proposed that there

was a negative control or **repressor**. Later studies isolated the protein repressor that *inhibits* transcription of the *lac z*, *lac y*, and *lac a* genes. The repressor is determined by another gene, *I*, which is not part of the same operon. Its transcription is independent of the other three genes under consideration. Initiation of transcription of the *lac* operon is prevented when the repressor binds to a specific DNA region, called the **operator**. See Figure 17.16(a).

Note that operon includes the adjacent control elements, the promoter and operator, as well as the region that is transcribed as a unit.

The Inducer
If the repressor turns off transcription of these genes, then the repressor must be removed from the operator region to turn on transcription. The affinity of the repressor for the operator region is dependent upon the repressor's physical conformation. The repressor is an **allosteric protein**; that is, a protein whose conformation and active site is altered by the presence or absence of a small molecule (effector) at a second site. In other words, the repressor has two different binding sites. One binding site is for the operator; the other, for an effector. In this case the effector acts as an **inducer**. When the inducer is bound to the repressor, the repressor has a conformation with a low affinity for the operator. Thus, in the presence of the inducer the repressor is removed from the operator and RNA polymerase can bind to the promoter. See Figure 17.16(c).

Not surprisingly, lactose will act as the inducer of the *I* repressor. In this way, the repressor can be removed when suitable substrate for beta-galactosidase is present. However, any molecule that can bind to the effector site and cause the appropriate conformation change will serve as an inducer.

Constitutive and Other Mutations
Mutations characterized by the continued transcription of the three genes, regardless of the presence or absence of the inducer, are called **constitutive mutations**. They can be alterations either in the operator region or in the gene for the repressor. The mutant operator (o^c) will no longer bind the repressor. The mutant i^- gene determines an altered repressor no longer able to bind to the operator. In either case, the repressor cannot prevent initiation of transcription.

Not all mutations affecting regulation are constitutive. For example, consider a mutant repressor no longer able to bind the inducer at its effector site. It

Figure 17.16
As shown in (a), the lac *operon consists of three structural genes and their control elements; i.e., the promoter and operator regions. The promoter is the binding site for RNA polymerase. The operator is the binding site for the repressor protein. The repressor is* *determined by another operon. In (b), binding of the repressor to the operator region prevents RNA polymerase binding to the promoter region and therefore blocks transcription. In (c), binding of the inducer to the repressor prevents the repressor from binding to the operator and therefore allows transcription.*

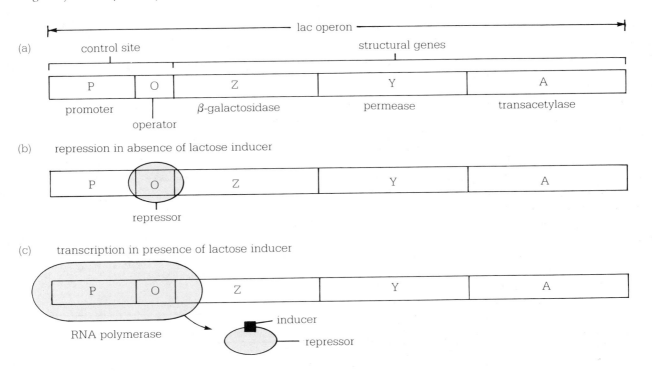

would have the opposite phenotype; that is, it would be *repressed* in the presence *or* absence of the inducer. Once the mutant repressor is bound to the operator, the inducer cannot remove it. The mutation is called a superrepressor and designated i^s.

Catabolite Repression—A Positive Control Mechanism
When glucose is readily available, there is repression of the *lac* operon even in the presence of its inducer, lactose. This repression is consistent with the needs of the organism. If there is sufficient glucose already present, it would be wasteful to utilize lactose as a source of glucose. The question was how this regulation is achieved. The answer revealed a second mechanism for regulating the *lac* operon involving a positive control.

A positive control enhances transcription. The active agent in this case is a protein called the *catabolite activator protein (CAP)*. The CAP protein binds specifically to the region immediately in front of the binding site of RNA polymerase (Figure 17.17). In this position, it helps the RNA polymerase bind, probably by a direct interaction between the two proteins. Indeed, if the CAP protein is not bound, the level of transcription is only two percent of the maximum, even when the glucose concentration is low and lactose (the inducer) is present. The consequence of the failure of the CAP protein to bind can be shown with mutations altering either the protein itself or its binding region.

What prevents the CAP protein from binding in the presence of glucose? The CAP protein is an allosteric protein, similar to the repressor. In this case, unless *cyclic AMP (cAMP)* is bound to form a cAMP-CAP protein complex, there is a low affinity for its DNA binding site. The intracellular concentration of cAMP is determined by the glucose level.

Thus, when glucose levels are high, cAMP levels are low. As a consequence, cAMP-CAP protein complex levels are low and transcription of the *lac operon* is low, even in the presence of the inducer, lactose.

Figure 17.17
Catabolite repression. In the absence of the inducer, the repressor will block transcription regardless of the presence (a) or absence (b) of glucose. In the presence of glucose and the inducer (c), the inducer prevents the repressor from binding. However, there is still little binding of RNA polymerase without the help of the CAP protein. Only in the absence of glucose and the presence of inducer (d) is there maximal transcription.

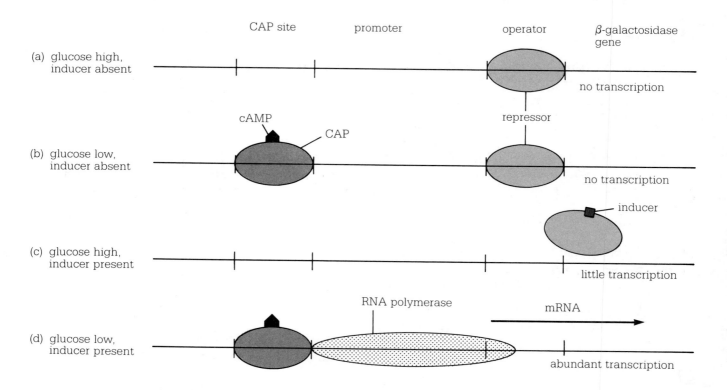

See Figure 17.17(c). By contrast, when glucose levels are low, cAMP levels are high. The cAMP-CAP protein complex is formed and binds to the DNA. Note in Figures 17.17(a) and (b) that when the repressor is bound to the operator, transcription is turned off regardless of the glucose levels. Only in the presence of low glucose and the inducer is there maximal transcription. See Figure 17.17(d).

Corepressor

The *lac* operon is turned off under normal conditions and only activated (induced) in the special situation of low glucose and high lactose. There are other operons that are turned on under normal conditions, but need to be turned off in special situations. For example, the *E. coli* cell needs a continuous supply of amino acids to synthesize its proteins. Thus, the biosynthetic pathways for the amino acids are in constant need under normal conditions. However, it would be wasteful to synthesize an oversupply of amino acids. Even these operons must be under some kind of regulation. Consider the *trp* operon, which contains the genes determining the enzymes involved in the biosynthesis of tryptophan.

Note in Figure 17.18 the presence of an operator region that will regulate transcription. The product of the *trp R* gene acts as a repressor; when it is bound to the operator region, transcription is blocked. The repressor has a low affinity for the operator, permitting continued transcription under normal conditions. However, if there are *high* levels of tryptophan, then tryptophan can bind to the repressor molecule. The tryptophan acts as an effector, binding to the second site. This binding causes an allosteric change in the repressor's conformation, which greatly *increases* the repressor's affinity for the operator. Thus, the tryptophan acts as a **corepressor**, helping to prevent transcription.

Figure 17.18
As shown in (a), the trp *operon of E. coli contains five genes coding for enzymes involved in the biosynthetic pathway of tryptophan. At very high concentrations (b)* tryptophan acts as a corepressor, enhancing the binding of repressor to the operator and thereby preventing most transcription. If the concentration of tryptophan is low (c), then high levels of transcription occur.

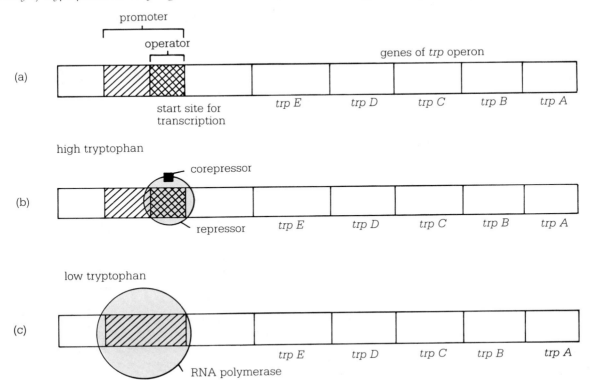

17.7 REGULATION OF GENE EXPRESSION IN HIGHER EUKARYOTES

The study of regulation of gene expression in higher eukaryotes was hampered by several additional obstacles, not present in prokaryotes. Higher eukaryotes have many more genes, typically distributed among numerous different chromosomes. The structure of eukaryotic chromosomes is more complex (section 16.4), including the presence of nucleosomes. Do the histones affect gene expression?

Recent studies of eukaryotes show numerous examples of gene families. Each **gene family** is a group of structurally similar genes, likely a result of duplication of a common ancestral gene. Human globin is a striking example (Figure 17.19). Other members of this group, differing from those determining adult hemoglobin, are expressed during embryonic development. How are these related genes regulated?

Multicellular eukaryotes show cellular differentiation, even though all the somatic cells of the organism have the same genes. Why are the globin genes only expressed in the erythrocytes? Each cell type in the body represents different genes being expressed at different times and/or in different amounts. Despite these differences, there must be total integration to yield the normal, functional organism.

Faced with these complexities in eukaryotes, prokaryotes presented a much simpler test system for the study of regulation. Understanding of the molecular genetics of eukaryotes progressed at much slower rate. Some general observations included the chemical modification of the DNA (methylation) and of the histones (phosphorylation, methylation, acetylation). Such changes could affect the distribution of nucleosomes either to inhibit or to stimulate transcription. Active gene expression is associated with some structural changes in the chromosome, as can be detected by an increased sensitivity of active DNA to degradation.

Figure 17.19
The family of human globin genes and their time of expression during development. The chromosome maps (a) show the family of alpha-like and beta-like genes. Shown in (b) is their time of expression in embryonic, fetal, and adult hemoglobin.

(a)

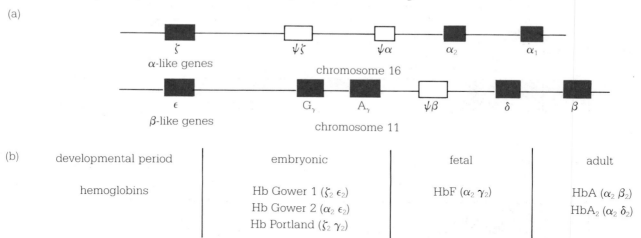

(b)

developmental period	embryonic	fetal	adult
hemoglobins	Hb Gower 1 ($\zeta_2 \epsilon_2$)	HbF ($\alpha_2 \gamma_2$)	HbA ($\alpha_2 \beta_2$)
	Hb Gower 2 ($\alpha_2 \epsilon_2$)		HbA$_2$ ($\alpha_2 \delta_2$)
	Hb Portland ($\zeta_2 \gamma_2$)		

Another avenue of inquiry was to consider the role of hormones known to stimulate synthesis of specific proteins. Steroid hormones, such as estrogens and androgens, are extracellular chemical messengers that enter specific target cells. There, they form a complex with specific cytoplasmic receptor proteins. These activated receptor proteins then bind to specific sites on the chromatin in the nucleus. In some way, still unknown, this binding turns on transcription of the appropriate genes.

With the recent advent of recombinant DNA (Chapter 18), new insights into eukaryotic regulation are now being reported at an increasing rate. Nucleotide sequences upstream of eukaryotic genes have been determined, yielding information about the promoter. One unexpected finding was that regions as far away as several thousand base pairs could greatly stimulate transcription. How these so-called **enhancers** can regulate gene expression at such distances remains uncertain. One suggestion is that the enhancer regions bind specific proteins, causing a local folding in the chromosome. The protein then could help bind the RNA polymerase. Alternatively, the protein bound to the enhancer could in some way alter the DNA conformation to indirectly facilitate the binding of RNA polymerase — for example, by affecting the local distribution of the nucleosomes.

Perhaps the steroid hormone receptor proteins bind to such specific enhancer regions, thereby influencing the rate of transcription initiation. Is the role of the steroid hormone analogous to the prokaryotic effectors that bind to the allosteric repressor protein or CAP protein? There are likely to be many similarities between prokaryotes and eukaryotes. However, the details of transcription and translation serve to caution us also to expect some differences.

Certainly there is a greater use of post-transcription regulation in eukaryotes. The processing steps in the production of mature eukaryotic mRNA provide additional steps at which a control mechanism could be introduced. One interesting example is the use of alternative splicing (Figure 17.20). For example, the mouse gene for myelin basic protein, which has seven exons, can be used to make four different forms of the protein. These proteins differ in which exons are retained. By use of the 5'-end of one intron together with the 3'-end of a different intron as splice points, the intervening exon can also be removed. This process is another way of making related proteins in different kinds of cells or under different conditions.

As previously stated, the stability of the mRNA is much greater in eukaryotes and there are mechanisms of controlling translation. Although these mechanisms are poorly understood, most of them seem to act to limit the initiation of translation. This is seen in the control of hemoglobin synthesis by heme (the iron-containing porphyrin group of hemoglobin which binds oxygen and carbon dioxide). High levels of hemoglobin synthesis require high heme concentrations. The heme acts to inactivate an inhibitor. When the heme levels are low, this heme-controlled inhibitor phosphorylates and inactivates one of the protein factors needed for translation initiation.

Figure 17.20
Alternative splicing patterns for the mouse myelin gene. As shown in (a), the DNA sequence encoding the myelin gene contains seven exons (represented by boxes) and six intervening introns (represented by lines). The splicing patterns are indicated below by the lines joining the lower corners of the exons. In (b), all seven exons are retained in the mRNA. In (c), exon 1 is spliced to exon 3 with the loss of exon 2 in the resulting mRNA. Other splicing patterns demonstrated are represented in (d) and (e).

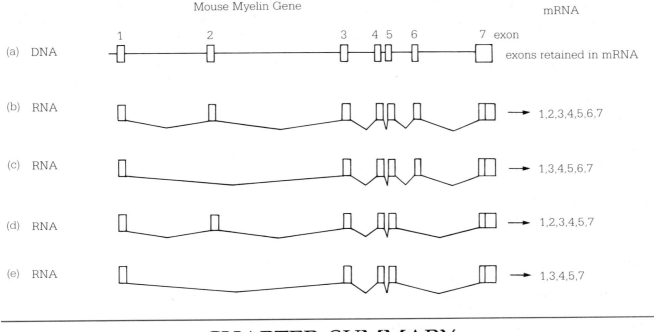

CHAPTER SUMMARY

Gene expression is achieved by the capacity of DNA to determine specific proteins, many of which function as enzymes. The specific nucleotide sequence of the gene encodes the specific sequence of amino acids of a protein.

The first step in gene expression involves the transcription of specific genes, thus creating discrete mRNAs. These single-stranded mRNAs are then translated to protein to complete the transfer of information. Each step involves cellular machinery to ensure the needed accuracy. There must be specific signals to indicate where to start and end both transcription and translation. These processes must have a high level of accuracy to ensure that the protein product has the correct amino acid sequence.

To a large extent, prokaryotes and eukaryotes share many features of this genetic machinery. However, one unexpected finding was that eukaryotic genes are discontinuous, containing intervening nucleotide sequences (introns). The introns are transcribed, but spliced out of the RNA transcription product to create the mature mRNA.

This major difference has alerted biologists to the likelihood that there could be significant differences between prokaryotes and eukaryotes in the regulation of gene expression. In prokaryotes, regulation is primarily at the level of transcription. Rates of transcription initiation are subject to both negative controls (repressors) and positive controls (for example, CAP protein). The situation in eukaryotes seems more complex and less is known about the details.

Objectives

Having completed this chapter, you should be able to do the following:

1. Describe in general terms how the genetic information encoded in DNA controls the activities of the cell.
2. Compare the structure of DNA and RNA and describe the relationship between them.
3. Outline the synthesis of mRNA by the process of transcription.
4. Describe how proteins are synthesized by the process of translation and outline the involvement of tRNA and ribosomes in this process.
5. Interpret an electron micrograph of DNA in process of being transcribed.
6. Describe the modification and processing of eukaryotic mRNA, including the excision of introns.
7. Describe, using the *lac* operon of *E. coli* as an example, how binding of repressor proteins at operator sites on DNA can regulate gene expression.
8. Describe, using the effect of glucose and lactose on expression of the *lac* operon in *E. coli* as an example, how environmental factors can influence gene expression.
9. Compare regulation of gene expression in eukaryotes and prokaryotes.

Vocabulary

transcription
translation
RNA polymerase
promoter
peptide bond
transfer RNA (tRNA)
anticodon
aminoacyl-tRNA synthetase
ribosomal RNA (rRNA)
A site

P site
polysome
intron
exon
splicing
spliceosome
small nuclear RNA (snRNA)
5' cap
poly(A) tail
operon

repressor
operator
allosteric protein
inducer
constitutive mutations
corepressor
gene family
enhancer

Review Questions

1. Compare DNA and RNA, listing
   (a) three similarities
   (b) three differences.
2. What is the difference between transcription and translation?
3. What would be the sequence of the product if the top strand of the DNA given below was transcribed?

   G C G A T G A A C T A G T
   C G C T A C T T G A T C A

4. Describe the structure and function of a promoter region in *E. coli*.
5. State the function of the anticodon of tRNAs.
6. Outline the function of ribosomes in peptide bond formation.
7. Describe the initiation complex formed at the start of protein synthesis.
8. Messenger RNA (mRNA), transfer RNA (tRNA), and ribosomal RNA (rRNA) all are transcribed from the DNA. How do they differ?
9. (a) What are introns?
   (b) Are they transcribed?
   (c) Are they found in mRNAs? Explain.
10. What is the difference between a gene and an operon?

11. (a) Under what conditions is the *E. coli lac* operon turned *off*?
    (b) What mechanism is used to turn off its expression?
    (c) Under what conditions is this same operon turned *on*?
    (d) What mechanism is used to turn on its expression?

Advanced Questions

1. Can you suggest some advantages to the cell in its having mRNA as an intermediate in protein synthesis?
2. What is meant by asymmetric transcription?
3. Describe how specific amino acids become associated with specific tRNAs.
4. The figure below is an electron micrograph showing transcription of ribosomal RNA in *Drosophila*.
    (a) Is the arrow at the beginning or end of the gene? Explain.
    (b) Where are the DNA and the RNA?
    (c) Are ribosomes present? Explain.

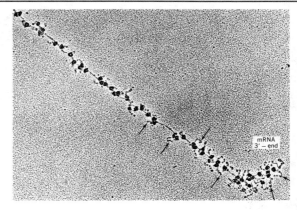

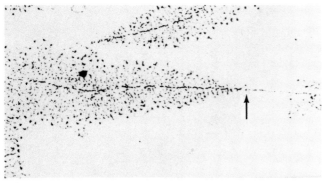

5. The following figure is an electron micrograph showing translation of mRNA in the silk gland of the silkworm.
    (a) Where are the mRNA and the ribosomes?
    (b) Why is DNA absent?
    (c) To what structure are the arrows pointing?

6. Which of the following strains of *E. coli* would produce beta-galactosidase in the presence of an inducer? in the absence of an inducer? (Note that the *i* gene determines the repressor, the *o* region is the operator, and the *z* gene determines the enzyme.)
    (a) i^+ o^+ z^+
    (b) i^+ o^+ z^-
    (c) i^+ o^c z^+
    (d) i^- o^+ z^+

7. (a) Under which of the following conditions would you expect maximal transcription of the *lac* operon? Explain.
     (i) high glucose, inducer present
     (ii) high glucose, inducer absent
     (iii) low glucose, inducer present
     (iv) low glucose, inducer absent
    (b) If the *E. coli* strain carried an o^c mutation, would that affect your answer?

CHAPTER 18

GENETIC RESEARCH AND TECHNOLOGY

If you do not think about the future,
you cannot have one.

John Galsworthy, *Swan Song* (1928)

The giant mouse you see here is a product of genetic engineering. The gene for growth hormone from a rat was injected into the nucleus of a fertilized mouse egg. The purpose was not to make a "supermouse," but to test the feasibility of a new mode of manipulating genes.

There is a long history of human intervention into the genetic make-up of various species. Following the domestication of plants and animals, many farmers used selection to improve their farm stocks. "Good" lines were maintained, while "bad" lines were discontinued.

Applied genetic research in agriculture now provides the necessary information to proceed in a systematic and productive manner. Plants have been bred that are more resistant to diseases and pests, have increased nutrient value, and have greater crop yield per hectare. Perhaps more subtle, but equally important, are improvements in plant features that facilitate harvesting, such as more uniform ripening or dwarf fruit trees. These current varieties often are the result of complex breeding schemes that combine many different traits. There are comparable breeding programs seeking increased viability, fertility, and productivity for farm animals.

To achieve these results, there are standard techniques such as seed storage, cross-pollination, and grafting. Analogous techniques for farm animals include sperm banks, artificial insemination, and the use of surrogate mothers. More recently, gene manipulation has been achieved by means of such techniques as recombinant DNA and cloning.

Do these techniques sound familiar? Do they remind you of some recent medical headlines? To what extent could similar programs be applied to prevent, treat, or cure human genetic defects? What are the social and moral implications for such interventions? This chapter explores how research in genetics has direct application to humans. Some applications seem highly desirable, others quite questionable. The more complete our knowledge and understanding of genetics, the easier it will be to make these distinctions and to make wise decisions.

18.1 EARLY EUGENIC PROGRAMS

Eugenics refers to the attempt to improve future generations of the human population through the selection of parents. The eugenics movement began in England during the late 1800s, a period following Darwin's publication of his theory of natural selection as the mechanism of evolution, but before the advent of Mendelian genetics. In the absence of much knowledge of genetics, advocates of eugenics were free to express the socioeconomic prejudices of their time. Individuals condemned to institutions because they were habitual criminals, feeble-minded, insane, drunkards, or simply paupers were all assumed to be genetically defective. The implication was that rich and successful people were "well-bred" and therefore genetically superior.

The eugenic movement advocated the sterilization of individuals in institutions to remove these undesirable traits from future generations. The advent of

Mendelian genetics in the early 1900s initially only seemed to support these convictions. As the continued absence of any evidence about the hereditary nature of these specific conditions was ignored, stress was placed upon the general importance of heredity. Thousands of individuals in institutions were sterilized during this period in North America. Immigration laws, with clauses discriminating against specific races and nationalities, were justified on eugenic grounds.

The danger of such thinking became shockingly apparent during the Nazi regime in Germany (1933–1945). The mass extermination of millions of people in Europe to maintain the "purity of the master race" should not be forgotten. Against this abhorrent background, is there any valid justification for a eugenic program?

How Different Are The Human Races?

The concept of race assumes that there are subpopulations whose members tend to mate only with each other and who are readily distinguished from members of other subpopulations. The basis for making such distinctions is very difficult to define; different anthropologists have subdivided the human species into as few as two or as many as 30 races. Such studies isolate and stress any differences found. However, genetic studies of these human subpopulations find very little biological difference when the total genome is considered. The same genes, with the same set of alternative forms (alleles), are present in all human beings. Typically, the subpopulations differ only in that certain alleles may be more common in one population than another. Most noteworthy, the genetic variation *among individuals within a "race"* exceeds the variation *between "races."* There are no "pure races." Any selection would have to be done on an individual basis and not on the basis of race, nationality, or culture.

What Human Traits Are Inherited?

The list of genetic defects numbers in the thousands. Absent from the list are such personality traits as "laziness" or "criminality," which are complex, ill-defined, and heavily influenced by environmental factors. Intelligence is poorly defined by any so-called "I.Q." test and is also absent from such a list.

As would be expected from knowledge of how genes function, the listed genetic defects are quite specific. There are some particular inherited metabolic defects associated with a mental handicap, such as

phenylketonuria, an infant disease caused by an accumulation of toxins in the body. However, the cause of many other cases of handicap remains unknown. Certainly environment, or even improper diagnosis, could account for many of the cases. Thus, much greater care must be taken even in the choice of what traits might be improved by a selective process.

How Effective Was The Eugenic Program?

Most genetic defects are both rare and recessive. When the frequency of an allele is low, the likelihood of an individual's being homozygous recessive is extremely small. Much more common are carriers, heterozygous individuals *not* expressing the defect. Sterilization of "unfit" homozygotes would have only a very slight effect on the allele frequencies. Thus the eugenic program to "improve" the human species was unrealistic and ineffective even when applied to specific detrimental alleles; it was very dangerous when applied to specific subpopulations.

18.2 GENETIC COUNSELLING

Even though the eugenic program is discredited, there are still important roles for some forms of genetic intervention that can alleviate individual human suffering. The biggest help for prospective parents concerned about hereditary conditions is more information. They may be concerned because they or other family members are affected. They may wish to know the likelihood of their having an affected child. Because a number of steps are involved, the counselling often involves a team of experts.

The first step must be a *medical diagnosis* to determine whether a genetic disorder is, indeed, involved. Many conditions (for example, embryonic malformations, deafness, and mental handicap) could also have a non-genetic basis. A correct diagnosis is essential. Biochemical analysis of the blood, urine, or cell culture often is needed. For some conditions, examination of the chromosomes (karyotyping) should be done.

Next, *genetic diagnosis* based upon a complete family pedigree, including stillbirths, abortions, and deaths, is needed. This information may be used to distinguish between similar disorders with different patterns of inheritance; for example, one dominant and the other recessive.

The third step is to *estimate the risk*. Sometimes the diagnosis is inconclusive or incomplete so that the calculation is not simple. Some well-known diseases such as diabetes show a familial association, but the genetic mechanism is not clear. If the situation is complex, some empirical estimate of the risk still may be calculated. This information, together with all of the options available, is then conveyed to the parents. The explanation must be given in terms the parents can understand, correcting any misconceptions about the condition and its inheritance.

Finally, the *decision* must be made by the parents. If there is a risk, should they have children? Is a selective or therapeutic abortion warranted? How great must the risk be, or how serious the condition, to make such a decision? This situation can be very stressful; thus the supportive role provided by the genetic counsellor is important.

18.3 SOME REPRESENTATIVE GENETIC DISORDERS

Genetic counselling deals with many types of disorders. Five representative cases are Tay-Sachs disease, hemophilia, the Down syndrome, Klinefelter's and Turner's syndromes, and spina bifida.

Tay-Sachs Disease

Tay-Sachs disease is a severe disorder of the nervous system. Although the newborn appears normal, the infant begins to lose nervous control of muscles by about six months. Additional effects may include blindness, deafness, paralysis, and mental handicap. Death usually occurs before the age of five.

Tay-Sachs disease is an example of a gene mutation causing a metabolic disorder. As a result of an autosomal recessive mutation, the activity of the enzyme *hexoseaminidase A* is missing. This enzyme is responsible for the breakdown of specific lipids (sphingolipids). Blocking the degradation process leads to the accumulation of the lipid, G_{M2} *ganglioside*. Elevated levels of this lipid in the brain account for loss of nervous function.

If individuals are concerned that they may be heterozygous and might be carrying the recessive allele, they can be tested for the level of hexosaminidase A activity in their blood plasma. Most heterozygotes show a level intermediate between that for normal individuals and patients with Tay-Sachs disease (Figure 18.1). The ability to detect heterozygotes among seemingly normal individuals has been a tremendous help to the genetic counsellor. There are numerous other examples of clinical tests for heterozygosity for other genetic diseases such as sickle-cell trait.

Figure 18.1

Levels of hexosaminidase A activity in the serum of (a) patients homozygous for Tay-Sachs disease, (b) individuals heterozygous for Tay-Sachs disease, and (c) normal individuals.

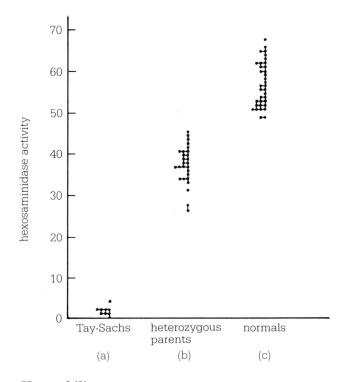

Hemophilia

This sex-linked recessive condition used to be called the "bleeder's disease" because affected individuals have very slow blood clotting times. Normal blood usually clots within five minutes after being placed in a test tube, whereas hemophilic blood may require several hours to clot. Without treatment, even common bruises could lead to serious hemorrhaging and internal bleeding in the hemophilic individual.

What is the basis of the slow clotting time? The clotting is a consequence of a complex cascade of events following cell damage at a wound (Figure 18.2). These steps lead to the conversion of a soluble protein, fibrinogen, into the insoluble *fibrin*. The mesh of fibrin strands helps trap blood platelets to form a clot at the wound. The majority of bleeders lack the key protein, *factor VIII*, and are said to suffer from hemophilia A. Individuals lacking *factor IX* suffer from hemophilia B.

The gene determining factor VIII is sex-linked, which explains why most hemophiliacs are male. Why would female hemophiliacs be uncommon? Of course,

Figure 18.2
Blood clotting and hemophilia. Cell damage at a wound initiates a series of events that ends as thrombin converts fibrinogen into a fibrin clot. The typical hemophiliac lacks factor VIII and therefore has a much slower blood clotting time.

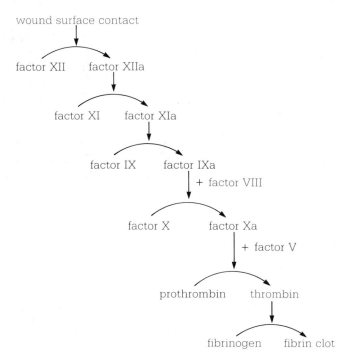

sex-linkage greatly affects the nature of genetic risk to the parents. Does it make a difference whether the gene for hemophilia is carried by the mother or father?

Before the middle of this century, hemophiliacs rarely survived beyond their teens. Medical treatment now extends their life expectancy to almost normal. They can be given concentrated factor VIII isolated from normal blood or manufactured using recombinant DNA (section 18.5). The availability of treatment obviously lessens the concern of some parents about their having an affected child. If the mother is known to be heterozygous, parents might still wish to know early in the pregnancy (by prenatal diagnosis, section 18.4) whether the fetus is male or female. As a sex-linked trait, male offspring have a 50 percent chance of being hemophilic. In contrast, none of the female offspring should be hemophilic. Why? What is the likelihood that they are heterozygous?

Other serious sex-linked conditions include Duchenne muscular dystrophy and the nervous disorder, Lesch-Nyhan syndrome.

The Down Syndrome

Individuals affected by the Down syndrome often exhibit mild to severe mental handicap. Moreover, many die relatively young because of the greater tendency to have serious malformation of the heart, gastrointestinal disorders, and acute leukemia. Early diagnosis is relatively easy because of a number of characteristic physical features. They have short stature, short broad fingers and toes, distinctive finger and palm prints, round face with almond-shaped eyes, and a long protruding and furrowed tongue.

The Down syndrome is associated with the presence of an extra copy of chromosome 21. Instead of the normal 46 chromosomes (2N), there are 47 chromosomes (2N + 1). This is an example of an abnormal chromosomal condition called **trisomy** (Figure 18.3).

Figure 18.3
Karyotype of a male with the Down syndrome. Note the presence of an extra chromosome 21, a condition referred to as trisomy-21. Because the chromosomes were at metaphase, each chromosome consists of two sister chromatids.

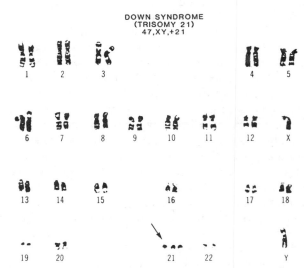

DOWN SYNDROME
(TRISOMY 21)
47,XY,+21

Table 18.1 gives the classification of some of the basic types of variation in chromosome number. **Euploidy** refers to the situation where there are complete sets of chromosomes (*genomes*) present. **Polyploidy** refers to the presence of extra sets of chromosomes. **Aneuploidy** refers to the situation where one or more chromosomes (but not a complete set) is added or missing.

Table 18.1 Some Basic Variations in Chromosome Number

EUPLOIDY (COMPLETE GENOMES)

haploidy (1N)
diploidy (2N)
polyploidy (<2N); e.g., triploidy (3N), tetraploidy (4N)

ANEUPLOIDY (INCOMPLETE GENOMES)

nullisomy (2N − 2; i.e., missing one pair of
    chromosomes)
monosomy (2N − 1; i.e., missing one chromosome)
trisomy (2N + 1; i.e., one extra chromosome)

The presence of a third copy of chromosome 21 (*trisomy-21*) causes an imbalance in the dosage of many genes, accounting for the many and varied symptoms. The more genes involved in the trisomy, the greater the phenotypic effect. Trisomies involving the larger chromosomes are thus rarely found among *live* births; rather, they are found in miscarried fetuses. Note that chromosome 21 is one of the smallest human chromosomes.

What is the origin of trisomy? About 95 percent of Down syndrome children have parents with the normal number of chromosomes; that is, their occurrence is sporadic (without any prior evidence within the family history). Presumably, the extra chromosome arises as a consequence of a nondisjunction involving chromosome pair 21 during meiosis (Figure 18.4). Note that such nondisjunction events should yield gametes lacking chromosome 21, as well as the gametes with the extra chromosome 21. Most likely, all potential cases of monosomy-21 (2N − 1) fail to survive beyond the early stages of development. The genetic imbalance created by a missing chromosome usually is far greater than that caused by an extra chromosome.

Figure 18.4
Nondisjunction of chromosome 21 and its consequences. Failure of the chromosome pair to segregate during meiosis yields gametes either having an extra chromosome or lacking the chromosome. Fertilization of an egg with an extra chromosome 21 results in a zygote with trisomy-21.

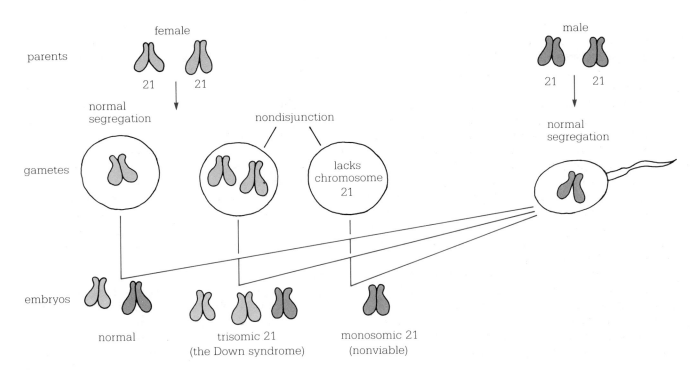

Figure 18.5

Translocation 14/21 is associated with familial Down syndrome. A chromosomal translocation involves breakage and transfer of part of one chromosome to another nonhomologous chromosome. A reciprocal exchange of parts leaves all of the chromosomal material present, but in a new arrangement. In the case illustrated, virtually all of chromosomes 14 and 21 are joined as one chromosome, leaving minute fragments to form the other chromosome 14-21 combination. Presumably, the second combination has no essential genes and was lost.

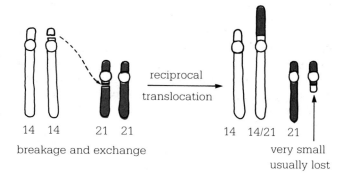

The *familial Down syndrome* refers to those cases in which there are several affected individuals within a single family. Although both parents are phenotypically normal, examination of the chromosomes of the parents usually reveals that one of the parents has only 45 chromosomes. Further study shows that a chromosome 21 is attached to another chromosome, thereby reducing the total number of chromosomes without a major loss of chromosomal material. Note in Figure 18.5 that a chromosome 21 is attached to a chromosome-14.

The joining of these two chromosomes is a result of a chromosomal **translocation**; that is, the transfer of part of one chromosome to another non-homologous chromosome. Figure 18.5 shows how the translocation could arise, following chromosome breaks in both chromosome 14 and chromosome 21. A reciprocal exchange of fragments leaves all of the chromosomal material present, but in a new arrangement. In the case illustrated, virtually all of chromosomes 14 and 21 are joined as one chromosome, leaving minute fragments to form the other chromosome 14-21 combination. Presumably the second combination has no essential genes and was lost.

The parent with the chromosome 14-21 has virtually the equivalent chromosomal content as the normal diploid and is phenotypically normal. Then why do such individuals tend to have affected offspring?

Chromosome 14-21 is transmitted as a single chromosome during meiosis. Therefore, the gametes could contain 14 and 21, 14-21, 14 and 14-21, or 21 and 14-21. Figure 18.6 shows the types of offspring that would result.

Figure 18.7 compares translocation to some of the other basic types of variation in chromosome structure. **Deletion** and **duplication** refer respectively to the loss or doubling of a chromosome segment. **Inversion** involves two breaks in the same chromosome that rejoin improperly to leave the internal segment in the reverse orientation.

Klinefelter's Syndrome and Turner's Syndrome

Klinefelter's and Turner's syndromes are examples of aneuploidy involving the sex chromosomes. Klinefelter individuals have 47 chromosomes, with an XXY composition. Turner individuals have only 45 chromosomes with an XO composition. Their origin is attributed almost entirely to nondisjunction of the sex chromosomes in one of the parents. Are XXY individuals males with an extra X or females with an extra Y chromosome? Clinical studies of these types of conditions have contributed to the understanding of human sex determination.

Individuals with Klinefelter's syndrome (XXY) are phenotypically male, but are characterized as having very small testes, sparse body hair, and are sterile. Many are thin and long-legged and have some female-like breast development. On the other hand, individuals with Turner's syndrome (XO) are phenotypically female but are characterized as having improperly developed ovaries, lack of secondary sexual characteristics, and sterility. Other physical features may include short stature, webbed neck, and a broad chest.

Although these individuals are not normal, the rule seems to be that the presence of a Y chromosome results in a male phenotype, whereas the absence of Y chromosome results in a female phenotype. Some other aneuploids that have been studied include 47,XXX (fertile female), 47,XYY (fertile male), and 49,XXXXY (sterile male). Clearly, the Y chromosome must carry one or more genes that play an important role in determining maleness in human beings.

Spina Bifida

Spina bifida is a genetic defect in which the bone, muscle, and skin fail to develop normally over the spinal cord. The severity is quite variable, from defects that can be treated by surgical closure of the neural tube to mental handicap, paralysis, and early death.

Figure 18.6
Possible consequences of matings between a 14/21 translocation carrier and a normal parent. One third of the *live births should have the Down syndrome and another third should be translocation carriers with a normal phenotype.*

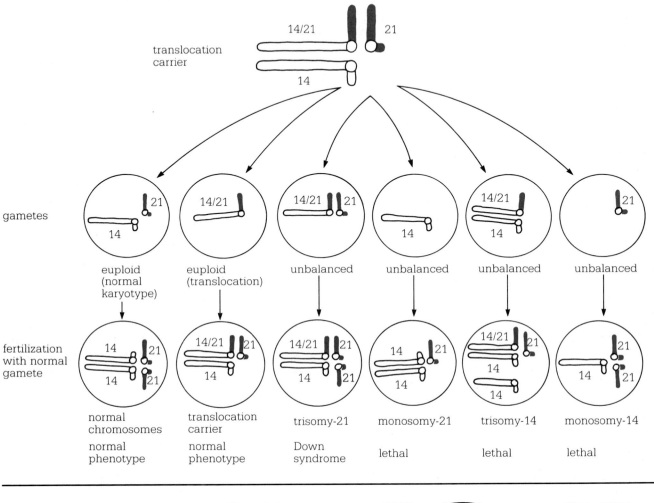

Figure 18.7
Mutations altering chromosome structure: (a) deletion, (b) duplication, (c) inversion, and (d) translocation

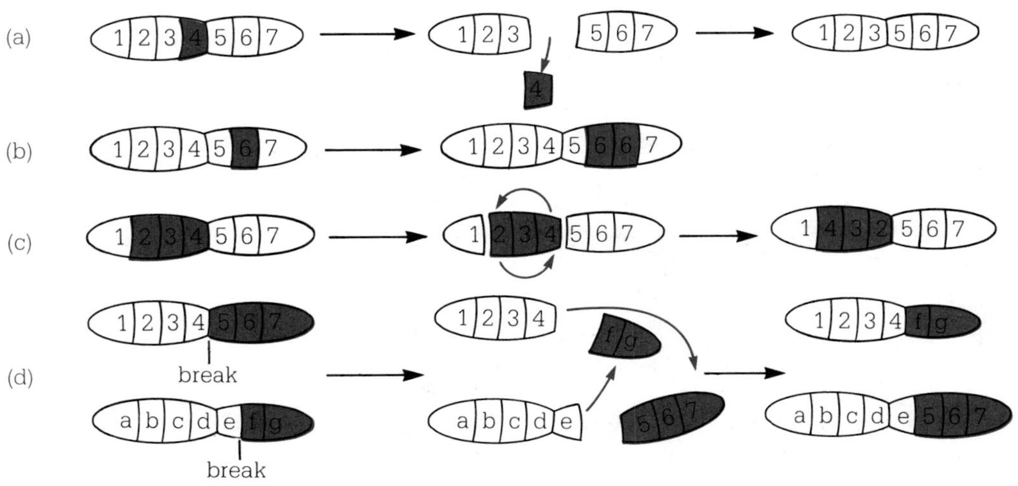

Pedigrees involving spina bifida do not show a simple Mendelian pattern. Some geneticists have suggested that more than one gene may be involved (a situation referred to as *polygenic inheritance*). For parents having a prior pregnancy involving a neural tube defect, there is about a five percent chance that they will have another.

Clinical tests are available to determine whether the fetus likely is affected (prenatal diagnosis). High levels of the protein *alpha fetoprotein* are indicative of neural tube defects. However, such tests do not indicate the severity of the defect. Even when given all of the possible information, many parents will find any decision related to possible therapeutic abortion extremely difficult.

18.4 PRENATAL DIAGNOSIS

For certain genetic disorders, the medical diagnosis of the fetus (*prenatal diagnosis*) can be a significant component of genetic counselling. Because the pregnancy is already in progress, prenatal diagnosis is generally associated with a decision for selective abortion if, indeed, the fetus is affected. However, prenatal diagnosis can serve other purposes. It can allow parents time to prepare emotionally for an abnormal child and to make any needed financial or medical arrangements for the child's care. In over 90 percent of the cases, prenatal diagnosis helps reassure parents about the well-being of their future child. Many high risk parents would not consider having a family without this option.

How can a medical diagnosis be done on a fetus still within its mother's womb? Several methods are now available. Three prominent ones are amniocentesis, chorion villus sampling, and ultrasonography.

Amniocentesis

Amniocentesis refers to the technique of removing a sample of the amniotic fluid that surrounds and protects the fetus. See Figure 18.8(a). A needle is inserted through the abdominal wall, through the uterine wall, and on into the amniotic sac. Accurate localization of the placenta and the fetus is required prior to insertion of the needle. This localization is aided by ultrasonic scanning examination.

From 5 mL to 20 mL of fluid is removed, depending upon the age of the fetus and the total amount of fluid in the amniotic sac. The amniotic fluid contains both fetal urine and sloughed-off fetal cells that can be tested. The fetal cells are separated from the fluid by centrifugation and are grown in culture medium.

Some tests can be done using the fluid. However, most tests are done on the cultured fetal cells. Chromosomal analysis can detect abnormalities such as trisomy-21 (the Down syndrome). Biochemical assays for some enzymes and other gene products can test for such conditions as Tay-Sachs (lack of hexosaminidase A) or neural tube defects (high levels of alpha fetoprotein). DNA analysis can detect the gene for HbS (sickle cell anemia) using specific restriction enzymes (section 18.6). It is anticipated that fetal DNA

Figure 18.8
Prenatal Diagnosis. Amniocentesis (a) involves taking a sample of amniotic fluid surrounding the fetus. Chorionic villus sampling (b) involves removal of a sample of the fetal membrane that extends into the uterine wall. In both methods, the fetal cells in the sample are cultured (c) for biochemical and chromosomal analysis.

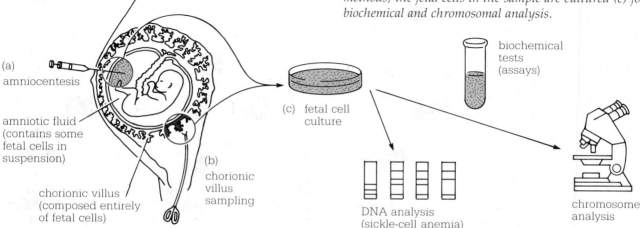

(a) amniocentesis

amniotic fluid (contains some fetal cells in suspension)

chorionic villus (composed entirely of fetal cells)

(b) chorionic villus sampling

(c) fetal cell culture

biochemical tests (assays)

DNA analysis (sickle-cell anemia)

chromosome analysis

Figure 18.9
The relationship between the age of the mother and the
frequency of Down syndrome births. Note the significant
increase in risk for mothers over age 35.

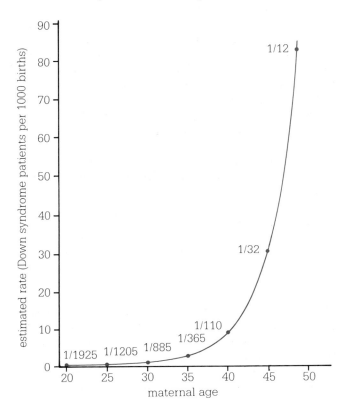

Figure 18.10
Ultrasonograph of a normal fetus. Ultra-high frequencies
of sound waves are beamed through the mother. The
reflection of the sound waves from the different tissues of
the mother and fetus can be transformed into visual
images of light and dark areas on a screen.

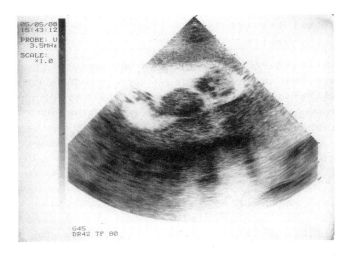

diagnosis can be extended to such important conditions as hemophilia, Huntington's disease, cystic
fibrosis, and Duchenne muscular dystrophy.

Amniocentesis is not without risk. There is about a
one percent higher chance of complications occurring,
including spontaneous abortion. It is not a procedure
to be done with most pregnancies. However, it is considered to be warranted in cases of proven high
genetic risk; for example, when the parents already
have an affected child or when the mother is known
to be heterozygous for a serious sex-linked recessive
disorder. The risk of the Down syndrome increases
with the mother's age (Figure 18.9), suggesting amniocentesis for women over 35.

Amniocentesis is not usually done until 15 to 18
weeks of gestation, when there is sufficient amniotic
fluid present to remove a sample. Because the fetal cells
first must be cultured, the test results may not be available for another month. If the fetus is affected, little
time is left for a decision about therapeutic abortion.

Chorion Villus Sampling

In contrast to amniocentesis, sampling of the chorionic
villi from the fetus can be performed at 8 to 12 weeks
of gestation. The chorionic villi are finger-like projections of the outermost membrane surrounding the
fetus. See Figure 18.8(b). Since the sample contains a
large number of rapidly dividing cells, the tests results
usually are ready within a few days.

The procedure is relatively simple and requires no
anesthesia. Early indications are that it is a safe procedure; this method of prenatal testing may ultimately
replace amniocentesis.

Ultrasonography

As mentioned, the procedures of amniocentesis and
chorionic villi sampling are considered safe, but are
not without some risk to the mother and fetus. That
is why their use is restricted to cases where there is a
known high probability that the fetus is affected. In
ultrasonography, which can be usefully performed
after the 16th to 20th week of pregnancy, a low intensity of high frequency sound waves is used to penetrate the body. The sound waves reflected from the
internal body structures can be displayed on a screen
to give a visual image of the fetus (Figure 18.10). Ultrasound has been reported to be completely safe and
can be used to detect a number of congenital physical

malformations, such as spina bifida, as well as malformation of the brain. Some other defects that are visible include short-limbed dwarfism, severe congenital heart disease, and some kidney abnormalities. Such "non-invasive" approaches to prenatal diagnosis are becoming routine for normal pregnancies.

18.5 RECOMBINANT DNA TECHNOLOGY

In the mid-1970s new techniques were developed that provided the means to cut and splice together pieces of DNA; that is, to create **recombinant DNA**. Imagine having a DNA fragment corresponding to the gene for human insulin. Also imagine you could insert that "gene for insulin" into a "DNA vector" capable of growing in the bacterial cell *E. coli*. Thus, when the DNA vector multiplied, so would the gene for insulin. The culture of *E. coli* has become a living factory for synthesis of the gene for human insulin. Moreover, if the gene for insulin is transcribed and translated within *E. coli*, then the bacterial cells become factories for the synthesis of human insulin protein. Imagination is not needed for all this! It has already been done for several human genes, including those determining insulin, growth hormone, and interferon (an antiviral protein).

Figure 18.11

An overview of how recombinant DNA is prepared and cloned. The process involves (a) generation of DNA fragments, (b) creation of recombinant DNA by covalent linkage of the fragment to a DNA plasmid, (c) introduction of the recombinant DNA into a host cell for multiplication (cloning), and (d) identification of the clone of host cells with the desired recombinant DNA.

How is this done? The ability to splice together specific DNA pieces takes advantage of several laboratory techniques developed in pursuit of quite different lines of genetic research. The relative ease with which recombinant DNA can now be obtained makes the prospect for the future very exciting. Major pharmaceutical companies have invested heavily and new companies have been formed with funding in the hundreds of millions of dollars to create the new "biotechnology industry" (section 18.6).

The four general steps in producing recombinant DNA (Figure 18.11) are generation of DNA fragments, creation of recombinant DNA by covalent linkage of the fragment to a DNA vector, introduction of the recombinant DNA into a host cell for multiplication, and identification of the **clone** of host cells with the desired recombinant DNA.

Generation of DNA Fragments

Generation of DNA fragments can happen in either of two ways: by random breaks or by sequence-specific cuts.

Random Breaks in the DNA

Physical methods such as ultrasonics or shearing can be used to generate random breaks in the DNA. In this manner, the entire DNA genome of human cells could be broken into pieces. If enough of these fragments were cloned, it is likely that all DNA sequences would be represented in the collection.

Sequence-Specific Cuts in the DNA

To isolate large amounts of a specific fragment the DNA must be cut at specific nucleotide sequences. In this way, each of the many millions of identical DNA molecules in the test tube will be cut at the same sites.

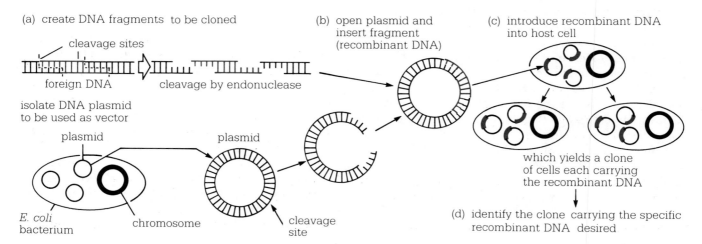

(a) create DNA fragments to be cloned

cleavage sites

foreign DNA   cleavage by endonuclease

isolate DNA plasmid to be used as vector

plasmid   plasmid

E. coli bacterium   chromosome   cleavage site

(b) open plasmid and insert fragment (recombinant DNA)

(c) introduce recombinant DNA into host cell

which yields a clone of cells each carrying the recombinant DNA

(d) identify the clone carrying the specific recombinant DNA desired

Enzymes known as **restriction endonucleases** provide the means of making these exact cuts. For example, the enzyme *HaeIII* (isolated from the bacterium *Haemophillus aegyptius*) recognizes the sequence GGCC. It makes a nick in the chain precisely between the Gs and Cs (Table 18.2). Notice that in the double-chained DNA molecule, this sequence is present in both chains. Read the top chain from left to right and the bottom chain from right to left; that is, the sequence has a *two-fold symmetry*. Therefore, both chains will be nicked and the DNA molecule cut.

Table 18.2 Some Restriction Endonucleases and
Their Cleavage Pattern.

ENZYME	RECOGNITION CLEAVAGE SEQUENCE	SOURCE
EcoR1	↓ GAATTC CTTAAG ↑	*E. coli*
*Hind*III	↓ AAGCTT TTCGAA ↑	*Hemophilus influenza*
*Bam*III	↓ GGATTC CCTAAG ↑	*Bacillus amyloliquefaciens*
*Taq*I	↓ TCGA AGCT ↑	*Thermus aquaticus*
*Alu*I	↓ AGCT TCGA ↑	*Arthrobacter luteus*
*Hae*III	↓ GGCC CCGG ↑	*Hemophilus aegyptius*
*Bal*I	↓ TGGCCA ACCGGT ↑	*Brevibacterium albidum*
*Sau*3A	↓ GATC CTAG ↑	*Staphylococcus aureus*

Source: Klug/Cummings

Figure 18.12

Shown in (a) are fragments with cohesive ends. Cohesive ends are created when the restriction endonuclease (e.g., EcoRI) makes staggered cuts in the DNA molecule. Shown in (b) are fragments with flush ends. Flush ends are created when the restriction endonuclease (e.g., HaeIII) cuts both chains at the axis of symmetry.

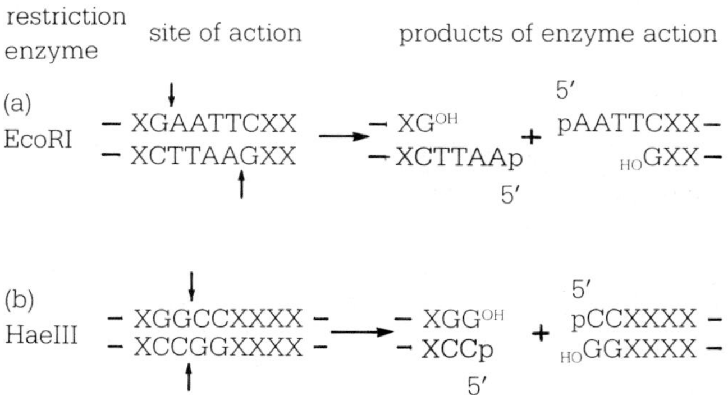

As indicated in Table 18.2, different restriction endonucleases have been isolated from various bacterial species. Each has its own specific target site at which it cuts the DNA molecule. Notice that each target sequence shows a two-fold symmetry.

The fragments created by the restriction enzyme EcoRI have short single-stranded projections or "tails" at both ends. See Figure 18.12(a). Because the two ends are complementary and can base pair, such tails are also referred to as "cohesive ends." The staggered cuts in the DNA made by the enzyme created these ends. Contrast these cohesive ends with the "flush ends" created by HaeIII. See Figure 18.12(b). The nature of the ends of the fragment become important when one wishes to covalently link fragments to the DNA vector to make recombinant DNA.

Creation of Recombinant DNA

Two steps are involved in the creation of recombinant DNA. The first is to locate a suitable vector; the second, to insert the DNA into this vector.

Plasmid Vectors

DNA replication requires a specific starting region (the **replication origin**) to initiate replication. Most fragments would lack the replication origin and be unable to replicate themselves in the host cell. It is therefore necessary to insert the fragment into a vector before introducing it into a host cell for multiplication (cloning). The vector is a DNA molecule with its own replication origin, and consequently can replicate in the host cell. After the fragment is inserted into the DNA vector, it behaves as if it were a part of the vector. Each time the vector replicates, it does too.

Where can suitable DNA vectors be found? Potential ones are commonly found in the normal host cell. For example, *E. coli* harbours viruses and other *plasmids* that can serve as a vector. Plasmids are small, extrachromosomal, circular DNA molecules that can replicate independently of the host chromosome. They are present in one to a hundred copies per cell. Before plasmids are used as vectors, they are often greatly modified. Non-essential regions of the plasmid can be deleted and additional DNA segments that are useful can be inserted. Such segments might be another specific insertion site for the fragment or a special promoter for gene expression. Whatever modifications are made, the vector must retain the replication origin.

Insertion of the DNA Fragment
For the DNA fragment to be inserted, the circular vector must first be cut open. The preferred method is to use a specific restriction endonuclease that will cause a specific single break in the circular plasmid to give a temporary linear structure (Figure 18.13). Note how the closed circular structure is restored when the fragment is linked to the two broken ends of the vector.

The method of joining the ends depends somewhat upon how the DNA fragments were produced and how the vector was opened. For example, if all of the breaks were made by EcoRI, then the cohesive ends shared by both the fragment and the vector can be used (Figure 18.13). The base pairings between the short single-stranded tails help hold the ends together until a proper joining can be completed. Note that the nicks created by the EcoRI enzyme must still be mended by the re-formation of phosphodiester bonds. This reaction requires the enzyme DNA ligase.

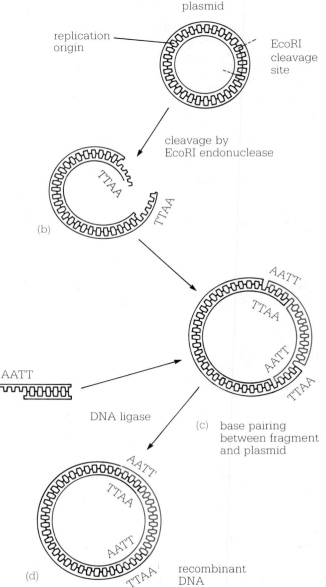

Figure 18.13
Insertion of a DNA fragment into a plasmid. In (a), the DNA to be cloned is cut into fragments by restriction endonuclease, EcoRI. Each fragment has the same short cohesive ends. In (b), EcoRI endonuclease is used to cleave the circular plasmid, leaving it as a linear structure also with the EcoRI cohesive ends. In (c), the cohesive ends of a DNA fragment can pair with the plasmid ends. In (d), the ends can then be joined together by DNA ligase, yielding a stable recombinant DNA.

Figure 18.14
Insertion of a fragment with flush ends into a plasmid. Fragments created by physical shearing (a) do not have cohesive ends. Homopolymer tails, e.g., poly(C) tails, can be added to the fragments by using terminal transferase plus only dCTP. (Terminal transferase can add nucleotides only to single-stranded DNA, so the DNA fragment must

first be treated with an exonuclease.) After cleaving open the plasmid (b), complementary poly(G) tails can be added to the plasmid by using terminal transferase plus only dGTP. In (c), the ends of the fragment can now pair with the ends of the plasmid. In (d), any gaps are filled in by DNA polymerase and the DNA ligase is used to complete the linkage.

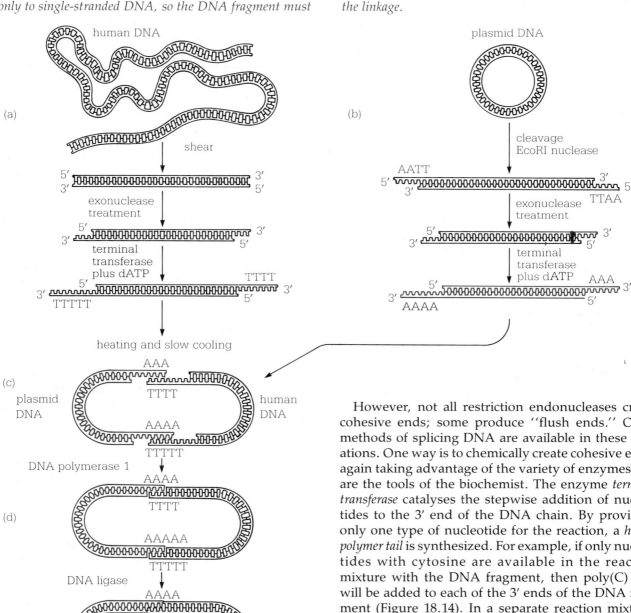

However, not all restriction endonucleases create cohesive ends; some produce "flush ends." Other methods of splicing DNA are available in these situations. One way is to chemically create cohesive ends, again taking advantage of the variety of enzymes that are the tools of the biochemist. The enzyme *terminal transferase* catalyses the stepwise addition of nucleotides to the 3' end of the DNA chain. By providing only one type of nucleotide for the reaction, a *homopolymer tail* is synthesized. For example, if only nucleotides with cytosine are available in the reaction mixture with the DNA fragment, then poly(C) tails will be added to each of the 3' ends of the DNA fragment (Figure 18.14). In a separate reaction mixture, poly(G) tails can be added to the ends of the opened vector. The fragment will then have ends that can pair with the ends of the vector. Any gaps created can be filled in using DNA repair enzymes (DNA polymerase and DNA ligase).

Cloning: Introduction of Recombinant DNA into a Host Cell

The process just outlined involves the creation of recombinant DNA *in vitro*; the cells are broken, the DNA extracted, and the manipulations done in test tubes. Now the vector with the inserted fragment (recombinant DNA) must be placed back into intact cells to multiply. One advantage of using a modified virus as the vector is that viruses possess a mechanism for injecting their DNA into the host cell. When plasmids are used as vectors, the DNA can be introduced into the cell only with difficulty. Even when cold solutions of calcium chloride are used to favourably alter the permeability of the bacterial cells, relatively few cells take up the DNA. Those few bacterial cells now harbouring recombinant DNA must be identified and isolated.

Identification of Clones with Specific Recombinant DNA

Clone selection involves two steps. The first step is selection of all cell lines which harbour recombinant DNA, as distinct from those which do not. Such a collection of cell lines is called a **DNA library**, the nature of which can vary. The second step is to select a cell line with a specific kind of recombinant DNA from the DNA library.

General Selection for Clones with Recombinant DNA
After exposure to the recombinant DNA preparation, the bacterial cells are grown on a solid medium. The progeny of each cell forms a discrete colony or clone. If the bacterial cell harboured a recombinant DNA molecule, then all its progeny should carry copies of that recombinant DNA. However, most of the colonies lack recombinant DNA. How, then, can the clones with recombinant DNA be identified?

Vectors that carry an easily detected gene — a **genetic marker** — are used. For example, the plasmid pBR322 carries the gene determining resistance to the antibiotic tetracycline. If tetracycline is added to the medium, only the transformed cells harbouring the pBR322 plasmid will survive and grow. Plasmid-free bacterial cells are tetracycline-sensitive and are killed. This method provides a very efficient selective procedure for the isolation of bacterial clones with the plasmid. Some very elaborate screening schemes have been devised to isolate specific recombinant DNA clones.

Recombinant DNA Libraries
A DNA library refers to a random collection of clones, each carrying a vector with a DNA fragment from the same organism. There are extensive libraries of DNA from such diverse organisms as *E. coli*, yeast, *Drosophila*, chickens, mice, and humans. As the term library implies, it is a collection of clones to which a researcher can go when seeking a specific recombinant DNA. There are two types of such libraries: the genomic and the cDNA.

The **genomic DNA library** is so called because it is genomic DNA (extracted from cell nuclei) that is cloned. If one wants a DNA library that contains the entire sequence of a mammalian genome, it must be very large. Typically, the size of each DNA fragment is about 1.5×10^4 base pairs, whereas the haploid set of chromosomes (*genome*) of a typical mammalian cell contains about 3×10^9 base pairs. Many separate clones would have to be isolated in the hope that a given region of the genome has been cloned. Moreover, when such libraries are made, there is no way to assure that each clone isolated will be different. In a large library, many DNA sequences are likely represented more than once, whereas other sequences may still be absent. If the entire human genome were to be cloned, a DNA library of several million clones would be needed.

A **cDNA library** is so called because it involves a DNA *copy* — a cDNA — of an RNA molecule. To synthesize the cDNA, an RNA template is used. See Figure 18.15(a). The mRNA is first isolated from the cells. By means of the enzyme **reverse transcriptase**, DNA chains complementary to the mRNA can then be synthesized. See Figure 18.15(b). In the next step, the mRNA template is removed, leaving the single-stranded DNA copy. See Figure 18.15(c). Before this complementary DNA can be inserted into the DNA vector, it must be made into double-stranded DNA. This step is done with the use of DNA polymerase. See Figure 18.15(d).

Since the mRNA was a copy of a portion of genomic DNA, cDNA (as a copy of a copy) should reflect the genomic DNA. However, there are some very striking differences between cDNA and genomic libraries! Three of these differences might be considered.

First, inactive genes not transcribed in a specific cell type are still present in the genomic DNA library. In contrast, cDNA libraries will reflect only the mRNAs that were present in that cell. There will be some special genes transcribed and expressed in brain cells that are not transcribed and expressed in liver cells, and

Figure 18.15

Making double-stranded cDNA from mRNA. Reverse transcriptase (a) uses mRNA as a template to make a complementary strand of cDNA. In (b), the RNA chain is removed by alkaline treatment. In (c) and (d), the single-stranded cDNA is converted to double-stranded cDNA using DNA polymerase. This description omits some steps that involve additional technical aspects of the synthesis. The double-stranded cDNA can be inserted into a plasmid and cloned.

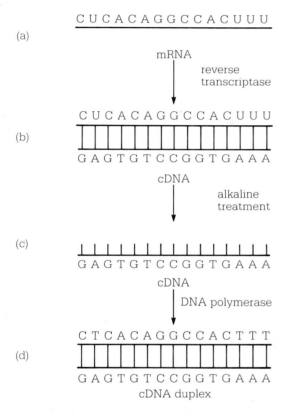

There were extra nucleotide sequences (introns) *within the gene* of the eukaryotic genomic DNA that were not present in the corresponding cDNA gene (Chapter 17). The introns are spliced out of the transcription product in the process of making mature mRNA.

Suppose a pharmaceutical company wants to clone the mammalian gene for growth hormone in *E. coli*. They hope to use these bacterial cells to manufacture the protein, assuming the cloned gene will be transcribed and translated. Should they use cDNA or genomic DNA? The gene from the genomic DNA library will contain the introns, which *E. coli* cannot remove from the transcription products. Consequently, such transcription products would not be processed to the proper mRNA sequence (without the introns) and the desired protein would not be made. This problem does not exist if cDNA is used.

There are other situations where the use of cDNA has advantages. Through a comparison of cDNA libraries made from different tissues of the same organism (for example, brain and kidney), similarities and differences in gene expression can be demonstrated. Each cDNA library contains only copies of those genes that are transcribed. On the other hand, genomic DNA libraries have all the DNA, whether or not that DNA is transcribed.

Screening a DNA Library for a Specific Clone

Imagine trying to find a specific reference book in a library where several million books are randomly shelved and none has a title. The greatest task in recombinant DNA studies is to identify the specific clone that you want in the DNA library. There are two basic approaches, either to identify the protein product of the DNA sequence or to identify the sequence itself.

Screening for the protein product requires that the cloned gene be expressed in the host cell; that is, the gene must be both transcribed and translated. Special vectors (*expression vectors*) that provide the needed promoter and other expression signals must be used. Some proteins can be identified by their known enzymatic activity. Another means of identifying the protein product uses specific antibodies made fluorescent for easier detection.

At present, the only way to recognize a specific DNA sequence is to have a short radioactive piece of complementary DNA or RNA, referred to as a **probe** (Figure 18.16). Cell samples from the clones are transferred to nitrocellulose filter paper. Their location left undisturbed, the cells are gently broken open and the

vice versa. Thus, different cell types will vary in the kinds and amounts of mRNA present, even though they all share the same DNA. Sometimes this variation can be useful in finding a specific gene, such as that for globin. Red blood cells would be an excellent source of globin mRNA; liver cells would not.

Second, DNA regions involved in regulation of transcription (that is, promoters or enhancers) will not be present in the cDNA library. To study such regions genomic DNA must be used.

Third, eukaryotic cDNA lacks the intron sequences that are present in the genomic DNA. Indeed, the existence of introns was first discovered by a comparison of genomic DNA and cDNA for the same gene.

Figure 18.16

Identification of bacterial clone carrying a specific recombinant DNA by use of a probe. Cell samples from the clones are transferred to nitrocellulose filter paper. Without their location being disturbed, the cells are gently broken open and the DNA denatured (by using alkaline solution). The radioactively labelled probe is then added. The probe should only bind to its corresponding DNA, thereby identifying the desired clone.

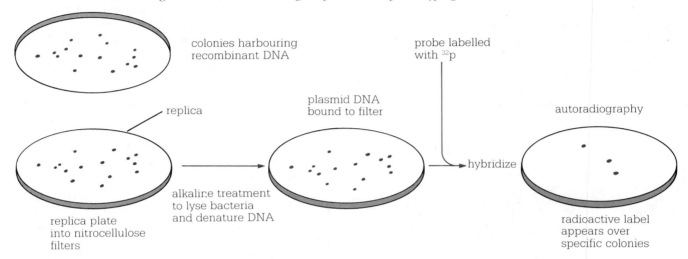

colonies harbouring
recombinant DNA

probe labelled
with ^{32}p

replica

plasmid DNA
bound to filter

autoradiography

replica plate
into nitrocellulose
filters

alkaline treatment
to lyse bacteria
and denature DNA

hybridize

radioactive label
appears over
specific colonies

DNA denatured by using alkaline solution. The radioactively labelled probe is then added. The probe should only base-pair with its corresponding DNA, thereby identifying the desired clone.

Only with extreme difficulty can specific probes be obtained. If the amino acid sequence of the protein gene product is known, the probe can in some cases be synthesized. A short sequence of codons corresponding to an unusual part of the protein is chosen. Another common source is the cDNA library. After the cDNA gene has been identified (by its expression), a portion of it can be used as a probe to help find its counterpart in the genomic DNA library.

If portions of gene can be synthesized as a probe, why not synthesize the entire gene and clone it? Indeed, such chemical methodology was used to clone the gene for somatostatin, a small peptide hormone normally secreted by the hypothalamus. However, for most genes this approach is far beyond the capacity of present day chemical technology. The somatostatin protein is only 14 amino acids long, whereas the typical protein is hundreds of amino acids long.

18.6 APPLICATIONS OF RECOMBINANT DNA TECHNOLOGY

The giant mouse (see page 354) is a good illustration of an application of recombinant DNA technology. The gene for rat growth hormone was injected into the pronuclei of fertilized mouse eggs, which were then re-implanted into foster mothers. Through the introduction of the DNA at this early stage, all of the cells of the embryo might carry the foreign gene. Mice that have integrated foreign DNA into their germ line are called **transgenic** mice.

Alternative means of introducing foreign DNA into mouse cells include the use of modified viruses as a vector. Use of retroviruses that insert their genetic information into the host cell chromosome has been extensively explored. The vector is injected into the fluid-filled cavity (blastocoel) of the early embryo.

The source of the rat growth hormone gene was a recombinant DNA clone. By use of restriction endonucleases, a fragment of the cloned gene without its 5' regulatory region was removed and inserted into another plasmid. In this plasmid, the fragment was fused to the 5' regulatory region of the mouse metallothionine gene. Because of this fusion, production of growth hormone is under the control of the metallothionine gene promoter. The hormone is produced predominantly in the liver, the tissue that normally synthesizes metallothionine. Moreover, the hormone is no longer subject to its own normal feedback control mechanisms. The serum concentration of the hormone in the fast-growing mice was up to 800 times the normal level.

DNA has a number of practical applications in agriculture, industry, and medicine.

CANCER GENES

There are many different kinds of diseases called cancer. The common feature of all cancer cells is their freedom from the normal constraints on cellular growth. When cancer cells are cultured in the laboratory, they seem to have achieved immortality; cell lines can be maintained indefinitely.

Cancer cells can be readily differentiated from normal cells by changes in their morphology, cell surface, and growth properties. Normal cells lie flat and grow as a single cell layer, keeping their distance from each other. In contrast, cancer cells round up, rapidly proliferate, climbing onto and over each other to form a solid mass or tumour.

Cancer can occur when there is a malfunction of one or more key genes involved in basic cell growth and regulation. Genes capable of causing cancer are called *oncogenes*. The malfunction may result from mutation or from the functioning of the normal gene at the wrong time, in the wrong cell, or in the wrong amount. For example, Burkitt's lymphoma, a cancer of the plasma cell specialized for antibody production, is associated with a chromosomal translocation between chromosomes 8 and 14. Chromosome 8 carries an oncogene (*myc*) involved in cell proliferation. Chromosome 14 carries an antibody-producing gene that is regulated by a strong enhancer of transcription. The enhancer helps the cell make vast amounts of antibody when needed. The chromosomal translocation places the *myc* gene under the regulation of the enhancer. In this circumstance, a signal in the body to make more antibody in the plasma cell will lead the enhancer to cause exces-

Shown are (a) normal cells and (b) cancer cells.

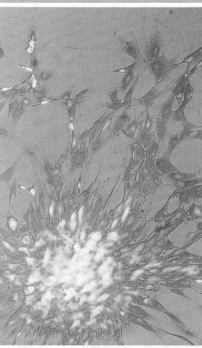

(a) (b)

sive transcription of the *myc* gene. The result is a rapid cell proliferation and cancer of that specific cell type.

How do viruses cause cancer? Some insert their own viral genes into the host chromosome. In that way, the virus will be transmitted whenever the host cell multiplies. If the viral DNA is inserted next to an oncogene, it could upset the normal oncogene function. In other instances, the cancer-causing virus has accidentally picked up a host oncogene during its passage through different host cells. When the virus inserts the oncogene into a new host cell, the oncogene may function improperly to upset normal cell regulation.

Identification of these oncogenes in the virus greatly helped researchers to find the oncogenes in normal hosts. The method used has three basic steps. In the first, DNA from cancer-causing viruses is cloned, using recombinant DNA technology. Next, oncogenes are identified as being distinct from the normal viral genes. Finally, DNA fragments from these cloned oncogenes can be labelled and used as probes to identify similar DNA sequences in the host genome.

Several dozen oncogenes have now been identified and are being intensively studied to determine what their normal functions are in the cell. These studies not only should help in the treatment of cancer, but also should provide significant insights into how normal cell growth is regulated.

Agriculture

Agricultural uses of recombinant DNA involve both farm animals and plants.

Farm Animals

Experiments with transgenic mice, such as the one described above, serve as testing grounds for similar applications with farm animals. Could larger pigs, sheep, and cattle be produced in the same manner? If the growth hormone gene can be transferred, can other genes for disease resistance, overall fitness, or reproductive capacity also be manipulated?

Although the biological principles may seem straightforward, the extension of this technology from mice to farm animals has not been easy. Obtaining and micro-injecting fertilized eggs from livestock has proved to be much more difficult. The level of successful genetic integration following microinjection has also been much lower than in mice. Nevertheless, even this limited success shows that the process is feasible.

Even after the technical difficulties are resolved, such genetic engineering programs will proceed slowly and cautiously. There have been side effects caused by the excess levels of growth hormone in the transgenic mice; for example, the fertility of the females was impaired. At present, the levels of gene expression are unpredictable. Basic research in regulation of eukaryotic genes should help. Genes associated with disease resistance will likely be among the first to be tested. Such genes are more readily identified and less likely to have other physiological repercussions.

Plants

The economic significance of using recombinant DNA to augment current programs of plant breeding is obvious. The initial barrier seemed to be finding a suitable vector. Attention soon focussed on the Ti plasmid found in the soil bacterium, *Agrobacterium tumefaciens*. This bacterium was known to cause tumours (crown gall disease) in plants, usually near the junction of root and stem. The tumour actually is caused by the integration of the T-DNA segment of the Ti plasmid into the nuclear genome of the plant. To use Ti plasmid as a vector, the T-DNA segment has been "disarmed" by removing the detrimental tumour-causing genes. Now by insertion of the foreign gene into the modified T-segment, *Agrobacterium* infection can be used to introduce genes into the plant cell.

At the same time, alternative methods of gene transfer to plants have been pursued. *Agrobacterium* is a pathogen of many dicotyledonous, but not monocotyledonous, plants. However, most of the major food crops are monocots, including rice, wheat, corn, barley, and sorghum. The first step in the transfer of genes into cereals is removal of the cell wall. The next step is introduction of the DNA by use of other vectors or by microinjection.

Early attention was focussed on the possibility of introducing the ability to fix atmospheric nitrogen into crop plants. Nitrogen fixation is restricted to only some prokaryotic cells; for example, the bacterium *Klebsiella pneumoniae*. Some plants, like clover and alfalfa, have evolved a symbiotic relationship with nitrogen-fixing bacteria as a ready source of fixed nitrogen. Most crop plants require extensive application of costly nitrogen-containing fertilizer each year. Could the bacterial genes for nitrogen fixation be transferred to the plant cell? There are at least 17 genes involved in nitrogen-fixation in *Klebsiella*, grouped into seven or eight operons. The mechanism for regulation of this cluster of genes is complex. Therefore, any attempt to transfer this complete genetic system would at present be beyond existing technical capacities.

Promising starts have been made in engineering single-gene traits such as storage proteins (such as in soybean beta-conglycinin) and resistance to weed killers (such as in the herbicide glyphosate) or insect pests (such as in bacterial delta-toxin genes or protease-inhibitor genes). Ultimately, genetic engineering should also contribute to improved resistance to stress conditions like drought, to increased photosynthetic efficiency, and thus to better crop yields. The economic dividends will then be enormous.

A different approach to agricultural problems uses genetic engineering not to produce transgenic plants but to modify microbes that can be added to the environment. For example, the bacterium *Pseudomonas* has been engineered so that it no longer is able to nucleate ice crystal formation. It is hoped that plants sprayed with this microbe will be more resistant to frost damage. Other microbes are being engineered to kill a variety of insect pests such as the gypsy moth larva.

Industry

The pharmaceutical industry was quick to apply the new biotechnology to the production of practical products. One of the first such products was human insulin to replace the pig or cow insulin previously used by diabetics. Animal insulin is effective, but not identical to the human insulin; some patients had adverse allergic reactions. Cloning the human gene in *E. coli* provided a means for mass production of the human protein.

Some of the other products being engineered include human growth hormone, interferon, factor VIII, and viral proteins. The first of these is otherwise only available in small amount from human cadavers. Human interferon is an antiviral factor produced by the body; cloning the gene has provided the supply of this protein necessary to test its actual or potential therapeutic actions. Other similar substances are interleukins, urokinase, and tissue plasminogen activator. Factor VIII is the blood clotting factor lacking in hemophiliacs. Obtaining the protein from bacterial clones could remove the risk of viral infection from contaminated blood supplies. Viral proteins for vaccines such as that for hepatitis B virus have been attempted. Usually vaccines are made from inactivated viral cultures that will elicit the immune response. Cloning the gene for a single viral protein can avoid the risk of virulent viruses contaminating the vaccine preparation.

Industrial applications are not limited to the pharmaceuticals. For example, genes that determine enzymes to break down hydrocarbons have been introduced into a marine bacterium. This engineered organism has been used to help clean up oil spills in the ocean. Conceivably, microbes could be engineered to degrade other toxic chemicals in the environment such as polychlorinated biphenyls (PCBs).

Medical Applications

Recombinant DNA has proven uses in diagnosis, in forensic science, and in gene therapy.

Diagnosis

Recombinant DNA and other related methods provide a means to detect defective genes in advance of their medical symptoms. Such early detection would contribute greatly to genetic counselling of prospective parents. For example, Huntington's disease is an extreme neurological condition that usually is not apparent until middle age. Imagine the value of being able to detect the presence of this dominant mutant gene among potential carriers.

Early detection also could permit special medical treatment of affected infants. For example, children with sickle cell disease have a 15 percent chance of dying from infection in the first few years of their life.

If they could be identified at birth, early treatment could significantly reduce that mortality rate.

How can this molecular diagnosis of mutant DNA be made? The first successful diagnosis involved sickle cell anemia, where the gene sequence was known. Restriction endonucleases provided the means to detect the mutant gene. The base substitution of this mutation also happens to affect a specific restriction cleavage site, changing the size of the restriction fragment containing the globin gene.

Mutations at restriction cleavage sites *outside* the gene, but near it, can also be used. Such variations in the restriction cleavage sites are used as "linked genetic markers" of the allele in question. For example, HpaI restriction endonuclease has a cleavage site about 5000 bases beyond the 3' end of the beta-globin locus for 87 percent of the Hb^S gene in the general population, but only 3 percent of the Hb^A gene. When done as part of a family study, early diagnosis can be facilitated by the presence or absence of this cleavage site.

Forensic Science

The number of potential mutations at restriction cleavage sites is sufficiently high so that individuals can often be identified by their unique pattern of restriction cleavage sites. This identification is called *DNA fingerprinting*. The process requires only a small sample of tissue or blood as the source of DNA. Identification of a certain person often plays an important role in solving crimes (forensic genetics). Widespread application of DNA fingerprinting likely will occur as some of the labour-intensive procedures are simplified and automated.

Gene Therapy

Perhaps the most widely discussed application of genetic engineering is *gene therapy*, the procedure by which defective genes in humans are replaced with their normal alleles. In principle, it may sound like a simple extension of the recombinant DNA technology. Of course, human diseases that might be treated by gene therapy would be restricted to those associated with single gene differences. Possible examples would include pituitary dwarfism (growth hormone gene), sickle-cell anemia (beta-globin gene), hemophilia (factor VIII gene), Lesch-Nyhan disease (hypoxanthine phosphoribosyl transferase gene) and phenylketonuria (phenylalanine hydroxylase gene).

However, the delivery of the gene is a difficult problem. The methods used to produce transgenic laboratory and domestic animals are not readily applicable to human beings. Gene replacement in a human fertilized egg or fetus is not expected in the foreseeable future. General use of a viral vector is still far too unpredictable to assure regulated expression in the proper cells. The most promising approach involves use of bone marrow cells. They can be taken from the patient, genetically manipulated during growth in culture, and then re-implanted into the patient. This approach would be suitable for disorders of the bone marrow cells, such as anemia. However, such therapy would be extremely difficult because so little is known about the regulation of the globin genes. Perhaps the bone marrow cell could be used to correct deficiencies of proteins such as blood clotting factors or hormones that are normally circulated through the bloodstream.

At present, gene therapy is still not possible for technical reasons. Before such applications come into use, a number of ethical questions will have to be carefully examined and decisions made. In the interim, numerous guidelines are being established. One recommendation is that any genetic modification be limited to the somatic cells so that the genetic change would not be transmitted to any future generations.

CHAPTER SUMMARY

The early attempts to selectively ''improve'' the human population by eugenic programs were guided primarily by social and political biases, rather than by proper genetic information. After these programs were discredited, the general public became aware of the caution needed when considering any intervention in the genetic system.

On the other hand, medical prevention and treatment of disease is based upon intervention. Great benefits have been derived from the increased knowledge of the genetic basis of many disorders. Some disorders, such as Tay-Sachs disease and hemophilia, are due to base substitutions in the gene. Knowledge of the structure and function of the mutant and normal gene products often can suggest better methods of treatment. Other genetic disorders, such as the Down syndrome, Klinefelter's syndrome and Turner's syndrome, are caused by chromosomal mutation. Much of this information now is potentially available to parents by consultation with professional genetic counsellors. In addition, many genetic disorders in the fetus can now be detected by prenatal diagnosis, using amniocentesis or chorion villus sampling.

The recent advent of recombinant DNA technology has provided the means to study the structure and regulation of specific genes. Recombinant DNA refers to the insertion of a ''foreign'' DNA fragment into a plasmid. When the recombinant DNA (plasmid + DNA fragment) is then inserted into a host cell, such as *E. coli*, it can replicate. A colony (clone) descendant from such a host cell therefore can be an excellent source of large quantities of the gene and/or its product. Many research laboratories maintain thousands to millions of colonies harbouring random DNA fragments from a common source. Such collections are called DNA libraries. A genomic DNA library contains DNA fragments derived from DNA extracted from the nuclear DNA. A cDNA library contains DNA copies of the mRNA obtained by the use of the enzyme reverse transcriptase. The major hurdle in the study of a specific gene is the ability to identify the colony in the library having that specific fragment. Identification is possible if the gene product is produced and readily detected or if a probe is used.

There is often a close relationship between advances in basic science and advances in technology. Significant applications of recombinant DNA technology are being made in such fields as agriculture, industry, and medicine.

Objectives

Having completed this chapter, you should be able to do the following:

1. Describe various programs of intervention into genetic systems and the biological and social implications of these programs.
2. Describe the cause of, effects of, possible solutions to, and treatments for such human genetic diseases as Tay-Sachs disease, hemophilia, the Down syndrome, Klinefelter's syndrome, Turner's syndrome, and spina bifida.
3. Describe chromosomal mutations.
4. Describe some of the techniques of genetic research that make genetic engineering possible.
5. Describe the applications of recombinant DNA technology to agriculture, industry, and medicine.

Vocabulary

eugenics	duplication	DNA library
trisomy	inversion	genetic marker
euploidy	amniocentesis	genomic DNA library
polyploidy	recombinant DNA	cDNA library
aneuploidy	clone	reverse transcriptase
translocation	restriction endonuclease	probe
deletion	replication origin	transgenic

Review Questions

1. List the common steps taken in genetic counselling.
2. (a) Give at least two examples of genetic disorders caused by
     (i) point mutation
     (ii) chromosomal mutation.
   (b) Describe the effect of each mutation.
3. (a) What is
     (i) euploidy?
     (ii) aneuploidy?
   (b) Of which one is the Down syndrome an example? Explain.
4. (a) What is
     (i) translocation?
     (ii) inversion?
   (b) Is a chromosomal mutation creating an inversion an example of aneuploidy? Explain.
5. (a) What is amniocentesis?
   (b) What types of information can be gained by amniocentesis?
6. How could the following genetic disorders be clinically detected in prenatal diagnosis?
   (a) Tay-Sachs disease
   (b) spina bifida
   (c) the Down syndrome
   (d) Turner's syndrome
7. Identify or explain the following:
   (a) recombinant DNA
   (b) restriction endonuclease
   (c) plasmid
   (d) reverse transcriptase
   (e) clone
   (f) probe
8. How is cDNA made?

9. How can a DNA fragment with blunt ends be inserted into a plasmid?
10. (a) What is a "DNA library"?
    (b) What is the difference between a "genomic DNA library" and a "cDNA library"?

11. Give an example of an application of recombinant DNA technology in each of the following areas:
    (a) agriculture
    (b) industry
    (c) medicine

Advanced Questions

1. What do you think would be good qualifications for a professional genetic counsellor?
2. (a) Why is amniocentesis not recommended for most pregnancies?
   (b) Under what circumstances has amniocentesis been recommended?
3. The study of a genomic DNA library reveals information that the study of a cDNA does not, and *vice versa*. Give examples of the kind of knowledge that can be gained by a study of each.
4. Should genetic research be restricted and controlled? If so,
   (a) What types of genetic research would you limit and why?
   (b) How should these decisions be made?

UNIT SIX

EVOLUTION

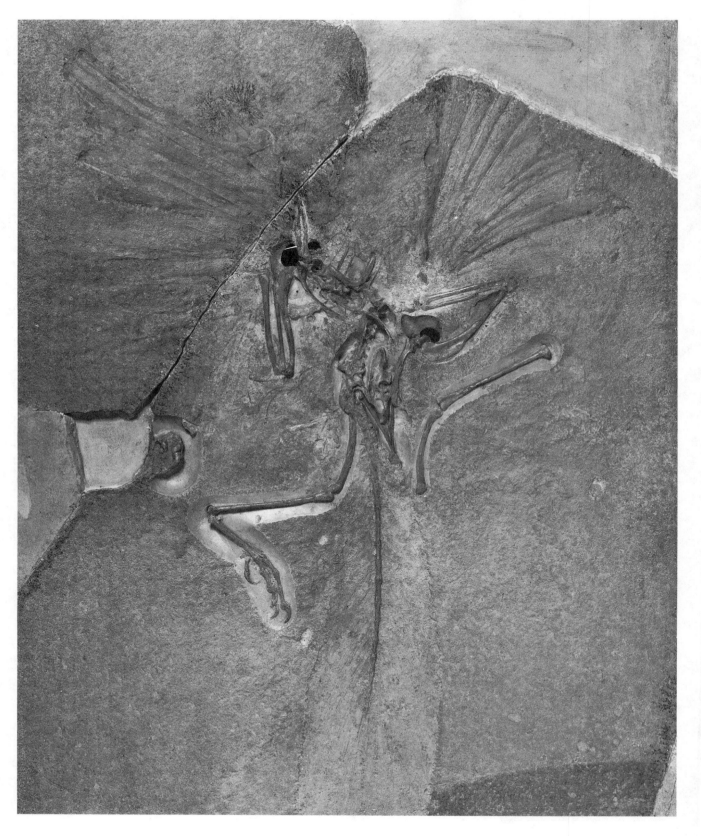

CHAPTER 19

EVIDENCE FOR ORGANIC EVOLUTION

Seen in the light of evolution, biology is, perhaps,
intellectually the most satisfying and inspiring science.
Without that light it becomes a pile of sundry facts—
some of them interesting or curious but making
no meaningful picture as a whole.

Th. Dobzhansky, 1973

*A*rchaeopteryx was a creature which lived in the time of the dinosaurs. Its fossilized form shows that, although feathered, it had teeth and a long, bony tail. In short, *Archaeopteryx* showed characteristics both of reptiles and of birds. It has led scientists to conclude that modern birds came from reptilian ancestors. In other words, some reptiles changed over time into birds.

This type of change, organic evolution, is one of the most interesting, controversial, and emotionally charged issues in science. It is also the single most important unifying concept in biology.

19.1 THE BACKGROUND OF THE THEORY OF EVOLUTION

Evolution—the idea that species of organisms might change through time — is not a recent notion. Even some thinkers of ancient Greece had proposed theories of organic evolution. Yet for the most part, it was not until the Enlightenment of eighteenth century Europe that the idea of biological change began to gain widespread acceptance in the scientific community. Not until the middle of the next century did the evidence for the mechanism of this change really come to light. What questions did scientists ask as they searched for this evidence? What methods did they use to find their answers?

Asking the Questions

The three basic questions asked by scientists with respect to evolution centered respectively on the three notions of organic *diversity*, *adaptation*, and *distribution*.

1. Why was there such a great diversity of organisms in the world? As merchants and colonists from Western Europe expanded their activities around the world, they brought back a bewildering diversity of plants and animals. It became evident that there existed thousands, perhaps even millions, of different kinds of organisms. Scientists began to ask why there were so many different kinds. Why was there so much variety in structure and behaviour among them? Why were different regions of the world occupied by different kinds of organisms?

2. How could the many and often quite remarkable adaptations of many living things be explained? As scholars carefully studied living things, they became increasingly impressed with how precisely structure, physiology, and behaviour seemed to be adjusted to fit the way of life of each creature. For example, they remarked that while most terrestrial vertebrates have heavy, thick bones, birds have hollow, light bones, that make it easier for them to fly (Figure 19.1). How could these adaptations have come to exist?

Figure 19.1
Sagittal section of a raven's humerus. Aerial birds, which fly, have hollow bones which are much lighter than bones of terrestrial animals. It is important for flying animals to be light in weight; the evolution of hollow bones in birds is apparently an adaptation for flight.

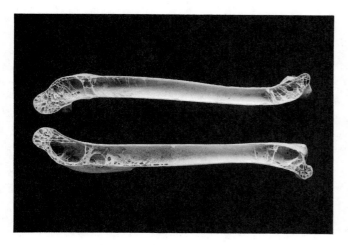

3. *Why were species of organisms distributed in the way that they were (and still are)?* As the world opened up to exploration and trade, people began to notice that there were different kinds of plants and animals ''doing the same thing'' in different parts of the world. For example, in the desert regions of the world there are many different kinds of plants well adapted to live in hot, dry conditions. But only in the Americas are the members of the cactus family found. Why is this so? Why is there not just one group of plants adapted to live in all deserts?

Finding the Answers

It is often difficult to make observations or devise experiments on the basis of a question. Rather, it is easier to provide a provisional answer or **hypothesis** which can then be tested. Scientists could not directly answer the question as to why are there so many different kinds of animals. Rather, they proposed an explanation. One's thinking might run something like this:

''I propose that the reason that there are so many different kinds of animals is [hypothesis]. If that is true, then I predict that [test of hypothesis.]''

The traditional answer to the question of why different kinds of creatures existed was *special creation*. In every human culture, there is a traditional explanation of the origin of life, specifically of human life, and of organic diversity. The Judeo-Christian tradition proposed that God created the diversity of organisms according to a general plan. Each species was precisely adjusted to the way of life for which it was created, and was *permanently fixed in form and characteristics through time.*

As scientists gathered more information about living things, it became increasingly evident to them that species were not fixed in form, but were changing, or *evolving*. The argument was put forth (1) that species were changing through time, and that modern species had evolved from extinct ancestral species. It followed (2) that similarities among organisms existed because they had descended from a common ancestor and dissimilarities were due to modification.

These notions exemplify an essential tool of the scientific method: the hypothesis. The notion of organic evolution (or descent with modification, as it is sometimes called) was not originally proposed as a hard, immediately verifiable answer to the questions of organic diversity. Rather, it was offered as a tentative answer, subject to verification. The validity of this hypothesis would depend on whether or not predictions made according to it could be verified. If so, the hypothesis was supported.

In the following sections of this chapter, you will study the predictions that scientists have derived from the hypothesis. The chapter will examine predictions based on the evidence from five sources: the biochemical similarities, the fossil record, geographic distribution, comparative anatomy, and embryology of organisms.

19.2 EVIDENCE FROM BIOCHEMICAL SIMILARITIES AMONG ORGANISMS

Prediction No. 1. If contemporary organisms are descended from a common ancestor, they should be highly similar at the molecular level.

Although there is tremendous diversity in the structure, behaviour, and physiology of organisms in the five kingdoms, there is a remarkable amount of molecular uniformity among them. Consider the following:

1. All cells are made up of the same basic types of organic compounds: nucleotides, proteins, lipids, and carbohydrates.

2. In all organisms, reactions involving these organic compounds are controlled by proteins known as enzymes.

3. In all cells, proteins are synthesized from about 20 known amino acids (even though other such acids may exist).

4. The major carbohydrate molecules of cells consist of six carbon sugars (such as glucose) and polymers of these (such as cellulose and starch).

5. All cells obtain energy by the breaking down of compounds (such as sugars) through the process of glycolysis (see Chapter 5). In most organisms, oxygen can be used as an electron acceptor in the breakdown of pyruvic acid to carbon dioxide and water. More energy is thus provided to convert ADP to ATP; in turn, glycolysis is made more efficient.

6. All cells contain DNA, a molecule that carries the coded information controlling the metabolism of the cell. This DNA also transmits the coded information to new cells.

7. DNA in all organisms determines the specificity of proteins through intermediate compounds (mRNA).

8. In all organisms, the structures of important lipids, proteins, and specialized molecules such as DNA, RNA, ATP, and some co-enzymes are similar.

9. The *genetic code* is virtually universal. In recent years, this biochemical unity has been dramatically shown in experiments in which the genes of structurally complex eukaryotes, such as human beings, have been incorporated successfully into the DNA of bacteria (see Chapter 18).

These biochemical similarities and others all point to a unity of life based upon descent with modification. The concept of organic evolution *predicts* that there will be molecular and metabolic similarities found among all living organisms, yet that there will be some molecular differences found as well. For example, some of the earliest organisms to live on the earth doubtless used anaerobic fermentation as a means of obtaining energy from organic compounds. Modern organisms retain this metabolic capability, but most have added to it. Aerobic metabolism was not possible on the surface of the young earth because the atmosphere was oxygen-free. As oxygen accumulated, however, aerobic respiration developed. The efficiency of this pathway provided cells with sufficient energy to grow larger and to become structurally more complex. Respiration was a prerequisite to the development of eukaryotic cells that would become the basic units of multicellular organisms. The eukaryotes carry the molecular fingerprint of their prokaryote origins; all eukaryotes possess a similarity of cell structure and metabolism that is evidence of their common origin.

Descent by modification is also exemplified by a comparison of the molecular structures of certain chemicals common to organisms. For example, consider the variation in the chemical structure of the hormone insulin. Insulin consists of two polypeptide chains bound to one another; one has 21 amino acids; the other, 30. The insulins of cattle and sheep—both hooved mammals in the same order—differ by only one amino acid. Cattle and horses, also both hooved animals but in different orders, differ by three amino acids. Among species less closely related than cattle and horses, there are greater differences in insulin molecules. For example, there are 16 different amino acids between mammals and cod fish. The shorter the time over which two species have been on separate evolutionary paths, the fewer the differences in such amino acid structures; by the same standard, the longer that time has been, the greater those differences. For example, the fossil record shows that horses and cattle probably shared a common ancestor less than 70 million years ago. Mammals and codfish, however, diverged from a common ancestor over 400 million years ago.

Cytochrome *c* is a respiratory enzyme that occurs in all eukaryotes as well as in some prokaryotes. The amino acid sequences of cytochrome *c* molecules have been determined for many species of organisms that are not closely related. From organism to organism, the length of the enzyme varies from 103 to 112 amino acids. Of these, 20 are the same in all of the organisms studied to date. However, there is variation in other amino acids (Figure 19.2). As is the case with insulin molecules, organisms thought to be closely related on the basis of their morphology have very similar cytochrome *c*, whereas those thought to be distantly related are more dissimilar in their amino acid sequences. For example, consider these three pairs. The chimpanzee and rhesus monkey are both in the same order of mammals, the primates; the chimpanzee and horse are both mammals, but in different orders; the chimpanzee and dogfish are in different vertebrate classes — one a mammal and the other a cartilaginous fish. In the first case, there is a difference of only one cytochrome *c* molecule; in the second case, of 11; in the third case of 24 (Figure 19.2).

Figure 19.2

The amino acid sequences of the cytochrome c molecule in 20 different organisms. Each letter refers to a different amino acid (e.g., G = glycine, V = valine). The cytochrome c of wheat is the longest molecule, with 112 amino acids; the others are numbered according to the wheat sequence. All vertebrates lack the first eight amino acids. At 20 positions, the same amino acid occurs in all of the organisms. The degree of similarity in sequences is very great between closely related species. For example, rhesus monkey and human differ only at position 66.

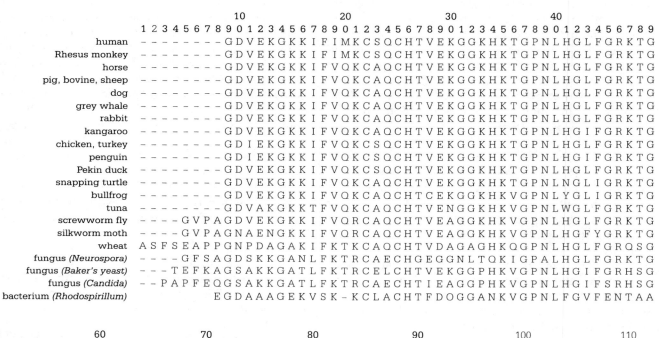

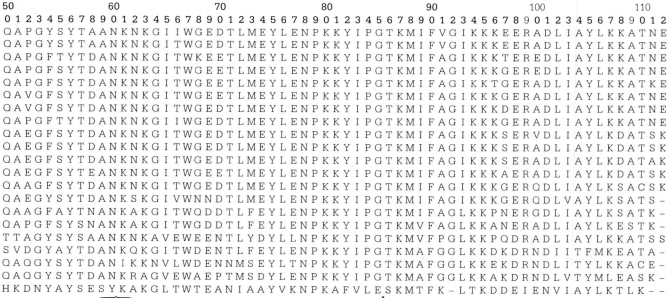

In general, closely related species are very similar at the molecular level. Indeed, for some molecules they are often identical. More distantly related species are more dissimilar at the molecular level, yet even they show some molecular similarities. This pattern of similarities and differences is as would be predicted if living organisms were evolving, each derived at some past time from the same ancestor. The similarities point to the historical unity of life, whereas the differences reflect the independent changes that have occurred in each *lineage* (ancestral species to descendant species) since its separation from other lineages derived from that common ancestor. This pattern would not be predicted to occur if each living species had been uniquely created for a specific purpose.

19.3 EVIDENCE FROM THE FOSSIL RECORD

Prediction No. 2. If life on earth has been evolving through time, then many extinct organisms would have been different from those living today.

These fossils provide a record, called a **fossil record**, of the kinds of organisms that lived in the past. Though some fossilized forms are very similar to those living today, most are different. For example, the fossils show that during the Carboniferous Period (Table 19.1), there were great forests of large tree-like club mosses and other spore-producing plants, unlike modern forests, which consist primarily of angiosperms or gymnosperms (Figure 19.3). The only ter-

Table 19.1   Geological Periods and Major Changes in Life on Earth

PERIOD/EPOCH	MILLIONS OF YEARS AGO	MAJOR CHANGES IN LIFE ON EARTH
Pleistocene	1.8–0.01	appearance of most modern species
Pliocene	5–1.8	appearance of *Australopithecus* and *Homo* and most modern vertebrate genera
Miocene	24–5	diversification of great apes
Oligocene	37–24	appearance of first monkeys; diversification of carnivores and seals
Eocene	58–37	appearance of first bats and whales
Paleocene	65–58	diversification of mammals
Cretaceous	144–65	diversification of flowering plants, birds, and dinosaurs; appearance of first snakes
Jurassic	213–144	appearance of first birds and pterosaurs; domination of land by conifers
Triassic	248–213	diversification of marine reptiles; appearance of first mammals and dinosaurs
Permian	286–248	diversification of reptiles
Carboniferous	360–286	formation of widespread coal swamps; appearance of first reptiles
Devonian	408–360	appearance of first amphibians (invasion of land by vertebrates), first fossils of insects, first bony and cartilaginous fishes
Silurian	438–408	appearance of first jawed fishes, land plants, and land animals (scorpions and perhaps insects)
Ordovician	505–438	diversification of jawless fishes; appearance of first vertebrates with skeletons
Cambrian	590–505	appearance of many marine invertebrates with exoskeletons, first amphioxus-like chordates, and in late Cambrian, first jawless fish
Proterozoic	2500–590	diversification of soft-bodied marine invertebrates
Archean	4600–2500	appearance of first bacteria and cyanobacteria
	4600	origin of earth; no life

Figure 19.3
In the Carboniferous Period (360 to 286 million years ago) tree club-mosses (such as shown here) and ferns would have been dominant plants in a forest. Late in the Carboniferous Period, the first cone-bearing plants appear in the fossil record. Flowering plants did not become dominant until the Cretaceous Period (144 to 65 million years ago).

restrial vertebrates living during the Carboniferous Period were amphibians and a few reptiles — all very different from any animals living today.

On the other hand, most recent fossils (those from the Pleistocene or Pliocene epochs) are of organisms much like, or indistinguishable from, living species. This evidence supports the hypothesis of organic evolution. Those forms living long ago would have had time to greatly change; those living only a few million years ago would have had little time to change.

Prediction No. 3. If evolution is occurring, one would expect to find only the "simpler" organisms in the older fossil-bearing strata, with the postulated descendants appearing in more recent rocks.

The very oldest fossils so far discovered and identified are those of stromatolites that lived about 3700 million years ago (Figure 19.4). Stromatolite fossils are sedimentary rocks formed by communities of prokaryotes, primarily cyanobacteria.

Figure 19.4
Stromatolites much like these are the earliest known organisms. They are produced as mat-like layers of cyanobacteria ("blue-green algae") and other prokaryotes.

There are also fossils of approximately the same age of other prokaryotes. Eukaryotes do not appear in the fossil record until about 700 million years ago.

If evolution occurs, one would predict that probable ancestors would appear *earlier* in the fossil record than probable descendants. This sequence is what paleontologists have found. They have observed that prokaryotes, dating from the Archean Period, precede eukaryotes in the fossil record. In rocks from the Cambrian Period (Table 19.1), paleontologists have seen forms that easily could have been the ancestors of most of the animals living today, including the earliest known chordates. Found in deposits from the Cambrian Period these chordates are similar to amphioxus, a "primitive" chordate that still lives today (Figure 19.5). Late in the Cambrian, about 505 million years

ago, they find fossils of jawless fishes which might have been the ancestors of other vertebrates (Figure 19.6). These jawless fishes in turn gave rise to the fishes with jaws, which did not appear in the fossil record until about 430 million years ago, during the Silurian Period. The jawed fishes then diversified; one group, the lobe-finned fishes, apparently gave rise to the amphibians. Lobe-fins of the sort that probably were ancestral to the amphibians (Figure 19.7) first appeared about 390 million years ago, during the middle Devonian Period. The first amphibians appeared about 10 million years later (Figure 19.8). The amphibians in turn gave rise to reptiles (Figure 19.9); the earliest reptile fossils are about 319 million years old. The descendants of early reptiles—modern reptiles, birds, and mammals—appeared later. If these forms were evolving, one would predict finding fossils of them in the following sequence: early chordata, jawless fish, jawed fishes, lobe-fins, amphibians, and reptiles. In fact, the fossil record shows precisely that sequence.

Figure 19.5
The earliest known chordate resembles the amphioxus that lives today.

Figure 19.6
Jamoytius, *one of the earliest-known fossil jawless fishes*

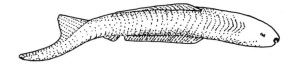

Figure 19.7
Eusthenopteron, *a Devonian lobe-finned fish*

Figure 19.8
Eryops, *an early amphibian*

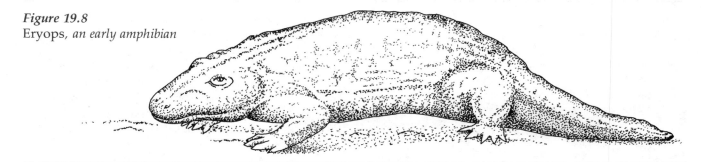

Figure 19.9
Cephalerpeton, *an early reptile*

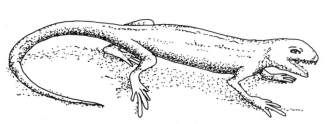

Figure 19.10
The structure of Ichthyostega *is intermediate between that of lobe-finned fishes and that of early amphibians. It has four legs with which it could have walked on land, but retains a tail fin.*

Prediction No. 4. If evolution has occurred, one would expect to find evidence that organisms living in the past have changed, producing those that live today. This evidence would consist of a fossil record for creatures intermediate in characteristics between very ancient ones and ones living today. If, for example, early amphibians evolved from certain lobe-finned fishes, one would predict finding fossils of animals intermediate between lobe-fins and amphibians, between amphibians and early reptiles, between reptiles and birds, and so on.

Although the fossil record is not complete, paleontologists have found many of these intermediate creatures, the so-called "missing links." The earliest amphibians were far different in structure from any that live today. The earliest known kind is *Ichthyostega*, found in Greenland in deposits from the Devonian Period (Figure 19.10). Apart from the absence of median fins and the presence of short, sturdy legs, these early amphibians closely resemble their lobe-fin ancestors.

Reptiles of the sort that gave rise to all modern reptiles and their descendants (such as birds and mammals) are long extinct. These are often called "stem reptiles" and are placed in the order Cotylosauria. Several major groups were derived from cotylosaurs, including the turtles, the archosaurs (including birds, alligators, and dinosaurs), snakes and lizards, mam-

mals, and some extinct groups such as ichthyosaurs and plesiosaurs. *Seymouria* (Figure 19.11) is a good example of an animal intermediate between amphibians and reptiles.

Fossils of *Seymouria* appear only as early as the Permian Period (about 340 million years ago), too recently for *Seymouria* to have been the actual ancestor of the reptiles. *Seymouria* does show us that animals intermediate between amphibians and reptiles once lived. What is known about *Seymouria* shows it to be so intermediate between these two groups that it cannot be placed with certainty in either one. If it were found that *Seymouria* laid its eggs on land, it would be a reptile *by definition.* Conversely, were *Seymouria* shown to have laid its eggs in the water, it would be an amphibian by definition.

Perhaps the most famous "missing link" is the reptile-bird, *Archaeopteryx* (page 378). It had characteristics both of birds and of a group of reptiles known as archosaurs. Archaeopteryx had feathers, and therefore by definition it was a bird. Yet the skeleton of *Archaeopteryx* is in general more like that of archosaurians than of modern birds. Although no *living* bird has teeth, Archaeopteryx and several other fossil birds from the Cretaceous Period did. Archaeopteryx had a long reptilian bony tail, while modern birds have most of their tail vertebrae fused into a single bone, with the "tail" being only feathers.

Figure 19.11
The earliest reptiles probably looked much like Seymouria, *shown here.*

There are many other examples of links in the fossil record. Most of the major groups of chordates, for example, are connected by intermediate species. *Eusthenopteron* (Figure 19.7) and *Cephalerpeton* (Figure 19.9) are other examples of species that link major groups. *Jamoytius* (Figure 19.6), resembles a "missing link," but appears too late in the fossil record to be an actual ancestor to jawless fishes. There are fossils that link the mammal-like reptiles with the earliest mammals; as well, many of the lineages of mammals can easily be followed in the fossil record (the horse lineage will be discussed in section 19.5). The record is not complete and probably never will be. Much of our fossilized past lies below inaccessible areas; some forms may have never been fossilized. The available record, however, is all consistent with the theory of evolution.

19.4 EVIDENCE FROM THE GEOGRAPHIC DISTRIBUTION OF ORGANISMS

Prediction No. 5. If the hypothesis of evolution is correct, then the organisms that live in any area (the biota of that area) would be made up of two different sorts: those that have moved into the area from the outside by dispersal (by flying, walking, swimming, floating in the water, or being carried in by other organisms); and those that have evolved from species already living in the area. It takes time for species to evolve major differences; therefore, one would predict closely related species to be usually found in areas geographically close to each other (that is, they would not have had time to disperse to distant parts of the world). Because it is difficult for species to disperse across an ocean, most of the species present on a given continent or island would be more similar to species that lived there in the past than to other species living in environmentally similar areas in other parts of the world.

The patterns of geographic distribution of organisms are complex, but as a general rule biologists find that closely related species occur in the same general region. For example, there are many groups of plants and animals that are only found in the Americas. As mentioned earlier, the cacti are native to the Americas in their distribution. The few cacti found in other parts of the world have arrived there only recently, either by people bringing the actual plants or by birds carrying the seeds. See Figure 19.12(a). Within the cactus family, the species in the genus *Cereus* are found only in the southwestern United States and in adjacent areas of Mexico. The giant saguaro and organ-pipe cacti are two members of this genus that you may recognize. See Figure 19.12(b).

Tanagers are medium-sized songbirds found only in the Americas. Living mostly in woodlands, they eat fruit, insects, and seeds. In other parts of the world, various species of birds not closely related to tanagers live in similar habitats, eat similar foods, and in general, "fill the tanager niche." The vast majority of tanager species are found only in South America. However, three species are found north of Mexico, and they are all closely related (Figure 19.13). This pattern of distribution would be predicted if the first tanagers evolved in South America and later moved northward. All three species of tanagers found north of Mexico almost certainly descended from a single species from Latin America.

If the biota were designed for the environment, and the species fixed in form, why would the species living in the Americas be so different from those living in Australia, Eurasia, or Africa? Why would not tanagers be in all tropical and temperate forests, and cacti in all deserts?

Figure 19.12
*Prickly-pear cacti such as in (a) have been introduced into arid regions of Africa and Australia, where they are thriving. However, prior to introduction, the members of the cactus family were virtually restricted to the Americas. Organ-pipe Cactus (*Cereus thurberi*) and the Saguaro (*Cereus giganteus*) (b) are closely related species, both living in the southwest United States and adjacent Mexico.*

(a)

(b)

Figure 19.13
*The scarlet tanager (*Piranga olivacea*) is the most common tanager in eastern Canada.*

Prediction No 6. Islands have been colonized most likely by organisms that dispersed from the nearest mainland. Once on an island, the colonizing species, which may be *isolated*, may evolve in different ways from its relatives on the mainland. Thus, one would generally expect island species to be different from adjacent mainland ones, but more similar to species in these areas than to those in other, more distant areas of the world. Because they would have had time to evolve, the species on very old islands may be quite different from mainland ones. Species on recently formed islands would be only slightly differentiated.

Madagascar, off the east coast of Africa, is a large island that has not been connected to the African mainland for a long time (Figure 19.14). Madagascar probably first split off the African continent over 150 million years ago. However, periodic fluctuations in the water level may have resulted in its being reconnected from time to time until the Eocene Period (about 50 million years ago). Today, the channel between Madagascar and the African mainland is nowhere less than 400 km wide, and is at least 1900 m deep. Thus, species reaching the island must have done so by crossing the water, at least during the last 50 million years.

Madagascar has 184 species of birds, divided into 133 genera. Of these, 125 species and 46 genera are not found anywhere else in the world and thus are unique or **endemic** to Madagascar (Figure 19.15). Many species of large waterbirds, such as ducks and herons, are found both in Madagascar and in Africa (400 km is not much of a flight for a duck). However,

Figure 19.14
The location of Madagascar and the Canary Islands

Figure 19.16
The ring-tailed lemur (Lemur catta) *is one of 20 species of lemurs living today on Madagascar.*

Figure 19.15
The brown mesite (Mesoenas unicolor) *is a member of a family of birds found only on Madagascar. Its nearest relatives are rails and cranes. Perhaps the most spectacular of the birds that were endemic to Madagascar were the now-extinct elephant birds. The largest species of elephant bird was about 450 kg, stood 3 m tall, and laid eggs that had a capacity of 9 L. They went extinct less than 1000 years ago.*

approximately 90 percent of the small land birds on Madagascar—those that would be the most unlikely to cross the water—are found only there. There are four families of birds endemic to the island. On the other hand, there are 12 families of birds found on mainland Africa that are absent from Madagascar *even though there is suitable habitat for them on the island*. Woodpeckers, for example, are not found on Madagascar even though many areas are extensively forested. Woodpeckers are birds that rarely fly very far over water and therefore apparently have not crossed from Africa to become established on Madagascar.

The mammals of Madagascar are also distinct, there being four endemic families and at least 34 endemic genera. For example Madagascar is today the only place in the world that the primates called lemurs (family Lemuridae) are found (Figure 19.16). The fossil record indicates that lemurs were once widespread, first appearing about 65 million years ago. At that time, there were no Old World monkeys on the earth; the lemurs seem to have occupied the ecological position that is today filled by monkeys. Again, the fossil

Figure 19.17
The chaffinch (Fringilla coelebs) is one of the most common birds of Europe. Chaffinches have invaded the Canary Islands at least twice. The descendants of the earlier invasion have evolved several noticeable differences from the mainland forms, and are recognized as a different species, the blue chaffinch (Fringilla teydea). The white wing bars that are distinctive on mainland chaffinches are greatly reduced in blue chaffinches, whose head, back, and breast are bluish-grey in colour. Male chaffinches have a bluish-grey cap, but the back and breast are rusty brown. The descendants of the more recent invasion of Chaffinches to the Canary Islands are little different from their mainland ancestors. Nonetheless, they have evolved slightly larger bills and shorter legs.

Chaffinch

Blue Chaffinch

record indicates that the monkeys did not come into existence until the Oligocene Epoch, about 35 million years ago. By that time, however, Madagascar was separated from Africa. The monkeys apparently have never been able to cross the water and colonize the island. It seems that the monkeys were more successful than the lemurs in other parts of the world and drove them to extinction. Lemurs are left only on Madagascar, where they did not have to compete with monkeys.

Unlike Madagascar, the Canary Islands off the northwest coast of Africa are of rather recent origin (10–15 million years old) and the forests on the islands are only about 5 million years old. There are 53 species of birds known to breed on these islands and only two of these are endemic there. There are no endemic genera or families of birds; all of the species are similar to species that breed in adjacent areas on mainland Africa (Figure 19.17). The Canary Islands are volcanic in origin and probably have never been connected to the mainland. There are no strictly freshwater fishes, snakes, or land mammals (except bats) on the islands. The eight species of lizards found there are all similar to west African species, though sufficiently different that some are recognized as different species. It is likely that the lizards drifted there from mainland Africa on floating pieces of wood but had little time to change.

If evolution were occurring, these are the patterns of distribution of animals on Madagascar and the Canary Islands that one would *expect* to find. Biologists have indeed found what the hypothesis predicts. Long isolated from mainland areas, the animals on Madagascar show evidence of having descended from mainland species, yet many are greatly modified. Animals on the relatively young Canary Islands are only slightly different from mainland forms.

19.5 EVIDENCE FROM COMPARATIVE ANATOMY

Prediction No. 7. If members of a group such as the chordates evolved from a common ancestor, then they should show many similarities in structure.

If species have descended from a common ancestor, within each lineage previously existing structures should show modifications to reflect new adaptations that have occurred through time within that lineage. In other words, the "old" structures should show modifications to meet new needs. **Vestigial** organs—reduced, often functionless remnants of organs that were more prominent in ancestors—would also show evidence of this descent. Consider the bones in the front legs (pectoral appendages) of terrestrial vertebrates. At first glance, these appear to be quite variable and very different from those of fish fins. However, the bones reveal remarkable similarities in basic structure among vertebrates. In all terrestrial vertebrates, the bones are divided into four major regions. Closest to the body, there is always a single bone (the humerus) that connects to the bones of the shoulder (the pectoral girdle). In the middle region, there are two bones (the radius and ulna). In the third region, the "hand," there are several bones (carpals and metacarpals). Lastly, there are the digits, or "fingers."

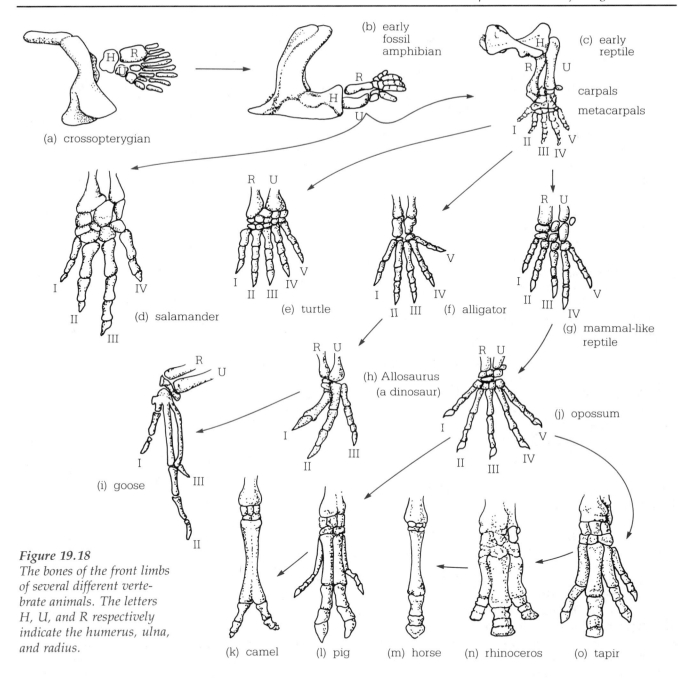

(b) early fossil amphibian

(c) early reptile

carpals

metacarpals

I II III IV V

(a) crossopterygian

R U

R U

(d) salamander

I II III IV

(e) turtle

I II III IV V

(f) alligator

I II III IV V

R U

(g) mammal-like reptile

I II III IV V

R U

(h) Allosaurus (a dinosaur)

I II III

R U

(j) opossum

I II III IV V

R U

(i) goose

I II III

Figure 19.18
The bones of the front limbs of several different vertebrate animals. The letters H, U, and R respectively indicate the humerus, ulna, and radius.

(k) camel   (l) pig   (m) horse   (n) rhinoceros   (o) tapir

As you learned earlier, the fossil record indicates that the ancestor to terrestrial vertebrates was a crossopterygian (lobe-fin) fish. If you look at the bones in the pectoral fin of a Devonian crossopterygian, you see a single bone, the humerus, connected to the shoulder girdle. See Figure 19.18(a). There are two other bones, the radius and ulna, which are connected to the humerus. Last, there are a number of small bones in the "hand" of the lobe-fin. Early fossil amphibians have a somewhat modified and enlarged humerus, radius, and ulna, as well as 12 bones in the hand (carpals and metacarpals), plus five fingers or *digits*. See Figure 19.18(b). The 12 bones of the hand consist of three that connect with the radius and ulna, one at the base of each of the five digits, and four in between. There are sometimes two but usually three bones in each digit. Because of the fusion of elements in all modern amphibians, there are fewer bones and one less finger. See Figure 19.18(d).

The forelimb of the earliest reptiles is very like that of the early amphibians. See Figure 19.18(c). From such an ancestor, there were several different lines of differentiation. See Figure 19.18(e), (f), and (g). The forelimbs of turtles, "primitive" archosaurs, and mammal-like reptiles are basically like the ancestor, with five digits, and some specialization, fusion, or loss of the carpals and metacarpals. The forelimb of the modern alligator is much like that of the earliest archosaurs. In many "advanced" archosaurs, such as the carnivorous dinosaur *Allosaurus*, there is a reduction in the number of fingers. See Figure 19.18(h).The ancestor to modern birds probably had only three fingers (like the flesh-eating dinosaur, *Allosaurus*). All modern birds have only three highly modified fingers, reflecting specialization for flight. See Figure 19.18(i).

The basic number of five digits is retained in many modern mammals, such as opossums, cats, and humans. See Figure 19.18(j). Within mammals, however, there have been many interesting modifications of the hand region. The earliest mammals were probably arboreal (that is, they lived in trees at least part of the time). For these mammals, the first digit (the thumb) became more or less opposable (capable of being placed opposite the fingers) and hence useful for grasping branches. As some mammals moved out of the trees, an opposable thumb was of little importance and was lost in many terrestrial, "running" species.

Consider the ungulates (hoofed mammals). There are two groups of ungulates, the artiodactyls (antelopes, cows, camels, pigs) and the perissodactyls (horses, tapirs, rhinoceroses). They have developed from different ancestors. In both groups specific modifications of the feet (front and hind) reflect adaptations to running. There is a considerable elongation of the metacarpals and a reduction in the number of digits. The ancestors to both groups originally lost the thumb and subsequently lost additional toes.

The foot of the pig, like that of an early artiodactyl, has four toes. See Figure 19.18(l). The foot of a camel is like that of a more "advanced" (and recent) artiodactyl. See Figure 19.18(k). Although both pigs and camels live today, the foot of the pig has evolved less than that of the camel because of different environmental pressures selecting for change. In the perissodactyls, the four-toed condition is still present in the tapir, an ungulate of the jungles of tropical America.

Figure 19.19

The front feet of four species of "horses." The Eocene ancestor was Hyracotherium *(a). Horse feet from the early and late Miocene Epoch are shown respectively in (b) and (c). The hoof of the modern horse (*Equus*) is shown in (d).*

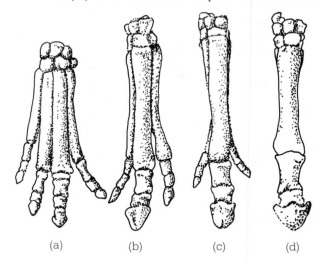

(a)   (b)   (c)   (d)

See Figure 19.18(o). In the tapir the third toe is the largest, and carries most of the weight of the animal. In the rhinoceros the fifth digit has been lost and the third digit is the largest, again bearing most of the weight of the animal. See Figure 19.18(n). In modern horses, the fifth toe has been lost, and the second and fourth toes have been reduced to virtually invisible vestigial splints in adults. See Figure 19.18(m). A few horses retain side toes as adults.

The general similarity in foot structure of all artiodactyls or perissodactyls is to be expected if living species have evolved from a common ancestor. These animals all carry some of the features of that ancestor. The *differences* among the feet of living ungulates indicate that each modern species has evolved feet that differ perhaps only slightly, but in some cases quite considerably, from those of that common ancestor.

The fossil record of the horses is extensive and clearly shows the changes that occurred through time in the feet of the horses. An early perissodactyl, *Hyracotherium*, lived during the Eocene Epoch. See Figure 19.19(a). On the basis of its structures, *Hyracotherium* could be ancestral to any modern perissodactyl—horse, rhinoceros, or tapir. It still retained four toes on its front foot, but had only three on its hind foot. Prior to the idea of evolution, the presence of vestigial toes in horses was difficult for people to understand. However, these vestiges are easily understood if horses were descended from a many-toed ancestor.

The many muscles that cover the bones of the limbs of tetrapods (animals having four limbs) can be shown to be essentially similar to the basic muscles on the upper and lower surfaces of a fish's fin. As well, the basic patterns of the nerves and blood vessels are comparable in all tetrapods. This pattern is what one would predict if all of these animals were descended from a common ancestor, each form modified to a specific habitat or lifestyle. Not all hoofed mammals are the same. Many have become independently specialized for speedy locomotion. But they started with the same basic limbs and the same five digits. In a parallel but different manner these features were modified to enable more efficient and rapid running in species in both groups.

19.6 EVIDENCE FROM EMBRYOLOGY

Prediction No. 8. If members of a major group such as the chordates evolved from a common ancestor, then their **embryology** (early development) should be similar. Related species would share not only adult features but also embryonic ones. This prediction has helped answer a number of questions. Why does development take what at times seems such a roundabout, indirect path to adult structure? Why do many structures that appear in the embryonic stage serve no apparent purpose? Why are these same structures absent in the adult?

In the embryonic development of fishes, the notochord appears as a "rod" of tissue like that present in Amphioxus. Later in development, bone develops in the area where the notochord had once held the developing embryo rigid. Within adult fishes, there is much variability in the extent to which the notochord has been replaced by bone. In some "primitive" forms, the notochord is still extensive.

During early embryology all vertebrates also develop a notochord as well as gill slits and a tail. Furthermore, they pass through stages in which they resemble larval amphioxus, then larval fishes. As the embryo develops, the gill slits are greatly modified; in adults, only one remains — the ear canal. The notochord becomes greatly modified and in adult mammals is retained only as the discs between the vertebrae.

During their embryology, baleen whales (toothless whales that filter food from the water using "whalebone") temporarily develop teeth as well as body hair. The appearance of these features in the embryos sup-

ports the hypothesis that the ancestors of whales had teeth and hair.

The details of the embryological development of some organ systems are impressive. During the embryology of all vertebrates, a series of aortic arches (generally six) develop as a major part of the embryo's circulatory system. Each runs unbroken from the ventral aorta to the dorsal aorta, much as do the numerous arches in both adult and larval amphioxus. In fishes, these six arches are modified in a number of different ways. During the development of the embryo, the arches become modified to form a bed of capillaries around the gill slits so that blood coming from the heart passes through the ventral aorta, through the capillaries, and into the dorsal aorta, from where it is distributed throughout the body. In the adults, it is mostly these gill capillaries that pick up oxygen from the water.

During the embryology of many vertebrates, various vessels become reduced in size and disappear. Others become diverted to different parts of the body. In lungfish, the sixth arch gives rise to the pulmonary artery, which supplies blood to the lungs. See Figure 19.20(a). In the lungfish, and doubtless in the ancestors of the terrestrial vertebrates, the lungs are the most important site of gas exchange in adults. The gills are non-functional (at least for gas exchange). In the terrestrial vertebrates, the first, second, and fifth arches are lost completely. Blood entering the sixth arch must come through the pulmonary artery. The third arch becomes the carotid artery that carries blood to the head. In mammals, the right side of the fourth arch is lost, leaving only the left side — the aortic arch. See Figure 19.20(g). The blood is pumped from the heart, through the aortic arch, and to the various organs of the body. In birds, the opposite occurs: the left side is lost and the right retained, but otherwise the pattern is the same. See Figure 19.20(f). The bird and mammalian systems evolved independently from different reptilian ancestors that possessed both left and right fourth arches.

The embryological development of vertebrate kidneys also provides an excellent example of how embryology can help us understand phylogeny (Figure 19.21). In the early embryos of all vertebrates, a kidney called the *pronephros* develops in the anterior portion of the body cavity. Later, the pronephros is replaced by a second, middle kidney, the *mesonephros*. In fishes and amphibians the mesonephros is retained in the adults, whereas in reptiles, birds, and mammals it is not. Near the end of the embryonic stage in these

Figure 19.20

During its embryology, any terrestrial vertebrate first develops a series of aortic arches; as the organism develops, these arches are modified so that at various stages in its embryology it progressively resembles many of the patterns illustrated here.

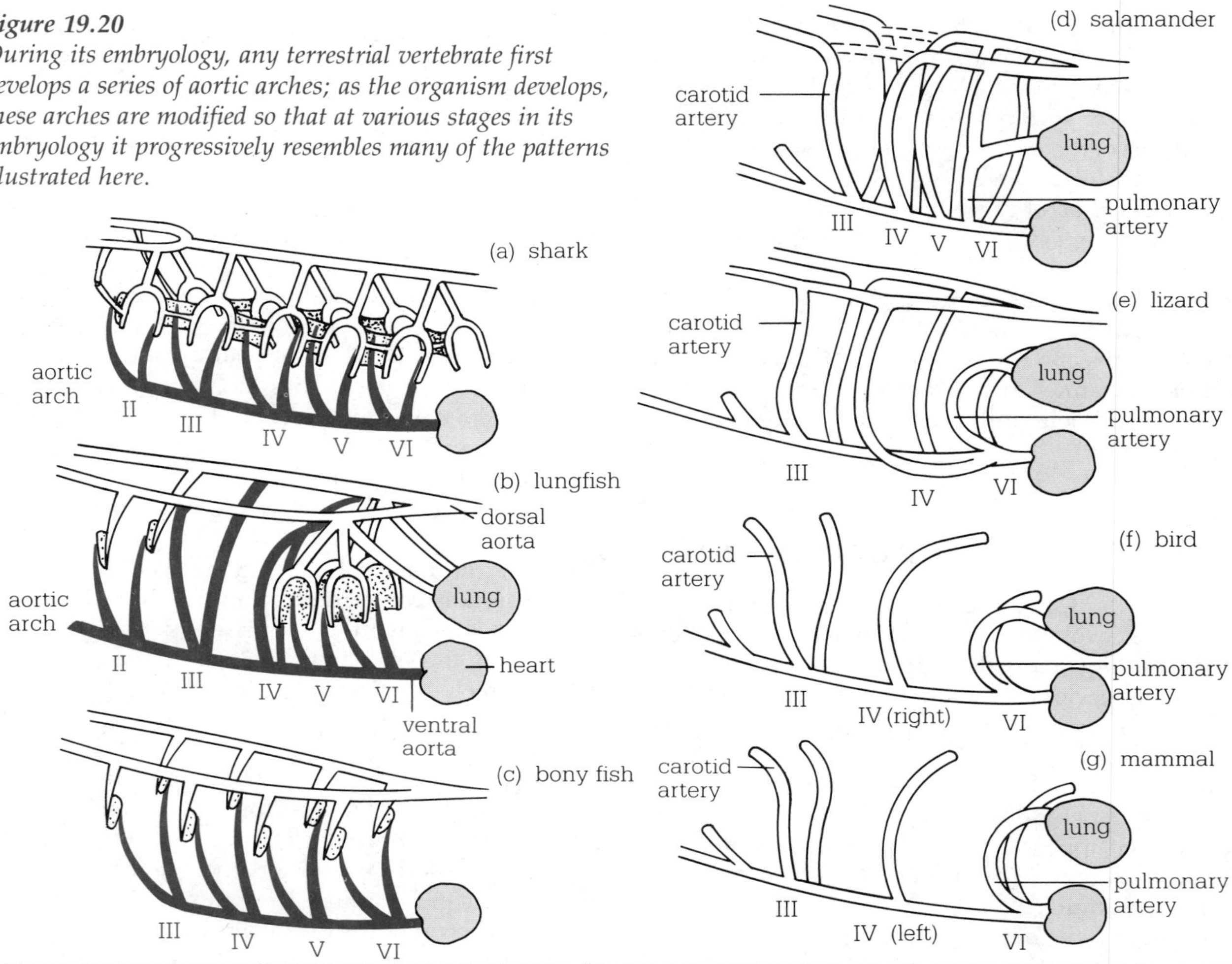

(a) shark

aortic arch

II   III   IV   V   VI

(b) lungfish

dorsal aorta

aortic arch

II   III   IV   V   VI

lung

heart

ventral aorta

(c) bony fish

III   IV   V   VI

(d) salamander

carotid artery

lung

pulmonary artery

III   IV   V   VI

(e) lizard

carotid artery

lung

pulmonary artery

III   IV   VI

(f) bird

carotid artery

lung

pulmonary artery

III   IV (right)   VI

(g) mammal

carotid artery

lung

pulmonary artery

III   IV (left)   VI

Figure 19.21 ▶

Shown here are pronephros (a), mesonephros (b), and metanephros (c). In male terrestrial vertebrates, the embryological mesonephric duct is retained in adults as the vas deferens, the duct that carries sperm from the testis. A new duct, the ureter, develops to carry the urine.

three classes, a third kidney known as the *metanephros* develops. It is the functional kidney in adult reptiles, birds, and mammals.

Without the concept of evolution, the development of the pronephros and metanephros kidneys observed in the embryology of reptiles, birds, and mammals would have no explanation. Neither would the development of gill slits, multiple aortic arches, or a notochord in the embryos of terrestrial vertebrates. The embryos indicate the ancestral condition, just as the embryology indicates the history of change in the species.

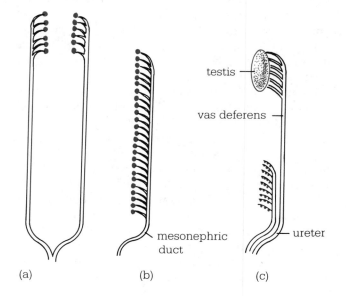

testis

vas deferens

mesonephric duct

ureter

(a)   (b)   (c)

19.7 THE CONCEPT OF EVOLUTION

From evidence such as that presented above, it is clear that organic evolution *has* occurred, is occurring, and presumably will continue to occur. People often refer to the "theory of evolution," and in some minds the word "theory" implies that organic evolution is a dubious proposition. Although some "theories" are no more than working hypotheses, the theory of evolution is not. Like the "cell theory" or the "theory of gravitation" it is a useful synthesis of knowledge from many different fields. The theory of gravitation tells us that there is a mutual attraction of bodies. This theory is a "fact" even though we do not understand just what it is that actually pulls bodies together. In a similar way, species of organisms have changed through time. We do not understand all of the mech-anisms that have caused this change; and we do not know and perhaps cannot discover many of the details. The theory of evolution has the same limita-tion as *all* theories in natural science: unlike theories in mathematics, it cannot be proven without any doubt. It can only be — and has been — demonstrated to be true beyond reasonable doubt. Because the word "theory" suggests something that is perhaps doubt-ful, it might be better to use the word "concept," and refer to the "concept of evolution." Organic evolution is not a dubious proposition. It is a logical and nec-essary deduction from the scientific study of the pat-terns of the diversity of living things and their features. Organisms have evolved and are evolving today.

CHAPTER SUMMARY

The idea of organic evolution has been fundamental to modern biology. It has sought to answer questions about the diversity, adaptation, and distribution of dif-ferent life forms on earth. These answers have arisen from the formulation of hypotheses — and the inves-tigation of predictions based on these hypotheses.

One prediction was for similarities at the molecular level in contemporary organisms. The supporting evi-dence has involved, among other things, the similarity of DNA structure and protein synthesis in all organ-isms. Another prediction concerned the differences between extinct and contemporary organisms; evi-dence confirming it has come from the fossil record. A third prediction, that closely related species would be found in areas geographically near each other, has been borne out by comparative studies of life forms in different parts of the world. Another prediction was for similarity of body structure in species descended from a common ancestor. Again, the fossil record sup-ports the prediction. A fifth prediction was for the similarity of embryonic development in species derived from a common ancestor. The confirming evi-dence here comes from studies of both extinct and contemporary life forms.

The evidence is all consistent with predictions based on the hypothesis that species of organisms evolve. There can be no reasonable doubt that organic evo-lution occurs.

Objectives

Having completed this chapter, you should be able to do the following:

1. Outline how the formulation of hypotheses was essential to the development of the notion of organic evolution.
2. Describe five predictions that support and are explained by the theory of organic evolution.
3. Discuss how the evidence for these predictions has established evolution as a biological fact.
4. Differentiate among empirical facts, hypotheses, and theories, and describe the origin and devel-opment of scientific theories.

Vocabulary

evolution	fossil record	vestigial
hypothesis	endemic	embryology

Review Questions

1. (a) What were the first organisms to live on the earth?
   (b) How might they, and organisms like them, have made it possible for eukaryotes to have evolved?
2. The respiratory enzyme cytochrome *c* occurs in all eukaryotes. Discuss how the differences in the sequence of amino acids that make up this molecule in different kinds of organisms help us understand evolution.
3. In what obvious ways would a forest in the Carboniferous Period differ from a forest today?
4. How do "missing links" help us to understand evolutionary events that have taken place in the distant past?
5. Why are cacti essentially restricted in their distribution to the New World?
6. Why are there many endemic forms on the island of Madagascar, but few in the Canary Islands?
7. How do vestigial organs help us understand the relationships among contemporary species?
8. Baleen whales, such as the grey whale (*Eschrichtius robustus*) of the Pacific Ocean, lack teeth and body hair as adults but possess these features while embryos. What does this fact indicate about their ancestry?

Advanced Questions

1. Sometimes similar structures or adaptations evolve independently in different lineages of animals that are not closely related. This pattern of development is called *convergence*. For example, both bats and birds have evolved the ability to fly; and in both cases, there has been special modification of some of the bones of the forelimbs and hands, although there are many differences in detail between a bird's wing and a bat's wing. The common ancestor of birds and bats probably lived early in the Permian Period, over 250 million years ago.
   (a) What are some other examples of convergence?
   (b) Given the hypothesis of evolution, would you have predicted that convergence would occur?
2. Starlings and house sparrows were introduced into North America. Both of these species nest in cavities in trees or in bird houses. Since their introduction, both species have become common in North America; they compete for nesting places with other hole nesting birds such as bluebirds and woodpeckers. Because of this competition, the numbers of bluebirds and some woodpeckers have greatly declined. Discuss what you would predict to be the consequences of the introduction of
   (a) cacti to the deserts of Africa
   (b) monkeys to Madagascar
   (c) woodpeckers to Madagascar.
3. In human organ transplants, the rates of success (that is, the acceptance by the recipient's body of the donated organ) are much higher in cases where the donor and the recipient are close relatives. Why?
4. Select one of the geological periods listed in Table 19.1 (page 383). Research what paleontologists have found about the organisms living during that period.

CHAPTER 20

THE DEVELOPMENT OF A THEORY OF EVOLUTION

. . . it at once struck me that under these circumstances [the struggle for existence] favourable variations would tend to be preserved, and unfavourable ones to be destroyed. The result of this would be the formation of new species. Here, then, I had at last got a theory by which to work.

Charles Darwin

Before the middle of the nineteenth century, the idea of organic evolution was present in Western thought but had failed to gain a wide acceptance. This failure was in most part attributable to three factors. First, the idea of an unchanging universe was entrenched in Western thought; for centuries, scholars had assumed that life forms stayed exactly as they were first created. Second, evolution was occurring so slowly that animal and plant species appeared to be fixed in form. Last, the mechanisms that had been proposed as causes of evolution were unconvincing.

It was the idea of natural selection, developed in the work of Charles Darwin (shown left) and Alfred Wallace, that would give the theory of organic evolution the element it needed to make its case convincing. In this chapter you will examine some of the discoveries and insights that ultimately led to the formulation of the theory of evolution by natural selection. Some of the modern refinements of Darwin's theory will then be discussed.

20.1 DARWIN'S THEORY OF NATURAL SELECTION

In 1858, when Darwin and Wallace proposed that *natural selection* was a mechanism by which evolution could occur, evidence of such change was accumulating. Astronomers had shown that the universe was not stable; new stars appeared and old ones vanished from view. Geologists had evidence that new mountains arose and old ones apparently wore away by the forces of erosion. More and more, it seemed that long term *change* rather than *stability* might be the norm. If the solar system and the earth's surface were ancient and gradually changing, perhaps species changed as well.

In 1858, Darwin and Wallace presented their theory of evolution by natural selection. Darwin's major work, *On the Origin of Species*, was published the following year. To state it briefly, Darwin and Wallace noted that there was variability in populations of organisms; not all individuals of a species were alike. Further, some individuals were better able to obtain food, mates, and other resources than others of the same species, and these individuals would produce more offspring than the less able individuals. Some characteristics were passed on to the offspring; consequently, the features of successful individuals would be disproportionately represented in future generations. Individuals in future generations would then tend to have the features of the successful individuals; through time, this process could bring about substantial changes, or *evolution*, in the population.

In many ways, the time was right for such a theory. Selective breeding was enabling farmers to create new vegetable crops and livestock strains. It was increasingly obvious that some species had, in the past, gone extinct. Geologists were arguing that the earth was millions of years old, not merely a few thousand. Perhaps most importantly, it was becoming clear that each different continent or island had its own unique species of plants and animals (a fact, as you will recall from the previous chapter, that is central evidence for the idea of evolution).

Nonetheless, Darwin and Wallace deserve considerable credit for brilliant and original insights. Because there was little physical evidence, the fact of evolution was much less clear then than it is today. At the time, the fossil record was only beginning to be uncovered and did not give a clear picture of the relationship between extinct and modern species. In many cases, it was not evident that these fossils were extinct species, some of them the ancestors of living ones. As well, since the mechanism of inheritance was not understood, there was no knowledge of the molecular basis of life; indeed, living species *appeared* to be unchanging. To the scientist and ordinary person alike, today's robins appeared to be just the same as last year's and just the same as they had always been.

Figure 20.1
Using his telescope, Galileo learned that objects in the heavens were in motion, not fixed and unchanging.

The general acceptance of the theory of natural selection was impeded by two implications of that theory. First, it implied that humans are not a "special" species. Copernicus (1473–1543) had demonstrated that the earth did not occupy a special position as the centre of the universe. A century later, Galileo (1564–1642) had further demonstrated that the universe was not stationary, but revolved (Figure 20.1). At the time, these ideas met widespread opposition because they showed that the earth was not the fixed centre of the universe. Just as the work of Copernicus and Galileo seemed to deny a unique position to the earth in the order of physical things, so Darwin's work seemed to deny a special place for humans in the order of living things. Second, natural selection flew in the face of attempts to explain organic diversity in terms of "purposes" or "final causes." The traditional thinking had been that every species existed to fulfill some important function — to play a vital role in a grand plan for the universe. For example, it was thought that wolves were created with the purpose of keeping the numbers of deer in check. Natural selection suggested that the hunting behaviour of wolves had evolved as a struggle among wolves for food. In short, just as Newton (1642–1727) had shown material causes to be sufficient to explain physical phenomena, natural selection implied that material causes were sufficient to explain organic phenomena.

20.2 THE IMPLICATIONS OF PLATONIC PHILOSOPHY

The idea of a dynamic world occurred to some of the ancient Greeks, but these scholars were not so influential as those who believed in a static, unchanging world. It was the philosophy of Plato (c. 428–348 B.C.) and his student Aristotle (384–322 B.C.) that, through its incorporation into Judeo-Christian theology, had the dominant influence on Western thought.

Plato believed that there existed **eidos**, transcendent ''ideas'' or ''forms.'' These ideal forms were specially created according to a plan ''from the region beyond the stars'' and were eternal and perfect. For example, triangles represented an ideal geometric form. Although triangles come in many different shapes, the sum of all of their angles is always 180°. This feature is the ''essential'' property of triangles that separates them from other geometric forms. Similarly, Plato believed there existed an *eidos* for each species; for example, there existed an ideal dog with its essential characteristics.

In this philosophy of **essentialism**, individual variation had no meaning. Aristotle thought that the essence of a species was given to the embryo during reproduction, and the embryo's development was guided by this essence. The ideal types were only imperfectly reflected in earthly things. The great variability among individual dogs thus represented accidents or errors in copying the ideal; each individual dog was just an imperfect copy of its *eidos* (Figure 20.2). Only the essences were important; through the study of them, the plan for the universe could be understood.

Figure 20.2
Dogs show a great deal of variation in form and colour.

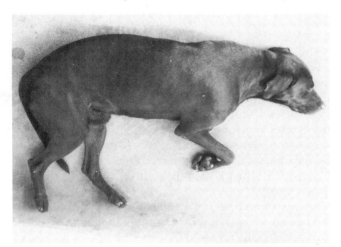

The implications of essentialism could, then, be summed up in three points. First, there is a plan for all objects, which are a part of a system. For Plato, the system is imposed from the outside. Second, the essential forms are permanent and do not change. Third, variation within a species is a consequence of imperfections in the copying process; the variability is uninteresting because it tells nothing about "essences."

After the decline of classical Greek and Roman civilization, learning in the Western world was for almost a millenium centered on interpretations of the writings of certain ancients, principally Aristotle. Then, with the emergence of the Renaissance in the late fifteenth century, European scholars began a new phase of learning. Leonardo da Vinci (1452–1519) is often considered the exemplary Renaissance person, with outstanding accomplishments not only in art, but also in science and technology. He and others such as Galileo and Newton did much to change the nature of European science. Their work inspired the efforts of scholars throughout Europe. However, the basic tenets of essentialist philosophy pertaining to the nature of living things remained unchallenged. For example, the scientist John Ray (1627–1705) was one of the earliest scholars to gather information about British plants and animals and wrote a number of books on the fauna and flora of northern Europe. Yet Ray, as did Newton, believed that the ultimate goal of the study of natural science was to discover the order given to life by God. He thus reaffirmed the notion of God as the creator of species, with each species eternally fixed in form and ideally suited for its role on the earth.

20.3 FOSSILS AND EXTINCTION

In the seventeenth century, it was generally accepted that the earth had been stable through time, but the study of fossils began to force a reassessment of this assumption. Robert Hooke (1635–1703) speculated on the nature of "figured stones," as fossils were generally called. He argued that they were of two types, "mineral deposits" (salts, crystals, precious stones) and the "petrifications" or impressions of organisms that had lived in the past. Today, we call only the latter type "fossils" (Figure 20.3).

This interpretation raised some questions. If fossils represented remains of dead plants and animals, how had these creatures become embedded in the earth? How had creatures such as clams, that live in the ocean, become embedded in stone at the top of mountains or deep in the ground? Hooke suggested that the surface of the earth had changed "since the Creation." Some land areas had once been covered by the sea and some areas underwater had once been dry land. As Hooke wrote, "Mountains have been turned into Plains and Plains into Mountains and the like."

Hooke's interpretation of fossils became generally accepted; it was made consistent with the idea of Creation by the belief that the individuals found fossilized had drowned during the Great Flood mentioned in the Bible.

Although the idea that fossils were the mineralized remains or impressions of dead organisms gained acceptance, it was not realized that many fossils were the remains of extinct species. Indeed, if the biota had been created according to some logical and perfect plan, there was no reason to suppose that species had become extinct. Extinction, after all, implies imperfection. However, with greater knowledge both of the fossils and of anatomy, it became increasingly obvious that extinction had occurred.

The French anatomist and paleontologist Georges Cuvier (1769–1832) ultimately convinced the scientific community of the reality of extinction. Cuvier was one of the most famous and influential scientists of his time. In addition to classical studies of anatomy, he did careful work on the fossils of the Paris Basin in France. He was able to create reconstructions of fossil animals based on fragmentary remains and to show that many of the fossils represented creatures that no longer existed on earth.

To explain extinction, Cuvier postulated that there had been a series of environmental catastrophes. Each local catastrophe resulted in the extinction of the existing organisms. Following each destruction of the biota, a new set of species recolonized the region from another part of the world. It was suggested that the Great Flood was simply the most recent of these catastrophes. Because of the paucity of the fossil record, it was not clear that species changed through time. Some thinkers, like the French scientist Jean-Baptiste Lamarck (1744–1829), thought that the new species were the descendants of previously existing ones. Others thought that they were truly new, having been created directly by God or indirectly by unknown natural causes for which God was ultimately responsible. Cuvier's **catastrophism** and the associated ideas offered a way to understand extinction in a manner that was consistent with many of the prevalent religious and philosophical views.

Figure 20.3
Early scholars did not realize that fossils were the remains of ancient, and sometimes even extinct, organisms.

20.4 AGE OF THE EARTH

Until the eighteenth century, the earth was believed to be much younger than it is known to be today. Using statements in the Bible, Archbishop James Ussher in 1650 calculated that the earth had been created in the year 4004 B.C. Although thinkers such as Newton accepted Ussher's calculations, not everyone did. (Much earlier, Leonardo da Vinci had calculated that the deposits in the Po Valley in Italy were 200 000 years old!) Still, the general idea that the earth was about only a few thousand years old was popularly held. During the eighteenth century the French thinker Georges Buffon (1707–1788) speculated from physical evidence that it must have taken tens of thousands or even millions of years for the earth to reach its present state.

The Scottish geologist James Hutton (1726–1797) argued that the earth was even older than that. Hutton postulated that natural forces had been responsible for sculpturing the surface of the earth. Mountains had been neither created nor destroyed by sudden, catastrophic events, but had been formed by uplifting and gradually worn down by erosion over immense periods of time. Such slow geological processes implied an earth of inconceivably great age.

The English scientist Charles Lyell (1797–1875), the foremost geologist of the nineteenth century, embraced and expanded Hutton's theory. It came to be called **uniformitarianism**. Through Lyell, uniformitarianism became widely accepted in the scientific world. Uniformitarianism does not imply that geological features change at a uniform rate. Rather, it holds that the "present is the key to the past." Mountains were uplifted in the past as they are today, a few centimetres or at most metres at a time. Floods in the past were of no greater power than those that occur today.

Figure 20.4
This sedimentary rock was deposited millions of years ago under some ancient sea.

Figure 20.5
Some cattle, such as the ones shown here, have been especially selected to produce large quantities of milk. Others are specifically bred for beef production.

Fossil clams, embedded in stone, were sometimes found high in mountains because they were elevated, a few centimetres at a time, from the bottom of the sea where they had been formed long before. Those buried deep in the earth had been covered by accumulated sediments (Figure 20.4).

Lyell's *Principles of Geology* (1830–1833) discussed a number of issues of not only geological but also biological interest. Although several of the ideas that he presented had previously appeared in the French literature, Lyell introduced them to the English-speaking public. One such idea was that fossils gave an imperfect record of the history of life. Another was that there was a "war in nature," a struggle for existence among organisms. As well, Lyell discussed the significance of changes in domesticated plants and animals. Breeders had learned that it was possible to change species by *selection*: removal of individuals that had undesirable characteristics would allow those with desirable characteristics to breed. This process, called "artificial selection," enabled breeders to create chickens that could lay larger or more eggs, cows that could produce more milk, and grain crops that had higher yields (Figure 20.5). Did this process imply that species were not immutable, and could be changed? Lyell argued that it did not, because if the domestic strains were returned to their natural environments they would "revert to the original type." Thus even in Lyell's scheme there was a retention of the Platonic concept of an original type or *eidos*.

20.5 LAMARCK AND HIS THEORY OF EVOLUTION

In addition to many important contributions in the fields of animal taxonomy and anatomy, Jean Lamarck was the first biologist to develop a theory of the causes and mechanisms of organic evolution. He first published his findings in 1802 and expanded them in his 1809 *Philosophie zoologique*. It was through the popularization of his work by Lyell that the English-speaking public was first exposed to his ideas. Lyell himself, however, did not accept Lamarck's hypothesis.

Lamarck did not propose that living species were descended from a common ancestor. Rather, he postulated that "lower" forms were spontaneously generated or created from non-living matter. These lower forms of life then progressed to more complex forms. He thought that it was a fundamental law of nature for organisms to go from the simple to the more complex. The actual path of progression that each species followed was determined by its interaction with the environment. As the environment changed, so did the needs and activities of the individuals of a species. Consequently, many structures were modified by use or disuse and to a certain extent these **acquired characteristics** were passed on to the individual's offspring.

To give an example used by Lamarck, the giraffe's long front legs and neck evolved by the transmission of acquired characteristics. The ancestral giraffes were

Figure 20.6
Lamarck postulated that giraffes evolved their long necks by stretching to reach leaves high in trees.

proposed to have had short necks. Since grass was scarce, they fed by browsing leaves from trees, habitually stretching their necks to reach the higher leaves and thus producing slightly longer necks which were passed on to their progeny. Consequently, the species through many generations evolved longer necks (Figure 20.6).

Lamarck's model does hold true for *cultural* evolution; language, for example, is a matter of acquired characteristics. But it does not hold true for *biological* evolution. Body structures may be modified by use. Weight lifters have larger muscles than most people, yet these larger muscles are not passed on to their children. The tails of certain breeds of dogs are cut off when the puppies are newborn, yet future generations of these breeds are still born with long tails. As you learned in the previous unit, it is an individual's genetic make-up that determines physical characteristics.

Lamarck is commonly remembered as ''someone who was wrong.'' This is not entirely fair because he did not originate the mistaken but widely held ideas of spontaneous generation and inheritance of acquired biological characteristics. Though he did not succeed in finding the cause of evolution, his insight that species might change without limit was a crucial one. (A similar theory was proposed, in a poetic and

speculative way, by Erasmus Darwin (1731–1802), grandfather of Charles Darwin.) It was largely because of Lamarck that organic evolution became a topic of great interest in the mid-nineteenth century. The evidence for evolution was plentiful, but Lamarck's mechanism unconvincing.

20.6 CHARLES DARWIN AND NATURAL SELECTION

Charles Robert Darwin (1809–1882) was one of the outstanding scientists of all time. His copious research in both biology and geology would have guaranteed him scientific immortality even if he had not proposed the mechanism for organic evolution accepted today — **natural selection**.

Darwin and the *Beagle*

As a boy, Charles Darwin loved the outdoors and the study of natural history. Upon his graduation from university, he was given the opportunity to become a serious *naturalist*, a student of living things in their natural environments. His chance came in 1831 when he was invited to travel on H. M. S. *Beagle*, which was to sail around the world and in particular to survey the coast of South America (Figure 20.7). During this voyage, which lasted nearly five years, Darwin kept very busy making observations in geology, botany, and zoology. Among the books that he took with him on the *Beagle* was the first volume of Lyell's *Principles of Geology*. The *Principles*, as well as his own observations, convinced Darwin of geological uniformitarianism. While in South America, for example, he witnessed a rather severe earthquake. After the quake, he found that the landscape had been noticeably altered. He reasoned that such earthquakes had been responsible for the uplifting of the nearby mountains, just as Lyell had hypothesized. At the same time, in keeping with uniformitarianism, Darwin was developing a theory on the formation of coral reefs, a view still held by geologists today.

In South America, Darwin spent much of his time ashore, studying the local plants and animals as well as the terrain. In Argentina, he unearthed the remains of extinct mammals. Though different from any living forms, these extinct forms more closely resembled contemporary South American mammals than animals from any other part of the world. Darwin thus concluded that ''the most important result of this discovery is the confirmation of the law that existing animals have a close relation in form with extinct

Figure 20.7
The voyage of the H.M.S. Beagle. *The young Charles Darwin was especially impressed with the unique animals and plants that he found on the Galapagos Islands.*

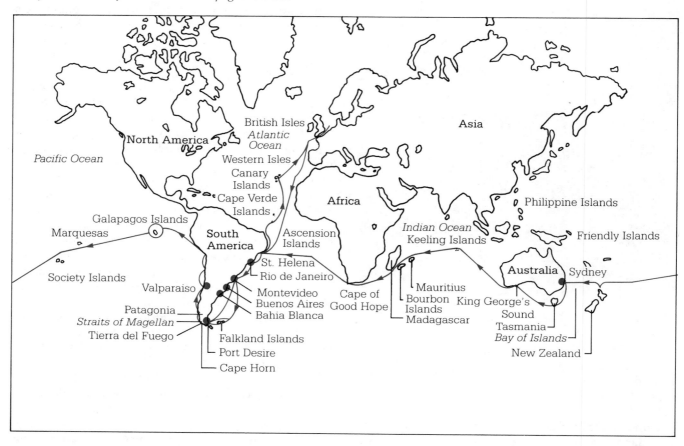

species." Darwin realized that this discovery would be expected *if the contemporary South American species had evolved from South American ancestors*, but not if there existed an ideal biota for each environment.

As the *Beagle* was leaving South America, it stopped in the Galapagos Archipelago, a group of islands about 800 km off the west coast of the continent. The islands of the Galapagos were all formed at about the same time and are similar to each other. Therefore, Darwin was surprised to find that each had certain unique forms of animals on them. Giant tortoises, for example, were common in the islands (Figure 20.8). Yet they were sufficiently different in appearance from island to island that it often was possible to tell which island a specimen was from simply by looking at it. This was also true of many of the birds that lived there. As Darwin wrote, "I never dreamed that islands, about fifty or sixty miles apart, and most of them in

sight of each other, formed of precisely the same rocks, placed under a quite similar climate, rising to nearly equal height, would have been differently tenanted [by animals]; but . . . this was the case." Darwin also noted that there were relatively few species of animals on the Galapagos. There was only one species of land mammal and there were no frogs or other amphibians. What species there were, however, most closely resembled those on South America — the nearest mainland. They were like South American species, but also different from them. This finding suggested to Darwin, and later to others, that the Galapagos species had originally come from South America and had changed after they arrived in the Galapagos. Also, once in the Galapagos, some species had become isolated on the individual islands and had changed in form from their close relatives on other islands. Animals that cannot fly, swim well, or be carried on drift-

Figure 20.8
Darwin was surprised that many of the Galapagos islands had distinctive forms of tortoises on them.

wood, such as land mammals and frogs, had not been able to cross the ocean and reach the islands. Darwin realized that what he had seen in the Galapagos made sense only if the ancestors of the Galapagos animals had come from South America and evolved their differences on the individual islands.

The Influence of Malthus

When Darwin returned to England, he began to contemplate his experiences on the *Beagle*. He decided that evolution must have occurred, even if in a way other than that proposed by Lamarck. Darwin thus began searching for a new mechanism to explain change in species. By his own account, the significance of natural selection first came to him in 1838 while reading *An Essay on the Principle of Population* by Thomas Malthus (1766–1834). Malthus was a clergyman who had noted that there was the potential for a rapid increase in the numbers of any species through reproduction. For example, if each human couple raised four children, then the number of people produced by a single couple would increase to four, then eight, then 16, then 32 in four generations. Because food cannot increase as fast as population can, the tendency for populations to increase in size leads to more deaths by starvation, disease, and warfare. (Malthus advocated a reduction in the human birth rate by late marriages and sexual restraint in order to decrease

the human suffering that arose as a consequence of these factors.)

As a naturalist, Darwin realized that, like humans, other animals also generally produced more offspring than were necessary to replace themselves. Logically, one would suppose that as a consequence the numbers of any species would eventually become too large to be supported on the earth. But in reality, this does not happen. It does not happen because as the numbers of any species increase so do the deaths due to factors such as starvation, disease, and fighting.

Today, such factors as these are called **density-dependent factors** because their significance corresponds to the density (number of individuals per unit area) of species. Given a constant amount of food, for example, a greater proportion of the individuals in a population would starve at high densities than at low ones. It is these density-dependent factors, not reproductive capabilities, that determine the numbers of most species of organisms. The number of oak trees living in a given region, for example, is limited by the amount of space available and the number of sites where seeds have been able to germinate, not by the number of acorns produced.

The ideas of Malthus led Darwin to a better understanding of "struggle in nature." The most important struggle in nature, Darwin realized, is not between predator and prey, but rather among individuals of the same species competing for limited resources. Seeds compete with each other for a place to germinate and grow. Animals that can obtain food, find a place to nest or breed, and escape predators are the ones that produce young for future generations. Those that cannot do not reproduce and thus are eliminated or "selected against." Malthus' insight was the missing piece in Darwin's puzzle. With this piece in place, Darwin was able to formulate his theory of natural selection (Figure 20.9). The crucial points of this theory could be summarized as follows:

1. Differences among individuals of a species are not an indication that individuals were imperfect copies of an ideal type as proposed by the long-standing notion of *eidos*. Rather, individual differences are essential to evolution.
2. The struggle in nature that is of the greatest consequence to evolution is not that between species. Rather, it is the competition within a population to obtain food, attract a mate, and escape predators.
3. Only those differences that are inherited are relevant to evolution.

4. Evolution generally takes a great deal of time and is ongoing.

5. Evolution does not inevitably progress from the less complex to the more complex. Rather, it has no necessary direction; species may become either more complex or less complex or may not change at all.

6. Natural selection is opportunistic and random. Species do not have a specific "purpose" in nature; predator and prey do not exist to keep each other in balance (Figure 20.10).

Figure 20.9
Some of the important facts and inferences that led Darwin to postulate his theory of evolution by natural selection. Malthus supplied Darwin with his first important inference, namely that there was a struggle among individuals of a species for limited resources.

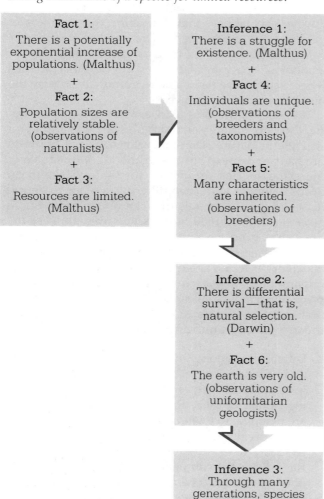

Fact 1:
There is a potentially exponential increase of populations. (Malthus)
+
Fact 2:
Population sizes are relatively stable. (observations of naturalists)
+
Fact 3:
Resources are limited. (Malthus)

Inference 1:
There is a struggle for existence. (Malthus)
+
Fact 4:
Individuals are unique. (observations of breeders and taxonomists)
+
Fact 5:
Many characteristics are inherited. (observations of breeders)

Inference 2:
There is differential survival — that is, natural selection. (Darwin)
+
Fact 6:
The earth is very old. (observations of uniformitarian geologists)

Inference 3:
Through many generations, species evolve. (Darwin)

Figure 20.10
A carnivore captures prey in order simply to obtain food, not to fulfill any larger purpose.

As an illustration of this last point, consider the predator–prey relationship between owls and rats (although any other relationship would serve just as well). The preying of owls on weaker rats means that the stronger rats have less competition for food. The owls' behaviour does, then, have the *effect* of helping the rat population weed out its weaker members, just as the availability of rats helps ensure a food supply for owls. However, while it has *effects* that benefit both rats and owls, this relationship does not have these mutual benefits as its *purpose*. As a consequence of efficient hunting, owls can survive and reproduce. Any benefit to other species — rats or otherwise — is incidental. Predator–prey relationships reflect random selection, not any design to keep nature in check.

20.7 THE PRESENTATION OF DARWIN'S THEORY

Although Darwin first conceived of his theory of evolution in the late 1830s, he did not present it to the public until 20 years later. During those years, he discussed his theory with a few close friends and sought confirmation for it in the study of nature. One difficulty that confronted Darwin was that neither he nor any of his contemporaries understood the nature of inheritance. Could acquired characteristics be passed on? The evidence seemed contradictory. Some features, such as human eye colour, seemed to be passed on without mixing. Others, such as stature or skin colour, seemed to be blended during reproduction. A

Figure 20.11
Alfred Russell Wallace (1823–1913)

Figure 20.12
A copy of the title page of the first edition of Darwin's major work on evolution and natural selection. Although this work is usually referred to as On the Origin of Species *the real title is much longer.*

tall and a short person generally produced children that were between them in height. During these two decades Darwin himself experimented with inheritance, but did not come up with a satisfactory explanation of the mechanism. Based on the evidence that was available to him, he was never able to abandon completely the idea of inheritance of acquired characteristics, even if he was unconvinced by Lamarck's particular explanation of it.

In 1858 Darwin was stimulated to publish his theory by another English naturalist, Alfred Russell Wallace (1823–1913). Wallace had done extensive field work in South America and southeast Asia. Like Darwin, he was convinced of organic evolution by evidence from his studies of the geographic distribution of plant and animal species. But he too did not think of the mechanism of evolution until he read Malthus and then, in 1858, wrote an essay in which he clearly outlined the principle of natural selection. Rather than first publishing his essay, he sent it to Darwin, who was by

that time the most respected naturalist in England. Despite his own already-formulated ideas on the subject, Darwin very justly believed that Wallace's independent and equally original contribution had to be recognized. Darwin thus submitted Wallace's paper to a journal to be published, while at the insistence of his friends simultaneously submitting his own papers. In recognition of the vast amount of work Darwin had already done, Wallace for his part insisted that the name "Darwinism" be given to the theory of natural selection (Figure 20.11).

In 1859, Darwin published *On the Origin of Species*, a much more detailed work than the first Darwin and Wallace papers (Figure 20.12). Darwinism was hotly debated, but because of the weight of evidence and the clarity of the arguments, scientists generally accepted the theory. Most acknowledged natural selection as at least a partial explanation of organic evolution, but many felt that there might be other, yet unknown explanations involved as well.

For many biologists, Darwinism was less than wholly convincing because the mechanism of inheritance was still to be discovered. It was thought that offspring demonstrated a blend of the characteristics of their parents. If, it was argued, an individual with a new, desirable characteristic appeared in a population, it would by necessity have to mate with an individual lacking this characteristic. In the offspring, characteristics would be blended, much as different colours of paint are mixed. The adaptive value of the desirable characteristic would be diminished. In the following generation, the offspring would again find as mates other "less fit" individuals. Thus, a desirable characteristic would over the generations be diluted rather than retained, just as consecutive mixings of paint would dilute the evidence of an original colour.

Today we understand that inheritance is "particulate" rather than the result of "blending," but that was not generally understood until the turn of the century, about two decades after Darwin's death, when the concept of the gene became established. A gene may be passed on through generations. It is not blended with other genes, although its phenotypic effects may be. In order to understand fully how species could change through time, it was first necessary to understand the working of the gene.

20.8 THE MODERN SYNTHESIS

The theory of evolution by natural selection had an immediate and substantial impact on biologists. It tied together observations from all areas of biological endeavour — embryology, anatomy, paleontology, biogeography, and systematics. Nevertheless, the theory was not widely understood; because of its failure to explain inheritance, many scientists questioned the importance of natural selection.

The discovery of Mendel's work in 1900 should have led to a general acceptance of Darwin's theory, but it did not. Biologists in the early part of this century tended to emphasize the importance of "mutation" — not selection — in evolution (Chapters 14 and 15). Many early Mendelian geneticists thought that "continuous variation" — features such as body size — was of little significance in the formation of new species and perhaps not even under genetic control. Many suggested that new species arose by "major mutations," not by the gradual divergence of populations.

Evolutionary theory has been somewhat modified to what is often called a neo-Darwinian theory, a modification that emerged in the 1930s and gave rise to the so-called "Modern Synthesis." Contributions from paleontology, biogeography, systematics, and especially genetics were synthesized with Darwin's theory. From this synthesis the great importance of natural selection in evolution and *speciation* (Chapter 22) became clear.

Geneticists have found that there exists a great deal of genetic variation in most species; there is good evidence that acquired characteristics cannot be inherited. They have also shown that continuous variation is inherited in the same way as the discrete characteristics studied by Mendel and that it involves the effects of many genes, each having only a small phenotypic effect. Thus, continuously distributed characteristics can also be influenced by selection and can evolve through time.

The modern synthesis is not essentially different from the theory put forth by Darwin in 1859, except that it incorporates the current understanding of inheritance. It is, however, much more complete because science has gathered a great deal of evidence that was not available to Darwin. The principles of inheritance and the molecular basis for the transmission of hereditary information are now understood. The fossil record is rich with examples and clearly reveals evidence of the change in species through time. Knowledge of anatomy, development, and distribution is also far more extensive than it was in Darwin's time, enhancing our understanding not only of evolution but also of the multiplication of species (Chapter 22).

The modern synthesis holds that variation is introduced into populations by random mutations. New genes accumulate and become common in populations primarily by natural selection. Selection "removes" most novelties because they reduce the fitness of the individuals that possess them; that is, they reduce their ability to compete for food or to reproduce. However, some mutations increase the fitness of the individual. Usually, characteristics that enhance fitness increase in frequency in populations because of natural selection. However, some mutations have little effect on fitness; these mutations may increase or decrease in frequency simply by chance. Populations evolve by changes in the frequency with which certain genes exist. Most genetic variants have only a slight phenotypic effect, so changes in average phenotype in a population generally occur only very slowly. Although factors other than selection do cause changes in gene frequencies in populations, neo-Darwinian theory remains based on the premise that *nat-*

ural selection is the primary factor causing adaptive changes in populations.*

The number of different kinds of organisms has increased through time. This diversification also generally has taken place slowly. Most often, different groups of individuals of the same species have become isolated in different places, such as the tortoises in the Galapagos Islands. Differences among such isolated populations accumulate through time as the populations adapt differently to the environments they encounter. After maybe thousands of generations, the differences among populations are sufficiently great to warrant recognition of the descendant populations as different species. After more time and divergence, they could be recognized as different genera, and so forth. The evolution of the major groups of organisms is thus seen as an extension of the multiplication of species. Natural selection is seen as the primary driving force in the origin of families and other "higher" groups just as it is in the origin of species. Just as mountains are built slowly, uplifted in many small steps, a new class of organisms becomes differentiated by the gradual accumulation of small differences, driven primarily by natural selection.

20.9 CHALLENGES TO THE MODERN SYNTHESIS

There is today a general consensus among biologists about the fact of evolution and its mechanism. That is not to say that there is no disagreement. There are several major areas of debate. The following are some of them:

1. Under certain circumstances new species can arise rapidly. Some argue that this is, in fact, what usually happens.

2. It is not always necessary for populations to be geographically isolated from one another to diverge. How frequently does speciation occur without this fragmentation?

3. As did Darwin, the modern synthesis has thought of selection as being among individuals in a population. Today, some argue that selection also operates among family groups, and perhaps as well among genes and groups of essentially unrelated individuals.

4. The events associated with speciation may not be sufficient to explain the diversification of higher taxa such as classes and phyla. Have the differences between, say, bats and mice arisen by the gradual accumulation of small differences, or are other mechanisms involved?

5. There is an increasing amount of evidence that there have been several brief periods of time during which many species have quite suddenly become extinct. It is debated whether or not these "mass extinctions" have been caused by major catastrophes, such as asteroids or comets colliding with the earth. The ongoing debate over the extinction of the last living species of dinosaurs is an outstanding case in point.

The contemporary theory of organic evolution, greatly bolstered by a knowledge of geology, inheritance, and molecular biology, differs from Darwin's in some details. Contemporary biologists still see natural selection, however, as the major force driving organic evolution. No other mechanism has been suggested which is supported by evidence rather than by speculation.

CHAPTER SUMMARY

Scholars of the ancient world generally believed that living species had been created according to some special design for the universe. It was also thought that the earth was much younger than we today know it to be, and that species of organisms did not change through time. It was commonly argued that the differences that existed among individuals of a species existed only because each individual was an imperfect copy of an "ideal type" for the species.

Several developments led to a questioning of the notion of unchanging species. Fossil studies offered evidence that some extinct species were different from any contemporary organisms. Geological evidence suggested that the earth was a great deal older than had been previously thought and that it was subject to ongoing change through natural processes. Botanical and zoological evidence of the geographic distribution of plants and animals did not seem to make sense if species had been created. The idea of organic evolution helped make sense of all this evidence.

Some early evolutionary biologists such as Lamarck postulated that changes acquired by organisms from their environment could be passed on to the offspring. However, evidence accumulated against such theories of evolution by acquired characteristics.

Charles Darwin and Alfred Wallace independently hit upon the idea that natural selection could explain evolution. They were both inspired by the ideas of Malthus on population growth, ideas that give rise to the notion of density-dependent factors. Competition for food, space, and mates "selected" only the most fit individuals within a species to survive. Darwin and Wallace argued that if the characteristics favoured by natural selection could be passed on to the young of the selected individuals, the evolution of the species would result.

There is evidence today for evolution from many different fields of study. While there are still considerable areas of debate, the great significance of natural selection as a mechanism of evolution is accepted by virtually all scholars of evolutionary biology.

Objectives

Having completed this chapter, you should be able to do the following:

1. Describe how his experiences on the *Beagle* as well as the writings of Malthus and Lyell helped Darwin develop his theory of evolution.
2. Describe the fundamentals of the theory of natural selection as set forth by Darwin and Wallace.
3. Outline the differences between Darwin's and Lamarck's theories of organic evolution.
4. Explain why the general lack of understanding of the mechanisms of inheritance before this century made it difficult to understand the concept of natural selection.

Vocabulary

eidos
essentialism
catastrophism

uniformitarianism
acquired characteristic
natural selection

density-dependent factor

Review Questions

1. (a) How did essentialism explain the significance of individual variation?
   (b) Why was this explanation incompatible with the idea of organic evolution?
2. (a) What is the difference between uniformitarianism and catastrophism?
   (b) Why does uniformitarianism imply that the earth is very old?
3. In what ways did the realization that extinction of species had occurred lead scientists to recognize the existence of organic evolution?
4. Prior to Darwin, the predator–prey relationship was believed to be the most significant "struggle" in nature. How did Darwin's thinking differ from this notion?

Advanced Questions

1. One tenet of uniformitarian geology has been that the present is the key to the past. In what way(s) might uniformitarian thinking have helped lead Darwin to his theory of evolution by natural selection?

2. While at university, Charles Darwin was trained as a clergyman. He once commented that "the voyage of the *Beagle* has been by far the most important event in my life, and has determined my whole career." On another occasion, he commented that had he not gone on the *Beagle* he doubtless would have led a quiet life as a country parson. Do some further reading to find out about Darwin's experience during the *Beagle* voyage and its influence on his theory of natural selection.

3. It is often argued that codfish have to lay millions of eggs to replace themselves because so many of the young are destroyed by predators. This argument implies that the fish are following a reproductive strategy that is designed to compensate for an anticipated (or at least predictable) loss and that their purpose is to replace themselves. Explain why Charles Darwin would not have accepted this argument.

412

CHAPTER 21

POPULATIONS AND NATURAL SELECTION

Nothing endures but change.

Heraclitus, 540–480 B.C.

I t is commonplace to hear that "no two individuals are exactly the same." Yet until the biological significance of this fact was appreciated, the evolution of species through time could not really be understood. The *variation* among individuals in populations is necessary for *natural selection*, and natural selection is an important key to evolution. Even a comparison of individual snails within the species *Nucella lapillus* illustrates the variability that occurs in populations in nature. Because of the variation among individuals in populations, it follows that some individuals can deal with environmental stresses better than others can.

Evolution is, however, a matter not of discrete changes within individuals but of cumulative change within a species. Only by a study of populations can evolution be understood. In this chapter you will learn how natural populations vary and how natural selection can change populations through time.

21.1 THE NATURE OF VARIATION IN POPULATIONS

An environmental condition may *select for* certain characteristics of some individuals and *select against* those of others. Consider, for example, that some individuals of a population tend to resemble their habitat and thus are camouflaged whereas others may not resemble the habitat so closely and thus are conspicuous (Figure 21.1). If there are predators that hunt by

Figure 21.1
This lizard is found near White Sands, New Mexico. It is much paler than other members of the same species living in areas where the ground colour is darker.

sight, they will see and therefore capture more of the conspicuous than of the camouflaged individuals. In this way, conspicuous individuals are *selected against* and camouflaged individuals are *selected for*. If there were no variability in the population, there could be no selection.

413

Biologists have long understood that the differences among individuals in a population are produced in two different ways. First, the appearance of individuals is affected by *environmental* factors such as the quantity and types of foods available, disease, crowding, and injury. Appearance is also influenced by *inheritance*, the characteristics that an individual has received from its parent or parents through genes. This latter variability in a population is called inherited variation or more often *heritable variation*. Because characteristics that are encoded in the genes of an individual may be passed on to future generations, it is heritable variation that makes organic evolution possible. The variation caused by environmental factors may be substantial and often is important to the success of the individual, but it is not important in evolution.

Environmental Variation

Environmentally induced changes often help an individual survive and reproduce. Many examples occur in nature. The water buttercup (*Ranunculus aquatilis*) lives in shallow pools. The leaves that develop under water are very different from those that are produced above the water (Figure 21.2). They are finely branched or dissected, while those above the water are shaped like more conventional leaves. It is important to the plant that a proper balance between light and water is maintained for photosynthesis to occur. Light is available in limited quantities to the submerged leaves. Their shape enables them to pick up more sunlight than the leaves growing above the water would if they were submerged. The underwater leaves, however, dry out relatively quickly if exposed to air.

"Environment" includes not only external conditions but also internal ones. For example, different phenotypes are also produced in populations by means of developmental or physiological differences. Thus, although the sex of an individual of many species is determined chromosomally at the time of fertilization, the physical differences between the sexes appear during development. A developing individual with, say, "female chromosomes" produces an internal hormonal environment that leads to the development of a female. Likewise "male chromosomes" lead to a male individual.

In some species, different types of individuals are produced as a consequence of environmental conditions. In many species of "social insects," such as honey bees, some individuals develop into "work-

Figure 21.2
*The white water crowfoot (*Ranunculus aquatilis*) grows in shallow water. Leaves submerged in water are greatly dissected, unlike the leaves above the water. All the leaves have the same genes, but grow to different shapes as they develop in different environments.*

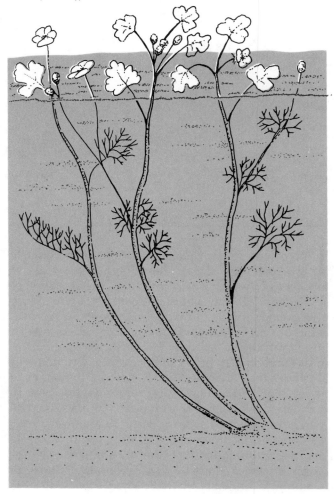

ers," others into "drones" (males), and still others into "queens" (Figure 21.3). The workers and queens are all females, but only those raised in a certain environment develop into queens, despite their being genetically the same as other females in the population that develop into workers.

Among others, the French scientist Lamarck proposed that many environmentally induced states, or *acquired characteristics*, could be passed on from generation to generation, and thus could play a pivotal role in evolution (Chapter 20). However, a great deal of experimental evidence indicates that Lamarck was wrong; indeed, our understanding of the molecular

Most of the genetic information that is transmitted from generation to generation in sexually reproducing species is carried in the nuclei of the egg and sperm cells. However, some features are also carried in the cytoplasm of the egg cell (there is little cytoplasm in the sperm cell). Most such *cytoplasmic inheritance* is carried in the self-replicating organelles, such as mitochondria, chloroplasts, and virus particles. Also, some diseases or immunities of the mother may be transmitted to the fetus, but these usually persist for only one generation. Some cytoplasmic particles of DNA (such as viruses) might also be incorporated into the nuclear DNA.

Although the significance of these factors is still not known, any change in the genetic make-up of the gamete by these means would not have been brought about by a change in the phenotype of the parent. There is no evidence that an adaptive response can be carried ''backward'' from the body to protein molecules and thus to the DNA of gametes.

Figure 21.3

The carpenter ants shown here are all members of the same species, are all females, and could all be found in the same colony. Each colony of carpenter ants is founded by a winged queen, shown as (a). She mates during a mating flight, after which the male dies. The queen then loses her wings and starts a colony. The workers in the colony, which are wingless, are her daughters and therefore all sisters. Some develop as large workers (b) who defend the colony. Others develop as small workers (c) who feed the queen and the young. A few of the females in the colony will be raised as winged queens, who in turn will go out and found new colonies. Whether a female ant develops into a queen, a large worker, or a small worker depends entirely upon the way she is raised—the environment.

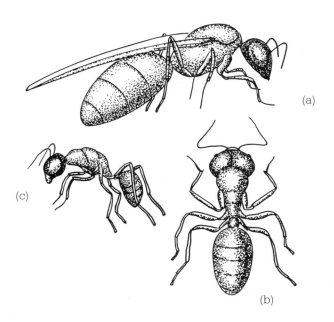

(a)

(c)

(b)

basis of heredity makes the notion of inheritance of acquired characteristics especially untenable. The heritable characteristics of individuals are determined by characteristics of their proteins. Specific proteins have specific sequences of amino acids; each amino acid is determined by only a few specific nucleotide base sequences which are present in the DNA of the chromosomes (Chapters 14 and 16). Environmental factors that influence a body cell (such as a muscle cell) would not change the nucleotide base sequence in that cell's DNA; even if that sequence were changed, it would not influence the sequence in an egg or sperm.

Heritable Variation

In order to discuss genetic variability in populations, it is important to review a few terms you learned in Chapter 14. A *gene* is a portion of a chromosome that is transmitted during reproduction and determines the hereditary traits of the offspring. A *locus* (pl. *loci*) is the position of a gene in a chromosome. At many *loci* several different genes may occur in a population. These alternative forms of the same gene are called *alleles*. Thus, I^A, I^B, and *i* are alleles of a gene that determines A, B, AB, or O blood type in humans. Generally, individuals have two sets of chromosomes, one that they received from their male parent and one that they received from their female parent. Thus, for each locus an individual may have two different alleles. An individual who has two different alleles at the same locus (for example, $I^A I^B$, $I^A i$, $I^B i$) is *heterozygous* at that locus; a person who has two of the same allele (for example, $I^A I^A$, $I^B I^B$, *ii*) is *homozygous* at that locus. If two or more alleles are present *in a population* that population is *polymorphic* at that locus. (The word polymorphic comes from two Greek words, *poly*,

Figure 21.4
The distribution of many features of organisms in populations approximates a bell-shaped curve. Most of the individuals are close to average; only a few are at the extremes of the distribution.

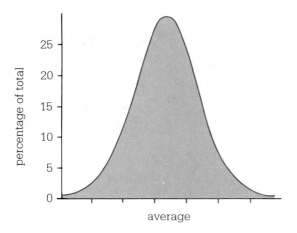

Figure 21.5
The mass of newborn babies shows an approximately normal distribution. Babies of approximately average mass had the greatest chance of living and thus of themselves producing children.

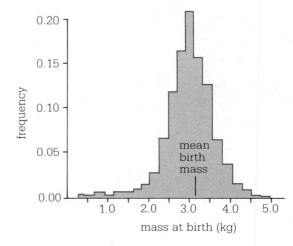

meaning many, and *morphe*, meaning form.) Thus, humans are as a group polymorphic at the I^A-I^B-i locus even though many individuals are homozygous for blood type. *Genetic variability thus occurs both within individuals (**heterozygosity**) and within populations (**polymorphism**).*

Phenotypic Variability in Populations
Phenotype, as you will recall, refers to the physical characteristics of an individual, which are influenced by both genetic and environmental factors. Consider the people in your classroom. They differ, for example, in the colour of eyes, hair, and skin. They also differ in many physiological ways not so easily observed, such as basic metabolic rate, normal body temperature, ability to metabolize certain foods, and tolerance of extreme temperatures. Type A blood, blue eyes, or an allergy to strawberries would be just a few examples of the great phenotypic variability in normal human populations.

The A-B-AB-O blood-type polymorphism is an example of a characteristic which is controlled by allelic variation at a single locus and for which there are distinct and different phenotypes. However, the genetic control of many other features is more complex. For example, the stature of humans is determined by allelic variation at many different loci and of course by environmental factors such as nutrition. The genetic blueprint is inherited. The environment affects

the expression of this blueprint. In the case of human stature, many different genes (as well as many different environmental factors) affect the phenotype. Therefore, we do not find populations where the individuals are of uniform stature. Rather, there is **continuous variation** in stature in all populations, with the majority of individuals being near the middle of the distribution (Figure 21.4). Average height does differ in different populations, but within each population the distribution is continuous.

Much of the phenotypic variation in populations such as weight of a newborn human (Figure 21.5) is continuously distributed. It is, however, easiest to study variation in discrete characteristics such as sex or blood type.

Polymorphic Variability in Populations
Polymorphisms occur frequently in populations. The A-B-AB-O human red blood cell polymorphism and Rh polymorphism are particularly familiar, but there are many others. There are, for example, no fewer than 17 different known red blood cell polymorphisms in humans.

Since the late 1960s, biologists have been able to assess the extent of genetic variation in populations through the technique of *electrophoresis* (Figure 21.6). Using the technique, they have found that there is a great deal of genetic variation in populations of almost all animals and plants. For example, in humans (one

The term *electrophoresis* comes from Greek words meaning electric-carrying. The technique allows the separation of different proteins extracted from tissues such as blood. A sample of tissue is placed in some supporting medium, commonly a sheet of gelatine-like material. Because some of the amino acids that make up a protein have an electrical charge, the protein will have a net charge. Therefore, in the presence of an electrical current, the protein will move through the medium to the positive or negative pole. The size, shape, and electrical charge of the protein molecule determine how far it will move through the gel in a given amount of time. Thus, electrophoresis will separate molecules that differ in any of these properties.

After the proteins have moved part way through the medium, the gel is stained with various protein-specific chemicals. After staining, the different proteins stand out as bands in the gel. The proteins that are studied by this method are often enzymes. They are stained by reactions coupled to the reactions that they catalyze. The amino acid sequences in these enzymes are encoded by the nucleotide base sequence in the DNA. Therefore, by looking at the protein variability in a population, a biologist can get an estimate of the genetic variability in that population. The estimate will, however, be a conservative one, since the method discriminates only among proteins that differ in size, shape, or charge, not in other features.

of the best studied species) at least 71 different enzyme loci have been examined; of these, 20 have been found to be polymorphic in populations. In surveys of electrophoretic variation in many species, an average of about 30 percent of the loci studied have been found to be polymorphic. These findings imply that in many species there is an immense reserve of genetic variability for natural selection to act upon.

Figure 21.6
Tissue extracts are applied to one end of the gel, which is then placed in an electrical current. After a certain period, the gel is placed in a bath containing a stain that is specific for a particular enzyme. The dark-staining areas indicate how far the enzymes have moved in the gel.

21.2 THE HARDY-WEINBERG PRINCIPLE

Early evolutionary biologists studied changes in populations resulting from natural and artificial selection. However, it was not until the turn of the century, with the recognition of Mendel's work, that quantitative models to describe changes in gene frequencies in populations could be developed. In 1908, the science of **population genetics** was initiated with the formulation of the Hardy-Weinberg principle, named after two of the four scientists who independently conceived it. Population genetics assumes the principles of inheritance first put forth by Mendel, and explores the statistical consequences of these principles. The Hardy-Weinberg principle may be briefly stated as follows. Note that it in effect defines the conditions under which evolution does *not* occur in a population.

The proportions of alternate forms of a gene (alleles) in a large population will not change from generation to generation, unless they are influenced by mutation, selection, emigration, or immigration of individuals from other populations. If these conditions have no effect and if mating is random, the proportions of genotypes in the population will also remain the same after one generation.

The Hardy-Weinberg principle is basic to population genetics. Using it, one can state precisely the conditions under which there will be no changes in the frequencies of alleles at a locus in a population; that

417

is, the alleles at a locus will be at *equilibrium* (hence, the principle is often called the Hardy-Weinberg equilibrium). In terms of the Hardy-Weinberg principle, the word *population* refers to a group of individuals that can mate with each other and produce viable and fertile young. In this sense, there may be a one-to-one correspondence of species and population, but a species also may be made up of several such populations living in different regions and physically isolated from each other.

It is easiest to understand the Hardy-Weinberg principle by using examples. In Chapter 14, you learned to calculate genotype frequencies among the offspring of a single pair of individuals. Say, for example, there are two alleles, A and B, at a single locus. If both of the parents are heterozygous (i.e., AB), then we would expect that the genotypes of their offspring would occur in a ratio of 1AA:2AB:1BB. In this case, the *frequency* of alleles in the parents is 50 percent A and 50 percent B; that is, half of the gametes that either parent produces will carry the A allele and the other half will carry the B allele. Also the expected allele frequencies among the offspring are also 50 percent A and 50 percent B; 25 percent of the offspring will be only able to produce A-carrying gametes; 25 percent will be only able to produce B-carrying gametes; the remaining 50 percent would produce A-carrying and B-carrying gametes in equal frequency. *The expected allele frequencies in the offspring are thus the same as those in the parents.*

If one parent were AB and the other AA, then the allele frequencies between them would be 75 percent A and 25 percent B. The expected ratio of genotypes would be 50 percent AA and 50 percent AB; you can calculate that the gametes produced by these offspring would be expected to carry the ratio of 75 percent A and 25 percent B. With just two parents, each carrying a maximum of two different alleles at each locus, the predicted genotype frequencies and allele frequencies are limited to a few.

However, in real-life populations any combination of gene frequencies may be possible. For example, assume that in a population of 100 individuals there are 20 with the genotype AA and 80 with the genotype BB (Figure 21.7). If these all produce gametes, the AA individuals could only produce gametes containing the A allele and the BB individuals could only produce gametes containing the B allele. Thus 20 percent of the gametes produced in the population will carry the A allele and 80 percent the B allele. Therefore, the frequency of the A allele in this population is 0.2, and

Figure 21.7

An example of genotype frequencies predicted by the Hardy-Weinberg principle.

		female gametes (eggs)	
		A (0.20)	B (0.80)
male gametes (sperm)	A (.20)	0.04AA	0.16AB
	B (.80)	0.16BA	0.64BB

the frequency of the B allele is 0.8. Assume that the individuals in this population mate randomly; that is, AA individuals do not tend to select either AA or BB individuals for mates, but rather choose a mate regardless of its AA or BB genotype. Because 20 percent of the individuals are AA, 20 percent of the males and 20 percent of the females in the population are AA and the probability that an AA female will mate with an AA male is 0.2 × 0.2, or 0.04. In other words, four percent of the matings will be between two AA individuals. Similarly, the expected frequency of matings between a BB male and a BB female is 64 percent (0.8 × 0.8). The remaining matings will be between AA females and BB males, and between BB females and AA males, each in a frequency of 16 percent (0.8 × 0.2).

It is common to refer to the frequency of one allele in a population as p and to the frequency of the other as q. Let the frequency of the A allele be p and that of the B allele be q. The frequency of the AA genotype would then be described as p^2 and that of the BB genotype as q^2. An AB genotype can be produced in two ways: an A sperm fertilizes a B egg, with an expected frequency of pq, and a B sperm fertilizes an A egg, with the same frequency. Therefore, the expected frequency of a heterozygote could be written as $2pq$. In terms of these notations, the F_1 offspring of the population described above would be 4 percent p^2, 32 percent pq and 64 percent q^2. The equation $p^2 + 2pq + q^2 = 1$ would then yield figures to describe the variations in a given population for a given pair of alleles, where 1 represents 100 percent of the population.

What happens to the allele frequencies in the population when the offspring (F_1 generation) reproduce? Again, assume random selection of mates. The four percent that have the AA genotype will produce only A-carrying gametes; the 64 percent that have the BB genotype will produce only B-carrying gametes. The AB genotypes will produce equal numbers of A-carrying and B-carrying gametes. Thus, the *frequencies of the alleles in the population have not changed*. Following the same method, take this another generation. You will find that p_2 will continue to be 0.2 and q_2 will be 0.8, and so forth, generation after generation. Neither the allele nor the genotype frequencies will change from generation to generation. That is the Hardy-Weinberg principle. It is true regardless of the allele frequencies, regardless of whether they are 19 percent and 81 percent or 0.2 percent and 99.8 percent.

To give an example of how the Hardy-Weinberg law can help one study evolution, consider a different human blood polymorphism, the M-N polymorphism. This polymorphism is controlled by two alleles, L^M and L^N. In a sample of 6129 American caucasians, 1787 were MM, 3037 were MN, and 1305 were NN. Given these figures, the frequency of the two alleles in the population can be calculated. Keep in mind that the 1787 MM individuals carry nothing but L^M alleles and that the 3037 heterozygotes carry half L^N and half L^N. The frequency of the L^M allele could be calculated thus:

$$[1787 + (.5)(3037)]/6129 = 0.54$$

Similarly, the frequency of the L^N could be calculated thus:

$$[1305 + (.5)(3037)]/6129 = 0.46$$

Following the Hardy-Weinberg equilibrium, these allele frequencies would lead one to *expect* the following genotype frequencies in the population:

p^2 MM, or $(0.54)^2 = 0.29$
$2pq$ MN, or $2(0.54)(.46) = 0.50$
q^2 NN, or $(0.46)^2 = 0.21$

In the sample, there were actually 29 percent MM individuals (1787/6129), 50 percent MN individuals (3037), and 21 percent (1305/6129) NN individuals. In other words, the *observed* frequencies and the Hardy-Weinberg *expected* frequencies were the same. Thus, on the basis of these data, there is no reason to suspect that natural selection favours individuals of one genotype over individuals of the other.

21.3 CHANGES IN ALLELE FREQUEN-CIES IN NATURAL POPULATIONS

The Hardy-Weinberg principle is important because it allows one to state precisely what gene and genotype frequencies are to be expected in populations *if the population is not evolving*. Deviations from the expected frequencies indicate that evolution could be occurring.

In fact, in natural populations it is often found that allele and genotype frequencies do change from generation to generation and are not in Hardy-Weinberg equilibrium. This deviation is because evolution *does* take place in natural populations. For example, what if each individual with the AA genotype produced twice as many offspring as individuals with either of the AB or BB genotypes? The frequency of the A allele would increase in the population in this case because of natural selection. In this hypothetical example, it is not known why the AA individuals are so successful. Perhaps they live twice as long as individuals with the other genotypes, or start to produce young at half the age of the others, and thus produce young for twice as long. Perhaps they have the same life expectancy, but produce young at twice the rate. Perhaps they live half as long, but still produce twice as many young. The reason(s) for their success could be determined by careful study; yet regardless of the reason, the AA individuals are selected for (they leave more of their alleles than the other genotypes) and the A allele increases in the population. This selection is shown graphically in Figure 21.8.

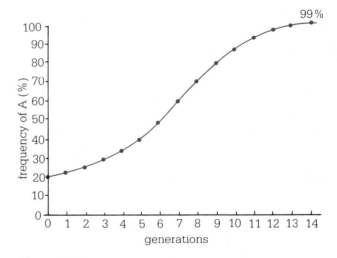

Figure 21.8
This graph shows the increase in 14 generations in the A allele in a population where individuals that were homozygous AA had fitness twice that of individuals with other genotypes. Starting with a frequency of 20 percent in the beginning generation, the frequency of the A allele is over 99 percent after 14 generations of selection. This level of selection is much higher than those levels generally found in nature; nonetheless, it accurately demonstrates that selection leads to rapid changes in allele frequencies in populations.

This evolution might be because of natural selection, but not necessarily so. The change may simply reflect chance (especially in small populations). Perhaps there are changes because of immigration of individuals from other populations in which the gene frequencies are different. Perhaps the individuals are not randomly mating (e.g., maybe BB individuals usually mate only with other BB individuals). These factors, especially natural selection, will be discussed in the following sections.

Fitness

Biologists often use the term **fitness**, or *Darwinian fitness*, to describe the relative life-long reproductive success of an individual; used in this way, the term means something quite different from its everyday meaning of physical health. An individual is said to have "high fitness" if it is more successful, relative to others in the same population, in producing many offspring that in turn survive to reproduce successfully. Its genetic characteristics will be proportionately more present in future generations of the species than will characteristics of other, less successful individuals in the species.

It is important to emphasize that fitness is *relative*. It is less a measure of an individual's characteristics such as strength, longevity, or vitality than it is a measure of its reproductive success. Those former characteristics may influence reproductive success and thus indirectly contribute to fitness. Yet they would not become more common in populations unless they were both transmitted genetically and possessed by individuals who produced young. Some individuals carry genetic characteristics that give them a fitness of 0. Such characteristics, known as "lethal" alleles, generally cause an individual to die before it reaches reproductive age, if not earlier. In humans (as well as in many other species) several lethals are known. Cystic fibrosis is an ailment that results from the presence of a lethal allele. It affects about 1 in 2500 newborn Caucasians, but is less common in other groups. The symptoms of cystic fibrosis are abnormal functioning of several glands, including the pancreas, liver, and sweat glands. Although many of the problems caused by this disease can be treated by modern medicine, most victims still die during childhood.

21.4 NATURAL SELECTION

There are many examples of selection taking place in nature. One well-known example from England involves a species of bird called the song thrush (*Turdus philomelos*) and a land snail, *Cepaea nemoralis*. The snails live in a variety of habitats, from open pastures to deep woods. The thrushes, however, live only in the woods, where they capture snails for food. Thrushes are unable to break snails' shells with their bills, so when a thrush captures a snail it carries it to a nearby stone and strikes the snail against the stone until the shell cracks. The thrush can then eat the snail's body, leaving piles of shells to accumulate next to the stones (Figure 21.9).

The shells of *Cepaea* shown on page 412 are *polymorphic*, occurring in a variety of colours and patterns. Some are banded with brown and yellow stripes and some are unbanded. By breeding these snails in the laboratory, biologists have been able to determine that this shell colour polymorphism (banded or unbanded) is inherited. There is, nonetheless, a great deal of variation among the banded snails; some of them appear at a glance to be unbanded because their bands are so indistinct.

To study the thrush predation on the snails, biologists gathered 863 broken shells found next to the stones. They then carefully searched for living *Cepaea* in the woods nearby, finding a total of 560 snails. They reasoned that the thrushes ate any snail that they could locate, but that the banded snails might be easier to see because the pattern could be easily seen on the shady forest floor. They compared the percentage of banded shells, unbanded shells, and obscurely banded shells that they found by the stones with the percentages of these types of snails they found living in the woods. Their results are given in Table 21.1.

Table 21.1   Percentages of Various Types of *Cepaea nemoralis* Snails Found Living and by Thrush Stones in a Woodland in England

	PATTERN		
	UNBANDED	OBSCURELY UNBANDED	DISTINCTLY BANDED
Percent Found Living	27.3%	25.5%	47.1%
Percent Shells Around Stones	23.6%	20.0%	56.3%

Although only about 47 percent of the snails living in the woodland were distinctly banded, over 56 percent of the snails eaten by the thrushes were distinctly banded. Statistical tests show that this difference is

Figure 21.9
The broken shells of Cepaea nemoralis *around this stone are a record of snails captured and eaten by song thrushes.*

Figure 21.10
*The black peppered moth (*Biston betularia*) is conspicuous against the lichens on a tree trunk (a), but camouflaged on the side of a soot-covered tree (b).*

(a)

(b)

"significant," that is, a difference that would probably not be found by chance alone. The thrushes find and eat the banded snails more often than they do the unbanded ones. Thus, the banded snails are *selected against* in the population of snails living in that woodland. On average, they would not live as long as unbanded ones; assuming that all snails reproduced at the same rate, they would thus not have as many offspring as the unbanded ones. Because the banded characteristic is passed on genetically, the percentage of banded snails would decrease from generation to generation in the woodland *unless* compensating factors were present. Such factors might include an advantage to the banding pattern that makes up for the cost of predation from thrushes, or an immigration of banded snails from other areas.

Indeed, because the banded snails are common in the woods, biologists thought that there in fact must be some compensatory advantage to the banding. Further studies revealed this advantage. Although banded snails in woodlands were *more* visible to the thrushes, those in pastures and meadows were *less* visible. Sunlight passing through grass creates a shadow pattern against which banded snails are not as visible as they are in woodlands. Thus, the predators in pastures and meadows eat proportionately more unbanded than banded *Cepaea*. Both kinds of snails are found in all habitats because they crawl from one habitat to the other. In the woodlands, banded snails are selected against, while in the pastures and meadows, unbanded snails are selected against. The different shell types are thus maintained in a dynamic equilibrium.

Another well-studied example of natural selection involves a polymorphism in the peppered moth, *Biston betularia*. As with *Cepaea*, there is a colour polymorphism. Some of the moths are greyish-white, sprinkled with black dots that resemble little flecks of pepper, while others are black (Figure 21.10). In the past, the black variety was extremely rare; the first known example was caught only in 1848, near Manchester, England. Yet by 1895, 95 percent of the peppered moths near Manchester were black! Why the sudden increase?

At night, peppered moths are active; in the day, they rest on the trunks of trees, during which time birds search the tree trunks for them and other insects. The flecked moths are camouflaged when they roost amongst the lichens on the trunk of a tree. On the other hand, the black moths are easily seen and thus easily preyed upon when they rest on the lichen-covered tree branches. However, because the lichens are extremely sensitive to air pollution, they often fail to survive in heavily industrialized areas such as Manchester. After the lichens die, the trunks of trees become darkened with soot from the air. When flecked moths rest against the blackened bark of such a tree, they are easily seen by birds, and a very large number of the moths are apparently eaten. By the same standard, the black moths are better camouflaged against the blackened bark.

In an attempt to further examine this selection of moths by birds, biologists raised both flecked and black moths in the laboratory and then released specimens of both types into polluted and unpolluted woodlands. Special traps were placed in the woods and an effort was made to recapture these moths during several nights following the releases. The numbers of the different types of moths released and recaptured are given in Table 21.2. In the unpolluted woodland, 12.5 percent of the flecked moths were recaptured, whereas only 6.3 percent of the black moths were; that is, about twice as many flecked moths were recaptured as were black ones. In the polluted woodland, the recapture rate for both kinds of moths was higher; yet the percentage of black moths recaptured was twice that of flecked moths — the inverse proportion to the situation in the unpolluted woodlands.

There are several reasons to account for the fact that not all of the moths that were released were recaptured. Some might have flown away from the woodland; others simply would not have gone to the traps. Many were of course found and eaten by predators.

Table 21.2   Numbers of Peppered Moths Released and Recaptured in a Polluted Woodland and an Unpolluted Woodland in England

		FLECKED	BLACK	TOTAL
Unpolluted Wood	Released	496	473	969
	Recaptured	62	30	92
	Percent Recaptured	12.5%	6.3%	
Polluted Wood	Released	137	447	584
	Recaptured	18	123	141
	Percent Recaptured	13.1%	27.5%	

Had the releases been made in only a single woodland, it would not have been possible to interpret the results. For example, a higher proportion of flecked moths might have been recaptured simply because they were easier to recapture than the black ones. Because two woodlands were used, however, that seems unlikely. If flecked moths were easier to recapture in one woodland, why not in both of them? These results, however, were as expected if the birds had been capturing a higher percentage of the black moths in the unpolluted woods and a higher percentage of the flecked moths in the polluted woods. The birds seem to be selecting for the black moths where the trees are soot-covered, and for the flecked ones where the trees are lichen-covered. By 1972, smoke control legislation in England reduced air pollution, and lichens again started to grow on the bark of some trees. As would be predicted by natural selection, there was a resulting increase in the relative frequency of flecked moths in industrial areas such as Manchester.

The examples you have observed raise the question as to why there is so much genetic variation in populations. In many cases, mutation has caused a new allele to arise in the population, but this mutation has not appreciably changed the fitness of the individuals carrying it. Such a **selectively neutral allele** may increase in the populations. (As you will see below, it may also by chance be lost.) There is, for example, no appreciable difference among the fitness of individuals of the various A-B-AB-O or M-MN-N phenotypes. In some cases, however, genetic variability is retained in populations because of the combination of selection for one enzyme in some areas and for other enzymes in other areas. Movement of individuals among the areas can also be a factor in retention of variability. Recall that the shell colour polymorphism in the *Cepaea* snails was maintained by the combination of selection and movement.

An example of an enzyme polymorphism that is maintained by selection and movement is known in the common edible mussel, *Mytilus edulis* (Figure 21.11). *Mytilus edulis* is found in the cooler marine waters of the northern hemisphere. Organisms that live in salt water tend to lose body fluids by osmosis to the seawater. Mussels and many other marine organisms possess mechanisms to reduce this loss of fluids. The concentration of salts in the seawater is balanced in mussels by their raising the concentration of amino acids in the fluids around the body cells. When the mussel is exposed to salt concentrations that are greater than those in its body fluids, it compen-

Figure 21.11
The adult edible mussel (Mytilus edulis) is permanently attached to sand, gravel, or rock. The larvae, however, may drift considerable distances before becoming attached.

sates by breaking down proteins into amino acids. One of the enzymes that is critical in this process is *aminopeptidase.*

Electrophoresis reveals that there are several different aminopeptidases in mussels that are coded by different alleles at the same locus. Three of these alleles are common in mussels that live in Long Island Sound, the body of sea water that is between Long Island, New York, and the south coast of Connecticut. These alleles are designated by the numbers ap^{94}, ap^{96}, and ap^{98}; they indicate how far the enzymes migrate in the starch gel (relative to the "fastest" allele, ap^{100}, which is not common in these mussels). The relative frequencies of these different alleles vary from place to place, but not in a haphazard manner. The ap^{94} allele is relatively scarce in populations that live in estuaries (where freshwater rivers flow into the ocean and dilutes the seawater) and relatively common where the salt concentrations are higher.

Laboratory studies show that these different aminopeptidase enzymes differ in their activity. Genotypes that contain the ap^{94} allele have significantly higher activities than genotypes that do not. Therefore, they are able to break down body proteins to

amino acids more quickly in all environments. Mussels with genotypes containing the ap^{94} are thus able to live in areas of high salinity without losing body fluids to their environment—but there is a cost. They break down proteins to amino acids and use energy and valuable elements such as carbon and nitrogen to make the proteins. Excess amino acids are lost to the environment by osmosis or are excreted. In areas such as estuaries, where salinities are low, mussels do not need the ap^{94} allele to be able to cope with osmotic loss. The presence of this allele causes them to produce an excess of amino acids which must be excreted, resulting in a waste of energy and elements. In estuaries, mussels with the other alleles are therefore favoured by natural selection.

Given these differences, why are all of the alleles found in all the mussel populations? The answer lies in the reproductive habits of the mussels. As adults, they live in shallow water, usually attached to gravel or coarse sand. When they reproduce, they release their sperm and eggs into the sea water, where fertilization takes place. After fertilization, the embryo develops into a tiny larva that is carried in the water currents until it is able to settle down and attach to the gravel. Studies have shown that these larvae (Figure 21.12) may be carried many kilometres by the currents. Therefore, although adult mussels in estuaries have the ap^{94} allele only infrequently (Figure 21.13), newly settled mussels have it relatively more frequently. Thus polymorphism is kept in the mussel population. The movement of the larval mussels between less salty and more salty environments prevents local mussel populations in estuaries from becoming optimally adapted to their environment.

Figure 21.12
A representation of the larval stage of the mussel. Microscopic in size, the larvae are carried in the ocean currents for three to seven weeks before they settle and develop into adult mussels.

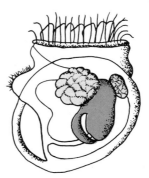

Figure 21.13
Variation in the frequencies of the three most common ap alleles in different populations of mussels in Long Island Sound and in the Atlantic Ocean along the south shore of Long Island, New York. The water in the western parts of Long Island Sound is not nearly as salty as that toward the eastern end of the Sound and in the ocean. The ap^{94} enzyme is important in enabling mussels to live in sea water.

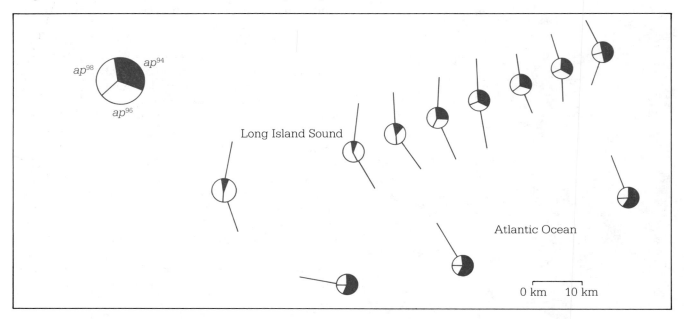

There are many good examples of selection operating on a quantitative characteristic as well. For example, the oil content of corn is not determined by alleles at a single locus, but is affected by variability at many loci acting together. One of the longest selection experiments ever conducted has involved selection for both high and low oil content in corn (*Zea mays*) (Figure 21.14). In both lines, the oil content was originally about 5 percent. After nearly 80 generations, oil content in the line selected for "high" has increased to about 19 percent, whereas oil content in the line selected for "low" has been reduced to less than one percent.

Figure 21.14
This graph shows the results of an experiment that has been carried on since 1896. One group of corn plants was selected for high oil content; that is, only the progeny that produced the most oil were picked to be the parents of the next generation. A second group of corn plants was selected in a similar way for low oil content. At first, the oil content was about 4.7 percent in both groups. After nearly 80 generations, however, the oil content in the low-oil group is less than 1 percent, whereas that in the high-oil group is nearly 19 percent.

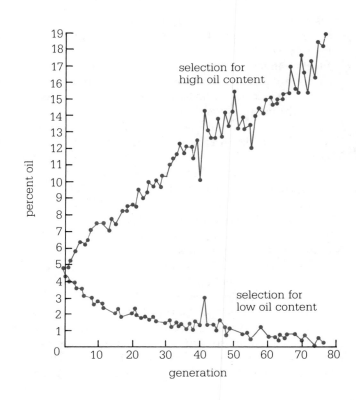

424

It is crucial to emphasize that natural selection may favour one genotype over another. However, natural selection also serves to maintain the physiological and morphological *status quo* in populations by selecting against individuals at the extremes of the range of phenotypic variation in a population. This sort of selection is often called **stabilizing selection**. Take another look at Figure 21.5 (page 416). The average birth mass is very close to the optimal birth mass; that is, it is close to the size at which the highest proportion of newborn babies survive. Very small or very large babies are selected against; giving birth to very large babies is also difficult for (and thus selects against) mothers. Stabilizing selection keeps the average birth weight of humans at about 3 kg to 4 kg.

21.5   OTHER FACTORS CAUSING EVOLUTION

There are factors other than natural selection that can cause the frequency of a characteristic to change in populations and thus potentially influence evolution. Two such factors are mutation and genetic drift.

Mutation

Mutations are the ultimate source of all of the genetic variability in populations. Most mutations reduce the fitness of the individuals carrying them, but some do not. If a new allele introduced into a population by mutation increases the fitness of individuals carrying it, it would be expected to increase in frequency in the population because of natural selection. Most mutations, however, decrease fitness and thus tend to be weeded out by selection. This selection is particularly efficient if the new allele is dominant. Selection against new alleles keeps new, harmful mutants from becoming more common in populations. If a new characteristic neither increased nor decreased fitness, there would be selection neither for nor against it. Such a "neutral" characteristic might increase in frequency simply because of repeated, similar mutations and the lack of selection against it. However, mutations are infrequent, perhaps occurring at each locus in only one in every 10^5 or 10^6 gametes. Thus, although mutations are the source of genetic variability they would without selection only slowly cause noticeable changes in allele frequencies in populations.

Genetic Drift

Allele frequencies can also change "by chance." The Hardy-Weinberg equilibrium describes ex-

pected results, not invariable ones. For example, if $p = q = .5$ at a locus, we would *expect* 50 percent of the individuals in a population to be heterozygous at that locus, but would often find some deviation from this figure that simply reflected chance. Such chance deviations would almost always be small in large populations — populations made up of many breeding individuals—but could be large in small populations. Think of tossing coins. When you flip a coin you expect to have it land heads half the time ($p = 0.5$) and tails half the time ($q = 0.5$). If you tossed this coin ten times, you expect it to land heads five times and tails five times, but would not be surprised to see some deviation from this expected frequency, such as six heads and four tails, or seven heads and three tails. Seven heads would occur less frequently than six, but would not be rare. On the other hand, if you tossed the coins 100 times, you would usually get very nearly 50 heads and 50 tails. Only rarely would you get 60 heads. The more times you tossed the coin, the smaller the magnitude of a chance deviation from the expected result.

In nature, as in games, chance events may be important. Actual allele and genotype frequencies may differ by chance from those predicted from the Hardy-Weinberg equation. However, chance events would lead to noticeable changes in allele frequencies only in small populations, and when natural selection was an unimportant factor. Indeed, in small populations of a species it is often found that some alleles are present in substantially different proportions than they are in larger populations of the same species. As well—and probably most importantly—we commonly find that many alleles are simply *not present at all* in small populations. They have, by chance, become lost in the population. This chance loss of alleles in small populations is often called **genetic drift**, so-called because some alleles seem to "drift" out of the population. Consequently, there is generally less genetic variability in small populations than in large ones.

Elephant seals (*Mirounga angustirostris*) illustrate genetic drift (Figure 21.15). These animals inhabit marine areas along the Pacific coast of North America. They used to be extensively hunted for their fat; by the 1890s, there were fewer than 20 individuals in existence. Today they are protected and their numbers have increased dramatically. Using electrophoresis, biologists have recently looked for genetic variability in the seals in 24 different enzymes and found the seals to have only one allele at each of these loci. This finding suggests that many alleles were lost by chance

Figure 21.15
Late in the nineteenth century, elephant seals (Mirounga angustirostris) were hunted to near extinction. Today, there is little genetic variation in the species, probably because the variation was lost by chance when the seals were rare.

Figure 21.16
Horseshoe crabs (Limulus polyphemus) are found in shallow waters along the Atlantic Coast of the United States and in other parts of the world. They are little different in general appearance from their ancestors that lived 160 million years ago.

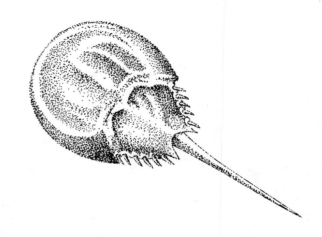

when the seals were so rare and that there has not yet been sufficient time for the variability to have been restored by new mutations.

21.6 RATES OF EVOLUTION

Although populations gradually evolve through time the actual rates of change vary considerably. There are doubtless some species that at a given time are not evolving at all. Evolution does occur, but it is not necessarily *always* occurring under *all* circumstances. For example, England has seen dramatic changes in the frequency of black moths in relatively few years. This change, however, is a rather simple one to understand and involves only the change in the allele frequencies at a single locus. This species has evolved with regard to this feature quite rapidly.

The fossil record indicates that rates of evolution vary greatly among different lineages. For example, the modern horse evolved from an ancestor that, about 50 million years ago, was the size of a fairly large dog. In addition to the great change in size, there were also fundamental modifications in structure in the horse lineage. The ancestor had four toes on its front feet and three on its hind feet, whereas modern horses have only one toe on each foot. There were great changes in the teeth as well.

On the other hand, the horseshoe crab (Figure 21.16) has evolved much more slowly than the horse. Contemporary ones are little different in external structure than those of 160 million years ago. The lampshell (Figure 21.17), still a common marine animal in some places, has changed little in external features for at least the last 550 million years.

Figure 21.17
*Lampshells (Lingula) superficially resemble clams, but
their internal structure shows that they are members of a
very different group, one called brachiopods. They have
changed little in external features for the past 550 million
years. Although brachiopods were once an important
group of marine invertebrate animals, they are rare today.*

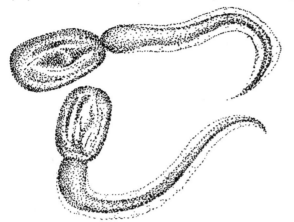

Two important factors affect rates of evolution: the amount of variability in the population and the intensity of selection. The more pronounced these factors are, the greater the rate; the less pronounced, the lower the rate. The bottom of the sea, the habitat of the horseshoe crabs and lampshells, has changed little for millions of years. Thus, there has been little selection for changes in the form of those species. On the other hand, horses changed greatly as they moved from woodlands into grasslands and went from a diet of leaves to one of grass. This transition took place as grasslands were becoming abundant on the earth and thus acted as an abundant source of food for animals that could graze. Selection strongly favoured individuals that were able to graze efficiently. Consequently, evolution of horses proceeded rapidly.

CHAPTER SUMMARY

Variations among individuals in a given population derive from both environmental and genetic factors. Genetic variability in an individual is known as heterozygosity and in a population as polymorphism.

The science of population genetics is based on the Hardy-Weinberg principle. This principle allows the prediction of allelic and genotypic frequencies in a hypothetical population where evolution is *not* occurring. Thus, deviations from the prediction can be taken as evidence of evolution which is occurring by means of natural selection or other factors.

There are abundant examples of natural selection in nature. Two well-documented studies, both done in England, involve land snails and peppered moths. Studies of the common mussel have demonstrated how allelic variations at the level of enzymes select for and against individuals within a species.

While natural selection is regarded as the central factor in evolution, other factors such as mutations and genetic drift may be important in some circumstances.

The rate of evolution is not a constant. It varies greatly according to the environment, the time, and the species.

Objectives

Having completed this chapter, you should be able to do the following:

1. Understand the nature of variability in populations.
2. Explain why evolution applies to populations, not individuals.
3. State the Hardy-Weinberg law and explain how it helps scientists study the process of evolution.
4. Give examples of selection occurring in nature.
5. Describe how selection, mutation, and genetic drift can affect genetic variability in populations.

Vocabulary

heterozygosity
polymorphism
continuous variation

population genetics
fitness
selectively neutral allele

stabilizing selection
genetic drift

Review Questions

1. Why must there be variability in a population be-ore organic evolution can occur?
2. What factors influence variability in populations?
3. (a) Explain what is meant by polymorphism in a population.
   (b) Give several examples of such polymorphism in humans.
4. How does the technique of electrophoresis help us understand genetic variability in populations?
5. (a) Distinguish between continuous and discrete characteristics.

   (b) Give examples of each.
6. What is the significance of the Hardy-Weinberg law?
7. Explain how the aminopeptidase polymorphism is maintained in mussels.
8. What factors *other than selection* might cause changes in gene frequencies in populations?
9. What accounts for the existence of "living fossils" (that is, species that have evolved very slowly)?

Advanced Questions

1. Although once a fairly common bird in North America, the whooping crane (*Grus americana*) suf-fered destruction of its habitat and was reduced in numbers to a low of 21 individuals in the wild in the winter of 1941–42. Today, fortunately, the cranes are responding well to habitat preservation and protection from hunting; their numbers have rebounded to approximately 100 wild birds. Suppose you were able to study the genetic variability in this species.
   (a) What do you predict that you would find, and why?
   (b) What would your findings indicate about the conservation and preservation of other species of plants and animals?
   (c) Do you think that the practice of exchanging animals between zoos is a good one? Explain.
2. Lamarck's now-discredited explanation for the evolution of the long front legs and necks of giraffes was given in the previous chapter. Using natural selection as a mechanism, explain how giraffes might have developed these structures.
3. *Panaxia dominula* is a polymorphic moth that occurs

in England. There are three different genotypes (AA, AB, and BB) that are caused by two alleles (A and B) at the same locus. The table gives data on the numbers of these genotypes in a population studied from four different years.
   (a) Using the data, calculate the frequency of the B allele in all four years.
   (b) Draw a graph illustrating any change that may be occurring.
   (c) Suggest what the data indicate about changes occurring in this population.

YEAR	NUMBER COUNTED	AA	AB	BB
1941	461	2	59	400
1947	1341	3	94	1244
1957	1612	5	138	1469
1968	131	0	3	128

4. During the 1970s, environmentalists in England organized a campaign to "bring back the grey-flecked moth." Why do you suppose they did so?

CHAPTER 22

THE ORIGIN OF SPECIES

The most curious fact is the perfect gradation of the beaks of the different species of
Geospiza [ground finches on the Galapagos Islands]. Seeing this gradation
and diversity of structure in one small, intimately related group of birds, one
might fancy that, from an original paucity of birds in this archipelago, one species
had been taken and modified for different ends.

Charles Darwin, 1842

Geospiza
scandens

Geospiza
fuliginosa

Geospiza
difficilis

Geospiza
fortis

Geospiza
conirostris

Geospiza
magnirostris

It is conceivable — it is even likely — that living things arose only once on earth. Whether life arose but once, or a few times from complex molecules, today there are millions of species existing in far greater diversity than existed on the surface of the young earth. Thus, since the origin of life there has been an enormous proliferation and diversification of species which evolution alone cannot explain. However, several models have been advanced that attempt to explain the multiplication of species. This chapter examines some of those models.

22.1 THE MULTIPLICATION OF SPECIES

A single species may change or evolve through time to become another species (Figure 22.1), but if this evolutionary path were true of all species, the total number and diversity of species in existence at any time would not change. In fact, there has been over time not only an evolution but also a *multiplication* of species. For example, the dog-sized Eocene mammal *Hyracotherium* is probably an ancestor not only of the several species of modern ''horses'' (horses, asses, zebras, donkeys) but also of the several species of rhinoceroses and tapirs. *Hyracotherium* (or a species much like it) has both changed through time and divided into many descendant lineages, each represented by several different species living today.

The process by which new species arise is known as **speciation**. It is of two types. One, as illustrated in Figure 22.1, is often called **phyletic speciation**. The other, as represented by the multiplication of species from a common ''horse'' ancestor (Figure 22.2), is termed **true speciation**.

Figure 22.1
How a species may change through time. The horizontal axis represents some measure of phenotype or appearance (for example, tooth size or coloration). The vertical axis indicates time. The species thus changes in phenotype through time. Fossils of this species taken at time a and at time b would be different in appearance; one might thus regard the two as different species. However, if a complete fossil record were available, one might observe that the species occurring at time a gradually evolved into that occurring at time b.

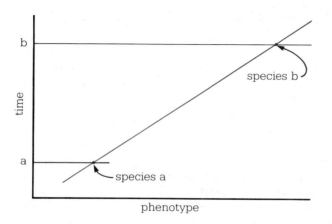

Figure 22.2
The small hoofed creature Hyracotherium of the Eocene Epoch, about 50 million years ago, was probably the ancestor to all living horses, tapirs, and rhinoceroses.

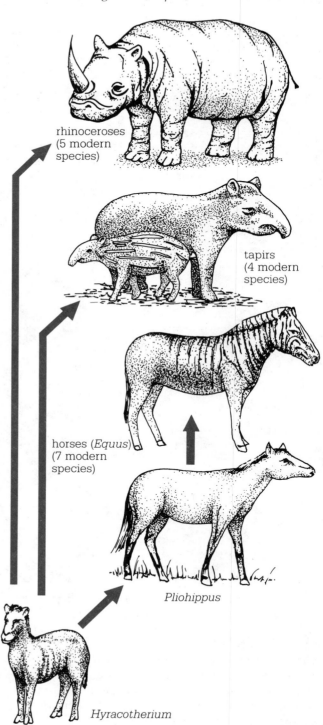

rhinoceroses
(5 modern
species)

tapirs
(4 modern
species)

horses (*Equus*)
(7 modern
species)

Pliohippus

Hyracotherium

SPECIES CONCEPTS

Most species were originally described on the basis of their morphological characteristics, but there are some obvious drawbacks to such a *morphological species concept*. Some very different-looking forms are really quite similar in their genetic make-up. Males and females of most species are different in morphology but certainly are not different species! Recall the polymorphic snails discussed in the previous chapter. Striped and unstriped snails are very different in appearance, but they readily interbreed with each other and quite successfully reproduce. On the other hand, some forms are very similar morphologically, but are so dissimilar genetically that they cannot produce young even if they do mate with each other. Many different species of budworm moths (*Choristoneura*) were originally described as a single species because they were virtually indistinguishable in appearance. Upon careful study, however, it was found that there were really several different species that did not interbreed with each other.

The *biological species concept* stresses the importance of interbreeding among individuals in a population as a defining criterion. Such a population could change through time; a biological species could be thought of as a unit of evolution. Yet there are also difficulties with the universal application of the biological species concept. It is often impossible to tell whether or not morphologically similar individuals from different parts of the world could or could not interbreed with each other because they do not occur in the same places. For example, can cactus finches (*Geospiza scandens*) from different islands in the Galapagos interbreed? The answer is uncertain, but it is a good guess that they could because they are so morphologically similar. Thus, a morphological species concept is in practice sometimes used for a biological one for lack of adequate information about interbreeding. As well, all species that reproduce asexually (such as dandelions, *Taraxacum officinale*) must be defined only on the basis of their appearance. In such species, each individual is an adaptively independent entity — a different biological species in that sense.

How true speciation occurs is a subject of much scholarly debate. Darwin's key work, *On the Origin of Species*, contains a brilliant discussion of the importance of natural selection in bringing about evolution in lineages. It does not, however, offer a clear hypothesis about the multiplication of lineages.

In discussing speciation, it is useful to define a *species* as a group of individuals that are reproductively compatible with each other, but not with individuals from other groups. In other words, an individual could mate or breed with another individual of the opposite sex and produce young that are themselves able to reproduce. Even though horses (*Equus caballus*) and donkeys (*Equus hemionus*) can mate and produce healthy offspring — mules — they are still considered separate species because the mules are almost always sterile. This view of species is often called the **biological species concept**. This concept cannot be used in describing many species in nature; it is, nevertheless, a useful concept for theoretical discussions of the process of speciation because it delimits a population that can evolve through time independent of other such populations.

In the previous chapter, you saw some examples of how natural selection can cause a local population to adapt to the local environmental conditions. Thrushes in woodlands select for snails with plain-coloured shells. The amount of salinity to which mussels are exposed selects for an appropriate aminopeptidase. Birds select for flecked moths in industrial areas.

In these examples, however, polymorphisms are maintained in populations as a consequence of two factors that in a sense counteract each other. On the one hand, there is selection for a particular phenotype in a local area. On the other, there is movement of individuals among areas, resulting in *gene flow* among local populations. There is selection for unbanded snails in woodlands and for banded ones in non-wooded habitats, but the snails move around among the areas and thus bring their genes with them. The possibility that a totally unbanded population of snails will evolve in the woodlands is therefore compromised by the flow of genes for banding selected for in the non-wooded habitats. The gene flow has prevented the evolution of two distinct populations of snails, one banded and the other unbanded. A single

431

species of snail has persisted in this case; both banded and unbanded individuals occur throughout England.

In order for two populations to become different through time it is necessary that there be little or no gene flow between them. The different hypotheses about how speciation takes place emphasize the importance of different kinds of *barriers* to gene flow. The barrier could be a physical one; for example, a river might separate the populations. It could be a behavioural one; for example, selective mating could occur, for example if banded snails were to mate only with other banded snails.

22.2 INSTANTANEOUS SPECIATION

Speciation can sometimes occur *instantaneously* (in a single generation) by major changes in chromosomes. Of the many types of chromosal change, that in chromosome number is likely the most significant.

Change in the number of chromosomes commonly occurs by the replication of an entire set of chromosomes. Individuals are generally thought of as having two sets of chromosomes; that is to say, two of each of the chromosomes that are characteristic of the species. An individual gets one set from its mother and the other from its father. As you learned in Chapter 14, such an individual is termed *diploid* or 2N. Normal sex cells (sperm and eggs) produced by diploid individuals are *haploid*, or 1N. Sometimes, however, an individual is formed by the fertilization of a 2N sex cell by a 1N sex cell. Such an individual is *triploid*, or has three sets of chromosomes, two from one parent and one from the other. Other combinations are possible, and in nature we find species that have three, four, or even more sets of chromosomes. One species of fern has 1260 chromosomes and is perhaps an 84-ploid (assuming a basic haploid number of N = 15). All combinations of more than two sets of chromosomes are collectively called *polyploids*.

Polyploid and diploid individuals generally cannot mate; if they do, they cannot produce offspring. The differences in the chromosome numbers in the germ cells produced are what prevent successful mating. For example, a 4N individual would produce 2N germ cells, whereas a potential 2N mate would produce 1N germ cells. Therefore, in order to reproduce, a polyploid would have to mate with another similar polyploid, or reproduce asexually. Triploids would have to reproduce asexually, because the three sets of chromosomes could not be divided equally into two dif-

ferent gametes during meiosis. In fact, many polyploids do reproduce asexually by a process known as *parthenogenesis* (from the Greek *parthenos*, virgin, and *genesis*, origin). Individuals that reproduce parthenogenetically are females that produce eggs with the same number of chromosomes as the maternal body cells. Thus a 3N individual produces eggs containing three sets of chromosomes that even without fertilization develop into other 3N individuals.

The many species of plants and invertebrates that are polyploids probably came into existence in a single generation. Each probably was first produced by diploid parents, but was able to reproduce only by parthenogenesis or by mating with another similar polyploid (very likely a brother or sister from the same brood). Because of the differences in chromosome numbers, polyploids generally would be unable to mate with diploid individuals. They thus would be *reproductively isolated* from 2N members of the species from which they came and by definition would be different species.

All species of birds and mammals are diploid, but there are a few lizards that are polyploid, such as the several species of whiptail lizards of the U.S. southwest and Mexico (Figure 22.3). Some of these lizards are 3N, some 4N; all of them reproduce asexually. Careful study of their chromosomes shows that many of these species were of hybrid origin. They were originally formed from the union of a 2N gamete from an individual of one species and either a 1N or 2N gamete from an individual of a second species.

There are other kinds of changes in chromosomes that might lead to instantaneous speciation. For example, sometimes two small chromosomes join to form a single large one, or a large chromosome may divide into two small ones. The house mouse *Mus musculus* has 20 pairs of chromosomes. The closely related tobacco mouse (*Mus poschiavinus*) in Europe has 13 pairs of chromosomes. The difference between the two is apparently because of chromosomal fusion and/or fission. For example, in the tobacco mouse, there may have been several instances where two small chromosomes fused to make a large one. Conversely, in the house mouse, large chromosomes may have divided. For a number of reasons, it is more likely that fusion occurred in this example (Figure 22.4). In the laboratory, these two mice can be hybridized. Yet because of the chromosome differences, the fertility of the hybrids is greatly reduced. Chromosomal changes such as these are probably less commonly involved in species formation than is polyploidy.

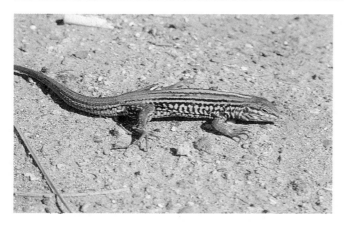

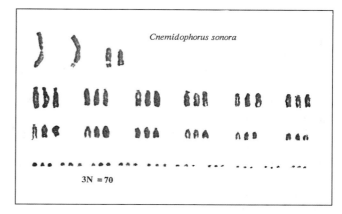

Cnemidophorus sonora

3N = 70

Figure 22.3
*There are several species of whiptail lizards
(Cnemidophorus) that contain only polyploid
individuals. These are all females that reproduce by
parthenogenesis.*

Figure 22.4
*The tobacco mouse (Mus poschiavinus) has a 2N
number of 26 chromosomes, whereas the house mouse
(Mus musculus) has a 2N number of 40. It is thought
that the tobacco mouse evolved from a house mouse
ancestor through seven instances of chromosome fusion.
Note that seven of the chromosomes of the tobacco mouse
are about twice as large as chromosomes of the house
mouse, suggesting that they were each formed by the
fusion of two small chromosomes.*

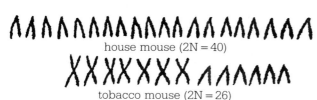

house mouse (2N = 40)

tobacco mouse (2N = 26)

22.3 GRADUAL SPECIATION

Although polyploidy has doubtless played an important part in the multiplication of species, especially plant species, it is generally thought that most species arose slowly as two populations gradually evolved differences through time.

The most commonly given model of how species may form gradually is generally called the **geographic speciation model**. It proposes that speciation can occur only if a population is first divided into two or more smaller populations (*daughter populations*) that are physically separated from each other. This separation prevents movement of individuals, and hence gene flow, between the two populations. Through evolution, each daughter population becomes adapted to the environment in which it lives. If the environments are different, the respective adaptations of each daughter population will also be different, provided that there is no movement of individuals between the different habitats (and hence no gene flow). According to this model, the two daughter populations will eventually become sufficiently different that they will be reproductively incompatible — and hence separate species. In effect, there could then be no gene flow between these populations *even if they were no longer physically isolated* (Figure 22.5). At this stage, these closely related species would be called a *species pair* or, if more than two species were involved, a *species group*. Through even more time, sufficient differences might have accumulated that they would be recognized as species in different genera.

Because the process of divergence and species formation is continuous, it is somewhat arbitrary whether two daughter populations are recognized simply as different populations in the same species, as different species in the same genus, or as different species in different genera.

Although biologists postulate that gradual speciation is a continuing process, they do not assume that divergence occurs at a constant rate. Rather, the evolution in each lineage could be taking place rapidly or hardly taking place at all. The concept of variation in rates of evolution is discussed in section 22.7.

Geographic speciation would generally occur in one of two ways. One would have a group of individuals (or perhaps only one pair) colonize a new area such as an island that is isolated from other individuals of the species. The next generation of individuals on the island would develop in physical isolation from individuals on the mainland. This process *might* explain

Figure 22.5
In the first stage (a) there is a single population. Within this population there is variability, but mating among individuals is more or less random. In the second stage (b), the population is divided into two or perhaps several daughter populations that are physically separated from each other. In the third stage (c), each isolated daughter population adapts to its environment, in the process becoming different from the others. In the final stage (d), speciation is complete. The physical barrier is no longer necessary to prevent the exchange of characteristics among the daughter populations. Each has become so different that it would not be able to produce fertile young even if it mated with individuals from another population.

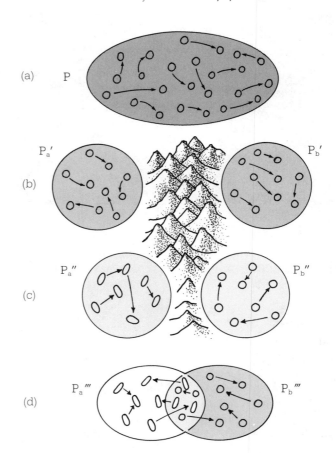

the divergent evolution of, for example, bird species on Madagascar and the African mainland (Chapter 19). The other way would have different groups of individuals become isolated in different areas as new physical barriers arise or as the range of the species changes. For example, during the Pleistocene Epoch (Ice Age) glaciers moved south across North America,

Figure 22.6
During the Ice Age (Pleistocene Epoch) glaciers moved south across North America, dividing woodlands into refuges in the southeast and the southwest. During this time, many species of trees and woodland-living animals were physically separated into different populations in the east and west, whereupon many evolved into separate eastern and western twin species. Some of these species hybridize at areas where they meet in the central part of the continent.

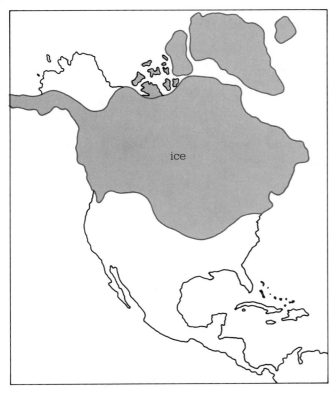

22.4 GRADUAL SPECIATION BY HABITAT SPLITTING

How can the present distributions of species give evidence about the process of speciation? The just-discussed example of the most recent ice age in North America could be considered. There is paleontological evidence that trees today growing in the north were pushed south into what today is the American midwest. Woodlands grew in the southeast and the southwest, but in the midwest there was apparently a dry, treeless area between the glaciers and the Gulf of Mexico (Figure 22.6). It could thus be predicted that many kinds of trees and animals that live in eastern woodlands would have evolved differences from those in the west, and *vice versa*. For several thousand years, the ice and desert between the eastern and western areas would have acted as a barrier to gene flow between species pairs in those two areas. While thus isolated, each of these ancestral populations would have had the opportunity to adapt to its respective environment.

To test this prediction, consider some species pairs and species groups of needle-leafed trees. In the east, one of the common trees of the boreal forest is the jack pine (*Pinus banksiana*). It is found on the Laurentian Shield, stretching across central Canada to the Rocky Mountains. In the Rocky Mountains and west of them, however, there are no jack pines, but rather the closely related lodgepole pine (*Pinus contorta*) (Figure 22.7).

In many eastern woodlands, the red pine (*Pinus resinosa*) is a common tree. In the west, the closely related ponderosa pine (*Pinus ponderosa*) is found. In the east, there is the eastern white pine (*Pinus strobus*) and in the west another, closely related western white pine (*Pinus monticola*). There are many other examples, often with more than two species involved. For example, the white spruce (*Picea glauca*) is found across the continent as far as the Rocky Mountains. In the Rocky Mountains, the Engelmann spruce (*Picea engelmannii*) grows. Along the Pacific coast, the closely related sitka spruce (*Picea sitchensis*) is common. These three species of spruce are all closely related to each other they probably diverged from a common ancestor in relatively recent geological times. These distributions provide indirect evidence that the ancestors of these trees were isolated in the east and the west and evolved differences while isolated. This finding supports the hypothesis that physical isolation is often a necessary prerequisite to speciation.

leaving much of the continent uninhabitable to most species of animals and plants. Many species that probably were widespread before the ice advance became isolated in little pockets of suitable habitat (*refuges*) in the southeast and the southwest of the continent. These populations would have been kept isolated from each other for thousands of years while ice was still south of the present day Great Lakes (Figure 22.6).

Because it takes a great deal of time to take place, gradual speciation is difficult to study directly. No one has seen it take place in nature, nor has it been simulated in a laboratory. Thus, the evidence for gradual speciation is indirect, and inferential, drawn primarily from the study of the present geographic distributions of species.

Figure 22.7
The jack pine (Pinus banksiana) *is a common tree in North America as far west as the Rocky Mountains. The closely related lodgepole pine* (Pinus contorta) *replaces it west of there.*

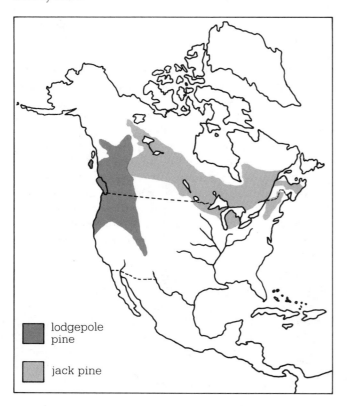

lodgepole
pine

jack pine

There are also many different species-pairs of animals in North America. The Baltimore oriole (*Icterus galbula*) is a common bird in the east; the closely related Bullock's oriole (*Icterus bullockii*) is found in the west (Figure 22.8). The ranges of these two orioles meet in the Great Plains, where they commonly hybridize. Many biologists thus consider them to be only a single species (called the northern oriole); that is, the two types are not sufficiently different to be considered separate species. Therefore, even though Baltimore and Bullock's orioles are quite different in their outward appearance, in most ways they must be very similar.

If there are two or more closely related species of woodland birds, one or more is generally found in the east and another or others in the west (Figure 22.9). On the other hand, most grassland birds have no east-west counterpart species. This second case is what would be predicted if the glaciation had divided woodland but not grassland areas into eastern and western pockets.

Figure 22.8
The Baltimore oriole (Icterus galbula) *is a common bird of open woodlands in the east. In the west it is replaced by the Bullock's oriole* (Icterus bullockii). *Although these two orioles differ in appearance, song, and environmental preferences, they can and commonly do interbreed where their ranges overlap in the Great Plains.*

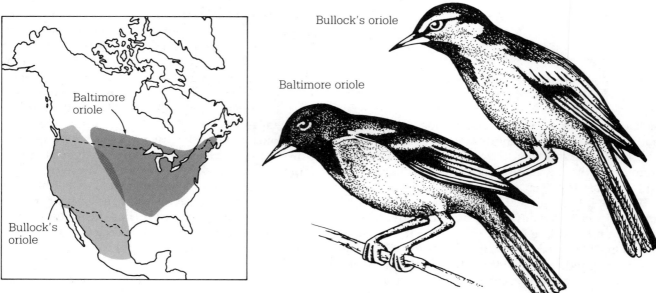

Bullock's oriole

Baltimore oriole

Baltimore oriole

Bullock's oriole

Figure 22.9
The eastern rose-breasted grosbeak (Pheucticus leudovicianus) (a) and the closely related black-headed grosbeak (Pheucticus melanocephalus) (b) are found in woodlands. They probably evolved into different species during the Pleistocene Epoch when their ancestors were isolated in pockets of woodland in the southeast and southwest. On the other hand, the grasshopper sparrow (Ammodramus savannarum) (c) and the vesper sparrow (Pooecetes gramineus) (d) live in grassland throughout much of North America. Their habitat was probably not divided during the Pleistocene, at which time they apparently did not undergo speciation. As a result, different populations of these sparrows have not evolved very different features.

(a) rose-breasted grosbeak

(b) black-headed grosbeak

black-headed grosbeak

rose-breasted grosbeak

vesper sparrow

grasshopper sparrow

(c) vesper sparrow

(d) grasshopper sparrow

Because the glaciation divided the woodlands in fairly recent geological times — most recently about 10 000 years ago—east-west counterpart species have not had many generations to evolve differences. They are still so similar to each other that in many cases there is hybridization where their ranges overlap. These populations are thus borderline cases between recently developed new species and well-marked populations of the same species. If there is hybridization, it occurs in only a few populations and only where the ranges of the two populations overlap. West of the Great Plains, there are no Baltimore orioles or jack pines. East of the Great Plains, there are no Bullock's orioles or lodgepole pines.

In short, the geographic speciation model involves first *isolation*, then *adaptation*, and finally *divergence*. In isolation, populations can evolve specific adaptations for their environment. These adaptations then lead to divergence between the populations in different areas. For example, Bullock's orioles are better adapted than Baltimore orioles to the relatively hot, dry conditions in the west. On the other hand, Baltimore orioles are better adapted to the relatively moist conditions in the eastern Plains and the northeast. If the ancestors of these birds had not been isolated from each other, the effect of selection for these different adaptations would have been offset to a certain extent by the movement of the birds from one environment to the other.

22.5 GRADUAL SPECIATION ON ISLANDS

Evidence for some of the most spectacularly known examples of species diversification is found on island archipelagos. (Again, the evidence is indirect and inferential.) Recall the importance of physical barriers to the prevention of gene flow. An island archipelago would therefore be an ideal place for speciation to take place because each island is surrounded by a barrier — the ocean. If the islands had been formed by volcanic activity in the ocean (rather than by splitting off and drifting away from the mainland), there would be no plants or animals on them. The first plant colonists would thus benefit from the absence of other kinds of plants on the islands. There would be no competition for water, minerals, or sunlight, and the colonizing species could increase in abundance rapidly. Thus both the climate and the organisms of the islands would be different from that of the nearest mainland; the colonizing population would, perhaps quite quickly, evolve new adaptations for its environment. As other plants became established, each species could become specialized in different ways. After land plants became established, land animals could then colonize the islands. A small flock of birds might become lost during migration, land on the island, and stay to breed there. A few lizards might drift out to sea on a log or on a mass of floating plants and become stranded on one of the islands. Again, the first colonists would find very little competition for the resources. Their populations could increase rapidly and evolve adaptations to the new environment.

The colonizing species would at first be confined to a single island, but occasionally would become established on the other islands in the archipelago. However, because of the water barrier between the islands, there would be little gene flow among islands. Distinctive species could therefore evolve on each island. The cycle of colonization, isolation, evolution, and recolonization would result in the multiplication of species on the islands (Figure 22.10).

RAPID EVOLUTION IN THE HAWAIIAN ISLANDS

When the first human populations arrived in the Hawaiian Islands from Polynesia about 1000 years ago, they brought with them the banana and other food plants which were unrelated to any plant forms already on the islands. There are today in the Hawaiian Islands 23 species of moths in the genus *Hedylepta*, all of which are endemic to the islands. At least five of these species, morphologically different from the other species of *Hedylepta*, feed exclusively on bananas. Therefore, they must have evolved within the last 1000 years.

Figure 22.10

A model of island speciation. At first (a) a population (perhaps only a single pair) reaches one of the islands in the archipelago. Once there, it may adapt to the new environmental conditions. Later, (b) colonists from the first island reach other islands, where they too become adapted to the local conditions. Then (c) colonists from these islands reach other islands in the archipelago. If they are no longer able to interbreed with their relatives on those other islands, the two species may cohabit the island while continuing to develop differences. In this way, there can be a great proliferation of closely related species on islands.

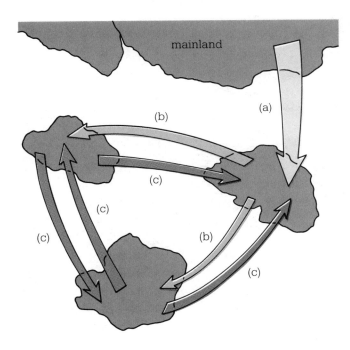

As predicted, there is a great deal of diversity of species on islands, at least within the groups of organisms that have been able to colonize them. Consider the Hawaiian islands, which are 4000 km from the nearest land mass. Only 17 percent of the 150 living families of birds and only 15 percent of the 1000 living families of insects have species that are found there. However, many of those species have undergone rapid speciation and show a great radiation of new types.

Various species of the fruit fly genus *Drosophila* are found virtually world-wide; they are one of the few groups of insects that have been able to colonize the Hawaiian Islands. There are today 346 different species of *Drosophila* in the Hawaiian Archipelago, about a quarter of all of the known species of *Drosophila*. Most of the Hawaiian species occur only on a single island. There are also in Hawaii at least seven other genera of insects that contain over 100 species.

Species in Hawaii are interesting from an evolutionary standpoint not only because so many different species have evolved there, but also because many of them have changed greatly from their probable ancestors. For example, measuring-worm caterpillars (which are moth larvae) are in North America all herbivores. In Hawaii, however, some species are carnivores—the only carnivorous butterfly or moth larvae in the world. There is a species of fly in Hawaii, related to the *Drosophila*, that preys on spider eggs.

Only a limited number of species of small land birds have been able to colonize the Hawaiian Islands. Yet in this group is one of the most remarkable examples of speciation and diversification that is known, the 43 species of Hawaiian honeycreepers. You can get some idea of just how diverse the honeycreepers are from looking at their bills (Figure 22.11). Many are slender-billed, feeding on the nectar of flowers and small insects. The downturned bills of the Kauai akialoa (*Hemignathus procerus*) and the beautiful, bright red iiwi (*Vestiaria coccinea*) fit perfectly into the curved flowers of several Hawaiian plants. See Figure 22.11 (a) and (b). Other honeycreepers, such as the apapane (*Himatione sanguinea*) and the crested honeycreeper (*Palmeria dolei*) augment their nectar diet with insects that they pick off foliage with their slender, straight bills. See Figure 22.11(c) and (d). Fruit and seed eating species, such as the Kona grosbeak (*Chloridops kona*), have heavy, triangular bills. See Figure 22.11(e). Using its heavy bill to tear the bark off branches, the Maui parrotbill (*Pseudonestor xanthophrys*) can expose its prey of larval insects. See Figure 22.11(f). The akiapolaau (*Hemignathus procerus*) pounds its straight, lower bill (which is only half as long as its curved upper bill) into a woody plant, then uses both bills to seize larval insects. See Figure 22.12.

Although the evolutionary relationships among these Hawaiian honeycreepers have not been determined, evidence from molecular studies suggests that they probably diverged from a single colonizing species from the mainland that reached the Hawaiian islands from 15 to 20 million years ago. Given the extremely interesting diversity of life on the Hawaiian Archipelago, it is no wonder that Charles Darwin put up a standing offer of 50 British pounds to any naturalist who would obtain good specimens from there.

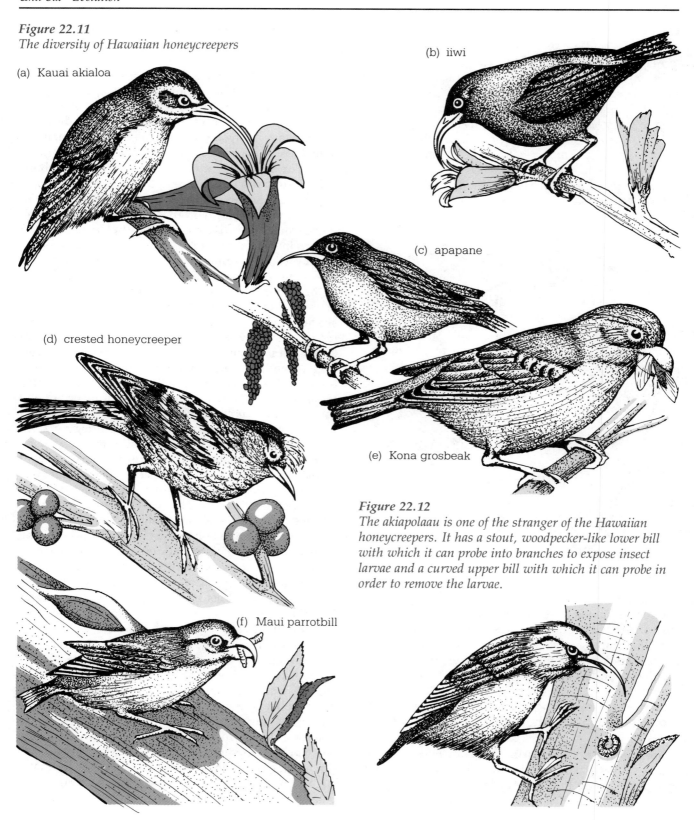

Figure 22.11
The diversity of Hawaiian honeycreepers

(a) Kauai akialoa

(b) iiwi

(c) apapane

(d) crested honeycreeper

(e) Kona grosbeak

(f) Maui parrotbill

Figure 22.12
The akiapolaau is one of the stranger of the Hawaiian honeycreepers. It has a stout, woodpecker-like lower bill with which it can probe into branches to expose insect larvae and a curved upper bill with which it can probe in order to remove the larvae.

22.6 SPECIATION WITHOUT PHYSICAL ISOLATION

The preceding sections have emphasized the importance of physical separation in the process of speciation. Is it always necessary for populations to be fragmented before speciation can occur? Probably not. In certain situations, new species could arise if mating did not take place at random. It has been suggested that this sort of speciation may be important in some groups of insects, especially those specialized to eat a few types of plants.

Consider, for example, the fly genus *Rhagoletis*. In general, flies in this genus both mate and lay their eggs on fruit in trees. After finding an appropriate piece of fruit, a male *Rhagoletis* fly will wait for a female to come to it. When she does, they mate; the female then lays her eggs in the fruit. When the young hatch, the larvae (maggots) eat the fruit.

Until the mid-nineteenth century, *Rhagoletis pomonella* was known only as a parasite of hawthorn trees (Figure 22.13). By 1864, some of these flies had become parasites of apple trees. They have spread widely through apple-growing areas in North America. Thus there are today two well-established groups of *Rhagoletis pomonella*, those that feed on apples and those that feed on hawthorns. (Recently, a third group that feeds on cherries has appeared.) If the apple-feeding flies mated only with their kind and the hawthorn-feeding flies mated only with their kind, there would be no exchange of genes between these two populations, even though there would be no physical barrier separating them. There is still little difference between the apple-maggots and the hawthorn-maggots, but in time more substantial differences may cause them to develop into different species.

There are examples of insect species that probably did speciate without isolation. Spruce budworm (*Choristoneura fumiferana*) do not interbreed with the closely related pine budworm (*Choristoneura pinus*). Inasmuch as the spruce and jack pine upon which these two kinds of budworms feed have broadly overlapping ranges, it could well be that these two diverged from a common ancestor without ever being physically separated. They are perhaps descended from two populations that were originally separated only because one fed primarily on spruce and the other on pine.

22.7 PUNCTUATED EQUILIBRIUM

There has recently been much debate as to whether species evolve through **phyletic gradualism** or through **punctuated equilibrium**. In the first case, evolution occurs at a more or less constant rate. In the second case, a local population rapidly evolves adaptations to the local environmental conditions to which it is exposed, then changes little for a long period of time (Figure 22.14). Proponents of the punctuated equilibrium model do not suggest that major changes in morphology appear instantly or that they become established in populations in only a few generations. Rather, they argue that these changes do occur quickly *in a geological sense*, that is, within a few 100 or 1000 generations.

Gaps in the fossil record make it difficult to determine which — if either — of these two models is more likely to describe what usually happens during speciation and evolution. Fossil-bearing deposits are usually separated by strata covering a time of at least 50 000 to 100 000 years; hence there is no evidence whether a species was evolving during that time (Figure 22.15).

Rather substantial changes in morphology could occur rather rapidly in lineages without requiring major changes in genetic make-up. Fossil ichthyosaurs provide a possible example. Ichthyosaurs are extinct marine reptiles that were common in the Jurassic Period, over 150 million years ago. Among the more specialized of the ichthyosaurs was a species called *Eurhinosaurus huenei*. It had a rostrum (snout) that extended far beyond its short mandible, or lower jaw; in this way, *Eurhinosaurus* resembles modern swordfish (*Xiphias*).

Figure 22.13
Rhagoletis pomonella *has become an important pest on apple and cherry trees. However, prior to 1864 it was known only as a parasite of hawthorn trees. The adult fly is about 0.5 cm long.*

Figure 22.14
Representations of phyletic gradualism and punctuated

equilibrium. In each, morphological change is indicated along the horizontal axis and time along the vertical axis.

(a) phyletic gradualism

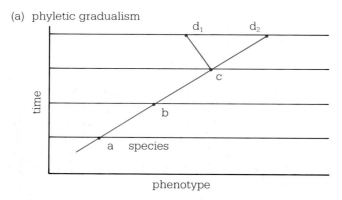

(b) punctuated equilibrium

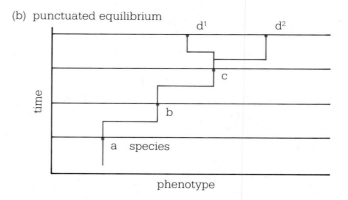

Figure 22.15
The change in tooth size (tooth length times tooth width) in the genus Hyopsodus, *mammals that lived during the Eocene Epoch. Tooth size is shown on the horizontal axis and time on the vertical axis. The samples of the geologically older fossils are toward the bottom and those of the younger toward the top. In all, it took about*

3.5 million years for these deposits to be made. At each time for which there is a sample of fossils available, the average tooth size is shown by the small vertical line, and the range of tooth sizes by the horizontal line. Where there is only one specimen, it is indicated by a single dot. These fossils indicate that evolution may take place at different rates.

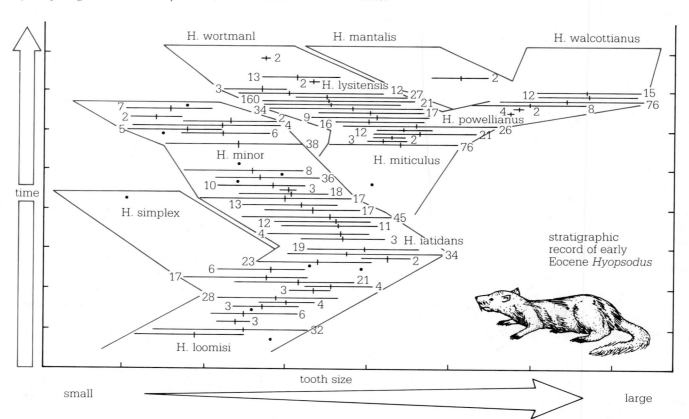

Figure 22.16
Excalibosaurus costini *was an unusual ichthyosaur because its rostrum was much longer than its mandible.*

In most ichthyosaurs found earlier than *Eurhinosaurus* in the fossil record the rostrum is about as long as the mandible. *Eurhinosaurus huenei* appears suddenly in the fossil record, as if it evolved rapidly from an ancestor like that shown in Figure 22.17(a). Recently, however, an intermediate species, *Excalibosaurus costini*, has been found. See Figure 22.16. Could *Ichthyosaurus tenuirostris* be the ancestor to an intermediate species such as *Excalibosaurus costini*, which then became an ancestor to *Eurhinosaurus huenei*?

In modern swordfish, the larvae have mandibles that extend to the tip of the rostrum resembling the jaw of *Ichthyosaurus tenuirostris*. During their maturation, however, the rostrum grows at a faster rate than the mandible, resulting in substantially different lengths of the mandible and rostrum in adult swordfish. The longer rostrum gives the swordfish an adaptive advantage in that it facilitates its catching of smaller fish. Perhaps in the evolution of *Eurhinosaurus huenei* there was slight change in the growth rate of the mandible relative to that of the rostrum, resulting in the great differences between *Eurhinosaurus* and

Figure 22.17
Eurhinosaurus huenei *(a) may have evolved from an ancestor such as* Ichthyosaurus tenuirostris *(c) through an intermediate species such as* Excalibosaurus costini *(b). A small change in the relative growth rates of the rostrum and the mandible would have been sufficient to bring about the great differences in the appearance of the adults of these species.*

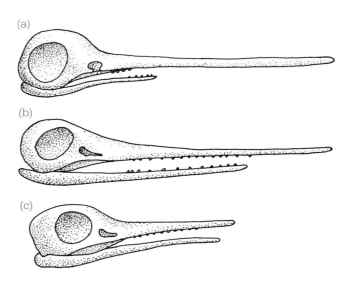

(a)

(b)

(c)

most other ichthyosaurs. Such a difference in growth rates would not require a major change in genotype in the *Eurhinosaurus* lineage. If the relatively long rostrum gave the ichthyosaurs an adaptive advantage, they could evolve rapidly.

The older model of phyletic gradualism and the more recent one of punctuated equilibrium are less opposing models than they are complementary ones. They differ most significantly in their respective emphases on the importance of speciation in the long-term evolutionary trends in a lineage. Phyletic grad-ualism stresses the importance of changes in a single lineage. It argues that species change through the accumulation of small differences. Punctuated equilibrium stresses the importance of changes that take place during speciation. It argues that local populations, often small ones, adapt rather quickly to local conditions to become distinct species. Rarely but significantly, some of these new species achieve an important "adaptive breakthrough," becoming widespread and replacing the species from which they originally evolved.

CHAPTER SUMMARY

During the history of life on earth, species have not only changed but also multiplied. New species may arise in a single generation through chromosomal changes, especially changes in chromosomes number. This sort of speciation may occur in either plants or animals, but probably has been more important in the diversification of plants.

Speciation may also occur gradually, through the slow accumulation of differences among populations over many generations. Physical barriers to gene flow among isolated populations of the same species make it easier for them to adapt to local environmental conditions and ultimately to become separate species. Speciation seems to take place particularly rapidly on island archipelagos, where there is little gene flow among islands.

Physical isolation is probably not absolutely necessary for speciation to take place. If individuals in a population mate only with others with whom they share a specific characteristic, such as a preference for a particular sort of food, new species could evolve in places where there is no physical impediment to random mating.

While gradual speciation has been the traditional model to explain how species emerge, the more recent model of punctuated equilibrium is also useful.

Objectives

Having completed this chapter, you should be able to do the following:

1. Outline both the morphological and biological species concepts.
2. Discuss the role of polyploidy in speciation.
3. Describe the origin of adaptations.
4. Explain the proliferation of species on some island archipelagos.
5. Outline the hypothesis of punctuated equilibrium.

Vocabulary

speciation
phyletic speciation
true speciation

biological species concept
geographic speciation model
phyletic gradualism

punctuated equilibrium

Review Questions

1. Distinguish between
   (a) organic evolution and speciation
   (b) the morphological species concept and the biological species concept
   (c) phyletic gradualism and punctuated equilibrium.
2. (a) Why do biologists attempt to define species on the basis of interbreeding among populations?
   (b) What difficulties are encountered in trying to define species of organisms that do not reproduce sexually?
3. (a) Explain speciation by polyploidy.
   (b) Give an example of a polyploid species.
4. Discuss the evidence for geographic speciation.
5. (a) Why are different islands in an archipelago often occupied by different but closely related species?
   (b) What conditions in the Hawaiian Islands might have enabled the evolution of such variation in the bill shapes of the Hawaiian honeycreepers?
6. (a) How might speciation occur without the existence of physical barriers to interbreeding?
   (b) In what kinds of organisms is this sort of speciation most likely to occur?

Advanced Questions

1. Compare the strengths and weaknesses of the morphological and biological species concepts.
2. In a geological sense, the Atlantic Ocean is a relatively young ocean. It was formed only after the separation of North America and Eurasia through continental drift. Offer an explanation for why there are many fewer species of marine organisms in the Atlantic Ocean than in the Pacific Ocean.
3. In the 1940s, chemical pesticides were first used on a large scale to control insect pests of crops in the United States and Canada. At that time, it was estimated that these pests destroyed about seven percent of the crops. Today, more than 400 pest species have evolved significant resistance to pesticides, and these destroy 13 percent of crops.
   (a) Explain how the use of pesticides and medicines could lead to speciation in insect pests.
   (b) Research some specific examples of the evolution of
      (i) insect resistance to crop pesticides; or of
      (ii) resistance to medicines by some diseases.
   (c) Suggest ways to reduce the evolution of this resistance.

ANIMAL BEHAVIOUR

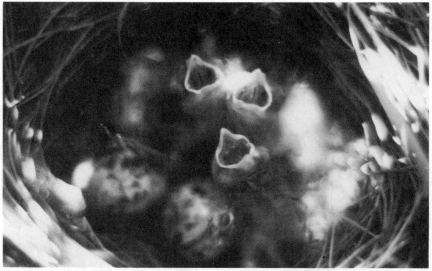

CHAPTER 23

THE BEHAVIOUR OF ANIMALS

*In the fields of observation, chance favours
only the mind that is prepared.*

Louis Pasteur, 1822–1895

T hese animals are all engaged in behaviours related to feeding, yet those behaviours are obviously quite diverse. Functional behaviour is as crucial to an animal's survival as are digestion, respiration, and reproduction. What determines how an animal behaves? What causes different species to respond differently, even to the same stimuli? These questions are among the most important ones asked by biologists who study animal behaviour.

23.1 WHAT IS BEHAVIOUR?

The Function of Behaviour

Behaviour can be defined as any external movement, action, or activity that changes the relationship between an organism and its environment including other members of its own species. In other words, it is what the organism "does." Behaviour includes both complex tasks that can last a relatively long time (for example, stalking prey or solving a math problem) and simple tasks that are almost instantaneous and unconscious (for example, blinking when an object suddenly approaches your eyes). As you learned in Chapter 10, behaviour is one of the mechanisms by which organisms maintain internal homeostasis. Drinking, for instance, is an act that restores water balance. Hibernation is a behaviour that lowers an animal's meta-

bolic rate, and thus its energy demand, during periods of cold stress.

Other behaviours are difficult to explain in these terms. Only a day after laying her egg, a female emperor penguin turns responsibility for it over to her mate and heads off to the ocean to feed. The male then incubates the egg for the next 62 to 64 days. During this time he fasts, living off his reserves of stored fat and losing a substantial proportion of his body mass. Obviously, this behaviour does not help him maintain homeostasis. It does, however, increase the likelihood that his young will survive. In fact, if the male did not behave in this way, the egg would not hatch and the pair would have no offspring. This particular behaviour therefore serves to increase reproductive output.

To increase the number of young raised is another major function of animal behaviour. It is the goal of a variety of activities, including those related to finding and courting a mate, as well as those involved with caring for eggs and/or young. Of course, behaviour that improves an individual's own welfare also helps to accomplish this end. An animal must obviously be alive and must usually be in good health if it is to reproduce.

Thus, in one way or another, the behaviour of animals living in their natural habitats is usually *adaptive*. Individuals that are ill or that have been removed from their usual environments may behave in ways that seem maladaptive (Figure 23.1). In normal circum-

Figure 23.1
Why whales become stranded on beaches is one of the biggest mysteries of animal behaviour. Examination of stranded whales often reveals an injury or infection of some sort that may have made normal, deep-water behaviour difficult. Faced with the risk of drowning, sick or weakened whales perhaps seek areas of shallow water to rest from the rigorous demands of swimming. (Whales are mammals; unlike fish, they must regularly come to the surface to breathe.) There is no way of knowing how often such behaviour might be successful; that is, how often a recovered whale returns unscathed to open water. Studies of the social behaviour of whales have led some to suggest that group-strandings may occur when healthy individuals attempt to help an ailing member of the population. Stranding therefore might be not an aberration but the result of a usually adaptive response. It causes death only when the animal is too ill to recover or if some miscalculation has been made.

stances, however, an animal's behaviour usually serves to maximize its chances of survival and/or reproduction. In short, an individual's behaviour increases its *fitness* (Chapter 20). As you will see in the following sections, the concept of fitness can provide a perspective from which to view the behaviour of all organisms — from protists to complex animals.

The Mechanism of Behaviour

The male meadowlark shown in Figure 23.2 is singing its courtship song. An inquiry into the cause of this behaviour might proceed at two levels.

First, *why* is the bird singing? This question addresses the *ultimate* cause of the behaviour. It is essentially asking about the function of song in male

Figure 23.2
A bird's song is often referred as an ''advertisement.''
Specifically, this individual is advertising that he is a male
meadowlark who owns a territory. His goal is to to attract
females to his territory and to discourage other males from
trespassing on it. He would prefer that the latter stay far
away from his mate!

meadowlarks; that is, how performance of the court-ship song increases the bird's fitness. The answer, in brief, is that singing helps him attract a female. If he did not sing, a male meadowlark would be unable to obtain a mate and would thus leave no offspring. Singing increases his reproductive output.

Second, *how* does the behaviour occur? This question gets at the *proximate* (more immediate) cause of a behaviour. It asks what occurred just before this individual started to sing that actually provoked the behaviour. Recall from Chapter 10 that at a very basic level, behaviour is produced by the action of *effectors* (in this case muscles and other structures in the bird's throat that produce song). The action is a *response* given to a *stimulus* that has been picked up by the individual's sensory *receptors*. The nervous system (Chapter 11) acts to filter and coordinate information running between receptors and effectors.

Types of Stimuli

The proximate cause of any behaviour is thus the detection of one or more stimuli. In the case of bird song, there are several different stimuli involved, some of which are internal. In many male birds, production of the hormone testosterone reaches a peak in spring. The presence of this hormone in the bird's bloodstream stimulates certain cells in its brain to initiate mating behaviour. The bird is thus *primed* (internally motivated) to perform a variety of courtship-related activities, including singing. It may then engage in these behaviours spontaneously.

In many cases, however, the animal must detect an additional but external stimulus before a given behaviour can be provoked. Often, internal and external stimuli interact closely, reinforcing or opposing each other. A meadowlark will sing even if he does not see a female but may increase his rate of singing if he does see one. On the other hand, an external stimulus may not provoke a behaviour if the internal stimulus is absent or weak. At certain times of the year, testosterone levels are low in the male meadowlark. In these periods, he usually will not sing even if he is surrounded by females. He is simply not interested in mating.

Changing levels of circulating hormones often cause individuals to shift their priorities, with the result that at different times of the year they may respond quite differently to the same stimuli. Since the level of hormone production is itself often determined by environmental events or conditions, there is thus a mechanism by which animals can alter their behaviour to accommodate changes in the environment (Figure 23.3). During times of the year when raising young is impossible, singing to attract a mate would be a waste of time and energy for male meadowlarks. The fact that testosterone production is much lower at this time ensures that they will not be stimulated to attempt courtship singing every time they see a female.

Other behaviours, such as those involved with escaping from danger, are appropriately performed at all times of the year. These types of behaviour are therefore usually not affected by circulating hormones but are elicited by external stimuli alone. Such responses must frequently be performed very rapidly if they are to be effective. They are usually more or less automatic responses, involving tight connections between sensory receptors, effectors, and the intervening neurons. The *startle reaction*, in which animals of various species draw or jump back immediately after detection of a stimulus such as a loud noise, is

Figure 23.3
Many of the behaviours exhibited by white-crowned sparrows occur predominantly or exclusively at certain times of the year and are linked to specific internal physiological states. Both behavioural and physiological cycles are produced by sequential changes in the levels of particular hormones released within the bird.

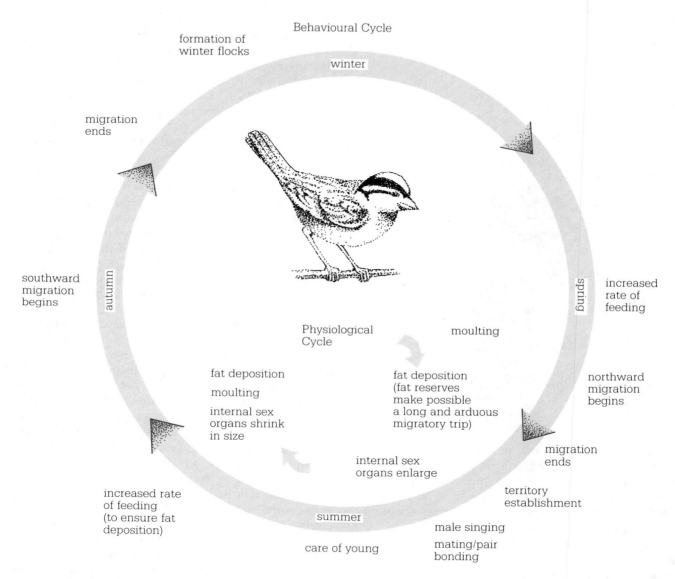

an example of such a response. It gives the responder time to escape and/or permits it to avoid the potentially dangerous source of the stimulus. The effectiveness of such behaviour would be reduced if hormones or other modifying stimuli intervened.

Still other types of behaviour seem to be independent of both hormones and outside influences. They are stimulated instead by cues from some sort of internal "clock." In other words, they occur in a regular pattern or cycle and are therefore referred to as *rhythmic behaviours*. There is evidence that all living things (plants, fungi, and protists as well as animals) possess internal *biological clocks*, set to a period of approximately 24 h, which govern their cycles of activity and rest. Termed **circadian rhythms** (from the Latin words *circa*, meaning about, and *dies*, meaning day), these cycles seem to occur even in the absence of all external stimuli (Figure 23.4).

Figure 23.4
The darker portions of the lines on this diagram indicate periods during which squirrels were active in their experimental chambers. During the first 17 days of this experiment, the animals were kept in total darkness. They still spent about 10 h foraging and 14 h resting, as they would in their natural environment. (As you may have noticed, the active period drifts slightly, with no external cues to set its beginning or end.) From day 18 to day 61, the chambers were lit for several hours starting at 2 p.m. real-time. The squirrels then gradually shifted their 10-hour activity period to coincide with this artificial day, as if 2 p.m. were actually dawn. When returned to total darkness, they continued on this new cycle for the remaining days of the experiment.

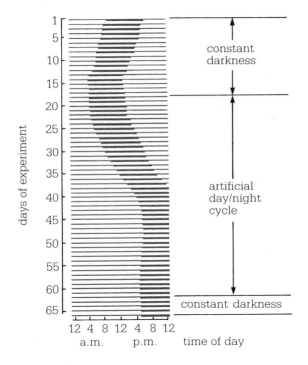

Figure 23.5
The brain of a rabbit. In all vertebrates, the hypothalamus is the portion of the brain that controls an animal's motivation to perform various behaviours, particularly simple responses such as eating and drinking. A very thirsty rabbit will ignore odours, sights, or sounds that might otherwise prompt it to eat, mate, or engage in a variety of other behaviours; it will concentrate exclusively on drinking or searching for water. Once the rabbit's normal balance of body fluids has been restored, the hypothalamus will no longer signal thirst; other types of behaviour may then take precedence.

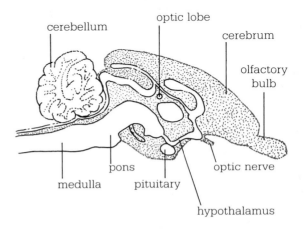

This is not to say, however, that external cues do not influence circadian rhythms in some way. Cycles can in fact be "reset" by a variety of such cues, the most important of which seems to be light. An experimental animal that is exposed to light several hours before dawn will have its clock shifted so that it is in tune with the new "environment." Depending on the difference between the animal's internal time and that of the environment, resynchronization of a circadian clock with altered external stimuli may take several days. This need for adjustment explains the "jet lag" that humans experience when they travel across time zones. The ability of organisms to reset their clocks allows them to stay in tune with alterations in environmental cycles such as seasonal changes in the length of day and night. Any behaviours controlled or influenced by a circadian rhythm will thus remain appropriately adapted to the local environment.

In addition to hormones and clocks, other types of internal stimuli exist. Hunger and thirst are two very basic cues that can provoke a variety of responses. Like other internal stimuli, these can act to alter an animal's behavioural priorities and thus control its actions. In mammals, the sensation of thirst is controlled by a small group of brain cells capable of measuring the salt content of the blood and thus the extent of an animal's need for water. When these cells register a high salt level, the animal feels thirsty; behaviour relevant to obtaining water then becomes very important (Figure 23.5).

Many types of behaviour are little more than automatic responses to these various internal and/or external stimuli. Although all types of animals exhibit at least some of these automatic behaviours, they are particularly common among less advanced organisms (section 23.2). Many of the responses exhibited by advanced animals such as birds and mammals are not similarly automatic. The behaviour of these more complex organisms can be modified in a variety of ways. Learning or experience can affect each individual differently (sections 23.3 and 23.4).

23.2 THE BEHAVIOUR OF SIMPLE ANIMALS

Much of the behaviour of simple animals consists of relatively automatic types of responses referred to as kineses, taxes, and reflexes. The uncomplicated nature of these behaviours reflects the simplicity of the nervous systems possessed by such animals.

Nervous Systems and Behaviour

One of the things that makes some animals "simple" is the structure of their nervous systems. Members of the phylum Porifera (sponges) lack anything resembling a nervous system, while animals in the phylum Cnidaria (for example, jellyfish and hydras) have only simple nerve networks (Figure 23.6). Lacking specialized nerve cells, a sponge has no way of conveying information quickly from one portion of its body to another. All of its responses are therefore very localized, involving only a few body cells at a time. The behaviour of sponges is correspondingly quite restricted. As adults they are sessile and able to perform only limited body movements.

Most members of the remaining "lower" animal phyla, such as Annelida (for example, earthworms) and Arthropoda (for example, insects, spiders, lobsters) do possess true nervous systems, including small brains, or ganglia (Figure 23.7). They also possess a variety of sensory receptors, as well as a number of different muscles and other body structures with which to effect responses. As a result, they are capable of many more responses and of more complex behaviours than are sponges or cnidarians. However, the range of behaviours they display is still no match for that of vertebrate animals. The relatively large brains and extensive nervous systems typical of birds and mammals, for example, permit an immense diversity of behaviours, from simple, automatic reactions to complicated, learned responses. To a very large extent, the complexity of an animal's behaviour is directly related to the size and complexity of its nervous system. It takes a great many neurons to be able to solve a physics problem, play basketball, or swat a

Figure 23.6
Cnidarians such as the jellyfish do not possess a true nervous system, which includes a brain and/or other centralized processing units (ganglia). They do, however, have primitive nervous networks such as the ring shown here. The connection of neurons into this structure allows the jellyfish to synchronize contraction of its muscles, thereby permitting it to swim more efficiently. Sensory cells in the tentacles are also connected to muscles in the central portion of the animal's body. As a result, the presence of food near a particular tentacle can stimulate contractions that move the jellyfish's mouth toward the potential prey.

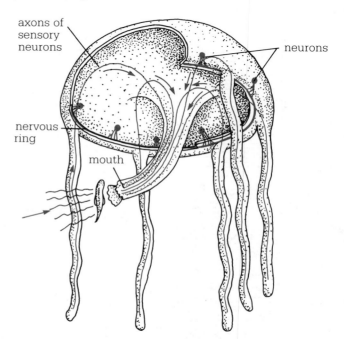

axons of sensory neurons

neurons

nervous ring

mouth

mosquito. Small, simple animals—like the mosquito—do not have enough nerve cells to accommodate the performance of such elaborate and diverse behaviours.

Simple animals nevertheless do exhibit a variety of responses which enable them to survive and reproduce successfully in their natural environments. Behaviour that allows animals to find food, shelter, or mates and to avoid predators or unfavourable environmental conditions is obviously of vital importance. Even small, simple animals have the behavioural means to cope with these problems—often simply by altering their position or location with respect to a particular stimulus. Two of the most common types of responses that accomplish this end are kineses and taxes.

Figure 23.7
The nervous systems of an earthworm (a) and a grasshopper (b). The possession of brains and/or ganglia permits the processing of larger amounts of sensory information and the coordination of many more responses.

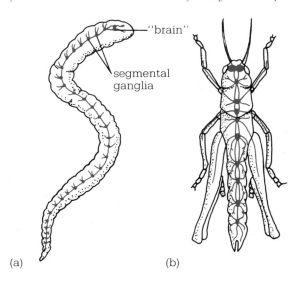

(a)   (b)

Figure 23.8
The path of a human body louse approaching a human. The louse follows a straight line in unfavourable conditions. Once on the host, the louse continues in the straight line until it reaches a less preferred zone, where it moves randomly.

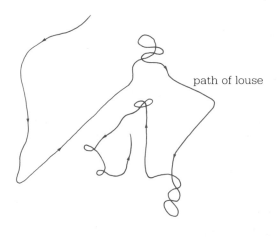

path of louse

Kineses

Kineses (sing. *kinesis*) involve a change in an animal's rate or pattern of movement following detection of particular stimuli. Different species respond in this way to different stimuli, depending on which cues are relevant to their particular lifestyles.

The flatworm *Planaria* spends its time in places that are fairly dark, such as under rocks or logs, where it is able to avoid predators and find suitable food. For a planarian, darkness is thus associated with safe and productive environments. It is hence not surprising that flatworms have the ability to sense light intensity, a stimulus to which they exhibit kinesis. A flatworm moves about randomly in lighted zones but slows down or stops in darkened areas. This behaviour increases its chance of moving out of the light and of encountering a more favourably dark environment. Once there, it tends to stay.

In the case of the human body louse, a change in the pattern rather than the speed of movement comprises the kinetic response. The louse exhibits kinesis in response to temperature, humidity, and odour stimuli rather than to light. These particular cues "tell" the louse whether or not it is on an appropriate host. While not on a host, and therefore in unfavourable conditions, the louse tends to travel in a straight line. Once a louse encounters a human, its environ-

ment suddenly takes on the temperature, humidity, and odour of its host. As long as it remains in this preferred habitat, the louse continues in a straight line. However, if the louse then suddenly enters a less preferred zone, it starts to turn in random directions (Figure 23.8). By starting to turn repeatedly after leaving a suitable environment, the louse increases its chances of re-encountering the conditions it has just left.

The mechanisms underlying the kineses of flatworms and lice are somewhat different. Yet in both cases, it can be seen that the response eventually brings the animal back into favourable conditions.

Taxes

Taxes (sing. *taxis*) involve the orientation of an organism toward or away from a stimulus. Animals that exhibit taxes can actually detect the location of the stimulus source, or at least determine its direction. This orientation is usually followed by locomotion; that is, the responding organism moves toward or away from the stimulus. Movement away from the stimulus is frequently referred to as a *negative taxis*, while movement toward it may be termed *positive taxis*. Taxes can also be classified according to the stimulus involved. For example, an orientation response to light is known as *phototaxis*; to chemical substances, as *chemotaxis*; to temperature, as *thermotaxis*.

Figure 23.9

In bacteria, specialized receptor molecules rather than sensory cells are responsible for detecting stimuli. Instead of sensory neurons, chemical messengers then carry information about these stimuli to the central processing unit—the nucleus. The ''decisions'' made by the nucleus (about whether to move or stay in a given environment) then appear to be conveyed to the effectors (the flagella) by some sort of electrical impulses, although not along motor neurons. This rather simplified view of stimulus–response connections in bacteria shows that the process is fundamentally similar (although different in detail) to that found in animals.

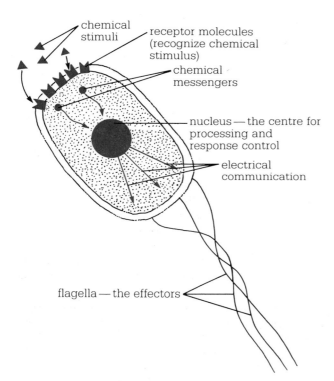

Many types of organisms display taxes, including single-celled protists and even some bacteria. These single-celled organisms, unlike animals, do not of course possess nervous systems or specialized sensory organs. Although the mechanisms underlying taxes in protists and bacteria are different from that of animals (Figure 23.9), the behaviour exhibited is much the same and is equally adaptive. The bacterial species *E. coli* exhibits chemotactic behaviour, orienting and then moving toward various sugars, amino acids, and other substances that it requires for survival and reproduction. Conversely, it displays negative chemotactic responses to potentially harmful chemicals.

Many types of photosynthetic protists, including *Euglena*, demonstrate positive phototaxis. They orient toward light, which provides them with the energy they need to manufacture food. On the other hand, house fly larvae, or maggots, exhibit negative phototaxis. When a maggot is finished feeding, it leaves its food source in order to seek a darkened (and therefore presumably enclosed and safe) location in which to pupate. Three or four days before pupation, such larvae will respond to the appearance of light by crawling directly away from it.

Reflexes

Simple animals also rely heavily on reflex behaviour. A **reflex** is an automatic, more or less *stereotyped* response to a particular external stimulus; that is, it is unvarying and fixed, performed in the same way each time by all members of the species. The uncomplicated nature of reflex behaviour is due to the simplicity of the neural mechanisms underlying it. In some organisms, reflex responses require the participation of only one nerve cell. Even complicated reflex responses involve little or no central nervous system control or coordination. They rely instead on direct connections between sensory neurons and effectors. Simply put, a reflex response involves only action, not ''thought.''

The importance of reflex behaviour to simple animals thus makes sense. The less complex its nervous system, the more the organism must rely on reflex behaviour. In cnidarians, the occurrence of adaptive responses such as tentacle withdrawal (in response to danger) depends on very simple connections consisting of only three parts: single receptor, conductor, and effector cells. See Figure 23.10(a). Some of the intermediate conductor cells are loosely interlaced, forming a *nerve net*. See Figure 23.10(b). Some nerve impulses can then travel from one part of the animal to another. However, most of a hydra's responses are very localized, involving only a few cells at a time. Because it lacks a true nervous system, there is, in effect, little communication among the parts of a hydra's body.

In a true nervous system conductor cells (called association neurons or interneurons) are grouped together into pathways (nerves) or centres of activity (ganglia and/or brains). This union of conductors allows incoming information from various receptors to be shared and integrated. Outgoing instructions (to effectors) can therefore be coordinated, modified, and finely tuned to specific situations. Organisms like hydra do not have such an ability to coordinate large

Figure 23.10
In hydra, there are separate receptor, conductor, and effector cells (a). The conductor cells interweave to produce a network (b), but definite pathways (like the large nerves or the spinal cord of vertebrate animals) are not formed. Nervous impulses simply spread slowly from the area first stimulated to nearby regions of the animal. There is no centralized control of behaviour and most responses are very localized.

Figure 23.11
The knee-jerk reflex is part of the body's automatic balance-control system. The sensory-motor connection shown constantly monitors the load on the thigh muscle and controls the activity of this muscle to compensate for any changes. The reaction that occurs when the tendon at your knee is tapped sharply is due to a brief overloading of the thigh muscle.

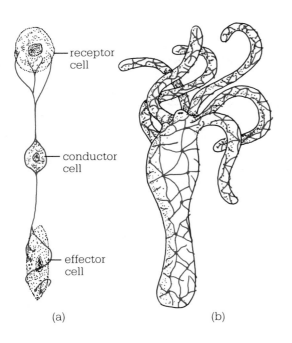

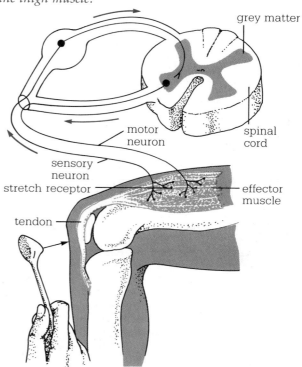

volumes of diverse sensory information and must hence rely heavily on reflex responses in order to survive.

Reflex behaviour is by no means restricted to simple animals. On the contrary, reflex arcs are a part of all vertebrate nervous systems and play an important role in the maintenance of internal homeostasis for these complex animals (Chapter 11). Consisting of a sensory neuron connected directly to a motor neuron, these arcs control behaviours that must occur quickly, such as the automatic responses that allow animals to maintain their balance. The familiar knee-jerk reaction in humans, for example, is a reflex that assists in the control of posture and equilibrium (Figure 23.11). Humans also possess a variety of emergency reflex reactions that permit very rapid responses, which occur long before the signals responsible for a conscious sensation of pain have been processed by the brain.

Not all reflex behaviours are based on neural pathways as simple as these two-neuron reflex arcs. Most in fact involve more extensive connections, with one or more interneurons between the sensory and motor cells. In addition, most reflex arcs make two types of connections with other nervous pathways.

First, the arcs almost always send information by way of nerves running up the spinal cord to the brain (Figure 23.12). The brain can then process information about the stimuli that initiated the reflex responses, produce conscious sensations (such as pain), and send additional instructions to the effectors involved.

Second, connections are often made to other reflex arcs, thus allowing the simultaneous participation of a number of muscles and/or body parts in a specific reaction. If you step on a thorn, a foot withdrawal response occurs. Stimulated sensory neurons in the foot pass impulses to motor neurons of the leg that must be raised. At the same time, these interneurons

Figure 23.12
In the central portion of the spinal cord, sensory neurons may connect with several interneurons. Some of these interneurons synapse with motor neurons on the same side of the spinal cord. Others cross the cord to synapse with additional interneurons that carry messages upward to the brain or with the motor neurons that serve effectors on the other side of the body.

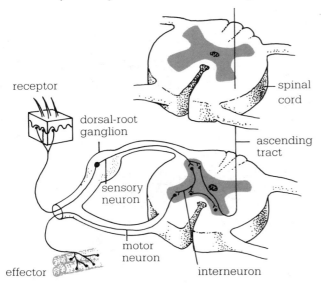

send messages across the spinal cord to the nervous pathways that control the other leg, preparing it to bear extra weight. A whole series of other responses are also generated throughout the body, making the muscular adjustments necessary for balancing on one leg. Meanwhile, the messages that have been sent to the brain are being processed. Part of the information goes to centres of the brain responsible for overall sensitivity to external stimuli. Another consequence of stepping on a thorn is increased awareness, which prevents a repeat of the same event! Still other parts of the message go to the cerebellum, which can then issue instructions if additional behaviour is necessary.

As you can see from this example, a single stimulus can set off a cascade of reactions. Reflex circuits can be quite complex and can control and coordinate a variety of simple behavioural responses. They may even provide the mechanism by which some kineses and taxes occur in complex animals. In addition, those reflex responses involved in the maintenance of balance are also to some extent part of even very complex behaviours. Most of these complicated responses do not, of course, rely on simple reflex circuits, but are the result of elaborate interactions between compli-

cated nervous pathways, hormones, external stimuli, and other factors such as learning. Just as it is not always possible to draw a firm line between simple and complex animals, it is not always possible to distinguish between what is a complex behaviour and what is merely a reflex response. It is perhaps most useful to think of the behaviour of animals as forming a continuum. At one end of this continuum lie the simplest reflex behaviours, in which only two neurons participate. Moving along the continuum are an array of behaviours of intermediate complexity: first reflexes that require the activity of extensive neural circuitry, then kineses, and then taxes. (In a variety of very simple animals, these types of behaviour can, of course, take place even in the absence of nervous systems.) Near the far end of the scale are behaviours that require intensive learning to be performed correctly. These behaviours are triggered by complicated combinations of internal and external stimuli and depend on neural pathways too complicated to be presently understood. It is these complex behaviours that are the subject of the following sections.

23.3 THE BEHAVIOUR OF COMPLEX ANIMALS

The behaviour of higher animals is a complex mixture of innate and learned components. There has been considerable debate about the relative significance of these two types of responses, particularly about how much each contributes to human behaviour patterns. This debate is often referred to as the ''nature-nurture controversy.''

Innate Behaviour
All the behaviours described so far in this chapter are examples of instinctive or **innate behaviours**. They have three major features. First, they are elicited or produced by relatively simple stimuli. Second, they are produced perfectly (or almost so) the first time they are performed; they do not need to be practised or learned from other individuals. Third, innate behaviours are stereotyped; they are carried out in the same fashion by all members of a particular species. (In the case of instinctive responses related to reproduction, all of the members of one sex perform the behaviour in the same way.) As these features imply, innate behaviour is *inherited*. The specific neural circuits and body structures necessary for performing these behaviours are coded for by genes; this coding determines the behaviours they produce.

Figure 23.13

The survival of this female digger wasp's offspring depends upon instructions for behaviour carried on her genes. These instructions are translated (during development) into the structure of her nervous system. She must have inherited the ability to recognize a male of her own species and to find a good site to dig her nest burrow. After digging a nest, the female covers the entrance with a pebble and flies off to find food. She learns the location of her own burrow by "studying" the surrounding landmarks. (She cannot relocate the entrance if an experimenter rearranges nearby objects.) However, she must have inherited the ability to see and to make use of such visual cues. Each species of digger wasp prefers a particular type of prey, the skills related to recognizing and paralyzing this prey having been genetically encoded. Returning to her nest, she uncovers it and draws the immobile food item inside, laying a single egg upon it. She then carefully closes the burrow and flies off to repeat the process as often as possible before dying. The still living prey will provide food for the young when it hatches—to repeat this cycle of behaviour.

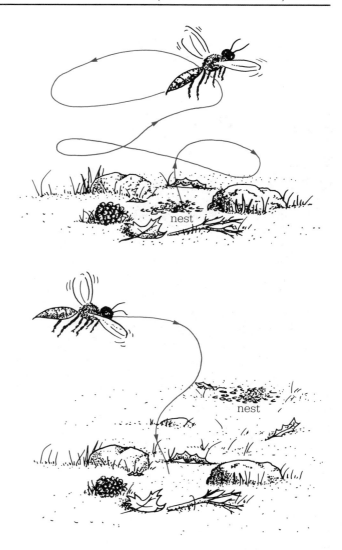

Innate behaviours are clearly adaptive for animals which have neither the time nor the opportunity to learn particular responses. In some species of wasp, for example, the female hatches alone (her parents having died the previous season) and often develops to adulthood in the absence of any contact with other members of her species. Her behaviours for finding a male, mating, building a nest, and laying eggs must be predominately innate; she has no one to learn them from and little or no opportunity to practise (Figure 23.13). Furthermore, since many wasp females have only one opportunity to mate, the behaviour must be performed correctly at the first appearance of the appropriate stimuli. The success of the behaviour is ensured only because the responses involved are innate. In other words, the reproductive behaviours are inherited, just as are the tissues, organs, and nervous systems that participate in these behaviours.

All animals possess at least some innate behaviours. As discussed, reflex responses are important in many situations; they are exhibited both by higher vertebrates (including humans) and by simple invertebrate organisms. Other, more complex behaviour patterns shown by advanced animals are also innate. Consider the responses which must be performed by very young animals who have not yet had much of an opportunity to learn. Newborn gull chicks crouch in the nest the first time they hear the alarm call of a parent warning them of danger (Figure 23.14). Newborn herring gull chicks are able to peck at the red spots on their parents' bills, a form of begging by which the chick secures food. Closely related to the gull is the kittiwake, a sea bird which builds its nest on cliff ledges so narrow that one misstep would result in a fall for the newborn chicks. Unlike gull chicks, which move about in and around their ground-level nests, the kittiwake chicks remain immobile until they are ready to fly (Figure 23.15).

The innate behaviours exhibited by these and other young birds are obviously vital for survival and must be performed as soon as the animal hatches. There is no time to learn them and mistakes can be very costly. The instinctive performance of these behaviours is clearly adaptive.

Figure 23.14
Attempting to reduce its conspicuousness, a chick crouches in the nest at the first sign of danger.

Figure 23.15
A young kittiwake must be born with the knowledge that it cannot move off its nest. It has neither the time nor the opportunity to learn this particular piece of information — one misstep would result in death.

Learned Behaviour

In contrast to instinctive responses, **learned behaviours** are not inherited. Although they do depend to some extent on possession of appropriate, inherited body structures, the neural circuits involved are not the relatively simple ones characteristic of innate responses. In fact, performance of the same type of learned behaviour can involve different nervous pathways in different individuals. Even within an individual, the specific neurons participating in the performance of a learned response may vary from one occasion to the next. Such behaviour is obviously not genetically controlled. Rather, it is learned — acquired (or eliminated) as a result of an individual's experiences.

Learning permits animals to use certain behaviours in order to adapt to changing environments. Advanced animals with relatively long life spans will likely encounter many habitat alterations and interact with many different individuals over their lifetimes.

Learning is therefore especially important to them. If their behaviour in a particular situation is adaptive, they learn to repeat the response when the same circumstances reappear. If it is not, they learn to avoid that response and perhaps try something else.

Learning is obviously necessary when the stimuli relevant to a particular behaviour are different for various individuals of a species. For example, animals that leave and later return to their own nests, dens, or burrows must learn how to find their way home using appropriate landmarks (Figure 23.16). Since the relevant cues will differ depending on where home is located and on where the animal has been, a completely innate home-finding mechanism would be inappropriate. It would force all members of a given species to respond in the same way to the same stimuli. Imagine, for example, the dilemma that would be faced by crabs trying to locate their own burrows by instinct from among all of the holes dug in a particular stretch of beach!

Figure 23.16
Wolf packs occupy a home range around their den that may be from 160 to 420 km² in area, at least during the summer. Within this area the pack travels along fixed trails following logging roads, rivers, lakes, and portages. Trails longer than 130 km have been discovered, along which the wolves navigate by using scent markings (urination posts) and other landmarks.

Figure 23.17
Within a baboon troop there is often a dominance hierarchy existing among the males. One individual, called the alpha male, is dominant over all others. Other male members of the troop may range below this one in dominance. This table shows the comparative frequency of copulation by three males in one troop with a female who was just coming into estrus (the physiological state necessary for conception). Notice that only the alpha male copulated with the female on August 29, the day she was in full estrus.

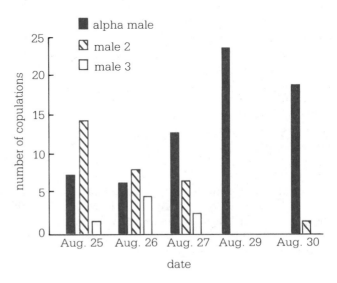

Learning is particularly important for animals that live in groups. In such environments, relationships among individuals can determine who will get a mate (Figure 23.17), who can feed (for example, at a lion kill), who will get the best den, or any number of other traits. Since these relationships are constantly changing, only if animals are able to learn new associations rapidly can they continue to behave appropriately in various situations.

The Nature-Nurture Controversy

How much of the behaviour typical of a particular species is instinctive, and how much of it is learned? What types of behaviour are controlled by heredity (that is, are innate) and what types can be modified by experience (that is, are learned)? These questions have generated considerable controversy, particularly with respect to species such as our own. This dispute, often called the **nature-nurture controversy**, was once quite serious, dividing scientists studying animal behaviour into two "camps." "Nature" implied that behaviours came naturally (that is, were inherited) and did not require training or experience in order to develop. "Nurture," on the other hand, meant caring for by feeding, protection, and/or education. The need of many young animals to be nurtured implied that most (if not all) behaviours needed to be learned before they could be expressed properly.

This debate has been largely resolved; most explanations of behaviour involve a compromise between these two views, allowing that the behaviour of almost every type of higher animal incorporates *both* learned *and* innate components. As you will see in the next chapter, much of the original controversy stemmed from the fact that researchers initially approached the study of animal behaviour from two distinctly different perspectives and employed contrasting methods of study. As a result, they produced what were often conflicting interpretations of animal responses. Yet both kinds of interpretations have contributed substantially to our knowledge of the functions and mechanisms of behaviour.

23.4 A BEHAVIOURAL CONTINUUM

Although some behaviours are clearly innate and others must be entirely learned before they can be performed, most animal responses do not fit neatly into either of these categories. Again, it is most useful to think of behaviour as forming a continuum. At one end lie the simple, purely innate responses that are genetically coded and controlled by a relatively few neurons. At the other end are those complex behaviours that must be learned and that involve the activity of a very large number of neurons. Although it is difficult to measure exactly the relative contributions of learning and instinct to any given response, it is helpful to have some way to arrange specific behaviours along this continuum. A number of schemes have been devised to classify behaviours in this way. One of the most useful, which is described below, categorizes the diversity of behaviour into four types: closed instincts, open instincts, restricted learning, and flexible learning.

Closed Instincts

Behaviours described as **closed instincts** are completely inherited and are susceptible to little or no modification through experience; that is, they are completely innate. Many reflex responses are closed instincts. This type of behaviour is particularly common in situations where it is adaptive for the response to be performed quickly and/or where the behaviour comprises a signal which must be made very clear to another animal. In these circumstances, the animals involved would benefit very little from any process (such as learning) that might modify the response; it must be performed rapidly, unambiguously, and correctly every time an appropriate stimulus appears.

Many courtship signals involve closed instincts. Upon encountering a female of his own species, a male wolf spider performs a stereotyped set of leg-waving movements (Figure 23.18). In many species, these courtship behaviours permit the female to recognize the performer as a potential mate. If the wolf spider fails to wave his legs correctly, and therefore fails to provide the appropriate signals, he will not attract the female. In some species, such a failure even leads the female to mistake the signaller for a member of a different species. She may then consider him to be a prey item and devour him before he has had a chance to copulate. Either result has disastrous consequences for his fitness, particularly for species in which males rarely have an opportunity to meet more than one

Figure 23.18
The courtship signals given by the male wolf spider permit females of his own species to recognize him as a suitable mate.

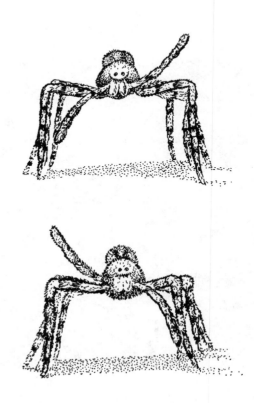

female during their lifetimes. This behaviour obviously selects for males that have inherited neural circuits enabling them to perform appropriate courtship behaviours correctly and completely the first time they meet a female.

Open Instincts

Types of innate behaviour that can be modified by experience are referred to as **open instincts**. The begging behaviour of herring gull chicks is an example of an open instinct. The movement and shape of the adult gull's bill and the red spot near its tip serve as stimuli to which the chicks respond by pecking (Figure 23.19). The behaviour is mostly innate; when it perceives these stimuli, a newly hatched chick begs sufficiently well to obtain a first meal. Over time, however, the chick's experiences teach it to modify (and thereby increase the efficiency of) its behaviour.

Figure 23.19
Herring gull chicks have an innate knowledge that pecking at a parent's bill is likely to produce food.

Figure 23.20
This graph shows the frequency with which laughing gull chicks in two different age groups pecked at different experimental models. Newly hatched gulls pecked at almost any pointed object. After three or more days in the nest, the birds became more selective. They pecked more often at model (a), which more closely resembles an adult laughing gull than do the others. (Unlike herring gulls, laughing gulls have a black head.)

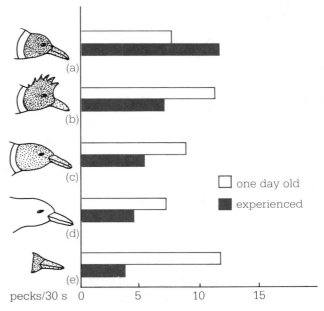

For example, it learns how to better judge the distance between itself and the red spot so that its pecks can be directed more effectively. In addition, the chick becomes more selective with respect to the stimuli needed to evoke the response. Although it will at first peck at any long, thin, moving object with a red tip, it soon learns that only pecking at an actual gull beak will secure food (Figure 23.20). Eventually, it even learns that it should beg only from its own parents. (Adult gulls will injure or even kill young that are not their own.) The animal's experiences thus allow it to alter its innate behaviour in beneficial ways.

Another way to alter open instincts is to suppress them or to reduce the frequency with which they occur. As mentioned previously, newly hatched gull chicks crouch in the nest when warned by a parent's alarm call. Whether performed in the nest or (as is the case when the bird grows older) in a chosen hiding place, this crouching behaviour is obviously a good defensive reaction to predators flying overhead. However, not all overflying birds are predators. Thus, after several experiences, the chick loses its generalized fear of birds passing overhead and ceases to crouch every time. This very simple type of learning is called **habituation**. It is essentially the reduction or elimination of responses that are followed by neither reward nor punishment. In normal circumstances, habituation is adaptive. In this case, the time and energy that the gull chick saves by not running and hiding from every

bird can be used for a variety of other purposes.

Gull chicks do not ignore *all* of the birds that pass overhead, however. This behaviour is appropriate, since the predatory species among them do in fact pose a threat. In this case, total habituation would be less beneficial than no habituation at all: all of the energy saved by not running and hiding might end up providing a meal for a hungry hawk. What the chick does habituate to is those bird species which it sees frequently — birds the size and shape of the ducks, shorebirds, and songbirds that share its environment (Figure 23.21). It does not similarly learn to ignore birds shaped like hawks (and other predatory species), since it sees these only rarely. As in the case of begging behaviour, the modifications of the defense response that occur as a result of learning are not haphazard or irregular. Rather, they are specific, positive changes, shared by most members of a particular species. Such changes increase the probability that an individual will survive and reproduce.

Figure 23.21
These models, representing the silhouettes of various types of birds, were used by Konrad Lorenz and Niko Tinbergen (who you will read about in the next chapter) to test habituation of young gulls to overflying predators.

Although the chicks initially crouched in response to any of the models, they eventually became habituated to (a) through (d). Models (e) to (j), however, which were shaped like various species of predatory birds, continued to evoke the crouching response.

Restricted Learning

Although its exact form is modified by experience, an open instinct can be performed the very first time an appropriate stimulus is perceived. On the other hand, behaviour involving **restricted learning** requires at least some environmental experience before it can be performed at all. The neural circuits participating in such responses are fairly simple, however, and can be modified to only a limited extent. In other words, restricted learning allows an animal to acquire a particular piece of information from the environment and to use this information to alter its behaviour in a relatively precise way.

Imprinting is one of the most familiar examples of restricted learning. Animals which exhibit imprinting have an innate ability to focus on certain stimuli during a specific period of their early development. In other words, their inherited nervous systems are primed to learn a particular behaviour at a particular time. The limited period during which this and certain other types of restricted learning can occur is referred to as the **critical period** (Figure 23.22).

Imprinting has been particularly well studied in ducks and geese. For these birds, as for many other animals, it is critical for the young to be able to follow their parents to feeding sites, hiding places, and so on

Figure 23.22
This graph shows the results of an experiment in which ducklings of various ages (in hours) were exposed to a moving model of a duck for 1 h, and then tested to see if they had become imprinted to the model. There is obviously a critical period during which this type of learning occurs most successfully. Ducklings less than 6 h or more than 22 h of age did not become imprinted to the model at all.

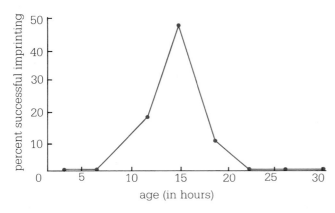

Figure 23.23
It is obviously adaptive for young birds to follow their parents, who in almost all cases will have been among the first things seen by the newly hatched chicks.

(Figure 23.23). This "following response" is learned through imprinting shortly after the young hatch. At this time, a young bird's nervous system is extremely sensitive to moving objects in its vicinity and responds to such stimuli by following them. Under normal circumstances, the only moving object which the chicks will see during the critical period is their mother. Her image is therefore what is imprinted in their memory.

Figure 23.24
Imprinted on a human, these birds follow him as if he were their parent. Although he will probably ensure that they get enough to eat (in a different way than their own parents would), the birds will still face some difficulties. Many types of animals also learn what their future mate should look like by imprinting on a parent. These particular birds may therefore meet with less success during their first breeding season than will others of their species who have had a more normal upbringing.

She becomes the stimulus which evokes the following response. In this instance, restricted learning is an efficient means of improving a young bird's chances of survival. If the learning involved was more flexible, they might learn to follow irrelevant objects—as they indeed do if their mothers are experimentally removed during the critical period (Figure 23.24). If the behaviour were wholly innate, all birds would require exactly the same stimulus to evoke a following response. The range of colour and size variation that exists among females (even within a single species) would make such limitations inappropriate.

Song learning in birds (and probably some features of language development in humans) is a further example of restricted learning. Many types of male birds sing songs that identify them as members of a particular species (Figure 23.25). They use these songs to attract females and/or to advertise their "ownership" of a particular area of habitat. This area becomes their *territory*, from which other males are excluded. It is usually here that the nest is built and the pair raises its young. Learning the song characteristic of their own species is thus vital to the reproductive success of the males.

Figure 23.25
Sonagrams are "pictures" of bird song. Produced by a machine which translates tape recordings of the songs (often made in the birds' natural habitat) into visual images, sonagrams show features of the notes that make up the song (their pitch and duration, for example) as well as characteristics of the song itself (how many notes it contains, etc.). Although the songs of individual birds may vary somewhat, each species has a more or less typical song, such as those shown for the Western meadowlark (a), the red-winged blackbird (b), the Northern oriole (c), and the white-throated sparrow (d).

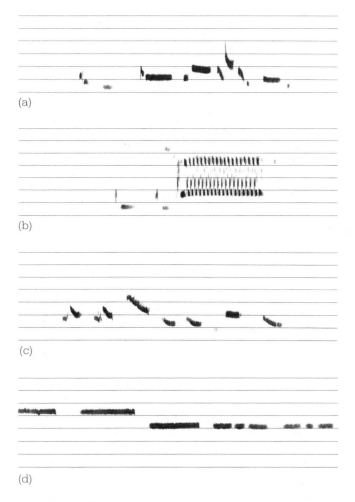

(a)

(b)

(c)

(d)

Figure 23.26
Sonagram (a) shows the song of a white-crowned sparrow raised under normal conditions in the wild. The song illustrated in (b) was produced by a bird reared in the laboratory, isolated from others of its own species.

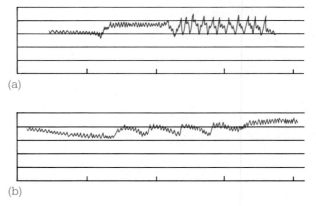

(a)

(b)

Individuals of some bird species appear to learn their songs by hearing their fathers sing. If a young white-crowned sparrow is raised in isolation in the laboratory (where it hears no songs), it will produce an abnormal song when it reaches adulthood (Figure 23.26). On the other hand, a sparrow that hears tape recorded songs of its own species during the critical period *will* learn to sing normally. If the song of a different species is played during this time, however, it is not learned: the bird will again sing an abnormal white-throated sparrow song an adult. It can apparently learn only the song of its own species. Thus, although these birds must *learn* to sing properly, they have been *innately* programmed to recognize and learn only certain things. Singing the wrong song would make it difficult or impossible for a bird to attract a female of its own species (and therefore successfully reproduce). Natural selection hence favours genotypes that prevent such mistakes from occurring, genotypes that code for neural circuits capable of recognizing and learning only certain types of song.

Flexible Learning

The difference between restricted learning and **flexible learning** is really one of degree. In the former, there are relatively strict limitations on what is learned, as well as on how and when it is learned. In the latter, many fewer limitations are involved. Behaviours that are the result of flexible learning can usually be continuously modified throughout the life of an animal as a result of new input from the environment. In addition, the range of environmental information that can affect behaviour is much broader. Four major types of flexible learning are exploratory, trial and error, insight, and imitation.

Figure 23.27
A chickadee hoarding food

Exploratory Learning

Exploratory learning, which enables a wide variety of animals to leave and later return to their homes or food storage sites, is one important type of flexible learning. Many different stimuli or features serve as cues which allow animals to learn a ''map'' of their environment by which they can find their way around. Such an ability is obviously vital for many species. Small rodents such as mice, rats, and voles usually build some type of nest in a safe, sheltered location. There, they can sleep in safety and often store food. A complex series of runways in the grass, the ground, or under the snow is then built to connect the nest with *foraging* areas (areas where they find, hunt, and/or catch food). The most successful mice are those that can find their way home quickly and accurately, especially if they are being pursued by predators. Laboratory experiments have shown that some white-footed mice can in only two or three days learn their way around an artificial maze with over 400 m of runways and 450 blind alleys. Similar feats of exploratory learning are shown by bird species such as the black-capped chickadee. Chickadees store food supplies to last them through the winter, hiding seeds and other edible items in the cracks and crevices of tree bark. They can remember the location of a surprising number of these hoards for quite a long time after they have hidden them (Figure 23.27).

Trial and Error Learning

Trial and error learning (about which you will learn more in Chapter 24) enables many types of animals to learn what and how to eat. Young toads will attempt to feed on almost anything. Successful capture of an edible prey item is rewarding; the toad's feeling of hunger diminishes. It will then incorporate this species into its regular diet. Conversely, food types that are difficult to catch, that taste bad, or that make the toad sick do not provide such a reward. The toad then tends to stop trying to feed on such items. Learning a food preference in this way produces adaptively flexible behaviour. Since the abundance of particular food types changes over time (certain species are available at only certain times of the year), it is advantageous for toads to be able to continually modify their foraging behaviour. Trial and error learning of this type can continue throughout an animal's life.

Insight Learning

Some of the most complex and least understood of all animal behaviours are produced by **insight learning**, or *reasoning*. Perhaps the most flexible of all learning processes, it is characteristic only of animals with very complex brains. Porpoises, apes, and humans are among the relatively few species which have been shown to be capable of insight.

Insight learning allows animals to respond appropriately to new stimuli or to new arrangements of old stimuli never previously encountered. An individual shows insight when it attempts to solve a problem by recalling relevant past experiences rather than by resorting to trial and error. It is this type of learning process that allows a chimpanzee to stack boxes in order to climb up to get at an out-of-reach banana, even if it has never done so before (Figure 23.28). The association of many separate previous learning experiences is necessary to accomplish such a task.

To a large extent, insight depends on the learning of *concepts*, or general principles. This learning involves recognition of the common elements in a number of items or phenomena. If a child can identify a poodle and a St. Bernard together as members of a single species, he or she has learned the concept ''dog.'' Similarly, studies on monkeys and other animals have shown that they can learn concepts such as oddity (Figure 23.29). Other types of animals do not display insight when solving experimental problems and apparently cannot master concepts. Rats do not appear to be able to learn the concept ''middleness'' (Figure 23.30). Instead, they seem to rely on trial and error to solve experimental problems.

Figure 23.28
The classic example of insight learning in animals comes from the work of Wolfgang Kohler, who placed chimpanzees by themselves in a room containing a number of boxes and a bunch of bananas hung too high to reach. After a period of time, some of the chimps piled up the boxes to make a stand from which they could get at the food. Although it is often difficult to distinguish insight from other types of learning, many mammals and some birds have been shown to apparently have some reasoning ability (like that of the chimps).

Figure 23.29
This monkey has learned that it can find food under the "odd" shape in each set of three presented. It therefore picks out the odd shape regardless of what objects are presented or where the odd item is located.

Figure 23.30
Unlike a chimp or a monkey, a rat does not appear able to learn concepts. In this test situation, a rat can obtain food by going through the middle of the three open doors, regardless of the position of these doors. Unable to learn the concept of "middleness," the rat usually goes first to whichever open door it obtained food from last; it is attempting to employ trial and error rather than concept learning.

Imitation

Among social animals, many complex responses are learned by **imitation**. While one individual may have hit upon the success of a particular behaviour through trial and error or through reasoning, others may have learned it simply by watching the behaviour and then copying it. Such behaviours are said to be culturally transmitted; that is, they are passed on within a species or population by tradition.

A group of Japanese macaques (monkeys) living in a semi-natural colony on the island of Koshima provide an interesting example of learning by imitation. Researchers regularly left sweet potatoes and wheat on the beach as food for the colony. Most individuals ate these foods as they were, covered with sand. One day, a young female, named Imo by the researchers, was observed using seawater to wash the sand off a sweet potato. Her behaviour was quickly copied by her mother as well as by other female macaques her own age, with whom she regularly played. When these individuals later became mothers themselves, their offspring copied the washing behaviour which the females continued to exhibit. The tradition had become firmly established within the colony.

Imo was an unusual macaque. As an adult, she later discovered that she could separate wheat from sand by throwing a handful of the two mixed together into the water. The sand would sink and she would then scoop up and eat the floating wheat. Within a few years this behaviour too had become a tradition within the troop. Cultural transmission of behaviour has been observed in a variety of social animals (Figure 23.31). The increased potential for the generation and subsequent learning of new responses is thought to be one of the benefits of group living.

Figure 23.31
For many years, English milkmen had been leaving their deliveries outside, on porches and front steps. In 1951, a few individual great tits (a species of bird found in England, which is related to the North American chickadees) suddenly learned how to open the milk bottles to drink from the top. Within a short period of time, many members of the species were performing this "trick." The behaviour became a tradition that people now have to guard against.

CHAPTER SUMMARY

The behaviour of animals living in their natural environments is almost always adaptive. In other words, its ultimate function is to increase an individual's fitness in some way. The proximate cause of a particular response is usually a stimulus, or a set of stimuli, that serve to provoke that behaviour. While many of these stimuli are external, internal cues such as hormones can also play a role. Certain responses, termed rhythmic behaviours, seem to occur independently of both hormones and external cues. They appear to be controlled instead by biological (for example, circadian) clocks.

To a large extent, the range of behaviours of which an animal is capable depends on the complexity of its nervous system. Lacking even specialized nerve cells, very simple animals exhibit only a limited number of responses. More complex organisms such as flatworms and arthropods do possess neurons and sim-

ple nervous systems. By coordinating the activities of sensory receptors and effectors, such systems permit more complicated and diverse responses. Kineses, taxes, and reflexes are categories of fairly basic responses by which all animals, simple and complex, cope with changes in their surroundings. Complex animals also display a wide range of learned behaviours which are not inherited. Learning permits animals to adapt behaviourally to changing environments and is particularly important for advanced animals with relatively long life spans.

Although some behaviours are completely innate and others are wholly learned, most animal responses do not fit neatly into either of these two categories. In fact, animal behaviour forms a continuum. At one end lie behaviours, such as some courtship displays, which can be described as closed instincts. These are purely innate. Open instincts involve responses which, although primarily or partly innate, can be modified by experience. Habituation is a very simple type of learning which serves to alter certain closed instincts. Further along the continuum lie behaviours which are the result of restricted learning. These behaviours depend on fairly simple neural circuits and can be modified to only a limited extent. Unlike open or closed instincts, however, they require at least some environmental experience before they can be performed at all. Flexible learning is different from restricted learning largely by degree. Behaviours that are the result of flexible learning are often quite complex and can be continually modified throughout the lifetime of an organism. Exploratory learning, trial and error learning, insight learning, and imitation are all types of flexible learning.

Objectives

Having completed this chapter, you should be able to do the following:

1. Discuss the general function of animal behaviour and describe the basic mechanism by which it occurs.
2. Describe the general types of stimuli that can give rise to behaviour and discuss how the nature of a particular stimulus is related to the function of the behaviour it elicits.
3. Discuss the relationship between the nervous system of an animal and the complexity of its behaviour.
4. Outline the similarities and differences between kineses and taxes and discuss how these types of behaviour relate to reflex responses.
5. Compare innate and learned behaviour, giving examples of each and describing the general circumstances in which one or the other is most adaptive.
6. Discuss how the behaviour of animals can be arranged into a continuum in terms of the relative contributions of instinct and learning to the development of particular responses.
7. Outline the differences and similarities between closed and open instincts, and restricted and flexible learning.

Vocabulary

circadian rhythms
kinesis
taxis
reflex
innate behaviour
learned behaviour

nature-nurture controversy
closed instinct
open instinct
habituation
restricted learning
imprinting

critical period
flexible learning
exploratory learning
trial and error learning
insight learning
imitation

Review Questions

1. What is the essential function of animal behaviour?
2. (a) What is the difference between the proximate and ultimate causes of behaviour.
   (b) Why is it useful to differentiate between the two?
3. (a) List three general types of internal stimuli, giving an example of each as well as describing the behaviour it evokes.
   (b) Describe two behaviours that require both external and internal stimuli.
4. (a) How can the influence of hormones on behaviour improve an animal's fitness?
   (b) How do circadian rhythms contribute to an animal's well-being?
5. What is the relationship between the structure of an animal's nervous system and the complexity of its behaviour? Explain your answer with the use of examples of species with differing sensory and nervous capabilities.

6. In what ways are kineses and taxes
   (a) different?
   (b) similar?

7. Which animals do you suppose have a higher proportion of reflex responses in their behavioural repertoires: earthworms or birds? Explain why you think this is so.

8. (a) Describe two examples of reflex behaviour in humans.
   (b) Suggest why it is adaptive for these behaviours to be controlled by relatively simple neural pathways.

9. (a) What three features are shared by all innate behaviours?
   (b) With respect to these three features, how do innate and learned behaviours differ?

10. What sort of circumstances select for
    (a) behaviour that is controlled by innate mechanisms?
    (b) learning?

11. (a) State how closed instincts differ from open instincts.
    (b) Give one example of a behaviour in each of these categories.

12. Give examples of and outline the similarities and differences between
    (a) restricted and flexible learning
    (b) restricted learning and open instincts.

13. Why is it adaptive for the courtship behaviour of many species to be innately controlled?

14. (a) Describe the process of habituation.
    (b) Suggest why behaviours modified by habituation might be called open instincts.
    (c) Give two examples of learning by habituation that are not described in the chapter.

15. List four types of flexible learning and describe what feature(s) they all have in common.

16. (a) Describe insight learning.
    (b) Suggest how an ability to learn concepts increases the speed with which an animal can solve problems that involve making choices.

Advanced Questions

1. Chemicals such as caffeine and nicotine have been shown to exert a significant influence (usually harmful) on driving ability. Why might such substances have a more substantial effect on the sorts of responses involved in driving than on behaviour related to solving a math problem?

2. (a) How might you use your knowledge of imprinting to tame a wild animal?
   (b) Why might this taming be harmful to the animal's ability to cope in the wild if you later released it?

3. Upon entering a classroom, or sitting down at a desk, you often find yourself irritated by a flickering light bulb, a low persistent hum, or a continuous noise coming from outside. Later, however, you may find that you no longer even notice what was originally a distraction.
   (a) What type of learning process is involved?
   (b) Why would you probably not be able to similarly ignore a sudden, loud noise or an irregular change in the environment?

4. Some women exhibit changes in their usual behaviour pattern just prior to their menstrual period, a phenomenon often referred to as *Premenstrual Syndrome* (PMS). What do you think causes this phenomenon?

5. A particular species of small parrot, *Agapornis personata*, uses its beak to carry nest-building materials (sticks, etc.) to its nest site. A closely related species, *Agapornis roseicollis*, instead carries such materials by tucking them into the feathers just above its tail. In the laboratory, these two species can be hybridized; the resulting individuals possess some of the genes of both of the parent species. When nest building, these hybrid individuals pick up material in their beaks, tuck it into their feathers, and then remove it again. They repeat this pattern several times until finally they pick up the material and carry it to their nests in their beaks.
   (a) Why do these hybrid individuals behave in this intermediate fashion?
   (b) Why would this behaviour be maladaptive in the wild? In other words, why would individuals that exhibit it have lowered fitness?

6. Do you think that the courtship behaviour of humans is primarily innate or mostly learned? Give examples to illustrate your point and describe why you think your postulated control mechanism is adaptive for humans.

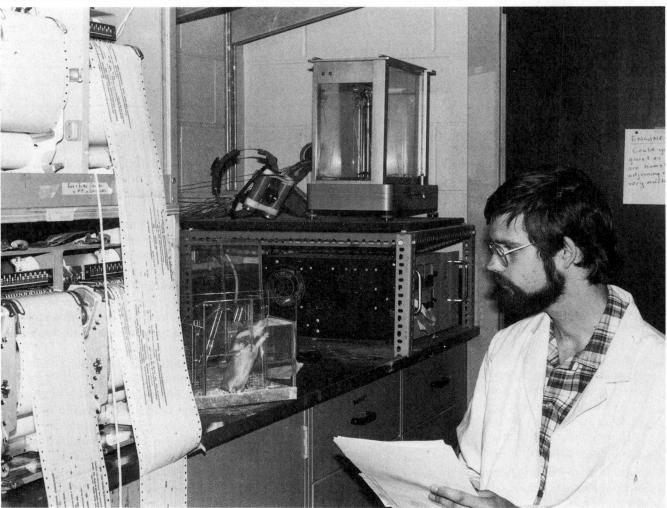

CHAPTER 24

THE STUDY OF ANIMAL BEHAVIOUR

The so-called, nature-nurture (genotype-environment) problem is not to distinguish which traits are genotypic and which are environmental, for all traits are genotypic and environmental.

Theodosius Dobzhansky

Although their activities may seem quite different, both of these researchers are investigating animal behaviour. One is studying her subjects in their natural habitat, observing their interactions with each other and the physical environment. By watching her subjects from a distance, she is minimizing the possibility that the animals will be disturbed (and therefore behave abnormally). The second researcher is taking quite a different approach. Working in a laboratory situation, he is carefully controlling as many aspects as he can of his subjects' physical and social environment. He can then experimentally manipulate the situation in order to study cause and effect relationships between particular stimuli and the responses they elicit. Although different in their approach and in the data they collect, both types of researchers actively contribute to our knowledge of animal behaviour.

24.1 STUDYING ANIMAL BEHAVIOUR

In a way, humans have always studied animal behaviour, a pursuit prompted by both curiosity and necessity. Since the evolution of *Homo sapiens*, human life has been intertwined with that of other animals. People have wondered about animals, domesticated them, hunted them for food and clothing, revered them as gods, and fought them in order to avoid being eaten by them. In the past, knowledge of the ways of animals was vital to human survival. It is no less so today, although this may be less obvious to many people, especially those living in cities. Various types of

insects and other invertebrates damage crops and infect domestic animals and humans. Many species of larger animals compete with humans for resources such as food, water, or space. Others provide food and a variety of products which are necessities of life for many people. The complex interconnections that exist within and among food chains (Chapter 26) ensure that almost all animals affect the lives of humans in some way.

It is still extremely important, therefore, to understand how and why animals behave as they do. The difference between the past and present in this respect lies primarily in how we go about achieving this goal. Biologists have developed methods to investigate the causes of animal behaviour and to observe its effects; they have devised various types of equipment to assist in the collection of behavioural data (Figure 24.1). They can now study animal behaviour with great rigour and in great detail. In recent decades, this scientific approach to the study of animal behaviour has produced some startling discoveries.

In their study of animal behaviour, modern researchers attempt to avoid **anthropomorphism**, the attribution of human characteristics (including emotions) to animals. (The term derives from the Greek words *anthros*, meaning man, and *morphe*, meaning form or shape.) It is anthropomorphic to say, for example, that a scolded dog slinks into a corner because it is ''ashamed,'' or that a bird sings because it is ''happy.'' Both behaviours are similar to the responses humans might make if they were experiencing these

Figure 24.1
The starlight telescope shown in (a) magnifies very low levels of light (for example, moonlight or starlight) so that researchers can observe the behaviour of animals even at night. The sound parabola shown in (b) collects sound *from a wide area and reflects it to a central point. With the use of this device, animal sounds can be focussed on a microphone to permit more effective recording than would be possible if the microphone alone were used.*

(a)

(b)

sentiments. The conclusion that particular actions are responses to human-like emotions does not, however, provide much useful insight into the function of such behaviours in other animals. It does not help to explain behaviours that bear no resemblance to human responses, that occur in situations never encountered by humans, or that involve body structures not possessed by *Homo sapiens*.

In fact, anthropomorphic interpretations of animal behaviour may be quite wrong. You are often not justified in interpreting someone else's actions in terms of what you might yourself have done in the same situation. Similarly, it is not always reasonable to explain the actions of other species in terms of what motivates human behaviour. The causes and effects of much human behaviour *may* be similar to those of other species. It is nevertheless more productive to avoid automatically assuming that this is so. An understanding of the behaviour of a particular animal species can be best achieved by a study of that species itself. Care must be taken to avoid biassing the study with human prejudices. For example, in explaining the dog's retreat into a corner, a behavioural scientist would take into account that such postures and actions are exhibited by many types of animals when they are faced by danger (Figure 24.2). These gestures act to appease their foes, thereby reducing the chances that they will suffer additional harm. Many studies have shown that bird song serves a variety of functions, few if any of which are related to human-like

Figure 24.2
A submissive dog

"happiness." In most species, bird song is important for mate attraction and is therefore vital for a bird's reproductive success (Figure 24.3). In short, as you learned in Chapter 23, such behaviours serve to improve the fitness of the animal in specific ways. They are not expressions of human-like emotions.

The Sensory World

One of the most important reasons for avoiding anthropomorphism is the fact that sensory capabilities differ widely among animal species. Few (if any) organisms are able to detect exactly the same types of stimuli as humans, and/or to detect them at the same levels. It is thus not surprising that response patterns also differ from humans to animals. In other words, it is not always reasonable to interpret an animal's

Figure 24.3
Bird song serves two primary purposes. It can be used to advertise the singer's territorial rights to a certain piece of habitat (and therefore to discourage rivals from coming too close) or it can be used to attract a mate (that is, as a signal that the singer is ready and willing to pair). In some cases the same song fulfils both purposes, depending on who is listening!

behaviour in terms of an apparently similar human response. Often, humans either cannot detect the stimulus to which the animal has responded or the animal cannot detect the stimulus that would have caused a human to exhibit a response similar to its own.

Even animals more closely related to *Homo sapiens* (those whose behaviour is most likely to be explained anthropomorphically) have quite different sensory worlds (Figure 24.4). For example, humans are quite visually oriented. A great deal of their behaviour occurs in response to stimuli perceived by their eyes.

Figure 24.4
This figure shows the limits of hearing in a variety of animals. Notice that many types of animals can hear high-pitched sounds (sounds of high wave frequency) that are inaudible to humans.

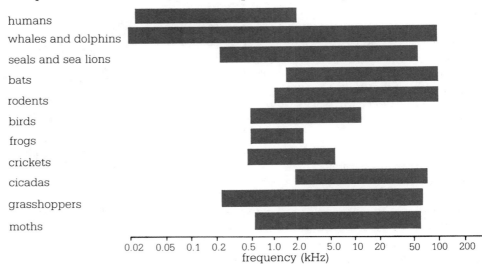

humans
whales and dolphins
seals and sea lions
bats
rodents
birds
frogs
crickets
cicadas
grasshoppers
moths

0.02   0.05   0.1   0.2   0.5   1.0   2.0   5.0   10   20   50   100   200
frequency (kHz)

Dogs, on the other hand, are colour blind and have poorer three dimensional sight than humans. Their activities are largely determined by their sense of smell. Dogs have as many as 225 million olfactory receptors in their nostrils, compared to the roughly nine million found in the human nose. Explanations of the behaviour of dogs based on human stimulus–response connections would therefore frequently be wrong.

The scientific elaboration of this concept — that the behaviour of an animal is largely a reflection of its sensory world—formed an important turning point in the study of animal behaviour. In the early 1900s the now-famous Austrian zoologist Karl von Frisch (1886–1983) discovered that honey bees had sensory abilities largely outside the range of our own. The experiments he conducted to arrive at this conclusion were among the first in what was to become a new field of scientific endeavour: **ethology**, the study of how and why animals in their natural environments behave as they do.

24.2 THE ETHOLOGISTS

Von Frisch became interested in the perception abilities of bees when he wondered why flowers are so colourful. At that time, it was felt that insects did not have colour vision. Accordingly, little credit was given to the notion that flowers might be brightly coloured in order to attract the bees that pollinate them.

Von Frisch, however, decided to rigorously test his hypothesis that bees *could* detect colour. He did so by designing some of the first behavioural tests. First, he repeatedly set out a series of disks filled with sugar solution, placing each disk on a blue card. The bees were trained to collect the sugar solution from the disks. As a next step, he set out a series of empty dishes, placing only one of them on a blue card and the others on cards that were various shades of grey (Figure 24.5). If they could see only in black and white, von Frisch reasoned, the bees would likely mistake at least one of the grey cards for a blue one. Yet the bees seemed to have no difficulty distinguishing the blue card; the majority of them flew to it immediately, expecting food.

Other experiments by von Frisch and his students showed that while bees are in fact blind to red they can see well into the ultraviolet end of the colour spectrum (Figure 24.6). They can also see polarized light, can smell carbon dioxide and other substances undetectable by humans, and can hear sounds inaudible to

Figure 24.5
After being trained to find food in a dish on a blue card, bees were presented with an array of empty dishes placed on cards of various shades of grey. At least some of these were close in colour to the blue, which was also included. The bees were not confused, however, and headed directly for the blue-card dish, expecting to find food.

Figure 24.6
After learning that bees could detect colour in the ultraviolet (UV) range of the spectrum, von Frisch looked at the world through UV filters in order to see what the bees were seeing. He discovered that many species of bee-pollinated flowers have a distinctive bulls-eye pattern, created by the presence of UV coloration at their centre (a). Since our eyes cannot detect such colours, we see the flower quite differently (b).

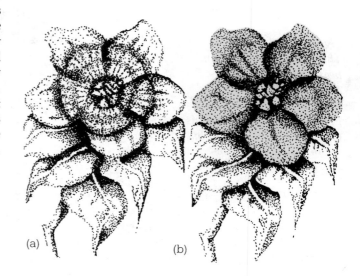

(a)   (b)

Figure 24.7
From left, Otto von Frisch, representing his father Karl, Konrad Lorenz, and Nikolaas Tinbergen make a toast at the 1973 Nobel Prize reception. These founding fathers of ethology shared the Nobel Prize in medicine for their contributions to the study of behaviour.

Figure 24.8
His usually friendly pet jackdaws would attack von Frisch whenever he carried a dangling black object. It apparently looked to them like a member of their own species in distress.

humans. In addition, they can detect the earth's magnetic field, and can sense changes in humidity.

The work of von Frisch and others, conducted on a variety of species, clearly showed that the sensory capabilities of animals are often closely adapted to the environments in which they live. In other words, their sense organs have evolved in ways that provide them with the range of sensory experiences they need in order to respond appropriately to, and therefore survive in, their natural habitats.

Konrad Lorenz and Niko Tinbergen

The discoveries of von Frisch and his colleagues inspired further studies of how animals respond to their environment, and to the other animals that are part of it (Figure 24.7). The German naturalist Konrad Lorenz (1903–1989) realized that although many animal species can perceive the same stimuli, their brains may interpret these stimuli quite differently. Lorenz noticed that whenever he dangled something black (such as a towel or swimsuit) from his hand, he was attacked by his pet jackdaws (Figure 24.8). Both he and the birds perceived the same black object, yet their brains obviously interpreted its meaning quite differently!

Jackdaws, which are themselves black, seem to see any black, hanging object as a member of their own

species in distress. Lorenz had watched these birds long enough to know that not only could they usually distinguish other black objects and other types of birds from jackdaws, but in fact they could recognize each other as individuals. Why was it, he then wondered, that in this situation they were ignoring most of what their eyes told them? Why were they focussing on only a small subset of the available stimuli, which in this case gave them misleading information?

Lorenz and others, most notably his colleague Niko Tinbergen (1907–1988), studied this question closely during the next 20 years. It became apparent that many animals are similarly responsive only to specific stimuli in certain situations (Figure 24.9).

Figure 24.9
A male English robin will furiously attack a bundle of red feathers glued on a stick (a) and placed in his territory. On the other hand, it will ignore a stuffed juvenile robin (b) placed in the same location. Even though this latter model looks much more like a real robin, it lacks the red breast characteristic of adult males in this species.

Figure 24.10
Even though the model labelled (a) looks much more like a stickleback than the other four, it lacks a red belly—the stimulus which excites male aggression. In Tinbergen's experiments, such realistic models were attacked far less often than models (b), (c), (d), and (e), which did have red undersides.

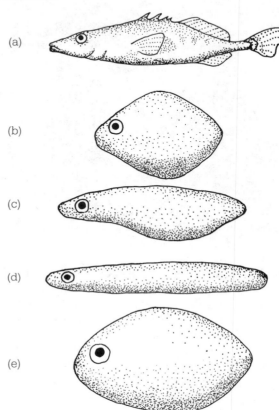

Tinbergen became particularly well known for his studies of this phenomenon in the stickleback, a small, minnow-like fish. At the beginning of the breeding season (in spring), the male stickleback acquires a bright red neck and belly. At the same time, he begins to defend a small territory, on which he will later build a nest. The preferred territory is a soft lake bottom (in which a male can dig a depression) with aquatic plants growing nearby from which he can construct the nest. Only males that have a territory can build a nest and thus later attract a mate. Since there are usually more males than there are good-quality territories, competition is keen. Territorial males must aggressively defend their "holdings" against other red-bellied males who have been less successful in acquiring space.

Both male and female sticklebacks recognize breeding males by their red bellies. Males respond to this particular stimulus aggressively since to them it signals the presence of another breeding male. He may be a territory holder who they can try to replace, or he may be a challenger against whom they must defend their own territories. In fact, males (and females) are so closely tuned to this single stimulus that they pay no attention to other cues which might assist identification, such as the size and shape of the red-striped object (Figure 24.10). Tinbergen found that sticklebacks defending territories in an aquarium near a window would even attempt to attack red mail trucks passing by!

Similarly simple stimuli seem to have a great influence on behaviour in all sorts of animals. Birds regu-

Figure 24.11
When a goose sees an egg outside her nest, she reaches out and rolls it back into the nest with her beak. Some female geese take advantage of this response to ''dump'' their eggs near the nests of other females, who will then recover and incubate them and subsequently care for the goslings *when they hatch. This behaviour is risky; perhaps the egg will get chilled too much, get broken, or fail to hatch before the nesting female leaves the nest with her own hatched goslings. Yet the behaviour permits some females to lay eggs without investing the energy required to build a nest and care for young themselves.*

larly turn their eggs during the incubation period. Unfortunately, this procedure (which is necessary to prevent embryos from sticking to the shell) sometimes causes the eggs of ground-nesting birds to roll out of the nest. A nearby egg lying outside a nest then becomes a stimulus to which a nesting female goose responds by carefully using her beak to roll the egg back to safety (Figure 24.11). However, only certain features of the stimulus seem relevant. Many females will also roll flashlight batteries, pop bottles, golf balls, or other egg-like objects into their nests.

Releasers and Fixed Action Patterns

The experiments of Lorenz, Tinbergen, and other ethologists showed that responses to such apparently inappropriate stimuli do not occur because the animals cannot see properly. They happen because at certain times, organisms possess an exaggerated sensitivity to specific stimuli which then serve to trigger specific behaviours. Because they serve to ''release'' these particular behaviours, such stimuli are often referred to as **releasers**. The bias imposed by the limits of the human sensory world makes humans most familiar with releasers that are visual stimuli (Figure 24.12). Yet many releasers involve auditory, taste, or olfactory stimuli (Figure 24.13).

Figure 24.12
Humans also respond to specific releaser stimuli. A baby who is between two and eleven weeks old will often smile if an experimenter moves toward it a two dimensional mask with black dots in the position of the eyes. A mask with more realistic eyes, or one with a nose and mouth included, is not likely to produce more smiles; a mask with only one dot is completely ineffective at triggering the same reaction. Adults respond to such smiles with smiles of their own, this facial response being very important for cementing ties of affection between parents and offspring.

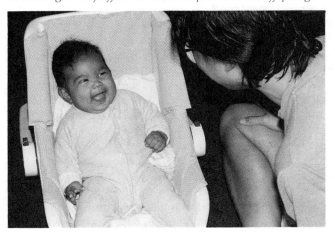

Figure 24.13
This figure shows audiograms, pictures produced by recording sounds into a microphone attached to an oscilloscope. Represented here are the songs of six cricket species. The song of a male cricket acts as a releaser for sexual behaviour by females of his own species. The ability of the females to detect differences among very similar songs allows them to select an appropriate mate even if several species of crickets sing at the same time and in the same area.

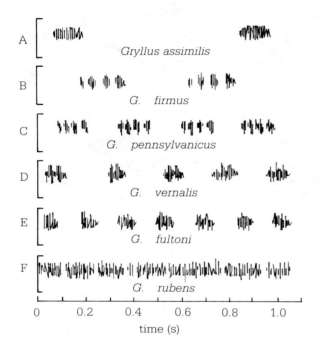

Fixed action patterns is the name sometimes given to the behaviours elicited by releasers. A fixed action pattern is a highly stereotyped behaviour that is performed almost the same way each time by all members of a species. It is, in short, almost purely the result of instinct; very little learning, if any, is involved. In the vast majority of cases, this narrow connection between a specific stimulus and the response it triggers is of great benefit to the animal involved. It is clearly adaptive, for example, for a goose to retrieve a lost egg during the nesting cycle. Since only rarely will batteries, golf balls, or other roundish objects be in the vicinity of her nest, it is appropriate that her perception of "egg" be based on only a few, important features. This perception lessens the possibility of confusion and reduces the amount of information processing that must take place before the behaviour occurs. The rate of reaction is thus accelerated. A speedy response is obviously vital if an animal is trying to save a member of its own species from death (as in the case of the jackdaws) or if it is trying to retrieve an egg before it cools (as in the case of the goose).

One of the key features of a fixed action pattern is that it is a complete behavioural unit. Once triggered by a releaser, it proceeds to its conclusion regardless of any change in (feedback from) the environment. If an egg is removed after the goose has begun to roll it, she will continue the behaviour as if nothing had happened, pulling an invisible egg into her nest.

Innate Releasing Mechanisms

In 1935, Lorenz introduced a model designed to explain how fixed action patterns were controlled. He proposed that an animal's nervous system is organized into many separate clusters of nerve cells that act to filter incoming sensations. Each of these clusters is responsible for the recognition of a particular releaser stimulus and for the initiation of the appropriate response. Lorenz believed that these nerve clusters were genetically determined (that is, inherited). He therefore termed them **Innate Releasing Mechanisms (IRMs)**. He considered IRMs to be much like doors: a releaser stimulus is a "key" that unlocks only one of the many such "doors" present in an animal's brain. Once the door (the IRM) is opened, the appropriate fixed action pattern is released.

In many cases, however, it is inappropriate for a particular releaser to trigger its associated response at *all* times in *all* members of a species. Egg rolling behaviour, for example, is adaptive only for females (male geese do not incubate) and only when they are sitting on eggs. It would obviously not benefit them to perform the rolling behaviour whenever they see an egg-like object. A variety of mainly internal mechanisms (for example, levels of circulating hormones) makes it possible for animals to have different behavioural priorities at different times of the year, month, or day, or at different stages of their development (Chapter 23). In a sense, it is as if many IRMs were "double-locked" at times, incapable of being opened by a releaser key alone (Figure 24.14). This double-locking is adaptive in that it prevents animals from wasting energy in the performance of behaviours inappropriate to the occasion.

Lorenz and other early ethologists felt that a great deal of behaviour, even that of very complex animals, could be explained by the operation of these innate mechanisms. According to them, an apparently

Figure 24.14
A diagrammatic representation of Lorenz's model of stereotyped behaviour

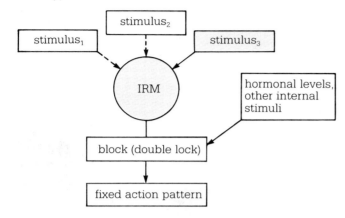

lengthy and/or complicated behavioural response simply consisted of a sequence of fixed action patterns strung together. Each pattern had its own IRM; the completion of one of these patterns was the releaser for the next.

This idea was in fact shown to be more or less true for a number of behaviours displayed by a variety of organisms. The studies of Tinbergen, for example, revealed that stickleback courtship behaviour consists of a series of behaviours performed by males and females, each of which is a necessary releaser stimulus for the next step in the sequence (Figure 24.15).

Figure 24.15
The courtship behaviour of sticklebacks. Each fish must respond to the correct cues at the proper time and behave appropriately if the sequence is to be completed.

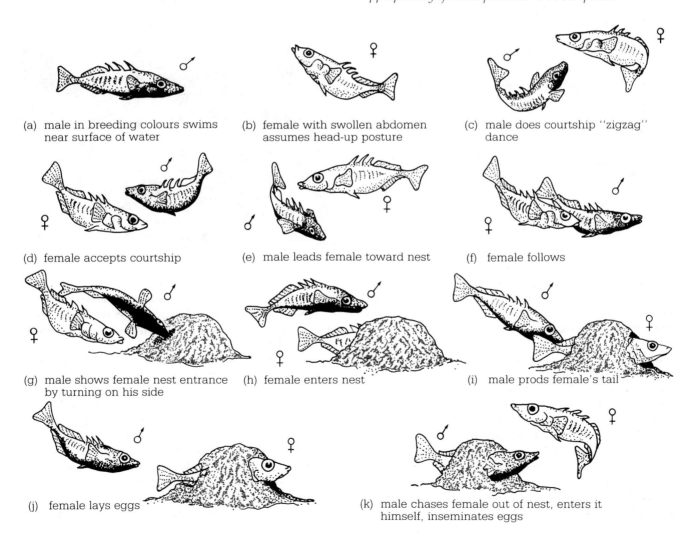

(a) male in breeding colours swims near surface of water

(b) female with swollen abdomen assumes head-up posture

(c) male does courtship "zigzag" dance

(d) female accepts courtship

(e) male leads female toward nest

(f) female follows

(g) male shows female nest entrance by turning on his side

(h) female enters nest

(i) male prods female's tail

(j) female lays eggs

(k) male chases female out of nest, enters it himself, inseminates eggs

Thus, an initial stimulus can trigger a whole chain of responses, producing what appears to be a quite complex behavioural pattern. All of the steps must be performed correctly, however, if the sequence is to be completed. If either participant in the sticklebacks' courtship dance behaves inappropriately at any point, the sequence is interrupted and fertilization fails to occur. This control system benefits each individual stickleback by the reduction of gamete wastage. A female will only lay eggs in the nest of a male who has proved his suitability as a mate by acquiring a territory, building a nest, and performing the elaborate species-specific zigzag dance. A male, in turn, will only release sperm after a female has also proven her suitability by exhibiting a correct response at the appropriate time.

Innate Behaviour and Learning

Upon closer inspection, many so-called fixed action patterns turned out to be less stereotyped than originally thought. For example, eggs which have escaped from different nests must be rolled varying distances and over varying terrains during the retrieval process. In order to recapture her egg safely in a specific situation, each female must deviate from the typical pattern at least to some extent. Her response cannot be completely preset by genes. The same is true of sticklebacks. While the actions of most individuals are similar to those shown in Figure 24.11, they do vary somewhat; the dance is not completely stereotyped. In addition, a male stickleback does not court *every* appropriate female, nor does every female he approaches necessarily respond. Although scientists are not completely certain of how mate selection is made, it likely involves past experience — learning — to some extent.

With the realization that many responses are not as stereotyped as originally thought, the term "fixed action pattern" has fallen into disfavour. Some ethologists recommend using "modal action pattern" or simply "action pattern." These terms indicate that, while such behaviours usually approximate some average pattern, they *do* vary.

As Lorenz himself observed, some of the most instinctive behaviours, such as the crouching response of gull chicks, can be modified by experience. Although a very simple type of learning such as habituation (Chapter 23) may be all that is involved, it is still learning. Its effect is to modify what might otherwise be thought of as a completely innate response. Imprinting — another primarily instinctive response — also requires some learning. An animal

Figure 24.16
In order to prevent young birds who are being raised by humans from imprinting on their caretakers, puppets resembling their real parents are often used when the birds are fed or otherwise cared for. This practice ensures that the birds will grow up with a normal idea of their species identity, without which they might be unable to find an appropriate mate.

may possess an action pattern for following behaviour, but the nature of what is to be followed must be learned. It is as if the IRM for following had a blank space in it on which something must be "imprinted" (Figure 24.16).

The IRM concept has also received much criticism. Part of this criticism stems from recognition of the fact that little behaviour, if any, is completely innate. Therefore, few IRMs are purely inherited in the way that Lorenz described them to be. In addition, neurobiologists (scientists studying the nervous system) have been unable to find any structures in the brain resembling IRMs. Instead, the central nervous system seems to operate as an integrated whole, rather than as a collection of discrete units each prewired to control a single motor response. However, even if the brain does not work this way, it often seems to. Lorenz did, therefore, provide a good *operational* model, even if not a good *structural* one, of how the brain controls action patterns. If not interpreted too strictly, the IRM concept is still useful to ethologists for understanding the coordination of relatively stereotyped responses.

24.3 THE BEHAVIOURISTS

The field of ethology was developed by scientists with a strong naturalistic bent, ones who were interested primarily in the behaviour of animals in the wild. For the sake of experimental technique, they often artificially manipulated an animal's environment. Nevertheless, their goal was to discover how a particular behaviour was adaptive. Toward this goal, they compared the responses of closely related species. Their finding that species which were similar genetically also exhibited many similar behaviour patterns confirmed their belief that most behaviour was innate (Figure 24.17).

A quite different view of animal behaviour was held by psychologists. Their focus of study was the operation of the mind, particularly the human mind. Unlike ethologists, who were interested in the *function* of behaviours (what they did to increase an animal's fitness), psychologists were concerned about the *mechanism* of behaviours (how learning occurred). Anatomists had already demonstrated that there were many structural similarities between the nervous systems of humans and other animals. Psychologists reasoned, therefore, that there should be corresponding similarities in the operation of these systems. In other words, the basic process of learning must be much the same in all animals. For this reason, comparative studies on a variety of species should yield, among other things, useful insights into human learning. Like the anatomists — and unlike ethologists — psychologists conducted these comparative studies almost exclusively in the laboratory. The field of science encompassing their search for general laws of learning came to be known as *comparative* or *behavioural psychology*, or more simply, as **behaviourism**.

Both the methods and focus of their research led many early behaviourists to believe that almost all animal behaviour was learned. In contrast to the ethologists, they regarded instinct as relatively unimportant, particularly for complex animals; they viewed even very stereotyped and/or simple responses as the result of some form of learning. They argued that almost all behaviour was the result of what they

Figure 24.17
Birds can scratch their heads by reaching either over or under their wings with one foot. As a general rule, all members of a particular species perform this behaviour the same way. Tennessee warblers (a) almost invariably scratch directly (under the wing), as do pigeons. Ruby-crowned kinglets (b) scratch indirectly (with a foot over the wing), as do house sparrows. Within a group (such as ''parrots'' or ''finches''), those species that are most closely related to each other tend to share the same scratching method. As a result, this characteristic has often been used to help classify bird species.

termed *conditioning*: an organism learns from its experiences with the environment what it needs to do in order to survive and/or reproduce. In other words, an animal is ''conditioned'' by the environment to behave in certain ways. Eventually, two different conditioning processes were identified: classical conditioning and trial and error learning.

Classical Conditioning

Classical conditioning was discovered in the 1920s by the Russian scientist Ivan Pavlov (1849–1936). As part of his studies on the physiology of digestion, Pavlov measured the quantity of saliva produced by dogs when they see food. He noticed that if an irrelevant stimulus such as a ringing bell regularly appeared just before a dog saw food, the animal came to associate this cue so closely with the appearance of a meal that the sound alone could stimulate salivation (Figure 24.18). In other words, the dog became conditioned to expect food when the bell rang. Upon hearing the sound, it began to salivate in anticipation — even before any food appeared. An ethologist looking at this stimulus–response connection would call the appearance of food a releaser for the fixed action pattern, salivation. Behaviourists, however, refer to the food as an **unconditioned stimulus**, a stimulus that doesn't elicit any learned behaviour. The salivation is termed **unconditioned response** (a response which has not been learned). The ring of the bell that triggers salivation is termed a **conditioned stimulus**, a stimulus to which the animal has been conditioned to respond in a new way. Salivation stimulated by the bell alone is then called a **conditioned response**, a response which the animal has been conditioned to exhibit when a particular stimulus occurs.

Timing is an important factor in classical conditioning. Learning will occur only if the conditioned and unconditioned stimuli occur simultaneously, or if the former slightly precedes the latter. No conditioning will take place if the normal releaser appears first. In Pavlov's experiment the dog became conditioned to salivate at the sound of a bell only if the ringing preceded the presentation of meat or if the two events occurred simultaneously. If the bell was rung after the meat had appeared, the dog did not learn to salivate in response to the sound alone.

A certain amount of repetition is also important: the stimulus that is to be conditioned and the one that is unconditioned must be paired a number of times before an animal can learn the association. Species (and even individuals within a species) vary with respect to how many repetitions are necessary or how close the timing must be before conditioning will occur. Given the proper procedure, however, animals as simple as earthworms and as complex as humans can be trained by classical conditioning techniques.

Indeed, early behaviourists held that any cue which a particular animal was capable of sensing could become a conditioned stimulus. As well, they believed

Figure 24.18
Studying his subjects in the laboratory, Pavlov was able to reduce the possibility that extraneous stimuli could be responsible for the responses he observed. Access to relatively sophisticated equipment permitted him to monitor fairly "invisible" responses such as salivation (which is being measured by the device on the dog's cheek). The controlled situation allowed him to repeat his experiment many times until he could be sure that what he observed was not attributable simply to chance.

that almost any response could be conditioned to occur after a previously irrelevant stimulus was given. Such thinking implied that any stimulus–response combination could be altered in a variety of ways; for behaviourists, therefore, innate behaviour was of relatively little importance and instinct was irrelevant to learning.

Trial and Error Learning

At first, some researchers claimed that linked chains of conditioned stimulus–response associations could explain even complex behaviours. However, it soon became clear that a variety of animals seem to "learn by doing" in many situations. That is, they learn through experience of the consequences of their actions rather than through recognition of associations between stimuli. The research of many behaviourists,

Figure 24.19

All animals with bilaterally symmetrical nervous systems exhibit some ability to solve maze problems; that is, to make consistent choices when presented with alternatives. Even earthworms can learn to repeatedly take the arm of a T-maze that leads to a reward rather than the one that leads to punishment (a). Although they make many mistakes at first, many ants can learn to run the maze shown in (b) after only 28 trial runs. Chimpanzees (c) seem to make some use of insight learning to solve even more complicated mazes. On occasion, they can solve mazes faster than can biology students!

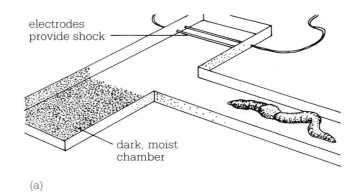

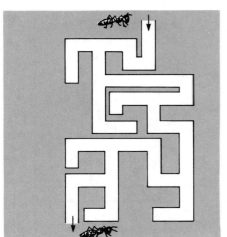

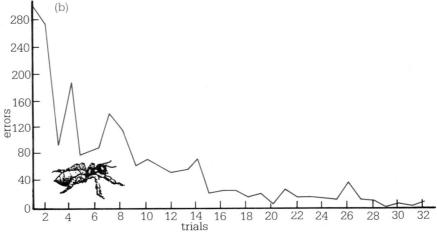

most notably the American scientists E.L. Thorndike (1874–1925) and B.F. Skinner (b. 1904), showed that classical conditioning in fact could not account for many behaviours such as maze learning (Figure 24.19). Instead, such tasks required what came to be known as **trial and error learning**.

It was found that in many situations, animals learn to associate responses with their results, rather than with the stimuli that preceded them. In other words, whether an animal learns to repeat or to forgo a particular behaviour often depends more on its consequences than on any particular environmental event. If a response leads to results beneficial to the individual, then **positive reinforcement** is said to take place. The animal soon learns to repeat the behaviour in similar situations. By contrast, if trial behaviours result in consequences *not* beneficial to the individual, then **negative reinforcement** is said to occur. These behaviours tend to decline in frequency because their consequences are unrewarding; animals therefore learn to avoid making these erroneous responses (Figure 24.20).

Figure 24.20
Placed in an enclosure often referred to as a "Skinner Box," the stimuli this pigeon encounters can be carefully controlled and its responses monitored and either rewarded or punished. In this case, it can move about and perform a number of behavioural activities. An experimenter training the bird will choose a particular one of these to reward—say, turning left—with a pellet of food obtained from a dispenser. By initially rewarding very slight movements to the left and then only progressively more complete turns, an experienced trainer can, in about two minutes, teach a pigeon to trace out a full circle. With a little more trial and error learning, the pigeon will travel a figure eight. By a comparison of the types of tasks different species can learn and the time it takes to learn them, psychologists have obtained a considerable amount of information about the learning process.

Thus, whereas classical conditioning depends on behaviours that are elicited by specific stimuli, trial and error learning relies on responses that are emitted spontaneously and then either positively or negatively reinforced. In other words, such behaviours do not usually require the appearance of a particular external stimulus. For this reason, classical conditioning is often termed *respondent conditioning*. Behaviours acquired by trial and error learning, however, frequently occur regardless of the environment. They are, in effect, "operations" that the animal performs *on* the environment rather than responses *to* it. This second type of learning is hence often called *operant conditioning*.

Learning and Genetic Programming
As mentioned, it used to be thought that animals could learn to associate any stimulus with any action pattern and that any behaviour could be taught by operant conditioning. It has since been discovered, however, that most animals have strong innate (and therefore species-specific) biases that limit their learning abilities in ways which are beneficial to them. Experiments have shown that pigeons can learn to associate a sound with an impending shock. The sound becomes a conditioned stimulus to which they respond by running or flapping their wings in an attempt to avoid the shock. They cannot, however, learn to respond to sound by pecking even when a sound stimulus is followed by the presentation of food — at which they *do* peck. Pecking easily becomes a conditioned response to a colour stimulus, once the pigeons have learned to associate this colour with a food reward (Figure 24.21). On the other hand, running or flapping behaviour cannot be elicited by the colour stimulus. In summary, the birds are unable to associate sound with food, or colour with an impending shock. In their natural environment, as you might expect, pigeons generally identify food by colour rather than by sound. Conversely, they usually recognize the approach of a predator by sound rather than by colour. As a result, the birds can be classically conditioned only in certain ways. These limitations to its neural processing abilities, which are imposed by its genetic material, have evolved as a result of natural selection.

Similar constraints have also been demonstrated for operant conditioning. For example, rats can learn to avoid drinking sugar-water when they are exposed to radiation (which causes nausea) afterwards. They cannot, however, learn to do so when the negative reinforcement consists of a shock. In a rat's natural

Figure 24.21
Pigeons can easily learn to peck at a coloured spot when such behaviour is rewarded with food.

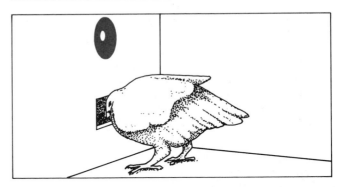

environment, nausea is a better indicator than is a shock of what is not good to eat. The rat's learning ability has therefore become constrained by natural selection. Because it ignores irrelevant stimuli when deciding what is good to eat it is more efficient at processing information needed to make such a decision. The ability to "learn" to avoid food which makes it sick is obviously vital to the survival of the rat.

In short, few animal behaviours are entirely without an innate component; the majority are influenced, even if only subtly, by genes. Just as very little of animal behaviour is wholly innate, very little (if any) is entirely learned.

THE SCIENCE OF ANIMAL BEHAVIOUR

Like researchers in other fields of science, students of animal behaviour employ the scientific method. In order to answer questions, they formulate *hypotheses* and collect *data* which will test *predictions* arising from these hypotheses. They then *analyze* the data objectively, usually with the use of statistical tests. Finally they *interpret* the results with respect to the original hypothesis.

As an example, consider two questions, the first general and the second specific. In what circumstances would it increase a male insect's fitness to stay with his mate and help her care for their young? (Males of many species leave soon after mating and females must raise their young alone.) What stimulates hamsters to run in the wheels that are commonly found in cages?

In seeking to answer the first question, researchers would need to decide on which insect species to study. A good approach would be to investigate one or more species in which males do exhibit parental behaviour and one or more in which they do not. The two species (or sets of species) could then be compared with respect to a variety of features such as size, habitat, number of females in the population, and number of young produced. Perhaps it is one of these features that explains why it is adaptive for males to help with the young (rather than leave and maybe mate again with another female). Subjects must also be chosen on the basis of how easy they are to study!

Once researchers have a specific question in mind, they formulate a hypothesis—a tentative answer to the question. A hypothesis related to the second question might be "hunger is what stimulates hamsters to run in their wheels." The validity of this hypothesis (its usefulness as an explanation of the behaviour) can be investigated by testing predictions arising from it. For example, if the hypothesis is true, then one would predict that hamsters will be more likely to run several hours after having a meal than after they have just eaten.

The researchers then collect data which will allow them to test this prediction. Perhaps they record the number of hamsters running at hour intervals after the animals have all had a meal of equal size. It is important that all but one of the variables be controlled, since any one might affect the behaviour in question. These variables could include the amount of food provided, the starting weight of the hamsters, the length of time since they were fed previously, and the cage conditions. It is also important that more than one hamster is tested; just as humans vary with respect to their responses to particular stimuli, so do other animals. The question is not "why does this individual hamster run?" but "why in general do hamsters run?" The answers may be quite different!

Based on a sample of ten hamsters, one researcher first collected data and then graphed the results, as shown in Table 24A.

The relationship between number of hours without food and wheel-running behaviour in hamsters

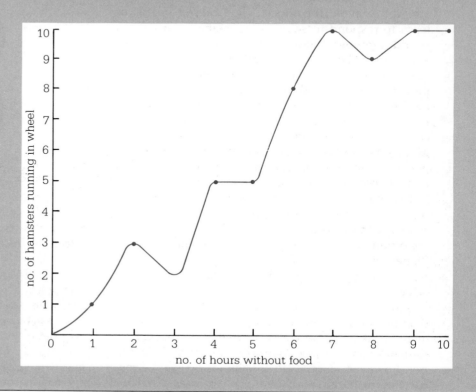

488

Table 24A Results of Experimenter #1's Test

NUMBER OF HOURS SINCE HAMSTERS WERE LAST FED	NUMBER OF HAMSTERS RUNNING (OUT OF 10)
1	1
2	3
3	2
4	5
5	5
6	8
7	10
8	9
9	10
10	10

A second experimenter, testing the same prediction, collected slightly different data. He compared two groups of ten hamsters each; the animals in one group had been fed 5 min previously, while those in the other group had been without food for 5 h. The results of this second test are shown below.

Table 24B Results of Experimenter #2's Test

GROUP	NUMBER OF HAMSTERS RUNNING
1	2
2	10

Both researchers then tested their results with appropriate statistical tests which allowed them to determine *objectively* (without bias) whether their results agreed with the prediction or not. In this case, the meaning of the results is obvious. Hungry hamsters use their wheels more than those that have just been fed. The data upheld the prediction. Both researchers therefore interpreted their results as support for the hypothesis that hunger is a stimulus that triggers wheel-running by hamsters. In looking for a reason why this might be so, they suggested that hamsters have probably been selected to start moving around in search of food when they become hungry. Under normal conditions, this movement would involve running through their natural habitat. Such a response to hunger would be adaptive because animals that exhibit it would be more likely to find food. Caged hamsters do not have a large habitat in which to run; instead, when hunger stimulates their running response, they make use of the wheel.

Finally, these researchers wrote a report so that others could see their data and think about their hypothesis. This stage too is important. Scientific knowledge is a result of the contributions made by many researchers. Studies that are not made public do not add to this body of knowledge and are therefore of little benefit.

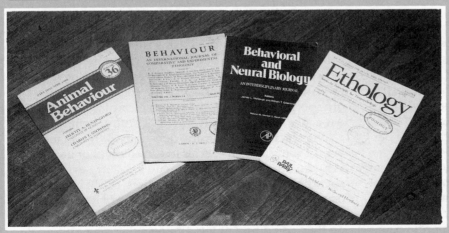

Most scientists publish their research findings in journals or books, or present them orally to other scientists at conferences.

Figure 24.22

The approach of a predator often causes a slight wind or change in air pressure which stimulates mechanoreceptors on the cerci of a cockroach. The mechanoreceptor neurons synapse in the sixth abdominal ganglion with a giant interneuron that then carries the impulses to the large metathoracic ganglion. It in turn synapses with motor neurons in each leg so that these appendages can be spurred into action. This series of interconnections, studied in detail by several scientists, including Jeffrey Camhi of Hebrew University, Jersualem, is responsible for what is termed "cockroach escape behaviour"—a highly adaptive response to the presence of a predator!

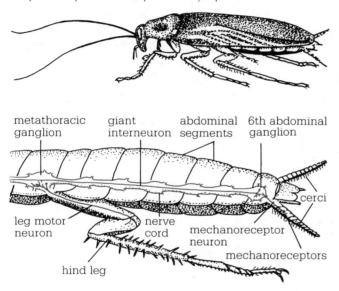

Figure 24.23

After only three training periods of 15 s, normal fruitflies can learn to avoid whichever of two odours is negatively reinforced by a shock; they can remember what they have learned for a period of 3 h to 6 h. However, flies with a single mutant allele on an identified gene cannot learn this same task. Referred to as dunce, *flies of the mutant strain seem to behave normally in all other ways. Another mutant strain (for which the chromosome location of the mutant allele has also been identified) is called* amnesiac. *These flies learn the odour task normally, but forget their training unusually rapidly.*

24.4 STUDYING ANIMAL BEHAVIOUR TODAY

In recent decades, the study of animal behaviour has advanced in several directions. In particular, it has become more "cross-disciplinary," taking advantage of the techniques and discoveries of a variety of scientific disciplines. Using the highly technical instruments and methods of *neurobiology*, researchers have been able to identify the parts of the brain (in some cases, even the specific neurons) involved in the performance of certain behaviours (Figure 24.22).

Behavioural genetics has used the mathematics of population genetics and the laboratory techniques of molecular genetics to demonstrate the importance of heredity to the performance of certain behaviours. In a few relatively simple organisms, the specific genes coding for a particular response have even been iso-

lated (Figure 24.23). Insofar as this is a comparatively new and rapidly developing field of science, there is still much that is not known. The role of natural selection in shaping much behaviour is still uncertain, particularly for complex organisms such as humans.

Behavioural ecology is the study of the relationship between an organism's behaviour and its ecology; that is, how both the physical and the social environment of a species affect the behaviour typical of its members. An active and productive field of study, behavioural ecology focusses on several questions. Why do members of some animal species live in colonies or groups? Why do other organisms pursue a solitary existence, spending time with other members of their species only when mating or caring for young? How do individuals decide when and with whom to mate? Why do they use different foraging techniques in different habitats? How do they choose their prey? Why are

Figure 24.24

The study of echolocation in bats and other animals that can emit ultrasound has benefitted enormously from advances in electronics technology. In the 1950s, the apparatus needed to ''hear'' and record bat calls filled the back of a pickup truck. Now, the equipment that does this job (and does it better) takes up only part of small car's trunk. Some versions even weigh less than 3 kg and can be easily carried. The increasing portability of such equipment has made it possible for researchers to follow bats through their natural habitats and to study their behaviour much more closely and carefully.

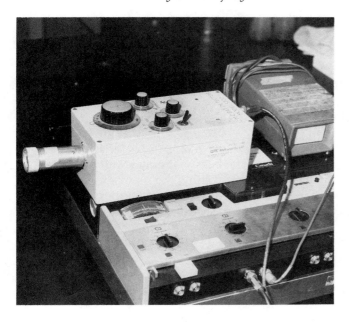

some individuals dominant to others? As is true for all scientific disciplines, behavioural ecology has benefitted from recent advances in computer and communications technology, advances which facilitate the collection and analysis of data (Figure 24.24).

Sociobiology

Closely linked to behavioural ecology, but focussing more specifically on the social aspects of an animal's environment, is **sociobiology**. One of the most interesting aspects of the biology of many animals is their social behaviour. This behaviour involves an individual's interactions with other animals, usually of its own species. The term ''social'' here implies *both* aggressive *and* cooperative behaviours. A major objective of sociobiology is to uncover the role of natural selection in shaping social behaviour. How do an organism's responses to other individuals serve to increase

its fitness? Why did this behaviour evolve?

One of the most challenging types of behaviour to explain in these terms is **altruism**. In a biological sense, altruism can be defined as any behaviour which increases the chances of survival or reproduction for other organisms, while decreasing these same probabilities for the performer. In other words, an altruistic act is carried out at some cost to the behaving animal, but provides some benefit to other individuals. Some of the workers in a honeybee colony will attempt to protect their hive by swarming out to sting intruders. Although this behaviour may be of considerable benefit to other members of the colony, it is lethal for the defenders; a portion of the bee's abdomen is left along with its stinger.

Altruistic behaviour is displayed by many invertebrate animals, particularly the social insects (bees, wasps, ants, *etc.*). It is also common in many vertebrate species. Musk-oxen gather to cooperatively defend their young from predators (Figure 24.25). Many species of birds and mammals utter ''alarm calls'' (squeaks, chatters, whistles, or some other easily heard sounds) when they see a predator approach. These calls provide a warning for nearby individuals, giving them time to escape. They also, however, attract a predator's attention to the caller, thereby putting it in great danger.

Since natural selection favours those individuals with attributes (including behaviours) that enhance survival and reproduction, the existence of altruism seems surprising. Would not the individuals selected for be those who sneak away at the sight of a predator, leaving others to fend for themselves? Selfish behaviour of this sort would certainly be more likely to increase an organism's chances of surviving and therefore its potential for passing on genes to the next generation. Why, then, do altruistic responses occur?

A special type of natural selection called **kin selection** offers part of the answer. Kin selection theory takes a broad view of how an organism can increase its *ultimate* fitness; in other words, can increase the number of copies of its own genes that will exist in future generations. According to this idea, alarm calling and other altruistic behaviour will be selected for if it ensures the survival of a certain number of the caller's relatives, each of whom carries some proportion of genes which are identical to the caller's own.

Altruistic behaviour has been carefully studied in Belding's ground squirrels, among other species (Figure 24.26). These small mammals live in Rocky Mountain meadows in colonies consisting of many burrows.

Figure 24.25
Musk-oxen defending their young

Figure 24.26
Once it detects the approach of a predator, a ground squirrel spreads the alarm.

When a squirrel spots a predator, it gives an alarm call which frequently causes other members of the colony to dive into a burrow for cover. The caller has made itself vulnerable to attack and is much more likely to fall prey to a coyote or weasel than is a non-calling squirrel.

To test whether altruistic behaviour evolved as a result of kin selection in this species, P.W. Sherman of Cornell University, and other investigators, set out to study the ground squirrels. By capturing, marking, and releasing individuals, and observing them for thousands of hours, they learned how colonies were formed and who was related to whom within them. Male squirrels leave their mother's home and establish new burrows elsewhere, usually about 400 m away. Females, on the other hand, usually settle within 50 m of their birthplace. As a result, the females in an area tend to be related to each other, whereas the males do not. After copulation, a male leaves the area of his mate's burrow. He is, therefore, far away not only from his mother, brothers, and cousins, but also from his offspring.

Based on their knowledge of kin selection, Sherman and his colleagues predicted that females should give an alarm call upon seeing a predator more often than should males, since an alarm calling male would be risking his life for non-relatives only. This prediction was borne out (Figure 24.27). In addition, it was discovered that females known to have close relatives living nearby gave an alarm call more frequently than did females whose relatives had died or moved farther away. These data strongly support the kin selection

hypothesis about the evolution of altruistic behaviour in this species.

Kin selection also explains the defensive behaviour of honeybees. The bees will only sting intruders that threaten their own colony, the members of which are all closely related. In other words, they will sacrifice themselves only for individuals who likely have at least some copies of genes just like their own, and not for bees with whom they have little in common genetically.

The kin selection hypothesis thus allows a somewhat expanded view of fitness. As you know, an organism's fitness depends on its contribution to the gene pool; that is, on its ability to spread its own genes (and therefore its successful characteristics) into succeeding generations. In the traditional terms of Darwinian fitness, fit individuals were by definition those who survived longer and/or left more offspring than less fit organisms. The idea of kin selection, however, takes into account the effect of individuals *and* their relatives (who by definition share a certain percentage of their genes) on gene frequencies. A new term, **inclusive fitness**, has been invented to refer to this broader concept. An individual's inclusive fitness is the sum of two things. One is its personal fitness, measured as its number of offspring (which carry genes like its own). The other is any increase it causes (by its actions) in the contribution made by its relatives to the gene pool (of genes like its own).

The inclusive fitness concept provides the basis for most sociobiological hypotheses about the evolution and/or function of particular social behaviours. As is

Figure 24.27

This figure shows the frequency with which Belding's ground squirrels in four age and sex classes were observed *to alarm call upon seeing a predator. Compared with this is the frequency with which they would have* been expected *to call if all types of squirrels were equally likely to do so; this expected frequency is calculated on the basis of how many times an animal from one of these categories was present when a predator arrived, multiplied by the percentage of times an approaching predator was met by any alarm call—from a squirrel of any age or sex. A comparison of observed with expected results thus allows researchers to test their hypotheses rigorously, excluding the possibility that chance alone was responsible for the results. In this case, it is obvious that males called much less than expected, whereas females called much more frequently than expected. Adult females have more offspring living nearby than do first-year females.*

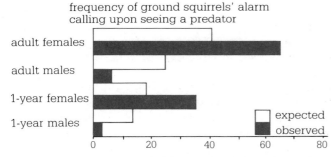

frequency of ground squirrels' alarm calling upon seeing a predator

adult females
adult males
1-year females
1-year males

☐ expected
■ observed

0   20   40   60   80

true of scientists in any field, sociobiologists formulate hypotheses, then make corresponding predictions which can be tested by study and/or experiment. The hypotheses are either refuted or supported by the results of such tests. Inclusive fitness is fundamental to most of these hypotheses; given that a particular type of social behaviour has an underlying genetic basis, sociobiological principles state that animals displaying this behaviour should do so in a way that maximizes their inclusive fitness.

For example, both zebras and wildebeests inhabit the savannas of Africa, often even travelling in the same herds (Figure 24.28). Both are preyed upon by lions and other carnivores. However, while zebras live in family groups (consisting of a male, his "harem" of females, and their young), wildebeests are much less "family oriented." Wildebeest males do not travel with their mates, and calves lose track of their mothers soon after weaning. Viewing the two species comparatively, a sociobiologist might hypothesize that zebras and wildebeests should respond differently when confronted by a predator. If lions threatened wilde-

Figure 24.28

A herd of zebra and wildebeest on the Serengeti plains of Africa

beests and zebras in the same way, male zebras should stand and attempt some defence of those around them (usually their mates and young), while male wildebeests should run. Field studies of these animals have confirmed this prediction, thus supporting the hypothesis. Both species behave in a way that maximizes their inclusive fitness. The contrast in their respective family organizations, however, means that they achieve this end using different strategies.

The Sociobiology Debate

Sociobiologists have had considerable success in explaining the evolution of social behaviour in many species. However, those who have tried to extend these concepts to human behaviour have frequently run into conflict. Human sociobiology deals with highly contentious questions. Are genes responsible for the human tendency to discriminate against outsiders? Do sexism and racism have a genetic basis? Does aggressive behaviour exist because it maximizes inclusive fitness? Questions like these have triggered an intense and often emotional debate between two major groups. They might be termed the *biological determinists* and the *environmental determinists*. Members of the latter school of thought deny that heredity plays any role in human behaviour. They feel that it is wholly shaped by the environment—by learning of some type. On the other hand, biological determinists, some of whom are sociobiologists, believe that learning plays a relatively minor role in shaping human behaviour. They claim that most human behaviours have a genetic basis and have evolved as a result of natural selection.

FIELD STUDY TECHNIQUES

It is frequently important to be able to identify the individuals in a group of animals under study. For example, a researcher may want to be able to see what happens to a particular individual over its lifetime. In the wild, the animal may be seen only irregularly and may look slightly different on each occasion. Alternatively, the study subjects may look very much alike or may be moving too quickly for a researcher to see subtle differences among them. Unless a field worker can identify individuals in some way, he or she will not know whether the particular response being studied is performed by the same animal many times (in which case the behaviour may be unique to this individual and perhaps abnormal) or by many different individuals (in which case the behaviour is probably of general importance). Other researchers may want to distinguish members of family groups to test hypotheses about the role of genes in controlling certain behaviours.

For a variety of reasons, therefore, field workers have had to devise methods of distinguishing their subjects as individuals. Usually the animals are captured, provided with some sort of identification badge, and then released. The markers must not harm the animals and should not alter their behaviour (or the way other organisms respond to them) in any substantial way. Many different types of identification badges are in use. Small mammals such as mice are often given a metal ear tag inscribed with a number. Larger animals such as bears can be tattooed. Workers may identify individual insects with small blobs of non-toxic paint or nail polish, while

fin-tags are often used for fish. Birds are commonly given variously coloured plastic leg bands. As well, millions of birds world-wide wear small, numbered aluminum rings, each of which is unique in some way. In North America, these bands bear an inscription, directing anyone who finds a banded bird to send the band (if the bird is dead) or information about the bird wearing it (where it was captured or seen, etc.) to a central data collection office in Washington, D.C. All such records are entered in a central computer, where they can be accessed for a variety of purposes. The information covers banded birds who have been recaught, found dead, or killed (by duck hunters, for example) anywhere in Canada, the United States, Mexico, and even further south. Most of what we know about the migratory patterns of

▲
Capturing the animals to be marked is often the most difficult part of the job. Birds can sometimes be caught in "mist nets," mesh nets made of very fine cord into which the birds fly — if they don't see them first!

A bird wearing a unique combination of coloured plastic bands as well as a numbered aluminum band
▼

birds and about how far individual birds move from where they were born has come from banding studies.

The movements of individual animals can be followed in much greater detail and on a smaller scale (within a habitat, for example) by using techniques of *biotelemetry*. Biotelemetry equipment consists of two parts: a radio transmitter attached to the animal being studied and a receiver which picks up the transmitted radio signals. Different individuals can be fitted with transmitters sending radio waves of differing frequencies. Techniques of biotelemetry give researchers the advantage of being able to monitor an animal's activities from a distance. The organism does not have to be examined or even seen in order to be identified. Although biotelemetry has been used in field research for decades, new innovations are making possible the manufacture of very small transmitters, which are light enough to be carried by a mouse or a songbird. In addition, transmitters have been developed that can send signals over long distances even under water. Scientists thus can follow the activities of marine animals such as whales that are virtually invisible at times. Perhaps most exciting of all, biotelemetry technology has now been developed that enables researchers to monitor the heart rate, body temperature, brain waves, and other body functions of the animals they are studying. In this way, scientists can determine the physiological state that accompanies behaviour and thus can investigate both the internal stimuli that trigger certain responses and the effect of particular behaviours on the body.

▲ This moose wears a collar equipped with a radio transmitter.

▲ Antennae attached to a radio receiver allow this researcher to pick up signals emitted by transmitters attached to the desert bighorn sheep he is studying. By tuning his receiver to different frequencies he can pick up the signals sent by the devices on various individual sheep — much as he would adjust his radio dial to tune in different stations.

Some people find biological determinism hard to accept because it implies (to them) that humans are more or less slaves to their genes. Some of their objections are philosophical rather than scientific; they fear that biological determinism could be used to "justify" some human behaviours (such as rape, racism, or even murder) as "unavoidable," or worse, as evidence of being "fit." Acceptance of such a theory, they suggest, will make it impossible for humans to alter their behaviour in order to improve social conditions. Extreme opponents of biological determinism advocate that study of the relationship between genes and human behaviour be avoided in case the results of such research are then used "unwisely."

This attitude has been criticized by those who believe that scientific inquiry should not be censored in any way. Still others argue that although the results of such studies *might* indeed be misused, they could also be used very productively to improve the understanding of human behaviour and thus to enhance our ability to change certain aspects of our behaviour for the better. The potential benefits of such research would far outweigh the possible liabilities.

Most scientists, including most sociobiologists, do not argue for either complete biological or complete environmental determinism. The real truth, as usual, probably lies somewhere in between. Humans are not machines whose thoughts and actions are completely programmed by genes. On the other hand, it is also unlikely that *Homo sapiens* is different from all other animals in this respect; as is true of other species, human behaviour is certainly affected by heredity to some extent.

Human social behaviour should be viewed as the result of a complex interaction of genes and environment. Much can probably be learned from attempts to discover the extent to which each of these factors affects human responses. The results of such studies might be used in a number of ways: for example, to prevent or treat mental illness, to decrease the frequency of aggressive behaviour (even of war), and to improve methods of education. Although there is no guarantee that it will provide these benefits, the sociobiological approach is probably worth investigating. It could provide a more complete—and potentially very useful — understanding of why humans behave as they do.

CHAPTER SUMMARY

Present day researchers attempt to avoid anthropomorphic interpretations of their observations of animal behaviour. This practice is important because most species of animals have sensory worlds different from that of *Homo sapiens*. There are two major schools of animal behaviour research: ethology and behaviourism.

Ethologists are interested in how a particular response increases an animal's fitness and how this response might have evolved. Most ethologists study their subjects in the natural environment. The founders of ethology (Konrad Lorenz, Niko Tinbergen, and Karl von Frisch) were in fact naturalists. On account of their conviction that behaviour, like morphology, is the result of evolution, early ethologists regarded almost all behaviour as completely innate or instinctive. They believed that learning played a relatively minor role in shaping responses. Most behaviours were held to be fixed action patterns, elicited by specific releaser stimuli and mediated by innate releasing mechanisms (IRMs). Complex or lengthy behaviours were chains of fixed action patterns, the completion of one step in the chain acting as a releaser for the next. Today, we realize that few behaviours are as stereotyped as fixed action patterns were originally proposed to be and that IRMs are not structural realities.

Behaviourism had its beginnings in psychology; some of its first proponents were Ivan Pavlov, B.F. Skinner, and E.L. Thorndike. Unlike ethologists, behaviourists placed great emphasis on the role of learning in determining behaviour patterns and worked primarily in laboratories. There, largely uninterested in the function or adaptive value of behaviours, they searched for general laws of learning. Their approach and methods thus led them to the conviction that genetics had little control over behaviour and that environmental factors were of primary importance. In other words, they felt that almost all behaviour was learned, either by classical conditioning or by trial and error learning. Recent studies, however, have shown that animals cannot learn to associate just any stimulus with any response; there are genetic constraints on learning.

Today, much of the research going on in animal behaviour is interdisciplinary. Ecology, genetics, neurobiology, psychology, and other fields all have much to contribute to the study of what shapes animal responses. New technology has facilitated the actual work of data collection and the investigation of previously inaccessible aspects of behavioural biology. Behavioural ecology and sociobiology are particularly active fields of study. The latter area of research focusses on the evolution of social behaviour. Altruistic behaviour is one of the many types of responses sociobiologists have investigated. Their explanations of such behaviour make use of kin selection and inclusive fitness, concepts central to understanding much of social behaviour. Sociobiological findings have sparked considerable debate between environmental and biological determinists. Nevertheless, sociobiology may ultimately provide a better understanding of many aspects not only of animal behaviour but also of human behaviour.

Chapter Objectives

Having completed this chapter, you should be able to do the following:

1. Define anthropomorphism and explain why it should be avoided in studies of animal behaviour.
2. Describe the methods and goals of ethology and discuss the views of ethologists regarding the functions and causes of behaviour.
3. Describe the methods and goals of behaviourism and discuss how they affect the behaviourist view of animal behaviour.
4. Discuss the interaction of genes and environment in the control of animal behaviour.
5. Outline the fundamental principles of sociobiology.
6. Discuss the sociobiology debate and explain why sociobiology has generated such controversy.

Vocabulary

anthropomorphism
ethology
releaser
fixed action pattern
innate releasing mechanism (IRM)
behaviourism

classical conditioning
unconditioned stimulus
unconditioned response
conditioned stimulus
conditioned response
trial and error learning

positive reinforcement
negative reinforcement
sociobiology
altruism
kin selection
inclusive fitness

Review Questions

1. (a) What is anthropomorphism?
   (b) Why should it be avoided in studies of animal behaviour?
2. A male flicker (a species of woodpecker-like bird) has a patch of black feathers on his face that resembles a moustache. If a similar black moustache is painted on his mate's face (females do not normally possess such a patch) he will attack her as if she were a rival male. Why?
3. Give two reasons an animal might not respond to a particular stimulus.

4. (a) In what ways are the methods and goals of ethologists different from those of behaviourists?
   (b) In what ways are they similar?
5. Stickleback courtship behaviour is quite elaborate and its performance requires the investment of a considerable amount of energy on the part of both male and female. Why is this energy nonetheless well spent? In other words, why has this behaviour evolved?

6. (a) What is Lorenz's model of how the brain controls stereotyped behaviour?
   (b) Why is this model useful?
   (c) Why must care be exercised when using it?
7. Your mouth waters when you smell a pizza. Is this an example of classical or operant conditioning? Explain your choice.
8. (a) When a dog is trained to obey certain commands, is classical or operant conditioning used? Justify your selection.
   (b) Explain, using the appropriate terminology, the steps in this learning process.
9. What is the relationship between
   (a) a releaser and an unconditioned stimulus?
   (b) an action pattern and an unconditioned response?
10. A rat cannot learn to perceive a shock as negative reinforcement for eating certain types of food.
   (a) What sort of treatment can act as a negative reinforcement in this case?
   (b) Why do these particular limitations on a rat's learning ability make sense in terms of the conditions and circumstances a rat usually

encounters in its natural environment?
   (c) Why might this type of constraint on learning be beneficial to an animal?
11. What is the relationship between a species' ecology and its behaviour?
12. Explain how the theory of kin selection can account for the evolution of altruistic behaviour, citing evidence from at least one scientific study to support your explanation.
13. (a) What is inclusive fitness?
   (b) How is it different from simple individual or "Darwinian" fitness?
14. Some sociobiologists hypothesize that many human attitudes (for example, racism and sexism) are at least partially determined by genes. Do you think that this suggestion is constructive or destructive? Explain your answer.
15. (a) What do the conflict between ethologists and behaviourists and the conflict between proponents and opponents of sociobiology have in common? Explain your answer.
   (b) How do these conflicts relate to the nature-nurture controversy described in Chapter 23?

Advanced Questions

1. Many people attach black silhouettes of falcons to their picture windows in order to discourage song birds from hitting the glass.
   (a) Using the information provided in this chapter, explain why this strategy works.
   (b) Discuss whether the strategy would continue to work after the silhouette had been up for some time.
2. Dog owners often enter their pets in shows or trials, during which the dogs demonstrate their skills at performing certain tasks — herding sheep, retrieving ducks, etc. Using your knowledge of both genetics and behaviour, explain how you could produce a champion dog.
3. On the outside, herring gull eggs are speckled with brownish spots which make them perfectly camouflaged against the backgrounds on which they are laid. These backgrounds are grassy nests on pebble-strewn ground. The inside surfaces of the eggs, however, are pure white. Herring gulls remove the egg shells from their nest soon after the young hatch. Explain how this behaviour might have evolved.

4. Explain how patriotism (a generalized type of behaviour exhibited by many humans) might have evolved.
   (a) Do you think that this type of behaviour is in fact genetically based?
   (b) If it is, does that mean that it cannot be altered in some way?
   (c) If your answer to the previous question was "no," then how might such behaviour be modified?
5. Suppose you were called upon to decide how rape behaviour might be reduced or eliminated from human activity — or even to speculate on whether it could.
   (a) What would you need to know about this behaviour in order to deal with it effectively?
   (b) How might you (or others) go about obtaining this information?
   (c) What sort of research would enable you to come to some decision about how to combat rape behaviour?

UNIT EIGHT

ECOLOGY

CHAPTER 25

THE BIOTIC NETWORK

*I've often heard people say, ''I wonder what it would be like
to be on board a spaceship,'' and the answer is very simple.
What does it feel like?
That's all we've ever experienced. We are all astronauts.*

R. Buckminster Fuller
Operating Manual for Spaceship Earth

The exploration of space during the second half of this century has provided the earth's inhabitants with a new perspective. The photographs sent back from spacecraft show no national boundaries dividing the continents. They illustrate clearly that water and air currents are global in nature. Although it has been known for several centuries that the earth is round, for the first time humans have truly understood that it is a single unit.

25.1 SPACESHIP EARTH: A CLOSED SYSTEM

Biosphere is a term used to describe the portion of this planet that supports all the living organisms within it. The biosphere includes the protective layers of the atmosphere to an altitude of about 30 km and the upper portion of the earth's crust to a depth of about 10 km. The materials needed to support life circulate among the organisms within this thin layer covering the planet. The study of all the interactions that occur within the biosphere has been given the name **ecology** from the Greek words *oikos*, house, and *logos*, study of. Athough this term was first used in 1866, it took over a century for people to recognize its significance.

During the past twenty years, this new understanding of the biosphere has resulted in a considerable increase in the number of people concerned about environmental issues. There are now over 5000 non-governmental international organizations and 80 000 regional groups focussed on a wide range of concerns. Millions of individuals have become affiliated with at least one of these groups. Canadians have become involved in activities as diverse as the preservation of the cloudforest in Costa Rica, the reduction of emissions causing acid rain, the curtailment of the whale harvest, and the establishment of new national parks. Now a World Conservation Strategy has been developed to coordinate priorities and establish global monitoring systems. Perhaps we have reached the stage predicted by native legends:

When the earth is sick and the animals have disappeared, there will come a tribe of peoples from all creeds, colours and cultures who believe in deeds not words and who will restore the earth to its former beauty. This tribe will be called the ''Warriors of the Rainbow.''

It has taken a long time for humans to develop even a limited understanding of the complex relationships among organisms on this planet. Prehistoric people survived by learning the habits and habitat of the plants they gathered and the animals they hunted. When agriculture began about 10 000 years ago, the first farmers learned even more about the plants and animals they domesticated. As people spread out across the world, each group had to learn about the new organisms that were encountered. This accumulated knowledge was passed on to successive generations of those who sought food from the land or sea.

Since the eighteenth century, efforts have been made to organize this information in ways that could lead to further understanding. These efforts have raised many new questions, resulting in an explosive increase in knowledge about individual species and their relationships to other species. The Industrial Revolution and later the Technological Revolution have released many pollutants into the biosphere. As their effects have been recognized, much more has been learned about the interrelationships among organisms.

As Buckminster Fuller noted, ''Now there is one outstandingly important fact regarding Spaceship Earth, and that is that no instruction book came with it.'' Modern industry considers problems from the viewpoint of the systems that are involved. Applications of this approach to the study of the movement of energy and materials within the biosphere has resulted in a greater understanding of how Spaceship Earth functions.

The Biosphere II experiment (Figure 25.1) is a test of our present understanding of how various systems are linked in the biotic network. If humans are to be

Figure 25.1
The Biosphere II experiment

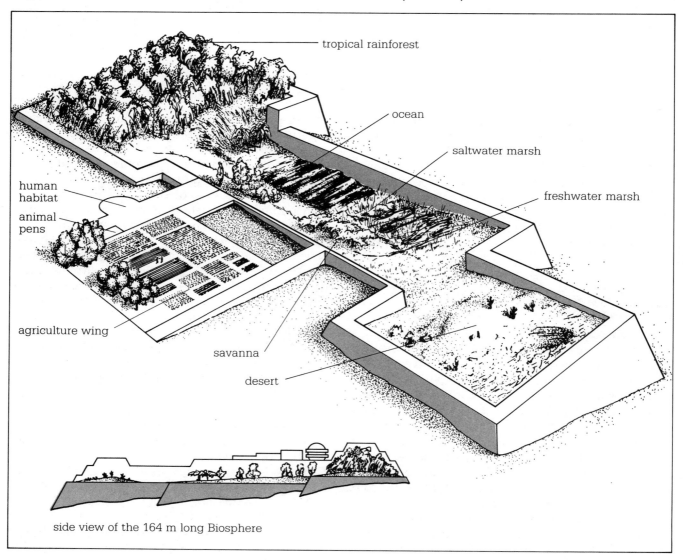

tropical rainforest

ocean

saltwater marsh

freshwater marsh

human habitat

animal pens

agriculture wing

savanna

desert

side view of the 164 m long Biosphere

able to colonize space, it will be necessary to establish a self-sustaining unit away from earth (Biosphere I). The Biosphere II structure, occupying about 1 ha of the Arizona desert, consists of living quarters, laboratories, an agricultural area, and five regions — savanna, marsh, desert, rainforest, and ocean. When it is completed, eight people will attempt to live in this sealed system for two years. It is hoped that this experiment will provide information that will be valuable in managing the earth's resources as well in furthering the space program.

25.2 INTERACTIONS

Living things both affect and are affected by their environment. Deer, for example, browse on the young green vegetation of the forest. As the forest matures, the larger trees shade the plants below, thus reducing the amount of food available for the deer. If beaver build a dam, flooding part of the forest, the trees in that area die. The plants that grow in the resulting marshy areas again provide suitable food for the deer. The deer, however, also affect the growth of the forest. If a large number of deer are feeding in a relatively small area, they can consume all the tree seedlings, preventing the forest from regenerating. If the deer trample the soil and strip it of all vegetation, the soil may dry and erode, thus becoming less able to support vegetation in the future.

Each of these changes, of course, also affects all the other organisms that share the forest habitat. The pattern of relationships between that species and all the living and non-living things within its habitat is called its **ecological niche**. A complete description of an organism's ecological niche includes where it lives, what it eats, what eats it, what it competes with, how and when it reproduces, what effect it has on its habitat, and what limits of environmental change it can tolerate. Many organisms such as the giant panda and the koala have a very narrow environmental niche. It is often their dependence upon a limited range of food that restricts them to a specific habitat. These species are called *specialists* and their degree of specialization often places them at the risk of extinction. Other organisms are quite flexible in their requirements and thus can occupy a wide range of habitats. Such organisms are called *generalists*. Generalist species are often found in habitats that are undergoing change and are much more likely to co-exist with humans. Cockroaches, rats, mice, raccoons, and squirrels are examples of generalist species as, of course, are

Figure 25.2
What would be the impact of building a dam this large?

humans. All the species that share a given habitat are said to form its **biological community**. In this sense, the biological community of a person includes not only the other people who live in the same area, but also the dogs, cats, snakes, birds, spiders, snails, insects, worms, and plants that are there.

Humans differ from other organisms in that they have learned to use energy and machines to affect the environment on a scale that is not possible for other organisms. Humans can level hills, drain swamps, excavate tunnels, or create lakes to suit their convenience (Figure 25.2). Only recently has concern emerged about the environmental consequences of such actions. The ability to transport water and food over considerable distances has allowed humans to live in ever larger urban groupings which permit them to ignore their link to the natural environment. Within cities, it is often possible to commute from home to business or recreational activities without leaving an artificial environment. Many people have no need for winter clothing. Yet a flood, or even a power failure, can immediately remind us that we cannot totally isolate ourselves from the environment.

The environment of any organism consists of all the **biotic** (living) and **abiotic** (non-living) factors that influence that organism's survival. Humans depend on the biotic and abiotic factors in the environment in ways that they often fail to realize.

Scientists exploring the possibility of life on other planets have investigated several hypotheses to explain how life originated on the earth. To test these hypotheses, it is necessary to simulate the conditions

Figure 25.3
A representation of conditions on the earth before life (a)
and with life (b). What process was responsible for the
decrease in carbon dioxide and the increase in oxygen?

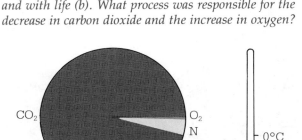

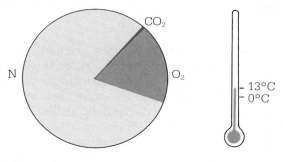

(a)   the earth without life

(b)   the earth with life

existing at that time in the earth's history. It is now
thought that, prior to the development of life, physical
conditions on the earth were very much different than
those that exist today. As shown in Figure 25.3(a), the
earth's average temperature was considerably colder
than at present; the atmosphere consisted largely of
carbon dioxide, with very little free oxygen. There
would have been no ozone layer to screen out ultraviolet radiation.

Thus it is assumed that the first forms of life evolved
in the shelter of the oceans, perhaps in layers of clay
or even ice. The first organisms capable of photosynthesis, probably similar to the prokaryotic cyanophytes (blue-green algae), slowly began to change
conditions in that early environment. These organisms consumed carbon dioxide and released oxygen,
thus changing the proportions of these gases in the
environment. Over millions of years, the ozone layer
began to form, filtering out the ultraviolet radiation
and permitting organisms to colonize the land.

It has required some three billion years of evolution
to reach the conditions that exist today. See Figure 25.3

(b). The maintenance and regulation of those conditions depend on a system of interacting organisms,
each of which has an effect on the composition of the
environment. Our present understanding of the
changes that have occurred in the nature of life on the
earth over millions of years suggests that this system
has undergone reorganization many times. There
have been periods of mass extinctions and of rapid
evolution of new species, interspersed with periods
of gradual change.

The hypothesis that life itself determines and controls the conditions that make the earth habitable is
called the **Gaia Hypothesis**. Species may come and
go, but the system undergoes reorganization and life
carries on. One conclusion that can be reached from
this hypothesis is that if humans become a threat to
life on this planet, they might become extinct while
more durable organisms such as cockroaches might
well survive. If humans wish to maintain the stability
of the present system and to minimize the adverse
effects that their activities have on other organisms,
they must strive for greater understanding of the complex networks of interactions that exist.

25.3 SUBSYSTEMS IN THE BIOSPHERE

Any change in one part of the biosphere produces a
ripple effect in other parts of it. For example, consider
a proposal to divert water southwards from Canada
to the United States. The effects of this diversion on
the ecological relationships of the whole continent
would have to be considered. Other actions, such as
the construction of a new expressway, may produce a
significant effect in a much smaller area.

Although the biosphere really is a single unit, at
times it is more useful to focus on a smaller portion.
The most obvious subdivisions of the terrestrial portion of the biosphere are those based on climate
patterns. The temperature range, the length of the
growing season, and the amount of precipitation
determine what plants can survive in an area. These
plants, in turn, determine which other organisms will
be present. The nature of the organisms inhabiting
aquatic portions of the biosphere is most strongly
influenced by whether the water is fresh or salt.
Within these two categories, it is possible to identify
large areas which will have a similar biotic composition. These areas are called **biomes** (Figure 25.4). The
distribution of the various biomes within the biosphere is largely determined by the earth's geology
and the patterns of air and water currents (Figure
25.5).

Figure 25.4
Which of these biomes are found in Canada? Which biomes found in the United States do not exist in Canada?

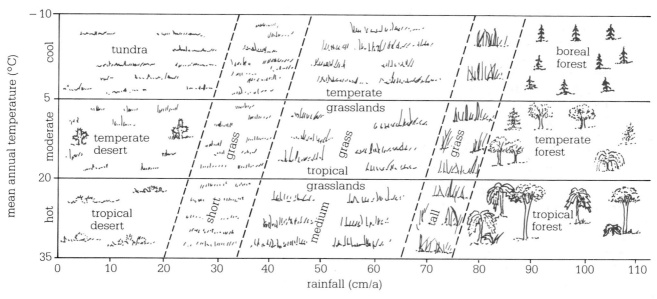

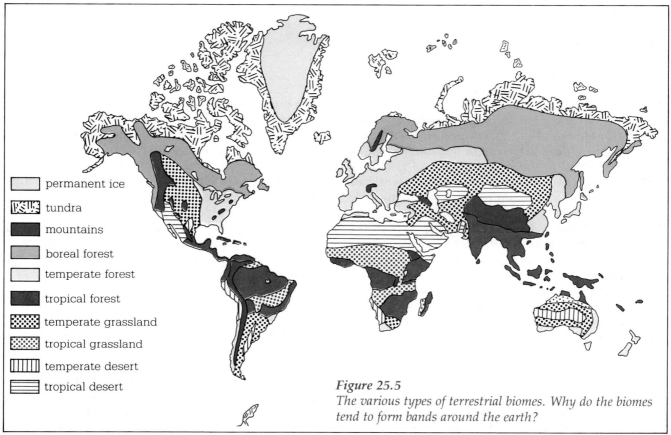

permanent ice

tundra

mountains

boreal forest

temperate forest

tropical forest

temperate grassland

tropical grassland

temperate desert

tropical desert

Figure 25.5
The various types of terrestrial biomes. Why do the biomes tend to form bands around the earth?

25.4 TERRESTRIAL BIOMES

Terrestrial biomes are generally identified on the basis of their dominant vegetation. The presence of closely spaced trees indicates a forest biome; if a mixture of grasses and annual plants predominates, then the area is described as a grassland; if neither trees nor grasses are abundant, the area is considered to be a desert biome. The transition from one biome to another is gradual. Suppose you drove from east to west across North America. West of the Great Lakes, you would notice the trees gradually becoming more widely spaced; suddenly, you would realize that you had left the forest and entered the grasslands. This transition zone between biomes is called an **ecocline**.

The Forest Biomes

Areas receiving precipitation in excess of 75 cm/a will generally support a dense enough growth of trees to be considered a forest. Frequent forest fires or poor forest management can, however, limit the ability of the forest to regenerate. Approximately 30 percent of the earth's land surface is covered by some type of forest. Another 10 percent receives adequate rainfall but fails to support forest cover. Figure 25.5 shows the pattern of these forests across the continents. In the north, extending from Alaska to Siberia, lie the vast boreal coniferous forests. The temperate zones support a variety of open woodlands and closed forest (more than 20 percent of the area is covered by the trees' crowns). These forests frequently contain a mixture of deciduous and evergreen species. The tropical forests that lie near the equator support the most dense and diverse of the forests (Figure 25.6).

The forest regions are major sites of photosynthesis and thus have an important role in the maintenance of the proportion of gases in the earth's atmosphere. They also stabilize the soil against erosion. Both the tree cover itself and the water vapour that evaporates from it influence the climate and rainfall patterns over a large portion of the globe.

Trees are also essential for a variety of human activities. Worldwide, humans consume in excess of 3×10^9 m³ of wood annually. About 55 percent of this is hardwood (from broadleafed trees) and the remaining 45 percent is softwood (from coniferous trees). The pattern of use is quite different from developed to developing countries. In the former, greater than 80 percent of the wood harvested is used for industrial purposes and less than 20 percent is used for fuel. In developing countries, these figures are reversed. A

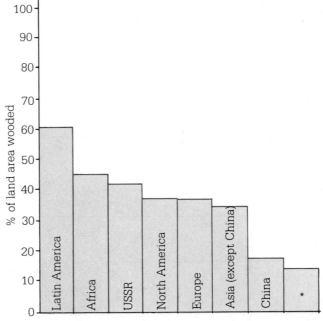

Figure 25.6
Although the developing countries appear to have adequate forests to supply their needs, their high rate of consumption is predicted to exhaust the supply by early in the next century.

*Australia, New Zealand, Japan, Israel, South Africa

large proportion of the wood harvested in developed countries is destined to become paper. It takes, for example, an average of 10 ha of forest to produce the paper used in one day's editions of a large city newspaper. As literacy increases in the developing countries, the demand for paper is doubling every decade. Yet, for some two billion people in those developing countries, the problem is more basic. They have difficulty finding the fuel wood needed for cooking and warmth. At present in much of the world, the forests are being harvested more rapidly than they are regenerating.

The Boreal Forests

The **boreal forests** form an irregular band about 950 km wide circling the continents north of a latitude of 50°. See Figure 25.7(a). Most of these forests lie on shield areas of Precambrian rock formed millions of years ago. During the Ice Ages, glaciers repeatedly scraped most of the soil from these rocks in Canada and Scandinavia. The shield area of Siberia was less heavily glaciated. The shallow soil that has developed

Figure 25.7
Boreal forests are found in the northerly regions of the earth (a). The mixture of land and water found in them makes road or rail transport difficult (b). Many areas such as ribbon bogs are accessible only by air or by winter roads.

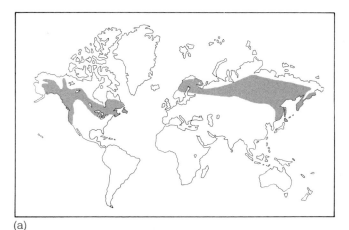

(a)

(b)

lichen covered trees that appear to struggle for existence. In the **taiga**, the ecocline at the edge of the tundra, the trees become stunted and more widely spaced and the ground between them is covered with a thick growth of lichen such as reindeer moss.

The most striking feature of the boreal forest, however, is **muskeg**. Some 1.3×10^6 km^2 of Canada consist of this strange mixture of land and water. The southern fringe of the boreal forests contains many *pond bogs*. These are often called *quaking bogs* because the spruce trees near shore grow on a mat of floating sphagnum moss. The trees move up and down with any wave action in the open water or when someone walks across the bog. Although these pond bogs are not typical of the major region of muskeg, they have been studied much more thoroughly since they are more accessible.

Although Canadians know little about the *raised bogs* of typical muskeg, Europeans have studied them quite extensively. Canadians have been able to ignore the resources of these regions, preferring instead to use those that were more accessible. The builders of the railroads and later of the Trans-Canada highway had tremendous problems dealing with muskeg. The stories of their achievements make us realize what difficult tasks they undertook.

The climatic condition that causes the formation of raised bogs is an excess of precipitation over evaporation. Although the annual rainfall is comparatively light, the weak sun in the short summers does not cause all of the water to evaporate. As a result, much of the soil is continuously waterlogged. Sedges, bullrushes, and horsetails grow in this soggy ground, forming a *fen*. If there is enough surplus to form pools of standing water, sphagnum moss begins to grow. The sphagnum acts as a sponge, absorbing the water, and spreads rapidly over the area, destroying most other plants. New layers of moss grow on top of the older ones, causing the bog to swell like a rising loaf of bread. Eventually the mound may split, forming ribbons of open water. These mounds are too thick to provide a foothold for trees.

Muskeg provides an ideal location for insects that are aquatic at some stage of their life cycle. Black flies are present in enormous numbers — one researcher counted five million larvae in a square metre of riverbed! In all, some ten thousand species of insects inhabit the boreal forest. There are many who believe that the mosquitoes, midges, and black flies are so numerous that people will never be able to fully exploit the resources of these areas. Migrating birds,

since is usually deficient in nutrients. The action of the glaciers also has left many depressions in the rock that collect water, forming lakes that often have no inlet or outlet.

The composition of the bedrock, the retention of water, and the nutrient deficient soil all affect the nature of the organisms that can survive in the boreal forest. The short growing season and harsh winters combine with these factors to form an environment that is inhospitable to most species. The boreal forests are a monotonous blend of black and white spruce, balsam fir, jack pine, tamarack, white birch, and poplar. These spruce are not the magnificent specimens found on suburban lawns, but short, scrawny,

however, travel long distances to raise their young in the boreal forest and tundra because of the ample food supply these insects provide. It is estimated that the boreal forest supports an average of 700 million warblers each season.

Much of the animal population of the boreal forest is concentrated in the treed areas. Most numerous are rodents such as mice, voles, lemmings, beaver, muskrats, otters, and porcupines that feed on seeds, nuts, and other plant material. Also common are carnivores such as marten, weasels, fishers, mink, foxes, lynx, wolves, and black bears. They prey largely on the rodents, although they supplement their diet with plant materials. The least numerous but largest animals of this biome are ruminants such as deer, moose, and caribou.

The animals of the boreal forest rely on special adaptations to enable them to survive the long, harsh winters. The relatively large size of many of the species reduces the ratio of heat loss to heat production. Long, dense coats of fur provide excellent insulation (and make the skins desirable to the fur industry). Smaller animals retreat to burrows for additional protection from the most severe weather. Reptiles and amphibians spend as much as eight months in a state of hibernation. The quest for food requires more time and energy in winter. Some animals solve this problem by hoarding food during the fall; others reduce their need for food through hibernation for at least some portion of the winter. Bats, skunks, some mice, ground squirrels, chipmunks, and woodchucks are true hibernators; bears are not, although they sleep through much of the winter.

A thick snow cover provides insulation for the hibernators. Small mammals tunnel through the base of the snow, insulated from the severe weather conditions above. Deer, moose, and caribou, however, have difficulty moving through a thick layer of snow. Thus, they can expend far too much energy in the search for food. Many animals die when the winter is unusually long or cold.

The Temperate Forests

The warmer average temperatures and longer growing season that give rise to the **temperate forests** also allow a much greater variety of organisms to survive there. Although the climate is not as harsh as that of the boreal forest, there are distinct seasons; in many areas, temperatures drop below freezing during the winter. Those plants not adapted to conserve water must shed their leaves to withstand the drought cre-

Figure 25.8
The temperate forest regions (a) and a deciduous woodland in spring (b). The small plants of the forest floor must grow, bloom, and produce seeds early in the spring before the trees above open their leaves and shade the ground-level plants.

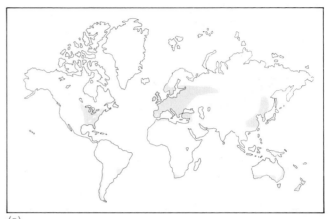

(a)

(b)

ated by winter. These forests generally contain a mixture of broad-leafed and needle-bearing trees, the proportions and species depending on local conditions (Figure 25.8).

The conditions that make these areas hospitable to so many organisms also make these areas desirable for human habitation. Thus, the portions of eastern North America, Europe, and western Asia that were originally covered by temperate woodlands have been largely cleared for habitation or agricultural and industrial use. The remnants are mostly protected and maintained by reforestation.

The mature temperate forests of Acadia and the Great Lakes Region are dominated by maple and beech trees with some red and white pine and hemlock. Younger forests contain a high proportion of red and white oak, basswood, and black cherry. Farther south, the forests also contain hickory, sassafras, pawpaw, and tulip trees. This Carolinian type of forest is found in Canada only in southwestern Ontario, close to Lakes Erie and Ontario. Point Pelee National Park preserves a sample of this forest.

Variations in the amount and timing of rainfall can result in quite different types of temperate forests. In the drier areas of southeastern North America, the dominant species may be the long-leaf pine, a species that is used to produce turpentine. The mild, moist climate along the west coast produces the temperate rainforests of British Columbia and the state of Washington in which Douglas fir and Sitka spruce predominate. Pacific Rim National Park was created to preserve a portion of this type of forest. Areas with mild, moist winters and hot dry summers produce a type of scrub forest called **chaparral**. Trees here are often stunted since the rain does not occur during the growing season. They are evergreen species with a thick waxy coating on the leaves to prevent drying. Scrub oak, olive, and eucalyptus trees are characteristic of this type of biome. Although fire occurs frequently during the summer, these species can regenerate rapidly. Animals often migrate from the chaparral to higher altitudes for the summer months. Chaparral is found in southern California, Mexico, South Africa, western Australia, and around the Mediterranean Sea.

Because the forested areas that remain tend to be small and isolated, many of the larger animals of the temperate forests are sparsely distributed or locally extinct. The establishment of hunting preserves in Europe many centuries ago did protect a number of species there. Other species survive in wildlife reserves or national parks. Many species, however, were hunted into extinction either as game or as pests. Most of the vertebrate animals found in these forests today are rodents, amphibians, reptiles, or other small species. The numbers of most bird species remain fairly high, although some have become rare or endangered. Some birds are resident full time in these forests. Others migrate southwards in the fall, returning to nest in the early spring. A great many other species pause in these forests during their spring and fall migrations.

The Tropical Forests

The high temperatures, heavy rainfall, and lack of seasonal variation typical of the tropics produce luxuriant forests. These **humid forests** grow in areas that receive from 200 cm/a to 400 cm/a of rainfall and have a dry season lasting less than two months. They form a belt around the earth, extending about 10° north and south of the equator. Although they account for only 8 percent of the land area of the earth, they comprise almost half of its heavily forested area and contain about half of its plant and animal species (Figure 25.9).

Undisturbed for millenia, the humid forests have evolved the most complex systems of interrelationships among species that are known. As many as 230 tree and 269 bird species have been recorded from a single hectare. A recent study in Peru found 41 000 insect species living in the canopy above a hectare of forest. It is estimated that these forests contain some two million species of which only about one sixth have been identified.

This diversity is both the strength and the weakness of the **tropical forests**. A humid forest survives small areas of disturbance well; the surrounding areas supply the species to fill in the gap. If a large area is cleared, however, the forest requires nearly 400 years to regenerate itself—twice the time required by a temperate forest. This is, to a large extent, due to the fact that the temperate plant species largely depend upon wind for seed dispersal, while most tropical plants are adapted for animal dispersal. The large number of animal species means that they, too, are rather sparsely distributed and thus can easily become threatened with extinction.

The tropical forests provide many useful products. More than half of modern medicines are derived from plants, largely tropical ones. From these forests are obtained oils, gums, resins, latexes, steroids, waxes, rubber, fibres, dyes, tanning agents, turpentines, rattan, bamboo, flavourings, spices, tea, coffee, cacao,

Figure 25.9

The tropical forest regions (a) and a forest scene (b). Most of the energy and activity of a humid forest occurs in the layers of the canopy rather than on the forest floor.

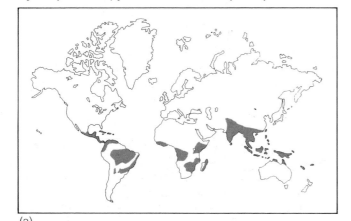

(a)

(b)

fruits, nuts, and pesticides. The world's food crops have been domesticated from wild plants. Of the dozen plants that provide 90 percent of human food, half are tropical in origin. Plant breeders depend on the gene pool of the wild relatives of these plants to develop strains that are well adapted to local conditions. There is still much to learn about the potential of these forests and the complex relationships among the organisms there.

Since World War II, over half of the world's humid forests have been destroyed. In many tropical countries, forest loss is accelerating to provide fuelwood and agricultural land. Much of the land is cleared to provide pasture for cattle, which in turn supply the North American demand for inexpensive hamburger beef. It has been calculated that one average hamburger represents the loss of about 5 m² of forest. Left as forest, that area would support one large tree, 50 saplings, several thousand insects, animals, and birds as well as a variety of mosses, fungi, and microorganisms.

These tropical forests are millions of years older than the temperate forests, yet they are supported by less soil. Here, the debris on the forest floor decomposes quickly and the nutrients are immediately absorbed by plant roots. If the trees are cleared, the resulting agricultural land is poor, since there is so little organic material in it. It does not hold water well and the few minerals quickly leach out. Without the sheltering canopy of the trees, the soil bakes hard in the tropical sun, forming *laterite*, a substance more useful for building than for farming.

At present, only about five percent of the global tropical forests are managed, mostly as national parks. There are many unique areas that require protection since their very existence is threatened. It is gradually being recognized that the logging practices used in the temperate forests cannot be transferred to the tropical forests without adverse consequences. New techniques are being developed that confine logging activity to the dry season and reduce damage considerably. Countries such as Thailand and Tanzania are modernizing the ancient techniques of *agroforestry*, a land use system that involves growing trees and food crops beside each other.

Some tropical areas receive enough rainfall to support trees, but also have long periods of drought. Here, the forest trees may be deciduous rather than evergreen. These are called seasonal (or *monsoon*) forests; they too support a great diversity of species. Still drier areas have more open forests of scrub trees and shrubs. Species that live in these forests are adapted to survive extensive periods of drought. Both types of forests tend to lie just to the north or south of the humid forests.

INDIVIDUALS CAN MAKE A DIFFERENCE

In the spring of 1987, teachers at Thornlea Secondary School in Thornhill, Ontario, asked their senior biology students to do more than just report on an ecological problem. They asked them to become involved—to do something that could make a difference.

Two students, Pam Hunt and Andrea Kopicki, became interested in the project of the World Wildlife Fund (WWF) to save the Monteverde Cloud Forest in Costa Rica. This forest reserve in the mountainous north-west is known to contain more than 2000 species of plants, 320 species of birds, and 100 species of mammals. A handful of landowners, farmers, and biologists banded together in an effort to triple the size of the reserve so that the entire river valley would be protected. They approached the WWF for assistance in obtaining the necessary funding.

In response to a reader's letter about an article he wrote for *Equinox*, naturalist Adrian Forsyth suggested that individual Canadians buy one or more acres of the projected reserve. Thus developed a campaign to persuade Canadians to purchase a portion of the forest at $25 an acre.

Pam and Andrea could not afford to purchase an acre but decided to encourage others to do so. They prepared a thirty-second radio announcement to publicize the campaign. It was broadcast on a community service program on a local CBC station. As a result, the WWF received some $300 000 in additional contributions. David Love, the education and membership director of the WWF, felt that these funds were in some part the result of Pam's and Andrea's

Each time relatively small areas of a forest disappear, several species, such as this wooly monkey, are lost. Forever.

efforts. He therefore asked them to make a second appeal on the CBC national network, this time one minute in length, in the spring of 1988. By the autumn of that year, a total of half a million dollars had been raised to save the Monteverde Cloud Forest.

The Grassland Biomes

Grasslands are found mainly in the interior of the continents, often in the rainshadow of mountain ranges. These areas receive from 20 cm/a to 70 cm/a of rainfall. While enough to support a dense growth of grasses, this amount is not enough for trees except in river valleys or other low-lying, moist areas. The *prairies* of North America, the *pampas* of Argentina, the *veldt* of Africa, the *savanna* of Australia, and the *steppes* of Asia are all grasslands, although each possesses a unique mix of species. The North American grasslands stretch for 1200 km across the centre of the continent, increasing in altitude from 240 m in the east to 1275 m in the foothills of the Rocky Mountains (Figure 25.10).

The dominant vegetation of grasslands is a mixture of as many as a hundred different species of grass. Grasses have fibrous root systems that may penetrate to a depth of six metres below the surface. These roots are very efficient at extracting the available moisture from the soil. They also hold the soil firmly, resisting erosion. Thus, grasses are well suited to climates in which most of the rainfall is in the spring. The stems of these plants lie close to or under the surface of the ground. The ability of the plants to regenerate from these underground stems enables them to withstand heavy grazing activity and to survive the fires that occur frequently in the dry summers.

Most of the animals of the grasslands are herbivores. On the North American prairies can be found bison, mule deer, pronghorn antelope, jack rabbits, ground squirrels, prairie dogs, and grouse. Their counterparts on the pampas of South America are viscacha, cavy, tuco tuco, rhea, guanaco, and pampas deer. The African grasslands support springhaas, ground squirrels, moles, ostrich, zebras, and springbok. On the Australian savanna live kangaroos, wallaby, wombats, marsupial moles, and emu. In Asia, one finds jerboa, hamsters, mole rats, saiga, and wild horses. Each of these regions also has characteristic carnivorous predators.

It would appear that the first human efforts at agriculture took place on the fertile grasslands in the river basins of the Nile, the Tigris/Euphrates, the Ganges/Brahmaputra, and the Yangtse. At first, these efforts probably involved little more than planting some of the seeds collected from wild plants. It gradually was recognized that if the poorer seeds were eaten and the best ones planted, the succeeding crops produced more abundant and larger seeds. Over centuries, the modern cereal crops of wheat, rice, oats, barley, maize (corn), rye, sorghum, and millet were developed from

Figure 25.10
The grasslands regions (a) and the pronghorn antelope (b). It is estimated that some 40 million pronghorn antelope once roamed the North American prairies. The numbers had declined to about 25 000 before conservation efforts began. Now, over a million of these animals again roam freely across the grasslands.

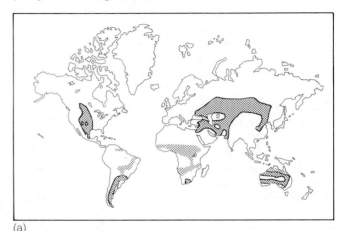

(a)

(b)

their wild ancestors. The seed heads of these early cereal crops resembled those found on wild grasses today. There were a small number of small seeds that ripened from the top down. The seeds were loosely attached so that the seed head tended to "shatter" when it was touched or blown, thus distributing the seeds. This characteristic made the grain very difficult to harvest and thus it was bred out of the species. The first cobs of maize were about 2 cm long and had 40 to 50 kernels. Table 25.1 lists the major food crops and their place of origin. Most, but not all, of these are grassland species.

Table 25.1   The Origin of Some Staples of the
World's Larder

EAST ASIA	NEAR EAST	LATIN AMERICA
adsuki beans	almonds	cocoa
bananas	apricots	chilies
coconuts	barley	lima beans
millet	chickpeas	manioc
oranges	dates	maize
rice	fava beans	peanuts
soybeans	figs	pinto beans
sugar cane	lentils	potatoes
yams	olives	pumpkins
	peas	squash
	raisins	sweet potatoes
	walnuts	tomatoes
	wheat	

What might account for the fact that most of the foods
we eat originated in these areas?

Some grassland areas have been cultivated or used
for grazing for about 10 000 years. Changing climate
patterns coupled with poor soil management practices
have resulted in the conversion of many of the early
farming areas into desert. Even today some 1.2 ×
10⁶ ha of agricultural land are lost to desert every year.
Arable land represents 40 percent of this total; the
remainder is grazing land. Part of this loss is caused
by attempts to grow crops in areas for which they are
not suited. Sorghum, for example, is a cereal that is
suited to the dry tropical grasslands of Africa and has
been a staple of the diet there for centuries. It has a
tough seed coat and is difficult to prepare. In addition,
sorghum is deficient in gluten, the protein that gives
bread its characteristic texture. Thus, wheat is deemed
to be a more desirable crop and many farmers cultivate
it in spite of frequent crop failures. When a crop fails
due to drought, the soil dries and erodes. The soil
organisms die and the ground is less able to support
a good crop the following season.

The native population of North America did little to
disturb the prairie biome. The establishment of the
outposts of the fur trade in the late eighteenth and
early nineteenth centuries produced the first significant changes. These posts depended on dried meat,
mostly bison, obtained by hunting the prairie herds.
The populations of large mammals were greatly
reduced. The building of the railroads and the resulting influx of farmers further contributed to the decline
by disrupting the habitat needed by these animals.
The bison were close to extinction by the time efforts

were made to preserve them. Today, large herds can
be found in several national parks as well as on a few
private ranches. The pronghorn antelope also
declined drastically, but they are now protected and
can frequently be seen grazing in the fields beside
highways.

The glacial history of the North American grasslands has left the landscape dotted with shallow
water-filled depressions called *sloughs*. Many of these
are surrounded by vegetation that provides ideal nesting sites for ducks. This area is often called the ''duck
factory'' of North America, in reference to the fact that
over half of the continent's ducks nest there. The
water that collects in sloughs contains a high concentration of mineral salts washed from the surrounding
soil. As a result, sloughs are quite alkaline. As the
water evaporates during the long, hot summers, they
become saturated and a rim of salts is deposited at the
shoreline. Few plants can survive these conditions.
Ranchers often use the less alkaline sloughs to water
their cattle. The cattle trample the vegetation at the
water's edge, spoiling the duck habitat. Farmers find
it a nuisance to have to detour around the sloughs
when working the fields, thus they prefer to drain and
fill them. Many duck hunters are involved in a group
called Ducks Unlimited that works to protect this habitat by paying farmers to leave the sloughs untouched.
They also encourage the farmers to leave some grain
in the fields in the fall to feed the migrating waterfowl.

Few grassland areas remain in their natural condition. Agricultural geneticists are becoming concerned
that, as the grasslands disappear, so do the native
grasses that carry genes enabling them to adapt to the
local conditions. These genes are a source of variability
that permits crop plants to be developed for specific
regions. Seed banks are being established all over the
world to maintain a supply of these plants. Canada
has now established Grasslands National Park in
southern Saskatchewan in order to preserve a sample
of the original prairies.

The Desert Biomes

Regions are considered to be **deserts** if they receive an
annual precipitation of less than 25 cm. In cold deserts
such as the **tundra**, some of this precipitation may be
in the form of snow. In hot, dry deserts, much of the
precipitation may evaporate even before it reaches the
ground. Plant and animal species that survive in these
regions must be well adapted to conserve the little
water that is available (Figure 25.11).

Figure 25.11
The desert regions of the earth (a) include both tundra (b) and hot deserts (c). What do these two kinds of regions have in common?

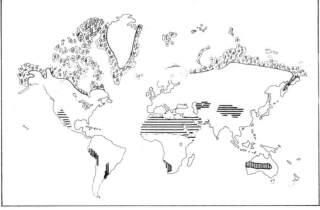

(a)

(b)

(c)

The Tundra

The mainland tundra presents a somewhat featureless landscape. Shallow lakes, covering about half of the area, lie between low eskers and drumlins of sand or gravel deposited by glaciers. The hard, dry snow that blows across the land in the winter forms drifts that level the area into a series of low ridges similar to those that form in sand on a beach. There is not a great deal of snow, but it tends to drift when the wind exceeds 16 km/h. This ground-drift decreases visibility and erodes snow that is not hard packed. This erosion effect is used in the building of winter roads and air-strips. Heavy rollers are used to pack the snow hard in the desired area. The surrounding snow then becomes wind-eroded, leaving the packed road or air-strip raised above the level of the surrounding snow. Snow will then continue to blow clear from these areas and thus they will not become closed by drifts.

Arctic soils are based on a mixture of various sized particles left by the glaciers. The finer particles are washed into the valleys by the spring meltwater, so the soil is a little better there. Soil formation processes occur slowly, with the result that the soil is thin and deficient in nitrogen. Any concentration of nitrogen, such as a dead animal carcass, an old encampment, bird or animal droppings, or sewage discharge pipes, results in an increased density, height, and variety of plant growth. These more vegetated areas are visible for some distance.

Permafrost underlies about one fifth of the earth's land area, mainly in the northern hemisphere. Close to half of the area of Canada lies over permafrost. This permanently frozen ground varies in depth from a few metres to as much as 360 m. A thin surface layer, the *active layer*, melts in the spring; it is in this layer that plants must grow. When the ground freezes again and heaves, the plants' roots are often torn or distorted. In consequence, trees may spread horizontally rather than vertically and become quite misshapen. Yet if it were not for the effect of the permafrost layer in trapping water close to the surface, the plants would not be able to survive in what would be desert-like conditions. In turn, the plant growth insulates the permafrost from the summer sun, ensuring that it does not melt except at the surface. Thus the biotic and abiotic factors work together to stabilize the biome.

During the brief summer, the tundra landscape is covered by plants. Lichens and mosses grow on the rocks; grasses and sedges grow in the moist depressions; saxifrage, poppies, heath, and other alpine flowers as well as dwarf birch and willow grow on the slopes. The air is alive with insects. Large numbers of migrating birds arrive to nest and raise their young. Caribou, musk-oxen, foxes, lemmings, and hares are also abundant.

The plants of the tundra must conserve heat in order for photosynthesis to occur. They grow close to the ground, away from the wind, often clustered together for additional protection. Many have leaves covered by felt-like hair that acts as insulation and reduces transpiration. Coloured petals absorb heat radiation to facilitate reproduction processes. Most plants are perennial and propagate themselves by various asexual means as well as by seed production. These plants are rich in sugars and starches which they store for the long winter. All tundra plants are edible, but they grow too sparsely to provide a staple in the native diet.

Few animals can survive the long, dry, cold winters of the tundra. Most birds migrate far to the south — only eight species remain: the raven, snowy owl, gyrfalcon, rock and willow ptarmigan, dovekie, black guillemot, and thick-billed murre. The caribou herds head for the protection of the trees in the taiga. The mammals that remain form a thick layer of fat under their heavy coats of fur. Most spend the harshest days sheltered in burrows or snow caves for additional protection. The winter is too long and too cold for hibernation to be a successful means of survival for most animals. Arctic animals must be able to conserve heat and water in the winter, yet dissipate them in the summer. The musk-ox is considered to be one of the best adapted of the arctic animals. Even its excretory processes vary to conserve needed materials.

The Hot Deserts

The world's major desert regions form two discontinuous belts that lie about 15° to the north and to the south of the equator. About one seventh of the earth's land area is occupied by a dozen large deserts. The Sahara is the largest, stretching across the entire width of North Africa. The North American desert covers approximately 1.3×10^6 km^2 of the southwestern portion of the continent, stretching from Mexico to British Columbia.

There is considerable temperature fluctuation in these regions. With little vegetation to insulate it, the ground becomes very hot (often as high as 50°C) as it absorbs solar radiation during the day. At night, there is no blanket of moist air to trap the heat released by the ground and the temperature may drop by as much as 30°C. Most desert areas have clearly defined summer and winter seasons. In some, what little rain there is falls in the winter; in others, the rain arrives during summer thunderstorms. Although these regions may receive amounts of precipitation similar to those of the tundra, there is no permafrost layer to hold the moisture close to the surface. Thus, it percolates down out of reach of plant roots. The warm and dry prevailing winds result in a high level of evaporation of any water remaining near the soil surface.

Desert soils usually contain an abundance of mineral salts. In moist areas, these salts move downward with the soil water as they are released from the rocks. As water evaporates from the soil of a desert, however, it carries these salts upwards and deposits them at the surface. In some deserts, these minerals are so concentrated that they prevent plant growth and can even be mined profitably.

In order to survive, desert plants must be very well adapted for water conservation. Most species have small leaves with heavy, waxy coatings that reduce transpiration. Their roots or stems may be swollen with cells that store water. They may have a dense network of fibrous roots that absorb rainwater very swiftly, or may have tap roots extending many metres underground to obtain water. Because of the competition for water, perennial plants grow widely spaced. The seeds of annual plants contain water-soluble growth inhibitors. These inhibitors keep the seeds dormant until sufficient rain falls to ensure that the plant can grow and produce seed. These plants grow swiftly when conditions are suitable. Many flower at night, when the larger number of insects enables cross-pollination to take place. Desert soils contain little organic matter. Some plants produce seeds with such a hard coating that they cannot germinate unless they pass through an animal's digestive system. The germinating seed will thus be provided with manure to supply suitable growing conditions.

Desert animals tend to be largely nocturnal. They avoid the heat of the day by burrowing underground, retreating to caves, or lying in the shade of vegetation. When plant growth is abundant, insects and other arthropods may be found in large numbers. These creatures leave a large supply of eggs and pupae to survive an interval of drought and to mature in the next moist period. Fish, of course, can survive only in the permanent water holes, but many amphibians have adapted to the dry conditions. They survive by burrowing into the muddy bottom of a drying pond and entering a period of *estivation*, a condition similar to hibernation. The desert reptiles (lizards, snakes, and tortoises) have evolved many successful adaptations for desert conditions. They conserve water by avoiding activity in the hottest part of the day; in addition, their metabolic processes permit them to convert some of their food to water. Many species of birds and bats live on the desert when it is most hospitable and migrate elsewhere when it is too cold or dry.

Seeds are the most important item in the diet of small desert mammals. They depend on the abundant supply to be found in the dry soil. Deer, pronghorn antelope, and rabbits browse on the plants themselves, wandering over large distances to meet their needs. Others such as gophers, ground squirrels, and prairie dogs subsist mainly on roots and underground stems. Foxes, coyotes, and various cat species such as the bobcat and puma prey on the herbivores.

Most desert species have evolved patterns of reproduction that initiate breeding whenever moist conditions prevail. The young develop quickly during the brief period when food is readily available. As adults they then survive until the next opportunity for reproduction occurs.

The Mountains

Mountainous regions exhibit very complex patterns of biomes. An increase in altitude produces changes that are very similar to those produced by changes in latitude (Figure 25.12). The biome at the base of the mountain will be that typical of the surrounding area. If you climbed a mountain in the northern hemisphere, you would pass through a series of biomes similar to those that you would encounter by travelling northwards.

Mountains also affect local rainfall patterns (Figure 25.13). Because winds must release their moisture as they rise over the mountains, the western slopes are moist and densely forested. The dry winds produce desert conditions in the mountain valleys, even though there are lakes and rivers formed from the meltwaters that run from the mountain snows. The warm, dry winds that flow onto the grasslands melt the winter snows, permitting cattle to graze, but these same winds are also responsible for summer droughts.

Figure 25.12
Why do changes in altitude and changes in latitude produce similar changes in biomes?

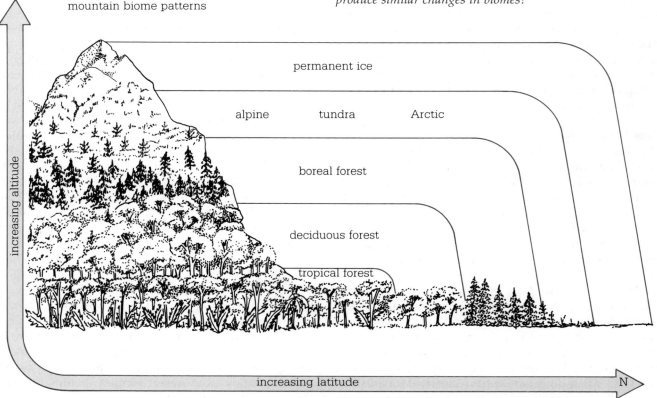

mountain biome patterns

increasing altitude

permanent ice

alpine   tundra   Arctic

boreal forest

deciduous forest

tropical forest

increasing latitude   N

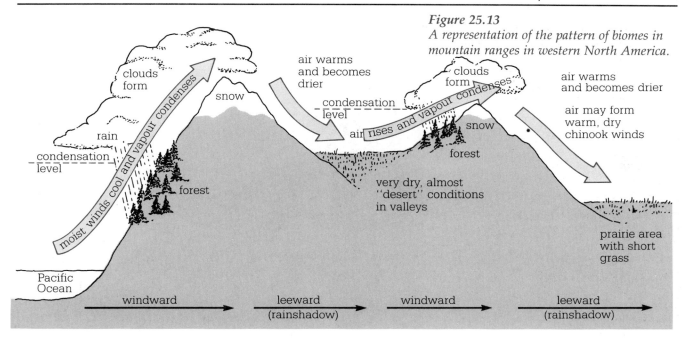

Figure 25.13
A representation of the pattern of biomes in mountain ranges in western North America.

25.5 AQUATIC BIOMES

Aquatic biomes are less strongly influenced by climate patterns than are terrestrial biomes. Abiotic factors such as the concentration of dissolved salts and gases, amount of suspended material, temperature, depth, nature of the material on the bottom, and rate of flow largely determine which organisms can survive in a given body of water.

Climate does, of course, have a major effect on the temperature of bodies of water. However, the capacity of water to gain or lose large quantities of heat with little resulting change of temperature moderates seasonal temperature changes both in the water itself and in the surrounding land area (see Figure 25.14 on the following page). The temperature of the water, in turn, determines the amount of oxygen dissolved in the water (Figure 25.15).

As is the case for most substances, water molecules become more densely packed during cooling. Water, however, reaches its maximum density at 4°C. This property produces three effects that are significant for aquatic biomes.

The first is that ice floats on water, effectively insulating it from the cold air above.

The second is an effect known as **seasonal turnover**. Warm (and therefore less dense) water floats upwards and cooler, more dense, water sinks (Figure 25.16). This movement carries new supplies of dissolved oxygen from the surface water to the lower regions. In

Figure 25.15
How much oxygen can be dissolved in water at 10°C? at 20°C? at 30°C?

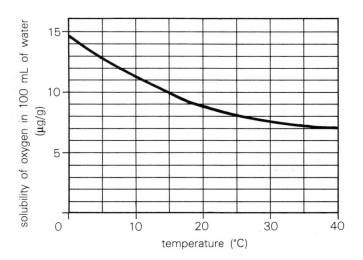

very deep lakes, such as Lake Superior, this process does not involve the deep, cold layers of water near the bottom and thus little oxygen is available there. At such depths, decay occurs slowly, if at all. Turnover also redistributes nutrients in the water, bringing a fresh supply from the bottom to the plants that must live near the surface to perform photosynthesis.

Figure 25.14
The presence of the Great Lakes moderates the temperatures of the surrounding area in both summer and winter.

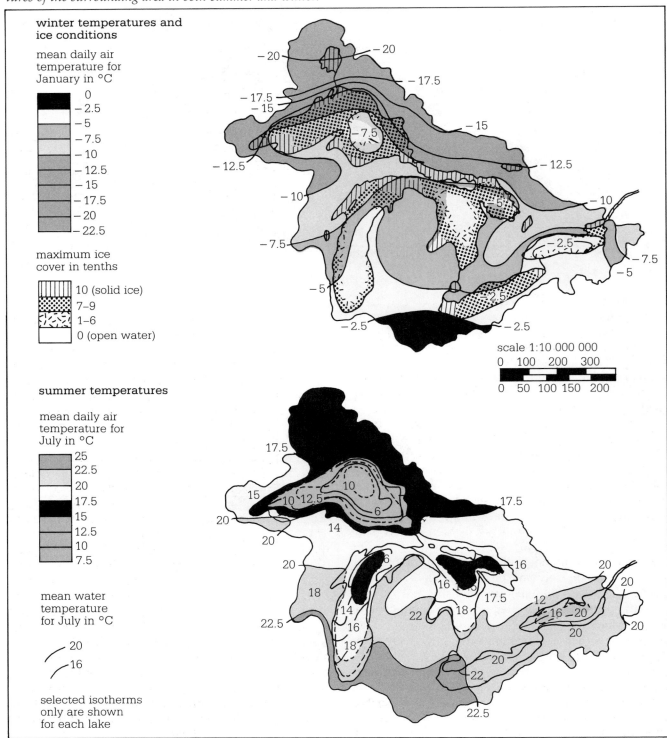

Figure 25.16
In winter (a) the ice remains at 0°C and the water does not freeze to the bottom. As the ice melts in the spring (b), the warmer water near the land rises and moderate currents produce circulation between the surface and the

depths. In summer (c) the warmest water floats in a layer on the surface. As the surface water cools in the fall (d), it sinks, pushing the water at the depths to the surface. A major turnover results.

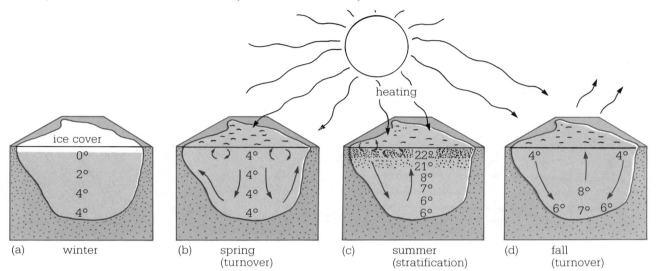

(a)   winter   (b)   spring (turnover)   (c)   summer (stratification)   (d)   fall (turnover)

The third effect, called **stratification**, occurs in bodies of water with a depth greater than 12 m. During the summer, a layer of warm water develops and floats on the cooler water below. Water currents produced by the wind tend to circulate only in this upper layer. A transition layer called the **thermocline** develops between the warm surface water and the cooler bottom water. Stratification plays a major role in the distribution of oxygen and nutrients and, therefore, also of pollutants. Consequently, the depletion of oxygen or the presence of toxins may have quite different effects, depending on the depth of the water and the time of year that pollution occurs.

Air and water currents also redistribute materials. Strong offshore winds push surface water away from the land, causing an upwelling of water from the bottom. This upwelling transports nutrients from the sediments back to the surface waters. The combined effects of wind, the rotation of the earth, and friction between the layers in the water produces major ocean currents that distribute warm and cold water and their accompanying nutrients over enormous distances (Figure 25.17). These currents influence not only the distribution of aquatic organisms, but also the nature of terrestrial biomes near the coastlines.

Based on the concentration of dissolved salts, aquatic biomes can be classified as fresh or saline. When rain falls, it is usually slightly acidic, since it

dissolves some carbon dioxide from the air as it descends. As this water runs across the surface or percolates through the soil, it dissolves minerals from the soil and rocks. Thus most surface and ground water is a dilute solution of various salts. Since the concentration of salts is well below the concentration found in cytoplasm, this water is considered to be fresh. If living cells are placed into fresh water, the process of osmosis will move water into them.

When water from the land finally reaches the oceans (or a lake without an outlet such as Great Salt Lake), it brings with it the salts it has absorbed. Since water can leave these areas only by evaporation, the salts accumulate there; such aquatic biomes are said to have salt (or saline) water. The concentration of salts in these bodies of water is above that of cell cytoplasm; thus osmosis moves water out of cells. In areas where salt and fresh water mix, the water is said to be *brackish*. Because much of the central portion of North America was once covered by a shallow sea, the soils of the Great Plains contain a high proportion of salts and ponds of water there are often brackish.

Living in fresh, brackish, or salt water requires different adaptations; thus, few species are found in all conditions. A few fish species such as salmon, shad, smelt, alewives, tomcod, striped bass, and sea lamprey do migrate from one to the other at different stages of their life histories.

Figure 25.17
The major ocean currents circulate nutrients and organisms in enormous eddies above and below the equator.

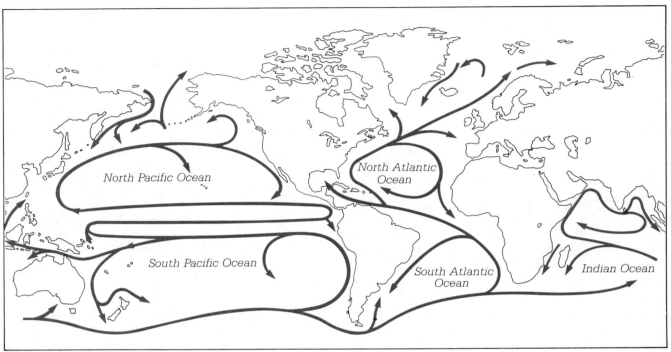

North Pacific Ocean

North Atlantic Ocean

South Pacific Ocean

South Atlantic Ocean

Indian Ocean

Freshwater Biomes

Each body of freshwater has unique characteristics that determine which organisms can survive there. Which organisms actually may be found there depends also on the opportunities that exist for organisms to migrate. Bodies of freshwater may be further subdivided into flowing water and standing water.

Flowing Water

When water falls on land, it flows downhill in tiny rivulets that eventually coalesce to form a stream. Since these areas are only temporarily wet, few aquatic organisms can survive there. If the ground remains moist, however, some micro-organisms, insects, and amphibians will become established.

The nature of life in a small but stable stream will depend upon its depth, the nature of the bottom, and the rate of flow. Plants must be able to anchor themselves firmly against the flowing water. The mud, sand, or gravel on the bottom of a turbulent stream is in constant motion, preventing plants from becoming established. When plants can anchor themselves to rocks, they provide a suitable habitat for many other organisms. Many insect larvae also have ways of attaching themselves firmly against the flowing water. Fish and other vertebrates can move against the force of the water. See Figure 25.18(b).

As various streams come together to form a young river, the volume and force of the water may increase considerably. Turbulent water is rich in oxygen, but is an inhospitable habitat. Only the strongest plants and animals can live there. These rushing rivers scour materials from the bottom and often carry such a load of suspended material that light cannot penetrate the water; photosynthesis is thus impossible. See Figure 25.18(a).

In flatter areas, called *riffles*, the rate of flow slows and the water releases its load of sediment. The sandbars formed by this sediment may cause the river to meander. The quieter pools of water are an ideal habitat for many organisms. The water is rich in oxygen and nutrients. Light can penetrate the water, permitting plants to carry out photosynthesis. There is usually a variety of depths and bottom conditions so that each organism can find a site to suit its needs. Some animals will skim across the surface; others will swim in the open water. Some will cling to the vegetation; still others will burrow in the muddy bottom.

Figure 25.18

Few organisms can survive in the rushing waters of the Athabasca River in Jasper National Park (a). The calmer water of the Bow River in Banff National Park (b) provides an ideal habitat for aquatic organisms.

(a)

(b)

Standing Water

Bodies of fresh standing water are usually called lakes or ponds. The distinction is somewhat arbitrary and is based on size and depth. In general, a pond is a body of water that is too shallow to develop stratification. Ponds may freeze to the bottom in severe winter conditions. Most lakes have an inflow and outflow of water. As a result, any lake will have a number of distinct current patterns. In most lakes and ponds, the pH of the water is neutral or slightly acidic. The prairie ponds, or sloughs, are somewhat alkaline. In mountains or other rocky regions, the ponds that may form tend to be quite acidic. These acidic ponds are called *tarns*.

The patterns of life are much the same in all of these bodies of water, although the specific organisms inhabiting them vary (Figure 25.19). Near the shore, *emergent* plants (such as pickerel weed) are rooted in the water but their leaves, stems, and flowers rise above the water. At greater depths are *submerged* plants (such as pondweeds) that are rooted on the bottom and are entirely under water. The depth at which they can live is limited by the clarity of the water. *Floating* plants, (such as waterlilies and duckweed) have their leaves on the surface of the water and may or may not be rooted to the bottom. Phytoplankton, single celled plants, have daily vertical migration patterns through the water down to the limits of light penetration.

Animals will be found on shore, on the surface, on or in the bottom sediments, or free swimming. Zooplankton (single celled animals) migrate along with the phytoplankton.

Lakes and ponds may be classified as **oligotrophic** (nutrient poor) or **eutrophic** (nutrient rich). Most lakes fall somewhere between these extremes and are said to be **mesotrophic**. More plants and animals can survive in mesotrophic or eutrophic conditions, but humans generally prefer the "cleaner" oligotrophic lakes for swimming and boating and as sources of drinking water. Eutrophication is a natural process that occurs in lakes as nutrients wash in from the shore or are carried in by rivers and streams. Unfortunately, the activities of civilization have greatly accelerated this process. Intensive agriculture results in considerable soil erosion. Excess fertilizer often washes into the surface or ground water as well. Even after full sewage treatment, the resulting effluent contains nutrients that increase eutrophication. The effluents from urban or industrial areas also frequently contain harmful chemical pollutants.

Figure 25.19
*Similar plants grow in lakes, ponds (a), and marshes (b).
As these plants grow more densely along shorelines, ponds
often change into marshes over a period of many years.*

(a)

(b)

Wetlands

Along the shores of many streams, rivers, ponds, and
lakes are areas that do not seem to be part of the land
or of the water but are a transition zone between the
two. Those areas that are periodically flooded and
contain mostly aquatic plants are called *marshes*. Moist

areas in which trees are found are usually called
swamps. These wetlands support a range of plants and
animals that are dependent upon these moist conditions. The depth, temperature, and salinity of the
water, as well as the nature of the terrestrial biome in
which the wetland is located, determine which species
may be found there. For example, the bogs and fens
of the boreal forest are usually quite acidic and thus
support the same plants and animals found in larger
areas of muskeg.

Wetlands in the temperate forest or grassland areas
are often ringed by trees such as alder, willow, poplar,
and aspen. Bullrushes and cattails are generally abundant, as are an assortment of rooted and floating
aquatic plants. The shallow, nutrient-rich water is an
ideal habitat for a great variety of micro-organisms,
insects, crustaceans, and amphibians. They in turn are
a source of food for fish, ducks, herons, grebes, and
other birds. Muskrats and mink also feed in these wetlands. Wetlands are spawning areas for many fish species and nesting areas for many bird species.

When wetlands are drained to provide agricultural
land or recreational sites, the species that are dependent upon these areas are often eliminated too. Many
of the species threatened with extinction depend on
wetlands for part, if not all, of their life cycles.

Draining of wetlands also eliminates their service
functions in the biome. Wetlands regulate water flow,
thus stabilizing the ground water supply and reducing
flooding downstream. When water flows through the
dense growth of plants, much of the sediment is fil-
tered out, as are many pollutants. For this reason, wetlands are often called the "kidneys" of aquatic
biomes.

Saltwater Biomes

The oceans contain most of the earth's salt water organisms. The salt lakes that form in arid regions are
the result of a high evaporation rate and the salt concentration in these lakes is so high that few organisms
can survive there.

The Oceans

Most people have an impression of the oceans as
rather uniform bodies of water. Although they may
appear that way from a ship, in fact there is as much
variety under the surface as there is on land. Some
areas correspond to deserts in the sparseness of the
life forms to be found there, while the concentration
of organisms in a coral reef rivals that of the tropical
forests.

Figure 25.20
The warm, clear waters of a coral reef can provide a
suitable habitat for an enormous variety of organisms.

Phytoplankton, the foundation of the ocean biomes, grow profusely in the surface waters, providing food for hundreds of other organisms. To do so they must, of course, have a rich supply of nutrients. Those nutrients are found primarily in the coastal zones that receive the sediments washed from the land. Areas where ocean currents or upwellings dredge materials up from the bottom will also produce abundant phytoplankton.

Zooplankton, jellyfish, crabs, shrimp, flatworms, small fish such as capelin, and even baleen whales feed on the phytoplankton. Most of these in turn provide food for fish such as cod, herring, mackerel, and tuna as well as for seals, porpoises, whales, and many sea-birds. Thus these species are also concentrated in the coastal areas.

In shallow areas, where light can penetrate to the bottom, a wide variety of plants can grow. These in turn supply food for a host of animals and their predators. Sponges, corals, shellfish, crabs, lobster, and starfish are typical inhabitants of these regions.

In certain places on the ocean floor are vents that release hot water and gases from the depths of the earth. Unique forms of bacteria found there are able to use the hydrogen sulfide in this hot water in an energy-generating process called **chemosynthesis**. These bacteria then serve as food for worms, clams, and crabs that have adapted to living at the pressure found at these great depths.

The Intertidal Zones

The actions of the ocean tides produce a most demanding habitat at the water's edge. Twice daily, the level of the water rises and falls by as much as 8 m to produce an **intertidal zone**. Organisms that live in this zone must be able to withstand several hours of immersion in salt water followed by several hours of exposure to conditions ranging from sun and wind to freshwater rain or snow. In addition, such organisms must be able to withstand the force of the waves pounding the shore. Where the shoreline is open and sandy, only those organisms that can bury themselves below the action of the waves can be found.

A rocky tidal shore provides a firm foundation for a variety of algal seaweeds that can glue themselves to the rocks with *holdfasts*. Barnacles, limpets, and other shellfish can grip the rock firmly enough to survive even storm conditions. Other organisms find safety in crevices and hollows that shield them from wave action and retain water at low tide (Figure 25.21).

Where temperate shorelines are muddy and gently sloping, salt marshes extend for considerable distances from shore. The sturdy but flexible stems of eelgrass and cord grass break the force of the wave action and trap the sediments that might otherwise wash away. These salt marshes provide a spawning ground for a variety of fish species, a "nursery" area for the young of many crustaceans and shellfish, and nesting sites for many species of waterfowl. Many land dwelling species such as deer and raccoons depend on the salt marshes for food.

To the early settlers of North America, the salt marshes represented the most rapid way to establish a farm. They could not clear the forests quickly enough to provide their cattle and other farm animals with hay. Thus the enormous marshes that once existed along the Bay of Fundy and Chesapeake Bay were

Figure 25.21
The organisms living on this rocky shoreline (a) must cope with all the forces of nature. The mangrove swamp along the coast of Florida (b) stabilizes the shoreline and provides a protected area for many species.

(a)

(b)

diked and drained. Rain quickly washed the remaining salt out of the soil. When the Acadian farmers were expelled from their rich marshland farms at the head of the Bay of Fundy in the mid-eighteenth century, they moved to other marshlands farther south. Some moved all the way to the Mississippi delta, where they became known as Cajuns.

Salt marshes stabilize the shoreline and control siltation. Where they have been drained to provide land for building or agriculture or simply to provide easier access to the water, many problems of erosion and siltation have occurred. In some areas, extensive destruction of wetlands has also reduced the catch of shrimp, lobster, and shellfish.

In warmer waters, the salt marshes are replaced by mangrove swamps. The mangrove is a small tree that can root in shallow salt water. Once established, it too collects silt and debris, thus stabilizing the shoreline and providing a habitat for a wide range of aquatic organisms and birds. Mangrove swamps have a vital function in protecting low, muddy, or sandy shorelines against the ravages of the circular storms common to tropical regions.

25.6 CONSERVATION EFFORTS

The reasons for protection of wildlife have varied considerably through the course of history. The civilizations of ancient Sumer and Babylon as well as those of Medieval Europe established hunting reserves. The purpose of these reserves was wildlife management rather than conservation, insofar as they existed to ensure that members of the nobility would have satisfactory hunting. Yet without these reserves in some areas of Europe and Asia, many species would long since have become extinct.

In the nineteenth century, natural history studies became a major recreational activity. As people began to identify and classify plants and animals, they began to recognize the immense diversity of species to be found in certain areas. Finally, it was acknowledged that certain areas were so unique that they should be preserved from development so that future generations could study and enjoy them. Yellowstone, established in Wyoming in 1872, was the first U.S. national park. Banff National Park, the first of Canada's seven mountain parks in Alberta and British Columbia, was established in 1885 after the building of the CPR made the area accessible. Canada now has some 30 national parks, plus another 56 national historic parks that preserve areas of historical rather than ecological significance. In addition, each province has established many provincial parks to preserve wildlife, historic sites, or recreational areas.

The national parks movement has gradually spread around the world, but even today less than three percent of the earth's surface is protected. Almost half of the total conserved area is found in North America and much of that is boreal forest or tundra. The citizens of industrialized countries now are beginning to recognize that countries that are having difficulty providing food, education, and health care for their populations need assistance to establish such reserves. Many groups are raising funds to purchase and maintain such areas. In other cases, banks and industries are permitting countries to ''buy back'' loans or debts by setting aside critical habitats. Assistance is also being provided in finding ways to permit these areas to contribute to the economy of the country.

National Park areas do not, unfortunately, protect all species. Migratory species are at risk when they move from breeding sites to feeding areas. Other species are at risk because of the commercial value of their hides, heads, horns, or tusks. Many concerned people have mounted conservation efforts on behalf of these species since the beginning of this century. The first agreements protecting migrating species were between Canada and the United States. These efforts became global in 1983 with the signing of the first Convention on Migratory Species of Wild Animals. Many countries have developed legislation to reduce or prohibit trade in animal products derived from wild species. Since 1983, 80 nations have signed the Convention on International Trade in Endangered Species. Unfortunately, this action will not be truly effective until it is supported by all nations. Many tourist destinations in the Caribbean sell products made from endangered species. When the tourists return to Canada or the United States, their purchases are confiscated. Many international airports now display the confiscated items in departure lounges to warn other tourists against purchasing them.

In the last half of this century, conservation efforts have taken a new direction. The realization that we share a common spaceship with all the other inhabitants of the earth has been coupled with an understanding that pollutants do not respect national boundaries. The problems caused by air, water, and land pollution must be attacked on a global basis if we are to be successful. This new perspective has resulted in the development of the World Conservation Strategy and the holding of global research conferences on such topics as acid precipitation and the depletion of the ozone layer.

Successful action focussed on these problems will require commitment from all nations. Much of the leadership and financial support will have to be provided by the industrialized nations. The remaining chapters in this unit will discuss the nature of some of the problems and their potential solutions.

CHAPTER SUMMARY

An increased understanding of the network of ecological relationships on the earth has led to the recognition that all life on the earth is interdependent. Changes in any portion of the biosphere affect other portions as well.

Variations in abiotic factors result in the formation of different biomes. The organisms that live in these biomes have various adaptations that help them cope with the abiotic factors. The terrestrial biomes are of four types: forest (boreal, temperate, and tropical), grassland, desert (including the tundra), and mountain. Aquatic biomes may be either freshwater or saltwater. The former may consist of flowing water, standing water, or wetlands; the latter can be either oceans or intertidal zones. Each of these biomes has economic importance to humans, but we must learn to manage them with respect.

Our growing understanding of the functioning of the biosphere has resulted in conservation strategies that are global in their focus.

Objectives

Having completed this chapter, you should be able to do the following:
1. State reasons why people now consider the earth to be a single biological unit.
2. Explain how the present composition of the earth's atmosphere is dependent upon living organisms.
3. Outline the general patterns of distribution of the various biomes.
4. Discuss why Canada's northern areas are largely undeveloped.
5. Outline why Canadians should be concerned about the destruction of tropical forests.

6. Identify the significance of the grassland areas in the maintenance of the world's food supply.
7. State the importance of wetlands in the maintenance of biomes.
8. Explain the importance of phytoplankton in aquatic biomes.
9. Discuss why conservation efforts must be global in nature.

Vocabulary

biosphere	boreal forest	tundra
ecology	taiga	seasonal turnover
ecological niche	muskeg	stratification
biological community	temperate forest	thermocline
biotic	chaparral	oligotrophic
abiotic	humid forest	eutrophic
Gaia Hypothesis	tropical forest	mesotrophic
biome	grassland	chemosynthesis
ecocline	desert	intertidal zone

Review Questions

1. Consider a situation in which a beaver builds a dam across a small stream in a narrow valley.
   (a) How does the beaver affect its habitat?
   (b) How does its habitat affect the beaver?
2. In what ways has an urban apartment dweller become isolated from the environment?
3. (a) What are the major terrestrial biomes?
   (b) What factors distinguish among them?
4. (a) Which forests are
      (i) the most diverse?
      (ii) the least diverse?
   (b) What factors cause these differences?
5. Explain how patterns of forest use differ between industrialized and developing nations.
6. Discuss the adaptations that permit plants and animals to withstand

(a) winter conditions
(b) very dry conditions.
7. Why do extended periods of drought in grassland regions often result in extensive wind erosion?
8. Why is it important that native grassland plant species be preserved?
9. Outline some factors that make the life patterns in mountainous regions so complex.
10. What properties of water are significant to aquatic organisms?
11. Explain why few organisms can live in both fresh and salt water.
12. How do human activities contribute to the eutrophication of aquatic biomes?
13. Why are saltmarshes and mangrove swamps essential to ocean biomes?

Advanced Questions

1. (a) What portion of Canada's economy depends directly or indirectly on the forest industries?
   (b) Does our present use of these resources exceed the rate at which the forests can regenerate? Explain.
   (c) What proportion of the harvested area is reforested?
   (d) Annually, in Canada, how much useful forest is destroyed by fire or pests?
   (e) What recommendations would you make for better management of our forests?
2. The fast food industry has many effects on the environment.

(a) Investigate such aspects of the industry as
   (i) the demand for beef
   (ii) the demand for potatoes suitable for frying
   (iii) the use of packaging materials
   (iv) waste management
   (v) the consumption of energy.
(b) Suggest how the effects of this industry could be reduced.

3. The plants and animals of Canada's North have not been domesticated. Develop a proposal for the utilization of these species to reduce the dependence of the northern communities on imported food.

4. One method used to rehabilitate polluted waterways is to create artificial waterfalls and rapids. Another is to widen the waterway and create a marsh.
   (a) What effect would each method have on water quality?
   (b) What other methods could be used to improve the habitat for aquatic organisms?

5. When silt accumulates at river mouths it often prevents navigation. Periodic dredging then becomes necessary to maintain a passage through the area.
   (a) What effect would dredging have on the aquatic organisms in the area being cleared?
   (b) Where is the dredged material deposited and what effect does it have on the organisms there?
   (c) What could be done to reduce the need for dredging?

6. Mangrove swamps form a barrier between the land and the water in tropical and semi-tropical areas. Tourists, however, want to be able to view the ocean and relax on the beach.
   (a) What has been the effect of the removal of the mangroves in the Caribbean tourist areas?
   (b) What solutions would you propose to these problems?

7. Select a non-governmental organization that focusses on environmental problems and investigate its activities. If possible, become directly involved. Evaluate such aspects as
   (a) the problem(s) it is attempting to ameliorate;
   (b) its sources of funding;
   (c) its sources of volunteers;
   (d) the strategies it employs to produce change;
   (e) the methods it uses to educate the general public;
   (f) the effectiveness of its programs.

8. What strategies are used by the oil industry to prevent destruction of the permafrost layer near its buildings, wells, and pipelines?

9. Select a local body of water that is exhibiting signs of accelerated eutrophication.
   (a) Identify the major sources of excess nutrients.
   (b) Evaluate the present methods of controlling the problem.
   (c) Develop strategies that would prevent most of the excess nutrients from entering the water.

CHAPTER 26

MATTER AND ENERGY FLOW IN THE BIOSPHERE

The sun is the external driving force of the biosphere.

Lee Durrell
The State of the Ark

A spaceship cannot function without a source of energy. The passengers must be fed and their wastes must be processed. The interior climate must be controlled to remain within acceptable limits. Each time materials are used, energy is needed. The many activities in which the passengers are engaged also require varying amounts of energy.

The assorted craft that have been sent from the earth to explore space rely on two types of energy sources. Some energy is stored on board before the craft is launched. There is, obviously, a limited supply of this energy, and it is carefully conserved for essential functions. Once the spacecraft has left the earth's atmosphere, solar collectors are extended to gather energy to supply less critical functions. The longer the duration of the flight, the greater the reliance on solar energy. Spacecraft destined for prolonged flight are usually provided with batteries to store excess solar energy for periods of high energy demand.

Like any other spaceship, the earth requires a constant supply of energy to maintain its processes. Some energy is stored on board in the hot core of the earth. This supply, however, has proved to be inconvenient to manage. Although hot springs are useful, they are not always located where they are needed. Volcanoes are unpredictable and often explosive in nature. The earth's satellite spaceship, the moon, causes gravitational forces that give energy to the tides. This energy is useful, but is not available in sufficient quantities in many parts of the world. As is the case with other spacecraft designed for extended flight, most of the required energy is delivered daily from the sun. The earth is equipped with several types of batteries (for example, water and fossil fuels) in which excess solar energy can be stored until required.

In order to understand the nature of many of the earth's problems, it is necessary to consider the characteristics of energy and the way energy and materials travel through the biosphere. This chapter will examine the nature of these processes and the effects that human activities can have upon them.

26.1 THE ROLE OF SOLAR RADIATION

Energy from the sun — **solar radiation** — sustains many processes (Figure 26.1). It is responsible for all the abiotic factors collectively called *climate*. The sun warms the air in some areas more than it does in others. The resulting air currents, influenced by the rotation of the earth, produce winds, major air currents, and storms. Similar currents develop in the ocean as a result of variations in water temperature. The heat from the sun is absorbed by bodies of water, thus cooling the surrounding areas in summer. As the temperature drops when winter approaches, this heat is released, again moderating the temperature change. The heat absorbed by water also causes some of it to evaporate. As this moisture accumulates in the atmosphere, it forms clouds and eventually precipitates as rain or snow. This distillation process returns pure

Figure 26.1
The pattern of energy distribution. What factors could alter this pattern?

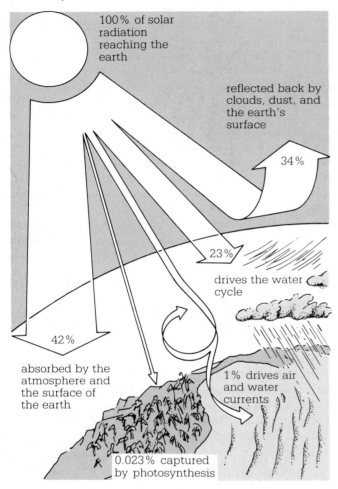

100% of solar radiation reaching the earth

reflected back by clouds, dust, and the earth's surface

34%

23%

drives the water cycle

42%

absorbed by the atmosphere and the surface of the earth

1% drives air and water currents

0.023% captured by photosynthesis

water to the land to start its downhill flow again. Some of the energy that the sun supplied to lift the water upwards can be retrieved by using waterwheels or turbines to transfer the energy of flowing water into mechanical or electrical energy.

Plants also use solar radiation. The chlorophyll they contain can absorb this energy and make it available for chemical processes. The sugars and starches that result from photosynthesis provide energy for all living organisms on spaceship Earth. Some of this chemical energy may not be required immediately. **Fossil fuels** are "storage batteries" for the earth. They are the energy-rich remains of plants that lived millions of years ago. At present, heavy withdrawals are being made from these "batteries" and many people are concerned about the consequences.

26.2 THE LAWS OF THERMODYNAMICS

Scientists have studied energy for hundreds of years. They have examined many situations in which energy was transformed from one form to another. In all that time, they have never discovered a situation in which energy was either created or destroyed. During this century, the study of the relationships among the various forms of energy has been organized into the branch of physical chemistry called **thermodynamics**.

The First Law of Thermodynamics states that *energy is neither created nor destroyed, but may be converted from one form into another.* In any system involving energy, the total amount of energy thus remains constant, although its distribution may vary. Another way to consider this concept is to recognize that the energy taken out of a system can never exceed the energy put into it. In fact, to convert energy to a different form, energy must be expended. For example, plants must use energy in order to perform photosynthesis. Animals must expend energy in order to eat and obtain energy from their food. Humans consume large quantities of energy to order to locate, extract, process, and transport fuels.

If energy cannot be created or destroyed, it is tempting to think that energy supply problems could be solved simply by recycling the energy that we now have. The efforts over the centuries to build perpetual motion machines (Figure 26.2) have demonstrated the futility of this quest. It is appealing, however, to think that one could be built; many inventors succeed in convincing unwary investors that they have achieved this miracle and simply require more funds to make it feasible on a large scale!

The problem lies in the fact that energy varies in its quality—that is, its ability to do useful work. Sunlight, wind, and fossil fuels are examples of high quality energy. When a substance has a high temperature, the heat within it is concentrated and thus is available to do useful work. This heat is considered to be high quality energy. On the other hand, the heat in a substance with a low temperature is too diffuse to be readily available. This heat is considered to be low quality energy. The oceans contain an enormous amount of heat energy, but it is of low quality and, therefore, not very useful. The Second Law of Thermodynamics states that *each time energy is converted to another form, some of that energy is degraded into lower quality energy.* The lower quality energy often occurs in the form of heat or sound. Consider, for example, the heat and

Figure 26.2
A perpetual motion machine. Why will it not continue to run indefinitely?

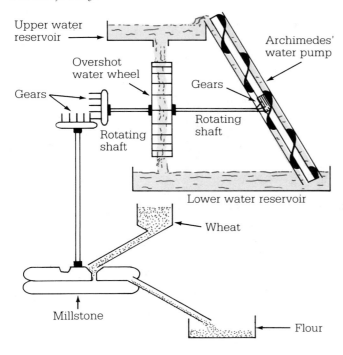

26.3 THE FLOW OF ENERGY IN THE BIOSPHERE

It is difficult to consider the flow of energy through the biosphere as a whole. Ecologists have found the energy transformations easier to analyze if they select a smaller functional unit for study. The term **ecosystem** is used to indicate a group of living organisms that, together with their non-living environment, form a self-regulating system through which energy and materials transfer. A forest, a desert, or a farmer's field are examples of terrestrial ecosystems. Aquatic ecosystems may be as small as the pool of water trapped inside a pitcher plant or as large as the ocean. Each ecosystem is unique, yet ecologists have learned that each seems to have the same underlying structure.

To identify the patterns of energy flow through any ecosystem, it is necessary to consider five basic questions:

1. What is the source of energy entering that ecosystem?
2. How does that energy enter the ecosystem?
3. How is energy transferred among the components of the ecosystem?
4. How is energy stored within that ecosystem?
5. How does energy leave the ecosystem?

noise caused by friction or a lightning bolt. The ability of a process to convert high quality energy to another form of high quality energy is referred to as its *efficiency*. In most situations, the efficiency of conversion is less than 40 percent. It is significant that the cellular processes that capture and release energy are more efficient than most processes devised by humans.

Another way of considering the Second Law of Thermodynamics is to recognize that energy has a tendency to change from a concentrated and ordered form to a dispersed and disordered form. This recognition leads to the concept of **entropy**—the theory that all matter tends to move to a state of greater disorder. (You may need only to consider your desk top or bedroom to become convinced of the validity of this theory!) Living systems can maintain an ordered, low entropy state by using energy to overcome this tendency toward disorder. The living system retains high quality energy and releases low quality energy to its surroundings. Nevertheless, even living systems conform to the Second Law of Thermodynamics if we consider them together with their environments and recognize that there is a net increase in entropy.

With few exceptions, the source of energy for the earth's ecosystems is the sun. As shown in Figure 26.1, 0.023 percent of the sun's energy that reaches this planet is absorbed by green plants during photosynthesis. It is converted into chemical energy, one of the few forms of energy that can be stored easily. Because green plants produce chemical energy for the ecosystem, they are called the **producers** of the ecosystem.

All the other living organisms of an ecosystem depend either directly or indirectly upon the producers for food. Animals that feed on plants are called **primary consumers**; the animals that feed on the plant eaters are called **secondary consumers**. **Parasites** obtain their energy by living on or in another organisms. **Scavengers** feed on dead animals. **Decomposers** extract the last remaining energy from dead plant and animal matter. These relationships are illustrated in Figure 26.3. The feeding level of each organism is said to be its **trophic level**. The sequence of organisms through the trophic levels is sometimes called a **food chain**. Few organisms, however, confine themselves to a single source of food. The network of organisms

Figure 26.3
A hypothetical (a) and an actual (b) food web. Consider the trophic levels of the ocean. Which organisms are the producers? the primary consumers? the secondary consumers? the decomposers? What advantage does the baleen whale gain by feeding on phytoplankton?

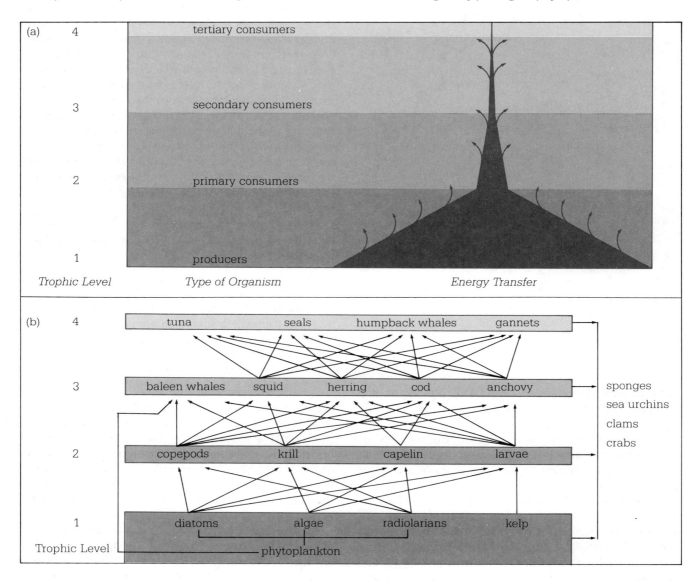

that is created by these feeding patterns is called a **food web**.

Most of the energy entering each trophic level of an ecosystem is consumed by the life processes of the organisms at that level. As can be predicted from the Second Law of Thermodynamics, that energy becomes low quality energy, much of which is dissipated as heat. The remaining amount, about ten percent, is high quality energy that is stored within the organism. It is that ten percent which sustains the organisms of the next trophic level of that ecosystem. The organisms functioning at the third and fourth trophic levels are thus in a somewhat precarious position with respect to their food supply. As a result, most of these organisms consume a widely varying diet so that they are not overly dependent on any one food source. These patterns of energy transfer also mean that an ecosystem can support very few organisms at the higher trophic levels (Figure 26.4).

Figure 26.4
Pyramid (a) illustrates the number of organisms required
to support one human at the fourth trophic level.
Pyramids (b) and (c) consider the energy units involved at
each trophic level. At which trophic level should humans
feed if an ecosystem is to support the maximum possible
number of humans?

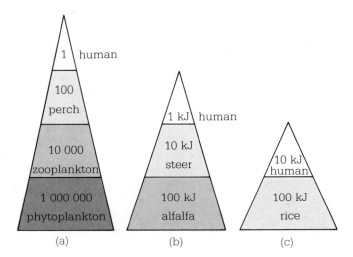

(a)   (b)   (c)

26.4 PRODUCTIVITY

A useful way to compare how effectively ecosystems process energy is to consider the rate at which energy is stored by their producers. This rate is called the **net primary productivity** of the ecosystem and it is usually stated in terms of the mass of living plant material (**biomass**) that the ecosystem forms in the course of a year. Not all tissues, however, contain the same amount of energy per kilogram. A more useful way of stating net primary productivity is to express it in terms of energy units. Table 26.1 shows the estimated net primary productivity for various Canadian ecosystems.

net primary productivity = rate at which plants produce chemical energy − rate at which plants use chemical energy

On the basis of these productivity figures, it might be tempting to assume that the earth's food requirements could best be met by farming the rain forests and coastal marshes. There are three problems with such an assumption. The first is that the productivity figures represent the total mass of plant material—not just the portion that humans consider edible. The second is that removal of the natural inhabitants of these

ecosystems would result in an environment inhospitable to the types of plants that one would want to grow as food. Finally, the "services" that these ecosystems provide would also have been lost. They are most valuable in terms of their contribution to climate and erosion control, conservation and filtration of water, and preservation of species.

Table 26.1   Estimated Net Primary Productivity of Major Canadian Ecosystems

ECOSYSTEM	NET PRIMARY PRODUCTIVITY	
	kg/m²/a	kJ/m²/a
coastal marsh	2.50	50 400
temperate rain forest	1.50	40 000
mountain coniferous forest	1.30	25 000
temperate deciduous forest	1.20	33 600
boreal forest	0.80	12 600
cultivated field	0.65	12 600
grasslands	0.60	10 500
continental shelf	0.35	8 400
tundra	0.15	840
open ocean	0.13	4 200
desert	0.13	840

26.5 SUCCESSION

Net primary productivity provides a way to examine the changes that occur in ecosystems over time. This process of change is called **succession**. Some changes in ecosystems occur in annual cycles and thus are referred to as **seasonal succession**. But the most important changes are those that develop over many years.

Consider what happens when a glacier melts and retreats from an area (Figure 26.5). As the ice begins to melt, the rock particles within the ice become more concentrated, making the remaining ice look dirty. These darker patches of ice absorb more of the sun's heat, creating tiny pools of water. Algae, perhaps carried there by the wind or on the feet of a bird, now colonize the habitat and begin to grow on the moist surface of the glacier. The productivity of this simple ecosystem is very low, but the algae do store a little energy. As the algae die, a small number of bacteria are able to obtain energy from the dead algal cells. As the glacier continues to melt, scattered pockets of algae and bacteria gradually add organic matter to the fine rock particles carried by the glacier, thus starting the long, slow process of soil formation.

WHAT IS THE NATURE OF THE WORLD FOOD PROBLEM?

Spaceship Earth can produce sufficient food to feed its passengers. Yet at present, some twenty million passengers are so undernourished (their food has insufficient energy content) or malnourished (their food has inadequate nutrient content) that they suffer severe health consequences. Many other passengers are overnourished to the point of requiring special programs of diet and exercise to control obesity.

In subsequent chapters, the problems caused by population growth itself will be considered in detail. There are other problems, however, that are the result of mismanagement of the resources of local ecosystems.

It is estimated that spaceship Earth carries a stock of some 80 000 edible plant species. Of these, the crew has selected only thirty for intensive cultivation. In fact, four crops—wheat, rice, corn, and potatoes—dominate food production. Although these crops give a high yield of useful food, they are not suited to all locations. In some areas, the major cause of crop failure is that the crop that was planted was not suitable for the area being cultivated. Although massive airlifts of food from other areas can provide short term relief from famine, they do not provide a permanent solution. Well-meant efforts to supply seed from other agricultural areas are also frequently doomed to failure. The best

possibility of long term solutions probably lies in current research efforts that are focussed on the development of crop plants specifically for the growing conditions in these famine-prone areas. In some cases, the crop plants traditionally grown there were lost because starving people were forced to eat the seed they had saved. Development of hybrid plants with the desired characteristics has traditionally been a tedious process. The cloning and gene-splicing techniques of biotechnology, however, are starting to accelerate this process.

A second aspect of the food problem is that the high agricultural yields typical of the developed countries have been achieved by the use of large quantities of energy and fertilizer. As shown in the figure on the right, the energy input in many cases far exceeds the food energy yield. Few countries are able to use energy resources in this fashion. In fact, many passengers question whether it is wise to use so much of spaceship Earth's "battery power" in this way. Some agricultural research scientists are focussing their efforts on the development of crops that give a better energy input:output ratio.

The diet of many of spaceship Earth's passengers is supplemented by fish, shellfish, meat, and other animal products such as eggs and milk or milk products.

Nine animal groups provide most of the meat: cattle, sheep, swine, goats, water buffalo, chickens, turkeys, geese, and ducks. Traditionally, these animals have served as "converters," consuming plant material that humans cannot eat and converting it into animal protein that is useful food. In the less developed countries, this is still the case. In the more developed regions, however, these food animals are often confined to small areas and fed on grain. Although this process does produce better quality meat more rapidly, it also changes the role of these animals. Rather than supplementing the human food supply, they are now competing for it with human assistance. In many cases, these food animals have been bred for this purpose so successfully that they can barely survive on pasture grasses. Thus, they too are of little value in food aid programs. Research efforts now are concentrating on the development of food animals that can flourish on poor pasture and crop plant waste. Efforts are also being made to domesticate some native species, such as insects and worms, that are not presently used as food.

Even if new techniques and new food sources are developed, considerable education efforts will still be required to convince people to abandon traditional ways or try new foods.

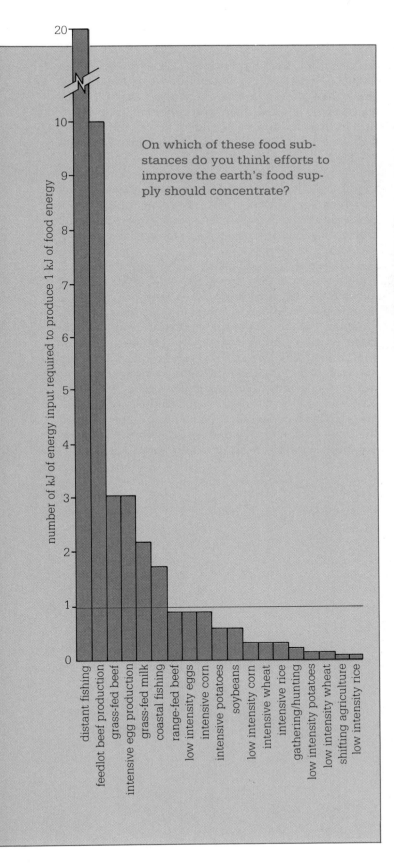

number of kJ of energy input required to produce 1 kJ of food energy

On which of these food substances do you think efforts to improve the earth's food supply should concentrate?

(bars left to right:) distant fishing · feedlot beef production · grass-fed beef · intensive egg production · grass-fed milk · coastal fishing · range-fed beef · low intensity eggs · intensive corn · intensive potatoes · soybeans · low intensity corn · intensive wheat · intensive rice · gathering/hunting · low intensity potatoes · low intensity wheat · shifting agriculture · low intensity rice

Figure 26.5
The process of succession is frequently interrupted in glacial valleys as the glaciers advance and retreat.

As the glacier continues to retreat, uncovering the rock surfaces and boulders beneath it, a second process of soil formation also begins. Lichens (an association of an alga and a fungus) colonize the bare rock surfaces. The algal cells carry out photosynthesis and their productivity is high enough to provide nourishment for the fungal cells with which they are associated. For their part, the fungal cells absorb minerals from the rock surface and provide protection against dehydration. When lichens die, they too provide energy for decomposers.

The organisms that can inhabit such inhospitable areas and start the process of succession are called **pioneer organisms**. The simple ecosystems they establish contain only a few species; the net primary productivity is typically very low. But these organisms have begun the process of soil formation and once soil is present other organisms can invade.

Mosses are often the next organisms to enter the developing ecosystem. These are slightly larger, more specialized plants with which the pioneer organisms cannot compete successfully. The mosses increase the net primary productivity of the ecosystem; as they do, a system is created that can support more organisms. Thus, small animals such as ants, mites, and spiders can now meet their energy requirements within the ecosystem.

Over a period of time, the mosses die and decay; meanwhile, a thicker layer of soil develops. Gradually the ecosystem is invaded by grasses and other small herbaceous plants that can compete successfully with the mosses. Again, as the productivity of the ecosystem increases, so does the number of animals that can be supported. Many types of insects and worms can now become part of the ecosystem. Birds and small rodents may move in to feed on these primary consumers. They in turn become sources of energy for birds of prey and carnivores.

Over many years this process of gradual change continues. Ferns and larger herbaceous plants invade, to be followed in turn by shrubs and eventually by trees. With the increase in food supply, many more animals and birds move into the area.

As the physical size of the major plant species increases, so does the net primary productivity of the ecosystem. The other inhabitants of the ecosystem increase in size, type, and number in a corresponding fashion. As conditions change, some plant and animal species are unable to compete with species better adapted to the new conditions. The less successful organisms often do not completely disappear; they simply become less numerous. In general, as an ecosystem matures, it supports an increasingly diverse community of organisms.

Eventually, the ecosystem stabilizes to form what is called the **climax community**. This community develops when two conditions have been met. One is that the ecosystem has reached the maximum net primary productivity for the given environmental conditions. The other is that the predominant plant species are those that can compete most successfully in the conditions they perpetuate. In the first case, the limitation is essentially one imposed by the climate; in the second case, by the ecosystem itself. In a climax temper-

ate forest, for example, the trees will be those such as maple, oak, and beech, whose seeds can germinate in shade. In a grasslands ecosystem, the dominant plant species will be those that can regenerate rapidly after fires or that can survive extended periods of drought.

A successional process such as that just described is called a **primary succession**. The basic process is always the same but the nature of the climax community will be determined by the nature of the biome in which the process occurs. Succession also takes place along the shore of bodies of water, gradually converting aquatic ecosystems to terrestrial ones (Figure 26.6).

Established ecosystems are sometimes destroyed, either by natural disasters (such as landslides, earthquakes, floods, hurricanes, or volcanic eruptions) or by human action (such as logging, farming, or construction). The processes of succession resume at the point of interruption and slowly rebuild the climax community. This process is referred to as **secondary succession** (Figure 26.7). Sometimes fires and other destructive events occur so frequently that the climax ecosystem never becomes established again. In such areas, called **barrens**, succession may progress only to the stage of small herbs and shrubs before the developing ecosystem is destroyed once more.

Figure 26.6
As mud and organic debris accumulate around the plants at the edge of a body of water, the area gradually becomes part of the land. Over a period of time the area becomes marshy, then a moist meadow, and finally a forest.

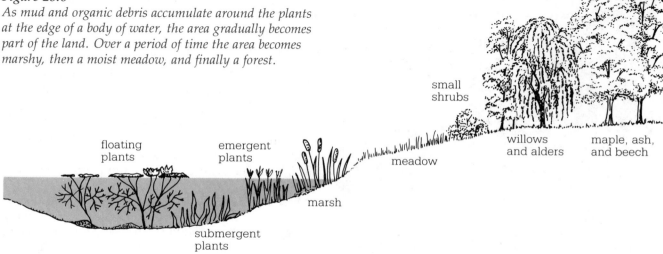

Figure 26.7
This rock face shows how organisms from the surrounding area gradually move into any vacant niche.

Figure 26.8
This map shows the frequency with which fires occur in Canada's six easternmost provinces.

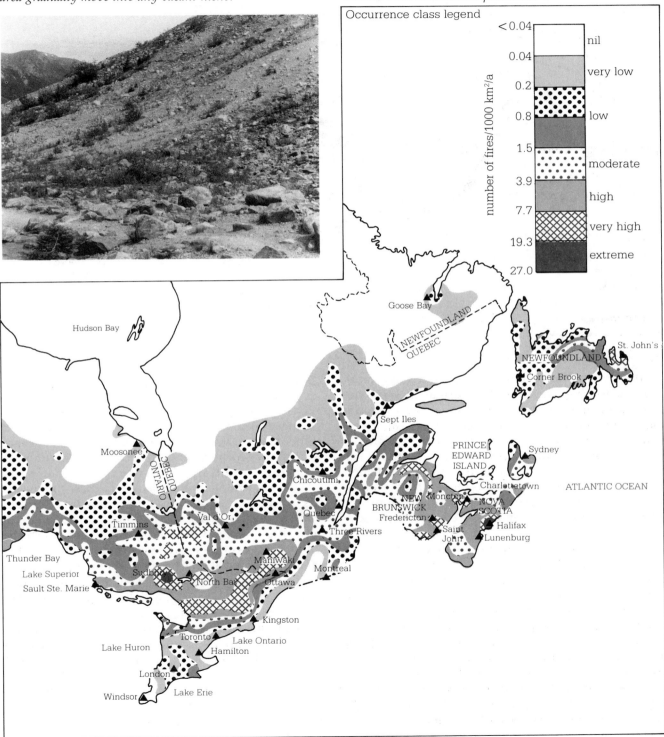

Figure 26.9

Chemical elements move from the air, soil, and water through the processes of photosynthesis to become part of living organisms. As these organisms carry out their life processes and eventually die, the various elements are gradually returned to the air, soil, and water to be used again.

nitrogen
water
oxygen
carbon

As shown in Figure 26.8 on the previous page, areas along major highways and high use areas show the highest incidence of wildfires. Although some fires are caused by lightning, the vast majority are caused by human carelessness and therefore are preventable. Ecosystems can benefit from occasional fires. For example, fire is needed to destroy the accumulated debris on the ground and release the nutrients for re-use in grassland ecosystems. The rapid development of new growth that follows a fire can rejuvenate the ecosystem.

Each ecosystem has plant species that have evolved an ability to recolonize the area after fire. Sawgrass, for example, enables wetlands to withstand fires. Jack pine and black and white spruce produce special cones at the top of the tree that do not open to release their seeds except after the intense heat of a fire. Other trees, such as red pine, Douglas fir, and sequoia have bark that resists burning and can survive most fires. Yet if fires occur too frequently, the organic material in the soil can be destroyed, making it impossible for seeds to germinate. In such cases, the process of primary succession must once more begin to rebuild the soil so that a new ecosystem can develop.

26.6 BIOGEOCHEMICAL CYCLES

Since spaceship Earth is essentially a closed system, chemical elements are neither gained nor lost, but rather are recycled continuously. Such processes are termed **biogeochemical cycles**. Organisms withdraw chemical elements from the environment in order to build and maintain their cells. When these organisms later die, decomposers break down the dead tissue to extract the remnants of energy and return the chemical elements to the environment. The rate at which the various stages of these processes occur determines the chemical composition of the environment.

Many of the pollution problems that humans face today are the result of a failure to fully understand the nature of these chemical cycles. Chemicals move through the air, water, and soil with little regard for political boundaries (Figure 26.9). When wastes are dumped without consideration of these processes, those wastes may be transported through the ecosystem along similar pathways. Thus a cooperative effort by all of spaceship Earth's inhabitants will be required to ensure that these cycles continue to operate as they should.

Figure 26.10
There are really two cycles involved within the hydrologic cycle—a ''short'' cycle which bypasses living organisms and a ''long'' cycle in which the water becomes part of an organism for a time.

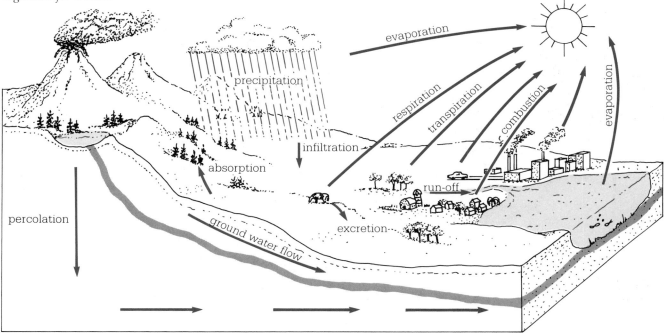

Six substances—carbon, hydrogen, oxygen, nitrogen, phosphorus, and sulfur—are responsible for 95 percent of the mass of living organisms. The movement of these materials through the biosphere is thus the key to understanding the role that biogeochemical cycles play in the maintenance of chemical balance. These cycles not only move materials through the biosphere but also ensure that these chemicals are delivered to plants in forms that they can use.

The Hydrologic Cycle

The hydrologic cycle not only moves hydrogen and oxygen through the biosphere, but also ensures that water is purified as it is recycled. Water is released from the atmosphere in the process of **precipitation**; rain, snow, hail, or sleet fall on the land or on bodies of water (Figure 26.10). Some of the water that falls on the land flows across the surface (often causing erosion) to join a body of water. Some of the water percolates into the soil to be held there for a time. Some of this soil water may be used by plants; some may evaporate from the surface of the soil; much of it may slowly filter down to form part of the water table.

This underground water also gradually flows downhill and eventually, over perhaps hundreds of years, becomes part of some body of water.

Wherever there are open surfaces of water, the sun's heat causes some of it to evaporate back into the atmosphere. Some of the water that is absorbed by plants is returned to the atmosphere through the process of transpiration. As plants and animals carry out respiration, the waste water from that process is also released to the environment through the various processes of excretion. Even organic matter that has become fossil fuel releases water when that fuel is burned.

Plants greatly influence the rate at which the hydrologic cycle functions. They reduce the force of the various forms of precipitation hitting the ground, thus in turn reducing erosion and run-off. Plant roots also hold the soil in place against the forces of erosion. Combined with the organic matter in the soil, these roots act as a sponge holding the water in the upper layers of the soil, where it is available to plants. The shade created by the plants reduces the soil temperature, thus slowing down the rate at which water evaporates from the soil. The plants act to reduce air

Figure 26.11
The carbon cycle. Note all the points at which human activities have an impact on it.

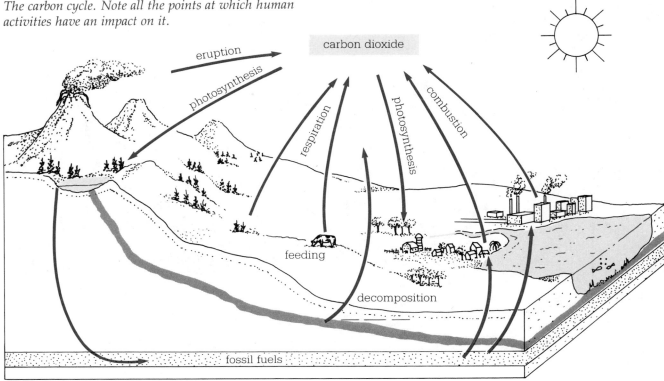

currents by helping to trap humid air around them; evaporation is thus slowed still further.

When areas of plants are cleared and the soil is left open or even paved, water is no longer retained but instead rushes on to the next stage of the cycle. Since they retain their leaves all year, the world's humid forests have a major influence on the functioning of the hydrologic cycle. There is great concern over the accelerating destruction of the forests of the Amazon Basin, the largest forested area on the earth. No one can accurately predict the effect of this loss. Most of this clearing is being accomplished by burning the forests, which in turn increases the amount of carbon dioxide and soot in the atmosphere. There is further concern over the effect that these atmospheric changes may have on global temperatures.

The water shortages in the south-central parts of North America have resulted from the fact that water is being withdrawn from underground supplies more rapidly than these supplies are being recharged through natural processes. The states of Colorado, Utah, Nevada, New Mexico, Arizona, and California depend heavily on irrigation and are already searching for new sources. Alberta and Saskatchewan have ade-

quate water supplies for normal conditions, but not for summers of extreme drought. Thus, North Americans must consider whether water is being used wisely and must investigate the possibilities of purifying and re-using it. Studies must also focus on how to increase the rate at which water is stored in the underground areas.

The Carbon Cycle

Plants obtain the carbon they require for photosynthesis by absorption of carbon dioxide from the air or water that surrounds them. The carbon becomes incorporated first in glucose and then in the various other macromolecules synthesized by plants. When plants or the animals that eat them later require energy, these macromolecules are broken down to release the energy locked in their chemical bonds. This process of cellular respiration returns carbon dioxide to the environment.

Some carbon molecules, then, may remain part of the plants' tissues for only a short period. Others may travel along food chains to the second or third trophic levels before being released. Still others may remain

Figure 26.12
The oxygen cycle. Note the many points at which human activities have a direct effect on it.

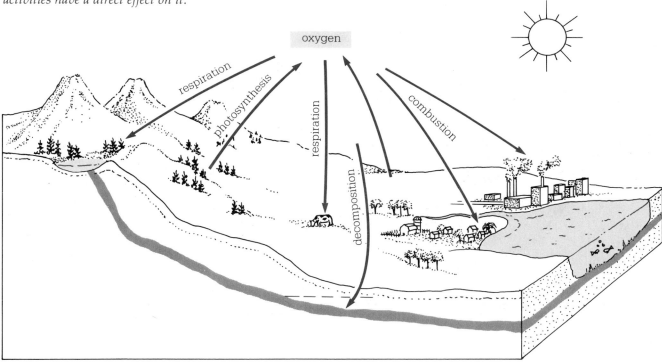

out of the atmosphere for a much longer time. As illustrated in Figure 26.11, some plant and animal tissues do not decay immediately, but may remain underground for even millions of years. These organic substances eventually form peat, coal, oil, or natural gas — the fossil fuels. When these fuels are burned, the carbon molecules they contain finally are returned to the active part of the cycle.

Human activities have had many effects on the carbon cycle. An increasing use of fossil fuels has resulted in a 30 percent increase in the amount of carbon dioxide in the atmosphere since 1850. This, one might think, could increase the rate of photosynthesis on spaceship Earth. Yet the spaceship's crew has also been busy felling the forests and paving the fields, thus reducing the global rate of photosynthesis. Many scientists believe that the increased level of carbon dioxide in the atmosphere will result in a phenomenon known as the *greenhouse effect* (Chapter 28). The carbon dioxide essentially acts as a blanket around our spaceship, reducing the amount of heat lost to space. There is much discussion about the potential consequences of even a two to three degree rise in average global temperatures. If polar ice caps melted and rainfall patterns changed, no nation would be immune from the effects.

The Oxygen Cycle

Oxygen molecules form a link between the carbon and hydrologic cycles, since both involve oxygen compounds. During photosynthesis, plants use energy from sunlight to split apart molecules of carbon dioxide and water, using the resulting elements to synthesize glucose. In this way, plants are able to store solar energy in the form of chemical energy. During this process, some of the oxygen that accompanies hydrogen in water is not required, and, therefore, is released to the atmosphere.

That oxygen is needed later, during cellular respiration, to release the energy contained in organic compounds. The total amount of oxygen that is released during photosynthesis is precisely the amount that is required to release energy from the macromolecules that were formed. As we use spaceship Earth's onboard fuel supplies, such as fossil fuels and even firewood, we also are consuming the store of oxygen that was produced when these substances were formed (Figure 26.12).

Figure 26.13
*The nitrogen cycle. Note the role of bacteria and
cyanophytes in the maintenance of it.*

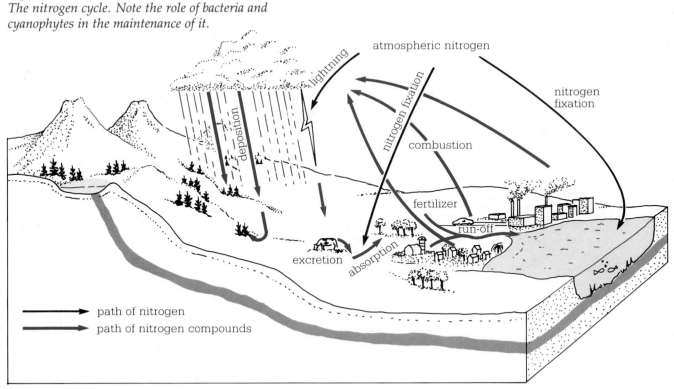

The Nitrogen Cycle

Nitrogen is essential for many biological processes, such as the synthesis of proteins and of DNA and RNA. Most plants obtain all of their nitrogen from the soil, and thus do not flourish in nitrogen-poor soils. Grasses in particular need generous quantities of nitrogen to grow well; therefore, lawn fertilizers contain a high proportion of nitrogen. Animals meet their need for nitrogen by obtaining it from the amino acids in their food. Because all animals require certain amino acids in order to synthesize protein, a lack of dietary protein, which is the only source of those amino acids, causes malnutrition in humans.

Although approximately 78 percent of the air consists of nitrogen gas, plants are unable to utilize it. Plants can absorb nitrogen only in the form of water-soluble compounds. One source of these compounds, strangely enough, is lightning. As an electrical discharge passes through the air, it causes some nitrogen to combine with oxygen to form compounds called nitrates. These dissolve in rain as it precipitates and are washed into the soil, where they become available to plants.

Most conversion of nitrogen into useable com-

pounds, however, is accomplished by three groups of micro-organisms. The first group consists of the soil bacteria known as nitrogen-fixing bacteria. They can absorb nitrogen from the air in the soil and convert it into various nitrates and nitrites. Other soil bacteria recycle the nitrogen-containing substances (such as ammonia, uric acid, and urea) excreted by other organisms back into useful forms.

A second group of micro-organisms is found in water and moist soil. They are the cyanophytes or the blue-green algae. These prokaryotic organisms also absorb nitrogen from the air and convert it into compounds useful to other plants. To a large extent, it is cyanophytes that are responsible for the high net primary productivity of swamps and marshlands and also of rice paddy agriculture (Figure 26.13).

The third group of organisms are the *Rhizobium* bacteria that live in swellings, called nodules, on the roots of legumes. Long before the chemistry was understood, farmers knew that if they grew a legume crop (for example, alfalfa, clover, lentils, peas, or beans) in their fields at least once every three or four years, their yield of other crop plants would be much higher. Legumes create conditions that attract these bacteria to their roots; the nitrogen that becomes available through nitrogen fixation not only enables the legume crop to flourish but also enriches the soil for future crops. This type of relationship, one in which both organisms benefit, is called **mutualism** or **symbiosis**. Almost all the legumes that have been domesticated are native to the temperate zones. There are many legumes that are native to tropical ecosystems, and much research is now being conducted with the aim of developing domesticated species that could enable tropical farmers to make similar use of them.

Many Canadian soils, particularly those of the Pre-Cambrian Shield, are deficient in nitrogen. Recent studies have shown that many native species (such as alder) that thrive in these soils appear to have similar relationships with soil organisms that can make nitrogen compounds available. Considerable research is being conducted to establish the potential for use of these organisms in forestry and agriculture. Already, it is possible to buy micro-organism cultures to add to soils that appear to be deficient in them.

Plants incorporate nitrogen in their proteins. Most animals obtain their nitrogen by eating plants or other animals. A few plants also obtain nitrogen in this way. Insectivorous plants, such as pitcher plants and sundew, can flourish in soils that are deficient in nitrogen. When plants and animals die, decomposers break down the proteins they contain into ammonia compounds which are then recycled by the soil bacteria.

When fossil fuels are burned, the nitrogen they contain is released into the atmosphere in the form of various oxides of nitrogen. Some of these dissolve in the moisture in the air to form nitric and nitrous acid, thus contributing to acidic precipitation while returning nitrogen compounds to the soil. Humans often deliberately add ammonia compounds to the soil as fertilizers. The use of such fertilizers has increased by twelve times in the past thirty years, although crop production has only doubled. Excess fertilizer tends to be washed off the land into the nearby aquatic ecosystems, thus stimulating growth there. Treated and untreated sewage also add a considerable quantity of nitrogen compounds to the ecosystem in which they are deposited. Rivers that receive the effluent from several urban areas in succession can become overloaded with organic nutrients. Growth may be stimulated to the point where the aquatic ecosystem becomes unbalanced and decomposers consume most of the available oxygen. The most modern sewage treatment processes remove much of this organic material from the effluent before it is released.

The Phosphorus Cycle

Phosphorus is required by both plants and animals. Among other things, phosphorus is an essential component of the ATP and DNA molecules. Phosphorus in the soil is absorbed by plant roots and incorporated in the plant tissues. Animals obtain their phosphorus by eating plants or other animals. Much of the phosphorus is returned to the soil in animal waste products. A particularly important source of phosphorus is *guano*, the wastes from fish-eating sea birds. Some coastal islands have large enough deposits that commercial industries "mine" them as a source of fertilizer. This industry is quite important to the economy of Peru.

Much of the phosphorus washes from the land to accumulate in the sea. There, it forms phosphate rock in the shallow coastal waters. Rocks of this sort were formed millions of years ago when central North America was a shallow sea. This phosphate rock is the basis of Saskatchewan's potash fertilizer industry. Heavy use of these fertilizers results in much of the phosphorus they contain being washed into the waterways. Sewage, treated or untreated, adds still more phosphorus.

The large quantities of nitrogen and phosphorus available in the water may cause an explosive growth of algae (an algal bloom). That growth quickly dies, consuming much of the oxygen in the water as it decays. This process accelerates eutrophication of the body of water (Figure 26.14).

The Sulfur Cycle

Sulfur is also a necessary constituent of some amino acids. Plants obtain the sulfur they require from sulfates in the soil. Animals, in turn, obtain their sulfur from plants or other animals. As plants and animals decay, the decomposers again release the sulfur to be recycled. If oxygen is available, the sulfur will be released in the form of sulfates. Under anaerobic conditions, the decomposers produce hydrogen sulfide ("rotten egg gas").

There is a considerable stockpile of sulfur underground. Some exists as compounds of metals; more is in the form of sulfur dioxide or hydrogen sulfide dissolved in the ground water. These gases are often released to the atmosphere through volcanoes, hot springs, and steam vents. They then dissolve in rainwater to form dilute acids. They may also react with ammonia in the air to form ammonium sulfate. This sulfur too then becomes available to plants.

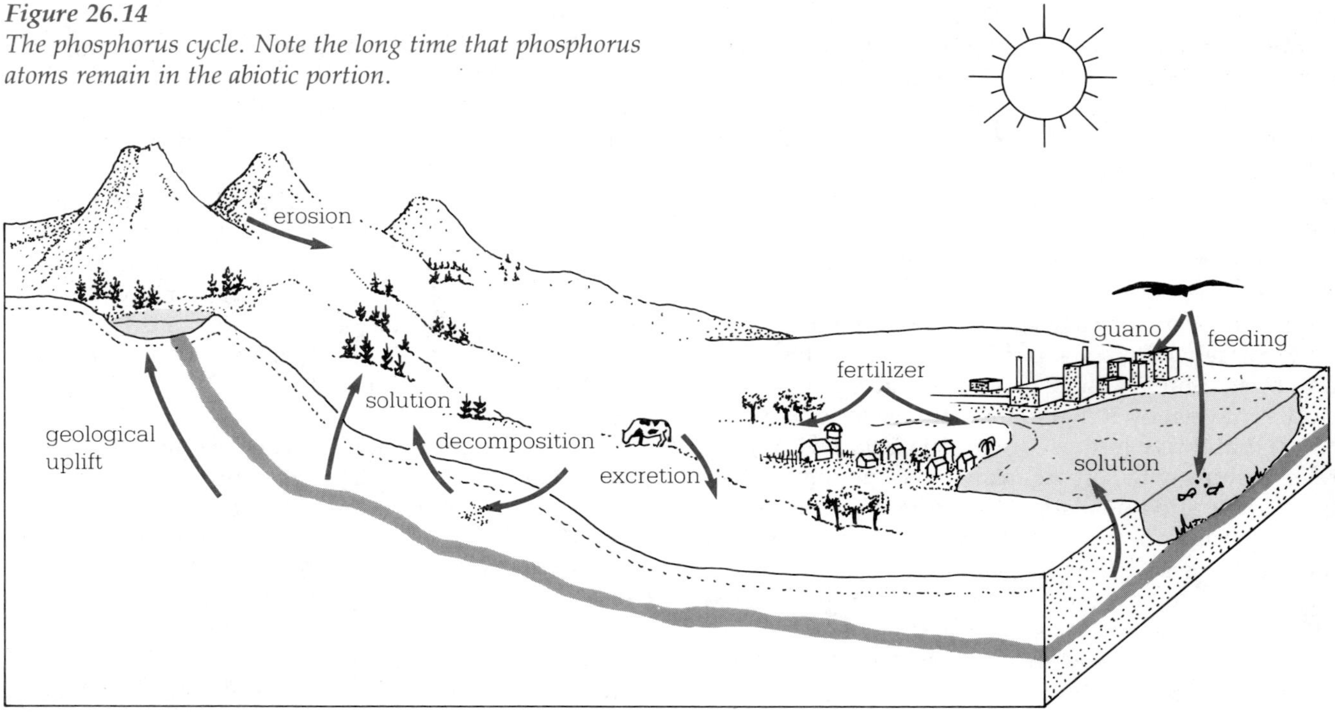

Figure 26.14
The phosphorus cycle. Note the long time that phosphorus atoms remain in the abiotic portion.

Figure 26.15
The sulfur cycle. The processes of industry have had a considerable impact on it.

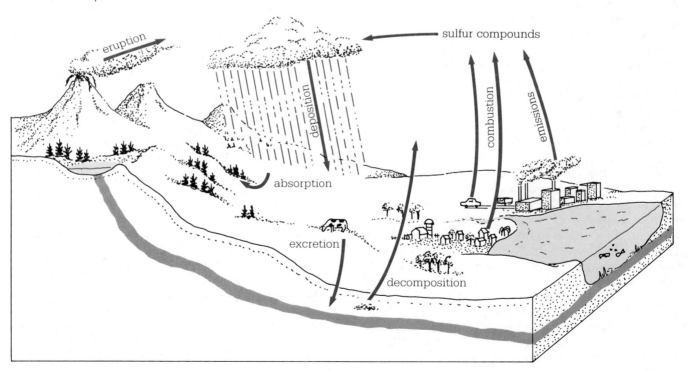

Combustion of wood or fossil fuels returns the sulfur they contain to the atmosphere. Smelting of ores separates the desired metal from sulfur and much of this sulfur also joins the atmospheric gases. Many other industrial processes, such as the refining of petroleum and the making of paper, contribute to the atmospheric concentration of sulfur (Figure 26.15). When all these factors combine, there may be sufficient acid dissolved in rainwater to give it a pH of 3.0! While plants and animals do need sulfur, they are damaged when the concentration is this high. The effects of acidic precipitation are considered more fully in Chapter 28.

26.7 EFFECTS OF COMPETITION

In any ecosystem, the supply of energy and materials is limited. As an ecosystem becomes more complex through succession, the competition for these resources intensifies. The organisms that are considered to be generalists solve their problem by being sufficiently flexible to use whatever resources are most readily available. On the other hand, the ''specialists'' compete by being better than any other organism at extracting the resources of a narrow segment of the ecosystem. The ''generalists'' therefore survive well in changing ecosystems and are most common during the early stages of succession. Many of the plants considered to be weeds are ones that can compete successfully in a wide variety of situations. The ''specialists'' are more suited to the stable conditions of a climax community and are most commonly found in such ecosystems. Many of these organisms, like the insectivorous plants, have become adapted to exploit a niche that is not available to others.

Competition for the resources of an ecosystem is of two basic types. The competition among organisms of different species for the same resources is said to be **interspecific**. If the competition is among members of the same species, then the competition is said to be **intraspecific**.

The plants that win in both interspecific and intraspecific competitive situations often do so simply by growing more rapidly than do the competing plants. As a result, their leaves create shade that prevents their competitors from obtaining sufficient sunlight for photosynthesis. In general, organisms may gain a competitive advantage by producing more offspring, by obtaining more food or energy, by defending themselves more effectively, or by having a greater tolerance for environmental change. Humans tend to

consider the organisms with which they (or their domesticated species) compete to be pests. A great deal of time and energy often is directed toward finding methods to eliminate pest species. These species, however, are quite resilient and can usually adapt to the methods used.

If two species attempt to occupy the same ecological niche, the competition becomes so intense that one species will eventually be eliminated. This is the principle of **competitive exclusion**. When two species do appear to be occupying the same niche, closer study reveals some subtle distinction between them. Hawks and owls, for example, appear to share the same niche. In fact, they do not; hawks are diurnal predators, whereas owls are nocturnal hunters. Thus, they are not competing for the identical food resource.

26.8 CITIES AS ECOSYSTEMS

When agriculture first commenced some 10 000 years ago, some groups of people abandoned their nomadic ways for at least part of the year and began to build more substantial shelters. Eventually those shelters became permanent dwellings to which people returned after hunting expeditions. The resulting villages were small and their inhabitants were very much a part of the ecosystem in which they lived. Like other animals, they consumed local plants and animals for food. Those parts that were inedible were returned to the surrounding ecosystem to be recycled by natural processes. When wood was burned for cooking or warmth, the ashes were spread on the fields to return minerals to the soil. Human and animal wastes were returned to the fields as fertilizer too. The activities of these people did little to disrupt the ecosystem and the wastes that they produced re-entered the biogeochemical cycles.

When the clusters of dwellings grew into towns and small cities, their inhabitants began to lose contact with the surrounding ecosystem. As specialization and division of labour increased, many people purchased their food and fuel rather than harvesting it themselves. The larger the cities became, the greater the area of the surrounding countryside that was needed to supply its inhabitants. Fuelwood supply became a major problem. With the exception of hunting reserves, most of the surrounding forests were cut for fuel or building material. The discovery of coal helped to reduce the dependence on fuelwood. By the time North America was being settled by Europeans, timber was a scarce commodity in some parts of Europe. Fish and, later, lumber were major exports from this continent in the early years of European settlement in eastern North America.

Until the development of the steam engine in the nineteenth century, cities were largely dependent on locally produced food. Crop failures produced widespread famine. The human diet was much less varied than it is today and malnutrition was common. During the winter, people were dependent on what could be preserved. Fruits were dried or preserved in sugar or honey. Vegetables that did not store well could be pickled. Meat was dried, smoked, or pickled in brine.

Wastes also became a problem in the larger cities. Although farmers returned most of their wastes to the fields, the materials that went to the cities generally remained there. Much of the waste was simply discarded in any place that was convenient, resulting, of course, in major sanitation problems. Human and animal wastes often were dumped into local bodies of water. Cities were filthy and infested with rats and other pests. Epidemics were frequent until the methods of disease transmission were recognized and sanitation measures were developed.

In 1900, only 14 percent of the world's population lived in urban areas. By 1950, this figure was 29 percent; by 1985, it was 43 percent. It is projected to be 62.5 percent by the year 2020. In 1900 only 1.6 percent of the earth's population lived in cities with more than one million inhabitants. In 1985, 16 percent lived in such cities. The ten largest urban areas in 1985 each contained more than ten million people.

Such cities no longer can function as part of the local ecosystem. Food is transported, often by air, from all over the globe. An immense amount of packaging is required to ensure its freshness and purity. Fuels, too, come from many sources. Although waste management systems have improved local sanitation, they rarely return the waste substances to an appropriate biogeochemical cycle. Many of the wastes now have been synthesized by humans and the natural cycles contain no organisms capable of processing them safely. The modern city has developed as though it could be independent of natural cycles. Yet, considering the biosphere as a closed system, it is easy to recognize that this kind of development cannot continue. If satisfactory solutions to the problems of waste management and the associated pollution are to be found, they must be within the context of the biosphere's natural processes.

26.9 WASTE MANAGEMENT

With the increasing difficulty of finding an "away" in which to throw wastes, people have begun to take a serious look at what they are discarding. Agricultural and industrial wastes form the largest proportion of the discarded material. Since these tend to be somewhat uniform in composition, they do not present the greatest challenge. Rather, it is the varied nature of urban solid waste that is the major barrier to more ecologically appropriate disposal (Figure 26.16).

Open dumping is not considered an acceptable method of disposal because of the pests it attracts. **Sanitary landfill** (covering the garbage each day with a layer of earth) does return materials to an ecosystem. There are, however, four major problems with this method. One is that the materials are generally returned to a different ecosystem than the one from which they were removed. Another is that the sheer quantity of waste involved tends to overwhelm natural systems. A third problem is that many substances found in today's urban waste stream cannot be decomposed by soil organisms and may, in fact, be toxic to them. Finally, urban waste may contain toxic chemicals that should not be allowed to move through the soil into the ground water.

Because landfill sites are increasingly difficult to obtain and because hazardous wastes may be present, many municipalities are now destroying wastes through **high temperature incineration**. The resulting heat can be used directly or used to produce steam to generate electricity. This method does reduce pollution considerably and leaves a much smaller quantity of ash.

Ideally, incinerator ash would be returned to farming areas to replace the minerals lost from the fields. Unfortunately, the ash may contain residues of heavy metals that could contaminate crops. A similar problem exists with sewage sludge which, theoretically, could replenish the organic matter in soil. Much more careful monitoring of what enters the waste stream would be necessary before these uses of waste could become reality.

Resource recovery processes may lead to a better solution to waste disposal problems. Although many attempts have been made to separate the components of urban waste at the receiving end, those attempts have been costly and inefficient. Currently emphasis is being placed on encouraging consumers to separate the wastes at source. Even a basic separation of paper,

Figure 26.16
The typical composition of urban solid waste. What proportion of municipal solid waste could be eliminated by composting? What proportion could be handled through a "blue box" recycling program?

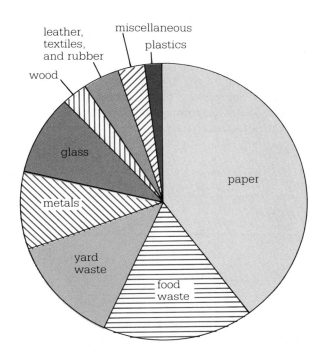

glass, and metal from the wastes of each household permits these materials to be collected separately and recycled. Many municipalities have initiated "blue box" **recycling** systems to accomplish this. Those with gardens are being encouraged to compost vegetable waste for their own use.

Little has yet been done to provide householders with alternative methods for the disposal of chemicals such as household cleaners and solvents, crankcase oil, pesticides and herbicides, paints, dyes, and glues. In general, these are flushed into the sewers or thrown into household garbage. Sewage treatment systems are based on providing ideal conditions for natural aquatic decomposition processes. These systems provide very effective treatment for human or animal wastes but may have little or no effect on chemicals that have been discarded into the sewers.

While considerable progress has been made in reducing pollution, it is still necessary to take the next step of considering all wastes as resources to be recovered and reused. Only then will spaceship Earth be operating effectively as the closed system it is.

CHAPTER SUMMARY

The earth is essentially a closed system. It must receive solar radiation to supplement its on-board energy supplies. Plants collect this energy and through photosynthesis make chemical energy available to all living organisms. This energy is then transferred to organisms at other trophic levels within the ecosystem. Each time energy is transferred from one form to another, however, some energy is converted to low quality forms that are no longer useful.

All living organisms are linked together in networks created by these patterns of energy transfer and by the recycling of chemical elements. Hydrogen, carbon,

oxygen, nitrogen, phosphorus, and sulfur move through biotic and abiotic components of ecosystems in predictable cycles.

As humans have clustered together in larger and larger groups, their activities have tended to remove materials from one ecosystem and return them to another. The result has been a considerable disruption of natural element cycles. The key to a solution of present resource and pollution problems is for humans to work within these cycles rather than independently of them.

Objectives

Having completed this chapter, you should be able to do the following:

1. Describe the significance of solar radiation for the earth.
2. Outline the importance of photosynthesis in making energy available to ecosystems.
3. State the significance of the First and Second Laws of Thermodynamics to living systems.
4. Discuss why the idea of an ecosystem is a useful concept.
5. Outline the concept of trophic levels.
6. Describe how net primary productivity can be used to analyze the functioning of an ecosystem.
7. Outline why ecosystems undergo succession and the factors that determine the nature of a climax community.
8. Explain why chemical elements must be continually recycled.
9. Describe the various biogeochemical cycles.
10. Discuss why large cities no longer function as part of the surrounding ecosystem.

Vocabulary

solar radiation	food chain	biogeochemical cycle
fossil fuel	food web	precipitation
thermodynamics	net primary productivity	mutualism
entropy	biomass	symbiosis
ecosystem	succession	interspecific competition
producer	seasonal succession	intraspecific competition
primary consumer	pioneer organism	competitive exclusion
secondary consumer	climax community	sanitary landfill
parasite	primary succession	high temperature incineration
scavenger	secondary succession	resource recovery
decomposer	barrens	recycling
trophic level		

Review Questions

1. Explain why the sun is really the source of hydro-electric energy.
2. Which of our energy sources can be traced back to photosynthesis?
3. Why is it so difficult to define the boundaries of an ecosystem?
4. How can the patterns of energy flow be used to analyze the structure of an ecosystem?
5. Explain why food chains in most ecosystems interlock to form food webs.
6. Why is net primary productivity more accurately expressed in energy units than in mass units?
7. (a) State the factors that might cause a developing ecosystem to remain at the pioneer organism stage.
   (b) Give an example of such a circumstance.
8. Poplars are among the first trees to move into a meadow, yet they are not found in mature forests. Suggest why.
9. Why can occasional fires be used to manage an ecosystem, while frequent fires can destroy it?
10. Why is the hydrologic cycle considered to be the earth's water purification system?

11. Why is a healthy population of micro-organisms an essential component of the nitrogen cycle?
12. What is the most rapid method of transferring phosphorus from the sea back to the land?
13. (a) How did the relationship of their inhabitants to the surrounding ecosystem change as small villages grew into cities?
    (b) What is your relationship to your ecosystem?

14. Summarize how the nature of waste management problems changed.
15. Evaluate various alternatives for waste management in terms of their relationship to the biogeochemical cycles.

Advanced Questions

1. Refer to the Biosphere II diagram (Figure 25.1). Evaluate this project in terms of its use of energy and recycling of chemical elements. Do you think these processes can be sustained over a period of years?
2. Consider the role of fire in creating the conditions that led to the establishment of Banff and Jasper National Parks.
    (a) How have these ecosystems changed since forest fires have become less frequent?
    (b) Why are parks managers now making judicious use of fire as part of their management policy?
    (c) What public relations problems does this cause?
3. Beavers do not always construct their dams in places that humans consider to be convenient. Yet it is generally acknowledged that their actions are essential for the survival of some other species. Explain why.
4. Does your community have a "blue box" recycling program?
    (a) If not, why not? Investigate these programs in terms of their economic viability.
    (b) What substances are being recycled?
    (c) Could other materials also be recycled in this way?
    (d) Could your school become involved in a recycling program?

5. (a) Select a region in which there are serious problems of undernutrition and/or malnutrition.
    (b) Investigate the historical and cultural roots of these problems.
    (c) Devise a program to alleviate these problems on a long term basis.
6. Undertake a study of the water supply in your community. Consider these factors:
    (a) the source of the supply
    (b) the agricultural, industrial, and public uses of it
    (c) the treatment of the water both before and after use
    (d) the real and potential sources of pollution
    (e) the consequences of a shortage
7. In the year 3000 a new planet is discovered with an atmosphere somewhat similar to that of the earth. The winters are long, however, with only three frost-free months during the year. Much of the surface water is locked in permanent ice. Only plants similar to algae and lichens are found there. There are many micro-organisms and a few worm-like animals. You have been given the task of establishing a permanent self-sustaining colony on this planet. Outline how you would do it.

CHAPTER 27

POPULATION DYNAMICS

*The power of population is infinitely greater than the power
in the earth to produce subsistence for man.*

Thomas Malthus

hat you see is a scene from an Australian ranch. At one time, it would not have been uncommon to see dozens of rabbits crowding around a waterhole on such a ranch. Yet rabbits are not native to Australia. In 1859, there were 12 pairs introduced from Europe to a few ranches near Victoria. Within six years, rabbits were so numerous that ranchers were hunting them in "drives," one of which yielded 10 000 rabbits from a single ranch! By 1895, rabbits were present 17 700 km from the sites where they were introduced. Today, although their numbers fluctuate, rabbits are only about as common in Australia as they are in the parts of Europe where they are naturally found. Populations of all organisms have the potential to "explode" like these Australian rabbits did. For the most part, however, such population explosions are uncommon.

27.1 DESCRIBING POPULATIONS

Ecologists use the term **population** to describe all of the members of one species found in a particular locality at a particular time. The study of the size and structure of populations is called **demography** (from the Greek *demos*, meaning the people, and *graphein*, meaning to write). Although originally applied only to the study of human populations, the term demography now applies to the study of populations of all kinds of organisms.

Some kinds of natural populations are easier to define than others. The population of fish in a lake or the population of a species of mammal on an island has quite distinct geographical limits. However, the limits of many of the kinds of populations that ecologists study must often be set rather arbitrarily. Wolves in an area such as Ontario's Algonquin Park frequently travel beyond the park's boundary. Nevertheless, it is possible to talk about the population of wolves in the park, with the understanding that the geographic limits of the population have been set for convenience. Although the way in which populations are defined may sometimes seem arbitrary, it is important to remember that populations are composed of very real individuals.

The terms used to describe how populations change over time differ from those used to describe changes in individuals. Individual organisms come into being when seeds germinate, eggs hatch, or offspring are born. A population comes into existence when individuals colonize a previously unoccupied area, or when part of a population becomes separated from an existing one. Although both individuals and populations can be said to grow, the ways in which they do so differ. In the case of individuals, growth is the result of an increase in either the number or the size of cells. The size of a population changes when individuals are born or die and when individuals **immigrate** (move into the population) or **emigrate** (move out of the population). Finally, death marks the end of an individual organism's life, but populations go extinct only when their last member disappears. Because a population is a collection of organisms, it is the rate at which individuals are born, die, immigrate, or emigrate that affects how its size changes over time.

Figure 27.1
Factors affecting the size of populations. A population's size is a matter both of how rapidly individuals are entering (through births and immigration) and of how rapidly others are leaving (through deaths and emigration).

In some ways, a population is like a reservoir or a rainbarrel. At any instant, a reservoir will contain a certain volume of water — just as a population will contain a certain number of individuals. The level of the reservoir will rise as water flows in and will fall as water flows out. In the same way, a population's size increases because new individuals immigrate or because those individuals already present reproduce. On the other hand, a population's size decreases when existing individuals die or emigrate. Therefore, like a reservoir, a population's size at any time is determined by the rate at which individuals are entering and leaving it. The study of **population dynamics** examines the effects of changes in **natality** (birth) and **mortality** (death) rates and in immigration and emigration rates on the size of populations. Figure 27.1 illustrates how the interaction of these factors with one another determines a population's size.

Estimating the Size of Populations

Before the dynamics of a population can be studied, certain features must be described. A vital one is the number of individuals that the population contains. In every country, government officials periodically conduct a **census** to calculate how its human population is changing and to determine the levels of resources required to keep its people healthy. Ecolo-gists attempt to estimate the sizes of natural populations for the same reasons. However, because censuses require an enormous amount of time and effort, ecologists only rarely attempt to count all the members of a population. More often, **population estimates** are made by counting the number of individuals in a sample and then extrapolating the results to the whole population. The methods used to obtain these estimates are different for populations of different kinds of organisms.

Estimating Numbers by Using Quadrats or Transects
For most plants and for sessile animals (such as barnacles, in which adults rarely move from the place where they settle), ecologists use **quadrats**—literally, squares or rectangles—to estimate a population's size. First several locations are randomly chosen within a study area and at each site a quadrat of known size (e.g., 1 m × 1 m) is marked out (Figure 27.2). All of the individuals contained within the area are then counted. Next, an estimate of the population **density** (the number of individuals in a particular area) is made by calculating the average number of individuals in all of the quadrats that were sampled (e.g., 0.5 individuals/m^2). If the total size of the study area (e.g., 1000 m^2) is known, an estimate of the size of the whole population can then be made (in this example, the estimate would be 500 individuals).

Figure 27.2
Quadrat sampling of a plant population

Figure 27.3
Transect sampling of plants in a forest

Another method used to estimate the density of stationary organisms is shown in Figure 27.3; it is called **transect** sampling. A transect is really just a long, rectangular quadrat. In transect sampling, a starting point and direction are randomly chosen and then a line of a specified length (e.g., 100 m) is marked out. Next, the occurrence of any individual within a certain distance (e.g., 1 m either side of the line) is recorded. Since the total area that was sampled is easily calculated (200 m² in this example), the population density can be estimated as it would be using quadrats. Transects are particularly useful for obtaining population estimates whenever small quadrats would fail to contain any individuals, as would be the case when the density of organisms is low.

An extension of these methods is used in aquatic ecosystems to estimate the size of populations of organisms such as plankton. In aquatic studies, samples

Figure 27.4
Marking a bird for later identification. Most ornithologists use distinctive combinations of small, coloured plastic rings that fit around a bird's leg to mark individuals. Once a sample is marked, the population size can be estimated or the behaviour of specific individuals can be studied.

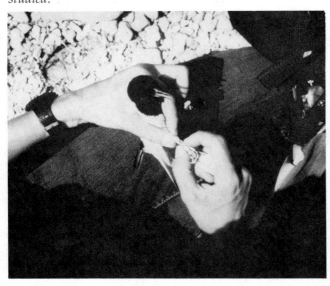

of a known volume of water are collected, the water is passed through a net or sieve, and then the number of organisms in each sample is counted. As with quadrats, the average density (the number of individuals per unit volume) is used to calculate the size of the population contained in the entire body of water.

Estimating Numbers by Capturing and Marking Individuals
It is difficult to use quadrats or transects to estimate the population size of mobile organisms such as birds or mammals. Individual animals might move between quadrats, in which case they could be counted more than once; as well, some individuals might move out of a quadrat before they were counted. Therefore, the size of a population of mobile organisms is frequently estimated using a different method — the **capture-recapture technique**. This method involves capturing a sample of the population, marking and releasing the captured individuals, and then capturing a second sample (Figure 27.4). The number of marked individuals in the second sample can be used to estimate the number of individuals present in the whole population. Formulas similar to the one which follows are often used to estimate a population's size.

$$\frac{\text{number of individuals caught and marked in the first sample}}{\text{total population size}} = \frac{\text{number of marked individuals recaptured in second sample}}{\text{total number in second sample}}$$

For example, if 40 animals were caught and marked in the first sample, and 20 of them were recaptured in a second sample of 100 animals, the population's size would be estimated to be 200 individuals using the following calculation:

$$\frac{40}{N} = \frac{20}{100}$$

$$N = 200$$

In both quadrat and capture-recapture sampling, changes in the population between successive sampling periods can be used to estimate the rate at which a population's size is changing.

27.2 DESCRIBING HOW POPULATIONS GROW

As noted earlier, populations grow when birth and immigration add more individuals than death and emigration remove. Immigration and emigration can definitely influence a population's growth. Although often described in studies of the dynamics of the human population, the effects of immigration and emigration are less often described in studies of other species. In natural populations, immigration and emigration rates are often assumed to be approximately equal; their effects, therefore, would tend to cancel each other out. Perhaps more importantly, however, the effects of immigration and emigration often seem extremely small in comparison to the effects that births and deaths have on a population's growth.

The Capacity for Exponential Growth
Consider the following example of the growth of a hypothetical bacteria population. If a single bacterium were placed in a beaker along with all of the nutrients it needed to live, after approximately 20 min it would reproduce by simply dividing in two. If it is assumed that all of the cells divide at the same time when reproduction occurs, it is a simple matter to calculate how large the population will be at some point in the future. Figure 27.5 shows how rapidly a population such as this one would grow. Notice that after only a few hours, the population is composed of many thou-

Figure 27.5
The growth of a bacteria culture

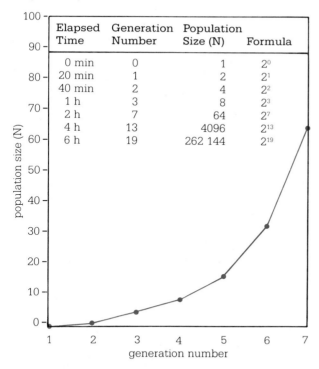

Elapsed Time	Generation Number	Population Size (N)	Formula
0 min	0	1	2^0
20 min	1	2	2^1
40 min	2	4	2^2
1 h	3	8	2^3
2 h	7	64	2^7
4 h	13	4096	2^{13}
6 h	19	262 144	2^{19}

Figure 27.6
Population growth rate for organisms that produce three offspring

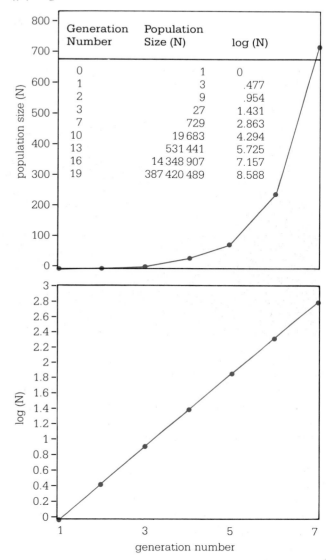

Generation Number	Population Size (N)	log (N)
0	1	0
1	3	.477
2	9	.954
3	27	1.431
7	729	2.863
10	19 683	4.294
13	531 441	5.725
16	14 348 907	7.157
19	387 420 489	8.588

sands of cells. If the future growth of this population is calculated, the results are rather frightening. After about 12 h, the population would number in the billions of cells. Thirty-six hours later, there would be enough bacteria to produce a ''blanket'' 10 cm thick over the entire earth. In the next hour, the blanket would be so thick it would be over our heads. Very soon thereafter, the population would be expanding out from the earth at close to the speed of light!

The rapidity with which this hypothetical population of bacteria expanded demonstrates that populations have an enormous capacity for growth. The pattern of growth exhibited by this population is called **exponential growth**. As shown in Figure 27.5, the number of individuals present at some point in the future can be calculated simply by taking the number of offspring each individual produces and raising it to the exponent of the number of generations that have elapsed. But why does exponential growth occur? For example, do populations in which individuals produce more than two offspring also grow exponentially? Figure 27.6 shows the growth of a hypothetical organism that produces three offspring after each interval of 20 min. Although in this example there are

more individuals in the population after each time interval, the graph of the changes in population size has the same shape as that in Figure 27.5. A simple way to determine whether a population is growing exponentially is to plot the logarithm of the population size against the number of generations that have elapsed. If the plot is a straight line, as it is for these data, then the population is growing exponentially. Therefore, this example shows that the tendency for exponential growth is *not* a matter of how many offspring each individual produces.

Figure 27.7

The growth of the human population since the year 1750 A.D. The population size for the year 2000 is an estimate.

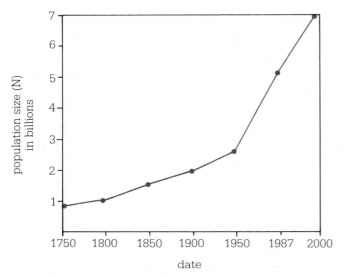

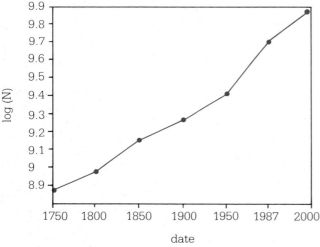

Does exponential growth only occur in populations with short time periods between generations? Figure 27.7 illustrates how the human population has changed over the last 250 years. The plot of the logarithm of population size versus time is very close to a straight line, showing that over this period the human population has indeed been growing exponentially. Thus, exponential growth is not only something that occurs in species that reproduce rapidly. In fact, populations of *all* organisms have the capacity for exponential growth.

There are several ways to describe how rapidly a population is growing. One way is to express the increase that occurs in a particular time period as a percentage of the population's size. For example, between 1981 and 1986 the population of Canada grew from 24 343 181 to 25 354 064. This net increase of 1 010 883 people represented both births and immigration minus both deaths and emigration. If this increase is averaged over the five year period, then the annual increase is approximately 202 177 people. In 1986, therefore, the **average annual increase** in population was approximately 0.8 percent. This figure is derived by the following formula:

$$\frac{\text{average annual increase}}{\text{total population size}} \times 100\% = \frac{\text{annual percent}}{\text{growth rate}}$$

or

$$\frac{202\ 177}{25\ 354\ 064} \times 100\% = 0.79\%$$

The rate of population growth as a percent of the population size is not, all by itself, very informative. Is 0.8 percent fast or slow growth? Percentage growth figures are most valuable as tools to compare the growth of two or more populations. For example, over the same period of 1981–1986, the annual growth rate of the population of Mexico was 2.6 percent, for Sweden it was 0.1 percent, and for the entire world it was 1.7 percent. It is therefore fair to say that compared with many populations, Canada is growing relatively slowly.

A more vivid description of the rate at which a population is growing is its **doubling time**, the time taken for a population to double in size. A simple way to calculate a population's doubling time is to divide the average lifespan (70 years) by the annual percentage growth rate. If Canada were to continue to grow at an annual rate of 0.8 percent, the population would double in approximately 87.5 years. If the world continues to grow at a rate of 1.7 percent annually, it will double in size in only 41 years. Since in 1987 the world contained approximately five billion people, this calculation suggests that it would contain ten billion by the year 2020.

The term **biotic potential** has been used to describe the capacity of populations for growth. This potential will increase both as the average number of offspring produced by an average individual increases and as the time between successive generations decreases. To state it another way, as the difference between a population's birth rate and death rate increases, so does its growth potential. Ecologists typically refer to this difference as the **intrinsic rate of increase**. In mathematical descriptions of population growth and in everyday conversation, ecologists use the term *r* as a symbol for the intrinsic rate of increase.

27.3 FACTORS LIMITING THE GROWTH OF NATURAL POPULATIONS

As illustrated with the bacteria example, the capacity of populations for exponential growth can produce some frightening projections. Can you imagine what would happen if even one natural population ever fully realized this potential? Since there is no evidence that any natural population has ever done so, something must hold the growth of natural populations in check. What is it?

As shown in Figure 27.8 **abiotic factors** (factors working independently of other organisms) such as blizzards, hurricanes, or floods can kill many living things. Therefore, the size of natural populations might be controlled by such catastrophes if they occurred frequently enough. Alternatively, it is a simple mathematical exercise to show that the number of individuals in a population only increases when birth rates exceed death rates. Therefore, the size of natural populations might be controlled by factors which naturally decrease birth rates and increase death rates. If these factors involve other living things such as competitors, parasites, or predators, they are referred to as **biotic factors**. In fact, both abiotic and biotic factors have been used to understand how the sizes of natural populations are regulated.

Density-Independent Population Regulation

Populations of insect pests (tent caterpillars, for example) occasionally come close to realizing their potential for exponential growth. Figure 27.9 illustrates how destructive explosions of some insect populations can be. Because of the economic effects of this destructiveness, ecologists have been very interested in the kinds of factors that normally regulate the size of pest populations. In many cases, it has been shown that an accurate prediction of a population's future size requires a knowledge not only of its current size and reproductive rate but also of past weather conditions. Studies of the effect of weather on mortality rates in several species indicate that adverse weather conditions such as dryness or cold often result in the death of a significant proportion of the existing population.

Figure 27.8
A late spring blizzard can kill many migrating birds.

Figure 27.9
Defoliation of trees in the Muskoka region of Ontario by tent caterpillars (Malacosoma americana)

If weather conditions remain favourable for long periods, populations of these organisms often grow quickly and achieve very large sizes. Although the *absolute number* of individuals that die during severe conditions is related to the population's size, the *proportion* dying is determined by the severity of the conditions, independent of the number of individuals in the population.

Ecologists have spent a great deal of time developing techniques to estimate immigration, emigration, birth, and death rates from data on natural populations. However, the effects of these factors on a population's growth are based on simple mathematical principles which vary according to whether the population has non-overlapping or overlapping generations.

Population Growth in Organisms with Non-Overlapping Generations
In many species, such as periodical cicadas, Pacific pink salmon, and all annual plants, individuals die after they reproduce. Organisms that reproduce in this way are described as having discrete or *non-overlapping* generations. The size of future populations of such organisms can be predicted using exponents, as was shown earlier with bacteria—but why? To calculate the size of a population in the future, one has to know only how many individuals there are at present (N_0, since the present is sometimes called time zero), the average number of offspring each current individual will produce (B), and the average number of offspring that will die before they get a chance to reproduce (D). For example, to calculate the population size one generation after observations began (N_1), the following formula is used:

$$N_1 = (B - D) N_0$$

In plain language, this equation says that the number of individuals in the next generation is simply the number currently present multiplied by the average number of surviving offspring that each individual produces. Frequently, the term (B − D) is replaced with the

THE PRINCIPLES BEHIND THE PATTERNS OF POPULATION GROWTH

term R, which is referred to as the *net reproductive rate*. When this replacement is made, the equation has the form:

$$N_1 = (R) N_0$$

The same reasoning can be used to predict the size of the population two generations in the future. The equation here would be:

$$N_2 = R (N_1)$$

If N_1 is replaced by its value in the first equation, then this equation becomes:

$$N_2 = R ((R) N_0)$$

or

$$N_2 = R^2 N_0$$

If t is used to denote the number of generations that have elapsed since observations began, the equation can be rewritten as:

$$N_t = R^t N_0$$

Since in the bacteria example N_0 was 1, this equation shows why simply raising the average number of offspring produced by individuals to the exponent of the number of elapsed generations can predict a population's future size.

Population Growth in an Organism with Overlapping Generations
Many organisms reproduce more than once before they die. Thus at any point, a population is made up of both adults and their offspring. Such populations are often referred to as having *overlapping generations* and are described as growing continuously. Because both births and deaths will occur in any time

interval, not just during distinct breeding seasons, overlap between generations makes a difference for how both population growth rates and future population sizes are calculated.

An example from banking can illustrate the difference between the growth of populations with overlapping and non-overlapping generations. Imagine that the rate at which individuals are added to the population is like the interest that a bank pays on the balance in an account. Populations with non-overlapping generations are like bank accounts for which interest is paid only once per year (that is, once per generation). If $100 were deposited in such an account and the annual interest rate was five percent, after one year the new balance would be $105.00 (100 + [100 × 0.05]; or 100 × 1.05); after five years the balance would be 127.63 (100 × 1.05^5), etc. If the same $100 had been deposited in an account for which an annual interest rate of five percent was calculated daily, the balances would have been $105.12 after one year, $128.40 after five years, etc. The figure (opposite page left) shows how the balances in these two accounts would change over a 50 year period. Although the balances at the start are rather similar, as time goes on they become more and more different. A particular bank balance (or in the case of populations a particular population size) will be reached more rapidly in populations with overlapping generations than it will in populations with non-overlapping generations.

With overlapping generations, exponential growth is described using the formula:

$$N_t = N_0 e^{rt}$$

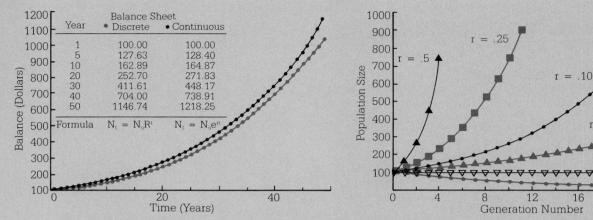

Year	Balance Sheet Discrete	Balance Sheet Continuous
1	100.00	100.00
5	127.63	128.40
10	162.89	164.87
20	252.70	271.83
30	411.61	448.17
40	704.00	738.91
50	1146.74	1218.25
Formula	$N_t = N_0 R^t$	$N_t = N_0 e^{rt}$

As in earlier equations, N_0 is the number of individuals at time zero and N_t the population size t time units later. Because reproduction goes on continuously, t can be a time interval of any length, not just the number of generations that have elapsed. In this equation, the term r is referred to as the *intrinsic rate of natural increase* and is similar to the term R used in equations for populations with non-overlapping generations. In populations that grow continuously, r represents the difference between instantaneous birth rates (b) and instantaneous death rates (d). Since births and deaths occur continuously in populations with overlapping generations, birth and death rates represent the probability that some individual will reproduce or die at a particular instant in time. Finally, the term e in the equation is the base of natural logarithms and has an actual value (2.71828 . . .). The term e is used in all equations for continuously growing populations so that populations with different rates of natural increase can be easily compared. The graph (right) shows that for different values of r, the steepness of the curve varies but its shape remains the same. When r is greater than zero, the population size *increases* exponentially; when r is less than zero, it *decreases* exponentially.

Because populations of organisms with overlapping generations grow continuously, it is important to be able to monitor their growth rates constantly. The "shorthand" of calculus provides a convenient way to determine how a population is changing at any given instant. Differentiating the population growth equation above with respect to time (t) gives the following result:

$$dN/dt = rN$$

In plain language, this equation says that the change in a population's size in a very short period of time (dN/dt) is equal to the per capita rate of increase multiplied by the population size at that instant of time. When a population is growing rapidly, dN/dt will be large; when its size is not changing, dN/dt will be zero; when it is declining, dN/dt will have a negative value. This form of the population growth equation is valuable because it can be used to make estimates of the absolute number of individuals that would be added to a population in a particular time interval.

Descriptions of Logistic Growth
Sigmoidal growth differs from simple exponential growth; different mathematical equations are therefore used to describe it. One such equation frequently used is the logistic equation. It contains a term that takes into account a population's current size when its growth rate is calculated. The most common form of the logistic equation is:

$$dN/dt = rN (K - N/K)$$

In this form, the logistic equation uses a term K to denote the population's carrying capacity in a particular environment. When a population's size is small relative to its carrying capacity, the value of the expression $(K - N/K)$ is nearly 1 and has little effect on the population growth rate. However, as a population's size increases and approaches its carrying capacity, the value of $(K - N/K)$ becomes smaller and smaller and only a fraction of its potential for growth is realized. The utility of this equation is that it not only can account for periods of near exponential growth but also can explain why a population's growth rate decreases as it gets larger.

Figure 27.10
*How the tent caterpillar (*Malacosoma americana*)*
population periodically erupts in Ontario

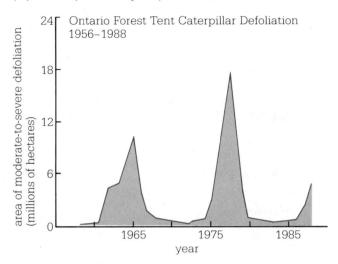

The regulation of population size by abiotic factors that result in the loss of a proportion of the population is known as **density-independent population regulation**. One characteristic of populations that grow in a density-independent fashion is that they have **J-shaped growth curves** (Figure 27.10). Such population growth curves typically result from periods of rapid exponential growth that are occasionally interrupted by periods of even more rapid population decline. For species that are apparently limited by density-independent factors, a population's size at any point in the future is determined only by the length of time that it experiences a positive population growth rate (that is, birth rates higher than death rates).

Density-Dependent Population Regulation

Unlike those of pest species, the populations of many other organisms often remain relatively stable generation after generation. This is particularly true of long-lived species. For example the size of many populations of songbirds remains about the same for long periods of time (Figure 27.11). Although severe weather conditions occasionally kill many individuals, long periods of exponential growth are rare, if they ever occur. What factors could be responsible for this sort of population regulation?

Studies of the dynamics of populations of laboratory animals such as protozoans have contributed greatly to an understanding of population regulation. Figure 27.12 shows how a population of *Paramecium* grows when it is provided with a constant daily food ration

Figure 27.11
The stability of a bird population in the City of Toronto.
Every year around Christmas, members of naturalist clubs
all over North America estimate how many individuals of
each bird species are present in their areas. This
information indicates that some bird populations are very
stable, but it can also give an advance warning about
species that are becoming endangered.

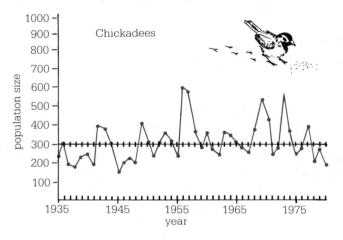

Figure 27.12
Growth of a laboratory population of Paramecium
aurelia

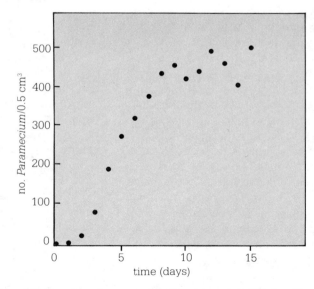

and its wastes are periodically removed. Under these controlled conditions, the population first exhibits a period of nearly exponential growth, but then the population size becomes stable. This sort of population growth has been called **sigmoidal growth**; it is characterized by an **S-shaped growth curve**. The reason that the numbers stabilize in such populations is that birth rates decrease and death rates increase as the population grows. Often these changes in the birth and death rates arise because of biotic factors such as competition, predation, or parasitism. This sort of control of a population's growth is called **density-dependent population regulation**.

Carrying Capacity
In populations that exhibit sigmoidal growth, the effect that density has on birth and death rates depends strongly on the population's size. When a population's size is small, the effect of density on birth and death rates may often be so small that it is difficult to distinguish sigmoidal growth from exponential growth. However, as the population's size increases, the difference between the two kinds of growth becomes larger. When the population's size becomes very large, it reaches a plateau rather than continuing to grow. At this point, the birth and death rates are equal. When population growth ceases due to density-dependent effects, it is said that the population has reached the environment's **carrying capacity**. As was the case for the term *r*, the term **K** is often used as a mathematical symbol for a population's carrying capacity.

One simple way to think about a population's carrying capacity is to picture it as a limited number of ''spaces'' in the environment; an individual must be able to occupy a space in order to survive and successfully reproduce. When the population's size is small, there are many living spaces still unoccupied; few individuals fail to find a space. However, as the population grows, an increasing proportion of the available living spaces are filled and individuals more frequently die before they reproduce. Once the environment's carrying capacity is reached, individuals can only reproduce if individuals that are already present die.

This description of an environment's carrying capacity is greatly simplified. In nature, the carrying capacity is not fixed but changes as a population's size increases. For example, as a population uses the resources in an environment, the more likely it is that its wastes will pollute the remaining resources. As a consequence, the environment's carrying capacity will decrease as the population grows. If an environment's resources were being polluted by wastes that accumulated over time, then a carrying capacity might decline even though a population's size remained

constant. One of the greatest threats to the future well-being of the human population is the current rate at which the environment's natural resources are being polluted. This pollution is decreasing the environment's carrying capacity for human life.

The Effects of Density on Survivorship and Fecundity
Since a population's growth rate reaches zero only when birth rates and death rates are equal, its size must somehow affect each individual's chance of survival and reproduction. Again, experimental laboratory populations have been particularly useful in understanding how population density affects birth and death rates. Figure 27.13(a) illustrates how the **fecundity** (the number of offspring a female produces) of microscopic crustaceans called *Daphnia* varies with population densities between 1 and 32 individuals per mL of water. High population densities affect fecundity in two ways. First, in dense populations, the total number of offspring produced by each female decreases. Second, high densities tend to delay the age at which females attain their maximum fecundity. Since *Daphnia* must feed and grow to a particular size before they are able to produce eggs, both of these effects are probably attributable to an increased competition among females for food.

In this laboratory population, the only organisms competing for food and other resources would have been other *Daphnia*. When individuals of the same species use and limit each other's ability to obtain resources, intraspecific competition is said to exist. In nature, there would undoubtedly have been many other species of organisms that would have competed with *Daphnia* for the food. If individuals of different species affect each other's ability to exploit a resource, interspecific competition is said to exist (Chapter 26). Since members of the same species would tend to use precisely the same kinds of resources and would tend to gather them in very much the same way, intraspecific competition is generally thought to affect a population's growth more strongly than does interspecific competition.

Figure 27.13(b) illustrates density-dependent changes in the **survivorship** (the proportion of individuals that survive to a certain age) in laboratory populations of *Daphnia*. Survival actually increases at densities of up to eight individuals per mL in these populations. However, at higher densities, death rates increase and survivorship decreases markedly. Although it is difficult to know precisely why death rates increase, individual body growth in crowded

Figure 27.13
How density affects (a) the fecundity and (b) the survival of Daphnia *in laboratory populations*

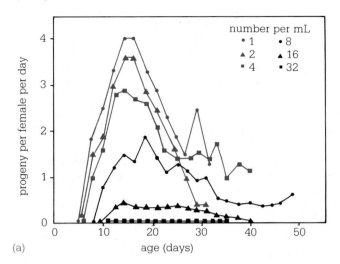

(a)

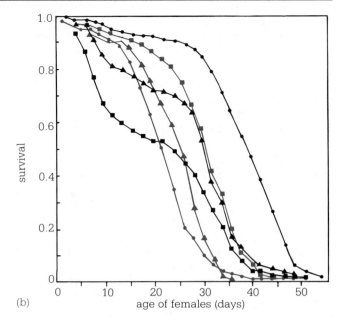

(b)

cultures is stunted. Again, this suggests that increased competition for food among females may be responsible for increased mortality at high densities.

The factors affecting the fecundity and survival of individuals in nature is probably more complex than it is in the lab. For example, in the last 20 years, the *rate* at which the world's human population has been growing has begun to decrease — as if it were approaching the environment's carrying capacity. (Note that population size is itself still increasing; it is the *rate* of this increase that has slowed.) But for humans, the decrease in the population's growth rate has not been because of an increasing death rate. In fact, death rates among humans have been *decreasing* constantly since the end of World War II. The slowdown in population growth has been the result of decreasing birth rates, especially in populations of Asia, Africa, and Latin America. Unlike *Daphnia*, decreases in the human birth rate have not been the product of poor nutrition. Despite the occurrence of catastrophic famines in recent years, the diets of people in these regions have generally improved in the last two decades.

The changes in the birth rates, and thus the growth of populations in developing regions of the world, are largely the result of cultural changes. History has shown that as the economy of a region becomes based more in industry and the population becomes more concentrated into cities, the traditional role and status

of women change. Since the cost of raising children in an industrialized society is high, many women obtain higher levels of education and many more women enter the work force. In addition, couples wait longer before starting a family. All of these factors tend to decrease birth rates.

In discussing human population dynamics, a distinction is usually made between fecundity and **fertility**. The physiological capacity to bear young (fertility) differs from the *actual* number of young produced (fecundity). Because of family planning practices, humans are probably the only species for which a distinction between the two terms is needed.

Cyclic Changes in Population Size
Populations that are near their carrying capacity often alternate between periods of growth and decline. At densities above the carrying capacity, decreased birth rates and increased death rates result in declines in populations; as the population size decreases below the carrying capacity, higher birth rates and lower death rates result in expansion of the population. Therefore, as a rule, most natural populations probably fluctuate around their carrying capacity rather than remain at a constant size.

Although the fluctuations in the size of many natural populations are often small and irregularly spaced, some species regularly exhibit large fluctuations in population size. A famous example of cyclic

Figure 27.14
Cyclic changes in the size of lynx and hare in the
Canadian North, as indicated by the purchase of furs from
trappers

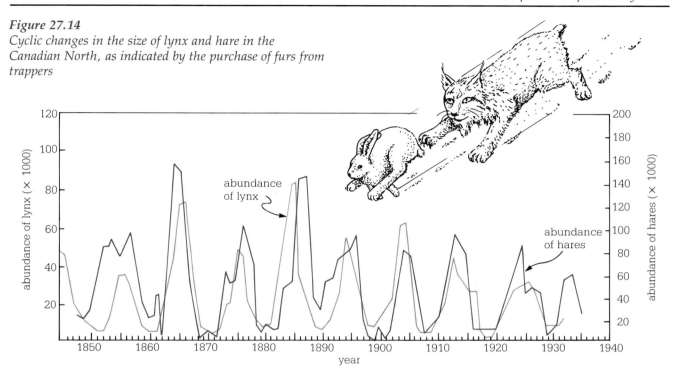

population changes involves the case of lynx and Arctic hare in the Canadian Arctic. Figure 27.14 shows the annual numbers of individual lynx and hare trapped over a 100-year period in the region around Hudson Bay. Notice that approximately every ten years the populations of both lynx and hare become very large, decline gradually, and then become large again.

Although ecologists are not completely agreed on the cause of population cycles, most concede that the cycles occur much too regularly to be caused entirely by abiotic factors. A different explanation for the lynx-hare cycle is that the density-dependent effects of growth by the hare population influence the growth of the lynx population. For example, an increase in the hare population would allow lynx to experience higher birth rates because the lynx would experience a relaxed competition for food. In addition, because well-fed lynx would likely survive longer, the lynx population would grow. However, the predation of hare by a large lynx population would decrease the survivorship of hare and thus ultimately lead to a decrease in the size of the hare population. As hare grow scarce, competition for food among the lynx would result in their own lower fecundity and survivorship. With a smaller predator population, death rates in the hare population would decrease and its high birth rate would lead to rapid population growth.

The cycle would then simply tend to repeat itself.

The link between predators and their prey cannot be the only explanation for the lynx and hare cycle. For example, hare populations exhibit cyclic changes on islands in the Arctic where there are no lynx. In addition, many populations of predators and their prey fail to exhibit regular population cycles. In the absence of natural predators and parasites, introduced species (such as the European rabbit in Australia) often realize their potential for exponential growth. This suggests that predation and parasitism are important factors that limit a population's growth. Interestingly, in the case of the Australian rabbits it was a virus purposely introduced by humans that brought about a stabilization of the population's size.

The Regulation of Natural Populations
From the examples presented here, it may seem that populations of some kinds of organisms (such as insects) are regulated by abiotic density-independent factors, whereas those of others (such as birds and mammals) are regulated by biotic density-dependent factors. This apparent difference led early ecologists to argue about which form of population regulation was more important, or at least more common. As is the case with most areas of biology, issues in ecology are seldom matters of black and white. For example,

Figure 27.15

The relationship between a species' biotic potential and the environmental resistance to population growth

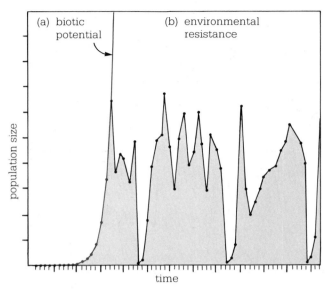

27.4 THE EFFECTS OF A POPULATION'S AGE STRUCTURE ON ITS GROWTH AND REGULATION

So far, it has been assumed that each individual in a population has an identical chance of survival or reproduction in a certain time interval. (This assumption is often made just to make the mathematics of calculating a population's growth rate simpler.) Clearly, such an assumption is *not* appropriate for populations in which individuals must first mature before they reproduce, or in which very young or very old individuals die more often than do middle-aged individuals.

Age-Specific Patterns of Survivorship and Fecundity

In many organisms, an individual's probability of survival and reproduction changes with its age. Figure 27.16 illustrates three different patterns of **age-specific survivorship**. The shape of a species' survivorship curve can often reveal a great deal about its life history. Curve (a) is typical of many long-lived organisms such as humans or elephants in which survivorship is high until old-age. Curve (b) is typical of the age-specific survivorship of many bird species. In this case, an individual's chance of survival from one year to the next stays the same but the proportion of the population reaching each successive age steadily decreases. Curve (c) shows the age-specific survivorship that is characteristic of many marine organisms such as oysters. These organisms produce an enormous number

much of the time a population of birds may be regulated by density-dependent factors that affect birth and death rates. However, occasional catastrophes may reduce a population to the point where density effects are relatively unimportant. Similarly, severe weather may regularly keep the size of an insect population low. Nevertheless, if protective sites are available but limited, the proportion of the population killed by a storm may not be altogether determined by its severity. Most populations are probably subjected to both density-dependent and density-independent regulation from time to time.

One way to think about the many factors involved with the growth and regulation of a population's size is shown in Figure 27.15. Curve (a) illustrates how a population would grow if it were able to realize its full biotic potential. Curve (b) shows the regulating effects that the environment might have on the population's growth. In this case, abiotic factors (that show up in the J-shaped portions of the curve) and biotic factors (that result in the saw-tooth changes) suppress the population's growth. Since the effects of both abiotic factors (such as weather) and biotic factors (such as the carrying capacity) can both be thought of as ways that an environment suppresses population growth, the combination of their effects can be called the **environmental resistance** to population growth.

Figure 27.16

Three hypothetical patterns of survivorship

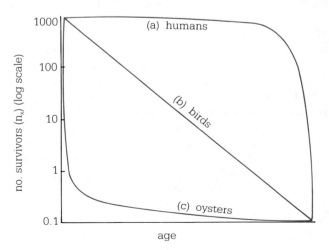

Figure 27.17

How age affects the reproductive capacity of North American men and women

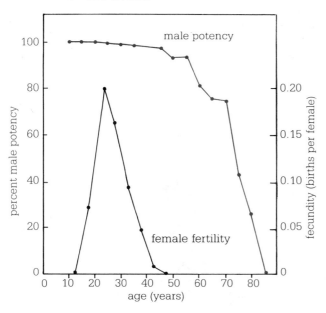

Figure 27.18

Changes in the total fertility rate of Canadian women between 1926 and 1976

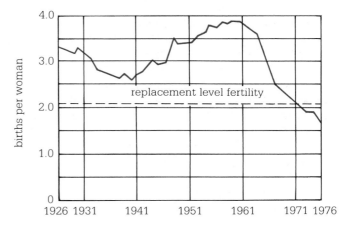

of eggs that they release into the open ocean. The curves drop rapidly for young individuals because only a tiny fraction of them survive long enough to settle in a suitable habitat.

In humans, many factors affect the probability of an individual's survival from one age to the next. For example, in times of war the chances that young individuals will die is higher than at other times. History affects the patterns of human survivorship in other ways as well. As was pointed out earlier, the birth rate commonly declines as a country switches from an agricultural to an industrial and technological economy. However, there is also commonly a shift from relatively low survival of young people to a very much higher survival. This change in the shape of the human survivorship curve most often occurs because readily accessible medical care prevents the spread of infectious diseases. This shift in survivorship will be discussed in more detail in the next chapter.

In short-lived organisms (such as many insects), an individual's age probably has little to do with how many eggs it lays or how many young it produces. More often, fecundity depends on factors that affect the physiological condition of individuals, such as the availability of food. However, in species that take a relatively long time to reach sexual maturity, the abil-

ity to produce young, often does vary with age. Figure 27.17 illustrates how the **age-specific fecundity** of American women (and the potency of North American men) change. Prior to puberty, conception is impossible and therefore female fecundity is zero. Women between 20 and 30 years of age have the highest age-specific fecundity, with approximately 20 percent of all babies being born to women in this age bracket. After 30 years of age, female fecundity declines rapidly. With the onset of menopause, usually between 45 and 50 years of age, female fecundity reaches zero again. In contrast, male potency remains constant from puberty until approximately 60 years of age. Because of this difference, females ultimately determine a population's birth rate and human demographic projections are based on estimates of the female segment of the population.

An important statistic used to describe human population growth is the **total fertility rate (TFR)**. This rate is defined as the average number of offspring a woman actually produces during her life. Although the onset and termination of female fecundity are set by puberty and menopause, the fertility rate is strongly influenced by cultural factors, such as those that affect the status of women in a society. Since approximately 0.1 percent of all infants die in childbirth, a total fertility rate of 2.1 percent is required for a couple to replace itself in the population. This figure is called the **replacement level fertility rate**. Figure 27.18 shows how the total fertility rate of Canada's population between 1926 and 1976 compared with replacement level fertility. During the peak of the baby boom years, the total fertility rate of Canadian women rose to 3.9 births per woman. To state it another way, Canadian women on average would have given birth to 3.9 children during their childbearing years.

At a fertility rate of 2.1 births per female, a human population will neither grow nor shrink; at that point birth and death rates become equal. Since the value for r becomes zero at this point, this level of fertility has been associated with what has been called **zero population growth (ZPG)**. Again, as will be dealt with in detail in the next chapter, many aspects of human ecology are affected by the population's size. Stabilization of the size of the human population through ZPG is an important goal that many feel must be achieved to guarantee the future welfare of the human population.

The Effects of a Population's Age Structure on its Growth

Age-specific survivorship and fecundity affect the number of individuals of different ages in a population and therefore affect the number of individuals in a population that will likely reproduce before they die. Information regarding the proportion of a population in each age class is often presented in **age pyramids** (Figure 27.19).

The age structures of the three hypothetical populations shown in Figure 27.20 differ dramatically. A consequence of the different age structures in these populations is that each one will tend to grow in a slightly different way. For example, in population (a), there are many more individuals in the younger age classes than there are in the older classes. This kind of age structure is fairly typical of many natural populations and characterizes the composition of many of the populations in developing countries. The abundance of young individuals in the population means that a large percentage of the population will have an opportunity to reproduce. The population will thus continue to grow and will continue to be composed of a large proportion of young individuals for quite some time. Populations such as this one are therefore described as having an **expansive age structure**. The persistent growth of a population with this type of age structure is sometimes referred to as a **population growth momentum**.

In population (b), the majority of the individuals are old; in nature, this type of age structure occasionally results from a catastrophe that kills predominantly

Figure 27.19
A population pyramid allows the sex and age structure of a population to be illustrated graphically. The male portion of the population is always shown on the left side of the pyramid and the female portion on the right. The width of each step shows the percentage of the population that lies in a particular age group. (Usually age groups represent five-year age intervals.)

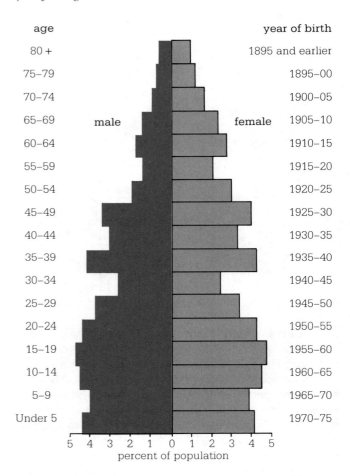

young individuals. In humans, it is typical for populations in which the total fertility rate has remained below the replacement level fertility for some time. In this population, the age structure is destined to change in the near future; gradually it will move toward being made up of an increasingly higher proportion of older individuals. In addition, since individuals are not being replaced when they die, the size of the population will decline. Populations of this type are hence said to have a **constrictive age structure**.

Figure 27.20
Three typical kinds of population pyramids

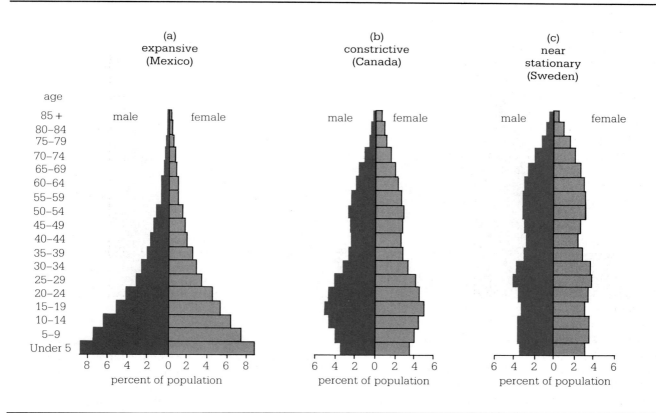

Population (c) has approximately equal numbers of individuals in each age class. Fish and game managers often aim to produce this sort of age structure in order to maximize the regularity of their harvests. The composition of this population will tend to remain about the same in future generations. This stability occurs simply because new individuals are being born at about the rate that old individuals are dying. Such populations are referred to as having a **stationary age structure**.

The age structure of the human population differs greatly in developing and industrialized regions of the world. Generally speaking, developing countries exhibit expansive age pyramids and industrialized countries stationary ones. Because the proportion of young people in developing countries is currently very large (37 percent of the current population is less than 15 years old), the developing countries of the world will contribute many more individuals to the next generation than will developed countries. In addition, even if couples in developing countries have

families that average only 2.1 children, the large proportion of young people in the population will translate into a momentum for continued population growth. See Figure 27.21(a). If future populations in these regions of the world do become this large, there will be enormous pressures on the nations involved. To deal with these pressures, these nations will have to develop viable economies and will have to ensure that their environments can supply the resources needed for this development.

Canada and other developed countries will face a different problem from that faced by developing countries—the aging of their populations. The increases in the population size of developed countries will be relatively small while the proportion of individuals in older age classes will be proportionately greater than it currently is. See Figure 27.21(b). As the population ages, relatively fewer people will be in the work force and contributing to the support of social services through taxes. The burden of care for the elderly will fall on the shoulders of a relatively small population.

Figure 27.21
*A comparison of the age structure and future growth of
developed and developing countries*

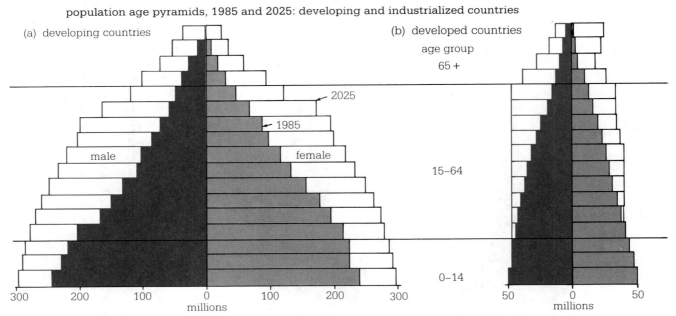

population age pyramids, 1985 and 2025: developing and industrialized countries

(a) developing countries

(b) developed countries

age group

65 +

2025

1985

male

female

15–64

0–14

Solutions to this problem are currently being sought by the governments of all developed countries. The Province of Quebec, with the lowest birth rate in Canada during the 1980s, is now providing incentives for couples to have larger families. Other countries, such as West Germany, have altered immigration policies in an attempt to provide a better balance to their work force.

The Evolution of Species-Specific Life Histories
Patterns of age-specific survivorship and fecundity give a population its characteristic age structure, but they are also responsible for each species' distinctive **life history**. For example, as described earlier, organisms can be divided into those with life histories in which individuals reproduce only once and then die (sunflowers, pink salmon, cicadas etc.) and those in which individuals survive between breeding seasons and reproduce more than once (oak trees, songbirds, humans, etc.). Another distinction can be drawn between species in which individuals produce relatively few young (for example, elephants) and those in which individuals typically produce many offspring (for example, rabbits). As well, while many short-lived organisms are also those in which individuals commonly produce numerous young, many organisms with long life spans produce comparatively fewer

young. These factors lead ecologists to examine how combinations of life history characteristics evolve.

Many ecologists believe that patterns of survivorship can account for several features of an organism's typical pattern of reproduction. For example, if an individual has only a small chance of survival from one breeding season to the next, regardless of how large or how healthy it is, natural selection will favour its reproducing only once. Individuals that produce numerous offspring and then die would leave more offspring than individuals that wasted their resources in growth. By contrast, if an individual has a substantial chance of survival between breeding seasons, then natural selection might favour individuals that use some of their available resources for growth and some for reproduction. This simple logic likely explains why many plant species in harsh and unpredictable environments (such as deserts) are annuals and why many that inhabit more benign environments (such as tropical forests) are perennials.

A similar logic based on the survivorship of offspring has been used to explain why some organisms produce many young and some produce only a few. If the mortality of young individuals is high and attributable mainly to density-independent factors, natural selection would favour parents that use their resources to produce many offspring. Such parents are more likely to have a few offspring survive. Since this sort of selection would result in a population with a high intrinsic growth rate, it is commonly called *r-selection*; the life history characteristics associated with it are called *r*-selected traits.

In contrast, if an offspring's survival depends mainly on its own ability to obtain limited resources, natural selection would favour parents that use their resources to produce a few, highly competitive offspring. If the same resources were used to produce many smaller, poorly competitive offspring, the resources would be wasted since few of them would survive. The competition responsible for this type of selection would be common in populations that are at, or near, their carrying capacity. For this reason, the selection for life history traits brought about by competition has been termed **K-selection**; the life history characteristics commonly associated with it have been termed K-selected traits. Table 27.1 lists a variety of traits that have been suggested to evolve in populations experiencing *r*- and K-selection.

As discussed earlier, few distinctions in ecology are absolute, and the distinction between *r*- and K- selection is no exception. Probably no organism's pattern of reproduction is entirely a product of either *r*-selection or K-selection; each species' particular life history likely reflects the consequences of both. Nevertheless, the recognition that very different life history characteristics evolve in different environments has been useful for understanding the ecology of organisms found in different habitats such as deserts or tropical rainforests. In addition, the determination of why certain life history traits evolve has been useful for understanding many aspects of ecological succession. For example, life history evolution can explain why species with high reproductive rates are typical of early stages of ecological succession (at which time competition is often low) and why those with lower reproductive rates are typical of later stages of succession (at which point populations are likely near their carrying capacity).

Humans produce relatively few offspring, individuals reach sexual maturity relatively late in their lives, and the lifespan of humans is comparatively long. All of these life history characteristics suggest that for much of its evolutionary history, the human population has been at, or near, its carrying capacity. There are several lines of evidence from archaeologists, anthropologists, and historians that support this viewpoint. Nevertheless, approximately 10 000 years ago the human population entered into a period of extremely rapid growth that is still underway. Many aspects of the present ecology of the human species have been altered by this recent period of growth. The future survival of *Homo sapiens* will depend on whether the growth of the world population can be brought under control in the near future.

Table 27.1 Some Correlates of *r* and *K* Selection

	r SELECTION	*K* SELECTION
climate	variable and/or unpredictable; uncertain	fairly constant and/or predictable; more certain
mortality	often catastrophic density independent	more directed, density dependent
survivorship	high juvenile mortality	long average lifespan
population size	variable in time, usually well below carrying capacity of environment; unsaturated communities or portions thereof, recolonization each year	fairly constant in time, at or near carrying capacity of the environment; saturated communities; no recolonization necessary
intra- and inter-specific competition	variable, often lax	usually keen
selection favors	rapid development; high maximal rate of increase; early reproduction; small body size; single reproduction; many small offspring	slower development; greater competitive ability; delayed reproduction; larger body size; repeated reproduction; fewer larger progeny
stage in succession	early	late, climax

Source: After Pianka (1970).

CHAPTER SUMMARY

In ecology, collections of individuals of the same species living in the same place at the same time are called populations. Populations grow when birth and immigration rates exceed death and emigration rates.

A variety of different methods have been devised to estimate the size of natural populations and to use data on changes in population size to estimate population growth rates. Even in the absence of immigration and emigration, a population has the potential to grow exponentially if its birth rate exceeds its death rate. If allowed to grow, any organism's population would become large enough to cover the earth. Natural populations never grow this large, in part because their numbers are occasionally reduced by abiotic factors and in part because biotic factors associated with competition, predation, and parasitism often decrease birth rates and increase death rates.

Differences in the chances that individuals of different ages reproduce or die often result in populations being composed of different proportions of young and old individuals. The number of individuals in different age classes affects how rapidly and how large a population will grow.

Two important aspects of each species' life history are the number of times an individual reproduces and the number of offspring it has each time it does so. Differences in life histories likely evolve because of species-specific differences in the survival of individuals. From one species to another, there may be differences in habitat, in stages of succession, or in population sizes.

Objectives

Having completed this chapter, you should be able to do the following:

1. Explain what a population is and describe how ecologists estimate the size of populations of different organisms.
2. Predict how rapidly a population would grow and how large it would become if its growth were not regulated.
3. Describe how both abiotic and biotic factors keep natural populations from growing indefinitely.
4. Discuss why organisms with different life histories evolve in different kinds of environments.

Vocabulary

population
demography
immigrate
emigrate
population dynamics
natality
mortality
census
population estimate
quadrat
density
transect
capture-recapture technique
exponential growth
average annual increase

doubling time
biotic potential
r (intrinsic rate of increase)
abiotic factor
biotic factor
density-independent population
    regulation
J-shaped growth curve
sigmoidal growth
S-shaped growth curve
density-dependent population
    regulation
K (carrying capacity)
fecundity
survivorship

fertility
environmental resistance
age-specific survivorship
age-specific fecundity
total fertility rate (TFR)
replacement level fertility rate
zero population growth (ZPG)
age pyramid
expansive age structure
population growth momentum
constrictive age structure
stationary age structure
life history
r-selection
K-selection

Review Questions

1. In what ways are the populations of Canada Geese *on* Lake Ontario and Lake Trout *in* Lake Ontario different from one another?
2. Describe the general conditions that would cause the size of a population to
   (a) increase
   (b) decrease
   (c) stay the same.
3. Populations of all organisms have the capacity for exponential growth and yet some populations grow more rapidly than others. Why is this so?
4. Use the data in this table to calculate each country's annual percentage growth rates and doubling time.

COUNTRY	POPULATION SIZE IN MILLIONS		ANNUAL % INCREASE	DOUBLING TIME
	1977	1987		
Sweden	8.2	8.4		
Canada	23.5	25.9		
Ethiopia	29.4	46.0		
USSR	259.0	284.0		
India	622.7	800.3		
China	850.0	1062.0		
World	4083.0	5026.0		

5. Give an example of an organism with population growth regulated by
   (a) abiotic, density-independent factors
   (b) biotic, density-dependent factors.
6. Discuss the relationship between a biotic potential for growth by a population and the environmental resistance exerted on this growth.
7. Why might an environment's carrying capacity for a particular species change as its population grows?
8. Discuss how competition with other members of one's own species might regulate population growth.
9. How might predation or parasitism explain why a population's size does not increase indefinitely?
10. Use the concept of density-dependent population regulation to explain why a population might be expected to fluctuate rather than to stay at a constant size.
11. If a large proportion of the young animals in a population were killed in a particular year, how would that population's subsequent growth be affected?
12. Discuss the difference between the terms fecundity and fertility as they are applied to human population dynamics.
13. Why will the populations of currently developing countries make up a larger proportion of the world's population in the year 2025 than they do today?
14. The life histories of different organisms reflect the results of different kinds of selection. Give an example of each type of organism below. In doing so, consider why some species are regarded as pests or weeds and why others are considered endangered.
    (a) an *r*-selected plant
    (b) an *r*-selected animal
    (c) a K-selected plant
    (d) a K-selected animal

Advanced Questions

1. Describe two methods a fisheries ecologist might use to estimate the size of a population of some fish species. Gather information from commercial fishermen about how much effort they put into fishing and from sport fishermen about whether any of the fish they have caught were tagged.
2. In order to estimate the size of a population of oak trees, a forester runs several 100 m transects through a 100 ha woodlot and counts the number of oaks whose trunks fall within 5 m of the line. Five transects produced the following results: 15, 17, 25, 16, 20.
   (a) What is the density of oaks in the woodlot?
   (b) How big would the population of oaks be?

3. Brewers' yeast is a type of ascomycete fungus that produces ethyl alcohol as a waste product of its metabolism. Reproduction most often occurs asexually, by the budding of one cell off another. For present purposes, consider this to be a case of the production of two offspring and the death of the parent. Under certain conditions, yeast reproduce every 15 min.

   (a) If a small amount of yeast (say 500 cells) were used to start a brew, how many cells would be present after 24 h of growing?

   (b) What do you think naturally limits the growth of yeast populations?

4. In British Columbia, pink salmon spawn in fresh water streams that connect with the Pacific ocean. The eggs hatch and the young fish migrate to the ocean, where they spend two years feeding and growing to sexual maturity. In the summer of their second year, the adults migrate back to the waters of their home stream, spawn, and then die. Female pink salmon produce an average of about 2000 eggs (of which about 1000 are female). Only about three percent of these eggs turn into salmon that successfully return to spawn two years later, in part because of natural predation and in part because of fishing.

   (a) How large would a stream's population be in ten years if it started out at 100 individuals?

   (b) What might keep pink salmon populations from realizing their potential for growth?

5. Canada's population in 1980 was approximately 23.8 million people. The birth rate was estimated to be 15.4 births per thousand persons and the death rate 7.2 individuals per thousand. If no immigration had occurred in 1980, how large should Canada's population have been in 1981?

CHAPTER 28

HUMAN ECOLOGY

We can change the world
Rearrange the world
We've got to: it's dying

Graham Nash

One thousand years ago an anonymous artist near Peterborough, Ontario pictured a day in his or her life in a rock painting. In its depiction of a small group of human hunters in pursuit of a variety of animal prey, the scene captures the essence of the close interaction that the human species has had with the natural environment for most of its history. Since the time when this picture was painted, the global human population has grown one thousand times. As a consequence of the relentless demands for food, energy, and materials that this population makes on the planet, reserves of some resources have been badly depleted and the supplies of others are threatened. With the prospect of the world population doubling or even tripling in the next century, a plan is urgently needed to develop and conserve natural resources and to protect the only environment that is known to support human life.

28.1 HUMAN DEMOGRAPHY

Ecology aims in general to understand how the biotic and abiotic components of a species' environment affect its abundance and distribution. Although it has this same basic goal, the science of human ecology in particular is faced with several unique problems, which have arisen from the human ability to modify environments. One such problem is that many environments are not naturally suited to human habitation, yet humans have learned to survive in them and to exploit their resources, often with adverse consequences for those environments. Another problem is that the human population has grown more rapidly and to a larger size than would have been possible without these environmental modifications. Consequently, severe pressures now exist both on the environments and on the human populations living in them.

Therefore, the study of human ecology focusses primarily on questions of how the resources available on the earth can support current and future human populations. Any discussion of human ecology must thus begin with an examination of the demography of the global human population.

Historical Changes in Human Population Growth

The world's population has changed greatly since humans evolved. Many of the changes have been shown to be the direct result of historical developments, such as the agricultural, industrial, or technological revolutions. In order to understand how the human population came to have its present make-up and how future populations are likely to change, the way human demography has been shaped by the events of the past must first be understood.

Any historical account of human demography cannot avoid a certain amount of guesswork. Although most countries have conducted censuses in recent decades, an enumeration of all of the people in the world has *never* been carried out. The size of the world population before the mid-twentieth century is even more uncertain because estimates are based on incomplete information; for example, the extremely large populations of India and China were not reliably censused until 1871 and 1953 respectively. Demographers have had to rely on even less complete information to estimate the size of earlier human populations. For example, the size of the population of the Roman Empire is most often estimated from administrative records such as taxation rolls. Estimates of the size of the human population before recorded history are lit-

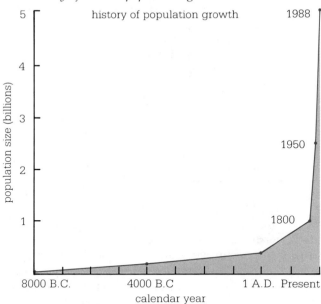

Figure 28.1
The history of human population growth

tle more than educated guesses. Scholars believe that the prehistoric environment could only have supported a human population of between five and ten million people that made a living by hunting and gathering food. Nevertheless what information is available has permitted demographers to piece together a history of the changes that the human population has experienced over the last 10 000 years. One point on which all demographers agree is that for most of its history the human population was relatively small (Figure 28.1).

Changes Brought about by the Agricultural Revolution
A benchmark for the history of the human population occurred in approximately 8000 B.C. Archaeological evidence shows that around this time, some human populations shifted from hunting and gathering food to the domestication of animals and the cultivation of crops. As agricultural practices spread, the human population grew continuously; in the 8000 years up to approximately 1 A.D., it increased from about ten million to around 300 million people.

Some disagreement exists concerning the effect that this **agricultural revolution** had on the early period of population growth. All that is known for certain is that during this period, the size of the world population increased dramatically. Some historians argue that these increases were caused by lower death rates attributable to the presence of assured supplies of food. Others contend that death rates would likely have remained high because infectious diseases and unforeseen crop failures would have killed large numbers of people. Instead, they argue that better nutrition would have produced a higher birth rate through higher female fecundity and would thus have offset a still persistently high death rate. Undoubtedly both factors had some effect.

Figure 28.1 shows that the increase in the size of the human population during this early period of expansion was modest compared to later increases. Indeed, the rate of increase up to about 1 A.D. can be calculated as only about 0.36 per 1000 persons. Most authorities agree that this rate of growth reflects both a high birth rate (a total fertility rate of approximately 6.5 to 8.5 births per female) and a high death rate (an average lifespan of only 15 to 20 years of age).

Between 1 A.D. and 1000 A.D., the human population either exhibited very little growth, or did not grow at all. Some historians attribute this apparent lack of growth to catastrophic losses of human lives that accompanied political upheavals. However, between 1000 and 1750 A.D. the human population is estimated to have more than doubled, from 300 million to approximately 750 million people. This increase would undoubtedly have been much larger had it not been for outbreaks of disease. For example, the Black Death devastated the population of Europe during the mid-fourteenth century; historians estimate that it wiped out about a third of Europe's population. When the entire period from 1 A.D. to 1750 is considered, the human population's growth rate was only slightly higher than it was during earlier periods. Most estimates of the growth rate are around 0.56 per 1000 persons. As during earlier periods of human history, high birth rates were balanced by high death rates.

Demographic Changes from 1750 to 1950

The year 1750 A.D. is another benchmark for human demographers. One reason why this date is considered so important is that it was the first year in which any country began conducting a census at regular intervals. This country was Sweden, and because continuous records are available, the transitions that occurred in growth of the Swedish population can be accurately charted (Figure 28.2). Perhaps more importantly, changes in the size of the Swedish population can be directly related to various sorts of social and cultural change, such as the growth of urban centres and the spread of knowledge about how to treat various sorts of disease. A second reason why 1750 is an

Figure 28.2
Both the birth and the death rates in Sweden have fallen more or less continuously since 1750; they have been converging since about 1900. Since the end of 1976, the size of the Swedish population has essentially stabilized; currently it remains very near zero population growth.

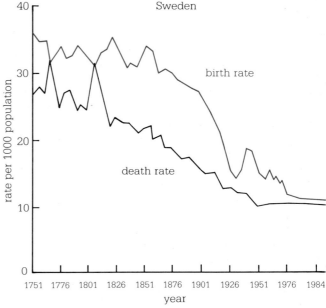

important date for demographers is that during the next 200 years, the global population was destined to double twice, in the process producing a population of approximately 2.5 billion people. Historians can, therefore, identify the combination of events on a global scale that led to this explosive period of population growth.

The growth rate of the human population increased from 4.4 per thousand people between 1750 and 1800 to approximately 7.9 per thousand in 1950. During the period 1750–1850, the European population and European colonies in North America and the South Pacific were responsible for much of this increase. However, in the period 1850–1950, the growth of the European population slowed; a much larger portion of the increase was because of the growth of populations in Africa, Asia, and Latin America.

The stabilization of the growth of the European population likely occurred because of distinct shifts in both death and birth rates. Between 1750 and 1850, death rates among Europeans decreased for three principal reasons. One was improved sanitary conditions; another was a developing medical technology that led to the prevention and treatment of several

Figure 28.3

Survivorship data for the City of Toronto. These data come from the records of Mount Pleasant Cemetery, one of the oldest cemeteries in Canada. Three ten-year periods were *chosen and the age-at-death was recorded for 1000 entries. True survivorship curves for these periods resemble these quite closely.*

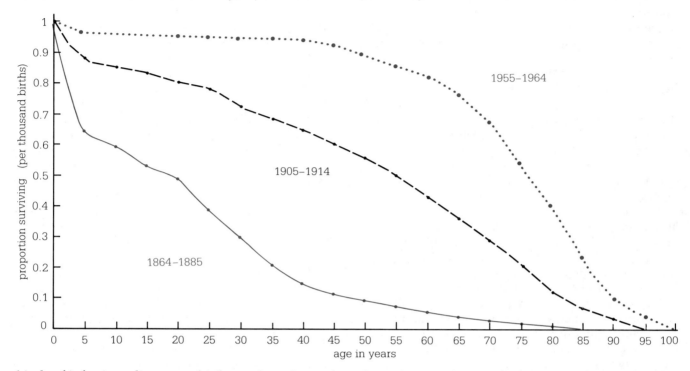

kinds of infectious disease; a third was the enhanced nutrition that came with the exchange among cultures of staple foodstuffs such as potatoes and corn. There was a corresponding decline in birth rates. In Sweden, between 1850 and 1950, the number of births fell from slightly more than 30 to slightly less than 15 births per thousand. This decline in the birth rate paralleled closely the growth of the **industrial revolution** and occurred, in part, because of a shift in the perceived benefits of having a large family in an industrial society. In rural societies, the cost of raising children is minimal and each child can contribute to the family's income and well-being from an early age. However, in an urban setting, education is compulsory and is costly, since child labour is prohibited. Both of these factors conspire against large families and thus lower the birth rate.

The **demographic transition** from high birth and death rates to very much lower ones is characteristic of the development of *all* industrialized societies. One reason for a decline in the death rate between the mid-1800s and the mid-1900s can be seen in the survivorship of the population of Toronto (Figure 28.3). During

the mid-1800s, this population showed the high infant mortality typical of many rural communities of that era. Over the next 100 years, the average lifespan gradually increased as both infant and adult mortality rates dropped. Figure 28.4 shows that this shift in survivorship was associated with a shift in the causes of death. Although the incidence of stillbirths and accidental death remained remarkably constant, death due to infectious diseases (such as typhoid) became much less common and degenerative diseases (such as heart disease) became a more frequent cause of death.

The decrease in the incidence of infant deaths between 1850 and 1900 came about to a large extent because of simple patent medicines that could control fever and diarrhea. The later decreases in the frequency with which adults were dying was mainly the result of improved sanitation and accessible hospital care. The development of a medical technology to treat some diseases (such as diabetes) and immunize against others (such as polio) also had a major effect on the age structure of Toronto's population.

The rapid increase in the size of the world popula-

Figure 28.4

Changes in the cause of death in the population of Toronto since the mid-1800s. The data used to produce this graph were the same as those used in Figure 28.3. Notice how in each decade, the incidence of stillbirths and accidental deaths remains more or less constant. What might cause this constancy?

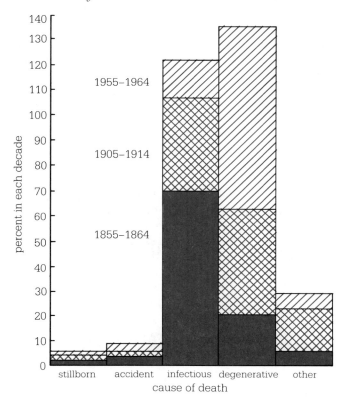

early 1970s the rate of increase (the difference between birth and death rates) was as high as 17 per thousand persons. This represented an annual rate of increase of nearly two percent. The enormous *number* of people added to the population (2.5 billion) occurred simply because this high growth rate was applied to populations that were already large. As much as 85 percent of this growth occurred in the populations of the developing countries of the world, again mainly in Asia, Africa, and Latin America.

Recently, the growth of the human population has been slowing down. Since 1970, the growth rates of most countries in the world have fallen steadily. At present, extremely high growth rates are typically found only among countries in tropical regions of the world. The decrease in growth rates in most others has been brought about because of decreases in the birth rate. As was the case with the European population in the last century, lower birth rates typically accompany a shift to an industrial economy; most developing countries are in the middle of such a shift. However, the transition to lower birth rates has been accelerated in developing countries for two additional reasons: an improvement in the status and education of women and more widespread access to information about family planning.

The greatest impact on the growth rate of the world population has come about because of dramatic changes in the birth rate in China. In the early 1970s the government of China came to believe that it had neither the resources nor the wealth needed to sustain its population's high growth rate. It therefore penalized couples that had more than one child. Not surprisingly, the fertility rate in China has fallen precipitously since those restrictions came into being. Since China accounts for such a large proportion of the world population (currently about one fifth), the decrease in the rate at which the Chinese population grows has a large effect on the statistics for the growth of the entire global population.

tion by 1950 was also associated with a decrease in the death rate — in this case affecting the populations in Asia, Africa, and Latin America. Undoubtedly the introduction of modern medical technology after World War II was a major factor in the decrease of deaths due to infectious disease in these areas of the world. Mainly because the shift from an agricultural to an industrial society has occurred only slowly in these regions, birth rates have remained higher than death rates. This difference produced the subsequent period of extremely rapid population growth.

Recent Patterns of Population Growth

Since 1950, the human population has doubled once again; on July 5th, 1987, the United Nations estimated that the size of the human population had reached the five billion mark. The world population doubled so quickly for a very simple reason: in the late 1960s and

Future Changes in the Size of the Human Population

The exact size of future human populations is impossible to predict accurately. As in earlier ages, changes in other aspects of human culture, such as medical breakthroughs, will influence the future birth and death rates. However, projections can be made by making certain assumptions about future birth and death rates.

Figure 28.5

Three projected patterns of growth for the population of Africa. Depending on the date one takes for the attainment of replacement level fertility, Africa's population may stabilize soon or not until the twenty-second century. How is the momentum for population growth in developing countries included in these predictions?

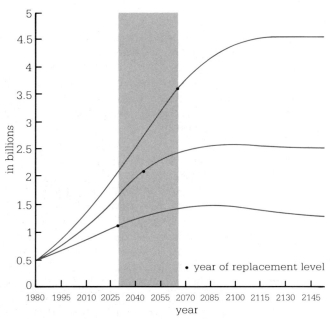

Figure 28.5 illustrates how projections about future size of the population in Africa will differ when different assumptions are made about future fertility rates. If replacement level fertility (2.1 births per couple) is reached by 2030, the population of Africa will stabilize at 1.2 billion people. However, if replacement fertility is not achieved until 2045, then the size of the African population will not stabilize until it has reached 2.5 billion people. If replacement fertility is not attained until 2065, the final population size in Africa will be 4.5 billion people—the size of the entire world population in 1980! Using similar calculations on a worldwide scale, demographers suggest that the world population will probably stabilize at between 7.5 and 10 billion people around the end of the twenty-first century. Again, the accuracy of these predictions is entirely dependent on the continuation of trends toward lower fertility rates.

Demography and the Technological Revolution
Currently the world is in the midst of its third great revolution — what has been called the **technological revolution**. The development of technologies to trans-port people and materials efficiently, to process and communicate enormous amounts of information, and to control both minute and massive manufacturing processes promises to change almost every aspect of human life. These changes will encompass everything from the harvest of untapped resources to the manipulation of the genetic code for life itself.

Some would argue that it has been technology, especially medical technology, that has permitted the world population to become as large as it currently is and that this technology therefore can support future increases. Many more contend that the technological developments needed to sustain a world population two to three times its current size cannot come rapidly enough to satisfy the population's needs.

One of the greatest challenges to human ecology is that the global population avoid future periods of growth such as the one that characterized the period between 1950 and 1980. To ensure that such growth does not occur will require that world leaders deal with some of the most difficult ethical issues humankind has ever faced. Nevertheless, it is essential that these issues are dealt with and not ignored. The global resources needed to sustain the world's human population are *already* limited and the well-being of *all* humanity, both today and in the future, depends on the stabilization of world population growth.

28.2 RESOURCE MANAGEMENT AND CONSERVATION

The ultimate size at which the world population stabilizes will depend on many factors, but one conclusion is certain: when it does stabilize, the human population will be larger than it has ever been before. As the human population grows, there will be an ever-increasing demand on the planet's ability to provide food, shelter, and energy resources. Our species has wrongly acted as if the supplies of these resources were inexhaustible; it cannot continue to do so.

The biosphere has a finite supply of non-living, **non-renewable resources** (such as minerals) and has a limited capacity to produce new materials (such as food) from its living, **renewable resources**. In many ways, the management of these resources to meet the needs of the world's population is a simple economic problem. Imagine that the earth's resources are like the balance in a savings account that pays interest continually. The demands of the population must not exceed the interest yielded by this balance; if its demands are too high, then the savings will have to be used to satisfy the demand. As the savings are depleted, those remaining will produce less interest and thus future populations will have to dip more deeply into the savings to satisfy their demands. Eventually the savings will be depleted completely.

In order to ensure an availability of resources sufficient to meet the demands of the current population, some of the planet's unexploited resources will have to be developed in the near future. However, to ensure that there will be a **sustainable yield** from those resources that remain, a portion of the earth's resources will have to be conserved. Only through conservation will the planet's resources be able to yield their bounty to future generations. The greatest challenge to the wise managment of the world's resources is to combine development with conservation. This challenge entails both taking an inventory of the supplies of goods and services that are available and understanding the demands that the current population is making on these supplies.

Production of Food for a Hungry World

The vast majority of the world's population currently depends on agriculture for food; as the population grows and becomes more concentrated into cities, this reliance on agriculture will become even greater. Nevertheless, only about 11 percent of the world's land area offers no serious limitation to agriculture; the remainder is subject to drought, mineral stress, shallow soils, permafrost, or excess water. To make matters worse, the best agricultural land is not evenly distributed—the regions of the world with the largest populations have the smallest proportions of arable land. Thus, either enormous amounts of energy will be required to move the products of agriculture to the people or the world's population will have to be dramatically redistributed.

Availability of Cropland and the Effects of Soil Degradation

The world's croplands currently occupy about 1.4×10^6 km². While it may be possible to double this area in the future, much of the most highly productive land is already under cultivation. Sadly, since humans prefer to live close to their breadbaskets, large areas of agricultural land are being lost to urban development. In developed countries alone, 3000 km² of prime agricultural land are being swallowed up every year by housing, industrial developments, and shopping malls. Even worse, it has been estimated that in the next 20 years one third of the world's arable land will

Figure 28.6
Erosion in prairie and coastal habitats. All terrestrial habitats are vulnerable to erosion.

be destroyed if current rates of land degradation continue! The greatest threats to future agricultural development come from the continued erosion of topsoil and the formation of deserts on grazing lands, a process called **desertification** (Figure 28.6).

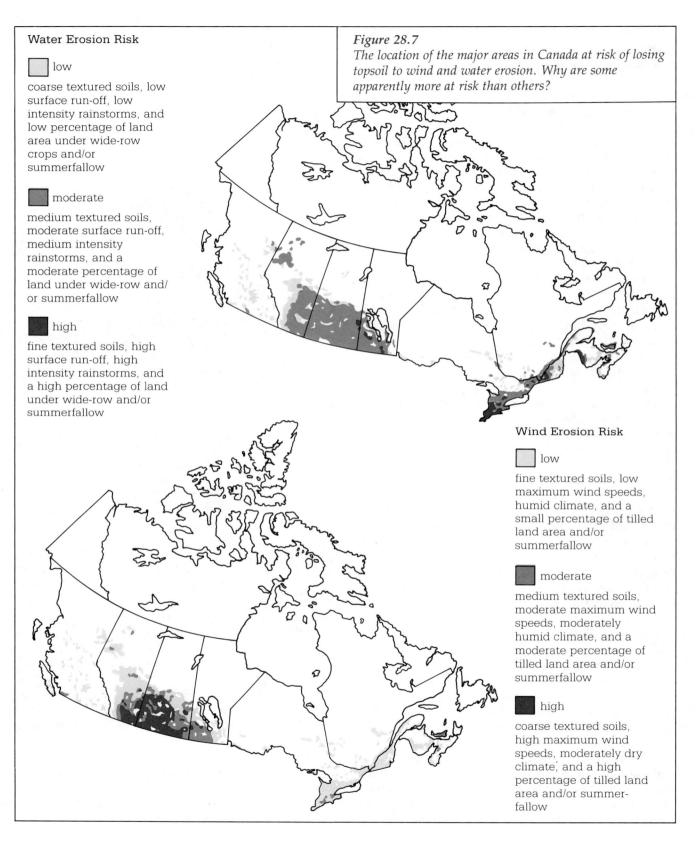

Water Erosion Risk

[ ] low

coarse textured soils, low surface run-off, low intensity rainstorms, and low percentage of land area under wide-row crops and/or summerfallow

[ ] moderate

medium textured soils, moderate surface run-off, medium intensity rainstorms, and a moderate percentage of land under wide-row and/or summerfallow

[ ] high

fine textured soils, high surface run-off, high intensity rainstorms, and a high percentage of land under wide-row and/or summerfallow

Figure 28.7
The location of the major areas in Canada at risk of losing topsoil to wind and water erosion. Why are some apparently more at risk than others?

Wind Erosion Risk

[ ] low

fine textured soils, low maximum wind speeds, humid climate, and a small percentage of tilled land area and/or summerfallow

[ ] moderate

medium textured soils, moderate maximum wind speeds, moderately humid climate, and a moderate percentage of tilled land area and/or summerfallow

[ ] high

coarse textured soils, high maximum wind speeds, moderately dry climate, and a high percentage of tilled land area and/or summer-fallow

Figure 28.8
The spread of desert in the Senegal region of Africa. The rate of this desert's spread is approximately 2 km per year —almost 1000 times more rapid than that of a glacier's spread.

Erosion occurs as wind and water move topsoil into rivers, lakes, and oceans; these agents also move soil into reservoirs of drinking water and hydro-electric dams. In undisturbed habitats, the roots of plants hold soil in place and topsoil is eroded at approximately the rate at which it is regenerated by dying vegetation. The accumulation of topsoil is, therefore, exceedingly slow; it would take about 1000 years to naturally generate a layer of topsoil the depth that this page is long. However, when the proportion of vegetation and soil fall out of balance, as they often do in poorly managed agricultural systems, erosion is accelerated. Figure 28.7 shows that the areas of Canada that are at the highest risk of wind and water erosion are also those that are the most valuable pieces of agricultural land.

The other major threat to the future of agricultural development comes from the mismanagement of land used for grazing domestic animals. Approximately 3×10^6 km² around the world are used for grazing. Much of this land is unsuitable for growing crops because of low or irregular rainfall. This area supports approximately 30 billion grazing animals that are responsible for most of the world's meat and milk production. In mountainous regions, particularly the Andes and Himalayas, the removal of grass and shrubs by livestock has accelerated soil erosion. In turn, this erosion has led to flooding and silt deposition, rendering several hydro-electric projects in the adjacent developing countries very expensive to maintain. Overstocking has severely degraded much of the grazing land in several areas of North Africa and is the major cause of the expansion of the Sahara and other desert regions (Figure 28.8). The United Nations has identified desertification as a major cause of famine in these regions of the world and as a threat to the well-being of all future generations.

Importance of Genetic Diversity for the Maintenance of High Yields
The selective breeding of wild plants and animals has led to the current high yields, nutritional quality, and resistance to pests and disease that are typically achieved by modern agricultural techniques. However, these qualities are rarely (if ever) permanent. In most cases, pests and disease organisms evolve new strains that overcome a particular variety's resistance. Modern agriculture relies heavily on continued research to keep farmers "one step ahead" in this

struggle. Nevertheless, in an attempt to maximize profits, agriculturalists have tended to concentrate on growing only the highest-yielding varieties. For example, only four varieties of wheat account for three quarters of the entire crop grown on the Canadian prairies; more than half comes from a single variety (Neepawa). The same can be said of almost any crop in high production. Such a concentration on single varieties is an invitation to disaster. If pests or disease-producing organisms get the upper hand, the production of an entire industry could be lost, with fatal consequences for much of the human population.

Such an agricultural disaster nearly happened to European grape producers in the last century. In the 1860s, an insect pest which lived on and destroyed the roots of the grape vine was introduced to Europe from North America. In many regions, every vineyard was destroyed before it was discovered that the native North American vines were naturally tolerant of the pest. Europe's grape and wine industry was saved only by grafting European vines onto American rootstocks, a practice that continues today.

The lesson to be learned from this example is that for future breeding programmes to be successful in combatting yet unknown threats to crops and livestock, a **genetic library** of characteristics must be available for selective breeding purposes. Ironically, many of the native varieties from which cultivated and domesticated stocks have been bred are themselves dangerously close to extinction, often because of the destruction of their natural habitats for agriculture!

Harvesting Food from the World's Oceans
The bounty of the sea has been traditionally viewed as inexhaustible. Figure 28.9 shows that in terms of the energy needed to produce protein from a variety of sources, seafood (mainly fish, crustaceans, and molluscs) is also one of the most economical forms of food. Indeed, seafood is the mainstay of the table in many cultures. There are 32 countries worldwide which currently obtain more than one third of the animal protein in their diet from marine organisms. Seafood is particularly important in developing countries where catches have traditionally been both more reliable and less expensive than many alternative agricultural products.

However the world's fisheries have not been managed as well as they should have been. Overfishing has been so heavy that the worldwide marine catch is now less than three-quarters of what its potential would otherwise have been; at least 25 of the world's most valuable fisheries are seriously depleted. The consequence of this overexploitation of the cod fishery in the northwest Atlantic is illustrated in Figure 28.10. Currently, this fishery is producing only about a third of its previously estimated potential.

Figure 28.9
The energy (in kilojoules) used to produce a gram of protein in unprocessed foods. Relatively speaking, various kinds of seafood are cheap to produce. Why is this so?

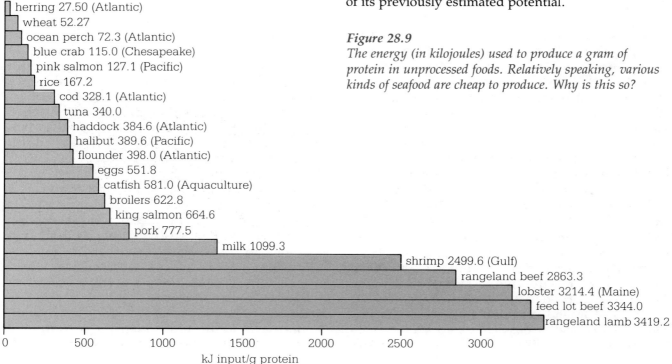

Figure 28.10

Changes in Canada's and the world's catch of cod in the northwest Atlantic. Canada's catch has actually increased slightly in the last 20 years, but much of this increase is due to a 1977 ruling that extended the territorial waters to *320 km offshore. The decline in the world's cod catch from these waters since the late 1960s is best explained by a decrease in the size of the cod population attributable to previous overfishing.*

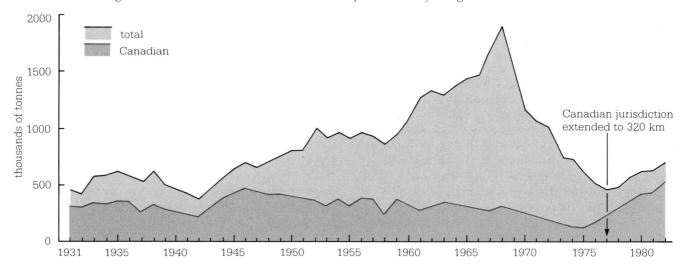

Another serious threat to the world's fisheries is the destruction of coastal wetlands that serve as spawning beds and nurseries for some of the most productive species. The main factors responsible for this destruction are the use of the wetlands for recreation and housing and their suffocation by silt from accelerated erosion. In addition, wetlands are used in many countries, either illegally or legally, as disposal sites for toxic chemicals and human sewage — both of which render these habitats unproductive for many of the most important commercial species.

One of the most tragic consequences of overfishing has been the **accidental take** of species not intended to be caught. The process is not only wasteful, destroying an estimated seven million tonnes of fish every year, but it also threatens to drive to extinction many species. The list of endangered species includes many marine mammals and several species of sea turtle. To many, the mismanagement of a resource as important as the world's fisheries has come to symbolize the disregard too many people have for living things.

It is a sad fact that because of past and present over-exploitation of the world's fisheries, the current level of the use of seafood as a protein source cannot be sustained, let alone expanded. Many believe that the ocean's fisheries are resilient enough to recover fully from the catches of the past century. Given sufficient

Figure 28.11

Farming fish in British Columbia. What might be some of the future problems with the use of aquaculture to meet the world's demands for food?

time, this recovery is a distinct possibility. It would, however, require a unified effort by all countries that have a fishing fleet; at present, this kind of international agreement seems unlikely. One alternative being explored with some success is fish farming (Figure 28.11). Experimental systems in several parts of the world are proving very productive. Yet the initial costs of establishing the industry are high and the endeavour will undoubtedly be plagued by problems analogous to those faced by other agricultural systems.

Development of Supplies of Material Resources and Energy

In both developing and industrialized countries, forests and woodlands have unquestioned importance for industry and commerce. These habitats provide lumber and construction materials that produce as much as $120 billion revenue annually. In addition, forests and woodlands produce the fuelwood for an estimated 1.5 billion people in developing countries. Wood is their only economical source of fuel for heat and for cooking. More than 10^9 m^3 of wood are consumed annually for these purposes.

However, forests also have a vital effect on processes that are of great significance to all living things. For example, forests and woodlands act on a local scale to protect soil from erosion. In so doing, these habitats also cleanse water supplies, an example of an **ecosystem service**. Some forests, notably tropical cloud forests (Figure 28.12), also increase the local availability of water by intercepting it from clouds. On a slightly broader scale, forests influence the climate; they generally make regional climates more moderate by screening the solar radiation from the ground. Because of the great amount of plant biomass they contain, forests are extremely important at the global level for their role in the production of oxygen through photosynthesis.

Figure 28.12
Part of the tropical cloud forest in Monteverde, Costa Rica. Among its many services, this forest produces an abundance of various sorts of food, makes wood available for fuel and building materials, captures and cleanses water supplies, and even contributes to the air we breathe. Isn't it about time it was treated with a little respect?

A large number of the drugs used to treat human ailments are derived from plants that grow in the tropical regions of the world. One example is *vincaleucoblastine*, a substance that is derived from the Madagascar periwinkle and used to treat leukemia.

The discovery that a particular substance has a property that is useful in the treatment of a disease is often linked to the fact that a particular plant has been used traditionally to treat related ailments with herbal medicines. This knowledge is used to chemically isolate the active ingredient and then to extract and purify it or to synthesize a chemical analog. With the almost infinite variety of ways that atoms can be rearranged to produce complex molecules, pharmacists need the sort of insight that comes from natural substances to produce a working product.

Research into the traditional use of plant substances to treat the symptoms of human ailments by tribal medicine practitioners and shamans will undoubtedly continue to provide insights into their applications in modern medicine. However, in order to provide these

All substances used to treat leukemia and other forms of cancer have complex chemical make-ups and complicated three dimensional "shapes" that interfere with the functioning of the diseased cells.

$$R = CH_3$$

insights, native plants must be available for chemical dissection. The development of tropical regions of the world is resulting in the loss of natural habitats. Along with the loss of the native plants that are thus driven to extinction are the lost possibilities that these plants could offer to treat human disease. This simple fact is just one justification for the conservation of all ecosystems, but particularly those in the tropics.

Despite these unquestioned benefits, the world's forests and woodlands are being destroyed at an alarming rate. The effects of an intensive demand for firewood in many developing countries has denuded large areas of woodland. In Gambia, for instance, it requires an average 360 days every year per family simply to gather enough fuelwood for cooking and heating. The clearing of rainforests in the tropics, both to produce lumber and to increase the amount of agricultural land, is occurring unbelievably quickly. Every minute of every day, an area the size of two ice hockey rinks is being bulldozed, burnt over, or flooded. The result is that every year an area of tropical forest the size of the United Kingdom is being lost. In Ontario

and Quebec, over 80 000 ha of temperate forest (producing approximately 5×10^6 m^3 of wood) are harvested annually; at present, only about one fifth of the area harvested is being replanted for the future.

The tragic irony of the development of rich tropical rainforests for agricultural land is that the soils that support these rainforests are extremely thin and nutrient-poor. Most of the nutrients in the rainforest are tied up in the living tissue of the plants above the ground. When the forest is cut and burned, the nutrients are either lost immediately to the atmosphere or washed away with the first rain. Crops are sustainable on such soils for only a few years, after which even more forest must be cleared. Since the original forest required thousands of years to generate, lost forever are both the services that this ecosystem provides and many of the unique life forms that it supports.

The World Wildlife Fund estimates that, mainly on account of the rapidity with which tropical forests are being destroyed, 1000 species of organisms are being driven to extinction every year (the number may be as high as 10 000). We will never know whether one of these disappeared species could have provided the key to breeding a disease resistance into a threatened crop variety or could have provided the raw material needed to cure a human disease. Currently, about three quarters of the pharmaceutical products manufactured in Canada use natural plant substances. In some cases, the plant substance is actually the active ingredient in a drug; in others, the plant substance provided the inspiration that led to the synthesis of the active ingredient.

Development and Conservation of Material Resources
Modern industry relies on a variety of different materials, all of which share one attribute: they originate from resources that are present only in finite quantities. For example, the manufacture of an automobile uses dozens of such materials, including steel, aluminum, glass, copper, nickle, chrome, and vinyl. Even platinum, mercury, and phosphorus are required for special tasks. Each of these substances is required because, by its particular chemistry, it has properties that make it useful for particular functions. However, this chemical uniqueness also means that substances are not interconvertible. (The alchemists of the Middle Ages tried to convert base metals into gold; modern metallurgy has only been successful in creating just a few sophisticated alloys.) Only those reserves in the earth's crust are currently accessible for development, and they are non-renewable; that is, once current supplies are used up the substance is gone forever (or at least a very long time).

For certain, the richest reserves of most minerals have not yet been exploited. The exact location of most of those on the earth are probably not even known because they lie beneath the oceans. Another potential source of raw materials lies beyond the limits of the earth. The moon, the other planets in this solar system, and all those in the galaxy are unexploited. The technology needed to develop these reserves commercially is not available and probably will not be in the near future. For now, the exploitation of these resources is still science fiction, not an engineering fact.

One characteristic of many metals forged from minerals is that they retain their particular physical properties long after they are cast in an original form. For example, steel retains the properties of iron. It only makes sense, therefore, that materials currently in use be re-used once the function served by their original casting has been fulfilled. Yet the record of industrial society in recycling has been less than admirable. For example, Metropolitan Toronto alone produces 5000 t of garbage annually. It has been shown that as little as 15 percent of this "waste" is non-recyclable (mainly plastics). The remaining categories of materials are present in the following quantities: 30 percent paper and paper products; 30 percent aluminum and other recyclable metals; and 15 percent degradable organic material.

The enormous amount of garbage that municipalities all over the world produce is dealt with in one of three ways: it is incinerated (in which case carbon dioxide, particulate matter, and hazardous chemicals are all injected into the atmosphere); it is buried in landfill sites (in which case water supplies are jeopardized); or it is simply dumped into a lake or ocean. Currently, landfill sites that were destined to be used until the turn of the century have been filled beyond capacity. In order to keep the costs of transporting the waste to a minimum, the proposed locations for future sites often lie on prime agricultural land near cities. The choice of a site does not always meet with the approval of people who would have to live near them (Figure 28.13). It has been estimated that if proper recycling measures had been instituted 15 years ago, landfills that are currently over their capacity would have lasted another 50 years!

As currently available reserves of non-renewable resources become more scarce and the costs of developing untapped reserves grows, recycling will become economically feasible. Indeed, today's garbage will be tomorrow's gold. However, recycling is currently perceived by many as more a matter of conscience than it is a matter of economics or necessity. Future generations will not be able to afford the luxuries of a "throw-away" society; ours cannot continue its wasteful practices, which use up precious supplies of another resource—energy.

Development and Conservation of Energy Resources
Whether it involves agriculture, fishing, forestry, or mining, the development of natural resources requires enormous amounts of energy. Industrial development makes additional demands for energy, both for man-

Figure 28.13
This community has something to complain about. Already this township in southern Ontario houses two landfill sites for Metropolitan Toronto and has disposed of 15.5×10^6 t of refuse. Many nearby residents object to the aromas from the decaying organic matter; the potential dangers from improperly disposed-of household cleaners, batteries, and hazardous wastes are a greater threat to health.

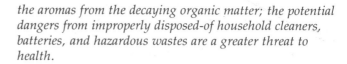

ufacturing processes and for transportation of its workers to and from the workplace. Finally, energy is required to heat or cool homes and to cook meals. As the world population grows and as the countries in the developing world make a transition to an industrial economy, the world's energy demands will increase even more rapidly. One of the greatest challenges for the future will be the meeting of these demands.

On a per individual basis, Canada's energy consumption has increased over the last two decades; its rate of consumption is currently among the highest in the world (Figure 28.14). Part of the increase is attributable to rapid industrial development, but the demand for energy has grown in each sector of the economy by about the same proportion. Although the populations in developing countries are large, each individual's demands are relatively small, much smaller than those of individuals in industrialized nations.

Currently, fossil fuels (mainly coal, oil, and natural gas) are the primary sources of energy for industrialized nations. In Canada, over 80 percent of the country's energy requirements are met by fossil fuels. However, as is the case with all other non-renewable resources, there is only a finite supply of fossil fuel contained in or below the earth's crust. The reserves currently being exploited were formed from biological and geological processes acting on the bodies of plants and animals over the past 200 to 300 million years. Large reserves of fossil fuels may exist under the polar ice or under the seas. Again, as current reserves are

Figure 28.14
The per capita energy demands of Canada and other countries. Only the energy demands of the countries with the highest consumption are illustrated. For reference purposes, most developing countries would have a per capita consumption roughly equal to that of the United Arab Emirates in 1965. Why have this latter country's energy demands risen so dramatically? How is it that the United Kingdom actually has a smaller per capita consumption now than it did in 1965?

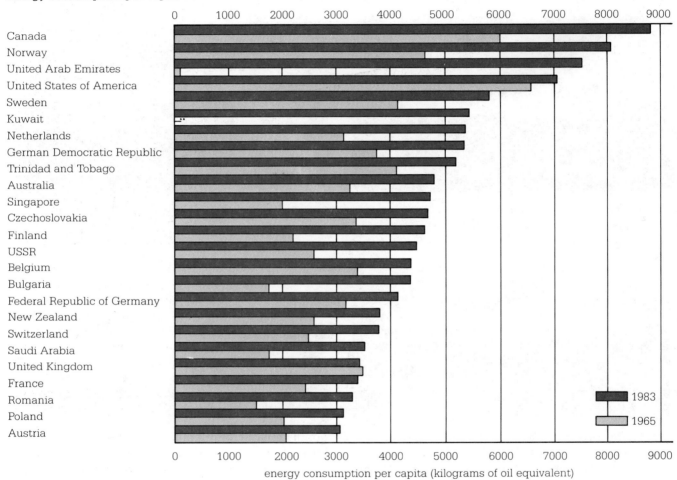

Energy consumption per capita in selected countries, 1965 and 1983

energy consumption per capita (kilograms of oil equivalent)

depleted, it may be economical to develop unexploited reserves. Yet the technology needed to extract those resources is in its infancy and may not mature as rapidly as will the world's needs.

The combustion of fossil fuels to provide energy results in the production of carbon dioxide and several by-products of impurities in the fuel. When human activities inject these compounds into the air, the ensuing **atmospheric contamination** threatens all life on the earth (Section 28.3). In addition, mining fossil fuels (particularly coal) often requires that the land overlaying the resource be cleared, thus making it unusable for agriculture, forestry, or other activities.

Finally, the transportation of supplies of fossil fuels, particularly the shipping of crude oil in tankers, has proven to be an accident prone endeavour. Oil spills have led to an enormous amount of environmental damage and to the loss of several important fisheries (Figure 28.15).

Since the reserves of fossil fuels are finite, and the extraction, transportation, and combustion of them are all environmentally dangerous activities, future generations cannot rely as heavily as does ours on these resources. The answer to the world's energy demands undoubtedly lies in the development of alternative energy resources. Nevertheless, each one

Figure 28.15
Seabirds are not the only victims of an oil spill. Spawning grounds, shellfish beds, and fisheries can be severely damaged as well as the economy of the affected seaside community. It can cost over ten million dollars to clean up an oil spill.

Figure 28.16
One of Ontario's largest hydro-electric generating plants, Sir Adam Beck, at Niagara Falls, Ontario.

of the current alternatives has drawbacks of its own.

Hydro-electric power has been a major source of energy in Canada for the past 50 years. In the generation of hydro-electric power, water turns turbines which generate electricity. The water may be naturally falling over a waterfall, moving through a dam, or pushed by a tide (Figure 28.16). Hydro accounts for approximately three quarters of Canada's electric energy generation; in turn, electricity accounts for about a quarter of the country's total energy budget. However, hydro-electric power cannot be effectively stored; any that is produced in excess of domestic needs must be transported and sold, or go to waste. Canada's sale of hydro power to the United States annually produces more than $1 billion in revenue.

The greatest environmental hazard posed by the development of hydro-electric power is the alteration of natural landscapes and habitats through the construction of dams and reservoirs. Large areas of land are removed from use for forestry or agriculture. Natural habitats are disturbed in order to transport the energy from the site where it is generated to its markets. World-wide, hydro-electric power may become more important, but only in those countries with accessible water resources.

Atomic energy is being exploited with increasing frequency, both in industrialized countries and developing ones; many believe that nuclear energy is the answer to the world's growing energy demands. The technology involved with the use of nuclear energy to produce power is relatively straightforward. As a fuel such as uranium undergoes nuclear fission (the breakdown of an atom's nucleus) the fuel becomes radioactive and the heat that is produced is used to turn water into steam. The steam is then used to turn turbines and generate electricity.

The ecological impacts of atomic power generation are not fully understood. However, heat from the water used to cool the reactor raises the temperature of rivers, lakes, and oceans in the vicinity of the reactor, thus altering the composition of the communities of aquatic organisms living there. (The release of radiation following the 1986 Chernobyl disaster illustrated how widespread the danger of radioactive contamination can be following a nuclear accident.) Finally, the fuel in the reactor does not last indefinitely. Once ''spent,'' the fuel is no longer useful in generating power; however, it remains highly radioactive for a long time—the half life for one isotope of plutonium (which is produced by reactors that use uranium for fuel) is 24 647 years! Currently, **radioactive wastes** are being disposed of at great expense in tightly secured underground caverns. As the use of atomic energy becomes more widespread, the disposal of nuclear waste will become an increasingly important environmental issue.

589

Figure 28.17
Ecology House is a demonstration home which uses both passive and active solar heating to fulfill its energy needs.

The energy from solar radiation is another source of power that will likely be developed commercially in the future. The technology to capture and use solar energy lies in two separate areas. On the one hand, the energy in sunlight can be captured by materials that retain the energy and later re-radiate it as heat. The design of homes that can have much of their energy requirements supplied by **passive solar heating** (Figure 28.17) will be an important step toward decreasing current energy demands. Sunlight can also be converted into electric energy using photovoltaic cells. This use of **active solar heating** to generate electricity puts solar energy in a form that can then be used directly or to charge batteries. One problem with solar power is that it has a limited value in regions where the sun is often obscured by clouds, as it is along many coastlines. Solar energy is currently being exploited most often to supply domestic needs; compared with its alternatives, it remains relatively expensive for commercial purposes.

It is inevitable that tomorrow's world will run in part on these and other kinds kinds of alternative energy, but it is also likely that all energy resources will be much more expensive. Many future sources will not be economically practical in the near future, when the demand for energy is likely to rise most dramatically. The first goal in the development of energy resources hence should be to avoid waste. In addition, it will be important to diversify the development of different energy technologies so that a particular region of the world can use its own resources to meet its specialized needs. Finally, the harmful effects on the environment caused by the development and use of energy resources must be controlled.

28.3 THE PROTECTION OF ENVIRONMENTS AND THE SERVICES THEY PROVIDE

There are many challenges that must be met if the resources needed to sustain the world's population are to be developed. However, none of these challenges is more urgent than to protect the environment from the adverse effects of development itself. Every human activity, whether it be driving an automobile or constructing a nuclear reactor, has an **environmental impact**. At the very least, human activities change natural habitats from ones in which many species flourish to ones in which only a few species survive. At the more frightening end of the spectrum, some activities (such as the release of toxic substances) make the environment unfit for any organism, including humans. To a greater or lesser extent, the environmental impact of human activities comes from the ways in which they disrupt ecosystem services such as the production of oxygen, the recycling of nutrients, and the cleansing of water supplies.

Assaults on the Atmosphere

The **atmosphere** is a thin layer of gases that envelops the planet and protects its surface from lethal ultraviolet and cosmic radiation. It does so by absorption of the energy contained in the rays into the molecular structure of its constituent gases. By filtering the radiant energy impinging on the planet, the atmosphere also maintains the climate. Life on the earth can only survive within a relatively narrow range of climatic conditions. Even within this range, minor changes have a profound effect on the types of organisms that survive. For example, there was a difference of only 5°C between the past ice ages and the intervening more moderate periods (Figure 28.18).

THE ENVIRONMENTAL EFFECTS OF NUCLEAR WAR

The middle part of this century saw the production and employment of nuclear weapons in warfare. Two generations of humans have now survived this technology. Yet the threat remains that nuclear conflict might destroy all life on the earth, either through the massive physical destruction of the initial detonation or through the subsequent poisoning of life with radiation. Thankfully, international agreements that limit the size of nuclear arsenals and the spread of this technology are reducing the probability that a global thermonuclear conflict will occur. However, ecologists are attempting to draw the attention of world leaders and the public to the environmental effects that even a "small" nuclear exchange would have. The effects of such an exchange on the global climate would very likely be as catastrophic as those of a full-scale thermonuclear war.

The detonation of a nuclear device produces an enormous cloud of dust from the explosion *per se* and from clouds of smoke accompanying the subsequent fire storms. Using computer models, scientists in several countries have independently conducted "experiments" that aim to predict the climatic effects that this dust and smoke would produce. Almost irrespective of the initial conditions, these models always yield the same answer: there would be very rapid global changes in the climate. The culmination of these changes has been called *nuclear winter*. The predicted climatic change is not the product of science fiction; it is the result of computer simulations conducted by physicists, meteorologists, and ecologists, some of whom have been awarded Nobel prizes for their science.

The computer models predict that with the detonation of as few as 5000 nuclear devices — the number that would be expected to be used in a conflict confined to the European continent — within two weeks the dust and smoke would be dispersed world-wide in the upper atmosphere. The most apparent effects of this dispersed particulate matter would be the following:

1. Since the particulate matter in the upper atmosphere would screen out most of the solar radiation, the temperature at the planet's surface would plunge to $-50°C$ within about two weeks, regardless of the season.

2. Since it would be nearly impossible to maintain supplies of fresh water at this low temperature, nearly all domestic animals would perish. Because the temperature would drop too rapidly for normal physiological changes (such as adaptations for hibernation) to occur, even the wildlife that naturally survives temperatures this low would succumb.

3. Although coastal habitats would enjoy the moderating effect of the oceans, they would drop to between $-20°C$ and $-30°C$ for several months. The loss of light would also mean that photosynthesis would effectively stop and the basis of all marine productivity would be at least temporarily lost.

The question of whether humans could adapt their behaviour to a world of darkness for a long period of time is still unanswered. The universal nature of these effects means that even the victor in a nuclear exchange would only be so for a very short time. However, the danger extends beyond the political arena; even an accident at a stockpile of weapons has the potential to destroy most, if not all, life on the earth. There is one undeniable imperative: the manufacture and spread of nuclear weaponry must stop and those nuclear weapons presently in existence must be dismantled.

Some of the substances that are now being released into the atmosphere as the result of human activities threaten to change the composition of this layer of gases. The levels of carbon dioxide have increased by 25 percent since the industrial revolution, mainly as a result of the combustion of fossil fuels. Other substances such as chlorofluorocarbons are not naturally present in the atmosphere; they are manufactured for use as propellants in aerosol sprays and as coolants in refrigeration processes. Studies of the atmosphere have shown that at least two major effects are occurring: the greenhouse effect and the depletion of the ozone layer.

Figure 28.18
Historic changes in the temperature on the earth. A change of only six centigrade degrees separated the ice ages from the warmer periods. The anticipated warming over the next 50 years could exceed anything that has existed since the evolution of the human species.

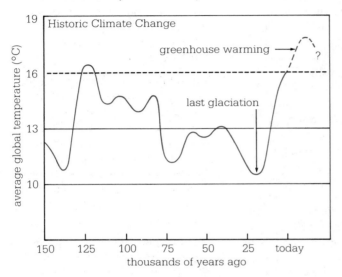

The Greenhouse Effect

Gases such as carbon dioxide are called **greenhouse gases** because they trap heat that would otherwise dissipate from the earth's surface. If the atmosphere did not perform this service, the temperature on the planet would likely fall to that experienced on the dark side of the moon ($-150°C$). It has been argued that as the amount of carbon dioxide in the atmosphere increases, its effectiveness at trapping heat will increase and the temperature of the earth will rise, much like temperature rises inside a greenhouse. If the abundance of the greenhouse gases were to double, it is estimated that the average global temperature would rise 1.5 to 4.5 °C as a result of this **greenhouse effect**.

If this change were to occur slowly, perhaps one tenth of a degree per decade, many ecologists believe that the effects on life on the earth might be relatively small. However, if the temperature changes were more rapid, perhaps eight tenths of a degree per decade, the results could be catastrophic. It has been predicted that the level of the seas would rise by as much as 10 m as the polar ice melted. Since the majority of the world's population and much of its arable land occurs along coastlines, many nations would have to relocate their populations and restructure their economies. In contrast, the level of the Great Lakes would

fall as rainfall patterns changed, hence depleting one of the world's largest sources of fresh water. The Canadian Prairies would undoubtedly experience hotter temperatures, so new varieties of agricultural crops would have to be produced. The forests of Canada would become drier and much greater losses due to natural forest fires would occur.

Depletion of the Ozone Layer

Figure 28.19 illustrates how **chlorofluorocarbons (CFCs)** cause the deterioration of the atmosphere. These compounds are responsible for the destruction of the **ozone layer**, a protective shield of ozone at the periphery of the atmosphere. This layer blocks **ultraviolet radiation** from penetrating to the planet's surface. Ultraviolet radiation is the component of sunlight that causes sunburns and induces skin cancer. In the laboratory, a one percent increase in the intensity of ultraviolet radiation causes a two percent increase in the incidence of cancer; a one percent decrease in the ozone layer causes a two percent increase in the intensity of ultraviolet light!

Heightened levels of ultraviolet light would probably affect all organisms. Some forms of plankton are particularly sensitive to ultraviolet light; relatively small increases in the intensity of this light might eliminate them altogether from the world's oceans. Because plankton forms the basis of the food web in all marine communities, such a loss would be catastrophic. At the very least, populations of many commercially important marine organisms would be devastated.

Canada is playing a leading role in the development of international agreements and laws to protect the atmosphere. In 1987, in Montreal, 24 nations signed an agreement to reduce the use of chlorofluorocarbons by half before the turn of the century. In 1988 an international conference in Toronto on air quality resolved that maintenance of the services that the atmosphere provides is as essential as the prevention of nuclear war.

Assaults on the Land and Water

The dangers posed by modern technology to aquatic and terrestrial environments come from three major sources: sewage and wastewater disposal, acid precipitation, and pesticides and herbicides.

Sewage and Wastewater Disposal

Life on the earth had its origin in the water and all organisms require clean water to survive. The world's

Figure 28.19
Deterioration of the ozone layer in the upper atmosphere by chlorofluorocarbons. Once CFCs reach the upper atmosphere, their effects are felt for 50 years. The upper diagram shows a step by step sequence of how CFC's reduce ozone molecules to oxygen molecules. In (a), ultraviolet light in the upper atmosphere breaks off a chlorine atom from a chlorofluorocarbon molecule. In (b), *the chlorine attacks and breaks apart an ozone molecule. In (c), a molecule of ordinary oxygen and one of chlorine monoxide are formed. In (d), once a free oxygen atom breaks up the chlorine monoxide, the chlorine is free to continue the process. The lower diagram illustrates how thin patches of the ozone layer will move in the upper atmosphere, distributing the harmful effects of increased intensities of ultraviolet radiation to all nations.*

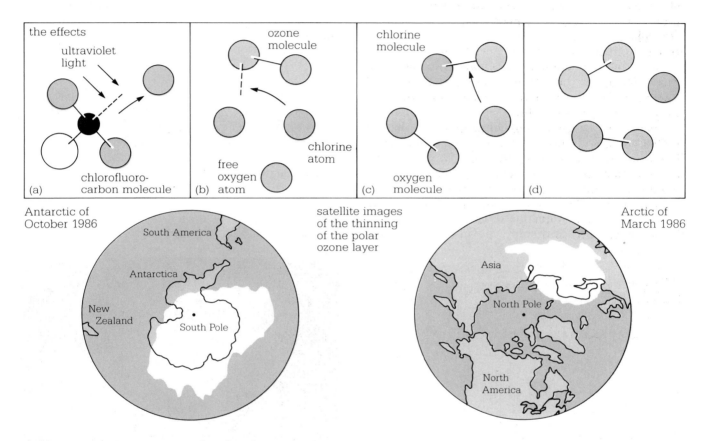

supplies of clean water are in grave jeopardy, largely because rivers, lakes, and oceans have traditionally served as the disposal sites for human wastes of all kinds. Human sewage poses a particular threat to the maintenance of clean water supplies. In addition to harbouring disease, raw sewage is decomposed by the action of bacteria which require oxygen. As a result, the supplies of oxygen in the water are not available to other organisms. The consequences of depleted oxygen reserves are illustrated in Figure 28.20. Fish kills are only one manifestation of the disposal of sewage. The nutrient enrichment or **eutrophication** that results from the injection of untreated human waste, fertilizers from agricultural land, and wastewater from domestic sources changes the fundamental composition of aquatic communities. Typical of eutrophic conditions are coarse fish (rather than game fish) and ''blooms'' of species of blue-green algae tolerant of low oxygen levels.

The chemical contamination of water can destroy life in different ways. In some cases, it occurs through the direct poisoning of the metabolic machinery of cells. One of the most effective of these poisons is mercury. Often along with other substances such as arsenic, mercury is produced as a by-product of several industries, particularly the pulp and paper industry. Mercury accumulates in the tissues of living organisms and is concentrated in the tissues of predators after they consume their prey. As a predator grows older, the amount of mercury accumulated over its life may become sufficiently high to kill it. Like other predators, humans also concentrate mercury. Health and Welfare Canada has therefore set a limit of 0.5 parts per million for commercially marketed fish; the Ontario Ministry of the Environment has developed guidelines for the frequency with which sport fish from certain lakes should be eaten. Several groups of Canada's native people that have traditionally relied on fishing to supply most of the animal protein in their diet can no longer do so.

Other chemical contaminants have been shown to cause damage to the genetic material present in all organisms. The effects of this damage range from sterility to developmental abnormalities to elevated frequencies of cancers. **Polychlorinated biphenyls (PCBs)** are one group of substances that are particularly offensive in this regard. They are given off mainly as by-products of the manufacture of plastics. Another highly toxic substance is **dioxin**. (Actually, dioxins are a group of about 75 different compounds that form as the result of the manufacture or combustion of other compounds.) Most commonly, dioxins find their way

into the environment through the improper disposal of electrical insulators, hydraulic fluids, or substances containing wood preservatives. Dioxins are also components of some widely used herbicides. It has been shown that dioxins are hazardous to human health at levels of only one part per billion; it has been estimated that a single drop could kill several million people. One of the largest accumulations of dioxin in the world is presently in a landfill site in New York State near Niagara Falls; it has the potential to contaminate *all* of Lake Ontario.

Figure 28.20
A fish kill and patterns of eutrophication in the Great Lakes. As water warms during summer months, it loses its ability to hold onto dissolved oxygen; as in a warm soft drink, dissolved carbon dioxide and oxygen go off as gases. When large populations of bacteria in eutrophic waters place an increased demand on these limited oxygen supplies, some fish species cannot survive. The map shows that eutrophication is common around very highly populated centres. Why, then, does it also occur toward the eastern end of Lake Ontario?

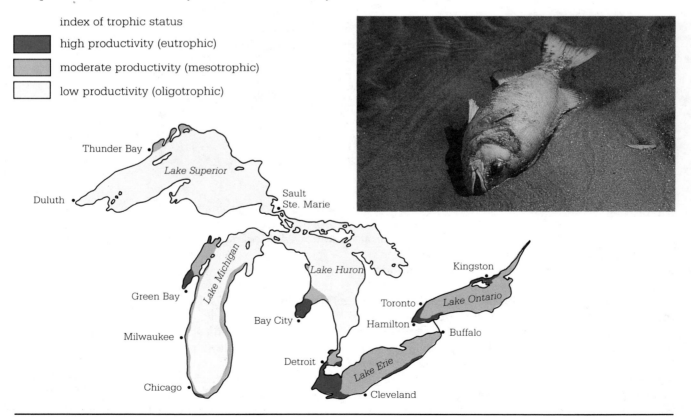

index of trophic status

high productivity (eutrophic)

moderate productivity (mesotrophic)

low productivity (oligotrophic)

Acid Precipitation

One form of chemical contamination that has become an important political issue is **acid precipitation**. The source of the acids in rain and snow are the oxides of nitrogen and sulfur that are injected into the atmosphere as by-products of the combustion of fossil fuels. When dissolved in water, these oxides produce nitric and sulfuric acids. The major sources of acid precipitation are automobile emissions and the coal-fuelled generation of electricity.

Because the contamination of the atmosphere rapidly spreads, the effects of one nation's activities often affect many others; the rains that fall on most of the Northern hemisphere are between 10 and 1000 times more acidic than the rains that fall from unpolluted skies. The record for acidity comes from the city of

Machin, China. In 1981, a rainfall with a pH of 2.25 was recorded; this rain was roughly as acidic as lemon juice! Figure 28.21 shows the pH of the rains that fell on the U.S. and Canada in the 1980s.

Figure 28.21

The pH of precipitation falling on the U.S. and Canada. The pH scale ranges from 0 to 14 and measures whether a liquid is acidic or alkaline (basic). A value of 7 is neutral; as values decline below 7, they indicate an increasingly acidic condition. Because the scale is a logarithmic one, there is a 10-fold difference between one number and the next. In the absence of any contaminants, rainfall is slightly acidic with a pH of 5.6. Factors such as windblown dust in the prairies raise the pH of rain or snow.

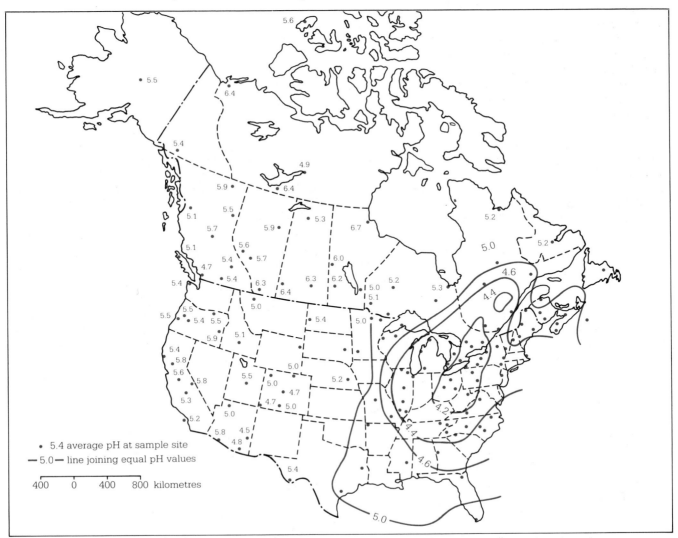

Figure 28.22
The angling catch of Atlantic Canada in Nova Scotia rivers. The data illustrated here are from 22 rivers that varied in their level of acid stress. The angling catch for each river was expressed as the percentage of the baseline catch (the average for the period 1936–1940); the rivers were then grouped by their average pH reading in 1980–81.

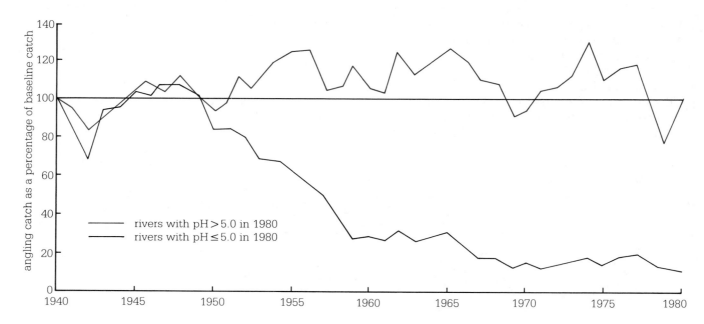

The full impact of acid precipitation is not fully understood, but what is known shows that it is a very real problem. For example, acid rains and snows falling on the Canadian Shield release large amounts of aluminum into the waters that run into rivers and lakes. It is known that high levels of aluminum affect both the normal development and the physiological function of fish gills. All of the fish populations in 300 lakes in the Adirondack region of New York State are extinct because of acid deposition; Canadian ecologists have identified 48 000 lakes that, if current trends continue, will not be able to support aquatic life. Figure 28.22 illustrates how Atlantic salmon's sensitivity to acid stress has decreased the catch of salmon in several of Nova Scotia's most productive rivers.

Terrestrial ecosystems are also affected by acid precipitation. Enough is known about the effects of acidity on biological systems to draw some preliminary conclusions about which ecosystem services might be affected most dramatically. One of the services threatened the most is the *nitrogen cycle* (Chapter 26). The reactions that are involved with the conversion of nitrogen from one form to another (for example, from ammonium to nitrates) by bacteria in the soil are extremely sensitive to pH. Since plant life depends on these sources of nitrogen, even a minor disruption of this service would be devastating to agriculture and forestry.

Pesticides and Herbicides
Every year hundreds (if not thousands) of new chemical compounds are developed which enable humans to improve their standards of living. Some are used to make stronger and safer construction materials; others are used in inexpensive and durable synthetic fabrics. Some are specifically developed to be used in the interminable war against pests, weeds, and diseases. The waters that irrigate agricultural crops carry some of these **pesticides** and **herbicides** into rivers and lakes that act as the main supplies of drinking water for wildlife and humans alike.

One of these substances, a pesticide called **DDT**, (dichlorodiphenyltrichloroethane), drew the attention of ecologists to the inherent dangers of unseen pollutants in the environment. When it accumulates in the tissues of vertebrate animals, DDT interferes with (among other things) the normal metabolism of calcium. The presence of residual DDT in the environment came to the public's attention early in the 1960s when the numbers of several species of birds of prey, especially peregrine falcons, bald eagles and osprey, began declining. When the reproduction of these and other species was examined in detail, it was found that the shells of their eggs were thinner than normal because of a lack of calcium deposition. Predatory birds had accumulated DDT to the greatest extent because, like humans, they were at the top of a food chain that concentrated the toxin at each step.

In 1969, the use of DDT for most purposes was banned in Canada. It was replaced by pesticides that have a much shorter lifespan. Many of the populations of birds affected by DDT have begun to recover, but most continue still to be small. Two decades after its use was banned, traces of DDT are still being detected in the breast milk of some Canadian women. Figure 28.23 shows that although its levels are measurably decreasing in some locations in Ontario, DDT is present in dozens of parts per billion in the tissues of some animals. This persistence should serve as fair warning about the perils of human-made substances in the environment. Yet DDT and related compounds are still being used widely in most developing countries!

Figure 28.23
DDT and PCB residues in herring gull eggs from selected Great Lakes nesting colonies. Due to the herring gull's metabolism, the concentration of residues in their eggs reflects the concentration of these substances in the bird's diet two to three weeks prior to egg laying. Since the time of exposure can be pinpointed in this manner, gulls can be used to monitor instantaneous changes in the levels of environmental pollutants.

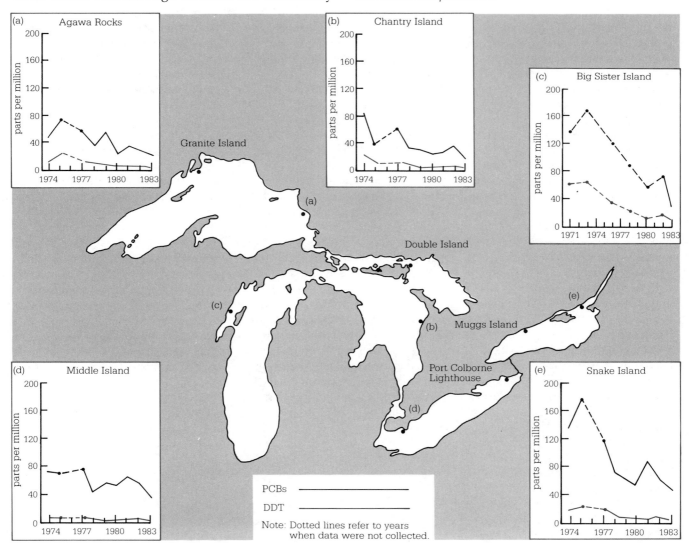

WHAT YOU CAN DO AND HOW YOU CAN MAKE A DIFFERENCE

The size of many of the environmental problems discussed in this chapter may seem overwhelming. You may wonder what you can do that will have any effect. If this or a similar question has crossed your mind, perhaps the most important point to realize is that the present environmental problems have not been created by any one person, nation, or part of the world. In every case, the problems are the cumulative effects of everyone's activities. Even if you did not design the process that produced a pollutant, you can be said to have helped cause the pollution if you purchased the product. Therefore, how one person behaves really does make a difference; every one of us is responsible for the environment's well-being.

How does one begin to have an effect? It starts with a consciousness of what is right and wrong with respect to the environment, with what has been called an *environmental ethic.* The first step is to identify how your behaviour affects the environment most strongly. In Canada, this behaviour has much to do with the relatively large amount of energy and material resources we consume in comparison with the rest of the world's population. The next step is to evaluate the effect that your behaviour has on a problem; the final step is to change your behaviour to lessen your impact.

Recycle, Reuse, and Reduce are the three R's of a resource conservation ethic.

Recycle. Instead of discarding a newspaper or junk mail, recycle it. With this small statement, you will be reducing the number of trees cut for pulp and paper and the total effect that paper production has on the environment. Many communities are providing a blue-box service to help with recycling paper and other materials (Chapter 26). To be effective, recycling must become a matter of habit.

Reuse. Many products have a finite lifespan, but with a little care their usefulness can be extended. For instance, the containers many products come in can be put to other uses. Each time a product is reused, the manufacture of another item to serve the same purpose is avoided. The energy needed to run that additional manufacturing process is also conserved.

Reduce. It costs a lot in money, energy, and materials to put products in attractive packages. Some of this packaging is needed; for example, some of the innovative packaging of foods allow a product to be stored for a long time. If what you are using will not be stored, or if you think there is too much packaging used on an item, you have the freedom to purchase an alternative that allows you to reduce the amount of material you consume.

In this country, we are fortunate enough to be able to join and meet freely with others that think as we do. In many nations, this is not the case. There are over 5000 international organizations with local chapters that represent environmental concerns. These organizations provide their newsletters either free or for a small membership fee. Since they represent the views of their members and hence of a block of both votes and consumer dollars, politicians and industrial leaders listen to the views of such organizations.

Finally, an environmental ethic simply means considering the impact that all of your activities have on the environment and acting in ways that minimize that impact. If everyone were simply to behave in just such a responsible manner, then many of the problems with the environment would be much less severe. To counteract the environmentally irresponsible behaviour of others, you can appeal to your political representatives to legislate against this behaviour. A single letter from a concerned voter is seen to represent the opinions of several thousand others who didn't write. Perhaps most importantly, a personal environmental ethic leads to a happier frame of mind, one in which you are confident that what you have done has made a difference.

28.4 ADDRESSING THE ISSUES

The issues of human ecology are complex. The questions may be asked from an economic, an ethical, or an ecological perspective, and the answers will accordingly be different. For most problems there probably are no simple solutions. In this area of biology, there are likewise few (if any) correct or incorrect answers—there are only opinions and viewpoints. Yet there is a difference between informed opinions based on consideration of the facts and different points of view and naive opinions based on personal prejudices and wishful thinking. In forming a viewpoint about any environmental issue, it is important to realize that you are part of a much larger global community. The decisions you make about environmental problems will affect all other members of your community. As illustrated in Figure 28.24, Canada is a nation that cares about environmental problems; traditionally, Canadians have been world leaders in seeking solutions to these problems. Many private citizens as well as politicians have been instrumental in important changes that have already had significant effects. This tradition is one to be proud of, but the urgency of current issues means that Canadians cannot rest on their laurels.

Some of the most urgent problems in human ecology must concern population control, resource management and conservation, and environmental protection.

Figure 28.24
A 1987 poll of the views of Canadians on environmental issues. Nine out of every ten Canadians surveyed said that they believed a clean environment is possible with our current technology. They expressed concern about the lack of action being taken to protect the environment. Four out of every five Canadians said they would be willing to pay higher product prices or higher taxes in order to improve environmental protection.

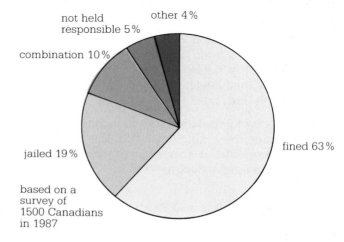

The Question: "If a company repeatedly pollutes the environment at unsafe levels, do you think that the company executives should be fined, jailed, or not be held personally responsible?"

not held responsible 5%
other 4%
combination 10%
jailed 19%
fined 63%
based on a survey of 1500 Canadians in 1987

The Question: "What do you consider to be the most serious environmental problem today?"	% responding				
	Canada	Atlantic Canada	Quebec	Ontario	Western Canada
"In Canada"					
water pollution	22	13	26	23	22
acid rain	18	24	14	18	18
air pollution	9	9	10	12	5
industrial pollution	8	6	9	6	12
pollution (unspecified)	7	7	8	8	4
air and water pollution	6	7	5	5	6
dump sites/chemical dumps	3	3	1	4	3
destruction of forests	2	4	4	1	2
destruction of animals	1	0	2	1	1
urbanization/no green spaces	1	1	1	1	1
land/soil pollution	1	1	2	1	2
don't know and other	22	25	18	20	24
total	100	100	100	100	100

based on a survey of 1960 Canadians in 1981

Population Control

The Problem
If the rate at which the human population is growing does not soon stabilize, then no amount of development will satisfy the population's demand for resources. In natural populations, high death rates occur in populations that chronically persist at or above their carrying capacity.

The Issues
1. Will the size of the human population stabilize only because of high death rates caused by starvation, pollution, and disease? Should this be allowed to happen if the means are available to prevent it?

2. Will the decrease in the birth rate that has traditionally accompanied industrialization occur rapidly enough to limit current population growth? Would it be justifiable for industrialized nations to retaliate against developing nations with a persistently high birth rate?

3. If some sort of population control is called for, who will enforce the regulations? Will the issues surrounding population control force changes in conventional religious doctrines?

Resource Management and Conservation

The Problem
As the population grows, the planet's resources will have to be developed. To ensure a sustainable yield, however, this development must consider the long term consequences of its actions. As well, parts of entire ecosystems will have to be conserved, both to supply a genetic library for future development and to provide the services crucial to all living things.

The Issues
1. How much conservation is enough? Are small pockets of natural habitat such as parks large enough to ensure the persistence of ecosystems, or are much larger areas needed? Are there certain kinds of designs for conservation areas that are better than others?

2. Who will be the appropriate stewards of those ecosystems identified as important enough to be conserved? Do the birthrights of some individuals give them the freedom to develop a resource at the expense of others in the global community? Can individual municipalities, provinces, or nations be trusted to be honest and effective custodians of the resources on the earth?

3. Should the responsibility for the protection and maintenance of ecosystems fall on the shoulders of an international organization? Will that international body have the power to intervene in disputes that arise between countries with different political and economic ideologies? What penalties will such a body be able to impose on a country that is too poor to pay? Who will pay for a body to police the management and conservation of its the world's resources?

Environmental Protection

The Problem
If the planet's resources are allowed to be suffocated and poisoned by current development, then no life will be able to survive on the earth for very much longer.

The Issues
1. At what point do the rights and freedoms of individuals to improve their own standard of living yield to the rights and freedoms of the global community? Should industries that earn a profit from a particular resource be forced to re-invest money in the protection of that resource or should the costs be shared by all individuals equally?

2. What agencies should be responsible for ensuring that individuals comply with regulations for the disposal of hazardous wastes? Are local concerns more important than national concerns in such matters?

3. What should the penalty be for knowingly releasing a toxic substance into the environment? Does any penalty match the crime?

CHAPTER SUMMARY

For much of its evolutionary history, the human population has been relatively small; high death rates have been traditionally balanced by high birth rates. With the advent of the agricultural, industrial, and technological revolutions, birth rates increased while death rates decreased. The currently large population is the product of this difference in birth and death rates. At present it has the momentum to double in size every 45 years. Although several recent changes point to a slowing of population growth for at least the near future, the population will be larger than it has ever been before.

The enormity of the human population places an ever-increasing demand on the planet's resources. Some resources have probably been exploited beyond recovery and others are threatened to be so exploited. The future of the human population depends on its ability to balance the development of resources with their conservation. But human activities are polluting the environment in ways that threaten to disable the services that ecosystems provide all living things.

The ecological answers to these environmental problems lie in conservation and in a change of attitudes to the protection of the environment. However, the immediate economic answers to the same problems are often different. The future well-being of humanity depends on the current generation's ability to deal with complex ecological, economic, and ethical issues.

Chapter Objectives

Having completed this chapter, you should be able to do the following:

1. Describe how historical changes have contributed to the recent explosive growth of the human population.
2. Understand why populations in different regions of the world are growing at different rates and why different estimates exist for the size of future human populations.
3. Discuss why the material and energy resources of the planet cannot sustain continued population increases of the magnitude recorded for the past two decades.
4. Identify how the exploitation of resources can affect services that ecosystems provide to all living things.
5. Use your own informed personal viewpoint to debate the crucial ethical issues affecting the ecology of humans.

Vocabulary

agricultural revolution	atmospheric contamination	ozone layer
industrial revolution	hydro-electric power	ultraviolet radiation
demographic transition	atomic energy	eutrophication
technological revolution	radioactive waste	polychlorinated biphenol (PCB)
non-renewable resource	passive solar heating	dioxin
renewable resource	active solar heating	acid precipitation
sustainable yield	environmental impact	pesticide
desertification	atmosphere	herbicide
genetic library	greenhouse gas	DDT
accidental take	greenhouse effect	
ecosystem service	chlorofluorocarbon (CFC)	

Review Questions

1. Why are there uncertainties about
   (a) the historical patterns of growth experienced by the human population?
   (b) the size at which the human population will stabilize?
2. Discuss the effects that the agricultural, industrial, and technological revolutions have had on human population growth.
3. Using an example from banking, discuss what is meant by sustainable yield.
4. What are the major problems that agriculture and fisheries face in providing food for future generations?
5. List and discuss the services that tropical forest ecosystems provide to all living things.
6. a) Distinguish between a renewable resource and a non-renewable resource.
   (b) Give an example of each.
7. (a) List at least five alternative sources of energy.
   (b) Describe the benefits and limitations of each one.
8. Both the greenhouse effect and the depletion of the ozone layer occur because of changes in the composition of the atmosphere.
   (a) What are these changes?
   (b) What causes them?
9. How might the improper treatment and disposal of human sewage affect the structure of the aquatic community in a lake or a river?
10. (a) Why do heavy metals such as mercury reach a higher concentration in the bodies of predators than in those of their prey.
    (b) How is the level of concentration related to the predator's age?
11. Discuss two different effects that acid precipitation might have on ecosystems.
12. Suggest three reasons why DDT is still detectable in animal tissues, despite its use being discontinued in Canada in 1969.

Advanced Questions

1. (a) Why did China impose limits to the number of children couples could have?
   (b) How were the laws worded and how were they enforced?
   (c) After they were put in place, what ramifications did these laws have on different aspects of Chinese culture?
2. Ontario is served by over 300 local naturalist clubs organized under one central body, the Federation of Ontario Naturalists.
   (a) What club is concerned with the affairs of your local community?
   (b) What is currently their most urgent conservation objective?
   (c) How are they dealing with it?
3. (a) About how much paper does your school use daily?
   (b) What happens to the waste paper?
   (c) How much money is being saved or might be saved by recycling this waste paper?
4. (a) Prepare a statement of your own personal viewpoint on one or more of the environmental issues raised in this chapter.
   (b) Criticize your own viewpoint by taking the opposite side of the issue.
5. Research a case in your community where there has been a legal dispute over the effects of a local industry on the environment. Consider factors such as
   (a) the industrial activity in question;
   (b) its environmental effects;
   (c) the group that initiated legal action;
   (d) the nature and length of the trial;
   (e) the legal judgement passed;
   (f) the fine (if any) levied and the consequences to the company involved.

GLOSSARY

A

A site – the site on the ribosome occupied by the incoming amino-acyl-tRNA during protein synthesis

abiotic – non-living or inorganic

abiotic factor – non-organic factors which work independently of other organisms

absorption spectrum – the graph of the efficiency of absorption of light as a function of the wavelength

accessory pigments – pigments such as the carotenoids which play an accessory role in the light-dependent phase of photosynthesis

accidental take – the accidental capture of an unwanted species

acetyl-CoA – a molecule composed of Coenzyme A and acetic acid

acid – a molecule from which a proton is easily removed, causing a relative increase in the hydronium ion concentration; having a pH in solution of less than 7

acid precipitation – precipitation that is very acidic; having a pH of less than 5, usually formed as a result of industrial pollutants such as sulfur dioxide and nitrous oxides reacting with water vapour to create sulfuric acid and nitric acid

acquired characteristics – the theory proposed by Lamarck stating that structures or traits that have been modified by use or disuse can be passed on to offspring

action spectrum – a graph depicting the efficiency of a process as a function of wavelength

activation energy – the amount of energy required to start a chemical reaction

active transport – an energy-requiring process in which molecules are transported across a membrane against the concentration gradient

active solar heating – using the energy of the sun to make electric energy in a photovoltaic cell

addiction – a compulsive and uncontrolled use of a chemical substance with characteristic withdrawal symptoms when its use is stopped

adenine – a purine base found in DNA and RNA

adenosine diphosphate (ADP) – a nucleotide found in living organisms to which inorganic phosphate may be added to make ATP, a chemical energy storage molecule

adenosine triphosphate (ATP) – a nucleotide which is used by living organisms to store chemical energy

adhesive – the ability of a molecule to form strong hydrogen bonds with other polar or charged substances, especially water

adrenal medulla – the area of the adrenal gland that produces epinephrine and norepinephrine

adrenal cortex – the area of the adrenal gland that produces steroid hormones

aerobic respiration – the breakdown of foodstuffs in the cell in the presence of oxygen

age pyramid – a horizontal bar graph which depicts the number of individuals in each age class

age-specific fecundity – the probability of an individual producing young at a specific age

age-specific survivorship – the probability of an individual surviving to a specific age

agricultural revolution – the change in a population lifestyle from hunting and gathering to domestication of animals and cultivation of crops

alcohol – a molecule having one or more terminal $-OH$ groups

alcoholic fermentation – the anaerobic conversion of glucose to ethanol by yeasts

aldehyde – a molecule having one or more terminal $-CHO$ groups

allele – one of several alternative forms of a gene

allosteric protein – a protein whose conformation and active site is altered by the presence or absence of a small molecule (effector) at a site

altruism – any behaviour which increases the chances of survival or reproduction for other organisms, while decreasing these same probabilities for the former

amine – a molecule having one or more $-NH_2$ groups

amino acid – a nitrogen-containing molecule with the formula $H_2N-RCH-COOH$, where R represents the side chain, different for each amino acid; the units from which proteins are made

aminoacyl-tRNA synthetase – an enzyme that activates and attaches a specific amino acid to its corresponding tRNA

amniocentesis – the removal of a sample of amniotic fluid surrounding a fetus for prenatal diagnosis

amphophilic – the characteristic of being attracted to basic and acid dyes

amphoteric – having the capacity to react in the presence of either acids or bases, or of behaving as either an acid or a base

anabolic steroid – one of a number of derivatives of male sex hormones used by some athletes to increase muscle mass

anabolism – the process by which smaller molecules are synthesized into larger molecules in a living organism

anaerobic – the breakdown of foodstuffs in the cell in the absence of oxygen

anaphase – the phase of nuclear division during which the chromatids are pulled to opposite poles of the spindle

androgen – a steroid which produces secondary male sexual characteristics

aneuploidy – the presence or absence of one or more whole chromosomes from the balanced set of chromosomes

anion – an ion which has taken one or more additional electrons and so has become negatively charged

antenna chlorophyll – the chlorophyll molecules in the photosynthetic unit which serve to absorb photons and pass the energy to the reactive centre

anthropomorphism – the attribution of human characteristics to animals

anticodon – the triplet of nucleotides found in the tRNA that pairs with the codon of the mRNA

antidiuretic hormone (ADH) – a hormone produced by the hypothalamus which causes the nephron to become more permeable to water

antiparallel – the term used to describe the opposite orientations of the two strands of a DNA molecule

association neuron – a neuron which connects sensory neurons to motor neurons

aster – a centrosome around which microtubules have formed

atmosphere – a thin layer of gases that envelopes the planet and protects its surface from ultraviolet and cosmic radiation

atmospheric contamination – the injection of impurities into the atmosphere

atom – the smallest unit into which a chemical element can be divided and still retain the properties of

the element; composed of a core of protons and neutrons, encircled by one or more electrons

atomic energy – the production of electrical energy using heat produced during the nuclear fission of uranium or other radioactive elements

atomic mass – the mass of a representative atom of an element relative to the mass of the most common isotope of carbon; equal to the sum of the number of neutrons and protons in an atom

atomic number – a number unique for each element which indicates the number of protons in the nucleus; also equal to the number of electrons in the element

autoradiography – a technique in which radioactive molecules are introduced into living cells, after which the cells are exposed to a photographic plate to show the distribution of the labelled molecules

autosomes – chromosomes similar in both sexes; chromosomes other than the sex chromosomes

autotrophic – an organism which is able to synthesize its own organic food using inorganic molecules

average annual increase – the percentage by which the population has grown in a year

axon – projections of the neuron that carry signals away from the nerve cell body

B

barrens – an area that cannot reach the climax community because of frequent disruptive actions

base – a molecule which easily binds a proton, causing a relative decrease in the hydronium ion concentration; having a pH in solution of greater than 7

base analogues – purines or pyrimidines structurally very similar, but still significantly different, from their normal counterparts

base pairing – the linking of complementary bases by hydrogen bonds

behaviourism – the study of the processes of learning

bilayer hypothesis – the theory of cell membrane structure in which the membrane is composed of a phospholipid bilayer

bioenergetics – the study of thermodynamics in the energy transformations in biological systems

biofeedback – the use of physiological monitors to teach a person to consciously control processes such as heart rate or skin tension

biogeochemical cycle – the cycling of matter within the biosphere

biological community – all of the species that are found within a given habitat

biological species concept – the definition of species as a group of individuals that can only mate with another individual within the group, of the opposite sex, to produce fertile offspring

biomass – the mass of living material

biome – an area with a characteristic geographic and climatic pattern which supports characteristic animal and plant populations

biosphere – the portion of the planet that supports life and the living organisms within it

biotic – living or at one time living

biotic factor – factors which are dependent upon other organisms

biotic potential – the capacity of a population for growth

bivalent chromosomes – paired homologous chromosomes observed during synapsis in meiosis

boreal forest – a biome that stretches across the northern area of the globe, characterized by a short growing season and harsh winters, and populated by several species of conifers

C

capture-recapture technique – a method of population estimation in which a group of organisms is captured, marked and released, and their subsequent rate of recapture used to estimate population

carbohydrate – a molecule containing carbon, hydrogen and oxygen in a 1:2:1 ratio, and having an alcohol group and at least one aldehyde or ketone group

carboxylic acid – a molecule having one or more terminal —COOH groups

carotenoid – a secondary pigment found in chloroplasts and involved in photosynthesis

carotenoids – orange and yellow plant pigments which play a part in the light-dependent stage of photosynthesis

carrying capacity (K) – the maximum population that an area can sustain

catabolism – the process by which larger molecules are broken down into smaller molecules in a living organism

catalyst – a substance which speeds up the rate of a chemical reaction by lowering the activation energy required; in biological systems a catalyst is usually a protein

catastrophism – the theory of change that proposes a series of environmental catastrophies has lead to the extinction of many species

catecholamine – a hormone derived from the amino acid tyrosine, such as epinephrine

cation – an ion which has given up one or more electrons and so has become positively charged

cDNA – complementary or copy DNA; DNA synthesized by reverse transcriptase, using an RNA molecule as the template

cDNA library – a DNA library involving copy DNA synthesized by using the RNA extracted from the organism as the template (see DNA library, genomic DNA library)

cell membrane – a selectively permeable boundary layer which separates the cell from its external environment

cell wall – a non-cellular layer found outside the cell membrane of plants and most prokaryotic cells which serves to protect and support the cell

cellulose – a complex carbohydrate which is the main constituent in the cell walls of higher plants

census – an official count of the population of an area, usually a country

central nervous system (CNS) – the portion of the nervous system composed of the brain and spinal cord

centrifuge – an apparatus which spins at high speed to separate the components of a mixture on the basis of mass

centriole – an organelle found in animal cells which organizes the spindle during nuclear division

centromere – the chromosome structure to which the spindle fibres are attached; required for chromosome movement during anaphase of mitosis or meiosis

centrosome – a pair of centrioles

cerebellum – the area of the hindbrain that coordinates and controls motor actions

cerebral cortex – the outer layer of the cerebrum, containing motor, sensory and associative areas

cerebrospinal fluid – the fluid found within the meninges of the CNS

cerebrum – the largest part of the forebrain, composed of two halves joined by the corpus callosum; coordinates sensory and motor information, provides memory and thought processes

chain termination mutation – a change in base sequence which causes early termination of the translation, resulting in an incomplete protein

chaparral – a scrub forest produced in areas with mild, moist winters and hot, dry summers

chemical bonding – the interactions of the electron orbitals of different atoms which hold the molecule together

chemiosmotic hypothesis – the theory of ATP synthesis which states that a proton gradient is created across a membrane using a proton pump, and as the protons return through the membrane via a chan-

nel, ATP is produced

chemosynthesis – the ability of an organism to produce food energy from inorganic matter

chiasma – a region of contact between pairs of homologous chromatids and associated with the occurrence of crossing over

chlorofluorocarbon (CFC) – an organic compound that causes the breakdown of ozone

chlorophyll – the main pigment found in chloroplasts and involved in photosynthesis

chloroplast – an organelle found in plants, algae and some protozoans which contains chlorophyll and carries out photosynthesis

cholesterol – a neutral lipid of the sterol group which constitutes part of the cell membrane of mammalian cells

chromatid – one of two copies of the replicated chromosome that are still joined at the centromeric region

chromatin – the form of chromosomes present during interphase; long strands of genetic information in which the DNA code is available for use

chromosomal mutation – a mutation which causes changes in the gross structure or number of chromosomes

chromosome theory of heredity – the concept that genes are located in chromosomes

cilium – a short hair-like structure usually found in large numbers on the external surfaces of cells, used for locomotion of unicellular organisms or the movement of substances across surfaces in multicellular organisms; contains microtubules

circadian rhythm – a pattern or cycle in an organism that centres around a biological clock roughly equal to a 24 h day

citric acid cycle – the second stage of aerobic respiration, in which pyruvic acid is completely oxidized

classical conditioning – the development of a conditioned response by the association of a conditioned stimulus to an unconditioned stimulus

climax community – a stable community of plants who have reached the maximum net primary productivity for the area and are able to compete most successfully in that area

clone – a group of genetically identical cells (or organisms) all descended from the same cell

closed instinct – a behaviour that is completely inherited and susceptible to little or no modification through experience

codominance – alleles whose gene products are both expressed in the heterozygote

codon – a sequence of three mRNA bases (or three base pairs in DNA) that code for either a specific amino acid or translation termination

coenzyme – a non-protein component which must be present for an enzyme to act

Coenzyme A – a derivative of vitamin B which is used in the citric acid cycle

cognitive therapy – learning to control moods through control of thought processes

cohesion-tension hypothesis – a theory which suggests that water moves through trees using two forces: the driving force of transpiration, which creates a concentration gradient, and the cohesive force of water molecules - within

cohesive – strong intermolecular attractions between molecules, especially water molecules

competitive exclusion – competition between two species for the same ecological niche that results in the elimination of one species

complementation test – a test to determine whether two mutants affect the same gene function based upon the phenotype of the heterozygote; a test to determine whether two mutant genes are alleles

condensation reaction – a chemical reaction in which a molecule of water is removed

conditioned response – a response which an animal has been conditioned to exhibit when a particular stimulus occurs

conditioned stimulus – a stimulus to which an animal has been conditioned to respond in a new way

constitutive mutations – mutations that result in continued transcription, regardless of the presence or absence of the inducer

constrictive age structure – a population with a large proportion of older individuals who are not being replaced when they die

continuous variation – a continuum of variation within a population, with most individuals being near the middle of the distribution

corepressor – a molecule that when bound to the allosteric repressor, enhances binding of the repressor to the operator region, thereby inhibiting transcription

corpus callosum – the band of nerves connecting the left and right hemispheres of the cerebrum

corpus luteum – a specialized group of cells located in the ovary which produce progesterone

cortex – the outer region of the kidney

covalent bond – the chemical bond between two atoms which results from the sharing of two or more atoms

cranial nerve – a nerve which leaves the central nervous system directly from the underside of the brain

cretinism – retardation of growth in young children due to low thyroxin production

crista – the folded inner membrane of a mitochondria

critical period – the limited time period during which some types of restricted learning can occur

crossing over – the reciprocal physical exchange of corresponding parts of homologous chromosomes during meiosis

cuticle – a layer of cutin formed by epidermal cells of plants and deposited on their upper surface to prevent water loss

cutin – a waxy substance formed on the upper surfaces of plants which prevents water loss

cyclic photophosphorylation – ATP generation associated with cyclic electron transport, which does not use an external source of electrons, but rather recycles them

cytochrome – an electron carrier molecule found in the electron transport chain

cytokinesis – the division of the cell cytoplasm which accompanies mitosis or meiosis

cytology – the study of cells

cytoplasm – the contents within a cell, excluding the nucleus

cytosine – a pyrimidine base found in DNA and RNA

cytoskeleton – a network of microtubules and microfilaments within the cell which serves to keep the cell shape

D

DDT – a pesticide that accumulates in the environment and causes many mutations

decomposer – an organism that breaks down dead organic matter

deletion – a mutation which results in the loss of a chromosomal segment

demographic transition – a change in the characteristics of a population

demography – the study of the size and structure of populations

dendrite – projections of the neuron that carry signals towards the nerve cell body

density – the number of individuals in an area

density dependent factors – the outcome of environmental limitations depends upon the density of organisms in the population

density-dependent population regulation – the regulation of population size by biotic factors such as competition or parasitism

density-independent population regulation – the regulation of population size by abiotic factors such as fire or flood that result in a loss of a proportion of the population

deoxyribonucleic acid (DNA) – the genetic material of all organisms, composed of two complementary strands of nucleic acid wound in a helix; contains the sugar deoxyribose

depressant – a chemical that slows down the muscular and nervous systems to abnormal levels

desert – a biome which receives an annual rainfall of less than 25 cm

desertification – the erosion of topsoil from grazing land, with the resulting formation of deserts

diabetes mellitus – a condition resulting from insufficient insulin production by the pancreas

diabetic coma – a loss of consciousness due to sudden lowering of blood glucose levels below the normal range

diffusion – the net movement of molecules from an area of higher concentration of molecules to an area of lower concentration of molecules

diglyceride – a molecule composed of glycerol and two fatty acids, with a functional group available for forming a phospholipid

dihybrid cross – crosses between individuals that differ at two gene loci; investigation of the combinations possible from the cross of two pairs of alleles

dimer – a molecule formed from the linkage of two molecules with only one functional group

dioxin – a highly toxic group of compounds that form as combustion by-products

diploid – presence of two sets of chromosomes in each nucleus (2n)

disaccharide – a molecule composed of two monosaccharides linked together

disulfide – a linkage formed between two sulfur atoms

diuretic – a substance that causes an increase in the amount of water excreted through the kidneys

DNA library – a large collection of clones, each clone having recombinant DNA with a random fragment from a common DNA source

DNA ligase – an enzyme which catalyzes the formation of a phosphodiester bond; required for closing nicks in the backbone of the DNA chain

DNA polymerase – an enzyme which catalyzes the synthesis of DNA using DNA chain as a template

dominant – an allele that is similarly expressed in both the heterozygous or homozygous form

double bond – the interaction of two atoms such that each atom provides two electrons to form the bond

double helix – a DNA molecule, composed of two chains of nucleic acid held together in a twisted length by hydrogen bonds between complementary bases

doubling time – the time taken for a population to double in size

duplication – a mutation which results in the presence of one or more extra copies of a genetic region

E

ecocline – the transition zone between ecosystems

ecological niche – the pattern of relationships between a species and all the living and non-living things within its habitat

ecology – the study of all the interactions that occur within the biosphere

ecosystem – a group of living organisms that, with their abiotic environment, form a self-regulating system through which energy and materials transfer

ecosystem service – a process beneficial to humans that occurs naturally in an ecosystem

effector – a structure that carries out an action in response to a stimulus

eidos – eternal and perfect ideas or forms

electron – a negatively charged particle with very little mass which orbits the positively charged nucleus of an atom

electron transport chain – the final stage of aerobic respiration in which the reduced electron carriers are oxidized to produce large quantities of ATP

electronegativity – the tendency of an atom to attract electrons

electrophoresis – a technique used to separate different types of molecules using differences in their electrical charges

element – a substance which consists of atoms of only one kind

embryology – the study of the prenatal development of an organism

Emerson enhancement effect – the amount of photosynthesis which occurs when both photosystems are active is greater than the sum of the two photosystems individually

emigrate – movement of an individual out of a population

endemic – restricted to a particular region or people

endergonic – a reaction which requires the input of energy to occur; a positive free energy change

endocrine gland – a gland which secretes its product directly into the bloodstream

endocytosis – the process by which the cell membrane engulfs a particle and forms a vacuole within the cell

endoplasmic reticulum (rough and smooth) – a system of tubes and channels formed from membranes within the cell; rough ER is covered with ribosomes, smooth ER lacks ribosomes

enhancer – a nucleotide sequence that increases the frequency of transcription in its vicinity

entropy – the portion of total energy not available to do useful work

envelope membrane – the double outer membrane of a chloroplast

environmental impact – the effect of a human activity on a natural environment

environmental resistance – biotic and abiotic ways in which an environment suppresses population growth

enzyme – a protein which acts as a catalyst in a living system

epidermal cell – the outermost layer of cells of an organism

epistasis – the interaction between non-allelic genes such that one gene interferes with the expression of another gene

ergogenic drug – a drug that is taken by an athlete to increase performance beyond his or her normal limits

essentialism – the philosophy that believes that each organism has its own perfect form with essential characteristics

estrogen – a hormone produced in high levels in females to induce secondary sexual characteristics and maintain normal female reproductive cycles

ethology – the study of how and why animals behave as they do in their natural environment

eugenics – the attempt to improve future generations of humans through the selection of parents

eukaryotic cell – a cell having membrane-bound organelles, particularly the nucleus, found in plants, animals, protists and fungi

euploidy – a condition in which there are one or more multiples of a complete set of chromosomes in the cell

eutrophic – a nutrient rich body of water

eutrophication – nutrient enrichment of water

evolution – the progressive genetic change of a group of organisms over time

exergonic – a reaction in which energy is given off; a negative free energy change

exocytosis – the process by which a vacuole in the cell fuses with the cell membrane, releasing the contents into the extracellular environment

exon – a nucleotide sequence that is transcribed and retained in the mature mRNA (see intron)

expansive age structure – a population with a large proportion of individuals of reproductive age

exploratory learning – a type of flexible learning in which the animal uses features or stimuli as cues to map their environment

exponential growth – growth of a population at rate equal to the number of offspring raised to the exponent of the number of generations

F

facilitated diffusion – the movement of large molecules through protein pores in a membrane in the direction of a concentration gradient

fatty acid – a molecule composed of a long chain of carbon atoms with a carboxylic acid group at one end

fecundity – the number of offspring a female produces

ferredoxin – a protein which captures displaced electrons in the light-dependent stage of photosynthesis

fermentation – the respiration of glucose under anaerobic conditions

fertility – the physiological capacity to bear young

first law of thermodynamics – energy can be neither created nor destroyed, it can only be converted from one form to another

fitness – the relative life-long reproductive success of an individual

5′ cap – the addition of a modified guanidine group to the eukaryotic transcription product (mRNA)

fixed action pattern – a highly stereotyped behaviour that is performed almost the same way each time by all members of a species

flagellum – a long hair-like structure found on the exterior surface of cells, used for locomotion and feeding; contains microtubules

flavin adenine dinucleotide (FAD) – a coenzyme that can be reduced to FADH to store energy or act as a reducing agent within the cell

flexible learning – learned behaviours that can be continuously

modified throughout the life of the organism as a result of new environmental input

fluid mosaic model – the theory of cell membrane structure which suggests there is a phospholipid bilayer with integral and peripheral proteins, all in constant motion

follicular cell – immature cells in the ovaries that will mature to form an egg cell

food chain – a chain of feeding relationships between organisms in the various trophic levels

food vacuole – an organelle surrounded by a single membrane which is formed when the cell membrane surrounds food and then pinches off within the cell

food web – a network of feeding relationships between organisms in the various trophic levels

forebrain – the largest area of the brain containing the thalamus, hypothalamus and cerebrum

fossil fuels – coal, oil and natural gas, produced from the breakdown of prehistoric plants

fossil record – a knowledge of the past that can be obtained by an examination of the fossils in that time period

frameshift mutation – a deletion or duplication of one or more nucleotides in the DNA that alters the reading frames of the codons during subsequent translation and protein synthesis

free energy – the portion of the total energy available to do useful work

functional group – a group of atoms that tend to react as a unit in a particular way

G

Gaia Hypothesis – the hypothesis that life itself determines and controls the conditions that make the earth habitable

ganglion – a collection of nerve cell bodies, in vertebrates, always found outside the CNS

gene – a segment of genetic material (DNA or RNA) that carries the information specifying the amino acid sequence of a polypeptide chain (protein); a DNA sequence coding for mRNA, tRNA or rRNA

gene family – in eukaryotes, a group of genes, related in structure and function, e.g., the globin genes

gene locus – the specific site of a gene in the chromosome or genetic map

genetic drift – the chance loss of alleles in small populations, resulting in less genetic variability in this population

genetic library – a collection of genetic material available for selective breeding

genetic marker – an allele whose presence is readily detected and so is used as an indicator for the presence of neighbouring region of the chromosome

genome – one complete set of non-homologous chromosomes

genomic DNA library – a DNA library which contains fragments of DNA extracted from a specific organism or cell (see DNA library, cDNA library)

genotype – the genetic makeup of an individual (see phenotype)

geographic speciation model – the concept that species form when a population is separated into two smaller populations by a geographical barrier so that no gene flow can occur

glomerular filtration – the forcing of the liquid portion of the blood from the glomerulus into the Bowman's capsule of the kidney

glucagon – a hormome produced in the pancreas which causes an increase in blood glucose levels

glycerol – a three carbon molecule with three hydroxyl groups; combines with fatty acids to form a lipid

glycolysis – the first stage of respiration in which glucose is broken down into pyruvic acid

goiter – an enlargement of the thyroid gland due to iodine deficiency

Golgi apparatus – an organelle composed of closely stacked flattened stacks which modifies and packages proteins

gonadotropin – a hormone such as FSH and LH which act on the ovaries and testes

Graafian follicle – the cell in the ovary which produces an egg cell during ovulation

grana – a stack of interconnected thylakoids found in the chloroplasts of higher plants

grassland – a biome characterized by moderate rainfall and a vegetation of grasses

greenhouse effect – an increase in the amount of heat trapped in the earth's atmosphere due to an increase in the levels of carbon dioxide in the atmosphere

greenhouse gas – a gas such as carbon dioxide that traps heat that would otherwise dissipate from the earth's surface

guanine – a purine base found in DNA and RNA

gyrase – an enzyme which catalyzes the temporary breakage and repair of bonds elsewhere in the DNA molecule to reduce physical stress on the molecule

H

habituation – the reduction or elimination of a response over time that is followed by neither reward or punishment

hallucinogen – a drug that alters the perception of reality of the user

haploid – having a single set of chromosomes; a genome

helicase – an enzyme which catalyzes the breakdown of hydrogen bonds to separate the two chains in a DNA molecule so that replication can occur

herbicide – a chemical that kills unwanted plants

heterotrophic – an organism which must consume other organic material to obtain its energy

heterozygosity – genetic variability within an individual

heterozygous – in a diploid organism, the condition in which the two alleles for a gene are different (see homozygous)

hexose – a six carbon monosaccharide which has six functional groups composed of alcohols and one aldehyde or ketone

high temperature incineration – burning of garbage at high temperatures, resulting in the formation of ash

hindbrain – the area of the brain just above the spinal cord which controls basic life processes such as breathing

homeostasis – maintenance of the internal environment of an organism within very narrow tolerance ranges

homeotherm – an animal in which the body temperature is maintained within a narrow range in spite of the external environment; sometimes called a "warm-blooded" animal

homozygous – in a diploid organism, the condition in which the two alleles for a gene are identical (see heterozygous)

hormone – a molecule required in very small amounts which is secreted directly into the bloodstream to effect a specific target cell's metabolism elsewhere in the body

humid forest – a forest with high temperatures, little seasonal variation and heavy rainfall

hydro-electric power – the production of electrical energy using the power of falling water

hydrogen bond – the bond formed between the hydrogen of one molecule and the oxygen, nitrogen or sulfur of another molecule

hydrolysis reaction – a chemical reaction in which a molecule of water is added

hydrophilic – water-loving; a molecule which is soluble in water

hydrophobic – water-hating; a molecule which is not soluble in water

hypertonic – a solution in which there is a higher concentration of solutes than the solution under comparison; water moves into the hypertonic solution

hypothalamus – the area of the forebrain which controls temperature and water balance, produces some hormones, and coordinates the nervous and endocrine systems

hypothesis – an explanation that is put forward to explain an observed phenomenon

hypotonic – a solution in which there is a lower concentration of solutes than the solution under comparison; water moves out of the hypotonic solution

I

imitation – copying the behavioural pattern of another animal

immigrate – the movement of an individual into a population

imprinting – a type of restricted learning in which the newborn recognizes any moving object as its parent

inclusive fitness – the sum of an individual's fitness plus the contribution made by its relatives to the gene pool of genes like its own

incomplete dominance – the expression of both alleles in the heterozygote, but the expression of one allele is more pronounced than the other

independent assortment – the random segregation of one pair of alleles in relation to a second pair of alleles: a consequence of the two pairs of genes being located in different pairs of chromosomes or very distant in the same chromosome

inducer – a small molecule that binds to and inactivates a specific repressor, and so increases the rate of transcription of a specific operon

industrial revolution – a change in a population lifestyle from agriculture to urban industrial living

inhalant – a volatile hydrocarbon produced from petroleum products that is inhaled to produce an alteration in consciousness

innate behaviour – an inherited response; a response elicited by an external stimulus that is performed properly the first time and characteristically by all members of a species

innate releasing mechanism (IRM) – a cluster of nerve cells that is responsible for the recognition of a particular releaser stimulus and for the initiation of the appropriate response

inner membrane – the folded inner membrane of the mitochondria which forms the cristae and contains a very high percentage of proteins

insight learning – the ability of animals with complex brains to respond appropriately to new stimuli using information taken from other situations

insulin – a hormone produced in the pancreas which causes a decrease in blood glucose levels by conversion of glucose to glycogen

intermembrane space – the area within the mitochondria which contains enzymes which use ATP and functions as a proton reservoir

intermolecular force – the forces which act to hold molecules to other molecules to form liquids or solids

interphase – the stage of a cell between reproductive cycles

interspecific competition – competition between organisms of different species for the same resources

intertidal zone – the area along the shoreline of oceans that is regularly immersed and exposed as the tide rises and falls

intramolecular force – the forces which hold the atoms in a molecule together

intraspecific competition – competition between organisms of the same species for the same resources

intrinsic rate of increase (r) – the difference between a population's birth rate and death rate

intron – a nucleotide sequence that is transcribed but is not present in the mature mRNA following RNA

splicing (see exon)

inversion – a mutation that reverses a linear sequence of a portion of the chromosome as a result of a 180° rotation of a chromosomal segment

ion – an atom to which electrons have been added or taken away, making the number of electrons and protons unequal

ionic bond – a bond formed between two ions of opposite charge

islets of Langerhans – endocrine cells in the pancreas which produce three hormones, glucagon, insulin and somatostatin

isotonic – a situation in which the concentrations of ions and water on both sides of a membrane are the same

isotope – an atom having the same atomic number but a different atomic mass as another atom of the same element

J

J-shaped growth curve – the growth curve typical of density-independent population changes

K

K-selection – natural selection which favours parents who use their resources to produce a few highly competitive offspring

kin selection – an altruistic behaviour that increases the survival of a number of the animal's relatives, and so increases the chances of common genes being passed on

kinesis – a change in an animal's rate or pattern of movement following detection of a particular stimulus

L

lactic acid fermentation – the anaerobic conversion of glucose to lactic acid by bacteria and animal muscle cells

lagging chain – the new chain of DNA that is being synthesized discontinuously in small sections as more DNA template is exposed

leading chain – the chain of new DNA that is being synthesized continuously in the 5'–3' direction

learned behaviour – a response that must be acquired as a result of the individual's experiences

lethal gene – an allele that causes death of the individual, often before birth or before sexual maturity

life history – the patterns of age-specific survivorship and fecundity of a population

light compensation point – the light intensity at which the net rate of carbon dioxide uptake is zero

light-dependent reactions – the formation of ATP and NADPH in the chloroplast, which requires light

light-independent reactions – the conversion of carbon dioxide to carbohydrates within the chloroplast, which does not require light

lipid – an organic molecule composed of carbon, hydrogen, and oxygen, with high concentrations of hydrogen; a combination of fatty acids and glycerol

lysed – a cell that has been ruptured

lysosome – a spherical organelle which is surrounded by a single membrane and contains digestive enzymes

M

macronutrient – a nutrient which is required in large quantities

malnutrition – an imbalance in the diet such that the body is not getting enough of a particular nutrient

map unit – the distance between two points within which an estimated one percent crossing over occurs

matrix – the central area of the mitochondrion, where the oxidation of foodstuffs occurs

medulla – the inner region of the kidney

medulla oblongata – the area of the hindbrain which connects the higher areas of the brain to the motor pathways

membrane potential – a difference in electrical potential across a membrane created by a difference in ion concentrations

meninge – a protective membrane which surrounds the central nervous system

menstrual cycle – the hormonally controlled female cycle of uterine and ovarian changes

menstruation – the periodic sloughing off of the uterine lining when pregnancy does not occur

mesophyll cell – the photosynthetic cells in a vascular plant, found under the epidermal layer

mesotrophic – a body of water that is neither oligotrophic nor eutrophic, but contains a moderate concentration of nutrients

messenger RNA (mRNA) – a single-stranded RNA molecule (transcribed from a DNA template) whose nucleotide sequence can be translated during protein synthesis

metabolism – the sum total of all chemical reactions within the cell

metaphase – the phase of nuclear division during which the nuclear envelope disappears, the chromatids move to the centre of the spindle, and each chromatid attaches to a spindle fibre

micelle – a cluster of molecules oriented with hydrophobic ends inward and hydrophilic ends outward in the water medium

microfibril – microscopic fibres made of cellulose which make up the cell wall of plant cells

microfilament – a long protein thread found in eukaryotic cells which is necessary for movement and alterations in shapes of cells

micronutrient – a nutrient which is required in very small quantities

microtubule – a long, hollow protein cylinder found in eukaryotic cells which assists in structure, support and movement of the cell

midbrain – an area of the brain which consists of four relay centres which control reflexes and connect the hind and forebrains

missense mutation – a base pair substitution mutation which changes the amino acid designation of one codon

mitochondrion – the organelle in which food energy is converted into ATP for use by the cell

mitosis – the division of the cell nucleus to form two identical copies of chromosomes

mitotic apparatus – microtubules in a spindle-like arrangement, seen during nuclear division; associated with the alignment of chromosomes during metaphase and anaphase

mole – the number of carbon atoms in 12 g of carbon-12; the mass of 6.022×10^{23} atoms of an element

molecular formula – a formula which indicates the number of atoms of each element in a molecule

molecule – the smallest unit of a substance that still possesses the chemical and physical properties of the substance, composed of two or more atoms

monohybrid cross – a cross between individuals that differ at one gene locus

monomer – the single units of which polymers are made

monosaccharide – a simple sugar that cannot be broken down further; the monomer unit of a carbohydrate

mortality – death rate

motor neuron – a neuron which carries information to effector cells to direct the action of the effector

motor cortex – a narrow band of nerve tissue in front of the central fissure of the cerebrum which controls the voluntary movements of the body

multiple alleles – the existence of three or more alternative forms of a gene within a population

Münch Pressure-Flow hypothesis – a theory which suggests that nutrients move through the phloem along a pressure gradient, from the leaf (source) to the non-photosynthesizing parts of the plant (sink)

muskeg – an area characteristic of boreal forests containing a thick deposit of sphagnum moss and partly decayed organic matter

mutagen – an agent that increases the frequency of mutation

mutualism – a relationship between two organisms in which both organisms benefit; symbiosis

myelin – a white, fatty lipoprotein found in cells forming the myelin sheath around neurons

myelin sheath – an axon covering composed of Schwann cells, which are high in the lipoprotein myelin

myelinated fibre – an axon which is covered with a myelin sheath

myxedema – a condition in adults caused by insufficient thyroxin production

N

natality – birth rate

natural selection – a theory which proposes that individuals whose genetic variations best adapt them to their environment will be most likely to survive and pass on their genotypes

nature-nurture controversy – the question of whether responses are inherited or learned

negative feedback – the buildup of products of a reaction inhibits the rate of further reaction

negative reinforcement – a situation in which the response to a stimulus leads to results not beneficial to the individual

nephron – the functional unit of the kidney, where the blood is cleaned, and water and ion balance maintained

net primary productivity – the rate at which energy is stored by producers

neuroglial cell – cells that help the neuron cells maintain their metabolic activities

neuron – animal nerve cells specialized to carry messages by electrical impulses

neuropeptide – a protein-like molecule produced by the brain which is associated with the immune system

neutron – a particle with no charge found within the nucleus of an atom

nicotinamide adenine dinucleotide (NAD) – a coenzyme that can be reduced to NADH to store energy or act as a reducing agent within the cell

node of Ranvier – the bare area on the axon where two Schwann cells meet

non-cyclic photophosphorylation – ATP generation associated with non-cyclic electron transport, which uses an external source of electrons

nondisjunction – failure of chromosomes in a bivalent to segregate during meiosis, resulting in aneuploidy

non-renewable resource – a non-living finite resource that once exhausted cannot be made again

nonsense mutation – an alteration in a codon to a triplet that specifies termination of translations, resulting in an incomplete and usually nonfunctional protein product

nuclear envelope – the double membrane which surrounds the nucleus of eukaryotic cells

nucleic acid – a polymer of nucleotides, the main types being DNA, which is a double strand of nucleic acid, and RNA, which is a single strand of nucleic acid

nucleoid – an area in prokaryotic cells which contains the genetic material

nucleolus – a spherical mass found in the nucleoplasm; site of ribosomal assembly

nucleoside – an organic molecule composed of a purine or pyrimidine base and a pentose sugar

nucleosome – a repeating unit of a section of DNA wrapped around a histone, found in eukaryotic chromosomes

nucleotide – an organic molecule containing a purine or pyrimidine base, a pentose sugar, and a phosphate group; a single unit of nucleic acid

nucleus – a prominent organelle found in eukaryotic cells which contains genetic information

O

obesity – the condition of being greatly overweight

oligotrophic – a nutrient-poor body of water

open instinct – a behaviour that is inherited but can be modified through experience

operator – a binding site on the DNA for a repressor protein that serves in the regulation of transcription

operon – a unit of transcription consisting of one or more adjacent genes along with their regulatory elements (promoter and operator)

organelle – a specialized structure or area within a cell, homologous to organs in multicellular animals

osmoregulation – the control of water and ion balance in the body

osmosis – diffusion of a solvent, usually water, through a selectively permeable membrane

osmotic pressure – the pressure in a cell caused by the movement of water into the cell; the pressure required to stop the movement of water into a solution

outer membrane – the smooth, outer membrane of the mitochondrion, which contains enzymes to convert fatty acids and allow small molecules through into the mitochondria

oxidation – the removal of an electron from an atom or molecule

oxidative phosphorylation – the process by which molecular oxygen is used to form ATP

oxidizing agent – an electron acceptor which causes an oxidation

ozone layer – a protective layer of ozone molecules found at the outer edge of the atmosphere

P

P site – the binding site on the ribosome for the tRNA that holds the growing peptidyl chain in protein synthesis

pancreas – a large gland found below the stomach which has both exocrine and endocrine functions

parasite – an organism that lives in or on a living host, to the detriment of the host and benefit of the parasite

parathyroid gland – four small glands located behind the thyroid gland which produce parathormone

passive solar heating – using the energy of the sun to heat an object and then re-radiating that heat

passive transport – spontaneous movement of molecules across a membrane with a concentration gradient

pentose – a five carbon monosaccharide which has five functional groups composed of alcohols and one aldehyde or ketone

peptide bond – a covalent linkage between the carboxyl group of one amino acid and the amino group of another amino acid

peptide hormone – a hormone composed of chains of amino acids

peripheral nervous system (PNS) – the portion of the nervous system composed of the nerve pathways outside the brain and spinal cord

permeability – the ability of a molecule to pass through a membrane

pesticide – a chemical that kills pests

pH scale – a scale measuring the relative concentration of hydronium ions in a solution; the negative of the logarithm to the base ten of the numerical value of the hydronium ion concentration, expressed in mol/L

phage – a virus which uses a bacterium as its host cell

phenotype – the appearance of an individual, determined by the interaction of genotype and the environment (see genotype)

phloem – a tissue found in vascular plants that carries nutrients from the leaves to other parts of the plant

phospholipids – a molecule composed of glycerol, two fatty acids and a phosphate group; found in cell membranes

phosphorylate – the addition of a phosphate molecule to a substance

photo-oxidation – the oxidation of a molecule as a result of energy absorbed from light

photon – a quantum of light

photosynthesis – the process by which chlorophyll uses light energy to convert carbon dioxide and water into glucose and oxygen

photosynthetic efficiency – the amount of net carbon dioxide taken up per unit of light energy absorbed

photosynthetic induction – the time necessary to restore the intermediates of the Calvin cycle and allow maximum photosynthesis to occur

photosynthetic unit – a collection of many chlorophyll molecules that work together to process the energy of a single photon

photosystem – a photochemical system that functions at a specific wavelength

phycocyanin – a blue accessory pigment associated with photosynthesis

phycoerythrin – a red accessory pigment associated with photosynthesis

phyletic gradualism – the constant but gradual change of a population over time

phyletic speciation – the formation and classification of species based upon evolutionary relationships

physical bonding – the forces which hold different molecules to each other to form liquids or solids

physical dependence – a condition whereby a person needs a drug for normal functioning after the body adapts to its presence and the body exhibits physical symptoms if the drug is stopped

pigment – a molecule that absorbs light; it reflects the colour it does not absorb

pioneer organism – the first organism to inhabit an area and start the process of succession

pituitary gland – a small gland located just under the hypothalamus and which produces many different hormones

placebo – an inert substance given in place of a drug without the user's knowledge

pleiotrophy – a situation in which an allele affects two or more seemingly unrelated traits

poikilotherm – an animal in which the body temperature changes according to the external environment; sometimes called a "cold-blooded" animal

point mutation – a mutation which alters a sequence of bases in a single gene; mutations too small in size to visibly alter the chromosome structure

polarized – a bond in which electrons tend to spend more time around one atom than the other

poly(A) tail – a sequence of adenine nucleotides which are added to the 3' end of eukaryotic mRNA after transcription

polychlorinated biphenol (PCB) – a group of substances that has been shown to cause damage to genetic material

polymer – a molecule which is composed of many small molecules of the same type linked together

polymorphism – genetic variability within a population

polynucleotide – a long chain of nucleotides linked together by phosphodiester bonds

polyploidy – a condition in which there are three or more complete sets of chromosomes in a cell or organism

polysaccharide – a molecule composed of many monosaccharides linked together

polysome – two or more ribosomes bound to and translating a common mRNA molecule

pons – the area of the hindbrain which connects the two halves of the cerebellum to each other, and the cerebellum to other areas of the brain

population – all of the members of one species found in a particular area at a particular time

population dynamics – the changes in a population over time

population estimate – an approximate count of the number of individuals in a population using a sample and extrapolation

population genetics – changes in the genetic makeup of a population due to natural and artificial selection

population growth momentum – the persistent growth of a population with an expansive age structure

porphyrin – a molecule containing a large ring system at the centre of which N-H groups can bind with a metal ion; hemoglobin contains a porphyrin group which binds with iron

positive feedback – the buildup of products of a reaction causing an increase in the rate of the reaction

positive reinforcement – a situation in which the response to a stimulus leads to results beneficial to the individual

potential energy – the potential ability of a substance to do work

precipitation – the release of water from the atmosphere, in the form of rain, snow, hail or sleet

primary consumer – an animal that feeds on plants

primary succession – succession from bare rock to a climax community

primase – an enzyme which catalyzes the production of RNA primer in discontinuous DNA replication

primer – a short segment of RNA that is used by the lagging chain in DNA synthesis

primer strand – a small area of duplex that is necessary for DNA synthesis to start

probe – a specific piece of radioactive, single-stranded DNA or RNA that is used to identify a particular mRNA or gene

producer – an organism that produces its own food

progesterone – a hormone produced by the corpus luteum of the ovary to prepare the uterus for pregnancy

prokaryotic cell – a cell having no membrane bound organelles or nuclear membrane, found in monerans

promoter – a segment of DNA which is involved in binding RNA polymerase and the initiation of transcription

prophase – the stage of nuclear division during which the chromosomes become visible and the spindle forms

protein – a large molecule composed of many amino acids joined by peptide bonds

proton – a positively charged particle found in the nucleus of an atom

proton pump – an energy-requiring process which moves protons from one side of a membrane to the other

psychoactive chemical – a substance that acts on the brain and affects the thought processes

psychological dependence – a condition in which a person has a compelling emotional need for a drug, and feels lost or desperate without it

punctuated equilibrium – the theory that proposes periodic rapid changes in a population followed by long periods of stability

Punnett square – a checkerboard-like grid used to determine all possible genetic combinations at fertilization for a given cross

purine – a nitrogenous base with a double ring structure, such as adenine or guanine

pyrimidine – a nitrogenous base with a single ring structure, such as cytosine, thymine or uracil

Q

quadrat – a rectangular or square area in which studies of sessile organisms occur

quantum – a particle of electromagnetic radiation; a discrete bundle of light as it behaves when it is emitted or absorbed by a substance

R

r-selection – natural selection which favours parents who use their resources to produce many offspring

radioactive waste – spent fuel from a nuclear generating station

reaction centre – a single chlorophyll molecule within the photosynthetic unit where transformation of light energy to stable chemical energy takes place

receptor – a structure capable of detecting change in the environment and passing that information on

recessive – an allele that is only expressed in the homozygous form, being otherwise masked by the dominant allele

recombinant DNA – DNA from two different sources that are spliced together

recombination – the formation of new genetic combinations as a result of crossing over or segregation of chromosomes

recycling – the re-use of garbage such as paper, glass, and metal after it has been made into new products

redox reaction – a reaction involving oxidation and reduction, resulting in the transfer of electrons

reducing agent – an electron donor; causes a reaction

reduction – the addition of an electron to an atom or molecule

reflex – an automatic stereotyped response to a particular external stimulus

reflex action – an involuntary response to a stimulus, such as blinking when something comes near the eye

reflex arc – a series of connected neurons which permit a reflex action

regulator – a structure that controls the levels of activity of the receptor and effector

relaxation response – a meditation technique used to control the fight or flight response

releaser – an exaggerated sensitivity towards a stimulus which then triggers a specific behaviour

renewable resource – a living resource that can be produced again

replacement level fertility rate – the fertility rate required for a couple to replace itself in the population

replication fork – a Y-shaped region created by the separation of the two strands of DNA during replication

replication origin – a specific DNA sequence that serves as the initiation site of replication

replisome – an assembly of proteins for DNA synthesis at the replication fork

repressor – a protein capable of binding to a specific operator region and inhibiting transcription of that operon

resource recovery – the return of resources such as glass, aluminum, and paper to use instead of disposing of them

respiratory control – regulation of the rates of glycolysis, the citric acid cycle and the electron transport chain using feedback loops

restricted learning – a behaviour that requires at least some environmental experience before it can be performed

restriction endonuclease – an enzyme which recognizes a specific DNA nucleotide sequence and makes cuts in both strands of the DNA molecule

reverse transcriptase – an enzyme that uses RNA as a template for the synthesis of a complementary DNA chain

reversion mutation – a second mutation that restores the codon to its original state, which was altered by the first mutation

rhizoid – cells on the lower surface of liverwort plants which extend and anchor the plant to the soil

ribonucleic acid (RNA) – a nucleotide chain containing the sugar ribose and the pyrimidine uracil (instead of thymine, which is found in DNA)

ribosomal RNA (rRNA) – a class of RNA molecules present in the ribosome which is involved in protein synthesis

ribosome – a small spherical organelle which synthesizes protein

RNA polymerase – an enzyme which catalyzes the synthesis of RNA from the DNA template

S

S-shaped growth curve – the growth curve typical of density-dependent population changes

saltatorial conduction – the process by which the nerve impulse jumps from one node of Ranvier to the next

sanitary landfill – a dump where the garbage is covered with a layer of earth each day

saturated fatty acid – a fatty acid chain which does not contain carbon-carbon double bonds

scavenger – an animal that feeds on dead animals

Schwann cell – a specialized neuroglia cell that wraps around an axon to form a myelin sheath

seasonal succession – an annual cycle of change within an ecosystem

seasonal turnover – the movement of water in lakes as warm water moves up and cooler, denser water sinks, causing a redistribution of nutrients

second law of thermodynamics – all energy in a reaction can be accounted for; $H = G-TS$, where H is the total energy of the system, G is free energy (the portion of the energy available to do useful work), S is entropy (the portion of energy which is not available) and T is the temperature of the system in degrees Kelvin

secondary consumer – an animal that feeds on plant eaters

secondary succession – succession that proceeds toward the climax community from a point of interruption due to natural disasters or human intervention

segregation – the separation of a pair of alleles as a consequence of the separation of paired chromosomes during meiosis

segregation test – crossing two mutations to see if the hybrid is heterozygous for only one gene

selectively neutral allele – an allele that does not appreciably change the fitness of individuals carrying it

semiconservative replication – the separation of the DNA chain during replication so that each new chain will contain one parental strand and one newly synthesized strand

sensory cortex – a narrow band of nerve tissue behind the central fissure of the cerebrum which receives sensory information from the body

sensory neuron – a neuron which carries information from receptor cells which are in contact with the environment

sex chromosome – chromosomes that determine the sex of the individual, such as XX or XY (see autosomes)

sex linkage – genes that are carried on the sex chromosomes and so their expression is determined by the sex of the individual

side chain – a part of an amino acid which differs for each of the 20 major amino acids

sieve plate – a perforated area at the end of a sieve tube which connects one tube to the next

sieve tube – a type of phloem cell which is living at maturity and forms long tubes connecting cells via sieve plates

sigmoidal growth – nearly exponential population growth followed by a levelling off and stability

silent mutation – a change in base sequence which does not result in an alteration of the amino acid designation of the codon

single bond – the interaction of two atoms such that each atom provides one electron to form the bond

sister chromatid – a pair of identical chromosomes joined in one or more places

small nuclear RNA (snRNA) – a specific small RNA molecule found in the nucleus and involved in the removal of introns from the transcription products

sociobiology – the study of the social aspects of an animal's environment

sodium-potassium pump – an active transport system in which sodium ions are moved out of the cell and potassium ions are moved in

solar radiation – energy from the sun

somatostatin – a hormone produced in the pancreas which is released when blood glucose or amino acid levels are high

speciation – the process by which new species form

spinal nerve – a nerve which leaves the central nervous system from the spinal cord

spindle – a network of microtubules formed during nuclear division which attach to the chromatids

spliceosome – an assembly of snRNA and proteins that is involved in the removal of introns from the transcription products

splicing – the removal of introns and joining together of exons during the processing of the RNA transcription products

spontaneous – a reaction that, once initiated, will continue to completion without further input of energy

stabilizing selection – natural selection that tends to select against phenotypes at the extremes of variation within a population, so maintaining the status quo of the population

stationary age structure – a population which is producing new individuals at approximately the same rate as individuals are dying

steroid hormone – a hormone derived from cholesterol

sterol – a group of neutral lipids such as cholesterol

stimulant – a chemical that speeds up the muscular and nervous systems to abnormal levels

stimulus – a change in the environment of an organism

stomate – a pore in the leaf surface of a higher plant through which gas exchange occurs

stratification – the layering of water created when warmer water sits on and insulates cooler water

stress – a change in an organism's internal or external environment which must be responded to so the organism can maintain homeostasis

stretch receptor – a neuron receptor which reacts to stretching of muscles

stroke – a blockage of the brain's circulatory system, which results in death of brain cells due to lack of oxygen

stroma – the enzyme-containing liquid in the chloroplast

stromal thylakoid – the single membranes which join the thylakoids in a grana

structural formula – a formula which depicts the bonding of each element in a molecule

substrate – raw material or initial ingredient

succession – the changes in the vegetation in an ecosystem that occur over time as each species creates conditions unfavourable for their own seedlings

survivorship – the proportion of individuals that survive to a certain age

sustainable yield – a balance between the level of production and use of a resource that can be maintained indefinitely

symbiosis – a relationship between two organisms in which both organisms benefit; mutualism

synapse – the area composed of the synaptic cleft and the ends of the two adjacent neurons

synapsis – the lengthwise pairing of homologous chromosomes during meiosis

synaptic cleft – the space between two neurons

T

taiga – the ecocline at the edge of the boreal forest

taxis – the orientation of an organism toward or away from a stimulus

technological revolution – the change in a population lifestyle to processing and communication of information

telophase – the phase of nuclear division during which the chromatids reach the poles of the spindle, the spindle disappears, the chromatids elongate into chromatin, and the nuclear envelope re-forms

temperate forest – a mixed deciduous and coniferous forest found in temperate regions

template – a molecule which serves as a pattern or mold for the synthesis of new identical molecules

test cross – a cross of a heterozygote with the corresponding recessive homozygote; progeny directly reflect the types and frequencies of gametes produced by the heterozygote

testosterone – a hormone produced in high levels in males to induce development of secondary sexual characteristics and maintain normal male reproductive functions

tetrad – a set of four homologous chromatids seen during meiosis

thalamus – the area of the forebrain which relays messages to the cerebrum and affects consciousness and pain perception

thallus – a flattened, lobed, leafless part of a liverwort

thermocline – the transition layer between two strata of water

thermodynamics – the study of the flow of energy

thermogenesis – a process by which the electron transport chain is used to produce heat instead of ATP

thermoregulation – the ability of an organism to maintain its internal body temperature within a very narrow range despite changes in its external environment

thiol – an organic molecule which contains a sulfur atom

thylakoid membrane – the inner membrane of the chloroplast, which forms many sac-like structures containing chlorophyll

thymine – a pyrimidine base found in DNA

tolerance – continuous use of a drug resulting in the need for more of the drug to produce the same effect

total fertility rate (TFR) – the average number of offspring a female actually produces during her life

tracheid – a type of xylem cell which has no protoplasm at maturity and forms long tubes with tapered ends

transcription – synthesis of a strand of complementary RNA using DNA as a template

transect – a long, thin quadrat that is used to study sessile organisms in low density areas

transfer RNA (tRNA) – a small RNA molecule that binds a specific amino acid and has a base sequence (anticodon) complementary to the mRNA

transformation – the genetic change in a cell as a result of the uptake of extraneous DNA from the surrounding medium

transgenic – the injection of foreign DNA into an early developmental stage to achieve a genetic change

translation – the process of protein synthesis using the nucleotide sequence of mRNA to determine the amino acid sequence

translocation – the transfer of part of one chromosome to another non-homologous chromosome

transmembrane pore – a theory which suggests that proteins wrap around the edges of the membrane bilayer to form channels through the membrane

transpiration – the evaporation of water through open stomates in the leaf

trial and error learning – the process of ''learning by doing,'' where, for example, animals learn to associate responses with their results, rather than with the stimuli that preceded them

triglyceride – a molecule composed of glycerol and three fatty acids, used for energy storage in the form of fat

triple bond – the interaction of two atoms such that each electron provides three electrons to form a bond

trisomy – a condition in which a diploid cell contains three copies of a particular chromosome instead of the normal two

trophic level – the feeding level of an organism

tropical forest – a forest found in areas near the equator, with little seasonal temperature variation

true speciation – an increase in the number of species from one common ancestor

tubular reabsorption – the recovery of water into the bloodstream in the kidney nephron

tundra – a cold desert found in northern regions

turgor pressure – a force created within the cell which pushes outward on the cell wall

U

ultraviolet radiation – a non-visible component of sunlight that causes sunburn and induces skin cancer

unconditioned response – a response to a stimulus that has not been learned

unconditioned stimulus – a stimulus that does not elicit a learned behaviour

undernutrition – insufficient energy present in the diet to satisfy the body's metabolic demands

uniformitarianism – the theory that changes in the earth have always occurred at the same rate as they do today

unit factor – a term used by Mendel to refer to the unit of inheritance, later replaced by the term gene

unsaturated fatty acid – a fatty acid chain which contains one or more carbon-carbon double bonds

uracil – a pyrimidine base found in RNA

V

valence electron – an electron found in the outermost orbital of an atom

ventricle – a fluid-filled space in the brain; a large muscular chamber of the heart which pumps blood out of the heart

vessel – a type of xylem cell which has no protoplasm at maturity and forms long thick-walled tubes with spiral bandings of lignin

vestigial – reduced, often functionless, remnants of structures that were more prominent in ancestors

W

wavelength – the distance between the crests of a wave of light as it travels through space

withdrawal reaction – physical disturbance or illness which occurs when the use of a drug is stopped

X

xylem – a tissue found in vascular plants, which lacks protoplasm at maturity, that carries water from the roots and supports the plant

Z

zero population growth (ZPG) – the point at which birth rates and death rates become equal

INDEX

sodium chloride 198
sodium-potassium ATPase 94, 98
sodium-potassium pump 92–3, 95, 207
soil 514, 516, 533, 535, 538, 543, 546, 585; *bacteria* 372, 542–3, 596; *erosion* 503, 506, 512–13, 521, 524, 533, 539, 579–80; *management* 513, 584–6; *minerals in* 519, 542–3; *moist* 159, 512, 539, 542; *nutrients in* 157, 161, 507, 510, 585
solar heating 154, 590
solutes 105, 108, 171–2
solvent 89, 90, 255, 261
somatic cell hybridization 299
somatic pathways 212, 221, 223
somatomedin 62
somatostatin 234, 235, 370
somatotropin 227, 231, 232
sonagrams 466
song, of birds 450–1, 463, 465–6
songbirds 560, 568
sorghum 182, 372, 512
sound 216, 217, 530–1; *as conditioned stimulus* 487; *as low-quality energy* 530–1; *heard by bees* 476–7
sound parabola 474
sound waves 363
soybeans 372, 513, 535
space program 502–3
sparrows 437, 452, 466, 483
spawning grounds 522, 523, 583
specialists (species) 503, 545
speciation 408–9, 430–44; *geographic* 434–40, 444; *gradual* 434–40, 444; *instantaneous* 434–5, 432–3, 444; *on islands* 434, 438–40; *phyletic* 430; *true* 430
species 398, 405, 409, 429–46, 525, 583, 586; *change in* 383, 388, 390–4, 398, 402–5, 408, 430; *endemic* 388, 438; *extinct* 380, 383, 386, 389, 395, 398, 400, 403, 409, 504, 524, 586; see also evolution; speciation
species groups 434, 435, 441
species pairs 434, 435, 436
specimen preparation 67–73
spectrum 142–3, 144, 148, 155, 159, 180, 476
"speed" (drugs) 255
spermatocyte 298
sperm cells 60, 108, 232, 282, 284, 394, 415, 418, 423, 432, 482
sphagnum moss 507
sphingolipids 357
spiders 439, 454, 462, 503, 535
spikes: see nerve impulses
spina bifida 357, 360, 362, 364
spinal column: see vertebral column
spinal cord 207, 211–16, 218, 221, 223, 360, 455–6
spinal nerves 215, 218, 220–1, 455
spindle apparatus 62–4, 65, 276, 277
spliceosome 344
splicing: *alternative* 350–1; *of*

DNA 364; *of RNA* 344, 345–6, 351, 369
sponges 454, 523, 533
spongy layer 131, 162
spontaneity, in thermodynamics 102, 103, 104, 107
spontaneous generation 403
sports, use of drugs in 261–2
spruce trees 435, 441, 507, 509, 538
squirrels 453, 491–3, 508, 512, 516; *as generalists* 503
stabilizing selection 425
Stahl, Franklin 318–19
staining, of specimens 67–8, 267, 276, 299, 417
starch 29, 110, 133–5, 137, 255, 381; *breakdown* 170; *in diet* 250–1; *in plants* 515, 530
startle reaction 451–2
starvation 251, 252, 405
stationary age structure, of population 567
steam vents 543
stem reptiles 386
stems 134, 161, 167, 372, 515; *as food* 516; *of aquatic plants* 521; *of grasses* 512
steppes 512
stereotyped behaviour 480–3, 496
sterility 360, 431, 594
sterilization (to prevent reproduction) 355–6
Stern, Curt 298
steroid hormones 41, 57, 123, 201, 228–30, 232, 237–8, 242, 261–2; *as oral contraceptives* 240
sterols 78, 80, 96–7
stickleback 478, 481–2
stigma, of flower 268
stillbirths 356, 576, 577
stimulation 218–19, 221–2, 228, 239, 247, 257
stimulus 191, 192–3, 195–7, 201, 208, 216–17, 253, 358, 451, 486, 496; *conditioned* 484, 487; *external* 451–59, 463–7, 470, 487; *hormones as* 233, 451–52, 469; *internal* 452–54, 458, 469, 480, 495; *irrelevant* 484, 487; *releasers* 479–81; *to behaviour* 449–70, 473, 475, 476–81; *to glands* 227; *unconditioned* 484
stomach 223, 230, 234, 256–7
stomate 131, 162–7, 183–4
stratification, in bodies of water 519, 521
streams 520, 522
stress 191–2, 222–3, 230–1, 237, 246–8, 252–3
stressors 192
stretch receptors 192, 195, 221–2, 455
strokes (CVAs) 213, 215, 247
stroma 60, 130–5, 137, 152–3, 179
stromal thylakoids 130
stromatolites 384–5
structural formula, of molecules 9–10, 19
strychnine 255
Sturtevant, Alfred 282

stylet, of aphid 171–2
subatomic particles 4
sublimation 12
substrate level phosphorylation 110, 112, 116, 121
substrates 34, 107, 110, 118, 157, 191, 302, 346; *carbon dioxide as* 181; *oxygen as* 136, 181
substrate saturation 181
succession, in ecosystems 533, 535–6, 545, 569, 570; *primary* 533, 535–6, 538; *seasonal* 533; *secondary* 536
succinate 122
sucrose 27, 110, 133–5, 137; *in sap* 172–3; *transport across membrane* 91; see also sugars
Sudden Sniffing Death 261
sugars 13, 41, 78, 104, 123, 381, 456, 487; *addiction to* 254; *as energy source* 530; *from photosynthesis* 131–2, 155, 171; *in DNA* 313–15, 319–20, 334–5; *in food* 246, 250–2, 255, 257; *in plants* 515; *in sap* 170, 172–3; *in urine* 235; *oxidation* 103; *refined* 250; *transport across membrane* 91; see also carbohydrates
sulfates 543
sulfur 4, 41, 158, 312, 544
sulfur cycle 543–5, 547
sulfur dioxide 543
sulfuric acid 595
sulfur oxide 595
sun: *and evaporation* 539; *as energy source* 103–4, 141, 154–5, 177, 185, 529–31, 533, 541, 547, 590; *light related to skin cancer* 592; *role in photosynthesis* 129, 132, 141
superior oblique muscle 220
supernatant 69–70, 107
surface receptors 33
surface tension 81–2
surrogate mothers, in animal breeding 355
survival 402, 405–6, 449, 456, 459, 463, 473, 483, 491–2, 508, 564
survivorship 561–3; *age-specific* 564–6, 568; *curve* 564–5; *in Toronto* 576; *of offspring* 568
Sutherland, Earl W. 228
Sutton, Walter 275, 279, 281
swamps 522, 542; *mangrove* 524
Swann, Theodor 47
sweat glands 197, 227, 420
sweating 257, 260
Sweden 567; *census* 575, 576; *energy demands* 588
swimming 454
symbiosis 372, 543
symbols, in genetics 291
symmetry, two-fold 365
sympathetic chain ganglia 222
sympathetic nerves 212, 222–3, 237, 239
sympathetic nervous system 221–2, 239
symport 94
synapses 209–10; *stimulatory* 218, 219
synapsis 278–80, 297, 458, 490

synaptic cleft 206, 210, 223
synaptic transmission 209
systematics 408

———————— T ————————

taiga 507, 515
tail 379, 386, 393, 403
tanagers 387, 388
tapirs 392, 430
target cells, for hormones 228–9, 231–3, 235, 239, 350
tarns 521
tars 256, 257
taste, sense of 217, 220
Tatum, Edward 301–2
taxis 454–56, 458, 470
Taylor, Herbert 319
Tay-Sachs disease 290, 294, 357, 362, 374
T-DNA 372
Technological Revolution 502; 574, 578
technology 565, 586–8, 590; *medical* 575–8; *nuclear* 589, 591
teeth 220, 379, 386, 427, 430, 442; *absence of* 393
telophase 62, 277, 279, 280, 281
temperate zones 506, 543
temperature 247, 416, 504, 529, 540; *and greenhouse effect* 592; *as sensory stimulus* 216–17, 455; *changes in* 191, 197; *effect on photosynthesis* 177; *effect on transpiration* 184; *in biomes* 504, 508, 509, 515, 517, 522; *in bonding* 7; *in nuclear winter* 591; *modified by bodies of water* 517–18, 529; *of the earth, before life existed* 504; *regulation of* 18; see also body temperature
temperature sensors 197–8
template 319–20, 322, 328, 333–7, 368
temporal lobe, of brain 214, 215
tendons 217, 218, 457
tension: *emotional* 258; *in muscles* 247
tentacles 454, 456
terminal transferase 367
territorial claim 465, 475, 478
territory 465, 478, 482
test cross 274–5, 291, 294, 296–7
testes 230–2, 239, 242, 360, 394
testosterone 41, 230–2, 239, 242, 261, 271, 449
tetracycline 368
tetrad 279, 298
tetranucleotide 310, 313
tetrapods 393
thalamus 213–14
thalidomide 30
thallus 160–1
therapy 251, 254
thermocline 519
thermodynamics 16, 101–4, 124; *first law of* 102, 124, 530; *second law of* 102–3, 124, 530–2
thermogenesis 119–20
thermoregulation 196–8, 202
thermotaxis 455
thiamine 254
thirst 214, 453
Thorndike, E. L. 485, 496

631

PHOTO CREDITS

All photographs not specifically credited to another source are courtesy of the authors.

Chapter 1 opener: R. DelMaestro, Victoria Hospital, London, Canada.

Figure Page 28: Osteoporosis Society.

Figure 3.1 (a): The Council of the Royal Society of London for Improving Natural Knowledge; (c): Robert Langille. Figure 3.2: Photo Researchers, Inc./Biophoto Associates. Figure 3.3: Photo Researchers, Inc./Biophoto Associates. Figure 3.5: Photo Researchers, Inc./Biophoto Associates. Figure 3.7 (b): Ontario Science Centre. Figure 3.9: Photo Researchers, Inc./Jeremy Burgess/Science Photo Library. Figure 3.10 (a): Bela Nagy. Figure 3.10 (b): Peter Lea/University of Toronto. Figure 3.11: Robert Langille. Figure 3.13: Ontario Science Centre. Figure 3.14: Robert Langille. Figure 3.16: Ontario Science Centre. Figure 3.17: Ontario Science Centre. Figure 3.18 (a): Ontario Science Centre. Figure 3.20: Bela Nagy. Figure 3.21: Robert Langille. Figure 3.22: Bela Nagy. Figure 3.23: Bela Nagy. Figure 3.24; Bela Nagy. Figure 3.25: Bela Nagy. Figure 3.26 (a): Bela Nagy; (b), (c): Carl Zeiss. Figure 3.28: R. Rajaraman, G. Johnston/Dalhousie University. Figure 3.33: Misa Ito. Figure 3.34: Stephen J. Hall.

Chapter 4 opener: Lennart Nilsson/Boehringer Ingelheim International.

Chapter 5 opener: British Tourist Authority. Figure Page 120: Dan Getz/N.R.C. Science Dimension.

Figure 6.4: Ontario Science Centre.

Chapter 7 opener: Alan Noon, Los Alamos National Laboratory. Figure Page 130: Ontario Ministry of Natural Resources.

Figure 8.3: Alan Noon. Figure 8.5: NASA. Figure 8.7: Photo Researchers, Inc. Figure 8.9: N. Dengler. Figure 8.13 (a), (b): Alan Noon. Figure Page 170: Ontario Ministry of Agriculture and Food, Ontario Ministry of Natural Resources.

Chapter 9 opener: United States Department of Agriculture.

Chapter 10 opener: Claude Latendresse/Athlete Information Bureau. Figure 10.4 (a): D. Cowl; (b): D. Gray/University of Alberta.

Chapter 11 opener: © Bruno Jarret 1989/VIS★ART Copyright Inc.

Chapter 12 opener: Photo Researchers, Inc./Bettina Cirone 1981. Figure 12.5: Photo Researchers, Inc./Paul Almasy. Figure Page 236: University of Toronto Archives.

Chapter 14 opener: E. Kassner. Figure 14.1: National Library of Medicine.

Figure 15.15: Photo Researchers, Inc./Omikron.

Figure 17.12 (a): B. Hamkalo/University of California.

Chapter 18 opener: R.L. Brinster/Peter Arnold, Inc. Figure 18.10: David Lynn. Figure Page 371: Cecil Fox/Masterfile.

Chapter 19 opener: British Museum of Natural History. Figure 19.4: J. W. Schopf/UCLA (Geology). Figure 19.13: Ontario Ministry of Natural Resources. Figure 19.16: E. C. Oaks/Mammal Slide Library/American Society of Mammologists.

Chapter 20 opener: National Library of Medicine. Figure 20.1: Yerkes Observatory Photograph. Figure 20.3: W. Poelman. Figure 20.5: Canada Packers. Figure 20.6: R. Harshman. Figure 20.8: R. Dengler. Figure 20.11: National Library of Medicine.

Figure 21.6: Misa Ito. Figure 21.9: British Trust for Ornithology.

Figure 22.3: R. W. Murphy. Figure 22.16: C. McGowan.

Chapter 23 opener (bottom right): Ontario Ministry of Natural Resources. Figure 23.1: W.A. Sheppe/Mammal Slide Library/American Society of Mammologists. Figure 23.15: Network/Derek Kirkland. Figure 23.23: Network/Barry Griffiths. Figure 23.24: Clyde H. Smith/Peter Arnold, Inc. Figure 23.27: Susan Bradnam.

Figure 24.7: The Bettman Archives. Figure 24.12: Michael Sukhdeo. Figure 24.16: Oklahoma Department of Wildlife. Figure 24.23: Bela Nagy. Figure 24.24: Brock Fenton/York University. Figure 24.25: R. Riewe/Mammal Slide Library/American Society of Mammologists. Figure 24.28: Valan/Jeff Foott. Figure Page 495: Ontario Ministry of Natural Resources.

Chapter 25 opener: NASA. Figure 25.2: Ontario Ministry of Natural Resources. Figure 25.9 (b): World Wildlife Fund, Toronto. Figure Page 511: World Wildlife Fund, Toronto. Figure 25.10 (b): C. Loeffler/Mammal Slide Library/American Society of Mammalogists. Figure 25.18 (a): Ontario Ministry of Natural Resources. Figure 25.19: Mississauga Diving Services Ltd. Figure 25.20 (b): R. Dengler.

Chapter 26 opener: Ontario Ministry of Natural Resources.

Chapter 27 opener: Ontario Science Centre. Figure 27.2: Bela Nagy. Figure 27.8: Ontario Ministry of Natural Resources.

Chapter 28 opener: IMS, University of Toronto. Figure 28.6 (top): Saskatchewan Agriculture; (bottom): John Luternauer. Figure 28.8: IDRC/G. Paulsen. Figure 28.11: Ian Fleming. Figure 28.15: Valan Photos/K. Ghani. Figure 28.16: Ontario Hydro. Figure 28.20: Ontario Ministry of Natural Resources.